Intellectual Property Law and Human Rights

Information Law Series (INFO)

VOLUME 34

General Editor

Prof. P. Bernt Hugenholtz, Institute for Information Law, University of Amsterdam.

Objective & Readership

Publications in the Information Law Series focus on current legal issues of information law and are aimed at scholars, practitioners, and policy makers who are active in the rapidly expanding area of information law and policy.

Introduction & Contents

The advent of the information society has put the field of information law squarely on the map. Information law is the law relating to the production, marketing, distribution, and use of information goods and services. The field of information law therefore cuts across traditional legal boundaries, and encompasses a wide set of legal issues at the crossroads of intellectual property, media law, telecommunications law, freedom of expression, and right to privacy. Recent volumes in the Information Law Series deal with copyright enforcement on the Internet, interoperability among computer programs, harmonization of copyright at the European level, intellectual property and human rights, public broadcasting in Europe, the future of the public domain, conditional access in digital broadcasting, and the 'three-step test' in copyright.

The titles published in this series are listed at the end of this volume.

Intellectual Property Law and Human Rights

Fourth Edition

Edited by

Paul L.C. Torremans

 Wolters Kluwer

Published by:
Kluwer Law International B.V.
PO Box 316
2400 AH Alphen aan den Rijn
The Netherlands
E-mail: international-sales@wolterskluwer.com
Website: lrus.wolterskluwer.com

Sold and distributed in North, Central and South America by:
Wolters Kluwer Legal & Regulatory U.S.
7201 McKinney Circle
Frederick, MD 21704
United States of America
Email: customer.service@wolterskluwer.com

Sold and distributed in all other countries by:
Air Business Subscriptions
Rockwood House
Haywards Heath
West Sussex
RH16 3DH
United Kingdom
Email: international-customerservice@wolterskluwer.com

Printed on acid-free paper.

ISBN 978-94-035-1304-1

e-book: ISBN 978-94-035-1314-0
web-PDF: ISBN 978-94-035-1320-1

Printed and bound by CPI Group (UK) Ltd, Croydon, CR0 4YY

Editor

Prof. Dr Paul L.C. Torremans is Professor of Intellectual Property Law, School of Law, Faculty of Social Sciences, University of Nottingham, United Kingdom.

Contributors

Prof. Dr David Felipe Alvarez Amezquita is Assistant Professor and Researcher at the University of Tolima, Colombia.

Dr Sven J.R. Bostyn is Associate Professor at the JUR Centre for Advanced Studies in Biomedical Innovation Law, Faculty of Law, University of Copenhagen, Denmark.

Prof. Abbe E.L. Brown is Professor in Intellectual Property at the School of Law, University of Aberdeen, United Kingdom.

Andrew T. Foglia is Associate at Winston & Strawn LLP, New York, United States.

Prof. Sharon E. Foster is Robert A. Leflar Professor of Law and Dean of Law, School of Law, University of Arkansas, United States.

Dr Giancarlo Frosio is Associate Professor of the Centre for International Intellectual Property Studies (CEIPI), University of Strasbourg, France and Non-residential Fellow at the Center for Internet and Society at Stanford Law School, United States.

Prof. Dr Dev Gangjee is Professor of Intellectual Property Law, Faculty of Law, University of Oxford, United Kingdom.

Dr Krzysztof Garstka is Lecturer at the British Law Centre, Poland and Research Associate at the Centre for Intellectual Property and Information Law, University of Cambridge, United Kingdom.

Prof. Dr Christophe Geiger is Professor of Law and Director of the Research Department of the Centre for International Intellectual Property Studies (CEIPI), University of Strasbourg, France.

Prof. Daniel Gervais is **Milton R. Underwood Chair in Law**, Vanderbilt University, United States and Director of Vanderbilt Intellectual Property Program.

Dr Henning Grosse Ruse-Khan is Reader in International and European Intellectual Property Law, Co-Director of the Centre for Intellectual Property and Information Law and Fellow and Director of Studies (King's College) at the University of Cambridge, United Kingdom.

Dr Naomi Hawkins is Associate Professor and Director of the Science, Culture and the Law Research Group at the University of Exeter, United Kingdom.

Prof. Laurence R. Helfer, is **Harry R. Chadwick** Sr. Professor of Law and Co-Director of the Center for International and Comparative Law, Duke University, United States.

Prof. Peter Jaffey is Professor of Law, Leicester Law School, University of Leicester, United Kingdom.

Dr Bernd Justin Jütte is Assistant Professor, University of Nottingham, United Kingdom and Senior Researcher, Vytautas Magnus University, Lithuania.

Nigar Kirimova, LLM is a tutor at Munich Intellectual Property law Centre, Irish and European Trademark Attorney, IP Lawyer at Brandstock Legal GmbH., Germany.

Prof. UAM dr hab. Katarzyna Klafkowska-Waśniowska is Professor at the European Law Chair in the European Law Department of the Faculty of Law and Administration, Adam Mickiewicz University in Poznań, Poland.

Prof. Marshall Leaffer is Distinguished Scholar in Intellectual Property and University Fellow, Maurer School of Law, University of Indiana, United States.

Prof. Dr Ida Madieha bt. Abdul Ghani Azmi is Professor at the Ahmad Ibrahim Kulliyyah of Laws, Civil Law Department, International Islamic University Malaysia.

Dr Patrick Masiyakurima is a Lecturer at Leicester Law School, University of Leicester, United Kingdom.

Dr Gemma Minero is Lecturer in Civil Law and Intellectual Property Law in the Civil Law Department of the University Autónoma of Madrid, Vice -Dean for Students, Faculty of Law UAM and coordinator of the Máster de Propiedad Intelectual, Industrial y Nuevas Tecnologías UAM, Spain.

Dr Jacqueline N. Nwozo is Visiting Researcher with The Dickson Poon School of Law, King's College London, United Kingdom.

Prof. Dr Alexander Peukert is Professor of Commercial and Intellectual Property Law, Faculty of Law and Cluster of Excellence 'Formation of Normative Orders', Goethe University, Frankfurt am Main, Germany.

Dr Andrea Radonjanin is Attorney at Law, Partner, Schönherr, Belgrade, Serbia.

Prof. Dr Marco Ricolfi is Professor of Intellectual Property Law, Turin Law School, Università degli Studi di Torino, Italy.

Prof. Dr Jens Schovsbo Professor is Professor in the Centre for Information and Innovation Law (CIIR) at the University of Copenhagen, Denmark.

Dr Sebastian Schwemer is Associate Professor in the Centre for Information and Innovation Law (CIIR) at the University of Copenhagen, Denmark.

Prof. Myra J. Tawfik is Professor of Faculty of Law at the University of Windsor and Senior Fellow at the Centre for International Governance Innovation, Canada.

Prof. Dr Geertrui Van Overwalle is Professor of IP Law at the University of Leuven, Belgium and Visiting Professor at the Grande École Sciences Po - School of Law in Paris, France.

Dr Karen Walsh is Lecturer in Intellectual Property Law at the University of Exeter, United Kingdom.

Prof. Peter K. Yu is Professor of Law, Professor of Communication, and the Director of the Center for Law and Intellectual Property at Texas A&M University in the United States.

Assoc. Prof. Dr Majdah Zawawi is Associate Professor at the Ahmad Ibrahim Kulliyyah of Laws, Islamic Law Department at the International Islamic University Malaysia.

Summary of Contents

Table of Contents

Chapter 9
Communication to the Public of Works and Freedom to Receive and Impart Information in the Charter of Fundamental Rights
Katarzyna Klafkowska-Waśniowska

Chapter 10
Guiding the Blind Bloodhounds: How to Mitigate the Risks
Article 17 of Directive 2019/970 Poses to the Freedom of
Expression

Chapter 11
The Conflict Between the Human Right to Education and
Copyright

Preface

Some sixteen years ago, I organized a conference on intellectual property and human rights at Canada House in London.[1] The papers dealt essentially with copyright-related issues and many of us present there felt that we were dealing with a niche topic. We were very happy when Kluwer Law International accepted to publish the papers as a book.[2] Soon afterwards we became aware that our niche topic started to mushroom and the book started to attract an increasing amount of interest. A much-expanded second edition followed in 2008 and a third edition in 2015.

The fourth edition that you have in front of you is once more an expanded edition. Together with the authors a decision was made that certain topics have not seen more interesting developments and as a result a couple of chapters from the previous editions were not retained. The other chapters were revised and fully updated where necessary. Other issues have arisen over the years and these are covered in-depth in nine completely new chapters or some 30% of the book. The book is therefore an exciting mix of the old and the new in this blossoming area of law.

In a first set of papers, the complex relationship between human rights and intellectual property as a whole is analysed. The starting point is that over the last couple of years these two disciplines had to learn to live together.

That brings us to the interaction with specific intellectual property rights. First, our attention turns to copyright.

Second, we address issues related to trademarks and similar rights. Folklore and commercial freedom of speech also fits into this category.

---

1. The support of the Canadian High Commission in London, my then colleagues in the BACS Legal Studies Group and especially Michael Hellyer in launching this project is gratefully acknowledged.
2. Paul Torremans (ed.), *Copyright and Human Rights: Freedom of Expression – Intellectual Property – Privacy*, Volume 14 Information Law Series, Kluwer Law International (2004).

Third, our attention turns to rights in information. New issues as diverse as artificial intelligence and climate change have joined the debate here, alongside privacy and breach of confidence.

Finally, we address issues in relation to patents for biotechnological materials. Some of the issues, many of them linked to morality, show up very sharply when living material, stem cells and gene patents are involved.

Human rights and intellectual property clearly remains a field in full expansion and development. On behalf of all the contributors, I hope that this book can make a substantial contribution to this development. Our thanks also go to Anja Kramer and her team at Kluwer Law International who made this expanded and fully revised fourth edition possible and who made editing it such a pleasant experience.

Part I

The Relationship Between Intellectual Property and Human Rights

Chapter 1

How Intellectual Property and Human Rights Can Live Together: An Updated Perspective

Daniel Gervais

1.1   INTRODUCTION

Intellectual property and human rights have learned to live together much better in the past decade. Traditionally, there have been, as Paul Torremans points out, two dominant views of this 'cohabitation', namely a conflict view, which emphasizes the negative impacts of intellectual property on rights such as freedom of expression or the right to health and security, and a compatibility model, which emphasizes that both sets of rights strive towards the same fundamental equilibrium. A somewhat different take on the cohabitation is to see it as both conflictual and potentially fruitful.[1] This chapter will take the dualist view that both are right, though there is now more truth to the second approach.

There are threads that weave intellectual property and human rights together. First, intellectual property rights claim to have roots in natural law, most famously as the Lockean moral desert theory, which held that property

---

1. *See* generally Willem Grosheide (ed.), *Intellectual Property & Human Rights: A Paradox* (E Elgar, 2010).

rights should be commensurate with 'the sacrifice actually incurred'.[2] According to this view, the property is justifiable as a (just) reward for work done to create new works from the existing inventory of ideas and public domain works, or on a significant, industrially useful improvement on the existing stock of technological knowledge.

Locke's original theory turned on the labour sacrifice of a particular landowner. He did not expressly advocate property rights in intangibles. Applying his theory to intangibles raises interesting questions. For instance, if one adopts a natural law justificatory theory for intellectual property, then one might ask whether the protection of intangible should be commensurate with the author's or inventor's efforts. If one were to argue for proportionality, a flood of both theoretical and practical questions immediately would race through one's mind: who could set and enforce the criteria to determine the value of a work or a patent? Which *kind* of value (societal, economic, etc.), and according to which set of metrics? How would temporal elements be factored into the equation (i.e., what is the value now and twenty years hence)? What would be the transaction costs of this determination? And the list goes on.

Is the invisible hand the best judge? Few would argue that the *market* value of a particular piece of music or patent (assuming the market value is a valid benchmark) is actually proportional to the efforts, time or money invested. The commercial success of poets, whose sweat and coffee stains are often the only visible result of a day's work, if and when it happens, will seem picayune compared to the latest techno or hip-hop hit. The same criticism could be addressed to many physical goods, whose market value bears little relationship to actual manufacturing costs or, indeed, the underlying R&D.

In spite of those differences between tangible and intangible property, natural law roots are something that intellectual property, and perhaps more acutely copyrights and patents, still share with traditional (Eurocentric) human rights theory.[3] One might disagree with the assertion that private property rights are human rights – at least in a universal conception. At the opposite end of the spectrum, French polemists asserted that authors' rights were 'the most sacred, the most legitimate, the most unassailable and … the most personal of all properties'.[4] That debate, however, is beyond the scope

---

2. Barbara H. Fried, *The Progressive Assault on Laissez Faire: Robert Hale and the First Law and Economics Movement* (Harvard University Press, 1998), 111.

3. Since at least Aristotle's Nicomachean Ethics, it has been argued that human rights underpin a moral order whose legitimacy precedes contingent social and historical conditions. According to this view, human rights are 'naturally' universal.

4. Le Chapelier, rapporteur before the Constituent Assembly, quoted in translation in Michel Vivant, 'Authors' Rights, Human Rights?', Revue internationale du droit d'auteur, RIDA 174 (1997): 60, 62. One could add Lakanal's amplification (quoted in idem): 'Of all properties, the least disputable, the one whose growth can neither undermine republican equality nor offend freedom, is unquestionably that of productions of genius.' The same

of this chapter.[5] Additionally, as Professor Torremans notes in his chapter, when applied to informational or ideational objects, the concept of property is imperfect. At the very least, in that context 'property' must have a different purpose and meaning,[6] because statutory intellectual property rights are not only non-excludable and non-rival;[7] they are also temporary.[8] Despite the imperfect match, it is worth noting, however, that property rights are the 'human rights' most often cited (by investors of course) in investor-state dispute-settlement proceedings (ISDS).[9]

---

was said of patents. That authors' rights are a property rights is formally recognized in Article L.111.1 of the Code de la propriété intellectuelle (France). The question whether this is still true in France is occasionally discussed. *See* M. Vivant, *supra*, at 81 et seq.

5. As Professor Yu demonstrates in his chapter, the synonymy between the reference to 'material interests' in the UDHR and other instruments (discussed below), on the one hand, and private property, which many often take for granted, on the other, has not in fact been established. That said, in a number of civil law jurisdictions, intellectual property forms part of incorporeal property and is considered as private property in the same way as chattels or land. The two classic divisions of property in those systems are between moveable and immovable and between corporeal and incorporeal (*see*, e.g., Article 899 of the Civil Code of Quebec). Article 458 of the Civil Code of Quebec is an illustration. It reads in part: 'Intellectual and industrial property rights are private property.' Article 909 reads in part as follows: 'Property that produces fruits and revenues, property appropriated for the service or operation of an enterprise, shares of the capital stock or common shares of a legal person or partnership, the reinvestment of the fruits and revenues, the price for any disposal of capital or its reinvestment, and expropriation or insurance indemnities in replacement of capital, are capital. Capital also includes rights of intellectual or industrial property.'

6. Property confers advantages by ensuring investment and development of resources. The social costs of excludability are acceptable because 'the losses that people suffer from exclusion are small compared to the gains that they get both from their ability to privatize their labour and from their ability to enter into trade'. In other words, the main propertization is a clear Pareto improvement, but copyright may be different. In classic property theory, for instance, possession is considered key and the law essentially reinforces the physical control that can be exerted by the owner (by fencing, etc.). No such metes and bounds exist in copyright law. This probably explains why property rights in intangibles have been the subject of many a scholarly debate.

7. Non-excludable means that it is impossible to prevent an individual who does not pay for that thing from enjoying the benefits of it. Non-rival goods may be consumed by one consumer without preventing simultaneous consumption by others. Those are the two traditional characteristics of public goods. The increasing recourse to Technological Protection Measures (TPMs) to prevent access to or use of copyright goods is, however, a form of enclosure that attempts to treat information object as excludable property. Tangible patented goods are also obviously excludable, but not the patented information itself, subject to the prohibition of its use to develop a commercial product that would infringe the patent. The level of patent protection in national law may go beyond this prohibition.

8. Except of course for trademarks that remain in commercial use.

9. *See* Jose Alvarez, 'The Use (and Misuse) of European Fundamental Rights Law in Investor-State Dispute Settlement', in F. Ferrari (ed.) *The Impact of EU Law on International Commercial Arbitration* (NYU Press, 2017) at 5. *See also* Daniel Gervais,

Leaving that debate aside, then, and against the backdrop of the traditional linkages based on natural law between intellectual property and human rights, section 1.2 of this chapter will argue that entering the pragmatic realm of trade law, as intellectual property norm-making has done over the past thirty years, might entail abandoning its claim to the property and/or human right status. This shift may be observed *inter alia* by the exclusion of moral rights from certain trade agreements concerning copyright, and the application of an effects-based test (the three-step test) as a common denominator for allowable exceptions to several intellectual property rights in the Agreement on Trade-Related Aspects of Intellectual Property (TRIPS Agreement).

Responding dialectically to section 1.2, section 1.3 will focus on copyright's internal balance as it relates to and mirrors human rights principles and suggests that copyright at least can (re)anchor itself normatively in such principles even if it abandoned traditional natural law-based claims by becoming a trade-related right. As was noted by other contributors to this book, including the editor and Professor Laurence Helfer, copyright can rely on both Article 27 of the Universal Declaration of Human Rights (UDHR)[10] and Article 15 of the International Covenant on Economic, Social and Cultural Rights, as well as regional instruments such as Article 13 of the American Declaration on the Rights and Duties of Man.[11] Those instruments provide a blueprint for cohabitation. The human rights principles they embody closely mirror the internal equilibrium of the copyright system, with its limited exclusive rights for authors and exceptions to such rights for users, including other authors.

Section 1.4 will suggest that the emergence of new normative conflicts between intellectual property and human rights, such as the right to health, and, in the field of copyright, face-offs with privacy, have fundamentally altered the landscape. There have always been perceived conflicts between copyright and rights, such as freedom of expression, but it was also argued in parallel that copyright was *intended* to be an engine of free expression.[12] Freedom of creation is a condition precedent to the existence of freedom of

---

'Intellectual Property: A Beacon for Reform of Investor-State Dispute Settlement', Michigan Journal of International Law 40 (2019): 289-325.
10. J.A.L. Sterling, *World Copyright Law* (Sweet & Maxwell, 2nd ed., 2003), 43.
11. Audrey R. Chapman, 'Approaching Intellectual Property as a Human Right (Obligations Related to Article 15(1)(c))', XXXV Copyright Bulletin nos 3 (2001): 4-36, at 11. *See also* Klaus D. Beiter, 'Establishing Conformity Between TRIPS and Human Rights: Hierarchy in International Law, Human Rights Obligations of the WTO and Extraterritorial State Obligations Under the International Covenant on Economic, Social and Cultural Rights', in H. Ullrich, R. M. Hilty, M. Lamping, and J. Drexl (eds.), *TRIPS plus 20: From Trade Rules to Market Principles* (Springer, 2016), 445–505.
12. This was the stated intention of the framers of the Constitution of the United States. *See* Michael Birnhack, 'Copyright Law and Free Speech after Eldred v. Ashcroft', Southern California Law Review 76 (2003): 1275, 1284. *See also* Patrick Masiyakurima's chapter in this book.

expression. Indeed, as is discussed in Professor Yu's chapter, censorship is at odds with the ability to access and contribute to the culture, and there is, therefore, a convergence of interests in having copyright as the economic underpinning of a free press and publishing industry. That case may be harder to make with respect to privacy and the right to health. The new environment is thus characterized, on the one hand, by human rights with increased visibility and status, and intellectual property 'reduced to' trade law status, on the other. Intellectual property rights holders ask for this linkage with trade essentially to benefit from the protection of trade sanctions and cross-sectoral trade-offs in trade agreements.[13] What they may have underestimated are the 'ontological costs' associated with what, for intellectual property, amounts to an existential shift. Whether trade remedies can compensate for those costs is discussed at the end of section 1.4.

1.2 INTELLECTUAL PROPERTY AS TRADE LAW

1.2.1 THE ALIGNMENT WITH TRADE

The progressive alignment of trade and intellectual property policy started in the United States (US) in the 1980s through successive amendments to section 301 of the *Trade Act*, which allowed the US Administration to impose trade-based sanctions on countries which, in the view of the US Trade Representative, did not adequately protect intellectual property rights of US citizens and companies. There is little doubt that this new weaponry bore fruit. It allowed US companies to obtain improvements in the protection of their intellectual property in several foreign territories, which agreed to increase protection lest they lose most-favoured-nation trading status with the US.

There ensued a well-documented[14] push by the US government, supported by the European Commission and the Japanese government, to link intellectual property and trade rules in the World Trade Organization (WTO) as part of the Uruguay Round of Multilateral Trade Negotiations, which ended in Marrakesh in April 1994 with the signing of the Agreement

---

13. By this, I mean that in trade agreement negotiations, concessions on intellectual property can be compensated by concessions in other areas, such as trade in cotton, cars or banking services.

14. Daniel Gervais, *The TRIPS Agreement: Drafting History and Interpretation* (Sweet & Maxwell, 2nd ed., 2003); Susan K. Sell, *Private Power, Public Law* (Cambridge University Press, 2003), 96-120; Christopher May, *A Global Political Economy of Intellectual Property Rights: The New Enclosures?* (Routledge, 2000); Peter Drahos & John Braithwaite, *Information Feudalism: Who Owns the Knowledge Economy?* (New Press, 2003); and A. Koury Menescal, 'Those Behind the TRIPS Agreement: The Influence of the ICC and the AIPPI on International Property Decisions', *Intellectual Property Quarterly* 2 (2005): 155.

Establishing the WTO, Annex 1C of which is the TRIPS Agreement. While critics opined that intellectual property was not a proper subject matter for the WTO, enter the house of trade it did, wholesale.[15]

This has at least two important consequences. First, unlike human rights, trade law is essentially pragmatic and results-based, something illustrated by such fuzzy notions under WTO law of 'nullification or impairment' of benefits or the doctrine of 'reasonable expectations'. Second, trade remedies are generally predicated on a showing of *actual* adverse impact on trade. The protection of intellectual property by trade rules does not seem to mesh with its ideological defence either as a 'property' or a human right.

A tort law analogy might be helpful in illuminating the difference. The tort of trespass to land occurs where a person enters or remains upon another's land without permission and is actionable per se without the need to prove damage. Trade law is closer to nuisance because a showing of damage (actual adverse impact) is required. Not surprisingly, since intellectual property trade law moved its home to the trade neighbourhood critics of intellectual property have tried to show that use of copyright works or patented goods (especially pharmaceuticals) in certain situations would lead to no demonstrable loss of income (i.e., no actual damage) for the rights holders. Logically, they say (if one accepts the premise of trade rules), use should be allowed. Linkage with trade thus reinforces the instrumentalist/ consequentialist approach to intellectual property regulation. Intellectual property rights serve a purpose, and when they no longer do (as a rule or in a given situation), they should cease to apply.

Rights holders may need to pick which legal horse they want to cross the intellectual property infringement river: if they choose a trade horse, they must accept pragmatism and the related need to show loss of reasonably available income streams. From that viewpoint, rhetorical reliance on 'property' is at odds with a strategy that was otherwise highly successful by copyright and patent lobbies to link intellectual property and trade. Perhaps the most direct and concrete illustration of the impact of trade rules on intellectual property is the omnipresence of the effects-based 'three-step test', increasingly viewed as a major normative vector to determine the appropriate scope of intellectual property rights, most notably copyrights, designs and patents in the TRIPS Agreement, as we shall now see.

1.2.2 THE THREE-STEP TEST

The three-step test has become the cornerstone for almost all exceptions to all intellectual property rights at the international level. It is the central test for exceptions to all copyright rights in the TRIPS Agreement (Article 13),

---

15. Jagdish Bhagwati, *In Defense of Globalization* (Oxford, 2004), 182-185.

to the rights created by two treaties negotiated under the auspices of the World Intellectual Property Organization (WIPO), namely the WIPO Copyright Treaty (WCT, Article 10) and the WIPO Performances and Phonograms Treaty (WPPT, Article 16). More recently, the test appears in Article 13(2) of the 2012 *Beijing Treaty on Audiovisual Performances* and Article 11 of the 2013 *Marrakesh Treaty to Facilitate Access to Published Works for Persons Who Are Blind, Visually Impaired or Otherwise Print Disabled*. It is also the basis for exceptions to industrial design protection (Article 26(2)), and patent rights (Article 30) in TRIPS.[16] The test, in its TRIPS Article 13 incarnation, requires that any exception be (1) a special case; (2) not interfere with normal commercial exploitation; and (3) not unreasonably prejudice the legitimate interests of rights holders. It achieves two objectives: first, the test canvasses the areas in which rights holders do *not* need rights to maximize their income; second, it provides a compensation mechanism (the third step) for exceptions that are considered desirable from a public interest perspective but could affect the material interests of rights holders, such as exceptions for private copying. As a result of this rather complete 'map' of rights holders' interests painted by the test, it has been suggested that the test should be reversed in the field of copyright to reveal the optimal scope of exclusive rights, thus greatly simplifying copyright law and aligning it with the economic purpose it embraced by inviting itself to the table of trade.[17]

Let us consider each of the three steps. This is only a rather cursory overview, and much more detailed commentaries are available elsewhere.[18]

1.2.2.1   'Certain Special Cases'

In the 2001 WTO panel decision concerning section 110(5) of the US Copyright Act,[19] the first part of the three-step test, namely the meaning of 'special', was interpreted for the first time by an international tribunal. The approach taken was essentially to look at the Oxford dictionary:

> The term 'special' connotes 'having an individual or limited application or purpose', 'containing details; precise, specific', 'exceptional in quality or degree; unusual; out of the ordinary' or 'distinctive in some way' [here was a footnote referring to the Oxford dictionary] This term

---

16. There is, however, a crucial difference in the case of patent rights: The last (third) step of the test [does] not unreasonably prejudice the legitimate interests of the patent owner, taking account of the legitimate interests of third parties.
17. Christophe Geiger, Daniel Gervais & Martin Senftleben, 'The Three-Step Test Revisited: How to Use the Test's Flexibility in National Copyright Law', American University Law Review 29, no. 3 (2104): 581-626.
18. Sam Ricketson & Jane C. Ginsburg, *The Berne Convention and Beyond* (Oxford, 2006), §§13.03 et seq.; and Christophe Geiger, Daniel Gervais & Martin Senftleben, 'The Three-Step Test Revisited: How to Use the Test's Flexibility in National Copyright Law', American University International Law Review 29, no. 3 (2014): 581.
19. Title 17, United States Code.

means that more is needed than a clear definition in order to meet the standard of the first condition. In addition, an exception or limitation must be limited in its field of application or exceptional in its scope. In other words, an exception or limitation should be narrow in quantitative as well as a qualitative sense.

The approach chosen by the panel is understandable. It followed the WTO Appellate Bod, which, for valid policy reasons, has preferred to stick with the ordinary meaning of words, in part to avoid introducing 'unbargained for' concessions in the WTO legal framework. As a result, however, the two steps in the test that can truly be operationalized as normative tools are the 'interference with commercial exploitation' and the 'unreasonable prejudice to the legitimate interests of the author'.

1.2.2.2   Interference with Normal Commercial Exploitation

What is the meaning of 'exploitation' in the context of this second step of the test? It seems fairly straightforward: use of the work by which the copyright owner tries to extract/maximize the value of her right. 'Normal' is more troublesome. Does it refer to what is simply 'common' (i.e., an empirical standard), or does it refer to a normative standard? The question is relevant in particular for new forms and emerging business models which have not thus far been common or 'normal'. During the last substantive revision of the Berne Convention (Stockholm, 1967), the concept was clearly used to refer to 'all forms of exploiting a work which had, or were likely to acquire considerable economic or practical importance'. As Paul Goldstein has noted, the purpose of the second step is to 'fortify authors' interests in their accustomed markets against local legislative inroads'. It thus seems that the condition is normative in nature: an exception is not allowed if it covers any form of exploitation which has, or is likely to acquire considerable importance. In other words, if the exception is used to limit a commercially significant market or, *a fortiori*, to enter into competition with the copyright holder, the exception is prohibited.

The WTO panel in the 110(5) case concluded as follows on this point:

> It appears that one way of measuring the normative connotation of normal exploitation is to consider, in addition to those forms of exploitation that currently generate significant or tangible revenue, those forms of exploitation which, with a certain degree of likelihood and plausibility, could acquire considerable economic or practical importance.

The test thus incorporates a dynamic notion of the normalcy of commercial exploitation. To be sure, to consider an exception incompatible with the second step because of conflict with a *potentially* significant source of revenue requires great caution.

1.2.2.3   Unreasonable Prejudice to Legitimate Interests of Rights Holders

The third step is perhaps the most difficult. What is an *'unreasonable* prejudice', and what are *'legitimate* interests'?

Let us start with 'legitimate'. It can have two meanings: (a) conformable to, sanctioned or authorized by law or principle; lawful, justifiable; proper; or (b) normal; regular; conformable to a recognized type. To put it differently, are legitimate interests only 'legal interests'?

The third step is a clear indication of the need to balance the rights of copyright holders and interests (under copyright law, not rights under other laws) of users. An analysis of the Records of the 1967 Stockholm Conference shows that the United Kingdom took the view that legitimate meant simply 'sanctioned by law', while other countries seem to take a broader view, meaning 'justifiable' in the sense that they are supported by social norms and relevant public policies. The WTO panel concluded that the combination of the notion of 'prejudice' with that of 'interests' pointed towards a legal-normative approach. In other words, it found that 'legitimate interests' are those that are protected by law. The interpretation might have been different if the third step had been formulated as 'the reproduction not contrary to the legitimate interests of the author'. With the 'unreasonable prejudice' element, however, the legitimate interests are almost by definition legal interests.

This leaves open one key question: what does 'unreasonable prejudice' mean? Clearly, the word 'unreasonable' indicates that some level or degree of prejudice is justified. For example, while a country might exempt the making of a small number of private copies entirely, it may be required to impose a compensation scheme, such as a levy, when the prejudice level becomes unjustified. To buttress this view, the French version of the Berne Convention, which governs in case of a discrepancy, uses the expression *'préjudice injustifié'*, which one would translate literally as 'unjustified prejudice'. The Convention translators opted instead for 'not unreasonable'. The inclusion of a reasonableness/justifiability criterion would allow legislators to establish a balance between, on the one hand, the rights of authors and other copyright holders and the needs and interests of users, on the other. This seems even clearer when the French term ('unjustified') is used. In other words, there must be a public interest justification to limit copyright.

In that vein, the WTO panel concluded that 'prejudice to the legitimate interests of right holders reaches an unreasonable level if an exception or limitation causes or has the potential to cause an unreasonable loss of income to the copyright owner'.

A public interest imperative may lead a government to impose an exception to copyright that may translate into a loss of revenue for copyright holders. It can nonetheless be 'justified'. Courts could consider human rights (such as freedom of expression) as a guide to determining exceptions to the proper scope of exceptions to trademark rights, for instance.[20]

A strictly economic approach (not factoring in human rights) may be seen as limiting the scope of exceptions by removing a significant part of their normative footing. That said, such an approach may also be a limitation of the scope of rights (which, in turn, reduces the need for exceptions). Perhaps this was unintended, but by focusing on economic harm, the panel may have considerably expanded the scope of some exceptions: it is not the fact that a user obtains some value that is determinative, but rather the fact that a rights holder can show that it stands to lose actual value (revenue) – the 'prejudice'. Exceptions to copyright are seen through a trade-related effects-based prism. By contrast, if the intellectual property and human rights learn to live together, as the title of this chapter in this and the previous edition of this book suggested, then both rights and exceptions can be infused and informed by human rights purposes, as in Article 27 UDHR which is discussed in the next section.[21] This has in fact arguably been done by the European Court of Human Rights in both a trademark case[22] and arguably at least also in a copyright case.[23] The situation in respect of patents may be somewhat different.[24] This dualist view is also reflected in some of the work done at WIPO, the WHO, and the tripartite collaboration between these two intergovernmental organizations and the WTO.[25]

---

20. *See* Lisa P. Ramsey, 'Free Speech and International Obligations to Protect Trademarks', Yale Journal of International Law, 35 (2010): 405, at 441.
21. *See* Hans Morten Haugen, 'Access Versus Incentives: Analysing Intellectual Property Policies in Four UN Specialized Agencies by Emphasizing the Role of the World Intellectual Property Organization and Human Rights', Journal of World Intellectual Property 13, no. 6 (2010): 697-728; and Martin Skladany, 'The Revolutionary Influence of Low Enlightenment: Weakening Copyright in Developing Countries to Improve Respect for Human Rights and the Rule of Law', Journal of the Patent and Trademark Office Society 95 (2013): 285.
22. *Anheuser Busch v. Portugal*, App. No. 73049/01, 45 *Eur. H.R. Rep.* 36 [830] (Grand Chamber 2007). For a discussion, *see* Laurence Helfer, 'The New Innovation Frontier – Intellectual Property and the European Court of Human Rights', Harvard International Law Journal 49 (2008): 3.
23. *Dima v. Romania*, App. No. 58472/00 (2005).
24. *See* Rochelle C. Dreyfuss, 'Patents and Human Rights: Where Is the Paradox', in W Grosheide (ed.) *Intellectual Property & Human Rights: A Paradox* (E Elgar, 2010), at 81.
25. The tripartite collaboration led to the publication of a joint study. *See* WIPO, 'WHO, WIPO, WTO Trilateral Cooperation on Public Health, IP and Trade', available at http://www.wipo.int/policy/en/global_health/trilateral_cooperation.html, accessed 6 October 2014. *See also* Kaitlin Mara & James Leonard (2009), 'Experts Aim to Balance Intellectual Property Rights and Human Rights', *Intellectual Property Watch*, available at http://www.ip-watch.org/2009/05/15/experts-aim-to-balance-intellectual-property-rights-and-human-rights/, accessed 6 October 2014.

1.2.2.4 European 'InfoSoc' Directive

The European Union's Information Society ('InfoSoc') Directive[26] contains two sets of exceptions. The first, and an only mandatory, exception is for transient copies 'forming an integral and essential part of a technological process'.[27] Otherwise, the Directive contains an exhaustive list of permitted exceptions (i.e., exceptions that European Union (EU) Member States may choose to use in their national copyright legislation). These are all purpose-specific exceptions. There is no set of criteria comparable to the US fair use doctrine.

However, the preamble to this Directive, which serves as a guideline for the interpretation of the operative part of the text, refers to permitting 'exceptions or limitations in the public interest for the purpose of education and teaching' and to the need to safeguard a 'fair balance of rights and interests between the different categories of rights holders, as well as between the different categories of rights holders and users' through exceptions and limitations, which 'have to be reassessed in the light of the new electronic environment'. Otherwise, the Directive refers to the three-step test as an overarching test for all permitted exceptions. Article 5(5) reads:

> The exceptions and limitations provided for in paragraphs 1, 2, 3 and 4 shall only be applied in certain special cases which do not conflict with a normal exploitation of the work or other subject matter and do not unreasonably prejudice the legitimate interests of the right holder.[28]

Interestingly, the reference to the test is seen as a 'guiding principle' rather than a means to effectively harmonize exceptions in the national laws of the twenty-five EU Member States. Indeed, at the level of national laws, the three-step test could be refined by enumerating certain specific cases, or by providing additional guidance on the interpretation of the three steps. It remains a flexible test which could, however, be used by courts in cases where no such specific exception exists, if allowed to do so under domestic law.

1.2.3 EXCLUSION OF MORAL RIGHTS

Article 9 of the TRIPS Agreement incorporates most of the substantive provisions of the Berne Convention (Paris Act, 1971) administered by the WIPO into TRIPS, though it also states that WTO 'Members shall not have

---

26. Directive 2001/29/EC of the European Parliament and of the Council of 22 May 2001 on the harmonization of certain aspects of copyright and related rights in the information society. OJ L 167/10, 22 June 2001).
27. *Ibid.*, Article 5(1).
28. *Ibid.*

rights or obligations under this Agreement in respect of the rights conferred under Article 6*bis* of that Convention or of the rights derived therefrom'. In other words, the moral right to claim authorship (or to remain anonymous) and the right to 'object to any distortion, mutilation or other modification of, or other derogatory action in relation to [a protected] work, which would be prejudicial to [the author's] honour or reputation' are excluded from TRIPS.

By excluding moral rights, the TRIPS Agreement split the copyright coin. One can adhere to a rather simplistic notion of moral rights (as implemented in common law jurisdictions) as a foreign, Continental, Kantian concept imposed on reluctant common law countries. Or one might see moral rights as forming a part of common law copyright – at least with respect to the right to claim authorship and the right to prevent first publication, which may conceptually be linked to a reputation-based right such as the right to oppose mutilation of a creative work. In either case, it seems fair to conclude that by removing the non-economic component from its normative frame-work, TRIPS has weakened the intrinsic equilibrium of copyright and, hence, the 'power to convince', rooted in natural law, which copyright had traditionally enjoyed. In other words, copyright is seen as a purely statutory entitlement enforced through trade rules, one set of rights, among many others, one designed to allow for limited market control.

Human rights and intellectual property were natural law cousins owing to their shared filiation with equity. Market optimization is not part of that family. Consequently, the policy debate has become not one of fairness to authors but rather of how much money it is fair for those companies (not authors) to make. This may explain part of the resistance of various user groups to copyright rules and their insistence that music or videos are too expensive, and the related, if generally intuitive, the perception that copyright works are public goods.

Because copyright claims were transplanted in the soil of trade, natural rights-based views – and with them, many of the perceived fairness – of copyright are no longer convincing. For user groups and developing countries implementing TRIPS and TRIPS Plus rules, it has become a numbers game, not one where players can defend a position strictly based on the propertization of creative works.

Nor can ethics guide us in a context of aggressive commercial exploitation: 'because of the breakdown of traditional social structure or matrix of social practices within which ethical questions have either been resolved or lack a motivation'.[29] In fact, social norms may be moving away from the industry control rhetoric and may give rise to other compensation.[30]

---

29. Mark Alfino (year, etc.), 'Intellectual Property and Copyright Ethics', http://guweb2.gonzaga.edu/faculty/alfino/dossier/Papers/COPYRIGH.htm (last accessed 6 October 2014), 10.
30. Daniel Gervais, 'The Price of Social Norms: Towards A Liability Regime for File-Sharing', Journal of Intellectual Property Law 12 (2004): 39.

The social norms do not reflect an understanding of downloading as *malum in se*, as a natural rights justification would suggest, but rather as a (sometimes annoying) *malum prohibitum*, and a prohibition that should be revisited (if not the norm itself then the way it is used and enforced). The lower level of internalization of the rule means that a higher degree of technical control or legal enforcement is required, i.e., exactly what can be observed in the marketplace.

Perhaps some forms of intellectual property that trace their origins to natural law can make claims to human rights status on that basis. It will not be at a greatly detailed level.[31] Yet, quite independently of where one draws the line of what constitutes a human right, the fact that trade rules do not qualify as human rights is beyond cavil. There is a cost to be paid in choosing a trade. To use rather loosely a Rawlsian analytical framework, one loses deontological pull. Perhaps this can be tied to the loosening of social norms concerning the use of copyright material.

Put differently, the trade link and the pragmatic nature of trade rules, and their enforcement in the WTO context, have forced copyright holders to find a new exposition of the principles according to which their investment should be protected, in what circumstances and to what extent. The term, scope (or rights and exceptions) and rights management are all on the Holmesian table set by the incorporation of copyright in trade. 'This is the age of the finance minister … The game of nations is now geo-monopoly.'[32] Copyright policy is not, or no longer, an exception. Whether that is for the best remains to be seen.

1.3	COPYRIGHT'S INTERNAL BALANCE IN THE MIRROR OF HUMAN RIGHTS

The ship of copyright policy is anchored more than ever in utilitarian waters now that it has jettisoned its property/natural law lineage by moving to the trade realm. Economic analysis is the sextant that can ensure that it avoids the Charybdis of rent-seeking and the Scylla of free-riding. A unified theory of copyright to navigate those shoals, one that applies to paintings, academic books, Harry Potter, Radiohead, and Windows Vista might seem somewhat murky to the purist. But, after all, this is the world of trade law, one in which bananas have been traded for educational services.

The point of this section is not to challenge the search for a justificatory theory.[33] Rather, in seeming contradistinction with section 1.1, it challenges

---

31. Costas Douzinas, *The End of Human Rights* (2000), at 7.
32. Thomas L. Friedman, quoted in John H. Jackson, *The World Trading System: Law and Policy of International Economic Relations* (MIT Press, 2nd ed., 1997), 4.
33. Indeed, it may very well that a federation of theories is a better outcome, one that recognizes the characteristics of each type of work. That being said, the search for a

15

the assumption that economic analysis must be the only toolbox and suggests that a cogent copyright theory can be based at least in part on a human rights analysis. It may also provide a more solid foundation because 'in generating rights to intellectual property on utilitarian grounds we are left with something decidedly less than what we typically mean when we say someone has a right'.[34]

Copyright could be defended on one of two bases as a human right. First, because it is seen as property and property in turn seen as a human right. This debate, as mentioned in the introduction, is beyond the reach of this chapter, though I return it briefly below.[35] There are, of course, questions as to the extent to which that human right protects private.[36] Even if one believes that internationally protected human rights include broad private property rights, the extent to which policy outcomes may be derived from such a finding is limited. For that reason, the issue is better left aside.

The other human right basis for copyright is, as René Cassin noted, '[h]uman beings can claim rights by the fact of their creation.'[37] The thesis explored in this part is thus that copyright should embrace the challenges posed by its deepening linkages with human rights and affirm its own (credible) justifications in human rights theory based on the creativity of authors and the universal cultural resonance of that role. In doing so, copyright might serve to show that intellectual property and human rights may indeed live together. This part also suggests that human rights principles and analogies are able to provide normative boundaries to the age-old quest for intrinsic equilibrium in copyright policy: the protection of interests resulting from expressed creativity, on the one hand, and the right to enjoy and share the arts and scientific advancement. In section 1.4, I will suggest that this analysis can inform the newer, extrinsic equilibria that are emerging in the world of intellectual property, namely the normative balance between intellectual property rights, on the hand, and other rights such as privacy and consumer protection, on the other.

---

theory may reveal with greater clarity the policy purpose of copyright and inform courts in (necessarily) case-by-case determinations. For example, a proper theoretical grounding might allow a court better to craft the proper scope of fair dealing or fair use in terms of societal outcomes: if fair use and fair dealing are designed to allow uses that maximize social welfare while not impeding normal commercial exploitation, a limit reminiscent of the omnipresent three-step test, then surely parody and transformative reuses should be allowed.

34. Adam D. Moore, *Intellectual Property & Information Control* (Transaction Publishers, 2001), 104.

35. *See infra* nn 43-44 and accompanying text.

36. Many non-Western legal systems recognize collective property in certain intangible creations. *See* Daniel Gervais, 'Spiritual but Not Intellectual? The Protection of Sacred Intangible Traditional Knowledge', Cardozo Journal of International & Comparative Law 11 (2003): 467-495.

37. Quoted in M. Vivant, *supra*, at 86.

The purpose of this exercise is not to dethrone economic analysis. After all, now that intellectual property lives in the house of trade law, it may not be possible to do so. Yet, in the very spirit of law and economics, it may be useful to question the *monopoly* of economic analysis on the theoretical discourse surrounding the foundations and evolution of copyright policy.

Article 27 UDHR, which saw the light of day 238 years after the *Statute of Anne*, is an interesting mirror for copyright's sleeping beauty, namely a solid justificatory theory beyond the practicalities of trade. Article 27 protects *both* the right to the protection of the moral and material interests resulting from and scientific, literary or artistic production of which he is the author *and* users' right to participate freely in the cultural life of the community, and to enjoy the arts and to share in scientific advancement and its benefits.[38] The objective of protection embraces at least indirectly the moral desert theory (protection of interests resulting from scientific, literary, or artistic production), while the objective of access is expressed teleologically as a tool to allow everyone to enjoy the arts and to share in scientific advancement and its benefits. By giving a purpose to exceptions, human rights may both serve as guidance to courts[39] and compensate for the excessively economic focus of trade law, as embodied in particular in the three-step test interpreted by a trade body, namely the WTO Dispute-Settlement Body.[40] It is interesting to recall François Dessemontet's words: '[T]he Universal Declaration and the UN Covenant [on Economic, Social and Cultural Rights adopted on 16 December 1966] mark the apex of the French vision of literary and artistic property, as opposed to the Anglo-American "mercantilist" view as ensconced in the TRIPS.'[41]

Indeed, human rights may compensate for an evolution (of copyright policy) that has not always been well thought through. As Peter Drahos aptly noted:

> The development of intellectual property policy and the law has been dominated by an epistemic community comprised largely of technically minded lawyers. In their hands, intellectual property has grown into a highly differentiated and complex system of rules. The development of

---

38. *See* Lea Shaver, 'The Right to Science and Culture', Wisconsin Law Review 2010 (2010): 121-184.
39. Daniel Gervais, 'The Role of International Treaties in the Interpretation of Canadian Intellectual Property Statutes', in O. Fitzgerald (ed.) *The Globalized Rule of Law: Relationships Between International and Domestic Law* (Irwin Law, 2006), 549-572.
40. United States – section 110(5) of the US Copyright Act, Document WTR/DS/160/R (WTO Dispute-Settlement Panel, 2000). *See* Jane C. Ginsburg, 'Toward Supranational Copyright Law? The WTO Panel Decision and the "Three-Step Test" for Copyright Exemptions', Revue internationale du droit d'auteur (RIDA) 187 (2001): 3.
41. François Dessemontet, 'Copyright and Human Rights', in Jan J.C. Kabel (ed.) *Intellectual Property and Information Law* (Kluwer Law, 1998), 113 at 114.

these systems has been influenced in important ways by the narrow and often unarticulated professional values of this particular group.[42]

Human rights approaches bring *values* back to the system. The emphasis on culture in human rights instruments, allow one, for example, to acknowledge the limits of economic analysis and theory as a policy-making machine. As Professor Julie Cohen suggests, we need a substantive balance, which concerns the ways in which copyright's goal of creating economic fixity must accommodate its mission to foster cultural play. Economic analysis can help us to understand some of the considerations relevant to the balance between economic fixity and cultural mobility, but both valuation and incommensurability problems prevent a comprehensive summing of the relevant costs and benefits. Modelling the benefits of artistic and intellectual flux is hard to do.[43] The copyright's 'mission to foster cultural play' may be read against the backdrop of Articles 27(1) UDHR and 15 of the Covenant, which enshrines the right to participate in cultural life. 'Cultural life must be regarded as a benefit to which every member of the community is entitled. Culture must not be viewed as an esoteric activity of a superior social elite.'[44]

Economic analysis is both useful and necessary and follows quite naturally from the shift to trade, but any complete analysis must be informed by broader, less tangible (and measurable) considerations. From copyright's viewpoint, culture is a two-way street: it provides the essential substratum upon which all creators draw to create, and their creations in turn feed and grow the culture. The phenomenon has taken on an additional layer of complexity with the globalization of Web culture, but a lot of cultural resonance remains local. 'Individual creators begin with situatedness and work through culture to arrive at the unexpected.'[45]

Copyright and culture need new works to be created, though for different reasons (the former to justify its existence, the latter to grow), and to be created, those new works need existing works. Conceptually, this can be framed as a 'freedom to create', which, to a certain extent at least, is the freedom to copy. Whether *copying* constitutes copyright *infringement* is a matter of degree. Professor Dessemontet suggested a list of factors to be taken into account: (a) whether the work copied from fades away in the new work; (b) whether the first work is recognizable and the degree to which it

42. Peter Drahos, 'The Universality of Intellectual Property Rights: Origins and Development', in *Intellectual Property and Human Rights* (WIPO, 1998), 10, available at http://www.wipo.int/edocs/mdocs/tk/en/wipo_unhchr_ip_pnl_98/wipo_unhchr_ip_pnl_98_1.pdf (last accessed 6 October 2014).
43. Julie Cohen, 'Creativity and Culture in Copyright Theory', U.C. Davis Law Review 40 (2007): 1151, 1196.
44. Yoram Dinstein, 'Cultural Rights', Israel Yearbook on Human Rights 9 (1979): 58, 76.
45. J. Cohen, *supra*, at 1183.

is; and (c) the proportionality of 'newness' (presumably assessed quantitatively but also, and perhaps mostly, qualitatively) to the amount that is borrowed.[46]

How can one reconcile human rights and natural law, the new and old sources of legitimacy for intellectual property? Is the question whether copyright is an instrument for stimulating creativity or property-like Lockean protection against the illicit appropriation of the work done and the investment made? Not quite. Let us remember that John Locke did not advocate a particular model for copyright.[47] He believed, to summarize his thought in a few words, that nothing in nature permitted the granting of a particular property right to a particular person. According to Locke, divine power imposed moral duties on each individual that could be discerned by reason, and this was what should guide the work of judges. Those duties are, in general, reciprocal: what I owe to others, they owe to me in return. Locke placed these duties in two categories: those dealing with liberty and those giving the right to make claims. One of the four great duties he describes was the duty not to impede others from profiting from what they have created or adapted from the public domain through their own efforts.[48] In other words, translated in Pareto-optimal terminology, the 'underlying rationale of Locke's proviso is that if no one's situation is worsened, then no one can complain about another individual appropriating part of the commons'.[49] That is the premise used to justify copyright: a new work after all is created from the 'public domain' – therefore from ideas and existing works. The rights are derived from intellectual efforts by sovereign moral agents, warranting non-interference claims.[50] This is indeed close to the rights flowing from the creative process recognized in international human rights instruments.

Natural law, as described by Locke, thus offers an interesting perspective, one that *can* be reconciled with an exegesis of Article 27 UDHR and Article 15 of the Covenant, and more recent instruments discussed by Professor Torremans, Professor Yu and Professor Helfer in their respective chapters. Human rights can, first and foremost, restore a degree of authorial dignity to copyright. '[H]uman beings have fundamental interests, which should not be sacrificed for public benefit, and ... society's well-being does

---

46. F. Dessemontet, *supra,* at 119-120.
47. Wendy Gordon, 'A Property Right in Self-Expression: Equality and Individualism in the Natural Law of Intellectual Property', Yale Law Journal 102 (1993): 1533. To return to the source, *see* John Locke, ed. Peter Laslett (Cambridge University Press, 2nd ed., 1967), 269-278 (vol. II, paras 4-15).
48. W. Gordon, *supra,* at 1542-1543.
49. A.M. Moore, *supra,* at 109.
50. *Ibid.,* 108.

not override those interests. Protecting those interests is deemed vital for maintaining individual autonomy, independence, and security.'[51]

Protection of copyright in the human rights framework can also be sourced in the continuum between an author and her creation. That is the basis in French and German doctrine,[52] for the moral right. One could perhaps consider that the prohibition contained in Article 12 of the WCT and Article 19 of the WPPT not to remove or alter Rights Management Information (RMI) can be justified on a similar basis, namely on the grounds that it identifies the author even after the transfer of economic rights.

It is essential to note, however, that this unbreakable link between author and work does not justify a perpetual *property* right or right to exclude all economically relevant uses. The fact that works fall into the public domain has consistently formed part of the human rights discourse concerning authors' rights since 1948.[53] True, it has been critiqued as a Western conception of authorship, rooted in individually authored, well-identified creations.[54] However, I would argue that the relevant human rights instruments do not embody this limited conception and could be extended to cover other forms of creation, thus adapting the extant intellectual framework to collective or traditional creations and inventions.[55]

I am not suggesting staking a vague claim to specific rights on dignity, but refocusing the policy efforts to operationalize the (supposed) value attached to the creation in the traditional conceptual edifice of copyright, recognizing that copyright works (arguably with the huge exception of software)[56] have a special status because of their cultural resonance.

Put differently, the trade-economic approach refocused copyright on the industries that produce and distribute copyright content. From a purely

---

51. Orit Fischman Afori, 'Human Rights and Copyright: The Introduction of Natural Law Considerations into American Copyright Law', Fordham Intellectual Property Media & Entertainment Law Journal 14 (2004): 497, 499.
52. Immanuel Kant, *Metaphysics of Morals, Doctrine of Right* (Cambridge University Press, 1996), § 31, II; Georg Wilhelm Fredrich Hegel, *Elements of the Philosophy of Right* (Cambridge University Press, 1991), §§ 43 and 69.
53. M. Vivant, *supra*, at 91-92.
54. *See* Alpana Roy, 'Intellectual Property Rights: A Western Tale', Asia Pacific Law Review 16 (2008): 219.
55. *See* Silke von Lewinski, *Indigenous Heritage and Intellectual Property* (Kluwer, 2003); and WIPO, Draft Articles on the Protection of Traditional cultural expressions, 22 January 2014, document WIPO/GRTKF/IC/27/5.
56. It was decided, first by the courts and then by many legislative bodies, that computer software should be considered literary works, an international consensus now reflected in Article 10.1 of the TRIPS Agreement. The entry of software in the house of copyright was to have major practical repercussions, but one must acknowledge that the conceptual shock was enormous, since it brought into the copyright family works created without any claim to artistic or aesthetic merit but rather on a purely functional basis. Another conceptual leap caused by the admission en masse of software was that the work being protected (i.e., the code) was not designed to be perceived by anyone. Its role was to make a computer function.

policy-oriented perspective, this 'de-centring' of copyright away from creators reduces the moral imperative of users, whose sympathy for large distribution multinationals (assuming for the sake of this discussion that this is a widespread perception of how the music and film industry are structured) is far from infinite. Conversely, copyright perceived as a right vested in and benefiting creators may have a different resonance, as the relative success of examples of 'pay as much as you feel this is worth' models tend to show. Industries that were quick to instrumentalize authors in the eighteenth century, with some benefit to creators, have lost much in moving to the trade arena and side lining creators. Phenomenologically, this was greatly reinforced by the introduction in international treaties and now many national laws of protection of Technological Protection Measures (TPMs), the use and/or circumvention of which is illegal in most cases independently of the underlying copyright. TPMs are rarely used by creators. It is an industrial tool, and its protection is generally viewed as such, thus further diminishing the perceived legitimacy of the copyright system.

Human rights, in providing a teleological framework for exceptions, can also guide courts[57] in interpreting whether a particular use should be covered by an exception whose interpretation is unclear, and policymakers in designing new exceptions. One might think this impossible owing to the presence of a three-step test straitjacket. However, the third step was interpreted as allowing public interest considerations (i.e., what constitutes an allowable 'justification' for the exception), and human rights principles might thus inform the determination of the proper scope of exceptions. In that respect, the UDHR, in particular, would allow exceptions that demonstrably augment access where such access (enjoyment) is not commercially reasonable or possible, and the right to reuse and thereby participate in the cultural life of the community. This seems to justify both consumptive use exceptions where commercial access is undesirable or impracticable, including exceptions such as those contained in the Appendix to the Berne Convention for access in developing countries, and exceptions for transformative uses (such as but not limited to parody), the principal element of the US fair use doctrine.[58]

The UDHR reference to moral and material interests is also fully consistent with the coin of traditional copyright, with its economic side and

---

57. As was done, e.g., by French courts. *See* JDI 1989, 1005 note Edelman; (1989) 143 RIDA 301, note Sirinelli).
58. Except, arguably, between *Sony Corp. of America v. Universal City Studios, Inc.*, 464 U.S. 417 (1984) and *Metro-Goldwyn-Mayer Studios Inc. v. Grokster, Ltd.*, 125 S. Ct. 2764 (2005). Sony was interpreted (wrongly in my view) as deciding broadly that private use was fair use (in fact, it says that some forms of time-shifting copying may be fair use). In Grokster, the Supreme Court arguably went back to traditional fair use jurisprudence and focused on transformative – instead of purely consumptive – uses.

its moral side. Copyright and human rights can indeed live together and learn from one another.[59]

1.4   INTELLECTUAL PROPERTY AND HUMAN RIGHTS: THE NEW CONFLICTS

A copyright holder who invades users' hard disks to search for unauthorized copies of music may run afoul of privacy laws.[60] Yet copies of the copyright content available for download will increasingly include codes to identify the purchaser of that copy, a tool to be used in the case that copy is later found circulating on the Internet. This information, whether expressed as full name, as a code or in the form of a hash or watermark, is protected by the WCT (WCT 1996) and WPPT (WPPT 1996), (and national implementations thereof), and cannot be removed or altered knowingly for the purpose of facilitating an infringement.

Copyright can live with human rights, and indeed reinforce its justification in human rights, but only if we can move the discourse away from property-based rhetoric, and treating any unpaid use as piracy. By moving away from the property, whether as a human right or as an economic tool, copyright can transcend this debate and find a new, balanced justification based on a human rights framework in which protection and access are seen as *complementary* objectives. The recognition that copyright is not 'ordinary' property led some scholars to argue that copyright was a 'hybrid property right'[61] or a 'transmuted right'.[62] There is a point where this type of debate may no longer provide a solid foundation for a justificatory theory for copyright that can withstand the need for detailed policy scrutiny and normative confrontations with other rights. From this perspective, the pragmatism of the three-step-test, infused with the human rights inspired the purposive approach to exceptions and limitations, could thus be seen as a significant step forward.

Can the same be said of patents? Patents are rights to prohibit even in the absence of a viable market. Would a refusal to make available a patented

---

59. It has also been suggested that copyright could be used as a model for human rights (i.e., the reverse analogical process). *See* John R. Morss & Mirko Bagaric, 'Human Rights as Copyrights: A Third Way in Human Rights Discourse', University of Baltimore Intellectual Property Journal, 13 (2005): 103.

60. *See* Bert-Jaap Koops, 'Law, Technology, and Shifting Power Relations', Berkeley Technology Law Journal 25 (2010): 973, at 1017-1018; and Mark H. Lyon, 'Technical Protection Measures for Digital Audio and Video: Learning from the Failure of Audio Compact Disc Protection', Santa Clara Computer & High Technology Law Journal 23 (2007): 643, 650-658.

61. C. Colombet, *Propri é t é litt é raire et artistique et droits voisin s* (Dalloz, 6th ed., 1992), § 20.

62. M. Vivant, *supra*, at 84.

product constitute only a potential abuse of patent rights, or is it also instead a violation of human rights? Here, denial of patented pharmaceuticals to patients who cannot afford them, when they, or their government, could afford those products at a generic rate (i.e., without patent rent) is confronted with the right to health and security. These are the new kinds of battles that are starting to emerge in our courts and in international discussions, in the WTO and elsewhere.

The battles with AIDS and public health activists advocating flexibility on behalf of developing countries has left scars on pharmaceutical companies, and impressions on public opinion. Their claims are based on the right to health and security, but also to the more controversial right to development.[63] Clearly, fighting not only human rights but spokespersons such as *Doctors without Borders* and Nelson Mandela against a backdrop of dying children to defend a 'trade-related' right was an unwinnable public relations battle, one which should never have been waged. An ethical, human rights approach to public health dictates limits on patent rights when no market is possible. No one is forcing patent holders to produce at or below cost.

At its most basic level, the argument is as follows: when the patent holder cannot reasonably hope to have a significant market in a territory for a product that has life-saving potential, there is no legitimate reason to prevent access to that product if someone (public or private entity) is willing to produce it at a cost that the country can afford. There are legitimate concerns on the part of patent holders about re-exportation, and those should be adequately addressed. It can be done, as the solution adopted by the WTO in amending TRIPS and adding Article 31*bis* demonstrates.

It must be stressed that the problem of HIV infection and other severe diseases affecting least-developed countries does not lie entirely with patents, far from it. In several African countries where patent protection would be available, antiretroviral drugs are not patented. Many others have until 2016 to adopt pharmaceutical patent protection under WTO rules.[64] Problems often lie elsewhere, such as in the absence of a capacity of production and the lack of distribution networks. The latter can be solved, though with colossal efforts, by setting up distribution mechanisms, local clinics, etc. Concerns about interrupted treatments and the possible emergence of more aggressive

---

63. Ruth Okediji, 'The Limits of Development Strategies at the Intersection of Intellectual Property and Human Rights', in D. Gervais (ed.) *Intellectual Property, Trade and Development* (Oxford University Press, 2007), 355-384; and Robert J. Gutowski, 'The Marriage of Intellectual Property and International Trade in the TRIPS Agreement: Strange Bedfellows or a Match Made in Heaven?', Buffalo Law Review 47 (1999): 713, 715.

64. Some commentators believe that this flexibility is 'merely academic' because many sub-Saharan countries comply with TRIPS even if they are under no obligation to do so. *See* Poku Adusei, 'Right to Health and Constitutional Imperatives for Regulating the Exercise of Pharmaceutical Patent Rights in Sub-Saharan Africa', African Journal of International and Comparative Law 21, no. 2 (2013): 250, at 262.

viruses must be taken seriously. The former problem required another series of solutions. One could reasonably suggest building public laboratories to produce antiretroviral, anti-malarial, or other drugs in each and every country where such products are needed. At the same time, no compulsory license could be issued predominantly for export under TRIPS Article 31 rules. This explains why this prohibition was waived, subject to a number of conditions in the new Article 31*bis*.

The ripple effect of the clash with human rights is far from over. The World Health Organization (WHO), for example, has actively entered the field and broadened the discussion to the entire financing of pharmaceutical research, questioning the predominance of private, profit-driven enterprises. There is indeed an enormous amount of publicly-funded research both in the US (e.g., the National Institutes of Health) and elsewhere, including in hundreds of universities worldwide. The recalcitrance of the pharmaceutical industry truly to engage may not be an optimal strategy.

Human rights also have a direct impact on the WTO itself. The WTO Appellate Body found that the WTO Agreement is 'is not to be read in clinical isolation from public international law'.[65] This principle was reflected in this and subsequent decision, which relied on the case law of other international tribunals, namely the International Court of Justice, the European Court of Human Rights cases, and the Inter-American Court of Human Rights, in interpreting the provisions of the WTO Agreement.[66] This could, of course, extend to TRIPS.

The panel report in the dispute concerning Australia's plain packaging of tobacco products offers a path for human rights to play a much greater role.[67] The panel put great emphasis on the fact that Australia invoked the guidelines to the Framework Convention on Tobacco Control (FCTC) to justify the adoption of measures that prohibited non-word marks entirely, and limited the use, format and size of word marks on cigarette packs.[68] This seemed to conflict with, *inter alia*, TRIPS Article 20 with provides that WTO Members cannot unjustifiably encumber the use of marks by special

---

65. US – Standards for Reformulated and Conventional Gasoline, WTO doc. WT/DS2/AB/R, para. III. B (Appellate Body, 1996).
66. *Supra* n. 36; and Japan – Taxes on Alcoholic Beverages, document WT/DS8/AB/R, part D, n. 19 Appellate Body, 1996).
67. *Australia – Certain Measures Concerning Trademarks, Geographical Indications and other Plain Packaging Requirements Applicable to Tobacco Products and Packaging*: Reports of the Panels, WTO document WT/DS435/R, WT/DS441/R, WT/DS458/R, WT/DS467/R (28 June 2018). This panel report was under appeal at the time of this writing.
68. World Health Organization, Framework Convention on Tobacco Control, Guidelines for Implementation of Article 11. The FCTC guidelines (though not the actual text of the FCTC) suggest that countries should 'consider adopting measures to restrict or prohibit the use of logos, colours, brand images or promotional information on packaging other than brand names and product names displayed in a standard colour and font style (plain packaging).' (para. 46).

requirements. While the panel reached the (fairly obvious) conclusion that the Australian measures were a prohibited encumbrance – and one the panel describes as extreme – it imposed on the complainants a burden to prove that such encumbrance was unjustified, noting that Australia's reliance on the guidelines provided a justificatory basis for their action despite somewhat shaky evidence about the efficacy of the measure.

The justification for this reliance by the panel of the guidelines might be (the panel does not make it entirely clear) that the FCTC has broad membership (181 parties as of this writing) – though it must be noted that three out of four of the Complainants at the WTO were not a party to the convention or had not yet ratified the Convention such that it did not apply to them, at least not fully.[69] Despite this, the panels took the Convention and its Guidelines on board with little, if any, discussion.[70] If FCTC *guidelines* are sufficient as a justification, then surely the main text of other key global instruments with near-universal membership, including the Framework Convention on Climate Change (FCCC), should also suffice.[71] The same might be said of human rights that have gained a board degree of acceptance.

Reliance by the Appellate Body on extrinsic (i.e., non-WTO negotiated) norms has thus far been limited to the application of well-accepted principles of international law, but the Australia panel report, if its findings are confirmed on appeal, will open the door much wider.[72] The traditional principle that another treaty should be used as a blueprint for the interpretation of, or to effect a reduction in the scope of the stated, negotiated obligations under, the TRIPS Agreement must be considered with utmost caution would thus be much weaker going forward.[73] This apparent shift was perhaps foreshadowed in the words of former WTO Director General, Pascal Lamy, at a conference on IP and global public policy issues:

---

69. I leave aside for now the somewhat complex issue of the effect of a signature not followed by a ratification.
70. The FCTC plays a central role in the panels' discussion of the Technical Barriers to Trade (TBT) arguments made by the Complainants, especially under Article 2.5 TBT. In the case of TRIPS and specifically Article 20 it seems accepted as the justification for the plain packaging measures. *See* Australia plain packaging report, n. 1, para. 7.2596.
71. The FCCC has 197 parties has of August 2019. *See* https://bit.ly/30MY9Tf (accessed 31 August 2019). Its Article 3(3), for example, provides that 'Parties should take precautionary measures to anticipate, prevent or minimize the causes of climate change and mitigate its adverse effects.'
72. *See* Susy Frankel, 'WTO Application of the "Customary Rules of Interpretation of Public International Law" to Intellectual Property', Virginia Journal of International Law 46, no. 2 (2005): 365-431.
73. *See ibid*; and Tatjana Eres, 'The Limits of GATT Article XX: A Back Door for Human Rights?', Georgetown Journal of International Law 35 (2004): 597-635, at 624-25.

The international intellectual property system cannot operate in isolation from broader public policy questions such as how to meet human needs as basic health, food and a clean environment.[74]

The tension between the right to health and IP is also visible in the joint work that the WTO has done in the area of public health with WIPO and the WHO. Together, they organized symposia on various aspects of public health and commissioned a joint study.[75] At a joint symposium in 2018, the Directors General of the three organizations pledged 'further cooperation on innovation and public health'.[76] Interestingly, at that symposium, the Director General of the WHO opined in his speech, echoing the WHO Constitution, that health was 'a *fundamental and universal human right*'.[77] Let us also recall that the 52nd World Health Assembly (WHA) – the Governing Body of the WHO – directed the WHO secretariat to monitor 'the impact of the TRIPS Agreement and other trade agreements and to help member states develop adequate health policies to, if necessary, mitigate the negative impact of trade agreements.'[78]

The question that remains is whether the tension that exists between patents and human rights can be effectively bottled up by (potentially major) adjustments to the interpretation of the TRIPS Agreement by the Dispute-Settlement Body and ongoing collaborative work between the WTO and the WHO.

1.5   CONCLUSION

Section 1.2 of this chapter explored the noble lineage of the intellectual property back to its natural law origins, and how an important group of IP rights holders was abandoned when they put their policy eggs in the trade

---

74. Pascal Lamy, Speech at the WIPO Conference on Intellectual Property and Public Policy Issues, Geneva, 14 July 2009, available at http://www.wipo.int/meetings/en/2009/ip_gc_ge/presentations/lamy.html, accessed 24 September 2014.
75. WHO-WIPO-WTO Technical Symposium on Sustainable Development Goals: Innovative Technologies to Promote Healthy Lives and Well-being: Summary of the Key Issues (WIPO, 2018); WHO, WIPO, WTO Joint Technical Symposium on Antimicrobial Resistance: How to Foster Innovation, Access and Appropriate Use of Antibiotics? (WIPO Publication WIPO/PUB/GC/13, 2017); Public Health, Intellectual Property, and TRIPS at 20: Innovation and Access to Medicines; Learning from the Past, Illuminating the Future (WIPO, 2015); and Promoting Access to Medical Technologies and Innovation – Intersections between Public Health, Intellectual Property and Trade (WIPO, WIPO/PUB/628, 2013).
76. WIPO, WHO and WTO Directors General Pledge Further Cooperation on Innovation and Public Health February 27, 2018, available at https://www.wipo.int/portal/en/news/2018/article_0003.html.
77. *Id.*
78. WHA, Resolution: WHA56.27: Intellectual property rights, innovation and public health (28 May 2003).

basket. It did so to obtain multilateral concessions that would likely not have been possible absent intersectoral bargaining. It incorporated all existing intellectual property norms essentially into trade rules, and a test, based on economic effects, was used as a filter for almost all exceptions to patent and copyright rights. By doing so, however, intellectual property holders left behind some of the doctrinal armour that could support its normative clashes with human rights. The move to trade also signifies a less persuasive reliance on property rhetoric, independently of whether the property is seen as a human right.

Section 1.3 suggested that copyright can reclaim its lost heritage, or develop a new normative framework, in keeping with its purpose of defending authorial dignity, by embracing the internal balance between protection of interests following from the production of new copyright works and the need to ensure adequate access and reuse of such works, especially in the absence of reasonable market conditions. In fact, the traditional balance between exclusive rights, on the one hand, and limitations and exceptions on the other, mirrors this dual objective of human rights legislation. In spite of occasional conflicts with free expression, for example, copyright and human rights share broadly similar objectives. This may not be true, however, of newer rights such as the protection of TPMs and RMI, which pull copyright policy further away from creators and may clash with privacy rights.

Section 1.4 explored whether a similarly harmonious solution may exist for extrinsic conflicts, those that do not affect the internal balance of the intellectual property (between protection and exceptions) but where exclusive protection clashes with a different set of norms. Courts may be able to address TPM or RMI, uses that infringe privacy, though the absence of a single set of privacy norms may lead to a variable geometry of national solutions. Then again, the pendulum could swing in the other direction in making it possible for human rights and well-calibrated para copyright measures to cohabit. For example, because it identifies the author (even if he or she is no longer the owner of the economic rights in the work), limited RMI protection could be justified under a human rights analysis using arguments similar to those justifying the moral right of attribution.[79]

Copyright more generally can be recast as the freedom to express oneself, to create, a (potentially perpetual) right (derived from the act of creation and authorial dignity) to be identified as the author (individual or collective) of a creation, and a limited economic entitlement to benefit materially from such creation. It is balanced against the freedom to participate in cultural life and rights to access information, to protect one's privacy and other such rights. Thus, a human rights framework can provide

---

79. See Daniel Gervais, 'The Right of attribution in literary works in three Acts, by W. Shakespeare', Vanderbilt Journal of Technology and Entertainment Law 22:1 (2019)39-70.

specific normative guidance in the elaboration and interpretation of copyright rules. This reasoning may be extended, though it has not traditionally been, to patents and other intellectual property rights, which, like copyright, are in search of a normative anchor as a result of moving into the trade realm and abandoning a (not very useful except as rhetorical tool) property status.

Patents on pharmaceuticals seem a harder case. In spite of agreeing to a solution in the WTO to allow compulsory licensing for export under strict conditions, important parts of the pharmaceutical industry are still trying to limit the use of export licenses. The great reluctance of the industry truly to engage has had several effects, including a significant involvement by the WHO. The response of the industry and a number of governments thus far, as illustrated by free trade agreements and recent multilateral efforts outside of WTO and WIPO, points to additional trade-enforced restrictions on existing flexibilities that would be successful in maintaining maximum protection and limiting access to products to be sold by the patent holder, but at a potentially high human and ethical cost. This seems like suboptimal cohabitation.

A note of caution must be added before we can end the analysis, however. As noted above, the way in which human rights affect intellectual property is a two-way street, as, for example, the conflict between the right to property (protection) and the right to health may clash in the area of pharmaceutical patents. As Professor Okediji noted, 'human rights framework for IP does not ineluctably facilitate socially desirable outcomes for all countries; slapping human rights ideals on IP regimes can, instead, actually strengthen IP rights in socially harmful ways.'[80] The individualistic nature of several human rights may actually make it harder to balance social welfare objectives and identify excessive or abusive use of IP rights. It may be that '[p]rogress toward attaining the highest levels of human flourishing will require novel approaches in the IP *and* in the human rights legal space'.[81] Still, human rights add analytical depth to the policy analysis by putting non-economic considerations, including human and cultural development, to the fore.

---

80. Ruth L. Okediji, 'Does Intellectual Property Need Human Rights', 51 New York University Journal of International Law and Politics 51 (2018): 1, at 4.
81. *Ibid.*, at 67 (emphasis in original).

Chapter 2

The New Innovation Frontier Revisited: Intellectual Property and the European Court of Human Rights

Laurence R. Helfer[*]

This chapter provides a comprehensive analysis of the intellectual property case law of the European Court of Human Rights ("ECHR"). Since the mid-2000s, the ECHR has issued several rulings applying the right of property protected by the European Convention on Human Rights to various types of intellectual property. These decisions, which view intellectual property through the lens of fundamental rights, have important consequences for the region's innovation and creativity policies. The cases are also emblematic of other controversies in domestic and international law over the intersection of human rights, property rights, and intellectual property. The chapter analyzes these trends, focusing on ECHR decisions through August 2019. The chapter develops three distinct paradigms to identify the proper place of intellectual property in the European human rights system. It concludes that the ECHR should find a violation of the right of property in intellectual property disputes only in cases of arbitrary government conduct.

---

[*] An earlier version of this chapter was published in 2008 as an article in the *Harvard International Law Journal*, volume 48, page 1-52. This revised chapter includes a discussion of European Court of Human Rights decisions relating to intellectual property issued through August 2019.

Chapter 2

2.1 INTRODUCTION

In Europe, human rights law is intellectual property's new frontier. This statement will no doubt surprise many observers of the region's intellectual property system, which has steadily expanded over the past few decades. The mechanisms of that expansion have included a litany of now familiar legal and regulatory tools—the negotiation and ratification of multilateral agreements, the promulgation of European Community ("EC") directives, the rulings of the powerful European Court of Justice, and the revision of national laws and administrative regulations. The result of these cumulative and interrelated initiatives is a highly developed intellectual property system that is strongly protective of creators, innovators, and businesses.

This regional intellectual property regime has developed in relative isolation from Europe's other judicial powerhouse, the European Court of Human Rights ("ECHR" or "Court").[1] The ECHR began its existence modestly as an optional judicial review mechanism for European states that had ratified the Convention for the Protection of Human Rights and Fundamental Freedoms[2] ("European Convention" or "Convention") and its Protocols. But in the half century since its creation, the ECHR has evolved into something far more momentous—the judicial guardian of a "constitutional instrument of European public order."[3] The Court now reviews tens of thousands of complaints each year, and its jurisdiction extends the length and breadth of the continent, encompassing 800 million people in forty-seven nations from Azerbaijan to Iceland and from Portugal to Russia.[4]

One might reasonably ask what an international human rights court and the human rights treaty it interprets has to do with intellectual property. The answer is the right of property, which appears in the European Convention together with more widely recognized civil and political liberties such as the prohibitions of slavery and torture, due process rights, and freedom of expression. Yet the protection of "the peaceful enjoyment of … possessions" in Article 1 of Protocol 1 ("Article 1")[5] has long been considered among the

---

1. For a detailed discussion of the ECHR's success and its influence on other international tribunals, *see* Laurence R. Helfer & Anne-Marie Slaughter, *Why States Create International Tribunals: A Response to Professors Posner and Yoo*, 93 Cal. L. Rev. 899, 917-22 (2005); Laurence R. Helfer, *Adjudicating Copyright Claims Under the TRIPs Agreement: The Case for a European Human Rights Analogy*, 39 Harv. Int'l L.J. 357, 399-410 (1998) [hereinafter Helfer, *Adjudicating Copyright Claims*]; Laurence R. Helfer & Anne-Marie Slaughter, *Toward a Theory of Effective Supranational Adjudication*, 107 Yale L.J. 273, 297-98 (1997).
2. Convention for the Protection of Human Rights and Fundamental Freedoms, November 4, 1950, 213 U.N.T.S. 222 [hereinafter European Convention].
3. *Loizidou v. Turkey*, App. No. 15318/89, 310 Eur. Ct. H.R. (ser. A) at 27 (1995) (preliminary objections).
4. *See* ECHR, Survey of Activities 2006, http://www.echr.coe.int/NR/rdonlyres/69564084-9825-430B-9150-A9137DD22737/0 /Survey_2006.pdf.
5. Article 1 of Protocol 1 states in its entirety:

weakest rights in the Convention system, affording government's broad discretion to regulate private property in the public interest.[6]

Partly for this reason, the ECHR and the European Commission of Human Rights ("European Commission" or "Commission") for decades gave intellectual property issues a wide berth. Intellectual property claimants did not file any complaints alleging violations of property rights until the early 1990s. And when these claimants did allege such violations, the ECHR and the European Commission summarily dismissed their challenges. Applying a restrictive interpretation of Article 1, the two tribunals eschewed searching scrutiny of national courts and administrative agencies and allowed Europe's intellectual property system to evolve largely unfettered by human rights concerns.[7]

This judicial reticence has now decisively ended. In the mid-2000s, the ECHR issued several important decisions holding that patents, trademarks, copyrights, and other economic interests in intangible knowledge goods are protected by the European Convention's right of property.[8] The 2007

Every natural or legal person is entitled to the peaceful enjoyment of his possessions. No one shall be deprived of his possessions except in the public interest and subject to the conditions provided for by law and by the general principles of international law.

The preceding provisions shall not, however, in any way impair the right of a State to enforce such laws as it deems necessary to control the use of property in accordance with the general interest or to secure the payment of taxes or other contributions or penalties.

Protocol to the Convention for the Protection of Human Rights and Fundamental Freedoms Article 1, March 20, 1952, 213 U.N.T.S. 262, [hereinafter Protocol 1]. Although the drafters of Article 1 "spoke of 'right of property' or 'right to property' to describe the subject-matter" protected by this clause, *Marckx v. Belgium,* App. No. 6833/74, 31 Eur. Ct. H.R. (ser. A), ¶ 63 (1979), the ECHR has consistently described this provision as guaranteeing the right of property. *See,* e.g., *Hutten-Czapska v. Poland*, App. No. 35014/97, 45 Eur. H.R. Rep. 4 [52], 129 (Grand Chamber 2007) (judgment of June 19, 2006) (holding that government had "failed to strike the requisite fair balance between the general interests of the community and the protection of the *right of property*.") (emphasis added) [Due to a change in 2000, recent volumes of the European Human Rights Report do not use standard citation formats for cases. For the reader's convenience, the Report's citation is given, along with the more traditional starting page number in brackets afterward.].

6. *See* Arjen van Rijn, *Right to the Peaceful Enjoyment of One's Possessions, in* THEORY AND PRACTICE OF THE EUROPEAN CONVENTION ON HUMAN RIGHTS 863, 864 (Pieter van Dijk et al. eds., 4th ed. 2006) ("[T]he right of property has lost a good deal of its inviolability, also in the Member States of the Council of Europe, under the influence of modern social policy (*Sozialstaat*). This fact is reflected in the very far-reaching limitations which Article 1 allows.").

7. *See infra* section 2.3 (reviewing intellectual property rulings of the ECHR and the European Commission).

8. *See Dima v. Romania*, App. No. 58472/00, para. 87 (2005) (admissibility decision) (in French only; unofficial English translation on file with author) (copyrighted works protected by Article 1); *Melnychuk v. Ukraine*, App. No. 28743/03, para. 8 (2005) (admissibility decision) (intellectual property protected by Article 1); *Anheuser-Busch Inc. v. Portugal*, App. No. 73049/01, 44 Eur. H.R. Rep. 42 [846], 855-56 (Chamber 2007) (judgment of October 11, 2005) (trademarks protected by Article 1); *see also Balan v.*

judgment of the Grand Chamber in *Anheuser-Busch Inc. v. Portugal* is especially striking.[9] The case involved a dispute between two corporations, the well-known American brewer and its longstanding Czech rival, Budějovický Budvar, over the exclusive right to market "Budweiser" beer in Portugal. The ECHR concluded that both registered trademarks and applications to register such marks fall within the ambit of the treaty's property rights clause. On the particular facts presented, however, the Court found that the Portuguese government had not violated Article 1.[10] Nevertheless, the analysis in *Anheuser-Busch* suggests that the ECHR recognizes the broader human rights implications of the region's innovation and creativity policies and that its future rulings may influence intellectual property protection standards in Europe.[11]

From just this brief description, the Grand Chamber judgment in *Anheuser-Busch Inc. v. Portugal* may strike many observers as misguided in several respects. First, the decision protects the fundamental rights of multinational corporations rather than those of natural persons. For reasons I explain below, the ECHR's adjudication of property rights claims by business entities is indisputably authorized by Article 1's text and the intent of its drafters.[12] Such cases nevertheless sit uneasily with a treaty whose principal objective is to protect the civil and political liberties of individuals. This is particularly true given that serious or systemic violations of those liberties are occurring in many countries.[13] In addition, with the accession to

---

Moldova, App. No. 19247/03 (2008) (finding a violation of Article 1 where the government refused to compensate a photographer for the use of a photograph on a national identity card).

9. *Anheuser-Busch Inc. v. Portugal*, App. No. 73049/01, 45 Eur. H.R. Rep. 36 [830] (Grand Chamber 2007).

10. The facts of the *Anheuser-Busch* case are complex. In essence, the ECHR concluded that Portugal had not interfered with the American brewer's application to register the trademark "Budweiser" because the application had been contested by Budějovický Budvar, the owner of a previously registered geographical indication for "Budweiser Bier." For a more detailed analysis of the case, *see infra* section 2.3.1.

11. Intellectual property owners have heralded *Anheuser-Busch* as a watershed ruling, suggesting that the case may trigger the filing of new complaints alleging violations of Article 1. *See,* e.g., Burkhart Goebel, *Geographical Indications and Trademarks in Europe*, 95 Trademark Rep. 1165, 1179 (2005) (describing the 2005 Chamber judgment as "remarkable and most important" in recognizing trademarks "as protected fundamental rights"); Arthur Rogers, *Anheuser-Busch Hails European Court Ruling that Trademark Applications Get Protections*, 24 Int'l Trade Rep. 72, 72 (2007) (characterizing the 2007 Grand Chamber judgment as a "landmark" decision).

12. *See* Protocol 1, *supra* note 5, Article 1 ("Every natural *or legal person* is entitled to the peaceful enjoyment of his possessions") (emphasis added).

13. *See,* e.g., Eur. Parl. Assemb., *Implementation of Judgments of the European Court of Human Rights: Supplementary Introductory Memorandum (Revised)*, AS/Jur (2005) 55 rev., 11-13 (2005), *available at* http://assembly.coe.int/CommitteeDocs/2005/20051220_Ejdoc55.pdf (assessing compliance with ECHR judgments involving widespread human rights abuses by the Russian military in Chechnya and massive structural failures of the Russian courts and the criminal justice system); Menno T. Kamminga, *Is*

the Convention of Eastern European states in the 1990s, the ECHR's caseload has exploded. The result is a mountainous backlog of pending complaints.[14] Adding intellectual property disputes to the Court's already vastly overburdened docket will only make it more difficult for the judges to adjudicate other complaints that allege violations of fundamental rights.

A second concern relates to the broader legal and political context in which the ECHR's recent intellectual property rulings are situated. The last several years have seen an explosion of competing human rights claims relating to intellectual property—in Europe, in the United States (U.S.), and in numerous international venues. There are two separate catalysts for these developments.

On the one hand, the expansion of intellectual property protection standards raises numerous human rights concerns relating to the right to life, health, food, privacy, freedom of expression, and enjoying the benefits of scientific progress. International experts, government officials, judges, and scholars are responding to these concerns by analyzing the interface between the two legal regimes[15] and, in particular, whether human rights should serve as "corrective[s] when [intellectual property] rights are used excessively and

---

the *European Convention on Human Rights Sufficiently Equipped to Cope with Gross and Systematic Violations?*, 12 NETH. Q. HUM. RTS. 153, 153-54 (1994) (analyzing past cases and suggesting that there will be an increasing number of systemic human rights abuses challenged before the ECHR); Paul Mahoney, *Speculating on the Future of the Reformed European Court of Human Rights*, 20 HUM. RTS. L.J. 1, 4 (1999) (predicting that the ECHR will increasingly be confronted with "serious human rights violations" such as "minorities in conflict with [a] central government" and cases relating to "terrorism, violence, and civil strife").

14. Lucius Caflisch, *The Reform of the European Court of Human Rights: Protocol No. 14 and Beyond*, 6 HUM. RTS. L. REV. 403, 404 (2006).

15. *See*, e.g., U.N. Econ. & Soc. Council [ECOSOC], Comm. on Econ., Soc. & Cultural Rights, *Substantive Issues Arising in the Implementation of the International Covenant on Economic, Social and Cultural Rights: Human Rights and Intellectual Property*, U.N. Doc. E/C.12/2001/15 (December 14, 2001) (analyzing conflicts between intellectual property and the International Covenant on Economic, Social, and Cultural Rights); The High Commissioner, *Report of the High Commissioner on the Impact of the Agreement on Trade-Related Aspects of Intellectual Property Rights on Human Rights, Delivered to the Sub-Comm'n on the Promotion and Protection of Human Rights*, U.N. Doc. E/CN.4/Sub.2/2001/13 (June 27, 2001); ECOSOC, Sub-Comm'n on the Promotion and Protection of Human Rights, *The Realization of Economic, Social and Cultural Rights*, at 3, U.N. Doc. E/CN.4/Sub.2/2000/L.20 (August 11, 2000) (identifying conflicts between intellectual property and "the right of everyone to enjoy the benefits of scientific progress and its applications, the right to health, the right to food, and the right to self-determination"). For more detailed analyses of these developments, *see*, for example, Christophe Geiger, *"Constitutionalising" Intellectual Property Law? The Influence of Fundamental Rights on Intellectual Property in the European Union*, 37 INT'L REV. INTELL. PROP. & COMPETITION L. 371, 382, 390-97 (2006) [hereinafter Geiger, *Constitutionalising Intellectual Property Law*] (analyzing recent intellectual property cases from Belgium, France, Germany, the Netherlands, Switzerland, and countries outside of Europe that raise non-trivial freedom of expression issues); Christophe Geiger, *Fundamental Rights, a Safeguard for the Coherence of Intellectual Property Law?*, 35 INT'L REV. INTELL. PROP. & COMPETITION L.

contrary to their functions."[16] On the other hand, litigants, lawmakers, and courts are increasingly invoking fundamental rights—including the right of property—as a justification for *protecting* intellectual property and the corporations and individuals that own it.[17] This countervailing trend is reflected in treaties,[18] reports of international expert bodies,[19] and judicial rulings in Europe[20] and the U.S..[21]

268, 277 (2004) [hereinafter Geiger, *Fundamental Rights Safeguard*] (analyzing "decisions in the field of copyright in which the freedom of expression has been invoked to justify a use that is not covered by an exception provided for in [intellectual property] law"); Laurence R. Helfer, *Toward a Human Rights Framework for Intellectual Property*, 40 U.C. Davis L. Rev. 971, 1001-14 (2007) [hereinafter Helfer, *Human Rights Framework*] (analyzing recent treaty-making initiatives in the United Nations Educational, Scientific and Cultural Organization, the World Health Organization, and the World Intellectual Property Organization concerning the relationship between human rights and intellectual property); Laurence R. Helfer, *Regime Shifting: The TRIPs Agreement and New Dynamics of International Intellectual Property Lawmaking*, 29 Yale J. Int'l L. 1, 26-53 (2004) (analyzing intellectual property standard setting in the biodiversity, plant genetic resources, public health, and human rights regimes).

16. Geiger, *Fundamental Rights Safeguard*, *supra* note 15, at 278; *see also* Helfer, *Human Rights Framework*, *supra* note 15, at 1017-18 (analyzing how international human rights law can be interpreted to impose "external limits on intellectual property").

17. *See*, e.g., Michael A. Carrier, *Cabining Intellectual Property Through a Property Paradigm*, 54 Duke L.J. 1, 1 (2004) (stating that "[o]ne of the most revolutionary legal changes in the past generation has been the 'propertization' of intellectual property"); Kal Raustiala, *Density and Conflict in International Intellectual Property Law*, 40 U.C. Davis L. Rev. 1021, 1032 (2007) (stating that "the embrace of [intellectual property] by human rights advocates and entities … is likely to further entrench some dangerous ideas about property: in particular, that property rights as human rights ought to be inviolable and ought to receive extremely solicitous attention from the international community").

18. *See* Charter of Fundamental Rights of the European Union Article 17, December 7, 2000 O.J. (C 364) 1 ("Everyone has the right to own, use, dispose of and bequeath his or her lawfully acquired possessions. … Intellectual property shall be protected."), *available at* http://www.europarl.europa.eu/charter/pdf/text_en.pdf.

19. *See* ECOSOC, Comm. on Econ., Soc. and Cultural Rights, *General Comment No. 17: The Right of Everyone to Benefit from the Protection of the Moral and Material Interests Resulting from Any Scientific, Literary or Artistic Production of Which He or She Is the Author (Article 15, Paragraph 1(c) of the Covenant)*, U.N. Doc. E/C.12/GC/17 (November 21, 2005) [hereinafter General Comment], *available at* http://www.ohchr.org/english/ bodies /cescr/docs/gc17.doc.

20. *See*, e.g., Joseph Straus, *Design Protection for Spare Parts Gone in Europe? Proposed Changes to the EC Directive: The Commission's Mandate and its Doubtful Execution*, 27 Eur. Intell. Prop. Rev. 391, 398 (2005) (discussing 2000 decision of the Federal Constitutional Court holding that patents constitute property under the German Constitution); Thomas Crampton, *Apple Gets French Support in Music Compatibility Case*, N.Y. Times, July 29, 2006, at C9 (discussing a ruling of the French Constitutional Council, the country's highest judicial body, which "declared major aspects of the so-called iPod law unconstitutional" and "made frequent reference to the 1789 Declaration on Human Rights and concluded that the law violated the constitutional protections of property").

21. *See*, e.g., *Zoltek Corp. v. United States*, 442 F.3d 1345 (Fed. Cir. 2006) (rejecting a claim that the federal government's uncompensated use of a patent amounts to a taking of private property in violation of the U.S. Constitution).

The ECHR's entry into this maelstrom of competing human rights-based claims to restrict or expand intellectual property raises important and difficult questions. For example, does intellectual property deserve to be treated as a fundamental right? And if it does, how does a human rights-inspired conception of intellectual property differ from existing rules that promote innovation and creativity? More concretely, what role, if any, should the ECHR play in shaping innovation and creativity policy in Europe? Should the Court favor the rights of corporate intellectual property owners over the rights of individual users and consumers, or should it strike a distinctive human rights balance among these actors with competing interests?

In this chapter, I consider one important dimension of these questions in light of the ECHR's recent intellectual property rulings. I provide the first detailed assessment of the European human rights tribunals' Article 1 intellectual property case law.[22] I also develop a comprehensive proposal for the ECHR to adjudicate intellectual property disputes under the European Convention's property rights clause.

The chapter begins in section 2.2 with an overview of the right of property in Article 1 and the decisions interpreting it. Section 2.3 develops a tripartite framework to analyze the ECHR's intellectual property case law, including decisions that commentators have not previously identified. I use this framework to link together a series of seemingly disconnected rulings and to expose the many points of intersection between Europe's human rights and intellectual property systems. Section 2.4 analyzes three distinct paradigms that the ECHR may apply in future intellectual property disputes. I label these approaches the rule of law paradigm, the enforcement paradigm, and the intellectual property balancing paradigm. Each paradigm finds support in the Court's case law and its interpretive methodologies. However, the three paradigms have radically different consequences for innovation and creativity policy in Europe. I analyze these consequences and emphasize the systemic effects of overlaying two previously unrelated legal regimes. I argue that the ECHR should follow the rule of law paradigm and restrict its review of Article 1 intellectual property claims to cases of arbitrary government conduct. Section 2.5 briefly concludes.

---

22. The few existing analyses of intellectual property in the European human rights system focus on treaty provisions that restrict intellectual property—such as the right to freedom of expression—or emphasize the European Convention's influence on the intellectual property laws of a specific country. *See* P. Bernt Hugenholtz, *Copyright and Freedom of Expression in Europe, in* EXPANDING THE BOUNDARIES OF INTELLECTUAL PROPERTY: INNOVATION POLICY FOR THE KNOWLEDGE SOCIETY 343 (Rochelle Cooper Dreyfuss et al. eds., 2001); Timothy Pinto, *The Influence of the European Convention on Intellectual Property Rights*, 24 EUR. INTELL. PROP. REV. 209 (2002). No comprehensive study of the European human rights tribunals' intellectual property jurisprudence under the Convention's property rights clause has ever been attempted.

2.2   EUROPEAN CONVENTION ON HUMAN RIGHTS
               AND THE RIGHT OF PROPERTY

This section surveys the property rights jurisprudence of the European
human rights tribunals, highlighting issues that are relevant to the more
detailed analysis of the intellectual property case law that appears in the next
section of the chapter. Before turning to this survey, however, a brief
introduction to the structure of the European human rights system and the
ECHR's interpretive methodologies is in order.

The European Convention enshrines a broad catalog of civil and
political liberties. The primary beneficiaries of these liberties are natural
persons, although certain rights of corporations also receive protection,
including the right of property.[23] In addition, the Convention is principally a
charter of negative liberties that constrain the behavior of state actors. But it
also imposes a limited set of positive obligations on European governments.[24]

When reviewing the actions of national governments, the ECHR gives
pride of place to the Convention's text, from which it has distilled a diverse
array of bright-line rules and multi-part balancing tests. But other interpretive
methodologies have been equally vital forces in shaping European human
rights jurisprudence. For example, the Court assesses the functional importance of particular rights in democratic societies, the rationale governments
advance for restricting those rights, the arguments for and against deference
to domestic decision-makers, and the need for the Convention to evolve in
response to legal, political, and social trends in Europe.[25] As explained
below, the Court has applied each of these doctrines and interpretive tools
when analyzing the right of property.

2.2.1   ARTICLE 1 OF PROTOCOL 1: PROTECTING PEACEFUL ENJOYMENT OF
               POSSESSIONS

The protection of "the peaceful enjoyment of possessions" for "every natural
or legal person" is one of the more controversial and obscure provisions in
the European human rights system.[26] The right appears not in the Convention's primary text, but in Article 1 of its first Protocol.[27] This placement, as

---

23. *See generally* MARIUS EMBERLAND, THE HUMAN RIGHTS OF COMPANIES: EXPLORING THE
    STRUCTURE OF ECHR PROTECTION (2006).
24. *See generally* ALASTAIR R. MOWBRAY, THE DEVELOPMENT OF POSITIVE OBLIGATIONS UNDER THE
    EUROPEAN CONVENTION ON HUMAN RIGHTS BY THE EUROPEAN COURT OF HUMAN RIGHTS (2004).
    For a discussion of "positive obligations" relating to the right of property, *see infra* section
    2.4.2.
25. *See* Helfer, *Adjudicating Copyright Claims*, *supra* note 1, at 407.
26. For more detailed analyses of the right of property in the European human rights system,
    see ALI RIZA ÇOBAN, PROTECTION OF PROPERTY RIGHTS WITHIN THE EUROPEAN CONVENTION ON

well as the absence of any mention of the word "rights" in Article 1, reflects a disagreement among European governments over the inclusion of a property rights clause in the treaty as well as the scope and extent of protection it provides.[28]

The Convention's drafters recognized that democratic governments need leeway to adopt or modify economic and social policies implicating private property without, in every instance, compensating adversely affected owners. On the other hand, the drafters also understood that the rule of law in general and the stability and predictability of property rights in particular would be undermined if governments could arbitrarily deprive owners of their possessions.[29] In attempting to reconcile these competing perspectives, the European Court and Commission have created a complex and intricate jurisprudence interpreting the right of property.

2.2.2   THE SUBJECT MATTER AND TEMPORAL SCOPE OF THE RIGHT OF PROPERTY

A preliminary issue the tribunals faced was defining Article 1's subject matter scope. The Court and Commission adopted a capacious interpretation of the word "possessions," extending it to a broad array of "concrete proprietary interest[s]" having economic value.[30] Whether such interests qualify as possessions does not depend on their status in domestic law.[31] Rather, Article 1 has an "autonomous meaning" that authorizes the ECHR to decide "whether the circumstances of the case, considered as a whole, may be regarded as having conferred on the applicant title to a substantive interest" protected by Article 1.[32] Applying this standard, the Court has adjudicated restrictions on most economically important types of tangible and intangible properties, including land, chattels, licenses, leases, contractual rights, corporate securities, business goodwill and, as described in detail below, intellectual property.[33]

HUMAN RIGHTS 124-25 (2004); CAMILO B. SHUTTE, THE EUROPEAN FUNDAMENTAL RIGHT OF PROPERTY (2004); Rijn, *supra* note 6.

27. *See* Protocol 1, *supra* note 5, Article 1.
28. *See* ÇOBAN, *supra* note 26, at 124-25 (reviewing Article 1's drafting history).
29. *See id.* at 127-37; Helen Mountfield, *Regulatory Expropriations in Europe: The Approach of the European Court of Human Rights*, 11 N.Y.U. ENVTL. L.J. 136, 146-47 (2002).
30. *See Kopecký v. Slovakia*, App. No. 44912/98, 2004-IX Eur. Ct. H.R. 125, 144 (Grand Chamber).
31. *Kechko v. Ukraine*, App. No. 63134/00, ¶ 22 (2005).
32. *Öneryıldız v. Turkey*, App. No. 48939/99, 2004-XII Eur. Ct. H.R. 79, 127 (Grand Chamber).
33. *See* ÇOBAN, *supra* note 26, at 152-55 (collecting recent decisions); David Anderson, *Compensation for Interference with Property*, 6 EUR. HUM. RTS. L. REV. 543, 546 (1999) (same).

Article 1's temporal scope extends to current and future proprietary interests. As the ECHR recently stated, "'Possessions' can be either (1) 'existing possessions' or (2) assets, including claims, in respect of which the applicant … has at least a 'legitimate expectation' of obtaining effective enjoyment of a property right."[34] The Court has extended the latter line of cases to enforceable debts, lease renewal options, final court judgments, and vested rights to social security and pension benefits.[35] By contrast, the mere "hope of recognition of a property right which it has been impossible to exercise effectively" is not protected, nor is "a conditional claim which lapses as a result of the non-fulfillment of the condition."[36] Future interests must also have a solid basis in domestic law, such as a statute or a judicial ruling that recognizes their existence.[37]

2.2.3   INTERFERENCES WITH PROPERTY

If the ECHR determines that a possession falls within Article 1's subject matter and temporal scope, it must then consider whether the government has interfered with the possession. The second and third sentences of Article 1 recognize two distinct categories of government interferences—deprivations of property and controls on its use.[38]

Deprivations are the more invasive of these two categories. They include expropriations, nationalizations, confiscations, and other comprehensive dispossessions. The ECHR has avoided finding a deprivation unless the

---

34. Kopecký, 2004-IX Eur. Ct. H.R. at 139-40 (enumeration added).
35. *See* ÇOBAN, *supra* note 26, at 152-55 (collecting recent decisions).
36. Kopecký, 2004-IX Eur. Ct. H.R. at 140; *see also Gratzinger v. Czech Republic,* App. No. 39794/98, 2002-VII Eur. Ct. H.R. 399, 419-20 (Grand Chamber). The ECHR has often applied these principles to complaints seeking restitution of real or personal property seized by socialist governments in Eastern Europe. The Court has held that former property owners have no "legitimate expectation" of receiving restitution if they do not have "a currently enforceable claim that was sufficiently established," for example because they do not meet "one of the essential statutory conditions" for recovery of previously owned property or because there is "a dispute as to the correct interpretation and application of domestic law by the national courts." *Rosival v. Slovakia*, App. No. 17684/02, para. 75 (2007) (admissibility decision) (internal citations omitted).
37. *See Zhigalev v. Russia,* App. No. 54891/00, ¶ 131 (2006); Kopecký, 2004-IX Eur. Ct. H.R. at 144-45.
38. *Hellborg v. Sweden,* App. No. 47473/99, 45 Eur. H.R. Rep. 3 [29], 43 (2007) (judgment of February 28, 2006) (explaining this distinction); *see also* ÇOBAN, *supra* note 26, at 174-86. The ECHR has also recognized a third category—interference with the substance of property. This category is reserved for government intrusions which, as a formal matter, "do[] not transfer the property to public authorities, nor … limit or control the use of the property … ." *Id.* at 187. In practice, however, the Court has not applied this concept consistently or coherently. Commentators have also noted that the cases decided under this rubric could easily fit under the first two categories. *See id.* at 189; Anderson, *supra* note 33, at 551-52. For these reasons, I do not give separate treatment to "substance of property" claims.

government has effectively extinguished the owner's property right. In contrast, controls on use encompass any lesser restriction on an owner's possessory interests. The ECHR has adopted "a very broad concept of 'control of use,'" thereby bringing "a wide range of regulatory measures within its jurisdiction ... ."[39]

2.2.4 Assessing the Legality of Interferences

Where a state interferes with a possession, the Court must assess the validity of its actions. For an interference to be compatible with the Convention, it must be "provided by law" and pursue "a legitimate aim" in the public interest.[40] Interferences must also achieve "a fair balance ... between the demands of the general interest of the community and the requirements of the protection of the individual's fundamental rights."[41] Striking this balance requires "a reasonable relationship of proportionality between the means employed" by the state and the objectives it seeks to achieve.[42]

Although this proportionality test is highly fact-specific, the ECHR has identified several considerations relevant to assessing whether the government has maintained the fair balance required by Article 1. These factors include the owner's reasonable expectations;[43] whether the restriction imposes an inequitable or excessive burden (especially on non-nationals);[44] the amount of compensation (if any) paid by the government;[45] the

---

39. Mountfield, *supra* note 29, at 146; *see also* Çoban, *supra* note 26, at 175-85 (analyzing deprivations and comparing them to controls on use).
40. *Jahn v. Germany*, App. No. 46720/99, 42 Eur. H.R. Rep. 49 [1085], 1103-04 (Grand Chamber 2006) (judgment of June 30, 2005).
41. *Kirilova v. Bulgaria*, App. No. 42908/98, ¶ 106 (2005).
42. *L.B. v. Italy*, App. No. 32542/96, ¶ 23 (2002).
43. *Pine Valley Dev. Ltd. v. Ireland*, App. No. 12742/87, 222 Eur. Ct. H.R. (ser. A) at 23 (1991).
44. The Court has justified this differential treatment on public choice grounds, reasoning that non-nationals lack representation in domestic political processes and thus risk bearing a disproportionate share of the costs of property deprivations. *See Lithgow v. United Kingdom*, App No. 9006/80, 102 Eur. Ct. H.R. (ser. A) at 49 (1986).
45. *See* Tom Allen, *Compensation for Property Under the European Convention of Human Rights*, 28 Mich. J. Int'l L. 287, 298-300 (2007). When the state deprives non-nationals of their property, Article 1's reference to "the general principles of international law" mandates the payment of prompt, adequate, and effective compensation. Protocol 1, *supra* note 5, Article 1; Anderson, *supra* note 33, at 548. By contrast, Article 1 does not require compensation to be paid to nationals. *Lithgow*, 102 Eur. Ct. H.R. (ser. A) at 47-49. In practice, however, the Court has applied an equivalent standard of compensation to both types of takings. As a result, where a state deprives its own citizens of their property, it must normally pay "an amount reasonably related to its value," and its failure to provide any compensation "can be considered justifiable under Article 1 of Protocol No. 1 only in exceptional circumstances." *Scordino v. Italy*, App. No. 36813/97, 45 Eur. H.R. Rep. 7 [207], 239 (Grand Chamber 2006) (judgment of March 30, 2005).

uncertainty created by the regulation;[46] and the speed and consistency with which the state acts.[47]

In assessing these factors, the ECHR affords governments considerable leeway to regulate private property in the public interest. Because states frequently impose property controls when implementing broader social and economic policies, "the national authorities"—which have direct knowledge of their society and its needs—"are in principle better placed than the international judge" to decide whether a regulation is necessary to achieve those policies.[48] As a result, the ECHR gives significant deference to "the legislature's judgment as to what is in the public interest unless that judgment is manifestly without reasonable foundation."[49] It also stresses the "wide margin of appreciation" that states enjoy "with regard both to choosing the means of enforcement and to ascertaining whether the consequences of enforcement are justified in the general interest for the purpose of achieving the object of the law in question."[50]

This deference does not, however, amount to a blank check for European governments. To the contrary, as the docket of property rights cases has expanded exponentially over the last decade,[51] the ECHR has pointedly refused to "abdicate its power of review" and has reserved the final authority to "determine whether the requisite balance was maintained in a manner consonant with" the right of property.[52] As a result of this European judicial supervision, the ECHR has found an increasing number of violations of Article 1 in the past few years.[53]

---

46. *Hutten-Czapska v. Poland*, App. No. 35014/97, 45 Eur. H.R. Rep. 4 [52], 108 (Grand Chamber 2007) (judgment of June 19, 2006).
47. *Kirilova v. Bulgaria,* App. No. 42908/98, ¶ 106 (2005); *Broniowski v. Poland,* App. No. 31443/96, 2004-V Eur. Ct. H.R. 1 (Grand Chamber).
48. *Draon v. France*, App. No. 1513/03, 42 Eur. H.R. Rep. 40 [807], 832-33 (2006) (judgment of October 6, 2005) (internal quotations omitted).
49. *Id.*
50. *Scordino*, 45 Eur. H.R. Rep. 7 at 239.
51. ÇOBAN, *supra* note 26, at 258 (stating that over the last decade "both the magnitude and variety of the applications regarding [Article 1] have escalated significantly and the number of the judgments rose consequently"). Not surprisingly, this expansion followed the accession of Eastern European countries to the Convention in the 1990s. These states have faced significant challenges to reallocating property rights during their transition from socialist to democratic systems of government. *See* Tom Allen, *Restitution and Transitional Justice in the European Court of Human Rights*, 13 COLUM. J. EUR. L. 1, 13-29 (2006/2007).
52. *Jahn v. Germany*, App. No. 46720/99, 42 Eur. H.R. Rep. 49 [1085], 1105 (Grand Chamber 2006) (judgment of June 30, 2005); *see also Fedorenko v. Ukraine,* App. No. 25921/02, ¶ 29 (2006) (asserting that the state's "margin of appreciation ... goes hand in hand with European supervision" which authorizes the ECHR to "ascertain whether the discretion afforded to the Government was overstepped").
53. *Kopecký v. Slovakia*, App. No. 44912/98, 2004-IX Eur. Ct. H.R. 125, 155 (Grand Chamber 2004) (Strážnická, J., dissenting) ("In the Court's case-law from 2000 onwards, a tendency may be discerned to subject the application of national law to supervisory

2.3   INTELLECTUAL PROPERTY AND THE
EUROPEAN CONVENTION'S RIGHT OF
PROPERTY: A TRIPARTITE FRAMEWORK FOR
ANALYSIS

In this section, I apply the general principles reviewed above to cases in which intellectual property owners alleged a violation of Article 1 of Protocol 1. The analysis consists of three questions: First, does Article 1 apply to the intellectual property at issue, either because it is an existing possession or because the owner has a legitimate expectation of obtaining a future proprietary interest? If neither type of property exists, the government's conduct, however egregious, cannot violate Article 1. In contrast, if the ECHR answers this question affirmatively, it must consider a second question: Has the government "interfered" with the possession? The absence of such an interference also requires a ruling for the respondent state. Conversely, the existence of an interference leads to a third and final question: Whether the interference is justified, i.e., has the state upset the fair and proportional balance that Article 1 requires between the interests of the public and the property owner's rights?

Analyzing the intellectual property jurisprudence of the ECHR and the European Commission using this tripartite framework helps to expose the numerous points of intersection—and of potential conflict—between the European human rights system and the region's intellectual property laws.

2.3.1   IS INTELLECTUAL PROPERTY PROTECTED BY ARTICLE 1?

In three decisions dating back to 1990s, the European Commission has consistently held that patents and copyrights fall within Article 1's subject matter scope.[54] The Court did not directly address this issue until 2005,[55] when it issued a trilogy of decisions applying Article 1 to intellectual property disputes.[56] *Anheuser-Busch Inc. v. Portugal* is the most well-known of these three rulings. In that judgment, analyzed in detail below, a

---

review by the Court."); ÇOBAN, *supra* note 26, at 258 (stating that the ECHR has found "more and more violations of [Article 1] in the last couple of years" and that it "is not as reluctant as it was before to find [a] violation").

54. *See Lenzing AG v. United Kingdom,* App. No. 38817/97, 94-A Eur. Comm'n H.R. Dec. & Rep. 136 (1998) (patent); *Aral v. Turkey,* App. No. 24563/94 (1998) (admissibility decision) (copyright); *Smith Kline & French Lab. Ltd. v. Netherlands,* App. No. 12633/87, 66 Eur. Comm'n H.R. Dec. & Rep. 70, 79 (1990) (admissibility decision) (patent).

55. In a 1995 ruling, *British Am. Tobacco Co. Ltd. v. Netherlands,* App. No. 19589/92, 331 Eur. Ct. H.R. (ser. A) (1995), the Court avoided deciding whether patent applications are possessions—an issue I discuss in greater detail below. *See infra* section 2.3.1.2.

56. *See supra* note 8.

seven-member Chamber of the ECHR concluded that "intellectual property as such incontestably enjoys the protection of Article 1 of Protocol No. 1."[57]

The case was reargued before a Grand Chamber of the ECHR in 2006. Review by this panel of seventeen judges is reserved for disputes which involve "a serious question affecting the interpretation or application of the Convention or the protocols thereto, or a serious issue of general importance."[58] In a judgment issued in early 2007, the Grand Chamber unanimously agreed with the Chamber's conclusion, holding that Article 1 "is applicable to intellectual property as such."[59] The Grand Chamber's statement is more measured than the language used by the Chamber. Nevertheless, its holding is an unequivocal endorsement of the view that the right of property protects the financial interests of intellectual property owners in their inventions, creations, and signs.

The ECHR's only justification for this conclusion is found in a brief quotation from the European Commission's first intellectual property decision, in which the Commission stated that:

> under Dutch law the holder of a patent is referred to as the proprietor of a patent and that patents are deemed, subject to the provisions of the Patent Act, to be personal property which is transferable and assignable. The Commission finds that a patent accordingly falls within the scope of the term "possessions" in Article 1 of Protocol No. 1.[60]

The Commission's reasoning in this passage is sparse. But it suggests that the European tribunals place significant weight on the exclusivity of the exploitation and transfer rights that national laws confer on intellectual property owners.[61] Inasmuch as these exclusive rights are standard features of national and international intellectual property systems, it is safe to predict that the ECHR will treat other forms of industrial and artistic property—such as new plant varieties, integrated circuits, performers' rights, trade secrets, and the like—as "possessions" protected by Article 1.[62] In addition, because

---

57. *Anheuser-Busch Inc. v. Portugal,* App. No. 73049/01, 44 Eur. H.R. Rep. 42 [836], 856 (Chamber 2007) (judgment of October 11, 2005). I discuss the complex facts and procedural history of the case below. *See infra* section 2.3.1.2.1.

58. European Convention, *supra* note 2, Article 43.

59. *Anheuser-Busch Inc. v. Portugal,* App. No. 73049/01, 45 Eur. H.R. Rep. 36 [830], 849 (Grand Chamber 2007). Both the concurring and dissenting judges agreed that Article 1 applies "to intellectual property in general and to a duly registered trade mark." *Id.* at 853 (Steiner & Hajiyev, JJ., concurring), 855 (Caflisch & Cabral Barreto, JJ., dissenting).

60. *Smith Kline & French Lab. Ltd. v. Netherlands,* App. No. 12633/87, 66 Eur. Comm'n H.R. Dec. & Rep. 70, 79 (1990) (admissibility decision).

61. *See* Laurent Sermet, The European Convention on Human Rights and Property Rights 13 (1998) ("patents have two characteristics—exclusiveness and transferability—which are also hallmarks of property").

62. In recent judgments, the ECHR has reaffirmed that "Article 1 of Protocol No. 1 is applicable to intellectual property as such." *Kamoy Radyo Televizyon Yayıncılık ve Organizasyon A.Ş. v. Turkey,* App. No. 19965/06, para. 37 (Chamber 2019) (registered

Article 1 applies to fixed claims to future revenue and compensation,[63] the Court will likely extend Article 1 to intellectual property rights that are subject to a statutory or compulsory license (i.e., a license that authorizes users to exploit protected works provided that they remunerate rights holders).[64] These logical extensions of prior Article 1 case law suggest that there are no obvious jurisdictional limits on the ECHR's power to review a wide array of intellectual property disputes under the rubric of the right of property.

Outside of these broad jurisdictional parameters, however, the scope of Article 1 is much less certain. This is particularly true where Article 1 intersects with intellectual property subject matter and ownership rules; for example, where ownership is contested or where it is unclear whether an inventor, creator, or business has satisfied the requirements for protection under domestic law. I analyze these unresolved issues below. I begin with literary and artistic works that are protected from the moment of their creation or fixation. I then discuss industrial property whose eligibility for protection is determined by a registration procedure.

2.3.1.1   Literary and Artistic Works

Consider first an easy case—literary and artistic works whose ownership and eligibility for protection in domestic law are undisputed. The creators of such works possess exclusive exploitation and assignment rights that fit comfortably within European jurisprudence protecting various forms of intellectual property under Article 1. In these cases of undisputed ownership and eligibility, the ECHR will simply defer to the national copyright or neighboring rights laws and conclude that Article 1 is applicable. Yet such deference may not always yield easy answers, particularly when domestic law provides limited guidance concerning a creator's proprietary interests.

2.3.1.1.1   Dima v. Romania

Dima v. Romania,[65] a 2005 admissibility decision previously unmentioned by commentators, highlights these complexities. The case concerned a

---

trademark); *see also SIA AKKA/LAA v. Latvia,* App. No. 562/05, para. 41 (Chamber 2016) ("The protection of musical works and the economic interests deriving from them thus fall within the scope of rights protected under Article 1 of Protocol No. 1.").

63. *See supra* section 2.2.2.

64. Compulsory licenses fit easily within the concept of Article 1 "assets," even where the amount of compensation is determined ex post by a government agency or royalty tribunal. *See Broniowski v. Poland,* App. No. 31443/96, 2004-V Eur. Ct. H.R. 1, 54 (Grand Chamber) (applying Article 1 to a right "to obtain … compensatory property" notwithstanding the fact that the "right was created in a somewhat inchoate form, as its materialisation was to be effected by an administrative decision allocating State property to" the applicant).

65. *Dima v. Romania,* App. No. 58472/00 (2005) (admissibility decision).

graphic artist, Victor Dima, who created the design for a new national emblem and seal shortly after the fall of Romania's communist regime in 1989. Dima developed a preliminary drawing of the state symbols in response to a public competition. A government commission selected his prototype over several other submissions and directed him to work with two history and heraldry experts to revise the design.[66]

The Romanian Parliament later adopted the revised design as the state emblem and seal, listing Dima as the "graphic designer" in a statute published in the country's Official Journal.[67] Inexplicably, however, the Parliament never paid Dima for his work. In addition to seeking to recover the compensation owed to him, Dima responded by asserting his rights as the graphic designer of the state emblem and seal.

He turned first to Romania's administrative agencies. The Patent and Trademark Office refused to register the design, relying on a provision of Romania's industrial design statute that excludes from protection designs "whose purpose and appearance are contrary to morality or public policy."[68] Dima had better luck with the Copyright Agency, whose director informed him in a series of letters that he was the author of the graphic design and enjoyed all of the rights in domestic copyright law. On the strength of these assertions, Dima filed three copyright infringement actions in the Romanian courts against two private businesses and a state-owned enterprise responsible for minting Romanian coins—all of which had reproduced and distributed the design for profit.[69]

The courts dismissed all three suits, holding that Dima did not own a copyright in the design of the state symbols. The decisive rulings were issued by the Romanian Supreme Court of Justice. The court acknowledged that Dima had personally created the design. But it held that the Parliament, which had commissioned the revision of the design, was the "author" of the

---

66. The ECHR does not indicate whether Dima prepared his initial design for the competition, although that is the most plausible interpretation of the facts. *See id.* at paras. 3-4.

67. *Id.* at para. 6 (*"auteur des maquettes graphiques"* in French).

68. The Patent and Trademark Office also based its refusal on an unpublished internal rule which provided that industrial drawings and models representing the emblem of a state were excluded from copyright protection (*"droit d'auteur"*). *Id.* at para. 9. The ECHR did not explain why an industrial property office believed itself competent to interpret an issue of copyright law. However, settled grounds for rejecting the registration of state symbols *as trademarks* appear in Article 6*ter* of the Paris Convention, which prohibits the registration and use of "armorial bearings, flags, and other State emblems" as such marks or as elements thereof "without authorization by the competent authorities … ." *Id.* at para. 27 (citing Paris Convention for the Protection of Industrial Property, Article 6 *ter*, March 20, 1883, 828 U.N.T.S. 305). Although the Patent and Trademark Office did not rely upon this provision in denying Dima's registration, Romania cited it in opposing his complaint to the ECHR. *See id.* at paras. 7, 18.

69. *See Dima,* App. No. 58472/00. at paras. 11-26.

works.[70] Alternatively, the Supreme Court concluded that "symbols of the State could not be the subject of copyright," neither under the 1956 copyright statute in effect at the time Dima created the design (which did not mention state symbols) nor under a revised 1996 statute (which expressly excluded such symbols from copyright protection).[71] Finally, the Supreme Court rejected Dima's argument that the lower courts had retroactively applied the 1996 statute to his design, since even under the earlier law Dima was not the author of "works of intellectual creation."[72]

Dima challenged these rulings before the ECHR, alleging that the Romanian courts had deprived him of a possession in violation of Article 1.[73] He invoked the subject matter and authorship rules of the 1956 copyright statute, which protected "all works of intellectual creation in the literary, artistic and scientific domain, whatever the contents and form of expression," including "works of graphic art."[74] The statute further provided that the "author" of such works "shall be the person who has created" them and that the copyright "arise[s] the moment the work takes ... concrete form."[75] Dima asserted that, as a result of these statutory provisions, his copyright in the graphic design arose at the moment he created it or, at the latest, when he was listed as the graphic designer in the Official Journal.[76]

The ECHR began its analysis by stating that Article 1 protects copyrighted works. But this conclusion did not resolve whether Dima had "a 'possession' or at least a 'legitimate expectation' to acquire a 'possession'" as the author of the graphic models he created.[77] To assess that issue, the

---

70. The Supreme Court emphasized the collective process of the models' creation and the decisive role played by the Parliament in selecting the final models. *See id.* at para. 14.
71. According to the ECHR, the 1996 statute was adopted to "modernize the field of copyright" after the fall of the socialist regime in 1989. *See id.* at paras. 61-62.
72. *Id.* at para. 13.
73. Dima's complaint to the ECHR also raised two other claims: (1) the government's failure to compensate him for his work, and (2) various procedural objections to the domestic infringement proceedings. As to the first claim, the ECHR ruled that Dima had failed to exhaust domestic remedies, thus precluding the Court from reviewing his allegations on the merits. *Id.* at paras. 78-81. As to the second claim, the ECHR rejected all of Dima's objections save one—a challenge to a report produced by an expert witness for one of the defendants. As to that issue, it declared Dima's complaint admissible. *Id.* at paras. 66-67. In November 2006, the ECHR concluded that Romania had violated the European Convention's right to a fair hearing when the Romanian Supreme Court dismissed his appeal without addressing Dima's challenge to the expert's report. The Court awarded Dima EUR 2,000 in damages. *See Affaire Dima c. Roumanie*, App. No. 58472/00 (2006); *see also* Press Release, Registrar, European Court of Human Rights, Chamber Judgments Concerning Azerbaijan, Bulgaria, Croatia, Italy, Lithuania, Romania and Russia (November 16, 2006) (summarizing the ECHR's judgment in English).
74. Decree No. 321 Relating to Copyright, June 18, 1956, Article 9 (Rom.) (copy on file with author).
75. *Id.* Article 2.
76. *See Dima v. Romania*, App. No. 58472/00, para. 38 (2005) (admissibility decision).
77. *Id.* at para. 87.

Court first turned to the subject matter rules of European copyright laws. It observed that "the majority of national legal systems, including that of Romania, provide that copyright arises upon the creation of an artistic work. Some jurisdictions require, in addition … that the work have a concrete form of expression."[78] These general principles, viewed in the abstract, appeared to support a ruling in Dima's favor.

Yet the Court also recognized that these principles did not answer all unsettled questions concerning the scope of national copyright law. In cases where the "existence or extent" of copyright is uncertain, the ECHR stated, it is the task of domestic courts to resolve any ambiguities.[79] Only once those ambiguities have been resolved can the Court determine the extent of the applicant's property right and whether the state had violated that right.

The key question, therefore, was whether Romanian courts had decided that a graphic design of a state emblem could be protected by copyright prior to the adoption of the 1996 statute that expressly denied such protection. On this issue, the facts did not favor Dima. Although he was listed as the graphic designer in the official gazette and the subject matter provisions of the 1956 copyright law were ambiguous, he could not point to "a judgment in his favor, nor could he rely on any favorable case law concerning the ability to copyright models of the State emblem and seal."[80] In addition, the Supreme Court of Justice ultimately rejected Dima's proposed interpretation of the 1956 statute (and, implicitly, that of the Copyright Agency, although the ECHR failed to mention this fact). In light of this rejection, Dima could not claim to have any "legitimate expectation" of acquiring a possession, since such an expectation cannot arise where there is "a dispute as to the interpretation and application of national law, and … the applicant's submissions [are] subsequently rejected by the national courts."[81]

The ECHR concluded by reaffirming its "limited power" to review allegations of legal or factual errors committed by national courts when interpreting domestic law. Applying this deferential standard, it found "no appearance of arbitrariness" in the Supreme Court's ruling. There was thus "no basis on which the [ECHR] could reach a different conclusion on the question of whether [Dima] … did or did not have a copyright" in the design he created.[82]

---

78. *Id.* at para. 88.
79. *Id.* at para. 89.
80. *Id.* at para. 91.
81. *Id.* at para. 92.
82. *Id.* at para. 93.

2.2.1.1.2 Implications of Dima for the Protection of Literary and Artistic Works

Dima v. Romania raises several important issues regarding the application of Article 1 to literary and artistic works. Perhaps, most significantly, the ECHR refused to second-guess the Romanian courts' interpretation of domestic copyright law in a case whose facts were sympathetic to the creator. Instead, it deferred to the authority of national courts of last resort to resolve contested legal issues that divide lower courts and administrative agencies. Yet the Court also signaled that its deference to these domestic decision-makers would not be unlimited. A close parsing of the judgment suggests several issues which may engender more searching scrutiny by the ECHR in future cases.

First, the ECHR in *Dima* did not address moral rights, a branch of copyright law that enables creators to control the attribution and integrity of their works. Inasmuch as moral rights protect the personal link between the creator and his or her intellectual creations, some commentators have argued that they have a stronger claim to protection as human rights than do copyright's economic exploitation privileges.[83] Scholars are divided over whether Article 1 extends to moral rights.[84] The Court did not resolve this debate, inasmuch as Dima's challenge focused solely on his economic rights in the graphic designs. However, creators may raise moral rights claims in future cases, for example, where the state misattributes authorship or distorts or damages a protected work.[85] In such cases, the Court will need to consider whether national decision-makers deserve less deference if they restrict moral rights.

Second, the ECHR refused to conflate subject matter standards from different branches of intellectual property law. In contesting Dima's allegations before the ECHR, the government argued against the *copyrightability* of state symbols by citing to a *trademark* provision of the Paris Convention

---

83. *See* Orit Fischman Afori, *Human Rights and Copyright: The Introduction of Natural Law Considerations into American Copyright Law*, 14 FORDHAM INTELL. PROP. MEDIA & ENT. L.J. 497, 524 (2004) (stating that "the center of copyright as a human right lies in the moral rights arena"). *But see* General Comment, *supra* note 19, ¶¶ 30-34, 44-46 (emphasizing importance of economic exploitation rights for creators and innovators and their interdependence with moral rights).

84. *Compare* ÇOBAN, *supra* note 26, at 149-50 (suggesting that Article 1 covers only the economic value of a possession), *with* Geiger, *Constitutionalising Intellectual Property Law*, *supra* note 15, at 383 & n. 54 (suggesting that Article 1 also protects moral rights).

85. Plausible illustrations of such claims include disputes over the government's removal or destruction of sculptures, murals, or other works of visual art from public buildings or parks. *Cf.* Rebecca Stuart, Comment, *A Work of Heart: A Proposal for a Revision of the Visual Artists Rights Act of 1990 to Bring the United States Closer to International Standards*, 47 SANTA CLARA L. REV. 645, 659-76 (2007) (reviewing cases decided under U.S. moral rights statute in which creators challenged the government's removal, destruction, or mutilation of works of visual art, and comparing U.S. law to the protection of moral rights in international agreements and in other countries).

and Romania's *industrial design* statute,[86] both of which exclude such symbols as protectable subject matter. The ECHR studiously avoided any mention of industrial property, however, restricting its analysis to copyright law. Had the Romanian courts relied solely on industrial property principles to reject Dima's copyright infringements claims, the case's outcome before the ECHR might have been quite different. A broader implication of this approach is that the ECHR will interpret Article 1 in a manner that is appropriately sensitive to the distinct subject matter and protection standards of different fields of intellectual property law.

Third, the ECHR signaled in *Dima* a concern with the retroactive application of domestic intellectual property laws. The ECHR recognized that copyright protection exists from the moment an author creates a work. Had the Romanian Supreme Court rejected Dima's authorship claim based solely on the subsequently enacted 1996 statute, the ECHR's recognition of this rule would have supported a finding that the retroactive application of the new law interfered with an existing possession.[87] On the facts presented, however, Dima did not have a reasonable basis for claiming copyright protection even before the new statute took effect. There was no final judgment, nor any favorable precedent that recognized the copyrightability of design models for state symbols. This raises the possibility that the ECHR may find in favor of authors and rights holders who rely on these legal authorities before a change in the applicable law.

Fourth, the ECHR did not dismiss Dima's complaint solely on the ground that he did not own a possession protected by Article 1. Although the Court emphasized that issue, it also considered whether the Romanian courts had acted arbitrarily, indicating that the Court was also implicitly addressing the second issue identified above—whether the government had "interfered" with a possession.[88] Had Dima not been the owner of such a possession, no amount of arbitrariness by the Romanian courts could have justified the ECHR in finding a violation of Article 1. The Court's willingness to consider the issue of arbitrariness suggests that in close cases it may assume *arguendo* that the complainant has an existing possession or a legitimate expectation in order to correct egregious errors of national courts in domestic intellectual property disputes.

---

86. *See Dima v. Romania*, App. No. 58472/00, para. 80 (2005) (admissibility decision). Dima challenged the government's reliance on these authorities.
87. In *Kamoy Radyo Televizyon Yayıncılık ve Organizasyon A.Ş. v. Turkey*, App. No. 19965/06 (Chamber 2019), the ECHR found such an interference from the retrospective application of a provision of the Turkish Patent Institute Act that precluded the owners of registered trademarks from preventing the publication of newspapers or periodicals that use their marks without authorization. *See id.* paras. 41-42.
88. *See supra* section 2.2.3.

2.3.1.2 Industrial Property

A different set of ambiguities arises with respect to the ECHR's treatment of industrial property. As mentioned above, the Grand Chamber's 2007 judgment in *Anheuser-Busch Inc. v. Portugal* definitively resolved the question of whether registered industrial property rights are existing possessions protected by Article 1.[89] The Court also concluded that applications to register trademarks are similarly protected, overruling the Chamber's conclusion that such applications are neither existing possessions nor legitimate expectations. This extension of Article 1 to trademark applications raises several important issues. I discuss those issues below, but first provide an overview of the case and the reasoning of the Chamber and the Grand Chamber.

2.3.1.2.1 Anheuser-Busch Inc. v. Portugal

The ECHR's judgment in *Anheuser-Busch* is one small skirmish in a longstanding litigation war between the American brewer of "Budweiser" beer and a rival Czech company, Budějovický Budvar ("Budějovický"), which also distributes beer under the "Budweiser Bier," "Budweiser Budvar," and similar brand names. Over the past quarter century, nearly fifty disputes between the two competitors have raged across Europe in industrial property offices, domestic courts, and regional tribunals.[90] These disputes raise difficult questions concerning the relationship between trademarks and geographical indications ("GIs")[91] and between national and international intellectual property laws.

The Portuguese legal system confronted these issues in 1981 when Anheuser-Busch applied to the National Institute for Industrial Property to register "Budweiser" as a trademark. Budějovický opposed the registration,

---

89. The ECHR reaffirmed this position in *Kamoy Radyo Televizyon Yayıncılık ve Organizasyon A.Ş. v. Turkey*, App. No. 19965/06 (Chamber 2019), finding that because "the applicant company was the owner of a registered trademark which had been recognised by the domestic authorities," there was "no dispute in the present case as to whether it could claim protection of its intellectual property rights." *Id.* para. 37.
90. *See European Rights Court Rejects Budweiser Bid for Protection Against Rival Czech Brand*, 70 PAT. TRADEMARK & COPYRIGHT J., 668, 668 (2005); Jeremy Reed, *ECJ Protects Simple Geographical Indications for their Bud-dy*, 27 EUR. INTELL. PROP. REV. 25 (2005); Budweiser Budvar, Disputes Concerning Registered Trademarks, http://www.budvar.cz/en/web/Znacka-Budvar/Znamka-Budvar.html (last visited November 14, 2007).
91. The World Intellectual Property Organization (WIPO) defines a GI as a "sign used on goods that have a specific geographical origin and possess qualities or a reputation that are due to that place of origin." World Intellectual Property Organization, About Geographical Indications, http://www.wipo.int/about-ip/en/about_geographical_ind.html #P16_1100 (last visited November 14, 2007). The TRIPS Agreement has a similar definition. Agreement on Trade-Related Aspects of Intellectual Property Rights, Article 22.1, April 15, 1994, Marrakesh Agreement Establishing the World Trade Organization, Annex 1C, Legal Instruments—Results of the Uruguay Round, 33 I.L.M. 1125 (1994) [hereinafter TRIPS].

citing its 1968 Portuguese registration of an appellation of origin[92] for "Budweiser Bier."[93] The industrial property office refrained from acting on Anheuser-Busch's application while the parties attempted to negotiate a licensing agreement. Eight years later, in 1989, after protracted negotiations proved unsuccessful, Anheuser-Busch asked the Portuguese courts to cancel Budějovický's registration. An additional six years elapsed before a lower court ruled in favor of the American company in 1995, cancelling the registration on the ground that "Budweiser Bier" was not a valid appellation of origin.[94]

In the wake of this ruling, the industrial property office promptly registered Anheuser-Busch's trademark.[95] It was now the Czech brewer's turn to petition the Portuguese courts, invoking a 1986 bilateral treaty between Czechoslovakia and Portugal that provided reciprocal protection for each country's indications of source and appellations of origin. Budějovický argued that the bilateral agreement required Portugal to register "Budweiser Bier" as a Czech GI. But the lower court held that only "ČeskoBudějovický Budvar"—a Czech phrase indicating a beer from České Budějovice, a town in the Bohemia region of the Czech Republic where the brewer is based—was an appellation of origin.[96] The German name of that town—"Budweis" or "Budweiss"—and the German translation of the phrase designating beer from that town—"Budweiser Bier"—were not.[97]

---

92. The Lisbon Agreement defines an appellation of origin as "the geographical name of a country, region, or locality, which serves to designate a product originating therein, the quality and characteristics of which are due exclusively or essentially to the geographical environment, including natural and human factors." Lisbon Agreement for the Protection of Appellations of Origin and Their International Registration, Article 2(1), October 31, 1958, last amended Sept. 28, 1979, 923 U.N.T.S. 205. For a discussion of the relationship between GIs and appellations of origin, *see* Felix Addor & Alexandra Grazioli, *Geographical Indications Beyond Wines and Spirits: A Roadmap for a Better Protection for Geographical Indications in the WTO/TRIPS Agreement*, 5 J. WORLD INTELL. PROP. 865, 867-69 (2002).

93. *Anheuser-Busch Inc. v. Portugal*, App. No. 73049/01, 45 Eur. H.R. Rep. 36 [830], 833-34 (Grand Chamber 2007). The 1968 registration was filed pursuant to the Lisbon Agreement for the Protection of Appellations of Origin and their International Registration, which was opened for signature on October 31, 1958. *Id.*

94. *Id.* at 834. The Lisbon Court of First Instance held that, under the terms of the Lisbon Agreement, appellations of origin were "reserved to the geographical name of a country, region, or locality, which served to designate a product originating therein … 'Budweiser' did not come within this category." *Id.*

95. *Id.* Budějovický had filed an opposition to the application to register the Anheuser-Busch mark with the industrial property office. Notwithstanding this opposition, the office issued a certificate of registration to the American brewer in June 1995. *See id.*

96. *Id.* at 834-35.

97. The translation from Czech to German is not serendipitous. Until the middle of the last century, a large German-speaking population resided in the Bohemia region of the Czech Republic (formerly Czechoslovakia and, before 1918, a province of the Austro-Hungarian Empire). According to the Budweiser Budvar website, "[s]ince the 14th century the official name of [České Budějovice] was Budweis. Only in 1918 was the name changed

An intermediate appellate court reversed this decision and ordered the cancellation of Anheuser-Busch's trademark. The Supreme Court of Portugal affirmed. It interpreted the 1986 bilateral treaty to protect each signatory's national products in translation as well as in their original language.[98] The German translation of ČeskoBudějovický Budvar—"Budweiser Bier"—was therefore eligible for protection as a GI under the 1986 treaty. Moreover, the refusal to register the American company's mark in reliance on that treaty did not violate the trademark priority rules in the Agreement on Trade-Related Aspects of Intellectual Property Rights ("TRIPS").[99]

With the Portuguese litigation at an end, Anheuser-Busch filed a complaint with the ECHR. The beer manufacturer alleged that Portugal had violated Article 1 by invoking the 1986 bilateral treaty to deny registration of its "Budweiser" trademark that the company had applied to register in 1981, six years prior to the treaty's entry into force.[100]

In their respective judgments, both the Chamber and the Grand Chamber began by surveying industrial property treaties, EU directives, and domestic laws. These sources treat registration as the key to obtaining protection of a trademark. But they also confer "certain rights" on trademark applications, such as fixing the beginning of the mark's period of validity and exclusivity. In addition, "in some countries, an application to register a mark … may be the subject of an assignment, security assignment or licence and (provided the mark is subsequently registered) create an entitlement to compensation in the event of fraudulent use by a third party."[101] These rights

---

into the Czech name of České Budějovice. However, the indication Budweis is today the official translation of the name of the city into many foreign languages." Budweiser Budvar, Information About Trademarks, http://www.budvar.cz/en/web/Znacka-Budvar/Znamka-Budvar.html (last visited November 14, 2007).

98. Anheuser-Busch disputed that the appellation of origin "Českobudejovicky Budvar" corresponds to the German expression "Budweiser," with the result that, even if the bilateral treaty applied to translations, it did not support the registration of "Budweiser Bier" as a geographical indication. The Supreme Court of Portugal rejected this argument. *Anheuser-Busch Inc. v. Portugal*, App. No. 73049/01, 44 Eur. H.R. Rep 42 [846], 848-49 (Chamber 2007) (judgment of October 11, 2005).

99. TRIPS, *supra* note 91, Article 24. Anheuser-Busch claimed a right of priority for its "Budweiser" mark application under Article 24(5) of TRIPS, which addresses a subset of the conflicts between geographical indications and trademarks. Article 24(5) gives priority to trademarks that have been applied for or registered in good faith before the entry into force of TRIPS or before the geographical indication is protected in its country of origin. The Supreme Court rejected the American company's claim of priority under this provision. Anheuser-Busch, 44 Eur. H.R. Rep. 42 at 848-49 (Chamber). For a more detailed discussion of the court's decision, *see* Antonio Corte-Real, *The Budweiser Case in Portugal*, 24 Eur. Intell. Prop. Rev. 43 (2002).

100. *Anheuser-Busch*, 44 Eur. H.R. Rep. 42 at 853-56 (Chamber). The 1986 bilateral agreement entered into force for Portugal on March 7, 1987. *Id.* at 848.

101. *Id.* at 852; *Anheuser-Busch Inc. v. Portugal*, App. No. 73049/01, 45 Eur. H.R. Rep. 36 [830], 840-41 (Grand Chamber 2007). The Portuguese courts had held that "the mere filing of an application for registration conferred on the applicant a 'legal expectation'

notwithstanding, most European states also authorize interested parties to oppose trademark applications and to bring actions to revoke or invalidate a mark within a set time period after its registration.[102] The key issue facing the ECHR was whether, in light of this palimpsest of legal rules, Article 1 protects not only registered marks but trademark applications as well.

The Chamber Judgment. By a five-to-two vote, the Chamber ruled that Article 1 was inapplicable to the dispute before it.[103] The majority offered two justifications for this conclusion. The first rationale was limited to the case's complex procedural history. Among the twists and turns of twenty years of litigation, two events stood out: First, that the American company's right to use its mark in Portugal "was already contested by Budějovický Budvar when [Anheuser-Busch first] filed its application" in 1981; and second, that the 1986 bilateral treaty had been in force for more than two years when the company first challenged Budějovický's GI registration in 1989.[104] As a result of these events, Anheuser-Busch:

> could not be sure of being the owner of the trademark in question until after final registration and then only on condition that no objection was raised by a third party. In other words, the applicant company had a conditional right, which was extinguished retrospectively for failure to satisfy the condition, namely that it did not infringe third-party rights.[105]

This narrow, fact-specific rationale was sufficient to support the Court's conclusion that Article 1 was inapplicable. The Chamber went further, however, holding that Article 1 applies only "after final registration of the mark, in accordance with the rules in force in the State concerned."[106] Prior to that time, while an application to register is pending, the applicant has "a hope of acquiring" a possession. But it does not have a "legally protected legitimate expectation" of a future proprietary interest.[107]

This second, categorical construction of Article 1 easily disposed of Anheuser-Busch's principal argument—that the Portuguese Supreme Court had expropriated its property when it invoked the 1986 bilateral treaty to reject the company's previously filed application to register "Budweiser." Under the majority's second, broader holding, the court's adherence to the

---

that warranted the protection of the law." *Anheuser-Busch*, 44 Eur. H.R. Rep. 42 at 852 (Chamber). This expectation was later codified in a provision of the Portuguese Code of Industrial Property—enacted after the conclusion of the domestic litigation between Anheuser-Busch and Budějovický—that provided "provisional protection" to trademark applicants and authorized them to bring infringement actions on the basis of that protection. *Id.*

102. *See Anheuser-Busch*, 44 Eur. H.R. Rep. 42 at 854-55 (Chamber); *Anheuser-Busch*, 45 Eur. H.R. Rep. 36 at 843 (Grand Chamber).

103. *Anheuser-Busch*, 44 Eur. H.R. Rep. 42 at 858 (Chamber).

104. *Id.* at 857.

105. *Id.* at 858.

106. *Id.*

107. *Id.*

later-in-time treaty was simply "irrelevant, since, when that Agreement entered into force ... the applicant did not have a 'possession.'"[108]

In contrast to the judges in the majority, the two dissenting judges believed that Anheuser-Busch had a legitimate expectation protected by Article 1.[109] That expectation was based on the Portuguese Code of Industrial Property, which conferred three rights on trademark applicants: (1) a right of priority over subsequent applications, (2) a right to compensation for illegal uses of the mark by third parties, and (3) a right to have their "application[s] examined in accordance with the rules" in force when they file an application.[110] The Portuguese courts had interfered with these rights by refusing to register the "Budweiser" mark in reliance on the 1986 bilateral agreement.[111] The refusal resulted in a "total inability to exploit the mark commercially" in Portugal without the payment of compensation. For this reason, the interference did not strike a fair balance between the company's property rights and the general interest.[112]

The Grand Chamber Judgment. Anheuser-Busch petitioned for a review of the Chamber's ruling before the Grand Chamber. The ECHR granted the company's request, received additional arguments from the parties, and issued a revised judgment in January 2007. By a fifteen-to-two vote, the ECHR held that Portugal had not violated Article 1. Unlike the Chamber judgment, however, the Grand Chamber advanced one-step further in the analytical framework outlined above.[113] Specifically, the majority held that property rights in the European Convention apply to trademark applications as well as to registered marks.[114]

To reach this result, the Grand Chamber reviewed the "bundle of financial rights and interests that arise upon an application" to register a mark. These rights and interests enable applicants to enter into transactions (such as assignments or licensing agreements) that may have "substantial financial value."[115] The majority categorically rejected Portugal's claim that these transactions have only "negligible or symbolic value," citing the numerous rights that domestic law grants to trademark applicants. The economic value of trademark applications was especially likely in the case of Anheuser-Busch's "Budweiser" mark, which the ECHR recognized as enjoying "international renown."[116]

---

108. *Id.*
109. *Id.* at 858-60 (Costa & Cabral Barreto, JJ., dissenting).
110. *Id.* at 859.
111. *Id.*
112. *Id.* at 859-60.
113. *See supra* section 2.3 (introductory paragraph).
114. *Anheuser-Busch Inc. v. Portugal*, App. No. 73049/01, 45 Eur. H.R. Rep. 36 [830], 850 (Grand Chamber 2007).
115. *Id.*
116. *Id.*

The Court next turned to the Chamber's conclusion that trademark applicants possess only conditional rights prior to registration, a status that precludes their protection under Article 1. The majority acknowledged the conditional status of the rights that attach to trademark applications. But it reasoned that:

> when it filed its application for registration, the applicant company was entitled to expect that it would be examined under the applicable legislation if it satisfied the other relevant substantive and procedural conditions. The applicant company therefore owned a set of proprietary rights … that were recognised under Portuguese law, even though they could be revoked under certain conditions.[117]

The Court thus held that Article 1 was "applicable in the instant case," a conclusion that made it "unnecessary … to examine whether the applicant company could claim to have had a 'legitimate expectation.'"[118]

2.3.1.2.2   The Significance of Anheuser-Busch's Extension of Article 1 to Trademark Applications

Before analyzing the next stage in the Grand Chamber's analysis, it is worth pausing to consider the significance of the Court's decision to overrule the Chamber and apply the Convention's property rights clause to Anheuser-Busch's application to register the "Budweiser" mark. In particular, the Grand Chamber's judgment raises at least three issues that will affect the future relationship between the European human rights system and national and regional intellectual property laws.

The first issue concerns the European-wide influence of the Court's ruling. As a formal matter, ECHR judgments only bind the parties to the dispute. They do not have binding precedential effect for future controversies involving other complainants or respondent states. In practice, however, many ECHR rulings have transjurisdictional consequences. These effects are especially pronounced when the Court departs from its normal practice of resolving cases on narrow, fact-specific grounds and includes general statements of principle in its judgments.[119]

---

117. *Id.*

118. *Id.* The majority's holding logically implies that trademark applications are "existing possessions," the only other temporal category of property rights protected by Article 1. *See supra* section 2.2.2. It is uncertain, however, whether the Grand Chamber placed trademark applications in this category, since it stated only that such applications "[give] rise to interests of a proprietary nature." *Anheuser-Busch*, 45 Eur. H.R. Rep. 36 at 850 (Grand Chamber). In contrast to the majority, the concurrence and dissent analyzed trademark applications under the rubric of "legitimate expectations." *Id.* at 853 (Steiner & Hajiyev, JJ., concurring), 856 (Caflisch & Cabral Barreto, JJ., dissenting).

119. *See* Robert Harmsen, *The European Convention on Human Rights After Enlargement*, 5 Int'l J. Hum. Rts. 18, 32-33 (2001) (discussing ECHR's common practice of issuing narrow, fact-specific rulings rather than broad statements of principle). The most recent

A close reading suggests that *Anheuser-Busch* is just such a case. Although the Grand Chamber refers to facts specific to the dispute between the two brewers, such as the claim that "Budweiser" is a well-known mark, several aspects of the decision suggest that the judges intend the case to apply more broadly. These include the Court's canvassing of international, regional, and national trademark treaties and statutes; its discussion of the economic value of trademark applications in a market economy; and the phrasing of its holding—that "the applicant company's legal position *as an applicant for the registration of a trade mark* came within Article 1."[120] The Court's inclusion of these general principles strongly suggests that its analysis of Article 1 applies to applications to register trademarks in all forty-seven European Convention Member States.

A second unsettled issue concerns the consequences of the Grand Chamber's analysis for applications to register other forms of intellectual property, such as patents, industrial designs, plant varieties, and integrated circuits. The Court's twin focus on (1) the priority, exploitation, and transfer rights that international, regional, and national laws grant to trademark applicants, and (2) the practical economic value that such applications possess, suggests that the ECHR will examine these same two factors to decide whether to extend Article 1 to applications to register other forms of intellectual property.

The Court's judgment does not expressly delineate the relationship between the two factors. Its analysis strongly suggests, however, that the legal recognition of these exclusive rights creates a presumption of economic value, even if the applicant did not itself assign, license, or otherwise derive financial benefit from the application.[121] Thus, to the extent that patent, industrial design, and similar laws confer such rights upon applications to register, those applications will fall within Article 1's ambit.[122] By contrast, if the relevant legal rules do not confer such rights, applicants will need to prove that they in fact engage in "legal transactions, such as a sale or license

past President of the ECHR has urged the Court to abandon this practice. *See* Luzius Wildhaber, *A Constitutional Future for the European Court of Human Rights*, 23 Hum. Rts. L.J. 161, 162-63 (2002).

120. *Anheuser-Busch*, 45 Eur. H.R. Rep. 36 at 850 (Grand Chamber) (emphasis added).

121. The fact that the ECHR did not reference Anheuser-Busch's attempt to license its trademark application to Budějovický Budvar in its analysis of the scope of Article 1 supports this view. *See id.* at 834 and 849.

122. *See,* e.g., European Patent Convention, October 5, 1973, 1065 U.N.T.S. 199, Article 67 (defining the rights conferred by a European patent application after publication) and Articles 71-73 (describing a European patent application as "an object of property" and enumerating rights of applicants including transfer, assignment, and licensing); Council Regulation (EC) No. 6/2002, Community Designs, 2002 O.J. (L 3) 1, 5, *available at* http://oami.europa.eu/en/design/ pdf/reg2002_6.pdf, Article 12 (term of protection exists from the date of filing of an application to register a Community design) and Article 34 (describing an "application for a registered Community design as an object of property").

agreement for consideration."[123] Such evidence demonstrates that applications to register these other forms of intellectual property are "capable of possessing ... substantial financial value" even in the absence of formal legal protection.[124]

A third consequence of the Grand Chamber's decision relates to the ECHR's jurisdiction to review the refusal of domestic industrial property offices and domestic courts to register trademarks on grounds such as consumer confusion or lack of distinctiveness.[125] These issues lurked in the background of *Anheuser-Busch*. The parties disputed whether the Portuguese courts had rejected the American brewer's 1981 application to register "Budweiser" not only because it conflicted with the 1986 bilateral agreement, but also because it was confusingly similar to the Czech brewer's appellation of origin.[126] Neither the Chamber nor the Grand Chamber addressed this issue. But its importance to the parties—and to future ECHR intellectual property disputes—is easy to explain.

Consumer confusion has long been accepted as a valid basis for refusing to register trademarks. Had such confusion in fact been the basis for the refusal to register "Budweiser," Anheuser-Busch could not have argued that Portugal had interfered with its statutory right of priority by enforcing the subsequently adopted bilateral treaty. Rather, the American brewer could only have complained that the domestic courts had misjudged the reputation and consumer associations of the two companies' brands in the Portuguese beer market.

It is here that the consequences of the different approaches adopted by the Chamber and Grand Chamber are illustrated most starkly. By deciding that Article 1 is not implicated until after a trademark registration is final, the Chamber adopted a bright-line rule that categorically precluded the ECHR from reviewing national court and administrative agency decisions that refuse to register trademarks. By extending Article 1 to trademark applications (as well as to applications for other registered rights) and holding that Anheuser-Busch was "entitled to expect that [its application] would be examined under the applicable legislation,"[127] the Grand Chamber expanded the ECHR's jurisdiction to review the denial of registrations on any ground recognized in national and regional intellectual property laws. The ECHR's

---

123. *Anheuser-Busch*, 45 Eur. H.R. Rep. 36 at 850 (Grand Chamber).
124. *Id.*
125. *See* Council Directive (EC) 89/104, Articles 3-4, 1989 O.J. (L 40) 1 (setting forth mandatory and permissive grounds for denying registration of a trademark).
126. Compare Anheuser-Busch's claim that during the domestic litigation, "there had never been any question of a risk of confusion with the Czech company's products," *Anheuser-Busch Inc. v. Portugal*, App. No. 73049/01, 44 Eur. H.R. Rep. 42 [846], 854 (Chamber 2007) (judgment of October 11, 2005) with Portugal's response that the Supreme Court considered both the risk of confusion and the 1986 bilateral agreement in refusing to register the American company's trademark, *id.* at 855.
127. *Anheuser-Busch*, 45 Eur. H.R. Rep. 36 at 850 (Grand Chamber).

review of complaints challenging refusals to register is likely to be quite limited.[128] It nevertheless creates an additional layer of European human rights scrutiny over domestic intellectual property registration systems.

2.3.2 HAS THE STATE INTERFERED WITH A POSSESSION?

After concluding that a particular form of intellectual property qualifies as an "existing possession" or a "legitimate expectation" protected by Article 1, the ECHR and the European Commission must next consider the second question identified above—whether the state has "interfered" with such a possession or expectation. The tribunals have identified two distinct types of interferences: (1) government restrictions on the exercise of intellectual property rights, and (2) interferences that result from domestic intellectual property litigation between private parties.[129]

---

128. See *CSIBI v. Romania*, App. No. 16632/12 paras. 4042 (2019) (admissibility decision) (rejecting a challenge to the refusal to register a trademark that the Romanian State Office for Inventions and Trademarks and Romanian courts concluded would undermine Romania's territorial integrity, national security, and public order).

129. The ECHR and the European Commission have also indirectly considered the interference issue in two other categories of Article 1 cases. In the first category, the tribunals decline to review a claim under Article 1 if they have already examined it under another provision of the Convention. See *British Am. Tobacco Co. Ltd. v. Netherlands*, App. No. 19589/92, 331 Eur. Ct. H.R. (ser. A) at 29 (1995) (refusing to consider Article 1 claim challenging denial of patent application where claim was "in substance identical to that already examined and rejected in the context of" complainant's Article 6 challenge to the independence and impartiality of the Appeals Division of the Dutch Patent Office); *Dimitrievski v. The Former Yugoslav Republic of Macedonia*, App. No. 26602/02, para. 7 (2006) (admissibility decision) (refusing to examine alleged violation of right of property where the complaint under Article 1 "relate[d] solely to the outcome of the proceedings" and was "in fact a restatement of the complaints under Article 6").

A second category of indirect interference has arisen in challenges to the authority of the European Patent Office ("EPO") to review patent applications and register patents. Inventors file applications directly with the EPO, whose examiners decide whether the applications meet the eligibility requirements of the European Patent Convention ("EPC"). If the EPO grants the application, the patent is automatically protected in all states that have ratified the EPC. National industrial property offices and national courts may not deny a patent that the EPO has granted nor grant a patent that the EPO has denied. In four cases, inventors whose patent applications were rejected challenged the state's delegation of decision-making authority to the EPO. In each case, the European Commission rejected the challenge. The Commission highlighted the numerous benefits of the EPO's centralized review and registration system and emphasized the EPC's "procedural safeguards," including an appeals procedure staffed by independent legal and technical experts. In light of these "equivalent protections" for the rights of patent applicants, the states' delegation of authority to the EPO to review patent applications and register patents did not interfere with a possession in a manner proscribed by Article 1. *Lenzing AG v. Germany*, App. No. 39025/97, para. 20 (1998) (admissibility decision); *Lenzing AG v. United Kingdom*, App. No. 38817/97, 94 Eur. Comm'n H.R. Dec. & Rep. 136, 144 (1998) (admissibility decision); *Heinz v. Contracting States* also Parties to the European Patent Convention, App. No. 21090/92, 76 Eur. Comm'n H.R. Dec. & Rep.

2.3.2.1 Restrictions on the Exercise of Intellectual Property Rights

As previously explained, government "interferences" with property rights take two principal forms—use controls and deprivations.[130] The European Commission and the ECHR have considered state interferences with intellectual property on several occasions, concluding that the government had restricted the exercise of intellectual property rights—that is, had controlled their use—but had not completely deprived rights holders of their possessions.

The first analysis of use controls appears in a 1990 decision of the European Commission on Human Rights, which considered whether a compulsory license issued by the Dutch Patent Office amounted to an interference within the meaning of Article 1.[131] The government argued that such licenses were not interferences because "patents are granted subject to the provisions of the Patent Act, which expressly limits the scope of the patent owners' rights by providing for the grant of compulsory licences … ."[132] The Commission disagreed. It reasoned that "a patent initially confers on its owner the sole right of exploitation. The subsequent grant of rights to others under the patent is not an inevitable or automatic consequence." The Patent Office's decision to grant a compulsory license thus "constituted a control of the use of property."[133]

In *SIA AKKA/LAA v. Latvia*, the ECHR analyzed use controls applied to a collective management organization established by the Latvian Authors Association to oversee the exploitation of copyrighted musical works.[134] After the organization was unable to conclude license agreements with several broadcasters in the country, it filed civil proceedings to enjoin the continued broadcasting of its members' music. The Latvian courts refused to grant the injunction and instead ordered the organization to enter into license agreements with the broadcasters and to set equitable royalty rates.[135] The ECHR rejected the government's contention that the compulsory licenses did

---

125 (1994) (admissibility decision); *Reber v. Germany*, App. No. 27410/95, 22 Eur. H.R. Rep. 98 (1996) (admissibility decision). The ECHR has never addressed this issue, although it has cited the Commission's case law with approval. *See Bosphorus Hava Yollari Turízm ve Tícaret Anoním Şírketí v. Ireland*, App. No. 45036/98, 42 Eur. H.R. Rep. 1 [1], 32, 45 (Grand Chamber 2006) (judgment of June 30, 2005) (analyzing the delegation of authority by the European Convention's Member States to the European Union).

130. *See supra* section 2.2.3.
131. *Smith Kline & French Lab. Ltd. v. Netherlands*, App. No. 12633/87, 66 Eur. Comm'n H.R. Dec. & Rep. 70, 79 (1990).
132. *Id.*
133. *Id.* The Commission's conclusion raises the question of whether such a control is justified. I address this issue below. *See infra* section 2.3.3.
134. *SIA AKKA/LAA v. Latvia*, App. No. 562/05, para. 6 (Chamber 2016).
135. *Id.* at paras. 7-21.

not amount to an interference with property. The Court held that the "terms and conditions ... set by the domestic courts ... attested to the limits imposed on the freedom to enter into contracts in relation to the broadcasting of music."[136] These limits "interfered with the functions and economic interests of the applicant organization" and thus amounted to a "control of the use of property."[137]

2.3.2.2 Interferences Resulting from Litigation Between Private Parties

A second category of interference cases arises from domestic litigation between private parties. It is axiomatic that only states parties to the European Convention can violate the rights and freedoms it protects. The ECHR thus has "no jurisdiction to consider applications directed against private individuals or businesses."[138] When those individuals or businesses turn to national courts to resolve their property disputes, however, the decisions of those courts trigger the application of Article 1.

The ECHR and the European Commission have thus recognized that domestic judicial rulings are a form of state action.[139] At the same time, they have been wary of treating those rulings as "interferences" with property. The tribunals have considered the interference issue in three types of intellectual property disputes involving private parties: (1) cases in which national courts adjudicate contract disputes involving the licensing or transfer of intellectual property; (2) cases in which national courts reject complaints alleging intellectual property infringement; and (3) cases in which national courts resolve competing claims of intellectual property ownership. I analyze these three categories of disputes below, highlighting the ways in which the Grand Chamber in *Anheuser-Busch Inc. v. Portugal* expanded Member States' obligations relating to domestic litigation between private parties.

2.3.2.2.1 Adjudication of Intellectual Property Contracts

Aral v. Turkey,[140] a previously unnoticed admissibility decision, reveals the tribunals' treatment of the first type of dispute—private contract claims

---

136. *Id.* at para. 58.
137. *Id.* at paras. 49, 59.
138. *Reynbakh v. Russia*, App. No. 23405/03, ¶ 18 (2005). The ECHR applied this principle to an intellectual property dispute in *Mihăilescu v. Romania,* App. No. 47748/99, paras. 22-28 (2003) (admissibility decision), dismissing an Article 1 claim by patent owner who was unable to enforce a domestic court damage award against a state enterprise which had been privatized and later declared bankrupt.
139. *See S.Ö. v. Turkey*, App. No. 31138/96, para. 20 (1999) (admissibility decision) (stating that a transfer of property ownership was "enforced by a court order and thus by an act of a State organ").
140. App. No. 24563/94 (1998) (admissibility decision).

involving the licensing or transfer of intellectual property rights. In *Aral,* the Commission dismissed a complaint filed by three artists who alleged that Turkey had violated Article 1 when its courts enforced a contract that governed the rights to cartoon characters that the artists had created.[141] The Commission held that:

> the case concerns a commercial dispute between private parties. The State's intervention in the case only occurred through its courts. ... [T]here is no interference with the right to peaceful enjoyment of possessions when, pursuant to the domestic law and a contract regulating the relationship between the parties, a judge orders one party to that contract to surrender a possession to another, unless it arbitrarily and unjustly deprives that person of property in favour of another.[142]

After briefly reviewing the domestic court decisions, which had interpreted the contract and Turkish intellectual property law to divide ownership of the cartoons between the parties,[143] the Commission found no evidence that "the courts acted in an arbitrary and unreasonable manner. Accordingly, there is no shortcoming attributable to the State."[144]

2.3.2.2.2   *Rejection of Domestic Infringement Claims*

Melnychuk v. Ukraine exemplifies the ECHR's analysis of the second category of private disputes—cases in which an intellectual property owner challenges a national court's dismissal of its infringement claims against a third party.[145] *Melnychuk* involved a dispute between a writer and a newspaper that published disparaging reviews of his books. The writer asked the newspaper to publish his reply to the reviews. When the newspaper refused, the author filed a complaint with the Ukrainian courts seeking "compensation for pecuniary and non-pecuniary damage caused by the publication" of the critical book reviews. He also claimed that the newspaper had violated his copyright, although he did not explain the basis for the alleged infringement.[146] The trial court dismissed Melnychuk's complaint in its entirety. As to the copyright claim, the court stated simply that his allegations were "unsubstantiated."[147]

---

141. *Id.* at paras. 7-17, 21.
142. *Id.* at para. 38.
143. *Id.* at para. 39. The Turkish court held that the magazine publisher owned cartoons which had been "published or which were unpublished but held in the archives of the magazines." But it also held that the artists "could continue to draw the same characters ... in association with other subjects and stories [and] in other magazines or newspapers." *Id.*
144. *Id.* at para. 40.
145. *See Melnychuk v. Ukraine,* App. No. 28743/03 (2005) (admissibility decision).
146. *Id.* at para. 7.
147. *Id.* at para. 9.

After exhausting all domestic appeals, Melnychuk filed a complaint with the ECHR. His complaint included a claim that "the newspaper articles about his books violated his copyright."[148] The Court rejected the claim, stating that "the fact that the State, through its judicial system, provided a forum for the determination of the applicant's rights and obligations does not automatically engage its responsibility under Article 1 of Protocol No. 1." Rather, the state's responsibility in such cases is only triggered in "exceptional circumstances" for "losses caused by arbitrary determinations." Melnychuk's complaint did not meet this high threshold. To the contrary, "the national courts proceeded in accordance with domestic law, giving full reasons for their decisions. Thus, their assessment was not flawed by arbitrariness or manifest unreasonableness."[149]

The European tribunal's limited scrutiny of national court rulings in *Melnychuk* and *Aral* indicates that challenges to garden variety infringement and breach of contract actions will rarely succeed. The ECHR did not simply dismiss Melnychuk's weak copyright claims out of hand, but instead emphasized the exceptionally narrow scope of review in such cases. This suggests that the Court will defer to domestic judges' resolution of infringement and breach of contract disputes even where an applicant's claims have greater merit. Such an approach is consistent with the European Convention's core objective—preventing governments and public officials from violating civil and political liberties. As stated above, the treaty has no "horizontal effect" between non-state actors.[150] The ECHR will thus only rarely find fault with "the determination of [property] rights in disputes between private persons."[151]

2.3.2.2.3   Resolution of Competing Ownership Claims

A third category of Article 1 interference cases arises when national courts resolve competing claims of intellectual property ownership. This issue arose in *Anheuser-Busch*, a case in which the Portuguese courts confronted "the conflicting arguments of two private parties concerning the right to use the name 'Budweiser' as a trade mark or [as an] appellation of origin."[152] As explained above, the courts ruled in favor of the Czech owner of the

---

148. *Id.* at para. 30.
149. *Id.* at para. 31.
150. This contrasts with many provisions of EC law, which have both a "vertical effect (between the State and the individual), [and] a horizontal effect (between individuals)." *Bosphorus Hava Yollari Turízm ve Tícaret Anoním Şírketí v. Ireland,* App. No. 45036/98, 42 Eur. H.R. Rep. 1 [1], 28 (Grand Chamber 2006) (judgment of June 30, 2005) (internal quotations omitted). It bears noting, however, that some national court decisions have given horizontal effect to certain provisions of the European Convention. *See* Geiger, *Constitutionalising Intellectual Property Law, supra* note 15, at 384.
151. *Voyager Ltd. v. Turkey,* App. No. 35045/97, para. 104 (2001) (admissibility decision).
152. *Anheuser-Busch Inc. v. Portugal,* App. No. 73049/01, 45 Eur. H.R. Rep. 36 [830], 852 (Grand Chamber 2007).

appellation on the basis of a 1986 bilateral agreement between the two countries. The American brewer challenged that ruling before the ECHR, alleging that Portugal had violated the right of priority attaching to its previously filed 1981 application to register Budweiser as a trademark.[153]

After concluding that trademark applications were protected by Article 1, the Grand Chamber considered whether the Portuguese courts had interfered with Anheuser-Busch's application to register Budweiser. In analyzing this issue, the ECHR struggled to knit together two previously unrelated strands of case law.

One line of decisions concerned "the retrospective application of legislation whose effect is to deprive someone of a pre-existing asset."[154] The retroactivity of such domestic laws "may constitute [an] interference that is liable to upset the fair balance that has to be maintained between the demands of the general interest on the one hand and the protection of the right to peaceful enjoyment of possessions on the other."[155] Previously, the ECHR had applied this principle to interactions between the government and private parties.[156] But in the year prior to the Grand Chamber's judgment, the Court extended the principle "to cases in which the dispute is between private individuals and the State is not itself a party to the proceedings."[157] These decisions provided support for Anheuser-Busch's claim that Portugal had violated Article 1 by applying the 1986 bilateral treaty retroactively to its 1981 trademark application.

The American brewer's complaint also intersected with a second strand of ECHR jurisprudence—cases challenging the interpretation or application of domestic law by national courts. When confronted with such challenges, the Court has consistently held that it cannot review errors of fact or law that domestic judges have allegedly committed. Rather, its jurisdiction is limited to ensuring that national court rulings "are not flawed by arbitrariness or otherwise manifestly unreasonable" and that their interpretations of domestic law do not violate the Convention.[158] To the extent that Anheuser-Busch's arguments were premised on the Portuguese courts' misinterpretation of the bilateral treaty and the Code of Industrial Property, the ECHR had solid jurisprudential grounds for rejecting its complaint.

The Grand Chamber reconciled these two lines of case law by emphasizing that the retroactive application of the 1986 bilateral treaty was itself an unsettled issue. Unlike prior decisions in which "the retrospective

---

153. *See supra* section 2.3.1.2.1.
154. *Anheuser-Busch*, 45 Eur. H.R. Rep. 36 at 851 (Grand Chamber).
155. *Id.* at 852.
156. *See Kopecký v. Slovakia,* App. No. 44912/98, 2004-IX Eur. Ct. H.R. 125, 142-43 (Grand Chamber 2004) (reviewing case law).
157. *Anheuser-Busch*, 45 Eur. H.R. Rep. 36 at 851 (Grand Chamber) (citing *Lecarpentier v. France*, App. No. 67847/01, ¶¶ 48, 51, 52 (2006); *Cabourdin v. France*, App. No. 60796/00, ¶¶ 28-30 (2006)).
158. *Id.* at 851.

effect of the legislation [was] indisputable … [and] intentional," the application of the bilateral treaty to pending trademark applications presented "difficult questions of interpretation of domestic law."[159] The complexities of the case were compounded by the fact that, at the time of the treaty's entry into force, the appellation of origin was still registered and the parties were attempting to negotiate a license agreement. Given these unique circumstances, the ECHR concluded that the Portuguese Supreme Court's rejection of Anheuser-Busch's claim of priority and its interpretation of the bilateral treaty were neither arbitrary nor manifestly unreasonable.[160] As a result, the Supreme Court's ruling did not "interfere" with the application to register Budweiser as a trademark and thus did not violate Article 1.

The ECHR's narrow, fact-specific disposition of the *Anheuser-Busch* case gives broad deference to national courts to interpret intellectual property statutes and treaties incorporated into domestic law. But the Grand Chamber did not limit its analysis to resolving the dispute between parties. In addition to affirming the difficulty of reconciling retroactive property restrictions with the Convention, the Court made the following general statement:

> [E]ven in cases involving litigation between individuals and companies, the obligations of the State under Art. 1 of Protocol No. 1 entail the taking of measures necessary to protect the right of property. In particular, the State is under an obligation to afford the parties to the dispute judicial procedures which offer the necessary procedural guarantees and therefore enable the domestic courts and tribunals to adjudicate effectively and fairly in the light of the applicable law.[161]

The Grand Chamber did not elaborate upon these seemingly basic due process requirements. As I explain below, however, the Court's statement has important implications for its future review of intellectual property disputes under Article 1. In particular, the ECHR may interpret these due process guarantees as requiring Member States to provide statutory, administrative, and judicial mechanisms to enable intellectual property owners to prevent private parties from infringing their protected works.[162]

---

159. *Id.* at 852. *Compare Kamoy Radyo Televizyon Yayıncılık ve Organizasyon A.Ş. v. Turkey,* App. No. 19965/06 para. 41 (Chamber 2019) (distinguishing *Anheuser-Busch* on the ground that "the retrospective application of section 31(2) of the Turkish Patent Institute Act," which interfered with a media company's "right of priority as the owner of the trademark," was "indisputable").

160. *See Anheuser-Busch,* 45 Eur. H.R. Rep. 36 at 852 (Grand Chamber).

161. *Id.* at 851.

162. *See infra* section 2.4.2.

2.3.3   HAS THE STATE ADEQUATELY JUSTIFIED ITS INTERFERENCE WITH A
        POSSESSION?

If the ECHR concludes that a possession exists and that the state has
interfered with that possession, it must then consider a third and final
issue—whether the state has adequately justified that interference. The
standard for assessing such justifications is well-settled. Every interference
must be specified by law, pursue a legitimate aim, and achieve a fair and
proportional balance between the rights of the property owner and the public
interest.[163] The European tribunals use this multi-part standard to assess the
social policies and values that underlie state regulations of property.[164]

2.3.3.1   Compulsory Licenses

In *Smith Kline & French Laboratories v. The Netherlands*,[165] the European
Commission applied this standard to uphold the grant of a compulsory
license to the owner of a dependent patent to use a previously registered
invention. After the company that owned the dominant patent refused to
negotiate a license, the dependent patent owner asked the Dutch Patent Office
to award a compulsory license. The Office issued the license, which the
Dutch courts upheld on appeal.[166]

The dominant patent owner then filed a complaint with the European
Commission, alleging that the compulsory license violated its exclusive
exploitation rights. The Commission agreed that the license interfered with a
possession, but it held that the interference was justifiable and thus did not
violate Article 1.

The Commission first found that the compulsory license was provided
by law—the Dutch Patent Act—and pursued the legitimate aim of "encouraging technological and economic development." The Commission then
emphasized that "many" European Convention Member States restrict a
patentee's exclusive rights to enable "other persons to make use of a
particular patented product or process ... for the purpose of preventing the
long term hampering of technological progress and economic activity."[167] As
to the crucial issue of proportionality, the Commission emphasized the social
benefits of granting compulsory licenses to dependent patent owners as well
as the protections such licenses afford to dominant patent owners:

> [T]he Commission notes that the provision only comes into effect where
> such license is necessary for the working of a patent of the same or later
> date and the license should be limited to what is required for the working

---

163. *See supra* section 2.2.4.
164. *See* ÇOBAN, *supra* note 26, at 195-210.
165. App. No. 12633/87, 66 Eur. Comm'n H.R. Dec. & Rep. 70 (1990) (admissibility
     decision).
166. *Id.* at 72-73.
167. *Id.* at 80.

of the patent. Further, the owner of the dominant patent is entitled to royalties in respect of each compulsory license granted under the legislation and receives reciprocal rights under the dependent patent. ... [T]he Commission finds that the framework imposed by the legislation is intended to prevent the abuse of monopoly situations and encourage development and that this method of pursuing that aim falls within the margin of appreciation accorded to the Contracting State. The Commission accordingly finds that the control of use in the circumstances of this case did not fail to strike a fair balance between the interests of the applicant company and the general interest ... .[168]

In 2016, the ECHR considered whether compulsory licenses of copyrighted musical works were legitimate and proportionate restrictions permitted by Article 1. In *SIA AKKA/LAA v. Latvia*,[169] discussed previously, the ECHR concluded that the court-imposed licenses interfered with the property rights of a collective management organization that represented the owners of the musical works. It then applied the three-part standard set forth above to determine whether that interference was justified.

The ECHR first held that the compulsory licenses were "prescribed by law" because the Latvian copyright statute, interpreted in the light of Article 11*bis* of the Berne Convention,[170] gave domestic courts "competence to order the parties to enter into a licence agreement and to set an equitable royalty rate."[171] The Court next concluded that the restrictions pursued a legitimate aim, deferring to the domestic courts' "efforts to maintain a balance between the rights of the applicant organisation to obtain equitable remuneration from the use of musical work, on the one hand, and the defendants' interest to obtain a licence allowing them to legally broadcast rights-protected work."[172] Finally, the ECHR turned to whether the particular compulsory licenses challenged by the collective management organization struck a fair and proportional balance between the general interest and the right of property, including whether the licenses "provided safeguards so as

---

168. *Id.*
169. *SIA AKKA/LAA v. Latvia*, App. No. 562/05 (Chamber 2016).
170. Article 11*bis* of the Berne Convention for the Protection of Literary and Artistic Works provides in relevant part:

(1) Authors of literary and artistic works shall enjoy the exclusive right of authorizing: (i) the broadcasting of their works or the communication thereof to the public by any other means of wireless diffusion of signs, sounds or images. ... .
(2) It shall be a matter for legislation in the countries of the Union to determine the conditions under which the rights mentioned in the preceding paragraph may be exercised, but these conditions shall apply only in the countries where they have been prescribed. They shall not in any circumstances be prejudicial to the moral rights of the author, nor to his right to obtain equitable remuneration which, in the absence of agreement, shall be fixed by competent authority.

171. SIA AKKA/LAA, App. No. 562/05, para. 64.
172. *Id.* para. 70.

to ensure that the functioning of the copyright protection system and its impact were neither arbitrary nor unforeseeable."[173]

Three considerations supported the Court's rejection of the organization's Article 1 challenge. First, the domestic proceedings gave the parties an opportunity to negotiate licenses voluntarily. Although the negotiations were unsuccessful, the compulsory licenses incorporated areas where the parties had come to terms, such as the method for calculating royalty rates.[174] Second, the ECHR gave weight to the fact that "the parties in principle were willing to enter into an agreement;" in these circumstances, "banning the broadcast of the music would not suit the best interests of copyright holders, that is to say to receive the maximum benefit from the oeuvres."[175] Third, the court-mandated licenses were limited in scope and time and did not preclude the parties from modifying the royalty rate. The resulting orders thus "minimally restricted the right of the applicant organisation to renegotiate terms and conditions with the defendants and other broadcasting companies."[176] Taken together, these factors led the ECHR to conclude that "the Latvian authorities did strike a fair balance between the demands of the general interest and the rights of the applicant organisation."[177]

2.3.3.2 Other Exceptions and Limitations to Exclusive Rights

The *Smith Kline & French Laboratories* and *SIA AKKA/LAA* decisions reveal fairly sophisticated understandings of patent and copyright policy for human rights tribunals with limited experience adjudicating intellectual property disputes. The decisions also give considerable leeway to national decision-makers to restrict exclusive rights to advance intellectual property's underlying social functions. However, the cases' precedential value for other Article 1 disputes over exceptions and limitations to intellectual property rights is uncertain.

The holdings in *Smith Kline & French Laboratories* and *SIA AKKA/LAA* were narrow and fact-specific. Both tribunals emphasized the limited scope of the compulsory licenses and the equitable remuneration that patent and copyright owners receive for the use of their works. Where these benefits are absent—such as for exceptions to exclusive rights that are more capacious or do not require remuneration—the ECHR may be less willing to defer to national decision-makers in striking a balance between private property and the public interest.

Both cases also upheld limitations that protect both the rights of other intellectual property owners and the public interest in technological progress

---

173. *Id.* para. 76.
174. *Id.* para. 77.
175. *Id.* para. 78.
176. *Id.* para. 79.
177. *Id.* para. 80.

and access to protected works. The European Convention repeatedly refers to rights of others as a justification for limiting civil and political liberties.[178] The tribunals' reasoning therefore suggests that other exceptions to intellectual property rights, such as private copying, parody, and noncommercial uses, are more likely to be upheld if the ECHR interprets them as safeguards for protecting the rights of users and consumers.

2.4   FORECASTING THE FUTURE: THREE PARADIGMS FOR ECHR ADJUDICATION OF INTELLECTUAL PROPERTY DISPUTES

The preceding sections of this chapter developed a tripartite framework to analyze the ECHR's intellectual property case law under Article 1. Such a framework has three benefits. First, it provides an organizing principle to explain the relationships among a group of diverse judicial rulings, including several decisions that commentators have not previously analyzed. Second, it exposes the numerous points of intersection between European human rights law and international and domestic intellectual property law. And third, it provides an informed basis for predicting how ECHR intellectual property jurisprudence will develop in the future.

This section forecasts the evolution of the ECHR's intellectual property case law in greater depth. It does so by developing and analyzing three paradigms that the ECHR may apply when deciding future disputes relating to intellectual property. I label these approaches the rule of law paradigm, the enforcement paradigm, and the intellectual property balancing paradigm.

These three paradigms, illustrated below with contemporary examples, provide competing visions of how to conceptualize intellectual property's place in the European human rights system. Each paradigm finds support in the Court's case law and in the interpretive methodologies that ECHR judges use to further the European Convention's objectives and values.[179] However, the three paradigms have radically different consequences for the region's innovation and creativity policies. I analyze these consequences below, emphasizing the sometimes-problematic effects of overlaying two previously distinct legal regimes.

---

178. *See* European Convention, *supra* note 2, Articles 8(2), 9(2), 10(2), 11(2) (all recognizing "the rights and freedoms of others" as a legitimate basis for restricting rights).

179. For an in-depth analysis of the three paradigms, *see* Jennifer W. Reiss, *Commercializing Human Rights: Trademarks in Europe After* Anheuser-Busch v Portugal, 11 J. World Intell. Prop. 176, 183 (2011).

2.4.1   THE RULE OF LAW PARADIGM

Many legal scholars and philosophers recognize the importance of protecting property as a fundamental right, although they differ on the appropriate justification for and scope of that protection.[180] As noted above, the decision to include a right of property in the European Convention was contested and controversial.[181] The drafters did not endorse any single philosophical or theoretical rationale for property rights. But the history and text of Article 1 reflects a consensus on the basic proposition that protection of private property is essential to preserving the rule of law.

The rule of law is a concept that suffuses the entire European Convention.[182] But it is expressed with particular forcefulness in Article 1, which provides that deprivations of property must be "subject to the conditions provided for by law" and requires controls on the use of property to be based on "such laws as [the state] deems necessary."[183] The ECHR has interpreted this dual reference to law as establishing Article 1's "first and most important requirement"—that "any interference by a public authority with the peaceful enjoyment of possessions should be lawful. ... [T]he principle of lawfulness presupposes that the applicable provisions of domestic law are sufficiently accessible, precise and foreseeable in their application."[184] By compelling states to regulate property pursuant to previously established rules with these characteristics, the Court prevents arbitrary and excessive exercises of government power.[185] The desire to uphold the rule of law also explains and justifies Article 1's application to corporations, since arbitrary deprivations of property do not affect only natural persons.[186]

Under a rule of law paradigm, therefore, the ECHR would treat intellectual property no differently than any other type of real, personal, or intangible property protected by Article 1. The Court would not consider the public good qualities of intellectual property rights, nor would it concern itself with the social and cultural policies which justify the state's protection of those rights. Instead, it would find fault only with arbitrary government conduct, such as *ultra vires* actions, failure to follow previously established

---

180. *See generally* JEREMY WALDRON, THE RIGHT TO PRIVATE PROPERTY (1990). For a comprehensive review of the literature, *see* ÇOBAN, *supra* note 26, at 35-77.
181. *See supra* section 2.2.1.
182. *See* EMBERLAND, *supra* note 23, at 44.
183. Protocol 1, *supra* note 5, Article 1.
184. *Edwards v. Malta*, App. No. 17647/04, ¶ 60 (2006). *See also Zlínsat, Spol. S R.O. v. Bulgaria*, App. No. 57785/00, ¶ 98 (2006) ("The requirement of lawfulness ... means not only compliance with the relevant provisions of domestic law, but also compatibility with the rule of law.").
185. EMBERLAND, *supra* note 23, at 46 ("When the Court invokes the rule of law as an interpretive argument, it emphasizes its capacity to prevent governmental arbitrariness and the excessive wielding of public power.").
186. *See id.* at 44 ("The rule of law also helps explain why corporate persons enjoy ECHR protection.").

rules and procedures, or laws that contravene the rule of law principles described above.[187] The Court's scrutiny of national decision-makers would thus be minimal and unobtrusive. It would allow governments' unfettered discretion to fashion their domestic innovation and creativity policies as they see fit, provided that they adhere to previously established rules embodying those policies.

Does the ECHR believe that intellectual property complaints should be analyzed under the rule of law paradigm? The Grand Chamber intimated as much in *Anheuser-Busch* when it emphasized that it could not "take the place of the national courts, its role being rather to ensure that the decisions of those courts are *not flawed by arbitrariness or otherwise manifestly unreasonable.*"[188] Similarly, in *Melnychuk*, the Court held that providing intellectual property owners with a judicial forum to adjudicate domestic infringement claims did not "automatically engage [the state's] responsibility" under Article 1. Only "in exceptional circumstances" could the state "be held responsible for losses caused by arbitrary determinations."[189] These quotations suggest that the ECHR will avoid using Article 1 as a vehicle to review the micro-foundations of domestic intellectual property laws.

The European tribunals have also addressed arbitrary government conduct involving other property rights. For example, the ECHR has found fault with a domestic law that authorized an executive branch official to obtain a court order quashing a final, executed judgment that restored nationalized real property to its former owner.[190] It has disapproved of a statute conferring unbounded discretion on a prosecutor to suspend a contract to privatize real property.[191] It has criticized the withdrawal of a banking license without prior notice or a procedure for subsequent administrative or judicial review.[192] It has condemned a state's arbitrary use of supervisory review to quash final judgments ordering it to pay disability pension benefits.[193] And it has found a violation of Article 1 when the eviction and continuing dispossession of a lessee was "manifestly in breach" of domestic law.[194]

Extrapolating from these cases, it is possible to predict how the ECHR would apply the rule of law paradigm to three categories of cases—infringements of intellectual property by state agencies, flagrant

---

187. *See* ÇOBAN, *supra* note 26, at 196-97 (reviewing case law).
188. *Anheuser-Busch Inc. v. Portugal,* App. No. 73049/01, 45 Eur. H.R. Rep. 36 [830], 851 (Grand Chamber 2007) (emphasis added).
189. *Melnychuk v. Ukraine,* App. No. 28743/03, para. 28 (2005) (admissibility decision).
190. *See Brumărescu v. Romania,* App. No. 28342/95, 1999-VII Eur. Ct. H.R. 201.
191. *Zlínsat, Spol. S R.O. v. Bulgaria,* App. No. 57785/00, ¶ 23 (2006).
192. *See Capital Bank AD v. Bulgaria,* App. No. 49429/99, 44 Eur. H.R. Rep. 48 [952], 984-85 (2007) (judgment of November 24, 2005).
193. *Chebotarev v. Russia,* App. No. 23795/02, ¶ 6 (2006).
194. *Iatridis v. Greece,* App. No. 31107/96, 30 Eur. H.R. Rep. 97, 116 (Grand Chamber 2000) (judgment of March 25, 1999).

misapplication of domestic laws by the judiciary, and statutes that authorize limited government uses of intellectual property without the rights holders' consent.

Government ministries that themselves infringe intellectual property rights arguably provide the strongest case for finding a violation of Article 1 under the rule of law paradigm. A ministry that installs copyrighted software on all of its desktop computers without obtaining a license from the software's owner provides a ready example. Equally problematic from a rule of law perspective would be a state-owned enterprise's failure to pay royalties to an inventor whose patented product or process it had previously licensed.

In 2008, the ECHR decided a case that fits squarely within this rubric. In *Balan v. Moldova*,[195] a photographer challenged as a violation of Article 1 the domestic courts' refusal to compensate him for the government's infringement of his photograph of Soroca Castle, a well-known historical site in Moldova. The Ministry of Internal Affairs used the photograph as a background for national identity cards without Balan's consent. Balan initiated court proceedings and received a modest damage award equivalent to USD 550. After the Ministry continued to use the photograph on identity cards without permission, Balan filed a second suit. The Moldovan courts confirmed Balan's copyright in the photograph but refused his request for additional compensation and for an order compelling the Ministry to enter into a contract for its future use.[196] Balan challenged these rulings before the ECHR, which upheld his complaint.

The ECHR applied the tripartite framework described in section 2.2. After concluding that the photograph was a possession protected by Article 1, the Court assessed whether the government had interfered with that possession, using language that emphasized the paramount role of national judges in interpreting and applying domestic intellectual property laws:

> [T]he Court reiterates that it is not its task to take the place of the national authorities who ruled on the applicant's case. It primarily falls to them to examine all the facts of the case and set their reasons out in their decisions. In the present case, the Court does not see any reason for questioning the domestic courts' application of a law adopted specifically to regulate intellectual property rights issues and which came into force before the alleged violation of the applicant's rights. ... The Court will therefore examine the case on the basis of the law as applied by the domestic courts.[197]

---

195. *Balan v. Moldova*, App. No. 19247/03 (2008).
196. The Supreme Court of Moldova distinguished the photograph from the identity card itself, which it concluded was an official document protected under the Moldovan Copyright and Related Rights Act. *Id.* at para. 18.
197. *Id.* at para. 37.

Moldova argued that Balan had "tacitly accepted the use of his protected work without remuneration" due to his failure to request an injunction against the Ministry's use of the photograph. The ECHR rejected this contention, noting that Balan had "continuously opposed [an] unauthorised use of his protected work" that was "expressly prohibited by law."[198] It thus found that the government had interfered with his possession.

The ECHR next considered whether the interference was lawful and proportionate to the legitimate aim of issuing national identity cards. Hewing closing to the text of Moldova's copyright statute, the Court noted that "neither the domestic courts nor the Government referred to any specific provision [in the law] which expressly provides for the termination of an author's rights in respect of his or her creation by virtue of a failure to prohibit its unauthorised use."[199] As to the issue of proportionality, the ECHR emphasized that the government could have distributed identity cards:

in a variety of ways not involving a breach of the applicant's rights. For instance, another photograph could have been used or a contract could have been concluded with the applicant. The Court is unaware of any compelling reason for the use of the particular photograph taken by the applicant or of any impediments to the use of other materials for the same purpose. ... It follows that the domestic courts failed to strike a fair balance between the interests of the community and those of the applicant, placing on him an individual and excessive burden.[200]

Having found a violation of the right of property, the ECHR awarded Balan "just satisfaction" in the amount of EUR 5,000.[201]

A second type of arbitrary government action involves the judiciary. A domestic court that refuses to consider a trademark applicant's plausible arguments in favor of registration illustrates one possible scenario.[202] Another involves domestic infringement proceedings that are inexplicably or

---

198. *Id.* at para. 39.
199. *Id.* at para. 42.
200. *Id.* at paras. 45-46.
201. *Id.* at para. 51. Article 41 of the European Convention authorizes the ECHR to "afford just satisfaction to the injured party" if national law "allows only partial reparation" for a violation of human rights. The Court considered two circumstances in support of the 5,000 Euro award. First, Balan "must have been caused damage as a result of the infringement of his rights ... and the refusal of the domestic courts to award compensation for that violation, the more so seeing that the photograph had been reproduced on a large scale, despite the authorities' awareness of the unlawful character of such use." *Balan*, App. No. 19247/03, at para. 50. Second, the national courts' more modest damages award was solely for the government's first infringement "and not for the subsequent use of the photograph taken by him." *Id.*
202. *Cf. Hiro Balani v. Spain*, App. No. 18064/91, 303 Eur. Ct. H.R. 23 (ser. A) at 30 (1995) (finding a violation of the right to a fair hearing where the Supreme Court failed to consider a trademark owner's argument that its mark had priority over the trade name of a competitor that had successfully applied to cancel the mark).

inexcusably prolonged, such that the right holder is effectively precluded from preventing unauthorized exploitation by third parties.[203] In both instances, the state has failed to provide the minimal procedural guarantees to which property owners are entitled under the ECHR's conception of the rule of law.[204]

The above examples must be distinguished from court decisions that invalidate a previously registered patent or trademark. It is an inherent feature of patent and trademark systems that third parties may challenge the validity and scope of inventions and marks after administrative agencies have registered them. In fact, roughly half of all patents whose validity is later tested in litigation are found to be invalid.[205] In this sense, registered rights are always conditional. Although it is therefore accurate to state that if a patent or trademark "is found invalid, the property right will have evaporated,"[206] the dissolution of that property right raises no Article 1 concerns.

Domestic laws that authorize governments to exploit intellectual property without rights holders' consent present a closer question under the rule of law paradigm.[207] On the surface, these statutes appear to sanction wholesale infringements similar to the software infringement and patent royalty examples described above. In fact, however, such laws allow governments to use private knowledge goods for the public's benefit under previously specified conditions and for particular purposes.[208] Because intellectual property rights are state-created monopolies, the ECHR should

---

203. *See Stele v. Slovenia*, App. No. 6549/02, para. 13 (2006) (friendly settlement) (approving the settlement of a complaint alleging a violation of Article 1 by a domestic court for failing to issue a judgment in a patent infringement action for nearly eleven years).

204. *See, e.g., Capital Bank AD v. Bulgaria,* App. No. 49429/99, 44 Eur. H.R. Rep. 48 [952], 984 (2007) (judgment of November 24, 2005) (stating that although Article 1 "contains no explicit procedural requirements," its provisions nevertheless imply that "any interference with the peaceful enjoyment of possessions must be accompanied by procedural guarantees affording to the individual or entity concerned a reasonable opportunity of presenting their case to the responsible authorities for the purpose of effectively challenging the measures interfering with the rights guaranteed by this provision.").

205. Mark A. Lemley & Carl Shapiro, *Probabilistic Patents*, J. Econ. Persp., at 76 (Spring 2005).

206. *Id.* at 75.

207. For summaries of such government use exemptions relating to copyright, *see*, for example, 2 Melville B. Nimmer & Paul E. Geller, International Copyright Law and Practice, GER § 8(2)(d)(iii) (2005) (Germany); *id.* ITA § 8(2)(b)(iii) (Italy); *id.* POL § 8(2)(c) (Poland); *id.* SWE § 8(2)(d)(iii) (Sweden); *id.* UK § 8(2)(c) (United Kingdom); LiLan Ren, Note, *A Comparison of 28 U.S.C. § 1498(a) and Foreign Statutes and an Analysis of § 1498(a)'s Compliance with TRIPS*, 41 Hous. L. Rev. 1659, 1664-69 (2005) (analyzing foreign statutes authorizing government use of patented inventions).

208. *See* Ren, *supra* note 207, at 1666, 1669 (reviewing European laws that provide for government use of patented inventions for purposes of, *inter alia*, national defense and producing or supplying drugs and medications).

reject rights holders' challenges to the application of these laws, provided that they are publicly available and drafted with sufficient prevision to enable rights holders to predict when the government may use their protected works.[209] By contrast, the ECHR should find a violation of Article 1 where the state fails to comply with the conditions specified in these statutes, for example, by refusing to pay the required compensation or by exceeding the scope of the privilege.

In summary, the rule of law paradigm has several virtues. It enables the ECHR to police arbitrary excesses of state power and unambiguous violations of national law without interfering with domestic intellectual property systems. Application of the Court's authority in such cases is fully consistent with the objectives of the European Convention and the shared intent of Article 1's drafters. These disputes thus merit a place on the Court's overloaded docket, whether the complaints are filed by individuals or by corporations. In addition, any violations that the ECHR finds in such cases would not exacerbate the adverse human rights consequences of overly capacious intellectual property protection standards.[210] On the contrary, a state would be free to either expand or reduce such standards without fear of violating Article 1, provided that the government did not itself infringe protected works and provided that the laws were precise, accessible, and foreseeable.

2.4.2   THE ENFORCEMENT PARADIGM

There is solid support for the rule of law paradigm in recent ECHR jurisprudence. But the cases also contain a broader vision for the Court's adjudication of intellectual property disputes. Embedded in the Grand Chamber's *Anheuser-Busch* ruling are the seeds of an enforcement paradigm, in which the ECHR interprets Article 1 to require states to provide statutory, administrative, and judicial mechanisms that allow intellectual property owners to prevent private parties from infringing their protected works.

Whereas the rule of law paradigm targets arbitrary government inter-ferences with possessions, the enforcement paradigm emphasizes the state's "positive obligations" to protect private property.[211] Positive obligations require public authorities to take affirmative steps to ensure that rights holders can effectively exercise their rights. It is the state's wrongful

---

209. *Cf. De Graffenried v. United States*, 29 Fed. Cl. 384, 387 (1993) (stating that a patent owner's rights "do not include the right to exclude the government from using his or her patented invention" because "the statutory framework that defines a patent owner's rights gives the government the authority to use all patented inventions.").

210. *See supra* note 15-16 and accompanying text.

211. *See Sovtransavto Holding v. Ukraine*, App. No. 48553/99, 38 Eur. H.R. Rep. 44 [911], 938 (2004). *See also Broniowski v. Poland*, 2004-V Eur. Ct. H.R. 1, 56 (Grand Chamber).

omission, not its wrongful action, that triggers its responsibility under international law.[212]

As applied to Article 1, positive obligations include "provid[ing] a legal system so that property rights can be enforced."[213] For example, the Court has required states to provide police assistance to landlords seeking to recover possession of leasehold property after the termination of a tenancy.[214] States must also "afford judicial procedures which offer the necessary procedural guarantees and therefore enable … domestic courts and tribunals to adjudicate effectively and fairly any [property] disputes between private persons."[215] The Grand Chamber in *Anheuser-Busch* quoted this language almost verbatim, although it did not acknowledge that it was implicitly referencing the Court's positive obligations case law.[216]

The ECHR's application of positive obligations to private intellectual property disputes is likely to generate a fresh set of complaints challenging the adequacy of domestic enforcement procedures. These complaints will require the Court to articulate with greater precision which mechanisms states must provide to enable rights holders to prevent and punish infringements by third parties. In determining Article 1's implicit affirmative requirements, the ECHR may draw inspiration from the domestic enforcement provisions of the TRIPS Agreement.[217]

TRIPS requires countries to establish "fair and equitable" procedures that "permit effective action against any act of infringement of intellectual property rights," including procedures to prevent and deter infringements.[218] The treaty also contains detailed rules for civil and administrative remedies,

---

212. *See* Mowbray, *supra* note 24. *See also* Clare Ovey & Robin White, Jacobs and White, The European Convention on Human Rights 51-52 (4th ed. 2006).

213. Çoban, *supra* note 26, at 164.

214. *See Immobiliare Saffi v. Italy*, App. No. 22774/93, 1999-V Eur. Ct. H.R. 73, 90-92 (Grand Chamber).

215. Sovtransavto Holding, 38 Eur. H.R. Rep. 44 at 916 ("positive obligations may entail certain measures necessary to protect the right of property even in cases involving litigation between individuals or companies") (internal citation omitted).

216. *See Anheuser-Busch Inc. v. Portugal*, App. No. 73049/01, 45 Eur. H.R. Rep. 36 [830], 851 (Grand Chamber 2007) ("[T]he State is under an obligation to afford the parties to the dispute judicial procedures which offer the necessary procedural guarantees and therefore enable the domestic courts and tribunals to adjudicate effectively and fairly in the light of the applicable law.").

217. As a formal matter, TRIPS protects only foreign intellectual property owners, whereas Article 1 protects the owners of all possessions regardless of nationality. As a political and practical matter, however, states rarely protect foreign intellectual property owners without extending equivalent protections to domestic creators, innovators, and businesses. *See* Helfer, *Adjudicating Copyright Claims*, *supra* note 1, at 367 & n. 38. As a result, the formal differences in scope between the two treaties are unlikely to deter the ECHR from consulting TRIPS when fashioning Article 1 positive obligations.

218. TRIPS, *supra* note 91, Article 41(2), 41(1).

provisional measures, border enforcement, and criminal penalties.[219] Tempering these obligations, TRIPS acknowledges that intellectual property enforcement measures may vary from country to country depending upon the resources available for law enforcement in general.[220]

Several factors suggest that the ECHR may refer to TRIPS when defining the positive obligation to protect intellectual property. First, TRIPS binds thirty-nine of the forty-seven European Convention members.[221] The Court has held that the Convention "must be applied in accordance with the principles of international law," including treaties to which the respondent state is a party.[222] For these thirty-nine countries, consulting TRIPS to interpret Article 1 would help harmonize the states' treaty obligations.[223] Second, the ECHR has held that the Convention must be interpreted in light of regional and international trends in law and social policy.[224] Thus, even for countries that are not World Trade Organization ("WTO") members, the ECHR may consult TRIPS to elucidate the domestic enforcement mechanisms that Article 1 requires.

To be sure, the Court is unlikely to incorporate every nuance of TRIPS into Article 1, especially in cases involving countries that are not WTO members. Rather, the ECHR would use the treaty as a rough benchmark to aid it in fashioning minimum enforcement standards that respect "the fair balance that has to be struck between the general interest of the community

---

219. *Id.* Articles 42-51, 61. These provisions have resulted in substantial changes to domestic enforcement procedures in many countries. *See* Jerome H. Reichman, *Enforcing the Enforcement Procedures of the TRIPS Agreement*, 37 Va. J. Int'l L. 335 (1997).
220. TRIPS, *supra* note 91, Article 41(5). For a detailed analysis of how WTO dispute settlement panels might draw on ECHR jurisprudence to interpret TRIPS' enforcement obligations, *see* Helfer, *Adjudicating Copyright Claims, supra* note 1, at 416-20.
221. *See* World Trade Organization, Understanding the WTO: The Organization—Members and Observers, http://www.wto.org/english/thewto_e/whatis_e/tif_e/org6_e.htm (last visited November 14, 2007); Council of Europe, Member States of the Convention for the Protection of Human Rights and Fundamental Freedoms, http://conventions.coe.int/Treaty/Commun/ChercheSig.asp?NT=005&CM=8&DF=2/23/2007&CL=ENG (last visited November 14, 2007). The eight European Convention members who have not yet ratified the WTO Agreement are Andorra, Azerbaijan, Bosnia and Herzegovina, Montenegro, the Russian Federation, San Marino, Serbia, and Ukraine. *Id.*
222. *Guichard v. France*, App. No. 56838/00, 2003-X Eur. Ct. H.R. 419, 431 (admissibility decision). *See also Paradis v. Germany,* App. No. 4783/03 (2004) (judgment of May 15, 2003) (admissibility decision).
223. The case for using TRIPS as a benchmark is strengthened by the fact that both treaties require states to use practical effective enforcement mechanisms to protect intellectual property rights. *Compare* TRIPS, *supra* note 91, Article 41(1) (TRIPS enforcement provisions aim "to permit effective action against any act of infringement of intellectual property rights"), *with Artico v. Italy*, App. No. 6694/74, ¶ 33 (1980) (holding that "the Convention is intended to guarantee … rights that are practical and effective … .").
224. *See* Alastair Mowbray, *The Creativity of the European Court of Human Rights*, 5 Hum. Rts. L. Rev. 57, 60-71 (2005).

and the interests of the individual" and that do not "impose an impossible or disproportionate burden on the authorities."[225]

Aware of the helpful analogies that TRIPS provides, rights holders are likely to invoke the treaty in three types of Article 1 enforcement cases. First, rights holders may contest the remedies awarded in individual infringement proceedings, even where a domestic legal system in the aggregate satisfies the Convention's rule of law requirements. These challenges are unlikely to succeed. Disputes over issues such as the amount of damages, the denial of injunctive relief, or the failure to impound infringing articles are precisely the sort of case-specific applications of domestic law with which the ECHR rarely finds fault.[226] In addition, nothing in TRIPS limits the discretion of national courts to tailor remedies to the facts and circumstances of individual disputes.[227] Only in extraordinary cases, such as where national courts refuse to award a remedy mandated by domestic law, might the ECHR plausibly intervene.

A second category of cases concerns a state's failure to provide one of the enforcement measures that TRIPS requires.[228] In the late 1990s, for example, the U.S. successfully challenged the lack of ex parte civil remedies in Denmark and Sweden.[229] Most European countries now authorize ex parte orders.[230] Some intellectual property owners claim, however, that the procedures for obtaining these orders are "unnecessarily complicated" and "costly" in some jurisdictions. These claims could be refashioned as arguments that the states concerned have failed to provide the effective enforcement measures required by Article 1.

The third and most serious non-enforcement claim concerns the wholesale failure to prevent private infringements of intellectual property. Cases of this nature target pervasive, systemic defects in civil, administrative, or criminal procedures which prevent intellectual property owners from enforcing their rights. Such system-wide enforcement deficiencies exist principally (although by no means exclusively) in Eastern Europe.[231] Piracy

---

225. *Özgür Gündem v. Turkey,* App. No. 23144/93, 2000-III Eur. Ct. H.R. 1, 21.

226. *See supra* section 2.3.2.2.2.

227. *Cf. eBay Inc. v. MercExchange,* L.L.C., 126 S.Ct. 1837 (2006) (emphasizing the discretionary nature of injunctive relief in patent infringement cases).

228. *See* Int'l. Intell. Prop. Alliance, Copyright Enforcement Under the TRIPS Agreement 5 (2004) (summarizing in chart form the TRIPS deficiencies found in national copyright laws and enforcement practices), *available at* http://www.iipa.com/rbi/ 2004_Oct19_TR IPS.pdf.

229. *See* Notification of Mutually Agreed Solution, *Denmark—Measures Affecting the Enforcement of Intellectual Property Rights,* WT/DS83/2 (June 13, 2001); Notification of Mutually Agreed Solution, *Sweden—Measures Affecting the Enforcement of Intellectual Property Rights,* WT/DS86/2 (December 11, 1998).

230. *See* Int'l. Intell. Prop. Alliance, *supra* note 228, at 3.

231. *See* Ed Bates, *Supervision of the Execution of Judgments Delivered by the European Court of Human Rights: The Challenges Facing the Committee of Ministers, in* European Court of Human Rights: Remedies and Execution of Judgments 49, 84-96 (Theodora

and counterfeiting in the Ukraine, Russia, and Turkey have been especially flagrant.[232]

The ECHR has established a "pilot judgment procedure" that is well suited to redressing widespread piracy of intellectual property rights. Under this aggregate litigation mechanism, the Court adjudicates a single case that represents a large number of similar human rights claims, and it uses the case to develop systemic reforms for the entire class. The ECHR first applied the procedure in a 2004 decision affecting nearly 80,000 real property claimants in Poland.[233] It later approved a settlement of the dispute, but only after the state had enacted legislation to prevent future Article 1 violations and provide remedies to all affected property owners.[234] The case publicized the Court's determination to scrutinize systemic problems that affect large numbers of similarly situated property owners.[235]

Intellectual property rights holders could invoke the pilot judgment procedure if they are unable, after reasonable diligence, to protect their works within a respondent state's territory. If rights holders prove that piracy in the jurisdiction is pervasive, the ECHR could require the government to adopt system-wide reforms. Depending on the nature and scope of the violations, such measures could include enacting domestic legislation, streamlining judicial procedures, or allocating additional resources to criminal or administrative enforcement actions. Here too the ECHR may turn to TRIPS' enforcement provisions for guidance in fashioning appropriate systemic remedies, although the Court should also be mindful of the

---

Christou & Juan Pablo Raymond eds., 2005) [hereinafter ECHR REMEDIES] (describing systemic and structural problems, including lack of resources, infrastructure, and slow or corrupt domestic judicial processes, leading to widespread violations of the European Convention in Turkey and in several Eastern European countries).

232. According to a U.S. government report, the deficiencies include the "lack of an effective and deterrent criminal enforcement system ... , the lack of effective plant inspection [for optical media production and distribution] ...; the lack of civil ex parte search procedures; an extremely porous border; delays in criminal prosecutions and adjudications; and infrequent destruction of seized pirate goods." OFFICE OF U.S. TRADE REPRESENTATIVE, 2005 SPECIAL 301 REPORT 32 (2005); *see also id.* at 24 (highlighting the need for Ukraine to "deter[] optical media piracy through adequate enforcement"), *id.* at 33 (highlighting "concerns over patent protection, copyright piracy, trademark counterfeiting, and IPR enforcement problems" in Turkey).

233. *Broniowski v. Poland,* App. No. 31443/96, 2004-V Eur. Ct. H.R. 1, 76 (Grand Chamber). The Article 1 violations in this case concerned the state's failure to meet its positive obligations and its interference with property rights. *Id.* at 57.

234. *Broniowski v. Poland,* App. No. 31443/96, 43 Eur. H.R. Rep. 1 [1], 19-20 (Grand Chamber 2006) (judgment of September 28, 2005) (friendly settlement).

235. *See* Philip Leach, *Beyond the Bug River—A New Dawn for Redress Before the European Court of Human Rights,* 10 EUR. HUM. RTS. L. REV. 148 (2005). The Court has since issued a pilot judgment involving an even larger number of property claimants. *See Hutten-Czapska v. Poland,* App. No. 35014/97, 45 Eur. H.R. Rep. 4 [52] (Grand Chamber 2007) (judgment of June 19, 2006) (holding that domestic legislation which prevented 100,000 landlords from raising rents to cover property maintenance for between 600,000 and 900,000 tenants violated Article 1).

statement that nothing in the agreement "creates any obligation with respect to the distribution of resources as between enforcement of intellectual property rights and the enforcement of law in general."[236]

Should the ECHR endorse the enforcement paradigm described above? The arguments in favor of its doing so are equivocal. On the one hand, once a government has recognized exclusive rights in knowledge goods, the owners of Article 1 possessions can reasonably expect that government to provide the means to prevent and punish infringements by third parties. This expectation is bolstered where the state is a WTO member and has accepted the obligation to conform its domestic laws to TRIPS. In addition, once a state has incorporated intellectual property enforcement mechanisms into its domestic legal system, rights holders can reasonably expect it to devote sufficient resources to make those mechanisms practical and effective.

Yet the enforcement paradigm also raises troubling issues. The first relates to the different judicial access rules of the WTO and the ECHR. In the WTO dispute settlement system, only states can file complaints alleging violations of TRIPS. This limitation on WTO standing acts as a key political filter that limits the number and type of TRIPS controversies[237] and colors how disputes are resolved.[238]

The enforcement paradigm bypasses this political filter by allowing private parties to litigate breaches of TRIPS' enforcement provisions in the guise of violations of Article 1's positive obligations. As the years of ceaseless judicial battles between Anheuser-Busch and Budějovický Budvar

---

236. TRIPS, *supra* note 91, Article 41(5).
237. *See* Alan O. Sykes, *Public Versus Private Enforcement of International Economic Law: Standing and Remedy*, 34 J. Legal Stud. 631 (2005) (analyzing "political filters" that allow states to limit WTO litigation to disputes that produce joint welfare gains). In the intellectual property context, governments litigate only a subset of TRIPS disputes that rights holders bring to their attention. In some cases, a state may decline to file a complaint because it fears a WTO countersuit. In others, it may refuse to do so because the probability of success is low or because victory will only marginally benefit domestic industries. In still others, geostrategic factors unrelated to trade or intellectual property may lead governments to refrain from litigating. In each instance, the "decision whether to challenge a practice of a member may be made only by another member government, not by the private party who is directly aggrieved by that practice." Judith H. Bello, *Some Practical Observations About WTO Settlement of Intellectual Property Disputes*, 37 Va. J. Int'l L. 357, 358 (1997).
238. When governments do file TRIPS complaints, they often prefer a politically palatable settlement or an ambiguous panel decision to a definitive WTO Appellate Body ruling. Such compromises allow both sides to claim victory and resolve the litigation in ways that both states are willing to accept. *See* Notification of a Mutually Satisfactory Temporary Arrangement, *United States—Section 110(5) of the US Copyright Act*, WT/DS160/23 (June 26, 2003) (notifying WTO of lump-sum payment by United States to the EC to settle TRIPS copyright dispute in which the EC prevailed); *see also* Eva Gutierrez, *Geographical Indicators: A Unique European Perspective On Intellectual Property*, 29 Hastings Int'l & Comp. L. Rev. 29, 48-49 (2005) (stating that both the United States and the EC claimed victory and did not appeal a WTO panel decision partially invalidating EC protection of GIs).

illustrate, many businesses have the incentive and the means to litigate in every available forum. The ECHR's adoption of the enforcement paradigm would thus presage an increase in litigation of intellectual property enforcement disputes framed as human rights complaints, including cases that, under the current system, would not have been litigated or would have been resolved through politically palatable settlements. It is highly questionable whether these cases warrant a place on the Court's already overcrowded docket.

A second concern of the enforcement paradigm relates to the dissimilar remedies that the WTO and the ECHR award. Although both tribunals recommend responses for states that have violated their treaty commitments, the ECHR's remedial powers are more expansive. Its recent judgments have included recommendations to reopen closed court proceedings, revise domestic statutes, and award restitution in kind.[239] In addition, the ECHR awards "just satisfaction" to "injured parties."[240] Damage awards are usually less than EUR 10,000, and the Court has discretion to award no monetary relief. In property rights cases, however, pecuniary damage awards sometimes "assume gigantic proportions" that run into the tens of millions of euros.[241]

The ECHR's award of these remedies when states violate Article 1's positive obligations could impose significant constraints on national legal systems. If countries do not adopt the remedies that the Court recommends, injured rights holders could file complaints with the Court seeking compensation. In addition, under the new pilot judgment procedure described above, the ECHR could recommend systemic reforms benefiting all similarly situated rights holders. In counterfeiting and piracy cases, for example, the Court may award large monetary awards to an entire class of rights holders if states do not improve their judicial procedures.[242] These concerns suggest, on balance, that the ECHR should avoid interpreting Article 1 to enable intellectual property owners to challenge the adequacy of domestic enforcement mechanisms.

---

239. *See* Leach, *supra* note 235, at 149-51 (describing evolution of ECHR's approach to remedies).

240. European Convention, *supra* note 2, Article 41.

241. Marius Emberland, *Compensating Companies for Non-Pecuniary Damage:* Cominger-soll S.A. v. Portugal *and the Ambivalent Expansion of the ECHR Scope*, 74 Brit. Y.B. Int'l L. 409, 412 (2003); *see also* Çoban, *supra* note 26, at 228. In addition, the ECHR has "awarded monetary compensation for moral injury in almost all of the property cases where it found [a] violation of" Article 1. *Id.* at 230. Moral damage suffered by corporations includes harm to business reputation, uncertainty in future planning, disruption in management, and inconvenience to directors and officers. Emberland, *supra* note 23, at 132.

242. *See Hutten-Czapska v. Poland*, App. No. 35014/97, 45 Eur. H.R. Rep. 4 [52], 139 (Grand Chamber 2007) (judgment of June 19, 2006) (Zupančič, J., concurring in part and dissenting in part) (stating that judgment finding a violation of Article 1 in a pilot judgment case "bind[s] the state to indemnify all" similarly situated rights holders).

2.4.3   THE INTELLECTUAL PROPERTY BALANCING PARADIGM

If the merits of the enforcement paradigm are at best ambiguous, the Court's adoption of an intellectual property balancing paradigm would have indisputably negative consequences for innovation and creativity law and policy. Such deleterious effects would result from the ECHR's inevitably ad hoc interventions at the upper and lower boundaries of intellectual property protection standards. Under the balancing paradigm, the ECHR would interpret the European Convention to impose both a floor and a ceiling on domestic intellectual property rights. The Court would police the lower limit of protection by reviewing whether the government's diminution of exclusive rights or expansion of exceptions and limitations satisfies Article 1's fair and proportional balance standard.[243] And it would police the upper boundary by assessing whether expansions of exclusive rights or restrictions on exceptions and limitations violate other European Convention provisions, such as freedom of expression and the right of privacy.[244]

The intellectual property balancing paradigm finds some support in recent European human rights jurisprudence. With respect to Article 1, the Court in *Anheuser-Busch* and *Dima* suggested that retroactive laws that restrict intellectual property rights may violate Article 1. This concern extends not only to interactions between the state and rights holders but also to disputes between private parties.[245]

With respect to other human rights, the ECHR has decided a string of cases challenging the Austrian Copyright Act's ban on public dissemination of "[p]ortraits of persons" that cause injury to "the legitimate interests of the persons portrayed."[246] In each case, the Court held that injunctions prohibiting newspapers from publishing photographs of politicians or individuals involved in matters of public interest violated the right to freedom of expression.[247] In reaching this result, the ECHR stated that freedom of

---

243. *See supra* section 2.2.4.
244. European Convention, *supra* note 2, Article 10(1) ("Everyone has the right to freedom of expression. This right shall include freedom to … receive and impart information and ideas without interference by public authority and regardless of frontiers."); *id.* Article 8(1) ("Everyone has the right to respect for his private and family life, his home and his correspondence.").
245. *See Anheuser-Busch Inc. v. Portugal*, App. No. 73049/01, 45 Eur. H.R. Rep. 36 [830] (Grand Chamber 2007); *Dima v. Romania*, App. No. 58472/00, paras. 87-92 (2005) (admissibility decision).
246. Urheberrechtgesetz—UrhG. Bundesgesetz über das Urheberrecht an Werken der Literatur und der Kunst und über verwandte Schutzrechte [UrhG] [Federal Law on Copyright in Works of Literature and Art and on Related Rights] Bürgerliches Gesetzbuch [BGB1] No. 111/1936, § 78 (1) (Austria) ("Portraits of persons may not be exhibited or otherwise distributed in a manner which would make them available to the public if legitimate interests of the person portrayed, or, should he have died without authorizing or ordering the publication of the portrait, of a close relative would be prejudiced.").
247. *See*, e.g., *Österreichischer Rundfunk v. Austria*, App. No. 35841/02, ¶¶ 72-73 (2006); *Verlagsgruppe News GmbH v. Austria* (No. 2), App. No. 10520/02, ¶ 29 (2006); *Krone*

expression "protects not only the substance of ideas and information but also the form in which they are conveyed."[248] The Court also conducted a detailed and fact-intensive balancing analysis, weighing the interests of the individuals whose images were disseminated against the media's interest in conveying information to the public.[249]

Several predictions follow from these two lines of decisions. The first concerns retroactive restrictions of property rights. When governments revise laws that protect intellectual property, they generally apply the revisions to works already in existence as well as to those yet to be created.[250] Where such modifications reduce the level of protection, they may upset rights holders' reasonable expectations and investments made in reliance on the prior legal regime.[251] Although expansions of exclusive rights have received the lion's share of attention, contractions are more widespread than is commonly believed.

Consider a few examples of diminutions of intellectual property protection. In the mid-2000s, Belgium introduced a research exemption and a compulsory license for public health uses of biotechnology patents.[252] The United Kingdom eliminated perpetual protection for unpublished copyrighted works in 1989.[253] Germany and Belgium amended their copyright statutes to implement a 2001 EC Directive on the harmonization of copyright.[254] The laws authorize users "to demand from the right holder any support required for the exercise of certain legitimate uses. This means that

---

Verlags GmbH & Co KG v. Austria, App. No. 34315/96, 36 Eur. H.R. Rep. 57 [1059], 1066 (2003) (judgment of February 26, 2002); *News Verlags GmbH & CoKG v. Austria*, 2000-I Eur. Ct. H.R. 157, 174-75.

248. *Verlagsgruppe News GmbH*, App. No. 10520/02, ¶ 29.

249. *See News Verlags GmbH*, 2000-I Eur. Ct. H.R. at 175-77; *Österreichischer Rundfunk*, App. No. 35841/02 ¶¶ 62-73; *Verlagsgruppe News GmbH*, App. No. 10520/02 ¶¶ 34-44.

250. Nothing in Article 1 or ECHR case law prohibits governments from limiting diminutions of intellectual property protection standards to inventions, creations, and signs that have yet to be created. In practice, however, states rarely limit protection in this way.

251. *See* Rochelle Cooper Dreyfuss, *Patents and Human Rights: Where Is the Paradox?*, in INTELLECTUAL PROPERTY AND HUMAN RIGHTS: A PARADOX 72, 82 n. 43 (Willem Groscheide, ed., 2009) (arguing against protecting patents as human rights but recognizing that "there is a grey area where investments made in reliance on a particular scheme of patent protection are frustrated by a change in regime; whether the change amounts to a taking of property is arguably a hard question.").

252. *See* Geertruii Van Overwalle, *The Implementation of the Biotechnology Directive in Belgium and Its After-Effects*, 37 INT'L REV. INTELL. PROP. & COMP. L. 889, 905-18 (2006) (describing the scope of the exemption and compulsory license in Belgium).

253. *See* R. Anthony Reese, *The New Property*, 85 TEX. L. REV. 585, 608 (2007). The law provides a fifty-year transition period, so that works unpublished in that year date will be protected until the end of 2039.

254. Council Directive 2001/29/EC, pmbl., 2001 O.J. (L 167) 10, 11. The Act of May 22, 2005 amended Belgium's copyright legislation to implement the directive. *See* 1 MELVILLE B. NIMMER & PAUL E. GELLER, INTERNATIONAL COPYRIGHT LAW AND PRACTICE, BEL § 1 (Belgium). The Amendment of September 10, 2003 implemented the directive in Germany. *See id.* GER § 1 (Germany).

if a technical measure hinders a user in a use permitted by law, the user can ask a judge to enforce his limitation."[255]

As applied to pre-existing works, each of these statutory revisions interferes with an existing possession, presenting the retroactivity concerns identified by the Grand Chamber in *Anheuser-Busch*. A challenge to these or similar laws under Article 1 would raise the third and most difficult issue in the tripartite framework described above—whether the laws strike a fair and proportional balance between the rights of intellectual property owners and the public interest.[256] The ECHR recently addressed precisely this issue in *Kamoy Radyo Televizyon Yayıncılık ve Organizasyon A.Ş. v. Turkey*,[257] a 2019 case challenging the retroactive application of a statute authorizing media companies to publish periodicals without regard to trademark rights.[258] The statute was subsequently annulled by the Turkish Constitutional Court as a violation of the right of property, but not before it was invoked by a rival media group to invalidate a registered trademark whose owner had previous filed an infringement action against media group.[259] Concluding that the retrospective application of the now-abrogated statute was neither legitimate nor proportionate, the ECHR stated:

> [T]he legislative intervention complained of by the applicant company, which definitively settled, in a retroactive manner, the substance of the dispute between the applicant company and the rival media group before the domestic courts, does not appear to have been justified by any grounds of general interest, as required, in particular, by the principle of the rule of law.[260]

The application of the fair and proportional balance standard to intellectual property raised other important and unresolved questions. For example, what is the relationship between the standard and the "three-step test" that TRIPS uses to regulate exceptions and limitations in national copyright, patent, and trademark laws?[261] If the standard is more *lenient* than the three-step test, rights holders whose complaints are rejected by the ECHR could petition their governments to challenge the exceptions as a violation of

---

255. Christophe Geiger, *Copyright and Free Access to Information: For a Fair Balance of Interests in a Globalised World*, 28 Eur. Intell. Prop. Rev. 366, 370 & n. 44 (2006).
256. *See supra* sections 2.2.4 & 2.3.3.
257. App. No. 19965/06 (Chamber 2019).
258. Section 31(2) of the Turkish Patent Institute Act, adopted in 2003, provided that "[t]hose who publish periodicals in accordance with the Press Act [Law no. 5680] at the time this Law enters into force cannot be prevented from publishing their periodicals owing to the provisions of Legislative Decree no. 556 on the Protection of Trademarks."
259. *Kamoy Radyo Televizyon Yayıncılık*, App. No. 19965/06, at paras. 9-17.
260. *Id.* para. 50.
261. For example, Article 13 of TRIPS confines exceptions and limitations to copyright to "certain special cases which do not conflict with a normal exploitation of the work and do not unreasonably prejudice the legitimate interests of the right holder." TRIPS, *supra* note 91, Article 13. *See also id.* Article 17 (trademark), Article 30 (patent).

TRIPS, taking what is, in effect, an appeal from the ECHR to the WTO. If the standard is more *restrictive* than the three-step test, rights holders will have an incentive to challenge exceptions and limitations before the ECHR, bypassing the WTO dispute settlement system's political filters[262] and adding more cases to the Court's docket. Even if Article 1 and the three-step test impose *equivalent* restrictions, their substantive application will undoubtedly differ. This will create complexity and uncertainty for both rights holders and users and increase opportunities for protracted, duplicative litigation and forum shopping.

These problems will only be compounded if the ECHR invokes other individual liberties to establish an upper human rights boundary on intellectual property protection standards. Although a detailed treatment of these issues is beyond the scope of this chapter, recent national court rulings and the writings of commentators suggest the kinds of cases that the ECHR may face.[263] As one scholar has predicted:

> [F]reedom of expression arguments are likely to succeed against copyright claims aimed at preventing political discourse, curtailing journalistic or artistic freedoms, suppressing publication of government-produced information or impeding other forms of "public speech." In practice, this might imply that the [ECHR] would be willing to find violations of Article 10 [protecting the right to freedom of expression] if national courts fail to interpret broadly or "stretch" existing copyright limitations to permit quotation, news reporting, artistic use or reutilization of government information. The Court might also be willing to find national copyright laws in direct contravention of Article 10 if they fail to provide exceptions for uses such as parody.[264]

In two cases decided in 2013, the ECHR took the first steps toward realizing this prediction. In *Ashby Donald and Others v. France*,[265] the Court rejected a freedom of expression challenge to the criminal prosecutions of photographers for the unauthorized distribution of fashion photographs of Paris runway shows. In *Neij and Kolmisoppi v. Sweden*,[266] the judges turned away a complaint by the founders of Pirate Bay, one of the world's largest file sharing websites, against prison sentences and damage awards for wilful infringement under Swedish copyright law.

---

262. *See* Sykes, *supra* note 237 (discussing how the restriction of judicial access to states functions as a political filter on WTO dispute settlement).
263. *See* Geiger, *Constitutionalising Intellectual Property Law*, *supra* note 15, at 394-96 (discussing court decisions from Austria, the Netherlands, and Germany in which freedom of expression and the public's right to information prevailed over claims for protection by copyright and trademark owners).
264. Hugenholtz, *supra* note 22, at 362.
265. App. No. 36769/08 (Chamber 2013) (in French only; unofficial English translation on file with author).
266. App. No. 40397/12 (Chamber 2013) (admissibility decision).

The outcomes of these cases is less significant than the ECHR's reasoning, which for the first time affirmed that the enforcement of national intellectual property laws interferes with the right to receive and impart information and ideas protected by Article 10 of the European Convention.[267] Such enforcement must therefore be prescribed by law and necessary in a democratic society for the achievement of certain societal aims, such as the rights and freedoms of others.[268] The decisions therefore suggest that ECHR may one day conclude that the enforcement of intellectual property laws transgresses these principles and violates the right to freedom of expression.[269]

There are several reasons to be concerned about the ECHR imposing upper and lower limits on intellectual property protection standards. First, the rights and freedoms in the European Convention, even when viewed collectively, do not provide a coherent blueprint for the Court to undertake such a sensitive and policy-laden function. Unlike the Universal Declaration of Human Rights[270] and the International Covenant on Economic, Social and Cultural Rights,[271] the Convention does not contain a single provision that expressly balances the rights of authors and inventors[272] against the public's right to benefit from the scientific and cultural advances that knowledge goods can engender.[273] In the absence of such a provision, the ECHR's interventions at the upper and lower boundaries of protection will inevitably be ad hoc. They also create a risk of both underprotection and overprotection,

---

267. *Donald Ashby*, App. No. 36769/08, at para. 34; *Neij and Kolmisoppi*, App. No. 40397/12, at 9-10.

268. *See Donald Ashby*, App. No. 36769/08, at paras. 35-45; *Neij and Kolmisoppi*, App. No. 40397/12, at 10-11.

269. The following passage from *Donald Ashby* is especially suggestive in this regard:

> In this case, the disputed photographs were published on a website belonging to a company run by the first two applicants, in particular to sell or give access against payment. The approach of the applicants was therefore primarily commercial. In addition, if one cannot deny the attractiveness of public fashion in general and haute couture in particular, it cannot be said that the applicants took part in a debate of general interest as they confined themselves to making fashion photographs accessible to the public.

> *Donald Ashby*, App. No. 36769/08, at para. 39.

270. Universal Declaration of Human Rights, G.A. Res. 217A, at 71, U.N. GAOR, 3d Sess., 1st plen. mtg., U.N. Doc. A/810 (December 10, 1948) [hereinafter UDHR].

271. International Covenant on Economic, Social and Cultural Rights, Articles 15(1)(b), 15(1)(c), December 16, 1966, 993 U.N.T.S. 3 [hereinafter ICESCR].

272. UDHR, *supra* note 270, Article 27(2) ("Everyone has the right to the protection of the moral and material interests resulting from any scientific, literary or artistic production of which he [or she] is the author."); ICESCR, *supra* note 271, Article 15(1)(c) (recognizing the same right in nearly identical language).

273. ICESCR Article 15 recognizes "the right of everyone" to "enjoy the benefits of scientific progress and its applications," and obligates states to take steps "necessary for the conservation, the development and the diffusion of science and culture." ICESCR, *supra* note 271, Articles 15(1)(b), 15(2). Similarly, the UDHR protects the right of everyone "freely to participate in the cultural life of the community, to enjoy the arts and to share in scientific advancement and its benefits." UDHR, *supra* note 270, Article 27(1).

depending on the vagaries of which cases are filed, in what order, and how the Court extends its jurisprudence over time.[274]

Second, and more fundamentally, the European Convention does not provide a mechanism to address the utilitarian and social welfare arguments that are central to intellectual property law and policy.[275] If the ECHR adopts the balancing paradigm, the disputes it reviews will be framed not in utilitarian terms but as clashes pitting one group of rights holders (intellectual property owners) against another (such as consumers or the media). The Court will respond to these competing claims by weighing one right against the other. Much has been written about the problematic nature of constitutional balancing methodologies.[276] These concerns are even more compelling when rights claims are infused with the myriad contestations of economic and social policy that intellectual property disputes inevitably engender.

A third and final reason to eschew the intellectual property balancing paradigm concerns the multiplier and feedback effects of ECHR rulings. Formally, the Court's judgments are only binding as a matter of international law and only upon the parties to each dispute.[277] But the influence of European human rights jurisprudence is far more sweeping in practice. In some countries, national courts give direct effect to ECHR judgments, a method of compliance that leaves little room for legislative compromises that preserve competing national values.[278] In addition, legislators and courts across Europe—including the Court of Justice of the European

---

274. The above statement does not imply that the authors' rights provisions of the ICESCR and UDHR provide a fully coherent framework for a human rights-inspired conception of intellectual property. To the contrary, such a framework remains to be specified through, for example, additional general comments of the ICESCR Committee, the decisions of national courts, and the writing of commentators.

275. *See* Dreyfuss, *supra* note 251, at 13-18 (critiquing human rights approaches to intellectual property as ignoring utilitarian concerns). *But see* Geiger, *Constitutionalising Intellectual Property Law*, *supra* note 15, at 388 (arguing that human rights "are effective tools to guarantee a balanced development and understanding of IP rights and a remedy for the overprotective tendencies of lobby-driven legislation").

276. *See, e.g.*, T. Alexander Aleinikoff, *Constitutional Law in the Age of Balancing*, 96 YALE L.J. 943, 972-83 (1987) (critiquing case-by-case or ad hoc balancing standards in constitutional adjudication). The difficulties with balancing tests include determining which factors a court should weigh against each other and whether those factors can be measured on the same scale. More generally, balancing "expands judicial discretion [and] frees it substantially from the need to justify and persuade. ... [I]t gives a view of judicial review that is intuitional, if not incomprehensible." Louis Henkin, *Infallibility under Law: Constitutional Balancing*, 78 COLUM. L. REV. 1022, 1047-49 (1978).

277. European Convention, *supra* note 2, Article 46(1) ("The High Contracting Parties undertake to abide by the final judgment of the Court in a case to which they are parties").

278. *See, e.g.*, Council of Europe, Committee of Ministers, Judgments by the European Court of Human Rights, ResDH(2006)27E (June 7, 2006) (quoting the government of Greece's statement that "the Convention and the Court's case law enjoy direct effect in Greek law," and citing a 2005 Court of Cassation decision that "recognised and stressed the supra-statutory force of Article 1 of Protocol No. 1 to the Convention"); *see also* Frank

Union[279]—consult ECHR case law when drafting or interpreting statutes and constitutions.[280] These consultations extend the Court's influence and further constrain the discretion of domestic decision-makers to set national intellectual property policies.[281] As a result, even if the ECHR intervenes in intellectual property issues only rarely, its rulings will likely have extensive regional effects.

2.5   CONCLUSION

This chapter provides a comprehensive analysis of the intellectual property jurisprudence of the European Court and Commission of Human Rights under the property rights clause of the European Convention on Human Rights. It organizes the tribunals' decisions interpreting Article 1 of Protocol 1 into a tripartite framework that exposes the many points of intersection—and of potential conflict—between human rights and intellectual property. It also provides a vision of how the ECHR's intellectual property jurisprudence may evolve in the future by developing three paradigms that the Court may follow, each of which has very different consequences for innovation and creativity policies in Europe.

The chapter concludes that the rule of law paradigm, which targets arbitrary government conduct, presents the strongest justification for the ECHR to find in favor of intellectual property owners. Such a minimalist approach serves the core European Convention values of promoting predictability, certainty, and adherence to the rule of law. And it does so without unduly constraining the discretion of national legislators and judges to tailor domestic intellectual property rules to local circumstances.

A more equivocal case can be made for the enforcement paradigm, which requires national governments to provide the minimal administrative, judicial, and criminal procedures necessary for intellectual property owners to challenge infringements of their protected works. Finding Article 1

Hoffmeister, *Germany: Status of European Convention on Human Rights in Domestic Law*, 4 Int'l J. Const. L. 722, 726-28 (2006).

279. *See, e.g., Regione Autonoma Friuli-Venezia Giulia v. Ministero delle Politiche Agricole e Forestali*, 2005 E.C.R. I-3785, ¶ 125 (referencing the "case-law of the European Court of Human Rights" as establishing the standard for assessing whether government controls on the use of property are compatible with European Community law); *Laserdisken ApS v. Kulturministeriet,* 2006 E.C.R. I-08089, ¶ 65 (stating that "intellectual property rights ... form part of the right to property").

280. *See* Tom Barkuysen & Michel L. van Emmerik, *A Comparative View on the Execution of Judgments of the European Court of Human Rights* 1, 15, 19, *in* ECHR Remedies, *supra* note 231.

281. *See id.* at 12 (describing Dutch legislative proposals that were modified to comply with Article 1 and stating that "in recent years the right to property, contained in Article 1 ... seems to have been discovered in legal practice" and "is gaining more attention in the legislative process").

violations where a state fails to adopt such procedures provides an alternative enforcement mechanism for rights holders to prevent widespread intellectual property piracy. It does so, however, by circumventing the political filter that prevents private parties from litigating intellectual property complaints in the WTO dispute settlement system.

The intellectual property balancing paradigm presents the least persuasive case for ECHR intervention. Under this approach, the Court determines the legality of diminutions of intellectual property by applying Article 1's fair and proportional balance standard. It assesses the legality of expansions of intellectual property under other European Convention provisions, such as freedom of expression and the right of privacy. Adoption of the balancing paradigm would create several interrelated problems, including greater complexity and uncertainty and increased opportunities for forum shopping. The paradigm would also transform the ECHR into an arbiter of intellectual property law and policy in Europe, a role that the Court is jurisprudentially and institutionally ill-suited to play.

Finally, the chapter highlights broader theoretical and doctrinal controversies over the intersection of human rights, property rights, and intellectual property. The boundaries between these three areas of law are increasingly overlapping, leading to contestations among rights holders, governments, consumers, and nongovernmental organizations. These contestations are playing out in multiple venues, including domestic courts, international tribunals, national legislatures, and intergovernmental organizations. As these controversies become more contentious and more pervasive, government officials, scholars, and policymakers in Europe and elsewhere would benefit from the cautionary lessons that the ECHR's intellectual property jurisprudence offers.

Chapter 3

Challenges to the Development of a Human Rights Framework for Intellectual Property

Peter K. Yu[*]

3.1 INTRODUCTION

Since the establishment of the World Trade Organization (WTO) and the entering into effect of the Agreement on Trade-Related Aspects of Intellectual Property Rights (TRIPS Agreement), government officials, international intergovernmental organizations, civil society groups, judges, academic commentators, and the media have focused considerable attention on the interplay of intellectual property and human rights. In the mid-2000s, scholars have begun advocating the development of a human rights framework for intellectual property law and policy.[1] As I pointed out in earlier works, such a framework will not only be socially beneficial but will also

---

[*] This chapter was abridged and adapted from P.K. Yu, 'Reconceptualizing Intellectual Property Interests in a Human Rights Framework', *U.C. Davis Law Review* 40 (2007): 1039-1149. The chapter also draws on research from P.K. Yu, '*Intellectual Property and Human Rights in the Nonmultilateral Era*', *Florida Law Review* 64 (2012): 1045-1100.

1. L.R. Helfer, 'Toward a Human Rights Framework for Intellectual Property', *U.C. Davis Law Review* 40 (2007): 977-1020; P.K. Yu, 'Reconceptualizing Intellectual Property Interests in a Human Rights Framework', *U.C. Davis Law Review* 40 (2007): 1039-1149. On the past two decades of scholarship on intellectual property and human rights, *see* P.K. Yu, 'Intellectual Property and Human Rights 2.0', *University of Richmond Law Review* 53 (2019): 1383-1399.

enable countries to develop a balanced intellectual property system that takes international human rights obligations into consideration.[2]

To help better understand the interplay of intellectual property and human rights, and how such a framework can be developed, the Committee on Economic, Social and Cultural Rights (CESCR) provided an authoritative interpretation of Article 15(1)(c) of the International Covenant on Economic, Social and Cultural Rights (ICESCR) in January 2006. In *General Comment No. 17*, the Committee distinguished the right to the protection of interests resulting from intellectual productions 'from most legal entitlements recognized in intellectual property systems'.[3] As the Committee elaborated:

> Human rights are fundamental as they are inherent to the human person as such, whereas intellectual property rights are first and foremost means by which States seek to provide incentives for inventiveness and creativity, encourage the dissemination of creative and innovative productions, as well as the development of cultural identities, and preserve the integrity of scientific, literary and artistic productions for the benefit of society as a whole.
>
> In contrast to human rights, intellectual property rights are generally of a temporary nature and can be revoked, licensed or assigned to someone else. While under most intellectual property systems, intellectual property rights, often with the exception of moral rights, may be allocated, limited in time and scope, traded, amended and even forfeited, human rights are timeless expressions of fundamental entitlements of the human person. Whereas the human right to benefit from the protection of the moral and material interests resulting from one's scientific, literary and artistic productions safeguards the personal link between authors and their creations and between peoples, communities, or other groups and their collective cultural heritage, as well as their basic material interests which are necessary to enable authors to enjoy an adequate standard of living, intellectual property regimes primarily protect business and corporate interests and investments. Moreover, the scope of protection of the moral and material interests of the author provided for by article 15, paragraph 1(c), does not necessarily coincide with what is referred to as intellectual property rights under national legislation or international agreements.[4]

To highlight the distinction and avoid confusion between the right protected in Article 15(1)(c) and the so-called intellectual property rights – a

---

2. Yu, 'Reconceptualizing Intellectual Property Interests', n. 1 above, at 1123.
3. UN Committee on Economic, Social and Cultural Rights, 'General Comment No. 17: The Right of Everyone to Benefit from the Protection of the Moral and Material Interests Resulting from Any Scientific, Literary or Artistic Production of Which He Is the Author (Article 15, Paragraph 1(c), of the Covenant)', para. 1, UN Doc. E/C.12/GC/17 (2006).
4. *Ibid.*, para. 2.

catch-all term for describing copyrights, patents, trademarks, trade secrets, and other existing and newly created intellectual property rights – the term 'the right to the protection of moral and material interests resulting from intellectual productions' – or, its shorter form, 'the right to the protection of interests resulting from intellectual productions' – is used throughout this chapter. Although these terms seem long and clumsy, they are superior to their shorthand counterparts, such as the human right to intellectual property. These shorter terms which tend to 'obscure the real meaning of the obligations that these rights impose'.[5]

While the development of a human rights framework for intellectual property is important, sceptics have warned about the danger of an 'arranged marriage' between intellectual property and human rights. Their scepticism is not new. During the drafting of Article 27(2) of the Universal Declaration of Human Rights (UDHR) and Article 15(1)(c) of the ICESCR, delegates already expressed concern over the inclusion of the protection of interests resulting from intellectual productions in human rights instruments. Some delegates found such protection redundant with the protection offered by the right to private property and other rights in the instruments. Meanwhile, other delegates considered such protection only secondary to such fundamental human rights as a prohibition on genocide, slavery, and torture; the right to life; or the right to freedom of thought, expression, association, and religion. Even today, commentators remain divided over whether the continuous proclamation of new human rights will undermine both the fundamental nature of human rights and the integrity of the process of recognizing those rights.[6]

Although the commentators' concerns are understandable, it may be too late to deny the protection of human rights-based interests in intellectual creations. The UDHR, the ICESCR, and many other international and regional instruments have all explicitly recognized the right to the protection of interests resulting from intellectual productions as a human right.[7] This chapter, therefore, does not seek to reopen this debate, which has been widely explored and documented elsewhere.[8] Rather, it examines three challenges

---

5. M. Sepúlveda, *The Nature of the Obligations under the International Covenant on Economic, Social and Cultural Rights* (Antwerp: Intersentia, 2003), 8.
6. P. Alston, 'Conjuring up New Human Rights: A Proposal for Quality Control', *American Journal of International Law* 78 (1984): 607-621.
7. *See*, for example, Article 27(2) of the UDHR; Article 15(1)(c) of the ICESCR; Article 14(1)(c) of the Additional Protocol to the American Convention on Human Rights in the Area of Economic, Social and Cultural Rights (Protocol of San Salvador); Article 13 of the American Declaration of the Rights and Duties of Man.
8. M. Green, 'Drafting History of the Article 15(1)(c) of the International Covenant', para. 45, UN Doc. E/C.12/2000/15 (2000); J. Morsink, *The Universal Declaration of Human Rights: Origins, Drafting, and Intent* (Philadelphia: University of Pennsylvania Press, 1999), 217-222; Yu, 'Reconceptualizing Intellectual Property Interests', n. 1 above, at 1047-1075.

that may confront the development of this framework, especially from a pro-development perspective:

(1) the 'human rights ratchet' of intellectual property protection;
(2) the undesirable capture of the human rights forum by intellectual property rights holders; and
(3) the framework's potential bias against non-Western cultures and traditional communities.[9]

To be certain, additional challenges exist. From the standpoint of intellectual property rights holders, there is a growing concern that the development of a human rights framework for intellectual property will undermine the balance of existing intellectual property systems. Just as public interest advocates are concerned about the *upward* ratchet of intellectual property rights through their association with human rights, rights holders are equally worried about the *downward* ratchet of intellectual property rights – that is, the potential degrading of the non-human rights aspects of intellectual property rights. Notwithstanding this worry, the present chapter focuses primarily on the pro-development concerns raised by the development of a human rights framework for intellectual property. It seeks to explain why this framework will benefit not only individual authors and inventors but also developing countries and traditional communities.

3.2   THE 'HUMAN RIGHTS RATCHET'

As intellectual property rights become increasingly globalized, there is a growing concern about the 'one-way ratchet' of intellectual property protection. As Laurence Helfer and Graeme Austin observed in their widely used textbook:

> Some in the human rights community … fear that intellectual property owners – in particular, multinational corporations – will invoke the creators' rights and property rights provisions of international instruments to lock in maximalist intellectual property rules that will further concentrate wealth in the hands of a few at the expense of the many.[10]

According to critics, the growing protection of intellectual property not only jeopardizes access to information, knowledge, and essential medicines throughout the world, but also heightens the economic plight and cultural deterioration of developing countries and traditional communities. To these

---

9. This chapter uses the term 'traditional communities', rather than 'indigenous communities', because the former captures a larger group of people who benefit from the protection of traditional cultural expressions and traditional knowledge, innovations, and practices. Yu, 'Reconceptualizing Intellectual Property Interests', n. 1 above, at 1047, fn. 18.

10. L.R. Helfer & G.W. Austin, *Human Rights and Intellectual Property: Mapping the Global Interface* (Cambridge: Cambridge University Press, 2011), 504-505.

critics, it would be highly undesirable to elevate the status of all aspects of intellectual property rights to that of human rights regardless of whether these aspects have human rights bases.

As Kal Raustiala noted, 'the embrace of [intellectual property] by human rights advocates and entities ... is likely to further entrench some dangerous ideas about property: in particular, that property rights as human rights ought to be inviolable and ought to receive extremely solicitous attention from the international community'.[11] An emphasis on the human rights attributes in intellectual property rights is also likely to further strengthen intellectual property rights, especially in civil law countries where judges are more likely to uphold rights that are considered human rights. As a result, the development of a human rights framework for intellectual property would result in an undesirable 'human rights ratchet' of intellectual property protection. Such development would exacerbate the already severe imbalance in the existing intellectual property system. It might also hamper the growing efforts to use the human rights forum to set maximum limits on intellectual property protection. Such hampered efforts would impoverish the public domain while impeding access to information, knowledge, and essential medicines.

While I am sympathetic to these concerns, the existing international instruments have recognized only *certain* attributes of existing intellectual property rights as human rights.[12] Because international and regional human rights treaties protect these attributes but not the remaining aspects, a human rights framework for intellectual property will recognize only these attributes as human rights. In the meantime, the status of those non-human rights aspects of intellectual property rights will not be elevated to that of human rights. As the United Nations (UN) Sub-Commission on Human Rights reminded governments in Resolution 2000/7 on 'Intellectual Property Rights and Human Rights', they have a duty to take human rights obligations into consideration in their implementation of intellectual property policies and agreements. In the event of a conflict between the two, they have the additional duty to subordinate these policies and agreements to human rights protection.[13]

Moreover, although States have obligations to fully realize the right to the protection of interests resulting from intellectual productions, their ability to fulfil these obligations is often limited by the resources available to these States and the competing demands of the core minimum obligations of *other* human rights. Indeed, the right to the protection of interests resulting from intellectual productions has been heavily circumscribed by the right to

---

11. K. Raustiala, 'Density and Conflict in International Intellectual Property Law', *U.C. Davis Law Review* 40 (2007): 1032.
12. Yu, 'Reconceptualizing Intellectual Property Interests', n. 1 above, at 1079-1092.
13. UN Sub-Commission on Human Rights, 'Intellectual Property Rights and Human Rights', Resolution 2000/7, para. 3, UN Doc. E/CN.4/Sub.2/RES/2000/7 (2000).

cultural participation and development, the right to enjoy the benefits of scientific progress and its applications, the right to food, the right to health, the right to education, the right to self-determination, as well as many other human rights. For instance, some commentators have suggested that the right to enjoy the benefits of scientific progress and its applications 'carries the inference that the right involved should promote socially beneficial applications and safeguard people from harmful applications of science that violate their human rights'.[14] Depending on the jurisdiction, such a right can be translated into *ordre public* exceptions that are similar to those found in Article 27(2) of the TRIPS Agreement and Article 53(a) of the European Patent Convention.

In fact, Article 5(1) of the ICESCR states:

> [N]othing in the present Covenant may be interpreted as implying for any State, group or person any right to engage in any activity or to perform any act aimed at the destruction of any of the rights or freedoms recognized herein, or at their limitation to a greater extent than is provided for in the present Covenant.

Thus, the ICESCR presumes that States would not be able to expand their protection of interests resulting from intellectual productions at the expense of both the existing protections for and the core minimum obligations of other human rights.[15] As *General Comment No. 17* declared:

> As in the case of all other rights contained in the Covenant, there is a strong presumption that retrogressive measures taken in relation to the right to the protection of the moral and material interests of authors are not permissible. If any deliberately retrogressive measures are taken, the State party has the burden of proving that they have been introduced after careful consideration of all alternatives and that they are duly justified in the light of the totality of the rights recognized in the Covenant.[16]

Notwithstanding these limitations, there remains a strong possibility that the status of all intellectual property rights, regardless of whether they have human rights bases, will be elevated to that of human rights in rhetoric even if not in practice. Indeed, intellectual property rights holders have widely used the rhetoric of private property to support their lobbying efforts and litigation,[17] despite the many limitations, safeguards, and obligations in the property system. These limitations and safeguards include adverse

---

14. R.P. Claude, 'Scientists' Rights and the Human Right to the Benefits of Science', in *Core Obligations: Building a Framework for Economic, Social and Cultural Rights*, ed. A. Chapman & S. Russell (Antwerp: Intersentia, 2002), 255.
15. 'General Comment No. 17', n. 3 above, para. 35.
16. *Ibid.*, para. 27.
17. On the use of the private property rhetoric to expand intellectual property protection, *see* T.W. Bell, 'Authors' Welfare: Copyright as a Statutory Mechanism for Redistributing

possessions, easements, servitudes, irrevocable licenses, fire and building codes, zoning ordinances, the rule against perpetuities, and doctrines concerning the eminent domain, waste, nuisance, and public trust.[18] The property gloss over intellectual property rights has also confused policymakers, judges, jurors, commentators, and the public at large, even though there are significant differences between real and intellectual property.[19] Using this line of reasoning, it is, therefore, understandable why some public interest advocates have been concerned about an 'arranged marriage' of intellectual property and human rights.

While their concerns are valid and important, the best response to alleviate these concerns is not to dissociate intellectual property rights from human rights or to ignore the fact that some attributes of intellectual property rights are indeed protected in international or regional human rights instruments. Rather, it is important to clearly delineate which attributes of intellectual property rights would qualify as human rights and which attributes or forms of those rights should be subordinated to human rights obligations due to their lack of any human right basis. In doing so, a human rights framework will highlight the moral and material interests of individual authors and inventors while exposing the danger of the increased expansion of the non-human rights aspects of intellectual property rights.

Consider, for example, the growing expansion of corporate intellectual property rights. Without any human rights basis, none of these rights would qualify as human rights. As Maria Green noted with respect to the ICESCR, '[t]he drafters do not seem to have been thinking in terms of the corporation-held patent, or the situation where the creator is simply an employee of the entity that holds the patent or the copyright'.[20] As pointed out at the

---

Rights', *Brooklyn Law Review* 69 (2003): 273-277; N.W. Netanel, 'Impose a Noncommercial Use Levy to Allow Free Peer-to-Peer File Sharing', *Harvard Journal of Law and Technology* 17 (2003): 22; S.E. Sterk, 'Intellectualizing Property: The Tenuous Connections Between Land and Copyright', *Washington University Law Quarterly* 83 (2005): 420; R.M. Stallman, 'Did You Say "Intellectual Property"? It's a Seductive Mirage', www.gnu.org/philosophy/not-ipr.html, 12 April 2020. On the use of the right to private property to provide an alternative human rights basis for intellectual property rights, *see* P.K. Yu, 'The Anatomy of the Human Rights Framework for Intellectual Property', *SMU Law Review* 69 (2016): 85-95.

18. W.W. Fisher III, *Promises to Keep: Technology, Law, and the Future of Entertainment* (Stanford: Stanford University Press, 2004), 140-143; J. Boyle, 'Foreword: The Opposite of Property?', *Law and Contemporary Problems* 66, nos 1-2 (2003): 32; M.A. Carrier, 'Cabining Intellectual Property Through a Property Paradigm', *Duke Law Journal* 54 (2004): 52-144; J. Lipton, 'Information Property: Rights and Responsibilities', *Florida Law Review* 56 (2004): 165-189; P.K. Yu, 'Intellectual Property and the Information Ecosystem', *Michigan State Law Review* (2005): 6.

19. On the differences between real and intellectual property, *see* M.A. Lemley, 'Property, Intellectual Property, and Free Riding', *Texas Law Review* 83 (2005): 1031-1075; Sterk, n. 17 above. On the controversy over the term 'intellectual property', *see* Yu, n. 18 above, at 11-16.

20. Green, n. 8 above, para. 45.

beginning of this chapter, the CESCR also emphasized the importance of not equating intellectual property rights with the human right recognized in Article 15(1)(c).[21] In distinguishing between the two, *General Comment No. 17* pointed out that, while human rights – including the right to the protection of interests resulting from intellectual productions – focus on individuals, groups of individuals, and communities, 'intellectual property regimes primarily protect business and corporate interests and investments'.[22] Because corporate entities remain outside the protection of human rights instruments, 'their entitlements … are not protected at the level of human rights'.[23]

The two strongest rebuttals corporate rights holders could make are as follows. First, because their intellectual property interests were initially derived from the human rights-based interests of individual authors or inventors, damage to corporate interests would jeopardize these individual interests by reducing the opportunities the protected individuals have and the remuneration they will receive. Second, corporate rights holders aggregate the disparate human rights interests of individuals, such as those of their shareholders. Because corporate rights holders are seeking protection on behalf of their individual shareholders of the human rights-based property interests in their investments, corporate intellectual property rights need to be strongly protected.

These rebuttals are rather weak, however. As *General Comment No. 17* reminded us in no uncertain terms:

> [O]nly the 'author', namely the creator, whether man or woman, individual or group of individuals, of scientific, literary or artistic productions, such as, inter alia, writers and artists, can be the beneficiary of the protection of article 15, paragraph 1(c). … Under the existing international treaty protection regimes, legal entities are included among the holders of intellectual property rights. However, … their entitlements, because of their different nature, are not protected at the level of human rights.[24]

The CESCR's position is understandable. Given the considerable disparity in power between transnational corporations and individuals – and oftentimes between these corporations and developing country governments – it is indeed repulsive to have a system whereby corporate actors can demand human rights protection at the expense of individuals.

Even if the corporate rights holders' claims are to prevail, there will be at least two counter-responses. The first counter-response concerns the fact that the reduction of opportunities and remuneration may not have reached

---

21. 'General Comment No. 17', n. 3 above, para. 3.
22. *Ibid.*, para. 2.
23. *Ibid.*, para. 7.
24. *Ibid.*

the level of a human rights violation. As the drafting history of the UDHR has shown, the right to the protection of interests resulting from intellectual productions was not designed to protect the unqualified property-based interests in such productions, but rather to protect the narrow interest of just remuneration for intellectual labour.[25] Thus, it is important to distinguish between full and just remuneration, as the rightholder may not receive the full value of the use of his or her protected content.[26]

Moreover, the core minimum obligation focuses mainly on protecting the 'basic material interests which are necessary to enable authors to enjoy an adequate standard of living'.[27] Thus, even if one subscribes to the view that property rights are the best means to protect these basic interests, there remains a need to define the amount of property rights needed to protect these basic interests. Article 23 of the American Declaration of the Rights and Duties of Man, for instance, states that 'every person has a right to own such private property as meets the essential needs of decent living and helps to maintain the dignity of the individual and of the home'. As Chilean delegate Hernan Santa Cruz observed during the UDHR drafting process, '[o]wnership of anything more than [what is required under this language] might not be considered a basic right'.[28] In other words, the right to the protection of interests resulting from intellectual productions only requires the protection of sufficient intellectual property-based interests; it does not cover those additional interests that are generally not required to meet the essential needs of decent living or to maintain human dignity.

To be certain, countries are free to extend through national legislation, human rights-like protection to corporations or other collective entities. As Craig Scott pointed out, '[w]ithin the European regional human rights system, powerful companies no less than wealthy individuals may bring, and have indeed brought, claims of violation of their "human" rights before the European Court of Human Rights'.[29] Although litigants 'have had very limited success invoking Article 1 of Protocol No. 1 due to the European Court's relatively "social conception of both the state and the function of property"',[30] their likelihood of success has been greatly enhanced by the 2007 judgment of *Anheuser-Busch, Inc. v. Portugal*, in which the Grand

---

25. Yu, 'Reconceptualizing Intellectual Property Interests', n. 1 above, at 1087-1088.
26. C. Krause, 'The Right to Property', in *Economic, Social and Cultural Rights: A Textbook*, ed. A. Eide, C. Krause & A. Rosas, 2nd rev. ed. (Boston: Martinus Nijhoff Publishers, 2001), 201.
27. 'General Comment No. 17', n. 3 above, para. 2.
28. Morsink, n. 8 above, at 145.
29. C. Scott, 'Multinational Enterprises and Emergent Jurisprudence on Violations of Economic, Social and Cultural Rights', in Eide, Krause & Rosas, n. 26 above, 564, fn. 3.
30. *Ibid.* As Uma Suthersanen pointed out, 'The property provision under the [European Convention on Human Rights] is qualified in that deprivation or third-party use of property is expressly allowed for "public interest" or "general interest" reasons.' U. Suthersanen, 'Towards an International Public Interest Rule? Human Rights and

Chamber of the Court extended the coverage of Article 1 to both registered trademarks and trademark applications of a multinational corporation.[31] *Anheuser-Busch* concerned a dispute over Portugal's cancellation of a multinational brewery's application for the Budweiser trademark in an effort to protect the appellation of origin Budějovický Budvar, which is owned by Budweiser's longstanding Czech rival.

Thus, to ensure that corporate intellectual property rights will not be ratcheted up through their association with human rights, it is important to distinguish between corporate actors that have standing to bring human rights claims and those that actually claim that their *human* rights have been violated. While it is acceptable, and may even be socially beneficial, to allow corporate actors to bring human rights claims on behalf of individuals whose rights have been violated, it is disturbing that these actors can actually claim that their human rights have been violated. As Jack Donnelly put it emphatically, '[c]ollectives of all sorts have many and varied rights. But these are not – cannot be – human rights unless we substantially recast the concept'.[32]

Moreover, if corporate actors have human rights, they should also have human rights responsibilities. As *General Comment No. 17* declared:

> While only States parties to the Covenant are held accountable for compliance with its provisions, they are nevertheless urged to consider regulating the responsibility resting on the private business sector, private research institutions and other non-State actors to respect the rights recognized in article 15, paragraph 1(c), of the Covenant.[33]

In the public health context, the preamble to the Human Rights Guidelines for Pharmaceutical Companies in Relation to Access to Medicines further states that '[p]harmaceutical companies, including innovator, generic and biotechnology companies, have human rights responsibilities in relation to access to medicines'.[34] Guideline 26, in particular, stipulates that these

---

International Copyright Law', in *Copyright and Free Speech: Comparative and International Analyses*, ed. J. Griffiths & U. Suthersanen (Oxford: Oxford University Press, 2005), 107.

31. *Anheuser-Busch, Inc. v. Portugal*, [2007] ECHR 73049/01 (Grand Chamber). On the increasing role of the European Court of Human Rights in innovation and creativity policies in Europe, *see* L.R. Helfer, 'The New Innovation Frontier? Intellectual Property and the European Court of Human Rights', *Harvard International Law Journal* 49 (2008): 1-52. On the emerging fundamental rights discourse on intellectual property in Europe, *see* C. Geiger, '"Constitutionalizing" Intellectual Property Law? The Influence of Fundamental Rights on Intellectual Property in the European Union', *International Review of Intellectual Property and Competition Law* 37 (2006): 371-406.

32. J. Donnelly, *Universal Human Rights in Theory & Practice*, 2nd ed. (Ithaca: Cornell University Press, 2003), 25.

33. 'General Comment No. 17', n. 3 above, para. 55.

34. Special Rapporteur on the Right of Everyone to the Enjoyment of the Highest Attainable Standard of Physical and Mental Health, 'Report of the Special Rapporteur on the Right

companies 'should make and respect a public commitment not to lobby for more demanding protection of intellectual property interests than those required by TRIPS, such as additional limitations on compulsory licensing'.

The second counter-response concerns the distinction *General Comment No. 17* made between fundamental, inalienable, and universal human rights and temporary, assignable, revocable, and forfeitable intellectual property rights. In making this distinction, the CESCR seemed to suggest that human rights instruments do not cover the protection of transferable interests.[35] Instead, the ICESCR focuses on what French delegate René Cassin, a key UDHR drafter, described as the right that would survive 'even after such a work or discovery has become the common property of mankind'.[36] Thus, the recognition of the human rights attributes of intellectual property rights may challenge the structure of the traditional intellectual property system. In the copyright context, for example, such recognition will encourage the development of an author-centred regime, rather than one that is publisher-centred. Many publishers may, therefore, find a human rights framework for intellectual property unappealing.

Indeed, the recognition of the human rights attributes of intellectual property rights may further strengthen the control of the work by individual authors and inventors, thus curtailing the corporate control of intellectual production as recognized by the ICESCR. The right to the protection of moral interests resulting from intellectual productions, for instance, already exceeds the standards of protection offered under most intellectual property laws. As Professor Helfer noted in relation to US laws:

> A human rights framework for authors' rights is ... both more protective and less protective than the approach endorsed by copyright and neighboring rights regimes. It is more protective in that rights within the core zone of autonomy [that is protected by human rights instruments] are subject to a far more stringent limitations test than the one applicable contained in intellectual property treaties and national laws. It is also less protective, however, in that a state need not recognize any authors' rights lying outside of this zone or, if it does recognize such additional rights, it must give appropriate weight to other social, economic, and cultural rights and to the public's interest in access to knowledge.[37]

---

of Everyone to the Enjoyment of the Highest Attainable Standard of Physical and Mental Health', UN Doc. A/63/263 (2008), 15-25.

35. 'General Comment No. 17', n. 3 above, para. 2.
36. 'Cassin Draft', Article 43, reprinted in M.A. Glendon, *A World Made New: Eleanor Roosevelt and the Universal Declaration of Human Rights* (New York: Random House, 2001), 275-280 (emphasis added).
37. Helfer, n. 1 above, at 997.

When the United States (US) pushed for the TRIPS Agreement, it paid special attention to ensure that 'Members shall not have rights or obligations under this Agreement in respect of the rights conferred under Article 6*bis* of that Convention or of the rights derived therefrom'.[38] In doing so, it successfully prevented the mandatory dispute resolution process from being used to resolve disputes over inadequate protection of moral rights, even though the WTO Member States continue to bear moral rights obligations under the virtually unenforceable Berne Convention.

While the strong protection of moral interests resulting from intellectual productions may surprise corporate rights holders, it may also limit access to protected materials and frustrate projects that facilitate greater unauthorized recoding or reuse of existing creative works.[39] Indeed, *General Comment No. 17* included a more stringent test than the three-step test laid out in the Berne Convention, the TRIPS Agreement, and the World Intellectual Property Organization (WIPO) Internet Treaties.[40] Article 13 of the TRIPS Agreement expressly stipulates that WTO Member States 'shall confine limitations or exceptions to exclusive rights to certain special cases which do not conflict with a normal exploitation of the work and do not unreasonably prejudice the legitimate interests of the right holder'. Article 30 further permits the Member States to

> provide limited exceptions to the exclusive rights conferred by a patent, provided that such exceptions do not unreasonably conflict with a normal exploitation of the patent and do not unreasonably prejudice the legitimate interests of the patent owner, taking account of the legitimate interests of third parties.

Compared to these two provisions, *General Comment No. 17* provided a much more stringent test. As the CESCR stated, the limitations 'must be determined by law in a manner compatible with the nature of these rights, must pursue a legitimate aim, and must be strictly necessary for the promotion of the general welfare in a democratic society, in accordance with Article 4 of the Covenant'.[41] In addition, these limitations must be proportionate and compatible with other provisions and must offer the least restrictive means to achieve the goals.[42] Thus, in certain circumstances, 'the imposition of limitations may … require compensatory measures, such as payment of adequate compensation for the use of scientific, literary or artistic productions in the public interest'.[43]

---

38. *See* Article 9(1) of the TRIPS Agreement. Article 6*bis* is the specific TRIPS provision providing for the protection of moral rights.
39. On the recoding or reuse of copyrighted works, *see* P.K. Yu, 'Moral Rights 2.0', *Texas A&M Law Review* 1 (2014): 881-895.
40. Helfer, n. 1 above, at 995.
41. 'General Comment No. 17', n. 3 above, para. 22.
42. *Ibid.*, para. 23.
43. *Ibid.*, para. 24.

3.3   INSTITUTIONAL CAPTURE

The second challenge to the development of a human rights framework for intellectual property relates to the undesirable capture of the human rights forum by intellectual property rights holders. Because these rights holders and their supportive developed countries are rich, powerful, and organized, their greater resources, tighter organization, and stronger negotiation skills may enable them to capture the human rights forum to the detriment of developing countries, traditional communities, and other disadvantaged groups. Such institutional capture would make the human rights forum less appealing for voicing concerns and grievances in the intellectual property area and for mobilizing resistance to increased intellectual property protection.

Indeed, it is not infrequent to learn that the lack of resources has forced governments of small developing countries to give up participation in international fora. As Gregory Shaffer recounted: 'One London-based environmental NGO, the Foundation for International Environmental Law and Development[,] ... negotiated a deal with a developing country, Sierra Leone, to represent it before the [WTO Committee on Trade and Environment]'.[44] Likewise, John McGinnis and Mark Movsesian pointed out that 'some developing nations lack the resources ... to send delegates to these fora and thus have resorted to using nongovernmental organizations ... to represent their interests'.[45]

Intellectual property rights holders can generally capture the human rights forum in two ways. First, they can lobby their governments to aggressively protect their interests. Indeed, because intellectual property-based goods and services remain key exports for many developed countries, the governments of these countries are likely to find a coincidence of their interests with those of intellectual property rights holders. A case in point is the aggressive push for the establishment of the TRIPS Agreement by the US and the European Communities. As Susan Sell described:

> In the TRIPS case, private actors pursued their interests through multiple channels and struck bargains with multiple actors: domestic interindustry counterparts, domestic governments, foreign governments, foreign private sector counterparts, domestic and foreign industry associations, and international organizations. They vigorously pursued their

---

44. G.C. Shaffer, 'The World Trade Organization under Challenge: Democracy and the Law and Politics of the WTO's Treatment of Trade and Environment Matters', *Harvard Environmental Law Review* 25 (2001): 62-63.

45. J.O. McGinnis & M.L. Movsesian, 'The World Trade Constitution', *Harvard Law Review* 114 (2000): 557, fn. 256.

[intellectual property] objectives at all possible levels and in multiple venues, successfully redefining intellectual property as a trade issue.[46]

Second, intellectual property rights holders can influence developments in the human rights forum through direct participation, collaborative efforts, or indirect participation – for example, through financial support or the establishment of front organizations. As two commentators noted concerns over the establishment of public-private partnerships in the public health area:

> In relation to the UN, fears arise that inadequately monitored relations with the commercial sector may subordinate the values and reorient the mission of its organs, detract from their abilities to establish norms and standards free of commercial considerations, weaken their capacity to promote and monitor international regulations, displace organizational priorities, and induce self-censorship, among other things. Interaction, it is argued, may result in these outcomes, not just because the sectors pursue opposing underlying interests, but because the UN, having very limited resources, may face institutional capture by its more powerful partners.[47]

Today, 'the movement towards human rights accountability of corporate actors has [remained] … an uphill battle'.[48] Thus, it is understandable why many commentators and activists are concerned that intellectual property rights holders may be able to capture the human rights forum, and thereby take away from developing countries an important venue to voice concerns and grievances in the intellectual property area. Such institutional capture would also significantly undermine a forum that countries can use 'to generate the political groundwork necessary for new rounds of intellectual property lawmaking in the WTO and WIPO'.[49]

There are several responses, however. First, to the extent that intellectual property rights holders, transnational corporations, and other hostile players are exploring strategies to create tactical advantages in the human rights forum, such political manoeuvring and strategic behaviours have

---

46. S.K. Sell, *Private Power, Public Law: The Globalization of Intellectual Property Rights* (Cambridge: Cambridge University Press, 2003), 8.
47. K. Buse & A. Waxman, 'Public-Private Health Partnerships: A Strategy for WHO', *Bulletin of the World Health Organization* 79 (2001): 750. On the roles and responsibilities of intellectual property-related public-private partnerships in the international human rights regime, *see* P.K. Yu, 'Intellectual Property, Human Rights and Public-Private Partnerships', in *The Cambridge Handbook of Public-Private Partnerships, Intellectual Property Governance, and Sustainable Development*, ed. M. Chon, P. Roffe & A. Abdel-Latif (Cambridge: Cambridge University Press, 2018).
48. Scott, n. 29 above, at 563.
49. L.R. Helfer, 'Regime Shifting: The TRIPS Agreement and New Dynamics of International Intellectual Property Lawmaking', *Yale Journal of International Law* 29 (2004): 59.

already taken place. Although the rights holders and transnational corporations continue to prefer such fora as the WTO and WIPO, they have paid growing attention to other fora, including the human rights forum. Thus far, these corporations have 'insist[ed] on the sufficiency of their own efforts, that is, self-implementation of human rights standards, and [remained] strongly resistant to the establishment of enforcement or even accountability and transparency procedures'.[50] Yet, they also try hard to persuade others of approaches that would benefit their interests while at the same time seeking to reduce the impact of human rights instruments on their business activities.

Their actions are understandable, considering that international and regional human rights instruments have created governmental duties to regulate the activities of private actors. As *General Comment No. 17* stated, 'While only States parties to the Covenant are held accountable for compliance with its provisions, they are nevertheless urged to consider regulating the responsibility resting on the private business sector, private research institutions and other non-State actors to respect the rights recognized in' Article 15(1)(c) of the ICESCR.[51] For instance, States can be found to violate the Covenant by action, such as when they 'entic[e transnational corporations] to invest by providing conditions which violate human rights, including tax-free havens and prohibition of trade union activities'.[52] States can also be found to violate the Covenant by inaction, such as when they 'fail[] to have the regulatory structures in place which prevent or mitigate the harms in question'.[53] As Professor Donnelly rightly observed, 'a State that does no active harm itself is not enough. The State must also include protecting individuals against abuses by other individuals and private groups'.[54]

Second, even if intellectual property rights holders try to capture the forum, it is unclear if they will ever succeed. The human rights forum is more robust than one would expect, and capturing a robust forum is not easy. At present, the forum provides significant safeguards to protect the poor, the marginalized, and the powerless. Thus far, non-governmental organizations and developing countries are well represented in the human rights forum. They have also been more active than transnational corporations and their supportive developed countries, which often find the structure of the human rights forum and the language used therein alien. Moreover, the discussion of human rights norms may even help developing countries make a convincing

---

50. R. Falk, 'Interpreting the Interaction of Global Markets and Human Rights', in *Globalization and Human Rights*, ed. A. Brysk (Berkeley: University of California Press, 2002), 65-66.
51. 'General Comment No. 17', n. 3 above, para. 55.
52. A. Eide, 'Obstacles and Goals to Be Pursued', in Eide, Krause & Rosas, n. 26 above, at 559.
53. Scott, n. 29 above, at 568.
54. Donnelly, n. 32 above, at 37.

case to their developed counterparts of the need for recalibration of interests in the existing intellectual property regime. As Professor Helfer pointed out:

> By invoking norms that have received the imprimatur of intergovern-mental organizations in which numerous states are members, govern-ments can more credibly argue that a rebalancing of intellectual property standards is part of a rational effort to harmonize two competing regimes of internationally recognized 'rights,' instead of a self-interested attempt to distort trade rules or to free ride on foreign creators or inventors.[55]

Third, it may not necessarily be bad to include intellectual property rights holders and transnational corporations in the forum. The human rights forum includes many different issues, which range from the right to health to the right to food to the right to education. Today, the development of intellectual property laws and policies is no longer just about intellectual production; it has affected many areas that are related to other human rights, including agriculture, health, the environment, education, culture, free speech, privacy, and democracy. The inclusion of intellectual property rights holders in the human rights forum would, therefore, create an opportunity to educate them on the adverse impact of an unbalanced intellectual property system. It would also broaden their horizon by encouraging them to develop a holistic perspective of issues concerning many different human rights – a perspective that is quite different from the one that narrowly focuses on profit maximization.

Fourth, even though States remain the central players in the human rights system, that system has been changing. As a result, there is a growing and conscious effort to directly engage private actors, in particular transna-tional corporations.[56] In the 1999 World Economic Forum, UN Secretary-General Kofi Annan challenged business leaders to join an international initiative called the UN Global Compact. This initiative brought hundreds of companies together with UN agencies and labour and civil society organi-zations to support universal principles in the areas of human rights, labour,

---

55. L.R. Helfer, 'Human Rights and Intellectual Property: Conflict or Coexistence?', *Minnesota Intellectual Property Review* 5 (2003): 58.
56. P. Alston, 'Ships Passing in the Night: The Current State of the Human Rights and Development Debate Seen through the Lens of the Millennium Development Goals', *Human Rights Quarterly* 27 (2005): 767-770. On the relationship between human rights obligations and private actors, *see* J.G. Ruggie, *Just Business: Multinational Corpora-tions and Human Rights* (New York: W.W. Norton, 2013); R.C. Bird, D.R. Cahoy & J.D. Prenkert (eds), *Law, Business and Human Rights: Bridging the Gap* (Cheltenham: Edward Elgar Publishing, 2014); A. Brysk, *Human Rights and Private Wrongs: Constructing Global Civil Society* (New York: Routledge, 2005); A. Clapham, *Human Rights in the Private Sphere* (Oxford: Clarendon Press, 1993); M. Emberland, *The Human Rights of Companies: Exploring the Structure of ECHR Protection* (Oxford: Oxford University Press, 2006); S.R. Ratner, 'Corporations and Human Rights: A Theory of Legal Responsibility', *Yale Law Journal* 111 (2001): 443-545.

the environment, and anti-corruption.[57] The following year, the Organisation for Economic Co-operation and Development (OECD) adopted the Revised OECD Guidelines for Multinational Enterprises in its annual ministerial meeting in Paris.[58] In August 2003, the UN Sub-Commission on the Promotion and Protection of Human Rights established the Norms on the Responsibilities of Transnational Corporations and Other Businesses, which states:

> Within their respective spheres of activity and influence, transnational corporations and other business enterprises have the obligation to promote, secure the fulfilment of, respect, ensure respect of and protect human rights recognized in international as well as national law, including the rights and interests of indigenous peoples and other vulnerable groups.[59]

While these developments remain in their early stages and their effectiveness has been questioned,[60] they are very likely to continue. They are also likely to expand as the world becomes increasingly globalized and transnational corporations become more important in the present State-centred system. Indeed, as the UN Sub-Commission recognized, 'new international human rights issues and concerns are continually emerging and that transnational corporations and other business enterprises often are involved in these issues and concerns, such that further standard-setting and implementation are required at this time and in the future'.[61]

Finally, despite the foregoing challenges, there are tremendous benefits to advancing a dialogue with intellectual property rightsholders in the human rights forum. For example, the language used in this dialogue may eventually find its way to other intellectual property-related fora, such as the WTO or WIPO.[62] Indeed, the new intellectual property lawmaking initiatives in the

---

57. UN Global Compact, 'The Ten Principles', www.unglobalcompact.org/what-is-gc/mission/principles,12 April 2020.
58. Organisation for Economic Co-operation and Development, *The OECD Guidelines for Multinational Enterprises: Revision 2000* (Paris: Organisation for Economic Co-operation and Development, 2000).
59. UN Sub-Commission on the Promotion and Protection of Human Rights, 'Norms on the Responsibilities of Transnational Corporations and Other Business Enterprises with Regard to Human Rights', UN Doc. E/CN.4/Sub.2/2003/12/Rev.2 (2003). On more updated developments, including the Ruggie Framework and the Guiding Principles on Business and Human Rights, *see* Ruggie, n. 56 above; Yu, n. 47 above.
60. On the UN Global Compact and corporate social responsibilities, *see* 'Holding Multinational Corporations Responsible under International Law', *Hastings International and Comparative Law Review* 24 (2001): 285-506; 'The U.N. Global Compact: Responsibility for Human Rights, Labor Relations, and the Environment in Developing Nations', *Cornell International Law Journal* 34 (2001): 481-554.
61. UN Sub-Commission on the Promotion and Protection of Human Rights, n. 59 above, Preamble, Recital 12.
62. P.K. Yu, 'Currents and Crosscurrents in the International Intellectual Property Regime', *Loyola of Los Angeles Law Review* 38 (2004): 428-429.

United Nations Educational, Scientific and Cultural Organization (UNESCO), the World Health Organization, and WIPO have already utilized approaches that 'are closely aligned with the human rights framework for intellectual property reflected in the [CESCR's] recent interpretive statements'.[63] The drafters of instruments developed in these initiatives not only cited to or drew support from international human rights instruments,[64] but also carried with them the usual scepticism among human rights advocates towards the benefits of strong intellectual property protection in the developing world.[65]

The language and the dialogue may also help countries in their negotiation of future intellectual property treaties. For instance, the CESCR's recommendations in *General Comment No. 17* 'provide[d] a template for countries whose governments already oppose expansive intellectual property protection standards to implement more human rights-friendly standards in their national laws'.[66] In the shadow of these templates, countries may be able to improve their negotiation positions and demand more access to protected materials. Those recommendations also

> may influence the jurisprudence of WTO dispute settlement panels, which are likely to confront arguments that the TRIPs Agreement should be interpreted in a manner that avoids conflicts with nonbinding norms and harmonizes the objectives of the international intellectual property and international human rights regimes.[67]

Indeed, countries have been relocating to more sympathetic fora to create tactical advantages for themselves.[68] As a result, intellectual property issues have been explored and discussed in many different regimes, thus forming what I have coined the 'international intellectual property regime

---

63. Helfer, n. 1 above, at 1001.
64. For example, the preamble to the UNESCO Convention on the Protection and Promotion of the Diversity of Cultural Expressions states that the instrument 'celebrat[es] the importance of cultural diversity for the full realization of human rights and fundamental freedoms proclaimed in the Universal Declaration of Human Rights and other universally recognized instruments'. Article 2(1) lists the principle of respect for human rights and fundamental freedoms among one of its guiding principles. That provision further states: 'Cultural diversity can be protected and promoted only if human rights and fundamental freedoms, such as freedom of expression, information and communication, as well as the ability of individuals to choose cultural expressions, are guaranteed. No one may invoke the provisions of this Convention in order to infringe human rights and fundamental freedoms as enshrined in the Universal Declaration of Human Rights or guaranteed by international law, or to limit the scope thereof.'
65. Helfer, n. 1 above, at 980.
66. *Ibid.*, at 1000.
67. *Ibid.*
68. *Ibid.*, at 974-975; Helfer, n. 49 above, at 59; Raustiala, n. 11 above, at 1027.

complex'.[69] This regime complex includes not only the traditional international intellectual property regime but also those other international regimes or fora in which intellectual property issues play a growing role or with which formal or informal linkages have been established.

In addition, a growing number of WTO and WIPO activities have explored the relationship between intellectual property and human rights. For example, in November 1998, WIPO conducted a panel discussion on 'Intellectual Property and Human Rights' as part of the effort to commemorate the fiftieth anniversary of the UDHR.[70] The WTO, in particular the TRIPS Council, has also paid closer attention to the lack of access to patented pharmaceuticals in light of HIV/AIDS, tuberculosis, and malaria pandemics in Africa and other developing countries.[71] Such attention eventually resulted in the adoption of the Doha Declaration on the TRIPS Agreement and Public Health, which delayed the formal introduction of the protection for pharmaceutical patents and undisclosed test or data for ten years. This Declaration, in turn, paved the way for the adoption of a protocol to formally amend the TRIPS Agreement by adding Article 31*bis*. Taking effect in January 2017, the new provision allows countries with insufficient or no manufacturing capacity to import generic versions of patented pharmaceuticals. Had the human rights-related activities not raised concerns and provided the needed counterbalancing language, the Doha Declaration that sparked off a number of changes to the international intellectual property system might not have been adopted.[72]

---

69. P.K. Yu, 'International Enclosure, the Regime Complex, and Intellectual Property Schizophrenia', *Michigan State Law Review* (2007): 1-291. The term 'regime complex' was derived from K. Raustiala & D.G. Victor, 'The Regime Complex for Plant Genetic Resources', *International Organization* 58 (2004): 279. David Leebron has also used the term 'conglomerate regime'. D.W. Leebron, 'Linkages', *American Journal of International Law* 96 (2002): 18.

70. World Intellectual Property Organization, *Intellectual Property and Human Rights: A Panel Discussion to Commemorate the 50th Anniversary of the Universal Declaration of Human Rights, Geneva, November 9, 1998* (Geneva: World Intellectual Property Organization, 1999).

71. On TRIPS developments in relation to access to medicines, *see* O. Aginam, J. Harrington & P.K. Yu (eds), *The Global Governance of HIV/AIDS: Intellectual Property and Access to Essential Medicines* (Cheltenham: Edward Elgar Publishing, 2013); P. Roffe, G. Tansey & D. Vivas Eugui (eds), *Negotiating Health: Intellectual Property and Access to Medicines* (London: Earthscan, 2006); F.M. Abbott, 'The WTO Medicines Decision: World Pharmaceutical Trade and the Protection of Public Health', *American Journal of International Law* 99 (2005): 317-358; P.K. Yu, 'The International Enclosure Movement', *Indiana Law Journal* 82 (2007): 827-907.

72. Yu, n. 62 above, at 414-415.

3.4   CULTURAL BIAS

The final challenge to the development of a human rights framework for intellectual property pertains to the framework's potential bias against non-Western cultures and traditional communities. In recent years, policy-makers and commentators have discussed how human rights instruments have failed to protect the interests of non-Western countries and traditional communities. As they noted, many of the rights included in the UDHR and the ICESCR articulate and reinforce values that have prior existence in the West and, therefore, limited applicability in non-Western countries.[73] The climax of this cultural relativist movement came when Asian countries adopted the Bangkok Declaration at the Asian preparatory regional confer-ence before the World Conference on Human Rights in 1993.[74] Although the Bangkok Declaration did not articulate the oft-discussed 'Asian values', it explicitly stated that, 'while human rights are universal in nature, they must be considered in the context of a dynamic and evolving process of international norm-setting, bearing in mind the significance of national and regional particularities and various historical, cultural and religious back-grounds'.[75]

This plea for cultural sensitivity is not new. Indeed, when the UDHR was being drafted, the American Anthropological Association sent a long memorandum to the UN Human Rights Commission, expressing their concern, or even fear, that the Declaration would become an ethnocentric document. As the Association's executive board put it in the now infamous 1947 memorandum:

---

73. On the tension between human rights and non-Western cultures, *see* A.A. An-Naim (ed.), *Human Rights in Cross-Cultural Perspectives: A Quest for Consensus* (Philadelphia: University of Pennsylvania Press, 1992), and other sources cited in n. 75 below.

74. World Conference on Human Rights, 'Report of the Regional Meeting for Asia of the World Conference on Human Rights', UN Doc. A/Conf.157/PC/59 (1993).

75. *Ibid.*, para. 8. On 'Asian values' and the Bangkok Declaration, *see* J.R. Bauer & D.A. Bell (eds), *The East Asian Challenge for Human Rights* (Cambridge: Cambridge University Press, 1999); D.A. Bell, *East Meets West: Human Rights and Democracy in East Asia* (Princeton: Princeton University Press, 2000); M.C. Davis (ed.), *Human Rights and Chinese Values: Legal, Philosophical, and Political Perspectives* (New York: Oxford University Press, 1995); W.T. de Bary, *Asian Values and Human Rights: A Confucian Communitarian Perspective* (Cambridge, MA: Harvard University Press, 1998); W.T. de Bary & W. Tu (eds), *Confucianism and Human Rights* (New York: Columbia University Press, 1998); M.C. Davis, 'Constitutionalism and Political Culture: The Debate over Human Rights and Asian Values', *Harvard Human Rights Journal* 11 (1998): 109-147; K. Engle, 'Culture and Human Rights: The Asian Values Debate in Context', *New York University Journal of International Law and Politics* 32 (2000): 291-333; R. Peerenboom, 'Beyond Universalism and Relativism: The Evolving Debates about "Values in Asia"', *Indiana International and Comparative Law Review* 14 (2003): 1-85; S.S.C. Tay, 'Human Rights, Culture, and the Singapore Example', *McGill Law Journal* 41 (1996): 743-780.

[T]he primary task confronting those who would draw up a Declaration on the Rights of Man is ... , in essence, to resolve the following problem: How can the proposed Declaration be applicable to all human beings, and not be a statement of rights conceived only in terms of the values prevalent in the countries of Western Europe and America?[76]

Notwithstanding these cultural concerns, human rights instruments do not seem to dictate a certain level or modality of protection, as far as the right to the protection of interests resulting from intellectual productions is concerned.[77] In fact, the drafting history of the UDHR strongly suggests that the drafters were determined to create a universal document and, therefore, reluctant to introduce language that was tailored towards a particular form of the political or economic system.[78] As John Humphrey, a key drafter of the UDHR and the director of the UN Division on Human Rights, at the time of drafting, recalled in his memoirs, Chinese delegate Chang Peng-chun 'suggested that [he] put [his] other duties aside for six months and study Chinese philosophy ... [implying] that Western influences might be too great'.[79] The drafters' eagerness and determination to create a universal document despite their cultural differences were indeed quite obvious.

Moreover, commentators have underscored the diverse cultural and religious backgrounds of governmental representatives participating in the drafting process. Based on one commentator's calculation, 'thirty-seven of the member nations stood in the Judeo-Christian tradition, eleven in the Islamic, six in the Marxist, and four in the Buddhist tradition'.[80] In addition, '"[w]estern" states ... made up only about a third of the votes for the Universal Declaration',[81] and the Soviet and Latin American countries dominated the discussion of economic, social, and cultural rights. A diverse

---

76. American Anthropological Association, 'Statement on Human Rights', *American Anthropologist* 49 (1947): 539-543.
77. Yu, 'Reconceptualizing Intellectual Property Interests', n. 1 above, at 1083-1092.
78. Morsink, n. 8 above, at 149.
79. J.P. Humphrey, *Human Rights and the United Nations: A Great Adventure* (Dobbs Ferry: Transnational Publishers, 1983), 29. Some commentators, however, disagreed with Dr Humphrey's assessment. For example, Glen Johnson noted, 'Those members of the [UN Human Rights] Commission who represented non-European countries were, themselves, largely educated in the European tradition, either in Europe or the United States or in the institutions established in their own countries by representatives of European colonial powers'. M.G. Johnson, 'A Magna Carta for Mankind: Writing the Universal Declaration of Human Rights', in M.G. Johnson & J. Symonides (eds), *The Universal Declaration of Human Rights: A History of Its Creation and Implementation, 1948-1998* (Paris: UNESCO, 1998), 46-47.
80. Morsink, n. 8 above, at 21.
81. Donnelly, n. 32 above, at 22, fn. 1. James Nickel also observed: 'When the International Covenants were finally approved by the General Assembly in 1966, they clearly reflected the concerns of Third World members in a way that the Universal Declaration did not.' J.W. Nickel, *Making Sense of Human Rights: Philosophical Reflections on the Universal Declaration of Human Rights* (Berkeley: University of California Press, 1987), 67.

array of governments, intergovernmental and non-governmental organizations, and private entities also participated widely in the drafting process.[82] Even when countries, in particular those from the Eastern bloc, abstained from voting on the final adoption of Article 27 of the UDHR and Article 15 of the ICESCR, they were able to influence the outcome by participating in the discussions and some preliminary voting and by submitting comments, drafts, and amendments.[83] As Lebanese delegate Charles Malik recounted, 'The genesis of each article, and each part of each article, [in the UDHR] was a dynamic process in which many minds, interests, backgrounds, legal systems and ideological persuasions played their respective determining roles'.[84]

In the end, the documents and their drafting processes were not marred by the delegates' differences but united by their commonalities. As Mary Ann Glendon pointed out, what was crucial for the principal UDHR framers 'was the similarity among all human beings. Their starting point was the simple fact of the common humanity shared by every man, woman, and child on earth, a fact that, for them, put linguistic, racial, religious, and other differences into their proper perspective'.[85] Thus, it is no surprise that *General Comment No. 3* stated that the ICESCR is neutral 'in terms of political and economic systems ... and its principles cannot accurately be described as being predicated exclusively upon the need for, or the desirability of a socialist or a capitalist system, or a mixed, centrally planned, or laisser-faire economy, or upon any other particular approach'.[86]

While the drafting history provides important evidence to dispel complaints about the fact that the right to the protection of interests resulting from intellectual productions has ignored the interests of non-Western countries, the concerns about its inability to accommodate the needs and interests of traditional communities require a different response. After all, indigenous groups are not what the drafters of the International Bill of Rights had in mind when they prepared the documents. As *General Comment No. 17* noted, the words 'everyone', 'he', and 'author' 'indicate that the drafters of that article seemed to have believed authors of scientific, literary or artistic productions to be natural persons, without at that time realizing that they could also be groups of individuals'.[87]

The double use of the definite article in 'the right freely to participate in the cultural life of the community', as compared to 'a right "to participate in the cultural life of his or her community"', also betrayed the framers'

---

82. Morsink, n. 8 above, at 9.
83. *Ibid.*, at 21.
84. Glendon, n. 36 above, at 225.
85. *Ibid.*, at 232.
86. UN Committee on Economic, Social and Cultural Rights, 'General Comment No. 3: The Nature of States Parties Obligations (Art. 2, Para. 1, of the Covenant)', para. 8, UN Doc. E/1991/23 (1990).
87. 'General Comment No. 17', n. 3 above, para. 7.

intentions.[88] As Johannes Morsink observed, 'Article 27 seems to assume that "the community" one participates in and with which one identifies culturally is the dominant one of the nation state. There is no hint here of multiculturalism or pluralism.'[89] In fact, Morsink has shown convincingly in his widely cited book why historical memories, political circumstances, concerns of the colonial powers, and the lack of political organization had caused the UDHR drafters to omit a provision on the right to protect minorities.[90]

To make things more complicated, many commentators have pointed out accurately that the existing intellectual property regime has ignored the interests of those performing intellectual labour outside the Western model, such as 'custodians of tribal culture and medical knowledge, collectives practicing traditional artistic and musical forms, or peasant cultivators of valuable seed varieties'.[91] By emphasizing individual authorship and scientific achievement over collective intellectual contributions, the UDHR and the ICESCR drafters seemed to have subscribed to the traditional Western worldview of intellectual property protection.

Nevertheless, the fact that the drafters might not have foreseen the extension of Article 27 of the UDHR and Article 15(1)(c) of the ICESCR to traditional communities or other groups of individuals does not mean that the documents cannot be interpreted to incorporate collective rights. To begin with, human rights instruments contain considerable language that allows one to explore collective rights. Although Article 27 of the International Covenant on Civil and Political Rights (ICCPR) is the only article in the International Bill of Rights that specifically addresses the cultural rights of minorities,[92] references to cultural participation and development appear in many international instruments, including the UN Charter, the UNESCO Constitution, the Declaration of the Principles of International Cultural Co-operation, the Convention on the Rights of the Child, the Convention on the Elimination of All Forms of Discrimination against Women, and the International Convention on the Elimination of All Forms of Racial Discrimination.[93]

---

88. Morsink, n. 8 above, at 269.
89. *Ibid.*
90. *Ibid.*, at 269-280.
91. Bellagio Declaration, reprinted in J. Boyle, *Shamans, Software and Spleens: Law and the Construction of the Information Society* (Cambridge, MA: Harvard University Press, 1996), 193.
92. Article 27 of the ICCPR provides: 'In those States in which ethnic, religious or linguistic minorities exist, persons belonging to such minorities shall not be denied the right, in community with the other members of their group, to enjoy their own culture, to profess and practise their own religion, or to use their own language'.
93. S.A. Hansen, 'The Right to Take Part in Cultural Life: Toward Defining Minimum Core Obligations Related to Article 15(1)(a) of the International Covenant on Economic, Social and Cultural Rights', in Chapman & Russell, n. 14 above, at 282.

In addition, the International Bill of Rights has undertaken a collective approach to specific rights, including 'self-determination, economic, social and cultural development, communal ownership of property, disposal of wealth and natural resources, and intellectual property rights'.[94] As Donald Kommers pointed out in his comparison of the German and US Constitutions, there can be two visions of personhood: 'One vision is partial to the city perceived as a private realm in which the individual is alone, isolated, and in competition with his fellows, while the other vision is partial to the city perceived as a public realm where individual and community are bound together in some degree of reciprocity'.[95] Drawing on this distinction, Professor Glendon suggested that the UDHR drafters might have embraced the latter vision:

> In the spirit of [this] vision, the Declaration's 'Everyone' is an individual who is constituted, in important ways, by and through relationships with others. 'Everyone' is envisioned as uniquely valuable in himself (there are three separate references to the free development of one's personality), but 'Everyone' is expected to act toward others 'in a spirit of brotherhood.' 'Everyone' is depicted as situated in a variety of specifically named, real-life relationships of mutual dependency: families, communities, religious groups, workplaces, associations, societies, cultures, nations, and an emerging international order. Though its main body is devoted to basic individual freedoms, the Declaration begins with an exhortation to act in 'a spirit of brotherhood' and ends with community, order, and society.[96]

Moreover, human rights continue to evolve and expand,[97] and a growing trend has emerged to extend human rights to groups, despite the original intentions of the UDHR and ICESCR drafters. As *General Comment No. 17* stated:

> Human rights are fundamental, inalienable and universal entitlements belonging to individuals and, *under certain circumstances, groups of individuals and communities.* … Although the wording of Article 15, paragraph 1(c), generally refers to the individual creator ('everyone', 'he', 'author'), the right to benefit from the protection of the moral and material interests resulting from one's scientific, literary or artistic productions can, under certain circumstances, also be enjoyed by groups of individuals or by communities.[98]

---

94. *Ibid.*, at 288.
95. D.P. Kommers, 'German Constitutionalism: A Prolegomenon', *Emory Law Journal* 40 (1991): 867.
96. Glendon, n. 36 above, at 227.
97. Sepúlveda, n. 5 above, at 81-84; A.R. Chapman & S. Russell, 'Introduction', in Chapman & Russell, n. 14 above, at 13.
98. 'General Comment No. 17', n. 3 above, paras 1, 8 (emphasis added).

The CESCR's interpretative comment is strongly supported by international law. As the International Court of Justice declared in the *Namibia Advisory Opinion*, '[a]n international instrument has to be interpreted and applied within the framework of the entire legal system prevailing *at the time of the interpretation*'.[99] Article 31(3) of the Vienna Convention on the Law of Treaties also requires subsequent agreement and practice to be taken into account in treaty interpretation.

In the context of cultural rights, the CESCR's interpretative comment also makes a lot of sense. As Asbjørn Eide aptly observed, 'the basic source of identity for human beings is often found in the cultural traditions into which he or she is born and brought up. The preservation of that identity can be of crucial importance to well-being and self-respect'.[100] Thus, it is no surprise that *General Comment No. 17* stated that 'States parties in which ethnic, religious or linguistic minorities exist are under an obligation to protect the moral and material interests of authors belonging to these minorities through special measures to preserve the distinctive character of minority cultures'.[101] As Article 31(1) of the Declaration on the Rights of Indigenous Peoples recognized:

> Indigenous peoples have the right to maintain, control, protect and develop their cultural heritage, traditional knowledge and traditional cultural expressions, as well as the manifestations of their sciences, technologies and cultures, including human and genetic resources, seeds, medicines, knowledge of the properties of fauna and flora, oral traditions, literatures, designs, sports and traditional games and visual and performing arts. *They also have the right to maintain, control, protect and develop their intellectual property over such cultural heritage, traditional knowledge, and traditional cultural expressions.*[102]

Likewise, *General Comment No. 21*, the CESCR's authoritative interpretation of Article 15(1)(a) of the ICESCR, declared:

> Indigenous peoples have the right to act collectively to ensure respect for their right to maintain, control, protect and develop their cultural heritage, traditional knowledge and traditional cultural expressions, as well as the manifestations of their sciences, technologies and cultures, including human and genetic resources, seeds, medicines, knowledge of the properties of fauna and flora, oral traditions, literature, designs,

---

99. Legal Consequences for States of the Continued Presence of South Africa in Namibia (South West Africa), Advisory Opinion, 1971 ICJ 31, para. 53 (June 21) (emphasis added).

100. A. Eide, 'Cultural Rights as Individual Human Rights', in Eide, Krause & Rosas, n. 26 above, at 291.

101. 'General Comment No. 17', n. 3 above, para. 33.

102. United Nations Declaration on the Rights of Indigenous Peoples, General Assembly Resolution 61/295, Article 31(1), UN Doc. A/RES/61/295 (2007) (emphasis added).

sports and traditional games, and visual and performing arts. States parties should respect the principle of free, prior and informed consent of indigenous peoples in all matters covered by their specific rights.[103]

Finally, compared to civil and political rights, economic, social, and cultural rights present less tension between Western and non-Western cultures and between traditional and non-traditional ones. Indeed, during the UDHR drafting process, many Western countries, in particular Britain and the US, were reluctant to recognize economic, social, and cultural rights as human rights. It is no accident that those rights were left out of the initial discussions of the now-abandoned Covenant on Human Rights, which was later split into the ICCPR and the ICESCR. In fact, '[w]ithin some societies in the West, cultural traditions persist based on a strong faith in full economic liberalism and a severely constrained role for the state in matters of welfare'.[104] The drafting history also showed that Britain and the US remained reluctant to embrace those rights because they seemed foreign to them. As Professor Glendon noted, 'The [relativist] label "Western" obscures the fact that the Declaration's acceptance in non-Western settings was facilitated by the very features that made it seem "foreign" to a large part of the West: Britain and the United States'.[105]

In sum, as far as the right to the protection of interests resulting from intellectual productions is concerned, the human rights regime is not as biased against non-Western countries and traditional communities as the critics have claimed. As indigenous rights strengthen, the use of the human rights regime may even help reduce the existing bias against those performing intellectual labour outside the Western model.

Nevertheless, there remains a considerable challenge concerning whether developing countries and traditional communities would be able to consider the right to the protection of interests resulting from intellectual productions as important as such other human rights as the right to food, the right to health, the right to education, the right to cultural participation and development, the right to enjoy the benefits of scientific progress and its applications, and the right to self-determination. This challenge exists notwithstanding the 'universal, indivisible and interdependent and interrelated' nature of human rights, as recognized in the Vienna Declaration and

---

103. UN Committee on Economic, Social and Cultural Rights, 'General Comment No. 21: Right of Everyone to Take Part in Cultural Life (Art. 15, Para. 1 (a), of the International Covenant on Economic, Social and Cultural Rights)', para. 37, UN Doc. E/C.12/GC/21 (2009).

104. A. Eide, 'Economic Social and Cultural Rights as Human Rights', in Eide, Krause & Rosas, n. 26 above, at 11.

105. Glendon, n. 36 above, at 227.

Programme of Action. There is also continuous tension between human rights protection and economic development.[106]

In addition, there is a growing concern that the development of a human rights framework for intellectual property will lead to the creation of the notorious one-size-fits-all templates that have been used to transplant intellectual property laws from developed to developing countries. Fortunately, the European Court of Human Rights has advanced a deferential approach that respects a considerable 'margin of appreciation'.[107] As Professor Helfer noted:

> [The Court] gives significant deference to 'the legislature's judgment as to what is in the public interest unless that judgment is manifestly without reasonable foundation.' It also stresses the 'wide margin of appreciation' that states enjoy 'with regard both to choosing the means of enforcement and to ascertaining whether the consequences of enforcement are justified in the general interest for the purpose of achieving the object of the law in question.'[108]

If this deferential approach is incorporated into the framework, countries are likely to be able to develop a balanced intellectual property system that takes international human rights obligations into consideration while at the same time maintaining the policy space needed for the development of a system that appreciates the divergent local needs, national interests, technological capabilities, institutional capacities, and public health conditions.[109]

3.5   CONCLUSION

With the continuous expansion of intellectual property rights, there is a growing need to develop a human rights framework for intellectual property. However, considerable conceptual and practical challenges remain. If policymakers are to ensure that these challenges will not ultimately undermine the development of this framework, they need to anticipate the challenges

---

106. On the tension between human rights and economic development, *see* Donnelly, n. 32 above, at 109-110, 194-203; P.K. Yu, 'Ten Common Questions about Intellectual Property and Human Rights', *Georgia State University Law Review* 23 (2007): 709-753. On how to recalibrate the concept of intellectual property in light of the development concept, *see* M. Chon, 'Intellectual Property and the Development Divide', *Cardozo Law Review* 27 (2006): 2821-2912.
107. On the margin of appreciation doctrine embraced by the European Court of Human Rights, *see* Laurence R. Helfer, 'Adjudicating Copyright Claims under the TRIPs Agreement: The Case for a European Human Rights Analogy', *Harvard International Law Journal* 39 (1998): 404-405.
108. Helfer, n. 31 above, at 10-11.
109. On the enclosure of the policy space developing countries have in designing intellectual property systems that fit their needs, interests, conditions, and priorities, *see* Yu, n. 71 above.

while at the same time advancing a constructive dialogue at the intersection of intellectual property and human rights. The successful development of the framework will not only offer individuals the well-deserved protection of their moral and material interests resulting from intellectual productions but will also allow States to harness the intellectual property system to protect human dignity and respect as well as to promote the full realization of other important human rights.

Chapter 4

Reconceptualizing the Constitutional Dimension of Intellectual Property: An Update

Christophe Geiger[*]

This chapter is an updated version of the chapter entitled 'Reconceptualizing the Constitutional Dimension of Intellectual Property' which appeared in the previous edition of the volume edited by Paul L.C. Torremans entitled 'Intellectual Property Law and Human Rights'. It draws on previous research published by the author on the ongoing 'constitutionalization' of intellectual property rights through the increasing use by legislators and courts of human rights to shape the contours of the exclusive rights. The paper incorporates the most recent judicial developments at the European Union (EU) level, which confirmed the full validity and legitimacy of the use of fundamental rights to interpret and adapt IP laws. Drawing on these developments, it advances several proposals in order to construct a satisfying and balanced clause for IP at the constitutional level, demonstrating thus a closer connection to the interests of society. First, the chapter proposes to link IP with the universally recognized right to culture and science, thereby mirroring a solution adopted at international and national levels in several countries. Second, it explores the protection that could be offered by the constitutional right to freedom of expression and information. Finally, the inclusion of IP within the protection of property at the constitutional level is analysed. It is demonstrated that the link with the property provision often guarantees that the social function of this right is extended to intellectual

[*] The author is thankful to Elena Izyumenko, Researcher at the CEIPI, for her excellent research assistance and editorial support.

property. When combined with the proportionality principle that mandates a fair balance between competing fundamental rights, intellectual property is far from absolute and can, on the contrary, be limited by the interest of the society at large.

4.1   INTRODUCTION

There is no longer any doubt: intellectual production is certainly the field of economic activity marked by the most significant evolution in the last few years. Indeed, it is undeniable that this new sector of activity progressively takes the place of traditional enterprises based on agriculture and the industrial revolution as a factor of development. The nations that are poor with respect to natural resources, as is the case for a majority of the European countries, have no choice but to innovate in order to survive. This is especially true if they want to maintain an advanced level of social protection for their populations since manpower in other parts of the world is much less expensive.[1] High hopes are, therefore, undoubtedly built on what economists call the knowledge economy or more recently the data economy,[2] and it is not surprising that the European Council in Lisbon, already in the year 2000, made this one of its priorities.

Intellectual property (IP) law, as it happens, will play an increasing role in the future, as it has the difficult task of regulating this rapidly expanding field, in which decision-makers see at least an important factor of development if not the guarantee that the competitiveness of the European economy will survive.[3] For example, cultural industries have become an important field of influence, and therefore, been at the centre of a philosophical and

---

1. *See* on this issue M. Vivant & P. Sirinelli, 'De l'irrésistible ascension de l'immatériel', RLDI (2005): 3.
2. *See*, for example, OECD, *Innovation in the Knowledge Economy, Implications for Education and Learning* (Paris: OECD Publishing, Centre for Educational Research and Innovation, 2004). *See* particularly D. Foray, *The Economics of Knowledge* (Cambridge, MA: MIT Press, 2004). *See also* more recently, European Commission, *The European Data Market Study: Final Report* (Brussels, European Commission, February 2017), Executive Summary, p. 5). 'Digital innovation, driven by the combination of Big Data, Cloud Computing, Mobile technologies and Social media, is one the most powerful drivers of change and the best opportunity for Europe to move back to a growth path (…), and is therefore a powerful value generator and constitutes a real benefit for Europe's economy as a whole'. On the issue *see* X. Seuba, C. Geiger & J. Pénin (eds.), *Intellectual Property and Digital Trade in the Age of Artificial Intelligence and Big Data*, CEIPI/ ICTSD publication series on 'Global Perspectives and Challenges for the Intellectual Property System', Issue No. 5, Geneva/ Strasbourg, 2018.
3. As a recent EPO/EUIPO study demonstrated, IPR-intensive industries generated 45% of the total economic activity (worth EUR 6,6 trillion) and 29.2% of all employment in the EU (63 million jobs) (EPO/EUIPO, *Intellectual Property Rights Intensive Industries and Economic Performance in the European Union*, Industry-Level Analysis Report, 3rd ed., September 2019.

cultural debate confronting, in particular, the United States (US) and the old continent. The famous question of the 'cultural exception', today renamed 'cultural diversity', is subject to a struggle on the international level,[4] the stakes of which extend from the control of the entertainment economy to the preservation of the very cultural identity and particularities of entire nations.[5]

It may seem astonishing that, at the same time, the more intellectual property rights have been at the centre of economic activity, the more their legitimacy has been contested by the public at large and by a great number of other circles: consumers are claiming their right to private copy;[6] researchers and libraries require the freedom to access research results;[7] the

---

4. On this question, *see* S. Regourd, *De l'exception à la diversité culturelle, Collection Problèmes politiques et sociaux* (Paris: La Documentation française, 2004). On the connections between cultural diversity and copyright, *see* A. Dietz, 'Cultural Diversity and Copyright', in *Mélanges Victor Nabhan, Hors série des Cahiers de propriété intellectuelle* (Québec: Les Éditions Yvon Blais Inc., 2004), 109, as well as, focusing on human rights, C.B. Graber, 'Traditional Cultural Expressions in a Matrix of Copyright, Cultural Diversity and Human Rights', in *New Directions in Copyright Law*, vol. 5, ed. F. Macmillan (Cheltenham, UK/Northampton, MA: Edward Elgar, 2007), 45.

5. On 20 October 2005, the General Conference of the UNESCO adopted with a sizable majority the Convention on the Protection and Promotion of the Diversity of Cultural Expressions, commonly called the 'Convention on Cultural Diversity' (only two countries voted against: the US and Israel). The consequences of this Convention, which does not provide for any dispute settlement body, are however not very clear, particularly regarding its connections to the agreements of the WTO. While Article 20(1) stipulates that the parties take into account the provisions of the Convention when they interpret and apply other treaties and when they enter into other international obligations – which is certainly encouraging – Article 20(2) specifies that 'nothing in this Convention shall be interpreted as modifying rights and obligations of the Parties under any other treaties to which they are parties'. Concerning this text and its deficits, *see* S. Regourd, 'Le projet de Convention de l'Unesco sur la diversité culturelle: Vers une victoire à la Pyrrhus', *Légipresse* 226 (2005): 115.

6. *See* on this issue C. Geiger, 'Legal or Illegal: That is the Question! Private Copying and Downloading on the Internet', IIC (2008): 597; and, C. Geiger, 'The Answer to the Machine should not be the Machine, Safeguarding the Private Copy Exception in the Digital Environment', EIPR (2008): 121.

7. In the field of research, several experts of high reputation, like Nobel laureate Joseph Stiglitz, plead for new models that are based on collaborative rather than exclusive innovation (open content or open source). Big European research institutions such as the Max Planck Society also favour these new models (*see*, for example, the 'Berlin Declaration on Open Access to Knowledge in the Sciences and Humanities' of 22 October 2003. On this declaration, *see* R.M. Hilty, 'Five Lessons about Copyright in the Information Society: Reaction of the Scientific Community to Over-Protection and What Policy Makers Should Learn', *Journal of the Copyright Society of the USA* 53 (2006): 103, at 127. More recently, the issue of text and data mining has become a pressing issue for many researchers. See on the issue, C. Geiger, G. Frosio & O. Bulayenko, 'Crafting a Text and Data Mining Exception for Machine Learning and Big Data in the Digital Single Market', in: X. Seuba, C. Geiger & J. Pénin (eds.), *Intellectual Property and Digital Trade in the Age of Artificial Intelligence and Big Data*, CEIPI/ ICTSD Series on 'Global Perspectives and Challenges for the Intellectual Property System', vol. 5, Geneva/ Strasbourg, 2018, 95. More generally on the access to knowledge movement (A2K) and

open source community has radically opposed software patentability;[8] patents on pharmaceuticals are increasingly said to hinder access to medicine in the poorest areas of the world;[9] strong apprehensions have been expressed concerning the development of a 'patent on life' (through the patenting of genetic material)[10] and the 'privatization', through IP rights, of the traditional resources of indigenous groups by large Western corporations.[11] This phenomenon has been aggravated by the fact that intellectual property rights are increasingly becoming perceived as a tool for industrialized countries to dominate developing countries.[12] Consequently, a large movement has been formed, contesting a law considered to privilege only the wealthiest

---

the conflicts with IP from a human rights perspective, *see* M. Beutz Land, 'Protecting Rights Online', *Yale Journal of International Law* 34 (2009): 1.

8. On this issue *see*, e.g., C. Geiger & R.M. Hilty, 'Towards a New Instrument of Protection for Software in the EU? Learning the Lessons from the Harmonization Failure of Software Patentability', in *Biotechnology and Software Patent Law: A Comparative Review on New Developments*, ed. G. Ghidini & E. Arezzo (Cheltenham, UK/Northampton, MA: Edward Elgar, 2011), 153; C. Geiger & M. Dhenne (eds.), *Computer-Implemented Inventions: Issues, Practices and Perspectives/ Les inventions mises en œuvre par ordinateur: enjeux, pratiques et perspectives*, Collection of the CEIPI, Paris, LexisNexis, 2019.

9. On this issue, *see* D. Matthews, 'Right to Health and Patents', in *Research Handbook on Human Rights and Intellectual Property*, ed. C. Geiger (Cheltenham, UK/Northampton, MA: Edward Elgar, 2015), 496; and, D. Matthews, 'Intellectual Property Rights, Human Rights and the Right to Health', Queen Mary University of London, School of Law Legal Studies Research Paper No. 24/2009, in *Intellectual Property Rights and Human Rights: A Paradox*, ed. W. Grosheide (Cheltenham, UK/Northampton MA: Edward Elgar, 2009). *See also* H. Hestermeyer, *Human Rights and the WTO. The Case of Patents and Access to Medicines* (Oxford/New York: Oxford University Press, 2007); E.B. Ituku, *Propriété intellectuelle et droits de l'homme, L'impact des brevets pharmaceutiques sur le droit à la santé dans le contexte du VIH/SIDA en Afrique* (Bruylant/Schulthess, Bruxelles/Genève-Zurich-Bâle, 2007); H.M. Haugen, 'Human Rights and TRIPS Exclusion and Exception Provisions', *Journal of World Intellectual Property* 5, no. 6 (2009): 345.

10. *See* on this issue, e.g., A. Plomer, 'Human Dignity and Patents', in *Research Handbook on Human Rights and Intellectual Property*, ed. C. Geiger, *supra* n. 9, 479; S. MacDonagh, *Patenting Life? Stop!* (Dublin: Dominican Publications, 2003); A. Stazi, *Biotechnological Inventions and Patentability of Life, The US and European Experience* (Cheltenham, UK/Northampton, MA: Edward Elgar, 2015).

11. *See*, e.g., on this issue S. Frankel, 'Using Intellectual Property Rules to Support the Self-Determination Goals of Indigenous Peoples'; and S. Farran, 'Human Rights Perspective on Protection of Traditional Knowledge and Intellectual Property: A View from Island States in the Pacific', both pieces in *Research Handbook on Human Rights and Intellectual Property*, ed. C. Geiger, *supra* n. 9, 627, 641.

12. *See* on this issue, e.g., A. Abdel-Latif, 'Right to Development: What Implications for the Multilateral Intellectual Property Framework?', in *Research Handbook on Human Rights and Intellectual Property*, ed. C. Geiger, *supra* n. 9, 605; P. Drahos, 'Developing Countries and International Intellectual Property Standard-Setting', *Journal of World Intellectual Property* 5 (2002): 789. More generally on international trade law and developing countries from a human rights perspective, *see* G. Moon, 'The WTO-Minus Strategy: Development and Human Rights under WTO Law', University of New South Wales Faculty of Law Research Series (UNSWLRS), March 2008, 10.

countries.[13] More than ever, intellectual property is going through a crisis of legitimacy; the issue of this crisis is still uncertain, as dissatisfaction is growing vis-à-visa system perceived as incapable of guaranteeing an equitable balance of the interests involved.[14] In what follows, we will attempt to show that a constitutionalization of intellectual property law can offer a remedy for the overprotective tendencies of intellectual property and can help this field of law recover its legitimacy (4.2). Several constitutional provisions, which could guide such a constitutionalization, will then be examined (4.3) with a view to identifying certain solutions for the interpretation and the adaptation of IP laws in the future (4.4). In the longer perspective, it will be argued that a reconceptualization of the constitutional framework for intellectual property through an ambitious redrafting of the currently existing provisions could be envisaged, in order to guarantee a better-balanced IP system (4.5).

4.2 'CONSTITUTIONALIZING' IP LAW: A WAY TO SECURE A JUST BALANCE OF THE INVOLVED INTERESTS

4.2.1 THE GUARANTEE OF A JUST BALANCE OF INTERESTS: THE CRUCIAL ISSUE

Even if the demand for a fair balance of interests within intellectual property has only quite recently been made, the idea is not completely new. Already in the thirteenth century, the theologian and philosopher Thomas Aquinas held the opinion that 'positive right' (*jus positivum*) could be regarded only as fair and legitimate as long as it aimed for general well-being. Thus, he also regarded private property as fair, though only because it served the interests of the public. Where this is no longer the case, property must be limited; otherwise, it will lose its legitimacy.[15] One already recognizes in these ideas

---

13. *See,* e.g., on this issue in the field of copyright, H. Sun, 'Copyright Law under Siege: An Inquiry into the Legitimacy of Copyright Protection in the Context of the Global Digital Divide', IIC 36 (2005): 192; U. Suthersanen, 'Education, IPRs and Fundamental Freedoms – The Right to Knowledge', paper presented at the ARHC Conference on Copyright, Corporate Power and Human Rights, London, 27 January 2006; C. Geiger, 'Copyright and Free Access to Information. For a Fair Balance of Interests in a Globalised World', EIPR 28(7) (2006): 366.
14. Indeed, as the results of the recent study on the IP perceptions of Europeans demonstrate, more than 40% of EU citizens, when asked who benefits the most from IP protection, mention large companies and famous artists, and not the creators or society at large: *see* OHIM Report, *European Citizens and Intellectual Property: Perception, Awareness and Behaviour* (November 2013), 66.
15. On the ideas of Thomas Aquinas, *see* G. Decker, 'Urheberrecht und Naturrecht – Grundfragen zum UrhG 1965', in *Urheberrechtliche Probleme der Gegenwart,*

the premises of a theory developed in the nineteenth century by two famous German scholars, Josef Kohler and Otto von Gierke, called 'the social function of private law', which refers on the one hand to the necessity for a fair reconciliation of the interests of a particular person with those of the other individuals, and with those of society on the other hand.[16] We know that to these authors, these principles also applied to copyright, which they regarded as 'a socially rooted right'.[17]

The perceptions of the philosophy of law go in the same direction; according to du Pasquier, it is the task of the law to secure the peaceful living together of the human group and to harmonize the different activities of the members of society. In a word: the law offers the basis of social order, which can be achieved only by a just balance of the different interests.[18]

Thus, one thing is certain: the law – in our case intellectual property law – does not exist as an end in itself but only has legitimacy as long as it fulfils a certain function. Hence, it is not surprising that the discussion about the legal nature of intellectual property (is it property or a monopoly?) has not supplied useful answers to the question of the concrete design of the law.[19] One may think of the continuing debate over the term 'intellectual property',

---

Festschrift für E. Reichardt, ed. A. Scheuermann & A. Strittmatter (Baden-Baden: Nomos, 1990), 13 et seq. *See also* J.-J. Rousseau, *Constitutional Project for Corsica*, 1765 (reprinted by Whitefish, MT: Kessinger Publishing, 2004): 'It is sufficient to explain my idea, which is not to destroy private property absolutely, since that is impossible, but to confine it within the narrowest possible limits […] and keep it ever subordinate to the public good.'

16. O. von Gierke, *Die soziale Aufgabe des Privatrechts* (Berlin: 1889; republished by Klosterman, Frankfurt, 1943); J. Kohler, *Das Autorrecht, eine zivilrechtliche Abhandlung* (Jena: Verlag von G. Fischer, 1880), 41: 'Property is not the bastion of egotism but rather the vehicle for social exchange.' On the social function of private rights, *see also* L. Josserand, *De l'esprit des droits et de leur relativité* (Paris: Dalloz, 1939; re-edited Bibl. Dalloz, 2006), 10 et seq.

17. These authors were the originators of the theory of the so-called social bounds of copyright. *See* J. Kohler, *Das Autorrecht, eine zivilrechtliche Abhandlung, supra* n. 16, at 40. The first use of this term is attributed to Julius Kopsch (J. Kopsch, 'Zur Frage der gesetzlichen Lizenz', ArchFunkR (1928): 201). On the theory of the social bounds of intellectual property, *see also* more recently F. Leinemann, *Die Sozialbindung des Geistigen Eigentums* (Baden-Baden: Nomos, 1998); E. Pahud, *Die Sozialbindung des Urheberrechts* (Berne: Stämpfli Verlag, 2000); C. Geiger, 'The Social Function of Intellectual Property Rights, Or How Ethics Can Influence the Shape and Use of IP Law', in *Methods and Perspectives in Intellectual Property*, ed. G.B. Dinwoodie (Cheltenham, UK/Northampton, MA: Edward Elgar, 2013), 153. On the social function of the general right to property *see* R. Libchaber, 'La propriété, droit fondamental', in *Libertés et droits fondamentaux*, ed. R. Cabrillac, M-A. Frison-Roche & T. Revet, 12th ed. (Paris: Dalloz, 2006), 659.

18. C. du Pasquier, *Introduction à la théorie générale et à la philosophie du Droit*, 4th ed. (Neuchâtel/Paris: Delachaux et Nestlé, 1967), 19.

19. *See also* in this sense M. Vivant, 'Le contenu du droit d'auteur', in *Le droit d'auteur aujourd'hui*, ed. I. de Lamberterie (Paris: Éditions du CNRS, 1991), 78, who considers that there is an element, which is not emphasized enough, namely that all properties are monopolies.

which so far has not been able to provide any information about the contents of the IP right, its duration and its restrictions. It has, strictly speaking, a purely symbolic character.[20] For example, you may hold the opinion that copyright is a property right; nevertheless, it is generally recognized that it concerns property *of a special kind*.[21] This debate is not getting us anywhere, because the question of the legal nature of intellectual property acts on the assumption of a postulate, which already gets in the way of a critical analysis: intellectual property *is*, we must only define its nature. A very good example of this approach can be found in the wording of the Charter of Fundamental Rights of the European Union (EU Charter),[22] which simply (in fact much too simply) states in Article 17(2): 'Intellectual property shall be protected'.[23] Intellectual property seems to stand as an end in itself.[24] We have seen, however, that the question of the legitimacy of a right must be based on whether the right fulfils its assigned function. To determine this, one must examine *why* there is intellectual property and which interests it protects. So we should not ask about the legal nature of the right, but search for its justification, even if both aspects may be linked with one another.

Having said that, it becomes evident that today we no longer know why we have intellectual property and why its scope should be increasingly extended. This really became obvious during the debate on the proposal for a directive on 'software patentability'. While economists were pointing out that an extension of the patent to software could harm innovation, the IT industry was underlining the need to have patents to compete with American companies and to build 'patent thickets' for defensive purposes.[25] Other examples could be given, like the extension of the duration of copyright in the US to the life of the author plus seventy years, just because Europe has

---

20. *See* A. Ohly, 'Geistiges Eigentum?', JZ (2003): 548, according to whom the reference to natural property is an 'argument with an intuitive persuasiveness which has often been used in the fight for a reinforcement of the protection of intellectual efforts. The reference to intellectual *property* has thus always had a function of judicial politics'.

21. *See* for further discussion on this C. Geiger, 'Copyright's Fundamental Rights Dimension at EU Level', in *Research Handbook on the Future of EU Copyright,* ed. E. Derclaye (Cheltenham, UK/Northampton, MA: Edward Elgar, 2009), 27; M. Vivant, 'Authors' Rights, Human Rights?', RIDA 174 (1997): 115, n. 41. On the flexible understanding of intellectual property in the constitutional sense, *see infra* 4.3.

22. European Union, *Charter of Fundamental Rights of the European Union,* 7 December 2000, OJ C 364/01, 18 December 2000.

23. On Article 17(2) of the Charter *see* C. Geiger, 'Intellectual "Property" after the Treaty of Lisbon, Towards a Different Approach in the New European Legal Order?', EIPR 32(6) (2010): 255; and, C. Geiger, 'Intellectual Property Shall be Protected!? Article 17(2) of the Charter of Fundamental Rights of the European Union: A Mysterious Provision with an Unclear Scope', EIPR 31(3) (2009): 113.

24. For further discussion, *see infra* 4.3.3.

25. On this issue *see* C. Geiger & R.M. Hilty, 'Towards a New Instrument of Protection for Software in the EU?', *supra* n. 8; and, C. Geiger & R.M. Hilty, 'Patenting Software? A Judicial and Socio-Economic Analysis', IIC 36 (2005): 615.

such a duration and American interests should be preserved in kind.[26] The foundations of intellectual property, and by consequence its legitimacy, are in a serious crisis. We will try to demonstrate this by taking copyright law as an example. But some of the conclusions we will draw below could easily be extended to other areas of IP law.

4.2.2   THE CRISIS OF THE CLASSICAL FOUNDATIONS OF IP LAW: THE
               COPYRIGHT EXAMPLE

As we have already mentioned, if one aims for a readjustment of the interests within the IP system, it is essential to ask oneself why a right exists, and thus to delve further into the question of the foundations of intellectual property. Only in this way can it be determined whether the law is properly conceived and which background the regulation has, above and beyond the question of which interests should be protected. Questioning the justification of a rule also makes it possible to evaluate critically whether the rule achieves its objective. If this is not the case, then it must be corrected. A return to the foundations is all the more necessary, as in the past this argument was very often carried out using catchwords; a systematic analysis was omitted (depending on which objective was to be reached, copyright was referred to as the 'holiest of all property rights'[27] or as the 'milder evil for the society'[28]). The seemingly never-ending battle against online file sharing is a good example. One could systematically observe the right holders resorting

---

26. Copyright Term Extension Act of 27 October 1998 (Pub. L. at 105-298). This extension encountered resistance on a large scale within American doctrine, which considered this long delay as being contrary to the constitutional clause on copyright, which only allows authors to be granted an exclusive right in their works for a limited period of time. A complaint of unconstitutionality was lodged before the Supreme Court, and was rejected by the renowned decision of 15 January 2003 (*Eldred v. Ashcroft*, 537 U.S. 186, 123 S. Ct. 769 (2003), rehearing denied, 123 S. Ct. 1505 (Mem. 2003)). *See*, e.g., W.J. Gordon, 'Do We Have a Right to Speak with Another's Language? *Eldred* and the Duration of Copyright', in *Copyright and Human Rights*, ed. P.L.C. Torremans (The Hague/London/New York: Kluwer Law International, 2004), 109 et seq. *See also* for neighbouring rights for phonogram producers, C. Geiger, 'The Extension of the Term of Copyright and Certain Neighbouring Rights – A Never-Ending Story?', IIC 2009, 78, and more recently, for press publishers C. Geiger, O. Bulayenko & G. Frosio, 'The Introduction of a Neighbouring Right for Press Publisher at EU Level: The Unneeded (and Unwanted) Reform', European Intellectual Property Review (E.I.P.R.) 2017, 202.
27. Consider the famous words of Le Chapelier, reporter of the French decree on copyright of 1791: 'The most sacred, the most legitimate, the most inattackable and the most personal of all properties, is the work which is the fruit of a writer's thoughts' (*Le Moniteur universel*, 15 January 1791), at 116 et seq.
28. *See*, e.g., Lord Macaulay's Speech before the House of Commons (*Hansard*, vol. 56, 5 February 1841), at 346 et seq.: 'For the sake of the good, we must submit to the evil. But the evil ought not to last a day longer than is necessary for the purpose of securing the good.' 'It is desirable that we should have a supply of good books; we cannot have such a supply unless men of letters are liberally remunerated and *the least objectionable* way

to the now classical analogy of online copyright infringement with the theft of tangible goods, according to which illegal downloading amounts to going into a shop and stealing an object.[29] Furthermore, the concrete design of the law in recent years was characterized more by the protection of private interests (legislators being put under pressure by strong lobby groups) than by systematic reasoning. A recent example is the EU Directive extending the term of neighbouring rights from 50 to 70 years,[30] which was based on no independent economic study and has been massively rejected by the majority of European academics.[31]

There is a traditional differentiation in copyright between the justifications of 'natural law' and 'utilitarian' justifications.[32] According to the natural-law approach, the law concretizes pre-existing rights of the author,

---

of remunerating them is by way of copyright.' The words of Le Chapelier and Macaulay were often quoted out of their context and instrumentalized to push certain interests.

29. On this rhetoric, *see* more generally P.L. Loughlan, '"You Wouldn't Steal a Car ... "
Intellectual Property and the Language of Theft', EIPR (2007): 401. Questioning the systematic referral to deterrence mechanisms to address the problem of the general disrespect for copyright on the Internet, *see* C. Geiger, 'Challenges for the Enforcement of Copyright in the Online World: Time for a New Approach', in *Research Handbook on the Cross-Border Enforcement of Intellectual Property*, ed. P.L.C. Torremans (Cheltenham, UK/Northampton, MA: Edward Elgar, 2014), 704. *See also*, C. Geiger, 'The Anti-Counterfeiting Trade Agreement (ACTA) and Beyond: Towards a Differentiated Approach to Criminal Enforcement of Intellectual Property Rights at Global Level', in *The ACTA and The Plurilateral Enforcement Agenda: Genesis and Aftermath*, ed. P. Roffe & X. Seuba (Cambridge: Cambridge University Press, 2014), 100.

30. Directive 2011/77/EU of the European Parliament and of the Council of 27 September 2011 amending Directive 2006/116/EC on the term of protection of copyright and certain related rights, OJ 2011, L 265/1 (for a comment, *see* V.-L. Benabou, *Propr. intell.* 41 (2011): 411). The Commission's proposal was for a term of 95 years (Proposal for a Directive of 16 July 2008 amending Directive 2006/116/EC of the European Parliament and Council on the terms of protection of copyright and certain related rights, COM(2008) 464 final), which was reduced to 70 years thanks to the intervention of the European Parliament (legislative resolution of the European Parliament of 23 April 2009 on the proposed Directive of the European Parliament and Council amending Directive 2006/116/EC of the European Parliament and Council on the terms of protection of copyright and certain related rights, P6_TA (2009)0282).

31. *See*, for example, the joint position adopted by a certain number of European academics: 'Creativity Stifled? A Joint Academic Statement on the Proposed Copyright Term Extension for Sound Recordings', EIPR (2008): 341; C. Geiger, J. Passa & M. Vivant, 'La proposition de directive sur l'extension de la durée de certains droits voisins: Une remise en cause injustifiée du domaine public', *Propr. intell.* 31 (2009): 146; C. Geiger, 'The Extension of the Term of Copyright and Certain Neighbouring Rights – A Never-Ending Story?' IIC (2009): 78.

32. For a detailed analysis of the justifications of copyright, *see also* C. Geiger, *Droit d'auteur et droit du public à l'information, approche de droit comparé* (Paris: Litec, 2004), at 22 et seq.; S. Dusollier, *Droit d'auteur et protection des œuvres dans l'univers numérique* (Brussels: Larcier, 2005), 216 et seq. *See also*, e.g., G. Davies, *Copyright and the Public Interest*, 2nd ed. (London: Sweet & Maxwell, 2002), 9 et seq.; A. Strowel, *Droit d'auteur et Copyright, Divergences et convergences* (Brussels/Paris: Bruylant & LGDJ, 1993), 174 et seq.; F. Fechner, *Geistiges Eigentum und Verfassung* (Tübingen: Mohr Siebeck, 1999),

which he (or she) is by nature entitled to. It is the property in one's own person that is extended to the fruits of one's work and the personal rights, which protect the work as an illustration of the personality of the author. In contrast to this, according to the utilitarian approach, the right does not exist from the beginning, but is granted by society with a view towards achieving certain goals and serves as a cultural or economic policy instrument. The author is to be motivated to create new works by the prospect of a reward in the form of a right, which he (or she) can make use of to receive remuneration. Copyright presents itself as a means of amortization of the investments the author must make to create the work and as a remuneration of his/her efforts. This already shows the deficits of the economic analysis: a remuneration results only in the case of exploitation of the work, thus when the work has already been created. In the creation phase, the author is dependent on the financial support of others, and therefore, has to put him-/herself in a position of dependence on an exploiter/ producer or on the state.

It must be stressed, however, that it is of substantial importance whether copyright is used as a cultural or an economic policy instrument, even if this distinction is often ignored in the literature.[33] In the first case, the main emphasis is on the aspect of the 'intellectual' enrichment of society, whereas in the second, it is on 'material' or 'economic' enrichment. In the first case, a diversity of opinions and the democratic dialogue with as many different works as possible is to be enabled, while in the second case, the exploitation of a work, meaning the monetary realization of profits, is at the centre of attention. Of course, both aspects are often very closely linked. Nevertheless, the distinction can be relevant, because cultural policy goals can require an emphasis on non-monetary incentives (e.g., a *'droit moral'*), if they have a larger incentive function for the author than just the prospect of profit. That will be especially the case if there is a very small market for the work ('avant-garde' art, science and so forth).

The classical principles of natural law and utilitarianism do not withstand a critical analysis.[34] As far as the justification of the IP right based on the personality of the author is concerned, its disadvantage consists in the fact that it is based on natural law. Natural law is difficult to outline; historians of law have shown that Aristotle's conception of natural law differs much from that of the Middle Ages, which again has very little in common

---

121 et seq.; S.T. Mcbribe Newman, 'Human Rights and Copyrights: A Look at Practical Jurisprudence with Reference to Authors' Rights', EIPR 31(2) (2009): 88.

33. On the reasons for such a distinction, *see also* in more detail C. Geiger, *Droit d'auteur et droit du public à l'information, supra* n. 32, at 27 et seq.

34. For a detailed critical analysis of copyright's classical justifications, *see* C. Geiger, *Droit d'auteur et droit du public à l'information, supra* n. 32, at 27 et seq. *See also* G. Davies, *Copyright and the Public Interest, supra* n. 32, 243 et seq.

with that of the French Revolution.[35] Today natural law would again look different. Because of its vagueness, natural law very easily provides the possibility for misuse and manipulation in favour of the opinion which one would like to uphold.[36] This can be best illustrated by the debate on intellectual property during the nineteenth century. While some authors[37] with reference to natural law wanted to protect the 'holiest, most legitimate, most unassailable and most personal of all property rights',[38] others argued that it was contrary to the laws of nature to grant property in an intangible asset.[39]

Another weakness of the concept of natural law is the fact that it offers only insufficient justification for protecting works with purely technical character that do not reflect the personality of their creator (computer programs, databases, works with a low level of creativity – the 'small change of copyright'). These works are often not created by particular authors working independently of each other, but within a team and according to certain predefined guidelines with little scope left for an author's creativity. Some '*droit d'auteur*' countries such as France even have the construction of the '*œuvre collective*', according to which the rights of the work are, under certain conditions, transferred to the exploiter.[40] Regarding computer programs, this has already become a legally binding rule.[41] For all these cases, the rationale of natural law does not suffice.

Turning to the utilitarian foundations, their weaknesses lie in the fact that they reduce creative activity to a strictly economic process. Numerous studies have shown, however, that the creator of a work often does not act out

---

35. P. Gaudrat, *Droit des auteurs, Droits moraux. Théorie générale du droit moral* (Juris-Classeur P.L.A., Fasc. 1210, 2001), at 8 et seq.
36. *See also* in this sense M. Vivant, 'Le contenu du droit d'auteur', *supra* n. 19, at 83.
37. *See*, e.g., Lamartine's pleadings for an eternal copyright, cited in: A. Strowel, *Droit d'auteur et Copyright, Divergences et convergences*, *supra* n. 32, at 597. On this issue, *see also* A. Götz von Olenhusen, '"Ewiges geistiges Eigentum" und "Sozialbindung" des Urheberrechts in der Rechtsentwicklung und Diskussion im 19. Jahrhundert in Frankreich und Deutschland', in *Festschrift für Georg Roeber zum 10.* Dezember 1981 (Freiburg: Hochschulverlag, 1982), 88.
38. This sentence comes from Le Chapelier, reporter of the first French Copyright Act (*supra* n. 27). But the sentence was later always cited out of its context, as Le Chapelier only referred to unpublished texts (*see* in this sense J.C. Ginsburg, 'A Tale of Two Copyrights: Literary Property in Revolutionary France and America', RIDA 147 (1991): 158).
39. *See*, e.g., A.-C. Renouard, *Traité des droits d'auteurs, dans la littérature, les sciences et les beaux-arts,* vol. 1 (Paris: Jules Renouard et Cie, 1838), 454. *See also* earlier Thomas Jefferson, writing in his famous letter to Isaac McPherson of 13 August 1813 (quoted in J. Cornides, 'Human Rights and Intellectual Property, Conflict or Convergence?', Journal of World Intellectual Property 7 (2004): 143, at 150: 'Inventions cannot, in nature, be subject of property.').
40. Articles L. 113-2 and L. 113-5 of the French Intellectual Property Code (IPC).
41. *See* Article 3 of the Directive on the legal protection of computer programs of 14 May 1991 (OJEC L 122, 17 May 1991, at 42); section 69b of the German Copyright Act; Article L. 113-9 of the French IPC.

of monetary reasons but with completely different motives (idealism, ability, self-fulfilment, desire for acknowledgement and so forth).[42] Evidence of this is the fact that numerous works were created before there was even any copyright protection at all.[43] Within certain domains like science, the fame and prestige connected with a work represent a much larger motivating factor than the prospect of remuneration (which is usually very small anyway).[44] Besides that, the remuneration – as mentioned above – benefits the author very late, that is, after the creation of the work. He (or she) must perform in advance and in the work phase is dependent on other earnings for a living. That is why a large number of works are financed indirectly by the state in the form of research jobs, scholarships and other support. If the state does not take over this financing, then it is an exploiter, or producer, who makes the creation of the work financially possible. He (or she) invests in a work and wants to see his/her investment amortized. Thus, copyright is much more of an incentive for the exploiter than for the creator.[45] With the increasing economic significance of the cultural industry, it is thus not surprising that the protection has progressively shifted from the author to the exploiter and (national and international) legislatures have, therefore, tried to build up the law in such a way that it would offer comprehensive protection for the producers.

It is, then, not surprising that copyright has evolved more and more into an investment-protection mechanism. It must be noted that copyright has gradually become an industrial right and the *investment has become the reason for protection.*[46] The copyright, which was originally intended to

---

42. *See,* e.g., A. Strowel, *Droit d'auteur et Copyright, Divergences et convergences, supra* n. 32, at 221 et seq.; and G. Davies, *Copyright and the Public Interest, supra* n. 32, at 249 et seq., with further references. *See also* A. Peukert, 'Die psychologische Dimension des droit moral', in *Die psychologische Dimension des Urheberrechts,* ed. M. Rehbinder (Baden-Baden: Nomos, 2003), 129 et seq.

43. *See* G. Boytha, 'The Justification of the Protection of Authors' Rights as Reflected in Their Historical Development', RIDA 151 (1992): 53 et seq.

44. M. Stojanovic, 'The Raison d'être of Copyright', RIDA 102 (1979): 128.

45. *See* in this sense, e.g., A. Plant, *The New Commerce in Ideas and Intellectual Property* (London: The Athlone Press, 1953), 13.

46. *See also* in this sense, e.g., M. Vivant, 'Propriété intellectuelle et nouvelles technologies, À la recherche d'un nouveau paradigme', in *Université de tous les savoirs,* vol. 5: *Qu'est-ce que les technologies?* (Paris: Odile Jacob, 2001), 201 et seq. This conclusion can equally be reached for patent law, where the protection of creativity and innovation seems to become subordinate to the protection of investment. As B. Remiche, 'March-andisation et brevet', in *Propriété intellectuelle et mondialisation,* ed. M. Vivant (Paris: Dalloz, 2004), 127, correctly emphasizes, we have been witnessing for several years a change in the centre of interest of the law 'turning from the inventor's person to the investing company'. This mutation can already be considered worrying since the perception of investment does not contain any human or ethical dimension. Compensation of the investment is not systematically a synonym for progress, and as Prof. Remiche recalls, 'to accent the investment – or even to make the nearly single element out of it – means to incite the research and the investment only there where they are the most

promote the interests of the public, presents itself increasingly as a protection of the interests of some few private entities. The bond between the author and society has loosened, and copyright has come to be seen by the public as a weapon in the hands of large companies.[47] The social dimension of the law is progressively disappearing in favour of a strictly individualistic, even egotistic conception. This means that the balance between the different interests within the system is threatening to tip in favour of the investors. It could even be argued that the continental term 'author's right' is no longer appropriate, since it suggests that the system of protection benefits above all the author.[48] In reality, only a small number of authors (the commercially most successful) benefit from copyright protection. The fact that an increasing number of authors no longer identify with the applicable system of protection can be seen in the increasing success of alternative models like the 'open source' and 'open content' movements, even if these are, technically speaking, also based on copyright.[49]

It is thus becoming urgent to give IP law a new legitimacy and to ensure the reconciliation of interests by searching for a new foundation for the system. In our opinion, fundamental rights and human rights can offer a suitable basis for a balanced system.

4.3   THE CONSTITUTIONAL FRAMEWORK FOR IP

The reason why fundamental rights and human rights are an ideal basis from which to start is that they offer a synthesis of the bases of natural law and

---

cost-effective and profitable!' (at 128). The public interest cannot be reduced to economic interest; the social justification for intellectual property is larger and should take into account certain fundamental values. *See also* in this sense C. Geiger, 'Copyright as an Access Right, Securing Cultural Participation through the Protection of Creators' Interests', in: *What If We Could Reimagine Copyright?*, ed. R. Giblin & K.G. Weatherall (Acton: Australian National University (ANU) Press, 2016), 73.

47. J.C. Ginsburg, 'How Copyright Got a Bad Name for Itself', Columbia Journal of Law & the Arts 26 (2002): 61; Y. Gendreau, 'The Image of Copyright', EIPR 28(4) (2006): 209; C. Geiger, 'Taking the Right to Culture Seriously: Time to Rethink Copyright Law', in *Intellectual Property and Access to Science and Culture: Convergence or Conflict?*, C. Geiger ed., (CEIP/ ICTSD publication series on 'Global Perspectives and Challenges for the Intellectual Property System', Issue No. 3, Geneva/ Strasbourg, 2016), 84.

48. *See* in this sense A. Strowel, *Droit d'auteur et Copyright, Divergences et convergences, supra* n. 32, at 276; A. Dietz, 'Transformation of Authors' Rights, Change of Paradigm', RIDA 138 (1988): 26. *See also* the very interesting study by M. Kretschmer, et al., *UK Authors' Earnings and Contracts 2018: A Survey of 50,000 Writers* (CREATe, 2019), showing that the current system of exclusive rights only rewards the top-selling authors and that other remunerations avenues have to be found: 'Surveys of creators' earnings consistently demonstrate the presence of winner-take-all markets' (at p. 19); '[T]here is a large gap between the earnings of successful writers and the rest. […] The top 10% of writers still earn about 70% of total earnings in the profession' (at p. 20).

49. *See* on this issue S. Dusollier, 'Les licences Creative Commons: les outils du maître à l'assaut de la maison du maître', *Propr. intell.* 18 (2006): 10.

utilitarianism and represent the values from which intellectual property developed.[50] The fundamental rights' framework hence can prove indispensable for a better understanding of the scope of intellectual property protection. Within such a framework, the 'balance of interests' considerations behind IP protection have found their way into three types of provisions.[51] First, certain[52] aspects of copyright but also patent protection are incorporated in the universally recognized right to culture and science.[53] Second, in direct link with its capacity to enable cultural access, intellectual property (and especially copyright) might be protected by the right to freedom of expression and information.[54]

Finally, the inclusion of IP within the protection of property at constitutional level[55] often guarantees that the social function of this right is extended to intellectual property.

4.3.1   COPYRIGHT AS A CULTURAL RIGHT

One of the best examples of a balanced framework for copyright protection is offered by Article 27 of the Universal Declaration of Human Rights

---

50. *See* P. Drahos, 'The Universality of Intellectual Property Rights: Origins and Development', in *Intellectual Property and Human Rights* (Geneva: WIPO Publications, 1999), 13, at 33; J. Cornides, 'Human Rights and Intellectual Property, Conflict or Convergence?', *supra* n. 39, at 138; P.L.C. Torremans, 'Copyright as a Human Right', in *Copyright and Human Rights*, ed. P.L.C. Torremans, *supra* n. 26, 9 et seq.; A. Chapman, 'Approaching Intellectual Property as a Human Right (Obligations Related to Article 15(1)(c)', Copyright Bulletin 35 (2001): 14; R.D. Anderson & H. Wager, 'Human Rights, Development, and the WTO: The Cases of Intellectual Property and Competition Policy', Journal of International Economic Law 9(3) (2006): 721 et seq.
51. For a detailed empirical study on how intellectual property provisions are currently incorporated in the leading international human rights treaties and national constitutions around the globe, *see* C. Geiger, 'Implementing Intellectual Property Provisions in Human Rights Instruments: Towards a New Social Contract for the Protection of Intangibles', in *Research Handbook on Human Rights and Intellectual Property,* ed. C. Geiger, *supra* n. 9, 661.
52. Further on the distinction that exists between the standard IP rights and the human rights protection given to creators in accordance with the right to science and culture, *see* UN Committee on Economic, Social and Cultural Rights (CESCR), *General Comment No. 17: The Right of Everyone to Benefit from the Protection of the Moral and Material Interests Resulting from any Scientific, Literary or Artistic Production of Which He or She is the Author (Art. 15, Para. 1 (c) of the Covenant)*, 12 January 2006, E/C.12/GC/17. *See* on this comment H.M. Haugen, 'General Comment No. 17 on "Authors" Rights', The Journal of World Intellectual Property 10 (2007): 53.
53. *See*, on the international level, Article 27 of the Universal Declaration of Human Rights (UDHR) and Article 15 of the International Covenant on Economic, Social and Cultural Rights (ICESCR.
54. *See* Article 19 of the UDHR and Article 19 of the International Covenant on Civil and Political Rights (ICCPR).
55. At the international level, *see* Article 17 of the UDHR. Note, however, that neither the ICESCR nor the ICCPR enshrine a similar guarantee of property within their human rights catalogues.

(UDHR) of 1948.[56] According to the first paragraph of this provision, '[e]veryone has the right freely to participate in the cultural life of the community, to enjoy the arts and to share in scientific advancement and its benefits', while according to its second paragraph, '[e]veryone has the right to the protection of the moral and material interests resulting from any scientific, literary or artistic production of which he [or she] is the author'. Although it is true that the UDHR does not have a direct binding effect, the same does not apply to Article 15(1) of the International Covenant on Economic, Social and Cultural Rights (ICESCR) of 19 December 1966,[57] which has adopted the wording of the UDHR almost verbatim.[58] Further-more, on the regional level, copyright is similarly conceived as enabling access to science and culture in Article 14 of the Additional Protocol to the American Convention on Human Rights (ACHR)[59] and Article 13 of the American Declaration of the Rights and Duties of Man[60] – the latter being in fact a precursor to the UDHR.

The classical foundations of IP are placed in a stable balance in these international human rights instruments: on the one hand, the foundation of natural law by acknowledging an exploitation right and a '*droit moral*' for the creator; and, on the other hand, the utilitarian foundation, because this acknowledgement has the promotion of intellectual variety and the spread of culture and science throughout society as a goal.[61] Further, both the UDHR

---

56. UN General Assembly, *Universal Declaration of Human Rights*, 10 December 1948, Resolution 217 A, UN Doc. A/810.
57. UN General Assembly, *International Covenant on Economic, Social and Cultural Rights*, 16 December 1966, 993 UNTS 3.
58. *See*, for further discussion of this provision, C. Sganga, 'Right to Culture and Copyright: Participation and Access', in *Research Handbook on Human Rights and Intellectual Property,* ed. C. Geiger, *supra* n. 9, 560; C. Sganga & L. Shaver, 'The Right to Take Part in Cultural Life: On Copyright and Human Rights', Wisconsin International Law Journal 27 (Winter 2010): 637; L. Shaver, 'The Right to Science and Culture', Wisconsin Law Review 1 (2010): 121; C. Geiger, 'Taking the Right to Culture Seriously: Time to Rethink Copyright Law', in *Intellectual Property and Access to Science and Culture: Convergence or Conflict?,* ed.C. Geiger (CEIPI/ ICTSD publication series on 'Global Perspectives and Challenges for the Intellectual Property System', Issue No. 3, Geneva/ Strasbourg, 2016), at 84 sq; C. Geiger, 'Copyright as an Access Right, Securing Cultural Participation through the Protection of Creators' Interests', in *What If We Could Reimagine Copyright?,* eds. R. Giblin & K. G. Weatherall, (Acton: Australian National University (ANU) Press, 2016), 73.
59. Organization of American States, *Additional Protocol to the American Convention on Human Rights in the Area of Economic, Social and Cultural Rights ('Protocol of San Salvador'),* 17 November 1988, OASTS No. 69.
60. Inter-American Commission on Human Rights, *American Declaration of the Rights and Duties of Man*, 2 May 1948, OAS Res. XXX, adopted by the Ninth International Conference of American States, reprinted in Basic Documents Pertaining to Human Rights in the Inter-American System, OAS/Ser.L/V/I.4 Rev. 9 (2003).
61. For further discussion of the classical foundations of IP law, *see* C. Geiger, '"Constitu-tionalizing" Intellectual Property Law?, The Influence of Fundamental Rights on Intellectual Property in Europe', IIC 37(4) (2006): 371, at 377 et seq.

and the ICESCR emphasize the link to the 'author', namely the creator, also referring to the words such as 'he [or she]' and 'everyone', thereby excluding protection of the legal entities' entitlements on the level of human rights.[62]

On the domestic constitutional level, an impressive number of national constitutions mirror the UDHR and the ICESCR in safeguarding creators' rights within the scope of the right to science and culture.[63] Most of such clauses are characterized by a balanced wording, directly referring to the 'public interest' dimension of copyright. To give just a few examples, Article 42 of the Lithuanian Constitution of 1992, for instance, ensures that the State *'supports culture and science'* while 'protecting and defending the spiritual and material interests of an author which are related to scientific, technical, cultural, and artistic work'.[64] A similar wording is adopted by many other constitutions worldwide, including Article 73 of the Constitution of Serbia of 2006, Article 98 of the Constitution of Venezuela of 1999, Article 46 of the Constitution of the Democratic Republic of Congo of 2006, and Article 40 of the Constitution of Tajikistan of 1994. Nevertheless, perhaps the most famous constitutional provision, explicitly referring to the general interest as a legislative motive behind copyright protection, is Article 1, section 8, Clause 8 of the US Constitution of 1787,[65] which reads as follows: 'The Congress shall have Power [...] *To promote the Progress of Science and useful Arts* by securing for limited Times to Authors and Inventors the exclusive Rights to their respective Writings and Discoveries.'[66]

---

62. *See* CESCR, *General Comment No. 17, supra* n. 52, at para. 7.
63. For examples of such constitutional provisions, *see* Article 54(3) of the Bulgarian Constitution 1991; Article 69 of the Croatian Constitution 1990; Article 34(1) of the Czech Charter of Fundamental Rights 1993; Article 113 of the Latvian Constitution 1922; Article 42 of the Lithuanian Constitution 1992; Article 43(1) of the Slovak Constitution 1992; Article 42 of the Portuguese Constitution 1976; Article 36 of the Armenian Constitution 1995; Article 44(1) of the Russian Constitution 1993; Article 73(2) of the Serbian Constitution 2006; Article 58 of the Albanian Constitution 1998; Article 64 of the Turkish Constitution 1982; Article 2(8) of the Constitution of Peru 1993; Article 98 of the Constitution of Venezuela 1999; Article I, section 8, Clause 8 of the US Constitution 1787; Articles 125 and 127 of the Constitution of Nicaragua 1986; Article 29 of the Constitution of Congo 2002; Article 46 of the Constitution of the Democratic Republic of Congo 2006; Article 94 of the Constitution of Mozambique 2004; Article 26 of the Constitution of Madagascar 1992; Article 47 of the Constitution of Afghanistan 2004; Article 49 of the Constitution of Kyrgyzstan 2010; Article 16 of the Mongolian Constitution 1992; Article 22 of the Constitution of the Republic of Korea 1948; Article 40 of the Constitution of Tajikistan 1994; Article 60 of the Constitution of Viet Nam 1992; Part 9, section 86 of the Constitution of Thailand 2007. For further discussion, *see* C. Geiger, 'Implementing Intellectual Property Provisions in Human Rights Instruments', *supra* n. 51.
64. Emphasis added. For an analysis of the Lithuanian Constitutional Court's interpretation of Article 42 IP provision, *see* V. Mizaras, 'Issues of Intellectual Property Law in the Jurisprudence of the Constitutional Court of the Republic of Lithuania', *Jurisprudence* 19(3) (2012).
65. The so-called Progress Clause.
66. Emphasis added.

The public interest considerations behind the grant of protection are made salient here: exclusive rights are conferred *insofar and inasmuch* as they facilitate cultural progress. The interests of society are a reason for granting protection but also a reason for limiting it – a premise that has been further interpreted and completed by the established judicial practice of the US Supreme Court. For instance, a decision dating from 1932 laid down that the 'sole interest of the United States and the primary object in conferring a monopoly lie in the general benefits derived by the public from the labour of authors'.[67] In addition, the Progress Clause explicitly refers to 'authors' as beneficiaries of copyright protection, thereby reinforcing, on a constitutional level, the primary role of the creator.

4.3.2   COPYRIGHT AS AN EXCEPTION TO FREEDOM OF EXPRESSION AND INFORMATION

The constitutional perception of copyright as an integral component of the right to freedom of expression and information is directly linked with its capacity to enable cultural access. Since its inception, copyright has maintained close links with freedom of expression and its corollary, the public's right to receive and impart information.[68] In fact, the access to information and copyright fully converge regarding both the rationale and the principles involved.[69]

---

67. *Fox Film Corp. v. Doyal*, 286 U.S. 123 (1932), at 127. Many cases reiterate the reference to the public interest and the public good. *See*, for example, *Fogerty v. Fantasy, Inc.*, 510 U.S. 517 (1994), at 526: 'We have often recognized the monopoly privileges that Congress has authorized, while "intended to motivate the creative activity of authors and inventors by the provision of a special reward," are limited in nature and *must ultimately serve the public good*' (referring to the landmark *Sony Corp. of America v. Universal City Studios, Inc.*, 464 U.S. 417 (1984), at 429, emphasis added). *See also Harper & Row, Publishers, Inc. v. Nation Enterprises*, 471 U.S. 539 (1985), at 558: 'The economic philosophy behind the clause empowering Congress to grant patents and copyrights is the conviction that encouragement of individual effort by personal gain is the best way to *advance public welfare* through the talents of authors and inventors in "Science and useful Arts"' (quoting *Mazer v. Stein*, 347 U.S. 201 (1954), at 219, emphasis added); *N.Y. Times Co. v. Tasini*, 533 U.S. 483 (2001), at 524 n. 20 (J. Stevens, dissenting): 'Copyright law is not an insurance policy for authors, but a *carefully struck balance* between the need to create incentives for authorship and *the interests of society in the broad accessibility of ideas*' (emphasis added).
68. *See* C. Geiger, *Droit d'auteur et droit du public à l'information, supra* n. 32, at 27 et seq; C. Geiger, 'Author's Right, Copyright and the Public's Right to Information: A Complex Relationship', in: *New Directions in Copyright Law*, vol. 5, 24 ed. F. Macmillan (Cheltenham (UK)/Northampton, MA (USA), Edward Elgar Publishing, 2007).
69. On the double-sided nature of the right to freedom of expression, *see* an interesting document by the Center for Studies on Freedom of Expression and Access to Information (CELE), *Libertad de Expresión versus Libertad de Expresión: La Protección del Derecho de Autor como una Tensión Interna* [Freedom of Expression versus Freedom of Expression: Copyright Protection Invokes Internal Tension], the study prepared by C.

A good illustration of this convergence is Article 20 of the Spanish Constitution of 1978, where IP is protected within the framework of the right to freedom of expression and information (paragraph 1(b)).[70] As put succinctly by F. Bondia in a comment on this provision, '[f]reedom of expression belongs to intellectual property, as its lack kills artistic creativity, scientific research as well as the philosophical search for the truth. Besides, intellectual property is the river bed or the iter where freedom of expression passes by, and that is perfectly understood in our Constitution when it gathers both rights in the same legal article [...].'[71] One can thereby infer from Article 20 of the Spanish Constitution that the goal of IP is, at least partly, to guarantee freedom of expression and the public's right to information – a logic that could be traced further in Article 15(e) of the Liberian Constitution of 1984, when it refers to 'the commercial aspect of expression in [...] copyright infringement', and Article 13 of the Central African Constitution of 2004, incorporating the protection of 'freedom of intellectual, artistic and cultural creation' within the broader freedom of expression guarantee.

Apart from domestic constitutions, in Europe, the European Convention on Human Rights (ECHR)[72] codifies the principle of freedom of expression and communication in Article 10(1), while Article 10(2) provides for restrictions in the protection of the rights of others, which include the rights of creators.[73] On the level of the EU, Article 11 of the EU Charter mirrors the Convention free expression provision, the meaning and scope of Article 11 being the same as those guaranteed by the ECHR.[74] As a result, the case law of the European Court of Human Rights (ECtHR) is paradigmatic for

---

Cortés & E. Bertoni (Faculty of Law, University of Palermo, 2014) (available only in Spanish), available at: http://www.palermo.edu/cele/pdf/La-proteccion-del-derecho-de-autor-como-una-tension-interna.pdf (accessed 28 May 2015).

70. For further discussion of this provision, *see* J.M. Otero, 'La protección constitucional del derecho de autor: Análisis del artículo 20.1 b/ de la Constitución española de 1978', *La Ley* Part 2 (1986): 370.

71. F. Bondia, *Propiedad intelectual. Su significado en la Sociedad de la Información* (Madrid: Trivium, 1988), at 94 and 105, cited in: J. Rodriguez, 'A Historical Approach to the Current Copyright Law in Spain', EIPR 28(7) (2006): 389, at 393.

72. Council of Europe, *European Convention for the Protection of Human Rights and Fundamental Freedoms, as amended by Protocols Nos. 11 and 14*, 4 November 1950, ETS 5.

73. For the examples of cases in which copyright was considered to fall under the 'rights of others' limitation of Article 10(2) ECHR, *see* ECtHR, *Neij and Sunde Kolmisoppi v. Sweden* (dec.), No. 40397/12, 19 February 2013, unreported; ECtHR, *Ashby Donald and Others v. France*, No. 36769/08, 10 January 2013, unreported; ECommHR, *Société Nationale De Programmes FRANCE 2 v. France* (dec.), No. 30262/96, 15 January 1997, unreported; ECommHR, *N.V. Televizier v. The Netherlands* (report), No. 2690/65, 3 October 1968, unreported.

74. *See* Article 52(3) of the EU Charter. *See also* Note from the Praesidium, *Draft Charter of Fundamental Rights of the European Union*, Text of the Explanations Relating to the Complete Text of the Charter as set out in CHARTE 4487/00 CONVENT 50 (Brussels, 2000), at 13-14.

shaping the European (i.e., both the EU and the Council of Europe) understanding of the freedom of expression protection.

It is hence of considerable importance that the recent judicial practice of the ECtHR regards creators' rights as an exception to the general rule of freedom of expression.[75] In particular, two important rulings from the Court rendered in early 2013 – *Ashby Donald* and *'The Pirate Bay'*[76] – clearly

---

75. Generally on the ECtHR approach towards deciding intellectual property cases, *see* C. Geiger & E. Izyumenko, 'Intellectual Property Before the European Court of Human Rights', in: C. Geiger, C.A. Nard & X. Seuba (eds.), *Intellectual Property and the Judiciary* (EIPIN Series vol. 4, Cheltenham (UK)/Northampton, MA (USA), Edward Elgar Publishing, 2018), p. 9 and from the same authors, 'Shaping Intellectual Property Rights through Human Rights Adjudication: The Example of the European Court of Human Rights', Mitchell Hamline Law Review 46(3) (forthcoming 2020).

76. ECtHR, *Ashby Donald and Others v. France, supra* n. 73; IIC 45(3) (2014): 354; ECtHR, *Neij and Sunde Kolmisoppi v. Sweden* (dec.), *supra* n. 73; IIC 44(6) (2013): 724. Further on these cases and – more generally – on the Court's approach towards copyright protection as an exception to the general principle of freedom of expression, *see* C. Geiger & E. Izyumenko, 'Copyright on the Human Rights' Trial: Redefining the Boundaries of Exclusivity Through Freedom of Expression', IIC 45(3) (2014): 316. Even though in the three recent judgments rendered in summer 2019 (CJEU, Case C-469/17, *Funke Medien* [2019], Judgment of the Court (Grand Chamber) of 29 July 2019, EU:C:2019:623; CJEU, Case C-476/17, *Pelham* [2019], Judgment of the Court (Grand Chamber) of 29 July 2019, EU:C:2019:624; and CJEU, Case C-516/17, *Spiegel Online* [2019], Judgment of the Court (Grand Chamber) of 29 July 2019, EU:C:2019:625) the CJEU seems to have taken a different position – namely, that freedom of expression is not allowed for an external application to EU copyright, such a position of the CJEU might turn incompatible with the European legal order including the ECtHR case law that mandates a case-by-case approach. Arguably, such a position will not be possible anymore when the EU accedes to the European Convention on Human Rights – a legal obligation that became binding on the EU with the entrance into force of the Treaty of Lisbon on 1 December 2009 (*see* Article 6(2) TEU as amended by Article 1(8) of the Treaty of Lisbon and Article 59(2) ECHR as amended by Article 17 of Protocol No. 14 to the ECHR). After the accession, the CJEU would need to take into account the precedents from the ECtHR case law. The CJEU's categorical exclusion of any external freedom of expression exception to copyright law, therefore, raises the questions of the 'constitutionality' of the Luxemburg Court's position in the sense of its compatibility with the EU treaties and the fundamental rights order in the EU. For further discussion of the CJEU judgments in *Funke Medien*, *Pelham* and *Spiegel Online*, *see* C. Geiger and E. Izyumenko, 'The Constitutionalization of IP Law in the EU and the *Funke Medien*, *Pelham* and *Spiegel Online* Decisions of the CJEU: Progress, but Still Some Way to Go!', International Review of Intellectual Property and Competition Law (IIC) 51(3) (2020): 282.; C. Sganga, 'A Decade of Fair Balance Doctrine, and How to Fix It: Copyright Versus Fundamental Rights Before the CJEU From Promusicae to Funke Medien, Pelham and Spiegel Online', EIPR 11 (2019): 683; T. Snijders & S. van Deursen, 'The Road Not Taken – the CJEU Sheds Light on the Role of Fundamental Rights in the European Copyright Framework – A Case Note on the Pelham, Spiegel Online and Funke Medien Decisions', IIC 50(1176) (2019) and B.J. Jütte & J.P. Quintais, 'Sample, Sample in My Song, Can They Tell Where You are From? The Pelham Judgment – Part I' [Blog post], Kluwer Copyright Blog, 6 November 2019, available at: http://copyrightblog.kluweriplaw.com/2019/11/06/sample-sample-in-my-song-can-they-tell-where-you-are-from-the-pelham-judgment-part-i/ (accessed November 2019). *See also* C. Geiger & E. Izyumenko, 'Freedom of Expression as an External

demonstrated the major change of perspective on copyright as being traditionally regarded immune from any external freedom of expression review. In both cases, the ECtHR held that the use of a copyrighted work should be considered as an exercise of the right to freedom of expression, *even if* the use qualifies as an infringement and is profit-motivated. Therefore, by verifying if in the given situation the interference can be justified with regard to other conflicting rights, the ECtHR advanced the idea that freedom of expression has to be considered as the point of departure and that no predetermined answer can be given by copyright law. Evidently, such understanding confirms that the exclusive right has to be considered as an exception to a broader principle of freedom of use.[77]

4.3.3   COPYRIGHT AS A (CONDITIONED) PROPERTY

Apart from Article 10, another provision under the ECHR might help to fill the missing link between copyright protection and its public interest justifications. Even if intellectual property is not explicitly named in the Convention, there is no longer any doubt (as the recent case law of the European Court of Human Rights has clearly demonstrated)[78] that the

---

Limitation to Copyright Law in the EU: The Advocate General of the CJEU Shows the Way', EIPR 41(3) (2019): 131; J. Griffiths, 'European Union Copyright Law and the Charter of Fundamental Rights – Advocate General Szpunar's Opinions in (C-469/17) Funke Medien, (C-476/17) Pelham GmbH and (C-516/17) Spiegel Online', ERA Forum 1 (2019): 35; C. Geiger & E. Izyumenko, 'Freedom of Expression as an External Limitation to Copyright Law in the EU: The Advocate General of the CJEU Shows the Way', EIPR 41(3) (2019): 131; D. Jongsma, 'AG Szpunar on Copyright's Relation to Fundamental Rights: One Step Forward and Two Steps Back?', IPRinfo 1/2019 (2019); and B.J. Jütte & J.P. Quintais, 'Advocate General Turns Down the Music – Sampling is not a Fundamental Right Under EU Copyright Law', EIPR 2019, 654.

77. C. Geiger, 'Fundamental Rights, a Safeguard for the Coherence of Intellectual Property Law?', IIC 35(3) (2004): 268, at 272 stating that 'intellectual property rights constitute islands of exclusivity in an ocean of liberty'. Further on the important implications of the right to freedom of expression for copyright law, *see* D. Voorhoof, 'Freedom of Expression and the Right to Information: Implications for Copyright'; for trademarks, M. Senftleben, 'Free Signs and Free Use: How to Offer Room for Freedom of Expression within the Trademark System'; for domain names, J.D. Lipton, 'Free Speech and Other Human Rights in ICANN's New Generic Top Level Domain Process: Debating Top-Down versus Bottom-Up Protections', all in *Research Handbook on Human Rights and Intellectual Property,* ed. C. Geiger, *supra* n. 9, 331, 354, 377.

78. *See*, in the field of copyright: ECtHR, *Neij and Sunde Kolmisoppi v. Sweden* (dec.), *supra* n. 73; ECtHR, *Ashby Donald and Others v. France*, *supra* n. 73; ECtHR, *Balan v. Moldova*, No. 19247/03, 29 January 2008, unreported; ECtHR, *Melnychuk v. Ukraine* (dec.), No. 28743/03, 5 July 2005, Reports of Judgments and Decisions 2005-IX; ECtHR, *Dima v. Romania* (dec.), No. 58472/00, 26 May 2005, unreported; ECommHR, *Aral, Tekin and Aral v. Turkey* (dec.), No. 24563/94, 14 January 1998, unreported; ECommHR, *A.D. v. the Netherlands* (dec.), No. 21962/93, 11 January 1994, unreported. In the field of trademarks: ECtHR, *Paeffgen Gmbh v. Germany* (dec.), nos. 25379/04, 21688/05, 21722/05 and 21770/05, 18 September 2007, unreported; ECtHR, *Anheuser-Busch Inc. v.*

exploitation right is furthermore protected by Article 1 of the First Protocol to the ECHR, which safeguards property.[79]

Even though such approach is not without the pitfalls,[80] the inclusion of intellectual property within the protection of property at the constitutional level can have visible advantages. In particular, it expands the social function of property to intellectual property,[81] as indeed the first paragraph of Article 1 of the First Protocol to the ECHR provides for the possibility of restrictions of the right 'in the public interest', while the second paragraph of the same provision allows the State 'to enforce such laws as it deems necessary to control the use of property *in accordance with the general interest* [...]'.[82]

Unlike the ECHR, the EU Charter of Fundamental Rights explicitly places intellectual property within its catalogue of rights. Thus, Article 17 of the Charter, dealing with the general right to property under its first paragraph, also contains a second paragraph specifying in a somewhat

---

Portugal [GC], No. 73049/01, 11 January 2007, Reports of Judgments and Decisions 2007-I. In the field of patent law: ECommHR, *Lenzing AG v. the United Kingdom* (dec.), No. 38817/97, 9 September 1998, unreported; ECommHR, *Smith Kline & French Lab. Ltd. v. the Netherlands* (dec.), No. 12633/87, 4 October 1990, Decisions and Reports 66, p. 70. For a detailed analysis of the intellectual property case law of the ECtHR, *see* L.R. Helfer, 'The New Innovation Frontier? Intellectual Property and the European Court of Human Rights', Harvard International Law Journal 49 (2008): 1; D.S. Welkowitz, 'Privatizing Human Rights? Creating Intellectual Property Rights from Human Rights Principles', Akron Law Review 46 (2013): 675.

79. *See* A. Peukert, 'The Fundamental Right to (Intellectual) Property and the Discretion of the Legislature', in *Research Handbook on Human Rights and Intellectual Property,* ed. C. Geiger, *supra* n. 9, 132; K.D. Beiter, 'The Right to Property and the Protection of Interests in Intellectual Property – A Human Rights Perspective on the European Court of Human Right's Decision in Anheuser-Bush Inc v Portugal', IIC 39(6) (2008): 714. Concerning moral rights, even if there is no case law on them yet, legal scholars are of the opinion that these can be protected by Article 8 of the Convention on the protection of privacy (*see* P.B. Hugenholtz, 'Copyright and Freedom of Expression in Europe', in *Expanding the Boundaries of Intellectual Property*, ed. R.C. Dreyfuss, D.L. Zimmerman & H. First (Oxford/Toronto: Oxford University Press, 2001), 343, at 346; and, more prudently, J. Drexl, 'Constitutional Protection of Authors' Moral Rights in the European Union – Between Privacy, Property and the Regulation of the Economy', in *Human Rights and Private Law, Privacy as Autonomy*, ed. K.S. Ziegler (Oxford/Portland, OR: Hart Publishing, 2007), 159 et seq.), or even by Article 10(1) ECHR protecting freedom of expression (*see* P. Leuprecht, 'Droit d'auteur et droits de l'homme au plan européen', in *Droits d'auteur et droits de l'homme* (Paris: INPI, 1990), 66).

80. Further on those, *see*, e.g., K.D. Beiter, 'The Right to Property and the Protection of Interests in Intellectual Property', *supra* n. 79.

81. *See*, for details on this issue, C. Geiger, 'The Social Function of Intellectual Property Rights', *supra* n. 17; T. Mylly, 'The Constitutionalization of the European Legal Order: Impact of Human Rights on Intellectual Property in the EU', in: *Research Handbook on Human Rights and Intellectual Property*, ed. C. Geiger (Edward Elgar, 2015), 103; C. Sganga, *Propertizing European Copyright: History, Challenges and Opportunities*, Edward Elgar, 2018, 191 et seq.

82. Emphasis added.

laconic way: 'Intellectual property shall be protected'.[83] Admittedly, the wording of Article 17(2) is surprising.[84] First of all, it rather strangely 'uplifts' an 'ordinary' economic right to the European constitutional level. Furthermore, the protection is not even linked to the creator and contains no visible limitations.[85] Even if we agree with one author that the ambiguous wording of Article 17(2) 'cannot be interpreted to imply a more absolute nature of intellectual property possessions'[86] – the position in fact shared recently by the Court of Justice of the European Union (CJEU),[87] – it would have been much better to underline the limited character of IP explicitly to prevent any abusive interpretations.

Anyhow, if analysed in the light of the first paragraph of Article 17, the IP clause of the Charter should be perceived as nothing more than a limited right, as long as the general property provision of the Charter reiterates: '[t]he use of property may be regulated by law *in so far as is necessary for the general interest*'.[88]

This limited nature of the right to property was clearly envisaged by the drafters of both the Charter and the ECHR. As the *travaux préparatoires* of the First Protocol to the ECHR demonstrate, a newly introduced property paradigm was viewed as being of a 'relative' nature as opposed to the absolute right to own property in the sense it was understood by Roman

---

83. On this provision, *see* C. Geiger, 'Intellectual Property Shall Be Protected!?', *supra* n. 23; 'Intellectual "Property" after the Treaty of Lisbon', *supra* n. 23. *See also* J. Griffiths & L. McDonagh, 'Fundamental Rights and European Intellectual Property Law – The Case of Art 17(2) of the EU Charter', in *Constructing European Intellectual Property: Achievements and New Perspectives,* vol. 1 ed. C. Geiger (EIPIN Series, Cheltenham, UK/ Northampton, MA: Edward Elgar, 2013), 75.

84. Notably, a similar approach towards safeguarding IP is adopted in the number of national constitutions, the most recent among which is certainly the Tunisian Constitution 2014. The latter states in Article 41 that 'intellectual property is guaranteed'. For an analysis of this provision, *see* A. Abdel-Latif, 'Egypt and Tunisia's New Constitutions Recognize the Importance of Knowledge Economy and Intellectual Property Rights', 3 March 2014, *cmimarseille.org* (accessed 19 March 2014).

85. For criticism, *see also* A. Dietz, 'Constitutional and Quasi-Constitutional Clauses for Justification of Authors' Rights (Copyright) – From Past to Future', in *Exploring the Sources of Copyright – Proceedings of the ALAI Congress 2005* (Paris: AFPIDA, 2007), 55; and J. Drexl, 'Constitutional Protection of Authors' Moral Rights in the European Union', *supra* n. 79.

86. T. Mylly, 'Intellectual Property and Fundamental Rights: Do They Interoperate?', in *Intellectual Property beyond Rights*, ed. N. Bruun (Helsinki: WSOY, 2005), 207.

87. *See*, e.g., CJEU, Case C-469/17, *Funke Medien* [2019], *supra* n. 76, para. 72; CJEU, Case C-476/17, *Pelham* [2019], *supra* n. 76, para. 33; and CJEU, Case C-516/17, *Spiegel Online* [2019], *supra* n. 76, para. 56; CJEU, Case C-314/12, *UPC Telekabel* [2014], Judgment of the Court (Fourth Chamber) of 27 March 2014, EU:C:2013:781, para. 61; CJEU, Case C-360/10, *SABAM v. Netlog* [2012], Judgment of the Court (Third Chamber) of 16 February 2012, EU:C:2012:85, para. 41; CJEU, Case C-70/10, *Scarlet Extended* [2011], Judgment of the Court (Third Chamber) of 24 November 2011, EU:C:2011:771, para. 43.

88. Emphasis added.

law.[89] A similar logic, clearly excluding an 'absolutist' conception of IP, accompanies the preparatory documents of the EU Charter, insofar as the drafters took care to specify that 'the guarantees laid down in paragraph 1 [of Article 17] shall apply as appropriate to intellectual property' and that 'the meaning and scope of Article 17 are the same as those of the right guaranteed under Article 1 of the First Protocol to the ECHR'.[90] Article 17(2) of the Charter could then be considered to be nothing more than a simple clarification of Article 17(1), with the consequence that there would be absolutely no justification to expand protection on this ground.

As already mentioned, it is this 'restrictive' understanding of IP protection that has recently accompanied the case law of the CJEU.[91] According to the latter, 'the protection of the right to intellectual property is indeed enshrined in Article 17(2) of the Charter of Fundamental Rights of the European Union. There is, however, nothing whatsoever in the wording of that provision or in the Court's case law to suggest that that *right is inviolable*

---

89. Council of Europe, *Preparatory Work on Article 1 of the First Protocol to the European Convention on Human Rights*, CDH (76) 36, Strasbourg, 13 August 1976 (*see,* e.g., presentation of Mr de la Vallée-Poussin (Belgium), at 12; consider also the statement made by Mr Nally (United Kingdom) at 16 that the 'basis of Europe's fight for survival is a struggle for the subordination of private property to the needs of the community').

90. Note from the Praesidium, *Draft Charter of Fundamental Rights of the European Union, supra* n. 74, at 19-20.

91. *See,* e.g., ECJ, Case C-275/06, *Promusicae* [2008], Judgment of the Court (Grand Chamber) of 29 January 2008, paras 65-68, ECR I-00271; ECJ, Case C-557/07, *Tele2* [2009], Order of the Court (Eighth Chamber) of 19 February 2009, paras 28 and 29, ECR I-01227; CJEU, Case C-461/10, *Bonnier Audio and Others* [2012], Judgment of the Court (Third Chamber) of 19 April 2012, para. 56, published in the electronic Reports of Cases; CJEU, Case C-145/10, *Painer* [2011], Judgment of the Court (Third Chamber) of 1 December 2011, paras 105 and 132, ECR I-12533; CJEU, Case C-70/10, *Scarlet Extended* [2011], *supra* n. 87, at para. 53; CJEU, Case C-360/10, *SABAM v. Netlog* [2012], *supra* n. 87, at para. 51; CJEU, Case C-314/12, *UPC Telekabel* [2014], *supra* n. 87, at para. 46; and CJEU, Case C-201/13, *Deckmyn* [2014], Judgment of the Court (Grand Chamber) of 3 September 2014, paras 26 and 27, not yet published. On some of these cases, *see* C. Geiger & F. Schönherr, 'Limitations to Copyright in the Digital Age', in *Research Handbook on EU Internet Law,* ed. A. Savin & J. Trzaskowski (Cheltenham, UK/Northampton, MA, Edward Elgar, 2014), 110, and, C. Geiger & F. Schönherr, 'Defining the Scope of Protection of Copyright in the EU: The Need to Reconsider the Acquis Regarding Limitations and Exceptions', in *Codification of European Copyright Law, Challenges and Perspectives,* ed. T. Synodinou (Alphen aan den Rijn: Kluwer Law International, 2012), 142; J. Griffiths, 'Constitutionalising or Harmonising? The Court of Justice, the Right to Property and European Copyright Law', European Law Review 38 (2013): 65; and, most recently, European Copyright Society (ECS), 'Limitations and Exceptions as Key Elements of the Legal Framework for Copyright in the European Union: Opinion on the Judgment of the CJEU in Case C-201/13 *Deckmyn*', 1 November 2014, available at: http://infojustice.org/wp-content/uploads/2014/11/Limitations-and-Exceptions-as-Key-Elements-of-the-Legal-Framework-for-Copyright-in-the-EU.pdf (accessed 12 November 2014), IIC 46(1) (2015): 93.

and must for that reason be absolutely protected.'[92] Moreover, to remove any ambiguity, in *Luksan v. Petrus* the CJEU directly referred to Article 17(1) of the Charter in the context of IP protection *before* discussing Article 17(2) – an explicit illustration on the part of the Court that IP clause of the Charter benefits from the more general wording of Article 17(1).[93]

The right to property in the Charter and in the ECHR is thus considered as a right having strong social bonds and its scope of protection is, therefore, limited by nature.[94] This leaves the States a large margin of appreciation in regulating property,[95] meaning that intellectual property – just like the right to physical property – can be restricted in order to safeguard the public interest.

This 'conditioned' reading of the constitutional right to property seems to have entered the IP-related practice of the national courts. For example, in a decision from January 2014, the Belgium Constitutional Court held[96] that the sanction that the patent has no effect on the Belgian territory without possibility of restoration, when failing to provide a translation within the strict three-month deadline, was a disproportionate deprivation of property in view of the legislator's aim to inform the public and a non-justified damage to the right to property of the patent holder. Interestingly, the latter right was interpreted by the Belgium judiciary not only in the light of the national Constitution's provision on the right to property, *but also* in the light of Article 1 of the First Protocol to the ECHR.

On the other side of the Atlantic, the first instance court of Argentina has explicitly relied in March 2013 on the public interest limitations of copyright in the decision concerning the abusive exercise of the co-heir's moral

---

92. CJEU, Case C-469/17, *Funke Medien* [2019], *supra* n. 76, at para. 72; CJEU, Case C-476/17, *Pelham* [2019], *supra* n. 76, at para. 33; and CJEU, Case C-516/17, *Spiegel Online* [2019], *supra* n. 76, at para. 56; CJEU, Case C-314/12, *UPC Telekabel* [2014], *supra* n. 87, at para. 61; CJEU, Case C-360/10, *SABAM v. Netlog* [2012], *supra* n. 87, at para. 41; CJEU, Case C-70/10, *Scarlet Extended* [2011], *supra* n. 87, at para. 43 (emphasis added).

93. CJEU, Case C-277/10, *Martin Luksan v. Petrus van der Let* [2012], Judgment of the Court (Third Chamber) of 9 February 2012, EU:C:2012:65, para. 68. For a comment, *see* E. Derieux, 'Titularité et partage des droits sur une œuvre cinématographique. Droits du réalisateur et du producteur', RLDI (82) (2012): 47.

94. *See* in this sense, C. Calliess, 'The Fundamental Right to Property', in *European Fundamental Rights and Freedoms,* ed. D. Ehlers (Berlin, De Gruyter, 2007), 456, stating that the social function 'serves as a justification for and limitation of the restrictions imposed on property utilisation'.

95. For example, in the *Smith Kline* case (ECommHR, *Smith Kline & French Lab. Ltd. v. the Netherlands* (dec.), *supra* n. 78), the European Commission of Human Rights stated that the grant under Dutch law of a compulsory license for a patented drug was not a violation of Article 1 of the First Protocol. It considered that the compulsory license was lawful and pursued the legitimate aim of encouraging technological and economic development.

96. Constitutional Court of Belgium, *BioPheresis Technologies Inc v. State of Belgium,* No. 3/2014, 16 January 2014.

rights.[97] In particular, the Court considered that the interest of the community in accessing unpublished works derived both from the social function provision of Article 21 ACHR on the general right to property and Article 15(1)(a) ICESCR (the right to take part in cultural life). The Court has also stated that an IP clause of the Argentine Constitution (incorporating exclusive owners' rights within the general right to property)[98] should be read in the light of these international human rights instruments, thus ensuring that a proper balance is achieved between the interests of society and the copyright owners' individual economic or moral rights. In a similar vein, the Brazilian Supreme Court has opined in its decision from March 2011 that each of the limitations foreseen in the national copyright law resulted from the legal incorporation of constitutional principles related, *inter alia*, to the right to culture, education and science. Moreover, the Court was of the opinion that such limitations themselves were not immune to external checks resulting from fundamental rights and guarantees. According to the Court, 'the effective scope of protection of the property right of authors is revealed after the consideration of the limitations contained in Articles 46, 47 and 48 of Law 9.610/98 [Brazilian Author's Rights Law], *interpreted and applied in accordance with the fundamental rights and guarantees*, and *after the consideration of the fundamental rights and guarantees themselves.*'[99]

4.4   CONSEQUENCES OF 'CONSTITUTIONALIZING' IP LAW

Opponents to any fundamental rights discourse within IP law often argue that these rights are vague and do not allow any conclusions to be drawn concerning the scope of IP rights – that the fundamental rights reasoning within IP is a merely theoretical exercise that does not have any practical impact. In our opinion, the contrary is true and we will hereafter try to demonstrate that a constitutionalizing of IP law would have numerous practical consequences.[100] In particular, fundamental rights would serve not

---

97. Court of First Instance in Civil and Commercial Matters (No. 12 of Rosario), *Ediciones de la Flor SA v. Fontanarrosa Franco*, Case No. 1420/08, 11 March 2013, unreported; IIC 44(7) (2013): 851.

98. Article 17 of the Argentine Constitution 1853.

99. Brazilian Supreme Court, Special appeal No. 964.404 – ES (2007/0144450-5), 15 March 2011, emphasis added. The author would like to thank Paula Westenberger who has kindly provided the English translation of this decision.

100. *See* in this sense P.L.C. Torremans, 'Copyright as a Human Right', *supra* n. 50, at 19, and J. Drexl, 'Constitutional Protection of Authors' Moral Rights in the European Union', *supra* n. 79, stating that 'constitutional considerations matter. They are crucial for building a legal system in a situation in which there is a growing feeling that something is wrong with existing copyright'. *See also* H. Porsdam, 'On European Narratives of Human Rights and Their Possible Implications for Copyright', in *New Directions in Copyright Law*, vol. 5, ed. F. Macmillan, *supra* n. 4, at 335 et seq.; C.

only as a guideline for the application of IP law, but also for a reorganization of IP law in the future.

4.4.1   Fundamental Rights as Guidelines for the Application of IP Law

There are several advantages involved in recognizing fundamental rights as a foundation for the IP system:

- Fundamental rights are included in the national constitutions and bind the legislature. They rank high in the hierarchy of norms. The reference to natural law is no longer necessary because the basis of natural-law values were codified in fundamental rights.[101] They form the roots of positive law and have to be considered by the lawmakers.[102] Fundamental rights therefore offer possibilities for a balanced development of intellectual property.
- The legislature has to consider all fundamental rights equally. There is no hierarchical relationship between them.[103] There is a basic tension between property and freedom, which the legislature must bring into a balanced relationship.[104] The property right and the personality right[105] must therefore always be confronted by different fundamental rights like the freedom of expression and information,

---

Geiger, 'L'utilisation jurisprudentielle des droits fondamentaux en Europe en matière de propriété intellectuelle: Quel apport? Quelles perspectives?', in *La contribution de la jurisprudence à la construction de la propriété intellectuelle en Europe*, vol. 193, ed. Ch. Geiger (Collection of the CEIPI, Paris, LexisNexis, 2013).

101. F. Fechner, *Geistiges Eigentum und Verfassung, supra* n. 32, at 135.
102. *See* T. Mylly, 'Intellectual Property and Fundamental Rights', *supra* n. 86, at 187 et seq., underlining that fundamental rights 'provide the basic set of the most fundamental norms and principles to which all areas of law are connected. They thus play a particular role in the pursuit of coherence. Accordingly, private law and fundamental rights should be seen in a dialogical relationship: rather than eliminating choice, autonomy and experimentalism, such a dialogue enables the realisation of certain basic values'.
103. Further on the 'complex issue of equality of human rights', *see* an excellent paper by P. Ducoulombier, 'Interaction Between Human Rights: Are All Human Rights Equal?', in *Research Handbook on Human Rights and Intellectual Property*, ed. C. Geiger, *supra* n. 9, 39. *See also*, P. Ducoulombier, 'Conflicts Between Fundamental Rights and the European Court of Human Rights: An Overview', in *Conflicts Between Fundamental Rights*, ed. E. Brems (Intersentia, 2008), 217.
104. *See also* in this sense D. Vaver, 'Intellectual Property: The State of the Art', Law Quarterly Review (LQR) 116 (2000): 636; S. Ricketson, 'Intellectual Property and Human Rights', in *Commercial Law and Human Rights*, ed. S. Bottomley & D. Kinley (Burlington: Ashgate, 2001), 192; J. Cornides, 'Human Rights and Intellectual Property, Conflict or Convergence?', *supra* n. 39, at 167.
105. The link between the moral right and the personality right is very clear in Germany, where moral rights are described as 'authors' personality rights' (*Urheberpersönlichkeitsrechte*). *See* on this issue J. Drexl, 'Constitutional Protection of Authors' Moral Rights in the European Union', *supra* n. 79. On the constitutional protection of copyright

freedom of arts and sciences, the right to privacy or the right to human dignity,[106] and a proportional balance between these rights must be found.[107] Importantly, not only national, but also the European legislature, is bound by them. The EU Charter has now acquired the status of primary law, thereby placing the rights enumerated in it at a higher status in the European hierarchy of norms than directives.[108] Furthermore, the rights listed in the ECHR, which have been hitherto

---

from a German perspective, *see also* H. Schack, *Urheber – und Urhebervertragsrecht*, 3rd ed. (Tübingen: Mohr Siebeck, 2005), 37 et seq.

106. This fundamental human right and principle, which is to be found in the preamble of the UDHR and of the Covenant, as well as in Article 1 of the EU Charter on Fundamental Rights, is very important to act as a limit for the existence of patent law in certain areas, like patents on genetic material. *See* on this subject the very interesting chapter of G. van Overwalle, 'Human Rights' Limitations in Patent Law', in *Intellectual Property and Human Rights, A Paradox*, ed. W. Grosheide (Cheltenham, UK/Northampton, MA, Edward Elgar, 2010), 236. *See also* in this sense recital 38 of the Directive of 6 July 1998 on the legal protection of biotechnological inventions (Official Journal L 213, 30 July 1998, at 13): 'Whereas the operative part of this Directive should also include an illustrative list of inventions excluded from patentability so as to provide national courts and patent offices with a general guide to interpreting the reference to *ordre public* and morality; whereas this list obviously cannot presume to be exhaustive; whereas processes, the use of *which offend against human dignity* [...] are obviously also excluded from patentability'. *See also* CESCR, *General Comment No. 17, supra* n. 52, stating that 'the States parties should prevent the use of scientific and technical progress for purposes contrary to human rights and dignity, including the rights to life, health and privacy, e.g., by excluding inventions from patentability whenever their commercialization would jeopardize the full realization of these rights' (para. 35). *See* more generally on the issue *Biotechnologies and International Human Rights,* ed. F. Francioni (Oxford, Hart Publishing, 2007); E.B. Ituku, *Propriété intellectuelle et droits de l'homme, supra* n. 9; J. Koopman, 'Human Rights Implications of Patenting Biotechnological Knowledge', in *Intellectual Property and Human Rights*, ed. P.L.C. Torremans (Kluwer Law International, Auston/Boston/Chicago/New York/The Netherlands, 2008), 533.

107. *See also* P.L.C. Torremans, 'Copyright as a Human Right', *supra* n. 50, at 17; M. Grünberger, 'A Constitutional Duty to Protect the Rights of Performers? Goldstein versus California and Bob Dylan – Two Different Stories', IIC 37 (2006): 277. More sceptical, R.L. Ostergard, 'Intellectual Property: A Universal Human Right?', Human Rights Quarterly 21 (1999): 156, arguing that to recognize IPRs as human rights is problematic because other human rights, like those relating to physical well-being, must take priority over the guarantee of IPRs as universal human rights. In our opinion, to recognize IPRs as human rights does not mean to give priority to these rights over those relating to physical well-being. On the contrary, it might even require that the latter prevail, because fundamental rights are always to be analysed in their interaction with other fundamental rights. Article 27(2) UDHR, for example, should always be contemplated with regard to Article 27(1).

108. The Treaty of Lisbon amending the Treaty on European Union and the Treaty establishing the European Community, signed at Lisbon on 13 December 2007 (OJEU 17 December 2007, 2007/C 306/01) gives the EU Charter of Fundamental Rights a legally binding force and integrates this text in the primary legislation of the European Union (Article 6(1) TEU).

recognized as the general principles of EU law,[109] will in the future bind the EU legislature (and other Union institutions) directly, as a result of the EU accession to the ECHR.[110] This means that in the future the Convention will become the highest binding source of law concerning fundamental rights, so that both primary and secondary EU law will have to comply with it. Directives should therefore always be interpreted 'in the light' of the European Convention.[111] Indeed, there have been more and more references to fundamental rights in the recitals (and, sometimes, even in the main text) of the latest directives on intellectual property, which also must be considered when interpreting the directives.[112] However, the nature of fundamental rights as objective principles implies that the obligation to interpret EU law in a manner compliant with fundamental rights is

---

109. *See* Article 6(3) TEU.
110. *See* Article 6(2) TEU as amended by Article 1(8) of the Treaty of Lisbon and Article 59(2) ECHR as amended by Article 17 of Protocol No. 14 to the ECHR.
111. In the case that a directive violates a fundamental right of the ECHR, Member States can bring an action before the CJEU and challenge the conformity of the text to the ECHR: action of annulment according to Article 263 TFEU (second indent) (ex. Article 230 (second indent) of the EC Treaty): the CJEU has 'jurisdiction in actions brought by a Member State, the European Parliament, the Council or the Commission on grounds of lack of competence, infringement of an essential procedural requirement, infringement of the Treaties or *of any rule of law relating to their application*, or misuse of powers' (emphasis added). Unfortunately, the delay for the action is only two months (Article 263 TFEU (sixth indent) (ex. Article 230 (fifth indent) EC Treaty)). Moreover, a natural or legal person can only initiate proceedings against a directive if it is of direct and individual concern (Article 263 TFEU (forth indent) (ex. Article 230 (forth indent) EC Treaty)). That is seldom the case, for example, when national legislators have absolutely no margin of discretion in implementing the directive. But after the directive has been implemented, the individual can claim that the implementation law violates his or her fundamental rights before a national court. If the court considers that the law could violate a fundamental right as embodied in the ECHR, it can refer the matter to the CJEU according to Article 263 TFEU (ex. Article 234 EC Treaty). That way, the CJEU can test the validity of a directive, even when the two months are over. On remedies before the CJEU, *see* P. Craig & G. de Búrca, *EU Law. Texts, Cases and Materials*, 3rd ed. (Oxford University Press, 2003), 482 et seq.
112. *See* recitals 3 and 31 of the Directive of the European Parliament and of the Council on the harmonization of certain aspects of copyright and related rights in the information society of 22 May 2001 (OJEC L 167, 22 June 2001, p. 10); recitals 2 and 32 of the Directive of the European Parliament and of the Council on the enforcement of intellectual property rights from 29 April 2004 (OJEC L 157, 30 April 2004, p. 45); recital 16 of the Directive 98/44/EC of the European Parliament and of the Council of 6 July 1998 on the legal protection of biotechnological inventions (OJEC L 123, 30 July 1998, p. 13); recital 12 of the Amended proposal for a Directive of the European Parliament and of the Council on criminal measures aimed at ensuring the enforcement of intellectual property rights of 26 April 2006, COM (2006) 168 final; recitals 19 and 34 of the Directive (EU) 2016/943 of the European Parliament and of the Council of 8 June 2016 on the protection of undisclosed know-how and business information (trade secrets) against their unlawful acquisition, use and disclosure (OJEU L 157, 15 June 2016, p. 1); recitals 70, 84, 85 and Article 17(10) of the Directive (EU) 2019/790 of the

not restricted to directives, but extends to the whole *acquis commu-nautaire*, including the articles of the EU Treaties.[113]

National legislatures also have, when implementing the direc-tives, to take into account the European standards of fundamental rights,[114] as well as the provisions of their national constitutions, when the directives leave some margin of appreciation.[115] Fundamen-tal rights therefore constitute a good framework for the development of IP protection. They are effective tools to guarantee a balanced development and understanding of IP rights and a remedy for the overprotective tendencies of lobby-driven legislation.[116]

– Fundamental rights and human rights represent ethical values, which enjoy widespread consent and acknowledgement under international law.[117] In the context of globalization, they offer a 'human' legal framework for the advancement of intellectual property, which so far has been regarded exclusively from an economic point of view.[118] Whereas, for instance, the different legal systems show various cultural differences despite their convergences, the moral and cultural

European Parliament and of the Council of 17 April 2019 on copyright and related rights in the Digital Single Market and amending Directives 96/9/EC and 2001/29/EC (OJEU L 130, 17 May 2019, p. 92).

113. *See,* e.g., the decision of the CJEU (Case C-260/89, ECR 1991, I-02925) in which the Court interprets the freedom to provide services in the light of the general principle of freedom of expression as embodied in Article 10 ECHR. For the use of fundamental rights as mandatory requirements that justify barriers to the fundamental freedoms, *see also* Cases C-368/95, ECR 1997 I-3689 and C-60/00, ECR 2000, I-6297.

114. P. Craig & G. de Búrca, *EU Law. Texts, Cases and Materials*, *supra* n. 111, at 337 et seq. *See* clearly in this sense ECJ, Case C-275/06, *Promusicae* [2008], *supra* n. 91, at para. 70.

115. *See,* e.g., the decision of the German Constitutional Court, 12 May 1989, 1989 EuGRZ 339, 340: 'The directive [...] leaves [...] a considerable margin of appreciation. The national legislature, when implementing the directive, is bound by the guidelines of the German Basic Law'. This has also been clarified in Germany by the German Constitutional Court in the context of a framework decision of 18 July 2005, 2005 NJW 2289.

116. *See* in this sense M. Grünberger, 'A Constitutional Duty to Protect the Rights of Performers?', *supra* n. 107, at 302, stating that if a fundamental rights analysis of IP law 'at first sight appears to be another twist to fortify the stronghold of right holders', it 'may well turn out to be the critics Trojan horse in the industry's citadel'.

117. According to M. Cassin, the UDHR has a very strong moral, political and practical impact (R. Cassin, 'L'intégration, parmi les droits fondamentaux de l'homme, des droits des créateurs des œuvres de l'esprit', in *Mélanges Marcel Plaisant* (Paris: Sirey, 1960), at 231).

118. In this sense also P. Drahos, 'The Universality of Intellectual Property Rights', *supra* n. 50, at 34; A. Chapman, 'Approaching Intellectual Property as a Human Right', *supra* n. 50, at 14 et seq.; A. Kéréver, 'Authors' Rights are Human Rights', Copyright Bulletin 32 (1998): 23; P.L.C. Torremans, 'Copyright as a Human Right', *supra* n. 50, at 16; C. Geiger, 'Fundamental Rights as Common Principles of European (and International) Intellectual Property Law', in: *Common Principles of European Intellectual Property Law*, ed. A. Ohly, (Mohr Siebeck, Tübingen, 2012), 223.

values of the UDHR are undisputed and could represent the basis of a worldwide harmonization.[119] It would thus be worth considering including a reference to the UDHR in the TRIPS Agreement, so that the Declaration could serve as a guideline for its interpretation.[120] This could prevent a systematic interpretation in favour of the right owners.[121] Furthermore, it would guarantee that economic reasoning is carried out with ethical considerations.[122] Such a reference could be

---

119. *See also* in this sense D. Beldiman, 'Fundamental Rights, Author's Right and Copyright – Commonalities or Divergences?', Columbia Journal of Law & the Arts 29 (2005): 60.
120. *See* Resolution 2000/7 of the UN Sub-Commission on Human Rights, 17 August 2000, on 'Intellectual Property Rights and Human Rights' (E/CN.4/SUB.2/RES/2000/7), where the 'Human Rights Commission requests the World Trade Organisation, in general, and the Council on TRIPS during its ongoing review of the TRIPS Agreement, in particular, *to take fully into account the existing State obligations under international human rights instruments*' (emphasis added). *See also* in this sense Resolution 2001/21 of the UN Sub-Commission on Human Rights, 16 August 2001 (E/CN.4/SUB.2/RES/ 2001/21). Unfortunately, these resolutions have no binding character for the Member States, but their political significance is not to be neglected. Furthermore, it is not excluded that these soft law principles evolve into customary international law (*see,* e.g., C.M. Chinkin, 'The Challenge of Soft Law: Development and Change in International Law', International & Comparative Law Quarterly 38 (1989): 856 et seq.). However, the interpretation of TRIPS in the light of the UDHR could already result from the General Rule of interpretation of treaties to be found in Article 31 of the Vienna Convention on the Law of Treaties of 23 May 1969, entered into force on 27 January 1980 (United Nations, Treaty Series, vol. 1155, 331). According to Article 31.3(c), for the interpretation of a treaty, 'any relevant rules of international law applicable in the relations between the parties' should be taken into account. Giving the numerous ethical questions involved, it is hard to deny that the UDHR can be such a relevant rule in the context of the TRIPS Agreement.
121. However, it has been suggested that the primacy of international human rights acts over trade liberalization rules already require that these rules have to be interpreted in the light of the UDHR (*see,* e.g., the article of G. Marceau, Counsellor for the Legal Affairs Division of the WTO Secretariat, 'WTO Dispute Settlement and Human Rights', European Journal of International Law 13 (2002): 753 et seq., and, G. Marceau, Counsellor for the Legal Affairs Division of the WTO Secretariat, 'The WTO Dispute Settlement and Human Rights', in *International Trade and Human Rights: Foundations and Conceptual Issues*, World Trade Forum, vol. 5, ed. F.M. Abbott, C. Breining-Kaufmann & T. Cottier (Ann Arbor: University of Michigan Press, 2005), Chapter 10; R. Howse & M. Mutua, *Protecting Human Rights in a Global Economy: Challenges for the World Trade Organization* (Montreal: Rights & Democracy, International Centre for Human Rights and Democratic Development, 2000). *See also* Resolution 2000/7 of the UN Sub-Commission, *supra* n. 120.
122. *See* A. Chapman, 'Approaching Intellectual Property as a Human Right', *supra* n. 50, at 15. *See also* A. Kur, 'A New Framework for Intellectual Property Law – Horizontal Issues', IIC 35 (2004): 1, at 14, underlining the need to take ethical issues more into account. Linking the interpretation of the TRIPS Agreement with international human rights, in particular in the context of its Articles 7 and 8, *see* C. Geiger and L. Desaunettes, 'Les articles 7 et 8, belle au bois dormant des accords sur les ADPIC', in: C. Geiger ed., *Le droit international de la propriété intellectuelle lié au commerce: L'accord ADPIC, bilan et perspectives*, Paris, LexisNexis, Collection of the CEIPI No. 65, 2017, 65 and from the same authors, 'The Revitalisation of the Object and Purpose

added via a Declaration or an Agreed statement without substantial changes to the Agreement and might draw more easily a consensus on an international level because of the high moral acceptance of the UDHR then a revision of TRIPS.[123]

– If legislation does not represent these values, the judges have to interpret the laws in the light of fundamental rights. In exceptional cases, they can even intervene without legal basis within IP law and correct certain excesses. Thus, in numerous decisions of European courts, the rights laid out in the ECHR have already been used in copyright disputes to limit the rights of the author (in these cases, fundamental rights act as 'external' limits of intellectual property).[124] In many countries, the application of the Convention is even recognized horizontally, that is in conflicts between two private persons,[125] so that without doubt a human rights reasoning has entered into the private-law discourse.[126] These values are also

---

of the TRIPS Agreement: The Plain Packaging Decision and the Awakening of the TRIPS Flexibility Clauses', in *Constitutional Hedges of Intellectual Property*, eds. J. Griffiths & T. Mylly (Oxford: Oxford University Press, 2020), forthcoming.

123. Favouring a link of the TRIPS Agreement to the human rights treaties, *see also* L.R. Helfer, 'Human Rights and Intellectual Property: Conflict or Coexistence?', Minnesota Intellectual Property Review 5 (2003): 47, at 61. According to this author, allowing greater opportunities for airing a human rights perspective on intellectual property issues will strengthen the legitimacy of the WTO and promote the integration of an increasingly dense thicket of legal rules governing the same broad subject matter. *See also* R.D. Anderson & H. Wager, 'Human Rights, Development, and the WTO', *supra* n. 50, at 707 et seq., underlining the complementarities of international trade law with human rights concerns: 'It remains that efficiently functioning markets, backed up by appropriate laws and institutions, are central to any realistic programme for development and hence to the fulfilment of human rights' (at 715). *See* further H. Wager & J. Watal, 'Human Rights and International Intellectual Property Law', in *Research Handbook on Human Rights and Intellectual Property*, ed. C. Geiger, *supra* n. 9, 149.

124. Consider, e.g., the above-discussed (*supra* 4.3.3) *Ashby Donald* and *'The Pirate Bay'* rulings from the European Court of Human Rights.

125. *See* A. Clapham, 'The "Drittwirkung" of the Convention', in *The European System for the Protection of Human Rights*, ed. J.St.R. Macdonald, F. Matscher & H. Petzold (Dordrecht/Boston/London: Martinus Nijhoff Publishers, 1993), 201; E.A. Alkema, 'The Third-Party Applicability or "Drittwirkung" of the European Convention on Human Rights', in *Protecting Human Rights: The European Dimension, Studies in Honour of G.J. Wiarda*, ed. F. Matscher & H. Petzold (Cologne: Carl Heymanns, 1988), 33 et seq. This evolution should be welcomed. Indeed, the fact that countries place increasing emphasis on their economic well-being has led to a certain transfer of power from the state to the industry. This cannot occur without consequences for positive law: As the misuse of power can now also emanate from economic actors, individual freedoms must from now on not only be protected vis-à-vis the state, but also vis-à-vis private persons. In this sense, *see also* T. Mylly, 'Intellectual Property and Fundamental Rights', *supra* n. 86, at 193.

126. According to F. Dessemontet, 'there will be in the future a tendency to emphasize the direct applicability of all fundamental provisions of the new European legal order to come, allowing, therefore, private individuals to complain about the behaviour of other

included in national constitutions, though. All provide equally for protection of property and personality on the one hand, and protection of the freedom of expression, of information and of art and science on the other hand.[127]

Admittedly, it is obviously not the ideal solution to fall back on rules from outside intellectual property. It would be preferable for these problems to be solved by IP legislation.[128] However, the difficulty here results from the fact that national legislatures are bound by an entire bundle of European or international regulation which does not necessarily incorporate sufficiently human rights concerns, leaving them a rather small margin of freedom. In addition, there is often a certain lack of political courage among legislators, as the question is sensitive and controversial. Thus, instead of taking any initiatives, national legislative bodies tend to prefer remaining quite passive.

Due to this lack of legislative development, the Courts in several countries and at EU level have tried to find some solutions in order to permit equitable readjustments. The judicial instruments to achieve this goal have been various, reaching from competition law (and the granting of certain compulsory licenses as in the *Magill* decision of the CJEU)[129] to media law,

---

private entities which could appear to be in violation of human rights. Why then should the Universal Declaration of Human Rights not benefit from the direct applicability of the European Convention on Human Rights?' (F. Dessemontet, 'Copyright and Human Rights', in *Intellectual Property and Information Law*, ed. J.J.C. Kabel & G.J.H.M. Mom (The Hague: Kluwer Law International, 1998), 116). In fact, according to the CJEU, the UDHR and the ICESCR are also part of the European framework concerning fundamental rights and have to be taken into account: *see*, e.g., ECJ, Joined cases C-20/00 and C-64/00, *Booker Aquaculture Ltd, Hydro Seafood GSP Ltd and the Scottish Ministers* [2003], Judgment of the Court of 10 July 2003, para. 65, ECR I-07411. *See also* ECJ, Case 4/73, *Nold KG v. Commission* [1974], Judgment of the Court of 14 May 1974, ECR 00491; and ECJ, Case 44/79, *Hauer v. Land Rheinland-Pfalz* [1979], Judgment of the Court of 13 December 1979, ECR 03727.

127. Nevertheless, the introduction of a balanced constitutional clause could permit the matter to be framed in a more readable way: *see infra* 4.5.
128. *See* in this sense, e.g., A. Lucas, 'Droit d'auteur, liberté d'expression et droit du public à l'information', A&M (2005): 21.
129. ECJ, Joined cases C-241/91 P and C-242/91 P, *Radio Telefis Eireann and Others v. Commission and Magill TV Guide* [1995], Judgment of the Court of 6 April 1995, ECR I-00743. It is clear that competition law can also be an effective judicial means to 'counter' certain abuses of intellectual property rights (*see* particularly C. Geiger, *Droit d'auteur et droit du public à l'information*, *supra* n. 32, at 306 et seq.; U. Bath, 'Access to Information v. Intellectual Property Rights', EIPR (2002): 138; P.B. Hugenholtz & R. Okediji, 'Conceiving an International Instrument on Limitations and Exceptions to Copyright', Study supported by the Open Society Institute (OSI), 6 March 2008; Amsterdam Law School Research Paper No. 2012-43; Institute for Information Law Research Paper No. 2012-37, at 32 et seq.). Paradoxically, its application to intellectual property law, while it is still contested by certain purists, is however less contested than the application of fundamental rights.

the theory of abuse of rights or the application of fundamental rights.[130] Some cases have entailed some very interesting decisions.[131] They mainly concern the conflict between an intellectual property right (especially copyright, but also trademark rights)[132] and freedom of expression or the public's right to information.[133] However, there is also a growing number of decisions on the intersection of IP rights with the right to privacy and data

130. On the judges' recourse to fundamental rights as external limitations, *see* C. Geiger, *Droit d'auteur et droit du public à l'information, supra* n. 32, at 382 et seq and, in the context of the interpretation of EU secondary IP law, C. Geiger, 'The Role of the Court of Justice of the European Union: Harmonizing, Creating and sometimes Disrupting Copyright Law in the European Union', in: *New Developments in EU and International Copyright Law*, ed. I. Stamatoudi, Alphen aan den Rijn (NL) (Kluwer Law International, 2016), 435.

131. For a presentation and analysis of those cases, *see* C. Geiger, '"Constitutionalizing" Intellectual Property Law?', *supra* n. 61. *See also* A.E.L. Brown, 'Guarding the Guards: The Practical Impact of Human Rights on Protection of Innovation and Creativity', paper presented at the 20th BILETA Conference, April 2005, Queen's University of Belfast.

132. To our knowledge, there are very few decisions on patents, which is surprising, as ethical questions play an important role in that field. However, see the two decisions of the CJEU on exclusion from patentability of inventions related to human embryonic stem cells/ human body on moral and human dignity grounds: CJEU, Case C-34/10, *Brüstle* [2011], Judgment of the Court of 18 October 2011, ECR I-09821; ECJ, Case C-377/98, *Netherlands v. Parliament and Council* [2001], Judgment of the Court of 9 October 2001, ECR I-07079. For an analysis of these and other decisions on the intersection of human dignity with patent protection, *see* A. Plomer, 'Human Dignity and Patents', *supra* n. 10.

133. On the conflict of copyright with freedom of expression and information *see*, e.g., P.B. Hugenholtz, 'Copyright and Freedom of Expression in Europe', *supra* n. 79; A. Strowel & F. Tulkens, 'Freedom of Expression and Copyright under Civil Law: Of Balance, Adaptation, and Access', in *Copyright and Free Speech*, ed. J. Griffiths & U. Suthersanen (Oxford University Press, 2005), 287; F. MacMillan Patfield, 'Towards a Reconciliation of Free Speech and Copyright', in *The Yearbook of Media and Entertainment Law 1996*, ed. E. Barendt (Oxford University Press, 1996), 199; C. Geiger, 'Author's Right, Copyright and the Public's Right to Information, A Complex Relationship', in *New Directions in Copyright Law*, vol. 5, ed. F. Macmillan, *supra* n. 4, at 24; C. Geiger, '"Fair Use" Through Fundamental Rights in Europe, When Freedom of Artistic Expression allows Creative Appropriations and Opens up Statutory Copyright Limitations', forthcoming in: *The Cambridge Handbook of Copyright Limitations and Exceptions*, eds. W.L. Ng-Loy, H. Sun, & S. Balganesh (Cambridge, Cambridge University Press, 2020), Center for International Intellectual Property Studies (CEIPI) Research Paper No. 2018-09, available at SSRN: https://ssrn.com/abstract=3256899 (accessed September 2019); E. Izyumenko, 'The Freedom of Expression Contours of Copyright in the Digital Era: A European Perspective', 19(3-4) Journal of World Intellectual Property 115 (2016); P. Akester, 'The Political Challenge – Copyright and Free Speech Restrictions in the Digital Age', IPQ (2006): 16; C.J. Angelopoulos, 'Freedom of Expression and Copyright: The Double Balancing Act', IPQ (2008): 328; D. Voorhoof, 'Freedom of Expression and the Right to Information', *supra* n. 77.

protection,[134] freedom to conduct a business,[135] and the due process guarantees.[136]

4.4.2 FUNDAMENTAL RIGHTS AS GUIDELINES FOR REORGANIZING IP LAW

Creating a human rights foundation for the IP system would also imply different consequences for the concrete design of the law. A new foundation

---

134. *See* for the examples of such decisions from the Luxemburg Court: CJEU, Case C-461/10, *Bonnier Audio and Others* [2012], *supra* n. 91; ECJ, Case C-557/07, *Tele2* [2009], *supra* n. 91; ECJ, Case C-275/06, *Promusicae* [2008], *supra* n. 91; but also CJEU, Case C-360/10, *SABAM v. Netlog* [2012], *supra* n. 87; CJEU, Case C-70/10, *Scarlet Extended* [2011], *supra* n. 87. And, from the Strasbourg Court: ECtHR, *Vorsina and Vogralik v. Russia* (dec.), No. 66801/01, 5 February 2004, unreported; ECtHR, *Chappell v. the United Kingdom*, No. 10461/83, 30 March 1989, Series A No. 152-A. For further insights into the relationship between IP and the right to privacy and personal data protection, *see*, e.g., R. Callender Smith, 'Discovery and Compulsion: How Regulatory and Litigation Issues relating to Intellectual Property Rights are Challenging the Fundamental Right to the Protection of Personal Data', Queen Mary Journal of Intellectual Property 3(1) (2013): 2.

135. *See*, e.g., in the context of the Luxemburg Court case law: CJEU, Case C-314/12, *Telekabel* [2014], *supra* n. 87; CJEU, Case C-360/10, *SABAM v. Netlog* [2012], *supra* n. 87; CJEU, Case C-70/10, *Scarlet Extended* [2011], *supra* n. 87. On the national level, *see*, for example, Hague Court of Appeal, *Ziggo and XS4ALL v. BREIN*, No. 200.105.418/01, 28 January 2014; *Cartier, Montblanc and Richemont v. BSkyB, BT, TalkTalk, EE and Virgin (Open Rights Group intervening)* [2014] EWHC 3354 (Ch), 17 October 2014. For the further analysis of the interplay between intellectual property and business freedom, *see* G. Ghidini & A. Stazi, 'Freedom to Conduct a Business, Competition and Intellectual Property', in *Research Handbook on Human Rights and Intellectual Property,* ed. C. Geiger, *supra* n. 9, 410.

136. *See*, e.g., in the context of the ECtHR judicial practice: ECtHR, *Rambus Inc. v. Germany* (dec.) [2009], No. 40382/04, 16 June 2009, unreported; ECtHR, *Rapos v. Slovakia* [2008], No. 25763/02, 20 May 2008, unreported; ECtHR, *Hiro Balani v. Spain*, No. 18064/91, 9 December 1994, Series A No. 303-B. For the CJEU case law examples, *see*: CJEU, Case T-542/10, *XXXLutz Marken v. OHIM* [2012], Judgment of the General Court (Third Chamber) of 13 June 2012, published in the electronic Reports of Cases; ECJ, Case C-385/07 P, *Der Grüne Punkt – Duales System Deutschland v. Commission* [2009], Judgment of the Court (Grand Chamber) of 16 July 2009, ECR I-06155. In the context of the quasi-judicial practice of the Boards of Appeal of the European Patent Office, *see* EPO, J 0015/04, *Possible reasons for exclusion/Mitsubishi Heavy Industries Ltd.*, 30 May 2006; EPO, G 0001/05, *Exclusion and objection*, 7 December 2006 (for an analysis, *see* A. Kupzok, 'Human Rights in the Case Law of the EPO Boards of Appeal', in *Research Handbook on Human Rights and Intellectual Property,* ed. C. Geiger, *supra* n. 9, 311). For further insights into the fair trial implications of intellectual property protection, in particular in the context of enforcement, *see* J. Griffiths, 'Enforcement of Intellectual Property Rights and the Right to a Fair Trial'; and P. Yu, 'Digital Copyright Enforcement Measures and Their Human Rights Threats', both in *Research Handbook on Human Rights and Intellectual Property,* ed. C. Geiger, *supra* n. 9, 438, 455.

could lead to a reorganization of IP legislation and set the course for the implementation of a fair and balanced system:[137]

- To start with, decisions that on principle favour the right-holder, like the principle of the restrictive interpretation of exceptions, would not be justified under a system based on fundamental rights.[138] A good illustration is the recent case law of the CJEU that, in view of the Union's fundamental rights obligations, departs from the long dominating its jurisprudence principle of restrictive reading of exceptions in favour of an interpretation that promotes the effectiveness of the exception.[139] In addition, the so-called three-step test (included in Article 5(5) of the InfoSoc Directive,[140] but also in the Berne Convention, the TRIPS Agreement[141] and the WIPO Treaties) needs to be understood in light of the fundamental rights and not in the sense of a preliminary decision for the author and inventor (or the right-holder). Rather, the test can offer greater flexibility for limitations to IP rights and their adaptation to changed social and technical circumstances. This requires, however, a new reading of the three-step test,[142] namely one that begins with the last step, which requires

137. *See also* in this sense H.L. MacQueen, 'Towards Utopia or Irreconcilable Tensions? Thoughts on Intellectual Property, Human Rights and Competition Law', SCRIPT- ed 2(4) (December 2005): 452, stating that human rights 'play a dynamic role in political debate about the content and effects of IPRs – and it is in that dimension, I suggest, that we should look to achieve their fullest effects'.

138. *See also* in this sense T. Mylly, 'Intellectual Property and Fundamental Rights', *supra* n. 86, at 208. *See* in this sense Supreme Court of Canada, 4 March 2004, *CCH Canadian Ltd. v. Law Society of Upper Canada*, 2004 SCC 13; IIC 35 (2004): 705: 'The fair dealing exception, like other exceptions in the Copyright Act, is a user's right. In order to maintain the proper balance between the rights of a copyright owner and user's interests, it must not be interpreted restrictively' (para. 48). For a comment on this important decision, *see* C.P. Spurgeon, 'Chronique du Canada', RIDA 207 (2006), at 209 et seq.

139. For an overview of such cases, *see* the Opinion of the European Copyright Society issued in *Deckmyn* case: ECS, 'Limitations and Exceptions as Key Elements of the Legal Framework for Copyright in the European Union', *supra* n. 91.

140. Directive 2001/29/EC of the European Parliament and of the Council of 22 May 2001 on the harmonisation of certain aspects of copyright and related rights in the information society (InfoSoc) (OJEC L 167, 22 June 2001, at 10).

141. The TRIPS Agreement contains such a test for the limitations of copyright, but also for limitations of trademark and patent rights (Articles 13, 17 and 30 TRIPS). For a horizontal approach to the three-step test, *see* M. Senftleben, 'Towards a Horizontal Standard for Limiting Intellectual Property Rights? – WTO Panel Reports Shed Light on the Three-Step Test in Copyright Law and Related Tests in Patent and Trademark Law', IIC 37 (2006): 407. *See also* on this topic, C. Geiger, 'From Berne to National Law, via the Copyright Directive: The Dangerous Mutations of the Three-Step Test', EIPR (2007): 486.

142. For such a new interpretation of the test, *see* C. Geiger, J. Griffiths & R.M. Hilty, 'Towards a Balanced Interpretation of the "Three-Step test" in Copyright Law', EIPR (2008): 489; C. Geiger, 'The Three-Step Test, A Threat to a Balanced Copyright Law?',

a balance of the concerned interests and fundamental rights positions with consideration of the principle of proportionality.[143] The second step would serve as a corrective, in order to prevent heavy losses for the right-holder. This means it would be necessary to reduce the term of normal exploitation to the core of the exclusive right, as has rightly been suggested by some scholars.[144] Otherwise, in practice almost every use could fall under this notion and other interests could not be considered.[145] In this understanding, the test would have to be applied from the bottom up. Another solution would be to read the test as setting out a number of factors that must be taken into consideration by the judge, following the model of the US doctrine of fair use. The

---

IIC 37 (2006): 683. *See also* C. Geiger, D.J. Gervais & M. Senftleben, 'The Three-Step-Test Revisited: How to Use the Test's Flexibility in National Copyright Law', American University International Law Review 29(3) (2014): 581.

143. *See* C. Geiger, 'The Role of the Three-Step Test in the Adaptation of Copyright Law to the Information Society', Unesco Copyright Bulletin (January-March 2007). *See* further the WTO Panel Reports of 17 March 2000 (WTO Document WT/DS114/R) and 15 March 2005 (WTO Document WT/DS174/R), interpreting the test in the field of trademark and patent law. According to the Panel, the term 'legitimate interests' has to be defined as 'a normative claim calling for protection of interests that are "justifiable" in the sense that they are supported by relevant public policies or *other social norms*' (WTO Panel Patents, para. 7.69; WTO Panel Trademarks, para. 7.663; emphasis added). Without a doubt, fundamental rights would be an example of such social norms. Further on the test of proportionality, including its role in the application to copyright law in Europe, *see* J. Christoffersen, 'Human Rights and Balancing: The Principle of Proportionality', in: *Research Handbook on Human Rights and Intellectual Property,* ed. C. Geiger, (Cheltenham, UK/ Northampton, MA, Edward Elgar, 2015), p. 19; O. Fischman Afori, 'Proportionality: A New Mega Standard in European Copyright Law', IIC 45(8) (2014): 889; C. Sganga & S. Scalzini, 'From Abuse of Right to European Copyright Misuse: A New Doctrine for EU Copyright Law', IIC 48(4) (2017): 405; P. Teunissen, 'The Balance Puzzle: The ECJ's Method of Proportionality Review for Copyright Injunctions', EIPR 40(9) (2018): 579; and T. Mylly, 'Proportionality in the CJEU's Internet Copyright Case Law: Invasive or Resilient?', in: *General Principles of EU Law and the EU Digital Order,* eds. U. Bernitz, X. Groussot, J. Paju, Jaan & S. de Vries (Kluwer Law International B.V., forthcoming 2020).

144. M. Senftleben, *Copyright, Limitations and the Three-Step Test* (The Hague: Kluwer, 2004), 193. *See also* S. Dusollier, 'L'encadrement des exceptions au droit d'auteur par le test des trois étapes', IRDI (2005): 220, who refers to the normal exploitation as 'the principal avenues of the exploitation of a work, those that provide for the author the major source of income'. In copyright, that could, for example, be the editing/publishing and selling of a book, meaning the exploitation of the work on the principal market.

145. Interestingly, the WTO Panel report in the patent case (*supra* n. 143), unlike the Panel decision of 15 June 2000 in the field of copyright (WTO Document WT/DS160/R), also accepted a normative understanding of the terms 'normal exploitation': it must be essential to the achievement of the goals of patent policy (para. 7.58). Therefore, policy considerations could be taken into account at the second step and the concept of normal exploitation would not only be understood in purely economic terms. Taking account of normative aspects also in the field of copyright, *see also* J.C. Ginsburg, 'Toward Supranational Copyright Law? The WTO Panel Decision and the "Three-Step Test" for Copyright Exceptions', RIDA 187 (2001): 23.

second step would then be only one of the criteria among others to be applied, one of the parameters to be taken into account in the analysis of the application of a limit.[146]

- A certain number of creations could be excluded from protection because of their importance for society by a positive definition of the public domain.[147]

Such exclusions, already known within patent law,[148] could clarify the existing regulations by identifying certain subjects that would be socially or economically undesirable to protect.[149] Of course, the list of excluded creations should be non-exhaustive to permit the law to adapt to technical and social evolution.[150] One could conceivably go one step further and limit

---

146. For such a reading, *see* K.J. Koelman, 'Fixing the Three-Step Test', EIPR (2006): 407. *See also* C. Geiger, 'The Role of the Three-Step Test in the Adaptation of Copyright Law to the Information Society', *supra* n. 143.
147. The notion and the content of the public domain is still not really clarified in legal literature. On this issue, *see*, e.g., J. Litman, 'The Public Domain', Emory Law Journal 39 (1990): 965; J. Boyle, 'The Second Enclosure Movement and the Construction of the Public Domain', Law and Contemporary Problems 66 (2003): 33; P.J. Heald, 'The Public Domain', in *Handb ook On The Economics Of Copyright: A Guide for Students and T eachers*, ed. R. Watt (Cheltenham, UK/Northampton, MA: Edward Elgar, 2014), 93; D. Barbosa, 'Domínio Público e Patrimônio Cultural', in *Direito da Propriedade Intelectual – Estudos em Homenagem ao Pe. Bruno Jorge Hammes* (Juruá: Curitiba, 2005), 117; P.B. Hugenholtz & L. Guibault (eds.), *The Public Domain of Information* (The Hague: Kluwer Law International, 2006); C. Waedle & H. MacQueen (eds.), *Intellectual Property, The Many Faces of the Public Domain* (Cheltenham, UK/ Northampton, MA: Edward Elgar, 2007); S. Dusollier, 'Le domaine public, garant de l'intérêt public en propriété intellectuelle?', in *L'intérêt général et l'accés à l'information en propriété intellectuelle*, ed. M. Buydens & S. Dusollier (Brussels: Bruylant, 2008); S. Dusollier & V.-L. Benabou, 'Draw Me a Public Domain', in *Copyright Law: A Handbook of Contemporary Research*, ed. P.L.C. Torremans (Chel- tenham, UK/Northampton, MA: Edward Elgar, 2007), 161. Unlike in the environmental sector, the preservation of informational resources has not been legally secured so far.
148. *See,* for example, Articles 52(2) and 53 of the European Patent Convention of 5 October 1973 (EPC); *see also* the possibility of Member States to exclude some subjects from patentability (Articles 27(2) and 3 of the TRIPS Agreement).
149. In the field of copyright, this could, for example, lead to the explicit exclusion of essential public information. *See also* in this sense V.-L. Benabou, 'L'étendue du droit d'auteur/Der Schutzumfang des Urheberrechts', in *Impulse für eine europäische Harmonisierung des Urheberrechts*, ed. C. Geiger & R.M. Hilty (Berlin/Heidelberg/ New York: Springer, 2007), 117 et seq. On the problem of the privatization of information through database rights from a human rights perspective, *see* S. Corbett, 'A Human Rights Perspective on the Database Debate', EIPR (2006): 83 et seq.; E. Derclaye, 'Database *Sui Generis* Right: The Need to Take the Public's Right to Information and Freedom of Expression into Account', in *New Directions in Copyright Law*, vol. 5, ed. F. Macmillan, *supra* n. 4, at 3. In many countries, some creations like official documents and official texts are explicitly excluded from copyright protection. This possibility is left open by the Berne Convention (*see* Article 2.4).
150. Compare, for example, the open wording of Article 53(a) of the EPC: 'European patents shall not be granted in respect of inventions the publication or exploitation of which

the scope of the exclusive nature of the right for creations of considerable social, cultural or economic importance. This kind of reasoning is already admitted in Europe by courts and legal scholars when applying principles of competition law to intellectual property.[151] For some creations, the scope of protection is restricted because they represent an 'essential facility'. Fundamental rights reasoning would help to extend this notion to other creations on moral and ethical grounds. A similar approach can be found in the European Television without Frontiers Directive of 30 June 1997,[152] which restricts the exclusivity of a right with regard to certain events of major importance for society.[153] The rationale behind this text was to guarantee fundamental rights

---

would be contrary to *"ordre public"* or morality, provided that the exploitation shall not be deemed to be so contrary merely because it is prohibited by law or regulation in some or all of the Contracting States.' This clause should allow patent offices (and judges when reviewing their decisions) to include a fundamental rights reasoning when granting a patent. However, it is to be doubted whether the narrow reading of this article by the EPO is compatible with fundamental rights obligations so far (*see* in this sense P. Drahos, 'Biotechnology Patents, Markets and Morality', EIPR (1999): 448, proposing that the EPO constitute a special Ethics Board with plural membership to hear matters in which Article 53 is being argued, decisions the appeal of which should lie to the European Court of Human Rights). In any case, the EPO Board of Appeal has clearly admitted in its Interlocutory Decision of 5 August 1998 (T 0377/95-3.3.4) that the European Convention on Human Rights should serve to interpret the patent provisions of the EPC. The court stated that 'the overall acceptance of the ECHR as guidance is shown by the fact that all Member States to the EPC adhere to the ECHR' (para. 36).

151. *See* the decision of the ECJ, Case C-418/01, *IMS Health* [2004], Judgment of the Court (Fifth Chamber) of 29 April 2004, ECR I-05039; IIC 35 (2004): 564, comment by B. Conde-Gallego & D. Riziotis. Numerous articles have been written on the application of the essential facilities doctrine to intellectual property; *see*, e.g., J. Drexl, 'IMS Health and Trinko – Antitrust Placebo for Consumers Instead of Sound Economics in Refusal-to-Deal Cases', IIC 35 (2004): 788; G. McCurdy, 'Intellectual Property and Competition: Does the Essential Facilities Doctrine Shed Any New Light?', EIPR (2003): 472; A. Narciso, 'IMS Health or the Question Whether Intellectual Property Still Deserves a Specific Approach in a Free Market Economy', IPQ 4 (2003): 445; B. Conde-Gallego, 'Die Anwendung des kartellrechtlichen Missbrauchsverbots auf "unerlässliche" Immaterialgüterrechte im Lichte der IMS Health – und Standard-Spundfass-Urteile', GRUR Int. 16 (2006).

152. Directive 97/36/EC of the European Parliament and of the Council of 30 June 1997 amending Council Directive 89/552/EEC of 3 October 1989 on the coordination of certain provisions laid down by law, regulation or administrative action in Member States concerning the pursuit of television broadcasting activities (OJEC L 202/60, 30 July 1997, at 60).

153. P.B. Hugenholtz, 'Copyright, Contract and Code – What Will Remain of the Public Domain?', Brooklyn Journal of International Law 26 (2000): 89: 'If legislatures were to contemplate legal measures to cure the negative effects of the wide-scale application of trusted systems, and to safeguard the public domain, comparable legislation outside the field of broadcasting law might be considered, for example, a right of access to (socially, culturally or economically) "important" scientific source material, works of art, etc.'

such as freedom of expression and the public's right to information.[154] Its Article 3a(1) holds that:

> each Member State may take measures in accordance with Community law to ensure that broadcasters under its jurisdiction do not broadcast on an exclusive basis events which are regarded by that Member State as being of major importance for society in such a way as to deprive a substantial proportion of the public in that Member State of the possibility of following such events via live coverage or deferred coverage on free television.[155]

Even though the Directive primarily referred to sporting events, it also covers other events of great importance.[156] This is how Article 3 has been perceived by certain national legislatures when transposing this Directive. Some of them have thus included several cultural events capable of being protected by copyright on the list of events the access to which cannot be restricted by systems of cryptography or other technical means of protection.[157]

More recently, the 'Trade Secrets' – Directive of 8 June 2016 provides for yet another example of limiting exclusive rights 'for exercising the right to freedom of expression and information as set out in the Charter, including respect for the freedom and pluralism of the media'.[158]

---

154. According to e.g., recital 18 of the Directive, 'It is essential that Member States should be able to take measures to protect the right to information and to ensure wide access by the public to television coverage of national or non-national events of major importance for society'.

155. *See also* in this sense Article 9 of the Convention of the Council of Europe on Transfrontier Television of 5 May 1989 that prescribed to signatory states that they 'examine and, where necessary, take legal measures […] to avoid the right of the public to information being undermined due to the exercise […] of exclusive rights'. Of course, the production of these events (or of information in general) sometimes requires substantial investments. It is then a question of public policy: If in a democratic society the access to information and to certain works is rated as an essential tool for citizens to participate in the public debate, the access costs should be kept very low (or even sometimes free of charge), like access to education. The production costs should then be partly covered by public funding, if the loss of income due to the reduction of the exclusivity could reduce the incentive for producing it.

156. *See* on this issue C. Geiger, *Droit d'auteur et droit du public à l'information, supra* n. 32, at 386 et seq.

157. For example, Austria and Italy included on the list some events related to national cultural and as well as other events. *See* N. Helberger, *Controlling Access to Content, Regulating Conditional Access in Digital Broadcasting* (The Hague: Kluwer Law International, 2005), 96 et seq.

158. Article 5 (a)(a) of the Directive (EU) 2016/943 of the European Parliament and of the Council of 8 June 2016 on the protection of undisclosed know-how and business information (trade secrets) against their unlawful acquisition, use and disclosure, (OJEU L 157, 15 June 2016, p. 1): 'Member States shall ensure that an application for the measures, procedures and remedies provided for in this Directive is dismissed where the alleged acquisition, use or disclosure of the trade secret was carried out in any of the

Limitations to intellectual property rights, which are based on fundamental rights and thereby represent basic democratic values within IP law,
are *rights* of the users (and not mere interests to be taken into account), which
are of equal value as the exclusive right.[159] The consequence of this is that
they should be considered mandatory (which means the user's exercise of
statutory limitations cannot be restricted by contract)[160] and should prevail
over technical measures. The national legislatures could introduce into their
acts a prohibition of technical devices that prevent a use privileged by law,

---

following cases: (a) for exercising the right to freedom of expression and information as
set out in the Charter, including respect for the freedom and pluralism of the media';
supra n. 112. *See also* Article 1.2, clarifying that 'the Directive shall not affect: (a) the
exercise of the right to freedom of expression and information as set out in the Charter,
including respect for the freedom and pluralism of the media'. For a comment on the
Draft Directive, *see* T. Aplin, 'A Critical Evaluation of the Proposed EU Trade Secrets
Directive', IPQ 4 (2014): 257; J. Lapousterle, C. Geiger, N. Olszak & L. Desaunettes,
'What Protection for Trade Secrets in the European Union? A Comment of the Directive
Proposal of November 2013', EIPR (2016): 255.

159. *See* for a more detailed analysis *see* C. Geiger, 'Die Schranken des Urheberrechts im
Lichte der Grundrechte – Zur Rechtsnatur der Beschränkungen des Urheberrechts', in
Interessenausgleich im Urheberrecht, ed. R.M. Hilty & A. Peukert (Baden-Baden:
Nomos, 2004), 143; C. Geiger, 'De la nature juridique des limites au droit d'auteur',
Propr. intell. (2004): 882; P. Chapdelaine, *Copyright User Rights: Contracts and the
Erosion of Property* (Oxford: OUP, 2017); C.J. Craig, 'Globalizing User Rights-Talk: On
Copyright Limits and Rhetorical Risks', 33(1) American University International Law
Review 1 (2017). *See also* Supreme Court of Canada, 4 March 2004, *CCH Canadian
Ltd., supra* n. 138 and in the EU the decisions of the CJEU *Funke Medien* and *Spiegel
Online supra* n. 76 (CJEU, Judgments in *Funke Medien*, at para. 70, and *Spiegel Online*,
at para. 54 (emphasis added), with further references to CJEU, Judgment in *Ulmer*, at
para. 43); *see also* CJEU, Judgments in *Telekabel*, at para. 57, In the context of patent
law and TRIPS, *see* D. Vaver & S. Basheer, 'Popping Patented Pills: Europe and a
Decade's Dose of TRIPS', EIPR (2006): 282. In this sense, *see also* L.R. Helfer, 'Human
Rights and Intellectual Property: Conflict or Coexistence?', *supra* n. 123, at 58, stating
that a human rights approach to intellectual property grants users a status conceptually
equal to owners and producers.

160. The Belgian law states this imperative character of copyright exceptions explicitly (*see*
Article 23 *bis* of the Belgian act of 30 June 1994, inserted by an Act of 31 August 1998,
which implemented the Database Directive in Belgian law). The mandatory character of
the exceptions was maintained in the new Belgian Act of 22 May 2005 (M.B., 27 May
2005, 24997; on this Act *see* M.-C. Janssens, 'Implementation of the 2001 Copyright
Directive in Belgium', IIC 37 (2006): 50), except for the works made available to the
public on agreed contractual terms (Article 7). In France, the imperative nature of
copyright exceptions could be deduced from the wording of Article L 122-5 of the
Intellectual Property Code, as it specifies that 'the author cannot prohibit' the uses there
stated. A decision of the Paris District Court of 10 January 2006, RLDI 13 (2006): 24,
even held explicitly that the private copy exception was '*d'ordre public*', meaning
mandatory, and therefore that a technical measure should not hinder the making of a
copy of a CD. But the French Supreme Court has then taken a different position (28
February 2006, D. (2006): 784). On this issue *see* C. Geiger, 'Effectivité et flexibilité:
deux impératifs de l'adaptation du droit des "exceptions"', RLDI (2013), Special issue,
No. 94: 41.

or at least grant the user judicial means to 'enforce' his or her exceptions (this would lead to the creation of a 'subjective right' to the exception). The InfoSoc Directive would not stand in the way of such a solution.[161]

Indeed, the idea of users' rights as enforceable rights of equal value has recently found its way into the practice of the CJEU.[162] For example, in its decision in *UPC Telekabel* from March 2014 the Court clearly adopted the language of users' rights as a counterbalance to the disproportionally extensive enforcement of copyright. The Court, by *obliging* the national authorities (albeit under a limited range of circumstances) to avail the users of the procedural opportunity to challenge copyright enforcement measures before the courts,[163] accepted the idea that fundamental rights (in the instant case – freedom of expression) may be invoked not as a mere defence but as a right on which action in the main case is based. Since then, the idea of users' rights has already reoccurred in *Ulmer* from September 2014. Notably, the CJEU referred in that case to the *'ancillary right'* of users to digitize works contained in publicly accessible libraries' collections.[164] In the Court's opinion, such a *right* of communication of works enjoyed by establishments such as publicly accessible libraries would stem from the exception in Article

---

161. According to Article 6(4), Member States shall take 'appropriate measures' to ensure the functioning of certain limitations. But the Directive does not say what these measures could consist of. It seems to us that one can hardly perceive it as an 'appropriate measure' if a user has to enforce the benefit of an exception before a court or an arbitration board, as the required efforts will deter most users. It could, therefore, be helpful to analyse the Directive in the light of Article 10 of the ECHR. *See also* in this sense P. Akester, 'The Political Challenge – Copyright and Free Speech Restrictions in the Digital Age', *supra* n. 133, at 33, according to whom the European Court of Human Rights could possibly declare national laws implementing Article 6 in contravention with Article 10 ECHR, at least if it is not assured that the beneficiaries of exceptions listed in Article 6(4) are able to benefit from them.

162. *See* CJEU, Case C-117/13, *Ulmer* [2014], Judgment of the Court (Fourth Chamber) of 11 September 2014, para. 43, not yet published; CJEU, Case C-201/13, *Deckmyn* [2014], *supra* n. 91, at para. 26; CJEU, Case C-314/12, *UPC Telekabel* [2014], *supra* n. 87, at para. 57; CJEU, Case C-467/08, *Padawan* [2010], Judgment of the Court (Third Chamber) of 21 October 2010, para. 43, ECR I-10055; CJEU, Case C-145/10, *Painer* [2011], *supra* n. 91, at para. 132. For the further discussion of these cases, *see* ECS, 'Limitations and Exceptions as Key Elements of the Legal Framework for Copyright in the European Union', *supra* n. 91.

163. CJEU, Case C-314/12, *UPC Telekabel* [2014], *supra* n. 87, at para. 57: '[I]n order to prevent the fundamental rights recognised by EU law from precluding the adoption of an injunction such as that at issue in the main proceedings, the national procedural rules *must provide* a possibility for internet users to assert their rights before the court once the implementing measures taken by the internet service provider are known' (emphasis added). For a detailed analysis of the *UPC Telekabel* decision, *see* C. Geiger & E. Izyumenko, 'The Role of Human Rights in Copyright Enforcement Online: Elaborating a Legal Framework for Website Blocking', 32(1) American University International Law Review 43 (2016); and C. Geiger & E. Izyumenko, 'Blocking Orders: Assessing Tensions with Human Rights', in *The Oxford Handbook of Intermediary Liability Online,* ed. G. Frosio (OUP, forthcoming 2019).

164. CJEU, Case C-117/13, *Ulmer* [2014], *supra* n. 162, at para. 43.

5(3)(n) InfoSoc for the purpose of research and private study. Finally and most importantly, in two recent judgments rendered in summer 2019, *Funke Medien* and *Spiegel Online*, the CJEU has unequivocally pronounced that, 'although Article 5 of Directive 2001/29 is expressly entitled "Exceptions and limitations", it should be noted that *those exceptions or limitations do themselves confer rights on the users of works or of other subject matter*'.[165]

Different rules should apply to different works: a work in which no elements of the personality of the creator can be found, cannot enjoy the same protection as those with such elements because the justification of personality protection is lacking. That means the extent of protection of creations with a low level of creativity (the so-called small change of IP-protected works) must be smaller than that of classical works (meaning, for example, a shorter term of protection, no '*droit moral*', that the employer can be the holder of the rights, registration, and so on).[166] Creativity or innovation must clearly be differentiated from investment. This would lead to the establishment of a graduated IP system.[167] It could also possibly lead to an outsourcing of the works with a low level of creativity from the classical

---

165. CJEU, Case C-469/17, *Funke Medien* [2019], *supra* n. 76, para. 70; and CJEU, Case C-516/17, *Spiegel Online* [2019], *supra* n. 76, para. 54 (emphasis added), with further references to CJEU, Case C-117/13, *Ulmer* [2014], *supra* n. 162, para. 43. *See* C. Geiger & E. Izyumenko, The Constitutionalization of Intellectual Property Law in the EU and the *Funke Medien*, *Pelham* and *Spiegel Online* decisions of the CJEU: Progress, but still some way to go!, *supra* n. 76.

166. *See also* in this spirit P.L.C. Torremans, 'Copyright as a Human Right', *supra* n. 50, at 19: 'The higher the level of creativity and the more important the input of the creator is, the stronger the Human Rights claim of copyright will be. Not all works and not all situations will give copyright the same strength in its claim to Human Rights status and in its balancing exercise with other Human Rights'; O. Fischman Afori, 'Human Rights and Copyright: The Introduction of Natural Law Considerations into American Copyright Law', Fordham Intellectual Property, Media and Entertainment Law 14 (2004): 500, at 524. *See also* in this sense M. Vivant, 'Authors' Rights, Human Rights?', *supra* n. 21, at 94 et seq.: 'It is thus far from being incongruous to say, at one and the same time, that authors' rights could be considered human rights and that this classification could remain a purely formal one in certain borderline cases (e.g., nuts and bolts and computer software).'

167. This would result in a system of different degrees of protection: (1) A creative work would be covered by normal protection; (2) Creations whose creative added value is inferior to external obligations that have to be observed by the creator (works with little margin of creative freedom because of technical, market or genre standards) would only benefit from weaker protection; (3) Non-creative results, which would not be protected by IP law. Such a graduated system has been suggested already by legal doctrine; *see*, e.g., M. Buydens, *La protection de la quasi-création* (Brussels: Larcier, 1993), 779 et seq.; C. Geiger, 'The Privatisation of Information by Copyright Law – What Are the Remedies?', in *Intellectual Property and Market Power*, ed. L. M. Genovese & G. Ghidini (Buenos Aires: EUDEBA, 2008), 567; C. Geiger, 'Copyright as an Access Right, Securing Cultural Participation through the Protection of Creators' Interests', *supra* n. 46, at 97 et seq.

IP regimes and to the establishment of a uniform sui generis right[168] (as has been proposed indeed for computer programs).[169] Where IP protection primarily aims at protecting an investment, the fundamental rights justification is very weak, and the balance should be drawn in a completely different manner than when creativity is the main goal for protection. Admitting a fundamental rights justification could then lead to a complete reshaping of existing IP laws, entailing rather broad protection when the creative input is high and rather narrow protection when the input is low. Such reshaping would surely help IP laws to regain their legitimacy because at present the public hardly understands why a salad basket, a telephone book, a trivial computer program or some isolated genetic material should deserve the strong protection offered by intellectual property as we know it.

The IP right has to be developed in such a way that the rights on already existing creations do not prevent the creation of new works.[170] On the one hand, there is no reason to put the creator who has already created in a better position than the creator who would still like to create.[171] Rather, the creation

---

168. For such an idea *see also* J.H. Reichman, 'Legal Hybrids between the Patent and Copyright Paradigms', in *Information Law towards the 21st Century*, ed. W.F. Korthals Altes, E.J. Dommering, P.B. Hugenholtz & J.C. Kabel (Deventer: Kluwer, 1992), 325 et seq. The author identifies a number of legal hybrids that form a third intellectual property paradigm and that should, therefore, not be protected by copyright or patent law, but by a distinct sui generis right.

169. C. Geiger & R.M. Hilty, 'Patenting Software?', *supra* n. 25. For such a proposal *see also* P.M. Samuelson, R. Davis, M.D. Kypor & J.H. Reichman, 'A Manifesto Concerning the Legal Protection of Computer Programs', Columbia Law Review. 94 (1994): 2308.

170. *See also* in this sense T. Mylly, 'Intellectual Property and Fundamental Rights', *supra* n. 86, at 219, n. 55, arguing that the original author should not necessarily be able to control derivative works. On the interaction of Freedom of Artistic creativity and copyright law, *see* C. Geiger, 'Freedom of Artistic Creativity and Copyright Law: A Compatible Combination?', 8/3 U.C. Irvine Law Review 413 (2018).

171. For such a reasoning, *see also* C. Geiger, 'Copyright and the Freedom to Create – A Fragile Balance', IIC 38 (2007): 707; 'Promoting Creativity through Copyright Limitations, Reflections on the Concept of Exclusivity in Copyright Law', *Vanderbilt Journal of Entertainment & Technology Law* 12 (2010) 3: 515; C. Geiger, '"Fair Use" Through Fundamental Rights in Europe', *supra* n. 133. In US law, such creative uses of protected material were sometimes considered as being a protected fair use (17 U.S.C. §107). *See*, for example, United States Court of Appeals for the Second Circuit, 26 October 2005, *Andrea Blanch v. Jeff Koons, The Solomon R. Guggenheim Foundation and Deutsche Bank*, No. 05-6433-cv, in the case of an artist's appropriation of a copyrighted image in a collage painting. The Court explored all statutory factors of the fair use clause, weighed them together in the light of the purpose of copyright and came to the conclusion that copyright law's goal of 'promoting the Progress of science and useful arts' would be better served by allowing the use than by preventing it. The problem of such an approach is that the fair use will always be a use free of charge. Moreover, the artist will never know in advance if his use can be considered 'fair' in a legal sense, which can affect his creative process as he might be reluctant to use copyright material in fear of a lawsuit. Therefore, it would be better to create a specific limitation with a clear scope to allow such creative uses. For a detailed exploration of how a 'fair use'-type provision can be structured and further introduced in the EU

of new material has to be privileged if we take intellectual property seriously as an instrument of cultural and technical progress and attach a high value to its social component. Therefore, the right has to be restricted if certain basic values (like the freedom of expression or information, privacy or the right to human dignity) are to be held higher than the rights of the creator. The compromise solution of the statutory license can help in these cases. One could, for example, consider converting the exclusive right into a remuneration right, with royalties paid every time the use of an existing creation makes it possible to create a new work.[172] In this way, problems like those of the *Magill* case could be prevented right from the beginning.[173] The exclusive right would, therefore, be limited to protection against piracy, and the exploitation rights could not be used to prevent the creation of new materials.[174] This might also reduce the number of cases in which IP rights

---

copyright framework, *see* C. Geiger and E. Izyumenko, 'Towards a European "Fair Use" Grounded in Freedom of Expression', 35(1) American University International Law Review 1 (2019); Centre for International Intellectual Property Studies (CEIPI) Research Paper No. 02-19, available at SSRN: https://ssrn.com/abstract=3379531 or http://dx.doi.org/10.2139/ssrn.3379531 (accessed September 2019).

172. C. Geiger, 'Statutory Licenses as Enabler of Creative Uses', in *Remuneration of Copyright Owners, Regulatory Challenges of New Business Models*, ed. K.-C. Liu & R.M. Hilty (Berlin/Heidelberg: Springer, 2017), 305. Patent law already provides a mechanism for this purpose: to prevent the holder of a patent (who is in a dominant position in view of a patent of improvement) from using his right to impede the exploitation of this improvement, the creator can sue for the issue of a compulsory license based on reasons of dependency (section 24(2) German Patent Act) or '*licence de dépendance*' (Article L. 613-615 IPC). Such compulsory licenses are also provided by the TRIPS Agreement (Article 31) and the members of the WTO have wide discretion regarding the reasons that may give rise to the grant of such a license. *See also* in this sense Article 12 of Directive 98/44, dated 6 July 1998, on the legal protection of biotechnological inventions (OJEC L 213, 30 July 1998, at 13), which also provides for compulsory licenses in cases of dependency. This situation is similar to the possibility (in theory) of obtaining compulsory licenses through antitrust law or via the theory of abuse of rights. The main disadvantage in all these cases is the fact that the license has to be ordered by a judge, a fact that favours those economic actors who have the resources to afford the associated legal costs of sometimes very long proceedings. In the meantime, innovation is blocked. Therefore, it seems that legal regulations for nonvoluntary licenses based on a right to remuneration should be preferred. In this sense in the field of software *see* C. Geiger & R.M. Hilty, 'Patenting Software?' *supra* n. 25, at 641 et seq.

173. *Supra* n. 129. In this case, the right holders were using their copyright to prevent the creation of a new TV guide.

174. For a detailed discussion of such a solution, *see* C. Geiger, *Droit d'auteur et droit du public à l'information, supra* n. 32, at 323-332. This would also be compatible with the three-step test (on this test *see supra*), provided that the second step related to the normal exploitation of the work is interpreted very restrictively. For such interpretation, *see* C. Geiger, 'Right to Copy v. Three-Step Test: The Future of the Private Copy Exception in the Digital Environment', Computer Law Review International (CRi) 1 (2005): 7, at 12. To avoid the radical implications of the statutory license and in regard of the current broad interpretation of the concept of normal exploitation, the option of the mandatory

are abused to hinder the expression of certain opinions. The idea of such an 'exception for creative uses' was present in draft legislation in the US concerning orphan works. According to this bill, when an author creates a derived work starting from an orphan work (i.e., whose right holders cannot be found after a reasonable search), the right holder to the first work who subsequently reappears will not be able to prevent the exploitation of the derived work post hoc, but can only demand fair compensation.[175]

Of course, adversaries of such a reshaping of the scope of IP rights would invoke the constitutional protection of property to oppose such a suggestion immediately. However, the constitutional sense does not, under any circumstances, prevent a balanced arrangement of the law.[176] On the

---

collective administration of the exclusive right in these cases of productive use could be followed (for a discussion of this option *see* C. Geiger, *Droit d'auteur et droit du public à l'information, supra* n. 32, at 333 et seq.). As has been asserted, the implementation of this solution would not be hindered by the three-step test, because provisions prescribing such administration should not be regarded as exemptions to the exclusive rights (*see* S. von Lewinsky, 'Mandatory Collective Administration of Exclusive Rights – A Case Study on Its Compatibility with International and EC Copyright Law', e-Copyright Bulletin (January-March 2004): 1; K.J. Koelman, 'The Levitation of Copyright: An Economic View of Digital Home Copying, Levies and DRM', in *Intellectual Property Law 2004*, ed. F.W. Grosheide & J.J. Brinkhof (Antwerpen/Oxford: Intersentia, 2005), 436 et seq.; C. Geiger, 'The Role of the Three-Step Test in the Adaptation of Copyright Law to the Information Society', *supra* n. 143).

175. Section 514, Orphan Works Act of 2006, 109th Congress, 2nd Session, H.R. 5439, introduced to the House of Representatives on 22 May 2006. On this bill *see* V. Bronder, 'Saving the Right Orphans: The Special Case of Unpublished Orphan Works', Columbia Journal of Law & the Arts 31(3) (2008): 409 et seq. Another very similar bill was introduced in April 2008 (Orphan Works Act of 2008, 110th congress, 2d session H.R. 5889, introduced 24 April 2008; for a comment *see* J. Ginsburg, 'Recent Developments in US Copyright Law. Part I 'Orphan' Works', RIDA 217 (2008): 99). *See also* the specific provision on orphan works in the Canadian copyright law (Copyright Act, R.S.C., ch. C-42, section 77 (1985) (Can.)), permitting anyone who wants to make a copyright use of a work and cannot locate the copyright owner to petition the Canadian Copyright Board for a license. *See also* on this point the study conducted by the IViR (Institute for Information Law) of the University of Amsterdam, 'The Recasting of Copyright & Related Rights for the Knowledge Economy', 185 et seq. (Amsterdam November 2006), which recommends the implementation in the countries of the EU of a system permitting a public authority to grant a compulsory license to the user of an orphan work. The study also envisages the creation of an exception for the use of such a work, which would have to provide for a payment to the right holder if he or she should reappear (at 188). *See also* the article of one of the author of this study S. van Gompel, 'Unlocking the Potential of Pre-Existing Content: How to Address the Issue of Orphan Works in Europe?', IIC 38 (2007): 669; and, S. van Gompel, 'The Orphan Works Chimera and How to Defeat It: A View from Across the Atlantic', Berkeley Technology Law Journal 27 (2012): 1347.

176. *See also* in this sense J. Griffiths, 'Copyright Law after *Ashdown* – Time to Deal Fairly with the Public', IPQ (2002): 240, at 263: 'The right to property is undoubtedly recognised internationally as a human right. However, states are typically accorded a wide margin of appreciation in regulating the right to property in order to advance the common good.'

contrary, the 'social function' of property (as laid down, for example, in Article 14(2) of the German Constitution) orders this reconciliation of interests.[177] The German Constitutional Court stated that very clearly at the beginning of the 1970s in its school book decision on copyright, holding that although the protection of property rights:

> implies that the economic exploitation of the work in principle rests with the author, the constitutional protection of property rights does not extend to all such exploitations. It is a matter for the legislature to determine the limits of copyright by imposing appropriate criteria, taking into account the nature and social function of copyright and ensuring that the author participates fairly in the exploitation of his work.[178]

The second paragraph of Article 1 of Protocol 1 to the ECHR also leaves, as demonstrated above, a large margin for the states to regulate property.[179] On the one hand, the constitutional right to property orders the fundamental allocation of the economic value to the creator, but it does not require that this value always be assigned to him or her by means of an exclusive right.[180] Sometimes a legal remuneration right (in the form of a

---

177. Admitting that intellectual property falls under the constitutional notion of property should then not be feared, on the contrary. *See* in this sense also P. Drahos, 'The Universality of Intellectual Property Rights', *supra* n. 50, at 34: 'Viewing intellectual property through the prism of human rights discourse will encourage us to think about ways in which the property mechanism might be reshaped to include interests and needs that it currently does not.'

178. German Constitutional Court, 7 July 1971, GRUR (1972): 481; IIC 3 (1972): 394, with comment by W. Rumphorst. On the relationship of intellectual property and Article 14 of the German Basic Law (protection of property), *see* B. Grzeszick, 'Geistiges Eigentum und Article 14 GG', 5 ZUM 344 (2007). *See also* on this issue C. Geiger, 'Promoting Creativity through Copyright Limitations, Reflections on the Concept of Exclusivity in Copyright Law', *supra* n. 171.

179. According to Article 1(2) of Protocol 1 to the ECHR, 'the preceding provisions shall not, however, in any way impair the right of a State to enforce such laws as it deems necessary to control the use of property in accordance with the general interest or to secure the payment of taxes or other contributions or penalties'. In his judgment in *Sporrong and Lönnroth v. Sweden* (23 September 1982, HRLJ 1982, 268 (284)), the European Court of Human Rights held that 'the Court must determine whether *a fair balance* was struck between the demands of the general interests of the community and the requirements of the protection of the individual's fundamental rights. [...] The search for this balance is inherent in the whole of the Convention and is also reflected in the structure of Article 1 of Protocol 1' (para. 69). For example, in the *Smith Kline* case (*supra* n. 78), the European Commission on Human Rights stated that the grant under Dutch law of a compulsory license in a patented drug was not a violation of Article 1 of Protocol 1. It considered that the compulsory license was lawful and pursued a legitimate aim of encouraging technological and economic development.

180. This is all the more the case in the context of the UDHR and the ICESCR which, as we have already pointed out, do not determine that the creators' material and immaterial interests should necessarily be protected by a right of intellectual *property*.

statutory license) can even be economically more favourable for the creator. This was emphasized by the German Federal Supreme Court explicitly in the field of copyright in its Electronic Press Review decision.[181] On the other hand, the legislature has a considerable scope of discretion.[182] It could, therefore, come to the conclusion that the creation of a new work has to be rated as being more important and introduce a remuneration right in the form of a statutory license. In our opinion, the protection of property prevents only a general transformation of the exclusive right into a mere levy.

The IP system must benefit the creators of works in a better way. They must participate more effectively in the exploitation of their works. How this can finally be reached is secondary. One could, of course, imagine a better contract law[183] (with some imperative rules, like the copyright contract laws of some European countries), but also an increase of statutory licenses if these offer financially more favourable solutions for the creators than the exclusive right. This latter course has so far remained relatively unexplored and still requires closer investigation.[184]

4.5   RECONCEPTUALIZING THE CONSTITUTIONAL
            PROTECTION FOR IP: THREE PROPOSED
            MODELS FOR A BALANCED IP CLAUSE IN
            HUMAN RIGHTS INSTRUMENTS

From the above observations, it appears that fundamental rights, far from being a danger for the rights of intellectual property, seem quite to the

---

181. German Federal Court, 11 July 2002, 2002 GRUR 963. The Federal Supreme Court of Switzerland came recently to the same conclusion in a very interesting decision of 26 June 2007; GRUR Int. (2007): 1046. *See* on this decision C. Geiger, 'Rethinking Copyright Limitations in the Information Society: The Swiss Supreme Court Leads the Way', IIC (2008): 943.

182. *See also* in this sense J. Cornides, 'Human Rights and Intellectual Property, Conflict or Convergence?', *supra* n. 39, at 141; P.L.C. Torremans, 'Copyright as a Human Right', *supra* n. 50, at 8. Much more restrictive in the German context, *see* H. Schack, *Urheber – und Urhebervertragsrecht, supra* n. 105, at 41.

183. *See,* e.g., R.M. Hilty, 'Five Lessons about Copyright in the Information Society', *supra* n. 7, at 137.

184. Such ideas have recently been formulated for the field of copyright. *See* C. Geiger, *Droit d'auteur et droit du public à l'information, supra* n. 32, at 318 et seq.; R.M. Hilty, 'Verbotsrecht vs. Vergütungsanspruch: Suche nach den Konsequenzen der tripolaren Interessenlage im Urheberrecht', in *Festschrift für Gerhard Schricker*, ed. A. Ohly, T. Bodewig, T. Dreier, H.-P. Götting, M. Haedicke & M. Lehmann (Munich: Beck, 2005) 348 et seq. In the context of the levy for private copying, *see also* K. Gaita & A.F. Christie, 'Principle or Compromise? Understanding the Original Thinking Behind Statutory License and Levy Schemes for Private Copying', IPQ (2004): 426; A. Dietz, 'Continuation of the Levy System for Private Copying Also in the Digital Era in Germany', *Auteurs et Médias* (2003): 348 et seq.; C. Geiger, 'Promoting Creativity through Copyright Limitations, Reflections on the Concept of Exclusivity in Copyright Law', *supra* n. 171.

contrary to be the very instruments to guarantee certain flexibility in IP law.[185] Of course, it is not to deny that fundamental rights, because of their very broad and sometimes imprecise wording, can sometimes be asserted in an abusive way. As we have seen above, using rules outside IP legislation to solve internal problems can be considered quite unsatisfying as well. However, such an external effect would be reduced substantially if fundamental rights were recognized as a foundation for the IP system because then a judge only would have to determine whether the application of the law is consistent with the fundamental rights objective of the regulation. Thus, the conflict would be 'internalized', and one would interpret the relevant regulations in light of the basic principles of IP law and its protected interests. This way, one could prevent the investors from arguing in the name of the creators or the users in order to promote their own interests.[186]

However, the introduction of a specific constitutional clause on IP, modelled on the fundamental rights foundations of intellectual property system, could permit the matter to be framed in a more balanced and transparent way.[187] Of course, adopting one single 'template' might be difficult in order to tailor to the needs of countries with fundamentally different histories, philosophies and legal traditions of intellectual property protection. However, the values behind human rights essentially represent the outcome of a worldwide agreement and could, therefore, offer room for a consensus at the international level. Three options are proposed hereafter for such internalization, grounding the constitutional IP protection in –

---

185. *See* on this issue C. Geiger, 'Flexibilising Copyright – Remedies to the Privatisation of Information by Copyright', IIC 39(2) (2008): 178. We thus cannot agree with A.E.L. Brown, 'Guarding the Guards', *supra* n. 131, when she concludes: 'It cannot be said, so far, that a human rights based approach to interpretation of IP is having any significant effect.' Even if the cases in which human rights have been used as external limits to intellectual property rights are still rare, which is rather a good sign, the interpretation of intellectual property 'in the light' of these rights has often had a considerable impact on the solutions elaborated by the judges.

186. In the context of the UDHR and the ICESCR, it has been argued, e.g., that the requirement of human creativity 'indicates that persons other than the initial creator of the subject matter may be outside the scope of protection guaranteed by these Articles' (T. Mylly, 'Intellectual Property and Fundamental Rights', *supra* n. 86, at 196); *see also* in this sense S. Ricketson, 'Intellectual Property and Human Rights', *supra* n. 104, at 192 and CESCR, *General Comment No. 17*, *supra* n. 52, stating that the 'the Committee considers that only the "author", namely the creator, whether man or woman, individual or group of individuals, of scientific, literary or artistic productions, such as, inter alia, writers and artists, can be beneficiary of the protection of Article 15(1)(c) [...]. The drafters of this article seemed to have believed authors of scientific, literary or artistic productions to be natural persons' (para. 7).

187. For such a clause *see* C. Geiger, 'Implementing Intellectual Property Provisions in Human Rights Instruments', *supra* n. 51. *See also* A. Dietz, 'Constitutional and Quasi-Constitutional Clauses for Justification of Authors' Rights (Copyright)', *supra* n. 85.

respectively – the right to culture and science, freedom of expression and the right to property conditioned to its social function.

In this light, the first, 'classical' (or 'conservative') model suggests (re)introduction of an IP provision within the framework of the (conditioned) right to property, thereby extending the social function of property to intellectual property. The objectives and conditions of the exercise of intellectual property would, therefore, always be examined in the light of the general interest. Furthermore, in contrast to 'unconditioned' IP rights subsumption under the general guaranty of property, the separate mentioning of IP within the broader constitutional clause on the protection of property would point out the *specificity* of intellectual property, underlining that it is a property *of a special kind*, which should not be equated with physical property and which has to be considered as having an even more limited nature than the latter.[188] Finally, an explicit reference to the applicability of the general constitutional clause on property protection to intellectual property avoids any risks of 'absolute' reading of existing constitutional IP provisions, as it would constitute a *lex specialis* with regard to the general right to property.

The second, more innovative model, advocates incorporation of IP provision into the right to science and culture, in the spirit of the universal framework for the protection of creators' rights set in Article 27 UDHR and Article 15 ICESCR. One of the prominent advantages of this approach lies in situating intellectual property in the category of cultural rights. In this manner, the social function of IP is placed at the very core of protection. This is very important since it is not without relevance whether IP is understood as a cultural or an economic right. The current overprotective tendencies might require an emphasis on non-monetary incentives in order to re-establish the balance between protection and cultural/ scientific access. Indeed, as has been aptly pointed out by some scholars, 'the continuing trend towards ever stronger' IP protection was partly 'supported by the fact that some Member States referred to the legal protection of IP as 'property' under their national Constitutions'.[189] Avoiding the privatization of information by IP law[190] and assuring that cultural and scientific creations are still available for future innovations might mean (re)conceiving IP as an access right,[191]

188. *See* for further discussion on this, C. Geiger, 'Copyright's Fundamental Rights Dimension at EU Level', *supra* n. 21.
189. A. Kur & T. Dreier, *European Intellectual Property Law: Text, Cases and Materials* (Cheltenham, UK/Northampton, MA: Edward Elgar, 2013), at 248. *See* further C. Geiger, 'The Construction of Intellectual Property in the European Union: Searching for Coherence', in *Constructing European Intellectual Property: Achievements and New Perspectives,* ed. C. Geiger, *supra* n. 83, at 5.
190. Further on this tendency, *see* C. Geiger, 'Flexibilising Copyright', *supra* n. 185.
191. Much in this line the last thematic report of the UN Special Rapporteur in the field of cultural rights was devoted to the issue of the impact of intellectual property regimes on the enjoyment of the right to science and culture, as enshrined in particular in Article 15

thus emphasizing the inclusive rather than the exclusive nature of IP protection.[192]

Finally, the third alternative underpins the strong social limits of protection by linking IP to the freedom of expression and information. Under this construction, it is the freedom of use that has to be considered as the principle, and exclusivity as the exception which has to be justified.[193] Freedom of expression would thus clearly be established as the principle from which IP law deviates. As we have seen, the third alternative is consistent with the recent tendency of the ECtHR to examine copyright disputes within the framework of Article 10 of the Convention[194] (to which Article 11 of the EU Charter corresponds).[195]

4.6   CONCLUSION

An investigation of the basis of intellectual property shows that the classical justifications have been displaced of protection of investment and that the balance within the system is threatening to break in favour of the exploiters of IP rights. This conclusion is not new, this 'paradigm shift' already having been stressed by the literature in the 1980s,[196] but no real conclusions were drawn at the time. Assuming, however, that the foundations of the system have changed, the same solutions cannot apply, and a reconceptualizing seems necessary in order to ensure a fair balance of interest. This chapter tries to demonstrate that fundamental rights can offer a suitable basis for a fair and equitable IP system. The search for a new foundation is already urgent since an unbalanced system is at risk of collapsing at any time. As Thomas Aquinas wrote in his works (referenced earlier in this chapter), positive law can only be regarded as legitimate as long as it aims for general societal well-being and ensures an appropriate balance between different interests. If this is no longer the case, then the system loses its legitimacy. The American writer Henry David Thoreau showed in the nineteenth century which attitude individual humans should have if they are confronted with a

---

ICESCR. *See* UN General Assembly, Report of the Special Rapporteur in the field of Cultural Rights, F. Shaheed, *Copyright Policy and the Right to Science and Culture*, Human Rights Council, Twenty-eighth session, A/HRC/28/57, 24 December 2014.

192. Further on this in more detail with regard to copyright, *see* C. Geiger, 'Copyright as an Access Right: Securing Cultural Participation through the Protection of Creators' Interests', *supra* n. 46.

193. C. Geiger, 'Fundamental Rights, a Safeguard for the Coherence of Intellectual Property Law?', *supra* n. 77, at 272.

194. *See* ECtHR, *Ashby Donald and Others v. France*, *supra* n. 73; ECtHR, *Neij and Sunde Kolmisoppi v. Sweden* (dec.), *supra* n. 73.

195. *See* Note from the Praesidium, *Draft Charter of Fundamental Rights of the European Union*, *supra* n. 74, at 13-14.

196. *See*, e.g., A. Dietz, 'Transformation of Authors' Rights, Change of Paradigm', *supra* n. 48, at 22.

law which is illegitimate. In his work 'On the Duty of Civil Disobedience', published in 1849, he maintains that everyone has the right to disobey an 'unfair' law. He writes: 'I think we should be men first, and subjects afterwards. It is not desirable to cultivate a respect for the law, so much as for the right',[197] and for justice. The massive rejection of intellectual property in the public opinion, unfortunately, seems to prove him right. It is, therefore, urgently necessary to bring intellectual property closer to the people again, to humanize the subject by binding it to the basic values of our juridical system: fundamental rights and human rights.[198]

---

197. H.D. Thoreau, *On the Duty of Civil Disobedience* (1849, republished by Applewood Books, Bedford MA, 2000).
198. Further on the tendencies towards such 'constitutionalization' of intellectual property law, *see* C. Geiger, 'Implementing Intellectual Property Provisions in Human Rights Instruments', *supra* n. 51; C. Geiger & E. Izyumenko, 'The Constitutionalization of IP Law in the EU and the *Funke Medien, Pelham* and *Spiegel Online* Decisions of the CJEU', *supra* n. 76; C. Geiger & E. Izyumenko, 'Intellectual Property Before the European Court of Human Rights', *supra* n. 75; T. Mylly, 'The Constitutionalization of the European Legal Order: Impact of Human Rights on Intellectual Property in the EU'; T. Dreier & M. Ganzhorn, 'Intellectual Property in Decisions of National Constitutional Courts in Europe'; D. Barbosa & C. Ávila Plaza, 'Intellectual Property in Decisions of Constitutional Courts of Latin American Countries'; T. Takenaka & L.P. Falcon, 'Human Rights and Intellectual Property in the United States: The Role of US Courts in Striking a Fine Balance Between Competing Policies', all in *Research Handbook on Human Rights and Intellectual Property,* ed. C. Geiger, *supra* n. 9, 103, 219, 236, 253.

Chapter 5

Intellectual Property Rights and Human Rights: Coinciding and Cooperating

Gemma Minero

5.1 INTRODUCTION

The debate on the interface between intellectual property rights and human rights is neither new nor ended. The roots of this interaction and its legal analysis emerged a long time ago. We can find several resolutions of international bodies – the World Intellectual Property Organization and the World Trade Organization, among others – that were adopted at the end of the 1990s, and early 2000s.[1]

---

1. *See*, among others, the documents cited by E. Derclaye in the second edition of this book (at 133). WIPO Panel Discussion, 9 November 1998, *Intellectual Property and Human Rights,* WIPO, Geneva, Publication No. 762(E)1999; United Nations Sub-Commission on the Promotion and Protection of Human Rights, Res. 2000/7 on *Intellectual Property and Human Rights,* 17 August 2000, Doc. E/CN.4/Sub.2/RES/2000/7; World Trade Organization, *Protection of Intellectual Property under the TRIPS Agreement,* DOC. E/C.12/ 2000/18, 27 November 2002. *See also* H. Cohen Jehoram, 'Freedom of Expression in Copyright and Media Law', 3 *European Intellectual Property Review* (1984); J. Cornides, 'Human Rights and Intellectual Property: Conflicts or Convergence?', *Journal of World Intellectual Property,* (2004), at 135; and P.B. Hugenholtz, 'Copyright and Freedom of Expression', in *The Commodification of Information,* edited by N. Elkin-Koren and N. W. Netanel (2002), at 239. In the national level, in the English law, this topic has been deeply discussed in case law and in the literature after the Human Rights Act was passed in 1998.

However, in recent years, those old approaches on the relationship between intellectual property rights and human rights have progressively separated from each other, at least in the national level, where these conflicts are sometimes mainly dealt from a political perspective.[2] As we will see, the United States is one the most ardent defender of stringent patent protection, but the US Government's position has changed depending on the case. In fact, some events have caused this issue to stand at the forefront of the international debate surrounding globalization.

The conflict between intellectual property rights and the access to medicine is and was dealt, for example, in discussions after pricing decisions of the patents' holders of medicines needed in developing countries or in the events surrounding the anthrax attack in the United States. The United States and the Canada Governments threatened to break Bayer's patent on the medicine used to treat with after the 2001 attacks – Cipro – that was still under patent in the United States and Canada – the protection had already expired in the European Union.

This national law entered into force in October 2000 and its main aim was to give further effect to rights and freedoms guaranteed under the European Convention on Human Rights, which was passed in 1950. *See*, among others, Case *Hubbard v. Vosper,* [1972] 2 Q.B. 84, 97 (CA), in which Lord Denning MR removed an injunction of a copyrighted work, holding that 'the law will not intervene to suppress freedom of speech except when it is abused', and Case *Times Newspapers Ltd v. MGN Ltd,* [1993] EMLR 445, in relation to a forthcoming unauthorized novel that contains quotes from the memoirs of a famous politician. In the US system, *see Rosemont Enterprises v. Random House Inc.* 366 F.2d 303 (2d Cir. 1966), cert. denied, 395 US 1009 (1067), in which the motion for a preliminary injunction was denied, basing its decision on a fair use defence. In that time, this defence was not codified, since it was included in the Copyright Act of 1976. The plaintiff, a famous aviator and film director, claimed that the biography about his life that was going to be published infringed his rights, since he had previously acquired the copyright in some articles published about him that were used in that forthcoming book. *See also* J. Griffiths, 'Copyright Law and Censorship: The Impact of Human Rights Act 1998', in *The Yearbook of Media and Entertainment Law 1996,* edited by E. M. Barendt (1996), at 3; and F. MacMillan Patfield, 'Towards a Reconciliation of Free Speech and Copyright', in *The Yearbook of Media and Entertainment Law 1996,* edited by E. M. Barendt (1996), at 199; and M.D. Birnhack, 'The Copyright Law and Free Speech Affair: Making-Up and Breaking-Up', 43(2) *IDEA: Journal of Law & Technology,* (2003), at 233.

2. More recently, human rights concerns have been raised in the international debates concerning access to medicines (Commission on Human Rights Res. 2004/26, *Access to Medication in the Context of Pandemics such as HIV/AIDS, Tuberculosis and Malaria,* 60th Sess. 15 March–23 April 2004, U.N. Doc. E/CN.4/RES/2004/26) and the protection of traditional knowledge and cultural expression (United Nations High Commissioner for Human Rights, *The Impact of the Agreement on Trade-Related Aspects of Intellectual Property Rights on Human Rights*, 11, U.N. Doc. E/CN.4/Sub.2/2001/13 (27 June 2001), para. 65).

Cancer medicines have also caused fierce debates.[3] The global situation explains the fact that in 2004 the United Nations Secretary General of the High-level Panel on Threats, Challenges and Change listed diseases like AIDS as a threat to international peace.[4] This statement can perfectly be extended nowadays to sanitary, political and economic circumstances around the combat of COVID-19 pandemic.

Besides, technological environments have generated new issues previously unexplored – such as protection of users' generated contents and regulation of the so-called graduated response systems to fight illegal activities. New technologies and new technical contexts challenge old notions. In the European context, EU Directive on the digital single market, recently passed by the European legislator, is proof that this is still a topical issue.[5]

The debate has traditionally been explained as follows: the public is interested in widening dissemination of works and patents, enabling easier access to them but, on the other hand, the author and the inventor wish to control his work or his patent – both in a reputational way and in an

---

3. *See* H. Hestermeyer, *Human Rights and the WTO: The Case of Patents and Access to Medicines,* (2007), Oxford University Press, at 1 (electronic paper). In 2003, an Indian pharmaceutical company launched a generic version of a well-known cancer drug for 10% of the price of the medicine protected by the patent owned by *Novartis*. In 2003, *Novartis* obtained marketing rights for its medicine in India, as well as some blocking injunctions against the Indian companies manufacturing the generic versions.

4. United Nations High-level Panel on Threats, Challenges and Change, *A More Secure World: Our Shared Responsibility* (2004), at 24.

5. Directive (EU) 2019/790 of the European Parliament and of the Council of 17 April 2019 on copyright and related rights in the Digital Single Market and amending Directives 96/9/EC and 2001/29/EC (OJ L 130, 17.5.2019, at 92-125). Among other things, this new Directive provides a new text and data mining exception to be used by research organizations and cultural heritage institutions with regard to contents to which they have lawful access, provided there is an open access policy database or because there is a contractual arrangement between right holders and research organizations or cultural heritage institutions. Besides, the Directive creates a new neighbouring right for press publishers in order to recognize their organizational and financial contribution in producing press publications and in order to ensure the sustainability of the publishing industry and thereby foster the availability of reliable information. Furthermore, this Directive clarifies that online content-sharing service providers perform an act of communication to the public or of making available to the public when they give the public access to copyright-protected works or other protected subject matter uploaded by their users. Thus despite the fact that the persons uploading the file with the work are the users of that service as such. The important parameter is that the service provider creates the platform and obtains profit therefrom, either directly or indirectly. Consequently, online content-sharing service providers should obtain an authorisation, including via a licensing agreement, from the relevant right holders. Where no authorisation has been granted to service providers, they should make their best efforts in accordance with high industry standards of professional diligence to avoid the availability on their services of the unauthorised works that were previously identified by the relevant right holders.

economic sense.[6] Intellectual property law is conceived as a means to enhance creative authorship and research. The intellectual property model has a flavour of indirect help by the State to the creation and commerce of scientific and cultural goods. The goal of intellectual property rights might be for the promotion of the common good, the 'encouragement of learning' (in the words of the Statute of Anne) and the promotion of 'the progress' (in the words of the American Constitution), but it does not mean that the intellectual property system provides absolute protection of the authors.[7] On the contrary, this system allows important limitations thereon in order to achieve a proper balance among human rights.[8] Therefore, the task of a country is providing the best protection to authors and inventors in equilibrium with public interests, that is, in a manner that would promote the exercise of human rights without undermining the authors and inventors' interests.

The conflict has its origin on the way of defining the private-public rights balance, being both rights – mainly, the freedom of expression and information and the intellectual property rights, or even all the human rights concerned in this debate – protected by a constitutional dimension in almost any country, as well as in the international background, as we will explain. On the one hand, the private exclusive right that is given to authors is a sort of general recognition of their contribution to society, and it has to be broad enough to incentive future creation. On the other hand, there is an interest to the public to have broad or adequate – or at least sufficient – access to the fruits of authors' creation. Professor Torremans concluded that consequently, we could not find a general consensus, but mere compatibility between these rights.[9] This concept – compatibility – is far away from the concepts of antagonism and/or general conflict, as we will see. There are zones of intersections or even controversy, as with many other human rights.

---

6. *See* M. Birnhack, 'Acknowledging the Conflict Between Copyright Law and Freedom of Expression under the Human Rights Act', *Entertainment Law Review* 24 (2003), at 28. This traditional view is influenced by the American reasoning regarding intellectual property rights to oppose the interests of consumers to the interests of authors and inventors. *See* for all P. Goldstein, *Copyright's Highway: from Gutenberg to the Celestial Jukebox,* (1994), New York, at 168.

7. The Statute of Anne, also known as the Copyright Act 1710, has as long title the following: 'An Act for the Encouragement of Learning, by Vesting the Copies of Printed Books in the Authors or Purchasers of such Copies, during the Times therein mentioned.' According to Article I section 8, Clause 8 of the American Constitution, 'Patent and Copyright Clause of the Constitution', [The Congress shall have power] 'To promote the progress of science and useful arts, by securing for limited times to authors and inventors the exclusive right to their respective writings and discoveries.'

8. *See* M. Birnhack, 'Acknowledging the Conflict Between Copyright Law and Freedom of Expression under the Human Rights Act', above n. 6, at 23.

9. P.L.C. Torremans, 'Copyright As A Human Right', in *Copyright and Human Rights. Freedom of Expression – Intellectual Property – Privacy*, edited by P.L.C. Torremans, Kluwer Law International (2004), at 2-3.

However, when examining those cases of interaction between intellectual property rights and human rights it has to be taken into account that one way or another intellectual property rights – or at least some attributes of intellectual property rights that are not close to an economic investment perspective – are also human rights. To that end, human beings must respect other human beings.[10] Therefore, the quid is the parameter or parameters to be taken into account in each dispute.

In other words, human rights and intellectual property rights share the same nature, without the hierarchical relationship between them, but it does not necessarily mean that they do have to follow the same goals or values in any single case.[11] The common aim is clear when applying copyright law and freedom of expression of that same author, for instance. In this case, each right or discipline has a common interest in the development of interaction with the other. However, it is not so obvious in case of conflict between the copyright of the author and the right of privacy of the offender or even in a dispute between the author – and his/her copyright – and the plagiarizer – and his/her freedom of expression – free speech, in American Law. In this case, each right or discipline seems to stand on its own.[12]

Therefore, as any conflict between human rights themselves, we have to analyse the facts, and rectify any excessive application or interpretation of the intellectual property right(s) and/or the other(s) human right(s),[13] in order to achieve the right balance in that specific case. Consequently, in case of conflict, courts have to look for cooperative answers in those extremes where intellectual property rights and other human rights do not coincide.[14]

In this sense, the World Trade Organization (WTO) has noted the potential for the intellectual property and human rights systems to coexist:

---

10. D.J. Gervais declared: 'Human Rights and Intellectual Property Were Natural Law Cousins Owing to Their Shared Filiation with Equity'. D.J. Gervais, 'Intellectual Property and Human Rights: Learning to Live Together', in *Copyright and Human Rights. Freedom of Expression – Intellectual Property – Privacy,* edited by P.L.C. Torremans, Kluwer Law International (2008), at 12.

11. For a philosophical view, *see* E. Derclaye, 'Eudemonic Intellectual Property: Patents and Related Rights as Engines of Happiness, Peace and Sustainability', *Vanderbilt Journal of Entertainment and Technology Law*, 14(3) (2012), at 495-543.

12. Helfer and Torremans wonder whether it is true though in a broader international context intellectual property rights and human rights are developed in virtual isolation. *See* L.R. Helfer, 'Human Rights and Intellectual Property: Conflict or Coexistence?', in *Minnesota Intellectual Property Review* 5 (2003), at 47 ff; and P.L.C. Torremans, 'Copyright As A Human Right', in *Copyright and Human Rights. Freedom of Expression – Intellectual Property – Privacy*, edited by P.L.C. Torremans above n. 9, at 1.

13. Alternatively, we may even ask for a revision in cases where those rules are not up-to-date any more.

14. For example, looking for a balanced interpretation of the originality requirement that ensures that some products do not come within the scope of copyright and they can, thus, be used by the public without having to ask for the creators' authorization; or regulating balanced parameters to be applied in cases of website blocking injunctions against internet service providers in copyright or trademark infringement cases.

Rights under article 27.2 of the Universal Declaration of Human Rights and article 15.1(c) of the International Covenant of Economic, Social and Cultural Rights together with other human rights will be best served, taking into account their interdependent nature, by reaching an optimal balance within the IP system and by other related policy responses. Human rights can be used – have been and are currently used – to argue in favour of balancing the system either upwards or downwards by means of adjusting the existing rights or by creating new rights.[15]

On the other hand, the United Nations High Commissioner for Human Rights has also declared that 'the balance between public and private interests found under [the international human rights instruments] is one familiar to intellectual property law'.[16]

Besides, we have to take into account that intellectual property rights, as any human rights, have intrinsic limits. The idea/expression dichotomy and term of protection are some of them. On the one hand, copyright cannot be used to avoid uses of the information contained in the work or those unsubstantial uses of a work that do not reproduce its originality, but just uses of the literal expression of a substantial part – an original part – of the work-. Besides, the author has no right to avoid the creation by a second author of a similar work that does not reproduce the originality of the expression of the first work, but just the idea behind that first work. Since copyright does not monopolize ideas, both copyright and freedom of expression are consistent, because they both generally promote speech.

On the other hand, there is no eternal intellectual property right. Besides, other limits are generally expressed in terms of legal exceptions or broad defences, such as the fair use defence.[17] Besides, when regulating and applying those exceptions to intellectual property rights, various links with the subject matter of human rights must be taken into account, such as the exercise of the freedom of expression and the promotion of public health, nutrition and general social development. In other words, exceptions to intellectual property rights are inspired, either explicitly or implicitly, in other human rights. Most countries allow, for example, news reporting, quotation, archival purposes, library and museum uses and online and offline teaching.[18] In those national systems where broad exceptions are applied –

---

15. United Nations Economic and Social Council, Commission on Economic Social and Cultural Rights, *Protection of Intellectual Property under TRIPS Agreement,* 24th session, 13 November–1 December 2000, U.N. Doc E/C.12/2000/18.
16. United Nations High Commissioner for Human Rights, *The Impact of the Agreement on Trade-Related Aspects of Intellectual Property Rights on Human Rights,* 11, U.N. Doc. E/CN.4/Sub.2/2001/13 (27 June 2001).
17. *Ibid.,* at 22.
18. In the European system, the list of exceptions and limitations is contained in Article 5 of Directive 2001/29/EC and this provision has an exhaustive nature. According to the Court of Justice of the European Union, 'exceptions and limitations provided for in Article

such as the United States, where the fair use defence is in force, in case of conflict, the judge applies a proportionality test. Consequently, the judge studies the proportionality whether on the portion of the creation which has been copied or on the market shares and on the power of substitution of the plaintiff's product by the defendant's product.

This system of protection mitigates the conflict among these human rights. In addition, it demonstrates that intellectual property laws' main or sole goal is not to maximize economic benefits but to incentivize innovation and social development. Therefore, intellectual property rights can be used to achieve human rights outcomes. International treaties, as we will see, provide national legislatures and judges with a wide margin of appreciation in balancing the human rights concerned both in the regulation of intellectual property rights systems and in their implementation. This flexibility is needed, especially in the dynamic environment of the Internet. Restrictions to any human right by other human rights are deemed necessary in a democratic society if they are proportional to the legitimate aim of the restriction.

5.2   INTELLECTUAL PROPERTY RIGHTS AS HUMAN RIGHTS: INTERNATIONAL AND EUROPEAN PERSPECTIVES

Intellectual property regimes seek to balance the moral and economic rights of authors, creators and inventors with the wider interests and needs of our

---

5(3)(c), second case, and (d) of Directive 2001/29 [reproduction by the press, communication to the public or making available of published articles on current economic, political or religious topics and quotations for purposes such as criticism or review] (...) are specifically aimed at favouring the exercise of the right to freedom of expression by the users of protected subject matter and to freedom of the press, which is of particular importance when protected as a fundamental right, over the interest of the author in being able to prevent the use of his or her work, whilst ensuring that the author has the right, in principle, to have his or her name indicated'. Judgment of the Court of Justice of the European Union of 29 July 2019, *Funke Medien,* C-469/17, EU:C:2019:623, para. 60, citing the previous judgment of 1 December 2011, *Painer,* C-145/10, EU:C:2011:798, para. 135. In relation to the exhaustive or *numerus clausus* list of exceptions to copyright in the European system, it has been said that 'freedom of information and freedom of the press, enshrined in Article 11 of the Charter, are not capable of justifying, beyond the exceptions or limitations provided for in Article 5 (...) of Directive 2001/29, a derogation from the author's exclusive rights of reproduction and of communication to the public, referred to in Article 2(a) and Article 3(1) of that directive respectively'. 'In that context, to allow (...) each Member State to derogate from an author's exclusive rights, referred to in Articles 2 to 4 of Directive 2001/29, beyond the exceptions and limitations exhaustively set out in Article 5 of that directive, would endanger the effectiveness of the harmonisation of copyright and related rights effected by that directive, as well as the objective of legal certainty pursued by it.' Judgment of the Court of Justice of the European Union of 29 July 2019, *Funke Medien,* C-469/17, EU:C:2019:623, paras 62 and 64.

societies.[19] Intellectual property laws are based in the utilitarian rationale: these rights are justified by the positive consequences they bring to the common well-being and by the fact that rewards to authors, creators and inventors result in the benefits for the society.[20] These rights, thus, are incentives to create and allow creators to recoup their investment and effort.[21] Besides, intellectual property regimes are not based in neutrality. Hence, laws do not foster all kinds of technology and creation, but only those that are not contrary to *ordre public,* human dignity and moral and ethical principles of our societies.[22]

Taking those parameters into account, our actual goal is to link intellectual property regimes with global human needs and interests. We have to bear in mind that even if intellectual property rights give exclusive rights which may sometimes confer a monopoly, it is always limited in time and scope. Therefore, these rights keep competition alive, and it leads to social welfare. The main instrument to insure or achieve a proper balance between

---

19. A.R. Chapman, 'A Human Rights Perspective on Intellectual Property, Scientific, Progress and Access to the Benefits of Science', WIPO Panel Discussion on Intellectual Property and Human Rights (8 November 1998), at 1, available at www.wipo.org. In this sense, as it has been indicated above, the United States Constitution vests the Congress with the power 'To Promote the Progress of Science and useful Arts, by securing for limited Times to Authors and Inventors the exclusive Right to their respectful Writings and Discoveries' (Article 1, para. 8, section 8). E. Derclaye noted that the underlying idea, which can be found in the US Constitution, is that 'patent and copyright are not ends in themselves but only tools to another greater end: progress' (E. Derclaye, 'Intellectual Property Rights and Human Rights: Coinciding and Cooperating', in the second edition of this book, at 136).

20. E. Derclaye, 'What Can Intellectual Property Learn from Happiness Research?' in *Methods and Perspectives in Intellectual Property,* edited by G. Dinwoodie, Elgar Publishing (2013) at 13.

21. *European Commission's Green Paper on Copyright in the Knowledge Society,* COM (2008) 466, at 4. For a clear legal and economic justification of the existence of intellectual property rights, *see* M. Lehman, 'Property and Intellectual Property – Property Rights as Restrictions on Competition in Furtherance of Competition', in *IIC* 1 (1989); and P.L.C. Torremans, 'Copyright As A Human Right', in P. L. C. Torremans, *Copyright and Human Rights. Freedom of Expression – Intellectual Property – Privacy,* above n. 9, at 12-13, and authors cited.

22. Article 53(a) of the European Patent Convention stipulates that patents cannot be granted for inventions the publication or exploitation of which would be 'contrary to *ordre public* or morality'. On the other hand, paras 37-40 of the Preamble of Directive 98/44/EC of the European Parliament and of the Council of 6 July 1998, on the legal protection of biotechnological inventions (Official Journal of the European Communities, 30.7.98, L 213/16) exclude from patentability any invention whose commercial exploitation offends against *ordre public* or morality, such as those related to processes for modifying the human germ line genetic identity of human beings and processes for cloning human beings. These paragraphs indicate that the list of inventions excluded from patentability has an illustrative nature and non-exhaustive character. Hence, national courts must take into account ethical or moral principles recognized in each Member State in order to decide whether a specific product may be excluded from patentability or not.

the various interests is by means of limitations and exceptions to intellectual property rights.

However, in the case of copyright, there is another internal mechanism to provide that equilibrium: the principle of originality as a requirement *sine qua non* for copyright protection. When interpreting this requirement, the Court of Justice of the European Union states: 'In order for an intellectual creation to be regarded as an author's own it must reflect the author's personality, which is the case if the author was able to express his creative abilities in the production of the work by making free and creative choices.'[23] The judge has to ascertain whether 'the author was able to make free and creative choices capable of conveying to the reader the originality of the subject matter at issue, the originality of which arises from the choice, sequence and combination of the words by which the author expressed his or her creativity in an original manner and achieved a result which is an intellectual creation'. 'The mere intellectual effort and skill of creating those reports are not relevant in that regard.'[24] The originality test has to take into account that originality cannot refer to just informative contents since information cannot enjoy the protection conferred by copyright. In words used by the Court of Justice:

> if military status reports, such as those at issue in the main proceedings, constitute purely informative documents, the content of which is essentially determined by the information which they contain, so that such information and the expression of those reports become indissociable and that those reports are thus entirely characterised by their technical function, precluding all originality, it should be considered, as the Advocate General stated in point 19 of his Opinion, that, in drafting those reports, it was impossible for the author to express his or her creativity in an original manner and to achieve a result which is that author's own intellectual creation.[25]

Besides, as a consequence of this principle, when it has been concluded that the creation is protected by copyright, only something which is the

---

23. Judgments of the Court of Justice of the European Union of 1 December 2011, *Painer,* above n. 18, paras 87-89, and of 29 July 2019, *Funke Medien,* above n. 18, para. 19. The creation studied in this second case consists of military status reports. The Court of Justice indicates that it is for the national court to determine whether the reports, or certain elements thereof, may be regarded as works and therefore be protected by copyright (para. 22).

24. Judgment of the Court of Justice of the European Union of 29 July 2019, *Funke Medien,* above n. 18, para. 23. The Court of Justice refers to its previous judgments of 16 July 2009, *Infopaq International,* C-5/08, EU:C:2009:465, paras 45-47, and of 1 March 2012, *Football Dataco and Others,* C-604/10, EU:C:2012:115, para. 33.

25. Judgment of the Court of Justice of the European Union of 29 July 2019, *Funke Medien,* above n. 18, para. 24, citing the previous judgments of 22 December 2010, *Bezpečnostní softwarová asociace,* C-393/09, EU:C:2010:816, paras 48-50, and of 2 May 2012, *SAS Institute,* C-406/10, EU:C:2012:259, para. 67.

expression of the author's own intellectual creation may be classified as a 'work' when analysing whether there was a copyright infringement or not.[26] Unprotected parts of a work can be used without infringing copyright on that work. If the part of the work that was used by the defendant when creating the second work does not reflect the original expression of the first work, then there is no violation of the plaintiff's copyright. Consequently, in that case, there is no sense in analysing whether an exception to copyright, such as the news reporting, may be applied to that case to resolve the conflict between copyright and other human rights, such as the freedom of information.

But sometimes, intellectual property standards texts are not sufficient enough to fulfil a real balance. In that case, there are external correction mechanisms that may help to achieve a balance in that particular set of circumstances. Hence, judicial and academic interpretation has to play a leading role. That objective cannot be reached without looking for a human rights approach to intellectual property, which takes an implicit balance between the moral and economic rights of authors, creators and inventors and the interest of the wider society within intellectual property paradigms.

In the case of copyright, it is clear because from a human rights perspective, the author assumes a lot of importance as his work may manifest itself an intrinsic value as an expression of human dignity and human creativity. Hence, there are several human rights concerned in the creation of the work and access to that work.[27] Moral rights, such as the right of paternity and the right of integrity, as part of copyright, are a recognition of that fundamental or human relationship between the author and his work or creation. They ensure proper identification and attribution of the creative work and prevent the work from being modified in a manner that would prejudice the author's honour or reputation. The United Nations Commission on Economic, Social and Cultural Rights has recognized that some attributes of intellectual property rights derive from the inherent dignity and worth of all persons.[28] Whereas economic or exploitation rights of the author can be transferable, moral rights always subsist or survive as rights of the author.[29]

---

26. Judgment of the Court of Justice of the European Union of 29 July 2019, *Funke Medien*, above n. 18, para. 20.
27. A.R. Chapman, 'Approaching Intellectual Property as a Human Right (Obligations Related to Article 15(1)(c)', XXXV(3) *Copyright Bulletin*, (2001), at 14. On the contrary, M. Vivant, 'Le droit d'auteur, un droit de l'homme?', *RIDA* 174 /1997), at 71, concludes that copyright falls under the constitutional right to the protection of property, as do the patents for invention.
28. United Nations Economic and Social Council, Commission on Economic, Social and Cultural Rights, *General Comment No. 17: The Right of Everyone to Benefit from the Protection of the Moral and Material Interests Resulting from Any Scientific, Literary or Artistic Production of Which He or She is the Author (Article 15, Para. 1 (c) of the Covenant)*, U.N. Doc. E/C.12/GC/17 (12 January 2006), at 1.
29. *See* M.P. Cámara Águila, *El derecho moral del autor. Con especial referencia a su configuración y ejercicio tras la muerte del autor*, Comares (1998), at 22-36; and P.L.C.

In contrast to economic rights, and according to (some) national legislation, some moral rights – as well as any human rights – are unlimited in time and cannot be revoked, licensed or assigned to someone else.[30]

This logic can also be extended to patents. The provisions on patents help ensure the recognition of inventors.[31] Besides, the provisions on geographical indications can help indigenous people and traditional communities obtain much-needed protection on their economic and cultural heritage of these individuals and communities, and therefore, it preserves their ways of life and it helps to promote the right to the benefits of scientific progress.[32]

However, it is much harder to justify human rights protection for neighbouring rights of broadcasters and phonogram and audiovisual producers and for databases makers, for trademarks and for any other right that mainly protects mere economic investments. Among them, it cannot be denied that trademarks are not granted to incentivize innovation but to prevent confusion of consumers and to protect the trademark owner's goodwill, even when these rights have limits as well.[33] Besides, no moral right attach to a database that is only protected by the sui generis right among the Member States of the European Union. This right cannot be considered

---

Torremans, *Holyoak and Torremans Intellectual Property Law,* Oxford University Press (2013), at 220-228. Intellectual property rights must thus be analysed with a double perspective. A report by the National Research Council of the United States Academy of Sciences comments as follows on this trend: 'Science operates according to a "market" of its own, one that has rules and values different from those of commercial markets. While protection of intellectual property may concern a scientist who is writing a textbook, that same scientist, publishing a paper in a scientific journal, is motivated by the desire to propagate ideas, with the expectation of full and open access to results. To commercial publishers (including many professional societies), protection of intellectual property means protection of the right to reproduce and distribute printed material. To scientists, protection of intellectual property usually signifies assurance of proper attribution and credit for ideas and achievements. Generally, scientists are more concerned that their work be read and used rather than that it be protected against unauthorized copying. These conflicting viewpoints pose challenging problems for science and the rest of society' (Report of the Committee on Issues in the Trans border Flow of Scientific Data of the National Research Council, *Bits of Power: Issues in Global Access to Scientific Data*, National Academy Press (1997), at 5).

30. United Nations Economic and Social Council, Commission on Economic, Social and Cultural Rights, *General Comment No. 17: The Right of Everyone to Benefit from the Protection of the Moral and Material Interests Resulting from Any Scientific, Literary or Artistic Production of Which He or She is the Author (Article 15, Paragraph 1 (c) of the Covenant),* U.N. Doc. E/C.12/GC/17 (12 January 2006), at 1-3.

31. *See* S. Ricketson, 'Intellectual Property and Human Rights', in *Commercial Law and Human Rights,* edited by S. Bottomley and D. Kinley, Ashgate (2002), at 189-191.

32. According to the *United Nations Declaration on the Rights of Indigenous Peoples*, G.A. Res. 61/295, Article 31(1), U.N. Doc. A/RES/61/295 (13 September 2007), indigenous people 'have the right to maintain, control, protect and develop their intellectual property over such cultural heritage, traditional knowledge, and traditional expressions'.

33. Such as the prohibition of protection of descriptive and misleading signs.

as such a human right because of its intrinsically economic nature.[34] The same rule applies to broadcasters and producers. Therefore, we cannot ignore that some attributes of intellectual property rights must be considered human rights while other attributes do not have any human rights basis.[35]

The vast majority of intellectual property rights' standard texts do not contain a reference to human rights. On the contrary, some important direct or indirect references to intellectual property rights can be found in some standard texts on human or fundamental rights. However, it has to be borne in mind that these international human rights instruments – their references to intellectual property rights – only deal with intellectual property rights as such. Thus, the determination of their scope and limitations is left to the legislatures of contracting parties.[36] On the other hand, it must be taken into account that human rights instruments are held to create obligations on the part of the governments of the contracting parts of these treaties, in order to take measures to protect these rights and make them effective.

In the international level, copyright – in its artistic perspective – is considered a fundamental or human right in Article 27 of the Universal Declaration of Human Rights, which means that it vested in each person by virtue of their common humanity.[37] According to the second paragraph of this provision, everyone has 'the right to the protection of the moral and material interests resulting from any scientific, literary or artistic production of which he is the author'.[38] It is clear that this provision covers both

---

34. S. Ricketson, 'Intellectual Property and Human Rights', in *Commercial Law and Human Rights,* edited by S. Bottomley and D. Kinley, above n. 31, at 201; and G. Minero, *La protección jurídica de las bases de datos en el ordenamiento europeo,* Tecnos, (2014), at 265.

35. P.K. Yu, 'Intellectual Property and Human Rights in the Nonmultilateral Era', *Florida Law Review* 64, no. 4 (2012), at 1062. *See also* United Nations Economic & Social Council, Commission on Economic, Social and Cultural Rights, *Implementation of the International Covenant on Economic, Social and Cultural Rights: Drafting History of the Article 15(1)(c) of the International Covenant on Economic, Social and Cultural Rights,* U.N. Doc. E/C.12/2000/15, at 45.

36. A.R. Chapman, 'A Human Rights Perspective on Intellectual Property, Scientific, Progress and Access to the Benefits of Science', above n. 19, at 2.

37. The first paragraph of Article 27 of the Universal Declaration of Human Rights provides the principle of freedom to create, as follows: 'Everyone has the right freely to participate in the cultural life of the community, to enjoy the arts and to share in scientific advancement and its benefits.' This provision is additional or complementary to those related to the freedom of thought, of speech and of opinion (Articles 18 and 19). At the national level, according to Hugenholtz, 'in Europe, the protection of copyright as a human right also is thought to be implicit in constitutional provisions that guarantee private property, right to privacy and personality, artistic freedoms, and so forth'. *See* P. B. Hugenholtz, 'Copyright and Freedom of Expression in Europe', in *Innovation Policy in an Information Age,* edited by R. Dreyfuss, H. First and D. Leenheer Zimmerman, Oxford University Press (2000).

38. There is a clear parallelism between this provision and Article 13 of the American Declaration of Rights and Duties of Man, which states 'Every person has the right to take part in the cultural life of the community, to enjoy the arts, and to participate in the

economic and moral rights, and therefore, the whole of copyright.[39] The economic or utilitarian perspective is also contained in this provision, as the enjoyment by the consumers of all the ensuing benefits of the creation. Second, we can conclude that the rights of authors must be understood as preconditions for cultural and scientific freedom, so the former facilitate cultural participation and access to scientific progress as a general rule.

This provision has sometimes been applied at the national level to extend copyright law. The well-known case of Charles Chaplin is an example of it. In 1959, the Paris Court of Appeal decided to grant to this British citizen the rights of a French citizen regarding a moral right: the right of integrity.[40] This assimilation was a direct application of Article 27(2) of the Universal Declaration. It was concluded that Chaplin's moral right of integrity on his film was violated by the defendant with the unauthorized addition of a soundtrack to the film.

In a very similar way and also in the international context, Article 15 of the United Nations Covenant of Economic, Social and Cultural Rights, adopted in 1966, imposes an obligation upon contracting parties to protect the moral and material interests of authors, inventors and creators – their rights to conserve, develop and make diffusion of science and culture; their freedom indispensable for research and creation; and their right to enjoy the benefits and to encourage the development of international contracts and cooperation.[41] Therefore, as a general conclusion, contracting parties of any of these international human rights instruments must regulate a level of protection of intellectual property rights sufficient enough to facilitate and

---

benefits that result from intellectual progress, especially scientific discoveries. He likewise has the right to the protection of his moral and material interests as regards his inventions or any literary, scientific or artistic works of which he is the author.' However, in 1950, Europe missed the opportunity to make a reference to intellectual property rights in the European Declaration of Human Rights.

39. P.L.C. Torremans, 'Copyright As A Human Right', in *Copyright and Human Rights Freedom of Expression – Intellectual Property – Privacy*, edited by P.L.C. Torremans above n. 9, at 7.

40. Judgment of the Paris Court of Appeal of 29 April 1959 in Case *Société Roy Export Company Establishment et Charlie Chaplin v. Société Les films Roger Richebé*.

41. Article 15(1) of the International Covenant of Economic, Social and Cultural Rights provides: 'The States Parties to the present Covenant recognize the right of everyone: (a) To take part in cultural life; (b) To enjoy the benefits of scientific progress and its application; (c) To benefit from the protection of the moral and material interests resulting from any scientific, literary or artistic production of which he is the author.' P. Cullet states: 'this international instrument provides a framework within which the development of science and culture is undertaken for the greater good of society while recognizing the need to provide specific incentives to authors for this to happen' (P. Cullet, 'Human Rights and Intellectual Property Protection in the TRIPS Era', *Human Rights Quarterly* 29, no. 2, (2007) at 408). For a comparison between Article 15 of the International Covenant of Economic, Social and Cultural Rights and Article 27 of the Universal Declaration of Human Rights, *see* A.R. Chapman, 'A Human Rights Perspective on Intellectual Property, Scientific, Progress and Access to the Benefits of Science', above n. 19, at 7-8.

promote cultural participation and scientific progress, in a way that benefits both individual authors, creators and inventors and members of society in a collective level.

Finally, in the international context we have to bear in mind some important references contained within trade treaties, such as the TRIPS Agreement – the Agreement on intellectual property of the WTO – with a mercantilist – more than an artistic or even human perspective. This non-human rights instrument includes some technology transfer provisions, whose application could promote the protection of human rights or, at least, the general right to the benefits of scientific progress.[42] For instance, Article 62, that outlines the obligation of developed countries to provide incentives to enterprises and institutions for the purpose of promoting and encouraging technology transfer to least-developed country Members 'in order to enable them to create a sound and viable technological base'.[43] Besides, Article 8(1) provides that 'Member may, in formulating or amending their laws and regulations, adopt measures necessary to protect public health and nutrition, and to promote the public interest in sectors of vital importance to their socio-economic and technological development, provided that such measures are consistent with the provisions of this Agreement'. Consequently, when implementing this treaty, Contracting Parties must respect both its intellectual property provisions and their human rights obligations other than intellectual property rights commitments.

On the other hand, in the European level, it has to be borne in mind that countries that are Contracting Parties of the Council of Europe must respect the obligations contained within the European Convention for the Protection of Human Rights and Fundamental Freedoms.[44] No reference to intellectual

---

42. It follows Article 7 of the TRIPS Agreement, which provides that intellectual property rights must 'contribute to the promotion of technological innovation (…) and in a manner conductive to social and economic welfare, and to balance of rights and obligations'.

43. Furthermore, Article 67 of the TRIPS Agreement outlines the obligation of developed countries to promote legal assistance in developing and least-developed countries (regarding the preparation of laws and regulations on the protection and enforcement of intellectual property rights and the establishment or reinforcement of national offices relevant to these matters, including the training of personnel).

44. This international instrument has the rank of national statutes for Contracting Parties, but it also influences the interpretation of national law, including higher-ranking national Constitutions. This issue came to light in the Caroline von Hannover Case (*Von Hannover v. Germany*, No. 59320/00, 24 June 2004, ECHR 2004-VI, 1 (2005) 40 EHRR 1 (2004), NJW 2647, 2649). The position adopted by the European Court of Human Rights in this case requires national courts to observe and apply the Convention while interpreting national law. *See* L. Fastrich, 'Human Rights and Private Law', in *Human Rights and Private Law. Privacy as Autonomy,* edited by K.S. Ziegler, Hart Publishing (2007), at 27-28. According to Article 6(3) of the European Union Treaty, fundamental rights, as guaranteed by the European Convention for the Protection of Human Rights and Fundamental Freedoms and as they result from the constitutional traditions common to Member States, constitute general principles of the European Union Law. Despite Article

property rights is directly regulated on this instrument. However, focusing on the right to property, the European Court of Human Rights has considered the term 'possessions' contained within this Convention to include trademarks and trademarks' applications in a case concerning a multinational corporation.[45] Following this decision, even an enterprise may receive human rights – like protection for its intellectual property.[46] On the other hand, Article 10(2) of this Convention is understood as a means to allow restrictions of freedom of expression if prescribed by the law and if necessary in a democratic society for the protection of the rights of others.[47] This provision can be interpreted as a bidirectional intersection between copyright law and freedom of expression, both of them affected by each other and involved in a complicated relationship.

6(2) of the EU Treaty made accession to the European Convention for the Protection of Human Rights and Fundamental Freedoms become a legal obligation, the European Union has not acceded yet. However, all the EU Member States are Contracting Parties of the Council of Europe, and thus, Contracting Parties of the European Convention for the Protection of Human Rights and Fundamental Freedoms.

45. Judgment of the European Court of Human Rights (Grand Chamber) of 11 January 2007, Case *Anheuser-Busch, Inc. v. Portugal*, 45 Eur. Ct. H. R. 36 (2007). In this judgment, the Court holds that Article 1 of Protocol No. 1 to the European Convention of Human Rights may be applicable to trademarks and trademarks application of an enterprise if such application gives rise to proprietary interests. The case concerned a dispute over Portugal's cancellation of an international brewery's application for the 'Budweiser' trademark in an effort to protect the appellation of origin 'Budějovický Budvar', which was owned by the Budweiser's Czech rival. The Court cited previous case law that also ruled in this direction: *Smith Kline and French Laboratories Ltd. v. The Netherlands*, No. 12633/87, Decision of 4 October 1990, Decisions and Reports (DR) 66, at 70 (in relation to patents); *Melnychuk v. Ukraine* (Dec.), No. 28743/03. ECHR 2005-IX (related to copyright).

46. P.K. Yu, 'Intellectual Property and Human Rights in the Nonmultilateral Era', above n. 35, at 1067. However, such an expansive view that allows corporate owners to demand human rights protection is problematic. The United Nations Economic and Social Council, Commission on Economic, Social and Cultural Rights, stated: 'Only the "author", namely the creator, whether man or woman, individual or group of individuals, of scientific, literary or artistic productions, such as, inter alia, writers and artists, can be the beneficiary of the protection of article 15, paragraph 1(c) (…) Under the existing international treaty protection regimes, legal entities are included among the holders of intellectual property rights. However, (…) their entitlements, because of their different nature, are not protected at the level of human rights' (United Nations Economic and Social Council, Commission on Economic, Social and Cultural Rights, *General Comment No. 17: The Right of Everyone to Benefit from the Protection of the Moral and Material Interests Resulting from Any Scientific, Literary or Artistic Production of Which He or She is the Author (Article 15, Paragraph 1 (c) of the Covenant)*, U.N. Doc. E/C.12/GC/17 (12 January 2006), at 7). We agree with P. K. Yu that 'It is one thing to give corporations standing to bring human rights claims on behalf of individuals, but quite another to allow corporate owners to claim that their human rights have been violated' (P.K. Yu, 'Ten Common Questions About Intellectual Property and Human Rights', *Georgia State University Law Review,* 23 (2007), at 730).

47. This provision indicates that the exercise of freedoms of expression carries with it duties and responsibilities.

Besides, the Charter of Fundamental Rights on the European Union which was signed and proclaimed on 7 December 2000 in Nice contains an important reference. For the first time in the history of the European Union, this Charter lays down the whole range of civil and social rights of European citizens, and it is based on the rights and freedoms as recognized by the European Convention for the Protection of Human Rights and Fundamental Freedoms and other international conventions to which the European Union or its Member States are parties, but also on the constitutional traditions of the EU Member States, and on the jurisprudence of the European Court of Justice and the European Court of Human Rights.[48] This Charter is to have the same legal value as the EU Treaties and is, thus, legally binding to the extent where the EU has specific competence.[49] As a consequence, the EU Member States must respect the rights and principles and promote the application thereof.

The main provision of the Charter of Fundamental Rights of the European Union related to intellectual property is laid down in Article 17(2). Protection of corporal general property is dealt with in Article 17(1).[50] According to Article 17(2), 'Intellectual property shall be protected.'[51] As fundamental rights, Article 52(1) of Charter must be applied to intellectual property rights by Member States. Intellectual property rights, thus, cannot be granted in an absolute basis, but any limitation to these rights must always be provided for by law – with an exhaustive or *numerus clausus* list of exceptions – and respect the essence of these rights and that limitation can only be made if it is necessary and protect the rights of others.[52]

It is surprising that, whereas Articles 37 and 38 of the Charter of Fundamental Rights of the European Union explicitly provide for a high level of environmental and consumer protection, there is no equivalent

---

48. *See* M.M. Walter, 'Fundamental Rights', in *European Copyright Law. A Commentary*, edited by M.M. Walter and S. Von Lewinski, Oxford University Press (2010), at 74.
49. Article 6(1) of the EU Treaty.
50. Please note that in some EU Member States neither intellectual property rights nor general or corporal property rights are considered fundamental rights in national constitutions. For a discussion on the nature of intellectual property rights as a part of the general property right or as a part of the freedom of expression, *see* R. Bercovitz Rodríguez-Cano, 'Comentario al artículo 1', en R. Bercovitz Rodríguez-Cano, *Comentarios a la Ley de Propiedad Intelecual,* Tecnos (2019); and G. Minero, 'Aproximación jurídica al concepto de derecho de autor. Intento de calificación como libertad de producción artística y científica o como derecho de propiedad', *Dilemata,* 12 (2013), at 215-245.
51. *See* P.L.C. Torremans, 'Article 17(2)', in *The EU Charter of Fundamental Rights. A Commentary,* edited by S. Peers, T. Hervey, J. Kenner and A. Ward, Hart/Beck (2014), at 489-517.
52. *See* S. Peters and S. Prechal, 'Article 52', in *The EU Charter of Fundamental Rights. A Commentary,* edited by S. Peers, T. Hervey, J. Kenner and A. Ward, Hart/Beck (2014), at 1455-1522.

provision with regard intellectual property rights.[53] However, this statement is contained in a lower-ranking provision: Recital 9 of the Information Society Directive, and it is commonly reminded by the Court of Justice of the EU case law.[54] That high-level protection rule does not disregard the necessity of balancing the rights of the owners of intellectual property rights and the interests of the public. That balance also follows from the recognition of other fundamental rights, meaning that the mere existence of other rights plays a role against any over-protective intellectual property legislation or any excessive interpretation of the intellectual property laws and statutes.[55]

The Charter of Fundamental Rights of the European Union is reflected in the European Court of Justice's case law in the context of intellectual property rights. In the judgment of 12 September 2006, it was held that intellectual property rights, which form part of the right of property, are to be observed by the Community courts, as well as freedom of expression.[56] In the case *ProMusicae v. Telefónica de España*, it was stated: 'It should be recalled that the fundamental right to property, which includes intellectual property rights such as copyright (…) and the fundamental right to effective judicial protection constitute general principles of Community Law.'[57] In this case, the dispute raises the question of the need to reconcile the requirements of the protection of different fundamental rights, namely the right to respect for private life, on the one hand, and the right of property, on the other hand. 'That being so, the Member States must, when transposing the Directives concerning intellectual property rights, take care to rely on an interpretation of the Directives which allows a fair balance to be struck between the various fundamental rights protected by the Community legal order. Further, when implementing the measures transposing those Directives, the authorities and courts of the Member States must strike a fair balance between the protection of copyright and the protection of the fundamental rights of individuals who

---

53. *See* M.M. Walter, 'Fundamental Rights', in *European Copyright Law. A Commentary*, edited by M.M. Walter and S. Von Lewinski, above n. 48, at 77.
54. Directive 2001/29/EC of the European Parliament and of the Council of 22 May 2001, on the harmonization of certain aspects of copyright and related rights in the information society. According to Recital 9: 'Any harmonisation of copyright and related rights must take as a basis a high level of protection, since such rights are crucial to intellectual creation. Their protection helps to ensure the maintenance and development of creativity in the interests of authors, performers, producers, consumers, culture industry and the public at large. Intellectual property has therefore been recognised as an integral part of property.'
55. *See* M.M. Walter, 'Fundamental Rights', *European Copyright Law. A Commentary*, edited by in M.M. Walter and S. Von Lewinski, above n. 48, at 78; and C. Geiger, 'Copyright's Fundamental Rights Dimension at EU level', in E. Derclaye, Research Handbook on the Future of EU Copyright, Edward Elgar Publishing (2007), at 30.
56. Judgment of the European Court of Justice of 12 September 2006, *Laserdisken v. Kulturministeriet*, C-479/04, EU:C:2006:549, parags 61-65.
57. Judgment of the European Court of Justice of 29 January 2008, *ProMusicae v. Telefónica de España*, C-275/06, EU:C:2008:54, para. 62.

are affected by such measures and other general principles of the EU law, such as the principle of proportionality.'[58]

Besides, no human rights are unlimited. Thus, when interpreting the freedom of information, the European Court of Human Rights has made it clear that information of a commercial nature is indeed protected, albeit to a lesser degree than political speech.[59] In this sense, in addition, the Court of Justice of the European Union indicates that for the purpose of striking a balance between copyright and the right to freedom of expression, it has to be taken into account the fact that 'the nature of the "speech" or information at issue is of particular importance, *inter alia* in political discourse and discourse concerning matters of the public interest'.[60]

Therefore, in the European level, there are various different steps to be taken. Moreover, if the concrete aspect of the intellectual property right is harmonized, national legislatures have to fulfil the proportionality test when transposing the IP Directives. Besides, when interpreting these rights, national courts have to look for a fair balance between intellectual property rights and the right to an effective remedy and other fundamental rights. On the other hand, if a specific aspect of an intellectual property right is not regulated at the European level, national legislatures and courts must also respect that fair balance in order to be consistent with the Charter of Fundamental Rights on the European Union.

Therefore, if intellectual property rights' aim is to promote progress and development, 'it may be assumed that if legislation on intellectual property corresponds to this purpose, there can be no true conflict between intellectual property and policy objectives, such as development, public health, or the fight against hunger'.[61] However, the flexibilities built into these international and European instruments have to be recognized. They left much space for Contracting Parties to implement these principles and rights, and also this common purpose of intellectual property rights and human rights. Consequently, when talking about intersections between human rights and non-human rights aspects of intellectual property protection and conflicts

---

58. *Ibid.*, para. 68. In the same way, judgment of the European Court of Justice of 24 November 2011, *Scarlet Extended v. SABAM*, C-70/10, EU:C:2011:771, paras 44-46 and judgment of 16 February 2012, *SABAM v. Netlog NV*, C-360/10, EU:C:2012:85, paras 41-43. *See* M.M. Walter, 'Fundamental Rights', in *European Copyright Law. A Commentary*, edited by M.M. Walter and S. Von Lewinski, above n. 48, at 77.

59. *See* judgments of the European Court of Human Rights of 25 March 1985, Case *Barthold v. Germany*, of 24 February 1994, Case *Casado Coca v. Spain*, and of 25 August 1998, Case *Hertel v. Switzerland*. *See* P.B. Hugenholtz, 'Copyright and Freedom of Expression in Europe', in *Innovation Policy in an Information Age*, edited by R. Dreyfuss, H. First and D. Leenheer Zimmerman, above n. 37.

60. Judgment of the Court of Justice of the European Union of 29 July 2019, *Funke Medien*, above n. 18, para. 74, citing the judgment of the European Court of Human Rights of 10 January 2013, *Ashby Donald and Others v. France*, para. 39.

61. J. Cornides, 'Human Rights and Intellectual Property: Conflict or Convergence?', *Journal of World Intellectual Property* (2004), at 159.

between human rights attributes of intellectual property and other forms of human rights, it has to be noted that much depends on how these treaties are actually implemented by their Contracting Parties.

One crucial aspect is the way in which exceptions to intellectual property rights are regulated. Taking into account that their regulation looks for the maximum respect to human rights – for example, the quotation exception promotes criticism and educational purposes; it must be noted that intellectual property rights and human rights do not conflict as such, but converge. In the next section, some common interferences between intellectual property rights and other human rights are identified and analysed from a legal point of view. Some of them are the result of unbalanced intellectual property rights legislation. In these cases, the solution has to come from the courts. Judges must interpret these rights in a restrictive manner in order to restore the necessary balance with their human rights obligations.

5.3 ANALYSING THE POTENTIAL OR APPARENT CONFLICTS

It is useful to analyse the areas where intellectual property rights may conflict with human rights – or areas where intellectual property rights at least have posed important challenges to the protection of human rights – in order to prove or disprove the conflictive nature of their relationships. The following potential conflicts are analysed below: (i) conflicts between copyright and related rights (including the sui generis protection of databases, among the European countries), on the one hand, and freedom of expression (including the right of the public to receive information), right to privacy, right to education and right to the respect of one's property, on the other; and (ii) conflicts between patents rights and protection of new varieties of plants, on the one hand, and right to health, e right to food, right to a safe and clean environment, right to freedom of speech, and right of the public to receive information, on the other.

In the vast majority of cases, the analysis will show that there are no real but only apparent conflicts, which are resolved internally, within the intellectual property laws – in particular, applying the provisions on terms of protection and the exceptions or limitations to intellectual property rights – or externally, by national courts, when interpreting those intellectual property laws from a human right perspective.

5.3.1 Conflicts Between Copyright and Freedom of Expression, Right to Privacy, Right to Education and Right to the Respect of One's Property

It cannot be admitted that there is an actual general conflict between copyright and freedom of expression, which contains the public's right to information.[62] As a consequence of the limited term of protection of copyright, and provided that paternity and integrity rights are observed, uses of works that have fallen in the public domain –after the term of protection expiration – need no authorization. Besides, because of the idea/expression dichotomy logic of copyright, anyone can freely use the ideas that are behind a work.[63] Third, exceptions and limitations to copyright and related rights, such as the parody, allow individuals to express themselves freely.[64] Finally, it has to be taken into account that copyright owner can decide whether to sue the infringer or not. Consequently, copyright ownership just provides a right to decide to litigate and claim damages in case of unauthorized use.

It has to be noted that copyright is closely linked with freedom of expression. The former is a means to allow a broad expression of people's beliefs. Consequently, there is an area of coincidence between copyright and related rights and freedom of expression and the right to freedom of thought, conscience and religion.[65]

Furthermore, there are at least two more areas of coincidence between freedom of expression and intellectual property rights: the moral right of

---

62. *See* A. Strowel and F. Tulkens, 'Freedom of Expression and Copyright under Civil Law: A Balance, Adaptation and Access', in *Copyright and Free Speech. Comparative and International Analyses*, edited by J. Griffiths and U. Suthersanen, Oxford University Press (2005), at 287.

63. Since the originality requirement implies that non-original expressions cannot be protected by copyright, it promotes the exercise of the freedom of expression and information. Individuals can express themselves freely by taking those unprotected expressions without having to ask previously for authorization.

64. The exception of parody is an appropriate way to express an opinion and its application must, consequently, strike a balance between, on the one hand, the interest and rights of the copyright holder of the work and, on the other hand, the freedom of expression of the user who is relying on the exception of parody (Judgment of the European Court of Justice of 3 September 2014, Case *Johan Deckmyn and others v. Helena Vandersteen and others*, C-201/13, EU:C:2014:2132, paras 25 and 27). The parody exception directly promotes the exercise of the freedom of expression since its application does not require that the parody made is itself original enough to be considered a work and, consequently, to be protected by copyright. When analysing the exercise of this exception, national court must draw attention to the principle of non-discrimination (Article 21(1) Charter of Fundamental Rights of the European Union), in order to safeguard that copyright holders have a legitimate interest in ensuring that the work protected by copyright is not associated with a discriminatory message (para. 31). In the drawing at issue, the people who, in the original work, were picking up the coins that the main character throws were replaced by persons wearing veils and people of colour. In the context of parody, we agree with F. Dessemontet, that states: 'It is our understanding that rules for parody, excerpt and fair use – when they exist – suffice to protect the freedom of the artist. There is at present no need to go beyond the clearly delineated exceptions to copyright as embedded in the copyright legislation.' The main problem is, therefore, the lack of real harmonization in the international level of exceptions to copyright. *See* F. Dessemontet, 'Copyright and Human Rights', in *Intellectual Property and Information Law: Essays in Honour of Herman Cohen Jehoram*, edited by J. Kabel and G. Mom, Kluwer (1998), at 10.

65. In the second edition of this book, E. Derclaye held that 'The Three Rights Form an Inseparable Trio', at 157.

divulgation, also known as the right to disclosure, and the moral right to retract or withdraw, in countries where they exist. This first right allows the author of a work to choose whether and in which conditions he or she prefers to divulge his or her work for the first time. Meanwhile, the author can keeps his or her work private – he or she can withhold the work if it is not finished or not ready for publication, and can prohibit anyone from divulgating it without his authorization. The moral right to retract or withdraw allows the author to recall a work where it no longer corresponds with his or her beliefs or views. It has to be taken into account that these moral rights are not harmonized, neither at an international nor a supranational level. Thus, their implementation depends on the national regulations.

However, the above-mentioned considerations and, consequently, the previous answer might not be the same when evaluating the European sui generis right over databases.[66] This special right has been seriously criticized by the literature because its broad economic goals may threat to override human rights considerations, in particular, the public's right to information.[67] Contrary to copyright, this new right does not focus on originality, but on the compiler's investment.[68] Consequently, this right applies to any database that fulfils the substantial investment requirement, irrespective of the eligibility of the structure of the database and/or of its contents for protection by copyright or any other intellectual property right.[69] No other criteria than that of the substantial investment is to be applied to determine the eligibility of a database on sui generis protection. This right protects database makers from unauthorized extraction or reutilization of all or a substantial part of the contents of the database, measured in a qualitative or in a quantitative manner. The burden of proof regarding the investment and its substantial nature lies with the maker of the database. Taking into account the lack of a

---

66. This right has its origin in Directive 96/9/EC of the European Parliament and of the Council of 11 March 1996, on the legal protection of databases (Official Journal of the European Communities, 27.3.96, L 77/20). According to Article 11, this right can only be applied to databases whose makers or right holders are nationals of a Member State or who have their habitual residence in the territory of the European Union. In the case of enterprises, the company must be formed in accordance with the law of a Member State and must have its registered office, central administration or principal place of business within the European Union.

67. *See* E. Derclaye, *Legal Protection of Databases. A Comparative Study,* (2008), Edward Elgar; G. Minero, *La protección jurídica de las bases de datos en el ordenamiento europeo,* above n. 34; and J. Phillips, 'Databases, the Human Rights Act and EU Law', in *Copyright and Free Speech. Comparative and International Analyses,* edited by J. Griffiths and U. Suthersanen, Oxford University Press (2005).

68. This protection lasts fifteen years from completion of the database, but any substantial change which implies a new substantial investment renews the protection for another fifteen years.

69. The European Court of Justice held that copyright and sui generis right over databases must be regarded as mutually independent and, thus, as cumulative protections. G. Minero, Judgment of the European Court of Justice of 1 March 2012, *Football Dataco Ltd and others v. Yahoo! UK Ltd and others,* EU:C:2012:115, para. 27.

harmonized set of rules acting as minimum threshold, the substantial nature of the protectable investment must be determined on a case-by-case analysis. Consequently, an undeniable risk of legal uncertainty is created. A case-by-case analysis is also needed regarding the use of a substantial part of the contents of the database – that is, a use of a sufficient significance or magnitude as to prejudice the database maker's investment – and, thus, regarding the existence of an infringement. Therefore, national courts have to look for a moderate and restrictive use of the qualitative criterion, in order to fulfil the principle that the sui generis right does not in any case give rise to the creation of a new right in the elements themselves.[70] In relation to mandatory exceptions and limitation to be applied to the sui generis right, the European legislature has recently regulated the text and data mining exception, with a mandatory implementation by EU Member States.[71]

On the other hand, in this judicial analysis, it must be borne in mind that in order to be consistent with the human rights balance, the legal protection of the technological measures that were introduced in the database cannot be disproportionate. The imbalance of the measures excludes their protection under Article 6 of Directive 2001/29/EC – or its national implementation-. Therefore, in the case the technical protection measure prevents any single use of the contents of the database – including those acts which do not require the database maker's authorization, there must be considered disproportionate and, consequently, this instrument – the technical protection measure – must remain unprotected by intellectual property law.[72]

---

70. This is the main criticism that can be made to the sui generis right. *See* J. H. Reichman and P. Samuelson, 'Intellectual Property Rights in Data?', *Vanderbilt Law Review,* 50 (1997). Whereas the quantitative examination of the substantial use of the contents of the database refers to the volume of the elements extracted from the database and/or reutilized and must be assessed in relation to the total volume of the contents of the protected database, the qualitative exam refers to the scale of the investment in the specific contents subject of the act of extraction and/or reutilization, regardless of whether it represents a quantitatively substantial part of the whole of the contents of the protected database. *See* judgment of the European Court of Justice of 5 March 2009, *Apis-Hristovich EOOD v. Lakorda AD*, Case C-545/07, EU:C:2009:132, paras 60 and 66; and judgment of 9 November 2004, *The British Horseracing Ltd and other v. William Hill Organization Ltd*, Case C-203/02, EU:C:2004:695, para. 71.
71. Article 3 of Directive (EU) 2019/790 of the European Parliament and of the Council of 17 April 2019 on copyright and related rights in the Digital Single Market introduces this mandatory exception, to be used by research organizations and cultural heritage institutions with regard to content to which they have lawful access. It has to be taken into account the fact that the vast majority of exceptions to copyright and related rights regulated in other previous EU Directives have a voluntary nature, since its transposition by national legislatures is not mandatory.
72. Following Advocate General Sharpston's Opinion, in the Case *Nintendo v. PC Box*, C-355/12, which was delivered on 19 September 2013 (paras 53-63 and 78), the Court of Justice of the European Union noted the fact that legal protection against acts not authorized by the right holder of any copyright must respect the principle of proportionality. Accordingly, that legal protection 'is granted only with regards to technological

Nevertheless, the conflict with freedom of speech is broader. It could extend to any work or other subject matter protected by copyright or related rights in which technical measures were inserted. That because disproportionate technological measures also interface with the exercise of exceptions and limitations to copyright and related rights – in practice, users could be impeded to benefit from these exceptions when the work is technologically protected – mainly regulated in Directive 2001/29/EC and implemented in the national intellectual property laws and regulations. This conflict was specifically acknowledged in Article 6(4) of this Directive, according to which Member States must provide means of benefiting from the exceptions and limitations.[73]

Moreover, extended global use of technical protection measures also interferes with the protection of private life, which includes the protection of privacy in the electronic communications sector and the processing of personal data. Some of these technical measures can monitor the contents that are being used by the user and, thus, it can identify what people listen to, view, read or access.[74] In this case, the answer must be the same: intellectual property laws cannot protect those technical measures that are

---

measures which pursue the objective of preventing or eliminating, as regards works, acts not authorized by the right holder of copyright'. In other words, 'those measures must be suitable for achieving that objective and must not go beyond what is necessary for this purpose'. Consequently, a case-by-case analysis must be made, in order to examine whether other measures could have caused less interference with the activities of third parties not requiring authorization by the right holder of copyright, while still providing comparable protection of that right holder's rights (Judgment of the European Court of Justice of 23 January 2014, paras 30-32). *See* S. Dusollier, *Droit d 'auteur et protection des oeuvres dans l'univers numérique. Droits et exceptions à la lumière des dispositifs de verrouillage des oeuvres*, Larcier (2005), at 119-120; U. Gasser, 'Legal Frameworks and Technological Protection of Digital Content: Moving Forward Towards a Best Practice Model', *Fordham Intellectual Property, Media & Entertainment Law Journal*, no. 17 (2006), at 71; and G. Minero, 'Videogames, Consoles and Technological Measures: The Nintento v. PC Box and 9 Net Case', *European Intellectual Property Review*, 36, no. 5 (2014), at 335-339.

73. '[I]n the absence of voluntary measures taken by right holders, including agreement between right-handers and other parties concerned, Member States shall take appropriate measures to ensure that right holders make available to the beneficiary of an exception or limitation provided for in the national law in accordance with Article 5(2)(a), (2)(c), (2)(d), (2)(e), (3)/a), (3)(b) or (3)(e) the means of benefiting from the exception or limitation and where that beneficiary has legal access to the protected work or subject-matter concerned'.

74. E. Derclaye also noted that such use of technical measures of protection may also 'endanger[s] free speech as people may be less inclined to express non-conformist opinions because they are aware their use is being monitored by copyright holders' (E. Derclaye in the second edition of this book, at 145). *See also* L. Bygrave, 'The Technologisation of Copyright: Implications for Privacy and Related Rights', *European Intellectual Property Review*, 24 (2002), at 53.

disproportionate and control the uses that go beyond those specific utilizations of works or other subject matters that the right holder of copyright or related rights can authorize or prohibit.

In case of information-society services which were used to infringe intellectual property rights, the European Court of Justice has stated that, according to Article 8(3) of Directive 2001/29/EC and Article 11 of Directive 2004/48/EC, holders of intellectual property rights may apply for an injunction against operators of an online platform, who act as intermediaries within the meaning of those provisions, given that their services may be exploited by users of those platforms to infringe intellectual property rights.[75] National courts are allowed to order the intermediaries to take measures aimed not only at bringing to an end infringements already committed against intellectual property rights using their information-society services, but also at preventing further infringements.[76] Although details such as conditions to be met and procedure to be followed are a matter for national law, those national rules must respect Article 15(1) of Directive 2000/31 (Directive on electronic commerce), which prohibits national authorities from adopting measures which would require a hosting service provider to carry out general monitoring of the information that it stores.[77]

Peer-to-peer platform can no longer benefit from the safe harbour defence established in Article 14(1) of Directive 2000/31. However, Directive (EU) 2019/790 of the European Parliament and of the Council of 17 April 2019 on copyright and related rights in the Digital Single Market did not introduce as such an *ex ante* filtering requirement for information-society services, but a mere general obligation for those services to act in a legal manner, asking for authorization of the copyright owners before their users upload works protected by copyright in those platforms – concluding licensing agreements – and acting expeditiously, upon receiving a sufficiently

---

75. Judgment of the European Court of Justice of 24 November 2011, *Scarlet Extended v. SABAM*, above n. 58, para. 30.
76. *Ibid.*, para. 31; and judgment of the European Court of Justice of 16 February 2012, *SABAM v. Netlog NV*, above n. 58, para. 29.
77. Judgment of the European Court of Justice of 24 November 2011, *Scarlet Extended v. SABAM*, above n. 58, para. 33; and judgment of 16 February 2012, *SABAM v. Netlog NV*, above n. 58, para. 31. The European Court of Justice noted that these Directives must be interpreted as precluding a national court from issuing an injunction against a hosting service provider which i) requires it to install a system for filtering information which is stored on its servers by its service users, ii) which applies indiscriminately to all of those users; iii) as a preventive measure; iv) exclusively at its expense; and v) for an unlimited period, vi) which is capable of identifying electronic files containing musical, cinematographic or audiovisual work in respect of which the applicant for the injunction claims to hold intellectual property rights, with the aim of preventing those works from being made available to the public in breach of copyright. In this case, such a disproportionate measure infringes not only the fundamental right to privacy (Article 8 Charter of Fundamental Rights of the European Union) but also the freedom to conduct a business enjoyed by operators as hosting service providers, which is contained within Article 16 Charter of Fundamental Rights of the European Union.

substantiated notice from the right holders, to disable access to, or to remove from their websites, the notified works or other subject matter, and made best efforts to prevent their future uploads.

Furthermore, the Court of Justice of the European Union has noted that Directive 2000/31/EC and Directive 2002/58/EC (Directive on privacy and electronic communications) do not preclude the Member States from laying down, with the view to ensuring effective protection of copyright, an obligation to communicate personal data which will enable the copyright holder to bring civil proceedings based on the existence of that right. However, when transposing those Directives, the Member States must take care to rely on an interpretation of them which allows a fair balance to be struck between copyright and related rights and right to privacy. Further, when implementing the measures transposing those directives, the national authorities and courts must interpret their national law in a manner consistent both with those Directives and fundamental rights and general principles of the EU law, such as the principle of proportionality.[78]

When talking about the right to education, we have to take into account the general exception or limitation for research and teaching contained within Article 5(3)(a) of Directive 2001/29/EC and Article 5 of Directive (EU) 2019/790 and implemented by national legislatures.[79] It includes any reproduction and communication to the public of works, including those involved in primary, secondary, vocational and higher education, provided the teaching activity has a non-commercial purpose.

---

78. Judgment of the European Court of Justice of 29 January 2008, *ProMusicae v. Telefónica de España*, above n. 57, para. 68. While Directive 2001/29/EC and Directive 2004/48/EC require the effective protection of intellectual property rights and the institution of judicial remedies for their enforcement, 'they do not contain provisions which require those directives to be interpreted as compelling the Member States to lay down an obligation to communicate personal data in the context of civil proceedings' (para. 60). The TRIPS Agreements do not contain provisions compelling their Contracting Parties to regulate such an obligation. They therefore leave Member States discretion to define transposition measures which may be adapted to the various situations possible (para. 67). Article 15(1) of Directive 2002/58 and Article 13(1) of Directive 95/46 authorize Member States to adopt legislative measures to restrict the obligation of confidentiality of personal data where that restriction is necessary *inter alia* for the protection of the rights and freedoms of others (para. 53).

79. According to Article 5(3)(a) of Directive 2001/29/EC, national legislatures may provide for an exception to 'use for the sole purpose of illustration for teaching or scientific research, as long as the source, including the author's name, is indicated, unless this turns out to be impossible and to the extent justified by the non-commercial purpose to be achieved'. Article 5 of Directive (EU) 2019/790 provides a mandatory nature to this exception in relation to the physical and digital environments. According to recital 22 of this Directive: 'The exception or limitation should cover both uses of works or other subject matter made in the classroom or in other venues through digital means, for example electronic whiteboards or digital devices which might be connected to the internet, as well as uses made at a distance through secure electronic environments, such as in the context of online courses or access to teaching material complementing a given course.'

Finally, we must refer to the potential conflict between the copyright holder and the owner of the physical work in those cases of destruction of the tangible medium of the work. The general property right is, thus, limited by the exercise of the author's moral rights, in particular the right of integrity.[80] Therefore, destruction of the work and any modification of that work must be authorized or can be prohibited by that author or his or her moral rights' holders after his or her death.

On the other hand, also related with the general property right, the principle of exhaustion (established in Article 6(2) of the WIPO Copyright Treaty, among other provisions) creates a coincidence between this general property right and the intellectual property rights on goods. After the first sale or the transfer of ownership of the corporal medium in which the intellectual property rights apply, the owner can dispose of it as he or she pleases, provided he or she did not infringe moral rights, so the intellectual property rights holder cannot interfere in the enjoyment of the product.[81] However, exhaustion is not absolute. If the good contains a work protected by copyright, rights of renting, reproduction, modification and communication to the public are not exhausted. In the case a good containing a patent, reconstructing is not exhausted as a consequence of the first sale. In the case of trademarks, the right to control the re-packaging does not exhaust. Besides, the principle of exhaustion can only be applied in the physical context, after the first sale of the physical device of the work, being software the only exception to this general rule.[82]

On the contrary, in the online context there is no equivalent exhaustion rule. However, according to European case law, once the copyright owner uploads his/her work on the Internet with free access, copyright does not

---

80. *See* M. Salokannel, A. Strowel and E. Derclaye, *Final Report of the Study Contract concerning Moral Rights in the Context of the Exploitation of Works through Digital Technology*, 2000, available at http://ec.europa.eu/internal_market/copyright/docs/studies/etd1999b53000e28_en.pdf.

81. E. Derclaye in the second edition of this book, at 155.

82. *See* the judgment of the Court of Justice of the European Union of 3 July 2012, *UsedSoft GmbH v. Oracle International Corp*, EU:C:2012:407. In the case of software, the Court of Justice of the European Union concluded that once the copy of the computer program has been brought into circulation in a physical medium or online, in the right holders' website, by or under licence of the copyright owner, subsequent acts of sale, both in the physical world and in the online world –rental not included – fall outside the scope of the copyright owner. The Court of Justice decided to apply the exhaustion rule to any sale, that is, to any agreement by which the customer who downloads the copy of the program and concludes with the seller company a licence agreement relating to that copy receives, in return for payment of a fee, a right to use that copy for an unlimited period. In this case, the copyright owner cannot prohibit subsequent sales of the software. The copyright owner can make use of technical protective measures to ensure that the original acquirer has not made copies of the program which he will continue to use after selling his material medium. On the contrary, the exhaustion rule cannot be applied to time-limited licenses.

allow him/her to prohibit or control linking that work in other websites.[83] The conclusion will not be the same in a case where the webmaster of the second website circumvents the technical measure inserted by the first webmaster in his/her website to restrict the access to the work, since in this second case the technical circumvention allows all Internet users to have free access to works that they previously did not have.

5.3.2   CONFLICTS BETWEEN PATENTS RIGHTS AND PROTECTION OF NEW VARIETIES OF PLANTS AND RIGHT TO HEALTH, RIGHT TO FOOD, RIGHT TO A SAFE AND CLEAN ENVIRONMENT AND FREEDOM OF SPEECH AND RIGHT OF THE PUBLIC TO RECEIVE INFORMATION

When talking about the interference between the right to health (Articles 25 Universal Declaration of Human Rights and 12(1) International Covenant of Economic, Social and Cultural Rights) and patents it must be taken into account that patent protection limits the enjoyment of the former because of the common high cost of medicines protected by patent rights. This topic has garnered an important amount of public attention in recent years. Two cases can be cited to illustrate the conflict: (i) a private British company obtained a patent on the use –oral administration- of a medicine – called *AZT*, but marketed under the trademark *Retrovir* – against AIDS in several countries – the United States, among them, where the patent was granted in 1988 – and priced the drug in such a way that many people could not afford it. For many years, *AZT* was the only drug available in HIV treatment and it causes an outcry by activists claiming that pharmaceutical patents result in higher prices thus reducing the accessibility to medicines.[84] (ii) The antibiotic *Cipro* was the only approved treatment for anthrax attacks occurred in 2001 and the patent on which the United States and Canada threatened to break to drive down the price.[85]

As patents grant a monopoly over a specific invention for a twenty years term, the price of those products or their results will generally be high. However, prices do not only depend on patent protection. Patent legislation's goal is to promote scientific progress and development. In order to fulfil it, patent right, right to health and right to food do cooperate. In other words, if patents rights did not exist, pharmaceutical companies and other inventors would probably not innovate, so there would be fewer medicines and innovations in our societies.[86]

---

83. Judgment of the Court of Justice of the European Union of 13 February 2014, *Svensson*, EU:C:2014:76.
84. The medium price for an annual supply of the medicine for one patient was USD 10,000.
85. *See* H. Hestermeyer, *Human Rights and the WTO: The Case of Patents and Access to Medicines*, above n. 3, at 2.
86. *See* E. Derclaye in the second edition of this book, at 148. 'Patents are therefore a necessary restriction on competition to enhance competition'.

This explains that, in the past, many developing countries did not allow patents on medical and pharmaceutical goods. However, after 1994, when the TRIPS Agreement was signed, all Member States are obliged to adopt a minimum standard of patent protection for medicines. This international treaty did not avoid the entry into force in South Africa of the Medicines and Related Substances Control Amendment Act, passed in 1997. The main aim of this act was to keep medicines affordable for South African people, thus protecting its citizens' right to health. This national act gave the Minister of Health the authority to limit patents rights, either authorizing parallel imports and providing compulsory licences. After strong US Government and EU Governments' critics and a suit filed by several multinational pharmaceutical companies, the pharmaceutical industry and the South African Government agreed a joint statement with their commitment to work together to further the health of South African population and the lawsuit was withdrawn.[87]

In the above-mentioned case related to the medicine used in HIV treatments, the patent owner – the British company – argued that the high price was justified by the cost of research, development and marketing of the drug, as well as the need to generate revenues before better therapies were introduced. The argument did not convince Congressional critics, since the United States Government made a significant contribution to the development of the drug, and the Congress put on the company attained a 20% cut in the medicine price.

Developing countries, such as South Africa, are struck severely with HIV, with an infection rate of almost 20% of the population.[88] After years, the World Health Organization concluded that treating AIDS merely with *Retrovir* was defective. Consequently, this organization recommended a therapy with three existing medicines combination in one pill. The Indian best-known generic manufacturer – *Cipla* – offered such combination. *Cipla* was granted a patent on the drugs combination in South Africa and in other countries where its components are not under patent or where the patent owners have granted licenses. Generic drugs brought down the prices significantly. However, besides India, the capacity to manufacture generic HIV medicines exists only in a few developing countries, so many of them have to import the components.

On the other hand, in relation to antibiotic *Cipro*, after the anthrax attacks in 2001, the US Government announced the desire to purchase a large amount of tablets. This medicine was protected in the United States by *Bayer's* patent. However, the Indian generics drug maker *Cipla* offered the

---

87. The Secretary General of the United Nations mediated in this conflict. The World Health Organization -the Sub-Commission on the Promotion and Protection of Human Rights- passed the resolution 'Intellectual Property and Human Rights' (Res 2000/7 (17 August 2000)).

88. *See* H. Hestermeyer, *Human Rights and the WTO: The Case of Patents and Access to Medicines*, above n. 3, at 7.

generic version for a lower cost. At first, the US administration defended a pro-patent position. Afterwards, Canada decided to buy the generic version manufactured by *Cipla,* for half the price that *Bayer* charged and, consequently, the US Administration threatened to do the same. As a result, *Bayer* decided to reduce the price of its patented medicine.

In general terms, it has to be taken into account that, apart from the protection requirements (novelty, non-obviousness and industrial application)[89] and the limited term of protection,[90] patents laws have intrinsic limits that help to balance this possible interference. First, there is a list of excluded subject matter, which cannot be protected (for instance, discoveries, scientific theories and mathematical methods, aesthetic creations, methods for doing business and presentations of information, but also inventions the commercial exploitation of which would be contrary to *ordre public* or morality, plant or animal varieties or biological processes for the production of them and methods for treatment of the human or animal body by surgery or therapy and diagnostic methods).[91]

Second, although international and European treaties and conventions do not regulate it, national legislatures have regulated some exceptions or limitations to patent rights that do not reasonably conflict with a normal exploitation of the patent and do not unreasonably prejudice the legitimate interests of the patent owner.[92] However, if those limits are not enough and patent law is over-protective, national courts may use competition law or the right to health to prohibit abuses of intellectual property rights.

Additionally, the area of coincidence between the right to a safe and clean environment and patents law has to be highlighted. The general aim of intellectual property – scientific progress and human welfare – is reflected in Article 27(2) TRIPS, which allows Contracting Parties to prevent the patenting of inventions which seriously prejudice the environment.[93]

On the other hand, the mandatory condition for patentees to disclose to the public their inventions once they have been patented is the price to pay to gain the patents rights. This requirement implies a real coincidence between patent law and the right to freedom of speech and the right of the public to receive information.

Finally, we have to take into account Article 15 of the Union for the Protection of New Varieties of Plants Convention of 1961, which provides

---

89. Article 27 TRIPS and Articles 52, 54, 56 and 57 of the European Patents Convention.
90. Article 33 TRIPS and Article 63 of the European Patents Convention.
91. Article 27 TRIPS and Articles 52 and 53 of the European Patents Convention.
92. Article 30 TRIPS leaves Contracting Parties discretion to define and regulate these exceptions and limitations. The most common are those for private uses and tests and experimental purposes with generic drugs.
93. *See* E. Derclaye, 'Patents Law's Role in the Protection of Environment – Re-Assessing Patent Law and Its Justifications', *International Review of Intellectual Property and Competition,* 40 (2009), at 249-273.

compulsory exceptions to protection for acts done privately and for non-commercial purposes, acts done for experimental purposes and acts done for the purpose of breeding other varieties. This provision also allows Contracting Parties to restrict the breeder's right in relation to any variety in order to permit farmers to use for propagating purposes.

5.4   CONCLUSION

This chapter tries to identify those possible or apparent areas of interference between human rights and intellectual property rights and to provide constructive guidelines. In particular, the tension or intersection between the imperative of copyright law and the core of the right to freedom of expression and information. The complexity of the relationship between these two areas must be emphasized.

This chapter shows the actual existence or not of these possible conflicts or even the very existence of a real cooperative relationship among them in those cases where both rights have the same goals or at least related aims. Moreover, in cases of conflict, this chapter analyses and provides possible solutions or parameters to be taken into account by legislatures and courts when balancing these rights and the interests of the intellectual property right holder and the public.

Therefore, we cannot agree with the categorical statement made by Lord Phillips M.R., in case *Ashdown v. Telegraph Group Ltd* [2001] EMLR 44 (CA): '[C]opyright is antithetical to freedom of expression. It prevents all, save the owner of the copyright, from expressing information in the form of the literary work protected by the copyright.'[94] Apart from other internal mechanisms such as the exceptions to copyright –that do not always imply a purely commercial or purely non-commercial uses of the work, but a mix of them,[95] the main copyright law doctrine that resolves much of the tension with other human rights is the principle of the idea/expression dichotomy, according to which copyright protects the expression rather than the idea or the content itself. The real logic behind this dichotomy is explained in one of the leading cases in the US of the eighties: *Harper & Row Publishers v. Nation Enterprises*, 471 US 539 (1985), which dealt with the unauthorized publication in *The Nation* news magazine of 300 words of a then-forthcoming biography of the President Ford. The US Supreme Court stated:

---

94. *Ashdown v. Telegraph Group Ltd* [2001] EMLR 44 (CA), at 30. For a comment on this case, *see* L. Joseph, 'Human Rights Versus Copyright: The Paddy Ashdown Case', 13(3) *Entertainment Law Review* (2002), 72.

95. In the case of a newspaper, for example, there is both a commercial and a non-commercial aim: the exercise the freedom of expression and the intention of profiting.

'In our haste to disseminate news, it should not be forgotten that the framers intended copyright itself to be the engine of free expression'.[96]

It has correctly been supported that the *idea v. expression dichotomy* and the existence of legal exceptions to copyright do not fully resolve the conflict between copyright and freedom of expression. However, maybe it is neither necessary nor preferable to provide an actual and complete response applicable to any case, but an adaptive mechanism of answer. In this sense, there is consensus that international treaties do not provide a general freedom to copy.

The vagueness of the demarcation between an idea and its expression is not always a disadvantage, but a mechanism to provide a case-by-case study and answer. Consequently, as an example, in case *Ashdown v. Telegraph Group Ltd*, it was concluded that the unauthorized use made by the newspaper – the defendant – of the work created by the plaintiff – a minute of a meeting between the plaintiff, Paddy Ashdown, then the leader of the Liberal Democrats, and the Prime Minister of the UK – was an infringement of copyright: a use of the expression, and not of the idea, that was beyond the necessary requirement for reporting the information, that is, a substantial and literal portion of the copyrighted work.

However, there are still important problematic interferences between intellectual property systems and other human rights, such as the potential imbalance provided by disproportionate use of technical measures for controlling access and use of works and other subject matters.

---

96. *Harper & Row Publishers v. Nation Enterprises*, 471 US 539, at 558.

Chapter 6

Proportionality and Balancing Within the Objectives for Intellectual Property Protection

Henning Grosse Ruse-Khan[*]

6.1   INTRODUCTION: PROPORTIONALITY, ARTICLE 7
TRIPS, AND HUMAN RIGHTS

The principle of proportionality is a concept with different connotations; it has distinct functions and is employed in various environments.[1] For example, it can be applied for the protection of human rights and fundamental freedoms to constrain the ways a state can exercise its power over its citizens. In this 'classic' case, the interference with a fundamental right affected must be proportional in relation to the legitimate public policy interests realized by the state measure.[2] It can further serve as a general mechanism for the balance of interests; as a standard for judicial review; a

*   I am grateful to Federico Ortino for some initial inspirations on the topic. All errors, of course, remain mine.
1. For an overview on these distinct contexts of application of proportionality, *see* M. Andenas & S. Zleptnig, 'Proportionality and Balancing in WTO Law: A Comparative Perspective', 20(1) (2007) *Cambridge Review of International Affairs*, at 2-3.
2. This can be further refined by requiring the state to pursue *suitable or appropriate* objectives, which it must implement in a way which is *necessary* (i.e., is least onerous to the citizen) and further *not disproportionate or excessive* in relation to the citizen's interests affected.

tool to determine the scope of legal norms or as a limit on the power of judges.[3] The role as a balancing tool can relate to state versus private interest – but can equally concern the weighting between any other type of (competing) individual or public interests.

It is this search for equilibrium between distinct values and objectives which will be at stake in this chapter: I plan to analyse the role of a proportional *balancing of interests* within intellectual property (IP) protection as part of international economic regulation. In this context, my scrutiny concentrates on the World Trade Organization (WTO) Agreement on Trade-Related Intellectual Property Rights (TRIPS). This is not only because it has – being a key element of the law of the WTO – an obvious link to the regulation of global trade and to international economic law. TRIPS, more than other international agreements on IP protection, contains several provisions which allow or even call for a balance of interests. Nevertheless, TRIPS has for quite some time been perceived by various (mainly developing) countries, civil society groups and Non-Governmental Organizations (NGOs) focusing on interests such as public health, the environment or human rights as overall biased towards the economic interests of (industrialized) countries and their industries. This raises the question whether the balancing provisions under TRIPS – in particular, in comparison to other regulatory systems of international economic law – are either not effective in itself, are not applied in an effective manner or, of course, whether the perception is incorrect. One needs to add that with the proliferation of free trade and other forms of bilateral or regional agreements (here commonly referred to as FTAs) which often contain chapters on IP that go beyond the minimum standards of TRIPS (i.e., are 'TRIPS-plus'), TRIPS increasingly does not look that bad after all.[4]

The analysis in front of the reader here needs to be understood as part of broader comparative research on balancing of diverging interests within international economic regulation. In the First Edition of this book, this chapter marked the starting point with a focus on Article 7 TRIPS as a tool for a (proportional) balancing of interests within International IP Law and its implementation in domestic IP rules. Further research took a closer look at the combined operation of Article 7 & Article 8 TRIPS, their application in the practice of WTO dispute settlement, and juxtaposed these IP-specific approaches to those in general exception clauses such as Article XX of the General Agreement on Tariffs and Trade (GATT) and Article XIV of the General Agreement on Trade in Service (GATS) (as the main operative provisions on international regulation on trade in goods and services which

---

3. *See* M. Andenas & S. Zleptnig, as n. 1 above, at 2-3.
4. *See* H. Grosse Ruse-Khan, *The Protection of Intellectual Property in International Law* (OUP, 2016) Chapter 5.

allow for weighing trade and non-trade interest).[5] Even around fifteen years after the First edition of this book had been published, I continue with comparative work in this context – for example, on international investment law and the role of customary international law for employing various balancing concepts in international IP law.

The focus on Article 7 in this chapter is motivated by the following considerations: Article 7 – together with Preamble, which will equally be analysed – provides evidence of the objectives of TRIPS. Under the principles of interpretation of public international law that inform the proper construction of WTO law, a treaties' objective is, next to the ordinary meaning and its context, a key source for determining the meaning of individual treaty provisions.[6] As the arguably most important expression of the TRIPS 'objectives', Article 7, therefore, can play a crucial role in interpretation. This is, in particular, the case when broad and open legal concepts within TRIPS treaty language are at issue. Here, the balancing objectives expressed in Article 7 are likely to have significant influence for the ability of WTO Member States to balance different interests addressed in, or affected by, IP protection.[7] As discussed further below, WTO members agreed in the Doha Declaration on TRIPS and Public Health that the principal way to achieve mutual supportiveness between the protection of public health and IP is by means of an interpretation and implementation of the agreement that is based on Articles 7 and 8 TRIPS.[8] In so far, this chapter aims to lay down a conceptual framework for interpreting individual provisions of TRIPS in light of the balancing objectives expressed in Article 7. As mentioned, it is especially useful when construing the meaning of broad and open terms in TRIPS – such as 'normal exploitation', 'legitimate interests', and (un)reasonableness in Articles 13, 17, 26 (2) and 30 TRIPS – as in those cases, the ordinary meaning of these terms is not necessarily decisive or even helpful.

Developments since the First Edition of this book call for a revision of this chapter. On the one hand, the continued proliferation of FTAs with TRIPS-plus commitments on the protection of IP to some extent challenges the normative role of TRIPS, and within it, of course, its provisions on

---

5. *See* H. Grosse Ruse-Khan, 'A Comparative Analysis of Policy Space in WTO Law', (2008) Max Planck Institute for Intellectual Property, Competition & Tax Law Research Paper Series No. 08-02, http://ssrn.com/abstract=1309526; H. Grosse Ruse-Khan, 'The (Non) Use of Treaty Object and Purpose in Intellectual Property Disputes in the WTO', Max Planck Institute for Intellectual Property & Competition Law Research Paper No. 11-15, (28 September 2011), http://ssrn.com/abstract=1939859 and H. Grosse Ruse-Khan, as n. 4 above, Chapters 10 and 13.
6. Compare Article 31(1) of the Vienna Convention on the Law of Treaties (VCLT) and the detailed discussion in section 6.3.2.4 below.
7. *See also* H. Grosse Ruse-Khan, as n. 4 above, Chapter 13.
8. *See Ministerial Conference*, Doha Declaration on the TRIPS Agreement and Public Health (WT/MIN(01)/DEC/2), 20 November 2001, para. 4, 5a).

'Objectives' (Article 7) and 'Principles' (Article 8). This revised chapter, hence, also addresses the role of the balancing concepts expressed in Article 7 for FTAs. On the other hand, WTO dispute settlement – which for a long time had effectively neglected Articles 7 (and 8) TRIPS – has, with the *Australia – Plain Packaging* Panel Report[9] now properly engaged with these provisions. The revised version of this chapter considers the role afforded to Articles 7 (and 8) in that dispute, and aligns this with broader conceptions of balancing public and private interests in international (economic) law, as expressed, for example, in the customary right to regulate.

One might wonder what all of this has to do with human rights. For a couple of years now, the narrative on TRIPS and perhaps IP, more generally, has shifted within the human rights community. From a confrontational approach that identified 'apparent conflicts' between IP and human rights – further reiterating that 'actual or potential conflict exists between the implementation of the TRIPS Agreement and the realization of economic, social and cultural rights, in particular, the rights to self-determination, food, housing, work, health and education'[10] – the tone has become much more accommodating.[11] Instead of insisting on conflict and the arguably not very strong legal arguments about a principal 'primacy of human rights obligations under international law over economic policies and agreements'[12] (what I have called the 'stick' approach), human rights advocacy has moved towards offering IP lawyers a 'carrot'. The carrot, in this case, is to show the international IP system and its lawyers a way out of the dilemma (of being potential perpetrators of human rights violations) by directing them to legal mechanisms and tools *within* their own system that can ensure human rights compliance: From early calls to 'protect the social function of intellectual property', human rights organs have come to learn the language of the IP system and to utilize it for their purpose. Already in a 2001 UN Report on the impact of TRIPS on human rights, a core section is devoted to a 'human rights approach to the TRIPS Agreement', while others deal with the 'Operational aspects of the IP system [vis-à-vis] access to drugs'.[13] These sections highlight TRIPS flexibilities such as compulsory licensing (Article

---

9. *Australia – Certain Measures Concerning Trademarks, Geographical Indications and Other Plain Packaging Requirements Applicable to Tobacco Products and Packaging (Australia – Plain Packaging)*, Panel Report, 28 June 2018 (WTO/DS435/P).
10. *See* UN High Commissioner for Human Rights – Sub-Commission on Promotion and Protection of Human Rights, *Intellectual Property Rights and Human Rights* (17 August 2000, Resolution 2000/7, U.N. Doc.E/CN.4/Sub.2/RES/2000/7), at para. 2; and the preamble of Resolution 2001/21 by the Commission on Human Rights, Sub-Commission on the Promotion and Protection of Human Rights on *Intellectual property rights and human rights* of 16 August 2001.
11. *See* the analysis in H. Grosse Ruse-Khan, as n. 4 above, para. 8.88-100.
12. Resolution 2001/21, at para. 3; *see also* Resolution 2000/7, at para. 3.
13. UN Economic and Social Council, 'The Impact of the Agreement on Trade Related Aspects of Intellectual Property Rights on Human Rights – Report of the High Commissioner', (27 June 2001, E/CN.4/Sub.2/2001/13), paras 20-28, 42-50.

31), exceptions and limitations to IP rights (Articles 30, 17, 13), measures against anti-competitive practices (Articles 8, 40) and international exhaustion (Article 6). They urge WTO members to 'use this operational flexibility in ways that would be fully compatible with the promotion and protection of human rights'.[14]

Over time, this approach has been fine-tuned by urging reliance on specifically identified, and comprehensively described flexibilities in TRIPS as essential from the human rights perspective.[15] Concerns about human rights compliance turn into 'concerns regarding the implementation of TRIPS flexibilities'; and restricting them, especially via 'TRIPS plus standards (...) in free trade agreements' is indicative for human rights violations.[16] The full use of TRIPS flexibilities, especially those mentioned in the Doha Declaration, hence, becomes the principal benchmark for human rights compliance. This shows that human rights organs have shifted focus towards the balancing mechanisms *within* the IP system.[17] The main reason for this is the cross-fertilization amongst critical IP and human rights scholarship (as, for example, represented in this book); as well as the increasing amount of IP-expertise amongst academics, NGOs and International Organizations (IOs) that deal with human rights. In a way, they have internalized, and perhaps re-constructed, tools such as compulsory licensing, exceptions to exclusive rights and limitations to the protectable subject matter for their own purpose and to maximize their own system's rationality: As means selected to give effect to human rights within the international IP system.

---

14. *Ibid.*, para. 28.
15. United Nations – Human Rights Council, *Report of the Special Rapporteur on the Right of Everyone to the Enjoyment of the Highest Attainable Standard of Physical and Mental Health* (31 March 2009, A/HRC/11/12), paras 25-55. *See also* United Nations, Report of the Special Rapporteur on the right to food, *The Right to Food. Seed Policies and the Right to Food: Enhancing Agrobiodiversity and Encouraging Innovation* (23 July 2009, A/64/170), paras 28-33.
16. United Nations, *Report of the Special Rapporteur on the Right to Food*, as n. 15 above, paras 56-67, 75-93.
17. *See also* the initiatives that eventually led to the Marrakesh Treaty to Facilitate Access to Published Works for Persons who are Blind, Visually Impaired, or Otherwise Print Disabled (Marrakesh Treaty). It has been placed in the 'human right to read' context (*see* the World Blind Union's 'Marrakesh Treaty – Right to Read' Campaign – online at http://www.worldblindunion.org/english/our-work/our-priorities/pages/right-2-read-campaign.aspx and is supported for 'its human rights and social development dimension' (*see* the statement made by India as the first country ratifying the Marrakesh Treaty (Geneva, 30 June 2014, PR/2014/761), http://www.wipo.int/pressroom/en/articles/2014/article_0008.html). Essentially, the Marrakesh Treaty aims to achieve *human rights objectives* by using tools of the international IP system – in particular by introducing *mandatory minimum exceptions* to facilitate (1) access to works by VIPs and (2) the cross-border exchange of copies made in formats accessible for VIPs. For a discussion on how this goes significantly beyond the idea of simply reading IP treaties with human rights glasses, *see* H. Grosse Ruse-Khan, as n. 4 above, para. 12.15-26.

From a technical legal perspective, this 'capture' or 'colonization' of key elements of the international IP system has to function by means of *interpretation* – an interpretation of TRIPS guided by human rights norms and considerations.[18] And that is where Article 7 TRIPS can play a major role as a tool for integration – in this case, opening the door for human rights considerations within its balancing objectives. Since WTO dispute settlement is traditionally rather cautious with regard to the reliance on external (i.e., non-WTO) norms,[19] an internal balancing mechanism which can be employed for human rights arguments then appears as the second-best solution. In the following, this chapter scrutinizes the role of Article 7 TRIPS as such a balancing mechanism: One which allows the incorporation of external interests, including human rights considerations. Combined with its role as treaty objective in the interpretation and implementation of TRIPS, it serves as the perhaps most important horizontal tool for integrating and accommodating competing concerns within IP protection and for tailoring the required balance to the domestic circumstances of individual WTO members.

6.2	THE ROLE FOR PROPORTIONALITY IN THE CONTEXT OF INTERNATIONAL ECONOMIC LAW

In order to point out the need for an effective balancing system, this review of the TRIPS objectives shall first be placed in the relevant global regulatory context: Common denominator in areas of international economic rule-making (such as trade, investment, IP) is their significant potential impact on domestic regulation of (non-trade and non-economic) societal interests for the sake of a harmonized global economy. While this certainly has its

---

18. A good example is the approach taken by L. Forman, 'An Elementary Consideration of Humanity? Linking Trade-Related Intellectual Property Rights to the Human Right to Health in International Law' 14(2) (2011) *Journal of World Intellectual Property* 155, 157-162.

19. While quite a bit depends on the factual and legal circumstances of the individual case at issue, WTO dispute settlement organs have generally avoided to apply non-WTO rules unless there is a specific reference or other means within WTO law to incorporate such rules – *see* generally L. Bartels, 'Applicable Law in WTO Dispute Settlement Proceedings' (2001) 35(3) *Journal of World Trade* 499; J. Pauwelyn, 'The Role of Public International Law in the WTO: How Far Can We Go?' 95(3) (2001) *American Journal of International Law* 535; D. McRae, 'The WTO in International Law: Tradition Continued or New Frontier?' 3(1) (2000) *Journal of International Economic Law* 27; J. Trachtman, 'The Domain of WTO Dispute Settlement Proceedings' 40(2) (1999) *Harvard International Law Review* 333; and G. Marceau, 'Conflict of Norms and Conflicts of Jurisdiction, The Relationship Between WTO Agreements and MEAs and Other Treaties' 35(6) (2001) *Journal of World Trade* 1081.

advantages[20] for those able to access and utilize the system for their own benefit and, at least in the area of classic trade liberalization, allows countries to rely on their 'comparative advantage';[21] by the same token, it can be detrimental for interests not sufficiently addressed and recognized within this increasingly comprehensive regulatory regime. This in itself may already provide for sufficient justification to incorporate balancing mechanisms such as proportionality tests in order to ensure due recognition of these (non-trade or non-economic) interests. One can further describe this common denominator among many areas of international economic law by the metaphor of extending, especially since the wave of economic liberalization since the early 1990s, international rules *'behind the border'*[22] of the nation state to affect various societal values, interests and lifestyles. Above all, this term has been used to paraphrase key developments in the transformation of the former GATT system mainly concerned with trade in goods towards the creation of the WTO with its comprehensive body of rules. Instead of increasing market access (for foreign goods) by simply binding and reducing the tariffs to be paid at the national border,[23] trade regulation in the last decades has moved beyond this and increasingly imposes obligations on national governments to adopt substantive rules in various areas traditionally not affected by international economic rule-making.[24] For example, freer

---

20. For example, by reducing transaction costs in international commerce, providing security and foreseeability on a global level as well as reducing various types of barriers to enter national markets.

21. A general explanation of the theory of comparative advantage, its origins in Adam Smith's and David Ricardo's work, its main argument for specialization and (free) international trade and its current implications can be found in P. Van den Bossche, *The Law and Policy of the World Trade Organization* (Cambridge, 2005) at 19-24; For an Economist's perspective *see* S. Brakman, et al., *Nations and Firms in the Global Economy* (Cambridge, 2006) at 63-95.

22. *See* generally C. Arup, *The New World Trade Organization Agreements* (Cambridge, 2000), at 5-13; TRIPS itself is often perceived as a prominent illustration of this trend to impose obligations in areas which where traditionally regarded in the purview of domestic regulation – also referred to as 'positive integration': *see* B. Hoekman & M. Kostecki, *The Political Economy of the World Trading System* (Oxford, 2001) at 283 as well as the further discussion on the role of TRIPS in this context below.

23. As it has been the 'classic' way of trade liberalization during the first six Rounds of Negotiations under the GATT 1947 – *see* a detailed history in A. Loewenfeld, *International Economic Law* (Oxford, 2003), at 46-55; M. Matsushita, T.J. Schoenbaum & P.C. Mavroidis, *The World Trade Organization* (Oxford, 2003), at 4-5; C. Arup, as n. 22 above, at 45.

24. *See* Matsushita, Schoenbaum, Mavroidis, as n. 23 above, at 595-596. While the initial rationale (during the Tokyo Round) was to counter the protectionists trade policies adopted by various key trading nations in the 1970s, this was extended to a much broader and deeper agenda for trade liberalization during Uruguay Round of Negotiations covering not only 'new areas' such as services, investment and intellectual property but also binding all Members of the newly established World Trade Organization to the so far voluntary codes on non-tariff barriers, subsidies and trade remedies; *see* A. Loewenfeld, as n. 23 above, at 54-67.

trade in goods has been realized by extending regulation and harmonization from reducing tariff barriers to eliminating *non-tariff barriers*[25] and turning attention towards so far untouched areas by considering them as *'trade-related'*.[26] Under these two concepts, basically, any field of domestic norm-setting may be subsumed provided it has a potential impact on trade: It, therefore, includes not only government procurement and subsidies policies[27] but also extends to (non-harmonized) domestic technical standards and safety regulations; diverging opinions on what constitutes a threat to plant, animal or human health and national measures adopted in their protection and further environmental, consumer protection as well as labour standards and workers' rights.[28] The overreaching and dominant notion is to perceive the world from a trade perspective and to aim for regulating all kinds of human activities as soon as they have a significant impact on free trade and economic globalization. As *C Arup* puts it: This tendency is sure to subject many more matters – at the core of economics, politics, cultures and law – to the influence of trade norms and processes.[29] The key areas of trade rules concerning goods and services within the WTO, however, do provide for some regulatory tools to recognize interests not motivated by trade liberalization.[30] Since there is, prima facie, no directly equivalent rule in TRIPS,[31] giving effect to these interests via an *interpretation* of key provisions then appears even more relevant.

The last decades of international IP regulation, in general, and the TRIPS Agreement, in particular, are, to a large extent, based on the very same trade perspective and should be analysed in this context.[32] One can find various examples for this increasing tendency to reach behind the border: To

---

25. *See* M. Trebilcock & R. Howse, *The Regulation of International Trade* (3rd edn, London 2005), at 24.

26. Compare C. Arup, as n. 22 above, at 11.

27. M. Trebilcock & R. Howse, as n. 25 above, at 24.

28. Compare on the societal issues Matsushita, Schoenbaum, Mavroidis, as n. 23 above, at 599-607.

29. C. Arup, as n. 22 above, at 5.

30. *See* Article XX GATT and Article XIV GATS in particular. For a discussion on the comparative policy space these provisions offer, *see* H. Grosse Ruse-Khan (2008), as n. 5 above.

31. This appears to be so especially in the case of Article 8 TRIPS as it requires 'measures necessary to protect public health and nutrition, and to promote the public interest in sectors of vital importance to their socio-economic and technological development' to be '*consistent with the provisions of this Agreement*' (emphasis added); on this issue *see* in particular H. Grosse Ruse-Khan, as n. 4 above, paras 13.03-16; C. Correa, *Trade Related Aspects of Intellectual Property Rights* (Oxford, 2007), 103-115; ICTSD/UNCTAD, *Resource Book on TRIPS and Development: An Authoritative and Practical Guide to the TRIPS Agreement* (Geneva, 2005), at Part 1, Ch. 6 (2.2, 3.2, 4. and 7.) – online available at www.iprsonline.org/unctadictsd/ResourceBookIndex.htm.

32. If this is so, it is reasonable to demand also in the area of *(trade-related)* protection of intellectual property for equivalent systems and regulatory tools for weighing distinct or competing interests – *see* the further discussion below.

some extent, the continuous move from mere obligations to provide national treatment and basic protections for foreign right holders towards more and more detailed and increasingly comprehensive minimum standards can be compared with the trend from reducing tariffs towards the regulation of non-tariff barriers.[33] However, even with an increasing amount of substantive minimum standards, especially in relation to copyright and neighbouring rights under the Berne and Rome Conventions, the international IP regimes did not necessarily have an extensive impact on domestic policies: First of all, countries could afford, if necessary, a rather lax implementation of the international agreements – and might do so whenever domestic interests seemed to be at stake or when domestic industrial policy demanded it.[34] While the key international IP regimes provided, in theory, for a system of resolving disputes in front of the International Court of Justice (ICJ), this option was subject to reservations and had never been exercised.[35] Second, the (more or less unlimited)[36] option to foresee exceptions and limitations to the exclusive rights in industrial property mandated by the international regime allowed to give due regard to various interests on the national implementation level. This, however, has changed since the TRIPS Agreement catapulted a provision imposing three conditions on possible exceptions to the reproduction right in copyright law to become the general template for limiting the ability of domestic policymakers to give effect to societal values and interests.[37] Post TRIPS, the 'three-step test' has continued to proliferate in the World Intellectual Property Organization (WIPO) (copyright and related rights) treaties, as well as bilateral and regional FTAs.

---

33. Here, the various revisions of the Berne Convention on the Protection of Literary and Artistic Works serve as prominent evidence (on the revisions of the Berne Convention *see* S. Ricketson & J. Ginsburg, *International Copyright and Neighbouring Rights*, Vol. I (2nd edn, Oxford, 2006), at 84-134. One, however, must contend that trade liberalization under GATT has – next to reducing tariffs also always consisted of an obligation to provide national treatment as well as most favourite nation (MFN) treatment, compare Articles I and III GATT 1947.
34. For historic examples for tailoring the level of IP protection to serve domestic industry interests, *see* N. Kumar, 'Intellectual Property Rights, Technology and Economic Development: Experiences of Asian Countries', Study Paper 1b to the Report of the Commission on Intellectual Property Rights (CIPR), Integrating Intellectual Property and Development Policy (London, 2002) – online available at www.iprcommission.org.
35. T. Cottier, 'The Prospects for Intellectual Property in GATT' (1991) *Common Market Law Review* 393.
36. For the limited harmonization in the area of patent law and the resulting freedom to provide for exceptions in national laws, *see* J. Straus, Implications of the TRIPS Agreement in the Field of Patent Law, in Beier & Schricker, *From GATT to TRIPS – IIC Studies* Vol. 18 (New York, 1996) at 170-175.
37. On the so-called three-step test with its origins in Article 9(2) of the Berne Convention and which can be found in Article 13 TRIPS as well as – in modified forms – in Articles 17, 26(2) and 30 TRIPS, *see* M. Senftleben, 'Towards a Horizontal Standard for Limiting Intellectual Property Rights?' 4 (2006) *International Review of Intellectual Property and Competition Law*, at 407-438.

Furthermore, TRIPS itself can be seen as evidence for the tendency for 'positive integration' and reaching 'behind the border':[38] As its name indicates, it addresses *trade-related* aspects of IP rights and thereby transports IP protection into the realms of world trade law where it is perceived mainly from a trade perspective.[39] This perspective on IP regulation is based on the insight that since the 1980s, more and more (high-tech) products and services are traded globally which require significant investment in their initial development but are easy to copy or imitate. The lack of harmonized and adequate protection for these products or services in export markets prevented right holders to access these markets: The fear of imitation or copying and thus effectively served as barriers to trade.[40] This focus on the interests of right holders and their home countries with a comparative advantage in innovation has not always been the prevailing view in trade theory and practice:[41] Interestingly, from a traditional 'GATT perspective',[42] IP rights have rather been viewed as (legitimate) barriers to trade: Due to their territorial nature, they allow the title-holder to prevent imports of goods containing the protected subject matter (or the provision of services building on it), in this way erect artificial barriers between countries and thereby prevent free trade.[43]

From the perspective of the main proponents of the new IP trade connection, TRIPS was to ensure a reliable, globally harmonized, and high

---

38. *See* B. Hoekman & M. Kostecki, as n. 22 above, at 283, further C. Correa, as n. 31 above, at 10: From the former GATT perspective with its focus on trade in (physical) goods, the mere fact that rules on IP protection became part of trade law implicated a significant extension of the scope of trade regulation and its interference with domestic policies.

39. *See also* A. Kur, 'A New Framework for Intellectual Property Rights – Horizontal Issues', 35(1) (2004) *International Review of Intellectual Property and Competition Law* 4-7; C. Arup, as n. 22 above, at 11-13 and especially H. Ullrich, Technology Protection According to TRIPS, in Beier & Schricker, *From GATT to TRIPS – IIC Studies* Vol. 18 (New York, 1996) 357 et seq.

40. Compare Matsushita, Schoenbaum, Mavroidis, as n. 23 above, at 396-397; M. Trebilcock & R. Howse, as n. 25 above, at 397-400.

41. For a compact analysis of global IP protection based on the trade theory of comparative advantage, *see* M. Trebilcock & R Howse, as n. 25 above, at 400-40: Depending on whether a country has – in any given field – a comparative advantage in innovation or imitation, overall welfare gains will be the highest if the domestic IP policies is tailored to this advantage; *see also* the discussion on the need for balancing tools to respond to the domestic economic and welfare interests in section 6.3.2.2 below.

42. Expression of this perception is Article XX(d) GATT which allows GATT contracting parties to justify inconsistencies with other GATT provisions (and thereby to restrict free trade) if necessary to secure compliance with laws protecting patents, trademarks and copyrights; for a detailed discussion, *see* H. Grosse Ruse-Khan, as n. 4 above, Chapter 10. *See also* P. Katzenberger & A. Kur, TRIPS and Intellectual Property, in Beier & Schricker, *From GATT to TRIPS – IIC Studies* Vol. 18 (New York, 1996) at 5.

43. Compare C. Correa, as n. 31 above, at 2-3; H. Ullrich, as n. 39 above, at 376. *See* the discussion of GATT disputes – in particular *United States – Section 337 of the Tariff Act of 1930 (US – Sec. 337)*, Report of the Panel adopted on 7 November 1989 – in the 1980s brought by the European Communities (EC) and Canada against what was perceived as

standard of protection – preferably for all subject matter where innovation is costly and imitation is cheap and (relatively) easy to perform. In order to achieve this, it had to overcome the perceived shortcomings of international IP property described above. This necessitated a significant curtailment of the freedom to tailor IP protection – in economic terms – to suit the domestic comparative advantage[44] and further to address non-economic domestic interests and societal values without interference from trade rules. Post-TRIPS, this trend has further accelerated: International IP law has, despite some early and some more recent multilateral advances negotiated at the WIPO in the field of copyright,[45] primarily developed via a network of bilateral and regional agreements. For reasons explained in detail elsewhere, since the mid-nineties, countries interested in further increasing IP standards have had much more success in negotiating IP (as well as other trade and trade-related issues) in fora outside the WTO and WIPO.[46] With multilateral solutions increasingly difficult to achieve, the world has, therefore, witnessed an unprecedented proliferation of FTAs. A brief look at the current numbers of bilateral and regional agreements provides a good indication of the scale of this phenomenon: On its website, the WTO, as of 4 January 2019, counts 291 so-called regional trade agreements (RTAs) that are currently in force (with a much higher number of around 700 for which notifications had been received by the GATT/WTO).[47] What all RTAs in the WTO have in common is that they are reciprocal trade agreements which further liberalize trade between two or more countries. As the data from WIPO below suggests, quite a lot of these agreements contain a chapter with obligations for the protection and enforcement of IP rights. Typically, IP obligations are requested for the benefit of IP-dependent export industries of one (or more) of the trading partners – and agreed by the other one(s) in exchange for commitments which benefit its own export industries, such as enhanced

---

trade-restrictive over-enforcement of IP rights at the US border (especially via exclusion orders issued by the International Trade Commission) in H. Grosse Ruse-Khan, as n. 4 above, paras 10.12-27.

44. Compare M. Trebilcock & R. Howse, as n. 25 above, at 400-401 and the brief explanations in n. 49 below.

45. *See,* for example, 1996 WIPO Copyright Treaty, 2186 UNTS 121 ('WCT') and more recently, for example, 2013 Marrakesh Treaty to Facilitate Access to Published Works for Persons who are Blind, Visually Impaired, or Otherwise Print Disabled, TRT/MARRAKESH/001 ('Marrakesh Treaty').

46. On the notion of 'regime shifting' in international IP law, *see* generally *see* L. Helfer, 'Regime Shifting: The TRIPS Agreement and New Dynamics of International Intellectual Property Lawmaking'. 29 (2004) *Yale Journal of International Law* 1, available online at http://ssrn.com/abstract=459740; K. Raustiala, 'Density & Conflict in International Intellectual Property Law' 31(6) (2006) *University of California, Los Angeles School of Law Research Paper,* online available at http://ssrn.com/abstract=914606.

47. *See* the WTO website on what it defines as 'regional trade agreements' (WTO (2019) Regional Trade Agreements, http://www.wto.org/english/tratop_e/region_e/region_e.htm).

market access for goods or services.[48] In early 2019, WIPO, in turn, counted 530 IP-related bilateral treaties – a significant portion of which are again agreements where enhanced IP protection and enforcement commitments accepted by one side function as a trade-off for concessions made by the other side.[49]

In comparison to TRIPS, today's IP provisions in bilateral or regional agreements are becoming ever more detailed, technology-specific, and prescriptive: They are often transplants of comprehensive IP protection or enforcement approaches that are extracted from the domestic law of the IP-demanding country – without considering whether they fit into the regulatory and technological environment of the receiving FTA partner country.[50] In addition, what is transplanted often leaves out the corresponding limits of IP protection and other checks and balances operating in the law of the transplanting country. All this led to IP regulation under TRIPS and especially its TRIPS-plus progeny reaching well beyond what had been known so far.[51] In summary, the following factors are indicative of the 'behind the border' effect of TRIPS: (1) A significant strengthening of the substantive protection of IP rights – especially patents and trademarks where previously almost no harmonized level of minimum rights existed on the international level; (2) expanding patents to cover pharmaceutical and agrochemical products, increasingly new uses and key areas of biotechnology, as well as introducing of new subject matter such as test data and patent term extensions; (3) potentially limiting the ability of national lawmakers to recognize and give effect to (non-trade) interests and societal values by introducing a set of conditions applicable to domestic exceptions to all key IP rights; (4) making TRIPS implementation subject to the new WTO dispute settlement mechanism and thereby ensuring not only the means to test the TRIPS compliance of domestic legislation, but also to retaliate by suspending obligations under WTO law in cases of non-compliance.[52] To that, TRIPS-plus provisions in FTAs have added: (1) an often unsustainable trade-off where the trade preferences expected in exchange for agreeing to additional IP protections erode once trading partners offer equivalent or

---

48. *See* generally H. Grosse Ruse – Khan, et al., 'Statement of Principles for Intellectual Property Provisions in Bilateral and Regional Agreements', 36(4) (2014) *European Intellectual Property Review*, 207-211, para. 5 – online available at http://www.ip.mpg.de/en/news/principles_for_intellectual_property_provisions_in_bilateral_and_regional_agreements.html.

49. *See* WIPO (2019) Treaty Secretariat: IP-Relevant Bilateral, http://www.wipo.int/wipolex/en/treaties/index_bilateral.jsp.

50. *See* H. Grosse Ruse-Khan et al., as n. 53 below.

51. With regard to the impact of TRIPS, *see* J. Watal, *Intellectual Property Rights in the WTO and Developing Countries* (The Hague, 2001) at 1-7.

52. For another list of issues exemplifying the increase of IP protection and its relevance in today's economy *see* D. Vaver, 'Intellectual Property: The State of the Art', 116(10) (2000) *Law Quarterly Review*, at 624-627.

better preferences to competitors; (2) transplants from domestic IP laws which are not well-suited in a different national context; and (3) ever more detailed and comprehensive rules – which are even less suitable for dynamic development of domestic IP laws.[53]

One can conclude that IP protection under TRIPS and its progeny provides various examples of international economic regulation extending into areas so far left untouched to the domestic policymaker. This tendency in TRIPS fits well into the overall trend to 'reach behind the border' in other areas of WTO law and its more recent counterparts. It is the context against which I plan to assess the options for a balanced and proportional weighing of interests within the TRIPS Agreement and compare them with its equivalents under GATT and GATS. In this chapter, my focus will be on Article 7 TRIPS as the main balancing tool available to national policymakers. At this point, one might offer two hypothesizes, which then should be tested against the normative content of the balancing mechanisms in current international economic regulation:

(1) The increased impact of trade rules on a wide range of domestic policies calls for strong regulatory tools which allow the recognition, and if necessary, the *giving of preference*, to distinct or competing interests in a transparent and rational process of balancing. The more intense (reaching 'behind the border', impacting on other areas of domestic policies) international regulation becomes; the stronger is the need for including a comprehensive and flexible regime which takes into account all interests affected. Its inclusion in trade law is even more important since the forums in which a trade perspective prevails often have stronger and more effective mechanisms of regulation, monitoring of implementation and for ensuring effective enforcement than forums where competing interests are in focus.[54]

---

53. *See* the critique in H. Grosse Ruse-Khan, 'From TRIPS to FTAs and Back: Reconceptualizing the Role of a Multilateral Intellectual Property Framework in a TRIPS-plus World', *Netherlands Yearbook of International Law 2017*, (Springer, 2018), pp. 57-107 – online at: https://ssrn.com/abstract=3082718.
54. On the WTO Dispute Settlement Understanding compare P. Van den Bossche, as n. 21 above, at 173, 284-289, 299-304; This call should not be understood as intervening in debates about comprehensively integrating (or perhaps rather 'capturing') non-economic interests and concerns within laws and rules that are produced from an economic perspective, or broader concerns about coherence and fragmentation in international law (*see* 'Fragmentation of International Law: Difficulties Arising From the Diversification and Expansion of International Law', International Law Commission (U.N. Doc A/CN.4/L.682), 13 April 2006; M. Koskienniemi & P. Leino, 'Fragmentation of International Law?' 15(2002) *Leiden Journal of International Law* 553-579; G Teubner & A. Fischer-Lescano, Regime-Kollisionen: Zur Fragmentierung des Weltrechts (Frankfurt 2006) – an English version is available as 'Regime Collisions: The Vain Search for Legal Unity in the Fragmentation of Global Law' at www.jura.uni-frankfurt.de/ifawz1/teubner/dokumente/regimecollisions.pdf. My argument for fair balancing within the systems

(2) The need for proportionality exists as much in the area of international IP law as it does in other fields of international economic law with a similar potential impact on non-economic or non-trade interests. The mechanisms for balancing should, therefore, allow an *equivalent level* of recognition and enforcement of these interests.

6.3   TRIPS OBJECTIVES AS NORMATIVE INPUT FOR THE BALANCING EXERCISE

The TRIPS Agreement includes several provisions which are designed for or at least allow a balancing of interests. While they seldom refer directly to the principle of proportionality, contain an explicit proportionality test or require measures to be 'proportional', a number of norms include broad and undefined legal concepts such as reasonableness, legitimate interests, or necessity.[55] A key question then is how to conduct a proper balancing exercise under these concepts.

With Article 3.2 of the WTO Dispute Settlement Understanding (DSU) in mind, such ambiguous terms shall be clarified 'in accordance with customary rules of interpretation of public international law'. It is established WTO jurisprudence[56] that this provision calls in particular for the application of Articles 31 and 32 of the Vienna Convention on the Law of Treaties (VCLT) – even though the VCLT is not treaty law for all WTO Members.[57] The principal rule of treaty interpretation in Article 31(1) VCLT requires an interpreter to analyse the relevant treaty provisions 'in good faith in

---

which have a significant impact on 'outside' interests is not an implicit call for addressing all affected societal values from a trade or economic perspective. This may not solve the problem since the forum in which these values then are discussed is set up to deal with the regulation of global trade and (still) mainly occupied by trade experts and economists (instead of doctors, health officials, environmentalists, human rights advocates, unionists and other stake holders). My approach here should rather be seen as a pragmatic response oriented at current political realities in international rule-making. It focuses on how the existing system should be applied or modified to properly balance the interests at stake and to ensure that in the currently dominant trade forums matters are looked at also from a cultural, human rights, bio-diverse, public health, workers, etc. perspective. And that such balancing essentially occurs at the domestic level where the relevant interests overlap or even collide – hence, essentially calling for sufficient domestic policy space.

55. *See* Articles 3(2), 8(1) and (2), 13, 17, 26(2), 27(2), 30, 31, 34, 39(2), 62, 63 and 73 TRIPS, which rely on such concepts as well as Articles 46 and 47 TRIPS which both explicitly require proportionality.
56. *United States – Standards for Reformulated and Conventional Gasoline* (WT/DS2/AB/R), Appellate Body Report (29 April 1996), 3 at 16; *India – Patent Protection for Pharmaceutical and Agricultural Chemical Products* (WT/DS50/AB/R), Appellate Body Report (19 December 1997), para. 46; *United States – Countervailing Duties on Certain Corrosion-Resistant Carbon Steel Flat Products from Germany* (WT/DS213/AB/R) Appellate Body Report (28 November 2002), paras 61-62.
57. Several WTO Members, notably the USA, have not ratified the Vienna Convention.

accordance with the ordinary meaning to be given to the terms of the treaty in their context and in the light of its object and purpose'.[58] Thus, next to a determination of their ordinary meaning, a proper context analysis (whose elements are defined in Article 31(2) VCLT and to which the interpreter should add the further elements listed in Article 31(3) VCLT), and due regard to the treaty's object and purpose will have a significant impact on the interpretation of the concepts exemplified above.[59]

For this reason, the focus of this chapter on proportionality and balancing is a scrutiny of the meaning and interpretative role of the object and purpose of TRIPS. It begins by looking at the preamble and then moves on to discuss in more detail Article 7 TRIPS. After identifying the two poles in between which IP regulation must be balanced, the chapter attempts to answer the question on the WTO Members' ability to engage in a domestically tailored balance of interests. It then examines the traditional role of the (TRIPS) objectives in (WTO) treaty interpretation. A central issue here is whether the Doha Declarations have effectively strengthened the role of Article 7 TRIPS in the interpretative process – something on which the Panel Report in *Australia – Plain Packaging* has shed some light now. Before concluding with some general remarks which consider the relevance of the TRIPS objectives in an environment increasingly determined by bilateral and regional FTAs; and which again refer to the global (economic) context, the other main WTO dispute which has examined the role of TRIPS' objectives is re-evaluated on the basis of the consequences of Doha and *Australia – Plain Packaging*.

6.3.1 THE PREAMBLE OF TRIPS

Next to Article 7, which is explicitly entitled 'Objectives', the preamble of the TRIPS Agreement is generally perceived as an integral part of the agreement which often indicates its underlying principles, objectives and

---

58. For a detailed analysis on the interpretative role of a treaty's object and purpose in the context of the WTO *see* section 6.4 below.
59. In the context of TRIPS, the importance of the 'Objectives' and 'Principles' of TRIPS (as expressed in Articles 7 & 8 TRIPS) for interpreting its provisions has been stressed also by para. 5(a) of the Doha Declaration, as n. 8 above. For a more detailed discussion of its role for TRIPS interpretation and balancing of interests, *see* the analysis of Article 7 below. On the importance of the Preamble (in that case the Preamble to the WTO Agreement) for determining the intentions of the WTO Members *see United States – Import Prohibition of Certain Shrimp and Shrimp Products* (WT/DS58/AB/R), Appellate Body Report (12 October 1998). On the role of the context compare *United States – Countervailing Duties on Certain Corrosion Resistant Carbon Steel Flat Products from Germany*, as n. 56 above, at paras 65, 69 and 104.

purpose.[60] According to Article 31(2) VCLT, a preamble also forms part of the context of a treaty. The TRIPS preamble thus can play an interpretive role both as a relevant context for other TRIPS provisions as well as an indication of the objective and purpose of TRIPS. In its here relevant parts, the Preamble states:

> *Members, Desiring to reduce distortions and impediments to international trade, and taking into account the need to promote effective and adequate protection of intellectual property rights, and to ensure that measures and procedures to enforce intellectual property rights do not themselves become barriers to legitimate trade;*
>
> *Recognizing, to this end, the need for new rules and disciplines concerning:*
>
> *[...]*
>
> (b) the provision of *adequate* standards and principles concerning the availability, scope and use of trade-related intellectual property rights;
>
> (c) the provision of *effective and appropriate* means for the enforcement of trade-related intellectual property rights, taking into account differences in national legal systems;
>
> *[...]*
>
> *Recognizing the underlying public policy objectives of national systems for the protection of intellectual property, including developmental and technological objectives;*
>
> *Recognizing also the special needs of the least-developed country Members in respect of maximum flexibility in the domestic implementation of laws and regulations in order to enable them to create a sound and viable technological base.*[61]

At its core, the relevant sections of the preamble refer to the need for adequate and appropriate – but equally effective protection of IP; and ask us to keep in mind the underlying public policy objectives for IP protection. Three related observations can be drawn from this summation that – taken together – reflect a series of individual equilibriums addressed in the various (other) paragraphs of the preamble:[62] First, the terms 'adequate' and 'appropriate' imply an assessment on the basis of an individual situation and tailored to the specific circumstances of the case at hand. This has been argued as recognition of the need for policy space in the domestic

---

60. Compare *Canada – Patent Protection of Pharmaceutical Products* (WT/DS114/R), Panel Report (17 March 2000), para. 7.26; D. Gervais, *The TRIPS Agreement – Drafting History and Analysis* (2nd edn, London, 2003), para. 2.08; C. Correa, as n. 31 above, at 1.

61. Preamble of the TRIPS Agreement – certain paragraphs omitted and emphasis added.

62. On the distinct sets of complementary interests to be balanced *see* D. Gervais, as n. 60 above, at 2.10.

implementation of IP protection – in accordance with national policy objectives and for the premise that 'one size does not fit all'.[63] It further follows from the unequivocal call for maximum flexibility available to least developed WTO Members in the preamble.[64] While not explicitly mandating a balance of interests or proportional treatment, the recognition of policy space certainly *allows* this to take place – in line with the specific economic, technological and developmental needs of the society.

Secondly, the protection of IP shall be *effective*. While this hardly can be said to establish an absolute and uniform or common standard of protection (which then could be enforced globally); it nevertheless emphasizes the need for the domestic protection of IP which is efficient, is successful or has an effect[65] – both on the substantive-as well as the enforcement level. One could be tempted to view this as a clear statement in favour of strong IP rights which must be made available and enforceable for the right holders of IP protected subject matter. However, the effectiveness, success or efficiency so required is no end in itself but should relate to the underlying policy objectives (of national systems) for the protection of IP.[66] Among other provisions,[67] this follows from the third observation I wish to highlight from the preamble:

> Members, Recognizing the underlying public policy objectives of national systems for the protection of intellectual property, including developmental and technological objectives.

IP protection under TRIPS thus needs to be *effective in achieving its goals* – the *raison d'entré* for its existence.[68] According to the quotation from the preamble above, these underlying policy objectives, in turn, can include

---

63. 'Global Economic Prospects and the Developing Countries, 2002', World Bank (Washington DC, 2001), at 129; on the historical evidence for tailoring national IP policy and regulation to the domestic economic, technological and development needs of a country *see* further Commission on Intellectual Property Rights (CIPR), as n. 34 above, at 18-20; and especially the two related background papers Z. Khan, Study Paper 1a: Intellectual Property and Economic Development: Lessons from American and European History; and N. Kumar, as n. 34 above; For an economic justification on this point *see* M. Trebilcock & R. Howse, as n. 25 above, at 397-401.
64. *See* C. Correa (as n. 31 above, at 13) who, however, stresses several limitations of this maximum flexibility appeal. While this may be true in face of the often extremely burdensome substantive standards in TRIPS, it nevertheless fits within the general idea of policy space in implementing those standards and stresses this to the utmost extent in the case of LDCs.
65. *See Chambers Dictionary* (Edinburgh 1993), 535.
66. *See* ICTSD/UNCTAD, as n. 31 above, Part 1, section 1; C. Correa, as n. 31 above, at 101.
67. These are in particular Article 7 (Objectives). Its role in the balancing exercise is discussed in detail below in section 6.3.2.
68. For a further discussion of the purpose and objective of TRIPS, *see* the analysis of Article 7 below. The need to consider the objective of IP protection follows not only from the term effective itself which has no real meaning if not considered in relation to a specific goal or success to achieve. It is also confirmed by Article 31(1) VCLT as calls for the

(but are not limited to) developmental and technological objectives. Again, the reference to national systems indicates flexibility for the domestic legislator to choose and balance the interests which it wishes to pursue via a system for the protection of IP. Primarily it will be the broad and undefined legal concepts such as reasonableness, legitimate interests, or necessity where such a balancing of interests can be given effect. As indicated above, the rules of treaty interpretation applicable in the WTO allow referring to the preamble for this purpose under the notion of giving due regard to the treaty's context and, of course, its objectives.[69] In conclusion, the preamble of TRIPS supports a regime of IP protection which can be tailored to the domestic needs and gives effect to the underlying policy objectives. It thereby offers several parameters which open gates for a balancing exercise or a proportional recognition of different interests.[70] Together with the ordinary meaning of a TRIPS provision, these parameters must be taken into account in the interpretative process by virtue of Article 31(1) VCLT.[71]

6.3.2 THE OBJECTIVES UNDER ARTICLE 7 TRIPS

Even more than the preamble, Article 7 TRIPS will be an important source for determining the object and purpose of the TRIPS Agreement, thereby influencing the proper construction of those broad and undefined legal concepts which are the primary tool for a balance of interests. Article 7 states:

> Objectives
> The protection and enforcement of intellectual property rights should contribute to the promotion of technological innovation and to the transfer and dissemination of technology, to the mutual advantage of producers and users of technological knowledge and in a manner conducive to social and economic welfare, and to a balance of rights and obligations.[72]

---

effectiveness criteria (like any other term or provision of a treaty) to be understood 'in light of its objective and purpose'.

69. *See also* ICTSD/UNCTAD, as n. 31 above, Part 1, section 1.
70. Compare *D. Gervais*, as n. 60 above, at 2.10.
71. Next to the Preamble of TRIPS, also the preamble to the WTO Agreement expressing the objective to promote sustainable development (in context of expansion of production and use of natural resources) as well as recognition of different levels of development (in relation to actions to protect the environment) may be relevant for proportional recognition of competing interests. For a detailed analysis of sustainable development as treaty objective, *see* H. Grosse Ruse-Khan, 'A Real Partnership for Development? Sustainable Development as Treaty Objective in European Economic Partnership Agreements and Beyond' 13(1) (2010) *Journal of International Economic Law* 139, 162-167.
72. Article 7 of the TRIPS Agreement (emphasis added).

6.3.2.1   Balance of Interests

The text indicates that Article 7 comprises, next to the overarching goal of facilitating social and economic welfare, three sets of (competing) interests which need to be properly balanced in order to achieve that overarching aim: First and foremost, Article 7 represents a compromise between the objectives to *promote* (new) innovation on the one hand and to *transfer and disseminate* the resulting knowledge and technology on the other.[73] This is further confirmed by the call for *mutual supportiveness* of IP protection for both producers (which receive an incentive to innovate via IP rights) and users (which (later) should be enabled to access and utilize these innovations). Thirdly, the need to weigh different positions is directly addressed by the phrase that the protection and enforcement of IP rights should contribute to 'a balance of rights and obligations'. While this is broad enough to accommodate both rights and obligations from the perspective of all potential stakeholders in IP regulation,[74] the balancing will often occur primarily between the two poles of promoting new innovation and transferring as well as disseminating the results to the wider public. One could even attempt to link balancing between these two poles to economic theories on the justification and scope of IP protection: Depending on whether its comparative advantage lies more in innovation or more in imitation, a country is – from the perspective of trade theory – best advised to choose a level of IP protection individually tailored to its strengths in innovation and imitation.[75] Article 7 arguably supports this by focusing on innovations and producers on the one hand as well as on the transfer and dissemination of these innovations and user on the other.[76]

In essence, Article 7, therefore, encourages WTO Member States to build their IP systems in equilibrium between the two key interests at stake:[77] Providing an incentive for the creation of new innovations through rewards (usually via negative monopolies – that is rights to exclude others from exploiting the IP-protected subject matter – ensuring artificial exclusivity and

---

73. *See* C. Correa, as n. 31 above, at 91-92 who notes that Article 7 has been written in particular with technology-related IP rights in mind; but argues that since the balance of rights and obligations is an overriding principle in IP law (compare the Preamble of the WIPO Copyright Treaty, WCT) and also in general WTO law (*see* Article 3.5 DSU and the Preamble WTO Agreement), Article 7 is of key relevance for all IP rights. For a discussion on the negotiation history of Article 7, *see* H. Grosse Ruse-Khan, as n. 4 above, paras 13.35-37.
74. One here can think of, e.g., rights and obligations of IP owners, original creators and inventors, investors, competitors, (commercial) IP users, (private) IP consumers, specific interest groups such as researchers, libraries, new market entrants, state authorities, etc. or those related to general societal interests.
75. M. Trebilcock & R. Howse, as n. 25 above, at 400-401.
76. Also arguing for the – albeit limited to Article 7 and provisions like Articles 30 and 31 TRIPS – incorporation of economic theory in the TRIPS objectives: *Straus*, as n. 36 above, at 170.
77. D. Gervais, as n. 60 above, at 2.76.

market-lead).[78] But equally securing the transfer and diffusion of innovations to the public (via disclosure mechanisms, the idea-expression dichotomy in copyright, and exceptions to exclusive rights).[79] The proportional balance of these two interests should be determined in accordance with the overall aim of promoting progress in science, arts and technology and acting 'conducive to social and economic welfare' in a society. This reference to (social and economic) welfare in Article 7 again links to economic theory on the justification for IP rights which puts these welfare concerns at the centre for rationalizing IP protection instead of relying on normative assumptions of natural rights which are argued to be expropriated unless strong protection is available.[80] Against this clear textual evidence of the purpose and objectives of the TRIPS Agreement, statements which assert the 'main objective of the TRIPS Agreement to strengthen and harmonize IP protection throughout the world' seem rather to represent certain trading interests than the textual reality embodied in the provisions of TRIPS.[81]

6.3.2.2   WTO Members Discretion to Exercise Balancing

The balancing exercise envisioned under Article 7 must by its nature respond to the individual circumstances at hand and thus necessarily includes some degree of discretion for the Member States as to allow for tailored responses to the developmental, technological and economic needs of society.[82] Interpreting TRIPS in light of this may be difficult in cases of clear-cut provisions with a straightforward ordinary meaning.[83] Against this background, it is even more important to allow for a balance of interests whenever the interpretation of broader and vague legal concepts is at stake. A central question here will often be to what extent this weighing process has already been performed by the negotiators while drafting TRIPS provisions or is to be conducted on the implementation level by the individual WTO Member

---

78. *See,* for example, Articles 11, 14, 16, 6(1) and 28 TRIPS.
79. *See,* for example, Articles 29, 9(2), 13, 17, 26(2), 30 and 31 TRIPS.
80. *See* M. Trebilcock & R. Howse, as n. 25 above, at 398-399.
81. *See* European Court of Justice, 'Advisory Opinion on TRIPS Jurisdiction', reprinted in 27 (1996) *IIC*, at 503; referred to in *Straus*, as n. 36 above, at 161.
82. For a detailed discussion on this point, *see* H. Grosse Ruse-Khan, as n. 4 above, para. 13.35-45. Against this background one can hardly argue that 'TRIPS negotiating parties had taken societal interests into consideration when agreeing on the balance of interests which were enshrined in the TRIPS Agreement. Consequently, *individual WTO Members could not now rebalance these interests unilaterally*' (Arguments forwarded by the EC in *Canada – Patent Protection of Pharmaceutical Products*, as n. 60 above, at para. 4.30).
83. For the Panel and Appellate Body jurisprudence on interpreting WTO law, *see* section 6.3.2.4 below.

States.[84] While this will depend to some extent on the interpretation of the individual provision at hand, important general observations can be made: First, the language of Article 7 (The protection and enforcement of IP *should* contribute)[85] suggests that the desired effects are not achieved automatically and do not follow as such from protecting and enforcing IP rights.[86] Neither are these effects necessarily inherent and fully realized in all the individual TRIPS provisions. Had this been the case, Article 7 would be redundant which in turn contradicts a general principle of treaty interpretation according to which words are in a treaty for a meaning and one must give effect to all terms of the treaty.[87]

Instead, national legislators should consider the objectives and interests mentioned in Article 7 and choose a proper balance when implementing TRIPS. Further, the very objective mentioned in Article 7, to advance social and economic welfare, necessitates at least a certain amount of flexibility and policy space to give due regard to the domestic needs of the society. This follows not only from economic theory on IP protection.[88] Also historical evidence from the IP policies of industrialized countries in the nineteenth and early twentieth century as well as the more recent experience of far-eastern countries such as Korea, India and China clearly indicates that in order to facilitate technological development and economic welfare, IP policies must be tailored to circumstances at hand and respond to domestic problems at stake: One size does not fit all.[89] If TRIPS provisions would not allow any significant policy space on the domestic level, the central objective not only of TRIPS but also of the WTO itself[90] could not be properly implemented.

---

84. This issue has been discussed in particular in relation to Article 30 TRIPS: *see Canada – Patent Protection of Pharmaceutical Products*, as n. 60 above, at 7.26 and C. Correa, as n. 31 above, at 101-102. For a more detailed discussion of the *Canada – Patents* report *see* section 6.3.2.6 below.

85. Article 7 TRIPS, emphasis added.

86. ICTSD/UNCTAD, as n. 31 above, at Part 1 section 6.

87. Principle of effectiveness or *effet utile*: *see United States – Standards for Reformulated and Conventional Gasoline*, as n. 56 above, at 21; *Japan – Taxes on Alcoholic Beverages* (WT/DS8/ AB/R); Appellate Body report (4 October 1996) at 96(106); and ICTSD/ UNCTAD, as n. 31 above, at Part 1 section 6.

88. *See* the explanations in section 6.2 above as well as M. Trebilcock & R. Howse, as n. 25 above, at 397-401.

89. *See* M. Trebilcock & R. Howse, as n. 25 above, at 397, 400-401, H. Grosse Ruse-Khan, as n. 5 above, paras 13.35-45 and Commission on Intellectual Property Rights (CIPR), as n. 34 above, 18-20, and especially the two related background papers by Z. Khan, as n. 63 above and N. Kumar, as n. 34 above.

90. *See* the WTO preamble which states: 'The Parties to this Agreement, Recognizing that their relations in the field of trade and economic endeavour should be conducted with a view to *raising standards of living*, ensuring full employment and a large and steadily growing volume of real income and effective demand, and expanding the production of and trade in goods and services, while allowing for the optimal use of the world's resources in accordance with the *objective of sustainable development*, seeking both to protect and preserve the environment and to enhance the means for doing so in a manner

6.3.2.3 Legitimate Expectations of Interested Trading Partners in the WTO

A counterargument here might be that allowance for balancing of interests on the domestic level might lead to legal uncertainty and/or frustrate legitimate expectations of private parties or other WTO Members to benefit from a certain standard of IP protection which they might argue was reasonably foreseeable from TRIPS norms. However, this reasoning does not stand up to a detailed scrutiny: For once, legal certainty and foreseeability in trade and commerce are primarily to be dealt with on the municipal level for the benefit of private entities which have a valid interest to know the law in order to adopt (business) strategies and decisions accordingly. Since TRIPS is in principle not designed as an agreement that grants directly enforceable rights to private entities, they do not have a valid claim in relying on the substance of a particular TRIPS provision.[91] One example may illustrate this point: In a case involving a Swiss Pharmaceutical Company which tried to challenge a certain provision of the Indian Patent Act as violating TRIPS, the Madras High Court upheld the argument that neither could private companies challenge a law as being TRIPS non-compliant nor could an Indian court decide whether the Indian patent law is TRIPS compliant or not.[92] In the WTO, the appropriate forum for claims of inconsistencies with TRIPS is the System of Dispute Settlement, set out in Articles XXII, XXIII GATT and the DSU.

A more complex issue is whether WTO Member States may claim that (extensive) balancing of interests in the TRIPS implementation process frustrates its own legitimate expectations for their domestic industries to benefit from a certain standard of IP protection. A country may, for example, argue that patent protection regulated under Articles 27 and 28 TRIPS obliges other WTO Members to grant certain exclusive rights for pharmaceutical products and thereby includes legitimate expectations that its domestic Pharma Industry will be able to (freely) exploit its patented drugs in markets abroad. It may then consider national measures which rely on a broad reading of the provision on exceptions in Article 30 TRIPS in order to

---

consistent with their respective needs and concerns at different levels of economic development' (emphasis added).

91. For International IP law, this follows mainly from the principle of territoriality: The rights available to private entities always flow from the domestic, national IP statutes of the country where IP protection is sought and not from international obligations to provide such rights in the national law (compare Article 5(2) of the revised Berne Convention on the Protection of Literary and Artistic Works). While countries may, of course, decide to give direct effect to international IP rules, that only applies to those rules which provide for concrete rights or obligations that can be applied and exercised by private parties without the need for domestic implementation – *see* the discussion in H. Grosse Ruse-Khan, as n. 5 above, paras 7.91 et seq.

92. *See Novartis AG v. Union of India*, Madras High Court Judgment of 6 August 2007 (W.P. Nos 24759 and 24760 of 2006).

balance the interests of right holders against those of patients for easy and cheap access to essential medicines as frustrating these expectations.

In the WTO law on trade in goods, such types of claims (stemming from the GATT origins of the WTO) are accepted as *'non-violation complaints'* and regulated under Article XXIII:1(b)-(c) GATT 1994: A WTO Member may initiate dispute settlement proceedings if it feels that another Member's measure nullifies or impairs benefits accruing to it under the GATT – regardless whether the measure violates GATT provisions. The idea behind these non-violation complaints under the GATT is to ensure that legitimate market access expectations based on tariff concessions are not upset by (non-tariff) measures later introduced by the Contracting Parties.[93] In the Uruguay Round Negotiations, the extension of this type of complaints to the TRIPS Agreement had been controversial, and as a compromise, a five-year moratorium had been agreed to in Article 64(2) TRIPS.[94] As the differences over the applicability of non-violation complaints in the TRIPS context persist in negotiations of the TRIPS Council, Members have continued to extend the moratorium so that currently these types of complaints cannot be invoked in the TRIPS context.[95] Against this background, the Appellate Body has explicitly rejected interpreting TRIPS on the basis of a WTO Members' legitimate expectations unless these expectations find a sufficient expression in the text of the TRIPS Agreement.[96]

A proper and tailored balancing of interests on the level of domestic implementation thus is not in general curtailed by arguments for legal certainty and legitimate expectations. The latter can be invoked only if it is based on interpretation in accordance with the VCLT – in particular the ordinary meaning or the context of a provision. Then, however, these

---

93. Compare *India – Patent Protection for Pharmaceutical and Agricultural Chemical Products* as n. 56 above, at para. 41: '"Non-violation" complaints are rooted in the GATT's origins as an agreement intended to protect the reciprocal tariff concessions negotiated among the contracting parties under Article II. In the absence of substantive legal rules in many areas relating to international trade, the "non-violation" provision of Article XXIII:1(b) was aimed at preventing contracting parties from using non-tariff barriers or other policy measures to negate the benefits of negotiated tariff concessions.' For a comprehensive analysis of the concept of non-violation complaints and its applicability in the TRIPS context *see* UNCTAD/ICTSD, as n. 31 above, at Part Five, section 32(3.2) and *WTO Secretariat*, Non Violation and Situation Complaints, (IP/C/W/ 349/Rev. 1), 24 November 2004.

94. Countries disagreed on the overall applicability of non-violation complaints and their implications for obligations under TRIPS; *see* UNCTAD/ICTSD, as n. 31 above, at Part Five, section 32(3.2).

95. *See*, for example, para. 45 of the Hong Kong Ministerial Declaration in 2005 (*Ministerial Conference*, Ministerial Declaration on Doha Work Programme, (WT/MIN (05)/DEC), 22 December 2005) and generally the dedicated WTO website on background and current status of non-violation complaints under the TRIPS Agreement at https://www.wto.org/ english/tratop_e/trips_e/nonviolation_background_e.htm.

96. *India – Patent Protection for Pharmaceutical and Agricultural Chemical Products*, as n. 56 above, at 45 and 48.

arguments must be weighed against the TRIPS objective in favour of a balanced and proportional system of IP protection. One may, therefore, conclude that the weighting advocated by Article 7 TRIPS is primarily to be conducted by the WTO Members when implementing TRIPS obligations. Of course, the WTO dispute settlement process ensures another Member's right to request an independent review of the compliance of this implementation with the TRIPS obligations – as they are to be understood under accepted principles of interpretation applicable in WTO law. It is the role of the TRIPS objectives within these interpretative principles which I shall turn to now.

6.3.2.4 The Role of 'Object and Purpose' in WTO Treaty Interpretation

We have seen that the object and purpose of TRIPS as articulated in the preamble and Article 7 call for a balanced system of IP protection and that in general this weighing of the different interests at stake should be performed at and tailored towards the domestic level unless the ordinary meaning or context of individual TRIPS provisions are sufficiently concrete and specific so as to leave little or no room for balancing. The question remains – both on a general, abstract level as well as in relation to individual TRIPS provisions: How much weight, in comparison to the role of 'ordinary meaning' and 'context', should be attached to these objectives in the process of interpretation? In the jurisprudence of the WTO treaty interpretation, it is well established that:

- an answer regarding individual terms of an agreement necessitates, as a *'single combined operation'* a comprehensive analysis of its ordinary meaning and context as well as both the provisions' and the treaties' object and purpose;[97] and

---

97. *See* the order of Article 31(1) VCLT and its application in the jurisprudence of the Appellate Body: *Japan – Taxes on Alcoholic Beverages*, as n. 87 above, 97 (at 105); *European Communities – Measures Concerning Meat and Meat Products (Hormones)* (WT/DS26/AB/R), Appellate Body Report (16 January 1998) at 181; *India – Patent Protection for Pharmaceutical and Agricultural Chemical Products*, as n. 56 above, at 45; *United States – Import Prohibition of Certain Shrimp and Shrimp Products*, as n. 59 above, at 114; *United States – Final Countervailing Duty Determination with respect to certain Softwood Lumber from Canada* (WT/ DS257/AB/R), Appellate Body Report (19 January 2004), at 58-59; but note that this is merely a logical order of analysis and implies no ranking between the individual elements mentioned in Article 31(1) VCLT: The International Law Commission (ILC), in its commentary on the said provisions of the VCLT stressed: 'The article, when read as a whole, cannot properly be regarded as laying down a legal hierarchy of norms for the interpretation of treaties.' Instead, the drafters of the Vienna Convention called for treaty interpretation as 'a single combined operation' *See Yearbook of the International Law Commission*, The International Law Commission's Commentary on Articles 27-29 of its Final Draft Articles on the Law of Treaties, Vol. II (1966), 219-220; further I. Sinclair, *The Vienna Convention on the Law of Treaties* (2nd edn, Manchester, 1984), 117-119.

– provisions incorporating broad and open legal concepts (such as reasonableness, necessity, normality and legitimacy in Articles 3, 8, 13, 17, 27, 30 TRIPS) will lend themselves much more for an interpretation which needs to draw from their context, from an evaluation of the specific objective (if any), as well as a determination of its meaning 'in light of' the general purpose of TRIPS.[98]

Above this, some general observations can be made on the importance of the objectives as set forth in the Preamble and Article 7 TRIPS which in turn may have a particular impact on the interpretation of the broad concepts mentioned above.[99] One may begin looking a bit closer at the general approach to interpretation taken by the Appellate Body in WTO dispute settlement: In line with the intention of the drafters of the VCLT[100] the Appellate Body made clear that:

Article 31 of the Vienna Convention provides that the words of the treaty form the foundation of the interpretative process: interpretation must be based above all upon the text of the treaty.[101]

The Appellate Body confirmed this so-called textual approach to interpretation[102] in various occasions – for example, by stressing the 'fundamental rule of treaty interpretations requires a treaty interpreter to read and interpret the words actually used by the agreement [...]'.[103] On its face, this approach seems to allow little room for giving due regard, in the interpretative process, to the purpose and objective of any of the WTO agreements.

---

98. *Canada – Patent Protection of Pharmaceutical Products*, as n. 60 above, at 7.26; Compare also the commentary of the ILC (*Yearbook of the International Law Commission*, as n. 97 above, at 221) citing the Advisory Opinion of the International Court of Justice on the *Competence of the General Assembly for the Admission of a State to the United Nations*: 'If the relevant words in their natural and ordinary meaning make sense in their context, that is the end of the matter.'

99. As explained in sections 6.1 and 6.2, a detailed assessment of key TRIPS provisions embodying such concepts in light of the purposes identified here and in comparison with the scope for balancing in other areas of international economic cannot – for reasons of space and time – be included in this chapter. *See*, however, the discussion on the notion of 'unjustifiable' under Article 20 TRIPS and its interpretation by the Panel in *Australia – Plain Packaging*, as n. 9 above, in section 6.3.2.6 below.

100. As expressed in the ILC Commentary on the respective VCLT provisions where the Commission stresses that 'starting point of interpretation is the elucidation of the meaning of the text, not an investigation *ab initio* into the intentions of the parties'. *– see Yearbook of the International Law Commission*, as n. 97 above, at 220, 221.

101. *Japan – Taxes on Alcoholic Beverages*, as n. 87 above, 97 (at 105).

102. So described by the ILC (*Yearbook of the International Law Commission*, as n. 97 above, at 220); compare also C. D. Ehlermann, 'Six Years on the Bench of the "World Trade Court"' 36(4) (2002) *Journal of World Trade*, 605-639.

103. *European Communities – Measures Concerning Meat and Meat Products (Hormones)*, as n. 97 above, at 181.

However, a closer look may reveal an understanding of this textual approach which is (1) in line with the intended equality amongst the three elements mentioned in Article 31(1) VCLT;[104] and (2) finds support in the case law of the Appellate Body: *R Howse* has pointed out that emphasis on the exact words of a treaty does nothing more than taking those words as the necessary *starting point* for an interpretative exercise that also includes teleological dimensions and merely rejects tendencies to assume objectives without having engaged in careful study of the treaties' text.[105] This observation corresponds with the Appellate Body's findings in the *US – Shrimp* dispute:

> A treaty interpreter must begin with, and focus upon, the text of the particular provision to be interpreted. It is the words constituting that provision, read in their context, that the object and purpose of the state parties to the treaty must first be sought. Where the meaning imparted by the text itself is equivocal or inconclusive, or where confirmation of the correctness of the reading of the text itself is desired, light from the object and purpose of the treaty as a whole may usefully be sought.[106]

It follows that the Appellate Body (1) wishes to confirm the logical order of interpretation which should always begin with the text as such and a determination of its ordinary meaning;[107] (2) above this, views the treaty text as the Archimedean Point for determining a treaties' objectives;[108] and (3) denounces any attempts to assert (*ab initio*) a treaty purpose not supported by the treaties' text.[109] This certainly leaves room for teleological considerations – as long as they are text-based. However, some argue that the Appellate Body seems to suggest that, in the first instance, *the purpose must be sought in the concrete provision at stake*: Only if that text is vague or inconclusive (as to its particular objective), one can move on to consult the objectives of the treaty as a whole.[110]

---

104. The ILC emphasized that ordinary meaning, context, object and purpose 'are all of obligatory character' and by their very nature not inferior to another, *see Yearbook of the International Law Commission*, as n. 97 above, at 220.
105. *See* R. Howse, Adjudicative Legitimacy and Treaty Interpretation in International Trade Law, in J. Weiler (ed.), *The WTO, the EC and the NAFTA* (Oxford, 2000).
106. *United States – Import Prohibition of Certain Shrimp and Shrimp Products*, as n. 59 above, at 114 (emphasis added).
107. As already briefly indicated above (*see* n. 84 and *Yearbook of the International Law Commission*, as n. 97 above, at 220).
108. Thereby countering accusations of 'overreaching' and 'judicial activism' which claim that the Appellate Body has not acted consistent with Article 3.2 DSU which prohibits the quasi-judicial organs of the WTO to 'add or diminish the rights and obligations provided in the covered agreements'.
109. Compare also A. Qureshi, 'Interpreting World Trade Organization Agreements for the Development Objective', 37(5) (2003) *Journal of World Trade*, at 866.
110. This has been criticized as unduly establishing a hierarchy (similar to the Articles 31-32 VCLT relation) between the objective as following from the treaty provision at stake and

Applying these standards to our scenario, the objectives expressed in the preamble and in particular in Article 7 TRIPS clearly are derived from the text of the Agreement and not speculative. They, therefore, are text-based and can be relied upon in the interpretation of TRIPS. Furthermore, especially the broader and more open concepts in several of the TRIPS provisions – for example, 'normal exploitation' and 'unreasonable prejudice (of) the legitimate interests' in Article 13 TRIPS – could still be available for an interpretation on the basis of the general objectives in Article 7 TRIPS. Nevertheless, a hierarchy where individual objective trump over general objectives may seriously curtail the number of instances in which the balance of interests advocated by Article 7 TRIPS will be able to guide the understanding of individual TRIPS provisions.

While this hierarchy amongst (potentially) different objectives may actually still be in line with the International Law Commissions argument against a legal hierarchy between ordinary meaning, context and purpose in Article 31(1) VCLT, it is inconsistent with the actual wording of that provision: 'A treaty shall be interpreted in good faith in accordance with the ordinary meaning to be given to the terms of the treaty in *their* context and in the light of *its* object and purpose'[111] 'Their' on the one hand clearly refers to the context of the terms (plural); 'its' on the other hand surely refers to the treaty (singular) – and not to the terms of the treaty which are to interpreted: 'Ordinary meaning' and 'context' thus relate to the individual terms at stake while 'object and purpose' relate to the treaty as a whole.[112] While this understanding of Article 31(1) VCLT may not necessarily prohibit recognition of an evident purpose of the individual provision interpreted, it nevertheless clearly establishes the overarching importance of the general objectives of the treaty.[113] On this basis, the TRIPS objectives, clearly expressed in the text of Article 7 and the preamble, will preserve their interpretative role on an equal standing next to the ordinary meaning and context of the TRIPS provision at stake.

6.3.2.5 The Doha Declarations: Increasing the Relative Importance of TRIPS Objectives?

The interpretative importance of proportionality and balancing under Article 7 TRIPS may be further amplified by two acts of WTO Members, both

---

the overall purpose of the treaty; *see* D. Shanker, 'The Vienna Convention on the Law of Treaties, the Dispute Settlement of the WTO and the Doha Declaration on the TRIPS Agreement', 36(4) (2002) *Journal of World Trade*, at 725-726.

111. Article 31(1) VCLT – emphasis added.
112. Compare also *Yearbook of the International Law Commission*, as n. 97 above, at 220 and 221, which seems to support this reading as the Commission always relates purpose to the treaty and not to its individual provisions.
113. Therefore, in so far as one aims to establish a *general* hierarchy which gives precedence to the purpose of the individual terms at stake, this has to be rejected as inconsistent with the wording of Article 31(1) VCLT.

adopted by consensus of all WTO Members at the fourth Ministerial Conference in Doha (Qatar). First, the Doha Declaration on TRIPS and Public Health, in its relevant parts, states:

> 4. We agree that the TRIPS Agreement does not and should not prevent Members from taking measures to protect public health. Accordingly, while reiterating our commitment to the TRIPS Agreement, we affirm that the Agreement can and should be *interpreted and implemented* in a manner supportive of WTO Members' right to protect public health and, in particular, to promote access to medicines for all.
>
> *In this connection, we reaffirm the right of WTO Members to use, to the full, the provisions in the TRIPS Agreement, which provide flexibility for this purpose.*
>
> 5. Accordingly and in the light of paragraph 4 above, while maintaining our commitments in the TRIPS Agreement, we recognize that these flexibilities include:
>
> (a) In applying the customary rules of interpretation of public international law, each provision of the TRIPS Agreement shall be read in the light of the object and purpose of the Agreement as expressed, in particular, in its objectives and principles.[114]

Secondly, the Ministerial Declaration adopted in Doha that kicked-off the so-called Doha Development Round of trade negotiations within the WTO contains two paragraphs which refer to the interpretation of TRIPS: Paragraph 17 refers to the Declaration on TRIPS and Public Health and states:

> We stress the importance we attach to implementation and interpretation of the Agreement on Trade-Related Aspects of Intellectual Property Rights (TRIPS Agreement) in a manner supportive of public health, by promoting both access to existing medicines and research and development into new medicines and, in this connection, are adopting a separate Declaration.[115]

Paragraph 19 then contains the mandate for further negotiations on key areas of concern related to the TRIPS Agreement and IP.[116] As to the implementation of this mandate, the WTO Members stressed:

---

114. Doha Declaration, as n. 8 above (emphasis added).
115. *Ministerial Conference*, Ministerial Declaration (WT/MIN(01)/DEC/1) 20 November 2001, at para. 17 (emphasis added).
116. This mandate includes an instruction of the TRIPS Council 'in pursuing its work programme including under the review of Article 27.3(b), the review of the implementation of the TRIPS Agreement under Article 71.1 and the work foreseen pursuant to paragraph 12 of this Declaration, to examine, *inter alia*, the relationship between the TRIPS Agreement and the Convention on Biological Diversity, the protection of

In undertaking this work, the TRIPS Council shall be guided by the objectives and principles set out in Articles 7 and 8 of the TRIPS Agreement and shall take fully into account the development dimension.[117]

Against this background, the question has been raised whether Articles 7 and 8 TRIPS now have a (formally) 'higher legal status' for the ongoing negotiations as well as the implementation and interpretation of TRIPS.[118] Regarding the substance of the Declarations, it has been suggested that the importance accorded to Articles 7 and 8 TRIPS may lead a WTO dispute settlement panel to 'take a longer look at how these provisions should be interpreted in the context of the Agreement as a whole, especially with respect to the need for "balance"'.[119] In order to engage in a comprehensive analysis of the Declarations' impact on Article 7 and on the idea of interpreting TRIPS with a balancing perspective, one needs to distinguish between the formal status of the Declarations and their substance. The main focus here will be on the Doha Declaration on TRIPS and Public Health since it refers to the interpretation and application of the existing body of WTO law – while the general Doha Declaration deals with negotiations on changing that body of law.

6.3.2.5.1   Formal Legal Status of the Doha Declarations

As to form, the legal status of Ministerial Declarations in the WTO seems ambiguous.[120] When attempting to qualify the ones adopted at the Doha Ministerial Conference under the rules of Decision-making in the WTO,[121] several options exist: Even though some key sections of the Doha Declaration on TRIPS and Public Health fulfil an interpretative function, the prevailing opinion[122] is that they do not amount to so-called authoritative

---

traditional knowledge and folklore, and other relevant new developments raised by Members pursuant to Article 71.1' – *see Ministerial Conference*, as n. 115 above, at para. 19.

117. *Ministerial Conference*, as n. 115 above, at para. 19 (emphasis added).
118. D. Gervais, as n. 60 above, at para. 2.80; compare also ICTSD/UNCTAD, as n. 31 above, Part 1, Ch. 6 (6.2.1).
119. D. Gervais, as n. 60 above, at para. 2.80; C. Correa speaks about a confirmation of the interpretative value of Article 7 TRIPS for each provision of TRIPS, *see* C. Correa, as n. 31 above, at 103.
120. *See* S. Charnovitz, 'The Legal Status of the Doha Declarations', 5(2) (2002) *Journal of International Economic Law*, 211.
121. These are in particular provisions in Articles IV, IX, X and XII of the Agreement establishing the WTO (WTO Agreement) – *see* H. Grosse Ruse-Khan, 'The Role of Chairman's Statements in the WTO', 41(3) (2007) *Journal of World Trade*, at 494.
122. *See* F. Abbot, 'The Doha Declaration on the TRIPS Agreement and Public Health: Lighting a Dark Corner at the WTO', 5(3) (2002) *Journal of International Economic Law*, 492; S. Charnovitz, as n. 120 above, at 210; ICTSD/UNCTAD, as n. 31 above, Part 1, Ch. 6 (6.2.1) – arguing in favour of classifying the Doha Declaration on TRIPS and Public Health under Article IX:2 WTO Agreement is D. Shanker, as n. 110 above, at 763.

interpretations[123] under Article IX:2 of the WTO Agreement,[124] which are generally considered binding upon WTO Members.[125] This is backed by the fact that no reference to the authority of Article IX:2 can be found in the Declaration and, more importantly, that the procedure required under Article IX:2 has not been adhered to.[126] Instead, most aspects speak for classifying both Declarations as 'decisions' under Article IV:1 and Article IX:1 of the WTO Agreement: They have been carefully negotiated and include reciprocal tradeoffs from all sides; they have finally been adopted by consensus of all WTO Members and are stated in the form of an agreement.[127]

While this qualification as such yet does not provide a general answer on the extent (if any) to which the Declarations have legally binding character,[128] the *formal status in the interpretation process* follows from another provision: In particular, the Doha Declaration on TRIPS and Public Health can be considered as a 'subsequent agreement between the parties regarding the interpretation of the treaty or the application of its provisions' under Article 31(3)(a) VCLT.[129] The relevant language in paragraphs 4 and 5 of the Doha Declaration on TRIPS and Public Health constitutes a consensual agreement of all WTO Members on the interpretation of TRIPS

---

123. The term 'authoritative interpretation' stems from Article 3.9 of the DSU. It allows discriminating interpretations under Article IX:2 from those adopted by a Panel or the Appellate Body which legally are only binding on the Parties to a dispute in respect to the case at hand.

124. This rule provides the Ministerial Conference and General Council with the exclusive authority to adopt interpretations of the WTO Agreements by a three-fourth majority of the Members.

125. *See United States – Tax Treatment for 'Foreign Sales Corporations'* (WT/DS108/AB/R), Appellate Body Report (24 February 2000), paras 112, 113; C.D. Ehlermann & L. Ehring, 'Decision-Making in the World Trade Organization', 8 *Journal of International Economic Law* (1/2005), at 58; J. Jackson, 'The World Trading System: Law and Policy of International Economic Relations' (2nd edn, Cambridge (MA), 1997), 123-124.

126. Article XI:2 requires that the Ministerial Conference, in the case of an interpretation of a Multilateral Trade Agreement in Annex 1 (as it is the case with TRIPS), shall exercise its authority on the basis of a recommendation by the Council overseeing the functioning of the WTO Agreement in question – in this case the TRIPS Council. The Doha Declaration, however, was not based on a recommendation from the TRIPS Council.

127. The records of the proceedings can be found at Ministerial Conference, 'Summary records of the Ninth Meeting of Ministerial Conference on 14 November 2001', (WT/MIN(01)/SR/9) 10 January 2002; compare also F. Abbot, as n. 122 above; at 491, S. Charnovitz, as n. 120 above, at 210; ICTSD/UNCTAD, as n. 31 above, Part 1, Ch. 6 (6.2.1).

128. Rejected by A. Sykes in TRIPS, Pharmaceuticals, Developing Countries, and the Doha Solution, J.M. Ohlin Law and Economics Working Paper No. 140 (February 2002), at 9 – online accessible at www.law.uchicago.edu/Lawecon/index.html.

129. Confirmed by F. Abbot, as n. 122 above, at 491-492; ICTSD/UNCTAD, as n. 31 above, Part 1, Ch. 6 (6.2.1). This, however, does not apply to para. 19 of the Doha Ministerial Declaration as it concerns the role of TRIPS objectives in the *ongoing negotiations* (which may lead to amendments of existing TRIPS provisions or new ones).

in general[130] and the application of its provisions in the public health context in particular.[131]

Considering paragraph 5 a) of the Doha Declaration and its reference to Articles 7 and 8 TRIPS, the Panel in *Australia – Plain Packaging* agreed that it must be seen as a subsequent agreement under Article 31:3 a) VCLT on the interpretation of TRIPS. The Panel stated with regard to paragraph 5 a):

> While this statement was made in the specific context of a re-affirmation by Members of the flexibilities provided in the TRIPS Agreement in relation to measures taken for the protection of public health, we note that paragraph 5 of the Doha Declaration is formulated in general terms, inviting the interpreter of the TRIPS Agreement to read 'each provision of the TRIPS Agreement' in the light of the object and purpose of the Agreement, as expressed in particular in its objectives and principles. As described above, Articles 7 and 8 have central relevance in establishing the objectives and principles that, according to the Doha Declaration, express the object and purpose of the TRIPS Agreement relevant to its interpretation.
>
> This paragraph of the Doha Declaration may, in our view, be considered to constitute a 'subsequent agreement' of WTO Members within the meaning of Article 31(3)(a) of the Vienna Convention. (...)
>
> In this instance, the instrument at issue is a 'declaration', rather than a 'decision'. However, the Doha Declaration was adopted by a consensus decision of WTO Members, at the highest level, on 14 November 2001 on the occasion of the Fourth Ministerial Conference of the WTO, subsequent to the adoption of the WTO Agreement, Annex 1C of which comprises the TRIPS Agreement. The terms and contents of the decision adopting the Doha Declaration express, in our view, an agreement between Members on the approach to be followed in interpreting the provisions of the TRIPS Agreement. This agreement, rather than reflecting a particular interpretation of a specific provision of the TRIPS Agreement, confirms the manner in which 'each provision' of the Agreement must be interpreted, and thus 'bears specifically' on the interpretation of each provision of the TRIPS Agreement.[132]

---

130. *See* para. 5(a) of the Declaration: 'In applying the customary rules of interpretation of public international law, each provision of the TRIPS Agreement shall be read in the light of the object and purpose of the Agreement as expressed, in particular, in its objectives and principles.'

131. *See* paras 4 and 5(b)-(d) of the Declaration.

132. *Australia – Plain Packaging*, Panel Report, as n. 9 above, paras 7.2408-10 (footnotes omitted). One might add that at the time of writing, this aspect of the Panel Report is under appeal. However, at the time of writing, it remains unclear if – given that the Appellate Body ceased most of its operations as of December 2019 – an Appellate Body Report will still be issued in the Plain Packaging dispute.

Because of the interpretative relevance of the main operational paragraphs in the Doha Declaration, it has further been argued as a 'substantive equivalent of an interpretation of the TRIPS Agreement and, from a functional standpoint, indistinguishable from an authoritative interpretation under Article IX:2 of the WTO Agreement'.[133] However, a word of caution should conclude this formal analysis. The *interpretative function* of the respective sections of the Doha Declaration may be equivalent to an authoritative interpretation. But the *legal weight* in the interpretation process is certainly distinct: An authoritative interpretation under Article XI:2 is *lex specialis* to Articles 31, 32 of the Vienna Convention. Since it amounts to an interpretation which is – as the Appellate Body puts it – 'generally binding', its legal relevance in the process of interpretation cannot be re-evaluated by applying the rules in the Vienna Convention.[134] Doing so would effectively lead to the possibility for the organs of the dispute settlement system to overrule a decision taken by the WTO legislator under Article IX:2.[135] As an agreement under Article 31(3)(a) VCLT, however, the Doha Declaration on TRIPS and Public Health is (only) one element (of potentially many) to be 'taken into account, together with the context' in the process of interpretation.[136]

6.3.2.5.2   The Substance of the Declaration on TRIPS and Public Health

Having its formal status as an additional and self-standing element in the interpretative process under the Vienna Convention in mind, we can now evaluate the *substance* of the Declaration on TRIPS and Public Health. Of particular importance for the concept of balancing on the domestic level is the second sentence of paragraph 4 (where WTO Members 'reaffirm the right of WTO Members to use, to the full, the provisions in the TRIPS Agreement, which provide flexibility for this purpose') and paragraph 5a (stating that '[a]ccordingly and in the light of paragraph 4 above, while maintaining our commitments in TRIPS Agreement, [WTO Members] recognize that these flexibilities include: In applying the customary rules of interpretation of public international law, each provision of the TRIPS Agreement shall be read in the light of the object and purpose of the Agreement as expressed, in particular, in its objectives and principles.') of the Doha Declaration. Taken together, one of the TRIPS flexibilities is the right of individual WTO Members to interpret and implement TRIPS in light of its purpose, as

---

133. F. Abbot, as n. 122 above, at 491-492.
134. Compare also C.D. Ehlermann & L. Ehring, as n. 125 above, at 59.
135. By giving legal weight to other elements recognized under the Vienna Convention rules a Panel or the Appellate Body could arrive at a distinct result as when relying exclusively on the authoritative interpretation as the sole source of guidance, compare H. Grosse Ruse-Khan, as n. 121 above, at 515-516.
136. *See* the wording of Article 31(3) VCLT.

particularly expressed in its Articles 7 (and 8). This allows the following deductions:

(1) It confirms the notion that a balance of interests as the main objective under Article 7 is to be conducted at the *domestic level* of implementing TRIPS.[137] Within the limits of the ordinary meaning and (other) context, Members are free to implement TRIPS in light of its central purpose of providing a balance – tailored to the domestic circumstances – between encouraging new innovations and transferring/disseminating the results for the benefit of the society.[138] By the same token, it provides evidence against the view that Article 7 is merely a declaratory expression of the balancing already performed in the drafting of TRIPS.

(2) It backs the view that the *overall objectives* of TRIPS are decisive – not the ones which may relate to the interpreted provision in particular.[139]

(3) Within those overall objectives, the Declaration places specific emphasis on the ones expressed in Articles 7 and 8 TRIPS. It has been argued that 'this may have the effect of elevating those provisions above the preamble of TRIPS for interpretative purposes'.[140] In any event, it places specific emphasis on Article 7 and thus on the key objective of a balanced level of protection advocated therein.

(4) An interpretation in light of TRIPS' object and purpose is obligatory for each provision of the Agreement – not only selected ones. It may nevertheless be of particular importance for those which contain broad and open legal concepts and/or which relate to exceptions of exclusive rights.[141]

(5) Finally and from a broader perspective on the overall interpretative process, the fact that of the three central elements of interpretation[142] the Declaration only focuses on the object and purpose (as expressed in Articles 7 and 8 TRIPS) could be understood as placing more emphasis on – or even giving the latter priority over – the ordinary meaning and context in the process of interpretation.

---

137. *See* above at 6.2.
138. *See* above at 6.3.2.1 and 6. 3.2.2.
139. *See* above at 6.4.
140. ICTSD/UNCTAD, as n. 31 above, Part 1, Ch. 6 (6.2.1): The latter effect is deemed relevant since the preamble 'might be understood to place a somewhat greater weight on the interests of intellectual property owners than on public interests'. This, however, is not necessarily the case – compare the interpretation of the preamble and its role for proportionality and balancing above.
141. *See* C. Correa, as n. 31 above, at 103; compare also D. Gervais, as n. 60 above, at 2.80 (p. 120).
142. Ordinary meaning, context and object and purpose, *see* Article 31(1) VCLT.

Recalling that the text is the starting point for treaty interpretation[143] which should be a single combined operation and include all relevant elements in a holistic manner,[144] this extra weight on the TRIPS objectives, however, should not lead to results which are contrary to the ordinary meaning or context of the provision at stake. Such a reading would raise questions as to the extent the Doha Declaration can authorize Members to depart from the accepted principles of treaty interpretation in public international law, as advocated in Article 3.2 of the WTO DSU.[145] Instead, the extra emphasis placed on the treaties' object and purpose will be of central importance where the ordinary meaning and context of the TRIPS provision at hand *allows* for an interpretation focusing on the objective of a balanced system of IP protection: That is, whenever the interpretation of broad and open legal concepts such as necessity, reasonableness and legitimacy is at stake.[146]

6.3.2.5.3   Conclusions: Double Counting and Single Most Important Element

In conclusion on the role of the Doha Declaration on TRIPS and Public Health for the interpretation of TRIPS provisions, one may emphasize the following points: Formally, the Doha Declaration is an agreement on the interpretation of TRIPS within the meaning of Article 31(3)(a) VCLT and thus an additional element relevant in the interpretative process. To illustrate, one could say that this amounts to a 'double counting' of the object and purpose of TRIPS in relation to ordinary meaning and other contexts: Once in the application of Article 31(1) and another time under Article 31(3) – there being considered an equivalent to the treaties' context. This is confirmed in *Australia – Plain Packaging*, where the Panel refers to Articles 7 (and 8) TRIPS as providing 'important context' for the interpretation of, in that case, Article 20 TRIPS.[147] As to its substance, the Declaration places emphasis on Articles 7 and 8 TRIPS as tools for an interpretation and implementation of TRIPS tailored to the domestic needs for a balance between incentives for new innovations and their transfer and dissemination

---

143. *United States – Import Prohibition of Certain Shrimp and Shrimp Products*, as n. 59 above, at 114; *Yearbook of the International Law Commission*, as n. 97 above, at 220; compare also R. Howse, as n. 105 above.
144. *Yearbook of the International Law Commission*, as n. 97 above, at 219-220; I. Sinclair, as n. 97 above, at 117-119.
145. Arguably, the Doha Declaration not being an authoritative interpretation under Article IX:2 or an amendment to existing WTO rights and obligations under Article X of the WTO Agreement, cannot have the character of adding to or diminishing existing obligations – in this case following from Article 3.2 DSU.
146. This result is confirmed by C. Correa, as n. 31 above, at 103.
147. *Australia – Plain Packaging*, Panel Report, as n. 9 above, para. 7.2411.

to the public. Overall, while the concrete interpretative result will certainly depend on the individual TRIPS provision, especially for broad and open legal concepts, taking proper account of the balancing objective advocated by Article 7 TRIPS is the single most important element in the process of interpretation and implementation of the TRIPS Agreement.

Against these conclusions, the findings of the Panel in *Canada – Patents* dispute as they regard Article 7 TRIPS cannot be upheld. The following section will, in summarizing the main points of this chapters' analysis on Article 7 TRIPS, critically address some of these findings as they concern the general role of Article 7 in the interpretation of the TRIPS Agreement.[148]

6.3.2.6 Re-evaluating *Canada: Patents* in Light of *Australia – Plain Packaging*

The dispute *Canada – Patents*[149] initiated by the European Communities (EC) against Canada concerned the TRIPS consistency of two provisions in the Canadian Patent Act, which allowed certain exceptions to the exclusive rights of the Patent holder. These exceptions concerned pharmaceutical patents and authorized the making and use of the patented invention (1) in order to carry out tests necessary to obtain marketing approval for generic versions of the patented drugs (bolar exception); and (2) in order to manufacture and stockpile generic versions for a period of six months before the end of the patent term so that generic copies would be readily available as soon as the patent term of the original drug expired (stockpiling exception). The EC challenged the compliance of these two exceptions with Article 27(1) 2nd sentence and Article 30 TRIPS. With regard to the objectives of TRIPS, the main issue was to what extent they influence the interpretation of the relevant terms in Articles 27 and 30. The following excerpts from the Panel report nicely summarizes the Arguments of Canada, the EC, as well as the legal reasoning of the Panel:

> 7.24 In the view of Canada, the italicized text of Article 7 above declares that one of the key goals of the TRIPS Agreement was a *balance* between the intellectual property rights created by the Agreement and other important socio-economic policies of WTO Member governments. Article 8 elaborates the socio-economic

---

148. It is, however, beyond the scope of this chapter to assess the main question, regarding Article 30 TRIPS, at issue in that Panel Report (in this vein, compare M. Senftleben, as n. 37 above). The interpretation of provisions such as Articles 30, 26(2), 17 and 13 TRIPS, in light of the objectives analysed here and in comparison to the scope for domestic policies in other areas of international economic law making, will be addressed in follow on research publications.
149. *Canada – Patent Protection of Pharmaceutical Products*, as n. 60 above.

policies in question, with particular attention to health and nutritional policies. With respect to patent rights, Canada argued, *these purposes call for a liberal interpretation of the three conditions stated in Article 30 of the Agreement*, so that governments would have the necessary *flexibility* to adjust patent rights to maintain the desired balance with other important national policies.

7.25 The EC did not dispute the stated goal of achieving a balance within the intellectual property rights system between important national policies. But, in the view of the EC, *Articles 7 and 8 are statements that describe the balancing of goals that had already taken place in negotiating the final texts of the TRIPS Agreement.* According to the EC, to view Article 30 as an authorization for governments to *'renegotiate' the overall balance of the Agreement would involve a double counting of such socio-economic policies.* In particular, the EC pointed to the last phrase of Article 8.1 requiring that government measures to protect important socio-economic policies be consistent with the obligations of the TRIPS Agreement. The EC also referred to the provisions of first consideration of the Preamble and Article 1.1 as demonstrating that the basic purpose of the TRIPS Agreement was to lay down minimum requirements for the protection and enforcement of intellectual property rights.

7.26 In the Panel's view, Article 30's very existence amounts to a recognition that the definition of patent rights contained in Article 28 would need certain adjustments. On the other hand, *the three limiting conditions attached to Article 30 testify strongly that the negotiators of the Agreement did not intend Article 30 to bring about what would be equivalent to a renegotiation of the basic balance of the Agreement.* Obviously, the exact scope of Article 30's authority will depend on the specific meaning given to its limiting conditions. The words of those conditions must be examined with particular care on this point. *Both the goals and the limitations stated in Articles 7 and 8.1 must obviously be borne in mind when doing so as well as those of other provisions of the TRIPS Agreement which indicate its object and purposes.*[150]

Assessing this passage and, in particular, the Panel's reasoning highlighted in italics against the main conclusions of the analysis the object and purpose of TRIPS after Doha, one certainly cannot agree with the position of the EC and further needs to criticize several points made by the Panel: As already indicated above, Article 7 cannot be viewed as merely declaratory of

---

150. *Canada – Patent Protection of Pharmaceutical Products*, as n. 60 above, at 7.24-7.26 (emphasis added).

a balance inserted into the individual norms of TRIPS. Apart from the wording of Article 7 as well as the principle of effectiveness, the very objective of balancing itself and the promotion of socio-economic welfare requires this to be tailored towards domestic needs and thus to be performed on the domestic implementation level.[151] It is on this stage only where a proportional balance between the protection of new innovations and their transfer and dissemination to the public can be performed effectively.[152] Within the process of treaty interpretation, established principles – as codified in the Vienna Convention Articles 31 and 32 – place the object and purpose of a treaty as elements of interpretation on equal footing next to ordinary meaning and context of the provisions at stake. In this regard, the Arguments of the EC are in complete denial of one of the three core elements of treaty interpretation included in Article 31(1) VCLT.

These principles of interpretation equally stand against the reasoning of the Panel in paragraph 7.26: While it is correct that the limiting conditions in Article 30 (as well as those in Articles 13, 17, 26(2) TRIPS) certainly have to be 'borne in mind' when exercising the balance Article 7 calls for, they, in turn, have to be interpreted in light of the object and purpose of TRIPS. In fact, it is the meaning of the limiting conditions in Article 30 that the interpretation exercise, which includes giving due regard to the treaty's object and purpose, that is at issue. Here we may recall that the starting point is the text of the treaty provision and its ordinary meaning.[153] If giving due regard to the provision's context, that meaning leads to an evident result and leaves few (if any) room for different understandings, the impact of the treaty's objectives is likely to be marginal.[154] If, however – as in the case of Article 30[155] – the interpretation of broad and open terms and concepts is at stake, the role of Article 7 will be much greater: affording WTO members with an option to balance competing interests within their own, domestic context and thereby giving effect to every state's right to regulate in the public interest (which, as the discussion below alludes to, has not been contracted out when TRIPS was agreed). One should keep in mind that paragraphs 4 and 5(a) of the Doha Declaration constitute a subsequent agreement of all WTO Members on the interpretation of TRIPS which one

---

151. *See* section 6.2 above.
152. This is further supported by historic evidence as well as economic theory on intellectual property protection – *see* section 6.1 above.
153. Compare section 6.3.2.4 above. *See* in particular *United States – Import Prohibition of Certain Shrimp and Shrimp Products*, as n. 59 above, at 114; *Japan – Taxes on Alcoholic Beverages*, as n. 87 above, 97 (at 105); *Yearbook of the International Law Commission*, as n. 97 above, at 220.
154. It nevertheless should be considered since para. 5 (a) of the Doha Declaration on TRIPS and Public Health, as n. 8 above, requires the objectives to be taken into account for every provision of TRIPS; *see* section 6.5 above.
155. 'Unreasonable conflict', 'normal exploitation', 'legitimate interests of the patent owner' and 'legitimate interests of third parties'.

could even see as effectively leading to double counting of the TRIPS objectives in the process of interpretation. Whenever the ordinary meaning and context allows, the objective of a proportional balance of interests will then be the single most important factor in the interpretation and implementation of TRIPS.[156] As this is certainly the case for several key terms in Article 30 TRIPS, these terms and the conditions they set out as such cannot be relied upon to limit the role of Article 7 *a priori*. These terms do, of course, serve as the object of the interpretative enterprise (and in that way could be said to 'condition' the interpretative outcome, primarily via an assessment of their ordinary meaning). But the point is that the broader and open-ended these terms are, the less of the overall outcome actually follows from a mere consideration of the ordinary meaning.

These insights also contradict another key passage in the Panel Report which deals with the relation between terms in individual provisions and Article 7 TRIPS and which has been criticized by commentators:[157]

> Article 27 prohibits only discrimination as to the place of invention, the field of technology, and whether products are imported or produced locally. Article 27 does not prohibit bona fide exceptions to deal with problems that may exist only in certain product areas. Moreover, to the extent the prohibition of discrimination does limit the ability to target certain products in dealing with certain of the important national policies referred to in Articles 7 and 8.1, that fact may well constitute a deliberate limitation rather than a frustration of purpose. It is quite plausible, as the EC argued, that the TRIPS Agreement would want to require governments to apply exceptions in a nondiscriminatory manner, in order to ensure that governments do not succumb to domestic pressures to limit exceptions to areas where right holders tend to be foreign producers.

Again, the specific terms of Article 27 TRIPS – the prohibition of certain types of discrimination – cannot be utilized to limit the impact of the general objectives in Article 7 *a priori*. Instead, while a careful assessment of the ordinary meaning of 'without discrimination' may certainly amount to a limited option for giving effect to a balance of interests, it is the terms of Article 27 which in turn must be interpreted in light of the object and purpose of TRIPS. In this case, 'without discrimination' is sufficiently open and broad to allow for various understandings.[158] One must, therefore, choose an interpretation which gives due regard to the increased importance attached to

---

156. Compare section 6.5 above.
157. *See* ICTSD/UNCTAD, as n. 31 above, Part 1, Ch. 6 (4.); D. Shanker, as n. 110 above, at 742.
158. This follows not only from the terms itself but especially in comparison to the established interpretations on very similar terms in the chapeau of Article XX GATT which is perceived mainly as a safeguard against the abusive reliance on GATT exceptions; *see United States – Standards for Reformulated and Conventional Gasoline*, as n. 56 above, at 22 and P. Van den Bossche, as n. 21 above, at 616-617.

Article 7 after Doha and at the same time prevents an *abusive* reliance on public policy objectives from furthering protectionist interests not recognized under Article 7 TRIPS.[159] In fact, the approach chosen to interpret the concept of (de facto) discrimination by the Panel in *Canada – Patents*, in the end, is one that accounts for exactly this balance between policy space and the proper protection of the interests of IP right holders.[160] But it does so without accepting or properly engaging with the conceptual framework TRIPS provides for this purpose and, in that way, appears arbitrary and without proper explanation.

This analysis of the *Canada – Patent* Report as well as other TRIPS-related decisions in WTO dispute settlement until recently indicated that the interpretation of TRIPS in accordance with all elements recognized under Article 31 VCLT and giving due regard to the extra emphasis placed on the objectives of Article 7 TRIPS was still to be realized in WTO jurisprudence.[161] However, already since 2005, we can observe a gradual shift towards a generally more flexible approach to construing broad and open terms in the TRIPS Agreement.[162] While this trend towards more flexibility was initially not (explicitly) based on Articles 7 and 8 TRIPS,[163] the most recent IP-related Panel Report in *Australia – Plain Packaging* reinforces not only a flexible approach towards IP commitments in TRIPS but also bases this squarely on an interpretation based on Articles 7 and 8 TRIPS. This is most apparent in the interpretation of Article 20 TRIPS and its notion of 'unjustifiable', applied to Australia's plain tobacco packaging rules which effectively prohibited the use of trademarks on tobacco packaging – except the brand name and variant in a standardized form. Based on

---

159. Compare the established interpretation of the discrimination clause in Article XX GATT; *see* P. Van den Bossche, as n. 21 above, at 616-617.
160. *See* Canada – Patents, as n. 60 above, para. 7.101, where the Panel construes the notion of (de facto) discrimination under Article 27(1) TRIPS as to include a requirement for a disadvantageous effect, and the lack of justification for such a disadvantage in practice. The latter element quite apparently allows a WTO member to justify disadvantages by public policy grounds, including, of course, public health (as addressed in the Doha Declaration) or the protection of the environment (as the Preamble to the WTO Agreement emphasizes).
161. *See* for a detailed discussion of the WTO case law on TRIPS and its avoidance of Articles 7 and 8: H. Grosse Ruse-Khan (2011), as n. 5 above.
162. *See* the discussion in H. Grosse Ruse-Khan, Protecting Intellectual Property Through Trade and Investment Agreements: Concepts, Norm-setting, and Dispute Settlement, in Christophe Geiger (ed.), *Research Handbook on Intellectual Property and Investment Law*, Cheltenham (UK)/Northampton, MA (USA), Edward Elgar Publishing, forthcoming 2020, University of Cambridge Faculty of Law Research Paper No. 14/2019, Max Planck Institute for Innovation & Competition Research Paper No. 19-09 – online at https://ssrn.com/abstract=3393645.
163. *See* in particular the flexible determination of 'commercial scale' under Article 61 TRIPS in *China – Measures affection the Protection and Enforcement of Intellectual Property Rights (China – IPRs)*, Panel Report (26 January 2009, WT/DS362/R), para. 7.577.

Articles 7 and 8 TRIPS,[164] the Panel understood the notion of 'unjustifiable' as reflecting a balance between the protection of legitimate interests of the trademark owner to use its mark and the 'right of WTO Members to adopt measures for the protection of certain societal interests that may adversely affect such use'.[165] Importantly, the Panel did not attempt to second-guess Australia's balancing exercise and eventually decided that the complainants had not shown that Australia acted 'beyond the *bounds of latitude available to it* under Art. 20' – hence, concluding that there had been no breach of Article 20 TRIPS.[166] Despite this gradual development, we only have very few TRIPS decisions in WTO dispute settlement that address, let alone explore in more detail the policy space (and its limits) WTO members have when implementing TRIPS. One might say that there is still a need for a more detailed, concrete elaboration of the content and implications of the objectives under Article 7 TRIPS and their impact on the meaning of individual TRIPS provisions.[167] In this chapter, I have tried to outline the overarching purpose of TRIPS to balance IP protection between the two poles of promoting innovation on the one hand and transferring and disseminating these innovations on the other. In order to actually be 'conducive to social and economic welfare',[168] this balancing must be performed on the domestic implementation level and tailored to domestic needs – without, however, contradicting the ordinary meaning and context of the TRIPS provisions implemented.

6.4   CONCLUDING REMARKS: THE CASE FOR A
           BALANCE OF INTEREST IN ITS WIDER
           CONTEXT

In light of an international IP framework that is increasingly determined by a global network of bilateral and regional FTAs which often contain IP chapters with 'TRIPS-plus' obligations to protect and enforce IP, one might wonder what role is left for TRIPS, and hence, also for its objectives? As I have argued elsewhere, the fact that most of these FTAs are concluded among WTO members means that TRIPS provisions, including Articles 7 (and 8) TRIPS, form 'relevant rules' that are 'applicable in the relations

---

164. *Australia – Plain Packaging*, as n. 9 above, paras 7.2397-2411.
165. *Ibid.*, para. 7.2429. As I have argued elsewhere, this is best understood as a recognition of the continued existence and relevance – within TRIPS – of a right to regulate; *see* H. Grosse Ruse-Khan, Intellectual Property and International Law, in I. Caboli & M.L. Montagnani, *Handbook on Intellectual Property Research*, Oxford University Press, forthcoming 2020 (10 September 2018). University of Cambridge Faculty of Law Research Paper No. 56/2018. Available at SSRN: https://ssrn.com/abstract=3246900.
166. *Australia – Plain Packaging*, as n. 9 above, para. 7.2604.
167. *See also* C. Correa, as n. 31 above, at 102.
168. Article 7 TRIPS.

between the parties', and hence, can inform, via Article 31(3)c) VCLT, the proper interpretation of IP rules in FTAs.[169] In addition, a lot of FTAs contain clauses (1) which either aim to uphold the contracting parties' (rights and) obligations under the WTO Agreement (including TRIPS), (2) refer to the Doha Declaration (which, of course, includes a reference to Articles 7 and 8 TRIPS in its paragraph 5 a), or (3) include references to specific TRIPS flexibilities, not least the TRIPS objectives.[170] Two examples shall suffice here. The Anti-Counterfeiting Trade Agreement (ACTA) states in its Article 2:3 (NATURE AND SCOPE OF OBLIGATIONS): 'The objectives and principles set forth in Part I of the TRIPS Agreement, in particular in Articles 7 and 8, shall apply, *mutatis mutandis*, to this Agreement.' The Comprehensive and Progressive Transpacific Partnership Agreement (CPTPP) goes one step further by including the full text of Articles 7 and 8 TRIPS, entitled 'Objectives' and 'Principles' as in TRIPS.[171] Since these objectives and principles embodied in Articles 7 and 8 TRIPS apply horizontally to all TRIPS obligations, their application in TPP (or ACTA, should it ever enter into force) via reference equally affects the understanding of all provisions of the treaty.[172] The nature and scope of TPP and ACTA obligations is, *inter alia*, determined by an interpretation and implementation based on the principles and objectives embodied in Articles 7 and 8 TRIPS. In sum, the main effect of the reference to Articles 7 and 8 TRIPS will again be on open and ambiguous provisions in the treaties that contain such a reference – while it is less likely to impact on most of the concise and detailed TRIPS-plus provisions. With these various types of linkages between TRIPS and FTAs in mind, the role for the balancing objectives in Article 7 TRIPS, therefore, is not limited to the proper construction of obligations under TRIPS. Of course, it remains to be seen whether the domestic implementation of FTA IP obligations or their international adjudication (should dispute settlement under FTAs become more prominent) actually engage with these balancing objectives.

To conclude this discussion, one can bring two further reasons for a proportional balancing as a guiding principle in the interpretation of TRIPS: First, international obligations to protect human rights have been relied upon to provide additional normative justifications for a balance of interest. Some point to the fact that WTO Members are generally bound by the UN Charter to comply with fundamental principles of human rights as enshrined in the

---

169. *See* H. Grosse Ruse-Khan, as n. 4 above, paras 5.81 et seq. One, however, also has to note that this 'systemic integration' of the TRIPS object and purpose for construing FTA IP rules is likely to have little effect when the increasingly detailed and specific IP commitments in those agreements are at issue.

170. For a detailed discussion, *see* H. Grosse Ruse-Khan, as n. 4 above, paras 5.61-5.80.

171. *See* Articles 18.2 & 18.3 CPTPP.

172. Since the ACTA Preamble refers to the Doha Declaration, one can safely conclude that the role para. 5 a) of the Doha Declaration foresees for Articles 7, 8 TRIPS also applies for ACTA.

Universal Declaration of Human Rights and the two International Covenants.[173] As already alluded to in the introduction, human rights approach to IP increasingly emphasize that such compliance can be achieved by strengthening the balancing mechanisms within TRIPS which then give effect to public interests protected by international human rights law and place those interests at the heart of the objectives of IP protection.[174] As long as the interests to be balanced fall within the broad paradigms of Article 7 TRIPS, the method of interpretation proposed in this chapter should give sufficient effect to the human rights considerations at stake. If this is not the case, one could consider giving effect to these 'additional' interests by integrating them into the interpretation process via Article 31(3)(c) VCLT: a rule of treaty interpretation that calls for the recognition of 'any relevant rules of international law applicable in the relations between the parties'. Even though its exact scope of application, in general, and in the context of WTO law, in particular, is (still) not clear,[175] good arguments can be forwarded for its application in relation to well-accepted rules of customary or conventional international (human rights) law. Especially regarding the Universal Declaration of Human Rights,[176] this should certainly be the case.

Second, the observations on the extension of various fields of international economic regulation into areas so far left untouched to the domestic policymaker (reaching behind the border)[177] merit an increased emphasis on balancing mechanisms within these systems. As stated in the hypothesis above: the more 'intense' and far-reaching international regulation becomes, the stronger is the need for the inclusion of a comprehensive and flexible regime which takes into account all interests affected. Within International IP law, as far as the domestic interests affected by global rule-making from a trade perspective fall within reach of the balancing advocated by Article 7 or the preamble of TRIPS, the method of interpretation proposed here may offer a proportional solution. If this is not the case, one should assess in detail

---

173. C. Correa, as n. 31 above, at 100.
174. UN Sub-commission on the Promotion and Protection of Human Rights, 'The Impact of the Agreement on Trade related Aspects of Intellectual Property protection on Human Rights', (E/CN.4/Sub.2/2001), 13 June 2001, at paras 16-28; *see also* C. Geiger, Constitutionalising Intellectual Property Law, 37(4) (2006) *IIC*, at 382-389 – as well as the contribution of C. Geiger in this book.
175. *See* generally I. Sinclair, as n. 97 above, at 138-140, and in the WTO context, for example, *European Communities – Measures Affecting the Approval and Marketing of Biotech Products* (WT/DS293/R) Panel Report (29 September 2006) at 7.52, 7.65-7.68, 7.72-7.75 as well as *European Communities – Measures Affecting Trade in Large Civil Aircraft (EC – Aircraft)*, Appellate Body Report, 18 May 2011 (WT/DS316/AB/R), para. 845. In a more general way the Appellate Body has stressed that WTO law should not be 'read in clinical isolation from public international law'; *see United States – Standards for Reformulated and Conventional Gasoline*, as n. 56 above, at 16.
176. Adopted and proclaimed by the United Nations General Assembly resolution 217 A (III) of 10 December 1948 – available at www.un.org/Overview/rights.html.
177. *See* section 6.2 above.

options of giving effect to these interests via any relevant rules of international law recognized under Article 31(3)(c) VCLT.[178] Support for such an approach also comes from the proper recognition and application of the customary international law right to regulate – in particular, since there is no evidence that WTO members have contracted out of this right when they entered into TRIPS.[179]

One must, however, always keep in mind that this *merely opens a door* for integrating the interests and concerns at stake into the overall process of treaty interpretation. It certainly does not guarantee that these interests will prevail. The likelihood that such interests actually do prevail in a given situation decreases, the more detailed and comprehensive the provisions that are giving effect to the trade interests are: Those provisions demand to be recognized under the notion of textual interpretation starting with the ordinary meaning of the treaty terms. Non-trade interests which are either neglected, or merely recognized as (limited) exceptions to the rule, or have to be imported from other regulatory systems to become a part of the recognized context for interpretation cannot compete effectively with de-tailed 'codifications' of trade interests. In the end, this observation provides evidence of the disadvantages which non-trade and non-economic interests are likely to face when competing with trade and economic interests in a regulatory framework dominated by trade rules and applied in a trade forum.

The question, then, is whether the incorporation of non-trade values into the global trading system, for example, by an interpretation focusing on the balancing objectives of TRIPS or by a broad understanding of norms such as Article XX GATT or Article XIV GATS, can really solve this problem. On the one hand, such an internalization of these non-trade interests could if properly implemented, lead to a more balanced international system of economic regulation and support coherence between distinct areas of public international law. On top of this, a more detailed 'codification' of these interests within the body of trade law would certainly enhance their importance in a balancing exercise and may offer (optional) guidance in their implementation on the domestic level. In the field of IP, especially for developing countries, a more detailed codification of interests in favour of the *transfer and dissemination* of innovations[180] could not only be helpful in guiding implementation but may also operate as a safeguard against

---

178. In this regard, one may look at the arguments put forward by the EC and various environmental NGOs of the effect on human health of imported Genetically Modified Organisms (GMOs), via international regulations such as the Cartagena Protocol on Bio-Safety; *see European Communities – Measures Affecting the Approval and Marketing of Biotech Products*, as n. 175 above.
179. *See* the discussion in H. Grosse Ruse-Khan, as n. 170 above.
180. One may recall that this objective represents one of the two poles between which the balancing under Article 7 TRIPS should be performed, *see* section 6.3.2 above.

unilateral, bilateral or regional pressures to adopt more stringent IP protection, for example, in FTAs.[181] On the other hand, the internalization of non-trade interests within the body of global trade rules bears the danger of subjecting the former to the latter. The regulatory, administrative and judicial forum would still be a trade-focused forum – unless, of course, over time, the relevant actors were to take non-trade interests as serious as trade interests.

---

181. This safeguarding function, however, implies a binding character of provisions promoting non-trade interests (ceiling rules) which might imply an amendment of Article 1(1) 2nd Sentence TRIPS. It further raises issues of how these ceiling rules could be enforced in the WTO dispute settlement context which is primarily driven by national *trading* interests.

Chapter 7

Copyright (and Other Intellectual Property Rights) as a Human Right

Paul L.C. Torremans

7.1   INTRODUCTION

When the Canada House conference in which the first edition of this collection of essays was rooted was set up, and subsequently when the topics and the essential components of a book treating the issue of copyright, and other intellectual property rights, and human rights were discussed it seemed obvious to think of the issue as one involving copyright and intellectual property rights, in general, on the one hand, and human rights, on the other hand. The first impression was inevitably one of two elements being involved and of the task ahead being the study of the interaction between these two elements.

That interaction between copyright and intellectual property rights, on the one hand, and human rights, on the other hand, is in truth, not a new phenomenon. This essay will demonstrate that the roots of this interaction go back a long time and are of a fundamental nature, but at least in the UK, it gave the impression of being something new. No doubt this was a consequence of the introduction of a formal Bill of Rights in the form of the Human Rights Act 1998, which provided a sharp focus on human rights in the English legal system. It is true though in a broader international context that copyright and intellectual property rights, on the one hand, and human rights, on the other hand, for quite a while seemed to develop in virtual isolation.[1] Each discipline seemed to stand on its own and had very little interest in the development of the other, let alone in the development of any interaction. It is in this respect sufficient to have a look at the vast majority of copyright and intellectual property rights standard texts. No reference to human rights is found,[2] and similarly, most standard texts on human rights law do not seem to refer to the copyright and intellectual property rights either. In other words, the interaction between the two areas of law may well not be a new phenomenon, but it is one the study of which has only attracted attention in earnest in recent years.[3]

Two approaches to this interaction can be distinguished.[4] The first approach is based on the conflict model and sees copyright and intellectual property rights as in fundamental conflict with human rights. The proponents of this approach argue that strong intellectual property rights are bound to undermine human rights and, in particular, economic, social and cultural aspects of human rights. This leads to an incompatibility that can only be resolved through the recognition of the primacy of human rights whenever a conflict arises. This solution imposes itself in the view of its proponents because, in normative terms, human rights are fundamental and of higher importance than intellectual property rights.[5] It is submitted that this approach focuses, maybe unduly so, primarily on the practical effects of certain forms of intellectual property rights in specific situations. In doing so, it does not address the broader picture involving the function and nature of the elements involved in the interaction. The second approach comes to the

---

1. Helfer, 'Human Rights and Intellectual Property: Conflict or Coexistence?', (2003) *Minnesota Intellectual Property Review* (forthcoming), *Loyola-LA Public Research Paper No. 2003-27; Princeton Law & Public Affairs Working Paper No. 03-15, 3.*
2. P.B. Hugenholtz, 'Copyright and Freedom of Expression in Europe', in R. Cooper Dreyfuss, D. Leenheer Zimmerman & H. First, *Expanding the Boundaries of Intellectual Property: Innovation Policy for the Knowledge Society*, Oxford University Press (2001), 343-363, at 350.
3. *See,* e.g., the expansion of the treatment in the second edition of J.A.L. Sterling, *World Copyright Law*, Sweet & Maxwell (2003) in comparison to the first edition of the book (1999). *See also* G. Schricker (ed.), *Urheberrecht: Kommentar*, Verlag C.H. Beck (2nd ed., 1999), § 97, Nos 19-25, 1500-1504 to which P.B. Hugenholtz, 'Copyright and Freedom of Expression in Europe', in R. Cooper Dreyfuss, D. Leenheer Zimmerman & H. First (ed.), *Expanding the Boundaries of Intellectual Property: Innovation Policy for the Knowledge Society*, Oxford University Press (2001), 343-363 refers as an example at 351 and Vivant, 'Le droit d'auteur, un droit de l'homme?', (1997) RIDA 174, 60.
4. Helfer, 'Human Rights and Intellectual Property: Conflict or Coexistence?', (2003) *Minnesota Intellectual Property Review* (forthcoming), *Loyola-LA Public Research Paper No. 2003-27; Princeton Law & Public Affairs Working Paper No. 03-15, 1-2.*
5. *See,* e.g., United Nations, Economic and Social Council, Commission on Human Rights, Sub-Commission on the Promotion and Protection of Human Rights, Resolution 2000/7 on Intellectual Property Rights and Human Rights, E/CN.4/Sub/2/2000/L.20, preamble § 11 and R. Howse & M. Mutua, *Protecting Human Rights in a Global Economy: Challenges for the World Trade Organisation,* International Centre for Human Rights and Democratic Development, Policy Paper, (2000), at 6.

interaction between intellectual property rights and human rights from this broader perspective. Looking at it from that perspective, both intellectual property rights and human rights deal with the same fundamental equilibrium. On the one hand, there is a need to define the scope of the private exclusive right that is given to authors as an incentive to create and as recognition of their creative contribution to society broadly enough to enable it to play its incentive and recognition function in an appropriate and effective way, whilst on the other hand, there is the broader interest of society that the public must be able to have adequate access to the fruits of authors' efforts. Both intellectual property law and human rights law try to get the private-public rights' balance right, and as such, there is no conflict. Both areas of law may, however, not define that balance in exactly the same way in all cases. There is, therefore, compatibility between them, rather than a consensus.[6]

The other essays in this collection will deal in detail with the various aspects of the interaction between intellectual property rights and human rights. In this essay, I would like to examine whether or not it might be too restrictive to see intellectual property rights and human rights solely as two sets of distinct rights between which there is an interaction along the lines of any of the two approaches or models set out in the previous paragraph. Maybe we are overlooking the fact that one way or another intellectual property rights and more specifically copyright may be considered as a Human Right. We will, therefore, have to examine whether or not copyright (or any other intellectual property right) can indeed be considered as a Human Right, both at international and at the national level. Additionally, we will need to examine whether any conclusion on this point necessarily applies to the whole of copyright or only to certain aspects of copyright and whether it applies to all aspects in the same way. And we will need to examine whether other intellectual property rights are different in this respect. Whatever the outcome of such an analysis may be and wherever it may lead us, we will inevitably have to come back to the issue of the interaction between copyright (and other intellectual property rights) and human rights. The question will have to be answered whether our findings can be reconciled with the idea of interaction as defined above. And if the interaction idea involves a balancing of interests, we will have to determine where and how balancing is to take place. The question of whether the balancing of interests can maybe also take place inside a broadly conceived human rights portfolio will arise unavoidably. But let us now first turn to the

---

6. *See,* e.g., United Nations, Economic and Social Council, Commission on Human Rights, Sub-Commission on the Promotion and Protection of Human Rights, 52nd session, Item 4 of the Provisional Agenda, Economic, Social and Cultural Rights – The Impact of the Agreement on Trade-Related Aspects of Intellectual Property Rights on Human Rights, Report of the High Commissioner, E/CN.4/Sub/2/2001/13, at 5.

question of whether there are indications in international legal instruments that allow us to define copyright as a Human Right.

7.2 THE HUMAN RIGHTS APPROACH TO COPYRIGHT IN INTERNATIONAL INSTRUMENTS

Let us for a moment leave behind legal concepts and consider the factual starting point. Broadly speaking, we are essentially concerned here with creative works, creations of the mind and elements of cultural heritage which are of particular value to society. Society finds it is, therefore, in its best interest to offer some form of protection to the creators of these works. Interests in material goods are protected by means of physical possession of the goods, which then gains legal recognition in the form of a property right. Whoever produces the goods and has them in his or her possession will be given a property right in the goods. Similarly, protection for creative works is offered along the property route. As these works are immaterial in nature,[7] the factual element of physical possession is not available here and cannot form the basis of the property right. That (intellectual) property right is, therefore, created as a legal fiction, but it serves the same purpose. It is important to note though that the way society and the legal system on its behalf deal with creative works is to turn them into property rights. Behind any property stands an owner and it is important to also note at the outset that the legal fiction that copyright as a property right refers in this respect to the creator or author behind the work in the absence of the concept of a person having the physical goods in his or her possession in relation to the immaterial property. This is important to keep in mind in a human rights context. Apart from the obvious references to copyright as such, the debate will also need to deal with the human rights aspects of property rights and personality rights.[8]

The importance of the act of creation and the link with the creator in relation to rights that may flow from it has also been emphasized by René Cassin, one of the architects of the current human rights framework. In his view, the ability and the desire to develop intellectual and creative activities from which copyright works may result is potentially found in all human beings. As such, it deserves, therefore, respect and protection in the same way as all other basic faculties that are common to all men. This would mean that creators can claim rights by the very fact of their creation. This is a broad statement, and it is by now clear that such rights are by definition human rights and that they must cover all creations and necessarily take the format

---

7. They are indeed to be distinguished from their material support of carrier.
8. *See* Chapman, 'Approaching Intellectual Property as a Human Right (obligations related to Article 15(1)(c))', (2001) Copyright Bulletin, XXXV, no. 3, 4-36, at 5.

of an exclusive right in such creations.[9] Further analysis is, therefore, warranted.

7.2.1   THE UNIVERSAL DECLARATION OF HUMAN RIGHTS

The first key provision in an international instrument that identifies copyright as a Human Right is found in Article 27 of the Universal Declaration of Human Rights.[10] According to Article 27, everyone has first of all 'the right to the protection of the moral and material interests resulting from any scientific, literary or artistic production of which he is the author'. But it is equally important to note another element of the same article where it is stated in its first paragraph that 'everyone has the right freely to participate in the cultural life of the community, to enjoy the arts and to share in scientific advancement and its benefits'.

This first paragraph of Article 27 clearly has historical roots. The Universal Declaration of Human Rights was drafted less than three years after the end of the Second World War, and science and technology, as well as copyright-based propaganda, had been abused for atrocious purposes by those who lost the war. Such an abuse had to be prevented for the future, and it was felt that the best way forward was to recognize that everyone had a share in the benefits and that at the same time those who made valuable contributions were entitled to protection. That process was of a human rights nature, as the series of rights and claims made in Article 27 are considered to be universal and vested in each person by virtue of their common humanity. It should, in this context, also be remembered that the human rights that were articulated in the Universal Declaration of Human Rights are held to exist independently of implementation or even recognition in the customs or legal systems of individual countries. They are after all such important norms that they create prima facie obligations to take measures to protect and uphold these rights. This obligation particularly applies to governments, as they are supposed to act in the common interest of humanity.[11] And '[b]ecause a human right is a universal entitlement, its implementation should be measured particularly by the degree to which it benefits those who hitherto have been the most disadvantaged and

---

9. Cassin, 'L'intégration, parmi les droits fondamentaux de l'homme, des droits des créateurs des oeuvres de l'esprit', in *Mélanges Marcel Plaisant: Etudes sur la propriété industrielle, littéraire et artistique*, Sirey (1959), at 229 and Vivant, 'Le droit d'auteur, un droit de l'homme?', (1997) RIDA 174, 60, at 87.
10. *See* J.A.L. Sterling, *World Copyright Law*, Sweet & Maxwell (2nd ed., 2003), 43.
11. *See* J.W. Nickel, *Making Sense of Human Rights: Philosophical Reflections on the Universal Declaration of Human Rights*, University of California Press (1987), 3.

vulnerable'.[12] It should not simply serve one group in society that already occupies a privileged position. The benefit that is produced for 'everyone' should also go beyond the ability to draw some benefit from the applications of intellectual property, i.e., the better goods and services that are made available as a result. Enjoyment of the arts and especially participation in the cultural life of society are clearly broader concepts that go further and involve elements of sharing at all levels and stages.

That brings us back to paragraph two of Article 27. This is not inasmuch a tool to implement paragraph one as a complimentary provision that sets up a right to the protection of moral as well as material interests. The protection of moral and material rights of authors and creator is clearly exactly what is covered by the area of law known as copyright and this second paragraph of Article 27 of the Universal Declaration of Human Rights must, therefore, be seen as elevating copyright to the status of a Human Right, or maybe it is more appropriate to say that the article recognizes the human rights status of copyright. The roots of this second paragraph of Article 27 go back to two influential elements. In the first place, there was the original suggestion made by the French delegation, which had a double focus. On the one hand, the emphasis was placed on the moral rights of the author, which centred around his or her ability to control alterations made to the work and to be able to stop misuse of the work or creation. On the other hand, there was the recognition of the right of the author or creator to receive a form of remuneration for his or her creative activity and contribution.[13] Second, the Mexican and Cuban members of the drafting committee argued that it made sense to establish a parallelism between the provisions of the Universal Declaration of Human Rights and the American Declaration on the Rights and Duties of Man that had at that stage been adopted very recently.[14] Article 13 of the latter dealt with intellectual property rights by stating:

> *[E]very person has the right to take part in the cultural life of the community, to enjoy the arts, and to participate in the benefits that result from intellectual progress, especially scientific discoveries. He likewise has the right to the protection of his moral and material interests as regards his inventions or any literary, scientific or artistic works of which he is the author.*[15]

---

12. Chapman, 'A Human Rights Perspective on Intellectual Property, Scientific Progress, and Access to the Benefits of Science', (8 November 1998) *WIPO Panel Discussion on Intellectual Property and Human Rights*, at 2, available at www.wipo.org, (last accessed 23 April 2008).

13. *See* J. Morsink, *The Universal Declaration of Human Rights: Origins, Drafting and Intent*, University of Pennsylvania Press (1999), at 220.

14. Chapman, 'Approaching Intellectual Property as a Human Right (Obligations Related to Article 15(1)(c))', (2001) Copyright Bulletin XXXV, no. 3, 4-36, at 11.

15. American Declaration of the Rights and Duties of Man, Approved by the ninth International Conference of American States, Bogota, Colombia, 30 March to 2 May 1948, Final Act of the Ninth Conference, 38-45.

Despite these rather clear and explicit roots, it is not necessarily clear what motivated those who voted in favour of the adoption of the second paragraph of Article 27 of the Universal Declaration of Human Rights. What we know is that the initial strong criticism that intellectual property was not properly speaking a Human Right or that it already attracted sufficient protection under the regime of protection afforded to property rights, in general, was eventually defeated by a coalition of those who primarily voted in favour because they felt that the moral rights deserved and needed protection and met the human rights standard and those who felt the ongoing internationalization of copyright needed a boost and that this could be a tool in this respect.[16]

This is, of course, not the strongest basis for a strong argument that copyright is beyond doubt a Human Right and in theory, things are not helped a great deal either by the fact that as a United Nations General Assembly action, the Universal Declaration of Human Rights is merely aspirational or advisory in nature. But where initially the Member States were not obliged to implement it on this basis, it has now gradually acquired the status of customary international law and of the single most authoritative source of human rights norms. That has, in turn, greatly enhanced the standing of copyright as a Human Right, even if the economic, social and cultural rights, of which copyright is one, are still seen as weaker provisions than those dealing with basic civil and political rights.[17] The exact ramifications of Article 27 of the Universal Declaration of Human Rights are also not always clear,[18] but what is clear is that copyright as a Human Right requires there to be a balance between the concepts expressed in Article 27(1) and those expressed in Article 27(2) as they are linked in the drafting of the provision.[19] Nevertheless, national courts have used it to protect the interests of authors on a couple of occasions.[20] For example, in a judgment dated 29 April 1959, the Court of Appeal in Paris granted Charlie Chaplin, a British national, the rights of a Frenchman in France in relation to his moral rights on the basis of assimilation based on Article 27(2) of the Universal

---

16. J. Morsink, *The Universal Declaration of Human Rights: Origins, Drafting and Intent*, University of Pennsylvania Press (1999), at 221.
17. Chapman, 'A Human Rights Perspective on Intellectual Property, Scientific Progress, and Access to the Benefits of Science', (8 November 1998) *WIPO Panel Discussion on Intellectual Property and Human Rights*, at 7, available at www.wipo.org, (last accessed 23 April 2008).
18. Cassin, 'L'intégration, parmi les droits fondamentaux de l'homme, des droits des créateurs des oeuvres de l'esprit', in *Mélanges Marcel Plaisant: Etudes sur la propriété industrielle, littéraire et artistique*, Sirey (1959), at 225.
19. *See* Villalba, 'Volviendo a justificar el derecho de autor – Revalidating Copyright', paper delivered at the ALAI 2007 conference in Punta del Este, to be published in the proceedings of that conference, at para. 8.
20. *See* F. Dessemontet, 'Copyright and Human Rights', in J. Kabel & G. Mom, (ed.), *Intellectual Property and Information Law: Essays in Honour of Herman Cohen Jehoram*, Kluwer Law International (1998), Volume 6, Information Law Series, 113-120.

Declaration when he wished to object to the unauthorized addition of a soundtrack to one of his movies.[21] Similarly, Article 27(2) played a prominent role in the granting of the status of author and with it moral rights in the first judgment in the John Huston – Asphalt Jungle saga where colour rather than sound was added to the movie.[22] Whilst both cases deal primarily with moral rights, the concept of authorship also has economic rights aspects, and it is clear that Article 27 covers both economic and moral rights and, therefore, the whole of copyright.

7.2.2   THE INTERNATIONAL COVENANT ON ECONOMIC, SOCIAL AND CULTURAL RIGHTS

This Covenant is to be seen as a follow-up action on the Universal Declaration of Human Rights. Important though is the fact that this follow-up action took the form of a Treaty and that as such, it can impose legally binding obligations to implement its provisions on States that became contracting parties to it. Article 15 of the Covenant is very clear in this respect and imposes a number of responsibilities and steps to be taken on the Contracting States in the following way:

(2) The steps to be taken by the States Parties to the present Covenant to achieve the full realization of this right shall include those necessary for the conservation, development and the diffusion of science and culture.

(3) The States Parties to the present Covenant undertake to respect the freedom indispensable for scientific research and creative activity.

(4) The States Parties to the Present Covenant recognize the benefits to be derived from the encouragement and development of international contacts and cooperation in the scientific and cultural fields.

These obligations apply to the substantive rights granted in paragraph one of Article 15 of the Covenant and which are very much based on Article 27 of the Universal Declaration of Human Rights. As such, they comprise the rights of everyone (a) to take part in cultural life; (b) to enjoy the benefits of scientific progress and its applications and, most importantly for our current purposes; and (c) to benefit from the protection of the moral and the material interests resulting from any scientific, literary or artistic production of which he is the author. However, this provision no doubt gains in importance in the light of the absence in the Covenant of a provision dealing with property,

---

21. *Société Roy Export Company Establishment et Charlie Chaplin c/. Société Les Films Roger Richebé*, 28 (1960) RIDA 133 and [1960] *Journal du Droit International* 128, annotated by Goldman.

22. *Tribunal de Grande Instance de Paris*, judgment dated 23 November 1988, 139 (1989) RIDA 205, annotated by Sirinelli and (1989) *Journal du Droit International* 1005, annotated by Edelman.

which at the time of the Universal Declaration was still seen as clearly the stronger and more obvious Human Right and which could also cover most of the intellectual property issues.

If we look in a bit more detail at the substantive provision contained in Article 15.1(c) of the Covenant, the clear starting point is that an obligation is imposed upon the Contracting Parties to protect the moral and material interests of authors and creators.[23] In essence, there is, therefore, an obligation to implement copyright as a Human Right and to put in place an appropriate regime of protection for the interests of authors and creators.[24] But a lot of freedom is left to the Contracting States in relation to the exact legal format of that protection. The human rights framework in which copyright is placed does, however, put in place a number of imperative guidelines:

- Copyright must be consistent with the understanding of human dignity in the various human rights instruments and the norms defined therein.
- Copyrights related to science must promote scientific progress and access to its benefits.
- Copyright regimes must respect the freedom indispensable for scientific research and creative activity.
- Copyright regimes must encourage the development of international contacts and cooperation in the scientific and cultural fields.[25]

In looking at this framework, it should not be forgotten that its genesis was troubled and cumbersome. Various proposals were made to include intellectual property rights in the Covenant, all of them attracted severe criticism, and some were rejected. However, whenever a draft Covenant without an intellectual property rights clause in it was submitted for further discussion, a new proposal to include intellectual property rights was tabled, and in the end, the incorporation into the International Covenant on Economic, Social and Cultural Rights of an intellectual property clause was approved by a vote of thirty-nine to nine, with twenty-four Member States

---

23. Chapman, 'A Human Rights Perspective on Intellectual Property, Scientific Progress, and Access to the Benefits of Science', (8 November 1998) *WIPO Panel Discussion on Intellectual Property and Human Rights*, at 15, available at www.wipo.org, (last accessed 23 April 2008).
24. *See also* A. Bertrand, *Le droit d'auteur et les droits voisins*, Dalloz (2nd ed., 1999), at 81.
25. Chapman, 'A Human Rights Perspective on Intellectual Property, Scientific Progress, and Access to the Benefits of Science', (8 November 1998) *WIPO Panel Discussion on Intellectual Property and Human Rights*, at 13, available at www.wipo.org, (last accessed 23 April 2008).

abstaining.[26] The Covenant then came into force several years later on 3 January 1976.[27]

It is, of course, interesting to look back at these instruments that enshrine copyright as a Human Right and the way in which they came into being, especially as the copyright community all too often simply ignores this aspect of copyright. However, one should not look at this simply as a historical accident. One should also try to identify its implications for copyright and the conclusions that should be drawn from it. The first thing to note is that copyright has a relatively weak claim to human rights status, as its inclusion in the international human rights instruments proved to be highly controversial. And in the end, the copyright and intellectual property components of the various articles were only included because they were seen as tools to give effect to and to protect other stronger human rights. The second conclusion flows from this first one. The various elements in the Articles dealing with copyright and intellectual property are interrelated, which means, for example, that the rights of authors and creators must be understood as essential preconditions for cultural freedom and for the participation and access to the benefits of scientific progress. The fact that the rights of authors and creators can also stand in their own right is instead an ancillary point. The third point takes this interaction one step further. Copyright and intellectual property rights are not simply preconditions. Not only do they need to exist to facilitate cultural participation and access to the benefits of scientific progress but also to make sure that the other components of the relevant articles in the international human rights instruments are respected and promoted. In this sense, the rights of authors and creators should not only enable but also facilitate rather than constrain cultural participation and access to scientific progress. The fourth implication of all this is that the international human rights instruments deal with copyright and intellectual property rights as such.[28] They do no delineate the scope and the limits of copyright. The determination of the substance of copyright is an issue that is left to the legislature.[29]

Perhaps it is worth adding at this stage that one can only talk in terms of a Human Right when the pre-normative state of a claim has been turned into a normative state that is recognized by the social group concerned. Additionally, the norm must fit the existing normative order in a coherent

---

26. M. Green, 'Background Paper on the Drafting History of Article 15(1)(c) of the International Covenant on Economic, Social and Cultural Rights', submitted for the Day of General Discussion on Article 15(1) of the Covenant, 9 October 2000, E/C.12/2000/15, at 8-12.

27. The International Covenant on Economic, Social and Cultural Rights, 993 U.N.T.S. 3, G.A. Res. 2200 (XXI), 21 U.N. GAOR Supp. (No.16), 49, U.N. Doc. A/6316 (1966), was adopted on 16 December 1966.

28. Chapman, 'Approaching Intellectual Property as a Human Right (obligations related to Article 15(1)(c))', (2001) *Copyright Bulletin* XXXV, no. 3, 4-36, at 13.

29. *See* H. Schack, *Urheberund Urhebervertragsrecht*, Mohr Siebeck (1997), at 40.

way; it must be considered to represent basic freedom, that is, an essential social condition for the better development of the individual, and finally it must be perceived as being of universal reach.[30] Broadly speaking, copyright seems to meet these requirements, and its inclusion in the international human rights instruments seems justifiable on that basis, but it remains to be seen how all these elements really fit together in practice in relation to copyright.

The common theme that seems to emerge and an understanding of which seems to be essential to understand how copyright operates as a Human Right is that of the balancing of rights and interests. Two kinds of balancing acts appear to be necessary. The first one relates to the balance that is inherent to copyright itself, and that involves both the private interests of authors and creators and the wider public interests of society as a whole.[31] We will now briefly look at other intellectual property rights, and we will then turn our attention to this particular balancing act. But on top of that, one has to acknowledge that copyright as a Human Right is just one element in the international human rights instruments. Surely, copyright as a Human Right will also have to be seen in relation to other human rights. Here again, a balancing of rights, albeit of a different nature, will be unavoidable, and we will deal with this at a later stage.

7.3 OTHER INTELLECTUAL PROPERTY RIGHTS

Article 27 of the Universal Declaration of Human Rights gives one a right to the protection of the moral and material interests also from the scientific production of which he is the author. Similarly, Article 15 of the International Covenant refers to science on top of culture. There is, of course, no reason to exclude scientific works from the scope of copyright, especially as Article 2(1) of the Berne Convention 1886 specifically includes scientific works in the scope of copyright. It is nevertheless arguable that the wording of the human rights instruments is broader and goes beyond the field of copyright. From an intellectual property perspective, the field covered traditionally by patent law could also be involved. The link is much weaker though, and apart from a broad statement that the interests of an inventor should be protected, there is very little guidance to be derived from these provisions for the exact scope and content of patent law. Trademarks, as the third major intellectual property right, seem to be entirely unaffected.

More interesting in this respect is the link to human rights through the property provisions in the European Convention. It should, in this respect, be kept in mind that property was also seen as a key element in the Universal Declaration of Human Rights, but that it had shrunk away when the

---

30. Vivant, 'Le droit d'auteur, un droit de l'homme?', (1997) RIDA 174, 60, at 73.
31. *See* J.A.L. Sterling, *World Copyright Law*, Sweet & Maxwell (1998), 40.

International Covenant came along. Article 1 of the First Protocol to the European Convention of Human Rights is the key provision on this point. Its role in relation to intellectual property rights was examined carefully by the Grand Chamber of the European Court of Human Rights in *Anheuser-Busch v. Portugal.*[32] Anheuser-Busch had applied to register its 'Budweiser' trademark in Portugal. This was opposed by their rivals Budejovicky Budvar, who relied on a bilateral treaty between Portugal and the Czech Republic protecting geographical indications. The Portuguese Supreme Court eventually ruled in favour of Budejovicky Budvar. Anheuser-Busch argued that they had acquired a property right through their application and that the retrospective application of the bilateral treaty interfered with their property right in a way that is prohibited by Article 1 of the first protocol.

For our current purposes, it is important to note that the European Court of Human Rights accepts that property or the concept of 'possession' in Article 1 of the first protocol is not limited to material property and can also include immaterial property such as intellectual property rights. In relation to patents, the Court referred to its judgment in *British-American Tobacco Company v. Netherlands.*[33] In relation to copyright, reference was made to the judgment in *Melnitchouk v. Ukraine*[34] and the Court then applied the same logic to trademarks in the case at issue.[35] Slightly more controversial was the issue of whether a mere application for an intellectual property right could also come within the scope of Article 1 of the first protocol. The Court argues that economic interests flow from the mere application, despite the fact that it is at best provisional and that a successful opposition can annul any interest. But under Portuguese law, a mere application makes licences and transfers of rights possible, as well as infringement proceedings. Despite the fact that it remains precarious and dependent on the eventual success of the registration this is in the view of the Court sufficient to bring the mere application also within the scope of Article 1 of the first protocol.[36]

The next step was then to examine whether the actions of the Portuguese State, effectively the judgment of the Portuguese Supreme Court, amounted to the kind of interference with a property that Article 1 of the first protocol rules out. The Court came to the conclusion that it did not, as the judgment of the Supreme Court was based on law and had nothing arbitrary or manifestly unreasonable in it. There was, therefore, no interference with the property right in a sense required by Article 1 of the first protocol.[37] As

---

32. *Anheuser-Busch v. Portugal*, Case 73049/01, judgment of 11 January 2007, European Court of Human Rights.
33. *British-American Tobacco Company v. Netherlands,* judgment of 20 November 1995, A Series No. 331.
34. *Melnitchouk v. Ukraine*, Case 28743/03, judgment of 5 July 2005, CEDH 2005-IX.
35. *Anheuser-Busch v. Portugal*, Case 73049/01, judgment of 11 January 2007, European Court of Human Rights, at para. 72.
36. *Ibid*., at para. 78.
37. *Ibid*., at para. 87.

a result, Anheuser-Busch was unsuccessful in the end. Interesting as the case may be on its facts, it adds little to the debate for our current purposes. On the positive side, we learn that intellectual property is also, for human rights purposes, a form of property and that as such, the human rights instruments will grant it some form of protection. That also seems to apply to applications to register intellectual property rights. On the negative side, we learn little, if anything at all, about the scope of form these intellectual property rights themselves, should take. The influence on the shape of substantive patent or trademark law seems negligible. Nothing is also said about the interaction with other aspects of human rights law.

7.4   CHARTER OF FUNDAMENTAL RIGHTS OF THE EUROPEAN UNION

The Charter of Fundamental Rights of the European Union also adopts an approach that applies across the board to all intellectual property rights. In its Article 17 which deals with the right to property, one finds a brief paragraph 2 that guarantees the protection of intellectual property as a fundamental right, by including it in the fundamental right to property:

Article 17
Right to property

1. Everyone has the right to own, use, dispose of and bequeath his or her lawfully acquired possessions. No one may be deprived of his or her possessions, except in the public interest and in the cases and under the conditions provided for by law, subject to fair compensation being paid in good time for their loss. The use of property may be regulated by law in so far as is necessary for the general interest.
2. Intellectual property shall be protected.[38]

The text of Article 17 of the charter is clearly based on Article 1 of the Protocol to the European Convention on Human Rights (ECHR). Let us, therefore, turn our attention to the question of how the addition of paragraph 2 changes matters. Article 17(2) covers 'intellectual property'. Our attention will, therefore, turn to the definition of the concept of intellectual property, but due to Article 51, which specifies that the provisions of the Charter are addressed to the institutions and bodies of the Union with due regard for the principle of subsidiarity and to the Member States only when they are implementing Union law, Article 17(2) only has relevance to the extent that EU law affects intellectual property rights.

---

38. Charter of fundamental rights of the European Union, [2000] OJ C-364/1. *See* P. Torremans, 'Article 17(2)', in S. Peers, T. Hervey, J. Kenner & A. Ward (eds), *The EU Charter of Fundamental Rights: A Commentary,* Hart/Beck (2014), 489-517.

Whilst the core of intellectual property is fairly well defined, there is no single accepted definition of the concept of intellectual property. The text of the explanations does not help either, as it merely restates the core intellectual property rights by referring to copyright, patents and trademarks. To these core rights are added 'associated rights'. Two forms of associated rights could be suggested in the absence of any definition or indication in the article and the explanations to it. On the one hand, there are rights that are linked to the core rights, in the sense that supplementary protection certificates are closely linked to patents, appellations of origin are linked to trademarks, and artistic design rights are closely linked to literary and artistic property. On the other hand, there are peripheral intellectual property rights that are associated with the core rights, as they equally protect intellectual or artistic creation. Here, the examples of the design right, the sui generis database right and the right in semiconductor topographies come to mind. It is probably fair to say that these are all 'intellectual property', as they are treated as such by the European Commission and in a number of international instruments. There is, however, no universally accepted definition[39], and it is, therefore, not clear where intellectual property stops. It is unlikely that Article 17(2) was ever intended to cover things such as breach of competence, passing-off and unfair competition. These may be too peripheral, and they do not involve property in the sense as set out by Article 17. But Article 17(2) does not provide certainty on this point.

Article 51 of the Charter is less of a restriction than may seem to be the case at first glance. Article 17(2) does not seem to cover the complex cases such as breach of competence, unfair competition and passing-off, and there is a fair bit of EU legislation affecting intellectual property rights outside these complex cases. Both in the area of trademarks and design rights, there are unitary Community rights put in place by means of Regulations, i.e. Community Trade Marks[40] and Community Designs.[41] These exist in parallel with national rights, but the latter have been harmonized on virtually every point by a Directive whose provisions run parallel with those of the relevant Regulation.[42] That leaves very little to purely national provisions that can use the escape route of Article 51. Copyright presents a more complex picture. There is no Community Copyright, and there are merely Directives dealing with certain aspects of copyright, even if these Directives increasingly are of a horizontal nature.[43] But in interpreting the provisions of these Directives,

---

39. Compare the definitions found in Article 1 TRIPS Agreement 1994 and the WIPO Intellectual Property Handbook (wipo.int/about-ip/en/iprm/) respectively.
40. Council Regulation (EC) 207/2009 on the Community trade mark [2009] OJ L78/1.
41. Council Regulation 6/2002 on Community Designs [2002] OJ L3/1.
42. Directive 2008/95/EC to approximate the laws of the Member States relating to trade marks [2008] OJ L299/25. EC Parliament and Council Directive 98/71/EC on the legal protection of designs [1998] OJ L289/28.
43. EC Council Directive 93/98 harmonizing the terms of protection of copyright and certain related rights (1993) OJ L290/9, now codified as Directive 2006/116/EC on the term of

the Court of Justice of the European Union increasingly feels obliged to define general copyright concepts, such as what amounts to a 'work', and what meets the 'originality' standard, even if they have no place in the Directive. Add to that, concepts such as 'communication to the public' which are in the Directives, and it becomes clear that EU law now affects the whole of the core aspects of copyright. Related issues such as the database right[44] and the right in semiconductor topographies[45] originate entirely in EU Directives, and for them, Article 51 has no relevance at all as a potential escape clause. In the patent area, things used to be more of a problem. There were Supplementary Protection Certificates[46] and a directive on biotechnological patents,[47] but the core instrument, the European Patent Convention, was never an EU instrument. All that is set to change radically, with the adoption in 2012 of Regulations creating a unitary patent for the EU, which will link that Convention to the EU legal order and which are expected to enter into force in 2015, although the unitary patent does not cover Italy and Spain.[48] Add to that, the impact of free movement law, competition law[49] and

---

protection of copyright and certain related rights (codified version) [2006] OJ L372/12; EC Council Directive 91/250 on the legal protection of computer programs [1991] OJ L122/42, now codified as Directive 2009/24/EC of the European Parliament and of the Council of 23 April 2009 on the legal protection of computer programs (Codified version) [2009] OJ L111/16; EC Council Directive 92/100 on rental rights and lending rights related to copyright in the field of intellectual property [1992] OJ L346/61, now codified as Directive 2006/115/EC on rental right and lending right and on certain rights related to copyright in the field of intellectual property (codified version) [2006] OJ L376/28; EC Council Directive 93/83 on the coordination of certain copyright and rights related to copyright applicable to satellite broadcasting and cable re-transmission [1993] OJ L248/15; EC Parliament and Council Directive 2001/29/EC on the harmonization of certain aspects of copyright and related rights in the information society [2001] OJ L167/10.

44. EC Parliament and Council Directive 96/9 on the legal protection of databases [1996] OJ L77/20.

45. EC Parliament and Council Directive 87/54 on the legal protection of topographies of semiconductor products [1987] OJ L24/36.

46. EC Council Regulation 1768/92 concerning the creation of a supplementary protection certificate for medicinal products [1992] OJ L182/1, now codified as Regulation (EC) 469/2009 concerning the supplementary protection certificate for medicinal products (Codified version) [2009] OJ L152/1.

47. EC Parliament and Council Directive 98/44/EC on the legal protection of biotechnological inventions [1998] OJ L213/13.

48. European Parliament and Council Regulation (EU) No. 1257/2012 implementing enhanced cooperation in the area of the creation of unitary patent protection [2012] OJ L361/1 and Council Regulation (EU) No. 1260/2012 implementing enhanced cooperation in the area of the creation of unitary patent protection with regard to the applicable translation arrangements [2012] OJ L361/89. *See also* the Agreement on a Unified Patent Court [2013] OJ C 175.

49. *See,* e.g., Joined Cases C-241/91 P and C-242/91 P *Radio Telefís Éireann & Independent Television Publications Ltd v. EC Commission* [1995] ECR I-743, [1995] 4 CMLR 718. A detailed and complete analysis is found in Chs 18 and 27 of P Torremans, *Holyoak and Torremans Intellectual Property Law*, 7th edn, OUP (2013).

the common commercial policy[50] on intellectual property rights, as well as the fact that the EU increasingly becomes a party to international intellectual property instruments[51] and it is clear that the impact of Article 51 of the Charter as a restriction on the scope of Article 17(2) is minor, or should one say (almost) a minute.

Be that as it may, Article 17 contains only one fundamental right amongst others, and we will have to return to the interaction between the fundamental rights in the Charter shortly.

7.5   BALANCING PRIVATE AND PUBLIC INTERESTS

7.5.1   THE NEED FOR A BALANCING ACT

As Audrey Chapman put it:

> To be consistent with the full provisions of Article 15 [of the International Covenant on Economic, Social and Cultural Rights], the type and level of protection afforded under any intellectual property regime must facilitate and promote cultural participation and scientific progress and do so in a manner that will broadly benefit members of society both on an individual and collective level.[52]

The emphasis here is on the broad public interest of society, but any level of intellectual property protection will also give rights to the individual right holder. The private interest of the author, creator and eventually of the copyright holder is an inevitable component of the equation. Somehow, a balance will need to be struck between these interests, as stronger individual rights inevitably impinge on the interests of society as a whole and vice versa.[53] This balance between public and private interests is not an external element for copyright or indeed any other intellectual property right. On the contrary, it has been internalized by copyright, and it is part of its fundamental nature.[54] Copyright is, therefore, familiar with this balance of

---

50. *See,* e.g., Case C-348/04 *Boehringer Ingelheim KG and ors v. Swingward Ltd and ors (No 2)* [2007] 2 CMLR 52. A detailed and complete analysis is found in Chs 18 and 27 of P. Torremans, *Holyoak and Torremans Intellectual Property Law,* 7th edn, OUP (2013).
51. Such as the TRIPS Agreement.
52. Chapman, 'Approaching Intellectual Property as a Human Right (obligations related to Article 15(1)(c))', (2001) Copyright Bulletin, XXXV, no. 3, 4-36, at 14.
53. *See* H. Schack, *Urheberund Urhebervertragsrecht*, Mohr Siebeck (1997), at 41.
54. Compare in this respect the wording of Article 1, para. 8, section 8 of the Constitution of the United States of America in which Congress is vested with the power 'To promote the Progress of Science and useful Arts, by securing for limited Times to Authors and Inventors the exclusive Right to their respective Writings and Discoveries'.

interests.[55] On the one hand, there is the need to protect the individual interest of the author in order to encourage further creation that results in the author being given a certain amount of exclusivity in relation to the exploitation and use of his or her work, and on the other hand, there is the public interest of society as a whole to have access to culture and to copyright works as a tool for progress and improvement.

The need for a balance that takes us away from granting a kind of unrestricted monopoly property right is also inherent in the wording of Article 15 of the International Covenant on Economic, Social and Cultural Rights where it requires States to make sure that everyone will be able 'to benefit from the protection of the moral and material interests resulting from any scientific, literary or artistic production of which he is the author'. Enjoying a benefit from such protection is clearly not the same as enjoying an unrestricted monopoly property right. In practice, copyright ensures the balance in many ways, for example, by means of limitations and exceptions to copyright infringement rules. This is an example of an attempt to strike a balance by drafting the rule in such a way that its effect in all practical cases is to achieve a proper balance between the various interests. On top of that, there are also external correction mechanisms that interfere whenever the rule would not achieve the balance in a particular, that is, peculiar, set of circumstances.

7.5.2   THE BALANCING ACT IN THE ECHR

The ECHR concerned itself with the conflict between copyright in photographs of fashion shows, held contractually by the fashion houses, and the freedom of expression of freelance photographers who took pictures without the permission of the fashion houses in the *Ashby Donald* case.[56] The court adopted a balancing of tights approach and did, in other words, and not surprisingly so,[57] go for the option to have a second stage in the balancing act. Even though (part of) the balancing act has been internalized by

---

55. United Nations, Economic and Social Council, Commission on Human Rights, Sub-Commission on the Promotion and Protection of Human Rights, 52nd session, Item 4 of the Provisional Agenda, Economic, Social and Cultural Rights – The Impact of the Agreement on Trade-Related Aspects of Intellectual Property Rights on Human Rights, Report of the High Commissioner, E/CN.4/Sub/2/2001/13, at 5.

56. *Ashby Donald and others v. France,* application 36769/08, ECtHR, 5th section, judgment of 10 January 2013. *See* Torremans, 'Ashby Donald and Others v France, Application 36769/08, ECtHR, 5th Section, Judgment of 10 January 2013', (2014) *Queen Mary Journal of Intellectual Property* 4, no. 1, 95-99.

57. *See* the reference to the 2007 Grand Chamber judgment in *Anheuser-Busch Inc. v. Portugal* in para. 40 of the judgment in Case *Ashby Donald and others v. France,* application 36769/08, ECtHR, 5th section, judgment of 10th January 2013: 'l'ingérence dans le droit à la liberté d'expression des requérants visait à la protection des droits d'auteur des créateurs de mode. Dès lors que l'article 1 du Protocole no 1 s'applique à la

copyright, there is still a need for an additional balancing act, taking account of the particular factual circumstances of each case. One could summarize this by saying that copyright's status as a fundamental right does not mean that Article 10 does not apply to it. That is a straightforward and obvious conclusion, and it should be so even from a 100% copyright point of view. It flows from the fact that there is a need for a balancing act when more than one right at the same level of fundamental rights are engaged. The conviction for breach of copyright and the award of damages is an interference with the rights protected by Article 10 of the Convention. Once that fundamental starting point is accepted, the interesting question of the criteria for the balancing of both rights arises and takes over.[58]

The court did not re-invent the wheel on this point. The criteria to judge the legitimacy of the interference was whether the interference was pre-scribed by law, pursued the legitimate aim of protecting the rights of others and was to be considered necessary in a democratic society. In a balancing exercise, there are, by definition, exceptions to Article 10, but these exceptions must be construed strictly, and the need for any restrictions must be established convincingly.[59] At first glance, copyright law and its exemp-tions fit in very well with these criteria. They are prescribed by copyright law, they protect the legitimate property rights of others, and copyright may play a necessary role in a democratic society.

In more detail, one needs to consider whether these criteria, which apply to all Article 10 cases, justify the interference in this case. The court has always given national authorities a margin of appreciation in this context. If the issue with which the exercise of the freedom of expression is concerned is related to an issue of general interest for society, the court tends to give the national authorities only a narrow margin of appreciation when it comes to justifying interferences with the right to freedom of expression. In this copyright context, i.e., the publication of the pictures of models at a fashion show and the fashion clothing shown on the catwalk in Paris, the court saw no issue of general interest for society. Instead, the court focused on the aim of the applicants to make a profit, and thus, the use of the freedom of expression happened in the context of commercial speech. The applicants, on the other hand, did not participate in a general interest debate. They were merely making the pictures available to the public to satisfy the individual curiosity of individual members of the public and to profit themselves

---

propriété intellectuelle (...), elle visait ainsi à la protection de droits garantis par la Convention ou ses Protocoles'.

58. *See* P. Torremans, 'Copyright (and Other Intellectual Property Rights) as a Human Right', in P. Torremans (ed.), *Intellectual Property and Human Rights,* Kluwer Law International (2nd ed., 2008), 195.

59. *Ashby Donald and others v. France*, application 36769/08, ECtHR, 5th section, judgment of 10 January 2013. Paragraph 38 of the judgment.

financially.[60] In such a context, the court gives the national authorities a very wide margin of appreciation.

In other words, the combination of the two elements, on the one hand, the commercial speech character of the publication of the pictures on the website, and on the other hand, the balancing exercise the Court needs to undertake between the conflicting rights guaranteed by Article 10 of the Convention and the right of property as protected by Article 1 of the First Protocol to the Convention, justify in the view of the court the award to national authorities of a very wide margin of appreciation.[61]

With that in mind, the court evaluates the decision of the Paris courts, which had in their exercise of the balancing act given preference to the enforcement of the property right of the fashion designers over the right to freedom of expression of the applicants. Taking account of the copyright in the pictures and the finding that the applicants had reproduced and represented the pictures without authorization by the copyright holders, hence infringing the rights of intellectual property of others, on the one hand, and the fact that mere commercial speech in search of a profit was involved, on the other hand, the court concluded that the Paris courts had not exceeded their very wide margin of appreciation.[62]

7.5.3 THE BALANCING ACT IN THE COURT OF JUSTICE OF THE EU

The balancing act can also be seen at work in the Court of Justice of the European Union and first of all in the court's judgment in the *Laserdisken* case. Laserdisken objected to the introduction in EU copyright of a right of distribution that was only exhausted once the recording of a cinematographic work had been placed onto the single market with the consent of the right holder (first sale). This restricted Laserdisken's ability to sell imported recordings and they argued that this also involved a violation of the right of the citizens of the EU to receive information and their freedom of expression. Having accepted that the right to freedom of expression, as well as the property right, are part of the EU legal order, the Court rejected Laserdisken's argument because the rights were not absolute and needed to be balanced with the interests of the owners of the copyright. Or as the Court put it:

> regarding the freedom to receive information, even if the exhaustion rule laid down in Art 4(2) of Directive 2001/29 may be capable of restricting

---

60. Paragraph 39 of the judgment.
61. The same approach was applied to the Pirate Bay case (decision of the 5th section of the court to declare application 40397/12 inadmissible, *Fredrik Neij and Peter Sunde Kolmisoppi v. Sweden*, 13 February 2013, available at http://hudoc.echr.coe.int/sites/fra/pages/search.aspx?i=001-117513).
62. *Ashby Donald and others v. France*, application 36769/08, ECtHR, 5th section, judgment of 10 January 2013, para. 42 of the judgment.

that freedom, it nevertheless follows from Art 10(2) of the ECHR that the freedoms guaranteed by Art 10(1) may be subject to certain limitations justified by objectives in the public interest, in so far as those derogations are in accordance with the law, motivated by one or more of the legitimate aims under that provision and necessary in a democratic society, that is to say justified by a pressing social need and, in particular, proportionate to the legitimate aim pursued (see, to that effect, Herbert Karner Industrie Auktionen GmbH v. Troostwijk GmbH (C-71/02) [2004] ECR I-3025; [2004] 2 CMLR 5 at [50]).
In the present case, the alleged restriction on the freedom to receive information is justified in the light of the need to protect intellectual property rights, including copyright, which form part of the right to property.[63]

The approach is not limited to the balance between freedom of expression and intellectual property. It applies to the balance with other fundamental rights too. The *Metronome Music* case is a good example as the Court held that the right of property and the freedom to pursue a trade might be restricted, here in order to achieve a balance with the rental and lending right of the copyright owner. This became very clear in paragraph 21 of the judgment:

Furthermore, according to settled case law, the freedom to pursue a trade or profession, and likewise the right to property, form part of the general principles of Community law. However, those principles are not absolute but must be viewed in relation to their social function. Consequently, the exercise of the right to property and the freedom to pursue a trade or profession may be restricted, provided that any restrictions in fact correspond to objectives of general interest pursued by the European Community and do not constitute in relation to the aim pursued a disproportionate and intolerable interference, impairing the very substance of the rights guaranteed.[64]

These cases were referring to the ECHR, but the same rights exist obviously under the Charter. The latter freedom to pursue a trade or profession is now guaranteed in Article 16 of the Charter, e.g., and there are more rights in the Charter with which a balance will need to be struck. There is also an interrelationship with the freedom of the arts and sciences, which is guaranteed in Article 13.[65] Artistic activity and scientific research may require the use of copyright material, and if reproduction or communication

---

63. Case C-479/04 *Laserdisken ApS v. Kulturministeriet* [2006] ECDR 30 [64]–[65].
64. Case C-200/96 *Metronome Musik GmbH v. Music Point Hokamp GmbH* [1998] ECR I-1953 [21].
65. Article 13 Freedom of the arts and sciences: 'The arts and scientific research shall be free of constraint. Academic freedom shall be respected.'

to the public is required, these may be withheld on the basis of the exclusive right of the copyright holder. The same can apply to trademarks, and scientific research may require the use of patented technology. It is then the right of the owner of the patent to grant or withhold a licence. The exercise of intellectual property can, therefore, restrict the freedom of arts and sciences. But in certain scenarios, the counterargument applies. There are indeed cases in which copyright and other intellectual property rights offer the protection that is necessary to attract the necessary investment of time and money that the arts and sciences need to flourish and that would not be made available in the absence of at least the potential of intellectual property protection.

Similarly, the right to education, as guaranteed in Article 14,[66] can be affected as the use of copyright and patented material may be required in the exercise of that right and that may clash with the power of the holder of intellectual property rights to withhold a licence, or even with the right to seek payment for the grant of a licence.

The right to the protection of personal data, as guaranteed in Article 8,[67] may also interact with intellectual property rights and a balance between both may need to be struck. This can occur, for example, when a copyright owner requests the identity of alleged infringers from an internet service provider, as demonstrated by the *Bonnier* case.[68]

A final but major interrelationship exists with the right to health care. Patents in particular (but to an extent also trademarks) tend to push up the price of pharmaceutical products that are vital in the context of health care. The right of access to health care provided for in Article 35[69] of the Charter may therefore potentially be impeded. Once more, a balancing act is called for.

There is, therefore, little doubt about the fact that this balancing act will also need to operate in the context of the EU Charter. Intellectual property as a fundamental right under Article 17(2) will need to be balanced with other

---

66. Article 14 Right to education: '1. Everyone has the right to education and to have access to vocational and continuing training … '.
67. Article 8 Protection of personal data: '1. Everyone has the right to the protection of personal data concerning him or her. 2. Such data must be processed fairly for specified purposes and on the basis of the consent of the person concerned or some other legitimate basis laid down by law. Everyone has the right of access to data which has been collected concerning him or her, and the right to have it rectified … '.
68. Case C-461/10 *Bonnier Audio AB v. Perfect Communication Sweden AB* [2012] 2 C.M.L.R. 42; [2012] E.C.D.R. 21. For a UK example in the context of the Norwich Pharmacal balancing act *see Golden Eye (International) Ltd, Ben Dover Productions and others v. Telefonica UK Ltd and another* [2012] EWHC 723 (Ch) and on appeal [2012] EWCA Cv. 1740.
69. Article 35 Health care: 'Everyone has the right of access to preventive health care and the right to benefit from medical treatment under the conditions established by national laws and practices. A high level of human health protection shall be ensured in the definition and implementation of all Union policies and activities.'

fundamental rights, such as the right to freedom of expression and the right to education. The relative strength of each right, the interests involved and the particularities of each case will play their role, as the same mechanism applies. As has already been seen on a couple of occasions, copyright cases are more prominent and more developed in this respect, but there is no reason to assume that when confronted with the question the courts will apply the same balancing exercise, using the same mechanism, in respect of trade-marks[70] and patents.[71] The EU Court of Justice was asked to apply its balancing approach in the context of the Charter in two cases that involved attempts by copyright owners to involve internet service providers in their attempt to enforce their copyright against acts of illegal downloading and sharing of their works. They wanted the personal data of the clients involved to be revealed. In other words, on the one hand, the right to property and Article 17(2) were engaged and on the other the right to private life and respect for personal data.[72] In the *Promusicae* case, the Court put it in the following way:

> 62. It should be recalled that the fundamental right to property, which includes intellectual property rights such as copyright (see, to that effect, *Laserdisken ApS v. Kulturministeriet* (C-479/04) [2006] ECR I-8089; [2007] 1 CMLR 6 at [65]), and the fundamental right to effective judicial protection constitute general principles of Community law (see respectively, to that effect, *R (on the application of Alliance for Natural Health) v. Secretary of State for Health* (C-154/04 & C-155/04) [2005] ECR I-6451; [2005] 2 CMLR 61 at [126] and the case law cited, and *Unibet (London) Ltd v. Justitie-kanslern* (C-432/05) [2007] 2 CMLR 30 at [37] and the case law cited).
>
> 63. However, the situation in respect of which the national court puts that question involves, in addition to those two rights, a further fundamental right, namely the right that guarantees protection of personal data and hence of private life.
>
> 64. According to recital 2 in the preamble to Directive 2002/58, the directive seeks to respect the fundamental rights and observes the

---

70. Canada: *British Columbia Automobile Association v. Office and Professional Employees' International Union* (2001) 10 CPR (4th) 423 (BCSC); South-Africa: *Laugh It Off Promotions CC v. Sabmark International et al.*, (2006) 1 SA 144 (CC). Compare the earlier Canadian Case *Michelin v. CAW Canada* (1996) 71 CPR (3d) 348.

71. For a critical approach that prefers not to qualify patents as fundamental rights, *see* R.C. Dreyfuss, 'Patents and Human Rights: Where Is the Paradox?,' in W. Grosheide (ed.), *Intellectual Property and Human Rights, A Paradox*, Edward Elgar Publishing (2009).

72. For a UK example in the context of the *Norwich Pharmacal* balancing act involving Article 8 of the Charter, as well as Article 17, *see Golden Eye (International) Ltd, Ben Dover Productions and others v. Telefonica UK Ltd and another* [2012] EWHC 723 (Ch) and on appeal [2012] EWCA Civ 1740.

principles recognized in particular by the Charter. In particular, the directive seeks to ensure full respect for the rights set out in Arts 7 and 8 of that Charter. Article 7 substantially reproduces Art. 8 of the European Convention for the Protection of Human Rights and Fundamental Freedoms signed at Rome on November 4, 1950, which guarantees the right to respect for private life, and Art. 8 of the Charter expressly proclaims the right to protection of personal data.

65. The present reference for a preliminary ruling thus raises the question of the need to reconcile the requirements of the protection of different fundamental rights, namely the right to respect for private life on the one hand and the rights to protection of property and to an effective remedy on the other.

66. The mechanisms allowing those different rights and interests to be balanced are contained, first, in Directive 2002/58 itself, in that it provides for rules which determine in what circumstances and to what extent the processing of personal data is lawful and what safeguards must be provided for, and in the three directives mentioned by the national court, which reserve the cases in which the measures adopted to protect the rights they regulate affect the protection of personal data. Secondly, they result from the adoption by the Member States of national provisions transposing those directives and their application by the national authorities (see, to that effect, with reference to Directive 95/46, *Lindqvist* at [82]).

67. As to those directives, their provisions are relatively general, since they have to be applied to a large number of different situations which may arise in any of the Member States. They therefore logically include rules which leave the Member States with the necessary discretion to define transposition measures which may be adapted to the various situations possible (see, to that effect, *Lindqvist* at [84]).

68. That being so, the Member States must, when transposing the directives mentioned above, take care to rely on an interpretation of the directives which allows a fair balance to be struck between the various fundamental rights protected by the Community legal order. Further, when implementing the measures transposing those directives, the authorities and courts of the Member States must not only interpret their national law in a manner consistent with those directives but also make sure that they do not rely on an interpretation of them which would be in conflict with those fundamental rights or with the other general principles of Community law, such as the principle of proportionality (see, to that effect, *Lindqvist* at

[87]; and *Ordre des Barreaux Francophones and Germanophone v. Conseil des Ministres* (C-305/05) [2007] 3 CMLR 28 at [28]).[73]

Having established the balancing exercise in a Charter context, the Court then applied it to a request to install a permanent filtering system to prevent copyright infringement. The Court ruled that such a request would distort the balance in favour of the intellectual property right:

> 43. *The protection of the right to intellectual property is indeed enshrined in art 17(2) of the Charter of Fundamental Rights of the European Union (the Charter). There is, however, nothing whatsoever in the wording of that provision or in the Court's case law to suggest that that right is inviolable and must for that reason be absolutely protected.*
>
> 44. *As [62]–[68] of the judgment in Productores de Música de España (Promusicae) v. Telefónica de España SAU (C-275/06) [2008] ECR I-271; [2008] 2 CMLR 17; [2008] ECDR 10 make clear, the protection of the fundamental right to property, which includes the rights linked to intellectual property, must be balanced against the protection of other fundamental rights.*
>
> 45. *More specifically, it follows from [68] of that judgment that, in the context of measures adopted to protect copyright holders, national authorities and courts must strike a fair balance between the protection of copyright and the protection of the fundamental rights of individuals who are affected by such measures.*
>
> ...
>
> 49. In those circumstances, it must be held that the injunction to install the contested filtering system is to be regarded as not respecting the requirement that a fair balance be struck between, on the one hand, the protection of the intellectual-property right enjoyed by copyright holders, and, on the other hand, that of the freedom to conduct business enjoyed by operators such as ISPs.
>
> 50. Moreover, the effects of that injunction would not be limited to the ISP concerned, as the contested filtering system may also infringe the fundamental rights of that ISP's customers, namely their right to protection of their personal data and their freedom to receive or impart information, which are rights safeguarded by arts 8 and 11 of the Charter respectively.[74]

A most recent example deals with the exception for parody in copyright. The court clearly recognized that that exception that authorizes parody needs

---

73. Case C-275/06 *Productores de Musica de España (Promusicae) v. Telefonica de España SAU* [2008] ECR I-271 [62]–[68].
74. Case C-70/10 *Scarlet Extended SA v. SABAM Scrl* [2012] ECDR 4 [43]–[45] and [49]–[50].

to be balanced with the right to non-discrimination. In the *Deckmyn* case,[75] the court put it as follows:

27 It follows that the application, in a particular case, of the exception for parody, within the meaning of Article 5(3)(k) of Directive 2001/29, must strike a fair balance between, on the one hand, the interests and rights of persons referred to in Articles 2 and 3 of that directive, and, on the other, the freedom of expression of the user of a protected work who is relying on the exception for parody, within the meaning of Article 5(3)(k).

28 In order to determine whether, in a particular case, the application of the exception for parody within the meaning of Article 5(3)(k) of Directive 2001/29 preserves that fair balance, all the circumstances of the case must be taken into account.

29 Accordingly, with regard to the dispute before the national court, it should be noted that, according to Vandersteen and Others, since, in the drawing at issue, the characters who, in the original work, were picking up the coins were replaced by people wearing veils and people of colour, that drawing conveys a discriminatory message which has the effect of associating the protected work with such a message.

30 If that is indeed the case, which it is for the national court to assess, attention should be drawn to the principle of non-discrimination based on race, colour and ethnic origin, as was specifically defined in Council Directive 2000/43/EC of 29 June 2000 implementing the principle of equal treatment between persons irrespective of racial or ethnic origin (OJ 2000 L 180, p. 22), and confirmed, inter alia, by Article 21(1) of the Charter of Fundamental Rights of the European Union.

31 In those circumstances, holders of rights provided for in Articles 2 and 3 of Directive 2001/29, such as Vandersteen and Others, have, in principle, a legitimate interest in ensuring that the work protected by copyright is not associated with such a message.

32 Accordingly, it is for the national court to determine, in the light of all the circumstances of the case in the main proceedings, whether the application of the exception for parody, within the meaning of Article 5(3)(k) of Directive 2001/29, on the assumption that the drawing at issue fulfils the essential requirements set out in paragraph 20 above, preserves the fair balance referred to in paragraph 27 above.

---

75. Case C-201/13 *Johan Deckmyn and Vrijheidsfonds VZW v. Helena Vandersteen, Christiane Vandersteen, Liliana Vandersteen, Rita Dupont, Amoras II CVOH and WPG Uitgevers Belgi ë*, 3rd September 2014, nyr, www.curia.europa.eu, [27]-[32].

What we are dealing with then bears a close resemblance to the abuse of rights scenario. The use of competition principles in relation to copyright can serve as a good example to clarify the concept of balancing interests in copyright.

7.5.4   COMPETITION PRINCIPLES AS AN EXAMPLE

7.5.4.1   Principles and Justification

It would indeed be a serious error to see copyright (and other intellectual property rights), as essentially a private monopoly right, and competition law, as a defender of the public interest against inappropriate behaviour, as irreconcilable opponents that fight for supremacy. Instead, one should start by looking at the way in which intellectual property rights and in particular copyright fit into our modern society and how their existence can be justified.[76] Why are these intangible property rights, such as copyright created? Economists argue that if everyone would be allowed to use the results of innovative and creative activity freely, the problem of the 'free riders'[77] would arise.[78] No one would invest in creation or innovation, except in a couple of cases where no other solution would be available,[79] as it would give them a competitive disadvantage.[80] All competitors would just wait until someone else made the investment, as they would be able to use the results as well without investing money in creation and innovation and without taking the risks that the investment would not result in the creative or innovative breakthrough it aimed at.[81] The cost of the distribution of the

---

76. *See* in general P. Torremans, *Holyoak and Torremans Intellectual Property Law*, OUP (5th ed., 2008), 10-24.
77. *See* R. Benko, *Protecting Intellectual Property Rights: Issues and Controversies*, American Enterprise Institute for Public Policy Research (AEI Studies 453) (1987), at 17.
78. Inappropriability, the lack of the opportunity to become the proprietor of the results of innovative and creative activity, causes an under-allocation of resources to research activity, innovation and creation: *see* K. Arrow, 'Economic Welfare and the Allocation of Resources for Invention' in National Bureau for Economic Research, *The Rate and Direction of Inventive Activity: Economic and Social Factors*, Princeton University Press (1962), at 609-625.
79. For example., a case where the existing technology is completely incapable of providing any form of solution to a new technical problem that has arisen.
80. *See* Ullrich, 'The Importance of Industrial Property Law and Other Legal Measures in the Promotion of Technological Innovation', (1989) *Industrial Property* 102, at 103.
81. One could advance the counterargument that inventions and creations will give the innovator an amount of lead time and that the fact that it will take imitators some time to catch up would allow the innovator to recuperate his investment during the interim period. In many cases this amount of lead time will, however, only be a short period, too short to recuperate the investment and make a profit. *See also* Mansfield, Schwartz and Wagner, 'Imitation Costs and Patents: An Empirical Study', (1981) *The Economic Journal* 907, at 915 et seq.

knowledge is, on top of that, insignificant.[82] As a result, the economy would not function adequately because we see creation and innovation as an essential element in a competitive free-market economy. In this line of argument, creation and innovation are required for economic growth and prosperity.[83] In this starting point, one recognizes very clearly elements of public interest, that is, as the needs of society. Property rights should be created if goods and services are to be produced and used as efficiently as possible in such an economy. The perspective that they will be able to have a property right in the results of their investment will stimulate individuals and enterprises to invest in further cultural and artistic creation as well as in research and development.[84] These property rights should be granted to someone who will economically maximize profits.[85] It is assumed that the creator or inventor will have been motivated by the desire to maximize profits, either by exploiting the creation or invention himself or by having it exploited by a third party, so the rights are granted to them.[86]

But how does such a legally created monopolistic exclusive property right fit in with the free-market ideal of perfect competition? At first sight, every form of a monopoly might seem incompatible with free competition, but we have already demonstrated that some form of property right is required to enhance economic development as competition can only play its role as a market regulator if the products of human labour are protected by property rights.[87] In this respect, the exclusive monopolistic character of the property rights is coupled with the fact that these rights are transferable. These rights are marketable; they can, for example, be sold as an individual item. It is also necessary to distinguish between various levels of economic activity as far as economic development and competition are concerned. The market mechanism is more sophisticated than the competition/monopoly dichotomy. Competitive restrictions at one level may be necessary to promote competition at another level. Three levels can be distinguished:

---

82. *See* R. Benko, *Protecting Intellectual Property Rights: Issues and Controversies*, American Enterprise Institute for Public Policy Research (AEI Studies 453) (1987), at 17.
83. *See* R. Benko, *Protecting Intellectual Property Rights: Issues and Controversies*, American Enterprise Institute for Public Policy Research (AEI Studies 453) (1987), Ch. 4 at 15, and US Council for International Business, *A New MTN: Priorities for Intellectual Property*, (1985), at 3.
84. Lunn, 'The Roles of Property Rights and Market Power in Appropriating Innovative Output', (1985) *Journal of Legal Studies* 423, at 425.
85. Lehmann, 'Property and Intellectual Property – Property Rights as Restrictions on Competition in Furtherance of Competition', (1989) *International Review of Intellectual Property and Competition Law* 1, at 11.
86. For an economic-philosophical approach *see also* Mackaay, 'Economic and Philosophical Aspects of Intellectual Property Rights', in M. Van Hoecke (ed.), *The Socio-Economic Role of Intellectual Property Rights*, Story-Scientia (1991), 1-30.
87. Lehmann, 'Property and Intellectual Property – Property Rights as Restrictions on Competition in Furtherance of Competition', (1989) *International Review of Intellectual Property and Competition Law* 1, at 12.

production, consumption and innovation. Property rights in goods enhance competition on the production level, but this form of ownership restricts competition on the consumption level. One has to acquire the ownership of the goods before one is allowed to consume them and goods owned by other economic players are not directly available for one's consumption. In turn, the intellectual property imposes competitive restrictions at the production level. Only the owner of the copyright in a literary work may, for example, produce additional copies of that work and exploit it in any other way. These restrictions benefit competition on the creation level. The availability of property rights on each level guarantees the development of competition on the next level. Property rights are a prerequisite for the normal functioning of the market mechanism.[88] Copyright and the restrictions on copying and communication to the public which it imposes are needed to enhance further creation of copyright work, which is clearly what is required and desirable from a public interest point of view. This is the only way in which copyright can in the words of the American Constitution play its public interest role 'to promote science and the useful arts'.[89]

Not only does this go a long way in demonstrating that the copyright system right from its inception is influenced heavily by public interest imperatives and that the balance which it tries to achieve between the interest of the right holders and of the users-public is based on public interest considerations. Competition law is also used as a tool to regulate the use that is made of copyright in a later stage. Excesses that cannot be reconciled with the justification for the existence of copyright, that is, that do not serve to achieve the public interest aims of copyright, will come to be seen as breaches of competition law. Yet again the public interest is involved, this time in regulating the use of the exclusivity granted by copyright.[90] The *Magill*[91] and *IMS*[92] cases are good examples in this area.

---

88. Lehmann, 'The Theory of Property Rights and the Protection of Intellectual and Industrial Property', (1985) *International Review of Intellectual Property and Competition Law* 525, at 539.

89. US Constitution, Article 1, section 8, clause 8.

90. *See* P. Torremans, *Holyoak and Torremans Intellectual Property Law*, OUP (5th ed., 2008), 297-312.

91. Joined Cases C-241/91 P and C-242/91 P *Radio Telefis Eireann and Independent Television Publications Ltd v. EC Commission* [1995] ECR I-743, [1995] All ER (EC) 4161.

92. Case C-481/01 *IMS Health v. NDC Health*, pending, the Advocate General delivered his opinion on 2 October 2003, available at http://curia.eu.int, (last accessed 23 April 2008). Order of the President of the Court of Justice of 11 April 2002 in Case C-481/01 P(R); Order of the President of the Court of First Instance of 10 August 2001 in Case T-184/01 R and Order of the President of the Court of First Instance of 26 October 2001 in Case T-184/01 R both available at http://curia.eu.int, (last accessed 23 April 2008).

7.5.4.2 Magill and IMS Health

Magill was concerned with the copyright in TV listings. The broadcasters that owned the copyright refused to grant a licence to Magill that needed it to be able to produce a comprehensive weekly TV listings magazine for the Irish market. The case shows clearly that there is nothing wrong with the copyright as such. The problem is clearly situated at the level of the use that is made of the copyright. Here again, the starting point is that it is up to the right holder to decide which use to make of the right and that as such a refusal to licence does not amount to a breach of competition law. But the Court of Justice argued that a refusal might in exceptional circumstances constitute an abuse.[93] These exceptional circumstances involved the following in this case. The broadcasters' main activity is broadcasting; the TV guides market is only a secondary market for them. By refusing to provide the basic programme listing information, of which they were the only source, the broadcasters prevented the appearance of new products which they did not offer and for which there was consumer demand. The refusal could not be justified by virtue of their normal activities. And, by denying access to the basic information which was required to make the new product, the broadcasters were effectively reserving the secondary market for weekly TV guides to themselves.

In essence, the use of copyright to block the appearance of a new product for which the copyright information is essential and to reserve a secondary market to oneself is abuse and cannot be said to be necessary to fulfil the essential function (reward and encouragement of the author) of copyright. Here again, one clearly sees the public interest input. Competition law is used to make sure that copyright is used according to its proper intention, that is, in the public interest. Any abuse of the right against the public interest, even if it would further enhance the exclusive monopoly style property right of the copyright owner by giving it full and unfettered control over the work and its use, will constitute a breach of competition law.[94]

IMS Health[95] is the complex follow-up case. IMS Health had developed a brick structure to facilitate the collection of marketing data on the German pharmaceutical market. It owned the copyright in that brick structure and refused to grant a licence to its potential competitors. In

---

93. Joined Cases C-241/91 P and C-242/91 P *Radio Telefis Eireann and Independent Television Publications Ltd v. EC Commission* [1995] ECR I-743, [1995] All ER (EC) 4161, at paras 54 and 57.
94. P. Torremans, *Holyoak and Torremans Intellectual Property Law*, OUP (5th ed., 2008), 297-312.
95. Case C-481/01 *IMS Health v. NDC Health*, ECLI:EU:C:2004:257 the Advocate General delivered his opinion on 2 October 2003, available at http://curia.eu.int, (last accessed 23 April 2008). Order of the President of the Court of Justice of 11 April 2002 in Case C-481/01 P(R); Order of the President of the Court of First Instance of 10 August 2001 in Case T-184/01 R and Order of the President of the Court of First Instance of 26 October 2001 in Case T-184/01 R both available at http://curia.eu.int, (last accessed 23 April 2008).

comparison with *Magill,* a number of complicating factors arise. First of all, it is not entirely clear whether there is a secondary market involved at all, as IMS Health and its competitors both wished to operate on the primary market for the collection of pharmaceutical data in Germany and secondly it is also not clear whether in the circumstances the emergence of a new product would be blocked, as the competitors were only interested in copying IMS's block structure without necessarily providing the user with a different product as a result of such use. The main point in *IMS Health* is however not as much the question whether the requirements of reserving a secondary market to oneself and of blocking the emergence of a new product can be defined in a more flexible way, but rather the question whether these two requirements need to be met cumulatively or whether meeting one of them is sufficient to trigger the operation of competition law. The definitional problems really come down to defining the boundaries of the public interest on this point, and the question whether the requirements apply in a cumulative manner defines when the threshold for intervention by competition law in defence of public interest concerns is met. This latter case shows clearly that striking a balance is not a straightforward or easy task and that the facts of any new situation may require further fine-tuning of the balance.

As *Magill* and *IMS Health* show clearly, society has a strong interest to have access to information and this interest can be impeded by the private interest of the right holder to enhance its exclusive monopoly style property right by giving it full and unfettered control over the work and its use. But it is not just passive access for society as a whole that is required. Each individual member of society also must have a right of access and a right to borrow (ideas and some expression) in order to exercise its fundamental freedom to create in order, in turn, to be able to exercise his or her Human Right to benefit from copyright in his or her creative effort. Copyright, therefore, simply cannot prohibit any and all borrowings.[96] This is another element that is to be taken into account in the fine-tuning of the balance.

7.5.4.3   Not Only Economic Considerations Count

Be that as it may, what is clear is that copyright has a number of built-in mechanisms to balance the private and public interests.[97] Further complications arise though as up to now, we have almost exclusively looked at economic interests on either side. This is, however, not the only interest

---

96. F. Dessemontet, 'Copyright and Human Rights', in J. Kabel & G. Mom, *Intellectual Property and Information Law: Essays in Honour of Herman Cohen Jehoram*, Kluwer Law International (1998), Volume 6, Information Law Series, 113-120.

97. United Nations, Economic and Social Council, Commission on Human Rights, Sub-Commission on the Promotion and Protection of Human Rights, 52nd session, Item 4 of the Provisional Agenda, Economic, Social and Cultural Rights – The Impact of the Agreement on Trade-Related Aspects of Intellectual Property Rights on Human Rights, Report of the High Commissioner, E/CN.4/Sub/2/2001/13, at 5.

involved.[98] From a human rights perspective, the author or creator also assumes a lot of importance. This manifests itself in the work produced by these authors or creators being acknowledged as having intrinsic value as an expression of human dignity and creativity.[99] In terms of copyright law, this is reflected by the balance between economic and moral rights, with the latter being a recognition of the fundamental link between the work and the author or creator. Moral rights survive as rights of the author or creator even when the latter transfers the economic rights in the work, thereby preserving the fundamental link.[100] The moral rights of paternity – that being the right to be identified as the author of the work – and integrity, that is, the right to object to the distortion or mutilation of the work that could affect the author's reputation,[101] operate as fundamental minimal rights that do not normally stand in the way of the normal exploitation of the work and the economic rights in it, but that allows the author to object to clearly abusive use of the work that would deny or distort his or her contribution as an expression of his or her human dignity and creativity.[102] This way, a fair balance with the economic rights is provided, but this is also clearly another important aspect of the overall balancing act that is required if copyright is to operate properly as a Human Right. '[T]he question essentially is [and remains] where to strike the right balance'.[103]

7.5.5   An Internal or an External Balance

We are back at our starting point, but this time the question is not whether copyright conflicts with other external rights such as the right of expression or whether the conflict has been fully internalized. As I indicated right from the start, the conflictual model whereby copyright and other intellectual property rights will have to give way to higher fundamental norms on a

---

98. *See* Chapman, 'A Human Rights Perspective on Intellectual Property, Scientific Progress, and Access to the Benefits of Science', (8 November 1998) *WIPO Panel Discussion on Intellectual Property and Human Rights*, at 2, available at www.wipo.org, (last accessed 23 April 2008).

99. Chapman, 'Approaching Intellectual Property as a Human Right (obligations related to Article 15(1)(c))', (2001) Copyright Bulletin, XXXV, no. 3, 4-36, at 14.

100. *See* P. Torremans, *Holyoak and Torremans Intellectual Property Law*, OUP (5th ed., 2008), Ch. 4, 218-226.

101. As enshrined in Article 6*bis* of the Berne Convention.

102. *See* P. Torremans, *Holyoak and Torremans Intellectual Property Law*, Butterworths (3rd ed., 2001), Ch. 13, 220-228 and P. Torremans, 'Moral Rights in the Digital Age', in I.A. Stamatoudi & P. Torremans (eds), *Copyright in the New Digital Environment*, Sweet & Maxwell (2000), Perspectives on Intellectual Property Series, 97-114.

103. United Nations, Economic and Social Council, Commission on Human Rights, Sub-Commission on the Promotion and Protection of Human Rights, 52nd session, Item 4 of the Provisional Agenda, Economic, Social and Cultural Rights – The Impact of the Agreement on Trade-Related Aspects of Intellectual Property Rights on Human Rights, Report of the High Commissioner, E/CN.4/Sub/2/2001/13, at 5.

number of occasions is too simplistic, as is the idea that copyright and other intellectual property rights have fully internalized the fundamental rights issues, meaning that no further issues arise. We are clearly coming to the obvious conclusion that a balance needs to be struck between fundamental rights, with copyright and other intellectual property rights as one fundamental right on the one hand and other fundamental rights on the other hand. I have tried to illustrate the basis for such a balancing act above.

The question that arises next is whether such a balancing act can result in additional ad hoc exceptions and limitations being introduced in intellectual property laws. Can, for example, the need to guarantee the freedom of the press and the freedom of expression in a certain case lead to the creation of a limitation or exception that is not in the copyright act? This could be called an externalization of the balancing act between copyright and other fundamental rights, and the same could apply to other intellectual property rights. The alternative model would be to internalize the balancing act. This is not to say that the legislator has already completely done the work when passing intellectual property legislation. But it does mean that the balance needs to be struck internally inside the intellectual property by making use of and interpreting the existing intellectual property exceptions and limitations in such a way as to strike a balance with the other fundamental rights concerned in a way that takes account of the interests of these other fundamental rights.

The Court of Justice of the European Union dealt with this question in two Grand Chamber judgments on 29 July 2019. In the *Funke Medien*[104] and *Der Spiegel*[105] cases, the court resolutely adopted the latter approach and rejected the creation of additional exceptions and limitations as a result of the balancing act. The balance between copyright and other fundamental rights needs to be struck inside copyright, by interpreting copyright exceptions and limitations in such a way as to take account of the interests of the other fundamental rights. Or as the court put it in *Funke Medien:*[106]

> Freedom of information and freedom of the press, enshrined in Article 11 of the Charter of Fundamental Rights of the European Union, are not capable of justifying, beyond the exceptions or limitations provided for in Article 5(2) and (3) of Directive 2001/29, a derogation from the author's exclusive rights of reproduction and of communication to the public, referred to in Article 2(a) and Article 3(1) of that directive respectively.
>
> In striking the balance which is incumbent on a national court between the exclusive rights of the author referred to in Article 2(a) and in Article

---

104. Case C-469/17 *Funke Medien NRW GmbH v. Bundesrepublik Deutschland* ECLI-:EU:C:2019:623.
105. Case C-516/17 *Spiegel Online GmbH v. Volker Beck* ECLI:EU:C:2019:625.
106. Case C-469/17 *Funke Medien NRW GmbH v. Bundesrepublik Deutschland* ECLI-:EU:C:2019:623, at para. 77.

3(1) of Directive 2001/29 on the one hand, and, on the other, the rights of the users of protected subject matter referred to in Article 5(3)(c), second case, and (d) of that directive, the latter of which derogate from the former, a national court must, having regard to all the circumstances of the case before it, rely on an interpretation of those provisions which, whilst consistent with their wording and safeguarding their effectiveness, fully adheres to the fundamental rights enshrined in the Charter of Fundamental Rights of the European Union.

The decision has now been made in principle, and there is no reason not to apply the approach also to other intellectual property rights, but it remains to be seen how national courts will put it into practice.

7.6   COPYRIGHT'S RELATIONSHIP WITH OTHER HUMAN RIGHTS

We already suggested above that a second part of the balancing act relates to the relationship between copyright and other human rights. Already intuitively one assumes that human rights must have equal value when compared to one another and that one cannot simply overrule the other. This must add yet another factor to consider when one works out the balance between public and private interests. The way we have looked at that balance up to now reflects very much the content of Article 27 of the Universal Declaration of Human Rights and Article 15 of the International Covenant on Economic, Social and Cultural Rights in both of which elements referring to the public as well as the private interest are brought together. But one needs to add to that that the balance between these interests must be struck with the primary objective of promoting and protecting human rights. That must be the overall aim of the international human rights instruments of which the clause considering copyright as a human rights forms part.[107]

Article 5(1) of the International Covenant on Economic, Social and Cultural Rights backs this up from a legal point of view by stating that:

> [n]othing in the present Covenant may be interpreted as implying for any State, group or person any right to engage in any activity or to perform any act aimed at the destruction of any of the rights or freedoms recognized herein, or at their limitation to a greater extent than is provided for in the present Covenant.

---

107. United Nations, Economic and Social Council, Commission on Human Rights, Sub-Commission on the Promotion and Protection of Human Rights, 52nd session, Item 4 of the Provisional Agenda, Economic, Social and Cultural Rights – The Impact of the Agreement on Trade-Related Aspects of Intellectual Property Rights on Human Rights, Report of the High Commissioner, E/CN.4/Sub/2/2001/13, at 5.

Copyright and its balance between public and private interests must, therefore, put in place a regime that is consistent with the realization of all other human rights.[108] The right to freedom of information and of access to information[109] provides a good example of another fundamental Human Right that needs to be respected, but the implementation of which alongside the implementation of copyright as an exclusive right in some of that information might create problems in a number of circumstances and will, therefore, call for a careful balancing of all the rights and interest.[110] The aim must be to respect both rights to the optimal or maximum extent possible. Maybe the suggestion of the German Constitutional Court that the freedom of access to information can still be guaranteed in those cases where whoever seeks access does not get that access for free but against the payment of a fee in respect of the copyright in the information can serve as an example here. Access is guaranteed, but it is not entirely free access, and on the other hand, copyright is respected by means of the remuneration whilst giving up the right to refuse to grant a licence as a part of the exclusive right in the work.[111]

The same kind of balance between various human rights is also found in a slightly different context when attention is turned to National Constitutions and the way in which they protect Copyright as a Human Right. Some of them such as the Swedish[112] and the Portuguese[113] Constitutions have a direct copyright clause, but most of them protect copyright as a Human Right by bringing aspects of it under other constitutional provisions covering other fundamental rights. The German Constitution is an example in point. The German Constitutional Court has intervened in copyright cases on many occasions despite the fact that the German Constitution does not have a copyright clause. Instead, there is a consensus in Germany that parts of copyright are covered by the property clause in the Constitution. Especially the economic rights part of copyright can be considered as immaterial property and is hence entitled to protection under the right of fundamental respect for property.[114] Moral rights, on the other hand, refer to the author and show strong overlap with personality rights.[115] The latter are also

---

108. Chapman, 'Approaching Intellectual Property as a Human Right (obligations related to Article 15(1)(c))', (2001) *Copyright Bulletin*, XXXV, no. 3, 4-36, at 14.
109. As found for example in Article 19 of the Universal Declaration of Human Rights.
110. A. Bertrand, *Le droit d'auteur et les droits voisins*, Dalloz (2nd ed., 1999), at 81.
111. H. Schack, *Urheberund Urhebervertragsrecht*, Mohr Siebeck (1997), at 42.
112. Chapter 2, § 19 of the Swedish Constitution of 1 January 1975.
113. Article 42 of the Portuguese Constitution of 2 April 1976.
114. H. Schack, *Urheberund Urhebervertragsrecht*, Mohr Siebeck (1997), at 40-43.
115. *See* G. Schricker (ed.), *Urheberrecht: Kommentar*, Verlag C.H. Beck (2nd ed., 1999), Vor §§ 12 ff., Nos 1-13, 243-247; A. Lucas & H.J. Lucas, *Trait é de la propri é t é litt é raire et artistique*, Litec (2nd ed., 2001), at 303, § 367; Poullaud & Dulian, 'Droit moral et droits de la personnalité', (1994) *Jurisclasseur P é riodique* G, I, p. 3780 and *Anne Bragance c/. Michel de Gr é ce*, Court of Appeal Paris, judgment dated 1 February 1989, (1989) RIDA, Issue 4, 301, annotated by Sirinelli.

specifically protected by the German Constitution.[116] These separate aspects of fundamental rights protection then have to be put together to come to overall protection for copyright as a Fundamental Human Right. This clearly does not simply amount to an adding up exercise.[117] The individual components may overlap, and they protect different interests which may enter into conflict with one another when pushed to extreme heights of protection. Here too, a balancing of these different fundamental rights will be required.

Exactly how this balancing works out and exactly where the balance lies also depends from case to case. The higher the level of creativity and the more important the input of the creator is, the stronger the human rights claim of copyright will be. Not all works and not all situations will give copyright the same strength in its claim to human rights status and in its balancing exercise with other human rights.[118]

7.7   CONCLUSION

This essay set out to demonstrate that copyright really has a claim to human rights status. We have shown that there clearly is a basis for such a claim in the international human rights instruments,[119] but it has also become clear that the provisions in these instruments that could be said to be the copyright clauses do not define the substance of copyright in any detail. Instead, one is left with a series of conclusions and implications for copyright and its substance as a result of its human rights status. The most important points are the balance that needs to be achieved between private and public interests and the equilibrium that needs to be achieved with other human rights.

This balancing of rights can be seen as inherently internal to copyright as a Human Right. The analogy – an example of the operation of competition principles in relation to copyright that was set out above demonstrates this clearly. Instead, it can also be seen in most instances as the impact of other human rights on copyright. It is with that impact or interaction in each specific case that the other contributions in this collection will deal in considerable detail.

---

116. H. Schack, *Urheberund Urhebervertragsrecht*, Mohr Siebeck (1997), at 39-40.
117. *See* G. Schricker (ed.), *Urheberrecht: Kommentar*, Verlag C.H. Beck (2nd ed., 1999), Vor §§ 12 ff., Nos 14-17, 247-249.
118. *See* Vivant, 'Le droit d'auteur, un droit de l'homme?', (1997) RIDA 174, 60, at 103 and 105.
119. Such a claim is confirmed in several jurisdictions, *see* e.g., Etheverry, 'Derecho de autorlibertad de creacion-libertad de expression', paper delivered at the ALAI 2007 conference in Punta del Este, published in shortened version as 'Opening speech' in ALAI Uruguay, The author's place in XXI Century Copyright: the challenges of modernization, ALAI-IUDA-UM (2007), 62.

Other intellectual property rights such as patents and trademarks are also covered by the international human rights instruments, be it only as a form of property for example under Article 1 of the first protocol to the ECHR. Apart from that, their position and that of intellectual property, in general, as a human right are far less developed. Copyright clearly stands out in this respect.

Part II
Copyright and Human Rights

Chapter 8

Copyright and Freedom of Expression in Canada

Myra J. Tawfik

Canadian courts have generally taken the view that conflicts at the intersection of copyright law and freedom of expression can be satisfactorily addressed within the four corners of the *Copyright Act*.[1] In the opinion of the Federal Court of Canada in *Michelin v. C.A.W Canada*: 'Copyright ... minimally impairs the Defendants' right of free expression by the very well-tailored structure of the Copyright Act with its list of exceptions ... '[2] The copyright statute to have internalized freedom of expression in a manner consistent with the Canadian *Charter of Rights and Freedoms* through its recognition of permitted uses and exceptions.[3] This 'internalized' approach has meant that courts have been reticent to look beyond the Act to reconcile conflicts between copyright and free speech.[4]

---

1. R.S.C, 1985, c. C-42 as amended (hereinafter 'the Act').
2. *Compagnie Générale des Établissements Michelin – Michelin & Cie v. National Automobile, Aerospace, Transportation and General Workers Union of Canada (CAW-Canada)* [1997] 2 F.C. 306, 71 C.P.R (2d) 348 Federal Court Trial Division (hereinafter '*Michelin*') at para. 111, p. 381.
3. Part I of the *Constitution Act, 1982*, being Schedule B to the *Canada Act 1982* (UK) 1982, c. 11 (hereinafter 'the Charter').
4. There have not been many cases in Canada in which the Charter right of freedom of expression has been advanced as a defence to a claim of copyright infringement. The two most notable decisions are the *Michelin* case, above at note 2 and *The Queen v. James Lorimer and Co.* [1984] 1 FC 1065, 77 C.P.R (2d) 262 (Federal Court of Appeal) (hereinafter '*Lorimer*'). For scholarly commentary on these decisions and on the constitutional dimension of copyright *see*, for example, the work of Graham Reynolds 'Reconsidering Copyright's Constitutionality' (2016) Osgoode Legal Studies Research

Section 2(b) of the Charter recognizes that everyone enjoys the 'freedom of thought, belief, opinion and expression, including freedom of the press and other media of communication.' As a constitutionally entrenched human right, it can be limited by State action only to the extent that any encroachment can be 'demonstrably justified in a free and democratic society'.[5] Given that copyright law encourages and safeguards individual expression, the law could, indeed, be said to have internalized the Charter. As Carys Craig has argued '[copyright] is an institution whose existence and maintenance encourage the kinds of communicative activity that lie at the heart of the rationale for freedom of expression … '[6]

However, copyright can also conflict with the constitutional guarantee in section 2(b) when it inhibits third parties from engaging in their own expression if that expression relies in whole or in part on underlying copyright work. In its assertion that the internal structure of the Act was sufficient to address free speech concerns, the court in the *Michelin* decision also took the position that: '[t]he Charter does not confer the right to use private property – the plaintiff's copyright – in the service of freedom of expression.'[7] Declaring that the property right of the copyright holder

---

Paper No. 30 and 'The Limits of Statutory Interpretation: Towards Explicit Engagement, by the Supreme Court of Canada, with the Charter Right of Freedom of Expression in the Context of Copyright' (2016) 41:2 Queen's Law Journal 455-500. *See also*, Jane Bailey, 'Deflating the Michelin Man: Protecting Users' Rights in the Canadian Copyright Reform Process' Chapter 5 in Michael Geist ed., *In the Public Interest: The Future of Canadian Copyright Law* (Toronto: Irwin Law, 2005); Carys Craig, 'Putting the Community in Communication: Dissolving the Conflict Between Freedom of Expression and Copyright' (2006) 56 University of Toronto Law Journal 75, David Fewer, 'Constitutionalizing Copyright: Freedom of Expression and the Limits of Copyright in Canada' (1997) 55 University of Toronto Law Review 175; Ysolde Gendreau 'Canadian Copyright Law and Its Charters' Chapter 10 in Jonathan Griffiths and Uma Suthersanen ed., *Copyright and Free Speech: Comparative and International Analyses* (Oxford University Press, 2005); Ysolde Gendreau, 'Copyright and Freedom of Expression in Canada' Chapter 8 in Paul Torremans ed., *Intellectual Property and Human Rights* (The Hague: Kluwer Law International, 2008). *See also* Brief –Statutory Review of Copyright, Pascale Chapdelaine on behalf of Canadian Intellectual Property Scholars submitted to the Standing Committee on Industry, Science and Technology, 22 October 2018 online at https://www.ourco mmons.ca/Content/Committee/421/INDU/Brief/BR10166923/br-external/ChapdelainePa scale01-e.pdf.

5. Section 1 of the Charter reads as follows: '1. The *Canadian Charter of Rights and Freedoms* guarantees the rights and freedoms set out in it subject only to such reasonable limits prescribed by law as can be demonstrably justified in a free and democratic society.' *See* generally, Richard Moon, *The Constitutional Protection of Freedom of Expression* (Toronto: University of Toronto Press, 2000).
6. Craig cited at note 4 at p. 108. *See also* Richard Moon, 'The Social Character of Freedom of Expression' (2009) 2 Amsterdam Law Reform 43.
7. *Michelin* cited at note 2 at para. 79, p. 362. For critiques of the property conceptualization of copyright *see*, for example, Michael Birnhack, 'Acknowledging the Conflict Between Copyright Law and Freedom of Expression under the *Human Rights Act*' (2003) Entertainment Law Review 24.

prevails over the freedom of expression rights of the copyright user is precisely the opposite of what a truly meaningful internalized approach should espouse. Copyright *is* and *should* be in the service of freedom of expression in that it must respect the expressive rights of both creators and users of copyright works. An overemphasis on the rights of the copyright holder over those of the user of copyright works challenges the legitimacy of the internalized approach. How contemporary constructions of copyright interfere with user rights of free expression has, therefore, become an important question of concern in Canada and elsewhere in the world.[8]

This chapter examines the evolution of the internalized approach to freedom of expression within Canadian copyright law. It traces the most recent legislative and jurisprudential developments that have simultaneously *broadened* and *restricted* the ability of the Act to address rights of free speech. Section 8.1 will explore the ways in which Canadian copyright law has expanded the range of exceptions and limitations to support the argument that permitted uses of copyright works to serve as the statutory manifestations of freedom of expression. Section 8.2 will then turn to an exploration of the structural threats to the internal approach by highlighting instances where the Act itself entirely undermines free expression considerations. These statutory contradictions require a second look at the legitimacy of addressing free expression solely within the four corners of the law of copyright. They require a reconsideration of the fundamental question of whether, in cases of conflict, the Charter should be invoked as an extrinsic and overarching instrument of constitutional oversight. This 'Charter approach' to copyright will, therefore, be discussed in section 8.3 of this chapter.

8.1   THE 'VERY WELL-TAILORED STRUCTURE' OF THE CANADIAN COPYRIGHT ACT: FREEDOM OF EXPRESSION INTERNALIZED

Historically, copyright laws arose out of concerns about encouraging the dissemination of knowledge consistent with Western enlightenment views of

---

8. In the Canadian context, *see* sources cited at note 4. Examples from Europe include Christophe Geiger & Elena Izyumenko, 'Copyright on the Human Rights' Trial: Redefining the Boundaries of Exclusivity Through Freedom of Expression' (2014) 45 International Review of Intellectual Property and Competition Law 316; Michael Birnhack, 'Copyrighting Speech: A Trans-Atlantic View' Chapter 3 in Paul Torremans, ed., *Copyright and Human Rights: Freedom of Expression – Intellectual Property – Privacy* (The Hague: Kluwer Law International, 2004); P. Bernt Hugenholtz 'Copyright and Freedom of Expression in Europe' in Rochelle C. Dreyfuss, Diane L. Zimmerman & Harry First, eds., *Expanding the Boundaries of Intellectual Property* (Oxford: Oxford University Press, 2001); Patrick Masiyakurima, 'The Free Speech Benefits of Fair Dealing Defences' Chapter 9 in Torremans cited at note 4; Alain Strowel and Françoise Tulkens, 'Freedom of Expression and Copyright under Civil Law: Of Balance, Adaptation and Access', Chapter 12 in Griffiths and Suthersanen cited at note 4.

the value of public education and the advancement of literacy and learning.[9] By encouraging authorship and book production, copyright was the policy vehicle through which ideas, knowledge and creativity could be widely shared. In its early iterations, the law achieved this objective by closely circumscribing copyright's scope of protection. The right was of very limited duration, and protection was contingent upon the fulfilment of mandatory formalities. The idea that the law must balance the competing interests of copyright holders and users of copyright works remains alive to this day even though registration requirements and other formalities have long been abandoned, and the duration of copyright continues to be extended.[10] Instead of formalities, a variety of copyright doctrines and statutory devices mediate the boundary between protection, permitted uses and the public domain. It is these doctrines and statutory devices that internalize freedom of expression within the 'well-tailored structure' of Canada's *Copyright Act*.[11]

Some of these rules relate to the determination of eligibility to protection in the first place, such as the requirement that a work be 'original',[12] that it be 'fixed in material form' and that its content reflects authorial expression rather than merely an idea. Works that cannot be protected by copyright do not interfere with the rights of free expression. Similarly, the fact that copyright protection is of limited duration means that, eventually, the work will enter the public domain and the constraints on its use by others will be eliminated.

Most importantly, for our purposes, even where copyright subsists, a variety of statutory defences, limitations and exceptions to infringement ensure the integration of freedom of expression considerations within the

---

9. *See* John Willinsky, *The Intellectual Properties of Learning: A Prehistory from Saint Jerome to John Locke* (Chicago: The University of Chicago Press, 2017); Ronan Deazley, *On the Origin of the Right to Copy: Charting the Movement of Copyright Law in Eighteenth Century Britain (1695-1775)* (Oxford: Hart Publishing, 2004). In the Canadian context, Myra J. Tawfik, 'History in the Balance: Copyright and Access to Knowledge' Chapter 3 in Michael Geist ed., *From Radical Extremism to Balanced Copyright* (Toronto: Irwin Law, 2010).

10. The first copyright statute, the Statute of Anne 1710, 8 Ann. c. 21, set the duration of copyright at fourteen years with the possibility of an additional fourteen years if the author was still alive at the expiry of the first term. Currently, in Canada, the duration of copyright is life of the author plus 50 years after the author's death. In European countries, the term is generally life of the author plus 70 years after the author's death. For a discussion of copyright term extension over the centuries, *see*, for example, Myra J. Tawfik, 'Copyright History as Book History: The Law in Multidisciplinary Context', in Torremans, P., ed., *Research Handbook on Copyright Law*, Second Edition, (Cheltenham, Edward Elgar, 2017).

11. *See* in this regard Gendreau in Torremans cited at note 4.

12. In Canada, the creator must have expended sufficient skill and judgment for the work to be considered original. Labour alone is not sufficient. *See CCH Canadian Ltd v. Law Society of Upper Canada* 2004 SCC 14.

copyright paradigm.[13] It is these statutory limitations, defences and exceptions that the courts have relied on to pay short shrift to the Charter as an extrinsic instrument of oversight, preferring the internalized approach to the resolution of any conflicts instead.

If, indeed, freedom of expression under Canadian copyright law is adequately served by the 'well-tailored structure of the Act', then the ways in which copyright exceptions are crafted, interpreted and applied become the measures through which to assess the validity of this assumption. What follows is a discussion of recent Canadian statutory and jurisprudential developments that have expanded the scope of permitted uses and exceptions, thereby legitimating the internalized approach.

8.1.1   THE SUPREME COURT OF CANADA AND THE CONCEPT OF USER
               RIGHTS

The Supreme Court of Canada has rendered a number of significant decisions in which it has emphasized the vital role that copyright law plays in advancing access to knowledge and encouraging individual creativity. Canada's highest court has recognized that copyright rights must be limited in their scope and balanced against the rights of users. Even as the international trend has been to strengthen copyright holders' rights, and perhaps precisely because of this phenomenon, the Supreme Court has clearly and forcefully articulated (or re-articulated) the foundational pillars upon which copyright law is based. In *Théberge v. Galerie d'Art du Petit Champlain*,[14] the court stated:

> The Copyright Act is usually presented as a balance between promoting the public interest in the encouragement and dissemination of works of the arts and intellect and obtaining a just reward for the creator (or, more accurately, to prevent someone other than the creator from appropriating whatever benefits may be generated) ....
>
> The proper balance among these and other public policy objectives lies not only in recognizing the creator's rights but in giving due weight to their limited nature ....
>
> Excessive control by holders of copyrights and other forms of intellectual property may unduly limit the ability of the public domain to incorporate and embellish creative innovation in the long-term interests of society as a whole, or create practical obstacles to proper utilization. This is reflected in the exceptions to copyright infringement enumerated in sections 29 to 32.2, which seek to protect the public domain in traditional ways such as fair dealing for the purpose of criticism or

---

13. In this chapter, I will use the terms 'defences', 'permitted uses', 'limitations' and 'exceptions' interchangeably.
14. 2002 SCC 34.

review and to add new protections to reflect new technology, such as limited computer program reproduction and 'ephemeral recordings' in connection with live performances.[15]

In its concern over 'excessive control', its desire to 'protect the public domain' and its striving for a fair 'balance' between competing interests, Canada's highest court was safeguarding the space within which free expression rights are to be exercised within the copyright framework. Two years later and building upon this earlier judgment, the Supreme Court rendered the seminal *CCH Canadian Ltd v. Law Society of Upper Canada* decision that characterized the limitations, exceptions and defences to copyright infringement as 'user rights' and placed them on equal footing with the rights of creators:

> The Copyright Act is usually presented as a balance between promoting the public interest in the encouragement and dissemination of works of the arts and intellect and obtaining a just reward for the creator ... The proper balance ... lies not only in recognizing the creator's rights but in giving due weight to their limited nature.[16]

The Supreme Court then made its most significant pronouncement:

> The fair dealing exception, like other exceptions in the Copyright Act, is a user's right. In order to maintain the proper balance between the rights of a copyright owner and users' interests, it must not be interpreted restrictively. As Professor Vaver ... has explained ... : 'User rights are not just loopholes. Both owner rights and user rights should therefore be given the fair and balanced reading that befits remedial legislation'.[17]

By affirming this need to balance competing interests and by invoking the language of rights to characterize the permissible actions of third parties in relation to a copyright work, the court made clear the equal treatment to be afforded to copyright holders and copyright users. In Canada then, fair dealing and other copyright limitations are integral to the overall policy underlying the legislation and the Act must be measured by the extent to which it recognizes and reinforces their importance.

Developments at the Supreme Court after the *CCH* decision have enhanced a 'user rights' conception of copyright limitations and exceptions. In 2012, the court rendered five copyright judgments simultaneously, each consistent with its position on the need for balance within the legal scheme and its concern over safeguarding user rights.[18] In *Society of Composers,*

---

15. *Théberge* at paras 30-32.
16. Cited at note 12 (hereinafter 'CCH') at paras 30-31.
17. *CCH* at para. 48.
18. *Entertainment Software Association v. Society of* Composers, Authors and Music Publishers of Canada, 2012 SCC 34, [2012] 2 SCR 231; *Rogers Communications Inc. v. Society of Composers, Authors and Music Publishers of Canada* 2012 SCC 35, [2012] 2

Authors and Music Publishers of Canada v. Bell[19] the court mused over the evolution of its understanding of the nature and purpose of the law from an 'earlier, author-centric view' to one that recognizes ' ... the importance copyright plays in promoting the public interest.'[20] The court's more nuanced view of the role of copyright recognized ' ... that the dissemination of artistic works is central to developing a robustly cultured and intellectual public domain'.[21] This conceptualization is bold, and its implications are far-reaching. For freedom of expression advocates, the characterization of the law as designed to foster a 'robustly cultured and intellectual public domain' is significant and profound. Indeed, the public domain is such an essential feature of the copyright balance that any attempts to restrict it challenges the very legitimacy of the law itself. As Jessica Litman has recognized, 'a vigorous public domain is a crucial buttress to the copyright system; without the public domain, it might be impossible to tolerate copyright at all.'[22]

The Supreme Court's pronouncements have had a significant influence on the policy discourse in Canada. Parliamentary action must now expressly take into account and effectively calibrate both copyright rights and user rights. The most recent amendments to the Act, *the 2012 Copyright Modernization Act,* attempted to adhere to this principle of 'balanced copyright'.[23] As we shall see in what follows, the 2012 amendments enhanced the rights of copyright holders while also introducing a number of new exceptions and limitations to bolster user rights.

8.1.2   FAIR DEALING AS A USER RIGHT IN CANADA: FOSTERING A
          'ROBUSTLY CULTURED AND INTELLECTUAL PUBLIC DOMAIN'

Fair dealing is the principal vehicle through which freedom of expression manifests itself within the internal structure of the Act. In characterizing this exception as the most important statutory embodiment of user rights, the Supreme Court rejected earlier lower court decisions that had construed fair

---

SCR 283; *Society of Composers, Authors and Music Publishers of Canada v. Bell Canada,* 2012 SCC 36, [2012] 2 SCR 326; *Alberta (Education) v. Canadian Copyright Licensing Agency (Access Copyright),* 2012 SCC 38, [2012] 2 SCR 345; *Re: Sound v. Motion Picture Theatre Association of Canada,* 2012 SCC 38, [2012] 2 SCR 376. For commentary, *see* Michael Geist, ed., *The Copyright Pentalogy: How the Supreme Court of Canada Shook the Foundations of Canadian Copyright Law* (Ottawa: University of Ottawa Press, 2013). *See also* Myra J. Tawfik, 'The Supreme Court of Canada and the "Fair Dealing Trilogy": Elaborating a Doctrine of User Rights under Canadian Copyright Law' (2013) 51 Alberta Law Review 191.

19. *Ibid.,* (hereinafter '*SOCAN*').
20. *SOCAN* at paras 9-10.
21. *SOCAN* para. 10.
22. Jessica Litman 'The Public Domain' (1990) 39 Emory Law Journal 965 at p. 977.
23. The *Copyright Modernization Act* S.C 2012 c. 20.

dealing very narrowly.[24] As a 'user right', the primacy of fair dealing as the statutory space for the exercise of free expression is assured. In Canada, it is not an infringement of copyright to deal with a copyright work for purposes of 'research', 'private study', 'education', 'parody or satire', 'criticism or review' and 'news reporting' as long as that dealing is fair.[25]

In *CCH*, the Supreme Court of Canada held that the various categories of dealings were to be interpreted broadly. As a result, in Canada, 'research' can be conducted for commercial purposes,[26] outside of educational settings[27] and without requiring that the research lead to a new or transformative work.[28] It can also encompass consumer research prior to purchase, as in the case of streaming online previews of songs before downloading.[29] Similarly, 'private study' can occur within a classroom setting, and teachers are acting within the purview of fair dealing when they make photocopies of excerpts of copyright works for their students' private study and research.[30] Assessments of the fairness of the dealing are to be conducted by taking into account a number of non-exhaustive factors, such as the purpose and character of the dealing, the amount reproduced, whether there were any viable alternatives to the dealing, the nature of the work reproduced and the effect of the dealing on the work.[31] These analytic factors allow the courts to gauge the dealing in light of a number of public interest concerns, including internalized free expression considerations.

The expansive treatment of fair dealing by the Supreme Court and the legislature lends credence to the argument that Canadian copyright law is sufficiently robust to integrate free expression within its internal structure. Although fair dealing is the most important feature of internalized freedom of expression, the Act also contains a number of other exceptions and limitations that further strengthen the legitimacy of this integrated analysis.

8.1.3   OTHER COPYRIGHT LIMITATIONS AND EXCEPTIONS THAT SUPPORT AN INTERNALIZED APPROACH

Without going through an exhaustive discussion of all these statutory devices, it is nevertheless worth highlighting those that have a more direct connection with freedom of expression. For example, the Act contains specific provisions designed to shield libraries, archives and museums from

---

24. *See Lorimer* cited at note 4 and *Michelin* cited at note 2.
25. Sections 29-29.2 of the Act. The categories of 'education' and 'parody and satire' were only recently added with the 2012 amendments.
26. *See CCH*.
27. *See CCH* and *SOCAN*.
28. *See SOCAN*.
29. *See SOCAN*.
30. *See Alberta (Education)* cited at note 18.
31. *See CCH* at para. 53.

copyright liability where they act on behalf of users whose activities would amount to fair dealing if they had performed the actions themselves.[32] The Act permits incidental and non-deliberate inclusion of a copyright work in another work without attracting liability.[33] Individuals with perceptual disabilities can translate, adapt or reproduce a work in a format that renders the work accessible to them if there is no commercially available equivalent.[34] Further, the 2012 amendments added exceptions that recognize new digital and technological uses of lawfully obtained copyright works.[35] One new and innovative measure stands out, in particular, as a strong affirmation of user rights of free expression.

The 'non-commercial user-generated content' provision, known colloquially as the 'YouTube Exception', allows individuals to incorporate all or part of an existing copyright work into their own work and disseminating it over the Internet if the use is solely for non-commercial purposes and the underlying copyright works are attributed. It is a stand-alone exception, not contingent upon the activity falling within an enumerated fair dealing purpose.[36] According to some, this provision has ' ... positioned Canada as the more forward-looking nation with respect to user rights ... .'[37]

Taken as a whole, fair dealing along with all of the other copyright limitations and exceptions, including the allowance for user-generated content, form the 'well-tailored structure' through which the right to freedom of expression is advanced. If one were to focus exclusively on these statutory features and their judicial interpretation, there is a good reason for confidence in the Act's capacity to integrate freedom of expression within it. However, given that the Act is designed to balance copyright rights with user rights, one must also look closely at the other side of the equation – on the copyright rights side – and assess the entire statutory scheme in light of freedom of expression considerations. The question then becomes whether, when viewed in its totality, the Act retains the structural integrity to effectively mediate freedom of expression concerns.

What follows is a review of some of the more significant intrinsic challenges to the internalized freedom of expression model of copyright law. These structural conflicts invite us to reconsider the extent to which even the

---

32. Section 30.2.
33. Section 30.7.
34. Section 32, as amended in 2016 to implement the *Marrakesh Treaty to Facilitate Access to Published Works for Persons who are Blind, Visually Impaired or otherwise Print Disabled*.
35. These provisions include allowances for 'Reproduction for Private Purposes' (space shifting) at section 29.22 and 'Fixing Signals and Recording Programs for Later Listening and Viewing' (time shifting) at section 29.23.
36. Section 29.21.
37. Daniel Rosen 'Electronic Dance Music, Creativity, and User-Generated Content – A Canadian Perspective' (2014) 26 Intellectual Property Journal 153 at p. 168. *See also*, Peter Yu 'Can the Canadian UGC Exception be Transplanted Abroad?' (2014) 26 Intellectual Property Journal 175.

most vigorous advancement of user rights is sufficient to ensure that the constitutional guarantee of freedom of expression is satisfactorily addressed within the four corners of the legislation. They challenge the very notion that copyright and free expression are reconcilable through the internal operation of the Act itself and ask us to re-examine the question of whether, at their points of collision, the constitutional guarantee in section 2(b) of the Charter should be invoked as an overarching instrument of oversight.

8.2	WHERE COPYRIGHT AND FREEDOM OF EXPRESSION COLLIDE: CASES OF STRUCTURAL FAILURE
8.2.1	PROVISIONS RELATING TO THE CIRCUMVENTION OF TECHNOLOGICAL PROTECTION MEASURES AND DIGITAL RIGHTS MANAGEMENT TECHNOLOGIES

The Act contains provisions that prohibit any person from circumventing a technological protection measure or from tampering with digital rights management information (hereafter referred to collectively as 'TPMs'). These prohibitions are not conditional upon whether the circumvention or tampering is done for infringing or non-infringing purposes. In other words, circumventing a TPM will always be actionable even if one is acting for fair dealing purposes such as, for example, for private study or for parody. Given that these anti-circumvention provisions purport to override the very mechanisms through which freedom of expression is integrated into the copyright system itself, the Act can no longer be said to be structurally well-tailored to advance this fundamental human right. On the contrary, the introduction of these provisions has undermined the ability of the Act to properly calibrate the intersection between copyright and free expression. As 'born-digital' works increasingly supplant works in print or other tangible media, the fail-safes or escape valves that internalize freedom of expression guarantees in the Act risk obsolescence, especially if copyright holders routinely embed TPMs in their digital works.

Granted, the statutory prohibition on circumvention is limited in certain respects. The prohibition is tied to access control technologies, and therefore, the Act does permit the circumvention of copy control technologies for non-infringing purposes.[38] However, this distinction is often specious given that digital works frequently embed both access control technologies and

---

38. The definition of technological protection measure at section 41 as ' … any effective technology … that, in the ordinary course of its operation … (a) controls access to a work … '. *See also* the recent Federal Court decision in *Nintendo of America v. King* 2017 FC 246 (CanLii).

copy control technologies such that the latter cannot be circumvented independently. The Act also recognizes certain exceptions to the blanket prohibition on circumvention such as, for example, for persons with perceptual disabilities, for encryption research and to ensure the interoperability of software.[39] That said, these limitations are very narrow and specific and do not come close to maintaining the structural integrity of the internalized approach to freedom of expression.

Finally, the Act mandates that the Governor in Council can make regulations to prescribe additional circumstances in which circumvention would be allowed taking into account a number of factors including, ' ... whether not being permitted to circumvent ... could adversely affect criticism, review, news reporting, commentary, parody, satire, teaching, scholarship or research that could be made or done in respect of the work ... '.[40] However, relegating fair dealing to case-specific regulatory redress denies it its heightened status as a Charter safeguard.

In fact, an earlier failed Copyright Bill had proposed limiting the prohibition on circumvention to cases involving infringing acts.[41] Government policymakers believed that this moderate approach would be more likely to pass Charter scrutiny.[42] This remained the view among Government legal experts at the time of the introduction of the current provisions.[43] It would seem clear then that in its failure to preserve fair dealing and other exceptions within the structure of the anti-circumvention provisions, the Act is vulnerable to a Charter challenge. And yet, policymakers remain unwilling to do a comprehensive constitutional review of copyright and TPMs. In the very recent report of the Standing Committee on Industry, Science and Technology ("INDU") on the Statutory Review of the Copyright Act, the Committee agreed that circumvention of TPMs should be permitted for non-infringing uses. However, its final recommendation was vague and open-ended. It suggested only that the Government of Canada 'examine measures to modernize copyright policy with digital technologies ...

---

39. Sections 41.12, 41.13 and 41.16.
40. Section 41.21(2)a)iii).
41. Bill C-60 – *An Act to Amend the Copyright Act* – (first reading, 20 June 2005) – Legislative summary at: http://www.parl.gc.ca/About/Parliament/LegislativeSummaries/Bills_ls.asp?ls=C60&Parl=38&Ses=1.
42. *See* Simon Doyle '"Prey to Thievery" The Canadian Recording Industry Association and the Canadian Copyright Lobby, 1997 to 2005' Master of Journalism Thesis, Carleton University, 2006 available at https://curve.carleton.ca/system/files/theses/29767.pdf.
43. A legal opinion of the Department of Justice, obtained through an access to information request, recognized that: ' ... legislation prohibiting anti-circumvention acts, devices and services would not be held unconstitutional (either they would not breach the freedom of expression rights or, if they did contravene, would be justified) where they are tied/linked to copyright infringement'. *See* Michael Geist 'Are the Canadian Digital Lock Rules Unconstitutional?' Huffington Post Online – posted 27 June 2012, updated 27 August 2012 available at http://www.huffingtonpost.ca/michael-geist/bill-c-11_b_1627604.html.

including the relevance of technological protection measures within copyright law ... '[44]

8.2.2 CONTRACTING OUT OF 'USER RIGHTS' ESPECIALLY FAIR DEALING

There is uncertainty in Canada over the question of whether some or all of the limitations and exceptions contained in the Act are to be interpreted as mandatory or whether they can be excluded by contract.[45] Obviously, permitting the contracting out of the statutory limitations and exceptions set out challenges the entire premise upon which the internalized approach to freedom of expression is based. There is a cogent argument to be made that, at the very least, those copyright exceptions and limitations that are directly tied to constitutional freedoms should be considered as mandatory.[46] Unfortunately, the Act remains silent on this question.

In contrast, other jurisdictions have paid attention to this crucial issue. A World Intellectual Property Organization Report, conducted in 2010, identified twenty-five member countries whose copyright statutes prohibited the contracting out of certain limitations and exceptions.[47] Recent amendments to the *UK Copyright, Designs and Patents Act*[48] introduced a clause after a number of specific permitted uses, including fair dealing, to the effect that: 'To the extent that a term of any contract purports to prevent or restrict the doing of any act which, by virtue of this section, would not infringe copyright, that term is unenforceable.'[49] Law reform initiatives have also tackled this question. For example, in its February 2014 report on Copyright and the Digital Economy, the Australian Law Reform Commission stated: 'In the Australian context, the existing fair dealing exceptions protect important public interests in education, the free flow of information and freedom of

---

44. *Statutory Review of the Copyright Act*, Report of the Standing Committee on Industry, Science and Technology, House of Commons, Parliament of Canada (June 2019) https://www.ourcommons.ca/DocumentViewer/en/42-1/INDU/report-16 (hereinafter 'INDU Report 2019').

45. *See* Pascale Chapdelaine *Copyright User Rights: Contracts and the Erosion of Property* (Oxford: Oxford University Press, 2017); Lucie Guilbault, *Copyright Limitations and Contracts: An Analysis of the Contractual Overridability of Limitations on Copyright* (The Hague: Kluwer Law International, 2001).

46. Jacques de Werra 'Moving Beyond the Conflict Between Freedom of Contract and Copyright Policies: In Search of a New Global Policy for Online Information Licensing Transactions' (2003) 25 Columbia Journal of Law & the Arts 239.

47. WIPO Standing Committee on Copyright and Related Rights, Report on the Questionnaire on Limitations and Exceptions, Twentieth Session, Geneva 21-24 June 2010 especially at pp. 10-11: http://www.wipo.int/edocs/mdocs/copyright/en/sccr_20/sccr_20_7.pdf. Canada did not participate in the questionnaire.

48. 1988 c. 48 as amended.

49. *See* for example sections 29)4B) and 30(4).

expression … . [T]he ALRC recommends that … limitations on contracting out should apply to these fair dealing exceptions.'[50]

Unfortunately, this issue was not specifically addressed in the INDU Report 2019 even though the Committee identified the question of contracting out of fair dealing as an area of concern.[51] No matter how robust the interpretation of fair dealing and other user safeguards might be, the fact that the statute remains silent on whether they can be eliminated by contract negates its ability to internalize freedom of expression considerations.

8.3   A CHARTER APPROACH TO CANADIAN COPYRIGHT LAW

What these two problem areas demonstrate is that the structure of the Act, both actively in the case of TPMs and passively in its silence on contracting out, undermines the efficacy of the internalized approach to free expression. In effect, what Parliament has given with one hand, in its enhancement of permitted uses and exceptions, it has taken away with the other. As a result, the Act cannot maintain the proper equilibrium between copyright rights and user rights that the Supreme Court of Canada has so painstakingly mapped out in its series of normative copyright decisions.[52] These structural failures necessitate a closer look at the Charter's role as an extrinsic mechanism to safeguard free expression rights in copyright cases.

8.3.1   A CHARTER CONSISTENT COPYRIGHT ACT: RESOLVING THE STRUCTURAL FAILURES

Over the course of the past three decades of Charter jurisprudence, Canadian courts have developed tests and interpretive models through which freedom of expression and other fundamental rights are balanced against legislative encroachments.[53] Where a statute or some of its provisions do not pass Charter scrutiny, the courts can strike down the impugned legislation or declare the offending provisions invalid and unenforceable. In the alternative and as a less drastic remedy, the courts could employ 'reading down' or

---

50. *Copyright and the Digital Economy*, Australia Law Reform Commission Report 122, 13 February 2004. http://www.alrc.gov.au/publications/copyright-report-122.
51. INDU Report 2019 cited at note 44 at p. 71. *See also*, submission to the INDU Committee by Pascale Chapdelaine et al., cited at note 4.
52. The Supreme Court of Canada continues to affirm the concept of balanced copyright. In its most recent decision in *Keatley Surveying Ltd. v. Teranet Inc.*, 2019 SCC 43, the court explained that user rights must be considered within the Act in its entirety, not only in relation to permitted uses and exceptions. In this case, the court interpreted the statutory provision on Crown copyright in light of both creator and user rights.
53. *See* Kent Roach & David Schneiderman 'Freedom of Expression in Canada' (2013) 61 Supreme Court LR 429.

'reading in' techniques to resolving the Charter conflict, which the Supreme Court of Canada has described as a 'Charter values' interpretive method.[54] 'Reading down' occurs in cases of textual ambiguity and dictates that where ' ... a provision is open to two possible interpretations and one interpretation would run afoul of a Charter right or freedom, the alternative interpretation is to be preferred.'[55] 'Reading in' involves reading Charter consistent provisions into the legislation. 'In the case of reading in the inconsistency is defined as what the statute wrongly excludes rather than what it wrongly includes.'[56] Regardless of which interpretive mechanism is the most appropriate in a given copyright infringement case, each of these methods offers a meaningful way of ensuring that the courts adopt Charter consistent constructions where the Act is in conflict with freedom of expression. This Charter approach – whether it takes the form of 'reading down' or 'reading in' – would, therefore, permit the courts to salvage the Act while tempering its overbroad contours.

How would this Charter approach be applied in the context of the two previously identified structural problem areas? Turning first to the anti-circumvention provisions, a Charter analysis would interpret the Act in a manner consistent with the ability of users to circumvent access control technologies for fair dealing or other free expression purposes, such as for non-commercial user-generated content. Although Canadian courts have yet to rule on this issue, this suggested line of reasoning has elicited mixed response in the United States where the anti-circumvention provisions in the American *Copyright Act*[57] raise similar concerns about their impact on the First Amendment right to free speech guaranteed by the American Constitution. American courts have been reticent to read the fair use exception into the anti-circumvention provisions. Nevertheless, some courts have been willing to restrict the scope of these provisions. For example, the 2010 appellate decision in *MGE UPS Systems Inc v. GE Consumer and Industrial Inc.*[58] recognized inherent limits to the anti-circumvention rules under American copyright law on the basis that the TPM provisions could not provide copyright holders with more rights than they already enjoyed:

> Merely bypassing a technological protection that restricts a user from viewing or using a work is insufficient to trigger the DMCA's anti-circumvention provision. The DMCA prohibits only forms of access that

---

54. *Bell ExpressVu Limited Partnership v. Rex*, 2002 SCC 42; *Québec (Commission des normes, de l'équité, de la santé et de la sécurité du travail) v. Caron* 2018 SCC 3.
55. *Allsco Building Products Ltd, v. UFCW Local 1288* [1999] 2 SCR 1136 at para. 26.
56. *R. v. Schacter* [1992] 2 SCR 679 at p. 698.
57. 17 USC §512 as amended by the *Digital Millennium Copyright Act* (DMCA) 112 Stat. 2860 (1998).
58. 622 F. 3d 361 (2010).

would violate or impinge on the protections that the Copyright Act otherwise affords copyright owners.[59]

Recent dicta of the United States Supreme Court in the decision in *Golan v. Holder*[60] confirmed the mandatory nature of fair use as a First Amendment safeguard, thereby calling into question any legislative constraints that purport to limit its exercise. Although not an anti-circumvention case, the court held that both the idea/expression dichotomy and the fair use exception contained in the US copyright statute were ' … recognized in our jurisprudence as "built-in First Amendment accommodations".'[61] The logical consequence of this argument is that any measures that undermine the internalized statutory recognition of freedom of expression should be subjected to constitutional oversight. According to Neil Netanel:

> Golan makes clear that copyright law's idea/expression dichotomy and fair use privilege both have constitutional import. Indeed … Golan strongly suggests that copyright law would not withstand First Amendment scrutiny but for those built-in First Amendment accommodations. Courts must, accordingly, interpret and apply the idea/expression dichotomy and fair use privilege in a manner consistent with their vital First Amendment role. Further … statutory provisions that disturb copyright's built-in First Amendment accommodations, or that otherwise abridge non-infringing speech, lie vulnerable to First Amendment challenge.[62]

This is a compelling argument and one that affirms the preeminent role of the fundamental right of free expression within the copyright paradigm such that only constitutional scrutiny could justify a statutory derogation.

Similar logic would apply in the Canadian context. Although the Supreme Court of Canada did not explicitly tie fair dealing or other exceptions to the Charter, it could be argued that it did so implicitly when it characterized permitted uses, especially fair dealing, as user rights. Taking these pronouncements and the recent statutory expansion of fair dealing together, it could be said that the Act has now 'constitutionalized' copyright by strengthening the most important internal mechanism for the advancement of free expression guarantees. Following this line of reasoning, to deny the user the ability to invoke fair dealing in cases involving TPMs is, in effect, to abrogate a 'built-in Charter safeguard'. Courts would, therefore, have to interpret the Act in a manner that preserved fair dealing in these circumstances.

---

59. *MGE UPS* at p. 6.
60. 132 S. Ct. 873 (2003).
61. *Golan* at p. 890.
62. Neil Netanel 'First Amendment Constraints on Copyright after *Golan v. Holder*' (2013) 60 UCLA Law Review 1082 at p. 1128.

This same kind of Charter analysis would be invoked in respect of the uncertainty surrounding contracting out of statutory permitted uses and exceptions. A Charter approach to this question would mandate that, given its status as a 'built-in Charter safeguard', fair dealing can never be overruled by contract and Canadian courts would interpret the Act accordingly.

That said, reinstating fair dealing and any other free expression safeguards into the structure of the Act is only a first step in the development of a meaningful Charter analysis of copyright. Beyond attending to the constitutional defects in the statutory treatment of TPMs and the question of contracting out of fair dealing, a more complete Charter approach would also assess the way in which the courts interpret and apply the Act in cases that raise freedom of expression concerns.

8.3.2   A CHARTER CONSISTENT INTERPRETATION OF THE ACT:
               RECOGNIZING COPYRIGHT'S CONSTITUTIONAL DIMENSION

The internalized approach to freedom of expression assumes that the policy objectives of copyright and of the constitutional guarantee of free expression are sufficiently similar such that, for example, a fair dealing analysis in a copyright infringement case would arrive at the same result as a Charter analysis. Although Canadian courts have already recognized the relevance of the Charter section 2(b) in copyright cases, they have subordinated the Charter to the four corners of the Act in the belief that the statute is itself a sufficient arbiter of free expression. However, this assumption needs to be questioned especially because of the Act's own internal inconsistencies. As Michael Birnhack notes:

> [t]he tendency to internalise the external sphere into the internal one by turning to copyright law mechanisms such as the fair dealing defence should be carefully inspected. Drawing quick conclusions may result in failing to take into account the constitutional dimension of the copyright law/freedom of expression intersection.[63]

Acknowledging the heightened constitutional dimension in copyright infringement cases would require a different kind of analysis than one based on the conflation of copyright principles with constitutional ones. In this respect, Canadian courts have, to date, taken a jaundiced view of the Charter's overarching importance.[64] Taking the Charter seriously would involve giving deference to freedom of expression as a constitutional guarantee.

One way of proceeding would be to recognize a robust set of normative principles around the concept of user rights so as to mitigate some of the

---

63. Birnhack cited at note 7 at p. 35.
64. *See Michelin* cited at note 2 and *Lorimer* cited at note 4.

weaknesses inherent in the internalized approach. As long as fair dealing and other statutory limitations and exceptions were interpreted broadly, an independent constitutional analysis would be unnecessary. The law of user rights would, by definition, cover the constitutional field. This perspective would be similar to the reasoning adopted by the United States Supreme Court in *Eldred v. Ashcroft*[65] wherein the court stated:

> The First Amendment securely protects the freedom to make – or decline to make – one's own speech; it bears less heavily when speakers assert the right to make other people's speech. To the extent such assertions raise First Amendment concerns, copyright's built-in free speech safeguards are generally adequate to address them. We recognize that the D.C Circuit spoke too broadly when it declared copyrights 'categorically immune from challenges under the First Amendment' … But when, as in this case, Congress has not altered the traditional contours of copyright protection, further First Amendment scrutiny is unnecessary.[66]

Certainly, the Supreme Court of Canada's expansive approach to fair dealing and other limitations and exceptions could justify the claim that the necessary constitutional safeguards are already in place without the necessity of further intervention. However, even acknowledging the great judicial strides that have been made to broaden the ambit of fair dealing, the constitutionalized nature of this user right may still require some extrinsic oversight. The internalized interpretive method may function effectively in the American context, where the First Amendment right to free speech is much more robustly constructed than freedom of expression is under the Canadian Charter. Indeed, the Act's Charter vulnerability remains despite the pronouncements of the Supreme Court of Canada. The evolving Canadian law in relation to fair dealing for purposes of parody or satire is a good illustration of the shortcomings of the internalized approach in the Canadian context.

As forms of creative expression, parody and satire necessarily require the conjuring up or invocation of the work being parodied or satirized. Denying a parodist or satirist the ability to engage in this type of activity on the basis that it constitutes an infringement of the underlying copyright work is an encroachment upon that individual's freedom of expression. Prior to the 2012 statutory amendments that introduced parody and satire as a separate category of fair dealing, individuals would have had to invoke fair dealing for criticism in their defence, on the basis that their parody amounted to fair criticism. However, in *Michelin*, the only Canadian case prior in which a question of parody was at issue prior to 2012, the court took a very restrictive view of what could constitute acceptable criticism for fair dealing purposes. There, the well-known tire manufacturer successfully sued its striking labour

---

65. *Eldred v. Ashcroft* 537 US 186 (2003).
66. *Eldred* at p. 221.

union for the latter's parodied depiction of the iconic 'Michelin man' on leaflets and other print material. The labour union argued that its use of Michelin's artistic work was fair dealing for criticism and that it was also protected under section 2(b) of the Charter. The court rejected each of these claims. It excluded parody as a form of fair criticism, and it paid short shrift to the separate Charter argument on the basis that the labour union was seeking to ' ... extend the scope of [its] right of free expression to include the use of another's property.'[67] Not surprisingly, the decision elicited much commentary, criticism and calls for legislative reform.[68] Parliament eventually intervened to reconcile this point of conflict by internalizing the freedom to parody within the fair dealing framework. This was an important statutory correction.

However, the first decision to consider the scope of this new category of fair dealing has left much to be desired from a freedom of expression standpoint. In *United Airlines v. Cooperstock*, the Federal Court of Canada dismissed a claim of fair dealing in a case involving a website critical of United Airlines.[69] This case is currently under appeal to the Federal Court of Appeal, but the lower court found that while the actions of the defendant amounted to parody, the dealing was not fair, largely because of the substantial amount of material that was copied from the plaintiff's website. The court accepted that parody could be a form of protected expression, but it limited its scope: 'Parody is not simply a defence to copyright infringement – it is also an aspect of free speech. However, like all free speech, it is not unrestricted.' That was the end of the court's musing on the interplay between copyright and freedom of expression. The court interpreted freedom of expression in the context of the primacy of copyright rights, never recognizing that copyright rights themselves are not unrestricted. What was missing from the decision was a heightened 'Charter values' interpretation of the *Copyright Act* consistent with the status of freedom of expression as a built-in human right. In the end, despite the significant statutory and jurisprudential strides in recognition of user rights under Canadian copyright law, the court's approach in *United Airlines* was not altogether that different from the court in *Michelin*.

A different interpretive approach is necessary in order to reconcile freedom of expression and copyright in a manner that ensures Charter consistent outcomes. Indeed, because of the significance of the issues at play, the Canadian Civil Liberties Association (CCLA) has been given leave to intervene in the *United Airlines* appeal. In its written submission, CCLA has argued that the trial court failed to 'balance the rights of copyright owners

---

67. *Michelin* cited at note 2 at p. 400.
68. *See* sources cited at note 4. For a comparative analysis of copyright, parody and freedom of expression *see* Amy Lai, *The Right to Parody: Comparative Analysis of Copyright and Free Speech* (Cambridge: Cambridge University Press, 2019).
69. 2017 FC 616.

with those of users, and chill[ed] critical commentary.'[70] Instead, the court should have adopted a 'charter values' approach to fair dealing for parody:

> A proper exercise of statutory interpretation, in accordance with Charter values, legislative intent and precedent, would have resulted in a broad interpretation of fair dealing generally, and parody in particular. It would also allow for an assessment of fairness that leaves room for critical and mocking parody and does not give undue preference to the commercial interests of copyright owners.[71]

A Charter values approach to copyright would be analogous to what European scholars have identified as an emerging human rights approach to freedom of expression and copyright in the decisions of the European Court of Justice and the European Court of Human Rights. For example, in the case of the European Court of Justice in the *Deckmyn v. Vandersteen*[72] and *Painer v. Standard Verlags GmbH and Others*[73] decisions, it was suggested that: ' ... in order to secure compatibility with Article 11 of the EU Charter of Fundamental Rights and Art. 10 of the ECHR, the Court adopted an interpretation that was broader than might have been appropriate in the cases of an [exception & limitation] without a comparably strong grounding in freedom of expression.'[74] Similarly, in *Ashby Donald e.a v. France,*[75] the European Court of Human Rights recognized that Member States' copyright laws must be explicitly assessed by the extent to which they respect the fundamental human right of freedom of expression guaranteed in Article 10 of the *European Convention on Human Rights.*[76] Christophe Geiger and Elena Izyumenko explain the implications of these rulings:

---

70. Memorandum of Fact and Law of the Intervener, Canadian Civil Liberties Association, at para. 19. Memorandum available online at https://ccla.org/cclanewsite/wp-content/uplo ads/2018/07/UA-v-Cooperstock-CCLA-Memo-of-Fact-Law-FINAL-July-3-2018.pdf.
71. *Ibid.*, at para. 47.
72. Case C-201/13 *Deckmyn v. Vandersteen*, 3 September 2014, *nyr, see* http:// curia.europa.eu/juris/document/document.jsf?text=&docid=157281&pageIndex= 0&doclang=en&mode=lst&dir=&occ=first&part=1&cid=421468. Ironically, the Federal Court in the *United Airlines v. Cooperstock* decision cited *Deckmyn* but not in respect of the heightened interpretive approach.
73. Case C-145/10 *Painer v. Standard VerlagsGmbH and Others*, [2012] ECDR 6.
74. European Copyright Society 'Limitations and Exceptions as Key Elements of the Legal Framework for Copyright in the European Union: Opinion on the Judgment of the CJEU in Case C-201/13 *Deckmyn*', 1 November 2014 available at http://infojustice.org/wp-content/uploads/2014/11/Limitations-and-Exceptions-as-Key-Elements-of-the-Legal-Framework-for-Copyright-in-the-EU.pdf at para. 27.
75. Application 36769/08, 10 January 2013 – http://hudoc.echr.coe.int/sites/fra/pages/ search.aspx?i=001-115845.
76. Convention for the Protection of Human Rights and Fundamental Freedoms (Rome, 4 November 1950) as amended http://www.echr.coe.int/Documents/Convention_ENG.pdf.

Practically speaking, this means that external factors can be applied to ensure a balanced protection beyond the already existing exceptions and limitations built into copyright legislation, in line with the underlying principle that the exclusive right constitutes an exception to a broader principle of freedom of use.[77]

What is being recognized in these decisions is that a reliance on copyright tests and analyses alone are insufficient in cases that involve freedom of expression concerns. The human rights dimension of copyright requires a broader, more heightened level of interpretation and of judicial scrutiny.

Returning to the Canadian context, a Charter approach would mean that copyright constraints on free expression would have to be evaluated according to Charter compatibility. Courts would not be able to assume that an internal copyright analysis would necessarily generate Charter consistent results or sufficiently account for the Act's constitutional character. An independent and purposive Charter analysis would have to be undertaken in which the courts explicitly recognize the overarching guarantee of freedom of expression within the copyright framework.

Whether Canadian courts are up to the challenge and will adopt a truly meaningful Charter approach to freedom of expression in copyright cases remains to be seen. As constitutional commentators Kent Roach and Schneiderman note, the courts, including the Supreme Court of Canada, have been fairly timid in giving freedom of expression its due weight: 'Despite its claim to being a "fundamental" freedom … much more work remains to be done in securing the central place that freedom of expression should occupy in the evolving Canadian constitutional landscape.'[78] The Federal Court of Appeal in the *United Airlines* case has been presented with the opportunity to provide judicious interpretive guidance that would recognize the centrality of freedom of expression within the Canadian copyright landscape. It is to be hoped that the court proves itself up to the challenge.

8.4   CONCLUSION

The question of how to reconcile the fundamental guarantee of freedom of expression within copyright law is one of the moments in the current legal landscape. Traditionally, courts in Canada have considered that the internal structure of the copyright statute was sufficiently responsive to free expression considerations. However, structural inconsistencies within the Act as well as restrictive judicial interpretive approaches bring to light the inadequacy of this internalized approach and the assumptions upon which it is

---

77. Geiger & Izyumenko cited at note 8, at p. 318.
78. Roach & Schneiderman cited at note 53, at p. 525.

based. A meaningful Charter approach to copyright must look *beyond* the 'well-tailored structure of the Act' to recognize the pre-eminence of Charter values in all cases that lie at the intersection of copyright and freedom of expression.

Chapter 9

Communication to the Public of Works and Freedom to Receive and Impart Information in the Charter of Fundamental Rights

Katarzyna Klafkowska-Waśniowska[*]

A simple answer to a question how the scope of exclusive rights and the scope of exceptions and limitations should be balanced in the light of Articles 11 and 17(2) of the Charter of Fundamental Rights (the Charter)[1] could be: favour freedom of expression. The answer, however, would not be complete. To offer a broader picture, this chapter undertakes the analysis of the role of the Charter in the interpretation and application of EU law, with a particular focus on the communication of works to the public.

In the case of a potential approach to intellectual property disputes by the European Court of Human Rights (ECtHR), L.R. Helfer raised concerns as to the engagement of the European Convention on Human Rights (ECHR) in balancing IP and other rights and freedoms, indicating that ECHR provides neither a coherent blueprint for the Court to impose upper and lower standards for intellectual property protection nor a mechanism to address

---

[*] Research for this chapter was financed in the framework of the Research Visits Program, by the Faculty of Law and Administration Adam Mickiewicz University in Poznan in 2019. The author's research stay at CREAT-e in Glasgow was also dedicated to this chapter.
1. Charter of Fundamental Rights of the European Union *OJ C 326, 26.10.2012, pp. 391-407.*

utilitarian and social welfare arguments, central to IP policy.[2] For the European Court of Justice (CJEU) this balancing approach is unquestionable and clearly developed in the case law addressing copyright and fundamental rights. Since the Lisbon Treaty, CJEU's reasoning is based on the Charter of Fundamental Rights as part of a primary EU law, with the references to the special significance of ECHR for EU law.[3] ECtHR role, as a court of human rights, is different from the role of CJEU in the European Union law. The latter includes fundamental rights analysis in the area of copyright law, as part of the review of the legality of secondary law and interpretation of secondary law in the course of preliminary rulings.[4] In its power to interpret EU law, the Court declared that all mechanisms necessary to ensure this balance are in the copyright directives, particularly the InfoSoc Directive.[5]

From the international perspective, P. Yu points that existing instruments have recognized 'only *certain* attributes of existing intellectual property rights as human rights', and highlights the distinction between the right 'to benefit from the protection of the moral and material interests resulting from any scientific, literary or artistic production of which he is the author',[6] and intellectual property rights, including copyright.[7] From the European perspective, C. Geiger notes how Article 17(2) of the Charter 'strangely "uplifts" "ordinary" economic right to the European constitutional level'.[8] The perspective originating in the Universal Declaration on Human Rights seems different from the European one, where, intellectual property protection is considered in the framework of the right to property, and its status of a fundamental right is not particularly strong.[9] These particular features of EU law, together with primarily economic objectives of harmonization of EU law intensify the debate on copyright protection in the context of freedom of expression. The preamble to the InfoSoc Directive underscores that 'any harmonisation of copyright and related rights must take as a basis

---

2. L.R.Helfer, *The New Innovation Frontier? Intellectual Property and the European Court of Human Rights*, in: P. Torremans ed. *Intellectual Property and Human Rights*, Edward Elgar, 2015. pp. 65 and 82-83.

3. Charter of Fundamental Rights became binding in 2009, when the Lisbon Treaty came into force. Article 6 of the TEU addresses the sources fundamental rights standard in the EU, and Article 52(3) of the Charter addresses relations between the Charter and the Convention.

4. Based on Article 263 TFUE, Article 267 TFEU.

5. Directive 2001/29/EC of the European Parliament and of the Council of 22 May 2001 on the harmonisation of certain aspects of copyright and related rights in the information society *Official Journal L 167, 22/06/2001 P. 0010 – 0019.*

6. Article 15(1)c International Covenant on Economic, Social and Cultural Rights.

7. P.K. Yu, *Challenges to the Development of a Human Rights Framework for Intellectual Property.* P.Torremans ed. *Intellectual Property and Human Rights*, Edward Elgar, 2015, p. 91.

8. C. Geiger, *Reconceptualizing the Constitutional Dimension of Intellectual Property,* in P. Torremans ed. *Intellectual Property and Human Rights*, Edward Elgar, 2015 p. 134.

9. P. Torremans, *Article 17(2) – Right to Property*, in: S. Peers, T. Hervery, J. Kenner & A. Ward ed. *The EU Charter of Fundamental Rights,* 2014, p. 503.

a high level of protection since such rights are crucial to intellectual creation.'[10] It is noted, that the approach found in the preamble of the InfoSoc Directive recognizes the potential of conflict between copyright and freedom of expression.[11] This potential conflict, embodied in the questions on the interpretation of the scope of rights on the one hand, and the scope of limitations and exceptions on the other, made its way to the Grand Chamber rulings in *Pelham, Spiegel-Online* and *Funke-Medien*.[12] Two of these cases concerned online publishing, and Pelham case has implications for the transformative works also popular online. The importance of the area of online 'expression', online communication and seeking knowledge, entertainment and information, cannot be overestimated. It shall be subject to the analysis, to what extent these rulings help answering key questions[13] on balance between expanding the right of communication to the public and limitations and exceptions in EU law.

The analysis starts with the GS Media ruling on the scope of the public communication right to demonstrate to what extent the Charter may serve to limit the scope of exclusive rights. The area of 'freedoms' safeguarded in Title II of the Charter is delineated by the scope of exclusive rights and the scope of limitations and exceptions. As the harmonization in the EU progresses, *i.a.,* with the new DSM Directive,[14] one problem to be dealt with in this Chapter is whether the Member States retain any discretion in the application of fundamental rights standards. If this discretion is substantially limited than CJEU's guidance on how to ensure proper safeguards for freedoms becomes crucial. What CJEU says about 'favouring "freedom of expression" and safeguarding the effectiveness of user's right', is particularly important for the development of EU law in the Digital Single Market Directive, addressing vital issues of the public communication of works on online content sharing platforms.

---

10. Rec. 9, it follows: ... Intellectual property has therefore been recognised as an integral part of property.
11. Noted on rec. 3 of the InfoSoc Directive '*The proposed harmonisation will help to implement the four freedoms of the internal market and relates to compliance with the fundamental principles of law and especially of property, including intellectual property, and freedom of expression and the public interest*' in: Y. Harn Lee, *Copyright and Freedom of Expression: A Literature Review*, 2015, p. 63; CREAT-e working paper 2015/4.
12. C-476/17 – *Pelham and Others v. Ralf Hütter and Florian Schneider-Esleben*, ECLI-:EU:C:2019:624; C-516/17 *Spiegel Online GmbH v. Volker Beck*, ECLI:EU:C:2019:625 C-469/17 – *Funke Medien NRW GmbH v. Bundesrepublik Deutschland* ECLI-:EU:C:2019:623.
13. C. Geiger, *supra.* pp. 146 and 150-152.
14. Directive (EU) 2019/790 of the European Parliament and of the Council of 17 April 2019 on copyright and related rights in the Digital Single Market and amending Directives 96/9/EC and 2001/29/EC; *OJ L 130, 17.5.2019, pp. 92-125.*

9.1 THE RIGHT OF COMMUNICATION TO THE PUBLIC AND FREEDOM TO RECEIVE AND IMPART INFORMATION

9.1.1 FREEDOM OF EXPRESSION AND THE DEVELOPMENT OF THE CJEU CASE LAW

After the Lisbon Treaty came into force, some questions were posed as to the future role of the ECHR and its relation to the Charter. One of the challenges identified with this change is the role of human rights in the interpretation and application of EU law.[15] The Charter is considered to bring both advantages and challenges[16] when conflicts between right holders and users are considered. The development of case law on the application of the Charter undoubtedly has a significant impact on copyright rules, especially as we observe the evolutionary shift from questions framed in the ECHR provisions, to questions referred for preliminary rulings solely in the context of the Charter.

In 2006, before the Lisbon Treaty came into force, the Grand Chamber of the Court addressed the issue of freedom of expression in the context of the ECHR In the Laserdisken case.[17] The question was important as it addressed the validity of Article 4(2) of the InfoSoc Directive, precluding national provisions on the international exhaustion of the distribution right in the light of the freedom to receive and impart information. The constraints on freedom to receive and impart information arose out of the restrictions on trade in imported 'cultural goods'. The Court underscored 'special significance' of ECHR for EU law,[18] and till now, the ECtHR case law remains the key point of reference for CJEU when it balances fundamental rights and freedom.[19]

---

15. W. Weiss, *Human Rights in the EU: Rethinking the Role of the European Convention on Human Rights after Lisbon,* p. 65 European Constitutional Law Review, 7: 64-95, 2011.
16. J. Griffiths, *European Union Copyright Law and the Charter of Fundamental Rights – Advocate General Szpunar's Opinions in (C-469/17) Funke Medien, (C-476/17) Pelham GmbH and (C-516/17) Spiegel-Online,* p. 35, ERA Forum, 20:35-50, 2019.
17. C-479/04 *Laserdisken ApS v. Kulturministeriet,* ECLI:EU:C:2006:549.
18. C-479/04 Laserdisken paras 62-65. CJEU reminded, that where freedom to receive information may be restricted, it may be justified by the rights of others and need to protect copyright as part of intellectual property.
19. The questions concerning Articles 17 and 44 of the Charter were referred by a national court in the case Promusicae C-275/06. Notwithstanding the importance of this case, and the subsequent Scarlet Extended Case (C-70/10) it concerned the question of balance between different Directives giving effect to different fundamental right and this chapter is narrowed to the questions of balance between exclusive rights and limitations and exceptions.

In Painer in 2010, the national court referred the question about the interpretation of both: the ECHR and the Charter.[20] It is interesting that when CJEU addressed the question of a national court, asking specifically about Article 17 of the Charter and Article 1 of the First Protocol to the ECHR, it did not refer expressly to any of those acts, focusing solely on the interpretation of EU Directives.[21] CJEU referred however to freedom of expression in its interpretation of the scope of exceptions and limitations in the Infosoc Directive. Rather than guiding what entails the balance between fundamental rights and freedoms, protected in Articles 11 and 17(2) of the Charter, CJEU simplifies the problem stating that Article 5(3)(d) of the InfoSoc Directive on permitted quotation serves to achieve a balance between one of the economic rights granted to authors (reproduction) on the one hand and freedom of expression of users of protected works on the other.[22] The Court concludes, that fair balance is struck in the case of publishing photos of a missing person by media, without the consent of the right holder, if the work was already lawfully published, and the name of the author, in principle, indicated. In this case, it requires favouring user's right to freedom of expression, over the interests of the author.[23]

In Deckmyn,[24] another case important for safeguarding freedom of expression, the national court did not include interpretation of any fundamental rights act in its question. This issue was however considered further, particularly in the AG opinion. The parties were also invited to submit comments on the possible impact of the interpretation of the concept of parody on certain fundamental rights referred to in the Charter, including freedom of expression. AG Cruz-Villalon reminded the importance of the Charter and its impact on the secondary law of the European Union. AG Cruz-Villalon invoked the *Fransson* case, where the Court said 'The applicability of European Union law entails applicability of the fundamental rights guaranteed by the Charter'.[25] In the case of publishing a parody of a drawing with a discriminatory context, AG Cruz-Villalon advised that the national court must take into account the prominent role of the freedom of expression in a democratic society, laid down in Article 11(1) of the Charter, relying on the case law of ECHR.[26] In its preliminary ruling, CJEU referred neither to the Charter, nor to the ECHR, confining its remarks to the interpretation of Article 5(3)(k), which must strike the fair balance between rights and interests of authors as protected by Articles 2 and 3 of the Infosoc

---

20. C-145/10 *Eva-Maria Painer v. Standard VerlagsGmbH*, ECLI:EU:C:2011:798.
21. Painer, paras 85-99.
22. Painer, para. 134.
23. Painer, para. 135.
24. C-201/13 *Johan Deckmyn and Vrijheidsfonds VZW v. Helena Vandersteen and Others*, ECLI:EU:C:2014:2132.
25. C-617/10, ECLI:EU:C:2013:105 Åkerberg Fransson, para. 21.
26. Opinion of AG Cruz-Villalon in C-201/13 Deckmyn, ECLI:EU:C:2014:458 para. 80.

Directive, and of the freedom of expression of users of the subject matter. The approach of the Court demonstrates the focus on 'internal' solutions, in the provisions of the InfoSoc Directive.

9.1.2   THE *GS MEDIA* RULING AND FREEDOM TO RECEIVE AND IMPART INFORMATION

Both *Painer* and *Deckmyn* cases addressed the problem of publishing certain content, but not the right of communication to the public that in fact, encompasses all forms of online publications. The development of case law on the public communication right highlighted the problem of how the broad interpretation provided by Court may adversely impact online communication, and eventually prompted questions on the scope of exceptions and limitations.

    The GS Media ruling[27] was awaited to clarify important uncertainties concerning linking to content online.[28] According to the CJEU's case law, the concept of communication to the public includes two cumulative criteria: an act of 'communication' and communication 'to the public'.[29] To test whether these conditions are fulfilled, the CJEU uses 'several complementary criteria, which are not autonomous and are interdependent'.[30] The application of those complementary criteria, may, on the one hand, serve as a tool to balance the interest of right holders and users, but on the other is the source of problems with determining the scope of the communication to the public right. In the broadly discussed Svensson ruling,[31] the Court provided for guidance on the scope of the making available right with respect to linking. CJEU confirmed, that in order to ensure a high level of the protection of authors, an act of 'communication' needs to be interpreted broadly. It is,

---

27. C-160/15 *GS Media BV v. Sanoma Media Netherlands BV and Others* ECLI:EU:C:2016:221.
28. On the development of the criteria for public communication, particularly with reference to linking, *see i.a.*: J.P. Quintais, *Untangling the Hyperlinking Web: In Search of the Online Right of Communication to the Public,* pp. 388-390 The Journal of World Intellectual Property, 21: 385-420, 2018. E. Rosati, *GS Media and Its Implications for the Construction of the Right of Communication to the Public Within EU Copyright Architecture,* pp. 1233-1238 Common Market Law Review, 54: 1221-1242, 2017; R. Markiewicz, Svensson a sprawa polska, ZNUJ 2014/126, p. 59.
29. The Grand Chamber ruling in the Case C-117/15 *Reha Training Gesellschaft für Sport- und Unfallrehabilitation mbH v. Gesellschaft für musikalische Aufführungs- und mechanische Vervielfältigungsrechte eV* (GEMA); para. 37.
30. C-117/15 Reha Training para. 35.
31. C-466/12 *Nils Svensson and Others v. Retriever Sverige AB* ECLI:EU:C:2014:76 The Svensson case was about posting links by the news aggregating site to articles published in the online version of a Swedish newspaper, without restrictions on content.; *see* Opinion of the European Copyright Society, Opinion on the Reference to the CJEU in Case C-466/12 Svensson, https://europeancopyrightsociety.org/opinion-on-the-reference-to-the-cjeu-in-case-c-46612-svensson/.

therefore, crucial that a link offers direct access to works published elsewhere.[32] Considering posting of a link as an act of communication to the public, the Court however clearly stated, that posting links does not require authorization from the right holder when it offers access to 'works freely available on another website'. In this ruling, the Court did not refer to any fundamental rights context, rights or position of users nor the technical aspects of internet communication. The judgment may, however, be read as aiming at achieving a balanced solution,[33] by excluding certain activities, constituting one of the cores of internet communication tools, from the need to obtain authorization. By declaring, that Article 3.1 of the InfoSoc Directive provides for the full harmonization, CJEU also reinforced its position to decide on any upcoming questions with regard to this balance. Among the questions left open, a notable one concerned the relevance of authorization for original uploading of a work.[34]

In the GS Media case, hyperlinks were posted by a Dutch portal to direct users to the photographs of an actress that leaked before they were published in a Playboy magazine. AG Wathelet, considering whether the Court should depart from its ruling in Svensson, pointed to the danger of significantly impairing the functioning of the Internet, and distorting the 'fair balance of rights and interests' between right holders and users, and thus undermining the objectives of InfoSoc Directive.[35] The 'Internet architecture' would be undermined if users were more reticent to post links, fearing copyright infringement.[36] AG Wathelet's argument was placed entirely in the context of the InfoSoc Directive's objectives. In its ruling, the Court emphasized, that InfoSoc Directive aims at maintaining the balance between the interest of rightholders as safeguarded by Article 17(2) of the Charter, and the protection of interests and fundamental rights of users of protected objects, 'in particular their freedom of expression and information, as safeguarded by Article 11 of the Charter (…)'.[37] In its interpretation of the scope of the public communication rights, CJEU referred to the particular

---

32. C-466/12, paras 24-27 and 30.
33. E. Rosati, *GS Media and Its Implications for the Construction of the Right of Communication to the Public Within EU Copyright Architecture*, p. 1241; According to M. Leistner the approach in GS Media allows to reach a balanced solution with one reservation: it 'overshoots the mark' and does not differentiate between different types of links, particularly inline links. In: *Copyright Law on the Internet in Need of Reform: Hyperlinks, Online Platforms and Aggregators*, p. 138, Journal of Intellectual Property Law & Practice 12(2), 2017,; Similar views, with a conclusion that GS Media failed to achieve the balance: R. Tarkiainen, *Tipping the Scale in GS Media: A Proposal to Restore the Balance Between Right Holders and Internet Users*, pp. 504-509 Journal of Intellectual Property Law & Practice 12(6), 2017.
34. Order of the Court in C-348/13 *BestWater International GmbH v. Michael Mebes and Stefan Potsch*.
35. Opinion of AG Melchior Wathelet para. 77.
36. Paragraph 78.
37. Paragraph 31.

importance of the Internet as such for freedom of expression, and to the importance of hyperlinks for 'its sound operation' and for the exchange of opinions and information 'in the network characterized by the availability of immense amounts of information'.[38] The analysis in this spirit, lead CJEU to create a sort of safe harbour for non-commercial users:[39] if a user did not know and wasn't reasonably expected to know, for example, upon a notice from right holders, that a link gives access to a work freely available, but posted without the consent of the right holders, the right holders may not enforce their right.[40] In the case of commercial users, when posting of hyperlinks is carried out for profit, it is presumed the user should have known if the work was published without the right holder's consent. This complicated solution apparently serves to safeguard freedom of expression without any reference to the concepts of limitations or exceptions to copyright.

Parallel to being an important judgment in the line of cases addressing public communication right,[41] *GS Media* judgment is also another step marking the importance of the Charter of Fundamental Rights when limits of copyright are considered. As in *Deckmyn*, the national court did not refer questions concerning fundamental rights. It was AG Wathelet to raise the point discussed earlier by academics, after the *Svensson* case.[42] In *GS Media,* however, the CJEU included interpretation of Article 11 of the Charter in its ruling, to limit the scope, or at least to limit the liability for certain acts of communication to the public.[43] It is thus important for any further consideration of giving effect to freedom of expression beyond the scope of Directive's limitations and exceptions. Indirectly, this case illustrates the link

---

38. Paragraph 45.
39. So-called safe harbour provisions in Article 14 of the E-commerce Directive foresees exemption of liability for host – service providers, if they had no knowledge nor control over the information and acted upon a notice by a right holder; M. Leistner points in the context of GS Media ruling to the 'effective notice and take down procedure on the side of person posting a link' *Copyright law on the internet in need of reform,* p. 139, and M. Senftleben notes that for commercial users GS Media results contrast with obligations resulting from Article 14 *Copyright Reform, GS Media and Innovation Climate in the EU – Euphonious Chord or Dissonant Cacophony?* Tijdschrift Voor Auteurs-, Media- & Informatierecht, 5/2016, p. 132.
40. Paragraphs 49-50. The court uses the phrase: right holders 'may act' against certain users. It is not entirely clear from the judgement what does it mean, if they may not act (enforce their rights) in certain circumstances.
41. In subsequent important cases in C-527/15 – Stichting Brein ECLI:EU:C:2017:300, C-610/15 – Stichting Brein (The Pirate Bay) ECLI:EU:C:2017:456 CJEU applied the broad concept of communication to the public right, but did not refer to fundamental rights, and the question of balancing in the light of freedom of expression.
42. ECS Opinion, Opinion on the Reference to the CJEU in Case C-466/12 Svensson, paras 3 and 37. https://europeancopyrightsociety.org/opinion-on-the-reference-to-the-cjeu-in-case-c-46612-svensson/.
43. This issue is unclear in EU law, the result to be achieved may be generally described as clarifying to users when hyperlinking entails no copyright liability, *see also* the analysis by J.P. Quintais, *Untangling the Hyperlinking Web,* p. 393.

between a full harmonization of the public communication right and giving effect to freedom of expression. The fact that communication to the public right is fully harmonized prompted the Court to ensure freedom of expression for users, this way declaring compliance with the Charter. For this purpose CJEU offered its reading of how freedom of expression is linked to the smooth functioning of the Internet, acknowledging the chilling effect implicitly that overbroad interpretation of the scope of a right may have on users.

In theory, this approach paves the way to mitigate the scope of exclusive rights when it is justified by any of the fundamental freedoms of users. Subsequent judgment in *Renckhoff.*[44] however, supports the view that hyperlinking, as a very particular form of communication to the public, requires the application of particular criteria. The criteria of a 'new public' and a new technological means of transmission were found to be inadequate to ensure the effectiveness of the right of communication to the public in the case of use of a photo in a school presentation, and its subsequent posting on the school website.[45] AG Campos Sánchez Bordona, apart from advocating that such an activity is not a communication to the public, pointed also to the need of a reasonable balance between protection of intellectual property (Article 17(2)) and the right to education (Article 14 of the Charter). The concluding remarks of the AG's opinion that in any event Article 5(3)(a) would apply to the situation in question were not followed by the Court. CJEU noted that a publication on a website does not contribute to the sound operation of the internet to the same extent as linking, therefore, there is no need to impose further limits in the light of Article 11 of the Charter. With reference to the need to balance Article 17(2) with Articles 11 and 14 of the Charter, the Court merely states there are provisions on the use for the purpose of teaching in the InfoSoc Directive, leaving further issues to the national court.

It may be concluded that by developing criteria *to* exempt certain acts of internet communication from copyright liability CJEU aimed at ensuring the same goal as addressed in Article 5(1) of the InfoSoc Directive. Interpretation of this provision in the case Meltwater[46] clarified that *browsing* as a typical internet activity of users is generally outside the scope of the control of a right holder. The problem identified with browsing and freedom of expression is similar: if users were not to browse without considering right holder's authorization, it would impose ' a significant restriction on the ability of ordinary Internet users to access, in a lawful manner, material that

---

44. C-161/17 *Land Nordrhein-Westfalen v. Dirk Renckhoff*, ECLI:EU:C:2018:634.
45. C-161/17 paras 20-31.
46. C-360/13 – *Public Relations Consultants Association*, ECLI:EU:C:2014:1195.

is available through the Internet'.[47] This problem was solved by CJEU favourably to freedom of expression but based solely on Article 5(1) of the Directive. It may be argued, that CJEU in the GS Media referred to the Charter, because the desirable solution was not provided for in the EU secondary law.

As was rightly observed, both the problem of the scope of rights and of the scope of exceptions and limitations, requires clarifying what copyright does not capture as justified by freedom of expression.[48] Along with the broad interpretation of fully harmonized economic rights of authors, in *Painer, Deckmyn* and *Renckhoff,* the Court suggests that the balanced solutions can be found in the InfoSoc Directive. It should be observed, however, that harmonization of limitations and exceptions was only complementary to achieving desirable solutions for the functioning of the internal market.[49] This leads straight to the question asked by the *Bundesgerichtshof,* in August 2017: 'In what way are the fundamental rights set out in the Charter of Fundamental Rights of the European Union to be taken into account when ascertaining the scope of protection of the exclusive right' (in this case of the phonogram producer) and when ascertaining the scope of the exceptions or limitations provided for in Article 5(2) and (3) of the Infosoc Directive, in the context of the public communication of so-called Afghanistan papers.

9.2	HARMONIZATION OF COPYRIGHT AND RELATED RIGHTS AND THE STANDARDS FOR PROTECTION OF FREEDOM OF EXPRESSION
9.2.1	PELHAM CASE AND THE SCOPE OF REPRODUCTION RIGHT IN THE LIGHT OF ARTICLES 13 AND 11 OF THE CHARTER

Both issues, the scope of rights, and the scope of limitations and exceptions were relevant in the Pelham case. The long dispute before the national courts concerned the practice of sampling,[50] and ultimately the questions referred to

---

47. Y. Harn Lee, *Copyright and Freedom of Expression: A Literature Overview. CREAT-e working paper 2015/4* p. 140; https://www.create.ac.uk/publications/copyright-and-freedom-of-expression-a-literature-review/.

48. C.Geiger & E. Izyumenko, *Freedom of Expression as an External Limitation to Copyright in the EU: Advocate General of the CJEU Shows the Way,* Centre for International Intellectual Property Studies Research Paper No. 2018-12. p. 13.

49. With reference to the harmonization of limitations and exceptions, recital 31 of the InfoSoc Directive provides that *The degree of their harmonization should be based on their impact on the smooth functioning of the internal market.*

50. L. Bently, et al., *Sound Sampling, a Permitted Use under EU Copyright Law? Opinion of the European Copyright Society in Relation to the Pending Reference Before the CJEU in* Case C-476/17, *Pelham GmbH v. Hütter;* IIC (2019) 50: 467-49, p. 472.

CJEU aimed at establishing whether reproduction right of a phonogram producer, as harmonized in the Article 2(c) of the InfoSoc Directive, was infringed by taking very short, two seconds, audio snatches (sample) from the work *Metal auf Metal* and using it in another recording *Nur mir,* by Pelham. AG Szpunar, in his opinion delivered in December 2018, offered a substantive analysis of what entails freedom of arts enshrined in Article 13 of the Charter, as a form of freedom of expression (Article 11 of the Charter). According to AG Szpunar, safeguarding freedom of arts requires creating space for interaction between existing and future works. This objective is attained through the provisions on the quotation, parody and pastiche in the InfoSoc Directive. Freedom of arts, however, is in the words of AG Szpunar: ' less extensive so far as concerns acquiring the means of their creation'. Advocate General was of the opinion that reproduction right of a phonogram producer encompasses the practice of sampling and that there is no need, in the light of Article 13 of the Charter, to introduce or recognize any limitations beyond those harmonized by the InfoSoc Directive. In the opinion of AG Szpunar, existing provisions of EU law 'facilitate dialogue and artistic confrontation through references to pre-existing works' creating sufficient space for artistic freedom'.[51]

CJEU was more favourable towards freedom of arts in its interpretation of the scope of reproduction right of a phonogram produces. It is clear from the judgment that taking a 'sound sample from a phonogram in order to use it, in a modified form unrecognizable to the ear, in a new work' does not constitute reproduction.[52] The CJEU did not focus on an initial reproduction from a previous recording, but on the artistic effect, on condition that is 'unrecognizable to the ear'. The CJEU finds that a user when exercising her freedom of arts, 'may decide to modify the sample' in the process of creating new works. Therefore, treating this effect of musical creation as a reproduction would run counter to the usual meaning of the term reproduction, and would not offer to serve as a balance between intellectual property rights enshrined in Article 17(2) of the Charter, and other fundamental rights, such as freedom of arts in its Article 13. The Court also points to the link between Articles 13 and 11 of the Charter, invoking the case law of Strasbourg court, that it is required under the ECHR to afford to the users 'the opportunity to take part in the public exchange of cultural, political and social information and ideas of all kinds'.[53]

The imminent question, what if a user, in exercising her freedom of arts and freedom of expression, does not decide to alter the sound sample, or does not achieve the desired effect of making it 'unrecognizable to the ear', was answered by the Court separately. Such a situation would, in principle,

---

51. Opinion of AG. M. Szpunar in *Pelham GmbH and Others v. Ralf Hütter and Florian Schneider-Esleben* ECLI:EU:C:2018:1002, paras 91-96.
52. C-476/17 para. 31.
53. C-476/17 para. 31.

amount to the infringement of reproduction right, but a fair balance, as an objective of the InfoSoc Directive, may be found in the provisions on quotations. On the condition, that ' a user of a protected work wishing to rely on the quotation exception must therefore have the intention of entering into "dialogue" with that work', such use may amount to the 'quotation', in the meaning provided by CJEU.[54] The answer to this particular question was provided without any reference to the fundamental rights;[55] however, the analysis was framed in the context of the questions of the German courts on the impact of fundamental rights on the interpretation of the InfoSoc Directive and the assessment of the validity of those national provisions that go beyond Article 5 of the InfoSoc Directive. CJEU's answer in *Pelham* that a Member State cannot establish any exception or limitation other than those provided for in the Article 5 of the InfoSoc Directive is accompanied by the Courts explanations in the Funke-Medien (Afghanistan Papers) and Spiegel-Online judgments issued on the same day.

9.2.2   Judgments in Funke-Medien and Spiegel-Online and the Impact of the Charter on the Interpretation of Provisions on Limitations and Exceptions

In the dispute concerning the publishing of military reports by the *Westdeutsche Allgemeine Zeitung*, scans of the reports that were unofficial, meaning: 'Classified documents – restricted', were made available online with an introduction, some additional links and an invitation to a discussion.[56] In the Spiegel-Online case, an article critical of some statements of Mr Beck, a German politician, was accompanied with links to a website where he published his controversial article in his version, and the version published in the 1980s in print. The politician added a statement that he distances himself from those articles, and publishing both versions served to sustain his argument on differences in the manuscript and published version.

In his opinion in the *Funke-Medien*, AG Szpunar invoked the ECtHR rulings in *Ashby Donald* and *Kolmisoppi* and the concept of an external limitation on copyright.[57] AG Szpunar pointed out that if there were 'systemic shortcomings in the protection of a fundamental right vis-à-vis copyright', it would entail the need for legislative amendments. It is clear, as the result of hierarchical relations between directives and primary EU law,

---

54. C-476/17 para. 72.
55. C-476/17 paras 66-74.
56. C-469/17 para. 10.
57. AG. M. Szpunar opinion in the Case C-469/17 *Funke-Medien*, ECLI:EU:C:2018:870 para. 41: Judgment of the ECtHR of 10 January 2013, *Ashby Donald and Others v. France* (CE:ECHR:2013:0110JUD003676908), and decision of the ECtHR of 19 February 2013, *Fredrik Neij and Peter Sunde Kolmisoppi v. Sweden* (CE:ECHR:2013:0219DEC00 4039712).

including the Charter.[58] AG Szpunar, however, also points to exceptional cases when copyright 'must yield to an overriding interest relating to the implementation of a fundamental right or freedom'.[59] This part of the opinion was praised, as supporting the proper perspective on the freedom of expression, as a rule, and copyright as its limitation, assessed in the framework of Article 10(2)[60] and for the analytical framework applied.[61] In *Funke-Medien*, AG Szpunar focused entirely on whether military reports should be protected by copyright and underscored that a state cannot invoke the fundamental rights protection, as a holder of the copyright in certain material.[62] It is only in subsequent opinion in *Pelham* and in the *Spiegel-Online* cases that AG Szpunar clarified its position with reference to the harmonization of exceptions and limitations in EU law. AG Szpunar stated that 'freedom of expression does not in principle have primacy over copyright beyond the limitations and exceptions for which copyright law provides', it is only possible, within the limits of judicial control, to depart from the wording of the relevant provision in cases of gross violation of the essence of fundamental rights.[63] AG Szpunar reasoning in those cases remains thus within the balancing exercise, with the major focus on the objectives of the Directive and uniform application of EU law, and his opinion in Pelham was criticized for a too restrictive approach.[64]

CJEU did not follow the opinions of AG Szpunar entirely, yet provided a negative answer, to the question whether the Member States can go beyond the list of exceptions and limitations of Article 5 of the InfoSoc Directive. In the *Funke-Medien* and *Spiegel-Online*, the Court declared that freedom of information, and freedom of the press, enshrined in the Article 11 of the Charter are not capable of justifying, beyond limitations and exceptions provided for in Article 5(2) and (3) a derogation from author's exclusive rights to reproduction and communication to the public. It is always possible to remove 'systemic shortcomings' of EU copyright law through legislative amendments. In this line, it should be noted that new exceptions and

---

58. The term for plea of illegality of the directive is two months, according to Article 263 TFEU. In the course of the preliminary ruling procedure, a national court may, at any time, ask about the validity of provisions of secondary law, for instance in the case of incompatibility with the Treaties or any rule of law relating to their application (Article 267 TFEU).
59. Opinion, para. 40.
60. Ch. Geiger & E. Izyumenko, *Freedom of Expression as an External Limitation to Copyright Law in the EU: The Advocate General of CJEU Shows the Way*, Centre for International Intellectual Property Studies Research Paper No. 2018-1; p. 6.
61. D. Jongsma, *AG Szpunar on Copyright's Relation to Fundamental Rights: One Step Forward and Two Steps Back?* IPRinfo 1/2019 p. 13.
62. Opinion in Funke-Medien paras 65-66.
63. Opinion in Spiegel-Online paras 65 and 98.
64. L. Bently, et al., *Sound Sampling, a Permitted Use under EU Copyright Law?* p. 470; D. Jongsma *supra* is critical particularly to interpretation of reproduction right, p. 5.

limitations are added and existing ones expanded in the Digital Single Market Directive.[65]

Both in the *Spiegel-Online* and in the *Funke-Medien* judgment, the CJEU invoked its rulings on the applicability of the Charter and limits of the Member States' discretion to apply national standards of fundamental rights protection. When a Member State is transposing a Directive, the level of protection of fundamental rights provided for in the Charter must be achieved irrespective of the Member States' discretion when transposing a Directive.[66] When the situation is not entirely determined by EU law and a Member State implements EU law, it may apply national standards of fundamental rights protection, provided that the primacy, unity and effectiveness of EU law are not thereby compromised.[67] The practical conclusion by the Court is that it is 'conceivable' only when implemented provisions are not the full harmonization.[68] In the area of copyright, if the provisions of the InfoSoc Directive on the exceptions and limitations do not harmonize fully, then it is theoretically possible to apply national standards, as long as it does not undermine EU law. It is the latter point that, in fact, limits the discretion of the Member States substantially.

9.2.3 FULL HARMONIZATION OF RIGHTS AND INTERPRETATION OF EXCEPTIONS AND LIMITATION IN THE LIGHT OF THE CHARTER

The CJEU found the communication to the public and reproduction rights as fully harmonized by the InfoSoc Directive[69] and also shaped the scope of these rights to ensure freedom of expression for internet users. I would argue that the Court's interpretation on linking, as discussed above, is going beyond the wording of the Directive to give effect to the freedom of expression, thus results in 'external' rather than 'internal' limitations.[70] It certainly is going beyond the existing list of exceptions and limitations, as demanded to ensure freedom to receive and impart information.

CJEU also considered whether the provisions on the exceptions and limitations, for now: Article 5(3)(c) and (d) of the InfoSoc Directive, constituted measures of full harmonization and answered in the negative. The

---

65. Articles 3-6 of the DSM Directive.
66. Pelham, para. 79; Spiegel-Online para. 20.
67. Pelham para. 80; Spiegel-Online para. 21. The court invokes its rulings in judgments of 26 February 2013, *Melloni*, C-399/11, EU:C:2013:107, para. 60, and of 26 February 2013, *Åkerberg Fransson*, C-617/10, EU:C:2013:105, para. 29.
68. Pelham, para. 81; Spiegel-Online para. 22.
69. Svensson; Pelham on Article 2c), and Funke Medien on Article 2a) of the InfoSoc Directive.
70. The wording of the judgments is blurred, but it seems that acts of communication to the public appear in the case of linking, and an act of initial reproduction in the case of sampling, but the scope of right is mitigated to give effect to the freedom of expression, encompassing freedom of arts.

margin of discretion for the Member States is, however, limited by the fact that the harmonization of limitations and exceptions is exhaustive. Exhaustive harmonization and establishment of the 'fair balance' as one of the objectives of the InfoSoc Directive prompt the Court to declare that all mechanism necessary to balance right to intellectual property in Article 17(2) of the Charter and freedom of expression in Article 11 are provided in the Directive. By those mechanisms, the CJEU means provisions on exclusive rights and provisions on possible limitations and exceptions.[71] This formally justifies why the Member States cannot provide for additional limitations or exceptions in the light of their constitutional standards of fundamental rights. In the words of AG Szpunar, another approach could result in 'a kind of "fair use" clause', that could be differently interpreted by national courts.[72] When it comes to the margin of discretion in the application of the harmonized exceptions and limitations, the CJEU offers an interpretation of what entails Articles 17(2), 11 and 13 of the Charter, in conjunction with the autonomous interpretation of the terms used in the InfoSoc Directive, such as 'reproduction', 'quotation' or even 'use of works ... in connection with ... reporting'.[73]

Ch. Geiger points that one of the results of applying fundamental rights framework to the interpretation of copyright should be the departure from the principle of a strict interpretation of the provisions on the exceptions and limitations as an alleged derogation from the 'rule' of protection of economic rights of authors.[74] CJEU confirms that Article 5(3)(c) and (d) derogate from Articles 2(a) and 3 of the InfoSoc Directive; nevertheless, all these provisions safeguard fundamental rights that need to be balanced. The exclusive rights of authors should be given a broad interpretation, but the rights of users recognized by the Court in its case law need to be effective.[75] As it is confirmed by the Court that Article 11 of the Charter corresponds to Article 10 of the ECHR, the national courts need to take into account the ruling of ECtHR in Ashby Donald, and the nature of the 'speech' or information at issue particularly for the political discourse and debate on matters of public interest,[76] to ensure full adherence to fundamental rights protection.[77]

According to the Court, in all three cases, it is possible to achieve a balanced solution without recourse to any exception or limitation going beyond the InfoSoc Directive. Exhaustive harmonization of exceptions and limitations, justified by the need to ensure full effectiveness of the exclusive rights, and removing any market distortions, does not, as such, contravene

---

71. C-476/17 para. 60, C-469/17 para. 58.
72. AG Szpunar's opinion in Spiegel-Online, para. 63.
73. C-469/17 para. 75.
74. Answer to question 3 in the Spiegel-Online and in the Funke-Medien case.
75. C-469/17 paras 70-71; C-516/17 paras 54-55.
76. C-469/17 paras 73-74; C-516/17 paras 57-58.
77. C-469/17 para. 59, C-516/17 para. 76.

the requirements of freedom of expression. The CJEU is of the view that exclusive rights on the one hand and exceptions and limitations on the other are indeed balanced in the Directive, though giving full effect to freedom of expression is nowhere mentioned as its primary objective. In contrast, ensuring a high level of protection of authors is.[78] Furthermore, when the Court emphasizes that all mechanisms for balancing are found in the Directive, it invokes Promusicae ruling, where it referred to balancing in the privacy Directive 2002/58/EC.[79] The objective of the latter Directive was, however, entirely different. According to Article 1, Directive 2002/58 harmonizes the provisions required to ensure an equivalent level of protection of fundamental rights and freedoms. For this reason, the answer of the Court cannot be welcomed without objections.

9.3   COMMUNICATION TO THE PUBLIC AND THE BALANCING OF RIGHTS AND FREEDOMS IN THE DIGITAL SINGLE MARKET DIRECTIVE: FAVOURING FREEDOM OF EXPRESSION?

Apart from the development of the important case law addressing freedom of expression concerns, 2019 was also the year of accepting new DSM, having for its principal objective contributing to the attainment of the internal market objectives.[80] Its answer to digital single market challenges includes 'clarifying' the concept of communication to the public and liability of online content sharing platform service providers (OCSSP). In the context of drafting new Article 17, concerns were raised as to the impact of the provisions on service providers' liability on users' rights to upload copyrighted material in the scope of exceptions and limitations, such as quotation, caricature or review.[81] It is possible that freedom of expression would be

---

78. Recital 4 of the InfoSoc Directive.
79. C-476/17 para. 60; C-275/06 para. 66.
80. Rec. 2 of the DSM Directive.
81. In the Impact Assessment it is noted that freedom of expression may be affected negatively when legal obligation to implement technological solutions identifying unauthorized content fail to identify the content correctly or when user uploads are limited in an unjustified manner. According to the impact assessment, this is mitigated by procedural safeguards that were developed in the course of trilogues. Commission Staff Working Document Impact Assessment on the modernisation of EU copyright rules Accompanying the document Proposal for a Directive of the European Parliament and of the Council on copyright in the Digital Single Market and Proposal for a Regulation of the European Parliament and of the Council laying down rules on the exercise of copyright and related rights applicable to certain online transmissions of broadcasting organizations and retransmissions of television and radio programmes, SWD(2016) 301 final PART 1/3, p. 169; Proposal for a Directive of the European Parliament and the Council on Copyright in the Digital Single Market. Preparation for trilogue. 4-column document of 26.09.2018, proposal for Article 13(7) p. 192; Proposal for a Directive of the

overly restricted by the automated means for content blocking and removal, especially with the use of algorithms.[82] Therefore, several measures safe-guarding the effective use of exceptions and limitations were included in the DSM directive. It is stipulated in recital 70 that 'The steps taken by online content-sharing service providers in cooperation with right holders should be without prejudice to the application of exceptions or limitations to copyright, including, in particular, those which guarantee the freedom of expression of users.' It is underscored that users should have the opportunity to upload and make available content 'for the specific purpose of quotation, criticism, review, caricature, parody or pastiche', as those exceptions are particularly important to strike a balance in the light of the Charter of Fundamental Rights. There are two main ways to ensure that objective. First, Article 17(7) indicates in a rather general way, that the Member States need to ensure that users 'are able to rely' on the exceptions listed in recital 70. According to recital 70, these particular exceptions 'need to be made mandatory', which seems to indicate what does an obligation to ensure the user's 'ability to rely' means in practice. Yet the language of Article 17(7) is unclear when read together with Article 1(2) of the DSM Directive, providing that except for the amendments introduced in Article 24 of the DSM Directive, the InfoSoc Directive remains intact, and the amendments listed in the Article 24 do not alter Article 5.3, where it is stated that the Member States 'may provide' for exceptions and limitation to the right of communication to the public from the list in Article 5.3.

Another set of obligations results from Article 17(9) and aims at ensuring that users can, in practice, assert their rights as conferred by the EU provision on limitations and exceptions. Therefore, complaint and redress mechanisms need to be established by platform service providers and Member States have to ensure access to out-of-court dispute settlement and access to court for users, to 'assert' their rights.[83] These two solutions,

---

European Parliament and the Council on copyright in the Digital Single Market – Outcome of the European Parliament's first reading, (Strasbourg, 25-28 March 2019) ST 7717 2019 INIT, Article 17 (7) and 17(9).

82. *See* E. Izuymenko, *The Freedom of Expression Contours of Copyright in the Digital Era: A European Perspective,* pp. 115-130, p. 123 The Journal of World Intellectual Property, 19(3-4), 2016; A. Kuczerawy on content recognition technologies in: *EU Proposal for a Directive on Copyright in the Digital Single Market: Compatibility of Article 13 with the EU Intermediary Liability Regime,* in: B. Petkova & T. Ojanen (eds.), *Fundamental Rights Protection Online: The Future Regulation of Intermediaries,* Edward Elgar, 2019, https://papers.ssrn.com/sol3/papers.cfm?abstract_id=3309099, p. 12. *See also* the review of empirical research with reference to potential for abuse and over-enforcement with the use of automated-systems, K. Erikcsson & M. Kretschmer, *Empirical Approaches to Intermediary Liability,* CREAT-e Working Paper Series, 2019/06, p. 9-12 yet concluding that potential for abuse is likely over-stated (p. 1) https://zenodo.org/record/3473215#.XcAIFNXdjD4.

83. Article 17(9), the debate how to achieve this goal is ongoing, *see,* for example: J. Quintais, et al., *Safeguarding User Freedoms in Implementing Article 17 of the Copyright*

provided for in Article 17(7) and 17(9) should be treated as complementary. The selected exceptions should be made mandatory,[84] and furthermore, there should be procedural safeguards to ensure that those exceptions and limitations are effectively invoked. Recent CJEU case law also points to the importance of the use of works for the reporting of current events from the freedom of expression perspective, however, this use is not mentioned in Article 17(7) of the DSM Directive, as it is typically not associated with individual users posting content.

The provisions of the DSM Directive, particularly the definition of an online content sharing service provider, including the definition of on online content sharing service, and Article 17 reflect the reality that users' uploads are essential for platforms existence. The content available on platforms includes works and other protected subject matter *uploaded by its users.*[85] Those uploads undoubtedly constitute communication to the public of works. It is recognized that some of these uploads may have a commercial purpose and some not and that some of those uploads are within the scope of permissible quotations, criticism, review, caricature, parody and pastiche. In those cases, users' freedom to impart information should be favoured. EU lawmaker thus also seeks the balance when assuring 'a well-functioning marketplace for copyright', but does so in a very complicated way.

For the reasons explained above, it is not entirely clear whether the implementation of these exceptions is mandatory.[86] Furthermore, doubts may arise as to the scope of these exceptions as the wording of Article 17(7) (a) 'quotation, criticism, review' is different from Article 5(3) (d): 'quotations for purposes such as criticism or review'. Article 17(7) refers to 'existing limitations and exceptions', but may cause doubts, whether 'quotation' is a separate use of work than criticism or review. According to the CJEU's interpretation of Article 5(3) (d) of the InfoSoc Directive, 'a quotation must *inter alia* be intended to enable criticism or review'.[87] In the Spiegel-Online case, CJEU points that the essential characteristic of 'quotations' is the use of a work, or an extract of a work, for the purpose of illustrating an assertion, defending an opinion, allowing an intellectual comparison between that work or an assertion by a user.[88] The CJEU then follows AG Szpunar's opinion that ' the user of a protected work wishing to rely on the exception for

---

    in the Digital Single Market Directive: Recommendations from European Academics, https://papers.ssrn.com/sol3/papers.cfm?abstract_id=3484968.

84. What is confusing, however, is the lack of reference to necessary changes in Article 5.3 of the InfoSoc Directive.

85. Article 2(6) of the DSM Directive.

86. *See,* however, remarks by J. Griffiths that some optional exceptions and limitations, like quotation, parody and reporting current events are in fact mandatory in general, and not only in platform context. *European Union copyright law and the Charter of Fundamental Rights* p. 47.

87. C-516/17 para. 79.

88. C-516/17 paras 77-78.

quotations must therefore necessarily establish a direct and close link between the quoted work and his own reflections, thereby allowing for an intellectual comparison to be made with the work of another'.[89] Yet, the quote does not need to be integrated into a work, thus a hyperlink, essential for online communications, may, according to the Court constitute a quotation.[90]

The CJEU confirmed that quotations are not permissible only in other 'works'; thus, it opens the way to treat hyperlinks posted by users as 'quotations' depending on their purpose and relation to statements (opinions, assertions) made online. Article 5(5) sets the limits for permissible quotation, as the use of a quoted work must be secondary to the assertions of the user.[91] Prior to the CJEU rulings, doubts were expressed on the possibility of application of quotation provisions to sampling, from the perspective of a three-step test.[92] After *Pelham* and *Spiegel-Online*, the provision on quotation appears as the key element to adapt copyright to the reality of online communication,[93] together with the provisions on parody and reporting current events.

To reinforce the arguments that a quotation may be made by a hyperlink, CJEU invokes the *GS Media* ruling and the importance of linking for the sound operation of the internet.[94] The CJEU does not offer a comprehensive analysis of linking as a restricted act of communication or permissible quotation, which is an issue of vital importance since case law on linking was not codified in the DSM Directive. For the national courts, it might be easier to apply the approach developed in the framework of provisions on quotations, measured against CJEU's interpretation to guarantee freedom of expression than to apply the complex analysis based on the knowledge factor from *GS Media*.[95] The ruling in *Spiegel-Online* should be read as supplementing and not superseding previous case law, but there is a certain degree of uncertainty as to how the interpretation on the scope of the public communication right and the scope of the permissible quotation will coexist. It seems the most important in the unclear area of assessment of the legality of a source a link leads to, and access control and preventive

---

89. C-516/17 para. 79.
90. C-516/17 para. 80.
91. C-516/17 para. 79.
92. B.J. Jütte & H. Maier, *A Human Right to Sample: Will the CJEU Dance to the BGH-Beat?* p. 792 Journal of Intellectual Property Law & Practice, 12, no. 9, 2017.
93. The use of quotation right to deal with the user generated content as a means to achieve more flexibility is suggested in P.B. Hugenholtz, Flexible Copyright. Can EU Author's Rights Accommodate Fair Use?, in: I.A. Stamatoudi ed. *New Developments in EU and International Copyright Law,* 2016. p. 287.
94. C-516/17 para. 81.
95. M. Senftleben also submits that for commercial users, the presumption of knowledge may be rebutted with reliance on limitations and exceptions, such as quotation *Copyright Reform, GS Media and Innovation Climate in the EU – Euphonious Chord or Dissonant Cacophony?* p. 133.

measures.[96] The conditions established for quotations include referring to a work already lawfully made available to the public.[97] Further, case law should clarify whether a work found not to be freely available under *Svensson* and *GS Media*, could be linked to base on Article 5(3)(d) of the InfoSoc. In both cases, the courts should pay particular attention to possible limitations to freedom to receive and impart information.

The final task of factual assessment and balancing belongs to the national courts. The framework of Article 17 of the DSM Directive integrates the assessment internally on platforms, and externally through out-of-court mechanisms as part of safeguards achieving that balance. It is clear from the CJEU's case law that the effectiveness of the rights of users' needs to safeguarded, and freedom of expression favoured. It is underlined in Article 17(9) of the DSM Directive, that in the case of out-of-court settlement of disputes over blocking or removing content, a user cannot be deprived of legal protection and her right to assert the limitation or exception in court. The emphasis is thus also, as in the CJEU's ruling, on ensuring the effectiveness of limitations and exceptions particularly important for freedom of expression. This should be achieved by national provisions implementing the objective of the DSM Directive.

9.4   CONCLUSION

Neither the InfoSoc nor the DSM directives have the protection of fundamental rights as their primary objective. It is, however, underscored by CJEU that implementation and subsequent application of relevant provisions of national law require giving full effect to the provisions of the Charter. CJEU's rulings discussed in this chapter, add 'freedoms' perspective to the primary market perspective of the directives. It thus supports the functional and systemic interpretation of provisions on exclusive rights and limitations and exceptions. The desired balance framed in the context of Article 17(2) and Articles 11, 13 and 14 of the Charter, is to be achieved through the interpretation of fully harmonized provisions on rights and exhaustively, yet not fully harmonized provisions on limitations and exceptions. This 'toolkit' is supplemented by the provisions of the DSM Directive, that aim at clarifying the scope of public communication right, and add new or expand existing limitations and exceptions.

The case law provides limited yet important guidance. It is limited by an *ad casum* interpretation of the directives, rather than offering a comprehensive analysis of the standards set by the Charter. At the same time, the role of the Court to incorporate the standards of the ECHR as the basis for the interpretation of the Charter, and to guard whether these standards are

---

96. J.P. Quintais, *Untangling the Hyperlinking Web,* pp. 399-400.
97. C-516/17 para. 93.

fulfilled in Member State's laws is reinforced. It is particularly important when it comes to the implementation of the DSM Directive, as it harmonizes further the area of limitations and exceptions. Even when this harmonization is not full, Member States should apply their constitutional standards, in the way that does not undermine effectiveness, unity and primacy of EU law.

In the area of the public communication right, the overall objective emphasized by the Court is to favour freedom of expression. It is not permissible for the Member States to include any kind of 'fair use clause' in their national law, nor to go beyond the limits of exhaustive harmonization. CJEU's case law signals, however, a departure from the principle of strict interpretation in the case of exceptions and limitations. The Court's interpretation seems to be in line with the recommendation made by academics that a restrictive approach to interpretation, cannot prevail in circumstances in which the use of a work is protected by a fundamental right.[98] More emphasis is put on identifying and safeguarding the interests of users. This issue is of paramount importance in the context of implementing Article 17(7) and (9). 'User's rights' and right to court are explicitly envisaged in the Directive. The link that CJEU does between exceptions and limitations and fundamental rights, supports, however, the view, that it is open for the Member States if they recognize enforceable rights, or safeguard freedom of expression otherwise.

Making exceptions of particular importance for freedom of expression mandatory results in further limiting the discretion of the Member States. A question, whether these exceptions become mandatory only in the 'platform context' in the framework of Article 17, should also be viewed from the perspective of freedom of expression. For example, would it be justified to introduce provisions on pastiche only for communication to the public on content sharing platforms?[99] Furthermore, though the harmonization of provisions on quotations or parody is not full, the Court develops an autonomous interpretation of these terms, in the light of ensuring freedom of expression. The CJEU's interpretation is broader than that offered by AG Szpunar. Article 5(3)(d) on quotations, as interpreted by the CJEU includes the use of works in sampling and linking. Broad interpretation is also offered in the case of the use of works in the reporting of current events online. It may be concluded that such an interpretation is what is demanded by the standards of the Charter, and therefore hardly any margin of discretion is left

---

98. L. Bently, et al., *Sound Sampling, a Permitted Use under EU Copyright Law?* p. 482.
99. With reference generally to parody exception T. Synonidou points CJEU is not clear if not implementing provisions on parody could amount to violation of the standards set by the Charter, as AG Szpunar suggests in his opinion (Pelham, para. 77); *Reflections on the CJEU's judgment in Spiegel-Online: is there a golden intersection between freedom of expression and EU copyright law?* Part I; posted on 23 September 2019, http://copyrightblog.kluweriplaw.com/2019/09/23/reflections-on-the-cjeus-judgment-in-spiege l-online-is-there-a-golden-intersection-between-freedom-of-expression-and-eu-copyrigh t-law-part-i/.

to the Member States.[100] Given the importance of ensuring the conformity with the Charter national courts have all the reasons to ask for more and more detailed guidance by the CJEU.

---

100. On the road to full harmonization *see also* conclusions in: *The Road Not Taken – the CJEU Sheds Light on the Role of Fundamental Rights in the European Copyright Framework – a Case Note on the Pelham, Spiegel-Online and Funke-Medien Decisions* T. Snijders, S. Van Deursen IIC October 2019 https://link.springer.com/article/10.1007/s40319-019-00883-0#Fn61_source.

Chapter 10

Guiding the Blind Bloodhounds: How to Mitigate the Risks Article 17 of Directive 2019/970 Poses to the Freedom of Expression

Krzysztof Garstka

10.1   INTRODUCTION

Following long months of a difficult legislative process, Directive 2019/970[1] (DSMCD) was adopted on 15 April 2019. One of the key provisions responsible for the difficulties in question is Article 17 (previously 13), providing the foundation for content filtering to be regulated and endorsed by European Union (EU) copyright law. In both the time available before the national implementation date as well as once the provision is live it is crucial to examine Article 17 closely, in order to ensure the Directive meets its legitimate aims, without causing undue side effects. And where this is not directly possible, it is crucial to balance the involved interests adequately, in order to clearly and consciously accept certain trade-offs.

This chapter seeks to contribute to such an exercise, through the use of the human rights perspective. It is now well established that online copyright enforcement takes place on a complex matrix of human rights-infused

---

1. Directive (EU) 2019/970 of the European Parliament and of the Council of 17 April 2019 on copyright and related rights in the Digital Single Market and amending Directives 96/9/EC and 2001/29/EC.

interests. Even though some of the stakeholders may not see it this way, as Common wrote,[2] the Court of Justice of the European Union (CJEU) is firm and clear on this point in decisions such as C-275/06 *Promusicae*[3] and C-314/12 *UPC Telekabel*,[4] where a website blocking injunction was seen as triggering a conflict between the right to property,[5] the freedom of expression and information[6] and the freedom to conduct a business.[7,8] Even more directly, the decision in C-70/10 *Scarlet Extended* provides that 'in the context of measures adopted to protect copyright holders, national authorities and courts must strike a fair balance between the protection of copyright and the protection of the fundamental rights of individuals who are affected by such measures'.[9] Angelopoulos and Smet aptly show how strongly the CJEU embraces the human rights lens in this context.[10]

And that is exactly what the chapter seeks to do in relation to the enforcement schemes warranted by Article 17 of the DSMCD Directive and freedom of expression, by analysing risks the former poses to the latter, as well assessing the degree to which it mitigates them. This is without undermining the fact that ensuring the Directive helps in reducing copyright infringement is a positive human rights outcome in itself, helping to protect the right to property, in its form of intellectual property; in line with Article 17(2) of the Charter of Fundamental Rights of the EU.[11]

The described exercise, however, is not conducted in a vacuum; with the stakeholder dialogues prescribed by the Directive and the implementation date growing closer, the article seeks to inform the national legislators on the challenges they are going to encounter, not only in preparing the national approach to Article 17 but also in honing it afterwards. To this end, the following structure is embraced.

Section 10.2 of the chapter outlines the concept of content filtering, explaining how it functions on a technical level, and what prevailing form it currently embraces in the world of online copyright enforcement. Section 10.3 moves onto the DSMCD, outlining the key elements of Article 17 and the regime it sets out. Section 10.4 looks at the nature of the risks posed by the discussed provision to the freedom of expression, arguably the key

---

2. Common MF, 'Fear the Reaper: How Content Moderation Rules Are Enforced on Social Media' (5 January 2019), at 4, available at https://ssrn.com/abstract=3405337 (NOTE: All weblinks cited in this chapter were accessed on 13 October 2019).

3. Case C-275/06 *Promusicae v. Telefonica* [2008].

4. Case C-314/12 *UPC Telekabel v. Constantin Film* [2014].

5. Protected by Article 17 of the Charter of Fundamental Rights of the EU.

6. Protected by Article 11 of the Charter of Fundamental Rights of the EU.

7. Protected by Article 16 of the Charter of Fundamental Rights of the EU.

8. *UPC Telekabel v. Constantin Film, supra* fn. 4, at para. [47].

9. Case C-70/10 *Scarlet Extended v. SABAM*, at para. [45].

10. Angelopoulos C and Smet S, 'Notice-and-Fair-Balance: How to Reach a Compromise Between Fundamental Rights in European Intermediary Liability' (2016) Journal of Media Law, vol. 8(2), at 300.

11. Which states directly that 'intellectual property shall be protected'.

interest vulnerable to interference by Article 17. Section 10.5 critically analyses the steps taken by the drafters of the Directive to mitigate the risks outlined in section 10.4, and proposed further solutions with this goal in mind. Next, section 10.6 looks at two broader aspects of Article 17 implementation, which could have a positive effect on the overall balancing of human rights involved. Finally, section 10.7 concludes the article.

10.2   CONTENT FILTERING

At its core, content filtering can be defined as using technical means to scour through digital content in order to find undesirable information and regulate access to it. Such technical means can be relying on, e.g., certain words (keyword filtering, sought, e.g., in the German case of *Atari v. Rapidshare*[12]), watermarks (sought, e.g., by book publishers[13]) or digital fingerprints attached to audio or video files.

The most prominent example of the last category and a direct source of inspiration for Article 17 is the Content ID system, developed by and implemented on YouTube. In an era where multiple courts in the EU pondered on whether diverse content filtering injunctions should be awarded against online platforms, YouTube (faced with a substantial claim from Verizon[14]) decided to integrate a filtering system into their own platform, in hope of avoiding liability and maintaining architectural and operational control over the whole process as well as obtaining further profits.

Content ID works in the following manner. First, copyright holders provide YouTube with digital reference files for their works. Such files are then used by a content filtering algorithm, to detect uploads copying the work in question (fully or in part). Upon finding a match, the system performs an action predefined by the rightsholder; the content is either blocked, monetised (by transferring the advertising revenue to the claiming rightholder), tracked (passing the data on the upload to the rightholder) or left alone.[15] Monetisation is the option which is most advocated by YouTube.

While Content ID is certainly the largest system if this kind – and one which received the justified lion's share of academic attention – mention ought to also be made of Audible Magic. It is a company which sells the identically named product, allowing platforms to develop and operate content filtering systems based on digital fingerprints from a single, global registry. Overall, it functions similar to Content ID, and Audible Magic's customers include Facebook, SoundCloud and Dailymotion.[16]

---

12. *Atari v. Rapidshare* (2010) OLG Düsseldorf, I-20 U 59/10.
13. *See* https://torrentfreak.com/researchers-crack-social-drm-ebook-watermarks-160625/.
14. *Viacom International Inc. v. YouTube, Inc.* (2010) No. 07 Civ. 2103.
15. *See* https://support.google.com/youtube/answer/2797370?hl=en.
16. *See* https://www.audiblemagic.com/customers/.

10.3   THE CORE TENETS OF ARTICLE 17

Inspired by the example of Content ID on YouTube, the DSMCD Directive is (among other things) seeking to make content filtering present on similar platforms as well as to introduce a larger degree of control over Content ID itself. The key provision in this regard is Article 17 (previously 13), and it is worth describing its core elements in detail.

Article 17 is focused on regulating the position of Online Content Sharing Service Providers (OCSSPs). Article 2(6) defines such an entity as one providing 'an information society service' with one of its main purposes being storage and giving access to a 'large amount of copyright-protected works' uploaded by the platform's users. The OCSSP should also be organising and promoting the said content, for 'profit-making purposes'.

Following Article 17(1), the OCSSPs are now clearly liable for the copyright-infringing user uploads made public via the platform, within the frame of the communication to the public right; a particularly fitting, yet troublesome cornerstone of EU online copyright law.[17] Hence, in order to avoid liability, OCSSPs should seek to obtain a licence from the rightholders, which by virtue of Article 17(2) is to cover the users' actions. Importantly, the liability limitation provision present in Article 14 of the E-Commerce Directive (ECD)[18] is excluded from application to infringing acts covered by Article 17 of the DSMCD Directive.[19]

However, the Directive sets out its own 'safe harbour' procedure, marking a significant leap from the 'expeditious removal' requirement known from Article 14 of the ECD. Article 17(4) lays out three, cumulative conditions which if met can absolve an OCSSP from liability under Article 17(1). First, the OCSSP should undertake 'best efforts' to obtain the authorisation from the rightholder.[20] Second, in observance of 'high industry standards of professional diligence' and using 'relevant and necessary information' provided by the rightsholders, the OCSSP should undertake 'best efforts' to prevent the infringement of the works in question.[21] While the definition of 'relevant and necessary information' is an open one (and to an extent flexible towards technological progress) for now, it is fairly clear

---

17. The steady stream of references to the CJEU being a good testimony to this – *see* a great chart at http://ipkitten.blogspot.com/2019/04/dsm-directive-series-4-article-17.html, as well as a reference from 2019 in the Case C-597/19 *M.I.C.M.* On further discussion of the connection with Article 3 of the Information Society Directive 2001/29 as well as the issue of licencing, *see* Husovec M and Quintais J, 'How to License Article 17? Exploring the Implementation Options for the New EU Rules on Content-Sharing Platforms' (2019), available at https://papers.ssrn.com/sol3/papers.cfm?abstract_id=3463011.
18. Directive 2000/31/EC of the European Parliament and of the Council of 8 June 2000 on certain legal aspects of information society services, in particular electronic commerce, in the Internal Market, Article 14.
19. DSMCD, *supra* fn. 1, Article 17(3).
20. DSMCD, *supra* fn. 1, Article 17(4)(a).
21. DSMCD, *supra* fn. 1, Article 17(4)(b).

that this part of Article 17 hints at content filtering, much in the manner of examples described in section 10.2 of this chapter. Third, and finally, the discussed provision obliges the OCSSPs to follow what could be categorised as a 'notice and stay-down' approach. Whenever a valid notice of infringement is made, the platform operator should block or remove the infringing content, as well as prevent its reuploads through the earlier described, preventive procedure;[22] one can assume that 'relevant and necessary information' would have to be enclosed in the notice itself.

The Directive moves on to attach certain modalities to the procedure(s) established by Article 17(4), in order to mitigate and/or manage the risks it carries to human rights of various stakeholders. Due to the goals and structure of this chapter, such modalities are presented in section 10.5 of the chapter. For now, it can be added that the noticeably broad and vague expressions such as 'best efforts' and 'high industry standards of professional diligence' are to be precised or rather given meaning through a series of stakeholder dialogues, which are to result in guidance published by the Commission.[23]

In a seminal study from 2016,[24] Urban, Karaganis and Schofield made a distinction on three strands of notice-related enforcement patterns applicable to online platforms. The first one was named 'DMCA Classic' – the initial concept of sending a notice of infringement, based on the Digital Millennium Copyright Act 1998,[25] the US legislation which inspired Articles 12-14 of the ECD and the idea of being immune to liability upon expeditious processing of copyright infringement notices. The second strand received the label of 'DMCA Auto' – it denoted the automatisation of the classic DMCA procedure, with thousands or even millions of notices being sent to platforms by bots, triggering automatic processing of notices on the side of the platforms, to even the scales. Finally, the third category was labelled as 'DMCA Plus' – it encompassed the procedures going beyond the classic notice and takedown procedure, such as 'filtering systems, direct takedown procedures for trusted rightsholders, hash-matching based "stay down" systems', as well as contractual agreements placing additional obligations on involved parties.[26] With the DSMCD, the EU copyright law is set to take a deep dive into the 'DMCA Plus' pool, swimming through the fishing nets

---

22. DSMCD, *supra* fn. 1, Article 17(4)(c).
23. DSMCD, *supra* fn. 1, Article 17(10).
24. Urban J, Karaganis J and Schofield B, 'Notice and Takedown in Everyday Practice', UC Berkeley Public Law Research Paper No. 2755628 (29 March 2016), available at https:// papers.ssrn.com/sol3/papers.cfm?abstract_id=2755628&rec=1&srcabs=2566364&alg=1 &pos=1.
25. Digital Millennium Copyright Act 1998 (US).
26. Urban, Karaganis and Schofield (2016), *supra* fn. 24, at 2.

which were placed on content filtering by Article 15 of the ECD[27] and the CJEU decisions in *Scarlet Extended*[28] and C-360/10 *Netlog*.[29]

10.4 IMPACT OF ARTICLE 17 ON THE FREEDOM OF EXPRESSION

Freedom to express oneself and receive information has long been recognised as a cornerstone of a healthy, democratic society, being enshrined into Article 11 of the Charter of Fundamental Rights of the EU. Looking back at the past two decades of the online copyright enforcement struggle, one seems inclined to agree with Yu, who wrote that 'out of all the internationally recognized human rights, the right to freedom of opinion and expression is most threatened by digital copyright enforcement measures'.[30] Article 17 of the DSMCD does hold the potential to assist the rightholders in protecting their works; but it also poses sizeable risks to the right protected in Article 11 of the CFREU. These risks are actually different aspects of the same concern – that legitimate content's presence on the OCSSPs' platforms will be diminished.

10.4.1 Overblocking of Existing Content

When it comes to content filtering, overblocking – that is removing access to more than one wishes to, or more than the law requires – is an in-built concern. While humans can also be the cause of overblocking (whether through intent, carelessness or honestly choosing a different interpretation of the law), it is the algorithmic systems which carry this risk to another dimension, for example, by being able to 'reason' only in terms of finding a matching keyword, digital fingerprint or another piece of data.

There are several key dimensions of the prima facie[31] overblocking problem, several interwoven factors which may contribute to the end result. Each of them received academic attention and had its existence supported by evidence; each of them deserves to be covered in turn.

First, the rightholders may ask for the removal of content which is legitimate – whether by virtue of being unrelated to the complaint, or as a

---

27. Which prohibits 'general monitoring' obligations, as well as general obligations to 'seek facts or circumstances indicating illegal activity'.
28. *Scarlet Extended*, *supra* fn. 9.
29. Case C-360/10 *Société belge des auteurs, compositeurs et éditeurs SCRL (SABAM) v. Netlog NV* [2012].
30. Yu P, 'Digital Copyright Enforcement Measures and Their Human Rights Threats' (2015) in Research Handbook on Human Rights and Intellectual Property (Christophe Geiger ed., Edward Elgar Publishing), at 456.
31. Before considering the role of appeal procedures – these received attention in section 10.5.4 of this chapter.

result of a failure to take account of factors nullifying the infringing character of the challenged content – such as copyright exceptions or existing consent. Speaking in terms of Article 17(4)(b), such an effect can occur at the moment of providing 'relevant and necessary' information (e.g., digital fingerprint for filtering systems) or when managing the actions which are supposed to be taken by the algorithm at the moment of detection (e.g., *removal v. 'red flag'* notification to the rightholder.)

Second, the OCSSPs receiving the request may take the content down, where they should have denied the request instead. This may happen due to the OCSSP failing to assess the notification, assessing it in an insufficient manner, or honestly misapplying the law. The threat of liability tied to time-related obligations (e.g., the well-known term 'expeditious removal') puts pressure on the online platforms, which can result in failure to assess the notification – e.g., one made via the procedure in Article 17(4)(c) of the DSMCD. Fiala and Husovec noted the existence of this problem and devised an empirical study which showed the decision-making processes leading to overblocking of content.[32] For another example, Elkin-Koren and Perel took note of the pressure which online platforms face when receiving a notification of infringement within the Digital Millennium Copyright Act 1998.[33] There are multiple authors who wrote convincingly about the relationship between pressure on platforms and over-removal of content.[34] Regarding the 17(4)(b) procedure, the OCSSP may fail in its potential duty to assess the digital reference files – moreover, given the opaque nature of the provision, there may be no such duty at all under the accepted 'best efforts' or actual agreements with the rightholders.

Third aspect of the overblocking concern is one which permeates through the previous two – it is the use of algorithms. Notifications/reference files generated by the rightholders' programmes may not only augment the previously identified concerns but also create new ones, by making new mistakes, tied to machine's 'reasoning'. This concern has long been recognised by the academia and verified by actual evidence. Jacques wrote (following the mass takedown of the Downfall movie parodies on You-Tube[35]) that 'algorithms work well when it comes to identifying when content such as the scene from Downfall is uploaded – but they have serious limitations when it comes to determining whether a particular use is

---

32. Fiala L and Husovec M, 'Using Experimental Evidence to Design Optimal Notice and Takedown Process' (2018), at 7. *See* https://ssrn.com/abstract=3218286.

33. Elkin-Koren N and Perel M, 'Accountability in Algorithmic Copyright Enforcement' (2016) Stanford Technology Law Review, vol. 19, 473, at 491.

34. For example, *see* Urban J and Quilter L, 'Efficient Process or "Chilling Effects"? Takedown Notices under Section 512 of the Digital Millennium Copyright Act' (2006) Santa Clara Computer and High Technology Law Journal, vol. 22, 621, at 641 or Edwards L, 'The Fall and Rise of Intermediary Liability Online' (2009) in Law and Internet (Edwards, L and Waelde, C, ed., 3rd ed.), at 66.

35. *See* https://www.cbsnews.com/news/hitler-downfall-parodies-removed-from-youtube/.

lawful'.[36] Elkin-Koren and Perel remarked that the Content ID system once took down the video of a cat purring on copyright infringement grounds.[37] On top of this, one could add a hefty amount of anecdotal evidence, such as when Professor Lessig uploaded a video of his lecture, which was then taken down by Content ID;[38] or where NASA's Mars Rover landing was claimed as well from the mission's *official* YT channel.[39] To reinforce this point even further, Urban, Karaganis and Schofield's seminal study found that even the rightholders themselves are aware of at least the accuracy problem with automated enforcement; though some of the ones interviewed saw it as an acceptable cost of mass-enforcement.[40]

10.4.2   CHILLING EFFECT PRECEDING ACTUAL CONTENT FILTERING

On top of the risk of content filtering systems directly overblocking legitimate content, it should also be mentioned that Article 17 carries two additional risks to the right protected under Article 11 of the CFREU, which may result in the diminished presence of legitimate content in an indirect manner.[41]

First, instead of being entirely at the mercy of procedures agreed under Article 17(b) and (c) with the rightholders, OCSSPs might conduct their own pre-emptive filtering, based on the idea that a platform can be governed by its own terms and conditions. This is particularly likely where the 'industry standards' for judging 'best efforts' under Article 17(4)(b) would be unduly burdensome on the operators. While this pre-emptive filtering could be understandable from the side of OCSSPs, Article 11 of the CFREU would still be relevant here, protecting fair use/difficult case from overly cautious platforms.

The second chilling effect element is tied to a specific element of Article 17(2), which states that the license obtained by the OCSSPs within Article 17(1) 'shall also cover acts carried out by users of the services falling within the scope of Article 3 of Directive 2001/29/EC *when they are not acting on a commercial basis or where their activity does not generate significant revenues*'.[42] In essence, this may mean that users creating content with the use of such copyrighted works should not be making it 'too good' – because, if we take YouTube's model as an example, the advertising profits they

---

36. *See* https://theconversation.com/the-eu-is-trying-to-protect-your-memes-but-its-a-battle-against-humourless-algorithms-112573.
37. Elkin-Koren and Perel, *supra* fn. 33, at 516.
38. *See*   https://www.eff.org/press/releases/lawrence-lessig-strikes-back-against-bogus-copyright-takedown.
39. *See*   https://arstechnica.com/tech-policy/2012/08/as-curiosity-touches-down-on-mars-video-is-taken-down-from-youtube/.
40. Urban, Karaganis and Schofield, *supra* fn. 24, at 35.
41. Again, before the role of the appeal procedure is considered.
42. (Emphasis added.).

receive if the content is good/popular might push them outside of the OCSSP's licence and into the 'commercial basis'/'significant revenue' territory. The end result of this may be a chilling effect on the quality of legitimate, transformative works. One could argue that those obtaining significant profits from their creations should have the money to pay for licenses; but unless credible data is available on the relationship between profits and licencing fees on such platforms, the chilling effect remains an uncontested concern here.

10.5 MITIGATING THE DAMAGE TO FREEDOM OF EXPRESSION

Just as there are multiple factors tied to the risk of legitimate content being removed/not appearing on the OCSSPs' platforms, there are multiple ways in which this risk could be mitigated. Some of them are, to an extent, placed within Article 17 itself – others are possible options to be undertaken. Both are covered under the following, thematic subsections.

10.5.1 THE 'WISHING WELL' PROVISION

The drafters of the Directive were well aware of the freedom of expression-related risks tied to Article 17 – either through their own reflection or through the massive protests against the (then) Article 13. The first clear sign of this is found in broadly worded Article 17(7), which states that the cooperative regime(s) put forward by Article 17(4) 'shall not result in the prevention of the availability of works or other subject matter uploaded by users, which do not infringe copyright and related rights, including where such works or other subject matter are covered by an exception or limitation'. As much as this can be seen as an indication of legislative desire, by itself, this provision does not do more than that, nor does it qualm the fears tied to freedom of expression, laid out clearly in section 10.4.1 of this chapter.

10.5.2 MAKING EXCEPTIONS MANDATORY (AND HARMONISED?)

The next freedom of expression-related provision is much more impactful, and unequivocally supportive of this fundamental right. Before the DSM-CD's arrival, the closed list of copyright exceptions put forward by Article 5 of the Information Society Directive 2001/29[43] was voluntary; the Member States could enable them in their frameworks, but they were under no direct

---

43. Directive 2001/29/EC of the European Parliament and of the Council of 22 May 2001 on the harmonisation of certain aspects of copyright and related rights in the information society, Article 5(2).

duty to do so. However, Article 17(7) of the DSMCD provides that users in every Member State should be able to 'rely on any of the following existing exceptions or limitations when uploading and making available content generated by users on online content-sharing services: (a) quotation, criticism, review; (b) use for the purpose of caricature, parody or pastiche'. Hence, those exceptions are – in the context of the Directive – made mandatory, as recital 70 of the Directive underlines.[44] This is a very good step towards protecting the main, publicly beneficial uses of copyrighted works on OCSSP platforms.

Unfortunately, it has to be stressed that the elevated exceptions are not harmonised (yet); every country can implement them in their preferred way, and CJEU judgments tied to the 'essence' of those exceptions, and their *de minimis* form, are likely to appear in the coming years.

Speaking of *de minimis*, one of the steps which was discussed during the legislative journey of the DSMCD was to agree on a specific percentage of the work used, below which the use would be legitimate. Within this logic, if less than, e.g., 3% of the work (e.g., a movie) would be used, then the use would be automatically seen as legitimate, without the need for a licence. Thus far, this concept has not entered any known legislative framework – while it is tempting to see this as a perfect way to legitimise gifs or use of extremely short excerpts from songs or videos, the core reasoning from the CJEU judgment in *Infopaq* invariably stands 'in the way' here. According to this decision, author's intellectual creation (which is the core of EU copyright protection) can subsist within the smallest, shortest excerpts of information.[45] While the *de minimis* percentage (or other)-based exception for user-generated content does have appeal, it would require cutting a bit out of the conceptual core of EU copyright protection, and that is rather unlikely to happen. On the other hand, designers of content filtering mechanisms have to set a certain threshold of data for triggering a 'match' within a system; and following Elkin-Koren and Perel,[46] it would be useful for someone (e.g., a supervisory body) to know what these are.

10.5.3   LIMITING THE OVERBLOCKING OCCURRING VIA MACHINE MISTAKES: KEEPING THE 'HUMAN IN THE LOOP'

As it was shown in section 10.4.1, overblocking of content is the main, tangible threat to freedom of expression in the discussed context. One of the distinct ways in which it can materialise within content filtering is due to the

---

44. It provides that 'Those exceptions and limitations should, therefore, be made mandatory in order to ensure that users receive uniform protection across the Union.'
45. Case C-5/08 *Infopaq International A/S v. Danske Dagblades Forening* [2009], at para. [51].
46. Elkin-Koren and Perel, *supra* fn. 33, at 514.

machine (algorithm) taking a different decision than a human moderator would.

One way to mitigate this is to set the filtering algorithm to detect-and-notify, as opposed to detect-and-block; thus introducing a human to the procedural loop. This approach was supported, e.g., by Boroughf, who saw this as a way to encourage communication between rightholders and uploaders.[47]

This approach has certainly a good amount of appeal for the freedom of expression – it highly decreases the likelihood of completely mistaken takedowns. This is of course assuming that the human in the loop does not just 'stamp' the removal without assessing the file, due to internal company guidance, prompted by, e.g., undue time expectations from rightholders' side. On the other hand, the burden tied to having a human verify and confirm every trigger from the filtering system may be disproportionately high, even for the large OCSSPs the Directive focuses on.

Perhaps the middle ground lies in the threshold approach – having a human confirm the takedown (or another action) whenever the match percentage is, e.g., below 3%. And here, a certain degree of categorisation of works may make sense; for a start, human review could be required for sound recordings below 1:00 minutes and audio-visual works shorter than 3:00 minutes. As we move on, further categories/lengths of works could be added/removed. In human rights jurisprudence terms, this approach could be justified by the logic of the difference between the *existence* and *exercise* of the right, which was strongly ingrained in EU intellectual property law by the decisions on the exhaustion of rights, such as *Centrafarm BV v. Sterling Drug*.[48]

Another way to diminish the risk of algorithmic overblocking could be in the notion of preliminary verification of algorithms that are to be used for Article 17 purposes. Now, in the era of machine learning, this can be quite challenging – an algorithm which learns based on the feedback to its decisions is in a constant state of flux. Hence, assessing its effectiveness or impact on various forms of freedom of expression cannot be really done with 100% accuracy; however, perhaps a 100% is not what the enforcement system should require. A supervisory body of sorts could be presented with a demonstration of the algorithm at work, on a selected sample of files, and if – for example – 98% of the takedowns would be accurate, then the algorithm can move onwards to play a part as an element of the 'best efforts' landscape. Such a verification procedure could act as a sieve for over-zealous/insufficiently prepared algorithms. And to take account of machine

---

47. Boroughf B, 'The Next Great YouTube: Improving Content ID to Foster Creativity, Cooperation, and Fair Compensation' (2014), at 17. *See* https://papers.ssrn.com/sol3/papers.cfm?abstract_id=2492898.
48. [1974] ECR 1183.

learning, perhaps a, e.g., tri-annual review of the algorithmic systems could take place.[49]

10.5.4   The Appeal Procedure

A well-designed and well-executed appeal procedure is a key, indispensable component of content filtering system employed in the service of copyright enforcement. As it was mentioned in the previous sections, 100% accurate content filtering systems are unlikely to be achievable and are not necessarily required in order to be seen as acceptable. A fast, balanced appeal procedure has to be there to mitigate any damage done to the freedom of expression. Moreover, even if the content is ultimately one that should be taken down, the right to a fair trial, protected by Article 47 of the CFREU[50] and Article 6 of the ECHR,[51] demands that the uploader should be given an adequate opportunity to challenge the actions of the filtering systems supported by Article 17 of the Directive.

These arguments have not escaped the drafters of the provision in question, as the latter itself provides certain requirements tied to the appeal procedure. First, Article 17(9) obliges the Member States to ensure that the OCSSPs 'put in place an *effective* and *expeditious* complaint and redress mechanism'. It is to be available to the latter's users 'in the event of disputes over the *disabling of access* to, or the *removal of*, works or other subject matter uploaded by them'. Right after this, the provision continues by stating that whenever rightholders request the removal (complete or access-based) of their works, they are to '*duly justify* the reasons for their requests'. Finally, complaints made with the indicated appeal procedure are to be 'processed without undue delay' and decisions on whether the takedown/access-removal request should be successful 'shall be subject to *human* review'.

Article 17(9) has several interesting components, and they deserve to be assessed in turn. First, the requirement for the appeal procedure to be 'effective and expeditious' is certainly a welcome one; this is how it should be. The real question is in the details, of course; how much time between complaint and reinstating the content is to be seen as 'expeditious'? Should there be a difference drawn here depending on the type of medium involved? Its size? Also, should redress include compensation of any sort? These

---

49. The author is well aware that this proposition would require much further work, choosing/updating the right data sets, etc. – but as a concept, it is too promising not to be tested in practice.

50. CFREU, *supra* fn. 5. Article 47 states that '(e)veryone is entitled to a fair and public hearing within a reasonable time by an independent and impartial tribunal previously established by law'.

51. European Convention on Human Rights 1950. Article 6 states that 'In the determination of his civil rights and obligations or of any criminal charge against him, everyone is entitled to a fair and public hearing within a reasonable time by an independent and impartial tribunal established by law.'

questions are, unfortunately, too detailed for this chapter. When answering them, however, it should be kept in mind (among other things) that oftentimes, certain types of content are relevant and sought after in certain specific periods of time. For example, a 'reaction video' to a game or movie trailer is in demand at a time when such a trailer appears. A parody video tied to a recent political scandal is to be normally seen right after the scandal is reported on.

On a different note, the provision seems to contain a gap when it comes to the availability of the appeal procedure. It is to be provided in case of 'disputes over the *disabling of access* to, or the *removal of*, works (...)'. What is missing here is disputes over monetisation claims. As written above in section 10.2, the Content ID system (conceptual protoplast of the Directive) heavily relies on the option of monetising content. It is quite likely that with time, this approach will be reproduced within systems appearing as a result of Article 17. Hence, in order to provide the uploaders (such as YouTube content creators, Twitch streamers[52]) with a proper possibility to defend their legitimate income, this should be rectified. In the implementation process, the Member States could perhaps take a wide reading of the notion of 'disabling access' and precise that it covers monetisation claims. That being said, this matter is likely to be the subject of CJEU judgments aimed at harmonising the implementations of the Directive, as well as the eventual, similarly aimed review of this legislative instrument.

Regarding the notion 'duly justified' removals, there are several points to note. First, the wording of the Directive is slightly misleading – it is not immediately clear whether reasons for the takedown should be given in relation to the *initial* takedown action, or *in response* to the appeal. Given that the first one is really fundamental and almost truistic (how is one supposed to support takedown action devoid of justifications?), and the statement appears in sub-paragraph on the appeal process, one can assume that the latter option was the legislative intention; still, clarification in wording would be helpful, perhaps within the Commission guidance. Setting this aside, the key question here is of course what justification would be defined as one made 'duly'. Would it be sufficient to simply state it is copyright infringement, or would more be needed, such as stating that no copyright exception applies in the discussed case, or perhaps even explaining why this is the case. From the freedom of expression perspective, the third option would be preferable; but even if this is not a statutory requirement, OCSSPs assessing the appeals should definitely take the robustness of takedown's justification into consideration.

The final element of interest here is the requirement for the appeal to be subjected to 'human review'. This is quite crucial; as the previous section argued, there is a need to keep a 'human in the loop', a need recognised by

---

52. Twitch is a video streaming platform focused on video games, *see* https://www.twitch.tv/.

major authors in the field, such as Urban, Karaganis and Schofield.[53] As Common argued, the unbridled view (often presented by the tech industry) that technology solves everything should be resisted in the realm of online content regulation.[54] The important question which emerges from this aspect of Article 17(9) is who that reviewing human should be. What sort of training should such a person receive? These are not new questions, as in the past few years, they began to be asked by various writers;[55] however, they gain importance in the face of the upcoming expansion of the copyright enforcement framework.

In this regard, perhaps a lesson could be taken out of the data protection law's book, and the requirements for larger entities to have a data protection officer (DPO) in their ranks, as Article 37 of the General Data Protection Regulation provides.[56] Just as companies process personal data and require a proficient individual in charge of this aspect of the business, so can companies hosting significant amounts of online content be required to provide a capable individual assessing the appeals *in line with the letter of the law*. In light of this, the stakeholder dialogues (conducted in order to precise many of the Directive's provisions) could eventually be tasked with developing the guidance documents for such appeal reviewers. And with time, the situation might reach the point arrived at by the French Data Protection Authority (CNIL), which published a list of seventeen characteristics, abilities and knowledge areas which a DPO should possess.[57]

Equally as important as characteristics of that person is the issue of their organisational belonging. Should this be an employee of the OCSSP, or an external agent, perhaps within a scheme akin to Alternative Dispute Resolution (ADR)?[58] The Directive does not lay out a clear and precise path here: it provides that 'Member States shall *also* ensure that *out-of-court redress mechanisms* are available for the settlement of disputes' and that the path to judicial redress stays open. In this regard, it is not certain whether the appeal process requires a decision from the OCSSP before further redress mechanisms (like ADR) are enabled, or whether the appeal process could be under the control of a third party straight away. A valuable study conducted by Fiala and Husovec demonstrated how valuable the presence of an ADR body could be in the process,[59] and hence, enabling this feature and placing it within a clearly framed appeal procedure would be advisable.

---

53. Urban, Karaganis and Schofield, *supra* fn. 24, at 5.
54. Common, *supra* fn. 2, at 13.
55. Common, *supra* fn. 2, at 3.
56. Regulation (EU) 2016/679 of the European Parliament and of the Council of 27 April 2016 on the protection of natural persons with regard to the processing of personal data and on the free movement of such data, and repealing Directive 95/46/EC (General Data Protection Regulation).
57. *See* https://www.cnil.fr/sites/default/files/atoms/files/d2019-092.pdf.
58. A solution strongly supported by Fiala and Husovec, *supra* fn. 32, at 14.
59. Fiala and Husovec, *supra* fn. 32, at 7.

There are certain challenges tied to the appeal procedure which do not flow directly from the text of the Directive but rather from existing experiences tied to such procedures. The first one of those challenges is the need to ensure that the users of OCSSP platforms are both aware of the appeal procedures and believe in their effectiveness and fairness. In the 'How Google Fights Piracy Report' from 2016, it was stated that fewer than 1% of Content ID notices were disputed. While this may be a more optimistic statistic for the system then say 70%, it does not translate directly to the algorithm being 99% accurate. It may be that users are not taking advantage of the appeal procedure in situations where they would at least have a chance of relying on, e.g., a copyright exception. As Fiala and Husovec write, challenging the content takedowns may be an unappealing option to users due to 'intimidation, high legal risks, and a weak prospect of a successful redress'.[60] Elkin-Koren and Perel also support this line of argument, stating that the potential reasons of this kind include the lack of will to disclose one's identity, intimidating language of notices, as well as a lack of sufficient awareness.[61]

Speaking of awareness, it can be argued that the users should be aware not only of the appeal opportunity but also of any takedowns which occurred. Some uploaders (e.g., YouTubers, SoundCloud users, Twitch streamers) may have multiple files uploaded on an OCSSP-qualifiable platform; they should not have to manually keep track of those files, to verify whether an enforcement action was taken. One of the 'best industry standards' should be ensuring that the content filtering systems inform the user about access limitations/monetisation claims. Content ID system on YouTube apparently does this fairly well[62] – but this voluntary step should be forged into a legal obligation.

Moving onto a yet another concern, as it was mentioned in section 10.4.2, there is a risk that instead of working within the unduly burdensome and uncertain systems emerging from Article 17, the OCSSPs might pre-emptively filter out files including copyrighted content, and avoid Article 17(1) liability in this way. What could be used to this end is reliance on the existing or adapted terms and conditions of a website. In fact this was one of the concerns raised by the SaveYourInternet campaign, protesting against Article 17 – its organisers stated that 'any complaint mechanisms will be easily bypassed if blocking is done under the pretence of a terms and conditions violation, rather than as a result of a specific copyright claim'.[63] In order to prevent such reality, the users should be able to challenge any terms and conditions which explicitly prohibit uploading content which uses another's work without consent, as this could result in a contractual override

60. Fiala and Husovec, *supra* fn. 32, at 2.
61. Elkin-Koren and Perel, *supra* fn. 33, at 525.
62. *See* https://support.google.com/youtube/answer/7002106?hl=en.
63. *See* https://saveyourinternet.eu/.

of copyright exceptions. This would be especially beneficial in instances involving parodies; rarely is the original creator happy with being parodied, but freedom of expression demands that this option should be available for the parodists.

Additionally, regarding contractual overrides – Elkin-Koren and Perel drew attention in their paper to a situation where a user who submitted a counter-notification to a copyright infringement notice on YouTube (classic, not Content ID) received a reply which denied the appeal on the basis that 'YouTube has a contractual obligation to this specific copyright owner that prevents us from reinstating videos in such circumstances. Therefore, we regretfully cannot honor this counternotification.'[64] Given the wide space Article 17 leaves to the confidential contracts between OCSSPs and rightholders, the national implementations of the Directive should expressly prohibit such contracts from obstructing the appeal mechanisms and limiting the space given by law to copyright exceptions.[65]

Another issue is the cost of the appeal procedure – should the users be required to pay, fully or partially, for the cost of the appeal procedure (through, e.g., a fee)? This is not the case with Content ID – and it would obviously be best to keep it this way within the whole realm of Article 17. However, should there appear evidence that operating the appeal procedure in a sufficiently precise and robust manner carries substantial, difficult to accept costs for the OCSSPs, the possibility of a minor fee, in an adversarial system, should be open to debate; while being avoided beforehand.

10.5.5   EXCLUDING CERTAIN PLATFORMS FROM THE SCOPE OF ARTICLE 17

While obtaining certainty on which exact entities fall into the definition of an OCSSP is a crucial element of the implementation (or more likely interpretation) process, the Directive does exclude from this definition certain entities acting as direct enablers of the freedom of expression. Article 2(6) states that operators of, first, 'not-for-profit online encyclopaedias, not-for-profit educational and scientific repositories' are not OCSSPs within the meaning of the DSMCD. Second, the same exclusion applies to entities which could be as indirect enablers of freedom of expression, namely 'open source software-developing and -sharing platforms', 'providers of electronic communications services as defined in Directive (EU) 2018/1972', as well as 'online marketplaces, business-to-business cloud services and cloud services that allow users to upload content for their own use'. Such exclusions are a welcome development from the freedom of expression's side, but the list should be monitored in both ways. Should there appear evidence that a

---

64. Elkin-Koren and Perel, *supra* fn. 33, at 507.
65. As to how it should be ensured that such contracts follow such guidance, *see* section 10.6 of this chapter.

different, specific class of entities requires protection in order to provide significant value to freedom of expression, the list should be expanded. Should there appear evidence that one of the excluded categories of entities is (mis)used for widespread copyright infringement, as a result of online pirates' migration, the list could be shortened, with different protections in place.

10.5.6   EDUCATING USERS ON WHAT CAN BE POSTED

While it may be traditionally seen as a step towards the goals of copyright enforcement regimes, educating users on what can and cannot be posted can also play a part in supporting freedom of expression. Apart from preventing instances of unjustified copyright infringement, a good set of educational measures may encourage users to create valuable secondary works relying on legitimate uses of copyrighted material, such as parodies, critiques.

The Directive does, to an extent, recognise the role of this approach, by stating in Article 17(9) that OCSSPs 'shall inform their users in their terms and conditions that they can use works and other subject matter under exceptions or limitations to copyright and related rights provided for in Union law'. While this is commendable, more can be done, and it is another place where copyright enforcement can rely on data protection law for inspiration. For a long time, the practice of burying privacy-related provisions in long T&Cs documents was regarded as inappropriate and undermining data protection goals, mainly that of obtaining informed consent to specific data processing activities. With the arrival of the General Data Protection Regulation, this can no longer be the case, as its Article 7(2) provides that if the request for consent is sought through a written declaration which deals with further issues, it 'shall be presented in a manner which is clearly distinguishable from the other matters, in an intelligible and easily accessible form, using clear and plain language'.

Following this logic, the highlighted information from Article 17(9) of the DSMCD could not only be present in terms and conditions of an OCSSP but also brought forward in a separate box, during events such as setting up of the account, uploading the file, and/or a dedicated monthly reminder. And while it is true that national definitions/interpretations of copyright exceptions may differ from one another, a section of the official stakeholder dialogues (or later activities) could be aimed at finding sufficient common ground between national systems for the purposes of putting an EU-wide guidance on OCSSP's websites. Alternatively, national systems could make sure that OCSSPs accessible in the former's countries proactively inform the users about not only what should not be uploaded in copyright terms but also about what *can* be uploaded.

10.5.7   Pre-upload Labelling by Users

Another copyright exceptions-supporting measure which is worth referring to is the idea of requiring uploading users who wish for their content to be seen as qualifying for one of the copyright exceptions, to have the option of labelling it as such, triggering a different treatment of that file.[66] Such treatment could take the form of, for example, automatic human review of the file upon a match being found by the content filtering system (as opposed to being directly blocked by the algorithm). This move could be very beneficial for the creators (and consumers) of transformative works based on copyright exceptions.

On the other hand, there are certain concerns surrounding this approach. It could be abused by the uploaders, with everyone pressing the 'fair use likely' button, in order to increase the chances of the file staying online longer, even when there is no actual legal ground for it (e.g., unchanged uploads of full, copyrighted movies). This would place an immense burden on the human reviewers, and in turn, would undermine the initial goal of the discussed mechanism. Another critique of it could be that the users should not be burdened with preventive labelling, and assessing whether their use of content qualifies as fair use, and – if such an option would be enabled – indicating what aspect of fair use do they have in mind.

In this author's opinion, the described burden would most likely be acceptable to those who wish to legitimately signal the presence of, e.g., a copyright exception. Regarding the risk of abuse, it could potentially be mitigated by making the discussed mechanism available only to those in possession of a user account on an OCSSP platform, one which was active for a sufficiently long period of time, with identity verification of sorts and/or remains in good standing. Should it appear that the account's 'fair use' labels are consistently denied by the human reviewers (and are not successfully appealed), then the privilege of using such labels could be frozen/removed. Regardless of the described implementation challenges, it is definitely a route worth exploring.

10.5.8   Legal Measures and Actions Taken for Violation of Freedom of Expression

Article 17 of the Directive is built around providing an opportunity to take specific, organised actions aimed at preventing copyright infringement. Given the presence of duties in the Directive tied to protecting the freedom of expression, one can ask the question whether Article 17 regime should be supported by a possibility for users to sue the OCSSPs and/or the rightholders for failing to fulfil such duties.

---

66. An idea discussed by Husovec M, during the European Copyright Society roundtable focused on the DSMCD – https://www.youtube.com/watch?v=hxN9ZO-KIEs, at 6:56:52.

Regarding the rightholders, this idea has been discussed and tested in the broader field of copyright enforcement. Fiala and Husovec noted the problem of lack of quality control by copyright notice senders, due to the lack of punishment for over-removal of content.[67] This argument is well supported by one of the limbs of arguably the most well-known legal saga tied to fair use, the US *Lenz* case, where it was stated that the copyright holders must consider fair use before submitting a takedown notice.[68] However, trying to prove that fair use was not considered can be exceedingly difficult, as Mrs Lenz found out herself.[69]

The idea of being able to sue the rightholders for failing to consider fair use in submitting the notification poses a range of difficulties in the context of Article 17 and content filtering. First of all, the whole 'notification' process can be seen as split here between the rightholders, platform operators and/or the designers of the content filtering system, with its surrounding procedures. Given that the process targeted by Article 17(4)(b) starts with the supply of a digital fingerprint, it is not really feasible to detect the lack of fair use consideration in this regard. Perhaps, if the earlier suggestion to introduce mandatory human review for matched secondary works using less than 3%-5% of the original work was introduced, then some form of action could be considered. Still, it is more likely that such a solution would be best implemented by the OCSSPs/content filtering system operators; thus further decreasing the feasibility of suing the rightholders in this context. Nonetheless, once the actual procedures under Article 17 begin to take shape, and rightholders do end up having certain concrete duties under the EU/national law, the opportunity to enforce those duties by the users/public could be sought.

Regarding OCSSPs, Sawyer argued in 2014 that the US DMCA regime could be amended, so that the platform operators would be liable for bad faith removals of content containing fair use. While this could be a somewhat effective response to the chilling effect problem discussed in section 10.4.2 of this chapter, there would be ample difficulties with this approach, particularly visible in the context of Article 17. Starting with the difficulty of correctly assessing various forms of fair use/dealing, through similar evidential problems as in *Lenz*, to the uncertainty regarding the specific shape of procedures warranted by Article 17 and the scope they leave for OCSSPs' assessment of fair use; for these reasons, the idea of enabling freedom of expression claims for inadequate content assessment should be, at this stage, set aside.

On the other hand, should the Commission's stakeholder dialogues result in guidance which would strongly suggest the presence of certain

---

67. Fiala and Husovec, *supra* fn. 32, at 2.
68. *Lenz v. Universal Music Corp.* (2013) WL 271673 (N.D. Cal. 24 January 2013).
69. *Lenz v. Universal Music Corp.* (2015) 801 F.3d 1126.

mechanisms in OCSSP-rightholder agreements, then a possibility to challenge the validity of agreements failing to meet them could open the path to enshrining such desirable mechanisms in law/judicial interpretation. Of course, this would require access to such agreements – an issue discussed thoroughly in section 10.6.1 of this chapter.

10.5.9 COPYRIGHT OWNERSHIP-VERIFICATION MECHANISMS

For the final measure discussed as a potential method of mitigating the negative effect of Article 17 on the freedom of expression, the well-known issue of copyright ownership verification can be discussed. In the various notice and takedown regimes, it happened on more than a few occasions that legitimate content was taken down/claimed on Content ID due to the fact that the notice sender/claimant did not actually have the copyright in the contested works. Elkin-Koren and Perel drew attention to this problem in the context of algorithmic copyright enforcement.[70]

The idea of such verification encounters an obvious barrier in copyright being a right which does not have to be registered. That being said, perhaps the use of very efficient, far-reaching content filtering procedures could require certain steps; maybe a form of identity verification could be among them? Drawing again on the CJEU's distinction on the existence and exercise of a right from *Centrafarm*,[71] controlling the use of certain high-calibre enforcement mechanisms which could pass through Article 17 gate could be seen as a justified limitation on the exercise of copyright and not on its existence and essence.

10.6 BROADER STEPS AIMED AT ENSURING THE ADEQUATE HUMAN RIGHTS BALANCE IN ARTICLE 17

While section 10.5 of this chapter presented and analysed the various ways in which the impact of Article 17 on the freedom of expression can be directly mitigated, there are also certain broader lines of implementation which, while not directly aimed at this freedom, could significantly enhance its presence within the content filtering systems enabled by the discussed provision.

---

70. Elkin-Koren and Perel, *supra* fn. 33, at 509.
71. *See* section 10.5.3 of this chapter.

10.6.1   Transparency

The first one of those gathers matters tied to the concept of transparency. Its value in the context of novel intellectual property enforcement mechanisms was well described in the EU Commission's report on the *Memorandum of Understanding on the Sale of Counterfeit Goods via the Internet* from 2013.[72] The report aptly states that '(e)xternal transparency increases credibility and ensures accountability and responsibility towards stakeholders, national authorities and Parliaments as well as to society as a whole'.[73] Conversely, as Urban, Karaganis and Schofield put it, 'secret, algorithmic decision making is difficult for Internet users to penetrate and challenge, rendering their expression rights vulnerable'.[74]

The debate on online copyright enforcement measures has often been host to concerns over the lack of transparency in this field. Urban, Karaganis and Schofield noted that one of the big challenges in studying the DMCA process was the lack of a legal requirement to publish the notices of infringement.[75] In discussing this issue with the rightholders, the cited authors found that the former were worried that such an increase in transparency could expose their practices and thus lead to further circumvention of enforcement efforts.[76] At the same time, the Online Service Providers (OSPs) receiving the notices were worried that exposing their practices may lead to increased attention from the public and rightholders, forcing the OSPs to change their procedures.[77] Writing in the broader field of content moderation, Common noted that the lack of transparency is 'one of the main weaknesses in the content moderation process developed by platforms and very few improvements can be initiated without a commensurate increase in transparency'.[78] Finally, Elkin-Koren and Perel's key work on accountability in algorithmic enforcement states that 'algorithmic implementations of N&TD [notice and takedown], and even more so voluntary measures applied to detect and prevent copyright infringement, fare poorly in accountability measures'.[79]

Given this hefty amount of commentary of the matter, one could expect the lawmakers behind the DSMCD to consider it in the context of Article 17. And indeed, Article 17(10) provides that 'for the purpose of the stakeholder dialogues, users' organisations shall have access to adequate information

---

72. Report from the Commission to the European Parliament and the Council on the functioning of the Memorandum of Understanding on the Sale of Counterfeit Goods via the Internet (2013), COM(2013) 209 final. *See* https://eur-lex.europa.eu/legal-content/EN/TXT/PDF/?uri=CELEX:52013DC0209&from=EN.
73. Report on the Counterfeit Memorandum, *supra* fn. 72, at 8.
74. Urban, Karaganis and Schofield (2016), *supra* fn. 24, at 4.
75. Urban, Karaganis and Schofield (2016), *supra* fn. 24, at 4.
76. Urban, Karaganis and Schofield (2016), *supra* fn. 24, at 4.
77. Urban, Karaganis and Schofield (2016), *supra* fn. 24, at 4.
78. Common, *supra* fn. 2, at 12.
79. Elkin-Koren and Perel, *supra* fn. 33, at 478.

from online content-sharing service providers on the functioning of their practices with regard to paragraph 4'. Now, in itself, this is a positive step; it is good that the non-governmental organizations (NGOs) representing users' interests will be able to obtain 'adequate information' from the OCSSPs. Of course, in order for this to work well, the phrase 'adequate' should translate into useful, legible and extensive information, and user organisations taking part in the stakeholder dialogues should both make good use of it, and be considered as one of the three pillars of the process, as opposed to a third wheel attached to the rightholders and OCSSPs.

However, one has to wonder whether more could be done in order to ensure transparency of this novel framework of enforcement, while giving due attention concerns such as competitive advantage or the risk of preventive measures being circumvented. To this end, the following propositions can be discussed.

First, contracts between OCSSPs and rightholders aimed at implementing the mechanisms warranted by Article 17 could be made available to the public. The vision which triggered many overblocking concerns raised during the legislative process was that of rightholders pushing OCSSPs to endorse technologies and procedures which care little about freedom of expression, through a series of secretive agreements. In order to prevent this vision from coming true, a database (EU-wide) or databases (national) of such contracts could be made. Due to the concerns over revealing information of competitive significance and facilitating circumvention, such a database could have two tiers. The first would be available to anyone, but sections of the agreements which are, on the balance of interests, not necessary for essential transparency purposes could be concealed. The second tier of the database would include the agreements in full but would be accessible only to certain entities, such as supervisory authorities and/or selected stakeholder organisations and researchers.

Second, the reference files used for content filtering could be organised in a centralised database or databases. This idea has often been raised by academics writing before the arrival of the DSMCD, perhaps as an extended, more organised form of the Chilling Effects archive.[80] Urban, Karaganis and Schofield argued in favour of creating a centralised repository of DMCA copyright infringement notices, for research purposes.[81] Similar suggestion was made by Elkin-Koren and Perel.[82] Common proposed developing a broader, case-study based, 'publicly-available body of precedents' in order to show 'how enforcement occurs on social media platforms'.[83] Finally, Boroughf considered the possibility of developing a Chilling Effects-like

---

80. First, key database of takedowns on Google – now known as Lumen; https://lumendatabase.org/.
81. Urban, Karaganis and Schofield (2016), *supra* fn. 24, at 4.
82. Elkin-Koren and Perel, *supra* fn. 33, at 531.
83. Common, *supra* fn. 2, at 20.

website for the purposes of the Content ID system, which, as it was earlier mentioned, is the conceptual inspiration for Article 17(4)(b).

A database of digital fingerprints for the purposes of Article 17 could have a positive effect on the freedom of expression. It could offer the opportunity to verify the connection between provided files and specific copyrighted works, deserving legal protection. Moreover, gathering the files in a specific format could foster the discussion on their use and further procedures, as well as provide research data. Rightholders found to be abusing the system could also be restricted from having their content filtered out, for example, through suspension; which would be applicable across all OCSSPs platforms. And of course, the database in question would bring multiple benefits of other kinds; the costs of operating the filtering systems could be decreased, due to all OCSSPs being able to rely on a single database. Moreover, smaller rightholders and platform operators could benefit in particular from the presented infrastructure. Admittedly, technical reports should be created at the development stage (as well as periodically renewed) on the threat of filtering systems being circumvented, as a result of the database's presence. However, unless such reports show with credibility that the database in question would significantly undermine the goals of Article 17(4), the broad, unverified concern over circumvention should not stand as a barrier to the discussed idea.

The final point to be reiterated in this section is that transparency measures should be aimed at providing the public and/or dedicated bodies with not only the quantity of information but also – more importantly – the *quality* of information. As Pasquale wrote, while 'sunshine truly is the "best disinfectant"', transparency 'may simply provoke complexity that is as effective at defeating understanding as real or legal secrecy'.[84] This reasoning can be seen as aptly transposed into the world of algorithmic regulation by Elkin-Koren and Perel, who noted that only a select few citizens would benefit (in transparency terms) from seeing the code behind content filtering systems such as Content ID. It is also worth citing Bamberger here, who wrote in a similar vein: 'programming and mathematical idiom can shield layers of embedded assumptions from high-level firm decision makers charged with meaningful oversight and can mask important concerns with a veneer of transparency'.

These concerns are especially evident nowadays in the context of machine learning, a matter discussed by Elkin-Koren and Perel as well.[85] It is difficult to draw conclusions, not to mention taking suitable actions, towards an algorithmic system which changes itself constantly through learning. However, instead of simply saying that nothing can be done due to the ever-changing nature of the algorithm, it is crucial to identify the

---

84. Pasquale F, *The Black Box Society: The Secret Algorithms That Control Money and Information* (2015) Harvard University Press, at 8.
85. Elkin-Koren and Perel, *supra* fn. 33, at 519.

elements of such a system which change little if at all: the input points which can be made transparent, and if need be, regulated as well the elements surrounding the machine-learning algorithm, which are unaffected by its nature, such as the procedures built around it, like an appeal procedure discussed in section 10.5.4 above. This last proposition can be seen as particularly fitting in the light of Wagner's words, who wrote that 'the danger in looking at the normative frameworks embedded in technology simply as "good" or "bad" algorithms, is that they are neither. Rather they are products of a socio-technical process that can only be understood by looking both at technology and human interaction with it'.[86] And finally, should the machine learning algorithm produce significant problems and the reason would be completely hidden inside the 'black-box', the option of shutting it down has to remain on the balancing scales.

10.6.2 INTRODUCING DEDICATED ADMINISTRATIVE BODIES

Back in 2016, the author published an article suggesting certain far-reaching reforms of the European online content regulation laws. Among the solutions proposed was a call for the establishment of an EU-wide administrative body which would be tasked with designing and updating specific obligations of intermediaries towards various types of illicit content online. This was suggested on the basis of the task being too detailed and fast-paced for the legislature, requiring more neutrality than industry self-governance carries, and requiring more proactive, comprehensive action than the judiciary can produce while acting on a case-by-case basis.[87]

Throughout this current chapter's study of the impact of Article 17 on freedom of expression, there were multiple signals indicating the need for a neutral, administrative body, which could help in ensuring the adequate implementation and functioning of the enforcement schemes enabled through the analysed provision of the DSMCD. To recapture and enhance, the potential list of tasks which could be placed on such a body could include:

- Preliminary verification/quality control of the algorithmic systems to be used for Article 17(4)(b) and (c) purposes, before they enter the copyright enforcement process – as suggested in section 10.5.3 above.

---

86. Wagner B, 'Algorithmic Regulation and the Global Default: Shifting Norms in Internet Technology' (2016) Etikk i praksis. Nordic Journal of Applied Ethics, 5-13, at 10.
87. Garstka K, 'Looking above and Beyond the Blunt Expectation: Specified Request as the Recommended Approach to Intermediary Liability in Cyberspace' (2016) European Journal of Law and Technology, vol. 7(3), at 13.

- Operating the suggested database of reference files used for content filtering practices enabled by Article 17 (as described in section 10.6.1 above).
- Operating the database containing official, Article 17-related contractual arrangements between OCSSPs and rightholders, as well as having access to full versions of those, so as to monitor compliance with, e.g., the freedom of expression-supporting requirements of the legislative provision in question, as well as any further interpretations of it; such as the inevitable CJEU judgments (as described in section 10.6.1 above).
- Taking on the interpretative role and publishing guidance building on the stakeholder dialogues, but with a more, regarding matters such as how should the content filtering algorithms be set (e.g., match percentages, human review enabling). Perhaps even more elusive, well-known, yet crucial questions, such as what expeditious removal in specific circumstances is or what should be the proper chain of events in an appeal procedure of system warranted by Article 17(4)(b). In this regard, the body could be playing a similar role to Article 29 Working Party/European Data Protection Board (EDPB) in the field of data protection law.[88]

The final suggestion of this chapter is to explore the possibility of establishing a dedicated, supervisory body (or, if an EU-wide one would be impossible, a series of national bodies, working together) for the purposes of Article 17 of the DSMCD, and its anti-infringement mechanisms. Elkin-Koren and Perel wrote that 'increasing the transparency of copyright enforcing algorithms must be supplemented with increasing the competence of the regulator'[89] – for transparency, freedom of expression and further benefits, such a regulator should accompany the upcoming, new chapter of online copyright enforcement in the EU. To draw the last comparison with data protection law, the national data protection authorities (DPAs) have been an integral and valuable part of European data protection regimes. While online copyright enforcement is admittedly a less far-reaching field of law than data protection and the General Data Protection Regulation (GDPR), the need for a DPA-like body/bodies accompanying the implementation, interpretation, and review processes of Article 17 seems to be strong. And given the narrower scope, the resources required for the functioning of the proposed body could be proportionally smaller.

---

88. *See* https://edpb.europa.eu/our-work-tools/consistency-findings/opinions_en.
89. Elkin-Koren and Perel, *supra* fn. 33, at 531.

10.7   CONCLUSION

Without forgetting the challenges that lie ahead, and the risks Article 17 poses to interests such as freedom of expression, the arrival of this provision should be seen as a welcome development. Not because it is a perfect, flawless and complete piece of legislation (it is not) – but because it puts 'clay' onto the previously empty regulatory wheel, clay which can now be shaped, chiselled and polished. Even though this process will take some time, there is an opportunity here to find the best possible place and shape for content filtering in the EU copyright regime; for too long this ship was allowed to drift between conflicting provisions of EU law on the one hand and voluntary measures such as Content ID on the other. As Husovec wrote, the normative goal of enforcement should be the long-term positive effect, not providing an instant benefit to the rights of an individual.[90] This is how DSMCD should be approached.

Of course, trade-offs between human rights involved will be necessary. At times, copyright protection will outweigh the freedom of expression; other times it will be the reverse. This relationship is practically as old as copyright itself, but the need for dialogue and compromise between the two should not be omitted in the considerations surrounding the short- and long-distance steps for Article 17.

This chapter is presented in hope that the risks posed by this provision to freedom of expression will be understood, together with a selection of steps to mitigate them, and that the latter will be adequately, consciously placed on the balancing scales, throughout the lifespan of the discussed legislative provision.

---

90. Husovec M, 'Accountable, Not Liable: Injunctions Against Intermediaries' (2016) TILEC Discussion Paper No. 2016-012, at 9. *See* http://papers.ssrn.com/sol3/papers.cfm?abst ract_id=2773768).

Chapter 11

The Conflict Between the Human Right to Education and Copyright

Sharon E. Foster

11.1 INTRODUCTION

"Teach the ignorant as much as you can; society is culpable in not providing a free education for all and it must answer for the night which it produces. If the soul is left in darkness sins will be committed. The guilty one is not he who commits the sin, but he who causes the darkness."[1]

Those familiar with the history of the Berne Convention for the Protection of Literary and Artistic Works (Berne) know the important role Victor Hugo's L'Association Litteraire et Artistique Internationale, played in drafting the propositions that provided the foundation for Berne[2] in 1886, the

---

1. Victor Hugo, Les Misérables, available at: https://www.goodreads.com/quotes/80246-teach-the-ignorant-as-much-as-you-can-society-is.
2. Martina Hinojosa, *Challenges for Emerging Art Forms under the Visual Artists Rights Act*, 11 J. TELECOMM. & HIGH TECH. L. 433, 450 (2013); Daniel Gervais & Dashiell Renaud, *The Future of United States Copyright Formalities: Why We Should Prioritize Recordation, and How to Do It*, 28 BERKELEY TECH. L.J. 1459, 1470-1471 (2013); Daniel Gervais, *Golan V. Holder: A Look at the Constraints Imposed by the Berne Convention*, 64 VAND. L. REV. 147, 150-151 (2011) (Victor Hugo recognized the need to balance authors' rights and public interest with the balance tipping in favor of public interest if necessary.); Deven R. Desai, *The Life and Death of Copyright*, 2011 WIS. L. REV. 219, 241-243 (2011); Lindsay Warren Bowen Jr, *Givings and the Next Copyright Deferment*, 77 FORDHAM L. REV. 809, 816-817 (2008).

first international treaty to deal with authors' rights. These authors' rights included moral rights and economic rights as reflected at the time, and today, in national copyright legislation. Copyright has always had a dichotomy of interests, public education and private economic rights sometimes referred to as material interests.[3] This is reflected in the above quotation from Victor Hugo, a staunch supporter of authors' rights who also seemed to recognize the public interest in free education which, of necessity, would require learning materials some of which would probably be copyright protected. Evidently, Hugo saw no conflict. More recently, there has been much discussion regarding the potential conflict between the realization of human rights and increased intellectual property protection, including copyright, as required by the Trade-Related Aspects of Intellectual Property Rights (TRIPS). This chapter focuses on the potential conflict between the human right to education and the protection of authors' rights, primarily through copyright.

There are quite a few treaties and conventions that address the issue of the human right to education; however, many of them deal with the issue of gender and racial discrimination in access to education.[4] While the elimination of discrimination and access is critical to the realization of the human right to education, this chapter discusses the particular problem of potential conflicts between the realization of the human right to free primary education and the human right of authors to material interests in their creations usually realized through domestic copyright legislation.

The problem of the potential conflicts arises from the fact that the instructional materials, in which authors may have a material interest, are critical to the realization of the human right to education. The World Bank in its World Development Report 2004 noted that the problems in the educational systems for some states were primarily due to unaffordable access, dysfunctional schools, low technical quality, low responsiveness and stagnant productivity.[5] While all factors need to be addressed, providing access to instructional materials has the greatest impact.[6] For example, in

---

3. Edward L. Carter, *Harmonization of Copyright Law in Response to Technological Change: Lessons from Europe about Fair Use and Free Expression,* 30 U. LA VERNE L. REV. 312, 317 (2009) (Carter).

4. For example, the Convention on the Elimination of all Forms of Discrimination Against Women, G.A. res. 34/180, 34 U.N. GAOR Supp. (No. 46) at 193, U.N. Doc. A/34/46 (September 3, 1981); and the International Convention on the Elimination of all Forms of Racial Discrimination, G.A. res. 2106 (XX), Annex, 20 U.N. GAOR Supp. (No. 14) at 47, U.N. Doc. A/6014 (1966), 660 U.N.T.S. 195 (January 4, 1969).

5. World Bank. 2003. World Development Report 2004: Making Services Work for Poor People. World Bank. World Bank (World Development Report, 2004) 111, available at: https://openknowledge.worldbank.org/handle/10986/5986.

6. *Ibid.,* at 112-116; Theme of the annual ministerial review: implementing the internationally agreed goals and commitments in regard to education, Report of the Secretary-General, Distr.: General (April 18, 2011), E/2011/83 para. 33 (the provision of affordable materials are necessary to meet the Millennium Goal of universal primary education.)

North East Brazil during the 1980s increases in test scores were measured based upon dollars spent on different inputs. Increased teachers' salaries resulted in an increase of 1; ensuring all teachers have three years of secondary schooling resulted in an increase of 1.9; providing tables, chairs and other hardware for the teachers and students resulted in an increase of 7.7; and providing a packet of instructional materials (access) resulted in an increase of 19.4.[7] In India during the 1990s a similar study was conducted. Increased teachers' salaries resulted in an increase of 1; facility improvements resulted in an increase of 1.2; one additional square foot of space per student resulted in an increase of 1.7; and providing a packet of instructional materials resulted in an increase of 14.[8]

Section 11.2 provides the historical context for the human right to education through an examination of the creation of the United Nations Charter and the Universal Declaration of Human Rights[9] (UDHR). Both of these documents created vague rights in order to achieve consensus and provide flexibility. But, as we shall see, it is the attempt to introduce normative rules through implementation required by subsequent treaties and trade agreements that tied intellectual property to trade and created the potential for conflict.

Although there are several treaties dealing with the human right to education,[10] this chapter focuses on the International Covenant on Economic, Social and Cultural Rights[11] (ICESCR). The ICESCR is intended to provide binding authority for the aspirations specified in the UDHR. Section 11.3 provides the relevant language from the ICESCR relating to the human right to primary education, which is compulsory and free of charge, and the available interpretations for these provisions. Specifically, what is meant by "primary education" "compulsory" and "available free?" These terms pose the most immediate possible conflict with the human right of authors to their

---

(Millennium Goal); Margaret Chon, *Intellectual Property "From Below": Copyright and Capability for Education*, 40 U.C. DAVIS L. REV. 803, 821-823 (2007) (Chon); LAURENCE R. HELFER & GRAEME W. AUSTIN, HUMAN RIGHTS AND INTELLECTUAL PROPERTY: MAPPING THE GLOBAL INTERFACE 318 (2011) (HELFER, MAPPING).

7. World Development Report, 2004, *supra* n. 5 at 116 Fig. 7.3.

8. *Ibid.*

9. Universal Declaration of Human Rights, G.A. res. 217A (III), U.N. Doc A/810 (1948) (UDHR).

10. *See*, generally, UNICEF, A Human Rights Approach to Education For All (2007), available at: unesdoc.unesco.org/images/0015/001548/154861e.pdf, at 7, specifying the United Nations Educational, Scientific and Cultural Organization (UNESCO) Convention against Discrimination in Education (1960); the International Covenant on Economic, Social and Cultural Rights (1966); United Nations Convention on the Rights of the Child (1989); and the Convention on the Elimination of All Forms of Discrimination against Women (1981).

11. G.A. res. 2200A (XXI), 21 U.N. GAOR Supp. (No. 16) at 49, U.N. Doc. A/6316 (1966), 993 U.N.T.S. 3, (January 3, 1976) (ICESCR).

material interests in their creations for their interpretation will tell us what potentially protected materials need to be made available for education and who, if anybody, is to pay for them.

In section 11.4 of this chapter, the author's human right to moral and material interests is discussed. Again, as in sections 11.2 and 11.3, the historical background, specific language and interpretations are addressed. While moral rights are mentioned, the main focus throughout this chapter is on the material interest as that interest presents the primary problem of conflict. Here we see that the UDHR and ICESCR provide the human right to education and the protection to authors' material interests creating the first potential conflict discussed in section 11.6, the internal conflict. An internal conflict is presented when two or more provisions in the same document appear to distract from the ability to comply with one or the other, or both.

The TRIPS[12] agreement is discussed in section 11.5 as it has been given much attention in academic circles and the international community regarding potential external conflicts with the human right to education. An external conflict exists when provisions in two separate documents have conflicting requirements. For example, TRIPS incorporates Berne[13] except for moral rights.[14] Berne provides for protection of authors' economic rights[15] which seems to basically equate to material interests.[16] This requirement may conflict with the requirement to provide primary education, for free, contained in the ICESCR. While TRIPS allows for certain limitations and exceptions such as fair use and compulsory licenses which may accommodate the human right to education, these limitations and exceptions by their very nature evidence a private, economic priority rather than a public priority in education and have proven to be ineffective.[17]

Sections 11.6 and 11.7 address the internal and external conflicts and how to resolve such conflicts when they occur. Here, there seems to be consensus in applying a balancing test, balancing the need for educational materials that may be necessary to fulfill the human right to education with

---

12. Marrakesh Agreement Establishing the World Trade Organization Annex 1C, 1869 U.N.T.S. 157; 33 I.L.M. 1125, (Marrakesh, April 15, 1994) (TRIPS).
13. Berne (Paris 1971) 828 UNTS 221.
14. TRIPS, *supra* n. 12 at Article 9; JAMES J. FAWCETT & PAUL TORREMANS, INTELLECTUAL PROPERTY AND PRIVATE INTERNATIONAL LAW 480 (1998) (FAWCETT & TORREMANS, IP).
15. Berne, *supra* n. 13 at Articles 8-9 and 13.
16. *See WTO Panel Report* in United States-section 110(5) of the Copyright Act, WT/DS160/R, para. 6.74, June 15, 2000 (WTO Panel Report).
17. For more information on limitations and exceptions *see* generally, RUTH L. OKEDIJI, EXCEPTIONS AND LIMITATIONS TO COPYRIGHT LAWS, COPYRIGHT LAW IN AN AGE OF LIMITATIONS AND EXCEPTIONS 429, 430 (Ruth L. Okediji ed., 2017); *Univ. of Oxford v. Rameshwari Photocopy Servs.*, (2016) RFA(OS) 81 (India), http://lobis.nic.in/ddir/dhc/RSE/judgement/16-09-2016/RSE16092016S24392012.pdf (allowing a broad educational use exception); Ruth L. Okediji, *Does Intellectual Property Need Human Rights?*, 51 N.Y.U. J. INT'L L. & POL. 1, 5-6, 34, 54-57, 61 fn 220 (2018).

the human right of authors to material interests. Finally, section 11.8 addresses the false conflict paradigm. The false conflict arises in situations where there is market failure; that is to say in situations where the market in question does not have the economic ability to pay for educational materials. In such a situation the authors of the educational materials have no material interest or economic rights because there is no commercial gain to be had.

11.2   THE FOUNDATION FOR THE HUMAN RIGHT TO EDUCATION: THE UNITED NATIONS CHARTER AND THE UDHR

Modern human rights originated with the creation of the United Nations in 1945 as a response to the human tragedies experiences during World War II. The United Nations Charter recognizes the need to protect and respect human rights but is vague as to what those rights are. The United Nations Charter specifies general principles and established the Economic and Social Council (ECOSOC) to provide recommendations for the specifics. Subsequent to the adoption of the United Nations Charter, an ECOSOC subcommittee was appointed to define and specify the human rights referred to in the United Nations Charter. The result was the UDHR. Compulsory, free, primary education was included as a human right. However, being a declaration, the binding authority of the UDHR is questionable.

The United Nations Charter was deliberately vague on the human rights issue, as it was believed that a consensus would never be reached in the short time period allotted at the San Francisco Conference to adopt the Charter.[18] Accordingly, all that was stated on the issue was:

Preamble: WE THE PEOPLES OF THE UNITED NATIONS DETERMINED ...

to reaffirm faith in fundamental human rights, in the dignity and worth of the human person, in the equal rights of men and women ... .

Chapter 1, Article 1, The Purposes of the United Nations are:

3. To achieve international co-operation in solving international problems of [a] ... humanitarian character, and in promoting and encouraging respect for human rights ... .

Chapter IV, Article 13, The General Assembly:

1. The General Assembly shall initiate studies and make recommendations for the purpose of ... b. assisting in the realization of human rights ... .

Chapter IX, International Economic and Social Co-operation. ...

Article 55

---

18. MARY ANN GLENDON, A WORLD MADE NEW 5 (Random House Inc., 2001) (GLENDON).

With a view to the creation of conditions of stability and well being. ... the United Nations shall promote: ... c. universal respect for, and observance of, human rights ... .

Chapter X, Composition of the Economic and Social Council ... . Functions and Powers ... . Article 62

2(A). It may make recommendations for the purpose of promoting respect for, and observance of, human rights.[19]

From this vague language we see that the concept of human rights was not an operative principle of the United Nations Charter when that document was created. Rather, it was a desideratum of the Charter as opposed to a legal obligation.[20] For example, the United Nations Charter is silent on identifying particular rights as human rights. Accordingly, after the United Nations Charter was approved a subcommittee, the Human Rights Commission drafting committee, was appointed by ECOSOC in 1945-1947 to address the issue of what were these "human rights" alluded to in the United Nations Charter. The result of the subcommittee's work was loosely articulated in the UDHR.[21]

John Humphrey, an international lawyer from Canada, prepared the first draft of the UDHR.[22] Humphrey gathered materials from all over the world in preparing what would be the first working draft.[23] The drafting group received the Humphrey draft in June of 1947.[24] René Cassin, the delegate from France, was assigned the task of revising the Humphrey draft in June 1947.[25] A working group then took the Cassin draft and made revisions producing what has been termed the Geneva Draft in December 1947.[26] The Geneva draft received comments, and the Human Rights Commission drafting subcommittee met again in early May 1948 to revise the Geneva

---

19. United Nations, Charter of the United Nations, October 24, 1945, 1 UNTS XVI, available at http://www.unwebsite.com/charter (last accessed October 27, 2014) (UN Charter).

20. *See* MICHLA POMERANCE, SELF-DETERMINATION IN LAW AND PRACTICE: THE NEW DOCTRINE IN THE UNITED NATIONS 9 (The Hague Kluwer Law International 1982) (Pomerance).

21. JOHANNES MORSINK, THE UNIVERSAL DECLARATION OF HUMAN RIGHTS 1-12 (University of Pennsylvania Press, 1999) (MORSINK).

22. GLENDON, *supra* n. 18 at 43, 48; HENRY J. STEINER & PHILIP ALSTON, INTERNATIONAL HUMAN RIGHTS IN CONTEXT: LAW POLITICS MORALS 138 (New York, 2nd 2000) (STEINER); MORSINK, *supra* n. 21 at 2, 5-6).

23. GLENDON, *supra* n. 18 at 49-50; Peter K. Yu, *Reconceptualizing Intellectual Property Interests in a Human Rights Framework*, 40 U.C. DAVIS L. REV. 1039, 1051-1052 (2007) (Yu, *Reconceptualizing*); Aurora Plomer, *The Human Rights Paradox: Intellectual Property Rights and Rights of Access to Science*, 35(1) HUM. RTS Q. 143, 159 (February 2013) (Plomer), available at: http://muse.jhu.edu/journals/human_rights_quarterly/v035/35.1.plomer.html (last accessed October 27, 2014).

24. GLENDON, *supra* n. 18 at 54, 58; MORSINK, *supra* n. 21 at 5.

25. GLENDON, *supra* n. 18 at 61; MORSINK, *supra* n. 21 at 8-9.

26. GLENDON, *supra* n. 18 at 79-94; MORSINK, *supra* n. 21 at 9-10.

draft.[27] The entire subcommittee met to further revise the Geneva draft in June 1948.[28]

Throughout the drafting process there were admonitions to avoid creating a document that reflected an emphasis on a particular culture, religion, socio-economic system, political or philosophical beliefs.[29] To avoid claims of bias and build consensus the drafters created a document that was envisioned as common standards and not rigid uniform practices.[30]

The UDHR passed on December 10, 1948 with forty-eight in favor and eight abstentions. There were no negative votes. Honduras and Yemen were absent.[31] The pertinent provision of the UDHR that relates to education is:

Article 26(1)
Everyone has the right to education. Education shall be free, at least in the elementary and fundamental stages. Elementary education shall be compulsory. Technical and professional education shall be made generally available and higher education shall be equally accessible to all on the basis of merit.[32]

In Article 26(1) education is understood to be, in a broad sense, the right to a free, fundamental education.[33] "Free" probably means free of charge but certain expenses may have to be covered by the students.[34] This fundamental education curriculum was to be left to the states to determine.[35] Elementary education is to be compulsory but there is no clear distinction between fundamental education and elementary education.[36] Most likely elementary education includes such things as reading, writing, arithmetic and other basic needs to function in a society.[37]

There have been attempts to assert that the UDHR is legally binding under international law through various mechanisms. Arguments based upon treaty law and customary international law[38] are the most prominent.

---

27. GLENDON, *supra* n. 18 at 107; MORSINK, *supra* n. 21 at 10-11.
28. GLENDON, *supra* n. 18 at 111-119; STEINER, *supra* n. 22 at 139; MORSINK, *supra* n. 21 at 11.
29. GLENDON, *supra* n. 18 at 38-43, 68-70, 73-78, 89-92, 140-142, 161, 222-223; STEINER, *supra* n. 22 at 139; MORSINK, *supra* n. 21 at 4-5, 24.
30. GLENDON, *supra* n. 18 at 230.
31. GLENDON, *supra* n. 18 at 169-170.
32. UDHR, *supra* n. 9 at Article 26(1).
33. THE UNIVERSAL DECLARATION OF HUMAN RIGHTS: A COMMENTARY 408 (Asbjörn Eide, Pentti Arajärvi, Gudmundur Alfredsson, Göran Melander, Lars Adam Rehof and Allan Rosas eds, with collaboration of Theresa Swinehart, Scandinavian University Press (1992)) (Commentary).
34. *Ibid.*
35. *Ibid.*
36. *Ibid.*, at 408-409.
37. *Ibid.*
38. Customary international law is evidenced by numerous sources such as diplomatic correspondence, policy statements, press releases, the opinions of official legal advisors, official manuals on legal questions, comments by governments on drafts, recitals in

Declarations, such as the UDHR, do not have the force of a treaty or convention,[39] but some core provisions of the UDHR may be considered customary and, thus, potentially binding.[40] However, the right to an education as well as the moral and material interests of authors reflected in copyright laws, discussed in section 11.4 below, have not risen to the level of customary international law. Not only is there a dearth of authority to indicate such customary international law, there is no general and consistent practice necessary for the distinction of customary international law. Indeed, in the current political environment, some commentators have suggested that this is a dark age for human rights as politicians are ineffective at protecting civil and human rights and some seem to be more interested in undermining civil and human rights.[41]

11.3	THE ICESCR ON THE RIGHT TO EDUCATION AND HOW IT HAS BEEN INTERPRETED

Recognizing the aspirational as opposed to binding nature of the UDHR there was a move to propose a binding treaty addressing the goals stated in

---

treaties and other international instruments, a pattern of treaties in the same form, practices of international organs, judicial decisions and United Nations resolutions. Although no particular duration of a practice is required to establish custom, a longer duration may help establish consistency and generality of the practice, which is required. With respect to consistency of the practice, substantial uniformity is required. As for generality, this compliments consistency and looks to the conduct of a state such as acquiescence. However, a state may contract out of custom in the process of its formation as a persistent objector. IAN BROWNLIE, PRINCIPLES OF INTERNATIONAL LAW 5-10 (5th ed. 2002) (BROWNLIE).

39. A treaty is an "international agreement concluded between states in written form and governed by international law", (Vienna Convention on the Law of Treaties, 1155 U.N.T.S. 331, Article 2(1)(a) (May 23, 1969) (Vienna Convention)); Restatement 3rd of Foreign Relations Law, Ch. 301 (1) (1987) (Restatement). A covenant, like a treaty, must be capable of legal enforcement. The term "declaration" has officially been defined by the United Nations Secretariat as: "a formal and solemn instrument, suitable for rare occasions when principles of great and lasting significance are being enunciated". GLENDON, *supra* n. 18 at 174 (citing to E/CN.4/L.610).

40. YEARBOOK OF THE UNITED NATIONS, SPECIAL EDITION UNITED NATIONS FIFTIETH ANNIVERSARY 1945-1995, 295 (Dept. of Public Information, United Nations, N.Y. (1995)) (YEARBOOK).

41. Leadership Conference on Civil & Human Rights, https://civilrights.org/2018/01/31/leadership-conference-education-fund-releases-report-trumps-civil-human-rights-rollbacks/. *See* Kavana Ramaswamy, *The Right to Education: An Analysis Through the Lens of the Deontological Method of Immanuel Kant*, 16 NW. J. HUM RTS. 47, 49-50 (2018); WITHOUT JUSTICE: TRUMP'S ACROSS-THE-BOARD ASSAULT ON CIVIL AND HUMAN RIGHTS CIVIL RIGHTS MONITOR, January 2018, Volume 27, http://civilrightsdocs.info/pdf/monitor/Without-Justice-2018.pdf; Klaus D. Beiter, *Is The Age of Human Rights Really Over? The Right to Education In Africa—Domesticization, Human Rights-Based Development, and Extraterritorial State Obligations*, 49 GEO. J. IL 9, 10-11 (2017).

the UDHR. It was urged by some that it would be best to create two separate treaties: one addressing economic rights and another addressing political rights.[42] This was the course taken by the subcommittee and the drafting of the ICESCR and the International Convention on Civil and Political Rights (ICCPR) commenced shortly after the passage of the UDHR. For purposes of the right to education, the ICESCR is the critical document and, thus, the one addressed in this section.

The provisions in the final version of the ICESCR that relate to the right to compulsory, free, primary education are:

Article 13 ... .

    2. The States Parties to the present Covenant recognize that, with a view to achieving the full realization of this right:
        (a) Primary education shall be compulsory and available free to all; ... .
        (d) Fundamental education shall be encouraged or intensified as far as possible for those persons who have not received or completed the whole period of their primary education; ... .

Article 14

Each State Party to the present Covenant which, at the time of becoming a Party, has not been able to secure in its metropolitan territory or other territories under its jurisdiction compulsory primary education, free of charge, undertakes, within two years, to work out and adopt a detailed plan of action for the progressive implementation, within a reasonable number of years, to be fixed in the plan, of the principle of compulsory education free of charge for all.[43]

The right to education articulated in Articles 13 and 14 is considered an economic right, a social right, a cultural right, a civil right and a political right given the fact that education is central to the realization of all of these rights.[44] Because of this critical importance, primary education is compulsory, meaning that neither parents, nor guardians, nor the state may treat primary education as optional.[45]

Primary education must be available without charge including hidden or indirect charges that may serve as a barrier to the right of the child to receive a primary education.[46] However, if a state party has inadequate financial

---

42. STEINER, *supra* n. 22 at 139.
43. ICESCR, *supra* n. 11 at Articles 13 and 14.
44. Committee on Economic, Social and Cultural Rights, Plans of action for primary education (Article 14): 10/05/99 E/C.12/1999/4, Substantive Issues Arising in the Implementation of the International Covenant on Economic, Social and Cultural Rights: General Comment No. 11, at para. 2 (GC11).
45. *Ibid.,* at para. 6.
46. *Ibid.,* at para. 7.

resources to provide free, primary education other state parties have an obligation to assist.[47] Just what is meant by "assist" has yet to be determined.

Primary education has been defined as: the basic learning needs of all children taking into account the cultural needs and opportunities of the community.[48] Basic learning needs are defined as:

> essential learning tools (such as literacy, oral expression, numeracy, and problem solving) and the basic learning content (such as knowledge, skills, values, and attitudes) required by human beings to be able to survive, to develop their full capacities, to live and work in dignity, to participate fully in development, to improve the quality of their lives, to make informed decisions, and to continue learning.[49]

States are primarily responsible for achieving human rights, such as the right to education, for their people but other actors are responsible as well including corporations.[50]

11.4   THE HUMAN RIGHT OF AUTHORS' MORAL AND MATERIAL INTERESTS

For better or worse the moral and material interests of authors were included in the UDHR and the ICESCR as a human right. This fact cannot legitimately be denied despite the questionability of the appropriateness for the inclusion of such rights as a human right.[51] Indeed, during the drafting of these documents the possible conflicts that could arise due to the inclusion of such rights were, briefly, discussed.

---

47. *Ibid.,* at para. 9.
48. Committee on Economic, Social and Cultural Rights, The right to education (Article 13): 08/12/99, E/C.12/1999/10, Implementation of the International Covenant on Economic, Social and Cultural Rights, Comment No. 13, at para. 9 (citing to The World Declaration on Education for All, at Article 1) (GC13).
49. *Ibid.*
50. *Economic, Social and Cultural Rights, Status of the International Covenants on Human Rights,* Report by Hatem Kotrane, independent expert on the question of a Draft Protocol For the ICESCR, E/CN.4/2003/53, para. 12, January 13, 2003; GLENDON, *supra* n. 18 at 69, 114.
51. Sub-Commission on Human Rights Resolution 2000/7, E/CN.4/Sub.2/2000/7, para. 1 (August 17, 2000) (Resolution 2000/7); Comm. on Econ., Soc. & Cultural Rights, General Comment No. 17: The Right of Everyone to Benefit from the Protection of the Moral and Material Interests Resulting from Any Scientific, Literary or Artistic Production of Which He or She is the Author (Article 15(1)(c)), U.N. Doc. E/C.12/GC/17 (January 12, 2006), available at: http://www1.umn.edu/humanrts/gencomm/escgencom 17.html (last accessed October 7, 2014) (GC17).

11.4.1   Article 27 of the UDHR Specifies That the Moral and Material Interests of Authors Are a Human Right

The dichotomy of rights provided for in the UDHR, Article 27, create the potential for a conflict between access to the benefits of arts and scientific advancement and moral and material interests. While the history of the drafting of the UDHR indicates some reluctance to include protection of moral and material interests of authors as a human right they were ultimately included. René Cassin the delegate from France who was assigned the task of revising the Humphrey draft of the UDHR in June 1947 included a provision protecting authors' rights.[52] A working group then took the Cassin draft and made revisions producing the Geneva Draft in December 1947.[53] In this draft the authors' rights provision was deleted. The Geneva Draft received comments and the Human Rights Commission drafting committee met again in early May 1948 to revise the Geneva Draft.[54] The entire subcommittee met to revise again in June 1948 and added back the authors' rights provision:[55]

> It has long been recognized that innovation and the dissemination of knowledge may be promoted through incentives such as the economic incentives created by laws protecting authors' rights.[56] This correlation and potential conflicts were discussed during the drafting of the UDHR where there was not much disagreement regarding the right to enjoy the benefits of scientific advances to be included in Article 27(1) of the UDHR[57] but there was more debate regarding the issue of authors' rights contained in what became Article 27(2). The French delegation proposed including moral and material interests but was more concerned with moral rights.[58] The French argued that, in addition to remuneration, an author should retain a right over his work that would not disappear

---

52. GLENDON, *supra* n. 18 at 61; MORSINK, *supra* n. 21 at 220; Yu, *Reconceptualizing*, *supra* n. 23 at 1052; Plomer, *supra* n. 23 at 168.
53. GLENDON, *supra* n. 18 at 61; MORSINK, *supra* n. 21 at 9-10.
54. GLENDON, *supra* n. 18 at 107; MORSINK, *supra* n. 21 at 9.
55. GLENDON, *supra* n. 18 at 111-119; MORSINK, *supra* n. 21 at 10-11.
56. For example, the United States Constitution, at Article 1, section 8: *To promote the Progress of Science and useful Arts, by securing for limited Times to Authors and Inventors the exclusive Right to their respective Writings and Discoveries*; ... FEDER-ALIST PAPERS, No. 43 (James Madison); James Madison, Letter to Thomas Jefferson (October 17, 1788), available at: http://userpages.umbc.edu/~nmiller/POLI100/MadisontoJefferson.htm (last accessed September 14, 2019).
57. Maria Green, *Drafting History of the Article 15(1)(c) of the International Covenant* para. 4, (Int'l Anti-Poverty L. Ctr.), U.N. Doc. E/C.12/2000/15 (October 9, 2000) (Green); MORSINK, *supra* n. 21 at 217-219; Yu, *Reconceptualizing*, *supra* n. 23 at 1054.
58. Green, *supra* n. 57 at para. 5; MORSINK, *supra* n. 21 at 219-221.

even after the work entered the public domain.[59] The Chinese delegate, Peng-Chun Chang, later stated that this moral right was not merely to protect the artist but also the public to ensure that the work was available in its original form.[60]

Although the Human Rights Commission rejected the provision, it passed in the Third Committee though objections were raised that these moral and material interests were not, properly speaking, a basic human right.[61] Some delegates from the Third Committee voted for this provision with the moral rights issue in mind and others voted for it in the hope that it would be a step toward internationalization of copyright.[62] Article 27 of the UDHR states:

Article 27

(1) Everyone has the right freely to participate in the cultural life of the community, to enjoy the arts and to share in scientific advancement and its benefits.

(2) Everyone has the right to the protection of the moral and material interests resulting from any scientific, literary or artistic production of which he is the author.[63]

Article 27(1) addresses enjoyment rights relating to the arts and scientific benefits and can be interpreted as applying to both groups and individuals.[64] However, it is limited to the enjoyment of arts and scientific benefits of the community and it is unclear if this means the domestic community or the international community. It is also unclear if these rights are to be interpreted as requiring free enjoyment, inexpensive enjoyment or just non-discriminatory enjoyment. This is the section that is associated with the access quotient in the copyright balance.[65] Indeed, in addressing the apparent conflict between education and authors' rights several commentators point to Article 27(1) for the proposition that it requires access to knowledge.[66]

---

59. Green, *supra* n. 57 at para. 5. Public domain is defined as expressions that are available for common use rather than owned. WILLIAM M. LANDES & RICHARD A. POSNER, THE ECONOMIC STRUCTURE OF INTELLECTUAL PROPERTY LAW 14-15 (2003) (LANDES).

60. Green, *supra* n. 57 at para. 5; MORSINK, *supra* n. 21 at 221-222; Yu, *Reconceptualizing*, *supra* n. 23 at 1057.

61. Green, *supra* n. 57 at para. 6; MORSINK, *supra* n. 21 at 220.

62. Green, *supra* n. 57 at para. 6; Yu, *Reconceptualizing*, *supra* n. 23 at 1058.

63. UDHR, *supra* n. 9.

64. Commentary, *supra* n. 33 at 430.

65. Resolution 2000/7, *supra* n. 51 para. 2.

66. Dr. Audrey R. Chapman (American Association for the Advancement of Science), *Implementation of the International Covenant on Economic, Social and Cultural Rights*, E/C/.12/2000/12, October 3, 2000 (Discussion Paper) at para. 29 (Chapman): Report of the High Commissioner—Commission on Human Rights, *Economic, Social and Cultural*

Article 27(2) is a declaration that authors' rights relating to moral and material interests which have been given the status of a human right.[67] It is an individual right delegated to states and, as such, is more similar to a civil and political right and has certain similarities with property rights.[68] It imposes on states' restrictions on creating obstacles to impede the ability of individuals to obtain these rights and has some similarities to the right to freedom of expression, freedom of thought, conscience and religion which are also civil and political rights.[69]

René Cassin observed in 1960 that Article 27(2) was still "shrouded in penumbra."[70] It is claimed that the UDHR and the ICESCR mark the apex of the French vision of literary and artistic property.[71] Such a statement gives an improper implication of a dominant philosophical view in these documents which runs counter to the *travaux préparatoires* expressing the desire to create, at least with respect to the UDHR, a document of a universal nature.[72] Still, Cassin was correct in asserting that Article 27(2) was then as it is now unclear regarding the reason for its inclusion. The language of Article 27(2) is, however, clear in granting authors' moral and material interests the status of a human right.

11.4.2   ARTICLE 15 OF THE ICESCR SPECIFIES THAT "THE MORAL AND MATERIAL INTERESTS OF AUTHORS ARE A HUMAN RIGHT"

As with Article 27 of the UDHR, Article 15 of the ICESCR has an apparent dichotomy of rights, which creates the potential for a conflict between access to the benefits of scientific advancement and moral and material interests. In drafting the ICESCR, the moral and material interests provision found in Article 15(1) was explicitly excluded from several drafts and only made its way into that document during the debate of the Third Committee of the General Assembly in 1957, three years after the Commission on Human Rights had completed its work and five years after it had last been debated.[73]

With respect to Article 15 of the ICESCR, there was some dissention regarding having its provisions dovetail the UDHR.[74] In particular, the

---

Rights, the Impact of the Agreement on Trade-Related Aspects of Intellectual Property Rights on Human Rights, E/CN.4/Sub.2/2001/13 (June 27, 2001) at para. 10 (HC Report).

67. Commentary, *supra* n. 33 at 431.
68. *Ibid.,* at 430-431.
69. *Ibid.,* at 432.
70. FRANÇOIS DESSEMONTET, COPYRIGHT AND HUMAN RIGHTS, IN INTELLEC-TUAL PROPERTY AND INFORMATION LAW: ESSAYS IN HONOUR OF HERMAN COHEN JEHORAM 113, 117 (Jan J.C. Kabel & Gerald J.H.M. Mom eds, 1998) at para. 4 (DESSEMONTET).
71. *Ibid.,* at para. 5.
72. GLENDON, *supra* n. 18 at 65, 69.
73. Green, *supra* n. 57 at para. 3.
74. Yu, *Reconceptualizing, supra* n. 23 at 1060-1061.

United States (U.S.) delegate, Eleanor Roosevelt, stated that the documents should not be a mirror image as these documents had very different legal effects.[75] Again there seemed to be little dissention over a provision that granted people the right to benefit from scientific progress,[76] but authors' rights were more contentious. The United Nations Educational, Scientific and Cultural Organization (UNESCO) and the French supported the inclusion of authors' rights. The UNESCO representative, Havet, stated that its inclusion would help to harmonize national and international legislation and practice in this field.[77] The French delegate argued that its inclusion stressed that the moral and material interest of creators should be safeguarded.[78] The U.S. delegate, speaking in opposition, pointed out that UNESCO was studying the issue of copyright and that until the study of the complexities of the subject had been completed it would be impossible to include the provision as a general principle.[79] The Chilean delegate, Hernan Santa Cruz, also voiced opposition with the concern that this was not a question of a fundamental human right.[80] The provision was rejected at this point seven to seven with four abstentions.[81]

A year later, in May of 1952, the issue again came up with the U.S., the United Kingdom (U.K.) and Yugoslavia against the inclusion of the authors' rights provision for the reasons articulated a year before by the U.S. France and UNESCO were still in favor of its inclusion.[82] The Chilean delegate, Valenzuela, articulated his state's concern in voting against the provision that the rights of the author should not be protected without safeguards for the underdeveloped states that would be harmed by such a monopoly as the developed states controlled a significant amount of the technical knowledge.[83] The French delegate did not believe such protection presented a *grave danger* and that, in any event, the absence of such protection was not a solution for underdeveloped states.[84] The representative from the U.K., Hoare, was not in favor of the inclusion of such rights but observed that the Chilean delegate's remarks shed a new light on his interpretation of the provision relating to the rights of all to the benefits of scientific advancements. If Mr. Valenzuela was reading that provision as in conflict with the proposed authors' rights, and, hence, reading it as an unqualified right, such

---

75. *Ibid.,* at 1061.
76. Green, *supra* n. 57 at para. 19; Yu, *Reconceptualizing, supra* n. 23 at 1062-1063.
77. Green, *supra* n. 57 at para. 21.
78. Green, *supra* n. 57 at para. 22; Yu, *Reconceptualizing, supra* n. 23 at 1063-1064.
79. Green, *supra* n. 57 at para. 23; UN Doc. E/CN.4/SR.229.
80. Green, *supra* n. 57 at para. 24; UN Doc. E/CN.4/SR.230.
81. Green, *supra* n. 57 at para. 25; UN Doc. E/CN.4/SR.230.
82. Green, *supra* n. 57 at paras. 26-28; UN Doc. E/CN.4/SR.292-93; Yu, *Reconceptualizing, supra* n. 23 at 1064.
83. Green, *supra* n. 57 at para. 29; UN Doc. E/CN.4/SR.292; Yu, *Reconceptualizing, supra* n. 23 at 1064-1065.
84. Green, *supra* n. 57 at para. 31; UN Doc. E/CN.4/SR.292; Yu, *Reconceptualizing supra* n. 23 at 1065.

a reading was far beyond the scope of the covenant and one to which the U.K. could not subscribe.[85] There appears to be no record of further discussion on this topic and the proposal was again rejected this time seven to six with four abstentions.[86]

The Human Rights Commission's final draft, without the provision protecting authors' rights, was sent to the General Assembly and then to the Third Committee for review. The Third Committee further reviewed the authors' rights proposal in October-November 1957. Again there was no dissent regarding the rights to enjoy the benefits of science. As for authors' rights, the French delegate, Juvigny, argued for its inclusion but did not make the proposal. This time it was made by the Uruguay delegate, Tejera.[87] Tejera argued that the rights of the public and the author were not contradictory but complimented each other. For example, protecting the author would ensure the authenticity of the work.[88] Chile was now in favor of the provision as were Sweden, Israel, the Dominican Republic and UNESCO. Indonesia and the United Socialist Soviet Republic were opposed for reasons already stated by the U.S. delegate to the Human Rights Commission. Saudi Arabia and Czechoslovakia also expressed concerns against its inclusion such as the fact that the provision seemed to protect individuals when much scientific work was completed by team effort and that such a delicate subject should not be included in haste without full debate and with an unsatisfactory text that could be misinterpreted.[89] In the end, the provision was voted in by a vote of thirty-nine to nine with twenty-four abstentions.[90] The provision in the final version of the ICESCR that relates to the moral and material rights of authors' issue is Article 15 which states:

Article 15

1. The States Parties to the present Covenant recognize the right of everyone:
   (a) To take part in cultural life;
   (b) To enjoy the benefits of scientific progress and its applications;
   (c) To benefit from the protection of the moral and material interests resulting from any scientific, literary or artistic production of which he is the author.

Given the vague language in Article 15 and the lack of attention paid to issues of conflicts between authors' rights and other human rights, such as

---

85. Green, *supra* n. 57 at para. 31; UN Doc. E/CN.4/SR.292; Yu, *Reconceptualizing, supra* n. 23 at 1065-1066.
86. Green, *supra* n. 57 at para. 31; UN Doc. E/CN.4/SR.292.
87. Green, *supra* n. 57 at paras. 33-35; Yu, *Reconceptualizing, supra* n. 23 at 1066.
88. Green, *supra* n. 57 at para. 35; Yu, *Reconceptualizing, supra* n. 23 at 1067-1068.
89. Green, *supra* n. 57 at para. 40; UN Doc. A/C.3/SR.798-799; Yu, *Reconceptualizing, supra* n. 23 at 1068-1069.
90. Green, *supra* n. 57 at para. 41; UN Doc. A/C.3/SR.799.

education, it is unlikely that the drafters imagined the key role intellectual property would play in the fields of trade, development or education.[91]

In interpreting paragraph 15(1)(c), the Committee on Economic, Social and Cultural Rights (the "Committee") issued General Comment No. 17 in 2006, a non-binding assertion of the Committee's interpretation of that paragraph protecting, as a human right, moral and material interests of authors. First, the Committee asserts that human rights are "inalienable"[92] and with respect to the ICESCR, Article 15(1)(c) "safeguards the personal link between authors and their creations."[93] Next, the Committee asserts that only natural persons or certain groups may claim a human right to moral and material interests as an author, not corporations.[94] It should be noted that some domestic legislation and regional human rights conventions conflict with General Comment No. 17 in that they recognize corporations as a "person" with human rights protections.[95]

Moral interests are defined as proclaiming the intrinsically personal character of every creation including:

> the right of authors to be recognized as the creators of their scientific, literary and artistic productions and to object to any distortion, mutilation or other modification of, or other derogatory action in relation to, such productions, which would be prejudicial to their honour and reputation.[96]

Material interests are proclaimed to have a close linkage to the right to own property as stated in the ICESCR at paragraph 17 and, while not directly linked to the author's personality, contribute to the right to an adequate standard of living as stated in the ICESCR at paragraph 11.[97] While this is a rather vague definition, it does not seem to require the type of economic and market analysis which is required under TRIPS as described below.

---

91. HC Report, *supra* n. 66 at 22, n. 4 (citing to Green, *supra* n. 57).
92. GC17, *supra* n. 51 at para. 1; but *see* Mirela V. Hristova, *Are Intellectual Property Rights Human Rights?; Patent Protection and the Right to Health,* 93 J. PAT. & TRADEMARK OFF. SOC'Y 339, 342-343 (2011)(Hristova) (arguing that human rights often conflict requiring a balancing approach and, hence, should not be categorically considered inalienable).
93. GC17, *supra* n. 51 at para. 2.
94. GC17, *supra* n. 51 at paras. 7 and 8; Laurence R. Helfer, *Toward a Human Rights Framework for Intellectual Property,* 40 U.C. DAVIS L. REV. 971, 993 fn. 81 (2007) (Helfer, *Framework*); Peter K. Yu, *Intellectual Property And Human Rights In The Nonmultilateral Era,* 64 FLA. L. REV. 1045, 1066-1068 (2012) (Yu, *Nonmultilateral*).
95. Helfer, *Framework, supra* n. 94 at 993 fn. 81 (2007) (citing to United States law 17 U.S.C. § 201(b) (2006)); Yu, *Nonmultilateral, supra* n. 94 at 64 1066-1068 (citing to *Anheuser-Busch, Inc. v. Portugal,* 45 Eur. Ct. H.R. 36 (2007) (Grand Chamber) interpreting the European Convention of Human Rights as providing human rights protection *to both registered trademarks and trademark applications of a multinational corporation*).
96. GC17, *supra* n. 51 at para. 13.
97. *Ibid.,* at paras. 15 and 16.

Although there is a potential for conflict between Article 15(1)(b) and (c),[98] a balanced approach could alleviate the conflict.[99] The problem of a conflict mainly arises through implementation. So a state that implements laws which over emphasize the human rights of moral and material interests of authors to the determent of core human rights, such as education, would not be meeting its human rights obligations.[100]

Finally, General Comment No. 17 states that the two provisions of Article 15, protecting the benefits of science and authors' moral and material interests do not necessarily conflict but may be mutually reinforcing.[101] This is an important observation as we have seen over the years the conflicts between human rights in terms of authors' moral and material interests and other human rights, such as education and health, arises more from the prioritization and implementation of intellectual property systems than from some inescapable, inherent conflict.[102] In this regard, it is important to keep in mind that while intellectual property systems may protect the human right to moral and material interests, they often go far beyond that including a property right for a term of years which is not required to comply with Article 15.[103] Intellectual property rights, as required by TRIPS, are not equal to human rights but they may contain the mechanism to protect certain aspects of human rights such as moral and material interests of authors.[104]

11.5   TRIPS INTERPRETED

The passage of TRIPS in 1994 tied intellectual property to trade and thus heightened the concern of a conflict between the human right to access to the benefits of the arts and scientific progress, education and other public concerns and the human right to moral and material interests. The TRIPS

---

98. U.N. Econ. & Soc. Council [ECOSOC], Comm. on Econ., Soc. & Cultural Rights, Substantive Issues Arising in the Implementation of the International Covenant on Economic, Social and Cultural Rights, U.N. Doc. E/C12/2001/15 (December 14, 2001), available at http:// www.unhchr.ch/tbs/doc.nsf/0/1e1f4514f8512432c1256ba6003b2cc6/ $FILE/G0146641.pdf (follow-up to day of general discussion on Article 15.1(c), Monday, November 26, 2001) at para. 1 (ECOSOC Issues).
99. ECOSOC Issues, *supra* n. 98 at para. 17; GC17, *supra* n. 51 at paras. 35 and 39(e).
100. ECOSOC Issues, *supra* n. 98 at paras. 10-12.
101. GC17, *supra* n. 51 at para. 4; Yu, *Reconceptualizing, supra* n. 23 at 1071-1072.
102. Hristova, *supra* n. 92 at 348 (*Theoretically, the two systems seem to coincide, but in practice they may diverge in certain areas due to the increasing levels of intellectual property protection* ...); Yu, *Nonmultilateral, supra* n. 94 at 1050-1051 (2012) (quoting Sub-Commission on Human Rights Resolution 2000/7).
103. GC17, *supra* n. 51 at para. 16.
104. GC17, *supra* n. 51 at para. 3; Yu, *Nonmultilateral, supra* n. 94 at 1053-1054, 1062 (*it is important to distinguish the human rights attributes of intellectual property rights from the non-human rights aspects of intellectual property protection.*); ECOSOC Issues, *supra* n. 98 at para. 4.

system adopted an intellectual property system, such as copyright as articulated in Berne. This is a more ridged system than that required under human rights law that merely requires the protection of moral and material interests. While the implementation of TRIPS may protect the human right to material interests, implementation and interpretation has the potential for prioritizing private economic interests over public human rights interests, including education, increasing the potential for conflicts.

Since at least the 1980s the U.S., supported by the European Union and Japan, sought to tie intellectual property to international trade policy.[105] The impetus was the increasing economic dependence for these economies on the sale of intellectual property, such as copyrighted goods.[106] This economic consideration, along with the fact that many developing states had weak or no intellectual property laws, caused concern in developed states. While Berne was an important step toward international copyright protection, it provided for national treatment. Many developing states had weak or no copyright law and had not ratified Berne evidencing a weakness in the international intellectual property regime.[107]

In 1994, at the Uruguay round of trade negotiations for the General Agreement on Tariffs and Trade (GATT) intellectual property was included under TRIPS and the World Trade Organization (WTO) was created.[108] In order to reap the benefits of free and open trade, in essence a most favored nation trading status, a state would have to join the WTO.[109] Membership in the WTO required agreeing to the requirements of TRIPS.[110] TRIPS incorporated Berne Articles 1 through 21 except for moral rights in Article 6*bis*.[111] Thus, many developing states had to agree to incorporate the requirements of Berne in order to reap free trade benefits.[112] But, unlike Berne, TRIPS provides for coercive measures for failure to comply through

---

105. DAVID C. RICHARDS, INTELLECTUAL PROPERTY RIGHTS AND GLOBAL CAPITALISM: THE POLITICAL ECONOMY OF THE TRIPS AGREEMENT 123 (2004).

106. *See* Ruth Okediji, *Toward an International Fair Use Doctrine*, 39 COLUM. J. TRANSNAT'L L. 75, 81 (2000) (Okediji).

107. Robert J. Gutowski, *The Marriage of Intellectual Property and International Trade in the TRIPS Agreement: Strange Bedfellows or a Match Made in Heaven?*, 47 BUFF. L. REV. 713, 720 (1999) (Gutowski).

108. Julie Cheng, *China's Copyright System: Rising to the Spirit of TRIPs Requires an Internal Focus and World Trade Organization Membership*, 21 FORDHAM INT'L L. J. 1941, 1948-1949 (1998) (Cheng); Jared R. Silverman, *Multilateral Resolution over Unilateral Retaliation: Adjudicating the Use of Section 301 before the WTO*, 17 U. PA. J. INT'L ECON. L. 233, fns 101 and 102 (1996) (Silverman).

109. Amy Nelson, *Is There an International Solution to Intellectual Property Protection For Plants?* 37 GEO. WASH. INT'L L. REV. 997, 1008 (2005) (Nelson).

110. *Ibid.*

111. TRIPS, *supra* n. 12 at Article 9; Fawcett & Torremans, *supra* n. 14 at 480.

112. From 1994 to 2006, fifty-seven additional states have ratified Berne. www.wipo.int/treaties/en/ShowResults.jsp?lang¼en&treaty_id¼15.

trade sanctions. Further, the WTO provides a dispute resolution mechanism.[113]

In 1999, around the time that the transitional arrangements provided for in Article 65 of TRIPS started to expire,[114] ECOSOC, the United Nations agency responsible for the oversight of the UDHR, and the ICESCR, was being petitioned by certain non-governmental organizations (NGOs) regarding the impact of globalization on human rights. In response to these concerns, several studies, reports and academic articles were published discussing the potential conflict between the realization of human rights and certain trade agreements, in particular TRIPS.[115]

In examining the potential conflict between TRIPS and the human right to education, because TRIPS incorporates Berne Articles 1 through 21, except for moral rights in Article 6*bis*,[116] it is necessary to examine some of the relevant provisions of Berne. For example, Article 8 of Berne provides authors with *the exclusive right of making and of authorizing the translation of their works throughout the term of protection of their rights in the original works*.[117] Article 9 of Berne provides authors with *the exclusive right of authorizing the reproduction of these works, in any manner or form* and further protects the *normal exploitation of the work* from exceptions to this exclusive right.[118] Accordingly, Berne protects what amounts to a means of

---

113. Gutowski, *supra* n. 107 at 714-715.
114. The language in Article 65 of TRIPS provides: "1. Subject to the provisions of paragraphs 2, 3 and 4, no Member shall be obliged to apply the provisions of this Agreement before the expiry of a general period of one year following the date of entry into force of the WTO Agreement. 2. A developing country Member is entitled to delay for a further period of four years the date of application, as defined in paragraph 1, of the provisions of this Agreement other than Article 3, 4 and 5." TRIPS, *supra* n. 12.
115. J. Oloka Onyango & Deepika Udagama, *The Realization of Economic, Social and Cultural Rights: Globalization and Its Impact on the Full Enjoyment of Human Rights, Final Report of the U.N. Sub-Commission on the Promotion and Protection of Human Rights*, U.N. Doc. E/ CN.4/Sub.2/2000/13 (2000) (Onyango and Udagama); David Weissbrodt & Kell Schoff, *Human Rights Approach To Intellectual Property Protection: The Genesis and Application of Sub-Commission Resolution 2000/7*, 5 MINN. INTELL. PROP. REV. 1, 26 (2003) (Weissbrodt and Schoff); *Globalization and Human Rights, Joint Oral Statement by Lutheran World Federation, Habitat International Coalition and International Commission of Jurists to the Sub-Commission on the Promotion and Protection of Human Rights*, August 8, 2000, UN DOC. E/CN.4/Sub.2/2000/NGO/14, at para. 2 (*Lutheran World*); Intellectual Property and Human Rights, Sub-Commission on Human Rights, UN Doc. E/CN.4/Sub.2.Res/2001.21 (August 16, 2001) (Resolution 2001/21); ECOSOC Issues, *supra* n. 98 at 2; Helfer, *Framework, supra* n. 94 at 997, 982, 985-986 (There is a potential for conflict) (citing to Resolution 2000/7, *supra* n. 51 recognizing potential conflict between human rights, such as education, and TRIPS and Resolution 2001/21, identifying "actual or potential conflicts" between human rights obligations and TRIPS, and asserting "need to clarify the scope and meaning of several provisions of the TRIPS Agreement").
116. TRIPS, *supra* n. 12 at Article 9.
117. Berne, *supra* n. 13.
118. *Ibid.*

achieving the material interests of authors. These exclusive rights are limited in time to the author's life plus fifty years.[119]

Although it has been observed that the principal object of Berne and TRIPS has been to protect private interests through a harmonized intellectual property system,[120] public interests, such as the human right to education, are protected as exceptions to the private rights. That said, the exceptions in Berne Articles 10 and 13[121] for education may not be *prejudicial to the rights of these authors to obtain equitable remuneration.* Accordingly, although TRIPS Article 13[122] allowing for exceptions (discussed below) does not contain the equitable remuneration language, exceptions are subordinated in Berne Articles 10 and 13 and incorporated by reference in TRIPS Article 9.[123]

TRIPS does protect access rights, which are necessary for education. For example:

> Article 7
> Objectives
> The protection and enforcement of intellectual property rights should contribute to the promotion of technological innovation and to the transfer and dissemination of technology, to the mutual advantage of producers and users of technological knowledge and in a manner conducive to social and economic welfare, and to a balance of rights and obligations.[124]

Article 7 addresses access, through language such as the "promotion of. … innovation" and "transfer and dissemination of technology." It also seeks a balanced approach focusing on the mutual advantages for owners and users.[125]

Further, Article 8 provides:

> Article 8
> Principles
> Members may, in formulating or amending their laws and regulations, adopt measures necessary to protect public health and nutrition, and to promote the public interest in sectors of vital importance to their socio-economic and technological development, provided that such measures are consistent with the provisions of this Agreement.
> Appropriate measures, provided that they are consistent with the provisions of this Agreement, may be needed to prevent the abuse of

---

119. *Ibid.*
120. For example, *see* HC *Report, supra* n. 66 at para. 22.
121. Berne, *supra* n. 13.
122. TRIPS, *supra* n. 12.
123. *Ibid.*
124. The US ratified TRIPS in 1994. The UK and France ratified TRIPS in 1995.
125. *HC Report, supra* n. 66 at para. 16.

intellectual property rights by right holders or the resort to practices which unreasonably restrain trade or adversely affect the international transfer of technology.[126]

Article 8 is sensitive to access issues advocated by human rights groups with regard to what amounts to a fair dealing provision.[127] Article 13 does, however, present an access problem in that it limits fair dealing to exceptions that do not unreasonably prejudice the legitimate interests of the rights holder.[128] Specifically, Article 13 has a three-part test applicable to the material interests of authors:[129] (1) the limitations or exceptions are confined to certain special cases; (2) they do not conflict with a normal exploitation of the work; and (3) they do not unreasonably prejudice the legitimate interests of the right holder.[130]

A limitation or an exception is consistent with Article 13 only if it fulfils each of the three conditions.[131] With respect to the first prong, the term "certain special cases" is defined by referring to the ordinary meaning of the terms in their context and in the light of its object and purpose.[132] This has been held to mean:

> a limitation or exception in national legislation should be clearly defined and should be narrow in its scope and reach. On the other hand, a limitation or exception may be compatible with the first condition even if it pursues a special purpose whose underlying legitimacy in a normative sense cannot be discerned. The wording of Article 13's first condition does not imply passing a judgment on the legitimacy of the exceptions in dispute.[133]

The second prong, that the exception not conflict with the normal exploitation of the work, has been held to mean:

> an exception or limitation to an exclusive right in domestic legislation rises to the level of a conflict with a normal exploitation of the work … if uses, that in principle are covered by that right but exempted under the

---

126. TRIPS, *supra* n. 12 at Article 8.
127. *See* Molly Land, *Rebalancing TRIPS*, 33 MICH. J. INT'L L. 433, 444-445 (2012) (Land) (addressing lack of use of TRIPS flexibilities relating to copyright and the human right to education).
128. Article 13 provides: "Members shall confine limitations or exceptions to exclusive rights to certain special cases which do not conflict with a normal exploitation of the work and do not unreasonably prejudice the legitimate interests of the right holder."
129. *WTO Panel Report, supra* n. 16. The Panel Report does not address moral rights nor economic interests of performers, phonogram producers and broadcasting organizations. Haochen Sun, *Overcoming the Achilles Heel of Copyright Law*, 5 NW. J. TECH. & INTELL. PROP. 265, 287 (2007) (Sun).
130. *WTO Panel Report, supra* n. 16.
131. *Ibid.,* at para. 6.74.
132. *Ibid.,* at para. 6.107; Sun, *supra* n. 129 at 305.
133. *WTO Panel Report, supra* n. 16 at para. 6.107; Sun, *supra* n. 129 at 306-307.

exception or limitation, enter into economic competition with the ways that right holders normally extract economic value from that right to the work ... and thereby deprive them of significant or tangible commercial gains.[134]

This includes actual or potential effects on that market.[135] Accordingly, economic evidence that the rights holder can or may, in the near future, extract economic value that is significant would be sufficient to create a conflict with an exception, such as one for educational materials.[136] Conversely, if there were little or no economic value to extract, this prong would not be met.

The third prong, whether the exceptions unreasonably prejudice the legitimate interests of the right holder has been defined as:

[W]hether the prejudice caused by the exemptions to the legitimate interests of the right holder is of an unreasonable level ... . [M]arket conditions [may be taken] into account, to the extent feasible, [in addition to] the actual as well as the potential prejudice caused by the exemptions, as a prerequisite for determining whether the extent or degree of prejudice is of an unreasonable level.[137]

The second and third prong are, perhaps the most troublesome as they both emphasize an economic analysis but do not provide states with much guidance. Accordingly, Article 13 has the same problem of a lack of certainty that domestic fair dealing/fair use doctrines, allowed in Berne and TRIPS via Article 10 of Berne,[138] have.[139] While this may lead to some uncertainty, it also has the benefit of being flexible enough to adjust to various needs in the international community.[140]

Finally, the provisions of Berne (the 1971 Appendix to the Paris Act Revision of the Berne Convention), incorporated in TRIPS provides for compulsory licenses intended to address some of the concerns the developing states expressed regarding the implementation of intellectual property laws

---

134. *WTO Panel Report, supra* n. 16 at para. 6.183-6.184. It has been observed that this may exclude a *de minimis* economic loss but that the second prong does not take public interests into consideration. Sun, *supra* n. 129 at 295.
135. *WTO Panel Report, supra* n. 16 at paras. 6.183-6.184.
136. *Ibid.,* at para. 6.180-6.187; Carter, *supra* n. 3 at 331-332.
137. *WTO Panel Report, supra* n. 16 at para. 6.236.
138. Berne, *supra* n. 13; *HC Report, supra* n. 66 at paras. 11 and 18; TRIPS, *supra* n. 12 at Articles 8(2), 27(3)(b) and 31; Chidi Oguamanam, *Beyond Theories: Intellectual Property Dynamics in the Global Knowledge Economy,* 9 WAKE FOREST INTELL. PROP. L.J. 104, 110-111, 140 (2009); Land, *supra* n. 127 at 444-445.
139. Chon, *supra* n. 6 at 837-839. Even the United States "fair use" doctrine (17 U.S.C. §110) hailed as being quite flexible (Carter, *supra* n. 3 at 327-328) has had limited application. (*See* generally L. Ashley Aull, *The Costs of Privilege: Defining Price in the Market for Educational Copyright Use,* 9 MINN. J.L. SCI. & TECH. 573 (2008) on some of the problems in applying a fair use exception for education.)
140. Land, *supra* n. 127 at 439-440.

conflicting with human rights obligations and public policies[141] such as advancing education. However, the compulsory license system under Berne/TRIPS has proven to be ineffective. The problem with the compulsory license system under Berne/TRIPS is three-fold: First, this system is dysfunctional due to unnecessary complexity[142] causing a lack of understanding.[143] Second, there is the TRIPS-plus problem where political pressure, economic pressure and nonmultilateral agreements circumvent the TRIPS system resulting in few developing states seeking the possible benefits of compulsory licenses and a greater potential for conflicts.[144] Third, compulsory licensing and other exceptions[145] require equitable remuneration even for educational purposes in states where this may be difficult if not impossible.[146] These problems have led commentators to state that compulsory licenses provided for in Berne have proven to be ineffective.[147]

11.6   THE INTERNAL CONFLICT

For purposes of this chapter, the internal conflict exists in situations where one document contains two or more provisions that appear to or do, in fact, conflict.[148] Potentially, the UDHR, ICESCR and TRIPS all contain internal conflicts. For example, Articles 26, 27(1) and 27(2) of the UDHR create a potential for conflict between the human right to education and moral and

---

141. HELFER AND AUSTIN, MAPPING, *supra* n. 6 at 338.
142. Dina Halajian, *Inadequacy of TRIPS & the Compulsory License: Why Broad Compulsory Licensing Is Not a Viable Solution to the Access to Medicine Problem*, 38 BROOK. J. INT'L L. 1191, 1202 (2013) (Halajian); on complexity *see* HELFER AND AUSTIN, MAPPING, *supra* n. 6 at 337, 340.
143. Chon, *supra* n. 6 at 806, 828-829 (2007); Molly Beutz Land, *Protecting Rights Online*, 34 YALE J. INT'L L. 1, 5-6 (2009) (Land, *Online*) (compulsory license ineffective regarding access to medicines).
144. Land, *supra* n. 127 at 434, 444 (2012) (stating threats of costly litigation and possible sanctions as a reason for over compliance and lack of utilization of TRIPS flexibilities); Halajian, *supra* n. 142 at 1204, 1212-1213 (2013); Sean Baird, *Magic and Hope: Relaxing TRIPS-Plus Provisions to Promote Access to Affordable Pharmaceuticals*, 33 B.C. J.L. & SOC. JUST. 107, 123-124 (2013).
145. Daniel Gervais, *Fair Use, Fair Dealing, Fair Principles: Efforts to Conceptualize Exceptions and Limitations to Copyright*, 57 J. COPYRIGHT SOC'Y U.S.A. 499, 515-517 (2010) (citing to *WTO Panel Report, supra* n. 16 at para. 6-180.
146. Chon, *supra* n. 6 at 835; Yu, *Reconceptualizing, supra* n. 23 at 1100-01.
147. HELFER & AUSTIN, MAPPING, *supra* n. 6 at 340 (2011) (citing to Ruth Okediji, *The International Copyright System: Limitations, Exceptions and Public Interest Considerations for Developing Countries*, at 29 (2006), available at: http://www.iprsonline.org; SAM RICKETSON & JANE GINSBURG, INTERNATIONAL COPYRIGHT AND NEIGHBOURING RIGHTS: THE BERNE CONVENTION AND BEYOND, at 957 (2006)).
148. Professor Yu has defined the internal conflict as conflicts within the human rights system and external conflicts as conflicts between intellectual property systems and the human rights system. Yu, *Reconceptualizing, supra* n. 23 at 1094.

material interests of authors.[149] Articles 13 and 14 of the ICESCR granting the human right to education appears to conflict with Article 15(1)(c) of that same document granting as a human right an authors' right to moral and material interests resulting from any scientific, literary or artistic production.[150] There have been attempts to prioritize these human rights, for example, by identifying core human rights obligations such as health, food and education.[151] The problem with such an approach is that it fails to recognize the interrelationship of some human rights such as between material interests creating an incentive to increase the quantity and quality of the works of authors including educational materials.[152] Rather than prioritizing, when such a conflict does arise, the conflict resolution approach suggested by General Comment No. 17 is a balancing test:

> The right of authors to benefit from the protection of the moral and material interests resulting from their scientific, literary and artistic productions cannot be isolated from the other rights recognized in the Covenant. States parties are therefore obliged to strike an adequate balance between their obligations under article 15, paragraph 1 (c), on one hand, and under the other provisions of the Covenant, on the other hand, with a view to promoting and protecting the full range of rights guaranteed in the Covenant. In striking this balance, the private interests of authors should not be unduly favoured and the public interest in enjoying broad access to their productions should be given due consideration. States parties should therefore ensure that their legal or other regimes for the protection of the moral and material interests resulting from one's scientific, literary or artistic productions constitute no impediment to their ability to comply with their core obligations in relation to the rights to food, health and education, as well as to take part in cultural life and to enjoy the benefits of scientific progress and its applications, or any other right enshrined in the Covenant. Ultimately, intellectual property is a social product and has a social function. States parties thus have a duty to prevent unreasonably high costs for access to essential medicines, plant seeds or other means of food production, or

---

149. Mirela V. Hristova, *Are Intellectual Property Rights Human Rights? Patent Protection and the Right to Health*, 93 J. PAT. & TRADEMARK OFF. SOC'Y 339, 346-347 (2011) (regarding the potential for conflict in general and relating to the human right to health.) (Hristova).

150. GC17, *supra* n. 51 at para. 35; Peter K. Yu, *"The International Enclosure Movement"*, 82 IND. L.J. 827, 866 (2007).

151. ECOSOC Issues, *supra* n. 98 at para. 12.

152. Yu, *Reconceptualizing, supra* n. 23 at 1078 (regarding overlapping nature of certain human rights).

for schoolbooks and learning materials, from undermining the rights of large segments of the population to health, food and education.[153]

Similarly, the TRIPS Preamble,[154] Articles 7 and 8, promoting innovation and dissemination arguably necessary for and, thus, encompassing the human right to education,[155] potentially conflict with authors' rights under Berne Articles 8 and 9,[156] incorporated in TRIPS, for exclusive rights of translation and reproduction. As seen above regarding the limitation or exception provisions in Article 13 of TRIPS a balancing test is applied.

Utilizing a balancing test as suggested, a state may implement domestic copyright laws that provide less protection in terms of years or more exceptions to protection for purposes of education in order to strike a balance that reflects that state's social and economic condition and priorities.[157] A state lagging in education may decide to provide weaker copyright laws than a state with relatively high education achievement but, perhaps, an economic dependence on copyright industries.

Such a balancing approach is not new and is similar to the balancing approach for internal conflicts in the domestic setting. For example, U.S. court decisions regarding conflicting constitutional rights provide an example of a balancing approach. The First Amendment of the U.S. Constitution, the right to free speech and freedom of the press, may conflict with the copyright provision in the same document but the courts balance the interests to be protected in these provisions based upon the circumstances of each case to determine which provision should prevail.[158] That said, the potential internal conflicts between human rights in the UDHR and the ICESCR may be easier to balance given the flexibility allowed for the provision of those rights. It is the moral and material interests that are accorded human rights status, not a property right as accorded under TRIPS.[159] While the external conflicts, discussed below, are more challenging in terms of human rights conflicting with intellectual property rights, as articulated in the TRIPS agreement, this does not mean to say there is a fundamental conflict.[160] The

---

153. GC17, *supra* n. 51 at para. 35. Also *see* GC17 at paras. 22-24 suggesting a balancing test for the conflicts between Article 15(1) and (2).

154. *Recognizing the underlying public policy objectives of national systems for the protection of intellectual property, including developmental and technological objectives ... .* TRIPS, *supra* n. 12.

155. Chon, *supra* n. 6 at 818-820 (citing to Ruth L. Okediji, *The International Copyright System: Limitations, Exceptions and Public Interest Considerations for Developing Countries* 2 (2006), available at http://www.unctad.org/en/docs/iteipc200610_en.pdf.).

156. Berne, *supra* n. 13.

157. Hristova, *supra* n. 149.

158. *Harper & Row Publishers, Inc. v. Nation Enterprises*, 471 US 539 (1985); *Eldred v. Ashcroft*, 537 US 186. 218-221 (2003).

159. Yu, *Reconceptualizing, supra* n. 23 at 1089.

160. *See* Yu, *Reconceptualizing, supra* n. 23 at 1075-1076 and Paul L.C. Torremans, *Is Copyright a Human Right?*, 2007 MICH. ST. L. REV. 271, 272 (2007) (Torremans) for an explanation of the fundamental conflict position.

flexibilities for intellectual property systems[161] articulated in TRIPS, specifically Articles 7, 8 and 13, provide for coexistence if the potentially conflicting interests are properly balanced.[162]

11.7   THE EXTERNAL CONFLICT

The external conflict exists in situations where the separate documents have potentially conflicting provisions. However, the possible conflict between TRIPS copyright protection and the human right to education as articulated in the UDHR and the ICESCR is less in the language of TRIPS, which provides for public interest exceptions as discussed above, than in the implementation and practices under TRIPS. TRIPS incorporates Berne, except for moral rights, which sets forth the minimal protection allowed. Domestic legislation may, and often does, set forth greater protections. For example, Berne requires a basic term of protection of the author's life plus fifty years.[163] Political and economic pressure, however, may be exerted on developing states to provide domestic legislation that gives more than the minimal protection to conform to the developed states copyright terms, in some cases the author's life plus seventy years and to limit exceptions allowed under TRIPS;[164] the TRIPS-plus problem.

The TRIPS-plus problem has been exacerbated by the digital era where dissemination is faster and easier. Like the advent of the printing press, we are attempting to adjust and balance public interests with private rights.[165] The response to the digital era has been more intellectual property restrictions to limit digital piracy, such as bans on circumventing technological

---

161. Yu, *Reconceptualizing, supra* n. 23 at 1093.
162. Torremans, *supra* n. 160 at 277, 280-281. On coexistence of the private material interests and the public dissemination interests *see* Estelle Derclaye, *Intellectual Property Rights and Human Rights: Coinciding and Cooperating*, in INTELLECTUAL PROPERTY AND HUMAN RIGHTS 133, 134 (Paul L.C. Torremans eds, 2008) ("[H]uman rights and [intellectual property rights] do not 'simply' coexist but in fact most of them coincide from the outset, that is, they have the same goal … and as a result, in most cases, because of this similarity or identity of goals, they even 'cooperate' … "); Daniel J. Gervais, *Intellectual Property and Human Rights: Learning to Live Together*, in INTELLECTUAL PROPERTY AND HUMAN RIGHTS, 3, 12 (Paul L.C. Torremans ed., 2008) ("Human rights and intellectual property were natural law cousins owing to their shared filiation with equity").
163. Berne, *supra* n. 13 at Article 7(1).
164. Lawrence Helfer, *"Regime Shifting: The TRIPS Agreement and the New Dynamics of International Intellectual Property Law Making"*, 29 YALE J. INT'L LAW 1, 24 (2003) (Helfer, *Regime Shifting*); *HC Report, supra* n. 66 at para. 27.
165. Court of Justice of European Union (ECJ), *Scarlet Extended SA v. SABAM*, CASE C-70/10 (November 24, 2011); Wenwei Guan, *When Copyrights Meet Human Rights: "Cyberspace Article 23" and Hong Kong's Copyright Protection in the Digital Era*, 42 HONG KONG L.J. 785, 793(2012); Yu, *Nonmultilateral, supra* n. 94 at 1079-1080.

measures to prevent infringement primarily through the use of nonmultilateral and plurilateral agreements which go beyond the requirements of TRIPS and reduce the flexibility in TRIPS creating a greater potential for conflicts with human rights obligations.[166] These TRIPS-plus type agreements further curtail access to knowledge, which directly implicates the human right to education in emphasizing protection of copyrights, databases and technological systems.[167] By circumventing the multilateral system, such as that utilized for TRIPS, the perception, if not the reality, is that of exerting undue influence by developed states over developing states to emphasize commercial rights in intellectual property systems over human rights obligations.[168] That said, while the promise of the digital era for increased access to knowledge is a distinct possibility, absent attempts to circumvent such access, it may not yet be a realistic option for some developing states which lack the supportive infrastructure.[169]

Further problems increasing the potential for conflicts include the global financial crisis of 2008 and the recent coronavirus pandemic of 2020 creating economic contraction. Limited resources often are directed to what are perceived as the most pressing needs, such as health care, food and shelter. This is understandable but problematic as education is necessary to reduce the need to divert resources to health care, food and shelter. It has long been recognized that the human right to education is tied to other human rights, such as health care, food and shelter[170] as well as reducing poverty and for a properly functioning democracy.[171] The importance of education as a human right and as necessary to achieve other human rights is reflected in the Millennium Development Goals established following the Millennium Summit of the United Nations in 2000 with the goal to *[e]nsure that, by 2015, children everywhere, boys and girls alike, will be able to complete a full course of primary schooling.*[172] While there has been some progress, there are still significant educational gaps between developed and developing

---

166. *See* generally Yu, *Nonmultilateral, supra* n. 94; Anti-Counterfeiting Trade Agreement, Chapter II, section 5, Article 27 (final version May 2011) available at: http://www.ustr.gov/acta. (As of the date of this paper not in force.) The Anti-Counterfeiting Trade Agreement does reference TRIPS at Article 1 so, theoretically, the education exception may be viable under its terms.

167. Yu, *Nonmultilateral, supra* n. 94 at 1079-1080 (2012); Carter, *supra* n. 3 at 314-315 (2009); Land, *Online, supra* n. 143 at 5-6.

168. Yu, *Nonmultilateral, supra* n. 94 at 1085-1091.

169. *See* HELFER AND AUSTIN, MAPPING, *supra* n. 6 at 360.

170. *Ibid.,* at 320-322.

171. *Ibid.,* at 321, 323-324 (2011); THOMAS PIKETTY, CAPITAL IN THE TWENTY-FIRST CENTURY, 70-71 (2014).

172. Millennium Goals, Goal 2: Achieve Universal Primary Education Target 2.A available at: http://www.un.org/millenniumgoals/education.shtml (last accessed September 14, 2019).

states as well as deficiencies in the quality of education.[173] The ability of states to achieve this human right goal has been greatly reduced by the financial crisis of 2008 which economic effects linger on today[174] as well as the coronavirus pandemic and its economic impact. This coupled with the increased costs associated with strong intellectual property law,[175] as required by TRIPS and nonmultilateral trade agreements, could reduce access to critical instructional materials and increase the conflicts between the human right to education and intellectual property laws, particularly copyright laws.

Some have argued that a solution to this problem is to change international intellectual property agreements to reflect a maximum standard of protection.[176] Yet, the history of international copyright law has taught that such a lack of flexibility inherent in this solution will lack consensus. The more realistic solution is political pressure through the international community directed toward those that attempt to gain TRIPS-plus protection in developing states. As Charles H. Malik stated with regard to the UDHR, more has been gained through such political pressure tactics for the

---

173. Barro, Robert J. & Jong-Wha Lee, *A New Data Set of Educational Attainment in the World, 1950-2010,* Working, Paper 15902, National Bureau of Economic Research, Cambridge, MA; Summary—Expert Group Meeting, "Expert review of draft reports of the Secretary-General for the 2011 ECOSOC High-Level Segment on education" (March 18, 2011, New York, UNHQ) (Ms. Lourdes Arizpe (CDP member and Professor, National Autonomous University, Mexico)) 3; Levy Santiago & Norbert Schady. *Latin America's Social Policy Challenge: Education, Social Insurance, Redistribution,* 27(2) J. ECON. PERSPS. 193, 197-200 (2013); Theme of the annual ministerial review: implementing the internationally agreed goals and commitments in regard to education, Report of the Secretary-General, Distr.: General (April 18, 2011), UN Doc. E/2011/83, paras. 29-31; HELFER AND AUSTIN, MAPPING, *supra* n. 6 at 332-335.

174. Education International, *Education and the Global Economic Crisis: Summary of Results of the Follow-Up Survey* (2009) 2, available at: download.ei-ie.org/.../ 05March10_Impactcrisisreport_followup_MDK; World Bank, World Development Report 2014, Risk and Opportunity: Managing Risk for Development, 49, 204, available at: https://openknowledge.worldbank.org/handle/10986/16092 (last accessed September 14, 2019); OECD Education Indicators in Focus (December 2013); Tenth meeting of the Working Group on Education for All (EFA), Concept paper on the Impact of the Economic and Financial Crisis on Education1, Paris, December 9-11, 2009, available at: www.unesco.org > High-Level Group > Ninth meeting; Summary—Expert Group Meeting (last accessed September 14, 2019), "Expert review of draft reports of the Secretary-General for the 2011 ECOSOC High-Level Segment on education" (March 18, 2011, New York, UNHQ) (Ms Lourdes Arizpe (CDP member and Professor, National Autonomous University, Mexico)) 3.

175. Chon, *supra* n. 6 at 833-834.

176. For example the Treaty on Access to Knowledge (May 9, 2005) (draft) at Articles 3-9 and 3-10 limits the term to the minimum term required by TRIPS under Articles 9-13, available at: www.cptech.org/a2k/a2k_treaty_may9.pdf (A2K) (last accessed September 14, 2019); *see* Helfer, *Framework, supra* n. 94 at 1013-1014 (discussing the A2K Treaty; Laurence Helfer, *Human Rights and Intellectual Property: Conflict or Coexistence,* 5 MINN. INTELL. PROP. REV. 47, 58-59 (2003) (discussing, the maximum standard of protection approach).

advancement of human rights goals than attempts to obtain consensus necessary for a binding convention.[177]

Assuming that there is a true conflict between TRIPS, or TRIPS-plus agreements, and the human right to education how might such a conflict be addressed? The balancing approach, as indicated above in General Comment No. 17 regarding internal conflicts in the ICESCR as well as the WTO balancing approach discussed above relating to TRIPS Article 13[178] seems to be the consensus. Additionally, the WTO has applied a balancing test regarding conflicting rights in Appellate Body in Korea—Various Measures on Beef[179] and U.S.—Measures Affecting the Cross-Border Supply of Gambling and Betting Services[180] where the WTO Dispute Resolution Panel articulated a three-part balancing test including (a) the importance of interests or values that the challenged measure is intended to protect. (With respect to this requirement, the Appellate Body has suggested that, if the value or interest pursued is considered important, it is more likely that the measure is "necessary"); (b) the extent to which the challenged measure contributes to the realization of the end pursued by that measure (in relation to this requirement, the Appellate Body has suggested that the greater the extent to which the measure contributes to the end pursued the more likely that the measure is "necessary"); and (c) the trade impact of the challenged measure (with regard to this requirement, the Appellate Body has said that, if the measure has a relatively slight trade impact, it is likely that the measure is "necessary." The Appellate Body has also indicated that whether a reasonably available WTO-consistent alternative measure exists must be taken into consideration in applying this requirement.[181] This is consistent with the balancing test suggested in by the ECOSOC in General Comment No. 17 for internal conflicts[182] and the balancing approach utilized by the WTO for limitations or an exceptions consistent with TRIPS Article 13[183] discussed in section 11.5 above.

Applying this test to the conflict between TRIPS and the right to education:

(a) The importance of the interest in education would be highly ranked given the social, political and economic ramifications of an educated public.[184] Additionally, the history of copyright indicates a strong interest in encouraging creation for the purpose of

---

177. GLENDON, *supra* n. 18 at 25.
178. *WTO Panel Report, supra* n. 16.
179. WT/DS19/AB/R, adopted January 10, 2001.
180. WT/DS285/AG/R, April 7, 2005.
181. United States—Measures Affecting the Cross-Border Supply of Gambling and Betting Services, WT/DS285/R at 236.
182. GC17, *supra* n. 51, at para. 35.
183. *WTO Panel Report, supra* n. 16.
184. GC11, *supra* n. 44.

education.[185] Finally TRIPS itself recognizes the necessity of the transfer of information, a function of the educational process.[186]

(b) Access to educational materials does contribute greatly to education according to the World Development Report 2004.[187] Therefore, making those materials available at a reduced cost or for free to realize the goal of education in a state with a depressed economy may be "necessary."

(c) Trade impact would be negligible in the situation of a depressed economy where neither the population nor the state have the ability to pay for educational materials as discussed in more detail below.

Accordingly, applying the above balancing test and the Article 13 balancing test of exceptions being limited in scope, and the two economic prongs of not conflicting with the normal exploitation of the work nor prejudicing the legitimate (material) interests it is apparent that, even under TRIPS with an emphasis on private rights there should be no TRIPS violation and no conflict in situations where there is no economic gain as in a market failure situation.

While the TRIPS balancing tests and the GC17 balancing test are phrased differently, they all generally require: (1) Addressing the importance of the competing interests, in context, so one interest does not unduly impede another. For purpose of the topics in this chapter, the interests would be education balanced with the material interest aspects of copyright. (2) Examining whether the reduction of authors' material interests is necessary to contribute to the realization of the human right to education. In a state where market conditions make such a trade-off unnecessary the balance would tip in favor of authors' material interests under copyright laws. But, in a state where it would be necessary to divert public or private funds from another important right, such as food, to pay for learning materials, the balance should tip in favor of a reduction of authors' material interests. (3) Establishing the amount of commercial gain or other economic value that has been lost by the author due to the reduction of authors' material interests necessary to achieve the human right to education. This third prong is critical because of the economic emphasis of TRIPS which correlates with the material interests of authors, a human right. If there is little to no commercial gain to be had in a state due to market failure there will be little to no material interests for authors, tipping the balance in favor of educational interests.

---

185. *Millar v. Taylor*, 98 E.R. 201 at p. 207.
186. *See* TRIPS, *supra* n. 12 at Articles 7-8.
187. World Development Report 2004, *supra* n. 5.

11.8   MARKET FAILURE AND THE FALSE CONFLICT
            PARADIGM

As indicated with the balancing tests above, the potential "conflict" between
the right to education and laws implemented to protect authors' moral and
material interests often does not exist due to market failure. Market failure
occurs when there is no market for a good either due to free riders or a price
beyond the market's ability to pay. In the free-rider situation, market failure
stems from the fact that information is non-rivalrous, that is, once it is
created it is inexhaustible; the making of a copy of information does not
deprive the owner of the original. However, if the cost of copying is
inexpensive, in terms of time and money, free riders (people who copy a
creation without paying for the right to do so) will reduce the material
interests of the author.[188] In the situation where a market does not have an
ability to pay, there can be no material interest, commercial gain or normal
exploitation due to market failure. In the case of market failure due to a
state's inability to afford to pay there would be a false conflict regarding
economic interests but moral interests would still have to be protected.

Certainly, from the perspective of the interpretation of the ICESCR the
false conflict paradigm would seem to comply with the General Comment
No. 17 balancing test, giving due regard to the importance of education while
at the same time recognizing that the material interests of authors of
instructional materials have little to no economic value in market failure
situations. This does not diminish the material interests of authors; rather it
accepts the economic reality of the market failure situation. In a market
where the population or the state has an ability to pay there would be an
adverse impact on authors' material interests and such interests would be
given more weight.

Even under the WTO balancing tests regarding TRIPS in the market
failure situation due to an inability to pay we see little to no conflict with a
normal exploitation of the work, economic competition or the deprivation of
significant or tangible commercial gains as required under the WTO
balancing test for TRIPS, Article 13.[189] Nor would there be a significant trade
impact as required in Various Measures on Beef[190] and Measures Affecting
the Cross-Border Supply of Gambling and Betting Services[191] as there can be
little to no trade with a market that cannot afford to buy the goods in
question.[192] The real problem in the false conflict because of market failure

---

188. Wendy J. Gordon, *Fair Use and Market Failure: A Structural and Economic Analysis of
     the Betamax Case and Its Predecessors*, 82 COLUM. L. REV. 1600, 1610-1612 (1982);
     see Linda J. Lacy, *Of Bread and Roses and Copyright*, 1989 DUKE L.J. 1532,
     1553-1554 (1989).
189. *WTO Panel Report, supra* n. 16 at paras. 6.183-6.184.
190. WT/DS19/AB/R, adopted January 10, 2001.
191. WT/DS285/AG/R, April 7, 2005.
192. *WTO Panel Report, supra* n. 16 at paras. 6.183-6.184.

for inability to pay situation arises from parallel imports due to free riders.[193] Accordingly, the state where there is such market failure would be allowed access to copyrighted materials for little or nothing, but would have to ensure that the protected instructional materials necessary for education are not exported for commercial gain to a state where there is no market failure.

Economic and political events arising from the financial crisis of 2008 and the coronavirus pandemic of 2020 have enhanced the probability of a market failure scenario. While enrollment in primary education has improved, the quality of primary education is on a downward trend due, in part, to decreased funding.[194] This lack of funding appears to be due to market failure in some states. Until there is an improvement in political and economic stability, market failure will persist and, indeed probably expand. If this is the case, there will be no material interests of authors to protect in market failure states. While increased enrollment is encouraging, achieving the human right goal of free primary education is more than just an enrollment head count; it requires a certain level of quality.[195] This quality may be met, in part, through educational materials which are copyrighted but in a market failure situation there is an inability to pay. As stated above, the alleged conflict between authors' material interests and the right to education in a market failure scenario is a false conflict but we have yet to see any case law which addresses the issue of false conflict.

11.9   CONCLUSION

While there is a potential for conflicts between the human right to education and the human right to material interests for authors, as realized through international and domestic copyright law, these conflicts seem to be more of a political or academic problem than a legal and economic one. Internal and external conflicts, when they do arise, may be resolved through a balancing test where the competing interests are weighed in a case-by-case situation. This provides the necessary flexibility to address the variety of factors that may have an impact, such as market conditions and educational needs. Many of the alleged conflicts will fall into the false conflict paradigm given the fact that most of the states with an acute need for imported, copyrighted instructional materials for educational purposes have partial or full market

---

193. Parallel imports in this context is the problem where copyrighted goods are created by without material compensation in one market, say a state where there is market failure, and imported to another state, where there is no market failure, for commercial gain. In that situation there would be an impact on trade.

194. MDG 2: Achieve universal primary education (2017) https://www.mdgmonitor.org/mdg-2-achieve-universal-primary-education/ (last accessed September 14, 2019); The University of Iowa Center for Human Rights (UICHR), #46—ACCESS TO EDUCATION HUMAN RIGHTS INDEX #46, 26 TRNATLCP 5 (2016).

195. Commentary, *supra* n. 33; GC13 *supra* n. 48.

failure due to an inability to pay. In such situations, there is little to no material interest to protect for authors as well as little to no trade impact. International law as well as most domestic laws provide for the economic reality analysis suggested under the false conflict paradigm. Accordingly, when at first blush a conflict appears, beware of the false conflict paradigm.

Chapter 12

Copyright and the Two Cultures of Online Communication

Alexander Peukert

12.1 COMMUNICATION CULTURES ON THE INTERNET

The relationship between copyright and the internet is often described as a conflict between exclusivity and access. Depending on whether one views this conflict from the perspective of copyright or of the internet, copyright optimists (or pessimists) stand in incontrovertible opposition to cyber optimists (or pessimists).[1] The solution then called for is 'fair balance'.[2] This article presents an alternative interpretation. It takes as a starting point the reality of online communication, which is characterized by two cultures of communication that relate to copyright in different ways.[3]

---

1. Goldstein, *Copyright's Highway: From Gutenberg to the Celestial Jukebox*, 10 (2d ed. 2003).
2. ECJ, Case C-275/06, paras 60, 70 – Promusicae; Geiger, *'Constitutionalising' Intellectual Property Law? The Influence of Fundamental Rights on Intellectual Property in the European Union*, 37 IIC 371 (2006).
3. Lehman, *Intellectual Property and the National Information Infrastructure, The Report of the Working Group on Intellectual Property Rights*, http://www.uspto.gov/web/offices/com/doc/ipnii/, at 14 (accessed 11 November 2014); Benkler, *The Wealth of Networks*, 395 (2006) (enclosure versus openness); Lessig, *Remix: Making Art and Commerce*

12.1.1 EXCLUSIVITY CULTURE

Let us call the first of these two cultures, the culture of exclusivity. It is primarily a business model whereby an entrepreneur provides paid access to works and other subject matter according to technical and contractual conditions. In 1994, Paul Goldstein predicted the advent of such a 'celestial jukebox' on the internet that would provide everyone at any time in any place with the desired content – though, of course, after automatically transferring a certain amount from the consumer's bank account to the copyright holder.[4] Today, examples of this model can be found in all copyright-related areas: the e-book market, access-controlled databases of academic publishers, newspapers behind pay-walls, proprietary software, music platforms such as Apple iTunes and Spotify, pay TV and video-on-demand providers like Netflix and so on.

Such business models implement a culture of exclusivity in the image of the analogue world. In a hierarchical model, information flows from one source to a great number of users whose activity is essentially limited to choosing and consuming the digital product. Many of the providers who operate in this mode today were already in the business of providing content before the advent of the internet.[5]

12.1.2 ACCESS CULTURE

The main characteristic of the access culture, in contrast, is that information is available without technical barriers and is not directly marketed in exchange for money. Certainly, the recipient normally may not do what he or she pleases with the data received. Indeed, many authors of works who make their works openly available in this way reserve certain rights, particularly moral rights. Still, temporary and permanent copies, as well as hyperlinks, are permitted free of charge in any case.[6] In this way, at least the exchange of unaltered data can take place without consideration of copyright in the sense of a prior consent requirement. The ideal of the open access culture is not Goldstein's celestial jukebox, but the wiki.[7] It allows information to flow through a network in which everyone who is connected to the net can, may and should take part as a sender and receiver of the information under equal conditions and without central control: heterarchical hypertext.

This model of communication can also be found in all copyright-related branches of the internet. There is text freely available on Wikipedia and on

---

Thrive in the Hybrid Economy, 105 (2008) (read-only versus read-write-culture); Cohen, *Configuring the Networked Self*, 6 (2012) (information-as-freedom versus information-as-control).

4. Goldstein, *supra* n. 1, at 22; Benkler, *supra* n. 3, at 41 (rights-based exclusion).
5. Litman, *Digital Copyright*, 171 (2001).
6. *See infra* 12.2.2.
7. http://de.wikipedia.org/wiki/Wiki (accessed 11 November 2014).

fan fiction platforms, in open databases like openjur.de for German legal information or in repositories for scientific and academic information[8] and, not least, in blogs. Free and open source software has become a serious rival of proprietary software in some fields. Finally, there are countless photos, audio and video files available on individual web sites and platforms like YouTube and Flickr, which range from professional works to amateurish 'user-generated content'.[9]

Unlike the exclusivity culture, the access culture cannot be reduced at the outset to a market transaction (content for money). While some open content offers are connected to commercial services, especially advertising and complementary offers, and are thus, indirectly commercialized,[10] for the most part, the access culture is fed by non-commercially motivated contributions that are financed in part by public funds (science, research, archives), and in part by private means (donations, not-for-profit hobby activities). The bulk of the necessary infrastructure is provided by companies like Google and Facebook, which, with their structuring and linking of the information, have developed the most dynamic, and presumably most profitable, business models on the internet.

The open, participatory and mostly non-commercial character of the access culture reflects the technical structure and the historical genesis of the internet.[11] The net of nets came into being in the 1960s in a unique military-scientific context that was shaped by the Cold War. The original impulse was the desire of the US military to possess a communications system that would survive an atomic attack.[12] The desired structure, therefore, had to have three features: stability, flexibility and de-centrality. If one or more nodes of the net failed, this should ideally not impact communication. To meet this challenge, the Advanced Research Projects Agency (ARPA) provided scientists with virtually unlimited funds and likewise, unlimited intellectual leeway. The scientists, in turn, used the net they were generating, ARPANet, with its strictly de-central conception, for their work, developing innovative forms of information exchange. If one working group reached a dead-end, it sent out a 'request for comments' and in this way put into practice the idea of the interactive network.[13] It went without saying that the researchers disclosed all source codes.[14]

---

8. Peukert, *Das Verhältnis zwischen Urheberrecht und Wissenschaft: Auf die Perspektive kommt es an!*, Goethe-Universität Frankfurt a.M., Fachbereich Rechtswissenschaft, Arbeitspapier Nr. 5/2013, http://papers.ssrn.com/sol3/papers.cfm?abstract_id=2268906 (accessed 11 November 2014).
9. *See* Naughton, *From Gutenberg to Zuckerberg*, 144, 245 (2012).
10. Benkler, *supra* n. 3, at 41 (non-exclusion-market versus non-exclusion-non-market).
11. Wielsch, *Zugangsregeln. Die Rechtsverfassung der Wissensteilung*, 243 (2008); Lessig, *Code*, 59 (2d ed. 2006); Abbate, *Inventing the internet*, 145 (1999).
12. Abbate, *supra* n. 11, at 43.
13. Abbate, *supra* n. 11, at 56, 74.
14. Abbate, *supra* n. 11, at. 70.

Scientific interests and communication norms became even more significant after the National Science Foundation succeeded the US military in the early 1980s as the primary source of funding for network research and development. It was scientists who programmed the underlying network protocols and applications like E-Mail and the World Wide Web, primarily for their genuinely non-commercial purposes. They even expressly waived all copyright protection for their computer programs.[15] Up until the early 1990s, the National Science Foundation's guidelines prohibited the use of the internet for non-scientific, in particular commercial, purposes. The state control of the infrastructural backbone of the net did not officially end until 30 April 1995.[16]

The result of this highly improbable, military-scientific genesis was a technology that is fundamentally different from previous means of communication: First, there exists no central authority to act as speaker or controller, and second, the network has a neutral relationship to the applications and contents located at the ends of the network (end-to-end principle).[17] Its function consists solely in transferring any and every binary data set from computer A to computer B as quickly and reliably as possible. Even technologies like packet switching and the multi-layer structure of network architecture are oriented fully towards the principle of most efficient and stable transmission of data while making it much more difficult to monitor those data for security reasons.[18]

Thus, the story comes full circle. A project that was increasingly driven by scientific interests brought forth a technology that facilitates means of communication that are ideally found in research groups, later in 'cyberspace'[19] and now, finally, in much-depleted amounts, in the access culture. These communication practices are characterized by the active involvement of all participants, openness towards new contributions and the lack of a central entity of control. Further, communication rules differ depending on the community at hand (i.e., military or science), whereas the culture of

---

15. Abbate, *supra* n. 11, at 111, 143, 214 ff. Cf. Statement Concerning CERN W3 Software Release into Public Domain, 30 April 1993, http://tenyears-www.web.cern.ch/tenyears-www/declaration/page1.html (accessed 11 November 201).
16. Abbate, *supra* n. 11, at 196, 199.
17. Post, *In Search of Jefferson's Moose*, 82 (2009); Naughton, *supra* n. 9, at 46.
18. Lessig, *supra* n. 11, at 144; Benkler, *supra* n. 3, at 412. This security shortcoming is not inconsistent with the military origin of the internet. The US military, indeed, thought in categories of a hermetic military network that was controlled by its hierarchically structured ends. If the authorization to participate in communication is dependent on military rank, and the content of the communication dependent on an order, any additional control of data transfer in fact seems superfluous. Security flaws did not become virulent, at any rate, until long after the US military had withdrawn and the internet was on its way to becoming the global net of nets.
19. Hoeren, *Das Internet für Juristen – eine Einführung,* Neue Juristische Wochenschrift 3295, 3298 (1995).

exclusivity is characterized by the formal, standardized legal rules of property and contract.

12.1.3   Freedom of Choice and Hybrids

The technology of the digital network allows for both a completely uncontrolled dissemination of data and the maximally regulated use of data.[20] Both variations co-exist on the internet, across which binary data are transferred without respect to their source, their destination or their content. This is how it can be that in some areas the access culture, and in others the exclusivity culture dominates. While Wikipedia has, for the most part, supplanted proprietary encyclopaedias, the information in the legal field is primarily made available and consulted through access-controlled databases like Westlaw. This variety follows from the freedom right holders enjoy in the digital world. They are free to market some subject matter exclusively while making other material available without any technical barriers. The status of a given work can change over time.[21] Even the simultaneous availability of content on closed and open platforms is technically and legally possible – consider, for example, so-called green open access in the academic area.[22]

The distinction between exclusivity culture and access culture draws upon the technology used. If someone makes a set of data unconditionally available, she is participating in the culture of open access. If, however, the access is technologically restricted, and dependent on an individual authorization, communication takes place in the exclusive mode.[23] The fact that digitized communication is by its nature, technologically processed communication makes technology the definitive criterion: *Code is law.*[24] Accordingly, the legal protection of technical protection measures has always been a core feature of copyright regulation of the net.[25] The German *Bundesgerichtshof* refers to technological criteria in deciding about the conformity of certain forms of online communication such as hyperlinks and search engines with copyright law.[26]

---

20. *See* National Research Council Committee on Intellectual Property Rights in the Emerging Information Infrastructure, *The Digital Dilemma: Intellectual Property in the Information Age* (2000); Litman, *supra* n. 5, at 12.
21. *See* Peukert, *A Bipolar Copyright System for the Digital Network Environment*, 28 Comm/Ent L.J. 1, 36 (2005), http://papers.ssrn.com/sol3/papers.cfm?abstract_id=801124 (accessed 11 November 2014).
22. Peukert, *supra* n. 8.
23. Efroni, *Access Right*, 490, 540 (Munich 2009).
24. Lessig, *supra* n. 11, at 24.
25. Wittgenstein, *Die digitale Agenda der neuen WIPO-Vertr äge*, 12 (2000).
26. *See Bundesgerichtshof*, Case I ZR 39/08, Gewerblicher Rechtsschutz und Urheberrecht 2011, 56 para. 27 – Session-ID (permissibility of hyperlinks depends on whether technical

The aspect of commercialization, instead, forms a merely subordinate distinguishing feature. It is true that an individual fee for the use of content can only be effectively enforced when access to that content is regulated by technology, which is why the fee-based, access-controlled online database is the paradigm of the exclusivity culture. And yet, open content is also commercialized in many different ways. Suffice it to refer to the marketing of complementary products and services in the case of Open Source Software and online games, live performances and merchandising of music or, last but not least, advertising other products in the context of freely accessible content.

There are numerous business models that populate the spectrum between the culture of exclusivity and the culture of access. It is hybrids like these that evoke the explanatory power of the distinction made here.[27] These hybrids are, economically and legally, just as interesting as they are contradictory and controversial because they cannot be placed in one or the other category. This observation provides an explanation, for instance, for the dispute over the new neighbouring right for press publishers in Germany, on both sides of which hybrids are involved. Press publishers have their roots in the exclusivity culture and run a business with a strict hierarchical organization, offline as well as online, with content that is in fact still for the most part freely accessible on the internet.[28] Commercial search engines and news aggregators, on the other hand, market freely accessible information in which, in their opinion, as few rights as possible should exist, whereas their centrally controlled search algorithm – a business model cast into code – represents the top-secret intellectual property. The newly implemented *Leistungsschutzrecht* for press publishers (Sections 87f-h German CA) is intended to help them to finally switch to the exclusivity camp to which they belong.[29]

In contrast to press publishers and Google, the operators of Spotify and Wikipedia clearly operate in one or the other model. That is why they provoke much less irritation. This has to do, in good measure, with each

---

measures are circumvented); *Bundesgerichtshof*, Case I ZR 69/08, Gewerblicher Rechtsschutz und Urheberrecht 2010, 628 paras 28, 33 – Vorschaubilder I (consent is implied for normal use if no technical measures are implemented to prevent it); on *Störerhaftung see Bundesgerichtshof*, Case I ZR 35/04, Gewerblicher Rechtsschutz und Urheberrecht 2007, 708 para. 47 – Internet-Versteigerung II (the limits of *Störerhaftung* are reached in any case when no features are included that are suited for use on a search engine); *Bundesgerichtshof*, Case I ZR 57/07, Gewerblicher Rechtsschutz und Urheberrecht 2009, 841 para. 34 – Cybersky (duties of care are normally reasonable if they can be automated. Otherwise the business model must be technically modified so as to no longer abet infringements.); Cf. Wielsch, *supra* n. 11, at 259 fn. 86.

27. Lessig, *supra* n. 3, at 179 (hybrids).
28. As regards online archives of newspapers, *see Bundesgerichtshof*, Case I ZR 127/09, Gewerblicher Rechtsschutz und Urheberrecht 2011, 415 paras 9 et seq. – Kunstausstellung im Online-Archiv.
29. §§ 87f para. 2, 87g German Copyright Act.

one's relatively clear relationship to copyright, which will be the focus of the following sections.

12.2 THE ROLE OF CURRENT COPYRIGHT LAW

12.2.1 COPYRIGHT AND EXCLUSIVITY CULTURE

The symbiosis alluded to above between the culture of exclusivity and copyright corresponds to the internal logic, and the primary historically developed purpose of this area of law. With exclusive exploitation rights,[30] copyright institutionalizes a market for the production and distribution of works and other intangible subject matter. Works, performances, phonograms, databases, etc. become tradable goods whose use is subject to prior authorization and, as a rule, payment of a fee. The entire purpose of copyright, in other words, is to commodify the input and output of the literary, scientific and artistic domain, and further branches of the digital economy.[31]

In the analogue world, this market communication flowed hierarchically from the author through a commercial middleman (publisher) to the public. On the internet, new actors have appeared on the scene. In particular, digital author-entrepreneurs are able to largely market their works themselves through online platforms.[32] And yet, even on the internet, they are able to operate in the exclusive mode because this market model has been applied to network communication via four legislative measures:[33] First, the exclusive right of reproduction was extended such that even a transient or incidental digital copy, and thus, every private enjoyment of a work on a computer, requires authorization.[34] Second, the making available of works and other subject matter was made subject to a separate exclusive right, irrespective of the location of the server.[35] Third, the option of online

---

30. Peifer, *Wissenschaftsmarkt und Urheberrecht: Schranken, Vertragsrecht, Wettbewerbsrecht*, Gewerblicher Rechtsschutz und Urheberrecht 22 (2009).
31. Cohen, *supra* n. 3, at 81.
32. For Apple iBooks, *see* http://www.apple.com/de/ibooks-author/ (accessed 11 Nov. 2014); on Kindle Direct Publishing *see* https://kdp.amazon.com/self-publishing/help?topicId=A3R2IZDC42DJW6 (accessed 11 November 2014).
33. European Commission, Green Paper on Copyright and Related Rights in the Information Society, 19.7.1995, COM (95) 382 final, at 44 ff.; Lehman, *supra* n. 3, at 19; Wittgenstein, *supra* n. 25, at 49.
34. *See* Agreed Statement on Article 1 para. 4 WCT; Article 7 WPPT; Article 2 Copyright Directive 2001/29; CJEU, Case C-360/13 – Public Relations Consultants Association.
35. *See* Article 8 WCT; 10, 14 WPPT; 3 Copyright Directive 2001/29; § 19a German Copyright Act. On the applicable law *see* CJEU, Case C-173/11, paras 18 et seq. – Football Dataco et al.; Reinbothe/v. Lewinski, *The WIPO Treaties 1996*, Article 8 WCT note 17 (2002/2007).

exhaustion, and thus, a secondary market for used digital goods, was ruled out.[36] Fourth, technological protection measures (digital rights management systems) were given legal protection against circumvention.[37] With this expansion of digital copyright, a pay-per-use business model – the 'celestial jukebox' – has been institutionalized as the 'normal' means of exploitation.[38]

This course was set by means of top-down regulation at a time when the internet was just emerging from the military-scientific context of its early development and was as yet barely commercialized.[39] As early as 1993, the Clinton administration appointed a working group to deal with questions of intellectual property in the context of the 'information highway'. In the fall of 1995, it presented its final report.[40] The legislative implementation of the four above-named pillars of digital copyright in the US failed in the following year, however, due in part to vehement criticism on the part of the US online community.[41] And yet, similar resolutions were attained shortly thereafter on the international level.[42] The European Council in July 1994 – even earlier than the Clinton administration – committed to a high level of copyright protection in the new networks.[43] In January 1995, a resolution of the G-7 Conference ran along the same lines, expressly referring to the already initiated efforts of the World Intellectual Property Organisation (WIPO).[44] The diplomatic consultations on applying copyright law to the internet lasted only three months. Already in December 1996, the agenda that had failed in the US was successfully implemented by the two WIPO 'internet treaties', the WCT or WIPO Copyright Treaty and the WPPT or the WIPO Performances and Phonograms Treaty.[45] The four principles of digital copyright set out therein found their way via the EC Directive 2001/29 'on the harmonization of certain aspects of copyright and related rights in the

---

36. *See* Articles 6 and 8 and Agreed Statement on Articles 6 and 7 WCT; recital 29 and Article 3 Abs. 3 Copyright Directive 2001/29; *Oberlandesgericht Stuttgart*, Zeitschrift für Urheber- und Medienrecht 2012, 81; *Landgericht Bielefeld*, Case 4 O 191/11, Zeitschrift für Urheber- und Medienrecht 2013, 688 f. Contra with regard to the Computer Program Directive 2009/24 CJEU, Case C-128/11 – Usedsoft.

37. *See* Articles 11, 12 WCT; 18, 19 WPPT; 6 para. 4 subpara. 4 Copyright Directive 2001/29; § 95b para. 3 German Copyright Act.

38. Peukert, in: Hilty/Peukert (eds), *Interessenausgleich im Urheberrecht*, 11, 24 (2004); European Commission, *supra* n. 33, 22.

39. Critical Hoeren, *Urheberrecht in der Informationsgesellschaft*, Gewerblicher Rechtsschutz und Urheberrecht 866, 874 (1997); Wittgenstein, *supra* n. 25, at 132.

40. Lehman, *supra* n. 3, at 14; Litman, *supra* n. 5, at 90.

41. Litman, *supra* n. 5, at 128.

42. On this forum shifting *see* Sell, *TRIPS: Fifteen Years Later*, (2011), http://papers.ssrn.com/sol3/papers.cfm?abstract_id=1900102 (accessed 11 November 2014).

43. EC Commission, Europe's way to the information society. An action plan, COM (94) 347 final, 19.7.1994, p. 3, 9; European Commission, *supra* n. 33, at 6; cf. recital 2 Copyright Directive 2001/29.

44. European Commission, *supra* n. 33, at 13.

45. Wittgenstein, *supra* n. 25, at 36, 44.

information society' into the copyright laws of the Member States of the then European Communities.

This swift victory march of copyright is particularly remarkable because it preceded the spread of the internet as a mass phenomenon. The net had formally only just been released from the care of the National Science Foundation onto the free market on 1 May 1995. In 1996, even in industrialized nations, only 11% of all households had internet access.[46] The European Commission stated quite frankly in its green paper of July 1995 that the 'issues which arise out of the development of an information society and its impact on systems of copyright and related rights' were 'still uncertain', and the new market structures 'largely hypothetical', as the development of the information society 'is still only in its infancy'.[47] Unlike in the US,[48] legal scholarship on the internet was also still evolving: In this decisive phase, German copyright lawyers were still grappling with the difference between online and offline[49] and opined that legal questions on the 'so-called' internet were not thoroughly researched.[50]

This ignorance can be seen as the very condition for the success of the political agenda of digital copyright. In the mid-1990s, there was simply no relevant civil society interest group outside the US that was able to articulate the concerns of the access culture.[51] The exclusivity culture, on the other hand, was powerfully represented by right holders. They had fully recognized not only the danger but also the potential of the internet for their business models.[52] And thus, dominated an orthodox copyright perspective on the 'information highway', which was completely detached from the discourse on the technological, social and cultural issues the internet presented. The internet was conceived of as a global highway on which hundreds of television channels and other content would be transmitted, if only it could be guaranteed that not a single unauthorized copy would find its way into this medium.[53] That the internet might represent a disruptive

46. http://en.wikipedia.org/wiki/Global_internet_usage (accessed 11 November 2014).
47. EC Commission, *supra* n. 43, at 19, 22.
48. *See Playboy Enterprises v. Frena*, 893 F.Supp. 1552 (M.D. Fla. 1993); Elkin-Koren, *Copyright Law and Social Dialogue on the Information Superhighway: The Case against Copyright Liability of Bulletin Board Operators*, 13 Cardozo Arts & Entertainment L.J. (1995), 345.
49. Schardt, *Multimedia – Fakten und Rechtsfragen*, Gewerblicher Rechtsschutz und Urheberrecht 827, 829 (1996).
50. Nordemann/Goddar/Tönhardt/Czychowski, *Gewerblicher Rechtsschutz und Urheberrecht im Internet*, Computer und Recht 645 (1996).
51. Hoeren, *Urheberrecht 2000 – Thesen für eine Reform des Urheberrechts*, Multimedia und Recht 3, 6 (2000) (users have no lobby); Dreier, *Urheberrecht an der Schwelle des 3. Jahrtausends*, Computer und Recht 45 (2000).
52. Wittgenstein, *supra* n. 25, at 133.
53. European Commission, *supra* n. 33, at 3; Lehman, *supra* n. 3, at 7-8.

technology just like writing or printing, and that it facilitates a completely different culture of communication, merited a footnote at best.[54]

The vision of a 'celestial jukebox', which in its basic features was thus already codified in 1996, further implies that copyright is changing from a tool to protect certain eligible aspects of communication only (namely 'works')[55] to a right that covers every potential asset, and thus, in the end, *every element of communication*.[56] When it becomes possible to market every data set, then the law should provide for this possibility: if value, then right.[57]

From this perspective, it is only logical that copyright first expanded in breadth, in the sense that requirements for protection were lowered and the scope of protectable subject matter was enlarged. Accordingly, every software marketed is a copyrightable work.[58] In addition, automatic protection is enjoyed under German copyright law by practically every piece of communication that is produced and conveyed by means of copyrighted software, namely: every photograph;[59] every particle, be it ever so small, of commercially produced audio and video recording;[60] texts consisting of at least two words;[61] as well as every part of a press product unless this pertains to individual words or the smallest of text excerpts.[62] Last but not least, the question of the copyrightability of single elements of communication becomes irrelevant when the obtaining, verification or presentation of these data or other independent elements requires a substantial qualitative or quantitative investment. In this case, the online database as such enjoys the

---

54. Lehman, *supra* n. 3, at 7-8. But *see* AG *Cruz Villalón*, Case C-314/12, para. 21 – UPC Telekabel Wien ('Few inventions have changed our habits and our media consumption as completely as that of the internet.'); Schmidt/Cohen, *The New Digital Age*, 1 (2013).
55. Schricker/Loewenheim, in: Schricker/Loewenheim (eds.), *Urheberrecht*, Einl. n. 7 (4th ed. 2010); Wielsch, *supra* n. 11, at 31.
56. Schricker, in: Schricker (ed.), *Urheberrecht auf dem Weg zur Informationsgesellschaft*, 5 (1997); critical *Hoeren*, *supra* n. 39, at 869; on scientific information *see* Hilty, *Das Urheberrecht und der Wissenschaftler*, Gewerblicher Rechtsschutz und Urheberrecht International 179, 181 (2006); Dreier/Leistner, *Urheberrecht im Internet: die Forschungsherausforderungen*, Gewerblicher Rechtsschutz und Urheberrecht 881 (2013).
57. Critically Peukert, *Güterzuordnung als Rechtsprinzip*, 132, 733, 765 (2008).
58. *Bundesgerichtshof*, Case I ZR 90/09, Gewerblicher Rechtsschutz und Urheberrecht 2013, 509 para. 24 – UniBasic-IDOS.
59. § 72 German Copyright Act.
60. On §§ 94, 95 German Copyright Act *see Bundesgerichtshof*, Case I ZR 42/05, Gewerblicher Rechtsschutz und Urheberrecht 2008, 693 para. 21 – TV-Total. On § 85 German Copyright Act *see Bundesgerichtshof*, Case I ZR 112/06, Gewerblicher Rechtsschutz und Urheberrecht 2009, 403 para. 14 – Metall auf Metall.
61. ECJ, Case C-5/08, paras 30 et seq. – Infopaq I; *Bundesgerichtshof*, Case I ZR 12/08, Gewerblicher Rechtsschutz und Urheberrecht 2011, 134 para. 33 – Perlentaucher; *Oberlandesgericht Frankfurt a.M.*, Case 11 U 75/06, BeckRS 2011, 27257 – Perlentaucher II (according to which such phrases as 'esoterical cock-and-bull story' and 'subsidized rediscovery' are protected by copyright, but not 'publishers ... which need no longer pay royalties').
62. § 87f para. 1 German Copyright Act.

three layers of digital copyright protection: law, technological protection measures and anti-circumvention rules.[63]

Second, in the world of the 'celestial jukebox', there is no such thing as out-of-print works because the marginal costs of keeping digital content in stock are negligible.[64] As a consequence, the expiry of a term of protection is perceived as destruction of assets, drawing complaint. A way out of this quandary is provided by the expansion of copyright duration. Following this logic, copyright in the US[65] and the related rights of performing artists and music producers in the European Union (EU) were extended by twenty years in 1998 and 2011, respectively.[66]

Third, enforcement of copyright shall be such that an unauthorized exchange of data can only take place under a high risk of legal consequences, in the hopes that the majority of average internet users will stay away from the darknet and find their way to the celestial jukebox. In this initially underestimated respect, digital copyright actually meets with considerable resistance, some of which is grounded in law.[67] For example, the liability of host and access providers, as well as search engine providers, is still the subject of intense debate. The EU Member States continue to have considerable leeway in establishing a 'fair balance' between the effective enforcement of copyright and the exclusivity culture on the one hand, and fundamental rights of users and intermediaries that tend to be associated with the access culture on the other hand.[68] Nevertheless, the German *Bundesgerichtshof* has done its part to improve the legal situation of right holders. Irrespective of express statements to the contrary in the legislative history of the Copyright Act, the court granted right holders a claim against internet access providers to reveal the identity of individual infringers, even if the infringement concerned only one single upload or download.[69] Further, service providers whose business model is based on copyright infringement or who promote the risk of infringing use of their otherwise neutral software by, for example, advertising 'free pay TV', are subject to extensive duties of care. Accordingly, a file hosting service can be under an obligation to search all external link lists that point to illegal files on the server of the company,[70]

---

63. §§ 85a et seq. German Copyright Act; ECJ, Case C-203/02, paras 28 et seq. – British Horseracing; ECJ, Case C-545/07, para. 73 – Apis.
64. Chris Anderson, *The Long Tail* (2007).
65. *See Eldred v. Ashcroft*, 537 U.S. 186 (2003); Hilty, *Eldred v. Ashcroft: Die Schutzfrist im Urheberrecht – eine Diskussion, die auch Europäer interessieren sollte*, Gewerblicher Rechtsschutz und Urheberrecht Int. 201 (2003).
66. Article 1 para. 2 lit. b, 3 para. 2 EU Directive 2011/77.
67. *See infra* 12.2.2.
68. ECJ, Case C-275/06, paras 47 et seq. – Promusicae.
69. *Bundesgerichtshof*, Case I ZB 80/11, Gewerblicher Rechtsschutz und Urheberrecht 2012, 1026 paras 22, 40 – Alles kann besser werden.
70. *Bundesgerichtshof*, Case I ZR 80/12, Gewerblicher Rechtsschutz und Urheberrecht 2013, 1030 paras 36 et seq. – File-Hosting-Dienst (a seventeen-member abuse team is not sufficient). Afterwards, the defendant modified its business model, introducing a cap on

and the company that promoted 'free pay TV' software had to modify the computer program so that it could no longer be used in infringing ways.[71]

12.2.2 Copyright and Access Culture

While copyright thus represents the legal basis for the exclusivity culture, its relationship with the access culture is at best neutral. The latter has its roots in a predominantly military-scientific 'cyberspace' that largely ignores core copyright norms of authorship, property and bilateral transactions.[72] It is not that copyright in any way prohibits an open communication culture. Rather, it merely creates the requirement of authorization by the right holder regarding whether, how, and with which of her works she would like to participate in network communication.[73] However, copyright does not have the purpose of creating or stabilizing conditions and norms of communication beyond commodity transactions.[74] Therefore, it is not surprising that the regulatory milestones in supporting and protecting the internet's original dominant culture of access are to be found outside copyright law.

This is true, first, of the limited liability of access and host providers pursuant to Articles 12-15 of the E-Commerce Directive 2000/31. These provisions are not intended to impact the effective enforcement of copyright on the internet.[75] And yet, the EU legislature thereby privileges technologies and commercial services whose purpose is to save and transmit third-party content without consideration of copyright protection.[76] Thus, different layers of the internet are subject to divergent, if not downright opposing, principles of regulation. The infrastructure and provider markets are supposed to function according to the principles of the open, heterarchical internet. The content markets, on the contrary, are regulated according to the hierarchical model of producing cultural goods in the analogue world. This contradiction plagues the 'networked continent' to this day.[77]

Second, communication on the open internet enjoys the protection of fundamental rights. These result in partly insurmountable hurdles for the

---

the amount of data transferable at maximum speed in the premium mode as well. The defendant lost many customers as a result; cf. http://www.heise.de/newsticker/meldung/Rapidshare-entlaesst-drei-Viertel-aller-Mitarbeiter-1865665.html (accessed 11 November 2014)).

71. *Bundesgerichtshof*, Case I ZR 57/07, Gewerblicher Rechtsschutz und Urheberrecht 2009, 841 paras 21, 32 – Cybersky (distribution of the software Cybersky TV is prohibited if it can be used to send or receive a decrypted pay TV content in the framework of a peer-to-peer system).
72. *Supra* 12.1.2.
73. Dreier, *supra* n. 51, at 45.
74. Wielsch, *Relationales Urheberrecht*, Zeitschrift für Geistiges Eigentum 274 (2013).
75. Recital 50 E-Commerce Directive 2000/31.
76. Recitals 40 et seq. E-Commerce Directive 2000/31.
77. *See infra* 12.2.1.

effective enforcement of copyright and the culture of exclusivity. Complete capture of online communication for preventive or repressive purposes would run counter to the constitutional identity of Germany, and therefore, could not be lawfully implemented, even via the roundabout route of international or EU law.[78] Processing dynamic IP addresses in order to identify an internet user as the infringer of copyright interferes with the fundamental rights of telecommunications privacy and informational autonomy.[79] The Court of Justice of the European Union (CJEU) has held that access and host providers may not be obligated to install as a preventive measure a system for filtering all electronic communications, indiscriminately to all their customers, at the provider's expense and for an unlimited period.[80] As the Court bases its holding not only on current secondary law but also on the Charter of Fundamental Rights, such a regulatory measure, which obviously would be especially favourable to right holders, is not feasible even for the future. Even after the *UPC Telekabel* decision, German courts deny blocking orders[81] and data-preservation orders against access providers.[82]

But it is not only data protection law that continues to stand in the way of digital copyright. Specifically, both EU and German high courts recognize that the business models of access and host providers, as well as other information society services (e.g., search engines), are allowed under the law and that their providers enjoy the protection of the fundamental right to freely conduct a business (Article 2(1) and Article 12(1) German Basic Law, Article 16 Charter). Their indirect liability for copyright infringements of third parties is, therefore, limited such that their business models are not called into question or disproportionately hampered.[83] This means, first and foremost, that the measures required of the defendant must be automatable: *Code is law.*

---

78. *Bundesverfassungsgericht*, Case 1 BvR 256/08, Neue Juristische Wochenschrift 2010, 833 paras 216, 218 – Vorratsdatenspeicherung.
79. *Bundesverfassungsgericht*, Case 1 BvR 256/08, Neue Juristische Wochenschrift 2010, 833 para. 258 – Vorratsdatenspeicherung; *Bundesverfassungsgericht*, Case 1 BvR 1299/05, Neue Juristische Wochenschrift 2012, 1419 paras 116, 122 – Bestandsdatenspeicherung; *Bundesgerichtshof*, Case I ZB 80/11, Gewerblicher Rechtsschutz und Urheberrecht 2012, 1026 paras 43, 45 – Alles kann besser werden.
80. CJEU, Case C-70/10, para. 29 – Scarlet Extended; CJEU, Case C-360/10, para. 26 – SABAM.
81. *Oberlandesgericht Köln*, Case 6 U 192/11, BeckRS 2014, 15246 (both highly efficient as well as less efficient blocking technologies unreasonable).
82. *Oberlandesgericht Düsseldorf*, Case I-20 W 121/12, I-20 W 5/13, Multimedia und Recht 2013, 392 – IP-Daten-Speicherung.
83. *Bundesgerichtshof*, Case I ZR 304/01, Entscheidungen des Bundesgerichtshofs in Zivilsachen vol. 158, 236, 251 – Internet-Versteigerung I; *Bundesgerichtshof*, Case I ZR 121/08, Entscheidungen des Bundesgerichtshofs in Zivilsachen vol. 185, 330 para. 24 – Sommer unseres Lebens; *Bundesgerichtshof*, Case I ZR 80/12, Gewerblicher Rechtsschutz und Urheberrecht 2013, 1030 para. 44 – File Hosting-Dienst; CJEU, Case C-324/09, para. 139 – L'Oréal.

As a consequence, the means and norms of communication that the internet makes possible do, in fact, influence digital copyright.[84] These opposing forces have as yet shown very little impact on black-letter copyright law, however. The first mention of the access culture in German copyright law was made in 2002 in the so-called Linux provisions. According to these, the author may, however – thus, as a departure from the copyright law standard – grant unremunerated non-exclusive exploitation right for every person.[85] With these provisions, the legislature acknowledges that open content models represent new and effective structures of communication and co-operation for which classical copyright contract law requirements of remuneration and written form are ill-suited.[86] As a matter of fact, licensing networks like open source and Creative Commons do not serve to secure equitable remuneration for the exploitation of the work,[87] but the widest possible dissemination of the respective work while preserving some rights, specifically, the moral rights of the author.[88]

However, only a fraction of the freely accessible content on the internet has a formal licence attached.[89] On personal home pages, but also on commercial platforms, there are countless texts, images, films etc. whose copyright status is not clarified or at best signalled with a ©. Since every text, audio or video file in case of doubt enjoys automatic legal protection, and every click encroaches on the exclusive reproduction right, the question arose whether the informal branch of the access culture operated by constantly infringing the copyrights involved. This possible conclusion of orthodox copyright thinking was already ruled out in the mid-1990s by the *Paperboy* decision of the *Bundesgerichtshof*. The Court held that hyperlinks to freely available copyright-protected content do not infringe the copyright or run afoul of unfair competition law.[90] It reasoned that the right holder herself makes the work available and that this access is merely facilitated by the hyperlink. She who takes advantage of the possibilities of the World Wide Web to offer her own content cannot complain when others also use this technology. After all, there exists a 'public interest in the well-functioning of

---

84. Wittgenstein, *supra* n. 25, at 133; Peukert, in: Bieber/Eifert/Groß/Lamla (eds), *Soziale Netzwerke in der digitalen Welt*, 225 (2009).
85. §§ 31a para. 1 section 2, 32 para. 3 section 3, 32a para. 3 section 3, 32c para. 3 section 2 German Copyright Act.
86. *See* Bundestags-Drucksachen 14/6433, 15; Bundestags-Drucksachen 14/8058, 19; Bundestags-Drucksachen 16/1828, 37; Bundestags-Drucksachen 16/5939, 44.
87. § 11 German CA.
88. Wielsch, *supra* n. 11, at 213.
89. On closer look, however, formal open content licences prove to be at least partly anachronistic hybrids, as they intend to put a dynamic access culture into operation by means of classic, that is, two-sided and inflexible, licensing agreements, whose effect is partially disputed; *see* Peukert, Der digitale Urheber, *Festschrift für Wandtke*, 455 (2013) = http://dx.doi.org/10.2139/ssrn.2268916 (accessed 11 November 2014).
90. *Bundesgerichtshof*, Gewerblicher Rechtsschutz und Urheberrecht 2003, 958, 961-2 – Paperboy; CJEU, Case C-466/12 – Nils Svensson.

the internet', the expedient use of which is practically impossible without search engines and hyperlinks.[91] In developing this point further, the *Bundesgerichtshof* decided in 2010 that a right holder who makes texts or images available on the internet without access or copy controls implicitly consents to the 'normal uses according to the circumstances'. It follows that non-commercial reproductions (downloads, printouts) and commercial image search engines are lawful on the basis of implied consent.[92]

Contrary to predominantly critical opinions in the literature, the *Bundesgerichtshof* deserves due respect for this courageous legal innovation.[93] With the doctrine of implied consent, the Court legalizes the social, inherently reciprocal norms of the access culture – and with them the public interest in their observation – by means of an informal, flexible and globally effective legal instrument. The *Bundesgerichtshof* likewise earns acclamation for making the validity of the access norms dependent upon there being no contradicting technical measures activated that make it recognizable on a technical level that the provider of the content does not want to participate in this mode of communication. Again, network communication is automated and requires automatable rules: *Code is law.*

Recently, the legislative branch has finally begun paying greater attention to the access culture. While the new German neighbouring right for press publishers, on the one hand, pursues the goal of bringing press products into the model of exclusivity,[94] its scope of application, on the other hand, has been limited to commercial providers of search engines and news aggregators, which moreover are still allowed to describe the linked content appropriately with single words and extremely short excerpts, so that 'the flow of information on the internet ... is not impacted by the proposed regulation'.[95]

Just a few months later, there followed the 'Act on the Use of Orphan and Out-of-Print Works and Another Amendment to the Copyright Act' of 1 October 2013,[96] containing three measures to actively promote the access

---

91. *Bundesgerichtshof*, Gewerblicher Rechtsschutz und Urheberrecht 2003, 958, 963 – Paperboy.
92. *Bundesgerichtshof*, Gewerblicher Rechtsschutz und Urheberrecht 2010, 628 paras 28 et seq. – Vorschaubilder I; *Bundesgerichtshof*, Gewerblicher Rechtsschutz und Urheberrecht 2012, 602 paras 16 et seq. – Vorschaubilder II.
93. Wielsch, *supra* n. 11, at 257; Wielsch, *Die Zugangsregeln der Intermediäre: Prozeduralisierung von Schutzrechten*, Gewerblicher Rechtsschutz und Urheberrecht 665, 617 (2011); critical Leistner/Stang, *Die Bildersuche im Internet aus urheberrechtlicher Sicht*, Computer und Recht 499, 507 (2008); Spindler, *Bildersuchmaschinen, Schranken und konkludente Einwilligung im Urheberrecht*, Gewerblicher Rechtsschutz und Urheberrecht, 785, 791 (2010); Senftleben, *Internet Search Results – a Permissible Quotation?*, 235 Revue International du Droit D'auteur 2, 59 (2013).
94. *Supra* 12.1.3.
95. *See* § 87f para. 1 section 1 German Copyright Act and Bundestags-Drucksache 17/11470, 5-6.
96. Bundesgesetzblatt 2013 I, 3728.

culture. The implementation of the EU Directive on orphan works is intended to benefit the development of a German Digital Library, whose goal is to make as much of the national cultural heritage as possible available online.[97] The provisions benefit only public institutions in the fulfilment of their cultural and educational objectives for the public good, however. These institutions may only charge fees to cover the costs of digitalization and making the material publicly available. The considerable effort needed for a thorough search for right holders must be paid for by public funds. It is highly doubtful whether these restrictive conditions will, at all, result in the desired mass digitalization of works.[98] The decidedly non-commercial orientation of the EU regulation furthermore prevents Google or any other company from making the digitized knowledge of the world accessible in the EU.[99] Orphan works are considered as cultural assets, as *res extra commercium,* under EU law.[100] This requirement made the promotion of the access culture politically acceptable. Google's hybrid business model, in contrast, meets with disapprobation, even though (or because?) it is technically and economically practicable. Here again, it becomes evident that hybrid forms between the cultures of exclusivity and access have a greater potential for conflict, but oftentimes also, the better potential for solving problems than make approaches that can clearly be assigned to one culture or the other.

Seen in this light, the new German regulation of out-of-print works appears not only more innovative but also more susceptible to dispute. According to these provisions, collective management organizations are endowed by means of a legal presumption with the legal power to allow public educational and cultural institutions to digitize and make publicly available all printed materials published before 1966 and now out of commerce for non-commercial purposes if the right holder does not object within six weeks after notification of the work's inclusion in a register of out-of-commerce works. This opt-out solution, which in the Google Books case was still vehemently fought by the German government, could, in fact, be an efficient instrument for mass digitization by public authorities, as it is possible to automatically determine a lack of availability and the expiry of the objection period.[101] The result will be an expansion of the pool feeding the access culture on both sides of the Atlantic. The only difference is in the

---

97. Bundestags-Drucksache 17/13423, 10.
98. Favale et al., *Copyright, and the Regulation of Orphan Works: A Comparative Review of Seven Jurisdictions and a Rights Clearance Simulation,* (2013), http://www.ipo.gov.uk/ipresearch-orphan-201307.pdf (accessed 11 November 2014), 82.
99. Bundestags-Drucksache 17/13423, 11. On the political economy of the EU orphan works regulation *see* Peukert, *Deutschland v. Google: Dokumentation einer Auseinandersetzung,* Archiv für Urheber- und Medienrecht 2010 II, 477. On U.S. law *see The Authors Guild, Inc. et al. v. Google Inc.,* 05 Civ. 8136 (S.D.N.Y., 14.11.2013).
100. If on the other hand a right holder is present, no objections are raised to the commercialization of literature, science and art.
101. Bundestags-Drucksache 17/13423, 11-2, 18.

parties benefiting from these changes: On the other side of the Atlantic, Google is attempting to snap up the world's collective knowledge, while in good old Europe, it is the public heritage institutions and collective management organizations that use tax money to generate tasks and income, each in its own interest.

Another goal of the amendment is to promote the open access movement in the academic field through a new copyright contract provision. According to Section 38(4) of the Copyright Act:

> The author of a scientific contribution which is the result of a research activity publicly funded by at least fifty percent and which has appeared in a collection which is published periodically at least twice per year has the right, even if he has granted the publisher or editor an exclusive right of use, to make the contribution available to the public in the accepted manuscript version upon expiry of 12 months after first publication, unless this serves a commercial purpose. The source of the first publication shall be indicated. Any deviating agreement to the detriment of the author shall be ineffective.

This provision gives publicly funded academic authors the opportunity to publish their texts primarily in the databases of the still dominant academic publishing houses, but to make the same content accessible after an embargo period in the open access mode.[102] This prevents at least a drying up of the access culture in the academy, and could even herald the transition of the academic communication system from the paradigm of the peer-review journal in the hands of a publisher to the open access repository.[103] A striking feature of these measures is that the German legislature only champions a non-commercial, ultimately tax-funded access culture, and thus, at the same time, rules out hybrid business models for the indirect commercialization of open content models. This approach institutionalizes only the hierarchical mode of commodification and thereby favours market participants, namely publishers, who operate on this basis. Innovative hybrids, on the other hand, have a rocky footing in Europe.

On the same day as the Orphan Works Act, the German parliament enacted another law, which can be taken as a kind of legislative admonishment to right holders to develop network-compatible business models, namely, the Act against Frivolous Business Practices.[104] The act sets a maximum attorney fee of approximately EUR 150 that private copyright

---

102. Hansen, *Zugang zu wissenschaftlicher Information – alternative urheberrechtliche Ansätze*, Gewerblicher Rechtsschutz und Urheberrecht International, 378, 383 (2005).
103. Peukert, *Ein wissenschaftliches Kommunikationssystem ohne Verlage – zur rechtlichen Implementierung von Open Access als Goldstandard wissenschaftlichen Publizierens*, Goethe-Universität Frankfurt a.M., Fachbereich Rechtswissenschaft, Arbeitspapier Nr. 6/2013, http://papers.ssrn.com/sol3/papers.cfm?abstract_id=2268901 (accessed 11 November 2014).
104. Bundesgesetzblatt 2013 I, 3714.

infringers have to reimburse if they receive a warning letter. The measure is intended to prevent copyright enforcement from becoming a lucrative business model for attorneys because such behaviour undermines the legitimacy of copyright.[105] One certainly cannot accuse the German legislature of wanting to make copyright infringement less risky, and thus, more attractive. And yet, the act does send a signal to right holders, in whose name the attorneys were, after all, acting, that they should provide more licensed services on the internet instead of simply invoking copyright. The attenuation of enforcement measures serves as an incentive to finally make the celestial jukebox a reality.

12.3   PERSPECTIVES

12.3.1   FURTHER PROMOTION OF THE EXCLUSIVITY CULTURE

And yet, such a negative sanction will likely remain an exception. More probable is further promotion of the exclusivity culture by strengthening and reinforcing copyright protection.[106]

The first possibility in this respect is the expansion of the scope of copyright protection, whether in the form of a generally related right for publishers,[107] or a further extension of the duration of neighbouring rights, particularly in the audiovisual area.[108] Further, the exclusivity model would become much more impervious if the notion of the 'primacy of contractual relations'[109] over the statutory limitations of copyright should prevail. According to this principle, all limitations and exceptions become inapplicable if the respective work can be licensed under equitable conditions via an access-controlled database. Lawful uses, for example, for the purpose of research or studying, would not only fail due to technical protection measures but would run idle before this stage for lack of necessity whenever the users have the celestial jukebox at their disposal.[110] Lawful access would

---

105. *See* Bundestags-Drucksache 17/13057, 10-1.
106. *See* e.g., Mazziotti, *Copyright in the EU Digital Single Market. Report of the CEPS Digital Forum*, (2013), http://www.ceps.be/book/copyright-eu-digital-single-market (accessed 11 November 2014); Benkler, *supra* n. 3, at 439.
107. Kauert, *Das Leistungsschutzrecht des Verlegers*, 226 (2008); Szilagyi, *Leistungsschutzrecht für Verleger*, 188 (2011); Rieger, *Ein Leistungsschutzrecht für Presseverleger*, (2013).
108. Article 3 EU Directive 2011/77.
109. *Bundesgerichtshof*, Gewerblicher Rechtsschutz und Urheberrecht 2013, 503 para. 18 – Elektronische Leseplätze with reference to recital 45 Copyright Directive 2001/29.
110. *See* Berger, *Die öffentliche Zugänglichmachung urheberrechtlicher Werke für Zwecke der akademischen Lehre*, Gewerblicher Rechtsschutz und Urheberrecht, 1058, 1064 (2010).

only be possible via this portal unless the respective licence conditions (including the price) are considered inequitable.[111]

As explained, the enforcement of digital copyright still faces considerable legal and practical hurdles.[112] And yet, many of these hurdles could be overcome by legislative action: The mass-prosecution of individual infringers would be made much easier if the law mandated that access providers were obliged to save dynamic IP addresses upon notice of infringement for a certain period and that this information had to be made available to right holders without a prior court decision.[113] The anonymous use of public wireless local area networks in hotels or cafes could be prohibited.[114] Platform and search engine operators could be declared liable to delete illegal content or links to this content and to use automated filters to prevent it from cropping up again.[115] Finally, German courts still have to implement the CJEU decision *UPC Telekabel*, according to which a court may even grant an unspecified injunction prohibiting an internet service provider from allowing its customers access to an illegal website.[116] Access providers could also be forced to participate in a system of graduated response.[117] Finally, hardcore commercial piracy could be combated effectively if credit card companies and advertising agencies were prohibited from contracting with these actors.[118]

All of these measures would contribute to the perception that the 'celestial jukebox' is the normal and the only reliably lawful source of information on the internet. At the same time, they would call into question the conditions of communication of the open internet, and with them the

---

111. Critical Sprang/Ackermann, *Der Zweite Korb aus Sicht der (Wissenschafts -) Verlage*, Kommunikation & Recht 7, 9 (2008).
112. *Supra* 12.2.2.
113. Dreier/Leistner, *supra* n. 56, at 893; Czychowski/J.B. Nordemann, *Grenzenloses Internet – entgrenzte Haftung?*, Gewerblicher Rechtsschutz und Urheberrecht 986, 995 (2013); *Bundesverfassungsgericht*, Neue Juristische Wochenschrift 2010, 833 para. 260 – Vorratsdatenspeicherung.
114. Czychowski/J.B. Nordemann, *supra* n. 113, at 993; contra *Landgericht Frankfurt a.M.*, Gewerblicher Rechtsschutz und Urheberrecht-Rechtsprechungs-Report 2013, 507 et seq. – Ferienwohnung.
115. Article 21 para. 2 E-Commerce Directive 2000/31. On the liability of host providers *see Landgericht Hamburg*, Zeitschrift für Urheber- und Medienrecht 2012, 596, 602 et seq. – GEMA/Youtube; Mazziotti (*supra* n. 106), at 24 f.; Dreier/Leistner, *supra* n. 56, at 895. On the liability of search engine operators *see* Czychowski/J.B. Nordemann, *supra* n. 113, at 992 (2013).
116. *Supra* n. 81. *See also* Senftleben, *Breathing Space for Cloud-Based Business Models*, 4 JIPITEC, 87, 94 (2013).
117. Giblin, *Evaluating Graduated Response*, (2013), http://papers.ssrn.com/sol3/papers.cfm?abstract_id=2322516 (accessed 11 November 2014).
118. Section 3 Preventing Real Online Threats to Economic Creativity and Theft of Intellectual Property Act of 2011 (Protect IP Act of 2011), p. 968, 112th Congress, 12.5.2011; Stop Online Piracy Act, H. R. 3261, 112th Congress, 26.10.2011. For EU law *see* Mazziotti (*supra* n. 106), at 23-4.

access culture. If internet users can be de-anonymized, and their communication reconstructed, then types of activity that today flourish in the grey zone of legality – just think of remixes, mash-ups and fan fiction – could become victims of precautionary self-censorship.[119] Automated procedures of 'cleansing' search engine results and platform contents, uncoupled from the controls of the rule of law, in what would then be a 'clean and safe' internet,[120] might also dispose of lawful content.[121] The significance of this automated and privatized enforcement is illustrated by a successful case that Lawrence Lessig and the Electronic Frontier Foundation filed in the wake of a purportedly ungrounded deletion of a lecture held by Lessig that had been available on YouTube. In the video at issue, Lessig presented several remix versions of a popular song to illustrate the creative potential of an access culture, and thus, became a target of the enforcement activities of the holder of the copyright in the music.[122]

Despite their severe effects, the enforcement measures listed above likely fall within the large discretion the legislative branch enjoys.[123] These instruments could become critical for the future of the open internet, and with it, the access culture if they were implemented on the technical layers of the network. This infrastructure is by no means a given. The anarchic internet as we know it can mutate to a perfectly controlled celestial jukebox.[124] The complexity that flows from the countless ends of the network and that undermines all aspects of IT security (confidentiality, integrity, authenticity) could be subjected to prior authorization if all machines capable of sending and receiving files over the network were required to meet the standards defined by the Trusted Computing Group.[125] That Trusted Computing is a real issue, is evidenced by a statement by the German government of August

---

119. *Bundesverfassungsgericht*, Case 1 BvR 256/08, Neue Juristische Wochenschrift 2010, 833 para. 258 – Vorratsdatenspeicherung.

120. *See* http://ec.europa.eu/internal_market/consultations/2012/clean-and-open-internet_en .htm (accessed 11 November 2014).

121. *Bundesgerichtshof*, Case I ZR 80/12, Gewerblicher Rechtsschutz und Urheberrecht 2013, 1030 para. 62 – File-Hosting-Dienst (that duties of care can in individual cases lead to the deletion of lawful back-up copies does not make their fulfilment unreasonable); but *see* CJEU, Case C-314/12 para. 56 – UPC Telekabel (injunctions against access providers must not affect internet users who are using the provider's services in order to lawfully access information).

122. *Lessig v. Liberation Music PTY Ltd.* (D. Mass. 2013), http://de.scribd.com/doc/ 162455224/Lawrence-Lessig-v-Liberation-Music-Pty-Ltd (accessed 11 November 2014).

123. ECJ, Case C-275/06, paras 61 et seq. – Promusicae; Peukert, *The Fundamental Right to (Intellectual) Property and the Discretion of the Legislature*, Goethe University Frankfurt am Main, Faculty of Law Research Paper No. 7/2013, http://dx.doi.org/ 10.2139/ssrn.2324132 (accessed 11 Nov. 2014).

124. Lessig, *supra* n. 11, at 57, 123; Benkler, *supra* n. 3, at 383.

125. *See* Bechtold, *Trusted Computing. Rechtliche Probleme einer entstehenden Technologie*, Computer und Recht 393 (2005); Benkler, *supra* n. 3, at 409; Zittrain, *The Future of the internet – And How to Stop It*, 36 (2011).

2012.[126] According to this document, an essential function of Trusted Computing consists of the 'permanent protection of digital content'. The German government states very clearly, however, that such measures have to respect the legal and social conditions governing access to knowledge. Further, it demands that public and private owners of computers alike must be able to fully control any implemented security architectures and to deactivate them at any time without negative consequences.

But even if the network's ends remain open for all types of applications and content, the technical and legal bases of data transmission can be changed in such a way as to make the internet a medium of the exclusivity culture alone. In this respect, the future of net neutrality plays a crucial role.[127] The principle of net neutrality reflects the original technical structure of the internet: operators of telecommunications networks have to make the best effort to guarantee non-discriminatory data transmission and non-discriminatory access to content and applications.[128] Under this principle, the cultures of exclusivity and of access receive equal treatment on the level of data transmission. Competition between proprietary and open content models, therefore, does not depend on the speed and quality of data transmission, but primarily on the functionality of the respective application or content transmitted. In other words, the principle of net neutrality guarantees on the technical level equal competitive and communicative conditions for all participants.

However, certain parties, specifically market-dominant access providers, have a strong vested interest in moving away from this principle. And indeed, Article 20(1) lit. b of the Universal Service Directive 2002/22 expressly proclaims that 'conditions limiting access to and/or use of services and applications' can be lawful.[129] Section 41a(1) German Telecommunications Act likewise merely prohibits 'an indiscriminate deterioration of services and unjustified blockage or retardation of data transfer in the networks',[130] so that one could justifiably argue that certain services, for instance, streaming services like Netflix, may be prioritized in order to

---

126. Eckpunktepapier der Bundesregierung zu 'Trusted Computing' und 'Secure Boot', August 2012, http://www.bmi.bund.de/SharedDocs/Downloads/DE/Themen/OED_Ver waltung/Informationsgesellschaft/trusted_computing.pdf?__blob=publicationFile (accessed 11 November 2014).

127. Wielsch, *supra* n. 11, at 249; Levine, *Free Ride*, 238 (2011); Cf. Article 8 para. 4 lit. g Directive 2002/21; Commission declaration on net neutrality, OJ 2009 C 308/2 ('The Commission attaches high importance to preserving the open and neutral character of the internet, taking full account of the will of the co-legislators now to enshrine net neutrality as a policy objective and regulatory principle to be promoted by national regulatory authorities'); § 2 para. 2 section 2 German Telecommunications Act.

128. Vgl. § 41a para. 1 German Telecommunications Act.

129. Brüggemann, *Abkehr von der Netzneutralität – Fluch oder Segen. Managed Services: Ausweg aus dem Datenstau oder Einstieg in das Zwei-Klassen-Netz?*, Computer und Recht 565, 569 (2013).

130. Bundestags-Drucksache 17/7521, 112.

guarantee their quality and security. In the Netherlands, in contrast, such measures are explicitly prohibited. Providers may only limit the data transmission capacity in a non-discriminatory manner and are obliged to advertise 'special services' separately from the general internet access.[131]

The currently pending EU regulation on a 'European single market for electronic communications and to achieve a Connected Continent' of 11 September 2013,[132] which is meant, to overcome these differences, threatens to become a true 9/11 for the principle of net neutrality in the EU. In contrast to what the EU Commission in a press release alleges,[133] it does not follow the Dutch example. Instead, end-users, providers of electronic communications to the public and providers of content 'shall be free to enter into agreements with each other to transmit ... data volumes or traffic as specialized services with a defined quality of service or dedicated capacity.' Although the provision of specialized services 'shall not impair in a recurring or continuous manner the general quality of internet access services', this right to establish 'specialized services' effectively does away with the principle of net neutrality in the EU.[134] If the Commission proposal became law,[135] the internet on the 'connected continent' would fundamentally change. In place of a uniform, the non-discriminatory medium of communication, in which proprietary and open content and applications co-exist and compete on equal terms, two painstakingly separate digital worlds would arise:[136] on the one hand, a premium internet, through which access-controlled services like IP-TV could be streamed with guaranteed quality and security,[137] and on the other, an open but insecure and slow remainder internet. The premium net would be controlled by access providers and

---

131. Article 74A paras 1 and 3 Telecommunicatiewet, available at http://wetten.overheid.nl/zoeken/.
132. Proposal for a Regulation laying down measures concerning the European single market for electronic communications and to achieve a Connected Continent, and amending Directives 2002/20/EC, 2002/21/EC and 2002/22/EC and Regulations (EC) No. 1211/2009 and (EU) No. 531/2012, COM(2013) 627 final, 2013/309 (COD).
133. *See* http://europa.eu/rapid/press-release_MEMO-13-779_en.htm (accessed 11 November 2014).
134. Article 23(2) Proposal Regulation Connected Continent, *supra* n. 132.
135. But *see* Article 23(2) European Parliament legislative resolution of 3 April 2014 – 2013/0309(COD) ('Providers of internet access, of electronic communications to the public and providers of content, applications and services shall be free to offer specialized services to end-users. Such services shall only be offered if the network capacity is sufficient to provide them in addition to internet access services and they are not to the detriment of the availability or quality of internet access services. Providers of internet access to end-users shall not discriminate between functionally equivalent services and applications.')
136. Siehe Renner/Renner, *Digital ist besser*, 225 (2011).
137. Recitals 49-50 Proposal Regulation Connected Continent, *supra* n. 132; Levine, *supra* n. 127, at 238; critical Litman, *supra* n. 5, at 14 ('shopping mall for copyright-protected material'); Zittrain, *supra* n. 125, at 178.

(potentially vertically integrated) content providers.[138] For the rest, access providers would retain their current role as intermediaries. It would suit the logic of the Commission proposal if access providers competed primarily over 'specialized services' and not over the heavily regulated transmission of the remainder internet. This competition could develop such a dynamic in favour of the premium internet and access-controlled 'specialized services'/ 'celestial jukeboxes' that the open internet, and with it, the access culture would drift steadily into oblivion.

Current copyright law is one factor contributing to this scenario becoming a reality. If access providers are, as under current CJEU jurisprudence, obliged to intervene in online traffic for the sake of copyright enforcement anyhow,[139] it indeed seems a logical step to allow them these measures as a business.[140] Thereby, the current contradiction between the regulation of provider markets and the regulation of application and content markets would be dissolved in favour of the latter option, which means controlled security on all layers of the network.

12.3.2   FURTHER REINFORCEMENT OF THE ACCESS CULTURE

In view of the commodification dynamic that radiates from the technically fulfillable wish to market and consume every binary element of potential value in a secure transaction,[141] the possibilities of reinforcing the access culture seem moot. Internet activists and their political offshoots like the Pirate Parties are for the most part fighting rear-guard battles, in which they defend the open internet and the access culture against restrictions. Where they succeed, as in the case of SOPA (the Stop Online Piracy Act), PIPA (the PROTECT IP Act (Preventing Real Online Threats to Economic Creativity and Theft of Intellectual Property Act)) and ACTA (the Anti-Counterfeiting Trade Agreement), it is celebrated as a great success.[142] Far-reaching proposals to weaken copyright immediately face the problem that they are incompatible with international copyright treaties, and therefore, require a –

---

138. Brüggemann, *supra* n. 129, at 567.
139. CJEU, Case C-314/12 para. 56 – UPC Telekabel.
140. *See* Frieden, *Internet Packet Sniffing and Its Impact on the Network Neutrality Debate and the Balance of Power Between Intellectual Property Creators and Consumers*, 18 Fordham Intell. Prop. Media & Ent. L.J. 633, 633 (2007-2008); *Wielsch, supra* n. 11, at 281; Brüggemann, *supra* n. 129, at 570.
141. *See* Cohen, *supra* n. 3, at 268; Zittrain, *supra* n. 125, at 101; Naughton, *supra* n. 9, at 285.
142. Lee, *The Fight for the Future: How People Defeated Hollywood and Saved the internet – For Now* (2013).

rather utopian – global consensus.[143] And even the call to boil down the EU copyright *acquis* to its international-law minimum is only expressed sporadically.[144] A reinforcement of the access culture is thus at best to be expected from outside copyright or as an accidental side result of developments within copyright.

One impulse promoting the participatory communication culture could come from fundamental rights. In particular, an interpretation of copyright law in light of the freedom of the arts could expand the scope of the remix culture.[145] Since adaptations or other transformations of a work may be published or exploited only with the consent of the author of the original work (Section 23 German CA), this widespread, creative and playful practice is generally held to be illegal, and therefore, has to be taken and stay down. A lawful 'free use' of existing work to create an independent work (Section 24 German CA) requires that the claimant's work was only used as a source of inspiration and that its protected elements are hardly recognizable in the independent creation.[146] Obvious borrowings of protected elements are only allowed if they concern parodies.[147]

If such anti-thematic treatment is not apparent, courts consider it infringing to reproduce or adapt recognizable parts of works and to sample even smallest excerpts of audio and/or video recordings, with the rare exception that the respective fragment cannot be recreated.[148] Under these conditions, fan fiction, mash-ups and remixes, as a rule, qualify as unlawful, as their hallmark is the re-use of recognizable, protected works.[149] It is irrelevant whether the contested use is suited or intended to replace the older

---

143. Litman, *supra* n. 5, at 182 and Lessig, *supra* n. 3, at 254 (application of copyright to commercial uses only); on the question or reintroducing copyright formalities *see* van Gompel, *Formalities in Copyright Law. An Analysis of Their History, Rationales and Possible Future* (2011).

144. But *see* Hargreaves/Hugenholtz, *Copyright Reform for Growth and Jobs – Modernising the European Copyright Framework* (2013), http://www.lisboncouncil.net/publication/publication/95-copyright-reform-for-growth-and-jobs-modernising-the-european-copyright-framework.html (accessed 11 November 2014).

145. Lessig, *supra* n. 3, at 28; Naughton, *supra* n. 9, at 253; Cohen, *supra* n. 3, at 247.

146. *Bundesgerichtshof*, Case I ZR 65/96, Gewerblicher Rechtsschutz und Urheberrecht 1999, 984 – Laras Tochter; *Bundesgerichtshof*, Case I ZR 12/08, Gewerblicher Rechtsschutz und Urheberrecht 2011, 134 para. 36 – Perlentaucher.

147. *Bundesgerichtshof*, Case I ZR 117/00, Entscheidungen des Bundesgerichtshofs in Zivilsachen vol. 154, 260, 268 – Gies-Adler; *Bundesgerichtshof*, Case I ZR 12/08, Gewerblicher Rechtsschutz und Urheberrecht 2011, 134 para. 34 – Perlentaucher.

148. § 24 para. 2 German Copyright Act and *Bundesgerichtshof*, Case I ZR 112/06, Gewerblicher Rechtsschutz und Urheberrecht 2009, 403 para. 21 – Metall auf Metall.

149. Alpert, *Zum Werk – und Werkteilbegriff bei elektronischer Musik – Tracks, Basslines, Beats, Sounds, Samples, Remixes und DJ-Sets*, Zeitschrift für Urheber- und Medienrecht 525, 530 (2002); Knopp, *Fanfiction – nutzergenerierte Inhalte und das Urheberrecht*, Gewerblicher Rechtsschutz und Urheberrecht 28, 29 (2010).

work.[150] According to this dominant view, the productive branch of the access culture must limit itself to material that has been licensed explicitly for this purpose[151] or for which the lawfulness of an adaptation follows from the implicit consent of the right holder.[152] The thousandfold playful treatment of popular cultural material that knows no rules of prior consent, therefore, depends entirely on the generous and intelligent forbearance of right holders like Ms Rowling.[153]

However, the prevailing restrictive reading of the principle of free use according to section 24 German CA[154] can no longer be upheld in view of the fundamental right to freedom of the arts. In a decision concerning the artistic technique of a text collage,[155] the German Federal Constitutional Court (*Bundesverfassungsgericht*) felt inclined to remind the *Bundesgerichtshof* of the 'fundamental' insight that a work once published is no longer at the disposal of its owner alone. Rather, over time it becomes intellectual and cultural common property. The social embeddedness and contextualization of a work is the prerequisite for its effectiveness and also the reason why artists are obliged to accept a 'certain measure of interference in their copyright on the part of other artists representing society interacting with the work of art'. To ascertain the permissible level of such interference, the limits of copyright must be interpreted in the light of artistic freedom, which protects the interests of other artists 'in being able to enter into an artistic dialogue and a creative process regarding existing works without the risk of interference on the level of finance or content'. These statements are likewise valid for fan fiction, mash-ups and remixes. The *Bundesverfassungsgericht* explicitly states that 'the artistic adaptation of others' texts is not limited to a critical annotation of the statement contained therein, but can take diverse

---

150. *Bundesgerichtshof*, Case I ZR 12/08, Gewerblicher Rechtsschutz und Urheberrecht 2011, 134 para. 45 – Perlentaucher.

151. 'Copyleft'.

152. This can only be referred to briefly here, and would have to be elaborated with regard to different circles of the public, in which different uses are 'normal' (cf. *Bundesgerichtshof*, Case I ZR 69/08, Gewerblicher Rechtsschutz und Urheberrecht 2010, 628 para. 36 – Vorschaubilder I). It seems obvious to distinguish between freely available artistic and other pictures, films and sound recordings, of which at least non-commercial adaptations can be viewed as implicitly legalized, on the one hand, and scientific works, where the scientific communication norms oppose such permission, on the other hand. *See* Peukert, *supra* n. 103.

153. *See*, for example, http://www.fanfiktion.de/FFs/c/103005001 (accessed 11 November 2014). *See also* Erickson/Kretschmer/Mendis, *Copyright and the Economic Effects of Parody: An Empirical Study of Music Videos on the YouTube Platform and an Assessment of the Regulatory Options*, http://www.ipo.gov.uk/ipresearch-parody-report3-150313.pdf, 9 (2013) (accessed 11 November 2014).

154. *Bundesgerichtshof*, Case I ZR 65/96, Gewerblicher Rechtsschutz und Urheberrecht 1999, 984, 987 – Laras Tochter.

155. *Bundesverfassungsgericht*, Case 1 BvR 825/98, Gewerblicher Rechtsschutz und Urheberrecht 2001, 149, 151 – Germania 3.

forms that the artist chooses according to his aesthetic conceptions.'[156] These adaptations are permissible as free uses pursuant to section 24(1) German CA if the recognizable borrowing of protected elements does not serve merely to enhance one's work with the intellectual property of another, but is an integral element of a new, artistic statement in its own right. Moreover, this exercise of freedom must not entail the risk of considerable economic harm (e.g., loss of profits).

Depending on the circumstances of the case, these requirements are met if fans continue fictional stories, in particular, if they change perspectives and dominant narratives.[157] The mixing of parts of other works and recordings into a new artistic whole, as well as the modification of digital works, can also qualify as a permissible 'free artistic use'. Whereas German copyright practice has long accepted these practices only if they form part of a parody, the *Bundesverfassungsgericht* made clear that copyright law has to be read in the light of the freedom of the arts, and therefore, has to accept artistic practices like collage and compilation films. EU copyright law refers to such practices under the heading of *pastiche*.[158] Precisely this positively connoted form of homage, of artistic emulation paying tribute to a masterpiece, characterizes the typical cases of fan fiction, mash-ups and remixes. Regardless of their aesthetic 'value', they are permissible under copyright law if they respect the moral rights of the author and exert no considerable economic harm on the works concerned.[159]

If this approach prevailed, the open remix culture could finally become formal and extend to the entirety of cultural goods. This mode of open communication would, however, still be accused of contributing very little to cultural diversity, or in fact of representing its downfall, if it only comprised amateurish 'user-generated content'.[160] An agenda favouring the access culture, therefore, has to comprise monetary incentives in order to increase the share of professional yet 'open' works. For also in an open internet, the investment of time and money requires amortization. Currently, professional authors finance their freely available works through sources of income not, or at best indirectly, related to copyright, such as income from other work, scholarships and prizes or complementary services, particularly live

---

156. *Bundesverfassungsgericht*, Case 1 BvR 825/98, Gewerblicher Rechtsschutz und Urheberrecht 2001, 149, 151 – Germania 3.

157. Contra *Bundesgerichtshof*, Case I ZR 65/96, Gewerblicher Rechtsschutz und Urheberrecht 1999, 984, 987 – Laras Tochter.

158. *See* Article 5 para. 3 lit. k Copyright Directive 2001/29.

159. *See* Erickson/Kretschmer/Mendis, *supra* n. 153, at 10 (no empirical proof that parodies of musical works are detrimental to the commercialization of the original).

160. *See* Lanier, *You are not a Gadget* (2010); Theisohn, *Literarisches Eigentum* (2012).

performances.[161] They have no share in the profits that hybrid business models – the Googles of the internet – generate. The standard copyright answers to this dilemma tend either toward combating hybrids in the interest of the exclusivity culture, thus undermining the access culture indirectly (*see* above), or toward introducing an alternative compensation scheme, in Germany labelled 'cultural flat fee'. The latter model, however, arouses considerable international-law concerns and in the meantime, enjoys only very little political support.[162]

However, it is possible to conceive a model that avoids these pitfalls and nevertheless funds the access culture via copyright law. The basic idea of the concept is to leave it up to the right holder to decide whether the work or the other subject matter of protection should be available in an exclusive or an open mode. Depending on this decision, uses would be remunerated either by individual licence fees (exclusivity culture) or by a statutory levy (access culture). The levy would be reserved exclusively for subject matter that is available without technical barriers on the internet. If instead, the author decided in favour of an exclusive marketing model, her copyright income would accrue only from individual royalties.[163] In both cases, the remuneration has to be 'equitable'.[164]

In such a model, the competition between the exclusivity and the access culture would receive an important economic twist: the more authors and users opt for one alternative (say the access culture), the greater becomes the share of the respective alternative (in this case the levy-based revenues) in the total copyright value, and the greater is the financial incentive for professional authors to prefer this option. Which way the scale will tip, and whether network effects will lead to the drying up of the communication culture that is marginalized, depends in part on the other regulatory conditions addressed in this paper. The more beneficial the regulatory environment is for one or the other communication culture, the more likely it is to prosper.

12.4   CONCLUSION

This final observation confirms that the dominant discourse about digital copyright is, in descriptive as well as prescriptive terms, too short-sighted.

---

161. Such sources of income have always been paramount for a majority of authors, even when they (want to) operate within the exclusivity model; cf. Kretschmer, *Does Copyright Law Matter? An Empirical Analysis of Creators' Earnings*, http://dx.doi.org/10.2139/ssrn.2063735 (2012).
162. *See* Peukert, *supra* n. 21.
163. Peukert, *Neue Techniken und ihre Auswirkung auf die Erhebung und Verteilung gesetzlicher Vergütungsansprüche*, Zeitschrift für Urheber- und Medienrecht 1050 (2003); Peukert, *supra* n. 21.
164. §§ 54h para. 1, para. 2 section 1 and §§ 32-32c German Copyright Act.

According to this reading, antagonistic conflicts are to be solved by balancing all interests involved. An either-or scenario disappears after a mystical balancing exercise. This counterintuitive narrative fails to recognize that the internet allows the co-existence of two paradigmatic communication cultures along with particularly interesting and contested hybrids between the two. Authors and users have the possibility to communicate in the copyright-secured, exclusive mode as well as the option to exchange information without technical and direct monetary access barriers. The preferred method can change at any time for every participant and content, which explains the unprecedented dynamic of online communication.

The approach taken here also has normative implications. First, it allows the analysis of copyright (and other) regulatory proposals according to their effects on one or the other culture of communication. Second, it releases from the ultimately fruitless quest for a harmonious solution on a higher level that will only trigger new conflicts in the future. Finally, the normative assessment of digital copyright can relax. Instead of professing to be a pro or contra digital copyright, it suffices to take the considerably less demanding normative starting point that in the interest of individual freedom and cultural diversity both cultures of communication are of equal value and that no regulation shall have the effect of threatening the existence of one of them. This approach is decidedly copyright affirmative, as it stresses the right of the original owner of the copyright to choose the proper mode of communication.[165]

These observations are not limited to copyright law but apply to the regulation of the internet in general. As has become evident in this paper, copyright law cannot be viewed in isolation from data protection, telecommunications and other information law.[166] Some of these rules are complementary (e.g., when access providers are liable for copyright infringements and are empowered by telecommunications law to commercialize 'specialized services'); others create tensions (e.g., when the enforcement of copyright is strengthened irrespective of data protection laws). As a whole, they provoke the question of what the internet of the future should look like.[167]

In this context, digital copyright, for the most part, supports a secure, exclusively controlled communication medium along the lines of Goldstein's 'celestial jukebox'. Despite all advantages that such a vision might entail, particularly to rights-holders, long-term implications of historical dimensions must also be considered. The open, participative internet, which is rightly

---

165. *See* Lehman, *supra* n. 3, at 14; Peukert, *supra* n. 89.
166. Komaitis, *Internet Society Issues Paper on Intellectual Property on the Internet*, http://www.internetsociety.org/doc/internet-society-issues-paper-intellectual-property-internet, 1 (2013) (accessed 11 November 2014); Wielsch, *supra* n. 11, at 254.
167. Schmidt/Cohen, *supra* n. 54, at 126 (in ten years the relevant question will no longer be whether a society uses the internet, but which version it uses). For different scenarios, *see* Komaitis, *supra* n. 166.

reckoned among 'the few things humans have built that they don't truly understand',[168] would become a kind of television. It could be controlled, monitored and potentially manipulated much easier than the internet in its current form.[169] Such a move would also bring to an end the innovative potential of the open internet and the access culture associated with it, manifesting itself in a stream of new applications, new business models, and last but not least countless new works.[170] The age of printing came about in spite of all-powerful resistance against the changes associated with that disruptive invention. The regulatory tendencies sketched out above make it seem plausible that the further development of the internet will take a different path.

---

168. Schmidt/Cohen, *supra* n. 54, at 1.
169. Lessig, *supra* n. 11, at xv; Naughton, *supra* n. 9, at 291 (Orwell-Huxley Scenario); Schmidt/Cohen, *supra* n. 54, at 162.
170. Cohen, *supra* n. 3, at 224; Lessig, *supra* n. 11, at 28, 146; Zittrain, *supra* n. 125, at 67; Brüggemann, *supra* n. 129, at, 568; Wittgenstein, *supra* n. 25, at 160; Litman, *supra* n. 5, at 102; Benkler, *supra* n. 3, at 63, 91; Post, *supra* n. 17, at 204. The 'copyright drag' is epitomized by the internet-based personal video recorder (PVR), whose admissibility under copyright law has been under dispute in Germany for eight years, outcome uncertain; cf. *Bundesgerichtshof*, Case I ZR 216/06, Gewerblicher Rechtsschutz und Urheberrecht 2009, 845 – Internet-Videorecorder I; *Bundesgerichtshof*, Case I ZR 152/11, Gewerblicher Rechtsschutz und Urheberrecht 2013, 618 – Internet-Videorecorder II.

Chapter 13

Fair Use, Transformative Use and the First Amendment

Marshall Leaffer

13.1   INTRODUCTION

The First Amendment of the Constitution of the United States (U.S.) declares: "Congress shall make no law ... abridging the freedom of speech, or of the press."[1] A few courts[2] and many commentators[3] have referred to a tension between copyright and the First Amendment that "Congress shall make no law ... abridging the freedom of speech. ... " If the First Amendment is taken literally, copyright appears to encroach on the freedom

---

1. U.S. Const. amend. I.
2. *See*, e.g., *Triangle Publ'ns, Inc. v. Knight-Ridder Newspapers, Inc.*, 626 F.2d 1171 (5th Cir. 1980); *Schnapper v. Foley*, 471 F. Supp. 426 (D.D.C. 1979); *Maxtone -Graham v. Burtchaell*, 631 F. Supp. 1432 (S.D.N.Y. 1986).
3. To mention a few: Neil Netanel, Copyright's Paradox (2008); Rebecca Tushnet, *Copyright as a Model for Free Speech Law: What Copyright Has in Common with Anti-Pornography Laws, Campaign Finance Reform, and Telecommunications Regulation*, 42 B.C. L. Rev. 1 (2000); Rebecca Tushnet, *Copy This Essay: How Fair Use Doctrine Harms Free Speech and How Copying Serves It*, 114 Yale L.J. 535 (2004); Robert C. Denicola, *Copyright and Free Speech: Constitutional Limitations on the Protection of Expression*, 67 Calif. L. Rev. 283 (1979); Paul Goldstein, *Copyright and the First Amendment*, 70 Colum. L. Rev. 983 (1970); Melville B. Nimmer, *Does Copyright Abridge the First Amendment Guarantees of Free Speech and Press?*, 17 UCLA L. Rev. 1180 (1970); Lyman Ray Patterson, *Private Copyright and Public Communication: Free Speech Endangered*, 28 Vand. L. Rev. 1161 (1975).

of speech and First Amendment values because it prohibits the right to reproduce the expression of others. Does this create an irreconcilable tension between the two constitutional provisions: the Patent and Copyright Clause and the First Amendment? Although the language of the First Amendment seems unqualified, courts have not interpreted it as such, and even scholars who argue for "absolute" free speech protection acknowledge significant limits on their theories. Courts have long recognized several critical exceptions to freedom of speech, including obscenity, fighting words, true threats, incitement, and child pornography. Additionally copyright law, which suppresses some forms of speech, is recognized as falling within the accepted restrictions on the First Amendment. Despite the amount of space devoted to this subject in law reviews, few courts have ever held that the First Amendment prevents the enforcement of copyright.[4] In fact, copyright and the First Amendment's guarantee of free speech have coexisted for two centuries with surprisingly little conflict.

How has this peaceful coexistence between copyright law and the First Amendment endured? Copyright, after all, allows the copyright owner to prevent others from legally reproducing, distributing, performing, displaying, or preparing derivative works from the copyrighted work. So what saves copyright from First Amendment condemnation? It is now universally accepted that copyright's idea-expression dichotomy supplies the necessary definitional balance, allowing access to and dissemination of ideas and facts while protecting the author's expression.[5] With equal vigor, courts recognize that the defense of fair use plays a critical role in reconciling copyright law with the First Amendment—fair use can be invoked where rigid application of the Copyright Act would unreasonably prevent the dissemination of information.[6] In addition to the idea-expression dichotomy and the fair use doctrine, several other aspects of copyright deserve mention in this regard. On the most basic level, the requirement of originality prevents copyright protection of anything that is in the public domain, and the requirement that copyright may not endure for more than limited times, in turn, ensures that all copyrighted matter will inevitably pass into the public domain. Moreover, the Copyright Act explicitly denies copyright protection to works of the U.S. Government,[7] and case law has held this to be true of state and local legislation and judicial decisions. The Copyright Act also contains a plethora of special exemptions from copyright protection that entail many situations that otherwise would raise First Amendment issues.[8]

---

4. *Triangle Publ'ns, Inc. v. Knight-Ridder Newspapers, Inc.*, 626 F.2d 1171 (5th Cir. 1980); *see also Schnapper v. Foley*, 471 F. Supp. 426 (D.D.C. 1979).
5. *See Sid & Marty Krofft Television Prods., Inc. v. McDonald's Corp.*, 562 F.2d 1157 (9th Cir. 1977).
6. *See Consumers Union of U.S., Inc. v. General Signal Corp.*, 724 F.2d 1044, 1046 (2d Cir. 1983).
7. 17 U.S.C.A. § 105.
8. *See* 17 U.S.C §§ 107-122.

Viewed in this way, copyright law optimizes First Amendment values by encouraging production of works of authorship without prohibiting the free communication of facts and ideas embodied in these works. In other words, copyright law does not impede the flow of information per se, and does not impede the free flow of ideas, but provides positive incentives to encourage the flow.[9] In *Eldred v. Ashcroft*, a case involving a First Amendment challenge to the Copyright Term Extension Act which increased the term of all existing copyrights by twenty years, the Supreme Court stated:

> The Copyright Clause and First Amendment were adopted close in time. This proximity indicates that, in the Framers' view, copyright's limited monopolies are compatible with free speech principles. Indeed, copyright's purpose is to promote the creation and publication of free expression. As Harper & Row, Publishers, Inc., v. Nation Enterprises] observed: "[T]he Framers intended copyright itself to be the engine of free expression. By establishing a marketable right to the use of one's expression, copyright supplies the economic incentive to create and disseminate ideas."[10]

In providing for copyright law the Constitution implicitly takes the position that protecting the creations of authors from exploitation by others enriches free expression. As one court put it: "The First Amendment is not a license to trammel on legally recognized rights of intellectual property."[11] If a copyright owner can demonstrate a substantial likelihood of copyright infringement, a court in its discretion can grant a preliminary injunction barring publication of the infringing work despite the First Amendment law that would preclude prior restraints on speech.[12]

In sum, the doctrine of fair use along with other fundamental doctrines within copyright law is said to save copyright from First Amendment condemnation. But when can fair use be asserted? In the most general of terms, fair use typically arises in two instances. The first involves the uses of copyrighted works for personal purposes such as excerpts from a book you

---

9. *See*, e.g., *Pac. & S. Co., Inc. v. Duncan*, 744 F.2d 1490 (11th Cir. 1984).

10. *Eldred v. Ashcroft*, 537 U.S. 186, 219, 1 (2003), quoting *Harper & Row* at 471 U.S. at 556 (1985). In *Golan v. Holder*, 132 S. Ct. 873, 889-890 (2012), the Court reiterated its observation, paraphrasing its statement in *Eldred*.

11. *Dallas Cowboys Cheerleaders, Inc. v. Scoreboard Posters, Inc.*, 600 F.2d 1184, 1187-88 (5th Cir. 1979).

12. *See ibid.*, at 1188; *Salinger v. Random House, Inc.*, 811 F.2d 90 (2d Cir. 1987) (enjoining publication of a biography of the writer J.D. Salinger); *see also Craft v. Kobler*, 667 F. Supp. 120 (S.D.N.Y. 1987) (enjoining a forthcoming biography of Igor Stravinsky, the composer, because the appropriations of copyrighted material were too extensive and important and their justification too slight to support an overall claim of fair use). *But see Sun Trust Bank v. Houghton Mifflin Co.*, 268 F.3d 1257, 1277 (11th Cir. 2001) (Vacating lower court's grant of temporary injunction against publication of defendant's parody. *See also* Mark A. Lemley & Eugene Volokh, *Freedom of Speech and Injunctions in Intellectual Property Cases*, 48 DUKE L.J. 147 (1998).

are reading for study purposes, whether by photocopying, digital copying, or scanning. The second general category of fair use, and the focus of this chapter, occurs when a third party reuses copyrighted material to make a new work under the doctrine "transformative use."

The purpose of chapter is not to examine the mechanics of fair use in all its manifestations but to concentrate on the aspect of fair use first adopted by the Supreme Court in *Campbell v. Acuff-Rose Music, Inc.* Known as "transformative use," this iteration of the fair use doctrine is defined as a use that has *transformed* the original, and, in so doing, adds value by creating "new information, new aesthetics, new insights and understandings."[13] The transformative use doctrine arose in the case law of the 1990s and its application is said to have enlarged the scope fair use. Indeed, if one reviews fair use case law since *Campbell,* one must conclude that transformative use has provided a basis for a more expansive application of fair use. However, determining what constitutes transformative use in a particular factual context is a question of some controversy as revealed in the case law and debate in literature. My goal is to examine to what extent the doctrine of transformative use in its current state of evolution allows the production of new works fulfilling the promise of copyright in support of First Amendments values as the engine of expression. Before delving into the evolution and intricacies of transformative use, section 13.2 which follows, provides a brief overview of the fair use doctrine. In section 13.3, I will examine the origins or transformative use doctrine and its application to issue of parody. In section 13.4, I will focus on the evolution and enlargement of transformative use. In sum, I will show how transformative use is a doctrine that has waxed and waned in the case law where the courts have essentially tried to First Amendment values with copyright law.

---

13. *See* Leon E. Seltzer, *Exemptions and Fair Use in Copyright Law* 24 (1978) (arguing statement that a fair use is a productive use). Instead of "productive use" some courts have adopted the term "transformative" use. The concept is the same. *See* Pierre N. Leval, *Toward a Fair Use Standard,* 103 Harv. L. Rev. 1105, 1111 (1990) (stating that a use is "transformative" if it is productive and employs the quoted matter in a different manner or for a different purpose from the original; it adds value to the original). For an application of Judge Leval's transformative use doctrine, *see Campbell v. Acuff -Rose Music, Inc.,* 510 U.S. 569, 579 (1994) ("[T]he goal of copyright, to promote science and the arts, is generally furthered by the creation of transformative works."). *See also* Judge Leval's opinion in *Am. Geophysical Union v. Texaco, Inc.,* 802 F. Supp. 1 (S.D.N.Y. 1992) (finding that reproduction of single copies from plaintiff's journals, even for research purposes, is not a transformative use and thus not a fair use). For a comprehensive discussion of the development of the fair use doctrine and the rise to prominence of the transformative use paradigm, *see* Neil Weinstock Netanel, *Making Sense of Fair Use,* 15 Lewis & Clark L. Rev. 715 (2011).

13.2 AN OVERVIEW OF FAIR USE

13.2.1 HISTORICAL PERSPECTIVE

Although codified in the 1976 Act, the doctrine of fair use has retained its nature as an equitable rule of reason to be applied where a finding of infringement would either be unfair or undermine "the Progress of Science and the useful Arts." Fair use has been defined as a "privilege in others than the owner of a copyright to use the copyrighted material in a reasonable manner without consent, notwithstanding the monopoly granted to the owner."[14] The current Act sets forth fair use in section 107, which contains a preamble, gives examples where fair use might apply, and provides four broad criteria that must all be applied to determine whether a use is "fair." It is by far the most important defense to an action for copyright infringement.

The defense of fair use becomes relevant only after the plaintiff has made out a prima facie case for copyright infringement by showing copying of the original work and substantial similarity between the works. Once this occurs, the defendant bears the evidentiary burdens of production and persuasion that the infringing use of the copyrighted work was privileged as a fair use.[15] Fair use is a mixed question of law and fact. If a reasonable trier of fact could reach only one conclusion, a court may conclude as a matter of law that the challenged use of the copyrighted work qualifies as a fair use.[16]

First articulated in case law in the mid-nineteenth century,[17] fair use was not given its first statutory recognition until the 1976 Act.[18] The 1976 Act, however, does not try to define the doctrine. Instead, in section 107, Congress codified past practice by incorporating an incoherent body of case law into the 1976 Act.[19] As a result, the fair use defense continues to defy precise definition and remains an ad hoc equitable rule of reason where finding an infringement would undermine the ultimate purpose of copyright law. As one court stated, "[t]he doctrine of fair use ... permits courts to avoid rigid application of the copyright statute when, on occasion, it would stifle the very creativity which that law is designed to foster."[20] The trade-off for this

---

14. *Rosemont Enters., Inc. v. Random House, Inc.*, 366 F.2d 303, 306 (2d Cir. 1966) (citing H. BALL, COPYRIGHT AND LITERARY PROPERTY 260 (1944)).
15. For a discussion of how liability for intermediaries affects the fair use privileges of individuals, *see* Joseph P. Liu, *Toward a Defense of Fair Use Enablement, or How U.S. Copyright Law Is Hurting My Daughter*, 57 J. COPYRIGHT SOC'Y 423 (2010).
16. *See Harper & Row, Publishers, Inc. v. Nation Enters.*, 471 U.S. 539 (1985); *Hustler Magazine, Inc. v. Moral Majority, Inc.*, 796 F.2d 1148, 1150 (9th Cir. 1986).
17. *See Folsom v. Marsh*, 9 F. Cas. 342 (C.C.D. Mass. 1841) (No. 4901).
18. 17 U.S.C. § 107.
19. For a discussion of the four criteria used in determining fair use, *see infra* section. 13.2.3.
20. *Iowa State Univ. Research Found., Inc. v. Am. Broad. Cos.*, 621 F.2d 57, 60 (2d Cir. 1980).

flexibility is an elusive legal doctrine reputed to be the most troublesome in copyright law.[21]

The doctrine of fair use is codified in § 107 of the 1976 Act. The statute, however, does not provide a tight definition of the doctrine. Instead, it sets forth in its preamble the kinds of uses that usually prompt the defense, followed by four criteria that must *all* be applied to determine whether the defense succeeds. The legislative history of § 107 indicates no intent to freeze the doctrine, but rather to allow its continuing development through the case law and its adaptation to changing times and technology.[22] The fact remains, where limitations and exceptions on copyright are concerned, that the U.S. does things differently from most of the rest of the world. In an era when "harmonization" has become the watchword in international copyright, will the U.S. continue to enjoy its unique position?

Elsewhere, particularly in civil law countries, the situation is different where the concept of fair use does not exist. For example, in sections of the German statute covering limitations of copyright, one can find the functional equivalent in certain exceptions specifically embodied in the German Act.[23] These specific exemptions include the making of single copies for strictly private use, reproducing small parts of works for instructional purposes, a narrowly restricted quotation privilege, copying in judicial opinions, reproduction of works in news reports, and certain reproductions of works of art in exhibition or auction catalogues. In addition, German law provides that other unlicensed private and educational uses of protected works may be permissible if the copyright owner's so-called right of remuneration is recognized. For example, home taping of broadcasts is exempt from liability for copyright infringement. A levy on equipment and blank media, however, creates a fund to remunerate copyright owners and creators through collective organizations. Treated similarly are exceptions and limitations that apply to photocopying, the creation of religious and instructional anthologies, and free, noncommercial performances.

Despite certain differences in conception, doctrines such as free utilization under certain civil law regimes may lead to similar results as one

---

21. *See Dellar v. Samuel Goldwyn, Inc.*, 104 F.2d 661, 662 (2d Cir. 1939); for a more positive view of fair use, *see* Pamela Samuelson, *Unbundling Fair Uses*, 77 FORDAM L. REV. 2537 (2009) (arguing that fair use is more coherent and more predictable than many commentators have perceived once one recognizes that fair use cases tend to fall into common patterns). For a discussion of the developments of fair use since 2004 and how James Madison's separation of powers metaphor applies in a preliminary way to copyright, *see* Michael J. Madison, *Madisonian Fair Use*, 30 CARDOZO ARTS & ENT. L.J. 39 (2012). For a discussion of the Second Circuit's invention of the concept of "fair use markets" and for an argument that fair use is possible even when licensing revenues are available, *see* Wendy J. Gordon, *Fair Use Markets: On Weighing Potential License Fees*, 79 GEO. WASH. L. REV. 1814 (2011).

22. H.R. REP. NOS. 94-1476, at 66 (1976).

23. Adolf Dietz, "*Germany*," *in* Paul Edward Geller & Melville E. Nimmer, *International Copyright Law and Practice* § 8[2][a], at GER-100 (1997).

would find under the fair use doctrine in U.S. law. For example, the German courts have given some leeway to forms of artistic expression, such as parody, that incorporate other protected works while only partially transforming them. Under these circumstances, the protected work remains clearly recognizable in the allegedly infringing work.[24]

Questions of form aside, how different in functional terms is the civil law system of specific exemptions from U.S. style fair use? Overall, the kinds of uses secured by fair use are significantly broader than their civil law counterparts. The U.S. conception of fair use is by its nature a dynamic rather than a static doctrine. As patterns of exploitation and consumption for copyrighted works change, courts can adapt the fair use doctrine to new circumstances as they have tried to do, for example, photocopiers, videocassette recorders, and software. Thus, the doctrine has the capacity to retain its relevance without the need for legislative enactment. By contrast, parliamentary action will be required to keep most civil law systems, such as that of Germany, abreast of current developments. The built-in flexibility of the U.S. fair use doctrine manifests itself in § 107 of the Copyright Act, which begins with a preamble followed in the statute by four broad criteria to be used in determining fair use.

No matter which legal regime one examines, copyright law was never intended to be a system that would extract every penny out of every use of copyright eligible work. In the U.S., copyright law defends certain limited exclusive rights but simultaneously recognizes that certain rights are not worth the costs they impose. The fair use doctrine implements that balance. It enables courts to consider the degree to which the enforcement of a given legal right would meaningfully encourage the type of creativity that copyright law was designed to foster as the engine of the First Amendment. Alternatively, it authorizes courts to weigh that consideration against whatever harms—First Amendment or otherwise—society could suffer if copyright law is enforced against use of copyrighted work.

13.2.2   The Preamble of the Statute

As a threshold, parties asserting the defense of fair use should show that they are engaged in an activity enumerated in the preamble to § 107.[25] The preamble reads as follows: "Notwithstanding the provisions of Section 106, the fair use of a copyrighted work, including such use by reproduction in copies or phonorecords or by any other means specified by that section, for purposes such as criticism, comment, news reporting, teaching (including

---

24. *Ibid.*
25. *See Ass'n of Am. Med. Colls. v. Mikaelian,* 571 F. Supp. 144 (E.D. Pa. 1983), *aff'd,* 734 F.2d 3 (3d Cir. 1984).

multiple copies for classroom use), scholarship, or research, is not an infringement of copyright."[26]

The examples listed are broad and overlapping. They are meant to be illustrative, not exhaustive, allowing for other contexts in which the fair use defense might arise.[27] For example, the preamble does not specifically mention parody, but the categories of criticism and comment are broad enough to include parody. Even if parody did not fall into the illustrative categories, one could nevertheless argue that it constitutes a context in which fair use should operate.[28]

13.2.3 THE FOUR CRITERIA

Whether or not the use falls into one of the enumerated categories of the preamble to § 107, the statute sets forth that one must apply the four factors to determine whether the use is fair. The four factors that follow the preamble are the heart of the fair use determination. Section 107 states:

> *In determining whether the use made of a work in any particular case is a fair use the factors to be considered shall include—*
>
> (1) the purpose and character of the use, including whether such use is of a commercial nature or is for nonprofit educational purposes;
> (2) the nature of the copyrighted work;
> (3) the amount and substantiality of the portion used in relation to the copyrighted work as a whole; and
> (4) the effect of the use upon the potential market for or value of the copyrighted work.

According to the legislative history, the four factors represent a codification of fair use.[29] One might ask why Congress would wish to codify the common law of fair use, with all its disarray and questionable applicability to a world of new technologies and nonprint media. The goal was not merely to incorporate the past but also to allow for a flexible and dynamic future. The House Report states:

> Beyond a very broad statutory explanation of what fair use is and some of the criteria applicable to it, the courts must be free to adapt the doctrine to particular situations on a case-by-case basis. Section 107 is

---

26. 17 U.S. C. § 107.
27. *See* 17 U.S.C. § 101. The terms "including" and "such as" are illustrative, not limitative.
28. *See infra* section 13.4 for a discussion of parody.
29. H.R. REP. NOS. 94-1476, at 66 (1976). One can trace the four-factor approach back to *Folsom v. Marsh* in 1841, 9 F. Cas. 342 (C.C.D. Mass. 1841) (No. 4901). In fact, the factors in § 107 differ from that early case only by the addition of the second factor, the nature of the copyrighted work.

intended to restate the present judicial doctrine of fair use, not to change, narrow, or enlarge it in any way.[30]

Despite Congress' intention to codify fair use, § 107 is, in some important ways, a departure from past practice. First, the major criteria in determining fair use are made explicit for the first time. Second, and more importantly, courts must consider *all* four enumerated factors in determining fair use. The inquiry, however, need not be limited only to those factors. The language "shall include" indicates that a court can, in its discretion, consider other factors as well,[31] such as lack of good faith[32] and industry custom or practice.[33]

Practical application of § 107's four factors has not led to predictable results. In a given case, one may find majority and dissenting opinions disagreeing completely on the application of each factor.[34] This is hardly surprising. The factors are broadly stated, overlapping, and vague, and the legislative history provides little insight as to their meaning, what weight to give them, or how they interrelate. Most post-1976 Act cases dealing with fair use apply the four criteria in a mechanical fashion.[35] Invariably, each factor is examined in sequence, the court focusing on one or more of the factors—often the fourth factor of market effect—in coming to a "reasoned" judgment.

Fair use analysis changed in the 1990s with the embrace of transformative use as a de facto fifth or super criterion applied in situations where the defendant has substantially copied the copyrighted work to produce a new work. As we will see in section 13.5 below, the courts have used the transformative use doctrine to allow a wider access to copyrighted works and as the discussion will show the doctrine has evolved in ways that have increased the access to copyrighted works. First, I will begin by describing the origins of the transformative use doctrine, with particular focus on its application in the parody context. As we will see from *Campbell v.*

---

30. H.R. Rep. Nos. 94-1476, at 66 (1976).
31. Section 101 defines "including" and "such as" as illustrative, not limitative.
32. *See Roy Export Co. Establishment v. Columbia Broad. Sys., Inc.*, 503 F. Supp. 1137 (S.D.N.Y. 1980), *aff'd*, 672 F.2d 1095 (2d Cir. 1982).
33. *See Use Triangle Publ'ns, Inc. v. Knight-Ridder Newspapers, Inc.*, 626 F.2d 1171 (5th Cir. 1980).
34. *Compare,* e.g., Justice O'Connor's majority opinion in *Harper & Row, Publishers, Inc. v. Nation Enters.*, 471 U.S. 539 (1985), *with* Justice Brennan's dissent in that case.
35. For a criticism of the standard mechanical application the process, *see* Judge Posner's opinion in *Ty, Inc. v. Publ'ns Int'l, Ltd*, 292 F.3d 512, 522 (7th Cir. 2002) ("The important point is simply that … the four factors are a checklist of things to be considered rather than a formula for decision; and likewise the list of statutory purposes. … Because the factors and purposes are not exhaustive, Ty can get nowhere in defending the judgment by arguing that some or even all of them lean against the defence of fair use. The question is whether … the use of the photos is a fair use because it is the only way to prepare a collectors' guide.").

Acuff-Rose,[36] the seminal case in fair use jurisprudence, finding that a use is transformative can be critical in a finding of fair use but the analysis does not stop there because the four criteria must also be applied as well.

The transformative use theory of fair use has its obvious limits and does not exhaust all the instances where fair use is appropriate. In *Sony Corp. of America v. Universal City Studios (Betamax)*,[37] the Supreme Court ruled that private, noncommercial taping of "free" television programming for time-shifting purposes[38] constituted fair use. The use made by the defendant did not fall into any of those listed in the preamble to § 107. It was clearly not a transformative use, but merely copying for the sake of convenience. Rather than limiting fair use to transformative use, the Supreme Court viewed fair use in much broader terms, as an equitable rule of reason to be determined case by case. In upholding the fair use defense, the Court focused on the economic impact of the use on the incentives to produce copyrighted works: whether the use was commercial or nonprofit. The Court found no harm to the market from defendant's private noncommercial use of the copyrighted material on "free" television broadcasts. In sum, *Betamax* shows that one can successfully assert fair use even if the use does not fall squarely within those listed in the preamble, and even if it is far from being a productive use that transforms the copyrighted work. Generally, however, the defense of fair use is much easier to prove when the defendant has made a transformative use, rather than an ordinary or reproductive use, of the copyright owner's work.[39]

13.3   THE ORIGINS OF THE TRANSFORMATIVE USE DOCTRINE

The concept of transformative use evolved in academic writings that attempted to provide a synthesis of fair use. Going back to basics, scholars have argued that the examples of fair use found in the preamble have one thing in common: each could be called a productive use that builds on the works of others by adding its own socially valuable creative element. Indeed, the uses listed in the preamble conveniently fit into the productive use concept, with the possible exception of "multiple copies for classroom use" to employ the copyrighted work in a different manner or for a different purpose from the original.

---

36. 510 U.S. 569 (1994).
37. 464 U.S. 417 (1984). The Supreme Court reversed the Ninth Circuit Court of Appeals, which rejected the fair use defense and had based its decision on a productive use theory of fair use. *See Universal City Studios, Inc. v. Sony Corp. of Am.*, 659 F.2d 963, 970 (9th Cir. 1981).
38. To "time-shift" means to copy a television program for viewing at a later, more convenient time.
39. *See Pac. & S. Co., v. Duncan*, 744 F.2d 1490 (11th Cir. 1984).

The concept of productive use reappeared with renewed vigor and a new name—*transformative use*—in an article written by Judge Pierre Leval, who reasoned that fair use of a copyrighted work is a use that has *transformed* the original, and, in so doing, adds value by creating "new information, new aesthetics, new insights and understandings."[40] Thus, critics, reporters, and biographers copy not for copying sake, convenience, or pleasure, but to produce separate works of authorship. Their use of the copyrighted work is productive or, in the current parlance, "transformative." On the other hand, a nonproductive use (*reproductive use*) occurs when a user copies the material to use it for the same intrinsic purpose for which the copyright owner intended it to be used, for example, when A copies B's download of a popular song from a peer-to-peer website rather than buying it. In sum, productive uses increase the number of original works of authorship, whereas reproductive uses merely increase the number of copies of a work to the detriment of the author, whose profits fall and whose incentive to create new works correspondingly diminishes.

Productive/transformative use synthesis of copyright law has had widespread appeal because it supports the underlying goal of copyright law by increasing our fund of knowledge and information. This view of copyright law seemed to correspond not only with the preamble of fair use but also coheres with the first fair use factor, "purpose and character of the use." In addition, the transformative use doctrine jells with the fourth criteria, "the effect on the market for the copyrighted work." Whether a work is transformative is significant for two reasons. First, all else being equal, a transformative work is less likely to harm the copyright owner. If an infringing work has the same purpose, meaning, or effect as does the original work, the infringing work is more likely to displace the need for the original work. If the infringing work is ostensibly different in purpose, meaning, and effect, the copyright holder's conventional business might remain fully unharmed despite the new, unlicensed use. The second reason is that a transformative work by definition is a work that provides something new and

---

40. *See* Leon E. Seltzer, Exemptions and Fair Use in Copyright Law 24 (1978) (arguing statement that a fair use is a productive use). Instead of "productive use" some courts have adopted the term "transformative" use. The concept is the same. *See* Pierre N. Leval, *Toward a Fair Use Standard*, 103 Harv. L. Rev. 1105, 1111 (1990) (stating that a use is "transformative" if it is productive and employs the quoted matter in a different manner or for a different purpose from the original; it adds value to the original). For an application of Judge Leval's transformative use doctrine, *see Campbell v. Acuff -Rose Music, Inc.*, 510 U.S. 569, 579 (1994) ("[T]he goal of copyright, to promote science and the arts, is generally furthered by the creation of transformative works."). *See also* Judge Leval's opinion in *Am. Geophysical Union v. Texaco, Inc.*, 802 F. Supp. 1 (S.D.N.Y. 1992) (finding that reproduction of single copies from plaintiff's journals, even for research purposes, is not a transformative use and thus not a fair use). For a comprehensive discussion of the development of the fair use doctrine and the rise to prominence of the transformative use paradigm, *see* Neil Weinstock Netanel, *Making Sense of Fair Use*, 15 Lewis & Clark L. Rev. 715 (2011).

potentially valuable to society. That a work is transformative, then, makes a finding of fair use more appealing. Otherwise, why weaken a copyright holder's exclusive rights if no real benefit to society results from doing so. By contrast, if society is getting something sufficiently new or valuable, a fair use finding is appropriate.

Thus, a transformative use should be impeded only when its use of the copyrighted work is so excessive as to undermine the incentive for others to produce copyrighted works.[41] Non-transformative (reproductive) use merely appropriates without creating anything of social value. Because transformative uses confer public benefits and reproductive uses do not, some would assert that the fair use privilege should be limited to uses one could characterize as transformative or productive.[42]

The transformative use doctrine was given explicit recognition by the Supreme Court in *Campbell v. Acuff-Rose*.[43] In this seminal 1994 fair use case, the Court attempted to synthesize the law concerning the use of a copyrighted work in creating a parody. The Court adopted, for the first time, the doctrine of transformative use. *Acuff-Rose* significantly changed the landscape of fair use and, if a court finds that defendant has used plaintiff's work "transformatively," the scales are tipped in favor of an ultimate finding of fair use. In the next section, I will focus on the question of parody as a fair use because it provides a most appropriate backdrop in understanding transformative use. I will follow in section 13.5 with a discussion of how transformative use has progressively enlarged to encompass a variety of uses that transcend its original origins and could hardly have been predicted after the Supreme Court's opinion in *Acuff-Rose*.

13.4 TRANSFORMATIVE USE AND THE PROBLEM OF PARODY

13.4.1 PARODY AS FAIR USE: ITS STATUTORY BASIS

A *parody*[44] is an imitation of a serious piece of literature, music, or composition for humorous or satirical effect. A "parodist" is a critic or

---

41. *See*, e.g., *Twin Peaks Prods., Inc. v. Publ'ns, Int'l, Ltd.*, 996 F.2d 1366 (2d Cir. 1993) (finding defendant's detailed report of the plots of a popular television program went far beyond merely identifying their basic outline for the transformative purposes of comment or criticism).
42. *See Sony Corp. of Am. v. Universal City Studios, Inc.*, 464 U.S. 417, 475 (1984) (Blackmun, J., dissenting); *Dow Jones & Co., Inc. v. Board of Trade*, 546 F. Supp. 113 (S.D.N.Y 1982).
43. 510 U.S. 569 (1994).
44. The term "satire" is often used synonymously with "parody."

commentator who exposes the mediocre and pretentious in art and society, forcing audiences to examine a serious text from a comedic standpoint.

Parody, by its very nature, makes use of another's work, sometimes extensively. Because the purpose of this use is satire and ridicule, there is a tension between the parodist and the copyright owner. As a result, some copyright owners are less than eager to see their work ridiculed and will not license their work for this purpose. Consequently, the parodist must rely on the defense of fair use where substantial use has been made of a copyrighted work and where biting criticism and ridicule may have offended the sensibilities of a copyright owner.

Whether parody, for these reasons, is entitled to a wider fair use privilege than other uses has been the subject of a long, on-going debate.[45] In one sense, a true parody is not just an ordinary taking because it is a transformative use, a form of criticism or comment—as such, a use specifically enumerated in the preamble to § 107. Moreover, the fair use defense is particularly important for the health of this genre because a copyright owner will seldom license a work to be satirized or ridiculed. One could say that the parody defense to copyright infringement exists precisely to make possible a use that generally cannot be bought.[46]

13.4.2   PARODY, TRANSFORMATIVE USE AND THE FOUR FACTORS: *CAMPBELL v. ACUFF-ROSE*

In *Campbell v. Acuff-Rose Music, Inc.*[47] the Supreme Court held that a commercial parody may qualify as a fair use. To decide the question of fair use, the court must subject the parody to an overall balancing process in which the parody's "transformative" character is more important than its commercial purpose. In this case, Acuff-Rose owned the copyright to Roy Orbison's 1964 hit song "Oh, Pretty Woman." The rap group "2 Live Crew" wrote and recorded a satirical version of the song also called "Pretty Woman" and in 1989 requested a license that Acuff-Rose refused to grant. 2 Live Crew released its satirical version of the Orbison classic anyway. Their version made use of the same drumbeat from the original and its distinctive bass line, repeating it eight times throughout the song while substituting its own words such as "big, hairy woman," "bald-headed woman," and "two-timin' woman" in place of Orbison's more genteel lyrics.

---

45. *See Berlin v. E.C. Publ'ns, Inc.*, 329 F.2d 541 (2d Cir. 1964). *But cf. Walt Disney Prods. v. Air Pirates*, 581 F.2d 751 (9th Cir. 1978).

46. *See Maxtone -Graham v. Burtchaell*, 803 F.2d 1253 (2d Cir. 1986). *But see Original Appalachian Artworks, Inc. v. Topps Chewing Gum, Inc.*, 642 F. Supp. 1031 (N.D. Ga. 1986) (finding bad faith was on part of defendant who asked for a license to use plaintiff's children's dolls (Cabbage Patch Kids) and was rejected).

47. 510 U.S. 569 (1994).

The Sixth Circuit found that 2 Live Crew had infringed Acuff-Rose's "Oh Pretty Woman."[48] Relying on the Sony presumption, in which all unauthorized commercial (for profit) uses of copyrighted works are presumptively unfair and have a harmful effect on the market for the work, the court disallowed the fair use defense. The Supreme Court rejected the Sony presumption, at least when a parody is at issue, opting for a balancing process that would apply all four fair use factors. As for the first factor, the purpose and character of the use, the Court held that the most important inquiry is not whether the use is commercial but whether it is "transformative." The focus should be on whether the work alters the original with "new expression, meaning, and message."[49] The more transformative the new work, the less will be the significance of the other factors, like commercialism, that weigh against a finding of fair use. After striking another blow against the Sony presumption, the Court then turned to an issue that has plagued the courts in determining whether a parody is a fair use: how much can parody take from the original?

13.4.3   How Much Can the Parody Take from the Original?

The third fair use factor, the amount and substantiality of the taking—how much a parody can copy from the original—remains the most controversial issue in determining fair use in the context of parody. The issue arises because the best parodies must take extensively from the original to create the humorous effect. A tension is created with the rights of copyright owners because extensive copying on the part of the parodist may supplant the need for the original. Should there be a wider privilege to take from the original to satisfy the needs of this art form? The issue was not resolved in *Acuff-Rose*. The Court repeated a familiar principle: "the parody must be able to 'conjure up' at least enough of [the] original to make the object of its critical wit recognized."[50] The Court added that the amount necessary to conjure up the original will depend on the persuasiveness of a parodist's justification for the particular copying done and will vary with the purpose and character of the use. Other than articulating these general principles, the Court refused to decide whether excessive copying of the music had actually taken place and remanded the case on this issue.[51]

Some statements in the case law[52] suggest a wider privilege for parody, but generally courts have not given the parodist carte blanche to take indiscriminately from the copyrighted work. In short, the right to make the

---

48. *Acuff-Rose Music, Inc. v. Campbell*, 972 F.2d 1429 (6th Cir. 1992).
49. *Acuff-Rose*, 510 U.S. at 579 (citing Pierre Leval, *Toward a Fair Use Standard*, 103 Harv. L. Rev. 1105, 1111 (1990)).
50. *Acuff-Rose*, 510 U.S. at 588.
51. *Ibid.*
52. *See*, e.g., *Berlin v. E.C. Publ'ns, Inc.*, 329 F.2d 541, 545 (2d Cir. 1964).

best parody is balanced against the rights of the copyright owner. The legal standard applied is that the parodist should be allowed to appropriate no greater amount of the original work than is necessary to recall or "conjure up" the object of his satire.[53] As a corollary, near-verbatim copying will rarely, if ever, be a fair use.

The "conjure up" test was reaffirmed but applied strictly in *Walt Disney v. Air Pirates*,[54] suggesting that the parodist can take only that which is minimally necessary to conjure up the original. In *Air Pirates*, defendants prepared two magazines of cartoons entitled the *Air Pirates Funnies*, an underground counter-culture comic book that made use of Disney characters by placing them in bawdy situations. The court rejected fair use of the Disney characters as the taking exceeded what was necessary to conjure up the original. The court suggested that the conjure up standard will vary from case to case and that a lesser taking was necessary for widely recognizable graphic images of the Disney characters than if the subject of the parody was a less concrete literary work such as a speech: "By copying the images in their entirety, defendants took more than was necessary to place firmly in the reader's mind the parodied work and those specific attributes that are to be satirized."[55]

Other courts, notably the Second Circuit, apply the "conjure up" test, allowing a greater taking than that minimally necessary if the parody builds on the original and contributes something new for humorous effect or commentary.[56] On the whole, determining "amount and substantiality" is a question of reasonability and proportionality. As the Supreme Court indicates, "[o]nce enough has been taken to assure identification, how much more is reasonable will depend ... [1] on the extent to which the [work's] *overriding purpose and character is to parody* the original or, in contrast, [2] the likelihood that the parody may serve as a *market substitute* for the original."[57]

13.4.4   Parody and the Fourth Fair-Use Factor: Market Effect

The fourth factor, the market effect of the use, will be decided in favor of the parodist absent near-verbatim copying.[58] The parody will usually not fulfill

---

53. *See ibid.*; *see also Sun Trust Bank v. Houghton Mifflin Co.*, 268 F.3d 1257, 1273 (11th Cir. 2001) ("A [parody] does not necessarily become infringing the moment it does more than simply conjure up another ... .").
54. 581 F.2d 751 (9th Cir. 1978).
55. *Walt Disney*, 581 F.2d at 758.
56. *See Elsmere Music, Inc. v. Nat'l Broad. Co.*, 623 F.2d 252, 253n.1 (2d Cir. 1980).
57. *Campbell v. Acuff-Rose Music, Inc.*, 510 U.S. at 588 (emphasis added).
58. *See Benny v. Loew's, Inc.*, 239 F.2d 532 (9th Cir. 1956).

the demand for the original, and rarely could the plaintiff argue that the market for this type of derivative work has been co-opted by the use.[59]

Thus, no presumption or inference of market harm is applicable unless the parody simply duplicates the original in its entirety for commercial purposes. However, when the second use is transformative, market substitution is less certain and market harm is not so readily inferred.[60] In determining market effect, it is not the impact of the parody as criticism but the economic effect of the use in fulfilling the demand for the original that is the issue.[61] Because of its devastating criticism, an effective parody may actually diminish the demand for the original. This is not the kind of market effect that justifies a denial of fair use.[62] The real issue for the fair use determination is whether the parody fulfills the demand for the original, that is, whether consumers are likely to purchase the parody rather than the original because it serves the same purpose as the original.

13.4.5   DOES THE PARODY HAVE TO TARGET THE COPYRIGHTED WORK?

Whether a parody, to qualify for fair use, has to target the copyrighted work itself, or whether it may use the copyrighted work for some other humorous purpose has been a point of controversy for some time.[63] The Second Circuit Court of Appeals, which has examined this question in greater depth than any other court, has vacillated on this basic issue, but the trend is to require that the parody comments in some way on the original.[64] The Supreme Court

---

59. *See Pillsbury Co. v. Milky Way Prods., Inc.*, 215 U.S.P.Q. (BNA) 124 (N.D. Ga. 1981) (finding fair use and no market harm for defendant's pornographic depiction in *Screw Magazine* of characters resembling plaintiff's *Poppin* and *Poppin Fresh* figures).

60. *See Campbell v. Acuff-Rose Music, Inc.*, 510 U.S. at 590.

61. *See Fisher v. Dees*, 794 F.2d 432 (9th Cir. 1986). The court held that a song parody, "When Sunny Sniffs Glue," based on the original song, "When Sunny Gets Blue," was a fair use, primarily because it did not supplant the need for the original. *Cf. Original Appalachian Artworks, Inc. v. Topps Chewing Gum, Inc.*, 642 F. Supp. 1031 (N.D. Ga. 1986) (discussing how defendant sold stickers resembling plaintiff's popular children's dolls, Cabbage Patch Kids, but which were much more grotesque in style; the district court rejected the fair use defense because of the commercial nature of defendant's use, emphasizing the *Sony* presumption of potential market harm, which could also be shown from the fact that the products competed for the same children's market. In addition, the court found defendant's principal purpose was to earn a profit rather than to engage in social commentary).

62. *See Campbell v. Acuff-Rose Music, Inc.*, 510 U.S. at 591-92 ("[W]hen a lethal parody ... kills demand for the original, it does not produce a harm cognizable under the Copyright Act").

63. *Compare Metro-Goldwyn-Mayer, Inc. v. Showcase Atlanta Coop. Prods. Inc.*, 479 F. Supp. 351 (N.D. Ga. 1979) (finding the musical stage version of *Gone with the Wind*, although comic, did not constitute a parody), *with Fisher v. Dees*, 794 F.2d 432, 436 (9th Cir. 1986).

64. *See Berlin v. E.C. Publ'ns, Inc.*, 329 F.2d 541, 542 (2d Cir. 1964) (finding *Mad Magazine*'s lyrics to be sung to the tunes of Irving Berlin and others a fair use even though

confirmed this view in *Acuff-Rose*, which sided with the traditional definition of "parody" as a literary or artistic work that imitates the characteristic style of an author or a work for comic-effect ridicule.[65] It rejected the contrary view that would allow use of the original work for humorous effect even though the original was not the object of ridicule or satire.

That a parody need be aimed at least partially at the original is justified by the principal purpose of granting to a parody a fair-use privilege—to criticize another text through satirical ridicule. When the original is used for general comic purposes or to criticize other targets, the same pressing need to encroach on the original does not exist. In other words, if the copyrighted song is not at least in part an object of the parody, there is no need to conjure it up. Thus, parody must do more than merely achieve comic effect but must make some critical comment or statement about the original work.[66] Otherwise, the parodist has simply created a derivative work based on the original and should be required to obtain permission from the copyright owner to use the work.[67]

---

the object of the humor was not the songs themselves but the "idiotic world we live in today"); *Elsmere Music, Inc. v. Nat'l Broad. Co.*, 623 F.2d 252 (2d Cir. 1980) (finding the primary question is whether the use is a valid satire or parody, not whether it is a parody of the song itself). *But see MCA, Inc. v. Wilson*, 677 F.2d 180 (2d Cir. 1981) (holding risque version of the Andrews Sisters' classic, "The Boogie Woogie Bugle Boy of Company B," entitled "Cunnilingus Champion of Company C," not a fair use). Generally, pornographic parodies have not received a fair use privilege. *See*, e.g., *Dallas Cowboys Cheerleaders v. Scoreboard Posters, Inc.*, 600 F.2d 1184 (5th Cir. 1979); *Pillsbury Co. v. Milky Way Prods., Inc.*, 215 U.S.P.Q. (BNA) 124 (N.D. Ga. 1981); *Walt Disney Prods. v. Mature Pictures Corp.*, 389 F. Supp. 1397 (S.D.N.Y. 1975); *Walt Disney Prods. v. Air Pirates*, 581 F.2d 751 (9th Cir. 1978).

65. *Campbell v. Acuff-Rose Music, Inc.*, 510 U.S. at 578; *see also Rogers v. Koons*, 960 F.2d 301 (2d Cir. 1992) (holding a three-dimensional wood sculpture in unnatural color scheme based on black and white photographs of puppies, was not a fair use; although it may be a satirical critique of the "materialist" society in which we live, there was no parody of the photograph itself).

66. Since *Campbell*, the lower courts have had several opportunities to consider what is and is not parody. *Compare Dr. Seuss Enter., L.P. v. Penguin Books U.S.A. Inc.*, 924 F. Supp. 1559 (S.D. Cal. 1996), *aff'd*, 109 F.3d 1394 (9th Cir. 1997) (holding that the use of Dr. Seuss rhymes, illustrations, and book packaging to take a fresh look at the O.J. Simpson murder trial did not attempt to comment on the text or themes of *The Cat in the Hat*), *with Mattel, Inc. v. Walking Mountain Prods.*, 353 F.3d 792 (9th Cir. 2003) (affirming summary judgment that seventy-eight photographs featuring naked Barbie dolls being menaced by kitchen appliances, baked in enchiladas, and in various other absurd positions, was a fair use). For a critique of *Dr. Seuss, see* Tyler Ochoa, *Dr. Seuss, the Juice and Fair Use: How the Grinch Silenced a Parody*, 45 J. COPYRIGHT SOC'Y 546 (1998).

67. *See* Julie Bisceglia, *Parody & Copyright Protection: Turning the Balancing Act into a Juggling Act*, 34 COPYRIGHT L. SYMP. (ASCAP) 1, 26 (1987); *see also* Richard A. Posner, *When Is Parody Fair Use?*, 21 J. LEGAL STUD. 67 (1992) (stating that parody is fair use when used to target the original, not when it is used as a weapon for humorous effect or to ridicule society at large). For criticism of this view, *see* Tyler T. Ochoa, *Dr. Seuss, the Juice and Fair Use: How the Grinch Silenced a Parody*, 45 J. COPYRIGHT SOC'Y 546, 610 (1998) (Drawing a distinction between "weapon" and "target" parody would ... allow

One explanation is rooted in the First Amendment for the disparate treatment of parody versus satire. The argument is that whereas copyright owner might be understandably wary of licensing a criticism or ridicule of his own work (a parody), he might be willing to license his work as a vehicle for broader social comment. The Campbell Court expressed this idea: "[T]here is no protectable derivative market for criticism. The market for potential derivative uses includes only those that creators of original works would in general develop or license others to develop."[68] The satire/parody distinction is consistent with the fourth criteria for fair use—the effect on the market for the copyrighted work. Thus, scathing parody may destroy the market for the original work, but its destruction stems from criticism, not usurpation by acting as a substitute. In addition, even if a copyright owner refuses to license a satirical use of the work, it is arguable that a pure satire still should not be considered a fair use, considering a satire benefits from the popularity of the original work and is more likely to act as a market substitute.

The Supreme Court in *Campbell* employed a flexible test that weighed the work's parodic character—i.e., the degree to which it criticized or commented on the original work—along with the other fair use factors in determining fair use. In subsequent cases, courts have become captivated by the ostensible dichotomy in *Campbell* between parody and satire. This dichotomy between parody and satire is less difficult to administer if the new work "criticized" or "commented" on the original. The result is that the other factors become less important and a finding of fair use likely. Alternatively, if the new work used the original work as a means to criticize something else, such as society in general, it is satire, not parody, and not fair use. The parody/satire distinction has become the central issue in many cases. Unfortunately, the proper dividing line between prototypical parody and satire is hazy at best. Resourceful lawyers and judges have taken advantage of this fuzziness in arguing for or against the parodic character of works.

Some parodies have satiric components; some satires have parodic components. As several commentators have observed, often works resist simple classification.[69] Even the Court in *Campbell* recognized the hybrid nature of many works, leading it to conclude that the fair use factors vary in

---

the copyright holder to censor satirical opinions with which he or she disagrees); Robert P. Merges, *Notes of Market Failure and the Parody Defense in Copyright Law*, 21 AIPLA Q.J. 305, 311 (1993) (arguing that Posner's assumption "seems wrong, at least in those cases where the target of the parody is a set of values or cultural assumptions deeply cherished by the copyright holder or at least widely shared by a segment of public loyal to her").

68. *See Campbell*, 510 U.S. at 592.

69. *See*, e.g., Annemarie Bridy, *Sheep in Goats' Clothing: Satire and Fair Use After* Campbell v. Acuff-Rose Music, Inc., 51 J. COPYRIGHT SOC'Y U.S.A. 257, 274-278 (2004); Bruce P. Keller & Rebecca Tushnet, *Even More Parodic Than the Real Thing: Parody Lawsuits Revisited*, 94 TRADEMARK REP. 979, 985 (2004); Tyler T. Ochoa, *Dr. Seuss, the Juice and*

importance depending on the level of commentary on the original work.[70] Other courts have blurred the distinction between parody and satire. For example, in *SunTrust Bank v. Houghton Mifflin Co.*,[71] the court upheld the parody defense for a book entitled, *Wind Done Gone* against a copyright infringement claim brought by the owner of *Gone With the Wind*, finding that the new work was a specific criticism of the depiction of slavery and relationships between blacks and whites in *Gone With the Wind*. Conversely, in *Dr. Seuss Enters., L.P. v. Penguin Books USA, Inc.*[72] the court discounted the defendants' argument that its book about the O.J. Simpson case parodied the original Dr. Seuss' works, and held that the work broadly mimicked Dr. Seuss' characteristic style to simply retell the Simpson tale. These two cases reveal another problem with the parody/satire distinction to determine what qualifies as a legitimate transformative use. The chilling effects of judges as final arbiters of the literary meaning of a work might be lessened if they carefully follow the guidance in *Campbell* to determine only whether a parodic character may be *reasonably* perceived. Under this framework, a "reasonably perceived" parody that predominantly criticizes matters external to the original work itself will be scrutinized more carefully under the other fair use factors. However, if courts insist on characterizing a work as "parody" or "satire," a traditional tenet of U.S. copyright is challenged, the oft-stated fear of judges acting as literary and artistic critics may come to pass.[73]

13.5   BEYOND PARODY: FROM TRANSFORMATIVE USE TO TRANSFORMATIVE PURPOSE

The judicial focus on the transformative use doctrine has challenged fair use analysis significantly, but the case law has hardly been transparent in relation to the role that transformative use plays in the overall analysis. The fact is that courts have differing views about what constitutes transformative use, which gives the impression that the doctrine is manipulated to achieve a desired result. Moreover, some courts appear to use the presence or absence of transformative use as a proxy for the fair use determination itself. The wholesale adoption of the transformative use doctrine highlights the need for

---

Fair Use: How the Grinch Silenced a Parody, 45 J. COPYRIGHT SOC'Y, 546, 557 (1998). Many works employ previous works to both criticize the work itself and myriad external matters.

70. *See Campbell*, 510 U.S. at 581.
71. 268 F.3d 1257, 1265, 1269 (11th Cir. 2001).
72. 109 F.3d 1394, 1401 (9th Cir. 1997).
73. *See Bleistein v. Donaldson Lithographing Co.*, 188 U.S. 239 (1903). (It would be a dangerous undertaking for persons trained only in the law to constitute themselves final judges of the worth of pictorial illustrations, outside of the narrowest and most obvious limits at 251).

clearly defining what constitutes a transformative use. Unfortunately, *Campbell*'s definition of transformative use—a use that "adds something new, with a further purpose or different character, altering the first with new expression, meaning, or message"—is prone to flexible or even capricious interpretations.

After *Campbell*, transformative use may arise in a multiplicity of situations where a third party has added new expression to the original, such as in writing a sequel to a work of fiction or placing a small excerpt of a song in a new composition. *Campbell* has also been extended to instances in which another user has transformed the meaning or message of the original, such as an audiovisual work that integrates an advertising logo to make an observation about consumerism. As courts and commentators have complained, the *Campbell* definition leaves ambiguous whether either, both, or some mixture of transforming content and transforming message are required to constitute a transforming use. In sum, the courts have differed on whether transformative use should be limited to instances where the copyrighted work has been altered or to other situations where the copyrighted work is used in an entirely different context than the copyrighted work.

As will be discussed below, the different expressive purposes that courts have recognized as transformative are wide-ranging. They have included the reproduction of literary or graphic works to serve as an information tool;[74] the reproduction of artistic works to illustrate a biography;[75] the reproduction of a fashion photograph originally made for a lifestyle magazine in a painting to make a comment about the mass media;[76] the scanning of millions of books for an online research function.[77] Despite its obvious ambiguities, the transformative use theory has appeal because it remains consistent with the underlying goals of copyright law while adding theoretical coherence to an amorphous fair use doctrine. Unfortunately, there seems to be little consensus in the case law concerning whether a third party's transformative use must truly alter the copyrighted work itself or whether the concept encompasses other uses of the copyrighted work.[78] While some courts insist on a substantial alteration of the copyrighted work,[79] the trend appears to construe the transformative use concept expansively. As the following examples will show the emphasis is placed on the distinction between the defendant's transformative purpose in using the work as distinct from that of the original.

---

74. *Perfect 10, Inc. v. Amazon, Inc.* 508 F.3d 1146 (9th Cir. 2007.
75. *Bill Graham Archives v. Dorling Kindersley Ltd*, 448 F.3d 605 (2d Cir. 2006).
76. *Blanch v. Koons,* 467 F.3d 244 (2d Cir. 2006).
77. *Authors Guild v. Google, Inc.*, 954 F. Supp. 282 (S.D.N.Y. 2013).
78. For a criticism of the productive/transformative use concept, *see* PAUL GOLDSTEIN, COPYRIGHT § 12.2.2(c) (3d ed. 2009).
79. *Leadsinger, Inc. v. BMG Music Publ'g*, 512 F.3d 522 (9th Cir. 2008).

13.5.1   On Line Research Tools: *Perfect 10, Inc. v. Amazon, Inc.*

In *Perfect 10, Inc. v. Amazon, Inc.*[80] the court excused the identical reproduction of plaintiff's work in thumbnails as being transformative in nature because they served an entirely different function than the copyrighted work. In the same case, the transformative use concept was also applied to the making of temporary cache copies of a copyrighted work in a computer because this mechanical process facilitated access to the Internet.[81] In holding that Google's display was fair use, the court specified that the use need not transform the original or add new creative expression so long as it serves a different purpose or function, one that promotes the objectives of copyright law, while serving the public interest. The court found that Google's image search engine provided a clear social benefit and was highly transformative. The plaintiff's images were created for purposes of art and entertainment; Google, on the other hand, used them as a means of directing the user to a source of information. Google did not display the thumbnails for aesthetic purposes; it incorporates them into its electronic reference tool.

The Court's decision in *Perfect 10 v. Amazon* is also significant for its treatment of the fourth factor, "the effect of the use upon the potential market for or value of the copyrighted work." After filing its lawsuit, Perfect 10 initiated marketing thumbnails of its images for downloading to cell phones. For the district court, this was sufficient to weigh the fourth factor against fair use. The Court of Appeals disagreed, refusing to consider Perfect 10's cell phone market as even a potential market that Perfect 10 would reasonably enter even though it had already done so. Viewed from this perspective, *Perfect 10* diminishes the scope and force of the fourth factor. Google's display of thumbnail images was highly transformative, and socially benefi- cial despite conceivable injury to the plaintiff's potential market for licensing thumbnails.

Of course, even transformative uses infringe if other factors weigh against the defendant. *Perfect 10* reveals that if transformative use trumps the fourth fair use factor it risks undermining copyright owner's right to control adaptations of the copyright work under § 106(2)'s derivative right.[82] Will any significant change in context, media, and scale merit the transformative use characterization? If so, the doctrine presents a threat to the continuing viability of the copyright owner's adaptation right. A case in point is *Bill Graham Archives v. Dorling Kindersley Ltd*,[83] where the court ruled that it was a fair use—a transformative use—for the defendant to reproduce seven of the plaintiff's copyrighted images of the Grateful Dead reduced in scale to fit the pages of a coffee table book on the band. The defendant, who could

---

80. 508 F.3d 1146 (9th Cir. 2007).
81. *Ibid.*
82. R. Anthony Reese, *Trasformativeness and the Derivative Work Right*, 31 Colum. J.L. & Arts 467, 485 (2008).
83. 448 F.3d 605 (2d Cir. 2006).

have negotiated a license with the copyright owner, added little if any original authorship to the copyrighted work. Nonetheless the court viewed the use as transformative because the book used the images of the posters as "historical artifacts" to document Grateful Dead's concerts, rather than for the posters' original aesthetic purposes. In addition to recognizing the distinct differences between the purposes of the respective works, the court ruled that the defendant took no more than was necessary for documentary purposes. *Bill Graham* illustrates once again that courts generally apply the transformative use doctrine along with weighing the other fair use factors. At the same time, the court gave short shrift to considering the fourth factor regarding the potential market for the copyrighted work.

In comparison with Dorling Kindersly, *Gaylord v. United States* indicates that the third party use must have a different expressive purpose than the copyrighted work. Gaylord created a sculpture of soldiers on a mission in the Korean War that was displayed on the National Mall in Washington D.C. The U.S. Postal acquired a photograph of the snow-covered sculpture, which it transferred as an image on to a postage stamp honoring Korean War veterans. Was the Postal Service's different expressive character and aesthetic aim sufficient to the make the use transformative? Although the stamp altered the appearance of the sculpture, it was not transformative. The court ruled that the expressive purpose of the sculpture and the stamp were identical that is to honor Korean War veterans.

13.5.2   APPROPRIATION ART

Some courts have expanded the concept of transformative use to embrace copying for an entirely different purpose and impact even when the copying does not significantly alter the copied work. In *Blanch v. Koons*,[84] the court held that "appropriation artist" Jeff Koons' use of a photographic image of a woman's feet was transformative because it used the image of the feet in a manner that was not the intent of the original photograph, in a way that was not merely a change of artistic media or venue.

Appropriation Art attempts to re-contextualize famous or not-so-famous images by juxtaposing them with new material. Whether this should be considered a transformative use has been a matter of long debate. This issue was central in *Prince v. Cariou*, a case that illustrates how far the doctrine of transformative fair use has developed since *Acuff-Rose*. In *Cariou*, the defendant reproduced images from the Plaintiff's book of Rastafarian photographs and incorporated them into his artwork, but he overpainted the images and collaged them with other images. The Second Circuit reversed the Districts Court's rejection of the fair use defense, holding that the law imposes no requirement that a work comment on the original or its author in

---

84. 467 F.3d 244 (2d Cir. 2006).

order to be transformative. The Second Circuit held that twenty-five of the thirty works at issue, primarily those that combined the plaintiff's photos with images from other sources, were fair use as a matter of law, despite evidence that another gallery had canceled a show of plaintiff's photographs after learning about defendant's paintings. Both *Blanch* and *Cariou* illustrate the greater breadth given to fair use in recent cases. Consistent with both *Perfect 10* and *Bill Graham*, these cases also demonstrate how the transformative use doctrine has undermined the importance of the fourth fair use factor concerning the potential market for the copyrighted work.

13.5.3   MASS DIGITIZATION AND FAIR USE: THE GOOGLE BOOK SEARCH PROJECT[85]

Since its debut at the Frankfort Book Fair in 2004, Google has made continued efforts to scan, archive, and digitize the contents of all books in major libraries with which it has concluded licensing agreements, including those of the University of Michigan, Harvard University, the New York Public library, and Oxford's Bodleian library.[86] The goal is to provide a searchable online database accessible to the public, containing all existing printed works. The general public will have access to view public domain works in their entirety. For copyrighted works, however, search results will be limited to snippets containing the search term, which Google continuously argues is fair use.

The Google initiative has unsurprisingly engendered much controversy and resistance among author groups in particular. In 2005, Google was sued in a class action by the Author's Guild, and the American Association of Publishers brought another action. In 2008, Google negotiated settlements for both lawsuits.[87] The change did not mollify the Authors Guild. In 2011, after comments from numerous sources, including the Antitrust Division of

---

85. For a discussion and a preliminary estimate of the economic impact of mass digitization projects, *see* Hannibal Travis, *Estimating the Economic Impact of Mass Digitization Projects on Copyright Holders: Evidence from the Google Book Search Litigation*, 57 J. COPYRIGHT SOC'Y 907 (2010).

86. For commentary on the Google Book Search Project and its ramifications *see* Randal C. Picker, *The Google Book Search Settlement: A New Orphan Works Monopoly*, 5 COMPETITION L. & E con. 383 (2009); Frank Pasquale, *Copyright in an Era of Information Overload: Toward the Privileging of Categorizers*, 60 VAND. L. REV. 135 (2007); Oren Bracha, *Standing Copyright on Its Head: The Googlization of Everything and the Many Faces of Property*, 85 TEX. L. REV. 1799 (2007); Siva Vaidyanathan, *The Googlization of Everything and the Future of Copyright*, 40 U.C. DAVIS L. REV. 1207 (2007); Hannibal Travis, *Google Book Search and Fair Use: iTunes for Authors or Napster for Books*, 61 U. MIAMI L. REV 87 (2006); Steven Hetcher, *The Half-Fairness of Google's Plan to Make the World's Collection of Books Searchable*, 13 MICH. TELECOMM. & TECH. L. REV. (2006).

87. Under the settlement Google would have paid USD 45 million to copyright owners for books already scanned, and an additional USD 35 million to create a Book Rights registry—a collective licensing organization for authors and publishers. The complex

the U.S. Department of Justice, the U.S. District Court for the Southern District of New York rejected the proposed settlement as not being "fair, adequate, and reasonable" with respect to the rights of the members of the relevant class.[88] In her statement before Congress, the Register of Copyrights criticized the settlement as a privately formulated compulsory license that compromises the rights of copyright owners of out-of-print books and encroaches on the responsibility of Congress to make copyright policy.[89]

After much legal jockeying concerning the plaintiff's class action, the district court was directed to decide the key issue in the dispute—whether Google's mass digitization of millions of books as part of its Google Book Search project (including scanning, indexing, and displaying "snippets" from most books in response to search queries) constitutes a fair use of the copyrighted works.[90]

Some nine years after the initial launch of the Google Book Search project, the district court in 2013 held that the use of the full text of millions of books for its online search function was a transformative use, and, thus, Google's mass digitization of those books without authorization from copyright owners constituted a fair use. The Court said that the book scanning amounted to fair use because it was "highly transformative" because it did not harm the market for the original work.[91] The Court argued that "Google Books provides significant public benefits," describing it as "an essential research tool" and noting that the scanning service has expanded literary access for the blind and helped preserve the text of old books from physical decay. The court also rejected the theory that Google was depriving authors of income, noting that the company does not sell the scans or make whole copies of books available, instead, that Google Books served to help readers discover new books and amounted to new income for authors. The Court found that Google Books should actually enhance the market for individual books, as users who find "snippets" on Google Books may want

---

385–page amended (2009) settlement agreement is available at www.googlebooksettle ment.com/agreement.html. For a discussion of the Google Books Settlement and an analysis of how the settlement should be characterized, *see* James Grimmelman, *The Elephantine Google Books Settlement*, 58 J. COPYRIGHT SOC'Y 497 (2011). For an overview of the Google Book Settlement, *see* Pamela Samuelson, *The Google Book Settlement as Copyright Reform*, 2011 WIS. L. REV. 479 (2011). For a comprehensive discussion of the Google Books Settlement and the surrounding legal and historical issues, *see* Jonathan Band, *The Long and Winding Road to the Google Books Settlement*, 9 J. MARSHALL REV. INTELL. PROP. L. 227 (2010). For a discussion of the settlement reached by Google books and the four ways that it differed from the "fair use" outcome that was predicted, *see* Matthew Sag, *The Google Book Settlement and the Fair Use Counterfactual*, 55 N.Y.L. SCH. L. REV. 19 (2010).

88. *Authors Guild v. Google Inc.*, 770 F. Supp. 2d 666 (S.D.N.Y. 2011).

89. *The Register of Copyrights Hearing before the H. Comm. on the Judiciary*, 111th Cong. 1st Sess. (2009) (statement of Marybeth Peters).

90. *Authors Guild v. Google, Inc.*, 721 F 3d 282 (2d Cir. 2013).

91. *Ibid.*, at 291.

to buy the entire work; in essence Google Books is acting as free advertising for the book.[92] This decision, which will certainly not be the last word on the matter, declares that fair use permits mass digitization of books for purposes that advance the arts and sciences, such as search, preservation, and access for the print-disabled.[93]

| 13.6 | TRANSFORMATIVE USE IN CONTEXT: STRIKING A BALANCE BETWEEN THE FIRST AMENDMENT AND COPYRIGHT |

The transformative use doctrine as attractively articulated in Judge Leval's influential article presented a cogent synthesis of fair use. Despite its surface appeal, the transformative use doctrine—like so many other comprehensive attempts to synthesize fair use—never provides a panacea for analysis but adds further layers of complexity to the already burdened fair use doctrine. In its latest iteration, transformative use has come to mean transformative purpose, which, if one empirically examines the case law, expands fair use significantly. When determining transformative purpose, the court attempts to compare the expressive purpose of the plaintiff's work with that of defendant's work. A finding of substantial differences between the two will often lead to a conclusion of transformative use. This is hardly a mechanical process and predicting fair use cases is as perilous a task as it has always been.

Since *Acuff-Rose*, the transformative use paradigm has come to govern fair use case law as the principal criteria in determining whether the defendant's use is fair. The evolving case law reveals that the crucial question for judicial determination of fair use is not whether the copyright holder would have reasonably consented to the use, but whether the defendant used the copyrighted work for a different expressive purpose from that for which the work was created. Courts ask, for example, does the defendant use the work for purposes of comment or criticism and, does the criticism target the work itself, the author or someone else associated with the work, or a general genre or social phenomenon? In some occasions the question is: Does the defendant use a work originally created for artistic, entertainment, or commercial advertising purposes, or for a different purpose, such as biographical or historical documentation? Yet in other instances, courts have questioned: Does the defendant use the copyrighted work as a reference

---

92. *Authors Guild v. Google, Inc.*, 954 F. Supp. 282 (S.D.N.Y. 2013).
93. In a parallel case upholding fair use for mass digitization *see Authors Guild, Inc. v. HathiTrust*, 902 F. Supp. 2d 445 (2d Cir. 2012) (holding project to systematically digitize copyrighted books to allow scholars to identify works more efficiently, to preserve universities' collections and to provide print-disabled individuals with access to library collections was protected by fair use doctrine).

guide or information location tool? If the answer to questions above is "yes," the use is likely to be transformative. Alternatively, if the defendant merely modifies the original or adds new expression for the same expressive purpose, the use will most probably qualify neither as a transformative nor as a fair use. The upshot of this turn to transformative use as transformative purpose reduces the importance of what was once the dispositive issue in fair use, that of the effect of defendant's use on the potential market for the copyrighted work.

Transformative use is often critical to a finding of fair use but it is not always dispositive. On finding a transformative purpose, the courts tend to apply the other four factors in sequence. Frequently, the emphasis is focused on the third fair use factor of section 107: whether the defendant has copied more than a reasonable amount for that purpose. Nonetheless, plausible rules of thumb concerning fair use are frequently contradicted, and it may sometimes be reasonable to copy the entire work without alteration. However, the defendant does best to preclude copying the most expressively rich dimension of the original work. For example, in both *Perfect 10 v. Amazon* and *Bill Graham,* the defendants' purposes were transformative despite identical copying to produce thumbnail images, because such reproduction were different in scale and aesthetic purpose when compared with the plaintiffs' full-sized copyrighted artworks. Similarly, the Google books litigation involved a novel use of massive amounts of information rather than a transformative use of copyrighted works in the strict sense of that term.

More recent cases suggest that evoking transformative use should not become a shortcut for a truncated analysis of fair use. For example, in *Fox News Network, LLC v. TV Eyes, Inc.,*[94] the Second Circuit rejected a fair use defense for an arguably transformative use involving a service that recorded all the content on approximately 1,400 television and radio stations, and imported the content into a database, which subscribers accessed for USD 500 per month. As to the effect of the use upon the potential market for or value of the copyrighted work, the court found that TVEyes' service undercut Fox's ability to profit from licensing searchable access to its copyrighted content to third parties, a market worth millions of dollars. Therefore, TVEyes deprived Fox of licensing revenues and from the opportunity to exploit the market for such its service.

Another recent case suggests a return to a more balanced approach to fair use in which the court applied the four criteria, emphasizing the importance of the fourth fair use factor, the potential market effect of the use on the copyrighted work. *Brammer v. Violent Hues Prods., LLC*, involved a time-lapse photo taken at night of the Adams Morgan neighborhood of Washington, D.C. Plaintiff brought a copyright infringement suit against Violent Hues Productions after discovering that defendant had used his

---

94. 833 F.3d 169 (2d Cir. 2018).

photograph on its website promoting a D.C.-area film festival. The lower court had ruled for the defendant, emphasizing defendant's transformative use of the work. In reversing the lower court's decision, the Court of Appeals found that neither defendant's cropping of the photograph not its use in an informational list of tourist attractions, constituted a transformative use of the photo because it provided no original new expression, meaning or message. In applying the four fair use criteria, the court noted that defendant's conduct, if widespread, would substantially reduce the value of the copyrighted work. Thus, the court found that the fourth factor, the market effect on the potential value of the copyrighted weighed against finding of fair use.

Both *TV Eyes* and *Brammer*, suggest a more balanced application of fair use, one that concentrates on the market effect of the defendant's use of the copyrighted work. Examining market effect in this manner curtails an overly broad application of transformative use as illustrated by *Cariou* and *Dorling Kindersley*. This newer tendency in regard to fair use keeps courts from encroaching on the copyright owner's right to make derivative works provided in 106(2) of the Copyright Act. In sum, the analysis in *TV Eyes and Brammer* recognizes implicitly that the principle of transformative use has an important role to play in supporting First Amendment values but is not a license to undermine the legitimate rights of the copyright owner.

Despite its seductive charm and approbation in the case law, the transformative use doctrine is neither supported by the language of the statute nor the legislative history. But this has always been the nature of the fair use, a doctrine that evolved over time to accommodate the most fundamental policies of copyright and First Amendment values. From its beginnings with *Acuff-Rose*, the case law has tried to provide more solid boundaries to the doctrine of transformative use first articulated in a law review article written by a famous judge. In general, it has enlarged the scope of fair use despite what appears to be a moderate retrenchment in the most recent cases.

It is easy to become so bemused by transformative use that one may overlook that there are sound reasons not to limit fair use to uses that transform or alter the copyrighted work. To do so would exclude some uses that are consistent with the law and policy of fair use and support First Amendment law and policy. Most important, a narrowly conceived reading fair use as transformative use would run at cross-purposes to the language of the preamble to fair use in § 107 such as the making of multiple copies for classroom use and copying in the furtherance of scholarship or research. Such copying is hardly "transformative," yet it clearly advances the Constitutional purpose of copyright law, that is, "to promote the progress of science and the useful arts."[95] Thus, fair use must support non-transformative but meritorious uses consistent with the public interest in the dissemination of information.

---

95. U.S. Const. Article I, section 8, Clause 8.

Chapter 14

After the Server Test: Embedded Content and the Digital Millennium Copyright Act

Andrew T. Foglia

14.1   INTRODUCTION

A young man snaps a cellphone photograph of a celebrity. He shares the photograph with friends via social media. One of those friends, without the photographer's permission, uploads the photograph to Reddit. The photograph goes viral. Twitter users post and retweet the photograph. Within hours, news media sites run articles embedding Twitter posts containing the photograph. That is, while the sites do not host the image on their own servers, they provide windowed images of Twitter pages showing the photograph. These "embedded" images allow visitors to view more-or-less full, color copies of the photograph. They also act as links to the underlying website. The original photographer looks around and asks, "who owes me money?"[1]

    For most of the past decade, the answer under United States (U.S.) copyright law would have been reasonably straightforward. The photographer could have sued the friend who uploaded the photograph and possibly the websites hosting the photograph (though sites hosting content at the

---

1. This fact pattern is drawn (roughly) from the Case *Goldman v. Breitbart News Network et al.*, 320 F. Supp. 3d 585, 586-87 (S.D.N.Y. 2018).

direction of users would have a defense based on § 512(c) of the Digital Millennium Copyright Act (DMCA)). But he could not have hoped to recover for *direct* copyright infringement from the news sites merely embedding social media posts featuring the photograph. That is because the "Server Test," developed in *Perfect 10, Inc. v. Amazon.com, Inc.* ("*Perfect 10*")[2] with reference to Google Image search, held that where a website embeds content hosted and transmitted from a third party server to the user, it is the third party that is actually displaying and distributing the content.[3]

The Server Test has had a profound impact on the development of modern Internet activity. Where linking is not "copying" or "displaying" content for purposes of the Copyright Act, any publisher can confidently share third-party content without concern about direct copyright liability. The rise of news articles aggregating content from Twitter, Tumblr, and Reddit is directly attributable to this legal regime. One study of prominent news sites found that 23% of news articles feature embedded content.[4]

But the Server Test is not as safe as it once seemed. In February 2018, in *Goldman v. Breitbart News Network*, a federal district court rejected application of the Server Test to facts like those described above, allowing direct infringement claims to go forward against media sites embedding a copyrighted photograph from Twitter.[5] The ruling cast doubt on the continued viability of the Server Test and raised alarm around the Internet.[6] Without the Server Test, could any site safely embed content from social

---

2. 508 F.3d 1146, 1156 (9th Cir. 2007).

3. *Id.* of a hyperlink to an authorized site, there is no "direct infringement.").

4. The State of Social Embeds, SAMDESK.IO (2016), https://cdn.samdesk.io/static-content/The-State-of-Social-Embeds.pdf.

5. *Goldman*, 320 F. Supp. 3d at 591. The *Goldman* decision followed a 2017 decision, *Leader's Institute, LLC v. Jackson*, No. 3:14-cv-3572-B, 2017 WL 5629514 (N.D. Tex. November 22, 2017) that also rejected application of the Server Test. If the *Leader's Institute* decision has received less attention than *Goldman*, it is perhaps because the Northern District of Texas is a less prominent venue for copyright litigation.

6. *See,* e.g., Brian Feldman, *How a Photo of Tom Brady Could Change the Way That You See the Internet*, N.Y. Mag. (February 16, 2018), http://nymag.com/selectall/2018/02/court-rulesthat-embedding-tweets-could-violate-copyright.html (Observing that the end of the server test "has the potential to shake the very foundation on which the modern internet is built, changing the way websites from huge publications to one-person blogs do business online"); Eriq Gardner, *Judge Rules News Publishers Violated Copyright by Embedding Tweets of Tom Brady Photo*, Hollywood Reporter (February 15, 2018), https://www.hollywoodreporter.com/thr-esq/judge-rulesnews-publishers-violated-copyright-by-embedding-tweets-tom-brady-photo-1085342 (reporting the decision could "potentially disrupt[] the way that news outlets use Twitter and causing many in technology to re-examine ubiquitous practices from embedding to linking"); Louise Matsakis, *A Ruling Over Embedded Tweets Could Change Online Publishing*, Wired (February 16, 2018), https://www.wired.com/story/embedded-tweets-copyright-law/ ("One of the most ubiquitous features of the internet is the ability to link to content elsewhere. Everything is connected via billions of links and embeds to blogs, articles, and social media. But a federal judge's ruling threatens that ecosystem [... and] could change the way online publishing functions.").

media without first tracing it back to the original owner (even if the original owner did not upload the content and was not known to the hundreds or thousands of individuals sharing the image online)? A defendant might have a fair use defense if the content were used for a news reporting purpose.[7] But fair use is formally an affirmative defense and also a fact-intensive inquiry, rarely available at the motion to dismiss stage,[8] and consequently less helpful to a news reporter or a publisher wishing to avoid the expense of prolonged litigation. What publishers require is another bright-line defense that can ward off suits before they are filed.

Fortunately, such a defense already exists in law—though it has not yet been tested in court. The Digital Millennium Copyright's safe harbor for "information location tools," U.S.C. § 512(d), shields online service providers from monetary liability for providing hypertext links, pointers, indexes, and other such references to third-party websites containing infringing content.[9] It is available to any website meeting simple preconditions and rarely requires significant factual development. And although § 512(d) has never been used in defense of embedded links, the statutory text, legislative history, and public policy interests involved all support its application in such circumstances.

This chapter will argue based on *Goldman* that, after the Server Test, § 512(d)'s safe harbor is the best defense available for embedding content. Section 14.1 will provide a brief summary of the *Goldman* litigation. Section 14.2 will walk through the application of § 512(d) to embedded media content. Section 14.3 will discuss the limitations of the § 512(d) defense.

14.2   GOLDMAN V. BREITBART NEWS NETWORK

14.2.1   THE PHOTOGRAPH

On July 2, 2016, around 2:00 p.m., 20-year-old Syracuse student Justin Goldman took a photograph of American football star Tom Brady walking in the Hamptons with several members of the Boston Celtics.[10] The timing of Brady's and the Celtics' visit to the Hamptons suggested to Goldman that

---

7. 17 U.S.C. 107. *But see Monge v. Maya Magazines, Inc.*, 688 F.3d 1164, 1172 (9th Cir. 2012) (distinguishing, for purposes of fair use analysis, news articles about particular photographs as objects in themselves from news articles about the underlying content of photographs).

8. *BWP Media USA, Inc. v. Gossip Cop Media, LLC*, 87 F. Supp. 3d 499, 505 (S.D.N.Y. 2015) (noting narrow circumstances under which "it is possible to resolve the fair use inquiry on a motion to dismiss").

9. *Id.*

10. *Goldman*, Dkt. No. 13 ("Amended Complaint") ¶ 5; Declaration of Justin Goldman ("Goldman Decl."), Dkt. No. 115-1, ¶¶ 2-3.

Brady was there to aid the Celtics' attempt to recruit NBA star Kevin Durant.[11] Goldman posted the photograph to his Snapchat account's My Story, a chronological feed of his in-app photographs accessible to his friends.[12] He added the text, "Celtics and Tom Brady roll thru to get Durant #Hamptons."[13]

Shortly thereafter, one of Goldman's friends (who happened to be the son of film director Spike Lee) took a screenshot of the photograph on Goldman's My Story.[14] He sent the photo to an acquaintance, who then posted the Photo to Reddit.[15]

The publication of the photograph broke the story that Tom Brady was helping to recruit Kevin Durant to the Boston Celtics. Within minutes, the photograph spread to Twitter and other social media networks, where it was shared and re-posted by numerous sports journalists.[16] Shortly thereafter, online sports media reported the viral photo on their own platforms.

14.2.2   EMBEDDED LINKS TO THE PHOTOGRAPH

Between July 2 and July 4, 2016, a collection of sports and general media websites ran articles containing embedded or "inline" links to Twitter[17] posts ("tweets") that contained the photograph.[18] An "inline" link is a method of directing the user's computer to content hosted elsewhere on the Internet.[19] When a user navigates to a particular webpage, his or her computer contacts the website's server, which sends back a data file containing any text that appears on the webpage, as well as instructions written in various computer programming languages, including HyperText Markup Language ("HTML").[20] Using the HTML instructions, the user's browser software

---

11. Goldman Decl. ¶ 3.
12. *Id.*
13. *Id.*
14. *Id.*
15. *Id.* at ¶ 4.
16. *Goldman*, Dkt. No. 113, ¶¶ 23-25.
17. Twitter is a social networking and online news website that allows members to post "tweets"—messages of 140 characters or less, which are then delivered to subscribers (called "followers") in a continuous "feed." *See* Twitter, *Getting Started with Twitter*, https://support.twitter.com/articles/215585. Each Tweet has its own URL (which typically appears as "https://twitter.com/[username]/status/[18-digit number]/." Users can also upload media content to accompany tweets, including photos, videos, and sounds.
18. *Goldman*, Dkt. No. 113, ¶¶ 30-39.
19. U.S. COPYRIGHT OFFICE, THE MAKING AVAILABLE RIGHT IN THE UNITED STATES 48 (2016), https://perma.cc/3JB9-AZYP (describing inline linking as a tool whereby "an image, audio file, or video seems to be part of the webpage being viewed, even though it is actually located on a different server").
20. *See also British Telecomms. PLC v. Prodigy Commc'ns Corp.*, 217 F. Supp. 2d 399, 406-07 (S.D.N.Y. 2002) ("HTML is the language in which Web pages are formatted. This

"builds" the page that ultimately appears on his/her screen. These instructions may include links to content on other websites and other servers. So, for example, the HTML code for Google Image Search instructs a user's browser to display a search results page incorporating framed previews of images hosted elsewhere on the Internet. These images are not hosted on Google's server. Were the linked site to delete the image, it would immediately disappear from Google image search as well.

In this case, staffers at each of the media sites found a tweet containing Goldman's photograph and then copied the URL for the tweet itself or copied embed code from Twitter.com and pasted it into their own webpage's source code. Twitter supports this linking and sharing of users' posts via its technology[21] and its Terms of Service.[22]

The result is that each of the news articles enclosed, between text passages, a windowed image of a tweet containing the photograph.[23] By clicking anywhere on the image, the user would be taken to the linked Twitter page.

With respect to these inline links, the photograph was not stored on, hosted by, or transmitted from servers owned or controlled by the news sites.[24] Instead, the photograph was hosted on and served from a server with the URL "pic.twitter.com", and the inline links on the news sites referred users to the appropriate address to find the photograph.

---

language is a kind of publishing mother tongue that all computers may potentially understand" (internal citation and quotation marks omitted)).

21. Twitter's development site explains that "An embedded Tweet brings the best content created on Twitter into your article or website. An embedded Tweet may include unique photos or a video created for display on Twitter or interactive link previews to highlight additional content. Author attribution, hashtags, mentions, and other key components of the Twitter experience helps your site's audience connect with the global conversation happening on Twitter." Twitter, *Embed a Single Tweet*, https://dev.twitter.com/web/embedded-Tweets. As Twitter explains further, an embedded tweet "may include a link to a Twitter-hosted photo, Vine video, or other content supporting a Twitter Card preview." Twitter may replace a link with a more visual experience including inline photo display, an inline video player, or a link preview display.

22. All users of Twitter must agree to the site's Terms of Service in order to register an account and use the site. *See* Terms of Service | Twitter, https://twitter.com/tos?lang=en. The Terms of Service in place at the time relevant to this case (July 2016) provide that posting content to the site grants Twitter a license to "use, copy, reproduce, process, adapt, modify, publish, transmit, display and distribute such Content in any and all media or distribution methods," which includes the right for Twitter to make that content "available to other companies, organizations or individuals who partner with Twitter for the syndication, broadcast, distribution or publication of such Content on other media and services, subject to our terms and conditions for such Content use." *See* Previous Terms of Service | Twitter, § 5, https://twitter.com /tos/previous/version_10?lang=en#yourrights. Users are also required to represent and warrant that they have "all the rights, power and authority" to grant that license to Twitter. *Id*.

23. *Goldman*, 320 F. Supp. 3d at 585.

24. *Id.*

There does not appear to have been any dispute that at the time the articles went live, none of the news sites was aware of any reason to believe the tweets they were linking contained infringing content.

14.2.3 GOLDMAN'S PROCEDURAL HISTORY

Goldman sued several news sites for embedding the photograph on April 28, 2017. In their defense, the news sites invoked *Perfect 10, Inc. v. Amazon-.com, Inc.*, which, addressing Google image search, held that Google's embedding of full-size images stored on third-party servers were not infringing because a publisher's direct liability for infringement turns entirely on whether the image is hosted on the publisher's own server.[25] Under this "Server Test," the news sites would not be directly infringing Goldman's copyright merely by embedding Twitter posts containing Goldman's photograph.

The *Goldman* court rejected the news sites' argument. It found the Copyright Act gave "no indication … that possessing a copy of an infringing image," i.e., hosting it on one's own server, "is a prerequisite to displaying it."[26] And it questioned whether the Server Test had any continuing application after the Supreme Court's decision in *American Broadcasting Companies, Inc. v. Aereo, Inc.*,[27] which warned that liability "should not hinge on invisible, technical processes imperceptible to the viewer."[28]

Despite throwing out the news sites' primary defense, the Court cautioned that even without the Server Test, the news sites had a "very serious and strong fair use defense, a defense under the DMCA, and limitations on damages from innocent infringement."[29] But Goldman ultimately voluntarily dismissed the case before any of these defenses could be tested.[30]

---

25. *Goldman*, Dkt. No. 57. All defendants filed an additional motion to dismiss on the grounds that the use of the Photo constituted fair use as a matter of law. ECF No. 59.
26. 302 F. Supp. 3d at 595.
27. 573 U.S. 431 (2014).
28. *Goldman*, 302 F. Supp. 3d at 595.
29. *Id.*
30. *Goldman*, Dkt. No. 235. What's more, this voluntary dismissal nullifies the court's prior order rejecting the Server Test. Voluntary dismissal of a suit "leaves the situation so far as procedures therein are concerned the same as though the suit had never been brought … thus vitiating and annulling all prior proceedings and orders in the case, and terminating jurisdiction over it for the reason that the case has become moot." *A.B. Dick Co. v. Marr*, 197 F.2d 498, 502 (quotation marks and citation omitted)*; see also Oneida Indian Nation v. Oneida County*, 622 F.2d 624, 629 n. 7 (2d Cir. 1980) ("Voluntary dismissal of a suit … vitiat[es] and annul[s] all prior proceedings and orders in the case, terminating jurisdiction over it for the reason that the case has become moot.").

14.3	THE UNTESTED ARGUMENT: DMCA SAFE HARBOR

Although it was never tested in court, there is considerable reason to think that the *Goldman* news sites would have succeeded had they claimed safe harbor under § 512(d) of the DMCA. Section 512(d) protects defendants from monetary liability "for infringement of copyright by reason of the [online service] provider referring or linking users to an online location containing infringing material or infringing activity, by using information location tools, including a directory, index, reference, pointer or hypertext link."[31] This safe harbor reflects a simple bargain: websites maintain agents to receive takedown notices for infringing content, comply with substantially complete takedown notices, and reasonably implement policies to terminate repeat infringers; in exchange, so long as they lack actual knowledge that the content they store, refer, or link is infringing, they cannot be liable for monetary damages[32] if the content stored, referred, or linked happens to be infringing. The DMCA relieves publishers of the obligation to trace the entire history of linked content—down to the circumstance of who posted it online and whether that person in fact had permission to do so.

14.3.1 GENERAL REQUIREMENTS FOR SAFE HARBOR UNDER § 512(D)

To qualify for § 512(d)'s safe harbor, a party must meet certain general requirements, including that (1) the party must be an online "service provider" as defined by the statute; (2) the party must have adopted and reasonably implemented a policy for the termination in appropriate circumstances of users who are repeat infringers; and (3) the party must not interfere with standard technical measures used by copyright owners to identify or protect copyrighted works.[33] These are standards that the *Goldman* defendants, and indeed most prominent websites, ought to be able to meet.

14.3.1.1 Who Is a Service Provider?

For purposes of the relevant safe harbors, the term "service provider" broadly means "a provider of online services or network access, or the operator of facilities therefor."[34]

---

31. 17 U.S.C § 512(d).
32. Although § 512(d) states that a qualifying service provider "shall not be liable for monetary relief," subsection § 512(j) clarifies that court may still grant injunctive relief requiring the service provider to remove an infringing link. In most cases, this form of relief will be moot because in order to qualify for safe harbor, the provider would have already removed the link as soon as it learned of the claim.
33. 17 U.S.C. §§ 512(c), (i); *Wolk v. Kodak Imaging Network, Inc.*, 840 F. Supp. 2d 724, 743 (S.D.N.Y. 2012).
34. *Wolk*, 840 F. Supp. 2d at 743-44 (quoting 17 U.S.C. § 512(k)(1)).

"The DMCA's definition of 'service provider' is intended to encompass a broad set of Internet entities."[35] It includes, for example, digital storefronts like Amazon,[36] real estate listing sites,[37] and message boards.[38] Indeed, one federal court has concluded that for purposes of safe harbor under § 512(d) "service provider" is "defined so broadly that [one] ha[s] trouble imagining the existence of an online service that would not fall under the definitions[]."[39] There is no reason to think that interactive news sites offering news, search functions, and "comment" tools would not qualify.

14.3.1.2   Repeat Infringer Policies

"To fulfill § 512(i)'s repeat infringer policy requirement, a service provider must (i) adopt a policy that provides for the termination of service access for repeat copyright infringers; (ii) inform users of the service policy; and (iii) implement the policy in a reasonable manner."[40] Courts have found that a "reasonably implemented [repeat infringer] policy can utilize a 'variety of procedures.'"[41] Factors that have been applied to determine whether a repeat infringer policy is reasonably implemented include whether the service provider "(1) has a system for responding to takedown notices, (2) does not interfere with the copyright owners' ability to issue notices, and (3) under 'appropriate circumstances' terminates users who repeatedly or blatantly infringe copyrights."[42]

Although this element appears to require some examination of the facts, as a practical matter courts rarely require an extensive showing. Indeed, courts and commentators alike have questioned whether this requirement even applies to search engines or other sites that "lack … subscribers or account holders."[43]

---

35. *Id.* at 744 (finding that Photobucket, likeYoutube.com and Veoh.com, is an internet service provider within the meaning of the DMCA).
36. *Corbis Corp. v. Amazon.com, Inc.*, 351 F. Supp. 2d 1090, 1100 (W.D. Wash. 2004) ("[There is] no doubt that Amazon fits within the definition [of a 'service provider']. … Amazon operates web sites, provides retail and third party selling services to Internet users, and maintains computers to govern access to its web sites.")
37. *Costar Group, Inc. v. Loopnet, Inc.*, 164 F. Supp. 2d 688, 701 (D. Md. 2001) (finding real estate listing site qualified as a service provider).
38. *See Totally Her Media, LLC v. BWP Media USA, Inc.*, No. 13-cv-8379, 2015 WL 12659912, at *8-9 (C.D. Cal. March 24, 2015) (web-based social discussion forum "unquestionably 'provides online services'").
39. *In re Aimster Copyright Litig.*, 252 F. Supp. 2d 634, 658 (N.D. Ill. 2002), *aff'd*, 334 F.3d 643 (7th Cir. 2003).
40. *Wolk*, 840 F. Supp. 2d at 744.
41. *Vimeo*, 2013 WL 5272932, at *10 (quoting *Perfect 10, Inc. v. CCBill LLC*, 488 F.3d 1102, 1109-11 (9th Cir. 2007)).
42. *Capitol Records, Inc. v. MP3tunes, LLC*, 821 F.Supp.2d 627, 637 (S.D.N.Y. 2011).
43. Miquel Peguera, *When the Cached Link is the Weakest Link: Search Engine Caches Under the Digital Millennium Copyright Act*, 56 J. COPYRIGHT SOC'Y U.S.A. 589, 614 (2009).

14.3.1.3 Interference with Standard Technical Measures

"Standard technical measures," which refer to "technical measures that copyright owners use to identify or to protect copyrighted works and: (1) have been developed pursuant to a broad consensus of copyright owners and service providers in an open, fair, voluntary, multi-industry standards process; (2) are available to any person on reasonable and nondiscriminatory terms; and (3) do not impose substantial costs on service providers or substantial burdens on their systems or networks."[44] Courts have never identified "standard technical measures" in this context, beyond suggesting, in *dicta*, that a service provider that "advises or encourages users to conceal a work's copyrighted status" might be interfering with such measures.[45] There is no reason to believe that this requirement would be an obstacle to any website obtaining safe harbor.

14.3.2 SPECIFIC REQUIREMENTS FOR SAFE HARBOR UNDER 17 U.S.C. § 512(D)

In addition to meeting the threshold requirements for DMCA safe harbor, defendants must also satisfy the specific requirements for safe harbor under § 512(d). Section 512(d) provides that:

> A service provider shall not be liable … for infringement of copyright: by reason of the provider referring or linking users to an online location containing infringing material or infringing activity, by using information location tools, including a directory, index, reference, pointer, or hypertext link, if the service provider—

> (1) (A) does not have actual knowledge that the material or activity is infringing;
> (B) in the absence of such actual knowledge, is not aware of facts or circumstances from which infringing activity is apparent; or
> (C) upon obtaining such knowledge or awareness, acts expeditiously to remove, or disable access to, the material;
> (2) does not receive a financial benefit directly attributable to the infringing activity, in a case in which the service provider has the right and ability to control such activity; and
> (3) upon notification of claimed infringement as described in subsection (c)(3), responds expeditiously to remove, or disable access to,

---

44. *Ellison v. Robertson*, 357 F.3d 1072, 1080 n.11 (9th Cir. 2004) (quoting 17 U.S.C. § 512(i)(2)).
45. *See Wolk*, 840 F. Supp. at 745. *Milo & Gabby, LLC v. Amazon.com, Inc.*, No. C13-1932 (RSM), 2015 WL 4394673, at *8 (W.D. Wa. July 16, 2015) (finding this element satisfied where the plaintiff did not allege that Amazon interfered with standard technical measures to identify or protect copyrighted works), *aff'd*, 693 F. App'x 879 (Fed. Cir. 2017).

the … the reference or link, to material or activity claimed to be infringing. [46]

14.3.2.1 Inline Links to Third-Party Media Content Are "Information Location Tools" Within the Meaning of 17 U.S.C. § 512(d)

In the past, websites have successfully invoked § 512(d) to evade liability for the provision of hyperlinks to infringing content.[47] But few courts have ruled—or evidently even considered—whether § 512(d) applies to inline links.

The statutory text and legislative history strongly suggest that it does. The plain language of § 512(d) defines "information location tool" to include "reference[s]," "pointer[s,]" and "hypertext link[s]."[48] These terms are not themselves defined in the statute, but a common sense reading of "reference" or "pointer" would have to include an inline link that, after all, points or refers the user to the content on a third-party site.

Moreover, § 512(d)'s legislative history demonstrates that Congress was interested in broadly promoting the use and development of information location tools. The purpose of the DMCA safe harbors, in the words of the House Report, was to protect certain common Internet activities by "clarif[ying] the liability faced by [online] service providers who transmit potentially infringing material over their networks."[49] Section 512(d) in particular reflected Congress's judgment that "[i]nformation location tools are essential to the operation of the Internet."[50] The House defined such tools to include:

> a directory or index of online sites or material such as a search engine that identifies pages by specified criteria, a reference to other online material such as a list of recommended sites, a pointer that stands for an Internet location or address, or a hypertext link which allows users to access material without entering its address.[51]

The list was non-exclusive and not limited to the then-current technology. And here again, it is difficult to distinguish the description of a "pointer"

---

46. 17 U.S.C. 512(d).
47. *See,* e.g., *Perfect 10, Inc. v. Google, Inc.,* No. CV 04-9484 AHM (SHx), 2010 WL 9479059, at *13 (C.D. Cal. July 26, 2010).
48. 17 U.S.C. 512(d).
49. S.Rep. No. 105-190 at 2 (1998), 19. Cf. *Distribuidora De Discos Karen C. Por A. v. Guerra Seijas,* 2015 WL 4496066, at *4 (S.D.N.Y. March 26, 2015) ("Congress enacted the DMCA in order to modernize the application of copyright law to the Internet and modern technology.").
50. *Id.*
51. H.R. Rep. No. 105-551 (II), at 58. The House Report cited as an additional example of a valuable information location tool a directory created by Yahoo! that functioned as a "card catalogue to the World Wide Web." *Id.*

or the function of a hypertext link from an inline link. Inline links do after all stand for Internet locations or addresses, and they allow users to access material without entering its address. There is nothing in the text or legislative history of § 512(d) to suggest that a link must be purely verbal rather than pictorial in order to warrant safe harbor. And indeed it is hard to see how sound Internet policy would be served by such an arbitrary limitation. Embedded images have the advantages of (a) more precisely previewing the content the viewer can expect to find at the destination and (b) not strictly requiring language proficiency. Including embedded links within § 512(d) is clearly consistent with Congress' evident agnosticism among forms of directors and hope to promote the development of new information location tools.[52]

The few courts to discuss the application of § 512(d) to inline links have treated them as information location tools. In *Flava Works, Inc. v. Gunter*, the Seventh Circuit stated that § 512(d)'s safe harbor would apply to a website's provision of embedded videos—subject to the site meeting the other requirements for safe harbor.[53] It added that Congress intended for § 512(d)'s safe harbor to be "as capacious as possible."[54] Similarly, in *Perfect 10, Inc. v. Google Inc.*, the court found that § 512(d)'s safe harbor protected Google's web and image searches' use of inline links.[55] No court has held that inline links are not information location tools. Although the law in this area is underdeveloped, the most plausible reading of the statutory text, the legislative history, and the available precedent suggests courts will find inline links, as used in cases like *Goldman*, are information location tools within the meaning of § 512(d).

14.3.2.2   Actual Knowledge of Infringing Activity

Section 512(d)'s "actual knowledge" criterion has been interpreted as referring to knowledge of specific instances of infringement—that is, the obligation to expeditiously remove or disable infringing material or else losing the safe harbor is triggered only by the service provider's subjective awareness that specific material is infringing.[56]

Prior to enacting the DMCA, Congress stressed that this knowledge requirement "should not be applied in a manner which would create a

---

52. Congress's stated goal was "to promote the development of information location tools generally." H.R. Rep. 105-551(II), at 58. Among other things, this meant that § 512(d) would apply "where information location tools refer or link users to an on-line location containing infringing material … without regard to whether the copyright infringement is technically deemed to have occurred at that location or at the location where the material is received."
53. 689 F.3d 754, 758 (7th Cir. 2012).
54. *Id.*
55. 2010 WL 9479059 (C.D. Cal., July 26, 2010).
56. *Viacom*, 676 F.3d at 31–32.

disincentive to the development of directories which involve human inter-vention. Absent actual knowledge, awareness of infringement ... should typically be imputed ... only with respect to pirate sites or in similarly obvious and conspicuous circumstances."[57] The point of the "red flag" knowledge standard is to ensure "on-line editors and catalogers would not be required to make discriminating judgments about potential copyright in-fringement."[58]

This standard would protect online publishers under circumstances captured in *Goldman*. There, the copyright owner never submitted a DMCA-compliant takedown notification to the news sites, and there was no evidence that anyone involved in the publication of the article thought that the photograph of Tom Brady might be infringing.[59] The same would likely be true in many cases involving viral content embedded from social media.

14.3.2.3 Financial Benefit Directly Attributable to the Infringing Activity

Nor would most online publishers need to worry about the safe harbor criterion that a defendant not "receive a financial benefit directly attributable to the infringing activity, in a case in which the[y] [had] the right and ability to control such activity."[60] Although most news sites are commercial and therefore in some sense expect to receive financial benefits from their content, Congress has explained that "[i]n general, a service provider conducting a legitimate business would not be considered to receive a financial benefit directly attributable to the infringing activity where the infringer makes the same kind of payment as non-infringing users of the provider's service."[61] In *Capitol Records, Inc. v. MP3tunes, LLC*, a federal district court found that there was no direct financial benefit where the service provider stored infringing and non-infringing songs free of charge.[62]

As to the right and ability to control infringing activity, the Court of Appeals for the Second Circuit has held that this "requires something more than the ability to remove or block access to materials posted on a service provider's website."[63] In *UMG Recordings*, there was no "right and ability to control" where a video-sharing website merely removed or disabled access to

---

57. H.R. Rep. 105-551(II), at 58.
58. *Id.*
59. *Goldman*, Dkt. No. 38; Dkt. No. 120, ¶¶ 41-45.
60. *Capitol Records, Inc. v. MP3tunes, LLC*, 821 F. Supp. 2d 627, 645 (S.D.N.Y. 2011), *partially reconsidered Capitol Records, Inc. v. MP3tunes, LLC*, No. 07-cv-9931 (WHP), 2013 WL 1987225 (S.D.N.Y. May 14, 2013).
61. H.R.Rep. No. 105-551(II) at 54.
62. 821 F. Supp. 2d at 645.
63. *Viacom Int'l v. YouTube, Inc.*, 676 F.3d 19, 38 (2d Cir. 2012).

infringing content but did not "exert[] substantial influence on the activities of users" by, for example, inducing copyright infringement.[64]

In cases like *Goldman*, where the defendants have embedded content and by happenstance included potentially infringing content, they can argue that they do not charge separately for infringing content. It is unlikely that any website's advertising revenue is directly related to embedded Twitter links, and in any case it is the nature of such links that the linking website would not have the right and ability to control the allegedly infringing upload. As soon as the hosting site alters or removes the content, however, it will be automatically altered on or removed from the linking site.

14.3.2.4   Takedown Notices

The final specific requirement for safe harbor under § 512(d) is that the website must not have failed to respond to any substantially complete DMCA takedown notice.[65] This is another fact-specific requirement. In *Goldman*, the defendants certainly met this requirement, because the copyright owner never submitted a DMCA-compliant takedown notice, and they took down the photograph anyway.[66]

Based on the above, it seems clear that the *Goldman* defendants, and those similarly situated, would satisfy all the requirements for safe harbor under § 512(d). Such a result would be consistent with Congress' intent when it created a safe harbor for information location tools. The news sites neither put Goldman's photograph online nor did they host it themselves; they merely provided inline links referring readers to tweets containing the

---

64. 718 F.3d 1006, 1030-31 (9th Cir. 2013) (citing *Viacom*'s explanation that "right and ability to control" "requires something more than the ability to remove or block access to materials posted on a service provider's website"); *see also Viacom*, 676 F.3d at 37 (pointing out that such a requirement would make qualification for 512(c)(1)(B) a *disqualifier* from the threshold requirement that a service provider remove or disable access to infringing material); *see also UMG Recordings, Inc. v. Shelter Cap. Partners LLC*, 718 F.3d 1006, 1027 (9th Cir. 2013) (same) (citing *Hendrickson v. eBay, Inc.*, 165 F. Supp. 2d 1082, 1093-94 (C.D. Cal. 2001)) (internal quotation marks omitted).
65. 17 U.S.C. § 512(d)(3).
66. 17 U.S.C. § 512(3) sets out the requirements for a DMCA takedown notice to be effective. The notice must, among other things, be sent, in writing, to the service provider's designated agent; and it must include "a statement that the information in the notification is accurate, and under penalty of perjury, that the complaining party is authorized to act on behalf of the owner of an exclusive right that is allegedly infringed." To the extent Goldman sent the news sites any notice at all, he did not send the notice to their designated agents, and his notice lacked the formalities to make it effective. "Substantial compliance with [the DMCA notification requirement] means substantial compliance with all of its clauses, not just some of them." *Perfect 10, Inc. v. Yandex N.V.*, 2013 WL 1899851, at *3 (N.D. Cal. May 7, 2013). Nonetheless, the news sites subsequently either removed the embedded tweet on their own, or when the photograph was removed from Twitter, it was no longer visible from their websites. *See Goldman*, Dkt. No. 120, ¶¶ 41-45.

photograph. They had no way of knowing at the time that the Twitter users who posted the photograph might not have authority to post it. To punish the news sites for the accident that the photographer's acquaintance may have uploaded the photograph to the Internet without permission would undo the bargain at the heart of § 512(d) and force news sites to abandon wide use of inline links.

14.4   LIMITATIONS

Recognition of § 512(d) defense for embedding content would create a substantial safety net, should additional courts reject the Server Test. The defense is, in theory, available to a wide variety of online service providers on relatively easy terms. And it does not require the same factual development as a fair use or innocent infringement defense. It does, however, have significant limitations compared to the Server Test.

First, an online service provider probably cannot invoke § 512(d) where the service provider's inline link refers to an authorized use of the copyright. By its terms, § 512(d) applies where the provider links to an online location "containing infringing material or infringing activity:"[67]

> Accordingly, a defendant who faces a claim of infringement of the rights of public display and performance by reason of providing an embedded link to *authorized* content—for example, the incorporation of a photograph originally posted to a news website which had obtained permission to display the photograph in connection with a particular article, or the "sharing" of a friend's photograph posted by the friend on a social media website—could not claim the protection of § 512(d).[68]

This may be a fair compromise. As Ginsburg and Budiarjo point out, this limitation protects photographers who wish to restrict access to their work,[69] but it still allows online service providers to safely aggregate from social media and other platforms whose terms allow it. Twitter, for example, requires uploaders to grant Twitter a license permitting sharing of their content—a license Twitter then extends to other Twitter users for the sake of wide sharing of content.[70] If, in *Goldman v. Breitbart News Network*, the photographer himself had uploaded the photograph to Twitter, there would have been no question that the news sites' links were authorized. It was only the twist that the photographer claimed not to have authorized the upload that put the news sites in legal danger. A legal regime in which § 512(d) protects

---

67. 17 U.S.C. § 512(d).
68. Jane C. Ginsburg & Luke Ali Budiarjo, *The Server Rule*, 42 Columbia J. L. & Arts 101, 130 (2019).
69. *Id.*
70. *See supra* note 22.

news sites from that sort of surprise but otherwise forces them to observe the terms of third-party sites would cover a large percentage of embedding activity. But it is also clearly more restrictive than the Server Test's blanket protection for inline linking in all circumstances.[71]

A second limitation of the § 512(d) defense is that it cannot be resolved as a matter of law. Although it is nowhere near as fact-intensive as a fair use defense, § 512(d) does require a claimant to adduce evidence that it is a service provider, that it maintains and reasonably applies a repeat infringer policy, that it lacked actual knowledge of infringing activity, and that did not derive a direct financial benefit from the infringing activity where it had the right and ability to control such activity.[72] This means undergoing at least some of the expense of discovery. By contrast, the great advantage of the Server Test is that it requires no facts at all and can be successfully invoked on a motion to dismiss.

But even with these limitations, § 512(d) is a substantial improvement over relying on fair use. Faced with the potential cost of litigating a fair use defense, some publishers might well decide that embedding content they don't control is not worth the risk. One thinks of the role a few court decisions played in diminishing the use of sampling in hip-hop music. The dense, multilayered samples of the late-1980s and early-1990s became uneconomical—and far too risky—in a culture of lawsuits and permissions. Similarly, here, without a bright-line defense, it is easy to imagine publishers reducing the role of embedding in their work, notwithstanding any expressive merit it might have. Section 512, by offering this bright-line defense, goes some way toward guaranteeing news outlets' reporting interest in embedding newsworthy images and the public interest in the development of new information location tools.

14.5   CONCLUSION

The erosion of the Server Test comes at a time when copyright suits based on the online use of photographs have come to occupy an increasingly substantial portion of U.S. federal court litigation.[73] The settlement value of such suits is rarely worth the cost of extensive litigation. Absent a way to win the suit quickly, defendants often have no reasonable choice but to settle. Section 512(d) offers a promising alternative. It is less fact-specific than fair

---

71. Suppose ESPN embeds a duly-authorized photograph from the Reddit, but it turns out that Reddit's terms no longer grant ESPN a license to use that content. The content was authorized on Reddit, so ESPN can't rely on § 512(d). ESPN will need another defense.
72. *See supra* text accompanying notes 59-69.
73. Anandashankar Mazumdar, *Photography Cases Spur Copyright Lawsuit Growth in New York*, Bloomberg BNA (November 7, 2017), https://www.bna.com/photography-cases-spur-n73014471850/.

use, permits a wider range of uses of embedded content, and arguably covers every kind of website. Although it cannot replace the full, presumptive immunity conferred on inline linkers by the Server Test, it may be the next best thing.

Chapter 15

Finding the Balance in Copyright Law: Internal and External Control Through Fundamental Rights

Bernd Justin Jütte

15.1   INTRODUCTION

The adoption of the Directive on copyright and related rights in the Digital Single Market (DSM Directive)[1] in 2019 was accompanied by unprecedented public attention.[2] During the three years of deliberations prior to its adoption, public interest groups and academia have commented extensively on the various draft versions of the directive.[3] A recurring argument stressed the implications the provisions of the new legislation would have on the exercise of fundamental rights. Whether it was the introduction of new exclusive rights, or the failure to systematically reform exceptions and limitations (E&L), commentators criticized the disregard for a proper

---

1. Directive (EU) 2019/790 of the European Parliament and of the Council of 17 April 2019 on copyright and related rights in the Digital Single Market and amending Directives 96/9/EC and 2001/29/EC, OJ L 130, 17.5.2019, pp. 92-125 (DSM Directive).
2. Aside from widespread media coverage, the process was accompanied by interventions from civil society organizations, artists and many different stakeholders; public demonstration against Articles 13 and 17 took place all over Europe.
3. A comparison table of the various draft versions has been compiled by the UK Copyright and Creative Economy Centre (CREATe) at the University of Glasgow and is available under: https://www.create.ac.uk/policy-responses/eu-copyright-reform/#table (last accessed on 14 September 2019).

balance between the various interests and fundamental rights in the drafting of the new rules.[4] Academic discourse on the relation between copyright and fundamental rights had been well established.[5] However, the discussion surrounding the adoption of the DSM Directive was the first opportunity to observe and discuss the legislative fixation of substantive copyright rules with the European Union (EU) Charter in force.[6]

---

4. *See,* for example, in the statements by the European Copyright Society (*see* here https://eur,opeancopyrightsocietydotorg.files.wordpress.com/2018/06/2018_european-copyright-societyopiniononpresspublishersright.pdf and here https://europeancopyrightsocietydotorg.files.wordpress.com/2015/12/ecs-opinion-on-eu-copyright-reform-def.pdf as well as a statement by academics at the 2018 *European Policy for Intellectual Property conference* (https://www.create.ac.uk/blog/2018/09/10/vote-for-a-balanced-european-copyright-law-statement-by-epip-academics/) *and the Initiative of Academics Against Press Publishers' Right* (https://www.ivir.nl/publicaties/download/Academics_Against_Press_Publishers_Right.pdf).

5. *See* only Geiger, C., Fundamental Rights, a Safeguard for the Coherence of Intellectual Property Law?, 35(3) *International Review of Intellectual Property and Competition* (2004), 268-280, Geiger, C., 'Constitutionalising' Intellectual Property Law? The Influence of Fundamental Rights on Intellectual Property in the European Union, 37(4) *International Review of Intellectual Property and Competition* (2006), 371-406, Geiger, C., Intellectual Property Shall Be Protected!? Article 17(2) of the Charter of Fundamental Rights of the European Union: A Mysterious Provision with an Unclear Scope, 31(3) *European Intellectual Property Review* (2009), 113-117, Geiger, C. & E. Izyumenko, Copyright on the Human Rights' Trial: Redefining the Boundaries of Exclusivity Through Freedom of Expression, 42(3) *International Review of Intellectual Property and Competition* (2014), 316-342, Peukert, A., The Fundamental Right to (Intellectual) Property and the Discretion of the Legislature, in: C. Geiger (ed.), *Research Handbook on Human Rights and Intellectual Property* (Cheltenham, Northampton: Edward Elgar Publishing, 2015), Voorhoof, D., Freedom of Expression and the Right to Information: Implications for Copyright, in: C. Geiger (ed.), *Research Handbook on Human Rights and Intellectual Property (Research Handbooks in Intellectual Property)* (Cheltenham, Northampton: Edward Elgar Publishing, 2015), Jütte, B.J., The Beginning of a (Happy?) Relationship: Copyright and Freedom of Expression in Europe, 38(1) *European Intellectual Property Review* (2016), 11-22, Griffiths, J. & McDonagh, L., Fundamental Rights and European IP Law: The Case of Art 17(2) of the EU Charter, in: C. Geiger (ed.), *Constructing European Intellectual Property: Achievements and New Perspectives* (Cheltenham, Northampton: Edward Elgar Publishing, 2013).

6. Other recent EU legislation on copyright law were either mandated by international agreements, such as the Marrakech Directive (Directive (EU) 2017/1564 of the European Parliament and of the Council of 13 September 2017 on certain permitted uses of certain works and other subject matter protected by copyright and related rights for the benefit of persons who are blind, visually impaired or otherwise print disabled and amending Directive 2001/29/EC on the harmonisation of certain aspects of copyright and related rights in the information society, OJ L 242, 20.9.2017, pp. 6-13 (Marrakesh Directive)), which was based on the Marrakech VIP Treaty (Marrakech VIP Treaty, Marrakesh Treaty to Facilitate Access to Published Works for Persons Who Are Blind, Visually Impaired or Otherwise Print Disabled, open for signature 27 June 2013, 52 ILM 1309), or were of a very technical or transactional nature (e.g., Directive 2014/26/EU of the European Parliament and of the Council of 26 February 2014 on collective management of copyright and related rights and multi-territorial licensing of rights in musical works for online use in the internal market, OJ L 84, 20.3.2014, pp. 72-98 (Collective Management

In parallel to the legislative process, the existing copyright rules were challenged for similar reasons. Three litigants, in particular, challenged the long-established dominance of exclusive rights and the inflexibilities of E&L. All three cases reached the Court of Justice of the European Union (CJEU) at the same time and were decided only briefly after the legislative process finally lead to the adoption of the DSM Directive.

The three litigations are symptomatic for a stronger reliance on fundamental rights to test the limits of copyright law and increasing attempts to reshape its substantive rules through challenging existing norms before the courts.[7] Whereas in some cases, national and European courts have relied on fundamental rights on their own initiative in order to interpret existing rules, the trilogy of preliminary references in *Funke Medien*,[8] *Spiegel Online*[9] and *Pelham*[10] challenged the scope of exclusive rights and E&L with fundamental rights.

Academic literature intensively discussed these developments at the legislative and the judicial levels. Most commentators advocated for a stronger and more influential role of fundamental rights in EU copyright law.[11] Internal and external challenges to copyright provisions were hoped to provide more flexibility in the absence of systematic reform, developments in technology and behaviour, and preferences of users could be accommodated by expanding existing E&L, and the EU copyright rules could be better legitimized through stronger reliance on fundamental rights

This contribution will briefly look at the role fundamental rights have played so far in the interpretation and application of the EU copyright rules, before discussing the three recent judgments and their implications in detail. In order to systematize the impact of fundamental right on EU copyright law, it distinguishes between internal and external effects of fundamental rights. To conclude, the role that fundamental rights might play in the future is examined.

Directive) and Directive 2012/28/EU of the European Parliament and of the Council of 25 October 2012 on certain permitted uses of orphan works, OJ L 299/5, 27.10.2012, pp. 5-12 (Orphan Works Directive)).

7. To use fundamental rights to reshape intellectual property law and copyright, in particular, has been suggested by Husovec, M., Intellectual Property Rights and Integration by Conflict: The Past, Present and Future, 18 *Cambridge Yearbook of European Legal Studies* (2016), 239-269 and Griffiths, J., Taking Power Tools to the *Acquis* – the Court of Justice, the Charter of Fundamental Rights and European Union Copyright Law, in: C. Geiger, C.A. Nard, & X. Seuba (eds.), *Intellectual Property and the Judiciary* (Cheltenham, Northampton: Edward Elgar Publishing, 2018).

8. CJEU, Judgment of 29.07.2019, *Funke Medien NRW*, Case C-469/17, EU:C:2019:623.

9. CJEU, Judgment of 29.07.2019, *Spiegel Online*, Case C-516/17, EU:C:2019:625.

10. CJEU, Judgment of 29.07.2019, *Pelham and others*, Case C-476/17, EU:C:2019:624.

11. *See* in particular Geiger & Izyumenko, IIC (2014), p. 339; Bently et al., Opinion of the European Copyright Society in Relation to the Pending Reference Before the CJEU in Case C-476/17, Hutter v. Pelham, 50(4) *International Review of Intellectual Property and Competition*, 474-475.

15.2   THE REACH OF FUNDAMENTAL RIGHTS

Fundamental rights are an essential part of the EU legal order. They were developed first as general principles, derived from the common constitutional traditions common to the Member States (MS),[12] and, since 2009, they are embodied in the EU Charter of Fundamental Rights (EU Charter),[13] and they enjoy a constitutional status equal to that of the Treaties. Pursuant to Article 51(1) EU Charter, its provisions are addressed to the EU institutions and its bodies and to the MS 'only when they are implementing Union law.' MS can have recourse to national standards of fundamental right only in situations not fully determined by EU law and provided that the level of protection provided by the EU Charter is not compromised.[14] This has been interpreted widely by the CJEU to the effect that even in areas not fully harmonized by EU law, the standard of protection offered by the EU Charter constitutes the absolute minimum of protection, and MS are only allowed to provide a higher level of protection based on their national standards of fundamental rights protection.[15]

The coming into force of the EU Charter saw the express recognition of intellectual property as protected rights under Article 17(2).[16] Prior to the EU Charter, the intellectual property had already been recognized as protected under Article 1 of the First Protocol to the European Convention on Human Rights (ECHR).[17] Due to their exclusive nature, intellectual property rights can be used by their rightholders or their assignees to prevent others in their exercise of fundamental rights.

---

12. CJEU, Judgment of 14.05.1974, *Nold*, Case 4/73, EU:C:1974:51, para. 14, in its first reference to fundamental rights in its case law, the European Court of Justice (as it then was) identified the right to property as a right common to the constitutional traditions of the Member States.
13. Charter of Fundamental Rights of the European Union, OJ C 326, 26.10.202, pp. 391-407 (EU Charter).
14. CJEU, C-516/17 *Spiegel Online*, para. 21.
15. CJEU, Judgment of 26.02.2013, *Melloni*, Case C-399/11, EU:C:2013:107, para. 60; CJEU, Judgment of 26.02.2013, *Åkerberg Fransson*, Case C-617/10, EU:C:2013:105, para. 29, *see* Jütte, B.J. & Maier H., A Human Right to Sample – Will the CJEU Dance to the BGH-Beat, 12(9) *Journal of Intellectual Property Law & Practice* (2017), 784-796, p. 786., *see* in relation to copyright CJEU, C-476/17 *Pelham and others*, para. 80.
16. The provision has been criticized by, amongst others, Griffiths & McDonagh, Fundamental rights and European IP law: the case of Article 17(2) of the EU Charter in: Geiger (2013), p. 76, Geiger, E.I.P.R. (2009), p. 115.
17. *See* on the case law Geiger, C. & Izyumenko, E., Intellectual Property Before the European Court of Human Rights, in: C. Geiger, C. A. Nard, & X. Seuba (eds.), *Intellectual Property and the Judiciary* (Cheltenham, Northampton: Edward Elgar Publishing, 2018).

In the field of copyright, the CJEU has stated that the exclusive rights contained, *inter alia*, in the Information Society Directive (InfoSoc Directive) constitute measures of full harmonization.[18] Other areas of copyright, including E&L, allow MS a certain margin of discretion when implementing a particular provision into national law, and are, therefore, not fully harmonized.[19] In these areas, MS are free to apply national standards of fundamental rights. However, MS are limited in the exercise of that discretion in several regards.[20] Therefore, when implementing a particular E&L, MS must comply with all the conditions established by the respective provision and the general principles of EU law,[21] cannot compromise the objectives of the relevant directive while ensuring the effectiveness of the particular E&L,[22] must comply with the three-step test,[23] and, finally, must strike a balance between the various fundamental rights provided for by the EU legal order.[24]

There remain areas of national copyright laws untouched by EU harmonization, including moral rights[25] and copyright contract law. Advocate General (AG) Szpunar argued in his opinion in *Spiegel Online* that the interpretation of E&L and exclusive rights by national courts must consider the interaction of harmonized areas with unharmonized areas.[26] This suggests that EU fundamental rights will, albeit indirectly, also have an influence on the interpretation of provisions of national law that are not the result of the implementation of EU law. Although the AG subsequently interpreted the negative exercise of the right to communicate a work to the public in the light of the right of freedom of thought, conscience and religion under Article 10 of the EU Charter, the argument which the CJEU had already used in *Deckmyn*[27] suggests that fundamental rights have a reach that extends beyond the fully or partially harmonized areas of EU copyright law.

The copyright rules enacted by the EU legislator constitute the balance between the various interest and fundamental rights concerned. Recital 3 of the InfoSoc Directive states that its provisions 'relat[e] to compliance with

18. CJEU, C-469/17 *Funke Medien NRW*, para. 38; CJEU, Judgment of 29.07.2019, *Pelham and others*, Case C-476/17, EU:C:2019:624, para. 85.
19. CJEU, C-516/17 *Spiegel Online*, para. 23 and CJEU, Judgment of 05.03.2015, *Copydan Båndkopi*, Case C-463/12, EU:C:2015:144, para. 57.
20. CJEU, C-469/17 *Funke Medien NRW*, para. 45.
21. CJEU, C-469/17 *Funke Medien NRW*, paras 46-49.
22. CJEU, C-469/17 *Funke Medien NRW*, paras 50-51.
23. CJEU, C-469/17 *Funke Medien NRW*, para. 52.
24. CJEU, C-469/17 *Funke Medien NRW*, para. 53; *see also* to that effect CJEU, Judgment of 27.03.2014, *UPC Telekabel Wien*, Case C-314/12, EU:C:2014:192, para. 46, CJEU, Judgment of 18 October 2018, *Bastei Lübbe*, Case CC-149/17, EU:C:2018:841, para. 45.
25. Recital 19, InfoSoc Directive and implicitly in Recitals 23 and 37 DSM Directive, *see* CJEU, C-469/17 *Funke Medien NRW*, para. 58 and CJEU, C-516/17 *Spiegel Online*, para. 57.
26. CJEU, C-516/17 *Spiegel Online*, para. 77.
27. CJEU, Judgment of 03.09.2014, *Deckmyn*, Case C-201/13, EU:C:2014:2132, paras 27-31.

the fundamental principles of law and especially of property, including intellectual property, and freedom of expression and the public interest'. The non-exhaustive enumeration of some fundamental rights must be read to include other interests rooted in fundamental rights, which must also be read into the requirement to strike a fair balance 'between the different categories of rightholders, as well as between the different categories of rightholders and users'.[28] When the Directive was passed and came into force the EU Charter had not yet been drafted, and the relation between fundamental rights as guaranteed by national constitutions and the general principles developed by the CJEU out of the common constitutional traditions had not been addressed, yet.

15.3 THE BALANCE BETWEEN EXCLUSIVE RIGHTS AND 'USER RIGHTS'

In 2017, the German Federal Supreme Court (BGH) referred three cases to the CJEU (the 'BGH-trilogy') which addressed a number of vital questions on the role of fundamental rights in EU copyright law. In *Pelham*, the most prominent of the three preliminary references,[29] a music producer sought to justify the use of a short sample with the exercise of his right to artistic freedom. In *Spiegel Online*, the operator of an internet news portal relied on the right to freedom of expression and information to publish two versions of a controversial paper written by a German politician. In *Funke Medien,* the German government attempted to block the leaking of secret military reports by invoking its alleged copyright over the documents.[30] All three cases had

---

28. Recital 31 InfoSoc Directive.
29. *See* for comments on the case in its various stages *see* e.g.: Apel, S., Unionsrechtliche Beurteilung des Tonträgersamplings 'Metall auf Metall' – Schlussantrag, 22(2) *Multimedia und Recht* (2019), 97-99; Bently et al., IIC (2019); Böttger, F. & Clark, B., German Constitutional Court Decides That Artistic Freedom May Prevail over Copyright Exploitation Rights (*'Metall auf Metall'*), 11(11) *Journal of Intellectual Property Law & Practice* (2016), 812, 814; Leistner, M., Die 'Metall auf Metall' – Entscheidung des BVerfG. Oder: Warum das Urheberrecht in Karlsruhe in guten Händen ist, 118(8) *Gewerblicher Rechtschutz und Urheberrecht* (2016), 772-777; Mezei, P., Thou Shalt (Not) Sample? New Drifts in the Ocean of Sampling, 11(2) *Zeitschrift für Geistiges Eigentum* (2019), 170-198; Jütte & Maier, JIPLP (2017); Jütte, B.J., New Perspectives for Sampling – US and German Developments and What Comes Next, 28(4) Entertainment Law Review (2017), 127-130; Jütte, B.J., Sampling of Sound Recordings in the United States and Germany: Revival of a Discussion on Musical Creativity, in: P. Torremans (ed.), *Research Handbook on Copyright Law* (2017); Quintais, J.P. & Jütte, B.J., *Thou Shalt Not Sample … Without Permission!*, available at: http://copyrightblog.kluwerip law.com/2019/01/02/thou-shalt-not-sample-without-permission/, accessed: 14 September 2019.
30. All three cases have been extensively discussed in the literature. For a summary of the facts for all three cases *see* Jütte, J. *Finding Comfort Between a Rock and a Hard Place – Advocate General Szpunar on Striking the Balance in Copyright Law*, available at:

in common that a rightholder relied on an exclusive right to prevent the use of subject matter protected by copyright or a related right to prevent acts in relation to which the user relied on a fundamental right. For example, in *Pelham*, when the case finally ended up before the German Federal Constitutional Court (BVerfG), the defendant argued that the application of German copyright law by the German courts,[31] which did not permit him to freely use a sample taken from a sound recording of the claimant, prevented him from exercising his right to artistic freedom.[32]

All three references were, therefore, similar in that the referring courts were uncertain whether fundamental rights could be used to interpret existing E&L flexibly or even to extend the exhaustive list of limitations and exceptions contained in Article 5 InfoSoc Directive. Formulated differently, the BGH asked whether fundamental rights are limited in their effects to an interpretation within the wording of EU copyright law, or whether fundamental rights can also be used to create room for the exercise of fundamental rights beyond the express wording of the harmonized area of copyright law.

15.3.1 Defining the Scope of Exclusive (Economic) Rights

Creative freedom exists outside the scope of the exclusive rights of copyright law. Whatever activity does not fall within the scope of Articles 2-4 InfoSoc Directive or the other exclusive rights provided for in other instruments, does not require authorization. Determining the scope of the rights has been notoriously difficult, and the CJEU has been asked to define some of the core concepts of EU copyright law on several occasions. In its heavily criticized case law on the right to right to communication to the public,[33] the Court has

---

https://europeanlawblog.eu/2019/02/28/finding-comfort-between-a-rock-and-a-hard-plac e-advocate-general-szpunar-on-striking-the-balance-in-copyright-law/, accessed: 14 September 2019; further *see* Jütte, B.J., Forcing Flexibility with Fundamental Rights, Questioning the Dominance of Exclusive Rights, in: T. Synodinou, P. Jougleux, C. Markou & T. Prastitou (eds.), *EU Internet Law in the Digital Era* (Heidelberg, Springer 2020).

31. The defendant relied in particular on §24 of the German Copyright Act, the so-called free use exception, *see* Jütte & Maier, JIPLP (2017), p. 785, Apel, MMR (2019), pp. 97-98, *see also* Maier, H., *Remixe auf Hosting-Plattformen: Eine urheberrechtliche Untersuchung filmischer Remixe zwischen grundrechtsrelevanten Schranken und Inhaltefiltern (Internet und Gesellschaft, Band 11)*, Mohr Siebeck, (Tübignen, 2018), pp. 43-46.

32. BVerfG, Decision of 31.05.2016 – 1BvR 1585/13 ('*Metall auf Metall*'), paras 26-32 *see* in particular Leistner, GRUR (2016); Schonhofen, S., Sechs Urteile über zwei Sekunden, und kein Ende in Sicht: Die 'Sampling'-Entscheidung des BVerfG, 8(16) *Gewerblicher Rechtsschutz und Urheberrecht. Praxis im Immaterialgüter- und Wettbewerbsrecht* (2016), 277-279; Wagner, K., Sampling als Kunstform und die Interessen der Tonträgerhersteller. Auswirkungen der BVerfG-Rechtsprechung auf die Kunstfreiheit, 19(8) *MultiMedia und Recht* (2016), 513-518.

33. *See* e.g., Hugenholtz, P.B. & van Velze, S.C., Communication to a New Public? Three Reasons Why EU Copyright Law Can Do Without a 'New Public', 47(7) *International*

made few references to the right to property under Article 17(2) and the right to freedom of expression under Article 11 EU Charter.[34] Even in the few instances in which the Court referred to the Charter, the judges did not engage in a thorough analysis of the balance between the different fundamental rights for the purposes of shaping the scope of exclusive rights.

In *Pelham*, however, the referring court asked explicitly how fundamental rights must be taken into consideration when interpreting the exclusive rights of the InfoSoc Directive. The formulation of the questions made it impossible for the AG and the Court to evade them.[35] AG Szpunar retreated to a conservative position, arguing that the balance struck by the legislator is reflective of fundamental rights and that a wide interpretation of the right of phonogram producers would not constitute an unjustifiable limitation to the right to freedom of expression, even in the absence of an applicable exception.[36] However, the AG had first determined the scope of the right of phonogram producers. In his interpretation of the exclusive right, he did not make reference to fundamental rights but based his argument on an investment-rationale.[37] Only much later in the judgment, he then turned to the question whether the right to artistic freedom and freedom of expression limits or can be used to justify an infringement of the right of phonogram producers.[38]

He argued that the legislature has a wide margin of discretion to strike the balance between the various interests. Only in exceptional circumstances would it be possible to control the balance outside of the wording of the laws.[39] As a result, an extensive interpretation of the right of phonogram producers would not allow for the use of even the smallest segments of their productions in the absence of an applicable exception. The AG seems to suggest that external control of the balance struck by the legislator would

---

Review of Intellectual Property and Competition (2016), 797-816; Quintais, J.P., Untangling the Hyperlinking Web: In Search of the Online Right of Communication to the Public, 21 *The Journal of World Intellectual Property* (2018), 385-420.

34. *See* CJEU, Judgment of 08.09.2016, *GS Media*, Case C-160/15, EU:C:2016:644, paras 31 & 45, and CJEU, Judgment of 07.08.2018, *Renckhoff*, Case C-161/17, EU:C:2018:634, para. 41.

35. The BGH referred similarly phrased question in *Funke Medien* and *Spiegel Online*.

36. In his opinion (Szpunar, AG, Opinion of 12.12.2018, *Pelham and Others*, Case C-476/17, EU:C:2018:1002) the AG had already rejected the legality of the German 'free use' provision of Article 24 of the German Copyright Act (paras 50-59) and had suggested that the right of phonogram producers under Article 2(c) InfoSoc Directive covers any reproduction of a phonogram or parts thereof, including the smallest extracts (paras 19-40).

37. Szpunar, C-476/17 *Pelham and Others*, para. 30, he then continued by addressing arguments of the parties for a more restrictive interpretation of the right of phonogram producers, all of which he rejected.

38. Szpunar, C-476/17 *Pelham and Others*, para. 82.

39. Szpunar, C-476/17 *Pelham and Others*, para. 94.

only be appropriate in cases where the application of the law would come to manifestly inappropriate results in the light of fundamental rights.

Instead of analysing the scope of the reproduction right and its compatibility with fundamental rights in two separate steps, the Court considered both questions together. Rather than establishing the scope of protection of the exclusive right and then asking whether certain fundamental rights could justify a derogation from the narrow scope of copyright exceptions, it construed the scope of the reproduction right of phonogram producers in the light of fundamental rights. Thereby, it internalized the balancing exercise, which also led the Court to a different outcome.

Post-*Pelham*, the reproduction of even short samples falls, in principle, within the scope of the reproduction right of Article 2(c) InfoSoc Directive. The Court relied on similar arguments as the AG, namely that a wide interpretation of the scope of the right is consistent with objective of the InfoSoc Directive, which is to provide rightholders with a high level of protection, and that 'the specific objective of the exclusive right of the phonogram producer' is to protect his investment.[40]

This is different, according to the Court, where a user in exercising his freedom of the arts, samples a part of a phonogram 'in a modified from unrecognisable to the ear, in a new work'.[41] Such an interpretation is mandated by the requirement to strike a fair balance between the interests of right holders, which are to enjoy the protection of their intellectual property, guaranteed by Article 17(2) EU Charter and the interest of users, including the exercise of their fundamental rights and the public interest.[42] A modified sample that is unrecognizable to the ear in a new work is not considered to be a reproduction within the meaning of Article 2(c) InfoSoc Directive for two reasons. First, the usual meaning of the word 'reproduction' does not support such an interpretation. Second, such an interpretation would not reflect a fair balance between the interest of right holders and users, because it would enable a rightholder to prevent the use of samples even if this use would not diminish the economic opportunities in the exploitation of his investment.[43]

In a methodologically questionable exercise, the right of phonogram producers is jurisprudentially curtailed. As a general rule, the exclusive right

---

40. CJEU, C-476/17 *Pelham and others*, para. 30, with reference to recitals 4,9 and 10 in relation to the high level of protection, and to recital 10 for the specific objective of the right of phonogram producers, *see* Szpunar, C-476/17 *Pelham and Others*, paras 28-30.
41. CJEU, C-476/17 *Pelham and others*, para. 31.
42. CJEU, C-476/17 *Pelham and others*, para. 32. Subsequently the Court mentions that Article 17(2) can under no circumstances be construed to provide absolute protection. In finding a proper balance in the interpretation of the right of phonogram producers the right to property must be weighed against the right to freedom of the arts and the right to freedom of expression, as guaranteed by Article 11 EU Charter and Article 10(1) ECHR (paras 32-33).
43. CJEU, C-476/17 *Pelham and others*, para. 38.

of Article 2(c) extends to very short extracts, and sampling of very short extracts can, therefore, constitute a reproduction. But when very short samples are used in the exercise of the right to freedom of the arts, a short sample unrecognizable to the ear does not constitute a reproduction. The conclusion of the Court on the first and the sixth question in *Pelham* also leaves room for an interpretation that, as a general rule, the use of samples in new works do not require authorization as long as the sample is modified an unrecognizable to the ear. Either way, what is striking about this argumentation is the relatively intensive balancing exercise compared to the Court's earlier case law. The balance within the scope of the exclusive right under Article 2(c) InfoSoc Directive is sought between the interest of the rightholder to exploit the economic potential of a sound recording, protected under the right to intellectual property under Article 17(2) and the cultural technique of sampling as a form of artistic expression. By marginally limiting the exclusive right the Court accommodates sampling as a non-rivalling use outside the scope of protection of the reproduction right.

15.3.2   IMPLEMENTING AND APPLYING 'USER RIGHTS'

In other situations, it is not possible to resolve conflicts between different fundamental rights by altering the scope of exclusive rights in order to permit acts that fall squarely within the scope of protection of exclusive rights. For such purposes, copyright law provides for E&L which govern acts that fall within the scope of the various rights. Article 5 InfoSoc Directive contains one mandatory exception[44] and a number of optional exceptions or limitations the MS can opt to implement. Although the aim of the Directive was to harmonize copyright, this 'shopping list' of E&L does not contribute to a full harmonization of copyright in the EU. Moreover, recital 32 InfoSoc Directive provides that Article 5 constitutes an exhaustive list of E&L. Accordingly, MS are barred from introducing exceptions to the exclusive rights harmonized in Articles 2-4 which are not contained in Article 5.

Moreover, E&L have historically been interpreted narrowly by the Court, which further decreased the room for manoeuvre for a flexible interpretation. To remedy this, the CJEU has supplemented the principle of narrow interpretation with the requirement to enable the effectiveness of E&L.[45] The Court has also applied a wider interpretation to enable the effective exercise of an exception beyond the express wording of the relevant

---

44. Article 5(1) InfoSoc Directive.
45. CJEU, Judgment of 4.10.2011, *FAPL/Murphy*, Joined cases C-403/08 and C-429/08, EU:C:2011:631, paras 162-163 and CJEU, C-201/13 *Deckmyn*, para. 23, *see* Jütte, B.J., *Reconstructing European Copyright Law for the Digital Single Market: Between Old Paradigms and Digital Challenges*, Nomos, (Baden-Baden, 2017) pp. 249-254.

provision.[46] Neither of these approaches could, however, possibly lead to a disruption of the copyright acquis and to a judicial creation of E&L where the law does not provide them.

How E&Ls had to be interpreted in the light of the tensions between different fundamental rights was not discussed until the CJEU had the opportunity in *Deckmyn*. In this case, a Belgian right-wing politician, Mr Deckmyn, had copied and altered a children's comic book cover to suggest that the major of the city of Ghent was showering immigrants with a distinctly oriental look with money, much to the shock of the local population. Deckmyn relied on the parody defence, and the referring court sought guidance from the CJEU whether the parody defence, as harmonized by EU law and implemented in Belgium, would apply in such a situation. The Court established that a concept contained in the directive that does not make reference to national law constitutes an autonomous concept under EU law. If this were not the case, different implementations in the MS would fail to realize the aim of the directive, which is to achieve harmonization.[47] In the following, the Court defined the autonomous concept of 'parody' in light of the wording and the purpose of that provision.[48] With reference to the fair balance that must be struck between the different interest of right holders and users of protected works, the Court argued that in a particular case the application of the parody exception must take 'all the circumstances of the case' into account.[49] One of the interests in this particular case was that of the heirs of the deceased author of the comic book not to have their ancestor associated with the particular message of the potential parody. Because the message Mr Deckmyn had inserted into the altered work was of a xenophobic and discriminatory nature, the Court had no difficulties linking to the principle of equal treatment irrespective of racial or ethnic origin under Article 21(1) EU Charter.[50] The national court would then have to take all these factors into consideration when applying the parody exception in a particular case.

In *Deckmyn*, fundamental rights seemed to have spill-over effects into unharmonized areas of copyright law, but the Court did not make it very clear whether it intended to interpret moral rights concerns into the application of a copyright exception as parts of the 'legitimate interests' of right holders.[51] Such interests could, in principle, also flow into the balancing exercise under

---

46. CJEU, Judgment of 11.09.2014, *TU Darmstadt*, Case C-117/13, EU:C:2014:2196, paras 43-47; here the CJEU granted libraries an ancillary right to digitize works to be able to effectively exercise the exception under Article 5(3)(n) InfoSoc Directive.
47. CJEU, C-201/13 *Deckmyn*, paras 14-16.
48. CJEU, C-201/13 *Deckmyn*, paras 20-24.
49. CJEU, C-201/13 *Deckmyn*, para. 27-28.
50. CJEU, C-201/13 *Deckmyn*, paras 29-30.
51. *See* critically Rosati, E., Just a Laughing Matter? Why the CJEU Decision in *Deckmyn* is Broader than Parody, 52(2) *Common Market Law Review* (2015), 511-530, pp. 527-528 and Jacques, S., Are National Courts Required to Have an (Exceptional) European Sense of Humour?, 37(3) *European Intellectual Property Review* (2015), 134-137, p. 137.

the third step of Article 5(5) InfoSoc Directive and thereby internalize moral rights, as an expression of fundamental rights.[52] Either way, the Court internalized the balancing of fundamental rights into the interpretation of the substantive rules of copyright law instead of considering fundamental rights as elements of external control of the rules themselves or their application.[53]

Since *Deckmyn* the CJEU has not departed from this position, although it did not have many opportunities to restate its position until the BGH-trilogy. With the BGH-trilogy on the horizon, Griffiths suggested that a national court should in some cases be compelled to give precedence to Charter rights other than the right to property. This could be the case in a situation where an act clearly covered by the right to freedom of expression is not permitted, even in an extensive interpretation, by any of the E&L contained in Article 5 InfoSoc Directive.[54] This could have also been read into the decision of the BVerfG in 'Metall auf Metall III', however, the court had also considered the option of a narrower interpretation of the rights of phonogram producers as a way to enable the effective exercise of artistic freedom.[55] Whereas AG Szpunar rejected this option, he left room for the possibility to use fundamental rights as correctives 'in cases of gross violation of the essence of a fundamental right.'[56]

The CJEU did not adopt this position. Instead, it ruled that the balance between the various fundamental rights has already been created within the EU copyright rules through the mechanism of exclusive rights and E&L.[57] The extension of copyright exceptions beyond the list contained in Article 5 would 'would endanger the effectiveness of the harmonisation of copyright and related rights'. The Court based this argumentation on the purpose of Article 5, which is to remove differences between the exceptions and limitations in national copyright laws, as such differences 'had direct negative effects on the functioning of the internal market of copyright and related rights'.[58] Hugenholtz[59] and Guilbault,[60] amongst

---

52. Rosati, C.M.L. Rev. (2015), p. 525.
53. Jacques argued, with reference to ECtHR terminology ('what is necessary in a democratic society') that other areas of the law are better suited to address clashes of fundamental rights that cannot be resolved within copyright law itself.
54. Griffiths, Taking Power Tools to the *Acquis* – the Court of Justice, the Charter of Fundamental Rights and European Union Copyright Law, in: Geiger et al. (eds.) (2018), pp. 161-162.
55. BVerfG, Decision of 31.05.2016 – 1BvR 1585/13 (*'Metall auf Metall'*), cf. Jütte & Maier, JIPLP (2017), pp. 789-791.
56. Szpunar, C-476/17 *Pelham and Others*, para. 98, *see also* CJEU, CC-149/17 *Bastei Lübbe*, para. 46.
57. Spiegel Online, paras 42-43.
58. CJEU, C-516/17 *Spiegel Online*, para. 47.
59. Hugenholtz, P.B., Why the Copyright Directive Is Unimportant, and Possibly Invalid, 22(11) *European Intellectual Property Review* (2000), 499-505, p. 501.
60. Guibault, L.M.C.R., Why Cherry-Picking Never Leads to Harmonisation: The Case of the Limitations on Copyright under Directive 2001/29/EC, 1(1) *Journal of Intellectual Property, Information Technology and E-Commerce Law* (2010), 55-66.

others,[61] had criticized the lack of a harmonizing effect of Article 5 at an early stage, and Hugenholtz was indeed not entirely incorrect to conclude that, in terms of harmonization, Article 5 constitutes a 'total failure'.[62]

The Court left at least a small window for further harmonization within the boundaries of existing legislation, yet one that it hid well in all of the trilogy-judgments. When stating that E&Ls are part of the mechanisms that constitute the balance between the interests of right holders and users of protected subject matter, it also states that MS 'may, or even *must*' transpose the E&Ls of Article 5 into their national laws.[63] This could either be a simple reference to Article 5(1), which makes the exceptions for temporary reproductions mandatory. However, a more convincing interpretation is that some exceptions that are reflective of fundamental rights must be implemented by MS. Support for this argument can be found in *Spiegel Online* and *Funke Medien*, where the Court stated that the exceptions for the reporting of current events and quotation 'are specifically aimed at favouring the exercise of the right to freedom of expression'.[64] Such exceptions would also include the exception for parody and arguably the exceptions for (analog) teaching and research,[65] for the benefit of people with disabilities,[66] the use of political speeches[67] and for the use during religious celebrations.[68]

---

61. *See also* Jütte, *Reconstructing European Copyright Law for the Digital Single Market: Between Old Paradigms and Digital Challenges* (2017), p. 244 for further references.

62. At least in the recent copyright reform the European legislator has learned from its past mistakes and made most of the new exception contained in the DSM directive mandatory. The directive provides for a new mandatory exception for digital and cross-border teaching (Article 5), which is however limited by a carve-out for available licensing solutions. *See* critically on the carve-out: Jütte, B.J., Uneducating Copyright: Member States Can Choose Between 'Full Legal Certainty' and Patchworked Licensing Schemes for Digital and Cross-Border Teaching, 41(11) *European Intellectual Property Review* (2019), 669-671.

63. CJEU, C-469/17 *Funke Medien NRW*, para. 58, and CJEU, C-516/17 *Spiegel Online*, para. 43 and CJEU, C-476/17 *Pelham and others*, para. 60 (emphasis added).

64. CJEU, C-469/17 *Funke Medien NRW*, para. 60 and CJEU, C-516/17 *Spiegel Online*, para. 45.

65. Article 5(3)(a) InfoSoc Directive.

66. Article 5(3)(b) InfoSoc Directive; for people with visual impairments the EU has passed a specific Directive which serves to implement the Marrakesh Treaty (Marrakesh Treaty to Facilitate Access to Published Works for Persons Who Are Blind, Visually Impaired or Otherwise Print Disabled, open for signature 27 June 2013, 52 ILM 1309): Directive (EU) 2017/1564 of the European Parliament and of the Council of 13 September 2017 on certain permitted uses of certain works and other subject matter protected by copyright and related rights for the benefit of persons who are blind, visually impaired or otherwise print disabled and amending Directive 2001/29/EC on the harmonisation of certain aspects of copyright and related rights in the information society, OJ L 242, 20.9.2017, pp. 6-13.

67. Article 5(3)(f) InfoSoc Directive.

68. Article 5(3)(g) InfoSoc Directive.

Accordingly, MS had to consider fundamental rights twice when implementing the provisions of the InfoSoc Directive – although some MS might now be required to reconsider whether their implementation complies with the Directive in the light of the CJEU's recent judgments.[69] In a first step, MS had to decide or will have to reassess, whether they are obliged to implement a particular E&L from the optional list of Article 5(2) & (3), and subsequently when giving concrete shape to a particular provision that implements an E&L into national law. The implementation of E&L in MS's copyright laws is far from uniform, and many national legislatures failed to expressly provide for exceptions that are aimed at enabling the exercise of freedom of expression.[70] Therefore, many MS might indeed be required to review the current implementation of the InfoSoc Directive to ensure that such E&L that enable the exercise of specific fundamental rights are provided for.

Another recent development, which the Court expressly confirmed in two of the cases of the recent trilogy is the elevation of E&L to user rights.[71] However, this terminological figure was only used to describe the exceptions in Article 5(3)(c) & (d), and the judgement in *Pelham* did not refer to rights of users at all. The reference to E&L as user rights is not unprecedented. Prior to *Spiegel Online* and *Funke Medien,* a similar terminology in relation to specific E&L was used, for example, in TU *Darmstadt*, where the Court recognized 'an ancillary *right* to digitise the works in question',[72] in *UPC Telekabel*, where the rights of 'internet users to assert their *rights* before the court'[73] and similarly in *Deckmyn*.[74] This is a terminological shift which is

---

69. The deadline for implementation passed on 22 December 2002, Article 13(1) InfoSoc Directive.

70. A 2015 European Implementation Assessment on the review of the EU copyright framework found, for example, that three out of the six countries assess had not expressly implemented an exception to the exclusive rights for purposes of parody (Ireland, Italy, Poland), I-127-132 (http://www.europarl.europa.eu/RegData/etudes/STUD/2015/558762/EPRS_STU(2015)558762_EN.pdf).

71. *See,* for example, CJEU, C-516/17 *Spiegel Online*, para. 59 and CJEU, C-469/17 *Funke Medien NRW*, para. 76.

72. CJEU, C-117/13 *TU Darmstadt*, para. 43 (emphasis added).

73. CJEU, C-314/12 *UPC Telekabel Wien*, para. 57 (emphasis added).

74. CJEU, C-201/13 *Deckmyn*, paras 25-26; although in *Deckmyn* the reference could be considered as one to fundamental rights in general, the context of the use suggest however that the Court recognized the parody defence, if implemented, as a right rather than an exception. On the appearance of this new terminology *see* Jütte, *Reconstructing European Copyright Law for the Digital Single Market: Between Old Paradigms and Digital Challenges* (2017), pp. 251-252, Geiger, C. et al., Reaction of CEIPI to the Resolution on the Implementation of Directive 2001/29/EC on the Harmonization of Copyright in the Information Society adopted by the European Parliament on 9 July 2015, *CEIPI* (2015), 1-23, p. 6 and Rosati, *Copyright Exceptions and User Rights in Case C-117/13 Ulmer: A Couple of Observations*, available at: http://ipkitten.blogspot.com/2014/09/copyright-exceptions-and-user-rights-in.html, accessed: 14 September 2019.

closely linked to the increased reference to fundamental rights and which could significantly strengthen the position of users vis-à-vis right holders.

It is safe to say that the growing recognition of E&L as user rights and the increased scrutiny by the courts of the application and interpretation of E&L in the light of fundamental rights has strengthened the position of users. A balance between the interest of holders and users of rights and other protected subject matter reflects better in the dialogue between national courts and the CJEU than compared to rights-centric rhetoric.

15.4 EXTERNAL DIMENSION: ENFORCEMENT

In the interpretation of exclusive rights and E&L, the CJEU restricts itself to an internal balancing exercise. Within this exercise, the Court relies predominantly on the fundamental rights in property and various types of expression.[75] The only other fundamental rights that make brief appearances in the CJEU's rulings and in AG opinions are the right to education, privacy, non-discrimination and the right to equal treatment.[76]

The situation is different in enforcement cases, in which the Court frequently and systematically includes other fundamental rights into the balancing exercise. This is unsurprising, considering the triangular relationship between 'rightholder – user – intermediary' in enforcement cases, opposed to the binary relation between user and rightholder in disputes on the interpretation of exclusive rights and E&L.[77]

The core provisions of the EU's copyright enforcement regime are contained in Article 8(3) InfoSoc Directive, which obliges MS to provide right holders with the possibility to request an injunction against intermediaries which services have been used to infringe copyright, in certain

---

75. These include, under the EU Charter, the right to freedom of expression (Article 11(1)), the right to freedom of the media (Article 11(2)), and the freedom of the arts and sciences (Article 13).
76. *See* e.g., CJEU, C-161/17 *Renckhoff*, paras 42-43, CJEU, C-201/13 *Deckmyn*, paras 28-32, and Szpunar, AG, Opinion of 19.01.2016, Case C-470/14, EU:C:2016:24, paras 15, 55.
77. *See* for a detailed discussion on the various interests involved: Geiger, C., Frosio, G. & Izyumenko, E. Intermediary Liability and Fundamental Rights, in: G. Frosio (ed.), *The Oxford Handbook of Online Intermediary Liability* (OUP, 2019); Centre for International Intellectual Property Studies (CEIPI) Research Paper No. 2019-06. Available at SSRN: https://ssrn.com/abstract=3411633 or http://dx.doi.org/10.2139/ssrn.3411633; specifically on blocking orders: Christophe Geiger and Elena Izyumenko, 'Blocking Orders: Assessing Tensions with Human Rights', in: G. Frosio (ed.), *The Oxford Handbook of Intermediary Liability Online* (OUP, 2019) Centre for International Intellectual Property Studies (CEIPI) Research Paper No. 2019-03.

provisions of the Intellectual Property Enforcement Directive,[78] and Articles 12-15 of the e-Commerce Directive on safe harbours for intermediaries.[79] The most recent addition to the rules governing online copyright enforcement and the liability of intermediaries for acts committed by their users is Article 17 DSM Directive.

The introduction of a third actor into the balancing exercise opens an external dimension in relation to copyright. Refusing external control of the fundamental rights implications of European copyright rules cannot be rejected with arguments that rely solely on effective harmonization and legal certainty. The questions whether to enforce and how to enforce require the balancing of copyright as such against other fundamental rights irrespective of the compatibility of substantive copyright law with fundamental rights.

The Court has struck a balance between the interest of right holders to enforce their rights, of intermediaries to operate their business without being instrumentalized as copyright police, and of users to receive and impart information on numerous occasions.[80] Even the European Court of Human Rights (ECtHR) was asked to decide whether the liability incurred by an intermediary for the acts of its users was in violation of its right to freedom of expression.[81]

Intermediaries can be exposed to three main types of liability. First, they can be asked to disclose information about their users, enabling rightholders to enforce their rights effectively. Second, intermediaries can be asked to take active steps to stop and prevent infringements by monitoring, filtering and deleting infringing content. Third, intermediaries can be held directly liable for content uploaded by their users. As the latter option internalizes enforcement into the normative structure of substantive copyright law, a brief description toward the end of this section will suffice. The balance struck by the CJEU in relation to the other two types of liability deserves closer scrutiny.

---

78. Directive 2004/48/EC of the European Parliament and of the Council of 29 April 2004 on the enforcement of intellectual property rights, OJ L 195, 2.6.2004, p. 16-25 (IP Enforcement Directive), in particular Articles 9(1) and 11 on injunctions.
79. Directive 2000/31/EC of the European Parliament and of the Council of 8 June 2000 on certain legal aspects of information society services, in particular electronic commerce, in the Internal Market ('Directive on electronic commerce'), OJ L 178, 17.7.2000, pp. 1-16 (e-Commerce Directive).
80. *See* only CJEU, Judgment of 29.01.2008, *Promusicae*, Case C-275/06, EU:C:2008:54; CJEU, Judgment of 24.11.2011, *Scarlet Extended*, Case C-70/10, EU:C:2011:771; CJEU, Judgment of 16.062012, *SABAM v. Netlog*, Case C-360/10, EU:C:2012:85; CJEU, C-314/12 *UPC Telekabel Wien*; CJEU, Judgement of 15.09.2016, *Mc Fadden*, C-484/14, EU:C:2016:689; CJEU, Judgment of 14.06.2017, *Ziggo*, Case C-610/15, EU:C:2017:456.
81. ECtHR, ECtHR (5th section) of 19 February 2013, case of *Fredrik Neij and Peter Sunde Kolmisoppi (The Pirate Bay) v. Sweden,* Appl. nr. 40397/12, Judgment (2013), 19.02.2013, on the developing relation between freedom of expression and the right to property *see* Jütte, E.I.P.R. (2016) and Geiger & Izyumenko, IIC (2014).

In its first judgment on intermediary liability, the Court asked whether an online intermediary could be required to provide personal data of potential infringers of protected works.[82] In a carefully balanced judgment, the judges argued that MS must exercise their margin of discretion when implementing and applying the various rules in combination and strike a fair balance between the various interests.[83] Pursuant to the ruling in *Promusicae*, neither of the fundamental rights enjoys primacy over the other, which was also expressly reiterated by the Court in the recent trilogy.[84] As long as the legislature exercises its margin of discretion with regard to a balance between the interests of all actors, national legislation is in conformity with the Charter. However, when a provision of national law does not provide the courts with sufficient room to strike a fair balance between the right to property and other fundamental rights, such provision does not conform to the requirements stemming from the EU Charter. The implementation of the EU enforcement rules must respect the essence of the various fundamental rights.[85]

The modalities under which intermediaries are exempted from liability are regulated in Articles 12-15 E-Commerce Directive. In general, intermediaries are exempted when they take a passive role and have no knowledge of infringements committed via their services.[86] Once intermediaries acquire knowledge of infringing activities, they can be asked to intervene by blocking or removing infringing content and by preventing future infringements. The CJEU has defined the extent of these obligations for the first time in *Scarlet Extended* and *Netlog*.[87] By balancing the interest in the above-mentioned triangular relationship, the Court ruled that broad blocking or monitoring injunctions which costs are carried entirely by the intermediary would disproportionately infringe the latter's right to conduct a business and the user's freedom to receive and impart information. Conversely, in *Mc Fadden*, the Luxembourg court ruled that in the absence of a less restrictive means, an injunction that obliges the operator to secure an open wireless network was considered proportionate in order to protect the essence of the

---

82. CJEU, C-275/06 *Promusicae*.
83. CJEU, C-275/06 *Promusicae*, paras 66-68, *see also* Kuczerawy, A., The Power of Positive. Thinking Intermediary Liability and the Effective Enjoyment of the Right to Freedom of Expression, 8(3) *Journal of Intellectual Property, Information Technology and E-Commerce Law* (2017), 226-237, p. 232 and Husovec, CYELS (2016), p. 11.
84. *See* to that effect only CJEU, C-516/17 *Spiegel Online*, para. 56: 'In that context, first, it should be added that the protection of intellectual property rights is indeed enshrined in Article 17(2) of the Charter. There is, however, nothing whatsoever in the wording of that provision or in the Court's case law to suggest that that right is inviolable and must for that reason be protected as an absolute right [references omitted].'
85. *See* CJEU, Judgment of 16.07.2015, *Coty Germany*, Case C-580/13, EU:C:2015:485, paras 35-37.
86. *See* CJEU, Judgment of 12.07.2011, *L'Oréal and Others*, Case C-324/09, EU:C:2011:474, paras 106-124.
87. CJEU, C-70/10 *Scarlet Extended*; CJEU, C-360/10 *SABAM v. Netlog*.

right of property.[88] In this case, the German Court, in its question for a preliminary reference, had suggested three possible measures to restrict infringement via the free wireless network operated by the defendant. AG Szpunar had still rejected all three measure as he considered them incompatible with EU law in general and fundamental rights in particular.[89]

The new vertical enforcement regime for online content-sharing service providers (OCSSPs) under Article 17 DSM Directive will partially shift the balance in the enforcement regime. On the one hand, it can be argued that the normative fixation of the case law on the right of communication to the public, which makes OCSSPs actors and not merely intermediaries in relation to content posted by their users impacts negatively on the freedom to conduct a business of the platforms concerned. On the other hand, the new licensing system, which obliges platforms covered by the provision to ensure that content uploaded by their users has been cleared with the relevant right holders, can be conducive to the exercise of freedom of expression by providing users with more legal certainty in relation to the legality of certain types of content.

This legislative choice, it can be presumed, should strike a fair balance between the interest of users under Article 11 EU Charter to receive and impart information and OCSSPs freedom to conduct their business. If these mechanisms create more legal certainty, more content will be available on platforms and both side benefit.

However, a part of the provision, which obliges OCSSPs to make 'best efforts' to prevent future uploads of infringing works or subject matter, has already been challenged by the Polish Government.[90] In the challenge, the Polish Government argues that the wording of the directive does not leave any other option, and thereby limits the margin of discretion for the MS to implement the contested provision of the Directive than to require OCSSPs to employ 'preventive filtering mechanisms'.[91] According to the Polish Government '[s]uch mechanisms undermine the essence of the right to

---

88. CJEU, C-484/14 *Mc Fadden*, paras 99-10.
89. Szpunar, AG, Opinion of 16.06.2016, *Mc Fadden*, Case C-484/14, EU:C:2016:170, paras 125-150.
90. CJEU, Application of 26.07.2019, Case C-401/19, *see* for first reactions: Targosz, *Poland's Challenge to the DSM Directive – and the Battle Rages On* … , available at: http://copyrightblog.kluweriplaw.com/2019/06/10/polands-challenge-to-the-dsm-directive-and-the-battle-rages-on/, accessed: 14 September 2019 and Mileszyk, *The Copyright Directive Challenged in the CJEU by Polish Government*, available at: https://www.communia-association.org/2019/06/01/copyright-directive-challenged-cjeu-polish-government/, accessed: 14 September 2019.
91. The Polish Government in particular challenges Article 17(4)(b) and Article 17(4)(c) DSM Directive. Article 17(4) in its entirety ready as follows:

> 4. If no authorisation is granted, online content-sharing service providers shall be liable for unauthorised acts of communication to the public, including making available to the public, of copyright-protected works and other subject matter, unless the service providers demonstrate that they have:
> (a) made best efforts to obtain an authorisation, and

freedom of expression and information and do not comply with the requirement that limitations imposed on that right be proportional and necessary.'

Even if Article 17 were to remain unaltered, or especially then, it would be interesting to see how the Court will balance fundamental rights in the application of this new provision. A strict departure from the liability regime of the E-Commerce Directive for OCSSPs would raise serious questions on the compatibility of the new rules with fundamental rights in the scope of application of Article 17.[92] It is yet unclear how the rights and interest of others will be safeguarded when OCSSPs are required to undertake 'best efforts' to offer content legally or ensure its unavailability on its services.[93] The murky language of this provision will most likely trouble national courts rather sooner than later, and eventually the CJEU.

The economically driven rules on copyright enforcement do not shape copyright from the inside but determine when and how exclusive rights can be effectively enforced. In an enforcement context, freedom of expression is regularly invoked but does not seem to be the determining fundamental right in the balancing of interests. Article 17 DSM has the potential to shift the attention more toward Article 11 EU Charter when over blocking and filtering by OCSSPs, in fulfilment of their obligations under Article 17, will impact on the exercise of legal expression that falls outside the scope of exclusive rights or which is covered by E&L.

15.5   FUNDAMENTAL RIGHTS AS DETERMINANTS AN EVER-SHIFTING BALANCE

The CJEU has made it clear that fundamental rights are reflected in the existing provisions of European copyright law and very little room, if any, exists for external control of these provisions in the light of fundamental rights. Exclusive rights and E&L are the parameters of the balance between the interest of rightholders and users. The conflicting interests must, therefore, be reconciled within the interpretative margins left by the

---

    (b)   made, in accordance with high industry standards of professional diligence, best efforts to ensure the unavailability of specific works and other subject matter for which the rightholders have provided the service providers with the relevant and necessary information; and in any event

    (c)   acted expeditiously, upon receiving a sufficiently substantiated notice from the rightholders, to disable access to, or to remove from their websites, the notified works or other subject matter, and made best efforts to prevent their future uploads in accordance with point (b).

92. Article 17(3) states that outside the scope of application of the Directive the liability exemption of Article 14(1) E-Commerce Directive continues to apply.

93. See for suggestion on the implementation of Article 17: Quintauis, J.P., Frosio, G., van Gompel, S., Hugenholtz, P.B., Husovec, M., Jütte, B.J. & Senftleben, M., Safeguarding User Freedoms in Implementing Article 17 of the Copyright in the Digital Single Market Directive: Recommendations from European Academics, (10(3) *Journal of Intellectual Property, Information Technology and E-Commerce Law* (2019), 277-282.

legislator. MS can take advantage of these margins and might be required to do so when implementing EU directives into their national laws. National courts can give effect to fundamental rights within these limits when applying national laws in the light of EU law.[94]

15.5.1 INTERNAL CONTROL

The Court has encouraged national courts to apply, but also seems itself more willing to scrutinize the application of, exclusive rights and E&L by 'having regard to all the circumstances of the case before it' in order to fully comply with the fundamental rights applicable.[95] A holistic appreciation of any specific situation enables the judiciary to explore the borders of EU copyright law and to adjust the balance between the various interests and fundamental rights on a case-by-case basis. This interpretation is limited by the wording of the applicable rules; an interpretation *contra legem* is not within the powers of national courts.[96]

External control of copyright through fundamental rights is, according to the Court, not foreseen. AG Szpunar had acknowledged that in extreme cases an external control of copyright through fundamental rights could serve to safeguard the essence of other fundamental rights.[97] Conversely, the right to property could support a claim that would protect copyright against an unjustified restriction based on other fundamental rights. However, it is difficult to determine the threshold that has to be passed with an infringement that would touch upon the essence of copyright as an intellectual property right protected under Article 17(2) EU Charter. Husovec argues that intellectual property, as a fundamental right, does not have a 'hard core' that constitutes its essence. Instead, the Court has relied on different concepts to identify 'crucial features of the legislative design of IP rights.'[98]

---

94. *See* for a discussion on recent cases that tested the borders of flexibility for artistic expression, and even went beyond statutory language of E&L in France: Geiger, C., 'Fair Use' through Fundamental Rights in Europe: When Freedom of Artistic Expression allows Creative Appropriations and Opens up Statutory Copyright Limitations (30 August 2018). Center for International Intellectual Property Studies (CEIPI) Research Paper No. 2018-09. Available at SSRN: https://ssrn.com/abstract=3256899 or http://dx.doi.org/10.2139/ssrn.3256899.
95. *See* e.g., CJEU, C-516/17 *Spiegel Online*, para. 59.
96. *See also* Husovec, CYELS (2016), p. 244, *see also* Rosati, E., Copyright in the EU: in Search of (in)Flexibilities, 63(4) *Gewerblicher Rechtsschutz und Urheberrecht, Internationaler Teil* (2014), 419-428, p. 428.
97. The AG remained silent on what constitutes the essence for any of the rights contained, *see* for an exploration of what constitutes this essence of intellectual property rights in general: Husovec, M., The Essence of Intellectual Property Rights Under Article 17(2) of the EU Charter, 20(6) *German Law Journal* (2019), 840-863.
98. Husovec, (2019), p. 855, such as 'substance', 'specific subject matter' and 'the very subject matter'.

Peukert supports relying on the balance struck by the legislator. However, he argues that intellectually, albeit protected by the right to property, does not enjoy an equal level of protection compared to the more traditional fundamental rights. Intellectual property rights only come into existence and take shape through acts of the legislature, and the rights are given shape through legislative intervention. This would suggest, at the very least, the right to property and other fundamental rights are not of equal rank.[99] This argument is convincing in the relation between the state and the individual, where fundamental rights serve to protect the latter against interference from the former. In striking a balance within copyright, the arguments lose some of its thrust. Nevertheless, it provides convincing reasons why courts should reflect more on the balance between the different interests reflected in substantive copyright law.

The balance between fundamental rights is only one factor that determines the interpretation of copyright law in the EU. The Court also stated that external control of EU copyright rules through fundamental rights could endanger the effectiveness of harmonization efforts.[100] Formulated differently, imperatives of effective harmonization prevent a more disruptive role for fundamental rights. Instead, the EU's interests to create legal certainty through effective harmonization mandate an interpretative role of fundamental rights within the EU copyright rules.

15.5.2   EXTERNAL CONTROL

External control of copyright is well established in the CJEU's case law on online enforcement. The Court has developed a jurisprudence which takes all relevant fundamental rights into consideration and exercises a thorough analysis in enforcement cases between the various interests in the triangular enforcement relationship. The balance created in the case law of the CJEU foresees relatively robust protection for right holders while intermediaries are shielded from excessive injunctions by the safe harbours contained in Articles 12-15 e-Commerce Directive.

The balance is about to be disturbed in the vertical relationship between right holders and OCSSPs by the introduction of Article 17 DSM Directive. The seemingly inevitable requirement to block and filter content in the absence of licensing solutions stands in stark contrast with the rulings in *Scarlet Extended* and *Netlog*. The provision abolishes Article 14

---

99. Peukert, The Fundamental Right to (Intellectual) Property and the Discretion of the Legislature in: Geiger (2015), pp. 138-139.
100. CJEU, C-476/17 *Pelham and others*, para. 63, already Szpunar, C-476/17 *Pelham and Others*, para. 56, *see* Jütte, B.J., The Limited Effects of Fundamental Rights on Copyright Exceptions, 16(2) *Medien und Recht International* (2019), 52-55, p. 54, *see also* CJEU, C-516/17 *Spiegel Online*, para. 47 and CJEU, C-469/17 *Funke Medien NRW*, para. 62.

e-Commerce Directive within the scope of the Directive and imposes an obligation on OCSSPs which had been excluded, with reference to fundamental rights, for intermediary service providers in general. The Polish challenge already indicated dissatisfaction with this development and is likely to spur more discussion even before the Court will render its judgment. Even if the Court does not annul the contested provisions of Article 17, the Court will then certainly be called upon by national courts to aid in the interpretation of the new liability regime for OCSSPs

15.6   CONCLUSION

As a general rule, copyright cannot be extended or restricted by fundamental rights; its scope has been written into law by the European legislator. Inside the scope of protection E&L, or what the CJEU now more frequently now refers to as 'user rights', provide room for the exercise of fundamental rights such as freedom of expression, freedom of the arts and sciences, and the right to education. Exclusive rights and E&L are interpreted in the light of fundamental rights as protected under the EU Charter. However, this is only one factor that serves to determine the balance within the framework of copyright norms.

The three judgements have clarified the role fundamental rights play in EU copyright law and how national courts must take them into consideration when interpreting and applying the EU copyright rules. The Court confirmed that the right to (intellectual) property is not absolute, but it must be weighed against other competing rights and interests. After *Pelham*, *Funke Medien* and *Spiegel Online*, external control of copyright within the harmonized area does not seem possible. This contradicts the position of the ECtHR. In *Ashby Donald* and *The Pirate Bay,* the ECtHR has adopted the position that the MS enjoy a wide margin of discretion in striking a balance between the right to property and freedom of expression in their national copyright laws. But it also ruled that, in principle, the right to freedom of expression could override certain provisions of copyright law.[101] Whereas AG Szpunar had expressly

---

101. ECtHR, ECtHR (5th section), 10 January 2013, case of *Ashby Donald and other v. France*, Appl. nr. 36769/08, Judgment (2013), 10 January 2013, paras 38-41, *see also* ECtHR, (2013). On these cases *see* Jütte, E.I.P.R. (2016), p. 11; *see* further Jones, J., Internet Pirates Walk the Plank with Article 10 Kept at Bay: *Neij and Sunde Kolmisoppi v. Sweden*, 35(11) *European Intellectual Property Review* (2013), 695-700, Voorhoof & Høedt-Rasmussen, *ECHR: Copyright v. Freedom of Expression*, available at: http://kluwercopyrightblog.com/2013/01/25/echr-copyright-vs-freedom-of-expression/, accessed: 14 September 2019; Voorhoof & Høedt-Rasmussen, *ECHR: Copyright v. Freedom of Expression II (The Pirate Bay)*, available at: http://kluwercopyrightblog.com/2013/03/20/echr-copyright-vs-freedom-of-expression-ii-the-pirate-bay/, accessed: 14 September 2019; Voorhoof, Freedom of expression and the right to information: Implications for copyright in: Geiger (2015), Izyumenko, E., The

adopted that position,[102] the Court has remained silent on the remote possibility that fundamental rights could have a more disruptive effect in some extreme cases.

So far, the Court has engaged with fundamental rights more intensively, mainly in enforcement cases. The trilogy is a welcome turn in the appreciation of the conflicts between different fundamental rights also within the core of EU copyright law. The cases have also demonstrated that it is difficult to strike a balance in complex situations with multiple fundamental rights involved. This is even more so when, as in enforcement cases, other actors and their respective interests must be taken into consideration.

The effect fundamental rights have on copyright in the context of enforcement resembles that of the early case law on intellectual property exhaustion in the internal market. In some cases, namely in such instances in which the interest of infringers or intermediaries outweighs those of the right holders, copyright cannot be effectively enforced. Injunctions can be refused if they unduly burden intermediaries or infringe the privacy of potential infringers. Therefore, fundamental rights, when they are referred to in the interpretation of the copyright enforcement provisions, cannot expand or reduce the scope of exclusive rights or exceptions and limitations. Instead, fundamental rights can be employed to restrict the enforcement of copyright, mainly online, when enforcement measures would infringe upon rights guaranteed under the EU Charter.

Fundamental rights affect copyright law at all stages, during legislation, implementation and interpretation. The closer a situation is to the national courts, the lesser the degree of flexibility or the margin of discretion. Remarkable is the intensity with which the Court now engages in detailed analyses on the conflict between the various interest and fundamental rights. This demonstrates the importance of the rights contained in the Charter in relation to copyright. It should also serve as a reminder for the legislature to reflect more consciously and transparently on the fundamental right implications during legislative processes.

Freedom of Expression Contours of Copyright in the Digital Era: A European Perspective, 19(3-4) *The Journal of World Intellectual Property* (2016), 115-130.

102. This position had been adopted by AG Szpunar in his Opinion in CJEU, C-476/17 *Pelham and others*, para. 98, but only with reference to the EU legislator within the harmonized area.

Chapter 16

Fair Dealing Defences

Patrick Masiyakurima

16.1 INTRODUCTION

A pervasive justification for copyright protection in Common Law legal systems is that it may incentivize the creation and dissemination of socially useful expressions.[1] Indeed, copyright has sometimes been referred to as a free speech engine.[2] The essence of that claim rests on the proposition that copyright works may be expensive or difficult to create, but their consumption may be non-exclusive and non-rivalrous.[3] According to that analysis, copyright works are public goods, which may be easily reproduced, thereby facilitating free riding behaviour. 'Free riding' itself refers to utilizing resources without incurring the costs associated with their production.[4] For our purposes, free riding might impede creativity. In order to stem free riding behaviour and its consequences on creativity, copyright confers various exclusive rights on authors.[5] Unauthorized uses which are inconsistent with these 'exclusive rights' constitute copyright infringement. Of course, the

---

1. For example, W.M. Landes & R.A. Posner, *The Economic Structure of Intellectual Property Law* (Cambridge, Massachusetts: Harvard University Press, 2003).
2. *Harper & Row v. Nation Enterprises* 471 US 539 (1985) 471.
3. *See* J.R. Minasian, 'Public Goods in Theory and Practice Revisited' (1967) 10 *J Law and Economics* 205.
4. T.C. Bergstrom & R.P. Goodman, 'Private Demands for Public Goods' (1973) 63 *Am Econ Rev* 280.
5. For example, sections 16-21 Copyright, Designs and Patents Act 1988 (CDPA).

economic justification for copyright protection is contested. For instance, quantifying the optimum incentives necessary for promoting creativity is problematical. In addition, alternative means for fostering creativity are abound.[6]

More importantly, copyright protection may generate rights which conflict with other public interests.[7] True, copyright itself possesses concepts, which can be deployed with the goal of promoting other interests, but these concepts harbour numerous drawbacks. For instance, while the idea/expression dichotomy excuses unauthorized uses of the ideas in a copyright work, its parameters are notoriously uncertain.[8] Similarly, copyright's temporal limits mean that eventually a work can be used freely, but this benefit has been eroded by progressive increases of the copyright term.[9] Equally, the evolving concept of 'originality', which requires a work to be its author's own 'intellectual creation'[10] may limit copyright's reach by excluding some works from protection but it is still embryonic. Besides, whether a particular work exhibits the necessary 'intellectual creation' is a fact-sensitive inquiry which sometimes yields inconsistent results. Lastly, exceptions to copyright infringement have their own problems. For example, the public interest defence is available to a defendant in 'rare circumstances',[11] and it is of no assistance to a defendant who unsuccessfully relies on the fair dealing defences.[12] In any event, some judges cannot even recognize it as one of the defences to copyright infringement.[13] Given these deficiencies, the question that is considered here is whether the fair dealing defences in the Copyright, Designs and Patents Act 1988 (CDPA)[14] fare any better – a discussion which is necessitated by relatively recent developments in this

---

6. E.C. Hettinger, 'Justifying Intellectual Property' (1989) 18 *Phil & Public Aff* 31.
7. For example., N.W. Netanel, 'Copyright and a Democratic Civil Society' (1996) 106 *Yale LJ* 283; R. Burrell, 'Reining in Copyright Law: Is Fair Use the Answer' (2001) 5 *IPQ* 361; J. Griffiths, 'Copyright Law after Ashdown: Time to Deal Fairly with the Public' (2002) 6 *IPQ* 240; R. Burrell & A. Coleman, *Copyright Exceptions: The Digital Impact* (Cambridge: Cambridge University Press, 2005); J. Griffiths & U. Suthersanen (eds) *Copyright and Free Speech: International and Comparative Perspectives* (Oxford: Oxford University Press, 2005).
8. M.B. Nimmer, 'Does Copyright Abridge the First Amendment Guarantees of Free Speech and Press?' (1970) 17 *UCLA L Rev* 1180; P. Masiyakurima, 'The Futility of the Idea/Expression Dichotomy in UK Copyright Law' (2007) 38 *IIC* 548.
9. For example, S. Ricketson 'The Copyright Term' (1992) *IIC* 753, 754; Term Directive 93/98 EEC; Copyright Term Extension Act, S 505 PL 105-298 11 Stat 2827 (USA); *Eldred v. Ashcroft* 537 US 186 (2003).
10. *See Infopaq International v. Danske Dagblades Forening* (C-5/08) [2009] ECDR 16 paras 30-39 (a work must be its author's own intellectual creation); E. Rosati, *Originality in EU Copyright* (Cheltenham: Edward Elgar, 2013).
11. *Ashdown v. Telegraph Group Ltd* (2002) Ch. 149.
12. *See Ashdown v. Telegraph Group Ltd* (2002) Ch. 149.
13. *Hyde Park Residence Ltd v. Yelland* (2001) Ch. 143 (CA) (Aldous LJ).
14. *See* sections 29-31 CDPA.

area.[15] The CDPA provides several fair dealing defences including criticism, review, quotation and news reporting, caricature, parody or pastiche[16] and research for a non-commercial purpose and private study.[17] In general, the fair dealing defences in the CDPA are available if a defendant's unauthorized use of a work falls within one or more of the prescribed categories, is fair, and, in some instances, if there is sufficient acknowledgement of the infringed work.[18]

It is argued that there are two key problems with the fair dealing defences in the CDPA. First, despite recent legislative reforms, the CDPA still provides a closed list of fair dealing defences; an approach which preserves authors' rights but yields uncertain results and fails to accommodate rapid technological advances. Crucially, the current fair dealing purposes are riddled with serious limitations. Second, the concept of 'fairness' is uncertain, thereby hindering the enforcement of rights. These difficulties have led to the suggestion that Britain ought to enact a general 'fair use' defence in its copyright law; a proposition which while quite attractive hinges on the interpretation of 'fairness'. It is argued that enacting a fair use defence into British copyright law will not eliminate the fact that judges will still need to evaluate competing interests in copyright law. In fact, the cases involving copyright exceptions are paradigm examples of the problems with balancing competing fundamental rights in borderline cases: the pendulum can legitimately swing in various directions. The structure of the article reflects these arguments.

16.2 NARROW STATUTORY PURPOSES

Unlike the USA,[19] Britain provides a closed list of fair dealing defences. In my view, a rigid list of exceptions interferes with other public interests and fails to respond to technological advances: a point that was best captured by Laddie J in *Pro Sieben Media v. Carlton UK Television*[20] when he referred to the 'extraordinary precision and rigidity' of copyright defences. Similar observations were made by the *Gowers*[21] and *Hargreaves*[22] Reviews. Unauthorized uses that fall outside the strict parameters of the prescribed fair

---

15. *See,* e.g., The Copyright and Rights in Performances (Personal Copies for Private Use) Regulations 2014 No. 2361; The Copyright and Rights in Performances (Research, Education, Libraries and Archives) Regulations SI 2014 No. 1372; The Copyright and Rights in Performances (Quotation and Parody) Regulations SI 2014 No. 2356.
16. Section 30A CDPA.
17. Sections 29-30 CDPA.
18. Section 30(1)-(3) CDPA.
19. *See* Copyright Act 1976 (USA), 17 U.S. Code section 107.
20. [1998] FSR 43, 48.
21. HM Treasury, *Gowers Review of Intellectual Property,* https://www.gov.uk/government/uploads/system/uploads/attachment_data/file/228849/0118404830.pdf, 39 para. 3.26.

dealing purposes constitute copyright infringement. However, the British approach to fair dealing defences can be justified because it recognizes the possibility that copyright is a property right. Consequently, in common with other property rights, copyright ought to have limited derogations. Apart from this, Britain's international obligations leave it with very little choice on the matter. The Berne Convention and the Information Society Directive require an exhaustive list of copyright exceptions.[23] In addition, it is sometimes suggested that a 'fair use' defence might yield uncertain results.[24]

Apart from failing to anticipate technological advances, the fair dealing defences that are in the CDPA still promote freedom of expression. For instance, criticizing or reviewing copyright works may disseminate expressions necessary for the discovery of the truth or democratic governance. A good illustration of that point can be gleaned from *Hubbard v. Vosper*[25] in which a disaffected congregant exposed the Church of Scientology's unorthodox practices. Another example of the value of fair dealing for the purpose of criticism or review to the discovery of truth can be obtained from *Time Warner v. Channel 4 Television*[26] in which the defendant broadcaster analysed the extreme violence in *A Clockwork Orange* and the decision by its director, Stanley Kubrik, to withdraw it from circulation in Britain. Similarly, in *Pro Sieben Media v. Carlton Television*,[27] there was criticism of the culture of 'cheque book journalism' which preyed on ordinary people facing unusual circumstances. In these cases, the courts interpreted the meaning of 'criticism or review' purposively, thereby securing other public interests. In addition, fair dealing for the purpose of criticism or review also facilitates freedom of expression by embracing criticism of: the work itself, the author of the work, or the work's underlying philosophy.[28]

The benefits of fair dealing for the purpose of criticism or review have been extended by the new 'quotation' exception.[29] That exception permits quotation of copyrighted material provided that 'the work has been made available to the public, the use of the quotation is fair dealing with the work, the extent of the quotation is no more than is required by the specific purpose for which it is used, and the quotation is accompanied by a sufficient

---

22. DBIS, *Digital Opportunity: Review of Intellectual Property and Growth*, https://www.gov.uk/government/publications/digital-opportunity-review-of-intellectual-property-and-growth, 3, 8.
23. Article 9(2) Berne Convention and Article 5 Directive 2001/29/EC of the European Parliament and of the Council of 22 May 2001 on the harmonisation of certain aspects of copyright and related rights in the information society [2001] OJ L 167/10.
24. *See* below.
25. *Hubbard and Anor v. Vosper and Anor* (1972) 2 QB 84 (CA).
26. [1994] EMLR 1 (CA).
27. [1999] 1 WLR 605 (CA).
28. *Hubbard and Anor v. Vosper and Anor* (1972) 2 QB 84 (CA).
29. *See* The Copyright and Rights in Performances (Quotation and Parody) Regulations 2014, 21 2014 No 2356.

acknowledgement (unless this would be impossible for reasons of practicality or otherwise).'[30] The main benefit of the quotation exception is that it addresses the problem that merely presenting expressions from an original work without comment does not amount to fair dealing for the purpose of criticism or review. However, a significant problem with that exception is that it excludes a wide range of unpublished material from its reach. These materials might possess expressions disclosure of which promotes various public interests.

The enactment of a new caricature, parody or pastiche limb to fair dealing for criticism or review;[31] a change that was recommended by the *Gowers*[32] and *Hargreaves* Reviews,[33] potentially broadens the circumstances in which a copyright work can be used for various purposes including freedom of expression. However, the utility of the proposed parody exception is limited. Although the European Court of Justice has held that to fall within the parody exception, a work must 'fulfil a critical purpose; ... show originality; display humorous traits; seek to ridicule the original work; and not borrow a greater number of formal elements from the original work than is strictly necessary in order to produce the parody',[34] it is notoriously difficult to define parodies.[35] While the factors that were enumerated by the European Court of Justice (ECJ) are helpful, they do not provide clear guidance on the meaning of a parody: humour is subjective. In addition, judicial attitudes to parodies in the UK have been problematical.[36] Apart from this, because parodies may interfere with the authors' economic and moral rights,[37] the new parody exception is likely to be subordinated to the authors' interests.

One of the major problems with fair dealing for the purpose of criticism or review is that it is confined to works which are 'made available to the public' with their author's consent.[38] Apart from public exhibitions of artistic

---

30. *Ibid.*
31. Section 30A CDPA.
32. HM Treasury, *Gowers Review of Intellectual Property*, https://www.gov.uk/government/uploads/system/uploads/attachment_data/file/228849/0118404830.pdf.
33. DBIS, *Digital Opportunity: Review of Intellectual Property and Growth*, https://www.gov.uk/government/publications/digital-opportunity-review-of-intellectual-property-and-growth.
34. Case C-201/13, *Deckmyn v. Vandersteen* (ECJ).
35. M. Spence, 'Intellectual Property and the Problem of *Parody*' (1998) 114 *LQR* 594.
36. *Suntrust v. Houghton Mifflin Co.*, 252 F. 3d 1165 (11th Cir. 2001).
37. G. Yonover, 'The Precarious Balance: Moral Rights, Parody and Fair Use' (1996) 4 *Cardozo Arts & Ent LJ* 79.
38. Section 30(1A) CDPA. A work is made available to the public 'if it has been made available by any means' including issuing copies of the work to the public, making the work available by means of an electronic retrieval system, renting or lending copies of the work to the public, and performing, exhibiting, playing, or showing the work in public, or communicating the work to the public. 'The requirement for the works to have been made available to the public was inserted by the Copyright and Related Rights

works or public performances of dramatic works, a work that is disseminated conditionally is not made available to the public. In addition, a work that is never disseminated at all cannot be criticized or reviewed. An implication of restricting fair dealing for criticism or review to a work, which has been made available to the public is that once a court decides that a work has not been made so available, the defence of fair dealing for criticism or review cannot be relied on. In such circumstances, the merit of the defendant's criticism or review of the infringed work is irrelevant: the unpublished status of a work can be an absolute bar to the availability of fair dealing for criticism or review.

HRH Prince of Wales v. Associated Newspapers Ltd,[39] the first reported case decided after the implementation of the *Information Society Directive* into British copyright law illustrates the restrictive nature of the current provisions on fair dealing for criticism or review. In that case, the Prince of Wales was in the habit of keeping handwritten travel journals. One of these journals recorded the handover of Hong Kong to China, and it criticized Chinese officials as 'appalling waxworks.' The journal was circulated to some of Prince Charles' confidants, but his secretary leaked it to the *Mail on Sunday* which published stories based on extracts from the unpublished journal. Prince Charles sued *Associated Newspapers Ltd* (owners of the *Mail on Sunday*) for infringement of his privacy, breach of confidence, and copyright infringement and successfully sought summary judgment on his copyright claim. The defendant argued that its unauthorized use of the Prince of Wales' journal amounted to fair dealing for the purpose of criticism or review: the newspaper was criticizing Prince Charles' intervention in controversial diplomatic matters, which was inconsistent with Britain's constitutional conventions. With respect to fair dealing for criticism or review, Blackburne J stated that:[40]

> The defendant's reliance on this provision is misplaced since it is plain that the Hong Kong journal has not been made available to the public. Circulation of copies of the journal to a number of carefully selected

---

Regulations 2003, Regulation 10 implementing Article 5(3)(d) of the Copyright Directive. The decision to exclude unpublished works from the ambit of fair dealing for criticism or review was based on Article 10(1) of the Berne Convention which provides that: '[i]t shall be permissible to make quotations from a work which has already been lawfully made available to the public, provided that their making is compatible with fair practice, and their extent does not exceed that justified by the purpose, including quotations from newspaper articles and periodicals in the form of press summaries. For the sake of resolving the threshold question of whether a work has been 'made available to the public', the focus is on the availability of the whole or a part of the work for public consumption. In common with the definition of 'publication', 'making available to the public' excludes unauthorized acts. *See* the Introduction to this thesis for the different meanings of publication.

39. *HRH Prince of Wales v. Associated Newspapers Ltd (No 3)* [2008] Ch. 57.
40. *HRH Prince of Wales v. Associated Newspapers Ltd (No 3)* [2008] Ch. 57, 100 D-H.

recipients, even if the overall total is as many as Mr Bolland claimed, does not amount to making it available to the public.[41]

There was no fair dealing for criticism or review in that case because although the work had been circulated widely, it had not been made available to the public. It might be argued that this restriction prevented a newspaper from disseminating expressions detailing the Prince of Wales' unconstitutional interventions in Britain's diplomatic affairs.

However, there is limited scope for criticizing or reviewing some unpublished works. The meaning of making available to the public includes public exhibitions of unpublished artistic works and public performances of unpublished dramatic works.[42] It, therefore, means that if a dramatic or artistic work is disseminated to the public (by performance or exhibition), it can be criticized or reviewed. The meaning of made available to the public in the context of fair dealing for the purpose of criticism or review demonstrates some differences of detail in the protection that is available to different categories of unpublished works. Works which have never been circulated or are disseminated privately receive the strongest protection because fair dealing for the purpose of criticism or review does not apply to such works. On the other hand, unpublished works which are disseminated by their public exhibition or performance can be criticized or reviewed or be quoted from.

Confining the availability of fair dealing for criticism or review to works which have been made available to the public with their authors' consent might constitute a significant barrier to exploitation of unpublished expressions and conflict with freedom of expression or the importance of facilitating derivative uses of authors' expressions. For example, an unpublished diary might contain explosive political expressions publication of which may facilitate freedom of expression and democratic governance. In addition, although other fair dealing defences may be applicable to unpublished works, unauthorized use of such material might be unfair. For the same reason, the public interest defence may be applicable to unpublished works, but its uncertainties reflect the significance of maintaining privacy or confidences. However, excluding some unpublished works from the ambit of fair dealing for criticism or review is justified because it might secure authors' economic and non-economic interests.

In common with the criticism or review exception, fair dealing for the purpose of reporting news or current events encourages the dissemination of material which might be essential for freedom of expression. A key benefit of this defence is that it embraces unpublished works. British courts have recognized the importance of fair dealing for the purpose of reporting news

---

41. *HRH Prince of Wales v. Associated Newspapers Ltd (No 3)* [2008] Ch. 57 100 D-F. Blackburne J's decision on the fair dealing issue was confirmed on appeal. *HRH Prince of Wales v. Associated Newspapers Ltd (No 3)* [2008] Ch. 57, 127 G-H (CA).
42. Section 30(1A) CDPA.

or current events to the public interest by interpreting 'news' purposively. In *NLA v. Marks & Spencer*, for example, information on groceries was held to be relevant for the purpose of reporting news or current events.[43] Similarly, 'current events' has been given a very wide meaning by the courts. For instance, the factual circumstances surrounding Diana, Princess of Wales' death constituted 'current' events even though the princess had been dead for some time.[44] Nevertheless, the Achilles heel of that fair dealing defence is that it excludes photographs from its ambit. Although the events recorded by a photograph can be presented by other means, excluding photographs from fair dealing for the purpose of reporting news or current events may interfere with the accuracy or poignancy of the expressions that are disseminated to the public. This point was best captured by Professor Nimmer when he stated that:

> Consider the photographs of the My Lai massacre. Here is an instance where the visual impact of a graphic work made a unique contribution to an enlightened democratic dialogue. No amount of words describing the 'idea' of the massacre could substitute for the public insight gained through the photographs. The photographic expression, not merely the idea, became essential if the public was to fully understand what occurred in that tragic episode. It would be intolerable if the public's comprehension of the full meaning of My Lai could be censored by the copyright owner of the photographs.[45]

The same can be said for the importance of photographs to democratic discourse in Britain. Excluding photographs from fair dealing for the purpose of reporting news[46] may dilute the accuracy or impact of the information that is presented to the public. Jacob J identified the importance of news photographs in *Hyde Park v. Yelland*[47] when he stated that photographs may leave an indelible impression on users, which words alone cannot achieve. In his view, the unauthorized first publication of a photographic still capturing the Princess of Wales' last movements was essential for refuting some of the conspiracy theories surrounding her death in Paris. Nevertheless, that view was not shared by the Court of Appeal, which seems to have been influenced by the unseemly intrusion into the claimant's private residence.[48] Apart from this, excluding photographs from fair dealing for the purpose of reporting news may also protect the commercial value of photographs. For example, unauthorized use of a substantial part of an unpublished photograph in a news report may fundamentally rob the photograph of its newsworthiness.

---

43. *See Newspaper Licensing Agency v. Marks and Spencer* [2003] AC 551.
44. *Hyde Park v. Yelland* (2001) 3 WLR 1172 (CA).
45. M.B. Nimmer 'Does Copyright Abridge the First Amendment Guarantees of Free Speech and Press?' (1970) 17 *UCLA LR* 1180, 1197.
46. Section 30(2) CDPA.
47. (1999) RPC 655 (HC).
48. *Hyde Park v. Yelland* [2001] 3 WLR 1172 (CA).

Another problem with fair dealing for the purpose of reporting news or current events is that 'distant' events are not sufficient to excuse a claim for copyright infringement. That problem manifested itself in *Associated Newspapers v. News Group* involving the unauthorized first publication of the Duchess of Windsor's private correspondence. The defendant relied on the reporting news or current events exception, but it was held that the scandalous affair between King Edward VII and Mrs Wallis Simpson was now in the distant past. However, although the events surrounding the abdication crisis were well known, the intensity of the romance between the king and his mistress could have been better understood if the letters had been published.[49]

Fair dealing for the purpose of non-commercial research or private study promotes freedom of expression by facilitating the cultivation of knowledge, the discovery of the truth, self-development and informed participation in a community's affairs: some copyright works including books, broadcasts, dramas and films possess expressions which may advance knowledge. Previously, dealings with sound recordings, films and broadcasts were excluded from the research or private study exception. Excluding such works from the research or private study exception might have reflected two things. First, exceptions to copyright infringement ought to be balanced with the authors' economic interests. Films, sound recordings, and broadcasts are valuable economically. Second, it is easy to reproduce and disseminate such works. However, the law has been changed. Fair dealing for research or private study now applies to films, broadcasts and performances;[50] an approach which recognizes the growth in importance of digital media and facilitates uses of valuable cultural expressions. Nevertheless, the new provisions must still meet the fairness test; a requirement which severely limits the fair dealing defences.

Fair dealing for research or private study has been expanded to include data mining;[51] a development which fosters scientific research, especially in the digital environment. However, there are a few problems with this exception. For instance, commercial research is still excluded from the ambit of fair dealing for the purpose of research and private study.[52] It is argued that there is no bright line between commercial and non-commercial research. As the *Royal Society* observed:

> non-commercial research is intrinsically difficult to define, and many research ventures or collaborations only become commercial subsequently. We believe that the limitation of fair dealing to non-commercial

---

49. [1986] RPC 515.
50. The Copyright and Rights in Performances (Research, Education, Libraries and Archives) Regulations 2014, SI 2014 No. 1372.
51. Section 29A CDPA.
52. Section 29-29A CDPA.

purposes gives rise to uncertainty, is not useful and is complex to operate.[53]

Although it might be argued that commercial researchers are better able to enter into voluntary agreements allowing them to use copyright works,[54] obtaining a license may be costly, owing to the market power of large collecting societies.

Another problem with the research or private study exception is that dealings on behalf of third parties are prohibited. That problem manifested itself in *Sillitoe v. McGraw Hill & Co.*[55] That exclusion is justified. Although the research or private study exception may advance the acquisition of knowledge necessary for self-actualization, wholesale copying on behalf of third parties might interfere with authors' economic interests. Besides, given the existence of collecting societies which can license mass reproduction of works, it is feasible for third parties who wish to reproduce copyright materials on behalf of other users to acquire the necessary licenses. The problem then has to do with whether the third party concerned has the resources to pay for licensed uses of copyright works; an issue which assumes some significance given, as we noted earlier, the market power of collecting societies.

Although the fair dealing defences in the CDPA may promote other public interests, a fundamental problem relates to the usefulness in the practice of the new exceptions. An old chestnut stands in the way of any new copyright exceptions. The new laws would need to be interpreted by the courts. If current judicial attitudes to 'fairness' prevail,[56] any new copyright exceptions are likely to be of limited value. It is to the issue of 'fairness' we now turn.

16.3   FAIRNESS

Apart from falling within any one of the recognized statutory purposes, the defendant's use of the claimant's work must also be 'fair'. The biggest impediment to reliance on the fair dealing defences in the CDPA is the requirement of fairness. The leading definition of 'fairness' was provided by

---

53. The Royal Society, 'Keeping science open: the effects of intellectual property policy on the conduct of science' www.royalsoc.ac.uk/displaypagedoc.asp?id¼411403, 20.
54. *Newspaper Licensing Authority v. Marks & Spencer* (1999) RPC 536, 547; *Princeton University Press v. Michigan Document Services Inc*, 99 F 3d 1381 (6th Circ 1996); *Haines v. Copyright Agency Ltd* (1982) 40 ALR 264.
55. *CCH Canadian Ltd v. Law Society of Upper Canada* (1999) 2 CPR (4th) 129 (Fed Ct); *Longman Group Ltd v. Carrington Technical Institute Board of Governors* (1991) 2 NZLR 574, *Television New Zealand Ltd v. Newsmonitor Services Ltd* (1994) 2 NZLR 91; *Sillitoe v. McGraw Hill Book Co (UK)* (1983) FSR 545; *Boudreau v. Lin* (1997) 75 CPR (3d) 1; *University of London Press v. University Tutorial Press* (1916) 2 Ch. 601.
56. *See* below.

Lord Denning MR in *Hubbard v. Vosper* in which he observed that 'fairness' is a matter of impression.[57] Because it is a matter of impression, the concept of fairness might give rise to uncertainty, especially in borderline cases, thereby preventing legitimate uses of copyright works. Of course, this argument has its limits. In *Designers Guild v. Russell Williams Ltd*, Lord Hoffmann stated that:

> When judges say that a question is one of impression, they generally mean that it involves taking into account a number of factors of varying degrees of importance and deciding whether they are sufficient to bring the whole within some legal description. It is often difficult to give precise reasons for arriving at a conclusion one-way or the other (apart from an enumeration of the relevant factors) and there are borderline cases over which reasonable minds may differ.

Lord Hoffmann's statement has equal relevance to the meaning of 'fairness'. The uncertainty of 'fairness' is constrained by the fact that judges use a defined list of criteria when deciding whether a particular use is fair. In *Hubbard v. Vosper itself*, Lord Denning MR relied on a variety of factors which have now assumed canonical status. Some of these factors require detailed discussion.

The quantity and quality of what is taken from the infringed work is an important benchmark for assessing 'fairness'.[58] That factor was prominent in *Newspaper Licensing Authority v. Marks & Spencer* in which the court suggested that a defendant who copies too much from a particular work ought to obtain a licence from the author.[59] Although copying an entire work may be necessary for the discovery of the truth,[60] as the Supreme Court of Canada stated in *Regina v. James Lorimer & Co Ltd*,[61] slavish copying adds little value to freedom of expression. However, certain genres rely on taking substantial amounts of material from the infringed work if they are to be successful. In my opinion, parodies present a specific example when the quantity and quality of what is taken from the infringed work ought to reflect the nature of the work. Otherwise, most parodies would constitute copyright infringement, thereby diminishing their utility as vehicles for criticism.

As *Associated Newspapers Group plc v. News Group Ltd* demonstrates,[62] commercial competition between the original and the infringing work is a significant 'fairness' factor. In that case, the defendant's unauthorized use of the Duchess of Windsor's letters interfered with the claimant's serialization rights. Once again, this fairness factor recognizes the economic

---

57. *Hubbard and Anor v. Vosper and Anor* (1972) 2 QB 84 (Lord Denning MR).
58. *Hubbard v. Vosper* (1972) 2 QB 84 (CA) and *Associated Newspapers Group plc v. News Group Ltd and Others* (1986) RPC 515, 517.
59. (1999) RPC 536 (HC).
60. (2001) 3 WLR 1368, 1381.
61. (1984) 1 FC 1065.
62. (1986) RPC 515, 518.

importance of copyright works, and it assumes greater significance if a work is unpublished. The commercial value of the expressions in a work might depend on their secrecy. However, secret or privately disseminated expressions might be vital to the discovery of the truth, especially in cases involving wrongdoing by public figures or organizations.

The manner of obtaining the infringed work is also a vital instrument for determining 'fairness'.[63] That factor was of some relevance in the *Distillers* case in which documents detailing the dangers of thalidomide were leaked to the media.[64] Similarly, in *Beloff v. Pressdram*, Ungoed-Thomas J referred to the 'vice of the leak' when discussing whether dealing with a leaked memorandum recording a secret meeting between a lobby correspondent and a cabinet minister was unfair.[65] In addition, in *Ashdown v. Telegraph Group Ltd*, dealing with an unpublished minute was held to be unfair partly because the minute had been leaked.[66] Furthermore, the contentious photographic stills in *Hyde Park v. Yelland* were obtained from a private residence[67] while the pictures in *Tennant v. Associated Newspapers*[68] were leaked to the media. In my view, when the courts rely on the manner of obtaining the infringed work, they are attempting to secure various interests, including the maintenance of confidences and protecting authors' privacy. However, this approach seems to be inconsistent with the argument that in general, the exercise of the right to freedom of expression does not depend on how the contentious information was obtained.

The unpublished status of a work is the single most important barrier to reliance on fair dealing defences. As we have already noted, Lord Denning MR observed that 'fairness' is a matter of impression.[69] Given that fairness is a matter of 'impression', the unpublished nature of the infringed work might render its unauthorized use unfair. Several cases demonstrate the significance of the unpublished status of a work when determining fairness issues. For instance, an important question that arose in some of the twentieth century fair dealing cases was whether dealing with an unpublished work for the purpose of criticism or review could ever be fair. This issue arose in *British Oxygen v. Liquid Air Ltd*[70] in which the defendant photographed the plaintiff's unpublished business letter and disseminated it without the plaintiff's consent. The plaintiff sought an injunction restraining unauthorized first publication of the letter and relied on both copyright infringement and breach of confidence to enforce its rights. The defendant argued that

---

63. *Associated Newspapers Group Plc v. News Group Newspapers Ltd* (1986) RPC 515, 518 but *cf. Hyde Park v. Yelland* (2001) 3 WLR 1172 (CA).
64. *Distillers Co v. Times Newspapers Ltd* [1975] QB 613.
65. *[1973] 1 All ER 241.*
66. *Ashdown v. Telegraph Group Ltd* [2002] Ch. 149 (CA).
67. *Hyde Park Residence Ltd v. Yelland and Others* [2001] Ch. 143 (CA).
68. *The Lady Anne Tennant v. Associated Newspapers* [1979] FSR 298.
69. *Hubbard v. Vosper* [1972] 2 QB 84 (CA).
70. *British Oxygen Co. Ltd. v. Liquid Air Ltd.* [1925] Ch. 383.

unauthorized first publication of the letter fell within the ambit of fair dealing for the purpose of criticism, review or newspaper summary.[71] Although the 1911 Act provided that 'fair dealing with any work for the purposes of private study, research, criticism, review, or newspaper summary'[72] constituted a defence to copyright infringement, it was held that the defendant's use of the business letter infringed the plaintiff's copyright and that the defendant's use of the letter was unfair.

In Romer J's view:

> it would be manifestly unfair that an unpublished literary work should, without the consent of the author, be the subject of public criticism, review or newspaper summary. Any such dealing with an unpublished literary work would not, therefore, in my opinion, be a 'fair dealing' with the work.[73]

The 1911 Act provided that fair dealing defences applied to published and unpublished works but the initial interpretation of the Act suggested that fair dealing for criticism or review was not available if a work was unpublished; a proposition that was established by Lord Cottenham LC in *Prince Albert v. Strange*.[74] Romer J's reasoning in the *British Oxygen* case might have been influenced by the limited exceptions to common law rights in unpublished works. Before the abrogation of common law copyright, the exceptions to infringement of copyright in unpublished works were confined to the vindication of personal reputation[75] and production of documents in legal proceedings.[76] In *British Oxygen*, we see courts' reluctance to sanctioning dealings with unpublished works.

The proposition that fair dealing for the purpose of criticism or review could not be relied on if a work was unpublished was qualified in *Hubbard v. Vosper*[77] in which Cyril Vosper took substantial extracts from L. Ron Hubbard's[78] unpublished manuals and incorporated them into his book, *The Mind Benders*. Hubbard's unpublished manuals had been disclosed to some of his followers. Hubbard relied on both copyright infringement and breach of confidence to restrain Vosper from publishing the extracts.[79] Hubbard's claim for breach of confidence failed because disclosure of his expressions was in the public interest. It was also held that the defendant's use of the extracts amounted to fair dealing for criticism or review. At first glance, Lord

---

71. Section 2(1) of Copyright Act 1911.
72. Section 2(1)(i) Copyright Act 1911.
73. *British Oxygen Co. Ltd. v. Liquid Air Ltd.* [1925] Ch. 383, 393.
74. (1849)2 *De G* & SM 293.
75. *Perceval v. Phipps* (1813) 2 V & B 19.
76. *Hopkinson v. Burghley* (1867) LR 2 Ch. App 447.
77. *Hubbard v. Vosper* [1972] 2 QB 84 (CA).
78. Ron L. Hubbard was the founder of the Church of Scientology.
79. *Hubbard v. Vosper* [1972] 2 QB 84 (CA) 92E.

Denning MR's decision constituted a major departure from Romer J's dictum in *British Oxygen v. Liquid Air Ltd.* In Lord Denning MR's view:

> Although a literary work may not be published to the world at large, it may, however, be circulated to such a wide circle that it is 'fair dealing' to criticize it publicly in a newspaper, or elsewhere.[80]

However, Romer J seemed to have accepted that criticizing a work that had been circulated widely was possible when he stated that:

> this permission of criticism would seem at first sight to extend to unpublished literary works. The permission was no doubt necessary in the case of unpublished dramatic and musical works, in as much as performance in public of such works is not publication for the purposes of the Act.[81]

It might be argued that both *British Oxygen* and *Hubbard v. Vosper* support the proposition that fair dealing defences might be available if the infringed work has been circulated widely. For our purposes, *British Oxygen* and *Hubbard v. Vosper* seem to suggest that fair dealing for criticism or review did not apply to a work which is never disseminated or to a work which is circulated privately; a position that is still maintained in the CDPA.[82] That restriction might limit the significance of fair dealing defences to the promotion of freedom of expression in that access to some unpublished material is severely circumscribed.

The idea that dealing with unpublished works which are not disseminated widely is unfair can be supported by Ungoed-Thomas J's obiter dictum in *Beloff v. Pressdram*.[83] In that case, Nora Beloff, *The Observer*'s lobby correspondent, sought to restrain unauthorized first publication of a leaked confidential minute recording her conversation with Willie Whitelaw, a cabinet minister, on the potential successor to Edward Heath, then British Prime Minister. The minute had been disclosed to some of Beloff's colleagues at *The Observer*. Beloff's claim failed because her employer owned the contentious minute. With respect to the fairness of the defendant's dealing with the minute, Ungoed-Thomas J stated that:

> the law by bestowing a right of copyright on an unpublished work bestows a right to prevent its being published at all; and even though an unpublished work is not automatically excluded from the defence of fair dealing, it is yet a much more substantial breach of copyright than publication of a published work.[84]

---

80. *Hubbard v. Vosper* [1972] 2 QB 84 (CA) 95A.
81. *British Oxygen v. Liquid Air Ltd* [1925] Ch. 383, 393.
82. *See* above.
83. *[1973] 1 All ER 241, 263.*
84. *Ibid.*

The gist of Ungoed-Thomas J's observation was that unauthorized use of an unpublished work was generally unfair, and it limits uses of vital unpublished material. However, confining the application of fair dealing defences to works which have been circulated widely can be justified on the basis that it preserves the right of authors to publish their works first.

The principle (established in *Hubbard v. Vosper*) that fair dealing for criticism or review was available to a work which had been circulated widely was confirmed by *Distillers Co. (Biochemicals) Ltd v. Times Newspaper Ltd*[85] in which the plaintiffs successfully restrained the defendant from publishing confidential documents detailing the side effects of *thalidomide*. The documents had been disclosed in civil proceedings. In the course of his judgment, Talbot J stated that:

> For my part, I doubt whether the plaintiff's documents could be said to have been circulated so widely that, though not published generally, it was fair dealing to criticise them.[86]

Talbot J's judgment illustrates the argument that courts are reluctant to find that unauthorized use of works which have never been circulated or privately disseminated works could amount to fair dealing.

The proposition that unauthorized dealings with unpublished works are generally unfair remained influential and was also applied to fair dealing for reporting news or current events in *Associated Newspapers Group plc v. News Group Newspapers Ltd and Ors*.[87] In that case, the *Daily Mail* obtained exclusive rights to the Duke and Duchess of Windsor's personal correspondence. The defendant, *The Sun*, printed one of the letters in its newspaper. The plaintiff sought an injunction restraining *The Sun* from infringing its exclusive rights in the unpublished letters. *The Sun* argued that its use of the unpublished letters fell within the ambit of fair dealing for the purpose of reporting news or current events. Walton J held that unauthorized first publication of the letters did not amount to fair dealing for the purpose of reporting current events because the events covered by the correspondence were distant.

The significance of the unpublished status of a work to the determination of fairness can also be gleaned from *Hyde Park Residence Ltd v. Yelland*[88] in which stills from a security video film owned by the plaintiff were published by *The Sun* without their owner's consent. A disgruntled employee had taken the stills and sold them to *The Sun*. The plaintiff sought to restrain the defendants from further publication of the stills based on copyright infringement and breach of confidence and sought an award of

---

85. *Distillers Co (Biochemicals) Ltd v. Times Newspapers Ltd* [1975] QB 613.
86. *Distillers Co (Biochemicals) Ltd v. Times Newspapers Ltd* [1975] QB 613, 625 G-H.
87. [1986] RPC 515.
88. *Hyde Park Residence Ltd v. Yelland and Others* [2001] Ch. 143 (CA).

additional damages.[89] The defendant maintained that its use of the stills was covered by the fair dealing and public interest defences; an argument which was successful before Jacob J. On appeal, Aldous LJ's reasoning confined *Hubbard v. Vosper* to its facts. In the course of his judgment, he stated that:

> Lord Denning MR had in mind the facts of that case where the works in which copyright was claimed had been widely circulated among the followers of the Church of Scientology. However, the general thrust of the conclusions of Romer J remained, namely that it was difficult to imagine that it could be fair dealing to use a work that had not been published or circulated to persons for the purposes of criticism, review or newspaper reporting.[90]

Aldous LJ's reasoning appears to confirm the position that dealing with an unpublished work can only be fair if a work is disseminated widely.

Apart from being a factor for determining 'fairness' in its own right, the unpublished status of a work also influences other 'fairness' factors. The manner of obtaining the infringed work is one of the factors for determining 'fairness', and it is affected by the unpublished nature of a work. This factor is of significant relevance to works which are never disseminated and privately disseminated works because it might be easier for claimants to prove that such works were obtained clandestinely. For instance, the fact that the contentious stills were taken from video footage of a private residence and leaked by a disgruntled employee seemed to influence Aldous LJ's reasoning in the *Hyde Park* case.[91] Similar considerations seem to have applied to the 'disclosed' journals in the *Prince of Wales* case. The documents had been disclosed to a limited audience and were leaked by a member of the Prince of Wales' staff. Therefore, in some instances, the unpublished nature of a work might tilt the balance of fairness in favour of the claimant.

The enactment of the Human Rights Act 1998 (HRA) did not dislodge the significance of the unpublished status of a work to exceptions to copyright infringement. For example, the freedom of expression provisions of the HRA were engaged in *Ashdown v. Telegraph Group Ltd,*[92] in which Lord Ashdown, a former leader of the Liberal Democrats made a confidential *aide memoir* recording his secret meeting with Tony Blair, then British Prime Minister. The *aide memoire* was leaked to the *Sunday Telegraph,* and it published stories based on the minute. The claimant sought to restrain further publication of the minute based on copyright infringement and breach of confidence and sought summary judgment on its copyright claim. The defendant relied on the public interest and fair dealing defences and averred

---

89. *Hyde Park Residence Ltd v. Yelland* [1999] RPC 655.
90. *Hyde Park Residence Ltd v. Yelland and Others* [2001] Ch. 143 (CA), 158 C-D.
91. *Hyde Park Residence Ltd v. Yelland and Others* [2001] Ch. 143 (CA), 159 D-E.
92. *Ashdown v. Telegraph Group Ltd* [2002] Ch. 149 (CA).

that even if the two defences did not excuse its conduct, it could rely on Article 10 of the European Convention on Human Rights as a defence to copyright infringement. At first instance, Sir Andrew Morritt V-C rejected the *Sunday Telegraph*'s arguments and held that existing copyright exceptions protected the defendant's freedom of expression adequately.[93] Sir Andrew Morritt V-C also stated that because the minute had not been published, dealing with such an unpublished work was unfair.[94] On appeal, the Court of Appeal did not disturb Morritt VC-s findings on the application of fair dealing defences to infringement of copyright in the minute. With respect to the freedom of expression point, it was held that circumstances might arise in which copyright exceptions might not accommodate a user's freedom of expression.[95]

The cases on fair dealing with unpublished works can be contrasted with those involving published ones. *Time Warner v. Channel Four PLC*[96] provides a striking example of the different treatment of published and unpublished works in the context of fair dealing for criticism or review. In that case, the defendants used Stanley Kubrick's *A Clockwork Orange* for the purpose of criticizing the film itself and the decision to withdraw the film from circulation in Britain. The film had been screened in the United Kingdom and in other countries. The plaintiffs successfully sought an interlocutory injunction restraining Channel 4 from using the film. However, the Court of Appeal reversed Harman J's decision and held that fair dealing for the purpose of criticism or review covered Channel 4's use of the film. Neill LJ observed that:

> There might be cases, particularly in relation to unpublished works, where the method by which the copyright material was obtained would be relevant to the issue of fair dealing. The defence of fair dealing was, however, primarily concerned with the treatment of the copyright material in the publication of which complaint was made. Criticism and review of a work already in the public domain which would otherwise constitute fair dealing would seldom if ever be rendered unfair because of the method by which the copyright material had been obtained.[97]

Fair dealing for criticism or review was successful in that case partly because *A Clockwork Orange* had been published.

Similarly, in *Pro Sieben Media AG v. Carlton UK TV Ltd*,[98] the Court of Appeal held that fair dealing for criticism or review was applicable to infringement of a published broadcast. In addition, in *Fraser-Woodward Ltd*

---

93. *Ashdown v. Telegraph Group Ltd* [2001] Ch. 685, 693 A-C, 693 G-694 A, 696 E-G.
94. *Ashdown v. Telegraph Group Ltd* [2001] Ch. 685, 699 E.
95. *Ibid.*
96. [1994] EMLR 1 (CA).
97. [1994] EMLR 1 (CA) 2.
98. [1999] 1 WLR 605 (CA).

v. BBC,[99] the BBC successfully argued that its use of David and Victoria Beckham's photographs for the purpose of criticizing the interaction between celebrities and the media was fair. The claimant owned the photographs, and they had been published in various tabloid newspapers. Mann J held that fair dealing for criticism or review was applicable to the facts of the case. It will be suggested that the purposive application of fair dealing defences to published works is justified because the privacy concerns that may be relevant in cases involving infringement of unpublished works might not be engaged by published works.

It might be argued that uncertainties surrounding the concept of fairness simply reflect the reality that freedom of expression ought to be balanced with authors' property rights; a proposition that might yield inconsistent results in some cases. In fact, some commentators have suggested that the vagueness of various copyright concepts might encourage voluntary transactions.[100] That claim is equally significant to 'fairness'. The absence of a litmus test for deciding 'fairness' may force defendants to obtain permission for using others' copyright material. The main thrust of that argument is that the public interest in disseminating socially useful expressions ought to be balanced with protecting authors' rights. Nevertheless, the argument that users ought to obtain licenses allowing them to use copyright material does not address the fact that in some instances, copyright owners might never want to compromise their privacy by publishing their material. In addition, an essential hallmark of copyright exceptions is that they allow users to exploit a work freely and without the author's consent.

Although the CDPA provides narrow fair dealing defences, the statutory purposes are often interpreted purposively. The effectiveness of fair dealing defences as a means for securing users' freedom of expression is often vitiated by the interpretation of 'fairness'. For the most part, economic and privacy considerations have meant that dealing with some works is generally considered to be unfair. Given the problems with 'fairness', it might be suggested that the Government ought to have adopted a general fair use defence to infringement of copyright. The question which remains for discussion is whether adopting a general fair use defence to claims for copyright infringement better secures the interests of users.

16.4   CONCLUSION

This chapter has highlighted some of the problems with the fair dealing defences in the CDPA and has argued that most of these problems simply reflect the fact that the cases that have been decided so far are a classic example of conflicts between fundamental rights. When such conflicts occur,

---

99. [2005] FSR 36.
100. M. Spence & T. Endicott, 'Vagueness in the Scope of Copyright' (2005) 121 *LQR* 657.

the decisions can legitimately swing in any direction. However, there are suggestions that Britain ought to enact a general fair use defence in the CDPA. The argument that Britain ought to have a general fair use defence to copyright infringement has been pursued in some quarters especially in the immediate aftermath of the Court of Appeal's judgment in *Ashdown v. Telegraph Group Ltd.*[101] Proponents of the introduction of a fair use defence in British copyright law have highlighted the possibility that the flexibility arising from having the equivalent of the USA fair use defence might allow judges to acknowledge other public interests in copyright cases. In addition, as the Australian Law Review Commission observed, a fair use defence is technologically sensitive in the sense that it can accommodate new methods of copyright exploitation.[102]

The Government's recent reforms eschewed the idea that there ought to be a fair use defence to copyright infringement.[103] There are two main reasons for the Government's attitude. First, a fair use defence might be uncertain because it might not give proper guidance on the kind of uses that may be fair.[104] In contrast, a delimitation of the permitted purposes may afford users the opportunity to determine whether unauthorized use of a work would interfere with the claimant's rights. Just like the exclusive rights that are granted to authors, users need specific and certain defences.

Another objection to having a general fair use defence to claims for copyright infringement is that it is inconsistent with Britain's international obligations. That point was put across by the Gowers[105] and Hargreaves Reviews.[106] However, given that the Australian Law Reform Commission recommended the adoption of a fair use defence in Australian copyright law,[107] the issue which arises here is the precise identification of the international obligations which prevent Britain from adopting a fair use defence. It is argued that introducing a fair use defence in British copyright law would fly in the face of the Information Society Directive which harmonizes the range of permissible exceptions in the copyright laws of the Member States of the European Union.[108] The latter argument has considerable force because the Information Society Directive permits a closed list of exceptions to copyright infringement.

---

101. *Ashdown v. Telegraph Group Ltd* [2002] Ch. 149 (CA).
102. Australian Law Reform Commission, Copyright and the Digital Economy (ALRC Report 122), http://www.alrc.gov.au/publications/copyright-report-122.
103. HM Government, *Consultation on Copyright*, http://www.ipo.gov.uk/consult-2011-copyright.pdf at 56.
104. HM Government, *Consultation on Copyright*, above Chapter 7.
105. *See* above.
106. *See* above.
107. *See* above.
108. Directive 2001/29/EC of the European Parliament and of the Council of 22 May 2001 on the harmonization of certain aspects of copyright and related rights in the information society OJ L 167, 22/06/2001 P. 0010 – 0019.

An additional limitation of enacting a general fair use defence into British copyright law relates to the issue of 'fairness'. As observed earlier, the unpublished status of a work is a prominent factor for determining whether unauthorized use of a work is 'fair'. In addition, the unpublished nature of a work might influence other 'fairness' factors, including the manner of obtaining a work and the impact of the infringing work on the market for the original work. Any new exceptions might not have much practical relevance if they cannot pass the 'fairness' hurdle. In any event, it might be argued that the proposition that 'fairness' is a matter of impression implicitly recognizes the need to balance infringement of copyright in unpublished works with authors' interests. Fair dealing defences are applicable in the event of genuine public interests necessitating unauthorized use of copyright works. That was the case in *Hubbard v. Vosper.*

The most serious objection to importing a fair use defence into British copyright law is that the availability of that defence in the USA has not diminished the numerous problems affecting exceptions to infringement of unpublished works in American copyright law. In fact, some of the leading cases on fair use in American copyright law involved the 'fairness' of using unpublished works.[109] In addition, the extensive literature on the fair use defence in American copyright law focuses on its application to unpublished works.[110] Moreover, the American Congress had to legislate in this area and specify that the fair use defence applies to unpublished works.[111] In the final analysis, judges interpret the law and having new exceptions might not displace judicial approaches to copyright infringement.

The gaps in exceptions to copyright infringement mean that in some instances, conflicts between copyright and freedom of expression remain unresolved. The British Government has attempted to address problems with fair dealing defences by expanding the statutory purposes. The introduction of a specific parody exception into British copyright law and the broadening of the research and private study exception will expand the fair dealing defences considerably thereby potentially aligning the rights attaching to copyright protection with other values. However, although the new exceptions will apply to the many published and publicly disseminated works, the

---

109. For example *Harper & Row v. Nation Enterprises*, 471 US 539 (1985); *Salinger v. Random House*, 811 F. 2d 90 (2d Cir. 1987); *ApS v. Henry Holt and Company, Inc.* 873 F. 2d 576 (2d. Cir. 1989).

110. For example J. Re, 'The Stage of Publication as A Fair Use Factor: *Harper & Row, Inc v. National Enterprises*' (1984) 58 *St John's LR* 597 P.N. Leval, 'Toward A Fair Use Standard' 1990) 103 *Harvard LR* 1105; L.L. Weinreb, 'Fair's Fair: A Comment on the Fair Use Doctrine' (1990) 103 *Harvard LR* 1137; M.S. Bilder, 'The Shrinking Back: The Law of Biography' (1991) 43 *Stanford LR* 299.

111. Fair use and unpublished works: joint hearing before the Subcommittee on Patents, Copyrights, and Trademarks of the Senate Committee on the Judiciary and the Subcommittee on Courts, Intellectual Property, and the Administration of Justice of the House Committee on the Judiciary, One Hundred First Congress, second session on S. 2370 and H.R. 4263 … 11 July 1990.

government's reforms are likely to make very little difference to infringe-ment of unpublished works. Apart from publicly exhibited artistic works and publicly performed dramatic works, the parody and quotation exceptions will be inapplicable to works that have not been made available to the public with their author's consent. In my view, the approach taken by the government to confine the parody and quotation exceptions to published and publicly disseminated works is a good one because a work whose very existence is not known need not be quoted from. Where a work has been circulated privately, there might be privacy issues at stake. Apart from this, Article 10 of the Berne Convention stipulates that the 'quotation' exception is only applicable to a work which has been made available to the public with its author's consent.

There is no obvious solution to the problems with the fair dealing defences in the CDPA. Copyright cases present the courts with conflicting public interests which can legitimately be resolved either way. Matters are not helped by the fact-specific nature of most copyright cases, which fail to provide opportunities for applying the law consistently.

Chapter 17

Fundamental Rights for Author's and Contractual Relations: A Comparative Perspective

David Felipe Alvarez Amezquita[*]

17.1   INTRODUCTION

In 2009, the Colombian Constitutional Court[1] ruled an action between two particulars in which the claimant demanded protection for his fundamental rights as an author against the musical publisher Edimusica.[2] The author, Mr Rafael Escalona, claimed the revision and eventual rescission of two

* This chapter is the result of the research developed as PhD Student at the University of Nottingham, sponsored by COLCIENCIAS and the University of Tolima. Email: dfalvareza@gmail.com.

1. *Sentencia T-367/09 (Corte Constitucional)* [2009] www.corteconstitucional.gov.co/relatoria.
2. Such kind of action, known as Tutela, protects citizen's fundamental rights through a fast procedure by which any court in the country is competent to take effective measures within ten days to protect the fundamental right at risk. The 'Tutela' is similar to the Spanish and Mexican figure of 'Amparo', a type of writ invoked to protect such rights. Nevertheless, this is a residual procedure, meaning that it only applies if there is no other possible legal mechanism to protect the fundamental right under jeopardy and/or if the affectation of the right is imminent. The Constitutional Court has a general competence to revise selectively the 'tutela' cases ruled by any other judge in the country in a final instance as superior court in constitutional matters. In this case, the Court selected the case as it refers to the protection of author's economic rights. *Sentencia T-367/09 (Corte Constitucional)* (n 1).

contracts he had signed with Edimusica in 1991 and 1999. By those contracts, the property of most of his musical compositions was transferred to the publisher. Mr Escalona argued that the poor management of his music by Edimusica[3] had diminished his income to the point that his life and well-being were in danger. The decisions from the Courts in the first and second instances denied the interests of the author. The case went for revision to the upper Court, but while the Constitutional Court was studying the case, Mr Escalona perished. In spite of this, the Court, arguing the importance of the case, decided to continue studying the case even when the person to be protected no longer exists.

The Court's decision can be summarized in these three determinations: first, the Court established that the contractual agreements about copyright should consider author's social security and his minimal material conditions of subsistence in congruence with his own normal economic conditions which should be ensured; second, Colombian copyright law is old and should be reformed in order to protect authors in their real conditions; and third, Escalona's heirs had to be informed about the judicial options they are entitled of in order to protect their own interests. Finally, the Court's decision recognizes the material impossibility of changing the state of things to protect claimant's interests as he no longer exists.[4]

The Court has proposed some reasons regarding the question of how the author's fundamental rights articulate with copyright laws. First, it recognizes that authors are normally in a weaker position against their counterpart, in this case, the musical publisher. This creates a defenceless circumstance in which the author is not able to address his counterpart while bargaining their contract. Second, such a weak position creates a situation by which the protection of fundamental rights has a horizontal effect among citizens with equal or similar rights in which the action of one citizen directly affects the fundamental rights of another.[5] As a consequence, if fundamental rights are under threat, the contracts in which copyright have been transferred could be revised by the Court and eventually rescinded. Third, the collision of

---

3. sociedad Editora Internacional de Música Ltda-EDIMUSICA.

4. For a complete revision of this case, *see*: Yecid Andrés Ríos, 'Problemas de La Predisposición Del Contrato de Edición En Colombia: Las Cláusulas Abusivas' (2014) 52 Revista de Derecho Privado 1.

5. Indeed, the theory of the horizontal effect has been proposed by Robert Alexy as another instance in which fundamental rights might be compromised, not because of the positive action of the State against citizens, nor even in the case of judges that violate those fundamental rights in benefit of other citizen, but in the case in which two individuals collide in their interests and the action of one affects the fundamental rights of the other. *See*: Robert Alexy, *A Theory of Constitutional Rights* (Julian Rivers tr, 1st edn, Oxford University Press 2002). p. 357 and ss. For a revision of the horizontal effect regarding private law, *see also*: Lorenz Fastrich, 'Human Rights and Private Law' in Katja S Ziegler (ed), *Human Rights and Private Law. Privacy as Autonomy* (Hart Publishing 2007); Alison L Young, 'Horizontality and the Human Rights Act 1998' in Katja S Ziegler (ed), *Human Rights and Private Law. Privacy as Autonomy* (Hart Publishing 2007).

interests in the horizontal effect can only be decided through the Constitutional forum if fundamental rights are under immediate threat. In the Escalona case, as the author had not the means to support his own subsistence despite the wealth his creations could have produced, his life was under evident jeopardy. In the case, the Court has argued that if an author's social security is under threat, even the economic rights of copyright are human rights. Finally, the Court has stated that the author's special role in society should be protected.

The following question arises from the case summarized above: Is that kind of argumentation congruent with the interaction between human rights and copyright regarding the protection of authors?

The interface between copyright and human rights has been studied often. Most of the studies on this matter have been made from the perspective of the interaction between right holders on the one hand and users on the other. Either the studies seek for collisions or contact points regarding the rights of one or another. However, less attention has been paid to the interaction between two stakeholders on the side of the right holders of the equation. It is simply assumed that the right holder is entitled to its copyrights, therefore, it would be entitled to human rights. Thus, such a premise should be reviewed as the entitlement for human rights differs when the subject is not a human being.

Traditionally, the protection of copyright as a human right has been argued from the point of view of the protection of property. However, the complex construction of the express recognition of copyright as a human right has had left aside the mere proprietary approach by stating one more related to the fact of creation and the person who has created the work, the author. Consequently, it looks more promising to draw the difference between the protection of copyright as property within the scope of human rights and the protection of the author's moral and material interests within the same scope.

Once such differentiation has been made, new questions should arise. This chapter will focus on one of those questions. Should human rights protection for authors affect the contractual relationships with those who acquire the copyright by any legal construction?

This chapter is aimed at copyright contract laws as these are the main mechanisms by which the author transfer her rights. It comprises two sections. The first section is aimed at the protection of authors as fundamental rights considering the constitutional development that some of the countries under study have created for that purpose. It will also explore how the concept of authorship and its connection with the requirement of originality can be linked with such protection of fundamental rights for authors. The second section identifies some mechanisms towards the protection of the author's moral and material interests in national laws, looking for a balance between eventual conflicting interests among authors and right holders of the copyright. Such mechanisms would be defined through the interest in protecting an author's dignity and autonomy as these serve to guarantee the author's freedom and independence in her creative process. It will be concluded that, although the concept of the author has been mainly constructed regarding the relationship between the author, the right holders or proprietary interests, and users; considerations have been made about the author as a natural person, and some principles improving the authors' position in contractual relationships have been developed.

Despite the attention given to the interface between copyright and human rights among the different perspectives, less attention has been paid to the interests of the author considered independently of the private interests of the successor in title of the copyright.

The role of the author should possess its own weight in the legal systems in order to conciliate both copyright and human rights towards the protection of the originator of the work. The General Comment 17th from the Committee on Economic, Social and Cultural Rights (CESCR) asserts that, at the level of human rights, only the entitlement granted by Intellectual Property (IP) systems to the authors of scientific, literary, or artistic productions as natural persons is protected. Therefore, other copyright entitlements should be considered below that level.[6]

The interaction between human rights and copyright based on a common background has to be tied to the interest of protecting the author. Such a common background relates, for instance, to the interest in democracy and the participation of the individual in the cultural life of society. As a notion, the author might be the result of historical construction, and as such, that notion could be reinterpreted to answer new conditions in the contemporary cultural environment. This functionality could relocate the author at the centre of copyright public policy debates, and this should produce an important impact on how copyright laws can be interpreted.

The study proposed here is part of larger research produced as a thesis for the PhD Degree in Laws from the University of Nottingham and supervised by Professors Paul Torremans and Nigel Gravells. Such study explored how the protection of the author can be articulated within constitutional democracies through the interaction of fundamental rights, copyright laws and international laws on copyright and human rights. Based on a comparative perspective, the analysis will be mainly horizontal and refer to the applicable law, case law, and constitutional context related to the problem within the countries under study.

The countries studied here are the United States (US), the United Kingdom (UK), Spain, Mexico, Colombia, and Argentina. Their selection responds to the interest in comparing different legal traditions, their evolution, and their connections. The Latin American countries are related to the

---

6. Committee on Economic Social and Cultural Rights, 'General Comment No. 17 (2005) (Article 15, Paragraph 1(c), of the Covenant) E/C.12/GC/17' (Committee on Economic, Social and Cultural Rights 2006).

civil law tradition through their Hispanic history of colonization; this will show an authors' based approach to copyright. The common law tradition, on the other hand, is related to protection based on the economic exploitation of the work, tradition that is shared by the UK and the US. Such legal traditions have shown some interactions that are interesting for comparative analysis. For instance, Mexico and Colombia have signed separated free trade agreements between them and with the US, these agreements include a component of copyright. In addition, Spain and the UK (to the date) are members of the European Union (EU); therefore, there are connections between the two systems through the EU Directives and their case law. Argentina has the oldest law in the region (dated 1954). While it maintains its structure, it has several reforms that added to and modified the original Law. Argentinian case law has had to adequate the interpretation of an old law to the context of a more recent Constitution in which the economic, social and cultural rights have been introduced.

17.2   COPYRIGHT LAWS ABOUT AUTHORSHIP FROM
            A FUNDAMENTAL RIGHTS PERSPECTIVE

Fundamental rights are often enacted as part of the constitutional charts of the countries. In the case of copyright, its constitutional assertion has been stated in two ways, as a mere property right within the concept of intellectual property, or as a complex right that involves the protection of author's interests and the protection of societal interests in accessing science and culture. Geiger proposes a similar division for the general concept of intellectual property, but splitting the latter into two separate branches, one following the Universal Declaration of Human Rights (hereinafter 'UDHR') by recognizing fundamental rights in the field of protecting the right to science and culture, and another constructed over the protection of freedom of expression.[7] However, as Geiger comments, this last is especially related to copyright. The distinction is relevant because it enables the possibility of understanding copyright in a more complex manner than mere property as it is related to other aspects of fundamental rights such as freedom of expression, dignity, privacy, and so on.

The first question to answer here would be about the position of copyright or author's rights in the scope of fundamental rights for the jurisdictions studied here. This would be only possible by understanding that the reference to author's rights is related to the protection of the person that has created the work and not to the right holder that has acquired the copyright by contracts or by the effect of the Law.

---

7. Christophe Geiger, 'Reconceptualizing the Constitutional Dimension of Intellectual Property' in Paul Torremans (ed), *Intellectual Property Law and Human Rights* (3d edn, Kluwer Law International 2015).

Authors exist because they propose expressions that add their own personal contribution to ideas in terms of originality. If the minds of authors prevail over machines and simple non-mindful efforts, and if a positive intention to produce a work is fundamental for the connection between the work and its authorship, also requiring some creation that, in fact, will separate the work from the mere idea, and if originality is a constant that is linked to the fact of human creation, then authorship is basically a matter of human individuals.[8]

Authorship becomes a promise in terms of fundamental rights. An author is not anyone, is a person who has created under the terms of originality a protectable work. Such protection comes in the form of a legal construction called copyright which is upheld on fundamental rights such as freedom of expression, free participation on the cultural life of society, freedom of creation, but also author's dignity. The complexity of such construction in the level of constitutional laws and fundamental rights will be explored in this section.

The study will show that beyond the mere economic interests represented in the protection of intellectual property as a fundamental right within constitutional laws, there are other fundamental rights immersed in the protection of author's rights related to culture and therefore to the very structure of societies as it is related to individual's freedoms and duties. Here it will be proposed that by the correlation between the concept of originality and the concept of authorship, as it has been proposed by Ginsburg,[9] the protection of the author in terms of her fundamental rights are to be taken into account when such rights seem under threat by action or omission of the rights holder of the work of such an author.

Differentiating the author from the rights holder of the copyright is relevant in terms of the fundamental rights each these subjects might be entitled of. It would support the idea of a possible prevalence for the protection of the moral and economic interests of the author over the protection of intellectual property as mere property. Given that most of the countries proposed here for study are members of the International Covenant on Economic Social and Cultural Rights (ICESCR),[10] in this regard is relevant the General Comment 17 from the Committee on Economic Social

---

8. The PhD Thesis from which this chapter derivate has a section related to examine the applicability of Gingsburg's principles for authorship from the comparative perspective studied there. *See*: David Felipe Alvarez Amezquita, 'Towards the Protection of Author's Moral and Material Interests through Copyright Laws. A Comparative Study' (University of Nottingham 2017) <http://eprints.nottingham.ac.uk/52552/>. Ginsburg proposes some important principles on which it is possible to support authorship based on human rationales. *See*: Jane C Ginsburg, 'The Concept of Authorship in Comparative Law' (2003) 52 DePaul Law Review 1063.

9. Ginsburg (n 8). p. 16.

10. The US has not *yet* ratified this Treaty, although it has signed it.

and Cultural Rights.[11] This document states the basic elements of protection of author's rights as present in Article 15.1.c of the ICESCR: First, the protection of author's moral interests is to ensure the link between the author and her work as a result of the expression of her personality. This has been explained here regarding the connection between authorship and originality. This protection regards the recognition as authors of the given work and the protection of its integrity in connection with the protection of the author's honour and reputation. Second, the protection of the author's material interests implies adequate remuneration, contributing to the right to an adequate standard of living. Finally, the Committee stresses that these rights contain the elements of availability, accessibility and quality of protection which entail the States responsibility of protection.

The second question to answer on this matter is how the comparative case law has constructed the relation between the author and the concept of originality within the constitutional protection of author's rights. Through this, it will be shown that the author's communicative and social powers are fundamental elements of copyright's constitutional protection.

17.2.1   THE CONSTITUTIONAL CLAUSES FOR COPYRIGHT

About how the countries under study in this research constitutionally enact the protection of copyright (or author's rights), four variables can be found.[12] Those variables are the absence of a constitutional provision, the constitutional provision in which the legislature is empowered to regulate copyright or intellectual property in general, the constitutional recognition of copyright or intellectual property as a singularized right, and the combination of programmatic and empowering clauses.

17.2.1.1   No Constitutional Provision

This is the case mentioned for the UK. This first variable is common for some European countries such as France, which do not have a constitutional clause for copyright or for intellectual property whatsoever. Dietz has identified some quasi-constitutional clauses that might be of consideration in some legislations.[13]

---

11. Committee on Economic Social and Cultural Rights (n 6).
12. The sources for this section, in the case of the Spanish speaking countries, have been consulted in its original language. In spite of possible fails in the translations, an English version of the constitutional texts referred here can be found in the following websites: www.constituteproject.org, or http://confinder.richmond.edu/. HeinOnLine provides an extensive database of world constitutions. Oxford University also provides full access to their database of constitutions of the world at: http://oxcon.ouplaw.com/.
13. Adolf Dietz, 'The Place of Copyright Law within the Hierarchy of Norms: The Constitutional Issue' in Pierre Sirinelli (ed), *Exploring the Sources of Copyright. ALAI 2005 Paris.* (ALAI 2005).

Nevertheless, in the case of the UK, according to Dietz, it is not possible to find a constitutional clause or even a quasi-constitutional clause in their copyright law (at least from the positive law perspective).[14] The old assertion enacted in the Statute of Anne which introduced the protection of authors and the protection of the public interest as the two basic elements commanding copyright laws[15] is no longer present in the British legal system, at least not within the statutes. The primary copyright British cases, *Millar v. Taylor* and *Donaldson v. Beckett*, support such an assertion and have been part of the case law and the doctrinal approaches about copyright since they were decided. It is possible to argue then, that these primary cases fix the main elements of UK's copyright.

17.2.1.2 Constitutional Provisions Empowering the Legislature

This was the case of the Spanish Constitution of 1931 in which the power to legislate on intellectual property was reserved to the State, and the duty of executing the law was situated in the hands of the autonomous regions.[16] None of the countries under study in this thesis uses this variable in their present systems. This variable is interesting, though, because it does not create or recognize a fundamental right by itself but enact a purpose that the legislature should develop. Nevertheless, the Colombian constitutional clause on intellectual property could be considered under this category: '*Article 61. The state will protect intellectual property for the relevant period using the means established by law.*' Due to its position among the list of other recognized fundamental rights, State's power to legislate about intellectual property acquires a qualified position as a right rather than a matter of mere definition of constitutional fora.

The Colombian Constitution protects copyright as part of intellectual property. The norm was introduced within the new Constitution for the Republic enacted in 1991. Its previous Constitution, from 1886, followed a tradition that came in 1858 when the literary property was recognized at the constitutional level for the first time in this country. The present Constitutional intellectual property clause has been repeatedly interpreted by the Colombian Constitutional Court as part of the constitutional bloc. On those

---

14. Dietz (n 13).
15. ' … for the encouragement of learned men to compose and write useful books … ' L Bently and M Kretschmer (eds.), 'Statute of Anne' <www.copyrighthistory.org>.
16. Article 15. Legislation [on the following subjects] is under the control of the Spanish state, and the execution may be under the control of the autonomous regions, to the extent of their political capacity, in the opinion of the Courts, on the following subjects: (…) Second. Legislation on intellectual and industrial property. Constitucion de la Republica Española 1931.

decisions, it has been stated that moral rights should be considered as fundamental rights and the economic rights are constitutionally protected.[17]

17.2.1.3 Constitutional Recognition as a Singularized Right

For instance, the Colombian 1886 constitutional clause stated this right as an extension of the property right: 'Literary and artistic property should be protected, as transferable property, for the life of the author and eighty more years, under the formalities established by the law.'[18] In other countries outside the scope of this study, the clause has been enacted as an independent right or in conjunction with other cultural rights.[19]

17.2.1.4 Combination of Programmatic and Empowering Clauses

The US constitutional clause is perhaps the best example of this possibility. It empowers Congress to legislate about the matter, and it states the purpose of such protection:[20] 'To promote the progress of science and useful arts by securing for limited Times to Authors and Inventors the exclusive Right to their respective Writings and Discoveries'.[21] In this type of clause, the persistence of the programmatic part is determinant in the interpretation of copyright law. However, the utilitarian approach commanding US's copyright laws might induce to think that there is some distance between protecting authors and protecting investments. Yet, the constitutional clause remains with a direct call for the protection of the author's interests and in some judicial cases, its application refers directly to their protection and the

---

17. For the concept of constitutional bloc and the development of Colombian Constitutional Court about intellectual property, *see*: Denis Borges Barbosa and Charlene de Avila Plaza, 'Intellectual Property in Decisions of Constitutional Courts in Latin American Countries' in Christophe Geiger (ed), *Research Handbook on Human Rights and Intellectual Property* (Edward Elgar Publishing 2015). The concept refers to the elements of the legal system that even if not mentioned in the constitution are part of it.
18. Constitucion de la Republica de Colombia 1886. Article 35. The 1886 text protected author's rights as literary property for eighty years in a separately manner from the protection of other types of intellectual property which were enacted as part of the presidential powers.
19. The Peruvian Constitution is an example of such clause: 'Article 2: Every person has the right: (...) 8. To freedom of intellectual, artistic, technical, and scientific creation, as well as to ownership of such creations and to any benefits derived from them. The State promotes access to culture and encourages its development and dissemination.'
20. Melville B Nimmer and David Nimmer, *Nimmer on Copyright* (Matthew Bender 2003). *See also*: Dietz (n 13).
21. United States Constitution, Article I, section 8. *See*: United States Copyright Office, *Copyright Law of the United States of America and Related Laws Contained in Title 17 of the United States Code. Circular 92.* (Library of Congress 2011) <www.copyright-.gov>.

implications on a culture that this has. The *Burrow-Giles* case[22] is a good example of such rationales.

However, this is not the only case, Argentina, Spain and Mexico have also introduced both formal and programmatic clauses even if they did it in a separate manner:

Argentinian 1994 Constitution:[23]

Article 17. Property is inviolable, and no inhabitant of the Nation can be deprived thereof except by virtue of a judgment supported by law. Expropriation for reasons of public utility must be authorized by law and previously indemnified. Congress alone imposes the taxes mentioned in Article 4. No personal service can be required except by virtue of a law or a judgment supported by law. Every author or inventor is the exclusive owner of his work, invention or discovery for the term granted him by law. The confiscation of property is stricken out forever from the Argentine Penal Code. No armed body may make requisitions, or demand assistance of any kind.

(...)

Article 75.

The Congress shall have power: (...)

19. (...)

To enact laws which protect cultural identity and pluralism, the unrestrained creation and circulation of the works of authors, the artistic heritage, and cultural and audiovisual spaces.

Spanish 1978 Constitution:

Section 20. 1. The following rights are recognized and protected: a. the right to freely express and spread thoughts, ideas and opinions through words, in writing or by any other means of reproduction. b. the right to literary, artistic, scientific and technical production and creation. c. the right to academic freedom. d. the right to freely communicate or receive truthful information by any means of dissemination whatsoever. The law shall regulate the right to the clause of conscience and professional secrecy in the exercise of these freedoms. 2. The exercise of these rights may not be restricted by any form of prior censorship. (...)

Section 149. (...)

---

22. *Burrow-Giles Lithographic Co v. Sarony* (1884) 111 US. *See also*: *Feist Publications v. Rural Telephone Service* (1991) 499 US 340., *Bleistein v. Donaldson Lithographing Co* (1903) 188 US., and *Eldred v. Ashcroft* 537 U. S.(2003).

23. Argentinian Constitution has been reformed in 1949 and in 1994. In spite of that, Article 17 has not been changed since 1853. The coherence between the programmatic part of the Argentinian constitutional clause and the effective protection of copyright has been asserted by the Argentinian judiciary in *Sentencia Sociedad Argentina de Autores y Compositores (Sadaic) C/ Crazy Confiteria S/ Recurso de Inconstitucionalidad (AST260P305).*

1. The State shall have exclusive competence over the following matters: (...)

9th. Legislation on copyright and industrial property.

Mexican 1917 Constitution:

Article 28. In the United Mexican States, all monopolies, monopoly practices, state monopolies and tax exemptions are prohibited. Protectionist policies are also prohibited. (...)

Privileges granted for a given period of time to authors and artists for them to produce their pieces of work and to inventors and those individuals who improve inventions will not be considered monopolies. (...)

Article 73:

The Congress shall have the power to: (...)

XXV. (...) legislate on copyright and other issues of intellectual property issues related to the same.

The examination of the different constitutional clauses regarding the protection of copyright from the countries mentioned above and the other Latin American countries shows that that either as a separated right or as part of the general protection for intellectual property, with the exception of Cuba, in almost all Latin American countries, copyright is constitutionally protected. Moreover, in some cases, constitutions include international instruments protecting human rights as part of its structure. That is the case of Colombian Constitution, in which Article 93 introduces the '[i]nternational treaties and agreements ratified by Congress that recognize human rights and prohibit the limitation of such rights in states of emergency' and therefore are part of the Constitution: 'The rights and duties mentioned in this Charter shall be interpreted in accordance with international treaties on human rights ratified by Colombia' the article continues.[24] That implies that

---

24. The Mexican Constitution shows a similar reference to the human rights treaties: 'Article 1: In the United Mexican States, all individuals shall be entitled to the human rights granted by this Constitution and the international treaties signed by the Mexican State, as well as to the guarantees for the protection of these rights. Such human rights shall not be restricted or suspended, except for the cases and under the conditions established by this Constitution itself.

The provisions relating to human rights shall be interpreted according to this Constitution and the international treaties on the subject, working in favour of the broader protection of people at all times.

All authorities, in their areas of competence, are obliged to promote, respect, protect and guarantee Human Rights, in accordance with the principles of universality, interdependence, indivisibility and progressiveness. As a consequence, the State must prevent, investigate, penalize and rectify violations to Human Rights, according to the law.'

The Argentinian Constitution expressively recognizes the constitutional character of certain human right treaties: 'The following [international instruments], under the conditions under which they are in force, stand on the same level as the Constitution, [but] do not repeal any article in the First Part of this Constitution, and must be understood as

in this case, as in the case of most of the American countries, the obligations from the UDHR (Article 27), the ICESCR (Article 15) and the American Declaration of Rights and Duties of Man (ADRDM) (Article 13) have direct application as part of the fundamental rights of these nations.

European law requires special mention. The question of whether the Treaty on the European Union (TEU) includes the protection of fundamental rights and in which manner, has been assessed by scholars such as Craig & de Burca[25] and Chalmers, Davies & Monti.[26] According to them, the EU Charter and the European Convention on Human Rights (ECHR) are part of the sources of the European Law, but its interpretation is subject to certain limitations in the case of the Charter as established in its Title VII.[27] European law, however, does protect copyright, particularly by the European Charter of Fundamental Rights through the protection of intellectual property as a type of property. This is one of the main conclusions expressed by Geiger in his article about the constitutionalization of copyright.[28]

---

complementary of the rights and guarantees recognized therein: The American Declaration of the Rights and Duties of Man; the Universal Declaration of Human Rights; the American Convention on Human Rights; the International Covenant on Economic, Social and Cultural Rights; the International Covenant on Civil and Political Rights and its Optional Protocol; the [International] Convention on the Prevention and Punishment of Genocide; the International Convention on the Elimination of all Forms of Racial Discrimination; the Convention on the Elimination of All Forms of Discrimination Against Women; the Convention Against Torture and other Cruel, Inhumane or Degrading Treatment or Punishment; and the Convention on the Rights of the Child. They may only be denounced, if such is to be the case, by the National Executive Power, after prior approval by two thirds of the totality of the members of each Chamber.'

Spain also introduces the supremacy of such treaties within their constitution: 'Part I. Fundamental Rights and Duties, Section 10: (...) 2. Provisions relating to the fundamental rights and liberties recognized by the Constitution shall be construed in conformity with the Universal Declaration of Human Rights and international treaties and agreements thereon ratified by Spain.'

25. Paul Craig and Grainne de Burca, *EU Law. Text, Cases, and Materials* (6th edn, Oxford University Press 2015).

26. Damian Chalmers, Gareth Davies and Giorgio Monti, *European Union Law* (3rd edn, Cambridge University Press 2014).

27. *See also* Geiger's recently published new version of the previously cited article: Geiger, 'Reconceptualizing the Constitutional Dimension of Intellectual Property' (n 7).

28. Christophe Geiger, '"Constitutionalising" Intellectual Property Law? The Influence of Fundamental Rights on Intellectual Property in the European Union' in Laurence R Helfer (ed), *Intellectual Property and Human Rights* (Edward Elgar Publishing 2013). Also: Christophe Geiger, 'Implementing Intellectual Property Provisions in Human Rights Instruments: Towards a New Social Contract for the Protection of Intangibles' in Christophe Geiger (ed), *Research Handbook on Human Rights and Intellectual Property* (Edward Elgar Publishing 2015). pp. 669-671. Recent advances from the CJEU decisions has been studied by Geiger and Izumenko. *See*: Christophe Geiger and Elena Izyumenko, 'The Constitutionalization of Intellectual Property Law in the EU and the Funke Medien, Pelham and Spiegel Online Decisions of the CJEU: Progress, but Still Some Way to Go!'

The matter is important because the Charter introduces intellectual property as a right within the general protection of property, while the ECHR does not, at least in express. The other source recognized by the TEU is the general principles of law, which are directly connected with two other sources, first and more important is the constitutional traditions of the members, which is relevant regarding the Spanish Constitution in this case. The second, according to Craig & de Burca, extends the general principles of law to the international treaties ' ... on which the Member States have collaborated or of which they are signatories' as guidelines to be followed within the EU Communitarian Law.[29] Consequently, it is possible to assert that copyright within the EU Charter and the ECHR is protected as a fundamental right. For example, in the Spanish constitution. European case law supports such an assertion also.

However, it is possible to apply the distinction the Court of Justice of the European Union (CJEU) has identified between the essential function of copyright and the scope of copyright. Such a distinction is relevant for the analysis in question here, that is, how programmatic can be understood the protection of copyright as a fundamental right towards the promotion of the communicative rationality of a given society. The discussion about to which extent copyright can satisfy the collective interests of society pertains to the scope of copyright and its limitations. Principles such as the no protection of ideas, the duration of the exclusive rights, or the limitations and exceptions to copyright moderate the interaction between interests collective and private. On the other hand, the essential function of copyright, which is 'to protect the moral rights in the work and ensure a reward for creative effort',[30] refers to those cases in which copyright and freedom of expression interact in what is referred to the interests of creators.[31] While the scope of copyright

---

(2019) IIC – International Review of Intellectual Property and Competition Law <http://link.springer.com/10.1007/s40319-019-00901-1>.

29. Craig and de Burca (n 25). p. 385.

30. *See Joined Cases C-241-242/91 P Radio Telefís Eireann and another v. European Commission (Intellectual Property Owners Inc and another intervening)*. *See also*: *Case C-275/06 Productores de Música de España (Promusicae) v. Telefónica de España SAU*. In *Promusicae*, the Court accepts the principle according to which 'The balance between the relevant fundamental rights must first be struck by the Community legislature and, in the interpretation of Community law, by the court. However, the Member States are also obliged to observe it when using up any remaining margin for regulation in the implementation of directives. Moreover, the authorities and courts of the Member States are not only required to interpret their national law in conformity with the Data Protection Directives, but also to ensure that they do not act on the basis of an interpretation of those directives which conflicts with the fundamental rights protected by the Community legal order or the other general principles of Community law'.

31. This perspective differs from the assessment of possible conflict between copyright and freedom of expression as, for example, in: Christophe Geiger and Elena Izyumenko, 'Copyright on the Human Rights' Trial: Redefining the Boundaries of Exclusivity Through Freedom of Expression' (2014) 45 IIC – International Review of Intellectual

points towards society, its essential function points to the creator himself and his rights and freedoms.[32]

In addition, the CJEU in the *Laserdisken* case has also made references to the TEU's Article 167 (former 151) which enacted the protection of culture as a principle within the EU. Such principle supports in part the Directive 2001/29, particularly regarding its recital 12th.[33] According to the CJEU, 'any harmonisation of copyright and related rights must take as a basis a high level of protection since such rights are crucial to intellectual creation and a rigorous, effective system for their protection is one of the main ways of ensuring that European cultural creativity and production receive the necessary resources and of safeguarding the independence and dignity of artistic creators and performers'.[34]

Property and Competition Law 316 <http://link.springer.com/10.1007/s40319-014-0181-3>. A recent decision on this matter from the CJEU confirms that it is even possible to consider by the courts that the exercise of freedom of expression, in particular freedom of the arts, must be protected as it 'affords the opportunity to take part in the public exchange of cultural, political and social information and ideas of all kinds' seeking to strike a balance between both the interests of the copyright owner and the user (who eventually will be entitled of a new copyright because of the exercise of such freedom). *Case C-476/2017 Pelham GmbH, Moses Pelham, Martin Haas v. Ralf Hütter, Florian Schneider-Esleben.*

32. Another recent case shows the other side of the coin related to the interaction between copyright and human rights. In *Funke Medien*, the CJEU acknowledges the priority of defining whether the content in question was a copyrightable material at all in order to then study if its publication under the protection of freedom of expression would affect any copyright at all. The matter of originality impacted the constitutional debate directly because the content in question was delicate information related to German troops from reports of which was questioned if in any case was possible to find any level of originality to then find rights to protect against freedom of expression. *See: Case C-469/2017 Funke Medien NRW GmbH v. Bundesrepublik Deutschland.*

33. *Case C-479/04 Laserdisken ApS v. Kulturministeriet (EC)* 549. The recital reads as follows: 'Adequate protection of copyright works and subject matter of related rights is also of great importance from a cultural standpoint. Article 151 of the Treaty requires the Community to take cultural aspects into account in its action.' Parliament and Council Directive 2001/29/EC of 22 May 2001 on the harmonisation of certain aspects of copyright and related rights in the information society [2001] OJ L167/10.

34. *Case C-479/04 Laserdisken ApS v. Kulturministeriet (EC)* 549 (n 33). At 75. Other cases have emphasised other areas of connection between the protection of copyrights as property and other fundamental rights. That is the *Metronome Musik* case in which the role of the free market of ideas have been also assessed as relevant for the purpose of the essential function of copyright. *See Case C-200/96 Metronome Musik v. Music Point Hokamp* (1998) I 1971. Paragraphs 22-24. *See also Case C-306/05 Sociedad General de Autores y Editores de España (SGAE) v. Rafael Hoteles SA* [2007] IP & T 521. At 67, in which it has been asserted that the expected remuneration for the communication to the public of a work is not related to the actual enjoyment of the work but to the legal possibility of enjoyment of such a work. The protection of privacy does not affect such a principle in the case of hotel rooms, as the potential enjoyment of works have been made possible by the Hotel not the costumer. Other cases have recognised that other fundamental rights can be restricted only in the case in which it is justified for the purpose of protecting the public interest. Under such idea, it has been considered that the essential

In sum, these findings taken together suggest a role for the constitutional clauses in the protection of copyright. However, it is important to consider that the mere introduction of copyright clauses of any kind within the constitutions of the states does not necessarily mean the recognition of such right as a fundamental right. Quite often, these rights along with others have been categorized as part of the second generation of human rights, those of which require the positive action of the State in its protection because they concern social, cultural and economic interests.[35] According to Osiatynski, the general theory about human rights differentiates between the classical human rights in which the protection is negative, safeguarding the individual from state's intrusion, and the social, cultural and economic rights, in which case the State should intervene to fulfil the aim proposed.[36] Even so, such an approach has been superseded as both kinds of rights require limitations and positive actions from the State. However, says Osiatynski, there is a subtle difference between the two: traditional rights require the 'creation of a general mechanism which facilitates the implementation of rights', while the second generation of rights implies the entitlement of a particular benefit by which resources are redistributed and allocated.

In terms of what Osiatynski has identified as a characteristic of social rights, would copyright implicate the transfer of resources from one individual to another? Such a transference was discussed in the very beginning of copyright. The *Millar v. Taylor* and *Donaldson v. Beckett* UK cases, the US case of *Wheaton v. Peters* and the French doctrinal discussion about the 'sacred' literary property, all of them have in common the indication according to which something should be left in the hands of the audience when the work has been published. The action of publishing implies the transference of certain resources from the individual control of the author to the audience. This is consistent with the idea of active access and participation in the cultural life of societies, the concept of a free market of knowledge and the availability of 'raw material' for ulterior creations.[37] However, knowledge is transferred, but copyright, as an asset, is not. That

---

function of copyright is of public interest. *See*, for example, *Joined Cases C-403/08 Football Association Premier League Ltd and Others v. QC Leisure and Others and C-429/08 Karen Murphy v. Media Protection Services Ltd.*

35. *See also*: Geiger, 'Implementing Intellectual Property Provisions in Human Rights Instruments: Towards a New Social Contract for the Protection of Intangibles' (n 28).

36. Wiktor Osiatynski, 'Social and Economic Rights in a New Constitution for Poland' in Andras Sajo (ed), *Western Rights? Post-Communist Application* (Kluwer Law International 1996). Cited by: Vicki C Jackson and Mark Tushnet, *Comparative Constitutional Law* (Foundation Press 1999). pp. 1486, 1487.

37. The two decisions from 2019 mentioned above, both related to freedom of expression, can show the importance of such structure. Either the content is not a protected work (as it should be assessed in *Funke Medien*) and it can be published without any copyright in the middle granting full access as it would be mere information not qualified with originality, or the use of the protected material (phonogram in the *Pelham* case) is of the kind that would not show in the result the origin of the extracted part (sampling).

creates a tension between the proprietary interests and the collective interests that copyright should be able to answer too. The complexities in such a balance have been studied widely by academics.[38]

As such, this would be sufficient enough to understand that even without its express manifestation, author's rights would have been considered as a fundamental element in the structure of the state. That would be the case for the US. Osiatynski's line of argumentation is a good example of such an assertion. After discussing in what extent the provisions for the protection of social and economic rights should be or not included within the post-communist constitutions, he concludes that the 'freedom of creative activities and scientific research, including the publication of results as well as the autonomy of academia, belong to the freedom of thought and expression'.[39] Consequently, the rights related to such freedom should be included in the constitutions with full protection.

Is the protection of authors' moral and material interest an aspect of such a core element of freedom of thought and freedom of expression as stressed by Osiatynski? The hinge between copyright and freedom of expression has been an aspect of wide analysis in the literature.[40] Often the case law and the scholars recognize the interaction of the two rights in a common level of fundamental rights. However, not so often they acknowledge the interaction between them both in a level of complementarity.

From such a level of complementarity, it is possible to argue that the mere constitutional introduction of copyright within the competences of the legislative branch is not enough in the case of copyright. Even in the case of hard approaches, like Osiatynski's thesis by which some of the social and economic rights do not require a constitutional assertion and should be left subjected to the competence of the legislature, in any case, copyright, due to its implications for freedom of expression should be considered beyond the proprietary reduction. The next part of this section will examine the mechanism by which the expression of the author has been asserted as an element of the constitutional protection of author's rights through the use of the concept of originality regarding the author.

---

38. *See,* for example, some of the articles published in these books: Lawrence R Helfer and Graeme W Austin, *Human Rights and Intellectual Property. Mapping the Global Interface* (Cambridge University Press 2011); Lawrence R Helfer, *Intellectual Property and Human Rights* (Lawrence R Helfer ed, Edward Elgar Publishing 2013); Paul Torremans, *Intellectual Property and Human Rights* (Paul Torremans ed, Kluwer Law International 2015); Christophe Geiger, *Research Handbook on Human Rights and Intellectual Property* (Christophe Geiger ed, Edward Elgar Publishing 2015) <http://www.elgaronline.com/view/9781783472413.xml>; Geiger and Izyumenko (n 28).
39. Osiatynski (n 36).
40. David Felipe Alvarez Amezquita, 'La Libertad de Expresión Como Resultado y Garantía Principal Del Derecho de Autor' (2007) 1 Revista Iberoamericana de Derecho de Autor.

17.2.2   THE CONNECTION BETWEEN AUTHORSHIP AND ORIGINALITY FROM A CONSTITUTIONAL PERSPECTIVE

The previous section in this piece has mentioned Ginsburg's six principles related to the concept of authorship. One of such principles, the one to stress here, is the apparent synonymy between the concept of authorship and the concept of originality. It will be studied here how the concept of originality, understood as the author's personal contribution, is immersed in the justification of protecting the author's rights as a fundamental right. Nevertheless, this is not a discussion about the concept of originality and its development, but a discussion of its position as a core element in the constitutional protection of the author's moral and material interests.

The concept of the author under the legislation studied in this work relates the act of creation, the product of such a creation, and the doer of such an action. The different approaches the legislations of the countries under study have adopted regarding the concept of author and authorship show that these concepts are attached to the natural or physical person who creates the work.[41] It can also be seen that the concept was not defined in previous legislations and it was introduced near to the date of US's adhesion to the Berne Convention in 1989. For example, in the case of the UK, the concept of the author was defined latter in the UK Copyright, Designs and Patents Act (1988) as the person who creates the work. Similar provisions have been adopted by other countries under study. That is the case of Colombia through the Andean legislation (1993), Spain (1987), and Mexico (1996). Nevertheless, the US's Copyright Act has a complex provision (section 101) in which the concept of an author is interlinked with the act of creation and the fixation of the work in a tangible form. In the case of Europe, only one of the European Directives on copyright identifies the author as the natural person who has created the work, in this case, the software.[42] The only exception, in

---

41. The author is defined as the person who creates the work (UK, section 9, Copyright, Designs and Patents Act 1988.); the physical person who has produced the intellectual creation (Colombia, Article 3, Law No. 23 – On Copyright 1982.); the first IP right holder (Argentina, Article 4); the natural person who has created the literary or artistic work (Spain, Article 5, Royal Legislative Decree No. 1/1996 of 12 April 1996. Consolidated text of the Law on [Copyright], regularizing, clarifying and harmonizing the Applicable Statutory Provisions 1996.); the natural person who has created the literary or artistic work (Mexico, Article 12, Federal Copyright Law, 1996 1996.). For the Argentinian copyright law *see* Leo G Koepfle, 'Copyright Protection Throughout the World. Part III The American Republics. Argentina.' in Guerra Everett (ed), *Industrial Property Bulletin*, vol III (The Division of Commercial Laws, Department of Commerce 1936). Although there is not a legal definition of the author in the US's Copyright Act, the concept is used often throughout the Act in relation with the concept of authorship and originality. For instance, sections 102 and 103 refers to the author and the originality in the case of works and in particular in the case of compilations or derivative works. *See* United States Copyright Office (n 21).
42. Parliament and Council Directive 2009/24/EC of 23 April 2009 on the legal protection of computer programs (Codified version) [2009] OJ L 111/16.

this case, is the Argentinian legislation which keeps the structure of the pre-war laws in which the concept of an author is not expressed but assumed as the initial owner of the work.

Potentially, any individual could be considered as an author under the studied jurisdictions. Once legal requirements are met, authorship rises as a consequence of human creativity in terms of what the concept of originality has been developed. Other kinds of authorships, e.g., corporative, would be considered a legal fiction towards the protection of economic interests. Thus, authorship is related to originality, and such requirement has a constitutional status or is attached to the constitutional protection of author's rights. The reason for this is that fostering creativity is an ultimate interest to promote the free participation of individuals in the cultural life of society, but also, and rather consequently because there is also a broader interest in fostering freedom of expression and therefore democracy. Those three elements (fostering creativity and freedom of expression and democracy) are often present in the decisions regarding the question of originality in the constitutional level of discussion and regarding the question of justifying of copyright.[43]

Is freedom of expression (and freedom of creation) a condition for originality? Does the lack of freedom minimize the author's creation? Such questions will be analysed in this section based on the comparative approach to the case law from the countries under study regarding their constitutional clauses or the absence of them. It will pay attention to the stream by which originality and the concept of authorship are connected, and a relationship between the author's communicative power and the concept of authorship can be found.[44]

---

43. A long examination of such decision has been made within the PhD Thesis from which this chapter has been extracted. *See*: Alvarez Amezquita, 'Towards the Protection of Author's Moral and Material Interests through Copyright Laws. A Comparative Study' (n 8).

44. The concept of communicative power has been drawn from Habermas who describes it as a motivating force which is capable of ' ... mobilizing citizens' communicative freedom for the formation of political beliefs that in turn influence the production of legitimate law, illocutionary obligations of this sort build up into a potential that holders of administrative power should not ignore'. Jürgen Habermas, *Between Facts and Norms* (Polity Press 1996). 147-148. Such a motivating force can be a copyrighted work. The original expression that an individual creates responds to such a characteristic. It comprehends both an idea and the original expression of such an idea. While the idea is not protected in terms of copyright, the expression could be protected as far as it complies with the requirements of originality. The importance of such a protection is that it responds to the intention of fostering individuals into creating other works, stimulating the exchange of ideas in the market of knowledge, improving the diversification of opinions, or in terms of communicative power, producing diverse sources of motivating forces, in the shape of cultural expressions. In this sense, an author's freedom is attached firmly to her position in society with the ability to participate through her creations in the rationality-producing communicative power, that is, by promoting consensus towards

17.2.2.1 The United Kingdom

In the case of the UK, due to the absence of Constitutional norms for copyright, the references to these elements, authorship, creativity and freedom of expression are not evident. The closer reference to the elements of creativity, freedom of expression in terms of originality and the concept of authorship can be found in at least two recent decisions: *Ray* and *Sawkins*.

That originality implies an expression and not a mere idea is common ground in the case law. This matter has been emphasized in the previous section of this chapter. However, such an expression should be an expression of thought and should be originated from the author, but also such an expression should be free. The *Sawkins'* Court has asserted this last element of freedom as a tool to assess claimant's authorship regarding his participation in the reconstruction of certain pieces of sheet music.[45] In fact, for Justice Patten, the effect of recognizing authorship was the result of the amount of freedom Mr Sawkins enjoyed when composing the missing elements of Lalande's work (an eighteenth-century French composer whose music was reconstructed by the claimant).[46]

The *Ray* case, on the other hand, shows that the test of originality recalls the author's responsibility for her own writings. In this case, the question of joint authorship leads to the question of what elements constitute authorship. The basic answer was the provision of significant input, but also that the co-author shares the direct responsibility for the expression in the way it was created.[47] If the author is responsible for his creation is because she has created freely and her creative decisions produced such a responsibility. In the absence of freedom, the responsibility would follow another path towards whoever has commanded such action.

Thus, these elements are present since the precursory cases of *Millar v. Taylor* and *Donaldson v. Beckett*. For the first one, in Lord Mansfield's opinion, is a matter of justice that the author exercises his right to decide whether to publish or not his work.[48] Once the work is published, the author loses his control over it: the public benefits of it and the law become the mechanism by which the author can control, for a limited time, if the work can be copied or published. In *Donaldson,* the structural principle of copyright by which the expression is protected but not the ideas is crucial in understanding the implications for freedom of expression that copyright can create.[49]

---

some interests. Alvarez Amezquita, 'Towards the Protection of Author's Moral and Material Interests through Copyright Laws. A Comparative Study' (n 8).

45. *Sawkins v. Hyperion Records Ltd* (2004) 418. At 439.
46. *Sawkins v. Hyperion Records Ltd* (n 45). At 430.
47. *Ray v. Classic FM plc* (1998) (D) 105. *See also: Brighton and another v. Jones* 247.
48. *Millar v. Taylor* 2303. At 2398.
49. *Donaldson v. Beckett* (1774) 1 Harv L Rev 953.

The following quote would serve the purpose of demonstrating the above:

> The resemblance holds only in this. As by the communication of an invention in trade, manufacture or machines, men are taught the art or science, they have a right to use it; so all the knowledge, which can be acquired from the contents of a book, is free for every man's use: if it teaches mathematics, physic, husbandry; if it teaches to write in verse or prose; if, by reading an epic poem, a man learns to make an epic poem of his own; he is at liberty.
> But printing is a trade or manufacture. The types and press are the mechanical instruments: the literary composition is as the material; which always is property. The book conveys knowledge, instruction, or entertainment: but multiplying copies in print is a quite distinct thing from all the book communicates. And there is no incongruity, to reserve that right; and yet convey the free use of all the book teaches.[50]

In conclusion, even if the UK does not state an evident correlation between copyright and freedom of expression, the elements of creativity, freedom, and responsibility over the creation of the work, and the implications for the dissemination of ideas that copyright has, are elements that have been considered under UK's case law.

Two elements can be highlighted in the decisions mentioned. First, freedom of expression, which regards not only the interests of access to knowledge but also the interests of publishing and dissemination of thoughts. The second element comprises the protection of proprietary interests provided *ab initio* discursively for the author, though extended more or less to third parties such as producers, publishers and other persons. Had these elements a constitutional recognition? Probably not, but this is a consequence of the peculiarities of the British system, and it should not undermine the importance of them within the British system of laws.

17.2.2.2   The United States of America

The next country to consider is the US. The first thing to establish is the scope of the concept of the author. For this purpose, four cases will be mentioned: The *Burrow-Giles*, the *Aalmuhamed*, the *Publications International* and the *Feist* cases.[51]

The US case of *Feist Publications v. Rural Telephone Service* asserts that the primary constitutional objective of copyright was stated in order to balance the weight given so far in the US tradition to the effort disregarding the amount the creativity of work. Even if it might seem unfair that the data

---

50. *Millar v. Taylor* (n 48). At 2331.
51. Another case regarding the constitutionality of the originality requirement was mentioned previously in section II. *See*: *Feist Publications v. Rural Telephone Service* (n 22).

gathered by the effort and economic investment of someone would be freely used, said the Court, copyright's primary objective is not to compensate such an investment: 'copyright is not to reward the labor of authors, but "to promote the Progress of Science and useful Arts."'[52] Instead, it gives weight to the public interest by stating that free access to enough raw material required for the free dissemination of ideas should be guaranteed.

In *Feist*, what is required is a 'minimal degree of creativity', or, what Justice O'Connor recognizes, quoting the *Burrow-Giles* case, as 'the existence of intellectual production, of thought, and conception'. Not gaining such a threshold means no copyright protection.[53] In this case, it has been analysed that the originality threshold serves the purpose of the US Constitutional clause. Justice O'Connor criticizes previous cases in which the prevalence of the principle of the 'sweat of the brow' has gone too far and states that the '"[s]weat of the brow" courts thereby eschewed the most fundamental axiom of copyright law – that no one may copyright facts or ideas.'[54]

In the *Burrow-Giles* case, the Supreme Court analysed the constitutional meaning of the concept of author and considered that it should be widened to other expressions and not only the mere authorship of writings as it was mentioned in the original text of the Constitution. The Court asserted that, according to the Constitution, 'the author' refers to "he to whom anything owes its origin; originator; maker; one who completes a work of science or literature.',[55] therefore, the author is entitled of the exclusive right to the production of his own genius or intellect.

In *Aalmuhamed,* the Court for the 9th Circuit narrowed the concept of the author in order to avoid the introduction of other contributors who might not have participated in the creation as such: 'Progress would be retarded rather than promoted, if an author could not consult with others and adopt their useful suggestions without sacrificing sole ownership of the work. Too open a definition of the author would compel authors to insulate themselves and maintain ignorance of the contributions others might make.'[56] Therefore, a concept of 'author' based on the principle of no protection of ideas also serves to the constitutional mandate of promoting the arts and sciences, and it would be based on communicative rationality of exchange of ideas. In this case, Spike Lee used claimant's advice in his film *Malcolm X*, but such

---

52. *Feist Publications v. Rural Telephone Service* (n 22). Section II.A.
53. *See also*: *Miller v. Universal City Studios, Inc* (1981) 650F.2d 13.
54. *Feist Publications v. Rural Telephone Service* (n 22). Section III.
55. *Burrow-Giles Lithographic Co. v. Sarony* (n 22). In fact, this case connects such rationalization to the English case, *Millar v. Taylor,* asserting that copyright is 'the exclusive right of a man to the production of his own genius or intellect'.
56. *Aalmuhammed v. Lee* (2000) 202F.3d 12. *See also*: *Burrow-Giles Lithographic Co. v. Sarony* (n 22). In fact, this case connects such rationalisation to the English case, *Millar v. Taylor* (1769) 98 ER 201, asserting that copyright is 'the exclusive right of a man to the production of his own genius or intellect'.

advice could not reach the threshold of creativity and originality required constitutionally for copyright protection, and consequently, Mr Aalmuhamed could not be considered by the Court as the author in the film.

In the previous case of *Publications International,* the Court of Appeals for the Seventh Circuit specifies that promoting the progress of science and art is possible by 'allowing others to build upon ideas or information', but the exclusive rights created by Congress 'shall accrue only to "Authors and Inventors" with respect to their "Writings and Discoveries"'. Given that the Constitutional requirement of copyright is originality, explained by Justice Kanne in this case as a 'minimum of creativity', then, if not present, there would not be authorship according to the Constitution.[57]

The author then is the originator of the work. However, a narrow definition of the author should avoid the inclusion of contributors who do not have decision power (communicative power) in the final creation at least with a minimum amount of own creation.

The second element to be considered in the US case law is the connection between the author's creativity and freedom of expression. In *Eldred v. Ashcroft,* the double purpose of the constitutional clause by which the function of copyright is to promote the useful arts and sciences and also to promote the creation and publication of free expressions has been asserted. The Court highlighted: 'The Copyright Clause and First Amendment were adopted close in time. This proximity indicates that, in the Framers' view, copyright's limited monopolies are compatible with free speech principles. Indeed, copyright's purpose is to *promote* the creation and publication of free expression.'[58]

This double purpose of the Constitutional clause in the US has also been asserted more directly by the 5th Circuit in *Miller v. Universal Studios.* In this case, the discussion refers to the protection or not of facts or ideas. The Court addressed such a discussion by interpreting the constitutional clause and stated that the difference between not protecting facts and protecting expressions is important for the purpose of balancing the interest of stimulating creativity and people's 'need for unrestrained access to information'.[59] 'The line drawn between uncopyrightable facts and copyrightable expression of facts serves an important purpose in copyright law. It provides a means of balancing the public's interest in stimulating creative activity, as embodied in the Copyright Clause, against the public's need for unrestrained access to information. It allows a subsequent author to build upon and add to prior accomplishments without unnecessary duplication of effort' (at 24).

---

57. *Publications International, Limited v. Meredith Corporation* 88 F3d 473 (7th Cir 1996).
58. *Eric Eldred et al. v. John D Ashcroft* 537 US (2003) 32. *See: Feist Publications v. Rural Telephone Service* (n 22). Also: *Bleistein v. Donaldson Lithographing Co.* (n 22).
59. *Miller v. Universal City Studios, Inc.* (n 53). Also *see: Publications International, Limited v. Meredith Corporation* 88 F.3d 473 (7th Cir. 1996) (n 57).

That the elements mentioned above are present in the US's constitutional framework has also been stated in the *Eldred* case. In this case, the Court has asserted the double purpose of the constitutional clause by connecting Article 1, section 8 and the First Amendment:[60] First, because 'copyright gives the holder no monopoly on any knowledge.' Second, because '[a] reader of an author's writing may make full use of any fact or idea she acquires from her reading'. And finally, because (quoting Harper & Row), 'the Framers intended copyright itself to be the engine of free expression. By establishing a marketable right to the use of one's expression, copyright supplies the economic incentive to create and disseminate ideas'. Moreover, the Court in *Eldred* recognized some 'built-in First amendment accommodations': The principle of no protection of ideas, and the fair use doctrine.

The case law shows that copyright within the US system cannot be treated in the same manner as any other property. An author's property over his work differs from the property that any other person might have over it. This is because the protection of the author's rights might imply the protection of their property, but such protection also responds to rationales that are distant from the mere economic interest and include fostering creativity, the protection of freedom of expression, and democracy.[61] A good example of this might be seen in the *Trademark Cases* in which the US's Constitutional level of protection for trademarks was distinguished from the constitutional copyright clause.[62] In this case, the Supreme Court found that the protection of trademarks does not correspond with the copyright Constitutional clause but with the commerce clause. Such a distinction is important because without changing the proprietary nature of both rights (trademarks and copyright), the US's Court was able to differentiate the origin of each right and the aims to which each clause responds.

17.2.2.3   Europe

The only existing definition of authorship in the European legislation is found on the Directive referred to software.[63] Paradoxically, some authors would consider the production of software as the antinomy of authorship, for the author's expression of personality might be difficult to support in these kinds of works.[64] The extension of how copyright participates within the concept of originality in fostering freedom of expression can be traced through the case law from the CJEU.

---

60. *Eric Eldred et al. v. John D. Ashcroft* 537 U.S. (2003) (n 58). At III.
61. *See,* for example: *Harper & Row v. Nation Enterprises* (1985) 471, 539.
62. *Trademark Cases 100 US 82 (1879).*
63. Article 2.1. Parliament and Council Directive 2009/24/EC of 23 April 2009 on the legal protection of computer programs (Codified version) [2009] OJ L 111/16.
64. Geiger, 'Reconceptualizing the Constitutional Dimension of Intellectual Property' (n 7). p. 125.

Within this framework, the application of elements protecting the author's moral and material interests in the discourse of fostering freedom of expression can be rich. Some cases are to be highlighted here regarding this matter.

In *Painer v. Standard VerlagsGmbH*, the Austrian Court requested the CJEU's opinion about the application of the ECHR and the EU Charter regarding the equality of protecting photographs within the Directive 2001/29. The CJEU, without referring to any of those two Human Rights instruments, recognized that the protection of copyright is subject to the concept of originality as a result of the author's expression of personality. Therefore, every expression that reaches the originality threshold should be protected equally as a copyrighted work. The Court considered the threshold of originality in terms of freedom of creativity. It argued that the degree of creative freedom that an author might have when shooting a portrait does not affect the general provision of protecting the author's intellectual creation. This provided that the author ' … can make free creatives choices in several ways and several points in its production'.[65]

Creative freedom has been assessed as well by the CJEU in the Football Dataco Ltd case. Here, the question is whether the skills and labour invested in a given database are enough criteria to determine its copyright protection. The Court first indicated that the protection related to databases is referred to the selection or arrangement of the database itself and not related to the data it contains. Second, that such selection or arrangement has to be original in the sense of the author's expression of 'his creative ability […] making free and creative choices'.[66] Given that, in such case, setting up the database was the result of technical criteria and certain rules, and there was no room for such creative freedom; therefore, no copyright protection can be allowed.

The connection between free creative choices and originality gives weight to the argument of the importance that the system gives to author's potential communicative power. Such freedom protects not only the copyright assets but the possibility of their existence. However, some could say that those are separated elements and that the protection of the author's freedom of creativity is not the protection of copyright or author's rights. That would be a contradictory statement towards the basic elements that support copyright in terms of incentive and dissemination of knowledge, as mentioned earlier.

Painer shows the weight given to freedom of choice as a central element for copyright protection. The CJEU left in the hands of the national courts the decision of defining the threshold of originality in which such a freedom can be exercised. In the Court's words, the national courts should decide if '[the work] is an intellectual creation of the author reflecting his

---

65. *Case C-145/2010 Eva-Maria Painer v. Standard VerlagsGmbH and Others.*
66. *Case C-604/10 Football Dataco Ltd and others v. Yahoo! Ltd UK and others.* Paragraphs 32-39.

personality and expressing his free and creative choices in the production of that photograph'.[67] The Court, however, did not utter a reference about the Human Rights instruments. There is not an evident reason for this in the case but is possible to speculate that the Court, first, tried to avoid a jurisdictional nightmare, and second, it considered that the Directive itself provides enough elements of interpretation to assess the principles protecting author's creativity. In fact, the Court refers to the recital 17th of the Directive 93/98 which states a general principle of copyright and, therefore, of the author's rights: a creation (in this case photographs) 'is to be considered original if it is the author's own reflecting his personality, no other criteria such as merit or purpose being taken into account'.[68]

The connection between the justification of protecting the author's rights as a fundamental right and freedom of expression has also been asserted in the *Luksan* case. There, the Court referred directly to Article 52(1) of the EU Charter guiding the interpretation of the rules regarding the assignation of rights in the case of films. This might be an initial response for a matter that will be analysed further below regarding the possible conflict of interests among parties for the protection of the fundamental right of property (horizontal effect). The Court, in this case, has stated that the author's rights prevail and cannot be 'undermined by the allocation of the exclusive exploitation rights to the film producer'.[69] Moreover, the Court weighed the public interest regarding the correct dissemination of the work within the interior market and the rights of the author (in this particular case, the principal director), and it has established that the director's rights could not be reduced without at least a fair compensation.[70]

The *Laserdisken* case is an interesting example on this matter. It reflects the importance given to freedom of expression *within* the internal market and its connection to the protection of copyright. The allegations from the claimant against the communitarian exhaustion of copyright and its implications on the free access to culture were denied by the Court with the simple argument that copyright ensures the author to introduce his work in the European market with no limitations. However, says the Court when referring to a previous decision from the European Court of Human Rights

---

67. *Case C-145/2010 Eva-Maria Painer v. Standard VerlagsGmbH and Others* (n 65). The Funke case mentioned above also reminds these premises: ' ... in order for subject matter to be regarded as a "work", two conditions must be satisfied cumulatively. First, the subject matter must be original in the sense that it is its author's own intellectual creation. In order for an intellectual creation to be regarded as an author's own it must reflect the author's personality, which is the case if the author was able to express his creative abilities in the production of the work by making free and creative choices'. *Case C-469/2017 Funke Medien NRW GmbH v. Bundesrepublik Deutschland* (n 32).
68. Council Directive 93/98/EEC of 29 October 1998 harmonizing the term of protection of copyright and certain related rights [1993] OJ L 290/9.
69. *Case C-277/10 Luksan v. van der Let.*
70. *See also*: *Case C-200/96 Metronome Musik v. Music Point Hokamp* (n 34).

(ECtHR), the right to free access to information 'prohibits a Government from restricting a person from receiving information that others *wish or may be willing to impart to him*'.[71] By doing so, the CJEU understands that copyright has two dimensions, the protection of author's rights and the promotion of the dissemination of original expressions, for those expressions enrich society but they dissemination is under the control of the author.[72] Therefore, the CJEU has weighed the originator's right to communicate or not his work into a particular market/society against the right of the members of such society to have access to such a communication, and it has acknowledged that the latter could only be achieved by protecting the first.

The protection of authors in the context of the exercise of freedom of expression is clear, for instance, in the recitals 10 and 17 of the Directive 93/98/EEC.[73] These assert two basic principles: first, that copyright is fundamental for intellectual creation, and second, that the intellectual creation is original as it reflects the author's personality. Perhaps where this connection is more evident is in the case of the Directive 2001/29/EC[74] which states the correlation of the four freedoms of the internal market with the protection of fundamental rights and principles of the Community, including intellectual property and freedom of expression (numbers 2nd, 3rd and 4th of the recitals). The Directive considers this as something possible through the aims stated in the subsequent recitals, particularly number 10th, 11th and 12th. Although utilitarianism has been enshrined in the 10th recital which protects a return for the investments made for the production of works, the 11th also refers to the role that copyright plays for author's (and performers') dignity and independence. Regarding the protection of author's interests in connection with their fundamental rights, those concepts are

---

71. *Case C-479/04 Laserdisken ApS v. Kulturministeriet (EC)* 549 (n 33). Paragraphs 64-66.
72. *Case C-479/04 Laserdisken ApS v. Kulturministeriet (EC)* 549 (n 33). At 63.
73. Council Directive 93/98/EEC of 29 October 1998 harmonizing the term of protection of copyright and certain related rights [1993] OJ L 290/9. The recitals read as follows: '(10) Whereas in its communication of 17 January 1991 "Follow-up to the Green Paper-Working programme of the Commission in the field of copyright and neighbouring rights" the Commission stresses the need to harmonize copyright and neighbouring rights at a high level of protection since these rights are fundamental to intellectual creation and stresses that their protection ensures the maintenance and development of creativity in the interest of authors, cultural industries, consumers and society as a whole; [...] (17) Whereas the protection of photographs in the Member States is the subject of varying regimes; whereas in order to achieve a sufficient harmonization of the term of protection of photographic works, in particular of those which, due to their artistic or professional character, are of importance within the internal market, it is necessary to define the level of originality required in this Directive; whereas a photographic work within the meaning of the Berne Convention is to be considered original if it is the author's own intellectual creation reflecting his personality, no other criteria such as merit or purpose being taken into account; whereas the protection of other photographs should be left to national law'.
74. Parliament and Council Directive 2001/29/EC of 22 May 2001 on the harmonisation of certain aspects of copyright and related rights in the information society [2001] OJ L167/10.

consistent with the protection of author's freedom of expression and their right to enjoy the material interests resulting from the use of their works. Finally, by mentioning Article 167 TEU (former Article 151 TEC), the Directive confirms the communitarian interest in shaping copyright in light of superior interests regarding the protection of culture.[75] This gives structure to a complex system in which copyright is aimed to play its role supporting the very democratic principle of the individual right to the benefit of equal conditions of participation in the public decisions.

17.2.2.4   Spain

The other European country in this study is Spain. Their Constitution has a very clear mandate regarding the protection of the author's interests and its connection with freedom of expression and therefore, democracy.[76]

In a case from the Civil Chamber of the Spanish Supreme Tribunal,[77] the judges argued that by creating an artistic work, the author develops a communicative process. Such a process requires the protection of author's moral rights. The case refers to the possible relocation of an artistic work placed in a public space. The use of the work was contractually agreed with the city government. Later on, new plans for the city indicate that the sculpture would be moved from its original place. The Tribunal considered the case regarding the communication that the author pursued in placing his work on that particular site. They found that such a right, part of author's moral rights to protect the integrity of her work, was in connection with the right to access to culture, for the public would not be able to access the work in the way the author wanted. Nevertheless, the Tribunal suggests, such a right could be limited in some particular cases,[78] though, in this case, the opposite right was the general interest of using public spaces. The Tribunal decided that the protection of the integrity of the work could be affected if the

---

75. In light of such principles, it is possible to assert, for example, that the Directive 2001/84/EC protects author's 'share in the economic success of their original works of art'. This example is interesting because the legal figure historically exists for years before as part of the legal systems of some European countries. However, the resale right (droit de suite) was not communitarian, therefore, for the communitarian interests, those principles stated above were applied regarding this particular right. *See also* recital 11th from the Directive 2006/116/EC (Term of protection) and recitals 2nd and 5th from the Directive 2012/28/EU (Orphan works).

76. Spanish Constitution, mentioned above. For the Spanish case *see also*: Gemma Minero Alejandre, 'Aproximación Jurídica Al Concepto de Derecho de Autor. Intento de Calificación Como Libertad de Producción Artística y Científica o Como Derecho de Propiedad' (2013) 5 Dilemata 215.

77. *Sentencia del Tribunal Supremo Sala de lo Civil No 458/2012* [2012] www.poderjudicial.es.

78. The Tribunal refers to a previous case in which a *fresco* had to be demolished due to the risk it posed for the community. In that case, the protection of author's interests had to bend in favour of the general public interest.

sculpture was moved and that implies 'an interference with the dialogue between the author and the audience'. But if that were not the case, added the Tribunal, meaning that such a communication was not present, the sculpture could be moved under the condition of not creating a disproportionate sacrifice for the author, which would imply abuse and yet, the moral right would not be affected.[79]

The element of communication in the above-mentioned case is important as the Tribunal linked such element with the concept of the social function of property (also enshrined by the Spanish Constitution), which in the case of copyright (*propiedad intelectual* from the Spanish use of the concept) means the satisfaction of the right to access to culture. This is important because in this case, such public interest was considered to be in the interest of protecting the integrity of the work as such, in the way the author had intended to communicate it.[80]

A previous case regarding this matter was decided in 1987 by the Supreme Tribunal in its Administrative Chamber (Contentious). In the case, a public office of the Basque Autonomous Government, called HABE, decided to publish the work of the plaintiffs with some sections severed and without the indication of their names as authors. The main issue was whether the fundamental right to scientific production could be alleged against an administrative decision. The Tribunal considered that such a discussion implied not only the legal connection between the author and her work as a matter of private law but also that such a link should be extended to the public law sphere. First, said the Tribunal, because scientific and artistic creations are protected by the Constitution, any conditions or constraints imposed to the author's creative activity by the administration are prohibited. Second, the Tribunal stated that the act of creation is directly connected with the right of dignity and the right to free development of personality and, therefore, those rights are also in connection with the author's moral rights. Furthermore, the Tribunal supported such an assertion on the applicability of the human rights instruments, particularly Article 27th from the UDHR, Article 15th of the ICESCR and the Berne Convention regarding the protection of the author's interests.[81]

The importance of these two cases, separated for almost fifteen years from one another, is the communicative element stressed by the judges within the constitutional perspective. It highlights that copyright is a legal framework surrounding the communicative action between authors and audiences. Protecting the author's freedom does not protect only her personal interests but also the audience interest in accessing the author's propositions

---

79. *Sentencia del Tribunal Supremo Sala de lo Civil No 458/2012* (n 77). Paragraphs 35 and 36. Free translation from the original in Spanish.
80. Regarding this matter, *see*: Minero Alejandre (n 76).
81. *Sentencia del Tribunal Supremo Sala de lo Contencioso No 499/1987* [1987] www.poder-judicial.es.

within the market of ideas. And that is a fundamental right that is worth to protect not only for economic purposes but also for the principle of freedom of expression, and the right to participate actively in the cultural life of society.

17.2.2.5 Colombia

Although Colombia belongs to the category of those countries in which their Constitution merely mentions the protection of intellectual property as a right that should be protected, their Constitutional Court has shaped the constitutional dimension of copyright through a series of decisions acknowledging its interaction with freedom of expression, the protection of author's dignity and social security, and the implications that these rights have for democracy and cultural diversity. Such a shaping activity comprises the examination of, first, special cases in which an author's rights have been considered under threat and their Constitutional protection was claimed,[82] and second, cases in which the constitutionality of certain pieces of legislation has been examined.

One of the first cases in which the Court assessed the scope of the constitutional protection of author's rights was the inclusion of the Phonograms Convention into the national legislation. In this case, the Court acknowledged that protecting intellectual property and therefore copyright, is connected to other fundamental rights protecting: (1) the cultural wealth of the nation, (2) the right to have a job as a social obligation, (3) the private property, (4) the obligation of fostering the access to culture recognizing that culture is the support of nationality, (5) and finally, the national cultural heritage. Therefore, for the Court, protecting copyright does not respond to a mere economic interest but also to a cultural one which reflects a humanistic, integral and cultural philosophy that supports the constitutional framework for this protection.[83]

The baseline for the recognition of author's moral rights as a fundamental right was created by the Court in 1998 when an article from the Law for the Promotion of Culture was attacked under claims of breaching the Constitution. This article establishes the inalienability of the moral and economic rights to protect the right of social security for authors, artists, and performers.[84] The decision of the Court discusses some questions which will be addressed in the next section of this chapter. For the interest of this section, it is important to highlight that the Court first asserted the

---

82. *See* n 2.
83. *Sentencia C-334/93 (Corte Constitucional)* [1993] www.corteconstitucional.gov.co/relatoria.
84. 'Articulo 33. Derechos de Autor. Los Derechos de Autor y conexos morales y patrimoniales de autores, actores, directores y dramaturgos, se consideran de carácter inalienable por las implicaciones que éstos tienen para la seguridad social del artista.' Ley 397 1997.

fundamental protection of moral rights as an evident consequence of protecting author's freedom of creativity, which is a rational expression of human nature. Therefore, moral rights should be inalienable as, in fact, the national copyright law recognizes. However, in the case of the economic rights, these are also protected by the Constitution as a mechanism to secure author's survival and dignity (in terms of an adequate standard of living) through the monetary utilities that her work can report.[85] However, those rights are not absolutely inalienable; their introduction into the market should be possible so they can produce the revenues they were created for. Therefore, the inalienability of economic rights should be accepted only in those cases in which an author's social security is under threat.

The consequences of such a decision are yet to be discovered; the only decision applying directly to such possibility is the *Escalona* case from the Constitutional Court.[86] In that case, the Court found that author's social security and dignity was in evident jeopardy and declared that had the author not died during the trial, the contracts he signed with the publisher would have been revised in order to protect the author's subsistence in congruence with his style of life. Nonetheless, other previous constitutional decisions are also based on those rationales.[87]

One of these decisions, the C-053/01, discusses the constitutional principle of social interest that creates conditions for Colombian copyright legislation. In that case, the norm attacked was part of an article that declares the author's rights of social interest and consequently states that such rights should prevail over other rights as in the case of the neighbouring rights. This prevalence was supported by the Constitutional Court based on the social function that fostering artistic and scientific creativity has in protecting the free development of personality, freedom of expression and the right to the recognition of own individual's work. The Court highlights the role that the protection of the author's moral and material interests plays for society. Such interests and their protection should not be considered absolute, though. The social function of property, as stated in the Colombian Constitution, creates a counterweight for the exercise of such rights to satisfy societal interests.[88]

---

85. *Sentencia C-053/01 (Corte Constitucional)* [2001] www.corteconstitucional.gov.co/relatoria.
86. *Sentencia T-367/09 (Corte Constitucional)* (n 1).
87. *See*: *Sentencia C-276/96 (Corte Constitucional)* [1996] www.corteconstitucional.gov.co/relatoria. *Sentencia C-1490/00 (Corte Constitucional)* [2000] www.corteconstitucional.gov.co/relatoria.
88. For an extensive analysis on this, *see*: Julio Cesar Padilla Herrera, 'La Función Social Del Derecho de Autor' [2015] Revista de Derecho, Comunicaciones y Nuevas Tecnologías 1 <https://derechoytics.uniandes.edu.co/components/com_revista/archivos/derechoytics/ytics218.pdf>.

Finally, the interaction between the right to creative freedom and the right to privacy were assessed in the case of *La Bruja*.[89] This is a book that narrates the relationships between a woman, politicians, and the drug cartels in the country. This woman sued the author arguing the book has infringed her privacy rights and asked for a modification of the book erasing any connection with her name. The first instance accepted this theory and ordered the modification and republication of the book. The Constitutional Court decided to examine the case and found instead that the author's creative freedom should be protected. Given that the facts mentioned in the book were publicly known, the Court's main argument was that the work is the expression of author's original thoughts and, as such, it has an unbreakable connection with him. Therefore, any modification of such a work ordered by an authority is basically a case of censorship, and it should be prevented.

By linking the protection of copyright with other fundamental rights through the integral interpretation of the Constitution, the Colombian Constitutional Court has assembled a complex system supporting the protection of authors fundamental rights. It recognizes the right to property but also determines that such a protection should be tuned in the scope of protecting the interests of society and authors themselves. Authors are protected through mechanisms that enhance their freedom of expression in connection with their personal contribution to the creation of an original work. But they should also be protected through mechanisms directed to their access to social security, well-being and dignity. Without these elements, no freedom of expression would be possible.

17.2.2.6   Argentina

The Argentinian constitutional clause, which dates from 1853, protects intellectual property within the protection of property as a fundamental right (Article 17). However, regarding the implementation of author's rights, Article 75.19 gives faculties to the Congress to legislate about the protection of 'cultural identity and pluralism, the unrestrained creation and circulation of the works of authors, the artistic heritage, and cultural and audio-visual spaces'.[90]

The Constitutional protection of copyright and the condition of originality have been stated by a few cases in the Argentinian case law. Unfortunately, some of those cases confused the concept of originality with novelty. For example, in *Gvirtz*,[91] the National Chamber of Appeals for the Criminal and Correctional connected the two concepts to assess the originality of a given TV Show. It found that the absence of novelty implied the

---

89. *Sentencia SU-056/95 (Corte Constitucional)* [1995] www.corteconstitucional.gov.co/relatoria.
90. *See* n 21.
91. *C 26734 Gvirtz, Diego s/Ley 11723 (CNCRIM Y CORREC Sala V)* [2005] elDial.com.

lack of originality to gain copyright protection. The Chamber, however, stated also that the concept of originality is derived from the constitutional protection of copyright. It is the result of the author's creative labour that expresses the 'fruits of her spirit'.

The constitutional protection of copyright and its relationship with the concept of originality has also been stated by the National Chamber of Appeals for the Commercial.[92] In this case, the chamber asserted that the principle of no protection of ideas serves the purpose of free discussion; thus, for a work to be protected, it must express ideas with originality. This would be the result of the author's intellectual creativity, and the Constitution and the law protect these works under such principles. Therefore, ideas alone are free to be used, and this upholds freedom of expression.

Another decision, this time from the Court of First Instance in Civil and Commercial Matters of Rosario, assessed the constitutional character of copyright regarding an alleged abusive exercise of the author's moral rights. Although in this case the protection of author's freedom of expression was not scrutinized, it is important to highlight that in this case the social function of the property has been weighed against the valid argument of protecting author's moral rights (as has been shown in Colombian case law). In this case, the Court decided that exercising the author's moral rights can be abusive if it affects the communicative (and therefore, social) function of the deceased author's work. This function determines that both the Argentinian Constitution and the human right treaties (included in the Constitution) concern the protection of the author's interests under limits that should protect the interests of society in accessing published works as well.[93] For this section, it is interesting to highlight how, in this case, the absoluteness of the author's moral rights has been relativized for the protection of the communicative function of the work.

17.2.2.7   Mexico

Mexican case law shows a strong approach to the protection of the author's interests. In a decision from the Plenum of the Supreme Court, it was assessed whether the right to receive royalties for the communication to the public of the work is an inalienable right or not. Although such a matter will be studied further below, in this section, the attention will focus on some of the constitutional principles the Plenum of the Court has stated for their decision. According to the Court, the connection between freedom of

---

92. *C Pedro E v. M y Cia y otros (CNC Sala A)* [1989] Cerlalc, Derecho Autor Reg.
93. *C 1420 Ediciones de la Flor SRL c/ Fontanarrosa Franco (CPICC Rosario)* [2013] https://es.scribd.com/document/135224740/Ediciones-de-la-Flor-SRL-c-Fontanarrosa-F-s-Accion-Mere-Declarativa-Expte-1420-08. *See also*: Maximimliano Marzetti, 'Ediciones de La Flor v. Fontanarrosa Franco' (2013) 44 IIC – International Review of Intellectual Property and Competition Law 851 <http://link.springer.com/10.1007/s40319-013-0115-5>.

expression (free emission, communication and reception of cultural information) and the protection of communication and publication of ideas should be considered essential for a constitutional state based on social and democratic principles. In addition, the protection of the moral and material interests of the author also has constitutional rank. Therefore, the interpretation of the law should consider these principles and balance the interests they protect. Those constitutional principles supporting copyright are: (1) the protection of the moral and material interests of the author, (2) the prohibition of any deprivation of property without a previous judicial decision, (3) the free emission, communication, and reception of cultural information, (4) the protection of communication and publication of ideas through any media (literary or artistic), (5) education as a mean for people's constant economic, social and cultural improvement, and (6) freedom of contract and autonomy. Further analysis of this decision will be developed in the next section.[94]

Although the concept of originality was not part of the considerations in the highest Court's decision,[95] one of the contested decisions that the Plenum has scrutinized did it (the one regarding the same problem adopted by the First Chamber of the Court).[96] In that decision, the Chamber studied the constitutional protection of creativity and originality. The Tribunal has begun analysing the concept of author stating that, under the Mexican copyright law, this would be the physical person who has created the work. Such a person would be anyone capable of complying with the conditions the law establishes for copyright protection, one of which is originality. The author is then the first owner of the copyright, both in its moral and economic dimensions. For the First Chamber, the protection established in the above-mentioned Article 28 of the Mexican Constitution refers to the protection of author's creativity and because of that, author's rights, constitutionally protected, depend on author's creativity, notwithstanding the fact the work was created under employment conditions, or made for hire or independently. Consequently, originality would be a constitutional condition for copyright that is directly related to the author's creativity and her freedom.

---

94. *Sentencia No 20709 (SCJ Pleno)* (2007) XXVII Sem Judic la Fed y su Gac 652.
95. The requirement of originality has been introduced in Article 3 of the Mexican copyright law. Surprisingly, there are less judicial decisions regarding this matter in the Mexican case law than in other jurisdictions. The concept of originality has been stated in opposition to the concept of novelty applicable for inventions regarding the personal print author affixes in his work (*Sentencia No 163309 (Tribunales Colegiados de Distrito)* (2010) XXXII Sem Judic la Fed y su Gac. *See*: Gabriel E Larrea, Ricardo E Larrea and Luis Schmidt, 'Alai Mexico Group, Questionnaire – Boundaries and Interfaces' (2011) <http://www.alaidublin2011.org/>.).
96. *Amparo en revision 581/2005 (SCJ Sala 1)* [2005] Cerlalc, Derecho Autor Reg. The two higher chambers of the Supreme Court decided separately and oppositely on the same case. This is why the Plenum has had the last word closing the case.

In line with the later, another axiomatic decision from the Mexican Supreme Tribunal in its First Chamber refers to the connection between the concept of freedom of creativity and the protection of author's moral rights.[97] In this decision, the Tribunal declared that moral rights are protected by the Mexican Constitution and by the international instruments in which Mexico is part (e.g., the ICESCR). Once the Tribunal analysed in detail the concept of culture in its complex dimension, it concluded that the right of access to culture includes: (1) person's right to express herself freely, (2) the freedom to exercise her own cultural practices, (3) the freedom of developing and sharing knowledge, and (4) the right to the protection of her moral and material interests related to the work's product of her cultural activity. The decision is axiomatic as it finds that such complex right of culture would be affected when the author's moral rights have been breached. By modifying the work and hiding the author's name, the infringement affects the right to culture as a whole.

Furthermore, the Tribunal explained that there is a hinge between freedom of creativity and the protection of the result of exercising such right through cultural expression, in this case, an expression protected by copyright. According to the Tribunal, moral rights also protect the right of society to access to the message the author has created without changes or mutilations that affect the author's own intention. Therefore, for the Tribunal, communicating a mutilated version of the author's work implies a breach of such moral rights affecting both author's and society's freedom of expression.

This is a case of horizontal effect. The mutilated version was communicated by a person who bought the copyright from a previous owner (not the author). Because such a publication comprises an action close to censorship, the clash between private interests is present. On the one hand, the right of the copyright owner of publishing the work of which he has bought the rights and on the other hand, the right of the author to see his work published integrally. In protection of author's rights, such publication could not be considered legal even if the copyright was legally bought.[98]

What is important to note here is the weight given by the Court to the communicative power that the author's work represents and how this should be protected at the constitutional level. The cases presented above coincide in a wider conceptualization of copyright and author's protection in which property rights play a fundamental role along, with moral rights in the protection of the author's interests.

Summarising, freedom of expression has a direct relation with the concept of originality, and therefore, with the author's communicative power. The protection of the author's moral and material rights through copyright

---

97. *Amparo directo 11/2011 (SCJ Sala 1)* [2011] Cerlalc, Derecho Autor Reg.
98. The consequences of such a horizontal effect are going to be studied in the next section of this chapter.

laws implies that such principles are to be present in the system. The case law studied so far supports such an assertion.

17.2.3 PARTIAL CONCLUSIONS

The concept of communicative power has been stated by Habermas as a *motivating* force which is capable of ' ... mobilizing citizens' communicative freedom for the formation of political beliefs that in turn influence the production of legitimate law'.[99] It is clear, therefore, that this concept is intrinsically connected with the potentiality of creativity described, for instance, by Rogel Vide as freedom of creation: freedom of creation is one step behind of authorship, is the potentiality of being an author, which is constitutionally protected.[100] Nevertheless, it would not be just the expectative to obtain the qualification of the author according to the law, the potentiality of creating something original what it would be protected. If authorship is the action by which a person became an author and if this is only possible when the author meets the threshold of originality according to the national rules of copyright, then, originality is a consequence of the free exercise of such a right. Therefore, originality can only exist if the author has creative freedom. Copyright creates the guarantees for such freedom and for the dissemination of the resulting expression. By doing so, it satisfies, more or less effectively, the expectations of authors and society. Protecting the authors' expectations should permit that society can satisfy theirs.[101]

By accepting that cultural expressions can be seen as communicative vehicles of thought, is possible to assert that protecting author's moral and material interests in the systems of laws could overcome the conceptualization of these rights as mere property rights. Because of their free exercise of creativity, authors should be able to hold and freely exercise their communicative power. They could even transfer part of the social power the work can carry,[102] but the author's communicative power should be innate, and the copyright is meant to protect it by guaranteeing their own dignity and social security. Accordingly, copyright would promote equal conditions of participation in the social life for authors so they can create autonomously. This would be a basic guarantee for democracy.

The connection between originality and authorship, as it has been described in this section, hinges on the communicative power of the author. Such power is not absolute, and it should be weighed against other interests,

---

99. Habermas (n 44). p. 147.
100. Carlos Rogel Vide, 'Libertad de Creacion y Derecho de Autor' in Luis Antonio Anguita Villanueva (ed), *Constitucion y Propiedad Intelectual* (1st edn, Reus 2014).
101. The immerse promise of protection that the copyright laws carry has been explained in an earlier work. *See*: Alvarez Amezquita, 'La Libertad de Expresión Como Resultado y Garantía Principal Del Derecho de Autor' (n 40).
102. For the concept of social power, *see* Habermas (n 44). p. 175.

even those that would serve for the protection of the author's own interests. As it is important to protect author's communicative power in order to maintain equal conditions of participation on the cultural life of a society, it is also important that such a communicative power is feasible and, in some cases, that means that the wealth a work can produce should be shared with enterprises who make possible such communication, e.g., the rationales created to support the distribution of copyrights in the case of films, or the examples in which the employer can hold in some extent the rights over the work the employee has created. However, such a balance, as unstable and idealistic as it appears, seems to be desirable, and in case of changes in the weight, either the courts or the law are called for actively assess and restore it. This will be revised in the next section.

17.3   HUMAN RIGHTS AND THE PRINCIPLE OF
        PRIVATE AUTONOMY IN COPYRIGHT LAWS

One of the principal characteristics of copyright is its transferability. Most of the laws since the Statute of Anne, recognize that at least the economic rights of the author can be assigned to a third party (in total or in part). Thus, once defined that the author enjoys constitutional protection regarding the creation of works, can an author challenge an assignment contract by claiming the protection of her moral and material interests? This is the question the Colombian Constitutional Court has addressed in the *Escalona* case as mentioned above.

The case law studied above has shown that author's rights have been constitutionally protected in some countries according to the general principles of freedom of expression and access to the culture which have demonstrated a clear connection with the communication of knowledge and ideas, and originality. Such a connection can be understood through the functioning of 'the market of ideas', and it is consequently related to the exercise of the author's communicative power.

Would the author's interests be really in a clash with other players in the chain of creation, production and dissemination of copyrighted works? Not necessarily, but, as the case law studied in this chapter suggests, authors may require, in some cases, additional protection when negotiating their rights. Nevertheless, quite often, the commercial relationships between authors and publishers or other corporations in charge of the dissemination of works are smooth enough to run quietly in the legal system.[103] In many cases, as it has been noted by scholars as Fisk,[104] the entrepreneurial association between the

---

103. An interesting analysis on this matter can be found on: Martin Kretschmer and others, 'The Relationship Between Copyright and Contract Law' (2010) <www.sabip.org.uk>.
104. Catherine L. Fisk, *Working Knowledge: Employee Innovation and the Rise of Corporate Intellectual Property, 1800-1930* (University of North Carolina Press 2009).

author and the corporation can create more balanced relations in which the author's freedom and creativity can be seen fostered.

But absolute freedom of contract is not possible in those relationships. In a study about how the protection of fundamental rights can affect private law, Lawrence Fastrich presents an interesting analysis that would help in understanding the variability of the interactions between the fundamental protection of author's moral and material interests and the exercise of proprietary interests of third parties in the exploitation of copyrights. According to Fastrich, unless there is a balanced exercise of bargaining power, freedom of contract should face some restrictions.[105] The law and the case law will present that such rationality in the case of copyright is often accepted under the premise that the author is the weaker part in such a contractual relation.

Thus, such a desirable balance between authors and producers, as described in the last part of the previous section, entails a range of possibilities and multiple scenarios, some of which might create cases of a horizontal effect between these two persons. The concept of horizontality regards the possible affectation of fundamental rights by the action or omission of one individual to another.[106]

Most of such a horizontal effect would occur around the contractual relationships between authors and others. The framework for the present section will be both, the contractual assignment of copyrights, and the transfer of copyrights as a result of commissioned works or in the case of works created under employment. The analysis will regard the required balance between possible conflicting interests in terms of protecting the author's dignity and autonomy.

Such an analysis will use two spheres of sources, the sphere of positive legislation and its evolution during the consolidation of modern copyright law (which include post-Berne laws until present times),[107] and the sphere of the case law related to the protection of the author's fundamental rights from the countries under study. Those cases have been selected in light of their connection to fundamental rights and their underpinning principles, and most of them have been mentioned in the previous sections of this chapter. Other cases, in which copyright entitlement has been solved in the scope of the applicable copyright law without considering either fundamental rights or

---

105. Fastrich (n 5).
106. Alexy (n 5). p. 359.
107. For this purpose, an analytical and historical comparison of the pertinent copyright laws from the jurisdictions under study was made. Due to its size, this will not be introduced in this document, but the most relevant examples will be indicated. The study comprised the changes in the national and regional (the Andean Community and the European Union) legislation since 1886 onwards. The compared data can be found published by the author David Felipe Alvarez Amezquita, 'Historical and Comparative Tables of Legislation Protecting the Author. Definitions, Main Contractual Issues and Constitutional Protection' (ResearchGate, 2017) 56.

principles, will not be considered as they do not show stress towards the constitutional framework.

Regarding the protection of the author's fundamental rights, the possible conflicts might arise from the core elements described in the General Comment 17, mentioned above. These are the protection of the author's moral interests (paternity and integrity) and the protection of the author's material interests regarding their impact on the author's adequate standard of living. Different choices may emerge depending on the nature of the right in question and the legal tradition in which such a right is inscribed.

In the case of moral rights, the possibility of a clash between stakeholders depends on the transferability and nature of such rights. For instance, the Anglo-Saxon tradition accepts that moral rights could be waived while the continental tradition considers moral rights either as one sole thing with the economic rights (monistic approach) or a separated branch (dualistic approach). In these two last possibilities, moral rights are not transferable nor waivable.[108]

In the case of economic rights, the situation is less evident. The variables are plenty in terms of whether the author is considered or not the first owner of the copyright, and the consequences of that might affect how the law is interpreted towards the author's fundamental rights. In this case, two options will be considered, one is the assignment or transfer of the copyright from the author to another person by a contract, and the other is vesting the copyright (or part of it) to another person by mechanisms such as the work made for hire (hereinafter WMH) doctrine or similar figures such as works created by employees. These variables will be discussed in the sub-sections below.

17.3.1   BALANCE

Copyright contractual relationships are often the result of a bargain between players with similar interests. Publishing or disseminate the work and obtaining some economic profit are the main interests at play. Fairness in these contractual relationships are desirable, and the copyright laws under study can show that they provide some tools for such an aim. For instance, in Europe, recital 31 from the Information Society Directive states that a fair balance is desirable for copyright relationships. The recent Directive on Copyright and Digital Single Market creates a direct response to such a

---

108. In this case, Rigamonti proposes that the differences between the two main copyright traditions rely more on the way these rights are recognized and applied in practice and not much on their substantive protection. *See*: Cyrill P Rigamonti, 'The Conceptual Transformation of Moral Rights' (2007) 55 The American Journal of Comparative Law 67. p. 72.

desirable balance and introduces a complex mechanism with the aim of improving such interest.[109]

How can this balance be achieved? The first thing to do is to acknowledge the conditions in the relationship. If the author is the weakest part on that bargain, in order to promote such a balance, the law should create some conditions improving the author's bargain position.[110]

17.3.1.1   Assignation or Transference

In the comparative perspective, the most immediate mechanism for the purpose of protecting the author's interests is the requirement of certain formalities for contracts. Such formalities help to avoid simple consensual agreements in cases in which the author might find herself under stress. In the case of the assignment of copyright, all the countries under study require a written contract, the absence of which, in some cases, would affect the validity of the contract (the UK, Colombia, Mexico, and the US) or its execution (the US and Spain[111]). Even greater formalities have been stated in particular cases such as in Mexico. In this case, the contract should also be attested by a notary public as a condition of execution. Argentina requires not only the written agreement as a condition of validity but also its registration.

Other requisites, such as the registration of contracts, not for their validity but for their publicity, have been created to protect other interests, (in particular, those of third parties in the property of the work). In these cases, the registration asserts assignee's property against such third parties.

Some other mechanisms for achieving balance are present in some of the legislation. For instance, when the contract does not mention certain elements, the law creates default conditions. Those elements are defined in the law. Examples of those are establishing the term of the assignment, the scope of rights assigned, or the territories in which the assignment will operate. The law from some countries supersedes the will of the parties if any

---

109. Parliament and Council Directive 2019/790 of 17 April 2019 on copyright and related rights in the Digital Single Market and amending Directives 96/9/EC and 2001/29/EC.
110. The weak position of the author has been often asserted, *see,* for example: William Cornish, *Cases and Materials on Intellectual Property* (5th edn, Sweet & Maxwell 2006). p. 391. Cornish quotes this case: *Schroeder Music Publishing v. Macaulay* (1974) 3 616. *See also*: Claude Colombet, *Major Principles of Copyright and Neighbouring Rights in the World. A Comparative Law Approach* (UNESCO 1987); Kretschmer and others (n 103); Martin Kretschmer, 'Creator Contracts ("Supply Side")' in Martin Kretschmer and others (eds), *The Relationship Between Copyright and Contract Law* (SABIP 2010) <www.sabip.org.uk>; Richard Watt, 'Economic Theory of Copyright Contracts' in Martin Kretschmer and others (eds), *The Relationship Between Copyright and Contract Law* (SABIP 2010) <www.sabip.org.uk>.
111. Although Spanish copyright law does not mention the execution of the contract, it mentions that the absence of a written contract would allow the author to request its resolution. *See: Sentencia de la Audiencia Provincial de Alicante Sección 8ª No 236/2006* [2006] Cerlalc, Derecho Autor Reg.

of such elements are not present in the contract, benefiting the author by creating those default conditions. For example, some laws can limit the term of the transfer to five years, reduce the scope of the rights assigned to only those required for the execution of the contract, and/or define the territories in which the transfer would take effect. Mexican, Colombian, and Spanish laws are examples of such mechanisms. However, these are the product of recent changes. In fact, Colombian copyright law was amended on this matter in 2011 and again in 2019; Mexico did it in 1996 and Spain in 1987.

However, other jurisdictions have shown a different approach. Under the premise of the prevalence of the economic interest, it is possible to imply the transfer of copyright under certain conditions, even as an exception to the written formality required in the UK Law. Torremans highlights the possibility of recognizing such implied terms in the case of assignment of copyright in the UK law.[112] Implied terms for assignment of copyright are subject to certain conditions stressed in *Fisher v. Brooker & Onward Music Ltd.* In this case, Mr Fisher participated in the recording of the final version of a song which, after its release, would be a hit in the music market. After the recording of a first version of the song, Fisher created and added his contribution. The question raised was whether Fisher was entitled to share the copyright in a second recording which included his contribution and which was finally the work published. The Court studied the possibility of accepting the existence of implied terms that would lead to the conclusion that Fisher had assigned his copyright to Essex Music and later Onward Music. In order to deny such implied terms, the Court assessed these three elements required for such alleged implication: (1) the existence of a previous agreement between the parties in conflict from which the implied terms can be derived; (2) business efficiency, which in this case was not alleged nor studied; and (3) the existence of customary usage in the particular industry that would lead to implying such assignment in the case (which was not proved).[113]

It is possible in certain limited cases to imply the assignment of copyright. The *Ray* case, mentioned in the second section of this chapter, shows a perspective in this matter.[114] The judgement analysed the possibility of assigning author's rights to a third party, or at least to concede a grant through implied terms in the contract giving attention to the investment related to the production of the work. In this case, the Court referred to the construction of the implied terms; it recalled the principles for such implied terms as mentioned above, and it recognized that this is an intrusion on the

---

112. Paul Torremans, *Holyoak and Torremans Intellectual Property Law* (6th edn, Oxford University Press 2010). p. 332. *See also*: William Cornish, David Llewelyn and Tanya Aplin, *Intellectual Property Patents, Copyright, Trade Marks and Allied Rights* (8th edn, Sweet & Maxwell 2013).

113. *Fisher v. Brooker and another* 306. At 58-60.

114. *Ray v. Classic FM plc* (n 47).

freedom of contract and therefore it should be constrained to strict conditions.[115] Although it is possible to consider that in certain cases the assignment of copyright might be implied, under certain conditions, the Court in Ray asserted that a minimalistic approach is desirable in order to not unreasonably affect the rights of the contractor and therefore the balance between the parties.[116]

In particular cases, a principle has been recognized that helps in the balance of the relationship above-mentioned. It is the principle of a restrictive interpretation of contracts.[117] In this case, the interpreter of the contract should understand that the assignment cannot go further than what has been mentioned in the contract. In practice, this means that no right, term, or territory is comprised in the transfer if not mentioned in the contract. This tends to discourage general clauses of transfer in the copyright contracts (Articles 77 and 78 of the Colombian Copyright Law, Law No. 23, 1982 and Article 31 of the Decision 351/1993 from the Andean Community of Nations).[118]

---

115. The Court in this case refers to Lord Bingham in the *Philips* case. *See*: *Ray v. Classic FM plc* (n 47). Paragraph VIII.a.(4). *See also*: *Cala Homes (South) Ltd and others v. Alfred McAlpine Homes East Ltd* (1995) 18. And also *Brighton and another v. Jones* (n 47).

116. The Court indicated: '(8) circumstances may exist when the necessity for an assignment of copyright may be established. As Mr Howe has submitted, these circumstances are, however, only likely to arise if the Client needs in addition to the right to use the copyright works the right to exclude the Contractor from using the work and the ability to enforce the copyright against third parties. Examples of when this situation may arise include: (a) where the purpose in commissioning the work is for the Client to multiply and sell copies on the market for which the work was created free from the sale of copies in competition with the Client by the Contractor or third parties; (b) where the Contractor creates a work which is derivative from a pre-existing work of the Client, e.g., when a draughtsman is engaged to turn designs of an article in sketch form by the Client into formal manufacturing drawings, and the draughtsman could not use the drawings himself without infringing the underlying rights of the Client; (c) where the Contractor is engaged as part of a team with employees of the Client to produce a composite or joint work and he is unable, or cannot have been intended to be able, to exploit for his own benefit the joint work or indeed any distinct contribution of his own created in the course of his engagement [...] In each case it is necessary to consider the price paid, the impact on the Contractor of assignment of copyright and whether it can sensibly have been intended that the Contractor should retain any copyright as a separate item of property; (8) if necessity requires only the grant of a licence, the ambit of the licence must be the minimum which is required to secure to the Client the entitlement which the parties to contract must have intended to confer upon him. The amount of the purchase price which the Client under the contract has obliged himself to pay may be relevant to the ambit of the licence.'

117. Colombet (n 110).

118. Article 31 reads as follows: 'Any transfer of the economic rights, and also authorizations or licenses for use, shall be understood to be limited to the forms of exploitation and other procedures expressly agreed upon in the relevant contract.' Decision 351 Common Regime on Copyright and Neighboring Rights 1993. Articles 77 and 78 of the Colombian Copyright Law read as follows: 'Article 77. The different forms of use of the

As it will be explained below, in the case of the UK and the US, their legislation in the dawn of the twentieth century protect authors or her heirs with the possibility of reversion of the assignment in the case of the UK and the renewal in the case of the US. This raises questions about the exercise of autonomy for contractual relationships which will be analysed further below.

17.3.1.2   Works Made for Hire or Similar Provisions

If the mechanism for the entitlement of the copyright is the work made for hire (WMH) or other similar mechanisms by which the employer or the commissioner of a work becomes the owner of the copyright, the comparative law shows different approaches. First, in this case, the weight given to author's will is reduced in favour of a presumption, in most of the cases, of transference. As a presumption, it flips the burden of proof in the case of disputed authorship, therefore, is the interested party, in this case, the author, who should demonstrate that the deemed transference should not apply.[119] However, even in these cases, the author is protected by some tools.

At first, it is important to mention that to the date, the laws under study accept the principle by which the author would be considered the first owner of the copyright.[120] This might not be a general principle historically, but for the analysis here, even in those cases where the copyright is not vested initially in the hands of the author, such a circumstance has been considered as an exception within the national legislation, and it can be understood as a legal fiction.[121]

The tools mentioned above seem to confirm this, at least theoretically. First, in most of the cases, a written contract is required for the purpose of this mechanism. Second, in all the legislations analysed, the author's will is safeguarded by stating that the effects of the presumed transfer of the copyright are subject to the absence of an agreement to the contrary. Even

---

work shall be independent of each other; authorization by the author of one form of use shall not extend to other forms.' 'Article 78. The interpretation of legal transactions concerning copyright shall always be restrictive. The recognition of rights broader than those expressly granted by the author in the instrument concerned shall not be allowed.' Law No. 23 – On Copyright. The recent modification to the Colombian Copyright Law introduces such a principle expressively as part of the regulations related to the transfer or assignment of copyrights. It modifies Article 183 from the original Law No. 23 by introducing the principle of restrictive interpretation of contracts in what is related to new forms of use unknown by the time of the contract which will not be considered as part of the contract. Ley 1955 de 2019 Por el cual se expide el Plan Nacional de Desarrollo 2018-2022. 'Pacto por Colombia, Pacto por la Equidad'. 2019.

119. Cornish, Llewelyn and Aplin (n 112). p. 523.
120. For the US case, *see*: *Burrow-Giles Lithographic Co. v. Sarony* (n 22). Moreover, the US has recognised this principle in Article 16.5.6 of its TPA with Colombia.
121. *See,* for example: HIL (Hugh Ian Lang) Laddie 1946-2008 and others (eds), *The Modern Law of Copyright and Designs [Electronic Resource] / Laddie, Prescott & Vitoria.* (4th ed., London: LexisNexis 2011). Paragraphs 22.23 and 22.24.

more, in the case of US section 101, for commissioned works, it is required that the author accepts that the work in question will be considered as a WMH.[122] Third, in some cases, the transfer is limited somehow (Colombia, Spain). Fourth, in other cases, the transfer only applies to certain kinds of works and not to all (the US for commissioned works). Fifth, in the case of Mexico, the WMH doctrine creates a sui generis condition by which both the author and the employer should share the benefits of the use of the work, but only the employer can decide the uses to be authorized. In the case of the US and the UK, the WMH applies for works created as a result of the employment conditions (*see* subsection 17.3.3 below).[123]

A very descriptive case of balancing interests with respect to the WMH doctrine is the case of the works created for advertisement in Mexico. In this case, the Mexican law establishes that the first six months of exploitation of the economic rights by the commissioner are covered by the first upfront payment; but once such a period terminates, any use of the work should be paid again to the author at least in the same amount paid originally. After three years, any use will require a new contract with the author.[124]

The most important conclusion here is that authors find it possible to contractually reverse the effect of the deemed transfer of the copyright. Nevertheless, if the postulate of author's weaker bargain position is accepted, the possibility of an author introducing a change in the employment agreement in order to retain the copyright is highly unlikely. There are cases, as in *Brighton*,[125] in which the defendant was able to retain her right in work since the beginning.

In general, the desired balance among parties in the contractual relationships finds some helpful tools in different jurisdictions: either statutory mechanisms or jurisprudential developments tending to protect author's weaker position in those relationships. In some cases, the support for such policy is clearly the protection of author's moral and material interests; in others, it is the principle of guaranteeing a proper reward for the creator.

---

122. In the US Copyright Law, the concept of Work Made for Hire (WMH) includes both works made under employment and commissioned works. For the latter it is referred to collective works, motion pictures, and other works enunciated within the definition. For these kind of works is required that the authors have agreed by a written contract that the work will be considered as a WMH (Sec. 101, Def. (2), United States Copyright Office (n 21).)

123. *See* Cornish, Llewelyn and Aplin (n 112). In the case of the US *see*: Robert A Gorman, Jane C Ginsburg and Anthony R Reese, *Copyright, Cases and Material* (8th edn, Thompson Reuters 2011).

124. Article 74. Federal Copyright Law, 1996.

125. *Brighton and another v. Jones* (n 47).

17.3.2   DIGNITY

The concept of dignity has been part of the integral view of human participation in society, and it is considered as the duty to respect another one's rights.[126] According to Habermas, this concept (assimilated to the concept of integrity) is the support of 'symmetrical relations of recognition' and regards the discourse theory explained in the previous chapter.[127] Alexy, for example, has set the concept in terms of the negative liberty co-related with the right to freedom which cannot affect the rights of others.[128] Protecting an author's dignity would mean that, in the protection of other interests, economic or of another kind, the author cannot result in a worse off situation than other members of society. That is to say, if copyright protects an author's rights to incentivize creativity, the creator should not be affected in his rights in a worse manner than others would if their own rights are not protected as a consequence of the protection of an author's fundamental rights.[129]

An example of this idea can be seen in practice in the US case of *Eldred v. Ashcroft*. In this case, the aim of protecting authors under equal and fair conditions lead the Court to recognize the tradition of extending the term of protection of copyright in favour of authors' interests. Quoting Huntington, the Court summarized the issue: '[J]ustice, policy, and equity alike forb[id]' that an 'author who had sold his [work] a week ago, be placed in a worse situation than the author who should sell his work the day after the passing of [the] act.'[130]

In view of the discussion and analysis proposed in this work, two interconnected dimensions of an author's dignity can be identified. One is the dignity in relation with well-being, understood as obtaining an adequate means of living, either in the modern concept of accessing social security, health, education, and other requirements or in the traditional concept by which well-being is the consequence of property.[131] This first dimension is

---

126. Philip Alston and Ryan Goodman, *International Human Rights. Text and Materials* (Oxford University Press 2013). pp. 182-183.

127. Habermas (n 44) p. 271.

128. Alexy (n 5). pp. 233-234.

129. Merges states this principle as follows: 'the creator of a work should be respected and recognized in ways that extend beyond the traditional package of rights associated with property: the right to exclude, to alienate (sell or license), to use as one wishes, and so forth. There is often a nonpecuniary dimension to situations where this principle is relevant, and indeed the interests it protects are often said to continue after a creator sells the rights to a given creative work.' Robert P. Merges, *Justifying Intellectual Property* (Cambridge University Press 2011). p. 156.

130. *Eric Eldred et al. v. John D. Ashcroft 537 U.S. (2003)* (n 58). At 13.

131. Based on a neutral approach to the concept, some markers of well-being have been suggested in these two connected articles: Estelle Derclaye and Tim Taylor, 'Happy IP: Replacing the Law and Economics Justification for Intellectual Property Rights with a Well-Being Approach' (2015) 37 EIPR 197; Estelle Derclaye and Tim Taylor, 'Happy IP: Aligning Intellectual Property Rights with Well-Being' (2015) Intellectual Property

important inasmuch as an author's well-being would be the consequence of the effectivity of copyright principles; thus, a given public policy for author's social security through welfare laws should not be required. The second dimension of an author's dignity is related to the practice of their freedom. In this dimension, an author's freedom of creativity is crucial as it has been indicated in the previous section of this chapter. Although their autonomy can be seen somehow reduced, as in the case of certain elements of the WMH, authors' creativity, and therefore the consequential originality of her work, continues to be a fundamental element of his communicative power. Due to its connection with an author's autonomy, this dimension will be analysed in the subsection below.

17.3.2.1   Dignity in Welfare

An author's dignity should not be different than anyone else's dignity. The problem here is not to define the content of an author's dignity, but rather to find how such a principle can be applied in the case of copyright contractual relationships.

The complex notion of dignity in the case of the author and her contractual relationships has been used in support of certain judicial cases. It also has been in the discourse of copyright scholars from both the common law and the civil law approaches. For example, in spite of the alleged utilitarian approach that characterizes US copyright law, in 1909, the country created a mechanism by which the term of protection would be renewed one time in favour of the author or her heirs. In this case, they would be able to recover control of his work once the first term of protection has ended (section 23, 1909 Act). In order to continue with such a benefit in the new 1976 Copyright Act, the US Congress created a mechanism by which the copyright returned to the author under previous notice after thirty-five years of assignment (section 203).[132] In supporting this mechanism, it has been

---

Quarterly 1. Although these markers are useful for measuring IP well-being capability, it is important to consider that these authors' suggestion is based on an utilitarian-only approach to the justification of IP, and, as they recognise, other justifications as those based on the natural rights might play a role there. Perhaps the fundamental effect of a (modern) natural rights approach is that protecting copyright (at least) should be paternalistic as there are individual subjects that reasonably require special treatments due to their position within society. *See* Dworkin's definition of paternalism at page 10 of 'Happy IP: Replacing the Law and Economics Justification for Intellectual Property Rights with a Well-Being Approach'.

132. Conditions provided, and notwithstanding the case of works made for hire, the transfer of copyright executed after 1 January 1978, is subject to termination in favour of the author (section 203.a). By such termination, all the rights transferred revert to the author (section 203.b). Conditions: (1) it should be effected by the author or if dead, the persons mentioned in section 203.a.2); (2) it should be effected within five years after thirty-five years of the execution of the transfer, or thirty-five years after the publication under the grant (if the right of publication was granted), or forty years (whatever happens first)

argued that the author and her heirs will find protected their income in the future, particularly in cases in which the work produces wealth after some time has passed since the assignment.

Protecting the author's income has been an issue of political interest since the earliest discussions regarding copyright. This was a point stressed by Justice Willes in *Millar v. Taylor*[133] when discussing the importance of the Statute of Anne. He claimed that the Statute purported the protection of authors and their families as publishing their works without their consent would create 'very great Detriment, and too often [...] the Ruin of them ... '. Even more, for Willes, the reference to the author's family clearly supports the idea that the Parliament in the Statute opts for protecting the author and not the proprietor (the assignee). Two basic principles can be drawn from this. First, that the author has the right to participate in the economic success of her work; second, that the author is the weaker party in the bargain.

In line with such argumentation, Lord Diplock reasserted that principle in *Schroeder Music Publishing v. Macaulay*.[134] In this case, an author entered into a contract at a young age in which he transferred all the copyright in his future creations for five years (or ten, if the contract continued), receiving only the amount of GBP 50 as compensation. The fairness in the bargain was under scrutiny, and the Court found that in this case author's weaker position, particularly in the case of standard contracts, affected the enforceability of the contract and would be considered unperformed.

In contrast with the cases mentioned above concerning implied terms for the assignment of copyright, this case shows that in the UK such line of argumentation in defence of the author as a weak party in the contractual relationship has at least been considered.

An example of how such principles have been made part of the policies is the recital 31 of the Information Society Directive which states that, as a principle among right holders, there must be a fair balance between rights and interests.[135] Author's dignity is mentioned in the same Directive (recital 9), and if those recitals are interpreted systematically, it would be clear that

---

(section 203.a.3); (3) an advance notice in writing should be produced stating the date of termination and shall be served not less than two years or more than ten before that date; (4) is should be recorded at the Register of Copyrights. Finally, no agreement to the contrary is valid about termination (section 203.a.5). United States Copyright Office (n 21).

133. *Millar v. Taylor* (n 48) at 2333 and 2334.
134. *Schroeder Music Publishing v. Macaulay* (n 110). Mentioned in Cornish (n 110). pp. 390-392.
135. Parliament and Council Directive 2001/29/EC of 22 May 2001 on the harmonisation of certain aspects of copyright and related rights in the information society [2001] OJ L167/10.

the aim proposed in recital 10, could not be achieved without the fair balance claimed in recital 31.[136]

Furthermore, the Directive 2019/790 has created a mechanism for such a balance to be achieved based on four pillars for the protection of the author's interests. One pillar is accepting the asymmetry between the parties in the contractual relationship and the principle of fair remuneration as established by the 2019/790 Directive, Article 18.[137] Another is the importance of transparency and accessing to the information related to the use and exploitation of the work for the author as a mean for the purpose of assessing the fairness in the development of the contract (Article 19). The third pillar would the possibility of revision or even revoke of the contract through the parties, meaning a remuneration adjustment mechanism (Article 20) and a right of revocation (Article 22). Finally, the fourth pillar is the possibility of enforcing such need to revise the contract or revoke it through either the judiciary or through an alternative dispute resolution mechanism, in case no agreement is reached on the remuneration adjustment, as it can be understood from recitals 78, 79 and 81 of the Directive.

The studied jurisdictions show some available mechanisms for the promotion of the author's dignity. In the case of the US, the above-mentioned termination of the contract of assignation is an example. In the case of Mexico, the limitation of the transference to fifteen years (with some exceptions) would be another. The adjustment mechanism and eventual revocation of contracts in Europe is the latest and perhaps the clearest legal initiative on the matter. Another example, though less strong than those mentioned previously, is the right for equitable remuneration for the authors who transfer their rental right in the case of films (Europe, Spain, the UK, and recently Colombia).

The Colombian Constitutional Court and some other courts have relied on this concept of a weaker position to assert the importance of protecting authors' interests, particularly in the case of protecting their income. The *Escalona* case, mentioned above, defines the scope of the author's dignity in connection with contractual practices and the judicial defence of the author's interests in case of a conflict as a result of the contract. For the Court, it is possible to consider that a person is defenceless not only if she cannot face another person's attack because there are no legal mechanisms at hand for

---

136. *See Case C-5/08 Infopaq International A/S v. Danske Dagblades Forening.* At 36-37.
137. Article 18: Principle of appropriate and proportionate remuneration. (1) Member States shall ensure that where authors and performers license or transfer their exclusive rights for the exploitation of their works or other subject matter, they are entitled to receive appropriate and proportionate remuneration. (2) In the implementation in national law of the principle set out in para. 1, Member States shall be free to use different mechanisms and take into account the principle of contractual freedom and a fair balance of rights and interests. Parliament and Council Directive 2019/790 of 17 April 2019 on copyright and related rights in the Digital Single Market and amending Directives 96/9/EC and 2001/29/EC.

her protection, but also in the case in which that person is weak in her contractual position and such mechanisms, if existent, are meaningless.

The precision in the concept of dignity helped the Colombian Court to define the scope of the Fundamental Jus, which would be the limit for the protection of fundamental rights through the Constitutional mechanism. What is not within the Fundamental Jus pertains to the ordinary jurisdiction and is out of the possibility of horizontal effect. Consequently, the author's dignity in the *Escalona* case was associated with the concept of his welfare and social security. The Court refers, in this case, to a previous decision that defines the inalienability of author's rights, which will be discussed in the next subsection.[138] Such a concept of dignity secures a minimal income for the author that would allow an adequate standard of living.

17.3.3 AUTONOMY

In terms of freedom of contract and the protection of author's will, the concept of autonomy creates some conundrums to analyse. These are related to the principle of freedom of contract against the protection of author's interests, the protection of author's freedom of creation in correlation with the concept of originality, and the problems that might arise from the protection of the author's moral interests towards the exercise of contractual assignment of rights, WMH, or works created by employees.

17.3.3.1 Freedom of Contract

The problem with the two principles stated above, the principle of dignity and the principle of freedom of creativity, is that for the law to protect such interests, the principle of autonomy that commands contractual relationships *inter pares* must be reduced in favour of one of the parties. In this section, the restrictions to such autonomy will be discussed in comparative law. The aim is to find trends in the different systems that would demonstrate the pertinence of such protections and its connection with the teleological principle of protecting the author's moral and material interests as a fundamental right.

The exercise of copyright, particularly in the case of economic rights, is based on the principle of private autonomy.[139] It should be possible for the author to freely transfer her rights to a third party in order to obtain economic

---

138. *Sentencia C-155/98 (Corte Constitucional)* [1998] www.corteconstitucional.gov.co/relatoria.
139. Kretschmer and others (n 103). *See* specially, Watt's section on the economic performance of copyright contracts.

benefits from his creation. However, the legislation about this matter shows that freedom of contract is not absolute in the case of copyright.[140]

17.3.3.1.1   Assignation of Copyright

Some countries restrict an author's freedom to contract more than others. Of the six countries under study, Mexico is the one that imposes more conditions in the contractual relationships. The UK and Argentina are probably the least interventionists. However, in the legislative history of the UK, certain limitations were adopted to protect the interests of an author's heirs. That is the case in section 5.2 in the 1909 Copyright Act which, under certain conditions, makes it possible to reverse the assignment of copyright to the author's estate twenty-five years after his death. Even if the author had agreed in life to dispose of such rights, the contract in those terms would be considered null and void. Colombian law from 1886 had a similar provision. However, since 1946, it was possible for Colombian authors to dispose of those reversionary interests in detriment of their heirs. The Copyright Act of 1956 in the UK eliminated the figure from the legislation. A similar situation occurred with a Spanish provision enacted in 1879.[141] Colombia and Mexico have similar provisions for reversion of assigned rights.

Colombian law intervened strongly in the author's contractual relationships through an unexpected statute. A law created for the promotion of culture included an article declaring authors' rights inalienable for the purpose of guaranteeing their social security. The Constitutional Court studied the statute and reduced its effect to those cases in which the author's social security is in jeopardy.[142] The decision argued both, the importance of economic rights' transferability, and the principle of protection of author's interests in the two dimensions mentioned above, author's freedom of creativity and the economic reward required for the guaranty of author's survival. This is why, in the final decision, absolute inalienability was denied and fitted to an unstable concept of risk in which protecting the author's social security should prevail over the assignment. Such a strong tool to destabilize the right holder's ownership has not been used as much as would be expected. Nevertheless, the tool exists, and it was alleged in the *Escalona* case, studied below. More research on the possible impact of such a tool is required.

---

140. The principle of freedom of contract is more evident, although not absolute in the UK. *See* for this matter: Patrick Selim Atiyah, *The Rise and Fall of Freedom of Contract* (Oxford University Press 1979).
141. For the comparative analysis of these provisions in both the UK and Spain, *see*: Paul Torremans and Carmen Otero Garcia-Castrillon, 'Reversionary Copyright: A Ghost of the Past or a Current Trap to Assignments of Copyright?' (2012) Intellectual Property Quarterly 77.
142. *Sentencia C-155/98 (Corte Constitucional)* (n 138). This case has been mentioned earlier in the discussion of the Constitutional approach to the concept of authorship.

Mexican highest Court examined a similar issue regarding the normative restriction to waiving author's royalties resulted from the communication to the public of her work.[143] The Plenum of the Court was required to decide whether such a rule would imply the inalienability of the royalty or not. For this purpose, the highest Mexican Court introduced an amplified concept of the beneficiaries of the Constitutional protection of copyright: they are not only the authors but also those persons who intervene in the development of copyright industries.[144]

As it has been mentioned above when analysing the Mexican approach to the fundamental protection of author's rights, the Court introduced a complex study which begins with the premise that copyright should not be reduced to a mere question of private (or civil) law. It has wider connotations in which the Constitutional protection of author's rights is coherent with the protection of freedom of expression in connection with the free emission, reception, and communication of cultural information and the protection of author's moral and material interests. The exercise of such a complex right has a direct implication in the author's autonomy, says the Court,[145] as it affects the principles of freedom of contract when the public policy finds that is necessary to restraint such autonomy in order to protect authors in their weaker position as much as it could affect the author's own interests. In its analysis, the Court found that the Mexican Congress deliberately decided to withdraw from the bill the inalienability of this right and leave enacted a non-waivable right. A wider analysis of Mexican copyright law would show that other mechanisms have been enacted to protect the author's rights, as it has been mentioned in the previous sub-sections. For example, by creating restrictions in the scope of the transferences, reducing the effect of the transfer in the case of works created for advertisement, and creating statutory implied terms, which would fill certain gaps in the contracts such as the definition of the duration of the transfer.

In Colombia, the *Escalona* case[146] has been the only case so far in which author's rights inalienability has been argued. The Court recognized as a principle that the law of the contract should be protected; otherwise, the consequent legal instability would be highly detrimental for the economy of the industry. However, the Court decided to address the case that challenged the assignation contracts an author signed, and, in spite of the death of the claimant, it first studied the legal feasibility of revising private contractual relationships from the perspective of the protection of fundamental rights. The Court analysed three basic elements for this purpose.

---

143. *Sentencia No 20709 (SCJ Pleno)* (n 94).
144. An analysis of these decisions can be found in: Roberto Garza Barbosa, 'El Artículo 1705(3) Del Tratado de Libre Comercio de América Del Norte y Su Interpretación Por La Suprema Corte de Justicia de La Nación' (2015) XLVIII Boletín Mexicano de Derecho Comparado 1231 <http://www.redalyc.org/articulo.oa?id=42741552010>.
145. *Sentencia No 20709 (SCJ Pleno)* (n 94).
146. *Sentencia T-367/09 (Corte Constitucional)* (n 1).

First, it analysed the horizontal effect of the constitutional protection of fundamental rights – in this case, the author's rights. As it was mentioned above, the effect of protecting the author's interests as a fundamental right in the system of laws is that it would clash with other fundamental rights, in particular the right to property. The literature in this area has been focused mostly on the interaction between societal interests (freedom of expression, access to culture, education) and the exclusive exercise of copyright. However, in the dimension proposed here, the clash would occur when the author's rights affect other proprietary interests. This would be only possible in the case of real and present danger to the fundamental interests of the interested party, in this case, the author.

Second, the principle of *pacta sunt servanda*. The horizontal effect, as it will be explained below, implies that the judiciary should consider that some individual's actions might affect another individual's fundamental rights. In virtue of such a possibility, the judge might be able to break the contract or amend it in order to restore the desired balance among parties.

Finally, the Court also considered the residual nature of the Constitutional action against contracts. The proper mechanism to solve disputes in the case of contracts would have been civil jurisdiction. However, the Court considered that if it is the case of a weak position of one of the parties and in the case of risk for this party's fundamental rights, the Constitutional action is viable as a mechanism to protect such rights.

The Court findings rely on those three elements to find that if alive, the revision of the contracts between Mr Escalona and the musical publisher would have been accepted in order to protect his dignity.

In the EU, the Directive 2019/790 takes into account the necessity of balancing the principle of freedom of contract and the rights of the author. Article 18.2 makes such necessity clear. It is, however, evident that such freedom has limitations as in the case of the revision of the contracts or their eventual revocation. Under very specific conditions, the EU law accepts the need for counterbalance the contractual relationship that shows has been unbalanced.

17.3.3.1.2   Works Made for Hire or Similar Figures

In the sphere of WMH, the situation tends to be stringent towards the author as this figure tends to protect the economic interests of the investor.

In the cases of WMH, the production of software and films, the legislations of the countries under study create presumptions in which the copyright is vested or assigned to the producer. However, as a manner of balance, those presumptions are constrained in certain conditions that more or less could protect the author's interests.

Nevertheless, not every employment relationship has, as a consequence, the transfer of the author's rights. There are some requirements that can be exemplified in some cases. In Spain, for instance, the First Chamber of the

Supreme Tribunal assessed the conditions required for the transfer of rights under cases of WMH. In that case, the Court discarded the publishing contract as a WMH as it lacked two elements: the intention of the parties to transfer the copyright and that there was not a concrete contractual specificity in the expected content of the work. Due to the obscurity of the clauses of the contract, the Court applied the rules of the Spanish Civil Code by which '[t]he interpretation of obscure clauses in the contract must not favour the party who caused the obscurity'.[147] Consequently, it declared that the contract was not of the kind of a WMH.

In other legislations, the financial muscle has a similar effect on the copyright entitlement. Colombia has rules related to works created under labour relationship and works made for hire. In these cases, only those rights required by the employer or commissioner at the moment of creation of the work would be deemed transferred. Nevertheless, if by the contract, the author retains his rights, the presumption stated in the law would be superseded.

The level of autonomy on these cases has also been assessed by the Colombian Constitutional Court with respect to the mechanism of presumptive transference of the copyright in the case of film productions and the WMH.[148] In this case, the plaintiff attacked the laws enacting such transfers under the argument of an unreasonable limitation to the freedom of contract. The Court highlighted that, even if the presumptive transfer is the rule, the author keeps the possibility to negotiate and retain his rights. The statute protects the economic interests of the corporations and investors who take the risk of producing and publishing or disseminating the work at their expenses. An author's contractual autonomy is safeguarded as she can introduce an agreement rejecting the presumptive transfer within the contract. The Colombian Court bore in mind that copyright can only be originated by the hands of the author; therefore, third persons who have not participated in the creative process can only own the patrimonial rights derivatively from the author. In the case of moral persons, the Court completely denies the possibility of authorship, as they do not have the creative capacity.[149]

The restrictive interpretation of the WMH has been assessed as well in the US. In *Community for Creative Non-Violence v. Reid* (*CCNV v. Reid*),[150] the scope of section 101 of the 1976 Copyright Act, when referring to the concept of WMH, is defined. First, in the case of commissioned works, the

---

147. *See*: *Sentencia del Tribunal Supremo Sala de lo Civil No 55/2005* [2005] www.poder-judicial.es. Codigo Civil 1889. Article 1288. Translation available: http://www.wipo.int/wipolex/en/text.jsp?file_id=221319#LinkTarget_6410.
148. *Sentencia C-276/96 (Corte Constitucional)* (n 87).
149. *Sentencia C-276/96 (Corte Constitucional)* (n 87). This principle has been also stated by the Andean Tribunal of Justice: *Proceso 24-IP-98* (1998) XV Gac Of del Acuerdo Cart 14.
150. *Community for Creative Non-Violence v. Reid* (1989) 490 US 730.

concept applies for certain types of work enumerated in the statute.[151] Second, the matter of what should be considered as ' … a work prepared by an employee within the scope of his or her employment' should be assessed when the case is referred to as a work created under employment. The protection for authors consists in that any other kind of works not considered under the statute would not be deemed transferred to the employer.

The UK shows a slightly different approach. First of all, in the current law, the commissioned works are not considered part of the WMH.[152] Second, in the case of employment, the transfer is subject to demonstrate three basic conditions as mentioned by Bently and Sherman:[153] that the author is an employee, that the work was created in the course of employment and that they are not in agreement on the contrary.

In the UK, *Ray v. Classic FM* mentioned above shows an interesting point of view about the matter under discussion. Notwithstanding the definition of conditions for authorship mentioned before in connection with the concept of originality, the case also explores the importance given to the economic muscle invested in the production of the work. Because the contract between the author (the claimant) and the corporation (the defendant) was not an employment contract, section 11.2 of the CDPA-UK would not apply. Consequently, no copyright would be in the hands of the defendant. However, Justice Lightman faced the problem of deciding in equity if the defendant is entitled to some amount of copyright. Given that the purpose of the contract was to obtain a certain work for the use of the company and some money was paid for such a work, the doctrine of implied terms in the contract was applied. As a consequence, it was accepted that permission to use the commissioned work would be implied, but 'the licence accordingly is to be limited to what is in the joint contemplation of the parties at the date of the contract, and does not extend to enable the Client to take advantage of a new unexpected profitable opportunity'.[154]

Comparatively, this is a similar reason to the one applied by the Argentinian courts. The lack of regulations on the matter led the judiciary to interpret the contract in equity. While protecting the interest of the author, the judiciary has also found a way to respond to the economic interest of the investor. The case law has analysed the possible consequences of contracts in which the creation is commissioned and has established that the transfer (or eventually the mere licence) for the use of the work would be the result of the parties' volition expressed on the written agreement that the law requires for these circumstances. Such an agreement would be interpreted restrictively in favour of the author. Therefore, no more rights than those

---

151. *See*: Gorman, Ginsburg and Reese (n 123). p. 325.
152. Torremans (n 112); Lionel Bently and Brad Sherman, *Intellectual Property Law* (4th edn, Oxford University Press 2014).
153. Bently and Sherman (n 152). pp. 133-135.
154. *Ray v. Classic FM plc* (n 47).

considered in the contract by which the work was commissioned would be considered assigned to the commissioner.[155]

In addition to the previous considerations, the principle of 'money talks' and the analysis of the rules in the protection of the elements of dignity and autonomy regarding the assignation of copyrights and the WMH doctrine leads to the conclusion that the protection of authorship, as established in the systems of laws of most of the countries under study, requires strong mechanisms of protection to produce a balance between the fundamental interests of authors and other copyright owners.

The trend is, in general, the limitations on the assignment of rights through different tools such as reversionary rights, limitation in time or in the scope of the transfer, or even, in some cases, by declaring the total or partial inalienability of the copyright. In the case of WMH or similar agreements, the author is affected by a presumed transfer that subsumes her will by the effect of the law. Nevertheless, in these cases, the causes for such presumption are usually restrictive and the law, in any case, opens the possibility for the author to contractually revert the effect of the presumption. The comparative study shows that freedom of contract is importantly restricted to secure higher aims such as the protection of author's rights, but also to guarantee a proper return on the investment the other party has incurred.

17.3.3.2　　　Freedom of Creativity

Another sphere of autonomy to be analysed is the freedom the author can exercise while creating the work. In this case, the complexities of creation and production would show some peculiarities. For instance, one can argue that there is not the same level of autonomy in the case of creating a computer program than in the case of poetry. However, both examples are protected under copyright. Should the rules of assignation or transference of right apply in the same way in both cases? Apparently, no. In the case of works created under commission or by employees, are they as free as independent authors who create their works by their own initiative?

Three examples serve to understand this problem. First, the case of WMH under the US Copyright Law (section 101 US Code) and *CCNV v. Reid*,[156] mentioned above. Second, the modifications to the rules applied for WMH in Colombia. And third, *Stevenson and others v. MacDonald and others* in the UK in which it has been distinguished between the employer's control and author's integration to the company.

In the first case, the distinction that the Supreme Court clarifies in the CCNV case between commissioned works and works under employment is important. In this case, the exercise of control in the creation of the work was

---

155. *C 393625 Santander De Santamaría María Cristina c/ López Gutiérrez Benilde y otros s/ daños y perjuicios (CNCIV Sala F)* [2004] elDial.com.
156. *Community for Creative Non-Violence v. Reid* (n 150).

considered in order to justify the WMH for commissioned works. 'Because a party who hires a "specially ordered or commissioned" work by definition has a right to specify the characteristics of the product desired, at the time the commission is accepted, and frequently until it is completed, the right to control the product test would mean that many works that could satisfy § 101(2) would already have been deemed works for hire under § 101(1).' However, the Court, in its analysis of how the statute was approved, found that such control was not the reason used in supporting the figure. Thus, control-based rationality would have affected the balance between the parties in the case of commissioned works.[157]

On the other hand, in the case of employment under the US copyright law, the Court has defined thirteen factors (in search for 'predictability') which have been enumerated by Nard et al.[158] Those factors would help to assess in which case, under the common law of agency, it could be claimed that the work created by the employee belongs to the employer. It has been argued by the cited authors that such a number of factors do not help for the predictability of the subject matter to be transferred as a single factor would do. Nevertheless, those factors are relevant in this analysis as they imply a general sense of the employer's control of the author's creation. Nard et al. summarize the factors from which is possible to highlight some that show such a level of control: (1) the hiring party's control over the 'manner and means' for the creation of the product; (2) the source of tools for the creation; (3) the right to assign more projects to the author under the same relationship; (4) author's scope of decision about hiring assistants and about the duration of the work; (5) whether the product is part of the hiring party's business and whether it is in business. These factors show that control is important for the CCNV Court regarding the employment situation to apply the WMH doctrine.[159]

The control issue has also been treated in the change in the legislation concerning WMH in Colombia. The original law from 1982 stated a specific rule for commissioned works that would not include the employment relationship.[160] Most of the argument about such a difference was that the

---

157. *Community for Creative Non-Violence v. Reid* (n 150). At 748. For the Court, 'importing a test based on a hiring party's right to control, or actual control of, a product would unravel the "carefully worked out compromise aimed at balancing legitimate interests on both sides."'

158. Craig Allen Nard, David W. Barnes and Michael J Madison, *The Law of Intellectual Property*, vol. 1 (2nd edn, Wolters Kluwer 2008). pp. 416-417.

159. Similar factors have been mentioned by Bently and Sherman regarding the employment conditions for the works created in the course of employment under UK Copyright Law. *See* Bently and Sherman (n 152). p. 134.

160. The original Article 20 in the 1982 Colombian Copyright Law was written only for the purpose of commissioned works made under a contractual plan for the creation of the work. Under such conditions, copyright would be transferred for the requesting party, and only author's moral rights (paternity and integrity) should remain in the hands of the author. Law No. 23 – On Copyright. Article 20.

presumption of transfer would only apply under certain conditions. Such conditions were that the work should not exist before the contract was signed, that the producer should be responsible for the production of the work, and most importantly, that a previous plan for the creation of the commissioned work should have been agreed on previously. The plan served two basic purposes: the possibility of identifying the work product of the commission (and therefore, the subject matter to be transferred) and that the plan determines the creation itself.

The reform adopted in 2011 changed Colombian legislation concerning WMH and included both the commissioned works and the works created under an employment relationship as in cases of WMH.[161] The statute, however, has abandoned the condition of a previous plan and it does not refer to any difference or qualification between commissioned works or employee's works whatsoever; it simply states the consequences for such kind of works, as it has been mentioned above.

Finally, the UK case of *Stevenson, Jordan and Harrison Ltd v. McDonald & Evans* calls attention to the fact that in some cases, control under a contract of service is not possible. Whether a work has been created under a contract of service or not, determines if such a work pertains to the employer or the employee. In the case, the question regarded if, while some sections of a book the author wrote were written because of lectures the author gave during his service to the plaintiffs, other sections were written for the purpose of a manual delivered by the company to its clients, all of those sections or only some of them would belong to the author's employer? According to the Court, while the sections written for the manual were an integral part of the company business and the author have worked as an employee, the copyright in such sections belong to his employer. The sections resulted from the lectures are not an integral part of the business, rather they would be considered an accessory to the contract of service. In the words of Denning, L.J., while the work created as an integral part of the business under the contract of service, even if created not necessarily under the control of the employer, would be considered anyhow as part of the business. However, the work created under a contract for services is accessory to such services, for instance, delivering a lecture, and therefore it

---

161. The reform to the Colombian Copyright Law introduced in 2011 states that When the work has been commissioned or has been made by an employee, the law presumes that only those rights the hiring party requires for its regular activities at the moment of creation would be deemed transferred. Those rights outside such regular activities would remain under author's control. The contracting parties could decide differently by consensual agreement. In any case, such a relationship (employer – employee or commissioner – commissioned) should be agreed by writing; otherwise no presumption would apply (Article 20, as it was amended in 2011 by the Law 1450, Article 28. *See* Law No. 1450 – by which the National Development Plan 2010-2014 has been established 2011).

would not belong to the employer.[162] The important part here is to highlight that control is not necessarily the only standard applicable upon works created by employees, if the work was created as an integral part of the business by the author, it would belong to the employer.

The factors considered under US and UK laws are helpful in assessing the cases in which a work should be considered owned by the employer. In general terms, control over the creation is the main factor that determines the allocation of the copyright. But if the work is the result of activities which are an integral part of the employer's business, this would also be a factor to consider for the allocation of the copyright as in the case of the UK. In the case of Colombia, the lack of determination of any factor lead to the Courts in the future to assess which cases the work might be exploited by the employer. However, it should be noted that, in the Colombian case under the new legislation, a work created under employment is not to be transferred in full to the employer but only those rights required at the moment of creation of the work would be assigned.

Although Argentinian law has not enacted general rules for the case of WMH, the case mentioned above about contracts in which the creation of work was commissioned requires the express assignation of the copyright within the contract. Thus, in the case of software, the conditions differ and are worth to mention it as an indication of the probable route the Argentinian law might follow. In this case, the software created under employment belongs to the employer only if the author was hired for such a purpose. That implies that some certainty should exist within the contract to identify in which cases the presumption would apply.

EU Law, in the case of software, makes those conditions more evident. Two mechanisms of creation might determine the transference. Either the work has been created under the execution of duties as an employee, which would be easy to prove, or the work was created following the employer's orders. In both cases, it is clear that the author lacks freedom in terms of her creation as is subjected to the constraints of the employment relationship.[163]

From the point of view of the authors, however, in the case of commissioned works, the control rule seems to be a two-edged weapon. On the one hand, the author is taking most of the risks in the creation and, as a consequence, it seems reasonable that in most of the cases the copyright would be kept in her hands (unless the law says otherwise). That would be the main conclusion of the *CCNV* Court in the US. On the other hand, the Colombian legislation has shown that it is possible to manage the control under commissioned works through the requirement of a previously agreed

---

162. *Stevenson, Jordan and Harrison Ltd v. McDonald and Evans* [1952] 69 RPC 10.
163. In addition, the Directive 2019/790, Article 23.2, allows the EU members to exclude the software from the application of any of the rules related fair contracts and remuneration to authors.

plan that would constrain author's creativity but also would provide certainty about whether a work falls under the WMH doctrine or not.

In the case of employment, certainty and control are factors at play. Employed authors normally are under the control of their employer and the clearer that relationship is, the more certain would be to define which creations belong to the author and which ones are deemed transferred.

On the other hand, if the author lacks control of the creative process, this will imply that the rights would be given to the employer. Fisk has explained this phenomenon in the US as a mechanism by which creativity has been bureaucratized.[164] The collectivization of creativity tends to reduce the scope of freedom that an employed author might have.

This could be seen as an extreme position, but it is undeniable that the fewer mechanisms the authors have to keep the control of their works in their hands, the lesser the principles that underline the protection of artistic and literary works are reflected in the practice of copyright.

In the same token of autonomy, the author's intent and will is openly protected. The best example of such protection is the ban on the assignment of future works of the author in a general clause. A statutory provision, in this case, has been often enacted. By such provisions, undefined future works cannot be transferred. This is the case of Colombia, Spain and Mexico. The Spanish law makes clear the incidence of this in terms of freedom: the prohibition is also extended to contracts in which the author agrees not to create.[165] In the UK, prospective copyright has a special treatment in terms of the effects of the assignment agreement. For this section, what is clear is that the prospective copyright is referred to copyright that will or may come into existence but in reference to a future work. This might imply that such a work should be expected.[166]

The conclusion of this discussion might lead to assert that if the author must relinquish his autonomy and/or his dignity somehow, her communicative power is also diminished, and therefore, the strength in the protection of the work in term of fundamental rights would also be diminished.[167]

---

164. Fisk (n 104). *See* particularly her Chapter 7.
165. The assignment of rights over the group of works that an author might create in the future, should be considered null (Article 43.3). Any contract by which the author accepts not to create some work in the future should be considered null (Article 43.4). Non-existent modes of exploitation at the moment of the contract are not part of the contract (Article 43.5). Royal Legislative Decree No. 1/1996 of 12 April 1996. Consolidated text of the Law on [Copyright], regularizing, clarifying and harmonizing the Applicable Statutory Provisions.
166. For further analysis of this, *see*: Laddie 1946-2008 and others (n 121) at 24.6.
167. A similar conclusion regarding the different uses that different kind of creators and their works can generate has been asserted by Gervais. *See*: Daniel Gervais, *(Re)Structuring Copyright* (Edward Elgar Publishing 2017) <https://www.elgaronline.com/view/9781785369490/9781785369490.xml>.

17.4   CONCLUSIONS

Author's moral and material interests are worth to be protected in a complex mixture of interests that supersede the mere rewarding-economic reasonability. Those interests are represented in the core elements of the author's fundamental rights indicated through General Comment 17 mentioned above. These elements respond to the principles of dignity and autonomy for authors.

The copyright system, then, operates in a twofold way in which freedom of choice applies for all society members and authors, but it is not absolute as it imposes certain limitations to both of them, for instance, in the case of protecting author's interests, certain limitations can be imposed to freedom of contract, but freedom of choice also implies that original creativity is a potentiality in every individual which if expressed would produce copyright.

Authorship requires creativity, and therefore, human intervention in the meaning of originality. The analysis of the relationship between authorship and originality in the constitutional perspective has shown that fostering authors and protecting freedom of creativity are core elements for the systems, for these protect equal conditions for all individuals to participate in the cultural life of society.

In the case law studied in the previous sections, it has been shown that freedom is an important precondition for the author's creativity. The exercise of freedom of creativity implies the potential originality in the creation and consequently, the existence of copyright. In the aftermath, the purpose of copyright guarantees a reward for the author, but the purpose of protecting the author's rights is, additionally, the guaranty of the author's communicative power. The laws under study here have shown that some national public policies have adopted certain mechanisms in order to provide balance for the author's contractual relationships.[168] Meanwhile, the case law should enter then in motion to promote and reshape the balance.

The answer to the question about how far a particular system can protect the author's rights depends on many factors. On the analysis proposed in this chapter, the factors considered are the two basic mechanisms for the transfer of copyrights, the assignment by contractual agreements and the WMH doctrine or other similar mechanisms.

From those two factors, the principles of dignity and autonomy were studied in the perspective of the desired balance between the interests of authors and other right holders of the copyright. For the analysis of how such a balance could be achieved, the case law and the comparative study of the

---

168. A good example of such a circumstance has been assessed for the reform of the European Copyright laws in the digital market. *See*: European Commission, 'Digital Single Market, Copyright' (*Digital Single Market*, 2016) <https://ec.europa.eu/digital-single-market/copyright> accessed 4 March 2017.

legal instruments of the countries considered were studied. This has shown that some restrictions have been implemented aimed to protect freedom of creativity and expression, the dignity of authors and the protection of their bargain position.

The disparities between different countries regarding the protection of this weak position creates a necessity of establishing a basic structure of principles that would support such decisions. On the one hand, it should support that authors benefit from the success of the works they created through the principles of dignity and autonomy. On the other hand, it should be possible that, while protecting those interests, others also benefit from the chain of creation, production, and dissemination of works, either because they make such dissemination possible or because they are members of society which, through the same idea, enjoy the right to freely access and participate in the cultural and scientific life of their societies.

Consequently, once those principles have been identified by the judiciary, their assessment would review the mechanisms that the statutes have been implementing, and then the courts should decide whether the desirable balance has been altered and the mechanisms to restore it.

In the cases in which those two principles, autonomy and/or dignity can be jeopardized, the judiciary would require intervening and protect such interests. In that case, horizontality for the protection of fundamental rights seems to be an option.[169]

In this work, the horizontal effect has been mentioned as a tool that might help in understanding the possible conflicts in protecting those principles. Horizontality can be, in fact, a very limited option in case of its application within the system of laws. This because most of those systems should have created legal mechanisms with enough effectivity for the solution of possible conflicts between stakeholders.[170]

The result of those legal mechanisms available in the systems of laws under study is the creation of certain limitations to contractual autonomy. Although most of those limitations have been created as statutory enactments, some have been the result of the judiciary's active participation in the protection of the author's interests. Then, some areas of action can be identified in order to further protect those principles and interests stated above: (1) the instance of legal policies in which the State could decide to structurally protect such interests; (2) the constitutional and international law's support of decisions from the judiciary when the legal instruments are not enough or have not been used correctly, and, finally; (3) the sphere of decision-making of stakeholders. In this last instance, the stakeholders' own policies of copyright management could achieve a better balance towards the author's interests.

---

169. Nevertheless, for certain countries, direct horizontality might not be the proper path as in the case of the UK. Young (n 5).
170. Alexy (n 5). *See also* Young (n 5); Fastrich (n 5).

The instance of legal policies can create mechanisms of protection of authors in their contractual relationships. However, the most important drawback is that the creation of limitations to contractual freedom would not be easily accepted. Bearing this in mind, two possibilities arise as the most likely.

The first would be the creation of provisions called to fill eventual gaps in the contracts, for example, in the case of assignment, if the contract does not define the scope of the transfer or its duration. The law could create statutory terms limiting the scope of the transfer to those rights related to the main interest of the assignee at the moment of the contract, or to limit the duration of the transfer for some years. In the case of WMH, some limitations in the scope of rights transferred could balance the relationship author-producer. Here, the rationality of the communicative theory could play an important role. The more communicative power a work has, the more protection its author/s would require. If the work has less communicative power, for instance, in those types of works in which the author's freedom of choice is limited, the effect of the transfer could be higher. Similar provisions as those shown in Mexico and Colombia, close to the doctrine of implied terms but bearing in mind not only the immediate purpose of the contract but also the superior interest in protecting the author could be adopted.

Other mechanisms within the possible introduction of legal reform of copyright contracts are the adoption of reversionary clauses limiting in time the duration of the transfer. Another is the introduction of mandatory limitations to the scope of the rights transferred, for instance, related to the nature of the commercial activities of the transferee at the moment of the contract.

Anticipating the activation of those legal mechanisms that would protect author's interests, stakeholders can assess their relationships and design contractual mechanisms in which, within the scope of action that private autonomy protects, some balanced clauses that protect author's interests could be created.

The position of the author in the contractual relationship can also be improved by extra-legal mechanisms such as collective bargaining of contractual relationships or by improving the role that in some countries agencies and agents play in negotiating contracts. In this case, agencies are not necessarily able to cover the whole spectrum of creators, though, and it is important that not all jurisdictions have or can develop those structures of the same kind.

The second option then relates more to the practice than to the contracts. It is possible to introduce figures of collective bargaining in certain sectors of the industry in which authors are not best sellers but rather contributors,[171] such as the sector of illustrations for books, writers, or musicians, who often

---

171. Kretschmer (n 110) p. 67.

have no power to negotiate their rights individually with long-time companies structured for the dissemination of works. The terms introduced by collective bargain could have the same effect, reducing the scope of rights transferred and/or creating limits to the duration of the transfer. For instance, the 'Fair Contract Initiative', developed by the Authors Guild Foundation in the US, proposes a series of principles towards the fairness in the contracts for book publishing.[172]

Collective bargain, however, has a drawback in the comparative perspective. Not all the countries have the same level of organization of guilds of authors. For instance, Latin American countries have not developed such structures enough yet.

Another mechanism between the legal and the private spheres is the promotion of managerial principles of administration of copyright. In not few of the cases studied above, the problems regarding authorship and the assignment of rights arise because of the informality in the practices of the industry and the lack awareness of the legal implications of certain decisions that authors and publishers and other parties have taken.

These possibilities operate on the national level of the law. The perspective of improving the author's contractual position through mechanisms in international law is another dimension to consider. Some factors are to be analysed in further studies. For instance, the interaction of international law on human rights with the treaties on copyright and intellectual property towards the protection of the author's moral and material interests. The applicability of these national mechanisms in cases of transboundary situations. Finally, the implementation of the regulation of principles for the protection of author's interests in the international arena, as it has been the case of the Directive 2019/790 is yet to be considered in a wider dimension.

---

172. The Authors Guild, 'Fair Contract Initiative' (*The Authors Guild*, 2015) <https://www.authorsguild.org/where-we-stand/fair-contracts/> accessed 24 October 2017.

Chapter 18

What Is Left of User Rights: Algorithmic Copyright Enforcement and Free Speech in the Light of the Article 17 Regime

Sebastian Felix Schwemer & Jens Schovsbo

Article 17 of the Directive on copyright and related rights in the Digital Single Market (hereinafter 'DSM Directive') has strengthened the protection of copyright holders. Moving forward, online content-sharing providers will be responsible for copyright infringement unless the use of works on their platforms is authorized or if they have made 'best efforts' to obtain an authorization and prevent the availability of unlicensed works. At the same time, the Directive has made it clear that users of protected works shall be able to rely on the existing limitations and exceptions regarding quotation, criticism and review and caricature, parody or pastiche. The Directive even casts these limitations and exceptions as 'user rights'. This chapter points out that copyright's limitations and exceptions have traditionally constituted a cornerstone in the internal balancing of the interests of users against rights holders and with a clear view of safeguarding the interests of free expression and information protected by the Charter. Given the overall purpose of the DSM Directive in strengthening the position of rights holders, there is a dire risk that the benefits of the limitations and exceptions evaporate in the attempts of platform operators to escape liability by use of algorithmic enforcement. The article uses the recent decisions of the Court of Justice of the European Union (CJEU) in Pelham, Funke Medien and Spiegel Online to draw attention to the central importance of the limitations and exception as the primary channel for fundamental rights analyses in copyright. It is finally pointed out how the DSM Directive – despite its on-the-paper recognition of users' rights – is most likely going to lead to a devaluation of those same rights.

18.1 INTRODUCTION

Article 17 of the Directive on copyright and related rights in the Digital Single Market[1] (hereinafter 'DSM Directive') aims to strengthen the position of copyright holders vis-à-vis online platform to fill an alleged *value gap* which has been argued to have arisen because of legal uncertainty and inefficient enforcement mechanisms. Seen from the perspective of fundamental rights, such an endeavour is in itself unproblematic or even laudatory: After all, the Charter of Fundamental Rights of the European Union's[2] (hereinafter 'Charter') Article 17(2) recognizes copyright as a fundamental right itself and mechanisms which ensure that copyright functions as anticipated by the legislator should be hailed as a natural extension of the acceptance of the system as such.

However, it is important to bear in mind that there is an intimate relationship between *substantive law* and *enforcement mechanisms*, or to phrase it more succinctly: between law as it appears in the books and law in action. As seen from such a perspective, legal analyses should include *i.a.* the *institutional setting* of the substantive law. This setting may either be 'too weak' in the sense that rights holders are not actually able to enforce their rights against users to the extent that the legislator has anticipated. Also, it may be 'too strong' in the sense that rights holders are able to overextend protection to claim more than their share, e.g., by limiting user rights. Both positions – the former of 'under enforcement' and the latter of 'overenforcement' – are problematic.

It is our starting point for the following, that whereas Article 17 may be seen as a response to a problem of 'under enforcement', the role which online sharing platforms are supposed to play implies a risk of 'over enforcement'.[3] These risks have been pointed out many times in the long, and at times, tumultuous process, which led to the adoption of Article 17 and the debate is far from over. By way of example, just a week after the Directive had been published in the Official Journal, Poland brought an action under Article 263 TFEU against Article 17 before the European Court of Justice (CJEU)

---

1. Directive (EU) 2019/790 on copyright and related rights in the Digital Single Market [2019] OJ L 130, pp. 92-125.
2. Charter of Fundamental Rights of the European Union [2012] OJ C 364, pp. 1-22.
3. *See* in this context, e.g., CJEU in C-360/10, *Belgische Vereniging van Auteurs, Componisten en Uitgevers CVBA (Sabam) v. Netlog*, ECLI:EU:C:2012:85, para. 50, that measures 'could potentially undermine freedom of information, since that system might not distinguish adequately between unlawful content and lawful content.'

seeking a partial annulment.[4] Specifically, the action is directed against the Article's provision regarding best efforts to ensure the unavailability unlicensed works as well as the prevention of re-uploads after takedowns, respectively.[5] The action is based on the Republic's view that the provision infringes the freedom of expression and the freedom of information guaranteed in Article 11 of the Charter.[6] In a similar vein, in March 2019, the UN Special Rapporteur on the promotion and protection of the right to freedom of opinion and expression, David Kaye, criticized the provision for its incompatibility with human rights, noting that '[m]isplaced confidence in filtering technologies to make nuanced distinctions between copyright violations and legitimate uses of protected material would escalate the risk of error and censorship'.[7] Also, the German Minister of Justice, Katharina Barley, had expressed concerns about the compatibility of Article 17 with fundamental rights but had given in to vote in favour nonetheless. Germany, in its extensive statement accompanying its Council vote, noted that '[t]he aim must be to make the "uploadfilter" instrument largely superfluous'.[8] Going even further, this is substantiated by the Council vote, where The Netherlands, Luxembourg, Poland, Italy and Finland voted against the Directive due to concerns that 'the final text of the Directive fails to deliver adequately on the above-mentioned aims' and '[m]ost notably [regret] that the Directive does not strike the right balance between the protection of right holders and the interests of EU citizens and companies'.[9] The scholarly community, too, has since early in the legislative process raised fundamental rights concerns in relation to the European Commission's proposal from September 2016 as well as the final text from May 2019.[10] Senftleben, for

---

4. Case C-401/19, *Republic of Poland v. European Parliament and Council of the European Union* (2019/C 270/24), OJ C 270, p. 22. The Polish action is also to be seen against the national political background. The Directive's Article 17 has been a prominent topic in the general public and during national elections.
5. Article 17(4)(b) and Article 17(4)(c), *in fine*.
6. Interestingly, the Republic chose not to invoke the right to conduct business.
7. UNHR, *EU Must Align Copyright Reform with International Human Rights Standards, Says Expert* (11 March 2019), https://www.ohchr.org/EN/NewsEvents/Pages/DisplayNews.aspx?NewsID=24298&LangID=E.
8. Council of the European Union, Statement by Germany, (5 April 2019), point 8, https://data.consilium.europa.eu/doc/document/ST-7986-2019-ADD-1/en/pdf.
9. Council of the European Union, Joint statement by the Netherlands, Luxembourg, Poland, Italy and Finland, (5 April 2019), https://data.consilium.europa.eu/doc/document/ST-7986-2019-ADD-1/en/pdf.
10. *See*, e.g., Sophie Stalla-Bourdillon et.al., *Open Letter to the European Commission – On the Importance of Preserving the Consistency and Integrity of the EU Acquis Relating to Content Monitoring within the Information Society* (30 September 2016), https://ssrn.com/abstract=2850483; Martin Senftleben et al., *The Recommendation on Measures to Safeguard Fundamental Rights and the Open Internet in the Framework of the EU Copyright Reform,* European Intellectual Property Review (2018) 40(3), 149-163; Christina Angelopoulos, *On Online Platforms and the Commission's New Proposal for a Directive on Copyright in the Digital Single Market,* (January 2017), https://ssrn.com/

example, criticizes the 'remarkable transformation of the function of copyright law ... [which] degenerates into a censorship and filtering instrument.'[11]

In this contribution, we join the conversation. Article 17 addresses the triangular relation between rights holders, online content-sharing service providers (OCSSPs) and users. Much of the criticism is related to the Article's interface with the E-Commerce Directive's[12] prohibition of general monitoring obligations[13] and fundamental rights. Here, we are not addressing the – principal – upstream question of compatibility of potential content filtering with fundamental rights. Instead, we focus on the relation between OCSSPs and the issues of freedom of expression, freedom of information and freedom of arts. More specifically, we focus on *the role of copyright's limitations and exceptions* in the scheme set up by Article 17. These provisions, which stem from the international copyright conventions where they are anchored in the three-step test, have traditionally constituted a centrepiece of copyright's *internal* safeguards of users' interests. In the following, we revisit the limitations and exceptions[14] in the light of Article 17, which has at the same time instituted a regime of algorithmic enforcement *and* bolstered the system of limitations and exceptions by recasting some of the limitations and exceptions as *user rights* and imposing procedural obligations on OCSSPs to safeguard those rights.

18.2   THE REGIME OF ARTICLE 17

18.2.1   Introduction

The background for Article 17 DSM Directive on the 'Use of protected content by online content-sharing service providers' is a peculiar one: the intermediary liability exemption rules of the E-Commerce Directive have

---

abstract=2947800; João Quintais et al., *Safeguarding User Freedoms in Implementing Article 17 of the Copyright in the Digital Single Market Directive: Recommendations From European Academics*, (11 November 2019), https://ssrn.com/abstract=3484968.

11. Martin Senftleben, *Bermuda Triangle – Licensing, Filtering and Privileging User-Generated Content Under the New Directive on Copyright in the Digital Single Market*, (4 April 2019), https://ssrn.com/abstract=3367219, p. 5.

12. Directive 2000/31/EC of the European Parliament and of the Council of 8 June 2000 on certain legal aspects of information society services, in particular electronic commerce, in the Internal Market [2000] OJ L 178, pp. 1-16 (hereinafter the 'E-Commerce Directive' or 'ECD').

13. Article 15 ECD.

14. The DSM Directive introduces several new limitations and exceptions. Given our focus on the specific Article 17-context, these are outside the scope of our contribution. Also, Article 25 DSM Directive on the relationship with exceptions and limitations provided for in other directives is outside the scope.

allegedly led to a failure in the copyright market.[15] Based on the notice-and-takedown regime, online content sharing platforms have been argued to have enjoyed an unfair advantage when negotiating (music) licensing deals with rights holders.[16] In a nutshell, this very specific issue of a potential 'value gap' in relation to the use of musical works on platforms like YouTube,[17] provides the context of Article 17.

According to Article 17(1) DSM Directive, Member States shall provide that an OCSSP performs an act of communication to the public or an act of making available to the public for the purposes of the Directive when it gives the public access to copyright-protected works or other protected subject matter uploaded by its users.[18] In other words, affected services are directly liable for copyright infringements by user uploads. In these situations, the horizontal liability exemption rules are thrown overboard.[19] Thus, affected platforms can no longer invoke Article 14 E-Commerce Directive for the copyright-relevant acts of their users and licensing becomes the legislative default option for the use of copyright-protected works in these situations, too.[20]

Instead of the traditional Article 14 E-Commerce Directive liability exemption regime for 'hosting',[21] Article 17(4) stipulates the new cumulative

---

15. It is notable that the question whether YouTube can be considered 'passive' and thus falls under the liability exemption rules of Article 14 ECD, has only recently been subject to a reference to the CJEU, *see* Case C-682/18, *YouTube* and Case C-500/19, *Puls 4 TV*. Related question had previously been answered by the Court in Joined Cases C-236/08 to C-238/08, *Google AdWords*, ECLI:EU:C2010:159, para. 107, and Case C-324/09 (eBay) ECLI:EU:C:2011:474, para. 113.

16. *See*, e.g., Stan Liebowitz, *Economic Analysis of Safe Harbor Provisions* (prepared for CISAC, 27 February 2018). *See also* the problem definition in the Commission's Impact Assessment: 'Rightholders have no or limited control over the use and the remuneration for the use of their content by services storing and giving access to large amounts of protected content uploaded by their users', European Commission, *Commission Staff Working Document, Impact Assessment on the modernisation of EU copyright rules*, Brussels, 14.9.2016 SWD (2016) 301 final, PART 1/3, p. 137 and p. 143.

17. Effectively, the scope of Article 17 is broader, though: 'online-content sharing service providers' (OCSSPs) defined in Article 2 nr. 6 DSM Directive, likely also encompasses other platforms like Facebook, Slideshare (sharing of presentations), Pinterest (image sharing), Snapchat, Instagram, erotic streaming sites like Pornhub, etc.

18. The unclarity of what constitutes a communication to the public has also been identified as obstacle by Commission in European Commission, *Towards a modern, more European copyright framework*, COM(2015) 626 final, p. 9. On case law on communication to the public more broadly, *see* João Pedro Quintais, *Untangling the Hyperlinking Web: In Search of the Online Right of Communication to the Public*, The Journal of World Intellectual Property (2018) 21(5-6), 385-420.

19. Article 17(3) DSM Directive.

20. On licensing, *see* Martin Husovec & João Quintais, *How to License Article 17? Exploring the Implementation Options for the New EU Rules on Content-Sharing Platforms*, IViR Working Paper (1 October 2019), https://ssrn.com/abstract=3463011.

21. Article 14(1) E-Commerce Directive on hosting reads: 'Where an information society service is provided that consists of the storage of information provided by a recipient of

conditions under which an OCSSP is not liable for content uploaded by its users.[22] First, Article 17(4)(a) DSM Directive stipulates that affected services need to demonstrate their *best effort* to obtain licences for user-uploaded content. This is the main trajectory foreseen by the Directive to achieve its goals.[23] Second, according to Article 17(4)(b), affected services also need to have 'made, in accordance with high industry standards of professional diligence, best efforts to ensure the unavailability of specific works and other subject matter for which the rightholders have provided the service providers with the relevant and necessary information'. Third, in any event, affected services need to have 'acted expeditiously, upon receiving a sufficiently substantiated notice from the rightholders, to disable access to, or to remove from their websites, the notified works or other subject matter, and made best efforts to prevent their future uploads in accordance with point (b)' according to Article 17(4)(c).[24]

In this way, it follows from Article 17 that it is the duty of OCSSPs to 'filter' unlicensed works and prevent their upload or re-upload. Compared to earlier versions in the legislative process, where technical means were directly mentioned, the final version of the Directive refrains from prescribing that the mechanism is implemented by using algorithmic solutions. Thus, there exists, in fact, no *ex lege* obligation for the affected parties to rely on algorithms. However, given the practical infeasibility of handling a large number of user uploads, the difficulty in identifying previously blocked content without technical means, as well as the reference to 'high industry standards' in the provision[25], the use of such algorithmic solutions is likely, akin to a de facto imposition.

---

the service, Member States shall ensure that the service provider is not liable for the information stored at the request of a recipient of the service, on condition that:

   (a)   the provider does not have actual knowledge of illegal activity or information and, as regards claims for damages, is not aware of facts or circumstances from which the illegal activity or information is apparent; or

   (b)   the provider, upon obtaining such knowledge or awareness, acts expeditiously to remove or to disable access to the information.'

22. On the one hand, Article 17(4) DSM Directive is somewhat awkward in the context of copyright, systematically it fits with much better within the E-Commerce Directive, where intermediary liability exceptions are horizontally addressed and to which Article 17 is represents a sector-specific carve-out. On the other hand, Article 17(1) DSM Directive introduces a substantive right and Article 17(2) DSM Directive a limitation of that right.

23. That is to 'foster the development of the licensing market between rightholders and ... .', *see* Recital 61 DSM Directive. *See also* Statement by Germany, *supra* note 8, para. 10, 'in the European compromise, licensing is the method chosen to achieve ... .'

24. Article 17(5) specifies that 'best efforts' have to be 'proportionate', meaning that the concept should take into account the type and size of the service, the type of content, and the costs of rights clearance given the existing licensing options on the market.

25. Youtube, for example, has had an algorithmic content regulation system, 'ContentID', in place since 2007. For an overview on content identification technologies, *see* Annex 12

Outside this novel liability exemption scheme in Article 17(4) DSM Directive, the sharing of user uploads is given Article 17(1) DSM Directive thus only permissible if a) permission has been granted or b) the use is covered by a *specific limitation or exception.*

18.2.2   ARTICLE 17's FUNDAMENTAL RIGHTS INTERFACE AND LIMITATIONS AND EXCEPTIONS

The protection of intellectual property rights (IPR) is enshrined in Article 17(2) of the Charter where after 'Intellectual property shall be protected [as property].' As it will be explained below on the 'constitutionalization' of EU IPR, the CJEU has established a reading where after IPRs are neither inviolable nor offer 'absolute protection'.[26] Instead, courts should balance the (property) rights of rights holders against the protection of other fundamental rights such as the protection of personal data and of private life (European Union (EU) Charter Articles 7 and 8) or the freedom of expression and information (Charter Article 11).

Compared to earlier IPR-related secondary EU legislation such as the InfoSoc Directive, fundamental rights are referenced explicitly in the DSM Directive.[27] In recital 84, for example, the DSM Directive stipulates broadly:

> This Directive respects the fundamental rights and observes the principles recognised in particular by the Charter. Accordingly, this Directive should be interpreted and applied in accordance with those rights and principles.[28]

---

in European Commission, *Commission Staff Working Document, Impact Assessment on the modernisation of EU copyright rules*, Brussels, 14.9.2016 SWD (2016) 301 final, PART 3/3, pp. 164-174.

26. *See* Case C-70/10, *Scarlet Extended SA v. Société belge des auteurs, compositeurs et éditeurs SCRL (SABAM)*, ECLI:EU:C:2011:771, para. 43. *See also* the EU Charter Article 17(1) *in fine* which makes it clear that the 'use of property may be regulated by law in so far as is necessary for the general Interest protection'. This also applies to IPR.

27. Since the Lisbon Treaty, also other recent secondary legislation unrelated to IPR, acknowledges explicitly fundamental rights and more specifically the freedom of expression, *see,* e.g., recitals 16 and 48 of Directive 2010/13/EU on the coordination of certain provisions laid down by law, regulation or administrative action in Member States concerning the provision of audiovisual media services [2010] OJ L 95, pp. 1-24 (Audiovisual Media Services Directive) and recital 153 of Regulation (EU) 2016/679 on the protection of natural persons with regard to the processing of personal data and on the free movement of such data, and repealing Directive 95/46/EC (General Data Protection Regulation) [2016] OJ L 119, pp. 1-88.

28. And in the same wording already in the Commission's proposal from September 2016, *see* European Commission, *Proposal for a Directive on copyright in the Digital Single Market*, COM/2016/0593 final – 2016/0280 (COD), (Brussels, 14.9.2016), recital 45.

In addition to the general acknowledgement of fundamental rights, the Directive comes with several specific references related to the Article 17-mechanism, notably in recital 70 (emphasis added):

> The steps taken by online content-sharing service providers in cooperation with rightholders should be without prejudice to the application of exceptions or limitations to copyright, including, in particular, those which guarantee the *freedom of expression of users.* Users should be allowed to upload and make available content generated by users for the specific purposes of *quotation, criticism, review, caricature, parody or pastiche.* That is particularly important for the purposes of striking a balance between the fundamental rights laid down in the Charter of Fundamental Rights of the European Union ('the Charter'), in particular the freedom of expression and the freedom of the arts, and the right to property, including intellectual property. *Those exceptions and limitations should, therefore, be made mandatory* in order to ensure that users receive uniform protection across the Union. It is important to ensure that online content-sharing service providers operate an effective complaint and redress mechanism *to support use for such specific purposes.*

Compared to the Commission's Proposal from September 2016, this constitutes a significant strengthening of user rights. In its Explanatory Memorandum, the Commission commented on the improved bargaining situation of rightsholders and noted that 'the Directive has a limited impact on the freedom to conduct a business and on the freedom of expression and information, as recognised respectively by Articles 16 and 11 of the Charter, due to the mitigation measures put in place and a balanced approach to the obligations set on the relevant stakeholders'.[29]

The most distinct feature relates to this latter point, namely the balancing within Article 17(7) and (9), which has only been introduced relatively late in the legislative process. As it has already been explained above, under the DSM Directive, sharing of user uploads is only permissible if a) permission has been granted or b) if the use is covered by a specific limitation or exception. Additionally, Article 17(7) stipulates:

> The cooperation between online content-sharing service providers and rightholders shall not result in the prevention of the availability of works or other subject matter uploaded by users, which do not infringe copyright and related rights, including where such works or other subject matter are covered by an exception or limitation.

---

29. *Ibid.*, Explanatory Memorandum, p. 9. *See also* European Commission, *Impact Assessment, supra* note 16, pp. 154-155, noting that '[t]he freedom of expression and information may be affected negatively in cases where the services limit user uploaded content in an unjustified manner (e.g., when an exception or a limitation to copyright applies or the content is in public domain) or when the technologies fail to identify the content correctly'.

Member States shall ensure that users in each Member State are able to rely on any of the following existing exceptions or limitations when uploading and making available content generated by users on online content-sharing services:
quotation, criticism, review;
use for the purpose of caricature, parody or pastiche.

As it can be seen (cf. the word 'shall'), the exceptions or limitations regarding quotation, criticism, review and use for the purpose of caricature, parody or pastiche, which we know from the InfoSoc Directive, are *mandatory* in the sense that the Member States shall ensure that users are able to rely on them.[30] Whereas it has been argued previously in the literature by Geiger that the CJEU had already in earlier decisions provided for (substantive) *'users rights',*[31] it is quite remarkable that recital 70 makes the point so clear.[32]

Apart from strengthening the specific limitations and exceptions by casting them as user rights, Article 17 also contains *procedural safeguards* of these rights, which we explore in depth below. OCSSP's are thus obliged to support users when they engage in quotations, etc., *see* recital 70. Additionally, these platforms are required to inform users in their terms and conditions of the user's right to use works under exceptions or limitations.[33]

---

30. It has been suggested that the concepts (quotation: Article 5(3)(d) InfoSoc Directive; caricature, parody or pastiche: Article 5(3)(k) InfoSoc Directive) in Article 17(7) should be considered autonomous EU concepts which are to be interpreted consistently across the directives and in line with CJEU case law, *see* João Quintais et al., *supra* note 10.

31. Christophe Geiger & Elena Izyumenko, *The Constitutionalization of Intellectual Property Law in the EU and the Funke Medien, Pelham and Spiegel Online Decisions of the CJEU: Progress, But Still Some Way to Go!*, Centre for International Intellectual Property Studies (CEIPI) Research Paper No. 2019-09, (21 October 2019), pp. 10 ff.; Senftleben, *supra* note 11, p. 8, more critically, notes that 'the scope of this obligation and the consequences of insufficient support for relevant copyright limitations remain unclear. The expression "are able to rely on" need not be understood in the sense of a hard obligation to ban filter systems that are incapable of distinguishing between a permissible parody and an infringing copy.'

32. In relation to consumer rights, it has been noted that 'consumers remained largely off copyright law's radar screen', *see* Bernt Hugenholtz & Natali Helberger, *No Place Like Home for Making a Copy: Private Copying in European Copyright Law and Consumer Law*, Berkeley Technology Law Journal (2007) 22, 1061, p. 1077. In 2014, the copyright unit within the European Commission was moved from its traditional proximity to other property rights in DG MARKT to the DG CONNECT, meaning a closer proximity to units working on Internet- and internal market related aspects, *see* Sebastian Felix Schwemer, *Licensing and Access to Content in the European Union*, (Cambridge University Press, 2019), pp. 15-16.

33. Article 17(9) para. 4 DSM Directive.

18.2.3   THE ROLE OF LIMITATIONS AND EXCEPTIONS IN THE LIGHT OF THE
                CASE LAW OF THE CJEU

In order to understand the background to the Directive, we now turn to the
case law of the CJEU on the interface between copyright and fundamental
rights and the 'constitutionalization'[34] of EU IPR. The literature on this topic
is abundant, and here we focus just on the most recent developments (namely
Pelham, Funke Medien and Spiegel Online). Suffice, therefore, to note that
following the decisions from the CJEU in *Promusicae,*[35] *Scarlet Extended,*[36]
UPC Telekabel[37] and *Deckmyn,*[38] the Court had established a *balancing of
interests* as the central mechanisms for the 'constitutionalization' of IPR.[39]
Unlike in a traditional IPR analysis, the constitutional balancing uses the –
as seen from a copyright perspective – *external* norms and values of
fundamental rights' norms to interpret copyright law. As seen in this
perspective, the weight on the rights holder's side of the scale is provided by
the right to property. On the other side of the scale, one might find the rights
to freedom of expression and information. The nature of the interests and
their weights cannot, however, be gauged once and for all but must be
determined through a case-by-case analysis. The test is based on a principle
of *neutrality* (no 'absolute protection of IPR'), and it's *open-endedness* lies
at the very heart of the test and enables the court to draw on arguments found
outside of the IPR framework and well-established basic assumptions (the
'author-centeredness of copyright').[40] These positions now have to be
re-evaluated in the light of the most recent developments in the case law
from the CJEU.

---

34. *See* on the term 'constitutionalization' the foundational paper Christophe Geiger,
    '*Constitutionalising' Intellectual Property Law? The Influence of Fundamental Rights on
    Intellectual Property in the European Union,* International Review of Intellectual
    Property and Competition Law (2006) 37(4), pp. 371-406.
35. Case C-275/06, *Productores de Música de España (Promusicae) v. Telefónica de España
    SAU*, ECLI:EU:C:2008:54.
36. *Supra* note 26.
37. Case C-314/12, *UPC Telekabel Wien GmbH v. Constantin Film Verleih GmbH and Wega
    Filmproduktionsgesellschaft mbH*, ECLI:EU:C:2014:192.
38. Case C-201/13, *Johan Deckmyn and Vrijheidsfonds VZW v. Helena Vandersteen and
    Others*, ECLI:EU:C:2014:2132.
39. On the 'fair balance' doctrine, *see,* e.g., Christina Angelopoulos & Stijn Smet, *Notice-
    and-Fair-Balance: How to Reach a Compromise Between Fundamental Rights in
    European Intermediary Liability,* Journal of Media Law, (2016), 8(2), 266 ff.
40. Based on Jens Schovsbo, '*Mark My Words' – Trademarks and Fundamental Rights in the
    EU*, UC Irvine Law Review (2018) 8, 555.

18.2.3.1 Pelham,[41] Funke Medien[42] and Spiegel Online[43]

The three judgments were handed down on the same day (29 July 2019) by the Great Chamber, and all were based on Opinions from Advocate General (AG) M. Szpunar. The facts of the 'trinity' of cases are quite diverse: *Pelham* (or *Metall auf Metall* case) concerned the sampling of a piece of music composed by the German band 'Kraftwerk';[44] *Funke Medien* dealt with the right to use allegedly copyright protected 'parliament briefings' ('the Afghanistan papers'); and *Spiegel Online* with hyperlinking to copyright-protected material as part of the reporting by a media outlet. However, the answers in all cases had to be found in the intersection between national and EU copyright and fundamental rights law.

As seen from the perspective of this contribution, the central aspect of the judgments was the way the CJEU limited the freedom of national courts to rely on the Charter to go '*outside*' of the catalogue of exceptions established by the InfoSoc Directive. By way of example in *Funke Medien*, the Court stated that the freedom of information and freedom of the press, enshrined in Article 11 of the Charter, 'are not capable of justifying, beyond the exceptions or limitations provided for in Article 5(2) and (3) of [the InfoSoc Directive], a derogation from the author's exclusive rights of reproduction and of communication to the public, referred to in Article 2(a) and Article 3(1) of that directive respectively' (paragraph 64).[45] In other words: The fair balancing between creators' interests and users' interests, which lies at the core of the 'constitutionalization', has been *internalized* via the limitations and exceptions. It is in interpreting *those* provisions that courts may draw on various legal sources, e.g., fundamental rights. In this way, one can describe the decision as leaving the door open to the constitutionalization but also making clear that the constitutional door only gives way to a room which has been built according to the blueprint found in the InfoSoc Directive.

When it comes to the interpretation of the limitations and exceptions themselves, the freedom of Member States depends on the wording of the individual provisions. Even if some discretion is left to national courts,

---

41. Case C-476/17, *Pelham GmbH and Others v. Ralf Hütter and Florian Schneider-Eschleben*, ECLI:EU:C:2019:624.
42. Case C-469/17, *Funke Medien NRW GmbH v. Bundesrepublik Deutschland*, ECLI:EU:C:2019:623.
43. Case C-516/17, *Spiegel Online GmbH v. Volker Beck*, ECLI:EU:C:2019:625.
44. The original Kraftwerk song can be accessed here: https://www.youtube.com/watch?v=JlatOPOMlyA. The sampling song 'Nur mit Dir' here: https://www.youtube.com/watch?v=_KQLxP-UX_Y. In the national German *Metall auf Metall* saga and music sampling *see also* Bernd Justin Jütte & Henrike Maier, *A Human Right to Sample–Will the CJEU Dance to the BGH-Beat?*, Journal of Intellectual Property Law & Practice (2017), 784-796.
45. And in the same wording in case C-516/17, *Spiegel Online GmbH v. Volker Beck*, para. 49.

however, the CJEU in *Funke Medien* made it clear that such freedom would often be (even at some points 'highly) 'circumscribed' in several regards (paragraphs 45 ff.), e.g., by 'the general principles of EU law, which include the principle of proportionality, from which it follows that measures which the Member States may adopt must be appropriate for attaining their objective and must not go beyond what is necessary to achieve it' (paragraph 49). Also, the Member States cannot rely on any discretion enjoyed by them according to a directive so as to 'compromise the objectives of that directive' (paragraph 50). At the same time, however, Member States must make sure that the effectiveness of the exceptions and limitations is safeguarded and a fair balance of rights and interests between the different categories of rights holders, as well as between the different categories of rightholders and users of protected subject matter, is secured (paragraph 51). Furthermore, a fair balance must be struck between the various fundamental rights protected by the EU legal order (paragraph 53). Importantly, even the 'three-step test' in InfoSoc Directive Article 5(5) – which here serves to limit the effect of the limitations– is seen as constituting an element of the overall *fair balancing* (paragraph 61).

The effectiveness of limitations and exceptions depends not just on their exact wording but also on the willingness of national courts to consider the conditions for the application to be fulfilled. As seen from a traditional and dogmatic view, Kur has pointed out that there is a 'normative drag' from IPR's inner structure and the hierarchy of norms and interests that, so to speak, compels a narrow interpretation of limitations and limitations.[46] Such an interpretation, of course, limits the impact of the limitations and exceptions and would as seen from a normative perspective furthermore stress the secondary importance of users' interests vis-à-vis those of rights holders. It has been argued that as seen from a 'constitutional' (and thus 'neutral') starting point one would need to give up on any presupposed modality for the interpretation of limitations and exceptions: If users' interests in access are as highly ranked as rights holders' interests in protection, then the baseline for establishing which is the 'main rule' – 'freedom of information' or 'exclusivity' – has evaporated, and one is left with empty scales and a balancing of interests.[47] In such a situation, one

---

46. *See* in particular Annette Kur, *Limitations and Exceptions under the Three-Step Test – How Much Room to Walk the Middle Ground?*, pp. 208-261 in: Annette Kur and Marianne Levin, *Intellectual Property Rights in a Fair World Trade System – Proposals for Reform of TRIPS*, (Edward Elgar 2011), pp. 212 ff.

47. *See* Christophe Geiger et al., *Limitations and Exceptions as Key Elements of the Legal Framework for Copyright in the European Union – Opinion on the Judgment of the CJEU in Case C-201/13 Deckmyn*, International Review of Intellectual Property and Competition Law (2015) 46(3), 93-101, points 23-27; Jonathan Griffiths, *Taking Power Tools to the Acquis – the Court of Justice, the Charter of Fundamental Rights and European Union Copyright Law*, pp. 144-174 in Christophe Geiger, Craig Allen Nard and Xavier Seuba, *Intellectual Property and the Judiciary* (Edward Elgar, 2018), and Jens Schovsbo,

cannot *a priori* indicate whether to interpret the norm favouring users or authors 'narrowly' (or 'broadly').[48]

The CJEU has, on several occasions, made it clear that limitations and exceptions should be interpreted narrowly based on what we called a 'traditional and dogmatic' argumentation above.[49] The Court revisited the issue in *Funke Medien* where it was asked to consider whether (as the Court decided to frame the question) a national court may under certain circumstances 'depart from a restrictive interpretation of [an exception] in favour of an interpretation which takes full account of the need to respect freedom of expression and freedom of information, enshrined in Article 11 of the Charter' (paragraph 65). In answering that question, the Court first remarks that 'is certainly the case, as the referring court notes, that any derogation from a general rule must, in principle, be interpreted strictly' (paragraph 89). This reconfirms the starting point of a strict interpretation of limitations and exceptions. It is only against this backdrop that the Court states that even the limitations and exceptions could be said to 'confer rights on the users of works or of other subject matter' (paragraph 70). Also, those rights, however, should be balanced in a fair manner against 'the rights and interests of rights holders, which must themselves be given a broad interpretation' (*ibid.*). Having thus established *narrowness* as the principle of interpretation for limitations and exceptions and *broadness* as the principle for the rights and interests of rights holders, the Court concludes that the interpretation of the exceptions and limitations involved in the case must allow 'their effectiveness to be to safeguarded and their purpose to be observed' in order 'to ensure observance of fundamental freedoms' (paragraph 71).

In this way, the Court would seem to assume the traditional hierarchal view on the interests of rights holders at the top and users' interest below. Thus, even though the Court apparently accepts that sometimes conflicts between IPR and fundamental rights may occur, one should – when *within the copyright system* – assume that priority has been given to the exclusionary powers of rights holders at the immediate expense of users. This is the

---

Constitutional Foundations and Constitutionalization of IP Law – A Tale of Different Stories?, Zeitschrift für geistiges Eigentum (2015) 7, 383, 391.

48. This view is even supported by the case law of the European Court of Human Rights in *Ashby Donald v. France* CE:ECHR:2013:0110JUD003676908, which according to Thom Snijders & Stijn van Deusen, *The Road Not Taken – the CJEU Sheds Light on the Role of Fundamental Rights in the European Copyright Framework – a Case Note on the Pelham, Spiegel Online and Funke Medien Decisions*, International Review of Intellectual Property and Competition Law (2019) 50, 1176-1190, 1185 'frames copyright enforcement measure in general as derogations from the freedom of information and freedom of expression' and as such open to external scrutiny via Article 10 ECHR.

49. For example, C-527/15, *Stichting Brein v. Jack Frederik Wullems*, ECLI:EU:C:2017:300, paras 62 f. and C-265/16, *VCAST Limited v. RTI SpA*, ECLI:EU:C:2017:913, paras 31 f. *See also* C-435/12, *ACI Adam BV and Others v. Stichting de Thuiskopie and Stichting Onderhandelingen Thuiskopie vergoeding*, ECLI:EU:C:2014:254, paras 20 ff.

baseline, and *that position,* which constitutes copyright's *pièce de résistance,* cannot be challenged on the basis of the Charter.[50]

Arguably these remarks, which seem to diminish the role and function of the limitations and exceptions and to subscribe to the traditional and dogmatic perception of copyright as being a system 'for the protection of rights holders', are not easy to align with the statements that the limitations and exceptions aim at securing an overall *fair balance* (above) and with the conceptualization of limitations and exceptions as *user rights.*[51]

18.2.4   SUMMING UP

At the same time that the Court canonized the inclusion of fundamental rights to copyright's *internal* analyses, it also gave a kiss of death to any attempts to rely on fundamental rights analyses to provide for an *external* system of checks and balances to be used to, e.g., expand or substitute the predefined system of copyright protection or to deviate from the settled practice of a narrow interpretation of limitations and exceptions.

In this way, and as pointed out by Geiger and Izyumenko, the judgments emphasize the central function of limitations and exceptions to the overall balancing of fundamental rights concerns into the copyright analyses.[52] The judgements primarily achieve this in two ways.

First, the CJEU states that the limitations in Article 5 of the InfoSoc Directive 'confer *rights of the users* of works or other subject matter':[53] limitations and exceptions, in other words, constitute *user rights.* What the Court had hinted at in earlier decision is here being unfolded. The decisions anchor the limitations and exceptions from the InfoSoc Directive rules on the use by the press (Article 5(3)(c)) and quotation for criticisms and review (Article 5(3)(d)) directly in the Charter. Arguably, Article 17 DSM Directive has already anticipated this development by making it clear that the specific limitations concerning quotation, criticism, review, caricature, parody or pastiche are mandatory ('unwaivable'), *see* above.

Second, the importance of limitations and exceptions is underlined by the Court's rejection of the use by national courts of fundamental rights as *external* balancing tools. The Court thus makes it clear that it is the *Directive* that in an exhaustive way indicates the pathway for finding a 'fair balance

---

50. On this central point, the CJEU may be on collision course with the ECtHR, *see Ashby Donald and Others v. France, supra* note 48 and to this point Geiger & Izyumenko, *supra* note 31, p. 26. This might also be the view of AG Spuznar in *Funke Medien, see* point 40: 'However, there may be exceptional cases where copyright, which, in other circumstances, could quite legitimately enjoy legal and judicial protection, must yield to an overriding interest relating to the implementation of a fundamental right or freedom.'
51. Geiger & Izyumenko, *supra* note 31, pp. 20 f.
52. *Ibid.,* p. 6.
53. *Funke Medien, supra* note 42, para. 70, and *Spiegel Online, supra* note 43, para. 54.

between, on the one hand, the interest of the holders of copyright and related rights in the protection of their IPR and, on the other hand, the protection of the interests and fundamental rights of users of protected subject matter as well as of the public interest'.[54] Therefore, the full lifting of the fundamental rights interests and concerns has to be done by the internal balancing tools, i.e., limitations and exceptions.

18.3   PROCEDURAL SAFEGUARDING OF LIMITATIONS AND EXCEPTIONS

Besides the copyright-internal balancing system of limitations and exceptions, Article 17 DSM Directive also foresees an institutionalized system of checks and balances in the form of procedural safeguards. These mechanisms do not concern substantive copyright, but rather its exercise and are foreseen at several levels: (1) at the platform level, (2) at the out-of-court level, and (3) at the judicial authority or court level.

At the platform level, Member States are in Article 17(9) DSM Directive mandated to provide that 'online content-sharing service providers put in place an *effective and expeditious complaint mechanism* that is available to users of their services in the event of disputes over the disabling of access to, or the removal of, works or other subject matter uploaded by them'.[55] The mechanisms of this first procedural safeguard are further circumscribed in Article 17(9) paragraph 2 DSM Directive, where after complaints 'shall be processed without undue delay, and decisions to disable access to or remove uploaded content shall be subject to human review'.[56] Especially the latter human review-criterion is interesting, as it implies that everything leading up to a dispute can be processed by the platform in an automated fashion by algorithms.[57] It is further specified in recital 70, that

---

54. *Pelham, supra* note 41, para. 59, no identical wording in *Funke Medien, supra* note 42, but *see* para. 57 and also para. 74 (with reference to *Ashby Donald and Others v. France* and on this *supra* note 48).

55. Emphasis added. Note that the requirement is on Member States, compared to the ensuring of unavailability which is on the platforms. This first aspect resembles the Commission's original proposal from September 2016, where it suggested in Article 13(2) that 'Member States shall ensure that the service providers … put in place complaints and redress mechanisms that are available to users in case of disputes over the application of the measures … .', *see* European Commission, Proposal for DSM Directive *supra* note 28.

56. Emphasis added. On a critique of the 'elastic timeframe' *see* Senftleben, *supra* note 11, p. 9. In its Council vote, Germany suggests the timeframe to be understood 'as rapidly as possible', *see* Statement by Germany, *supra* note 8, point 7.

57. *See* similarly Commission Recommendation (EU) 2018/334 of 1 March 2018 on measures to effectively tackle illegal content online, 6.3.2018, [2018] L 63/50, points 20 and 27 in relation to proactive measures on human oversight and in the context of data protection *see,* e.g., Article 22(3) GDPR.

these mechanisms should allow 'users to complain about the steps taken with regard to their uploads, *in particular* where they could benefit from an *exception or limitation* to copyright in relation to an upload to which access has been disabled or that has been removed' (emphasis added). Furthermore, the provision stipulates a justification-duty on rights holders. The reasons for a rights holder's request to make content unavailable needs to be 'duly justified'.[58] The decision at this level remains with the platform, but as Senftleben notes, '[t]he underlying legal assessment, however, is likely to be cautious and defensive ... [and] a generous interpretation of copyright limitations serving freedom of expression seems unlikely, even though a broad application of the right of quotation and the parody exemption would be in line with CJEU jurisprudence'.[59] In other words, there exists a risk of overenforcement.[60]

In addition to the platform-based procedural safeguards, also out-of-court redress mechanisms for the impartial settlement of disputes are to be put in place by the Member States.[61] Finally, this out-of-court mechanism is 'without prejudice to the rights of users to have recourse to efficient judicial remedies ....'[62] Specifically in relation to exceptions and limitations, 'Member States shall ensure that users have access to a court or another relevant judicial authority to assert the use of an exception or limitation to copyright and related rights.'[63] Member States enjoy a considerable amount of discretion when implementing the procedural safeguards, and such mechanisms might also be informed by the stakeholder dialogues and the Commission's guidance on the application of Article 17.[64]

---

58. Article 17(9) para. 2 DSM Directive.
59. Senftleben, *supra* note 11, p. 9.
60. For empirical work on overenforcement, *see,* e.g., Kris Erickson & Martin Kretschmer, *Empirical Approaches to Intermediary Liability,* CREATe Working Paper 2019/6, (2019), pp. 10 ff.; Jennifer Urban, Joe Karaganis, & Brianna Schofield, *Notice and Takedown: Online Service Provider and Rightsholder Accounts of Everyday Practice,* 64 Journal of the Copyright Society (2017); Sharon Bar-Ziv & Niva Elkin-Koren, *Behind the Scenes of Online Copyright Enforcement: Empirical Evidence on Notice & Takedown,* 50 Connecticut Law Review (2017); specifically in the context of YouTube and parodies, *see* Kris Erickson & Martin Kretschmer, *This Video Is Unavailable: Analyzing Copyright Takedown of User-Generated Content on YouTube,* Journal of Intellectual Property, Information Technology and Electronic Commerce Law (2018) 9, 75 and Sabine Jacques et al., *An Empirical Study of the Use of Automated Anti-Piracy Systems and Their Consequences for Cultural Diversity,* SCRIPTed (2018) 15(2), 277-312.
61. Article 17(9) para. 2 DSM Directive.
62. *Ibid.*
63. Article 17(9) para. 2 DSM Directive.
64. Article 17(10) DSM Directive reads: 'As of 6 June 2019 the Commission, in cooperation with the Member States, shall organize stakeholder dialogues to discuss best practices for cooperation between online content-sharing service providers and rightholders. ... When discussing best practices, special account shall be taken, among other things, of the need to *balance fundamental rights* and of the use of exceptions and limitations. For the purpose of the stakeholder dialogues, users' organizations shall have access to adequate

Conceptually, it is unclear whether these procedural safeguards should be understood as independent additions to the limitation and exception safeguards or rather as a further specification of those safeguards. Recital 70 of the DSM Directive puts Article 17(9) in the context of situations where '*in particular* [users] could benefit from an exception or limitation' (emphasis added). Thus, one the one hand, the existence of these specific procedural safeguards relating to the institutional setting can be interpreted as an admirable attempt to create procedural transparency and safeguards. Without such setup, user rights might end up under- or even unenforced. The existing regime under the E-Commerce Directive does not directly impose any restrictions on platforms on what content they remove. Seen in a broader European intermediary liability exemption perspective, where the notice-and-takedown regime based on Article 14 of the E-Commerce Directive has lacked a counter-notice idea or general procedural safeguards, such attempt is to be welcomed and strengthening the enforcement of user rights vis-à-vis content moderation practices by large online platforms. On the other hand, however, their very existence implies an understanding of Article 17(7) that the mechanisms foreseen in Article 17(4) DSM Directive will inevitably lead to false-positives, i.e., to situations where platforms will falsely take-down or block content which is covered by a limitation or exception.[65] In other words, it can also be understood as a confession that – in practice – automatically distinguishing copyright violations from legitimate uses will be a challenging exercise.

At least from the lawmaker's perspective, procedural safeguards *in themselves* are seen as a means of mitigating the negative impact on fundamental rights. Already the Commission's Impact Assessment accompanying the Proposal from 2016, for example, noted that procedural safeguards would mitigate the negative impact on freedom of expression and information.[66] Similarly, Germany in its Statement accompanying its Council vote notes that '[e]ach permanent "stay down" mechanism ("uploadfilter") must comply with the principle of proportionality. Procedural guarantees, in particular, could be considered, for example, when users notify that they are lawfully uploading content from third parties.'[67] In other words, the

---

information from online content-sharing service providers on the functioning of their practices with regard to paragraph 4' (emphasis added).

65. In the Council vote, Germany lays outs its reading of Article 17(7) and (8) 'that protective measures must not impede the permitted use of protected content', *see* Statement by Germany, *supra* note 8, point 7. To this point *see also* European Commission, *Impact Assessment*, *supra* note 16, pp. 153 ff.

66. European Commission, *Impact Assessment*, *supra* note 16, pp. 153-154, reading '[t] his negative impact should be mitigated by the fact that the services would be obliged to put in place the necessary procedural safeguards for the users which in the majority of cases already exist in the related context of notice and take down requests.'

67. Statement by Germany, *supra* note 8, point 8.

procedural safeguards are in itself a weight on the scale of the fundamental rights balance.

18.4   CONCLUDING REMARKS: WHAT IS LEFT OF USER RIGHTS?

The limitations and exceptions contained in Article 5 InfoSoc Directive constitute *user rights,* and the courts are obliged to interpret those in light of fundamental rights norms. In relation to these user rights, as seen, the DSM Directive's Article 17 contains both an *internalized* system of checks and balances with limitations and exceptions and a somewhat *externalized* system of procedural safeguards. For the specific limitations and exceptions consisting of 'quotation, criticism, review, caricature, parody or pastiche', the DSM Directive has made it clear that these are unwaivable and also that OCSSP's are under a specific obligation to safeguard those. The Commission's proposal for the Directive from September 2016 did not contain the reference to limitations and exceptions. Nor did it contain procedural safeguards to the same extent as the final provision in the DSM Directive from May 2019. Previous, optional limitations and exceptions from the InfoSoc Directive are fully harmonized within the Article 17-framework. And both, internalized and externalized safeguards, act as an expression of user rights as a balancing factor in the reconciliation of fundamental rights. But do these safeguards do enough to balance the tensions between conflicting fundamental rights?

On a more principal level, a first aspect relates to a more 'upstream' issue of the Article 17 mechanism. Both strands of safeguards, limitations and exceptions as well as procedural safeguards, come in at a relatively late stage: neither of them addresses the very central – upstream – challenge of Article 17 from a fundamental rights perspective: the *de lege* reliance on stay down mechanisms and *de facto* reliance on filtering algorithms in the first place.[68] As Elkin-Koren points out: 'Algorithmic copyright enforcement has tilted the balance of copyright law. It has changed copyright default: if copyrighted materials were once available unless proven to be infringing, today materials that are detected by algorithms are removed from public circulation unless explicitly authorized by the right holder.'[69] This principal

---

68. On the issue of notice and stay-down in relation to freedom of expression, *see,* e.g., Jennifer M. Urban, Joe Karaganis, & Brianna L. Schofield, *Notice and Takedown in Everyday Practice,* UC Berkeley Public Law Research Paper No. 2755628 (2016). On the applicability and compliance of the Commission's proposed Article 13 in relation to notice and staydown with Articles 8 and 10 of the ECHR, *see* Felipe Romero-Moreno, *'Notice and Staydown' and Social Media: Amending Article 13 of the Proposed Directive on Copyright,* International Review of Law, Computers & Technology (2019) 33(2), 187-210, 194 f.
69. Niva Elkin-Koren, *Fair Use by Design,* UCLA Law Review (2017) 64, 1082-1100, 1093.

issue is not directly dealt with by the two – downstream – safeguards we have addressed in this contribution. Instead, a third user-oriented safeguard is coming into play with Article 17(8), where it is stipulated in a somewhat declaratory fashion that the application of Article 17 DSM Directive may not lead to any 'general monitoring obligation'. This prohibition of general monitoring contained in Article 15 E-Commerce Directive[70] is again to be seen as a result of balancing between fundamental rights (in particular, Articles 7 and 8, 9, 10, and 14 of the Charter).[71] Could an explanation be that the 'downstream' balancing of interests in limitations and exceptions is also somehow relevant 'upstream' and 'overrides' or already contains the balancing of conflicting fundamental rights in relation to Article 15 E-Commerce Directive, too?

To further explore this argument, let us take one step back from the specific copyright system for a moment: The takedown of unlawful (or even unwanted) content has become topical in relation to a variety of subject matter such as hate speech,[72] terrorist content and others. In this development, there is a call for 'enhanced responsibility'.[73] In the Commission's Recommendation (EU) 2018/334, proactive – i.e., algorithmic content – mechanisms, akin the one introduced in Article 17 of the DSM Directive, are subject to a variety of safeguards and considerations.[74] Similarly, also the Commission's proposal for a Regulation on Terrorist Content,[75] compared to Article 17 DSM Directive, is much more reluctant as to the instances when intermediaries should rely on proactive mechanisms in the first place.[76] The DSM Directive, on the other hand, offers little discretion: once an online content sharing platform falls within the scope of the Directive, the Article 17 regime applies.

---

70. The prohibition of general monitoring in Article 15 ECD has been subject to a surprisingly low number of references before the Court of Justice. In a case unrelated to IP rights, the Court of Justice recently ruled that platforms can be ordered to remove information that is 'identical' or 'equivalent' to content which is declared unlawful, *see* Case C-18/18 *Glawischnig-Piesczek v. Faebook Ireland Limited*, [2019] ECLI-:EU:C:2019:821, para. 53.
71. In *Scarlet v. SABAM*, *supra* note 26, and *Sabam v. Netlog*, *supra* note 3, for example, the Court of Justice refers to the right to protection of personal information (Article 8 of the Charter) and the freedom to receive or impart information (Article 11 of the Charter).
72. On the freedom of expression and hate speech, *see* Federica Casarosa, *Freedom of Expression and Countering Hate Speech, Handbook on the Techniques of Judicial Interactions in the Application of the EU Charter* (European University Institute, 2019).
73. European Commission, *Communication on Tackling Illegal Content Online – Towards an enhanced responsibility of online platforms*, COM(2017) 555 final, (Brussels, 28.9.2017).
74. *See*, e.g., Commission Recommendation (EU) 2018/334, *supra* note 57, points 19 and 20.
75. On the proposed Terrorist Content Regulation, *see also* Alexandra Kuczerawy, *The Proposed Regulation on Preventing the Dissemination of Terrorist Content Online: Safeguards and Risks for Freedom of Expression*, CiTiP (5 December 2018).
76. *See* Thomas Riis & Sebastian Felix Schwemer, *Leaving the European Safe Harbor, Sailing Towards Algorithmic Content* Regulation, Journal of Internet Law (2019) 22(7), 12-16.

This raises the question, why the enforcement of copyright-protected works requires fewer safeguards to be reconciled with conflicting fundamental rights. Besides a political reality, which is outside our scope, a simple answer at hand is that limitations and exceptions, which are to be respected by and partly harmonized by the Directive, are already an expression of that internalized balancing of conflicting fundamental rights. Or put differently: in a copyright-specific context, limitations and exceptions are the 'only' tool for finding a fair balance between conflicting fundamental rights. And this, indeed, is in line with the Court of Justice's case law confirmed in *Pelham*, *Funke Medien* and *Spiegel Online* on these 'user rights' and the extent to which fundamental rights can (not) be invoked as external limitations to copyright.

On a more granular level, a second aspect relates to the importance of procedural safeguards in the Article 17-regime. If procedural safeguards in itself are relied upon as a weight in the balancing of fundamental rights as described above, the 'default'-scale (with limitations and exceptions as weight) is logically leaning towards rights holders' protection: users are, in a way, awarded secondary procedural protection in an attempt to find a new equilibrium (as an additional weight). As Frosio notes, 'the introduction of a complaint and redress mechanism turns a traditionally *ex ante* review mechanism into an *ex post* mechanism while content is taken down proactively regardless of the fairness of the use of the protected content, the application of exceptions or limitations or the public domain status of the works'.[77] But then, non-derogatory user rights and procedural safeguards –undoubtedly a good intention and a strengthening in itself – are hardly more than a drop in the bucket. If in the context of Article 17(4) DSM Directive, indeed, overenforcement is unavoidable, the system comes with great legal uncertainty and wiggle room in practice. Article 17 DSM Directive constitutes a change of perspective from alleged under-enforcement of copyright-protected works in certain situations, to a situation where overenforcement of content via automated algorithmic solutions is deemed acceptable given safeguards (limitations and exceptions and procedural). So, what is left of user rights?

According to the DSM Directive, Member States shall ensure that users are able to rely on the exceptions and limitations, *see* Article 17(7). Also, the Directive shall 'in no way affect legitimate uses' and platforms shall inform users that they can use works under limitations and exceptions, *see* Article 17(9). In this way, the DSM Directive provides users with procedural safeguards. It is, however, far from clear how users should enforce their rights under the Directive. The DSM Directive does not specify the legal consequences of a platform's failure to live up to its obligations to ensure user rights. This stands in stark contrast to the situation of rights holders,

---

77. Giancarlo Frosio, *Reforming the C-DSM Reform: A User-Based Copyright Theory for Commonplace Creativity*, (7 November 2019), https://ssrn.com/abstract=3482523, p. 17.

where both international and EU legislation have boosted enforcement during the past many years. The Agreement on Trade Related Aspects of Intellectual Property Right (TRIPS Agreement),[78] for instance, devotes a full part (No. III) to the 'Enforcement of IPR', which obliges members to ensure that enforcement procedures are available to permit effective action against any act of infringement of IPRs. In the same vein, the Enforcement Directive[79] explains that effective and harmonized enforcement mechanisms are necessary to ensure that the substantive law on IP is applied effectively in the community.[80]

Against this background, it is remarkable that the DSM Directive does not attempt to ensure that the *user rights*, which arise under the limitations and exceptions regarding quotation, criticism, review, caricature, parody or pastiche, are not backed up with enforcement tools *ad modum* those found in the Enforcement Directive. As seen in the light of the system set up by the DSM Directive and the general 'tilting of the balance' (as per Elkin-Koren) in favour of rights holders, the lack of attention to the enforcement of the rights and interests of users undermines not just the effects of the limitations and exceptions. It also serves as a reminder that no rights (be that for rights holders or users) are worth more than the level to which they can be enforced. The DSM Directive may have provided users with strong 'rights' but without matching duties for platforms or a harmonized system for the enforcement of those user rights.

---

78. Trade Related Aspects of Intellectual Property Rights, available at https://www.wto.org/english/docs_e/legal_e/27-trips_03_e.htm.
79. Corrigendum to Directive 2004/48/EC of the European Parliament and of the Council of 29 April 2004 on the enforcement of intellectual property rights, (2004) OJ L 195, pp. 16-25.
80. *Ibid.*, Preamble point 3.

Part III

Trade Marks and Human Rights

Chapter 19

Trademarks and Human Rights

Marco Ricolfi

19.1 INTRODUCTORY

Two separate features make the current relationship between trademark laws and human rights especially significant. First, the relationship is two-sided: human rights may not only form the ideological underpinning of intellectual property rights (IPRs), including trademarks but may also limit or restrict them, sometimes to a very considerable extent.[1] Second, trademarks are in many ways different from the two other main paradigms of IPRs, copyright and patents, so that their interface with human rights exhibits a number of special features which are not to be found in connection with other IPRs.

What do we understand by reference to the notion of human rights in the present context? As a European lawyer, I am induced to look at the notion of human rights in two complementary perspectives. The former is broader and looks globally at public international law norms and instruments which protect human rights; the latter specifically concerns European law dealing with those aspects of human rights which may interface IPRs.

---

1. *See,* e.g., F.M. Abbott, Th. Cottier & F. Gurry, *International Intellectual Property in an Integrated World Economy* 117-126, (Wolters Kluwer, Austin, Boston, 2015); G. Resta, *Nuovi beni immateriali e* numerus clausus *dei diritti esclusivi,* in G. Resta (ed.), *Diritti esclusivi e nuovi beni immateriali* 3 ff., 64-66 (Utet, Torino, 2010).

In the first global dimension, we should consider Articles 17, 19 and 27(2) of the Universal Declaration of Human Rights (1948)[2] and Article 15 of the International Covenant on Economic, Social and Cultural Rights (1966).[3]

In the second, specifically European, dimension we should consider:

– the European Convention for the Protection of Human Rights and Fundamental Freedoms (ECHR),[4] which today counts forty-seven Member States including all the twenty-seven European Union (EU) Member States (but not the EU). It is still doubtful whether the EU will – and may – eventually accede, as provided by Article 6(2) TEU;[5] in any event, under Article 6(3) TEU, 'Fundamental rights, as guaranteed by the European Convention for the Protection of Human Rights and Fundamental Freedoms and as they result from the constitutional traditions common to the Member States, shall constitute general principles of the Union's law'; and
– the Charter of Fundamental Rights (CFR), which is recognized under Article 6(1) TEU and in its content basically reflects the same principles as the ECHR,[6] expressly provides, in a single sentence, Article 17(2), rightly described as both 'laconic' and 'surprising',[7] that 'intellectual property rights shall be protected'. While Article 51 of the Charter states that the rights contained therein, including Article 17(2), are addressed to the institutions of the Union and to the Member States 'only when they are implementing Union law', this does not necessarily mean, by inference, that they never can be

---

2. GA Res. 217 A, at 71, UN, GAOR, 3d Sess., 1st plen. mtg., U.N. Doc. A/810 (10 December 1948) [hereinafter 'UDHR']. While Articles 17 and 19 deal with property and freedom of expression, Article 27(2) states that 'everyone has the right to the protection of the moral and material interests resulting from any scientific, literary or artistic production of which he is the author'. For background *see* P. Torremans, *Comment* to Article 17(2) in S. Peers-T. Hervey-J. Kenner-A. Ward (eds), *The EU Charter of Fundamental Rights* 489 ff., 495 ff. (Hart Oxford and Portland, Oregon, 2014).
3. 16 December 1966, 993 U.N.T.S. 3 [hereinafter 'ICESCR']. *See* P. Torremans, *Comment* to Article 17(2), *supra* n. 2, 498 ff.
4. For a full treatment of this instrument, *see* L.T. Helfer, *The New Innovation Frontier? Intellectual Property and the European Court of Justice* in P. Torremans (ed.), *Intellectual Property Law and Human Rights* 27 ff. (Wolters Kluwer, Alphen aan den Rijn, 2015).
5. The answer appears to be in the negative: *see* now the Opinion 2/13 of the Court of 18 December 2014.
6. *See* Article 52(3) CFR, according to which 'in so far as this Charter contains rights which correspond to rights guaranteed by the Convention for the Protection of Human Rights and Fundamental Freedoms, the meaning and scope of those rights shall be the same as those laid down by the said Convention. This provision shall not prevent Union law providing more extensive protection.' The Charter was originally proclaimed on 7 December 2000; its binding force dates from the date of coming in force of the Lisbon Treaty on 1 November 2009.
7. C. Geiger, *Reconceptualizing the Constitutional Dimension of Intellectual Property* in P. Torremans (ed.), *Intellectual Property Law and Human Rights*, *supra* n. 4, 134.

invoked 'horizontally' by private individuals. As the EU Intellectual Property Office (EUIPO) is an institution of the EU and Courts are institutions of the Member States, it is not surprising that a modicum of horizontal, inter-private effects is injected into the application of this provision.[8]

Symmetrically, in exploring the trademark/human rights interface, I shall give primary consideration to EU and EU-harmonized trademark law[9] while extending the perspective to non-EU situations where these may be helpful to illustrate European rules by way of analogy or opposition.

Instruments which protect and guarantee human rights at the European level to a large extent draw from 'fundamental rights as they result from the constitutional traditions common to the Member States' parties to them.[10] However, also, international human rights conventions are part of the EU legal framework[11] and have an international and global dimension: their

---

8. A good example of indirect horizontal effect is to be found in General Court 21 January 2015 (Second Chamber), Case T-587/13, *Miriam Schwerdt v. OHIM and Iberamigo*, 'cat&clean/clean cat', paras 51 ff. (the argument of applicant that refusal of his registration was abridging her freedom to conduct business was defeated by the counterargument that opponent's prior national trademark right was protected by Article 17(2)). Even though other decisions of the General Court (General Court 15 March 2018 (Ninth Chamber), Case T-1/17, *La Mafia Franchises v. EUIPO and Repubblica Italiana*, 'La Mafia', para. 36 and 5 October 2011 (Third Chamber), Case T-526/09, *PAKI Logistics GmbH v. OHIM and Vereinigtes Königreich Grossbritannien und Nordirland*, 'Paki', para. 15) could be interpreted as stretching the effects of (at least some of) the provisions of the CFR to horizontal applicability, the rationale behind the choice in favour of the applicability of the CFR in these decisions may also be found in the European approach which considers the decision whether to grant or to refuse a trademark application an action of a public institution, the EUIPO, rather than a response to the private request from the applicant (in this connection, *see infra* § 19.10). A discussion about the vertical or horizontal effects of the CFR is in L.T. Helfer, *The New Innovation Frontier? supra* n. 4, 59 ff.; A. Ohly, *European Fundamental Rights and Intellectual Property* in J. Pila-A. Ohly (eds), *The Europeanization of Intellectual Property Law. Toward a European Legal Methodology* 145 ff., 150-151 (Oxford University Press, 2013) and J. Griffiths & L. McDonagh, *Fundamental Rights and European IP law: The Case of Art. 17(2) of the EU Charter* in C. Geiger (ed.), *Constructing European Intellectual Property. Achievements and New Perspectives* 75 ff., 82 ff. (Edward Elgar, Cheltenham, 2013).
9. *See* respectively, the European Trade Mark Regulation No. 101/2017 [hereinafter referred to as 'EUTMR'] and the parallel provisions of the Directive (EU) 2015/2436 [hereinafter referred to as 'EUTM' Directive]. When necessary reference will be made to the older Community Trade Mark Regulation No. 207/2009 [hereinafter referred to as 'CTMR'] and to its amendment by the Regulation (EU) 2015/2424 as well as to the parallel provisions of the EU Directive No. 2008/95 [hereinafter 'TM Directive'].
10. *See* Article 52(4) CFR.
11. *See* with specific reference to UDHR and ICESCR C. Geiger, *Reconceptualizing the Constitutional Dimension of Intellectual Property, supra* n. 7, 115 ff., 143 and note 125 (quoting to this effect ECJ 10 July 2003, Joined Cases C-20/00 and C-64/00, *Booker Aquaculture Ltd., Hydro Seafood v. The Scottish Ministers*, 'Booker Aquaculture', para. 65).

yardstick is humankind; constitutions, on the contrary, are firmly rooted in the national polity. The two sets of values, to a large extent, overlap; if they do not, their interface may raise thorny issues.[12]

In certain contexts, human rights are qualified as 'fundamental'.[13] It is not easy to make out what is the reason for such a linguistic variation; one explanation may consist in the fact that the adjective may have the rhetorical virtue of announcing that, in the event of a conflict with other rights, the 'fundamental' right should prevail.

19.2	THE RESURGENCE OF THE HUMAN RIGHTS DISCOURSE AT THE TURN OF THE LAST CENTURY

The last two decades witnessed the growing importance of proposals and discussions concerning the relevance – and indeed the prominence – of human rights in various areas of IP. To name just a few, in the field of patents, the three imperatives of health, nutrition and the preservation of biodiversity have been underscored; in connection with copyright, the twin mandates of freedom of access and of expression have come to the fore; as far as trademarks are concerned, freedom of expression again as well as wide pro-competitive concerns have raised their head, in various ways which will be dealt with below.

To a very large extent, this resurgence of human rights in the area of IPRs has to be understood as reactive. In the previous decades, the level of protection of IPRs had been increased steadily and across the board. This substantial expansion – sometimes described as a protectionist wave –[14] may go back to a number of factors. Among the determinants of this surge, we may take into account both technological[15] and institutional factors. From this latter perspective, the mechanism of regulatory competition may, to a

---

12. *See,* e.g., the final footnote of § 19.10.
13. *See* the title of the CFR.
14. G. Ghidini, *Prospettive 'protezioniste' nel diritto industriale, Riv. dir. ind.* I, 73 ff. (1995). On the phenomenon of the ratcheting up of IP protection in the final decades of last century, *see* also P.K. Yu, *Challenges to the Development of a Human Rights Framework for Intellectual Property,* in P. Torremans (ed.), *Intellectual Property Law and Human Rights, supra* n. 4, 87 ff., 90 ff.
15. Valuable innovation has shown a tendency to bear the same know-how that makes it valuable 'on the face' of the products and services which incorporate it, as shown in the case of designs, plant varieties, semiconductor chips, data bases and even biotechnology, so that protection based on low access requirements has been seen as a prerequisite for investment. For a full treatment of this line of thought *see* the abundant work of J.H. Reichman, from *Legal Hybrids Between the Patent and Copyright Paradigms,* 94 *Columbia L. Rev.* 2432 ff. (1994) to *The Globalization of Private Knowledge Goods and the Privatization of Global Public Goods,* 7 *Journal of Int. Ec. Law* 279 ff. (2004) (written with Keith E. Maskus).

large extent, account for the fact that often the increase in protection of an IPR in a given jurisdiction – e.g., for trademarks, the extended protection for trademarks considered either 'famous' or enjoying some level of 'reputation', also for biotechnological and software patents – is quickly imitated in other jurisdictions, on the prompting of well-organized interest groups.[16] The phenomenon that political scientists describe as 'coercion'[17] may, in turn, explain why the global South was induced to agree to a generalized increase of the protection of IP assets, normally belonging to Northern businesses, through the reluctant acceptance of that component of the WTO package which is the TRIPS agreement.

The years which followed the adoption of TRIPS (1994) witnessed an effort towards 'rebalancing' IP by taking into greater account competing claims, particularly from users and from nations located at lower stages in the IP chain, and often by advancing them in terms of human rights before *fora*, such as the World Health Organisation (WHO), United Nations Educational, Scientific and Cultural Organization (UNESCO), Food and Agriculture Organization (FAO) and the United Nations (UN) Commission on Human Rights.[18]

This does not mean that resort to human rights arguments has been limited to the camp of the players favouring a limitation of IPRs in the name of 'rebalancing'. Indeed, human rights have also been often enlisted to carry out the opposite mission, by underpinning the interests and the rights of holders of IPRs under the umbrella of one of the most powerful, if controversial, human rights, the right to enjoyment of property[19] and, in

---

16. Triggering the phenomenon which presciently Justice Brandeis characterized as a 'race of laxity'. According to Justice Brandeis two famous dissents, regulatory competition may oscillate between two extremes. Either the different competing jurisdictions are seen as laboratories experimenting diverse legal rules to strike whatever balance between conflicting interests appears appropriate to the relevant constituencies (*New State Ice Corp. v. Liebmann*, 285 U.S. 262, 311 (1932); or, in the alternative, they may be seen as engaging in a 'race of laxity', *Louis K. Liggett v. Lee*, 288 *U.S.*, 517, 557-559 (1933), to favour concentrated interest's (typically: business interests) or to cut down on dispersed interests (typically: consumers').

17. J. Braithwaite & P. Drahos, *Global Business Regulation* 79 ff. (Cambridge University Press, Cambridge, 2000).

18. For an early and persuasive account of these developments, *see* L.R. Helfer, *Regime Shifting: The TRIPS Agreement and New Dynamics of International Intellectual Property Lawmaking*, 29 *Yale J. Int. L.* 1 ff. (2004). A follow up is in C. Geiger, *Reconceptualizing the Constitutional Dimension of Intellectual Property*, *supra* n. 7, 117 ff. Resort to human rights 'discourse' as a tool in campaigns directed to facilitating access to essential drugs is vividly illustrated by D. Matthews, *When Framing Meets the Law: Using Human Rights as a Practical Instrument to Facilitate Access to Medicine in Developing Countries*, in G. Ghidini- J.R. Peritz-M. Ricolfi (eds), *TRIPS and Developing Countries. Towards a New IP World Order* 12 ff. (Edward Elgar, Cheltenham, 2014).

19. On the reference to the notion of property as to the *Kampfbegriff* or battle-cry for IP expansion, *see* G. Resta, *Nuovi beni immateriali e numerus clausus dei diritti esclusivi*, *supra* n. 1, 14.

connection with trademarks, also of the same right to freedom of expression which otherwise may be invoked to restrict the right in question,[20] thereby confirming the just mentioned two-sidedness of human rights in their relationship to trademark rights.

19.3   IN WHICH WAYS ARE TRADEMARKS DIFFERENT FROM OTHER IPRs FOR PURPOSES OF HUMAN RIGHTS ANALYSIS?

While trademark rights share with other IPRs the peculiar 'two-sidedness', we just mentioned, they also exhibit a number of features which differentiate them from other IPRs in specific connection with human rights analysis.

Also, in this regard, the specificity of trademarks cuts both ways having an impact on their *protection* by means of human rights as well as on human rights-based *limitations* of their protection and scope.

From the first perspective, it may be suggested that trademarks and other IPRs share a common characteristic, in that in all of them, we may analytically distinguish the negative side of the right, the exclusivity feature which enables the right holder to prevent third parties from using the entity without authorization, from the positive side, which consists in the opportunity of directly using the entity in question. While this characterization is not unchallenged,[21] it is undisputed that a number of clear and significant functional and structural differences between trademarks and other IPRs go a long way towards explaining why the protection of trademarks under the umbrella of the right to property is much more problematic than for patents and, especially, copyrights.

To understand why this is so, we must go back to the circumstance that the signs protected as trademarks, differently from patentable innovations and copyrighted works or creations, are not what economists describe as public goods.[22] While it is commonly accepted that the grant of legal exclusivity in the form of a property right is required to give *ex ante* an incentive to innovations and creations which otherwise would not be forthcoming on the basis of markets mechanisms,[23] this is not the case with

---

20. *See infra* for both aspects §§ 19.5-19.11.
21. §§ 19.9-19.11; *see* E. Bonadio, *On the Nature of Trademark Rights: Does Trademark Registration Confer Positive or Negative Rights?* in A. Alemanno-E. Bonadio (eds), *The New Intellectual Property of Health. Beyond Plain Packaging*, 43 ff. (Edward Elgar, Cheltenham, 2016).
22. As indicated by W.M. Landes & R. Posner, *Trademark Law: An Economic Perspective*, XXX *Journal of Law and Economics* 265 ff., 274 (1987); according to them 'a proper trademark is not a public good; it has social value only when used to designate a single brand'.
23. For a classic treatment of this argument in favour of IP protection *see* J. Hirshleifer, *The Private and Social Value of Information and the Reward to Inventive Activity*, 61 *Am.*

the signs which are protected under trademark law. Indeed, there is no undersupply of signs as such, let alone of signs to be used in trade.[24]

This does not mean that trademarks do not give a remarkable contribution to the optimization of economic welfare. However, while the contribution deriving from the supply of patentable inventions and copyrightable works is direct, the contribution flowing from the functioning of trademarks in the marketplace is much more roundabout, even though as essential as for the other entities protected under an IP property right rule.[25] Indeed, economists have been able to show persuasively how trademarks provide an incentive for businesses to enhance the quality – or more accurately, the combination of quality and price – of the goods which they supply to the public;[26] to lower the information and search costs consumers face when looking for the goods they wish,[27] and finally to reward businesses providing goods which meet the public's demand while punishing, by expulsion from the market, the businesses which fail to do so. This complex mix of positive functions played by trademarks did not escape the attention of Courts, which on several occasions have underlined how, while 'the function of a trademark' is 'to distinguish the goods and services of various undertakings with the purpose of guaranteeing to the user or the consumer the identity of their respective origins, that immediate and specific purpose of trademarks is no more than a staging post on the road to the final objective, which is to ensure a system of genuine competition in the [internal] market'.[28]

However, the fact that all these positive functions are carried out by signs, or, in other words, language or even – as a great Italian scholar put it a long time ago – 'mere nomenclature of reality',[29] makes it more

---

Econ. Rev. 561 ff. (1971) and K. Arrow, *Economic Welfare and the Allocation of Resources for Invention*, in *The Rate and Direction of Inventive Activity: Economic and Social Factors* 609 ff. (National Bureau Committee for Economic Research, Princeton University Press, Princeton, N.J., 1962). A more updated – and less formalized – treatment now in M. Libertini, *Tutela e promozione delle creazioni intellettuali e limiti funzionali della proprietà intellettuale*, AIDA 299 ff. (2014).

24. As noted by W.M. Landes & R. Posner, *Trademark Law*, *supra* n. 22, 271 ff.
25. For similar points, *see* C. Geiger, *The Social Function of Intellectual Property Rights, or How Ethics Can Influence the Shape and Use of IP Law*, in G. Dinwoodie (ed.), *Methods and Perspectives in Intellectual Property* 153 ff., 166 (Edward Elgar, Cheltenham, 2013); M. Senftleben, *Trademark Protection – A Black Hole in the Intellectual Property Galaxy?*, IIC 383 ff., 384 (2011).
26. G.A. Akerlof, *The Market for 'Lemons': Quality Uncertainty and the Market Mechanism*, 84 Q. J. Econ. 488 ff. (1970).
27. For a review of this facet of trademark protection, *see* S.L. Dogan & M. Lemley, *Trademarks and Consumer Search Costs on the Internet*, 41 Hous. L. Rev., 777 ff. (2004).
28. The quotation is taken from the Opinion of the Advocate general Ruiz-Jarabo Colomer of 13 June 2002, Case C-206/01, *Arsenal Football Club plc v. Matthew Reed*, 'Arsenal', para. 42.
29. T. Ascarelli, *Teoria della concorrenza e dei beni immateriali. Lezioni di diritto industriale* 433 ff. (Giuffrè, Milano, 1960).

problematic to build an argument for their protection as property. To begin with, language as such is not appropriable, while specific creations and technological innovations may be reserved to their authors. Moreover, by depriving a business of the right of availing itself of a given sign nothing is detracted from its entitlement to supply the same identical goods or services under another (at least apparently) equivalent sign. This also explains why the relationship between trademark protection and freedom to conduct business is, to a certain extent, ambiguous. On the one hand, trademark rights may be seen part and parcel of the freedom to conduct business: their purpose is to institute a bi-directional link between that business and the goods and services originating from it. The case could, therefore, be made that the continued possession of trademarks should be safeguarded not only on the basis of property guarantees but also on the complementary ground that trademarks are essential tools to exercise the 'freedom to conduct business', as recognized under Article 16 of the CFR. On the other hand, it may also be argued – more or less plausibly – that even though the right to resort to a specific trademark belonging to a given firm is restricted or curtailed, this does not by itself mean that the business in question is denied its continued presence in the market place. However, again, to ask a business to compete in the market after giving up its trademarks might appear not very dissimilar to asking a swordsman to duel after tying one hand to his back. Sound as it may be, the argument has not cut much ice until now;[30] it not only does not appear anywhere in Courts' reasoning but also does not seem to have come up very often in pleadings before Courts.

In building a case for protecting trademarks as property, additional difficulties may arise. In the case of patents and copyright, the countervailing interests – of users and competitors – which may suggest a curtailing of the rights of IPR holders may occasionally be accommodated by reconfiguring the right in question as protected under a liability rule as opposed to a property rule. Compulsory licensing of patents on life-saving drugs comes to mind immediately; similarly, fair uses of copyrighted material providing for compensation or remuneration can be imagined – and indeed have been implemented with remarkable success.[31] However, it is widely felt that it is not possible to transform trademarks from signs protected under a property rule to entities protected under a liability rule, as – the case is made – the very

---

30. *See* §§ 19.8-19.11.
31. *See* P.B. Hugenholtz-João Pedro Quintais, *Towards a Universal Right of Remuneration: Legalizing the Non-Commercial Online Use of Works* in P.B. Hugenholtz (ed.), *Copyright Reconstructed. Reconstructing Rights: Rethinking Copyright's Economic Rights in a Time of Highly Dynamic Technological and Economic Change* 241 ff. (Wolters Kluwer, 2018) and C. Geiger, *Promoting Creativity Through Copyright Limitations: Reflections on the Concept of Exclusivity in Copyright Law*, 12 *Vanderbilt J. of Ent. and Tech. Law*, 515 ff. (2011).

moment the sign was to stop designating one and only one source, its information value and rationale would be totally destroyed.[32]

Moreover, trademarks share with patents a feature which differentiates them from copyright. While copyright protection of works is automatic, that is triggered by communication to the outside world and, in common law countries, fixation of the work without the need of the intervention from a public authority, trademarks, in parallel to patents, obtain protection to the full extent only after a sovereign grant of rights based on an application by the interested party.[33]

Finally, the idea that a ground for refusing registration of a given sign, e.g., for public policy reasons, may be overridden by free speech concerns may be greatly weakened by the same functional and structural features of trademarks we just discussed. After all, while technical innovations and intellectual creations come in limited numbers, signs under which to conduct business are potentially infinite. Therefore, it is difficult to see how freedom of expression may be invoked to claim not just the right to use a given expression or symbol but the *exclusivity* over them conferred by trademark registration; this is even more so if one takes into account that refusal of registration of a sign may be without prejudice of the right to use the same as an unregistered trademark.[34]

From the second (and opposing) perspective, concerning human rights-based limitations of trademark protection, it should be noted that the divide between the notion of infringement on the one side and of exceptions on the other is much blurrier in trademark law than in copyright and patent law.[35] There are many ways to express this divergence. It has been remarked that in patent and copyright law the perimeter of prohibited behaviour is neatly described by reference solely to reserved acts (manufacturing, selling or

---

32. At least if one accepts the idea that a trademark 'has social value only when used to designate a single brand', as argued by W.M. Landes & R. Posner, *Trademark Law, supra* n. 22, 274. The point may be disputed, however: *see* E.H. Chamberlin, *The Theory of Monopolistic Competition* 273 (Harvard University Press, Cambridge, Mass., 1962) and, in case law, the US Federal Trade Commission decision of 19 August 1976, *Borden Inc.* concerning the 'ReaLemon' trademark, as well as, in the EU, the decision by the ECJ of 16 July 2009 (Grand Chamber), Case C-385/07 P., *Der Grüne Punkt – Duales System Deutschland GmbH v. Commission, Intersoh Dienstleistungs GmbH*, 'Grüne Punkt'.

33. However, this feature has not been deemed controlling by the ECtHR in the 'Budweiser' Case: *see infra* § 19.6. On the difference between European and common law approaches concerning the role played by registration in trademarks' enforcement and on the implications this difference may have in granting protection to signs which are against public policy or *mores see infra* § 19.10.

34. On this group of issues, in which the EU position is, however, markedly different from the approach adopted in the US, *see infra* § 19.10.

35. This is one of the main arguments underlying the perceptive contribution by G. Dinwoodie, *Developing Defenses in Trademark Law*, 13 *Lewis & Clark Law School* 99 ff. (2009). The notion of infringement, as adopted in this writing, includes what US law designates both as infringement and dilution; EU law does not follow the differentiation between the two notions which is characteristic of US trademark law.

non-privately using the patented item; copying, distributing copies, communicating to the public the work) which may described as (proscribed) conduct. Characteristically, the prohibition in trademark law refers to a composite which is made by both conduct (use in commerce in connection with goods and services) and effect or outcome of the conduct itself (be it, in classic trademark law, the likelihood of confusion of the public as to the origin of the goods; or, in modern, post-expansionary trademark law, also the risk of dilution).[36] Therefore, behaviour which conforms to the description of the conduct, e.g., reproducing Campbell soup logos in a painting, but fails to effect the proscribed outcome, confusion as to the origin of the painting or dilution, is outside of the reach of the prohibition.

In a similar vein, it has also been said that patents and copyright confer comprehensive exploitation rights in that the exclusivity conferred by the law in principle enables the holder of the right in the innovation or work to extract – almost – all the fruits which can be derived by the work;[37] while the exclusivity conferred by trademark law is intended to stop short of conferring full exploitation rights, as (even commercial) uses which do not affect the messages which the sign is intended to convey (such as the use of the Campbell logo; or use of a corporate logo in images accompanying a journal article concerning the business in question),[38] are located outside the scope of the protection granted by the law to the trademark proprietor.[39]

Whatever characterization we may choose, the result is the same: while exceptions in patent and copyright law refer to behaviour which otherwise would neatly fall into the proscribed area, except that a specific provision may come to its rescue declaring that the same is by normative choice deemed lawful, in trademark laws permitted behaviour often fluctuates between conduct which is not exactly within the scope of the exclusivity and behaviour which is declared permissible under an exception in spite of being arguably covered by the grant conferred to the trademark proprietor.

In this respect, it is often noted that conduct which is considered non-infringing in a given legal system, may be deemed infringing in principle but absolved by an exception in another legal system. Two examples come to mind: the use of a sign which, while not authorized, does not take place *as a trademark*, i.e., is descriptive rather than distinctive or the case of 'referential' use of a trademark, where the sign is employed by a third party for the purpose of identifying or referring to the goods as those of the

---

36. G. Dinwoodie, *Developing Defenses*, *supra* n. 35, 103 ff.
37. The qualification in the text takes into account that not all legal systems reserve to the copyright holder the right to exploit all possible modes of employing works.
38. On the treatment of this occurrence, *see infra* § 19.17.
39. On the recurring fear that the limited protection characteristic of trademarks may be transmogrified into a copyright-like full exploitation right, *see* M. Senftleben, *The Trademark Tower of Babel – Dilution Concepts in International, US and EC Trademark Law*, *IIC* 45 ff., 59 ff. (2009) and A. Vanzetti, *Funzione e natura giuridica del marchio*, *Riv. dir. comm.* 16 ff., 64 (1961).

proprietor rather than her own. Both situations present a classic case of behaviour which may either be appreciated as altogether outside of the scope of exclusivity, and therefore, non-infringing in one jurisdiction or, in the alternative, infringing but permitted by a specific permissive norm in another jurisdiction.[40]

This characteristic feature of trademark law has a significant, if not immediately obvious, impact precisely at the interface between trademark protection and human rights and, more specifically, at the strategic level of delineating the options to deal with the question. There is a certain amount of consensus on the idea that the recent expansion of trademark exclusivity to encompass the publicity function of the sign, particularly in connection with trademarks which are considered famous or with a reputation, has brought with itself an enhanced risk of a conflict with human rights, including freedom of expression and of competition.[41] There is also agreement on the notion that the reconciliation between the conflicting values is to be sought by way of a balancing exercise. It is, however, striking to see how scholars – and judges – part company when the question arises whether the balancing should take place at the proscription end, i.e., in determining what exactly are the requirements which trigger a finding of infringement, or at the exception end, i.e., in devising which behaviour, while prohibited, may nevertheless be immunized by exceptions (or, as some scholars prefer to put it, by defences).[42]

A number of authorities and of commentators would appear to opt for the latter alternative. The case is eloquently made that the expansion of trademark exclusivity has brought it much closer to the copyright (and patent)-like mode of full exploitation rights and that this very development calls for the adoption of a countervailing and expanded 'new limitations infrastructure',[43] which indeed is an approach which makes a lot of sense and has been recently adopted by the EU (as we will *see* in greater detail below,

---

40. For a thorough treatment of the issue, *see* R. Knaak, *Markenmäßiger Gebrauch als Grenzlinie des harmonisierten Markenschutzes*, GRUR *Int.* 91 ff. (2008). It is not infrequent that within one and the same jurisdiction, the same behaviour is sometimes considered non-infringing, other times infringing but exempted.

41. *See* M. Senftleben, *Adapting EU Trademark Law to New Technologies: Back to Basics?* in C. Geiger (ed.), *Constructing European Intellectual Property, supra* n. 8, 137 ff., 143 ff.; W. Sakulin, *Trademark Protection and Freedom of Expression. An Inquiry into the Conflict between Trademark Rights and Freedom of Expression under European Law* 9 ff., 57 ff. and passim (Wolter Kluwer, The Hague/London/New York, 2010); J. Lipton, *Internet, Domain Names and Freedom of Speech* 97ff. (Edward Elgar, Cheltenham, 2010); R. Burrell & D. Ganjee, *Trademarks and Freedom of Expression: A Call for Caution*, 41 *Int'l Rev. Int'l Prop. & Competition L.* 544 ff. (2010); G. Dinwoodie, *Developing Defenses in Trademark Law, supra* n. 35, 102.

42. G. Dinwoodie, *Developing Defenses in Trademark Law, supra* n. 35, 119 ff.

43. M. Senftleben, *Adapting EU Trademark Law to New Technologies: Back to Basics? supra* n. 41, 137 ff. and *The Trademark Tower of Babel, supra* n. 39, 62 ff. In a similar vein G. Dinwoodie, *Developing Defenses in Trademark Law, supra* n. 35, 119 ff.

at § 19.18). However, other very distinguished scholars have begged to differ:[44] their idea is that working on exceptions concedes too much leeway to trademarks proprietors; offers too little to non-trademark interests; and may systematically lead to the judicial fashioning lines of cases based on apparent analogies but lacking a thought-through rationale.

19.4   IDENTIFICATION OF THE LEVELS OF THE
        INTERFACE BETWEEN TRADEMARK LAW AND
        HUMAN RIGHTS

While keeping in mind these peculiarities of trademark law may come handy in the process of dealing with specific issues of human rights analysis, the time has come to identify the specific areas where trademark law and human rights meet. To build a workable taxonomy, we should start by contrasting procedure to the substance. Human rights may become relevant also in connection with the procedure itself, which leads to the grant and the enforcement of trademark rights; however, their greater impact is to be registered at the substantive level.[45] Therefore, I will confine myself to

---

44. *See* particularly R. Burrell & D. Ganjee, *Trademarks and Freedom of Expression*, *supra* n. 41.

45. Indeed, the interface between human rights and procedural safeguards in the field of trademarks may well deserve thorough consideration, which would, however, exceed the scope of this article. However, in this connection it may be noted that EU cases stick to the notion that (i) the procedural provision of Article 6 ECHR (right to a fair trial) and of Article 47 CFR do not apply to proceedings before the EUIPO (formerly OHIM), as these are administrative rather than jurisdictional in nature (General Court 17 May 2018 (Ninth Chamber), Case T-760/16, *Basil BV v. EUIPO and Artex*, 'bicycle baskets', para. 26 (in the field of designs); 3 May 2018 (Eighth Chamber), T-463/17, *Raise Conseil v. EUIPO and Raizers*, 'Raise', para. 22; 23 September 2014 (Third Chamber), T-341/13, *Groupe Léa Nature SA v. OHIM and Debonair Trading Internacional Lda*, 'SO'BiOētic/So … ?', para. 25; 22 May 2014 (Ninth Chamber), Case T-228/13, *NIIT Insurance Technologies Ltd. v. OHIM*, 'Exact', para. 52; 25 April 2013 (Eighth Chamber), Case T-284/11, *Metropolis Immobiliarias y Restauraciones SL v. OHIM and MIP Metro Group Intellectual Property GmbH & Co. KG*, 'Metroinvest/Metro', para. 62 and 12 September 2012 (Fifth Chamber), Case T-295/11, *Duscholux Ibérica SA v. OHIM and Duschprodukter i Skandinavien*, 'duschy/DUSCHO', para. 21 where additional references); and (ii) the question of compliance of proceedings before EUIPO (formerly OHIM) with ECHR provisions is considered of little relevance anyhow, as the corresponding safeguards are already provided in the EUTMR and, previously, in the CTMR [on the equivalence between the obligation to state reasons under Article 6 ECHR and Article 75 CTMR, now Article 94 EUTMR, *see* General Court 23 September 2014 (Third Chamber), T-341/13, 'SO'BiOētic/So … ?', para. 26; 25 April 2013 (Eight Chamber), 'Metroinvest/Metro', para. 63; on the equivalence between the obligation to give grounds under Article 41(2)(c) CFR and Articles 62 and 75 CTMR *see* General Court 15 January 2013 (Fourth Chamber), Case T-237/11, *Lidl Stiftung & Co. KG v. OHIM and Lactimilk, SA*, 'Bellram/Ram', para. 21; accordingly in General Court 29 November 2016 (Third Chamber), Case T-617/15, *Chic Investments sp. Zoo. v. EUIPO*, 'e-smoking World', paras

discussing the substantive rules, which, as the quite abundant case law shows, may concern: (i) the applicability of the human rights guarantee of property (and of freedom to conduct business) to rules adversely affecting the prerogatives belonging to a trademark proprietor, an applicant for trademark registration or the owner of other signs used in trade (§§19.6-19.9 and 19.11); (ii) the relevance of a human rights dimension for the assessment to be conducted in connection with absolute grounds for refusal of an application for registration of a trademark or for invalidity of a registered trademark (§§19.10 and 19.12); and (iii) the relevance of human rights in respect of the conflict between a senior and a junior mark (§§ 19.13-19.18).

19.5 TRADEMARKS AS PROPERTY

Trademarks registrations and applications may claim human rights protection on several grounds. This is not in and by itself an uncontroversial claim. Indeed, it has been remarked that 'human rights have been answers to

---

102 ff. Article 41(2)(c) is mentioned but not specifically discussed; on the equivalence between the right of defence and a right to a fair hearing under, respectively, Article 41(2)(a) CFR and Article 6 ECHR on the one side and the safeguard of the opportunity to present comments on the issues on which the decision is based, provided by Article 75 CTMR, *see* General Court 16 March 2017 (Third Chamber), Case T-473/15, *Capella EOD v. EUIPO and Abus August Bremicker Söhne KG*, 'Apus/Abus', para. 49 (finding at para. 58 a violation of the corresponding provision); 8 February 2013 (Sixth Chamber), Case T-33/12, *Elke Piotrowski v. OHIM*, 'Medigym', paras 14 ff. (holding that the second part of Article 75 CTMR is an expression of the general right to be heard under Article 41(2)(1) CFR and is respected when OHIM's decision is based on generally accessible sources, as dictionaries, on which the applicant had an opportunity to comment) and 12 September 2012 (Fifth Chamber), 'duschy/DUSCHO', paras 22 ff.]. However, more recent cases, subsequent to the coming into force of the CFR, indicate that the EU Courts are now taking a more expansive view of the impact of the procedural provisions of the CFR, in particular in connection with the right to be heard under Article 41(2)(a) CFR and to a fair trial under Article 47: *see* EU Court 14 June 2018 (Sixth Chamber), Case C-35/18 P., *Carrera Brands v. EUIPO and Autec*, 'Carrera', paras 8 ff. (ruling out a violation af the right to a fair trial under Article 47 where the argument disregarded by the General Court confined itself to a mere reference to passages in writings submitted in prior stages of the proceeding before EUIPO); 14 January 2016 (Sixth Chamber), Case C-278/15 P, *Royal County of Berkshire Polo Club Ltd. v. OHIM and Lifestyle Equities CV*, 'Royal County of Berkshire Polo Club', paras 51 ff. (finding that the right to a fair trial under Article 47 had been respected); 27 March 2014 (First Chamber), Case C-530/12 P., *OHIM v. National Lottery Commission*, 'image of a hand', paras 53 ff.; General Court 13 December 2016 (Fourth Chamber), Case T-549/15, *Ramón Guiral Broto v. EUIPO and Gastro & Soul*, 'Café de Sol/Café de Sol', paras 30 ff. (finding a violation of Article 41(2)(a) CFR in deciding the matter without raising the issue of the incompleteness of a translation); 9 December 2014 (Third Chamber), C-176/13, *DTL Corporación SL v. OHIM and Mar Vallejo Rosell*, 'Generia/Generalia', para. 29 ff. Also the right to a reasonable duration under Article 41(1) CFR is deemed applicable to proceedings before EUIPO by General Court 13 July 2005 (Fourth Chamber), Case T-242/01, *The Sunrider Corp. v. OHIM*, 'Top', paras 47 ff.

specific and fundamental threats to individuals in human history. They establish specific zones of protection and cannot entail the design of an overall economic concept'.[46] In even more fundamental terms, it may be questioned whether and to which extent corporations, as artificial entities rather than natural persons, may enjoy human rights comparable to the ones which in our legal traditions belong to individuals.[47] Even admitting that human rights may be ascribed to legal entities, a separate question arises as to which protection may accrue to them under the human rights shield of IPRs in general and of trademarks in particular. IPRs amount to monopoly rights; they may be construed as an exception – and even as an abridgement – of fundamental freedoms, of competition and trade; in this perspective, it may appear difficult to argue that they exist independently of a sovereign decision to provide for their protection and of a specific grant of the protection itself. This objection may be sometimes countered, e.g., by the remark that human rights protection concerns not the patent but the invention; not the copyright but the copyright-protected work and that the safeguards ultimately benefit the individuals who are behind the invention and the work.[48] The counterargument is more difficult to articulate in connection with trademarks; first, because trademark protection may depend, to a certain extent, on registration (a condition which admittedly applies to patents too); second, because the contribution given to the society by trademarks is not as direct, immediate and intuitively visible as in the case of inventions and works; third, because there is a bi-univocal relationship between trademarks and businesses which is not apparent in connection with patents and works; and finally, because signs are language and it is somewhat difficult – and clumsy – to make a case for the private appropriation of a discrete portion of language.

All these misgivings have been overcome, at least in principle, in a number of cases. It is nevertheless remarkable, and possibly also a bit puzzling that in all the controversies which concern trademarks the ultimate practical outcome has not been especially satisfactory to the right holders.

---

46. F.M. Abbott, Th. Cottier & F. Gurry, *International Intellectual Property*, *supra* n. 1, 119.
47. For a discussion of the question, *see* P.K. Yu, *Challenges to the Development of a Human Rights Framework for Intellectual Property*, *supra* n. 14, 94 ff. and the *Report* of the Special Rapporteur to the United Nations High Commissioner on Human Rights in the field of cultural rights Farida Shaheed, 4 August 2015, A/70/279 available at http://www.concernedhistorians.org/content_files/file/TO/352.pdf.

    Intellectual property rights, including trademarks, may also considered an 'investment' under Article 8(1) of the (not yet 'concluded') Comprehensive Economic and Trade Agreement between Canada, of the one part, and the EU and its Member States, of the other part, signed in Brussels on 30 October 2016 (CETA), which may fall under Sec. F (Resolution of investment disputes between investors and states) of Ch. 8 (Investment) of the Agreement, with all the consequences discussed in the Opinion 1/17 by the EU Court of 30 April 2019 (Full Court), 'CETA'. The complex issues that this legal regime entails remain outside the scope of this article.
48. *See* Article 15(1)(c) ICESCR.

More specifically, ECHR and EU case law show how a human rights protection has been recognized in principle, but denied in practice, in connection with trademarks, trademark applications, as well as trade names germane to them, such as domain names and geographical indications. Hereafter are the details of the corresponding controversies.

19.6 THE ANHEUSER-BUSCH CASE

The decision by the Grand Chamber of European Court of Human Rights (ECtHR)[49] is just a chapter of the global Anheuser-Busch saga, which has so far resulted in innumerable Court decisions throughout the word.[50] The Grand Chamber dealt only with the Portuguese part of the ongoing dispute between the Czech firm which claimed to be heir to the tradition in brewing beer in the Bohemian locality of České Budějovice or, in German, Budweis, under the sign 'Budweis',[51] and the firm Anheuser-Busch, which, continuing the tradition of Czech immigrants in North America, had produced and sold beer in the United States (US) under the trademark Budweiser since 1876. The Grand Chamber was called to pronounce on the compliance of Portuguese proceedings with Protocol 1 of the ECHR.[52] Plaintiff Anheuser-Busch complained that the Portuguese Supreme Court had given precedence to a bilateral Czech-Portuguese treaty, signed in 1986, by which protection for the 'Budweiser' sign was reserved for indicating the geographic origin of beer brewed by the Czech firm Budějovický Budvar over the trademark application by Anheuser-Busch to the Portuguese trademark office made five years earlier. A Chamber of the Second Section of the Court reached the first decision in 2005, holding that, while trademark registrations were to be considered as 'property' in the meaning of Article 1 of the First Protocol; still, the guarantee under the ECHR did not extend to mere applications for registration. The Chamber had held in that regard that ' … while it is clear that a trademark constitutes a "possession" within the meaning of Article 1 of Protocol no. 1, this is only so after final registration of the mark, in accordance with the rules in force in the State concerned. Prior to such

---

49. Grand Chamber of the ECtHR 11 January 2007, *Anheuser-Busch v. Portugal*. A full discussion in L.T. Helfer, *The New Innovation Frontier? supra* n. 4, 47 ff., 60 ff.
50. Including the decision by the EU Court of 22 September 2011 (First Chamber), Case C-482/09, *Budějovický Budvar, národní podnik v. Anheuser-Busch, Inc.*, 'Budweiser'.
51. Which apparently went all the way back to the kingdom of the Bohemian Ottokar II, in the thirteenth century.
52. Article 1 of Protocol No. 1 reads as follows: 'Every natural or legal person is entitled to the peaceful enjoyment of his possessions. No one shall be deprived of his possessions except in the public interest and subject to the conditions provided for by law and by the general principles of international law.
   The preceding provisions shall not, however, in any way impair the right of a State to enforce such laws as it deems necessary to control the use of property in accordance with the general interest or to secure the payment of taxes or other contributions or penalties.'

registration, the applicant does, of course, have a hope of acquiring such a "possession", but not a legally protected legitimate expectation.'[53]

The Grand Chamber overruled that finding by holding that 'the concept of "possessions" referred to in the first part of Article 1 of Protocol no. 1 has an autonomous meaning, which is not limited to ownership of physical goods',[54] and may also cover intellectual property.[55] From there it proceeded to hold that the notion also included the rights deriving by a mere application for protection, in spite of their inchoate character. To reach this opposite conclusion, according to which also a trademark application gives 'rise to interests of a proprietary nature',[56] the Grand Chamber underlined that even an application might be transferred or licensed and, under certain conditions, obtain protection in the form of monetary compensation for unauthorized third-party uses.[57]

On this basis, the Grand Chamber examined 'whether there had been an interference with the applicant company's rights to the peaceful enjoyment of its possessions'.[58] In this regard, it confirmed the principle whereby 'the retrospective application of legislation whose effect is to deprive someone of a pre-existing "asset" that was part of his or her "possessions" may constitute interference that is liable to upset the fair balance that has to be maintained between the demands of the general interest on the one hand and the protection of the right to peaceful enjoyment of possessions on the other.'[59] This principle, however, did not lead to a finding of a violation of Article 1 of the Protocol, as the applicant company had complained that 'the courts wrongly gave retrospective effect to the Bilateral Agreement, rather than of the retrospective application of a law which deprived them of their pre-existing possessions' and that the rightful place for an answer to the former question is a domestic court rather than the ECtHR.

19.7   UNREGISTERED TRADEMARKS, TRADE NAMES
            AND DOMAIN NAMES: THE PAEFFGEN CASE

We might wonder whether the reasoning behind the Grand Chamber's decision in Anheuser-Busch would also assist in establishing whether the guarantee of 'the peaceful enjoyment of … possessions' under Article 1 of the Protocol to the ECHR extends to unregistered signs. In some – but not in all – Member States of the ECHR (and of the EU) unregistered signs may be

---

53. Paragraph 52 of the Chamber's decision.
54. Paragraph 63.
55. *See also* the decision of the Court of Human Rights No. 28743/03, *Melnychuk v. Ukraine*, in ECHR 2005-IX.
56. Paragraph 78 of the Grand Chamber's decision.
57. Paragraphs 76 and 77 of the Grand Chamber's decision.
58. Paragraphs 79 ff. of the Grand Chamber's decision.
59. Paragraph 82 of the Grand Chamber's decision.

transferred and licensed.[60] For sure EU law and EU-harmonized trademark laws confer on the owners of unregistered signs rights at least in part parallel to the ones conferred by registered trademarks.[61] Under Article 8 of the Paris Convention (1967), 'a trade name shall be protected in all the countries of the Union without the obligation of filing or registration, whether or not it forms part of a trademark.'

Thus, it may well be suggested that unregistered trademarks and trade names fall under the same rules as registered trademarks as far as human rights protection is concerned.

One might expect to find a confirmation of this approach in connection with domain names, that is, the unique names that identify an internet resource such as a website. Indeed, the Fifth Section of the ECHR was called to rule on the issue several years ago.[62] On that occasion, after repeating that the notion of 'possessions' is autonomous[63] and depends on factors such as the question 'whether the legal position in question gave rise to financial rights and interests and thus had an economic value', it went on to remark that the right at issue had contractual nature, as it was based on 'contracts with the registration authority' that:

> gave the applicant company, in exchange for paying the domain fees, an open-ended right to use or transfer the domains registered in its name. As a consequence, the applicant could offer to all internet users entering the domain name in question, for example, advertisements, information or services, possibly in exchange for money, or could sell the right to use the domain to a third party. The exclusive right to use the domains in question thus had an economic value. Having regard to the above criteria, this right, therefore, constituted a 'possession', which the court decisions prohibiting the use of the domains interfered with.[64]

As a result, it may be concluded that the notion of 'possession' for human rights purposes assists not only trademark rights granted by a sovereign (such as the EU or a State) and the application for such a grant but also contractual positions which are tradable and have a financial value.

---

60. Contrast the positive solution taken for granted, in Italy, by Trib. Torino 15 June 2005, *Astigiana Materassi s.n.c. di Silvano Ballardelli & C. v. Centro Arredo Casa di Cantamessa Marco & C. s.n.c.*, in *Sez. spec. PII* I, 402 f. (2005,) with the negative solution adopted by British Courts and reported in detail by L. Bently, et al., *Intellectual Property Law* 1169 (Oxford University Press, Oxford, 2015) (assignment of the unregistered mark without the business held impermissible).
61. *See* Articles 5(4)(b) of the EUTM Directive and 8(4) EUTMR.
62. Decision by Fifth section of the ECtHR of 18 September 2007, 'Paeffgen'.
63. Paragraph 1 of the decision by Fifth section of the ECtHR of 18 September 2007, 'Paeffgen'.
64. Paragraph 1 of the decision by Fifth section of the ECHR of 18 September 2007, 'Paeffgen'.

Court orders prohibiting the use of the 'possession' in question, as conflicting with prior trademarks, maybe, therefore, constitute a 'deprivation' for purposes of the second sentence of the first paragraph of Article 1 of the Protocol. Such interference may, however, be in full conformity with the State's right under the second paragraph of the same provision, provided that the interference in question is 'in accordance with the general interest' of protecting prior trade signs and of maintaining a functioning system of protection and provided that such a priority-based interference is supported by 'a reasonable relationship of proportionality between the means employed and the aim to be realized'.[65] The conclusion makes sense: it would be surprising that human rights guarantees for a later trade sign were to be used to overturn the – even more valuable – 'peaceful enjoyment' of prior and conflicting 'possessions'.[66]

19.8 GEOGRAPHIC INDICATIONS AS PROPERTY: THE TOCAJ CASE

Geographic indications (GIs) designate the territorial, rather than business, source of the goods they identify. Still, they are trade signs too; and have something to teach us about the quite marked limits of the human rights protection of identifiers.

It so happens that in the traditional wine-growing region of Friuli, in Italy, certain dry wines had been designated as Tocai for a very long time. However, the really famous Tocaj, spelt with a 'j' and not an 'i', was all along the Hungarian one, which is altogether different: it also is wine, but it is a sweet dessert wine. The conflict between the two denominations has remained latent, as long as the commercial ties between the two areas remained weak. The two signs went on a collision course as soon as the Iron curtain fell and EU-Hungarian trade soared.

The matter was swiftly taken care of by means of a (then) EC-Hungary Agreement on wines of 1991, which, in dealing with homonymous geographical indications, established that Italian wine producers would stop

---

65. Paragraph 1 of the decision by Fifth section of the ECHR of 18 September 2007, 'Paeffgen'.
66. It may be of some interest that, in a different context, contractual positions concerning the use of a trade name and trademark have obtained full protection for violation of constitutional limits on retrospective legislation: *see* the decision of the Italian Constitutional Court of 8 July 2009, No. 206, *Pubblikappa s.r.l. v. AGCOM*, 'radio Kiss'. [keep it as it is; this is the way the radio was named] The legislation in question had obliged a local licensee of the trade name 'radio kiss[keep it as it is; this is the way the radio was named]' to surrender its rights to another licensee, which had obtained at a later time a license to use the same sign at the national level, by providing that national users should prevail over local ones irrespective of the time of acquisition of their respective rights.

using the expression Tocai in a time frame of sixteen years, thus starting from 2007.[67]

The local authorities of the Friuli Region attacked Italian rules implementing the EC-Hungary Agreement; on request of the competent Italian administrative court, the European Court of Justice (ECJ) gave its ruling.[68] The Court tackled a number of issues; what is of specific interest here is that it also dealt with the question whether the deprivation of Italian operators of the right to use the geographical term Tocai was against the then applicable property guarantee. As at the time of the decision, the CFR had been adopted but was not yet in force; the Court looked at the ECHR to determine the scope of the fundamental right to property. In doing so, it took for granted that GIs are protected (intellectual) property; however, it also found that the prohibition against using the word Tocai was not a disproportionate and intolerable interference impairing the fundamental right in question under the second part of the first paragraph of Article 1 of the Protocol[69] and that the measure in question was pursuing aims of general interest in a proportionate way under the second paragraph of the same provision.[70]

The first conclusion was reached on the remarkable ground that the prohibition 'does not exclude any reasonable method of marketing the Italian wines concerned'.[71] This statement would seem to implicitly accept the idea that, even though the right to resort to a specific trade sign belonging to a firm is restricted or curtailed without compensation, this does not by itself mean that the business in question is altogether denied its presence in the market place; and that the possibility of continued access makes the prohibition to continue using the sign hitherto employed on the market tolerable in some meaning of the word.

The notion that trade signs may well be assets and proprietary, but still children of a lesser God for purposes of property protection, is reinforced by the second conclusion. The prohibition was deemed to be proportionate to the general interest aim,[72] 'since a transitional period of 13 years was provided for in the exchange of letters on Tocai and, as the Commission

---

67. It is worth reminding that the Tocaj/Tocai conflict was the only instance in a set of 116 situations of total or partial homonymity where the parties decided for the gradual phasing out of one of the two overlapping indications, while in all the other cases coexistence rules were devised to allow the simultaneous presence on the market of the expressions while – purportedly – avoiding consumer confusion.
68. ECJ 12 May 2005, Case C-347/03, *Regione Autonoma Friuli Venezia Giulia and Agenzia regionale per lo sviluppo rurale (ERSA) v. Ministero delle Politiche Agricole e Forestali*, 'Tocaj/Tocai'.
69. ECJ 12 May 2005, 'Tocaj/Tocai', paras 121 ff.
70. ECJ 12 May 2005, 'Tocaj/Tocai', paras 125 ff.
71. ECJ 12 May 2005, 'Tocaj/Tocai', para. 122.
72. 'To reconcile the need to provide the final consumer with clear and accurate information on the products concerned with the need to protect producers on their territory against distortions of competition': para. 128.

611

observed at the hearing, alternative terms are available to replace the name "Tocai friulano" and its synonym "Tocai italico", namely, *inter alia*, "Trebbianello" and "Sauvignonasse"".[73] It would seem that also the principle of freedom to conduct a business under a sign of one's choosing was here in question; however, the issue was not even raised.

In conclusion, also, geographical indications have proved to be a very vulnerable property right.[74]

All the decisions reviewed in the previous pages have been reached before the date of coming into force of the Lisbon Treaty which refers to the CFR. One might, therefore, wonder whether the standards to be applied to trademarks and other trade signs have, in the meantime, changed as a result of the relevance acquired by the CFR. The reply is plausibly in the negative. According to settled case law, including the one just discussed, under ECHR law the right of property is not absolute but must be viewed in relation to its social function; consequently, the exercise of the right of property may be restricted, provided that those restrictions, in fact, correspond to objectives of general interest and do not constitute in relation to the aim pursued a disproportionate and intolerable interference.[75] In a similar vein, EU Courts also hold in connection with the specific safeguard under Article 17(2) CFR that intellectual property is not absolute, and therefore, may be restricted, provided that, in accordance with Article 52(1) of the same CFR, these restrictions are proportionate in relation to the aim pursued[76] and are apt to

---

73. ECJ 12 May 2005, 'Tocaj/Tocai', para. 133.
74. A different issue concerns the question of the compatibility of the outcome with Article 345 TFEU (according to which 'The Treaties shall in no way prejudice the rules in Member States governing the system of property ownership'), which probably is to replied in the affirmative as the legal basis for the protection of the indication was EU legislation concerning quality wines. The provision in Article 345 falls outside the scope of this article, as it deals with the boundaries of EU and national law, rather than human rights protection, by indicating in the negative to which extent EU law may restrict Member States' choices concerning property regimes (EU Court 22 October 2013 (Grand Chamber), joined Cases C-105/12 to C-107/12, *Staat der Netherlanden v. Essent NV, Essent Nederland BV, Eneco Holding NC and Delta NV*, 'Netherlanden/Essent', paras 28 ff.) and, in the positive, to which extent EU law may adopt European property regimes, including in the field of IP (*see* B. Akkermans & E. Ramaekers, *Article 345 TFEU (ex Article 295 EC), Its Meanings and Interpretations*, 16 *Eur. L. J.* 291-314 (2010)). Accordingly, EU case law consistently holds that the EU Treaties do not affect the IP rights granted by Member States but may impact on their exercise: *see* General Court 21 January 2015 (Second Chamber), 'cat&clean/clean cat', *supra* n. 8, para. 40 and the references there.
75. *See* ECJ 12 May 2005, 'Tocaj/Tocai', para. 119 and quotations there.
76. *See* General Court 30 January 2014 (Eight Chamber), Case T-495/11, *Michael Streng v. OHIM and Fulvio Gismondi*, 'Parametrica/parameta', para. 38 (upholding the burden on the opponent to make available translations of certificates of his prior registered trademarks into the language of the proceedings in compliance with Article 17(2) CFR); 3 July 2013 (Third Chamber), Case T-06/12, *Cytochroma Development, Inc. v. OHIM and Teva Pharmaceutical Industries Ltd.*, 'Alpharen/Alpha D3', paras 45 f. (holding that applicant's right are subject to legitimate third part prior rights); Court of First Instance

strike a 'fair balance' between the competing fundamental rights involved.[77] As the EU Court put it even more bluntly, if in connection with a different IPR, copyright, 'There is ... nothing whatsoever in the wording of that provision or in the Court's case law to suggest that that right is inviolable and must for that reason be absolutely protected'.[78]

Therefore, in this respect, we cannot expect notable changes to follow as a result of the transition from ECHR to CFR.

19.9 THE TOBACCO AND PLAIN PACKAGING CASES

The human rights dimension of trademark protection has played a crucial role in the now quite extensive line of cases which, in a number of jurisdictions, have dealt with public health-based interventions on trademark owners' prerogatives in the field of tobacco products.

These initiatives are quite recent and find their basis in a public international law instrument, the Framework Convention on Tobacco Control, adopted on 21 May 2003.[79] Five are the major decisions at the intersection of trademark law and human rights which have been taken so far.

---

3 May 2006, Case T-439/04, *Eurohypo AG v. OHIM*, 'Eurohypo', para. 21. Article 52(2) CFR provides: 'Any limitation on the exercise of the rights and freedoms recognised by this Charter must be provided for by law and respect the essence of those rights and freedoms. Subject to the principle of proportionality, limitations may be made only if they are necessary and genuinely meet objectives of general interest recognised by the Union or the need to protect the rights and freedoms of others.' In this connection *see* the thoughtful analysis of C. Geiger, *The Social Function of Intellectual Property Rights, supra* n. 25, 183 ff., 162-163.

77. ECJ 29 January 2008 (Grand Chamber), Case C-275/06, *Productores de Música de España (Promusicae) e Telefónica de España SAU*, 'Promusicae', par. 66; EU Court 24 November 2011 (Third Chamber), Case C-70/10, *Scarlet Extended SA v. Société belge des auteurs compositeurs et éditeurs (Sabam) and Belgian Entertainment Association Video ASBL (BEA Video), Belgian Entertainment Association Music ASBL (BEA Music) and Internet Service Providers Association ASBL (ISPA)*, 'Scarlet Extended', paras 45 ff. In the literature, also in relation to the mandate of a 'fair balance' between competing fundamental rights and to the mechanisms on which the same is based, *see* C. Geiger, *Reconceptualizing the Constitutional Dimension of Intellectual Property, supra* n. 7, 134 ff.; P. Torremans, *Comment* to Article 17(2), *supra* n. 2, 504 ff.; J. Griffiths & L. McDonagh, *Fundamental Rights and European IP law, supra* n. 8, 79, 85 ff. and, also for additional quotations, my *Commento* all'art. 17, in R. Mastroianni-O. Pollicino-S. Allegrezza-O. Razzolin (eds), *Carta dei diritti fondamentali dell'Unione Europea* (Giuffrè, Milano, 2017) 337 ff., 345 ff.
78. EU Court 29 July 2019 (Grand Chamber), Case C-476/17, *Pelham GmbH, Moses Pelham, Martin Haas v. Ralf Hütter, Florian Schneider-Esleben*, 'Pelham', para. 33; 29 July 2019 (Grand Chamber), Case C-469/17, *Funke Medien NRW GmbH v. Bundesrepublik Deutschland*, 'Funke Medien', para. 71; 24 November 2011 (Third Chamber), 'Scarlet Extended', *supra* n. 77, para. 42.
79. By the World Health Assembly, the decision making body of the World Health Organisation (WHO); the Convention has 168 Signatories and entered into force on 27 February 2005.

We may begin with the judgement given by the High Court of Australia in *JT International SA v. Commonwealth of Australia*.[80] It is true that this decision may appear located at the periphery of the human rights debate, as in this instance the matter was dealt with only from the perspective of Australian constitutional law so that the discussion did not have a chance to take into account any international human rights provisions.[81] However, the issues decided by the Australian Court have relevance in this context as they deal head-on with the so-called tobacco plain packaging mandate, i.e., the prohibition to use on packaging relating to tobacco products the non-denominative components of the trademarks of tobacco firms, i.e., the figurative or device elements included in the same. In this connection, the Australian High Court ruled out that the prohibition amounted to an 'acquisition' according to section 51(xxxi) of the Australian Constitution, as an 'acquisition' requires 'receipt of something seen from the perspective of the acquirer'; according to the Australian judges, this was not the case in the situation before them, as the measure involved a mere 'deprivation of property', over the non-denominative components of trademarks, which does not trigger the constitutional clause.

Also, the two EU cases[82] are in a way located at the periphery of the debate concerning the guarantee of possession under the ECHR and CFR provisions. Indeed, the directives attacked by trademark proprietors[83] mandated labelling and packaging requirements which did not entail any prohibition to use the trademarks in question,[84] even though they mandated

---

80. High Court of Australia 5 October 2012, *JT International SA v. Commonwealth of Australia* [2012] HCA 43, 'Tobacco Plain Packaging'.

81. Which is obvious in some regards, as Australia is not part to the relevant European conventions; less to in connection with a possible reference to Article 17 UDHR (*supra* §19.1).

82. ECJ 10 December 2002, Case C-491/01, *The Queen and Secretary of State for Health ex parte British American Tobacco (Investments) Ltd and Imperial Tobacco Ltd*, 'BAT (labelling)' and European Court 4 May 2016 (Second Chamber), Case C-547/14, *The Queen, on the application of Philip Morris Brands SARL and Others v. Secretary of State for Health*, 'Philip Morris (labelling)'.

83. Directives 2001/37/EC and 2014/40/EU on the approximation of the laws, regulations and administrative provisions of the Member States concerning the manufacture, presentation and sale of tobacco and related products.

84. *See* ECJ 10 December 2002, 'BAT (labelling)', para. 132 (stating, in the proportionality analysis, that Article 5 of the 2001/37/EC Directive requires 'an increase in the percentage of the surface area on certain sides of the unit packet of tobacco products to be given over to those indications and warnings, in a proportion which leaves sufficient space for the manufacturers of those products to be able to affix other material, in particular concerning their trade marks'); on this basis, the Court found, at para. 148, that impact of the legislation was not on the national rules governing the system of property ownership in the Member States, but rather 'on the exercise by the manufacturers of tobacco products of their trademark rights over those products'; and went further to note, at para. 149, that the right of property 'is not an absolute right and must be viewed in relation to its social function'; therefore, 'it's exercise may be restricted, provided that those restrictions in fact

the inclusion of certain indications and warnings ('labelling') on an extensive portion of the packaging. Therefore, these provisions raised issues which ultimately concern freedom of expression,[85] rather than deprivation of possession.

The full brunt of the questions concerning the compatibility of the outright prohibition to use the figurative components of tobacco trademarks, adopted by the United Kingdom (UK) legislature,[86] with the property guarantees enshrined in the ECHR and the CFR, has fallen on the shoulders of UK Courts.[87] As regards the protection of the right to property, Lord Justice Lewison, who delivered the judgement of the Court of Appeals, made reference both to Article 1 of Protocol 1 of the ECHR and to Article 17(2) of the CFR. In determining the compatibility of plain packaging with the former, he acknowledged that the appellants had argued, 'no doubt rightly',[88] that the Regulations made their rights 'far less valuable than they were before'.[89] Nonetheless, he held, with a wording reminiscent of the position taken by the Australian judges a few years earlier, that the fact that in the corresponding 'negative' rights there is a residual utility means that it cannot be said that the trademark proprietors 'have been *deprived* of their national marks'.[90] Further, Lord Justice Lewison noted that the legislation allowed proprietors to use the world component of their trademarks, and therefore, concluded that Mr Justice Green, in the previous decision of the High Court, was indeed entitled to conclude that the Regulations adopted by the UK legislature under the umbrella of the EU Directive strike a 'fair balance' for the purposes of Article 1 of Protocol 1 of the ECHR.[91]

Concerning the second provision, the trademark proprietors had argued that Article 17(2) of the Charter goes further than Article 1 of Protocol 1 in protecting the right to possessions because, whereas under Article 1 of

---

correspond to objectives of general interest pursued by the Community and do not constitute a disproportionate and intolerable interference, impairing the very substance of the rights guaranteed'.

85. On which *infra* § 19.11.
86. The Standardised Packaging of Tobacco Products Regulation 2015 adopted in UK in part implements Directive 2014/40/EU, in part goes further than the directive; it is those additional restriction which were subject to judicial challenge.
87. *See* Court of Appeal, Civil Division, 30 November 2016, *British American Tobacco and Others v. Department of Health*, [2016] EWCA Civ 1182, 'Tobacco Plain Packaging', https://s3-eu-west-2.amazonaws.com/sqe-essexcourt/wp-content/uploads/2016/12/08152845/BAT-CA-Judgment.pdf, and High Court of Justice of England and Wales, Queen's Bench Division 19 May 2016, *British American Tobacco and Others v. Department of Health*, [2016] EWHC 1169, https://www.judiciary.uk/wp-content/uploads/2016/05/bat-v-doh.judgment.pdf, 'Tobacco Plain Packaging'.
88. Court of Appeal, Civil Division, 30 November 2016, 'Tobacco Plain Packaging', *supra* n. 87 at §106.
89. *Id.*
90. *Id.*
91. Court of Appeal, Civil Division, 30 November 2016, 'Tobacco Plain Packaging', *supra* n. 87 at §§ 115-123.

Protocol 1 'there can be exceptional situations where compensation need not be paid even in the case of deprivation, under Article 17 of the Charter, the right to compensation is absolute in the case of deprivation'.[92] Lord Justice Lewison, however, held that, since it was concluded that the case in question is one 'of control of use rather than deprivation',[93] the point does not arise, to begin with, and hence, the Regulations, just as they were found compliant with Article 1 of Protocol 1 of the ECHR, are indeed also compatible with Article 17 of the Charter.[94] The reasoning of the Lord Justice may appear at first blush formalistic; but may turn out to be ultimately quite acceptable if we pause to consider that the trademark proprietors were not altogether deprived of the right to use the entire mark, but only of the device. Nor should we forget that the asset which was subject to the prohibition after all was not a technical innovation or an intellectual creation, but consisted just in signs and symbols, also language. This may be important to the extent one accepts that the functional and structural features which make trademarks different from other IP rights we discussed earlier[95] justify that the former enjoy a lesser human rights safeguard than the latter; and that nobody in her right mind would dream that prohibiting the use of a harmful drug, such as thalidomide, is an unjustified deprivation of possessions.

Also, the recent WTO panel *Reports* of 28 June 2018 concerning Australian plain packaging legislation[96] deserve mention in the current context, even though strictly speaking, these decisions do not deal with the human rights protection of intellectual property and concentrate on compliance with a number of provisions of various relevant IP Conventions.[97] What should be remarked in this specific connection is that the reasoning of the *Reports* revolves around an issue which may be considered essential and overarching in the analysis of the compatibility of state intervention concerning trademarks: namely, the recurring question whether trademark

---

92. Court of Appeal, Civil Division, 30 November 2016, 'Tobacco Plain Packaging', *supra* n. 87 at §116.
93. Court of Appeal, Civil Division, 30 November 2016, 'Tobacco Plain Packaging', *supra* n. 87 at §117.
94. Court of Appeal, Civil Division, 30 November 2016, 'Tobacco Plain Packaging', *supra* n. 87 at § 125. On 12 April 2017 the Supreme Court refused permission to appeal the decision. The order (https://www.supremecourt.uk/news/permission-to-appeal-decision-12-april-2017.html) took pains to explain that the court below correctly identified the legal principles concerning the issue whether the trademarks gave applicants 'positive exploitation rights, whether the relevant preventive provisions deprived the applicants of the use of their trademarks or of their substance or essence'.
95. § 19.3.
96. *Report* of the WTO Panels 28 June 2018 *Australia – Certain Measures Concerning Trademarks and Other Plain Packaging Requirements Applicable to Tobacco Products and Packaging,* WT/DS435/R; WT/DS441/R; WT/DS458/R; WT/DS467/R. For commentary *see* M. Davison, *Plain Packaging of Tobacco Products and the WTO Challenge* in A. Alemanno-E. Bonadio (eds), *The New Intellectual Property of Health, supra* n. 21.
97. These include Articles 15(4), 16(1) and (3), 20, 22(2)(b) and 24(3) TRIPS and Article 6*quinquies* and 10*bis* of the Paris Convention (1967).

rights confer on their proprietors only negative rights, in the form of exclusivity or of an *ius excludendi alios*, against third parties using identical or similar signs, or may be said to entail, by necessary implication, also a positive right or privilege, that is the entitlement to use in commercial life the sign of their choice.[98]

A few notes may be sufficient for present purposes. It is unsurprising that the supporters of the idea that trademark protection concerns not only the negative but also the positive side of the right, i.e., the entitlement of their proprietor to actually use the signs in trade, are more likely to see an encroachment on these right *via* a prohibitive State intervention and a corresponding violation both of human rights guarantees and of the other safeguards mandated by international conventions, such as the Paris Convention (1967) and TRIPS. This position is open, however, to a number of objections.

Even cursory consideration of other IPRs would seem to suggest that the negative and positive side of any given right not necessarily go hand in hand. Certain inventions may well be patentable, but their use may be subject to authorization or altogether prohibited. A drug may be found to be dangerous and prohibited after the grant of exclusivity, as it was in the case of thalidomide after its side effects were disclosed. As earlier suggested, nobody ever imagined that this was a 'taking' of the rights of the holders of the patent. Similarly, a translation of a work gives it creator a negative right, to prevent the exploitation of the translation itself without her consent; but does not give the translator any positive right to commercialize the translation, unless the consent of the author of the original work is obtained. It is expected that this line of reasoning may apply *a fortiori* to trademarks, considering that these are just signs and symbols, rather than technical innovations and intellectual creations.

However, also the opposite position, whereby an intellectual property right technically only entails a negative side, an *ius excludendi*, may end up sounding disingenuous, if it is taken to the extremes and invariably leads to the conclusion that, while the right holder may prevent third parties from using the right, she may not do so herself; and, by implication, that legislation impacting only the positive side escapes scrutiny by definition.

It is suggested that the relevant question does not concern the 'nature' of the right itself, whether it is – in some metaphysical sense – negative, positive or both. After all, rights are not to be found in nature but are man-made. The question should rather be directed to the kind of assessment,

---

98. *See* in this connection S. Frankel-D. Gervais, *Plain Packaging and the Interpretation of the TRIPS Agreement*, 46 *Vanderbilt J. Transnat'l L.* 1149-1214 (2013) (arguing in favour of the existence of a positive side of TM rights); the opposite view was adopted by the WTO Panel 15 March 2005, *European Communities – Protection of Trademarks and Geographical Indications for Agricultural Products and Foodstuffs*, Complaint by Australia, WT/DS290/R at §VII.332.

or scrutiny, which comes into play when we ask whether the right in question also has a positive side.

Indeed, it would appear that the relevance of the positive side of the right, i.e., here, of the effective possibility of resorting to a sign in communication with the interested public, comes into the limelight when the State intervention under scrutiny concerns the safeguards of freedom of expression. After all, it is difficult to assert that the speech of the trademark proprietor is not abridged, if she is not allowed any commercially significant for of use of the sign of her choice. Conversely, it appears well open to question whether the protection of the trademark proprietor speech extends all the way to the negative right of preventing third parties to use a sign identical or similar to her trademark, as we will presently see.[99]

A different reasoning may come to the fore if we consider trademarks from the angle of the protection of property. Property tends to be considered as a negative right, an *ius excludendi alios*, even in connection with tangible property, including real estate and personal property. This leads to a presumption that the impact of legislation on the negative side of the trademark right is already by itself relevant for purposes of analysis under this perspective. However, in the perspective of businesses, assets may be seen in a complementary light, also as tools to compete. From this angle, even registration of a trademark which has not yet been used may be seen as a necessary prerequisite for planning an investment in the area. This suggests that the question whether legal restrictions on the positive side of trademark rights are compatible with human rights is best appreciated if we look at these restrictions not by asking the somewhat fuzzy question whether the 'positive' side of the right is affected, but whether the restrictions posed on the use of the trademark intolerably affect the freedom to conduct business of the proprietor. We shall have a chance to test this line of reasoning in the two paragraphs which follow.

19.10 ABSOLUTE GROUNDS FOR REFUSAL OF THE REGISTRATION OF A TRADEMARK AND HUMAN RIGHTS: TWO APPROACHES ON THE RELEVANCE OF FREE SPEECH

The special features of trademark protection play a certain role also in regard to the human rights dimension of the assessment of absolute grounds. In the EU legal systems, trademarks which are contrary to public policy or to accepted principles of morality may not be registered.[100] Similarly, the US Lanham Act barred, until recent times, the registration of trademarks that

---

99. *See infra* § 19.10.
100. And, if registered, may be found invalid: *see* Articles 4(1)(f) EUTM Directive and 7(1)(f) EUTMR.

'consist of or comprise immoral or scandalous matter' or that 'may disparage ... any person'.[101] Can a refusal by a trademark office to register a sign under this ground be considered as a restriction of freedom of expression?

In fact, brands may convey – and do convey – not only messages about the origin of the goods and their quality but also other messages, about lifestyles, values, attitudes towards society and the like. The question has found opposing solutions on the two sides of the Atlantic.

The diverging outcomes are not accounted for by different assumptions on the scope of the protection based on the principle of freedom of expression. Indeed, the notion that freedom of expression assists not only purely non-commercial speech but also commercial speech has been a foregone conclusion in the US legal system for quite a long time.[102] Meanwhile, in the European context, the belief that only speech conducted for non-economic purposes triggers human rights protection was followed for quite a long time at the Member State level.[103] Nevertheless, also at the European level, the conclusion that also information provided by economic players in connection with market transactions may be valuable to the public, and therefore, deserves some extent of protection has finally, if gradually, emerged.[104]

In spite of this shared assumption, when the principle of freedom of expression is applied to trademark registrations (and applications), a clear divergence between the two systems comes to light. The US approach is that as the choice of expressions intended as trademarks is entirely left to private parties, the resulting message has to be considered 'private' rather than

---

101. 15 U.S.C. § 1052(a). Under this provision the US Patent and Trademark Office (PTO) refused registration of the expressions 'FUCT' for clothing and 'Slants' (which employs a derogatory stereotype, 'slant-eyed', for people of Asian ethnicity) for a rock-band: *see* respectively U.S. Supreme Court 24 June 2019, *Iancu v. Brunetti*, 588 U.S. (2019), 'FUCT', and 19 June 2017, *Matal v. Tam*, 582 U.S. (2017), 'the Slants'.

102. US Supreme Court, 19 June 2016, 'the Slants' (finding that resort to the prohibition of registration of the trademark 'the Slants' under the disparagement clause of the Lanham act run afoul even of the relaxed scrutiny mandated for commercial speech and leaving open the issue whether trademarks may also have an expressive, non-commercial component) and 24 May 1976 *Virginia State Board of Pharmacy v. Virginia Citizens Consumer Council*, 425 U.S. 748 (1976). For other references *see* E. Bonadio, *Are Brands Untouchable? How Availability and Use of Trademarks Can Be Restricted for Furthering Public Interests*, Charlotte Intellectual Property Journal (2014), http://papers.ssrn.com/sol3/papers.cfm?abstract_id=2540848; W. Sakulin, *Trademark Protection and Freedom of Expression, supra* n. 41, 142 ff.

103. *See* the Italian case Cass. 14 September 2004, n. 18431, *A. Mondadori Editore s.p.a. v. A. Manzoni s.p.a ., Prefetto di Milano, Giur. it.*, 1189 ff. (2005), with annotation by N. Bottero, 'Camel Trophy-Merit Cup'.

104. *See* EU Court 4 May 2016 (Second Chamber), 'Philip Morris', *supra* n. 82, paras 147 ff.; 24 November 2011, 'Scarlet Extended', *supra* n. 77, paras 50-52; ECJ 25 March 2004, Case C-71/02, *Herbert Karner Industrie Auktionen GmbH v. Trostwijk GmbH*, in (2004) I-03025 ff., 'Herbert Karner' and ECtHR 20 November 1989 (Plenary), App. No. 10572783, *Markt Intern Verlag and Klaus Beerman v. Germany*.

'government' speech for purposes of constitutional analysis. Now, in accordance with the rather extreme approach which in the recent decades has come to prevail in American law in connection with the protection freedom of expression, legal prohibitions based on immorality or derogatory character of the trademark applied for have been invalidated. These prohibitions, in the form adopted at the time of the Supreme Court decisions, have been seen as not viewpoint neutral, even though possibly serving a substantial public interest; as such they have been deemed disproportionate, and therefore, invalid.[105]

On the contrary, in the EU, the grounds to oppose or invalidate registration on the basis of mores or public policy are firmly upheld.[106] What transpires from the EU case law is that the prohibition intends to take care of the governmental, not of the private speech, component of registrations. In the European perspective, what is controlling is that registration confers to the trademark proprietor a position of exclusivity against third parties, a 'negative' right fully enforceable *via* Court orders; from this viewpoint, it appears unjustified that justice should lend its strong arm to trademark proprietors when the sign invoked is contrary to mores or public policy.[107]

---

105. U.S. Supreme Court 24 June 2019, 'FUCT', and 19 June 2016, 'the Slants', *supra* n. 101.

106. *See* General Court 24 January 2018 (Sixth Chamber), Case T-69/17, *Constantin Film Production GmbH v. EUIPO*, 'Fack Ju Göhte', paras 20 ff., 29 (refusing the registration of the expression as vulgar and unacceptable for the relevant public; holding in passing that artistic freedom and freedom of expression do not apply in the field of trademark law); 15 March 2018 (Ninth Chamber), 'La Mafia', *supra* n. 8, paras 35 ff. (refusing the registration of the sign for clothing and bars on the basis of the deeply negative connotations of the reference to the criminal organization known under that name); General Court 26 September 2014 (Fifth Chamber), Case T-266/13, *Brainlab AG v. OHIM*, 'curve' (upholding the refusal to register a word which in Rumanian means 'whores' for hospital supplies); 9 March 2012 (First Chamber), Case T-417/10, *Federico Cortés del Valle López v. OHIM*, '¡que bunu ye!Hijoputa', para. 17 ff. (finding that the expression was undeniably shocking and insulting for the public concerned); 5 October 2011 (Third Chamber), 'Paki', *supra* n. 8, paras 12 ff. (holding that the sign is racially abusive whatever good or service it is used for) and 20 September 2011 (Fourth Chamber), Case T-232/10, *Couture Tech Ltd. v. OHIM*, 'Soviet emblem' (finding that a sign consisting of a hammer and sickle was contrary to *ordre public* in Eastern European States formerly subject to Soviet domination). For a (somewhat skeptical) discussion of this case law, as well as of the UK decisions in this area, *see* L. Bently, et al., *Intellectual Property Law*, *supra* n. 60, 1013-1014.

107. This line of reasoning is not altogether foreign to US decisions: *see* the Opinion, concurring in part and dissenting in part, by Justice Sotomayor in U.S. Supreme Court 24 June 2019, 'FUCT', 15 and 19 of the slip, pointing out that what is questionable is whether applicants for 'scandalous' signs should enjoy the 'additional benefit' deriving from registration. There may be a reason why the argument has not been taken up by the other Justices (except Breyer, who joined Sotomayor's Opinion): indeed, in the US legal system the protection of trademarks is still seen as based on use rather than registration, the role of the latter being confined to giving constructive notice of the registrant's claim of ownership and to supplying prima facie evidence of the validity of the mark: *see*

This approach appears confirmed by the recurring decisions which hold that a trademark office does not truly interfere with the freedom of expression of the applicant just by refusing registration, as that decision does not affect the right to use the trademark, which in principle survives even though registration is denied.[108]

The EU approach may be criticized by remarking that the refusal of registration still represents an indirect restriction of applicant's free speech as the corresponding businesses are discouraged from making an investment on signs which are likely to turn out not registrable.[109] A possible rebuttal to this further argument may be based on the notion that freedom of expression cannot be invoked to claim *exclusivity* of use: what is relevant for freedom of expression analysis is whether the speaker is still given the possibility of employing the expressions and symbols in question (positive right), which is left untouched by a refusal of registration; not whether she may prevent others from doing so (negative right), as, in a freedom of expression analysis, this latter behaviour entails a suppression rather than expansion of freedom of expression.[110]

Justice Alito's Opinion in US Supreme Court, 19 June 2016, 'the Slants', 4 of the slip. In continental Europe the reluctance to lend the arm of justice to enforce trademarks which are deemed against public policy or *mores* may be so strong to occasionally induce Courts to go all the way and deviate by the ordinary rule, whereby invalidity is not declared by Courts unless a request to the effect is made by the private parties, in connection with signs which are deemed repugnant to the polity: *see* Trib. Milano 17 dicembre 2005 (ord.), *Marco Bruns and other v. Flirt s.r.l.*, in *Giur. ann. dir. ind. 4990.*

It may be suggested that the decision by the EFTA Court (6 April 2017, Case E-5/16, *Municipality of Oslo v. Norwegian Industrial Property Office*, 'Vigeland') focuses precisely on this aspect of the ground of refusal of registration as a trademark. There, the signs for which registration was sought by the Municipality of Oslo, which consisted of works by the national icon Vigeland, were not by themselves objectionable, as they were neither vulgar nor offensive; rather, what was deemed to be against public policy was the fact that the Industrial Property Office would grant the exclusivity conferred by trademark registration over signs which, after the lapse of the term of copyright protection, were destined, by legislative option, to fall into public domain; given the exceptional stature of Vigeland's work, registration would have been detrimental to the nation's access to its cultural heritage (for the application of the principle *see* Board of Appeal for Industrial Property Rights 13 November 2017, *The Municipality of Oslo v. Norwegian Industrial Property Office*, 'Vigeland'; for a prescient discussion of the underlying issues *see* M. Senftleben, *Public Domain Preservation in EU Trademark Law – A Model for Other Regions? Trademark Reporter* 775 ff. (2013)).

108. General Court 9 March 2012 (First Chamber), '¡que bunu ye!Hijoputa', *supra* n. 106, para. 26, adding, somewhat disingenuously, that, where the contrast with public policy and *mores* concerns only one component of the sign – e.g., the denominative part, but not the images – the applicant's freedom remains unrestricted as far as the permitted component is allowed.

109. E. Bonadio, *Are Brands Untouchable?*, *supra* n. 102, 16-17. This argument could be further developed in the perspective of freedom to conduct business (as suggested at the end of § 19.9).

110. W. Sakulin, *Trademark Protection and Freedom of Expression*, *supra* n. 41, 21-22 and 223-224.

Even accepting the opposite idea, that registration should be understood as a necessary intermediate step or springboard for further diffusion, and that, therefore, refusal to register may finally entail a certain degree of interference with the right to commercial free speech, in the EU context this interference may still be justified. Indeed, Article 10(2) ECHR provides that the exercise of this freedom 'may be subject to such formalities, conditions, restrictions or penalties as are prescribed by law and are necessary in a democratic society, in the interest of national security, territorial integrity or public safety, for the prevention of disorder or crime, for the protection of health or morals ... '.[111]

Thus, interference, in order to be justified, should address pressing social needs, be proportional and accompanied by adequate reasoning.[112] In particular, the proportionality requirement opens the door to a delicate balancing exercise, taking into account, on the one hand, the right of traders to freely choose signs and claim trademark exclusivity over them and on the other hand the right of the public not to be exposed to outrageous signs.[113]

Unsurprisingly, in the EU, the outcome tends to favour the second interest.[114] In this respect, freedom of commercial expression would appear to assist prospective trademark proprietors' interest in obtaining and maintaining registration as little as the property guarantees. Also here, a claim to exclusive private appropriation of language through Trademark Offices would appear not to cut much ice.

19.11 PROHIBITIONS TO USE A TRADEMARK FOR PUBLIC POLICY REASONS

Let us consider now the obverse situation, which does not concern the refusal *to register* a sign on absolute grounds but a prohibition *to use* it. One could imagine that surely freedom of expression concerns should play a much bigger role here, as at stake is not only a claim to exclusivity over a given

---

111. For a complete treatment of the issue *see* J. Griffiths, *Is there a Right to an Immoral Trademark?* in P. L. C. Torremans (ed.), *Intellectual Property and Human Rights* 309 ff. (Kluwer, 2008).

112. E. Bonadio, *Are Brands Untouchable?*, *supra* n. 102, 17-19.

113. E. Bonadio, *Are Brands Untouchable?*, *supra* n. 102, 19. Of course, the notion of relevant public refers here not only to the consumers who may be interested in purchasing the goods but also to the bystanders who may come across them: *see* General Court 14 November 2013 (Seventh Chamber), Case T-52/13, *Efag Trademark Company Gmbh & Co. KG v. OHIM*, 'Ficken'.

114. *See* General Court 14 November 2013 (Seventh Chamber), 'Ficken'; 20 September 2011 (Fourth Chamber), 'Soviet emblem', *supra* n. 106. A certain attenuation to the rigors of the approach may derive from the fact that, also for Member States trademarks and trademark applications, it is arguable that the concept of public policy and morals should be distilled from EU, rather than Member State, notions.

sign or symbol (a negative right) but the very entitlement to employ it as a commercial message (a positive right).

To be sure, the existing case law in the EU does not support this more libertarian view. To begin with, the issue has come up rather tangentially in the EU Tobacco cases concerning labelling, i.e., the assessment of the rules mandating the inclusion of certain indications and warnings and conversely prohibiting the inclusion of certain features and elements in the information contained in tobacco products and packaging. It was easy for the Court to find that a fair balancing between the requirements of the protection of freedom of expression and information and those of human health protection had been achieved,[115] even more so as the issue was found to be ultimately only remotely related to the 'positive' rights to use trademarks, as the labelling requirements did not entail a prohibition to use the trademarks.[116]

Turning then to the prohibition to use immoral, scandalous, derogatory or otherwise insulting expressions, on the grounds of *mores* or of public policy, it is submitted that in the EU, the matter belongs to the ordinary laws of the Member States, of criminal nature or otherwise. It would appear that the fact that the from time to time prohibited expression is intended for use as a trademark may well be part of the factual context against which the applicability of the prohibition has to be assessed; however, the fact that the expression is used in commerce as a trademark does not seem by itself to suggests a redeeming feature.

This outcome is in line with the European human rights analysis of trademarks in the light of the functional and structural features of trademarks.[117] After all, as pointed out several times, trademarks are just signs and symbols, also language, rather than technical innovations and creations. Still, it is commonly accepted that use even of patented inventions, and copyrightable works may be prohibited on public policy grounds. This prohibition may be justified *a fortiori* in connection with trademarks, for which the human rights safeguards may arguably be lesser than in other IP cases. On the one side, exclusivity over language may appear (and indeed may be) a lesser form of property or possession; on the other, its 'taking' does not prevent the former trademark proprietor from remaining on the market after she has been

---

115. EU Court 4 May 2016 (Second Chamber), 'Philip Morris', *supra* n. 82, paras 149 ff.
116. As previously indicated in § 19.9. The matter would have been otherwise troubling if the freedom of expression had been raised in the Australian and UK cases (§ 19.9), which were decided only (except for a cursory reference to freedom of expression at paras 828-829 in High Court of Justice of England and Wales, Queen's Bench Division 19 May 2016, 'Tobacco Plain Packaging', *supra* n. 87) on the basis of the issue of deprivation of possession. It is, however, submitted that at least under the provisions applicable in the EU (Articles 10 ECHR and 11 CFR) a freedom of expression claim might have been rejected on the basis of the reasoning that the trademark proprietor is not altogether deprived of the right to use the trademark in its entirety but only in connection with the figurative, or 'device', part of it.
117. Discussed at § 19.3.

deprived of the identifier of the goods she supplies, so that it is arguable once more that also the freedom to conduct business is not altogether denied.

19.12   THE 'NEED TO KEEP FREE' IN A HUMAN RIGHTS PERSPECTIVE

While the just mentioned features of trademarks account for the limited human rights protection their proprietors enjoy in connection with deprivation of property, restrictions of freedom of commercial speech and of the freedom to conduct business, it might be expected that a more expansive approach is adopted when it comes to the reverse side of the coin, i.e., to designing a system of absolute grounds for refusal and invalidity which is consistent with the positive function trademarks may, as fully recognized, play in creating a competitive environment.

More specifically, it may be questioned whether the current approach of EU legislation and case law in connection with the imperative to keep signs free, which the German language aptly describes as *Freihaltebedürfnis*, is entirely consistent with a correct understanding of the principle of freedom to conduct a business which, as the EU Court recently reiterated in the 'Scarlet Extended' case (2011), has to be taken into account in granting protection to IPRs.[118] What is at stake here is not the freedom to conduct the business of the trademark proprietor, but rather the freedom of competitors and of the public at large to avail themselves of signs and symbols, i.e., language, which may serve purposes other than as an identifier of business origin.

In the 'Scarlet Extended' case, the Court underlined that legislatures and courts should 'strike a fair balance' between competing claims of IP holders and of freedom to conduct business. There are, however, reasons to doubt that the balance struck in Europe in connection with the appropriability and protection of signs devoid of distinctive character, descriptive or customary in the current language or in trade is fully in line with the freedoms of users, including traders, both competing and non-competing with the trademark proprietors. Two are the reasons for concern in this regard.

In a first perspective, what is most remarkable is that all the bars to registration identified in the letters b) to d) of paragraph 1 of Article 7 EU Trade Mark Regulation (EUTMR) and of Article 4 of the EU Trade Mark Directive (EUTM) are essentially impermanent. Their permanence or not depends to a large extent on the decision of the trademark applicant or proprietor to engage in a promotional investment significant enough to cause the symbol to acquire, on top of the original, non-distinctive meaning, a

---

118. EU Court 24 November 2011 (Third Chamber), 'Scarlet Extended', *supra* n. 77, para. 46.

'secondary meaning' as an identifier of commercial source.[119] If this is the case, then the grounds for refusal and for invalidity cease to apply. The rule has a clear rationale: once the sign has come to strongly signify commercial source, rather than its original non-distinctive meaning, the interest of the buying public not to be misled by other businesses using the same sign for goods of different origins prevails over the other interests, including of the same public, that the same sign remains in the public domain.[120] The rule is remarkably permissive if contrasted with the principles prevailing in the US where generic trademarks never and by no means can be rescued by the acquisition of secondary meaning.[121]

The European rule is unfortunate, in particular, in connection with descriptive signs where the need of competing and non-competing traders and of the public to have unrestricted access to the informational value of the sign is more obvious. Here is a case in which planning and investment of a firm on a given trademark, which might be described as 'strategic branding', are capable of turning a symbol which originally belonged to the public domain into a valid and enforceable trademark. This is a case of a law-made self-fulfilling prophecy. The firm registers or uses a symbol which cannot as yet be considered a trademark *as if* it could; acts in accordance with its belief in ways which, quantitatively and qualitatively, are fit to have the public go along with that belief in a more or less long period of time. Surely the firm takes a risk; but, it does so because the law provides that, if the registration is not attacked before the secondary meaning has set in, the prophecy is bound to turn into a reality.

This approach seems to be fully accepted by the ECJ, to the point that when asked whether *Freihaltebedürfnis* should be taken into account in giving protection against unauthorized use to a sign which had earned its validity through secondary meaning (the Adidas stripe motif), the Court emphatically denied this possibility and, uncharacteristically, gave a ruling broader than it was strictly necessary. Rather than confining itself to saying that once a sign has acquired secondary meaning, its scope of protection is equivalent to the one of an originally valid trademark, it went all the way to

---

119. Article 7(3) EUTMR and Article 3(4) of the EUTM Directive.
120. For a critical assessment of the rule, *see* M. Senftleben, *Public Domain Preservation in EU Trademark Law*, *supra* n. 107, 794 ss., 812 ff.; A. Kur, *Strategic Branding: Does Trade Mark Law Provide for Sufficient Self Help and Self-Healing Forces?* in I. Govaere, H. Ullrich (eds), *Intellectual Property, Market Power and the Public Interest* 191 ff. (College of Europe Series, Bruxelles, P.I.E. Lang, 2008).
121. *See* Ch.R. McManis, *Intellectual Property and Unfair Competition* 147 ff. (Thomson-West 2004). As the decision of the US District Court, Western District of Washington of Seattle of 22 January 2003, *Microsoft Corp. v. Lindows.com, Inc.*, 'Lindows', indicates, under US law the expression 'lite' for drinks never could acquire secondary meaning.

make the sweeping statement whereby *Freihaltebedürfnis* never plays a role in an assessment of infringement.[122]

The combined effect of this legal provision and of its judicial interpretation is pretty straightforward – and dangerous. If and to the extent the investment of a firm on a given descriptive sign is sufficient to re-orient the perception of a substantial part of the interested public, a language which originally was in the public domain is privately appropriated, and the descriptive, ordinary meanings of the sign may become inaccessible.[123] Such an outcome is questionable, as it occurs in spite of the fact that at the basis of the ground for refusal lay a judicially recognized public interest reason, i.e., that signs which are descriptive of the goods they refer to should remain free to be used by the public at large and specifically by all traders who may need the sign in question to refer to the goods or to a character of the same. Since the registration of a sign as a trademark confers on the proprietor an exclusive right which enables her to monopolize the sign without time limits, it is hard to reconcile this outcome with the assumption that the overarching rationale for trademark protection is to preserve competitive markets.[124]

Indeed, denial of access to the informational value of a trademarked descriptive sign specifically runs counter the specific functional feature of signs candidate to becoming trademarks, which enjoy protection not as creative or innovative contributions of their proprietors but only as linguistic entities which may be privately appropriated if and to the extent the grant of exclusivity over them contributes to the competitive openness of markets.[125] It is, therefore, somewhat surprising that the rule whereby the acquisition of secondary meaning may override the imperative to keep free also in connection with a descriptive sign has not been even challenged as a violation of the principle of freedom to conduct business. Of course, there are possible explanations for this neglect; the status of freedom to conduct businesses is not yet well established among human rights, in part because as a rule, it belongs to business entities rather than to individuals; in part,

---

122. ECJ 10 April 2008, Case C-102/07, *Adidas AG and Adidas Benelux BV v. Marca Mode CV, C&A Nederland, H&M Hennes & Mauritz Netherlands BV and Vendex KBB Nederland BV*, 'Adidas/Marca Mode', paras 25, 29-33, 43. This sweeping statement is contradicted by specific provisions of EU law: *see* Articles 74(2) EUTMR and 28(4), 29(3) of the EUTM Directive, concerning nominative fair uses provided in connection with geographical collective trademarks (on which I commented in *Geographical Symbols in Intellectual Property Law: The Policy Options,* in *Festschrift für Ulrich Loewenheim zum 75. Geburstag, Schutz von Kreativität und Wettbewerb* 231 ff., 235 (Verlag Beck, 2009)).

123. For a similar remark, *see* W. Sakulin, *Trademark Protection and Freedom of Expression, supra* n. 41, 216.

124. As underlined by the Opinion of the Advocate general Ruiz-Jarabo Colomer of 13 June 2002, 'Arsenal', *supra* n. 28 para. 42.

125. The dangers to competitive openness which may derive from privatization of language are well exemplified by D. Bollier, *Brand Name Bullies. The Quest to Own and Control Culture* 101 ff. (Wiley and Sons, Hoboken, N.J., 2005).

because even in the 'constitutional traditions common to the Member States',[126] it has gained full recognition only in comparatively recent times.

19.13   HUMAN RIGHTS AND THE CONFLICT BETWEEN SENIOR AND JUNIOR TRADEMARKS

Human rights analysis is also relevant in another fundamental aspect of trademark law: the conflict between senior and junior marks which may arise both in connection with the registrability and validity of the latter and at the infringement stage.[127]

In contemporary trademark law, trademarks are protected not only against the risk of confusion as to the origin of the goods they designate but also against acts which may negatively affect the messages concerning the quality and reputation of the signs they convey. While it is questioned whether the expansion of the protection to cover these further, non-origin functions may be supported by an overall economic rationale beyond the – obvious, but in this connection irrelevant – advantage conferred to firms which happen to be willing and able to invest on their own brands,[128] there is no doubt that this development entails a number of risks.

Some of these risks are directly relevant in the present context. Expanded protection may now impose far-reaching negative obligations – duties to abstain – on individuals and entities that are in no way competitors with the trademark proprietors. Trademark exclusivity may be employed to silence parody and satire, even though frequently brands themselves have taken the centre of the stage at the initiative of their own proprietors; it may also be harnessed to stifle artistic creativity in spite of the fact that the same may well have been stimulated by the ideological and expressive potential triggered by the signs themselves.[129] While it is clear that these developments may endanger freedom of expression, in the current legal context also freedom of commercial expression and its usual companion and ally – freedom of trade and to conduct business – may suffer at the hands of

---

126. Article 52(4) CFR.
127. The major difference between the two sets of situations resides in the fact that what is relevant in connection with relative grounds of refusal of registration and invalidity is the junior trademark's *anticipated* use, while in connection with infringement the focus is limited to the *actual*, precise, and concrete use of the later trademark which is alleged to be infringing: *see* ECJ 12 June 2008, Case C-533/06, *O2 Holding Ltd., 02 (UK) Ltd v. Hutchinson 3G UK Ltd.*, 'O2', paras 66 ff.
128. For a discussion of the literature *see* V. Di Cataldo, *The Trade Mark with a Reputation in EU Law – Some Remarks on the Negative Condition 'Without Due Cause'*, IIC 833 ff., 835-836 (2011). A review of older literature is in N. Bottero, A. Mangàni & M. Ricolfi, *The Extended Protection of 'Strong' Trademarks*, 11 *Marquette Int. Prop. Law Rev.* 265 ff. (2007).
129. *See* in this connection the eloquent indictment by D. Bollier, *Brand Name Bullies*, *supra* n. 125, 81 ff.

expanded trademark protection. Questions tend to arise also when commercial information is conveyed to consumers by means of reference to competitors' brands and, even more so, to the descriptive components of competitors' brands. Moreover, novel business models, enabled by the digital environment, may entail as their necessary building block the possibility of resorting to unauthorized uses of third-party trademarks. Now, if the exclusivity conferred by trademark law is unduly mobilized against these efficient and innovative uses of protected brands, search costs for consumers may increase, and the competitive structure may be ossified.

Of course, the worthy goals of preserving freedom of speech and of trade may not be attained one-sidedly and at the expense of the protection of trademark proprietors' legitimate prerogatives. Here again, the need to work out a reasonable balancing between the competing claims of freedom of expression and to conduct business, on the one hand, and of protection of (intellectual) property, including its very significant precompetitive features,[130] on the other hand, becomes crucial.[131] It is, however, commonly acknowledged that mutual accommodation of these two competing forces is not easy to figure out and to implement.

The difficulties in the balancing act and the possible solutions significantly vary along the spectrum of the three possible types of conflict between senior and junior trademarks (and signs) visualized by contemporary trademark law. Therefore, I will trace the steps of the efforts to balance trademark protection and human rights by separately looking at the solutions envisaged in each of these conflicts. There is an overarching theme, though, which cuts across all three conflicts and goes back to the two alternative approaches we came across earlier:[132] given the structural features which characterize trademark law (and make it different from patent and copyright law), it is possible to explore possible balancing techniques both in delineating the scope of the notion of infringement and in carving out limitations and exceptions. It should also be noted at the outset that the most recent EU legislation in the field of trademarks has addressed the issue in a way which is not usual, i.e., by adding a dedicated 'Recital' both in the EUTMR and EUTM Directive,[133] and certainly deserves careful scrutiny.

In a progression from simple to complex, I will start from the second conflict.

---

130. *See supra* § 19.3.
131. As exemplified by the approach adopted by EU Court 24 November 2011 (Third Chamber), 'Scarlet Extended', *supra* n. 77, paras 44 ff.
132. § 19.3.
133. *See* 'Recitals' 21 of the EUTMR and 27 of the EUTM Directive.

19.14   LIKELIHOOD OF CONFUSION AND HUMAN
          RIGHTS

The second conflict is based on the notion of infringement developed by classical trademark law. It concerns the use of a later sign which is identical or similar to an earlier trademark for identical or similar goods, which is prohibited to the extent such use entails a risk of confusion on the part of the relevant public as to the business origin of the goods stemming from the junior user. It is commonly accepted that the roots of the second conflict are to be found in prejudice to the original distinguishing function of trademarks, even though in the progress of time, the risk of confusion has been understood by courts as encompassing not only likelihood of confusion as to business origin but also as to association or sponsorship.[134]

Even in connection with the second conflict, difficulties may arise at the intersection between trademark law and human rights. Up to a point, these difficulties would appear amenable to reconciliation. This is the case with respect to *freedom of non-commercial expression*. When the Aqua pop group lashes out at the inculcation in young girls of a mix of consumerism and overdone sexiness conveyed by the Barbie icon, the trademark proprietors may well react by claiming infringement (also) in the form of risk of confusion.[135] However, the claim rings hollow. Even looking at the average 'consumer' of the satirical song, rather than at the smart one, the conclusion is pretty straightforward: the origin of the doll and of the song cannot be the same and the two are – so to say – disassociated one from the other, even though the latter refers back (or lashes out) to the former. This is a recurring feature of parody and satire targeting trademarks: they do not function unless there is a dose of critical distance between the original sign and the new context in which the same is recast; however, critical distance builds on non-confusion between the two and, even more to the point, on the underlined 'otherness' of the junior use vis-à-vis the earlier sign.[136] Of course, trademark proprietors argue that the very success of parody and satire assumes that consumers institute a 'link' between the earlier sign and the

---

134. *See* among the many EUC UE 18 September 2014 (Seventh Chamber), Cases C-308/13 P and C-309/13 P, *Società Italiana Calzature s.p.a. v. OHIM and Vicini s.p.a.*, 'Giuseppe by Giuseppe Zanotti/Zanotti', para. 60; ECJ 6 October 2005, Case C-120/04, *Medion v. Thomson multimedia Sales Germany & Austria GmbH*, 'Medion', paras 24 e 26; General Court 12 December 2014 (Fourth Chamber), Case T-591/13, *Groupe Canal + v. OHIM and Euronews*, 'News +/Actu+', para. 17.

135. *See* the decision of 24 July 2002 of the US Court of Appeals for the Ninth Circuit, *Mattel Inc. v. Universal Music International Ltd. and others and MCA Records*, 296 F.3d 894 (9th Cir. 2002), *cert. denied*, 123 S. Ct. 993 (2003), 'Barbie Doll'; on the dilution claims *see infra* § 19.15. A discussion of the different episodes in the 'Barbie' litigation is in D. Bollier, *Brand Name Bullies*, *supra* n. 125, 84 ff.

136. For an eloquent example *see* Trib. Milano 31 December 2009 (ord.), *Deutsche Grammophon GmbH and Universal Music Italia s.r.l. v. Hukapan s.p.a. and Sony Music Entertainment Italy*, in *Giur. ann. dir. ind. 5466*, 'Deutsche Grammophon'.

later take-up of the same; except that invoking a 'link' does not do the trick, as a link which distances rather than associating has little to do with confusion, be it in a narrow or wider sense. The same reasoning would seem to apply to other signs – in particular domain names – ridiculing a third-party trademark; in this connection, the decision handed down by a US Court, finding that the registration of a website (www.peta.org) run under the ludicrous title 'People eating tasty animals', caused initial interest confusion with the trademark of the animal rights organization People for the Ethical Treatment of Animals (PETA)[137] is not – to use a euphemism – beyond reproach.

It would appear that similar possibilities of reconciliation – and of balancing – are available also in connection with *freedom of commercial expression*. Indeed, the Barbie example itself is a mix between the two, as it combines non-commercial and commercial expression: even though the content itself of the Aqua's song may have been critical and even subversive, the song was sold rather than given away for free.

However, even purely commercial expression may claim protection on the basis of the ECHR, under Article 10(1) (right to impart ... information)[138] as well as of CFR-protected freedom to conduct business (Article 16 CFR), when third-party trademark rights are liable to prevent the conveying of information which would reduce consumers' search costs and thereby put another business at a competitive disadvantage.[139]

There are different options which can be resorted to in order to tackle the difficulty. One of these is to raise the threshold question whether the allegedly infringing sign is used 'as a trademark', that is to indicate the commercial origin of the goods in question. This route is barred, however, by EU case law.[140] Alternatives may be found either at the infringement level, by holding that the descriptive part (or content) of the senior mark is not protectable;[141] or at the level of limitations and exceptions, by holding that

---

137. *See* U.S. Court of Appeals, Fourth Circuit 23 August 2001, *People for Ethical Treatment of Animals v. Doughney*, 263 F.3d 359. For criticism of the outcome of the case *see* W. Sakulin, *Trademark Protection and Freedom of Expression*, *supra* n. 41, 255 and J. Lipton, *Internet, Domain Names and Freedom of Speech*, *supra* n. 41, 130-131.

138. *See also* Article 19 UDHR.

139. A prominent example of this situation is referential use, e.g., use of a sign to indicate that the junior user's goods are compatible with a product of the senior user, which also employs identical goods (e.g., pods for a coffee machine). As in this group of cases usually both the sign and goods are identical, I will consider the issue in the part concerning the third conflict (in the next two paragraphs).

140. For the reasons discussed at the end of § 19.14.

141. *See* for this conclusion Trib. Bergamo 12 December 1991, *San Carlo Gruppo Alimentare s.p.a. v. ETS Picard s.a. and Esselunga*, in *Giur. ann. dir. ind. 2895*, 'Pain Braisé', holding that, while the sign was valid, if of weak distinctive character, it still could not prevent the use of the descriptive expression on a competitor's products. But *see* the decision of 30 September 2008 by the Hof Den Hag, *The Bo-Dean Company & Lief! V. Prenatal*, 'Lief!' as summarized by W. Sakulin, *Trademark Protection and Freedom of*

the immunity under Articles 12(b) of the EUTM Directive and 14(1)(b) EUTMR applies. Either way, the interpretation of the relevant provisions might well be influenced by human rights analysis, which in either case favours a reading which allows for some breathing space for uses of signs which, while possibly interfering with senior trademarks, still convey significant information to consumers and maximize competitive freedom, to the extent these do not entail outright exploitation of confusion or obvious chicanery.[142] It is, therefore, confirmed here that both options for balancing may come in handy here.

| 19.15 | HUMAN RIGHTS, DILUTION AND 'ABSOLUTE' PROTECTION OF TRADEMARKS: THE ISSUE |

The biggest threats to freedom of speech and of trade, it is often argued, spring from the expansion of the scope of trademark protection to encompass dilution, reaching well beyond the boundaries of the requirement of risk of confusion. Indeed, for a long time trademark was seen as 'the least dangerous branch' of IP protection, having a narrow scope of protection tailored on its specific subject matter, which concerns linguistic entities (signs) and possessing a limited monopolistic potential which in turn enables and justifies potentially perpetual protection.[143] This characterization has in the meantime been overturned by the addition of a new layer of protection for

---

Expression, supra n. 41, 251-252, which inhibited, on the basis of a finding of a risk of confusion with the previously registered trademark for baby clothing, 'Lief!', the use by a third party in connection with baby clothing of the most common Dutch exclamation ('sweet!') used with respect to babies. The solution adopted by the Dutch Court may be questioned also when, in accordance with the case law discussed in § 19.12, the imperative to keep free is disregarded because the descriptiveness of the senior trademark has been cured by secondary meaning. Turning the attention to the junior trademark, it should be added that under EU trademark law descriptive uses of the same have been allowed under very restrictive circumstances: compare the decisions reached by ECJ 14 May 2002, Case C-2/00, *Hölterhoff v. Freisleben*, 'Hölterhoff' with ECJ 12 November 2002, Case C-206/01, *Arsenal Football Club plc v. Matthew Reed*, 'Arsenal'.

142. It has been pointed out that such human rights-oriented approach may also assist in a balancing exercise in respect of the rules governing the second conflict in different, but germane, areas such as (i) the uncontrolled and over-expansive use of the 'fiction' (W. Sakulin, *Trademark Protection and Freedom of Expression, supra* n. 41, 248) whereby a higher degree of distinctiveness enhances the risk of confusion, as the opposite conclusion may sometimes be true; and (ii) resort to the doctrine of initial interest confusion (on which *see*, also for references, W. Sakulin, *Trademark Protection and Freedom of Expression, supra* n. 41, 253-254; a thorough discussion of US case law is to be found in G. Dinwoodie, *Developing Defenses in Trademark Law, supra* n. 35, 123 and n. 86), which conceptualizes as confusion a state of mind which by definition has been dispelled at the time in which the consumer makes her purchase decision.

143. For a thorough treatment of the pro-competitive dimension of classic trademark law, *see* A. Kur, *Strategic Branding, supra* n. 120, 191-192.

the publicity function, which has brought with it a vast, 'expansive',[144] 'amorphous',[145] and even 'potentially overreaching'[146] notion of actionable harm to the interests of trademark proprietors, turning what used to be a merely 'defensive right' into a new sort of 'exploitation right'.[147] This trend towards overreach may have been exacerbated as harmonized EU trademark law would appear to have increasingly absorbed the role traditionally vested in national unfair competition, in particular, offering trademark proprietors a broader protection of goodwill accumulated by their signs and the occasion for striving for a growing control over some forms of referential (or nominative) uses.[148]

Also, the expansive protection of trademarks 'with a reputation'[149] under the *third conflict* is characteristically based on the two components consisting in conduct, on the one hand, and outcome of the conduct itself, on the other; except that in this connection the outcome itself does not consist in the risk of confusion but in the 'detriment' to 'the distinctive character or the repute' of the trademark or in the 'unfair advantage' taken thereof 'without cause'.

While it is unclear to many commentators what are the outward limits of protection structured in such an expansive way, what is quite obvious is that the potential for clash with human rights has vastly expanded. In the new context, Barbie's owners are no longer saddled with the burden of proving an – unlikely – likelihood of confusion; Deutsche Grammophon has a much greater chance of success in demonstrating that its long-standing and prestigious logo is indeed tarnished by having a rival imitate it with the addition of a ring of piglets.[150] This is even truer in legal systems, like the EU, which go well beyond the more restrained US approach and top the actions of dilution by blurring and by tarnishment with the separate tort of

---

144. J. Lipton, *Internet, Domain Names and Freedom of Speech*, *supra* n. 41, 99.
145. G. Dinwoodie, *Developing Defenses in Trademark Law*, *supra* n. 35, 101 and 124.
146. R. Burrell & D. Ganjee, *Trademarks and Freedom of Expression*, *supra* n. 41, 544.
147. M. Senftleben, *The Trademark Tower of Babel*, *supra* n. 39, 45 ff., 59 ff.
148. *See* M. Senftleben et al., *The Recommendation on Measures to Safeguard Freedom of Expression and Undistorted Competition – Guiding Principles for the Further Development of EU Trade Mark Law*, in *EIPR*, 337, 338 (2015). *See also* in this connection A. Kur, *Trademarks Function, Don't They? CJEU Jurisprudence and Unfair Competition Principles* in *Max Planck Institute for Intellectual Property and Competition Research Paper Series* No. 14-05, *http://papers.ssrn.com/sol3/papers.cfm?abstract_id=2401536* and A. Ohly, *Designschutz im Spannungsfeld von Geschmackmuster-, Kennzeichen und Lauterkeitsrecht*, in *GRUR* 731 ff., 737 (2007).
149. Or 'famous' under the – much more exacting – US standard: *see* B. Beebe, *A Defense of the New Federal Trademark Antidilution Law*, 16 *Fordham Intell. Prop. Media & Ent. L.J.* 1142 ff. (2006).
150. *See* Trib. Milano 31 December 2009 (ord.), 'Deutsche Grammophon', *supra* n. 136.

'free riding', which results from the 'taking advantage' 'without due cause' limb of the action.[151]

The potential for a clash between trademark law and human rights is even greater in connection with the *first conflict*, and this is particularly so in connection with free trade concerns. This risk may have gone unnoticed for a long while, because this hypothesis, which is based on the complete identity of the senior and junior sign and of the goods for which they are respectively protected and used, had originally been conceptualized mainly as a powerful weapon and quick fix against 'piracy', street vendors of false Louis Vuitton bags and their ilk. However, experience has taught us that the double identity of signs and goods is a much more extensive phenomenon than originally imagined. It is an – almost – unavoidable feature of comparative advertising, in which the party making the comparison has to refer to the sign under which the compared party's goods and services are known to the public. Also, there is no way for the vendor of pods compatible with the Nespresso machine to let the public know about this other than by referring to Nespresso's trademarks. Even the manufacturer of the generic version of a drug cannot effectively advertise its products without reference to the brand of the now off-patent incumbent.

These are instances of 'referential' use of a trademark: the third party employs the sign for the purpose of identifying the goods as those of the proprietor rather than her own goods;[152] it may be unclear whether such use amounts to infringement. This is so because, under EU laws, the notion of infringement in cases of double identity is characteristically truncated: reference is made only to conduct, i.e., to the acts which are reserved to the senior trademark's exclusivity, but not to any specific outcome, i.e., either likelihood of confusion or dilution. This is why the reference to 'absolute' protection in the case of double identity,[153] which, as we shall see, is in a way a misnomer or at least a misleading characterization,[154] immediately caught up when the case law brought up the disturbing possibilities of an uncontrolled reading of the provisions concerning the first conflict.[155] The unease has turned into real worry when a myriad of decisions handed down in multiple jurisdictions visualized the possibility that even keyword advertising, which consists in 'purchasing' advertising space for inserts to be

---

151. Only the first limb of the harm is actionable under US law (except for occasional lapses into a European-style anti-free riding rulings on which, critically, M.A. Lemley, *The Modern Lanham Act and the Death of Common Sense*, 108 *Yale L. J.* 1687 ff., 1706 ff. (1999)).

152. As earlier indicated: *supra* § 19.3.

153. *See* ECJ 18 June 2009, Case C-487/07, *L'Oréal SA, Lancôme parfums et beauté & Cie, Laboratoires Garnier & Ci. v. Bellure NV, Malaika Investments Ltd. e Starion International Ltd.*, 'L'Oréal', para. 58.

154. *See* § 19.16.

155. M. Senftleben, *Trademark Protection – A Black Hole in the Intellectual Property Galaxy?*, *supra* n. 25, 385.

shown when a trader's trademark is selected by a search engine user as a keyword, may be conceptualized as a case of double identity. Such characterization did not – and does not – please at all powerful digital intermediaries; therefore, the issue has ignited, as proved by the abundant literature which has sprung up in the last decade.[156]

19.16   THE OPTIONS

The need to find a way to reconcile principled enforcement of trademark rights with respect to human rights also in the new context has been widely recognized. What is still open is how the balancing exercise may be best carried out. As noted, one line of thought sees the remedies in a counter-vailing expansion of limitations and exceptions; the other cautions on the dangers which this approach might entail, and indicates a preference for finding solutions by importing some clarity into the requirements which have to be met before a finding of trademark infringement is reached.[157]

To appreciate the two options, a few remarks may be in place. The first approach has been advocated on the basis of the argument that the expansion of trademark scope calls for the adoption of a 'balanced and effective limitations infrastructure' based on 'clear and explicit language'.[158] This proposal was ultimately taken up, at least at the EU level, by the inclusion of the twin 'Recitals' in the EUTMR (No. 21) and in the EUTM Directive (No. 27).[159] In principle, a solution based on exception or limitations may suggest

---

156. *See* among the many L. Bently, et al., *Intellectual Property Law, supra* n. 60, 1120 ff.; S. Hühner, *Domain-Parking. Vertrags – und Haftungsfragen unter Zusätzlicher Berück-sichtingung suchwortabhängiger Werbung (Keyword Advertising/Ad-Words)* (Carl Heymanns Verlag, Köln, 2012) and E. Goldman, *Deregulating Relevancy in Internet Trade Mark Law*, 54 *Emory Law Journal*, 507 ff. (2005).

157. *See supra* n. 41-44 and accompanying text. A thorough discussion of the available alternatives against the background of the US and EU legal systems in L.P. Ramsey & J. Schovsbo, *Mechanisms for Limiting Trade Mark Rights to Further Competition and Free Speech*, in *IIC* 671 ff. (2013).

158. M. Senftleben et al., *The Recommendation on Measures to Safeguard Freedom of Expression and Undistorted Competition, supra* n. 148, 337, 342.

159. Recital 21 EUTM (which is mirrored by Recital 27 of the EUTM Directive) reads: 'The exclusive rights conferred by an EU trade mark should not entitle the proprietor to prohibit the use of signs or indications by third parties which are used fairly and thus in accordance with honest practices in industrial and commercial matters. In order to ensure equal conditions for trade names and EU trade marks in the event of conflicts, given that trade names are regularly granted unrestricted protection against later trade marks, such use should be only considered to include the use of the personal name of the third party. It should further permit the use of descriptive or non-distinctive signs or indications in general. Furthermore, the proprietor should not be entitled to prevent the fair and honest use of the EU trade mark for the purpose of identifying or referring to the goods or services as those of the proprietor. Use of a trade mark by third parties to draw the consumer's attention to the resale of genuine goods that were originally sold

two sets of reservations. First, there is always some danger that introducing novel limitations and exceptions may 'backfire', i.e., lead to outcomes opposite to the ones envisaged at the time of their adoption. In fact, as any exception draws boundaries to a rule and thereby contributes to defining the same, the scope of the rule itself may arguably be inferred backwards from the exception: the behaviour in question would be prohibited except in the cases specifically provided for. Thus, an exception immunizing non-commercial satire might well suggest that satire conducted in the course of business activity, such as journalism, may not be exempted; or that parody, be it for profit or not, is never immunized. Second, in the current lawmaking process where sectional interests dominate, there is reason to expect that it will be some special players – be they Internet Service Providers (ISPs) or digital platforms – that will be in a position to demand, and possibly obtain, limitations and exceptions which dovetail their own particular needs, possibly leaving open the question whether the adoption of the sectionally tailored exception may not have, wittingly or unwittingly, curtailed the availability of the exception in situations which are similar but not identical.

It is well possible that the solution adopted by the EU lawmakers avoids the first, 'technical', risk. 'Recitals' are not exceptions or limitations. Their normative value is incomplete: as the case law has several times clarified, 'while the preamble to an EU measure may explain the latter's content, it cannot be relied upon as a ground for derogating from the actual provisions of the measure in question'.[160] This feature may, on the one hand, entail certain disadvantages when it comes to invoking the 'Recital'; but, on the other hand, makes any reasoning *a contrario* based on the content of a provision contained in a preamble very doubtful or even impossible.

Also, the second option, focusing on the requirements which must be met in order to find an infringement, may turn out to be unsatisfactory in several regards. In particular, it may not deliver all the benefits it promises. It has been suggested that many difficulties could be taken care of if it were possible to insist that, in addition to the multiple requirements which must be

---

by or with the consent of the proprietor of the EU trade mark in the Union should be considered as being fair as long as it is at the same time in accordance with honest practices in industrial and commercial matters. Use of a trade mark by third parties for the purpose of artistic expression should be considered as being fair as long as it is at the same time in accordance with honest practices in industrial and commercial matters. Furthermore, this Regulation should be applied in a way that ensures full respect for fundamental rights and freedoms, and in particular the freedom of expression.'

It should be remarked that the proposal, originally made by the Commission in the process which lead to the adoption in 2015 of the new TM directive and regulation, to clarify that in case of double identity non-infringement is to be found unless the origin function of the trademark is affected, was rejected by the European Parliament; arguably the Recitals are intended to partly offset that negative choice.

160. EU Court 20 December 2017 (Second Chamber), Case C-397/16 and C-435/16, *Acacia s.r.l. v. Fall to Pneusgarda s.r.l. and Audi; Acacia s.r.l. and Rolando d'Amato v. Dr. Ing. F. Porsche AG*, 'wheel rims', para. 40.

met for a finding of infringement ((i) *use*, (ii) of a *sign*, (iii) *in commerce*, (iv) *in relation to goods and services*, (v) *without the consent* of the trademark proprietor), also *use as a trademark* by the defendant, to be understood as use indicating commercial origin, should be a necessary predicate for the action.[161] We may as well acknowledge that this would indeed be very nice, as this approach would automatically immunize from infringement claims a number of conducts which are free speech and free trade-friendly, such as the use of a third party's trademark to identify the target of parody or to indicate what is the bioequivalent molecule of the generic version of an off-patent drug. Except that one has to acknowledge that this solution truly is an impossibility under EU law. To begin with, the only possible legal basis for the approach would be a reading of Article 10(6) of the EUTM Directive whereby the appreciation of non-trademark use is left to the national laws of the Member States, which, as we earlier saw,[162] have vastly different approaches in this specific regard. Now, it would appear that our legal systems are not prepared to pay the price of such a significant dis-harmonization of EU trademark law just to remedy, and then only in part, the difficulty discussed here. Moreover, this solution has been flatly rejected by EU Courts,[163] which consistently held that the assessment of infringement does not depend on how the later sign is used but rather on the effect such use has on the legally protected interest of the proprietor of the earlier trademark.

Taking into account these twin *caveats*, we may consider the possibility that the balancing exercise may deliver better results if we try a combination of the two approaches.[164] What would appear to be called for is an 'integrated system' of balancing, which results from the combination of components – or building blocks – taken from both approaches.

19.17 THE FIRST THREE PILLARS OF AN 'INTEGRATED SYSTEM'?

It is arguable that an 'integrated system' capable of reconciling adequate trademark protection and human rights is taking shape under our eyes, particularly in the EU system.

Several steps towards an acceptable balancing may be made consider-ing that the provisions concerning the third conflict contain two general

---

161. *See* the closely argued position adopted by S.L. Dogan & M. Lemley, *Trademarks and Consumer Search Costs on the Internet, supra* n. 27.
162. Section 15.3.
163. In spite of the very strong case made for it by English judges: Chancery Division 12 December 2002, *Arsenal Football Club plc v. Matthew Reed*, [2002] EWHC 2695 (CH), 'Arsenal'.
164. As suggested by M. Senftleben-et al., *The Recommendation on Measures to Safeguard Freedom of Expression and Undistorted Competition, supra* n. 148, 337 ff.

clauses: first, the advantage gained by the junior user which is banned is only the one which qualifies as 'unfair'; second, taking advantage of the distinctive character or of the reputation or causing detriment to them may be justified when the conduct causing these outcomes is justified by a 'due cause'.

The case law has valiantly made its best of these two general clauses. The German Supreme Court resorted to the notion of 'due cause' to condone as non-infringing a postcard which established a clear link to the Milka chocolate brand by using an ironic combination of German high-brow poetical references with a very low-brow hint to cows and pastures.[165] Also, European Courts are adopting an appropriately nuanced approach.[166] We may surmise that European judges might well reach a similar conclusion if they happened to assess the treatment of the Barbie brand by the Aquas.

Similarly, the EU case law dealing with ad-words established quite firmly that we may draw a fine line between reference to a third party trademark which is not 'unfair', as it clearly indicates that what is on offer is a bona fide competitive alternative to the product supplied by the senior proprietor, on the one hand, and an imitation which is merely parasitic on the other hand.[167] The point made by this latter line of cases is important, e.g., in connection with the issue of compatible products (e.g., coffee pods which may also be inserted into another trader's machine and which, therefore, are substitutes of the products supplied by the trademark proprietor himself). While the reference to another trader's trademark may entail an advantage for the competitor, such an advantage is not automatically 'unfair'. Unfairness, it would seem, depends on the occurrence of an 'image transfer' whereby the positive appreciation by the market of the senior trader's products is appropriated by the way the products are offered by the junior firm.[168]

A judicious resort to the two general clauses may, therefore, constitute the *first pillar* of the integrated system. We should not overestimate,

---

165. BGH GRUR 2005, 583 ff., 'Lila Postkarte'. A discussion of decisions by other national Courts in Europe is in M. Senftleben, *Public Domain Preservation in EU Trademark Law*, *supra* n. 107, 811 and n. 132.
166. EU Court 6 February 2014 (First Chamber), Case C-65/12, *Leidseplein Beheer BV, Hendrikus de Vries v. Red Bull GmbH and Red Bull Nederland BV*, 'the Bull Dog/Red Bull'; a more restrictive, but still altogether reasonable, approach in EU Court 30 May 2018 (Tenth Chamber), Cases C-85/16 P and C-86/16 P, *Kenzo Tsujimoto v. EUIPO and Kenzo*, 'Kenzo Estate/Kenzo'.
167. EU Court 22 September 2011 (First Chamber), Case C-323/09, *Interflora Inc. and Interflora British Unit v. Marks & Spencer plc Flowers Direct Online Limited*, 'Interflora', paras 81 ff.
168. This opinion was first accepted in connection with comparative advertising: *see* ECJ 23 February 2006, Case C-59/05, *Siemens AG v. VIPA Gesellschaft für Visualisierung und Prozeßautomatisierung GmbH*, 'Siemens', para. 18 and 25 October 2001, Case C-112/99, *Toshiba Europe GmbH v. Katun Germany GmbH*, 'Toshiba/Katun', paras 57 e 60.

however, the role which may be played by this first element, which for sure would not by itself be sufficient if it was not complemented by other components. In fact, the two general clauses we just discussed are relevant in connection with the third conflict only but do not assist in respect of the characteristically truncated notion of infringement adopted by the provisions concerning the first conflict. At first blush, it would appear that in situations of 'double identity', all that is required to establish a finding of infringement is the conduct, use of identical signs for identical goods. Indeed, it is often repeated that here the protection is 'absolute'. However, since the 'Arsenal' case the ECJ made clear that this is not the case, by reading into the relevant provision a – quite reasonable, if only implied – requirement: there is no infringement unless at least one of the functions carried out by trademarks is 'adversely affected' or may suffer a prejudice. It is unsurprising that English judges have frowned upon on the 'invention' of this implied requirement, seeing it as an example of characteristic continental fuzziness.[169] Nevertheless, it should be acknowledged that this requirement, while not helping much to reach a reasonable outcome in some cases,[170] was crucial in establishing in the ECJ 'Google' decision under which circumstances a trader who had purchased sponsored links reproducing a trademark belonging to a third party could still be deemed not infringing even in double identity cases.[171] More specifically, the Court held that a sponsored link adopted in a context where the competitor is clearly identified and does not ambiguously hint at a commercial 'link' with the trademark proprietor does not affect the latter's origin function.[172] Even the publicity function may not be affected by sponsored links considering that search engines benefit proprietors by showing their trademarks as organic, non-sponsored, results of a keyword search.[173] We may, therefore, aptly characterize the requirement of prejudice to the interests of the trademark proprietor as the *second pillar* of the integrated system.

---

169. *See* England and Wales Court of Appeal (Civil Division) 21 May 2010, *L'Oreal SA, Lancôme parfums et beauté & Cie, Laboratoires Garnier & Ci. v. Bellure NV, Malaika Investments Ltd. and Starion International Ltd.*, 'L'Oreal', para. 31.
170. ECJ 12 November 2002, 'Arsenal', where the Court held that the fact that the Club's insignia might have been used as 'a badge of support' did not prevent the occurrence of prejudice to the functions.
171. EUC 23 March 2010, Cases C-236-238/08, *Google France SARL and Google Inc. v. Louis Vuitton Mallettier SA, Google France SRL v. Viaticum SA, Luteciel SARL and Google France SARL v. Bruno Raboin, Tiger SARL v. CNRHH, Pierre Alexis Thonet*, 'Google Ad-Words', para. 79 ('It is apparent from the case law cited above that in the situation envisaged in Article 5(1)(a) of Directive 89/104 … , in which a third party uses a sign identical with a trade mark in relation to goods or services which are identical with those for which that mark is registered, the proprietor of the mark is entitled to prohibit that use if it is liable to have an adverse effect on one of the functions of the mark, whether that be the function of indicating origin or one of the other functions').
172. EUC 23 March 2010, 'Google Ad-Words', paras 82 ff.
173. EUC 23 March 2010, 'Google Ad-Words', paras 92 ff.

While in identifying the first two pillars I confined myself to restating concepts which are fairly uncontroversial, I will deviate a bit from conventional wisdom in respect of the discussion on the *third pillar*. While several courts have held that websites reproducing and even distorting a trademark owner's signs to criticize the 'dark side' of their businesses are not infringing because they are 'of a polemical character which is alien to business life',[174] I am not persuaded that the finding may truly be based on the absence of the requirement for infringement that the use in question takes place 'in commerce'. From a technical standpoint, the notion of use 'in commerce' is very broad; according to the EU Court even a charity is acting in commerce, as it competes on the market with other Non-Governmental Organisations (NGOs), not in the provision of goods and services to its beneficiaries, which may well be supplied for free, but in the raising of funds to finance its mission.[175] From a policy standpoint, insistence on the relevance of the 'in commerce' requirement, whatever its scope of application, would not assist in most of the situations at the intersection between trademark infringement and human rights. Surely, newspapers and most of the media are for-profit organizations; so are music and book publishers and the sellers of t-shirts, where critical or subversive statements abound.[176] However, commendable the contribution to freedom of expression these outfits may make, their speech is not going to be shielded by the argument that they are not active in commerce. Even a doctor who is signing a prescription for a generic drug indicating the generic molecule by reference to the brand name would not be immunized.[177]

Now, quite often in these situations, the balancing cannot be effected on the basis of the two pillars we discussed. The general clauses come to the rescue to the extent the infringement action is based only on the provisions concerning the third conflict; also a finding of prejudice to the interests of the trademark proprietor may well be established. The brand image of Philips

---

174. *See* the French Cour de Cassation 8 April 2008, *Esso SA v. Greenpeace France IIC* 241 ff. (2009); Paris Court of Appeals 26 February 2003, *Assoc. Greenpeace France v. SA Sté Esso*, in *IIC* 342 ff. (2004) and Paris Court of Appeals 26 February, 2003, *SA SPCEA v. Assoc. Greenpeace France*, in *IIC* 342 ff. (2004). In very similar terms Paris Court of Appeals April 30 2003, *Assoc. Le Réseau Voltaire pour la liberté d'expression v. Sté Gervais Danone*, in *IIC* 342 ff. (2004).
175. *See* EU Court 9 December 2008 (Grand Chamber), Case C-442/07, *Verein Radetzky-Orden v. Bundesvereinigung Kameradschaft 'Feldmarschall Radetzky'*, 'Feldmarschall Radetzky', para. 47.
176. *See* Trib. Milano 4 March 1999, *AGIP Petroli s.p.a. v. Dig. It. International and v. Ambrosiana Serigrafia*, in *Giur. ann. dir. ind.* 3987/1, 'Agip/Acid' and the much discussed South African Case, SA Constitutional Court 27 May 2005, *Laugh It Off Promotions v. South African Breweries, Case CCT* 42/04, 'Carling Black'.
177. *See* the Benelux Case *Nijs et al. v. Ciba Geigy*, in *Ing. Cons.* 317 ff. (1984), 'medical prescription'. Even though many continental jurisdictions, including Italy, are reluctant to find that the medical profession ultimately is a trade, still they would have to admit that a private physician is engaging in economic activity.

and of the South African beer producer Carling Black is not likely to be enhanced by allegations of exploitation of slave and black labour.[178]

Maybe, to find the missing third pillar, we should look at a different requirement for a finding of infringement, which, in my opinion, is unduly neglected. I refer to the requirement that the allegedly infringing use is 'in relation to goods and services'. The case may reasonably be made that not any relationship between the sign and the goods or services will trigger this requirement. We should pause for a moment to consider why the fact that a logo incidentally appears in a movie sequence is not infringement; and why the same assessment applies to the reproduction of the Campbell soup brand in the famous Warhol's series of painting. The fact is that in neither case, the presence of the sign – of that sign – is a factor in the decision of the viewer or purchaser to view or purchase the movie or the painting. This argument does not lead to a resurrection of the argument made in 'Arsenal' that use of the sign which does not qualify as use as a trademark is outside the scope of trademark exclusivity. Indeed the purchase decisions by acquirers of Arsenal scarves, caps and shorts *was* influenced by the presence of the logo; so in that case, for sure there was a 'relation to the goods'. However, the fact that a doctor is going to write one specific prescription referring to a given brand of drugs is *not* a factor in the choice of the physician; the fact that a magazine carries a story featuring an alleged involvement of Philips in the exploitation of Nazi concentration camps labour and in doing so reproduces Philips's logo is *not* a reason to choose that magazine. The same principle applies to the NGO's cases: it cannot be said that the factor why they are able to raise funds is that they target Danone rather than Esso. This is the reason why the just mentioned French NGO cases are good law, even though these entities were acting in commerce, and the recent Italian decision, whereby Greenpeace was held to be infringing the electricity producer's trademark is bad law,[179] even though it is probably correct to say that the NGO is acting in commerce.

I, therefore, suggest that an important contribution to the balancing may come from an understanding of the requirement of use of the sign 'in connection to goods and services' as implying that reference to the sign is a factor in consumer's decision to choose the good or service in question. Reading this requirement into the notion of infringement is likely to be able to give its fair share of contribution to the exercise we are dealing with here.

---

178. SA Constitutional Court 27 May 2005, 'Carling Black'.
179. Trib. Milano 6 May 2013 (ord.) and 8 July 2013 (ord.), *Enel s.p.a. v. Greenpeace Onlus*, 'Enel/Greenpeace', *Il dir. ind.* 147 ff. (2014), with a comment by F. Paesan-M. Venturello, *Libertà di espressione e funzioni del marchio*. As it should be clear by now, I do not share the view adopted by M. Senftleben, *Public Domain Preservation in EU Trademark Law*, *supra* n. 107, 805 ff., that the requirements for a finding of infringement of use 'in trade' and 'in relation to goods' are recessive; my point rather is that resort to the former is too broad, and therefore, often untenable, while resort to the latter is on the contrary well below its potential scope of application, and therefore, insufficient.

It seems to me that a balancing carried out on the basis of these three pillars may take us quite a long way in the right direction, even though – as we will see in a moment – this mode of analysis may not take care of all the difficulties to be found at the intersection between trademark protection and human rights.

In the meantime, it should be noted that it is hardly surprising that the interpretive tools we went through turn out to be apt to deliver a reasonably good outcome in the task proposed. After all, they have to a large extent been fashioned and tested in the course of one important phase of the recent legal evolution, and precisely in the context of the adaptation of trademark law doctrines to the online environment, which has helped to bring into full focus the 'adverse effect' requirement which previously had remained to a large extent underdetermined.

Even the adoption of the Comparative Advertising Directive (CAD) would seem to confirm some of the conclusions reached in connection with the points previously made. First of all, the CAD is based on the assumption that, even if the comparison between the junior trader's good and the ones supplied by the earlier trademark proprietor may benefit the former, this advantage is not prohibited per se, as by its nature, the comparison provides information to the public unless it is 'unfair'; which is a quite important contribution toward the reading of the first of the two general clauses provided for in connection with the third conflict. Even more importantly, CAD case law has clarified that 'fair' comparison may well remain perfectly lawful, even though it is not strictly speaking indispensable or even necessary to describe the characteristics of the goods offered by the comparing party.[180]

19.18   EXCEPTIONS AND LIMITATIONS AS THE FOURTH PILLAR OF THE 'INTEGRATED SYSTEM'

All the three pillars of the proposed integrated system we discussed, so far concern, as it is by now apparent, the scope of trademark protection. This does not mean that they are by themselves sufficient to carry out in an optimal way the balancing in all the conceivable situations.

Resort to limitations and exceptions may still be necessary to complete the balancing exercise, as it may contribute several additional strong points to the integrated system. One is quite obvious: the situations which remain

---

180. ECJ 25 October 2001, 'Toshiba/Katun', paras 57 and 60. It is worth remarking that lett. f) of Article 4 CAD allows reference to a third party's trademark also in the absence of a 'due cause' and does not consider relevant 'unfair advantage' of the distinctive character of the same trademark. *See* now Articles 9(3)(f) EUTMR and 10(3)(f) EUTM Directive.

of problematic or ambiguous character under the analysis of the scope of infringement, which are likely to be recurring given the remarkable expansion of trademark protection,[181] may be sorted out and dealt with by the adoption of limitations and exceptions containing appropriately open-ended immunizing language. Resort to limitations and exceptions may also have a – possibly less obvious but certainly more significant – advantage: they may be drafted as bright-line rules which set forth in so many words precisely what conduct is immunized. This point is about user-friendliness. Analysis of the exact scope of trademark protection may possibly serve the purpose of prevailing in litigation, but a vibrant expressive and commercial environment requires more than that: it needs bright-line rules which are easy to use at the point of adoption and which provide prospective users assurance on what they may do without fear and tremors when considering incorporating in their communication third-party trademarks. This is necessary to avoid that an otherwise good balancing mechanism still ends up having an undesirable chilling effect, which may derive from the anxiety of incurring into an infringement.[182]

Pre-2015 EU law did not assist much in either respect. Even now, in the EUTMR and in the EUTM Directive limitations and exceptions[183] are still conceived as a closed catalogue, i.e., an exhaustive list which does not admit expansion by interpretation[184] and are drafted having in mind specific sectional interests rather than general concerns such as competitive openness, artistic creativity and freedom of commercial and non-commercial expression.

A *fourth pillar* of the integrated system is, therefore, still needed, even though it is arguable that a step in the right direction has in the meantime been taken, at the EU level, technically not by the adoption of exceptions and limitations in the traditional sense but of the twin 'Recitals' 21 and 27 of the EUTMR and EUTM Directive.

A detailed analysis of the twin 'Recitals', of their implication and of the areas of penumbra they still leave would lead us well beyond the scope of the present article. In this respect, I will confine myself to a few cursory remarks. To begin with, it is finally established that 'referential' uses are considered permissible, at least to the extent the reference by the third party to the trademark proprietor's goods is 'fair'. Both Recitals are quite adamant in

---

181. For example: how should we assess the case in which the Philips logo, associated to the Nazi swastika, is on the cover of the magazine and as such – differently from the situation discussed in § 19.17 – may be a factor in the decision to purchase of the relevant public? How about access to the informational value of a trademarked descriptive sign, in particular when assisted by secondary meaning? *See* in this connection the decision of 30 September 2008 by the Hof Den Hag, 'Lief!'.
182. For a similar point, G. Dinwoodie, *Developing Defenses in Trademark Law, supra* n. 35, 101, 112.
183. *See* Articles 14 EUTMR and 14 EUTM Directive.
184. ECJ 10 April 2008, 'Adidas IV', para. 47.

stating that a proper reading of trademarks exclusivity 'should ... permit the use of descriptive or non-distinctive signs or indications in general. Furthermore, the proprietor should not be entitled to prevent the fair and honest use of the EU trade mark for the purpose of identifying or referring to the goods or services as those of the proprietor. Use of a trade mark by third parties to draw the consumer's attention to the resale of genuine goods that were originally sold by or with the consent of the proprietor of the EU trade mark in the Union should be considered as being fair as long as it is at the same time in accordance with honest practices in industrial and commercial matters.'

What is even more important in a human rights perspective is that the twin Recitals provide a reasonable amount of flexibility. This is important because the rate of change of our societies has increased exponentially, and this is even truer when we consider the communication proper. So we cannot stay stuck with a closed list which does not enable adaptation and evolution as circumstances change, particularly as the experience coming from the US legal system has indicated what the advantages of combining a list of bright-line exceptions with an open-ended clause are.

Resort to an open-ended clause like the one embodied in the Recitals also has a further advantage. Even if we assume that sectional interests groups – the ISPs and platforms I mentioned before – may have obtained 'their own' exception or limitation[185] via the reference to 'freedom of expression', it is remarkable that this principle goes well beyond the servicing of these sectional interest. Moreover, it is arguable that an embryo of an open-ended clause is to be found in the language adopted. The combination of the reference to the 'full respect for fundamental rights' and of the adverb 'in particular' might indeed enable to incorporate into the mechanism an appropriate balancing also for those less powerful, if possibly essential to society, individual and collective interests who may not have had the clout to stake their claim in advance in the lawmaking process.[186]

Of course, we cannot know for sure whether such an integrated system, based on the four pillars which I tried to briefly sketch out, may indeed be sufficient to do the job of providing an appropriate balancing between trademark rights and human rights. It is my impression, however, that the approach may take us a long way in the right direction.

---

185. As it is the case in the 'facilitating' language inserted in the US revision of 1995: *see* G. Dinwoodie, *Developing Defenses in Trademark Law*, *supra* n. 35, n. 61 at 118.
186. An early example of resort to 'Recital' 27 of the EUTM Directive is to be found in Cassation Court (Criminal Chamber) 21 May 2019, n. 35166, *Limone Armando e Matera Gianmario*, 'Fake lab' (holding that a seizure on the basis of criminal provisions concerning trademark infringement, namely Article 473 f. of the Italian Criminal Code of original and creative clothing articles, parodying Gucci, Lacoste, Hermès and other well-known brands in an artistically inspired fashion, is not acceptable). In the literature *see* L. Bently, et al., *Intellectual Property Law*, *supra* n. 60, 1165.

Chapter 20

Folklore, Human Rights and Intellectual Property

Andrea Radonjanin

20.1   INTRODUCTION

Folklorists recognize that folklore[1] is not merely something from the past to be collected or something that exists only in isolated pockets of the world. Quite the contrary – the impulses to create and express that underpin it have not died. Particular traditions arise, are modified and come to an end; still, the folkloric process continues even as particular events, objects and forms of expression change and evolve.[2] These evolving and living expressions are ubiquitous: folklore can be found in both the developing and developed worlds, in indigenous communities and non-indigenous communities, in cities as well as rural environments.

At the same time, folklore is being increasingly exploited. Undeniably, exploitation of folklore was also possible in the past. However, the rapid development of technology, the ever-increasing ways of capturing and manufacturing expressions of folklore through audio-visual productions,

---

1. While there is a number of different terms used over the past years to describe the subject matter (folklore, traditional cultural expressions, indigenous heritage, etc.), this chapter will use the term 'folklore' or 'expressions of folklore' to describe the subject matter.
2. Palethorpe, S. and S.G. Verhulst. *Report on the International Protection of Expressions of Folklore Under Intellectual Property Law*. Study Commissioned by the European Commission, October 2000, p. 13.

phonograms, their mass reproduction, broadcasting, cable distribution, Internet transmissions and so on, have amplified the range and frequency of possible abuses.[3]

Over the past five decades since the subject of folklore and the question of its potential legal protection were first raised within the international community, much, without doubt, has been done in this field. Within this period, the tackled issues occupied considerable attention and acquired wide awareness, becoming one of the 'hot' law topics of the twenty-first century. While initially the topic was prompted by certain indigenous communities, it swiftly grew to become a widely recognized international problem and has, ever since, been a subject of interest of various local, regional and international governmental and non-governmental groups, among which the World Intellectual Property Organisation (the WIPO) lately plays the most important role. As a result, it is clear today, over fifty years after the Stockholm Diplomatic Conference for the Revision of the Berne Convention,[4] that the protection of folklore is a global problem which requires international attention and coordinated solutions.

Even though much has been done in the field of folklore protection to date, a number of questions remain unanswered. The attention of the experts was and still is primarily focused on the theoretical and practical problems related to achieving the most effective manner of protection of expressions of folklore and proposing solutions to this problem – a work in progress itself – however, a number of preceding questions have only just been asked. One cannot but conclude that there is an apparent lack of understanding and agreement on the ground aspects of any folklore related considerations. The pondering questions are not just a few, and they are fundamental: What is folklore? Who is the holder of folklore? Should it be protected? If yes, which law is the most appropriate for achieving such protection?

The last of these questions seems to have attracted most attention in the scholarly debates and legal literature since expressions of folklore can be dealt with under a number of available legal regimes. In addition to intellectual property laws, various international agreements concerning the

---

3. Ficsor, M. *The Protection of Traditional Cultural Expressions/Folklore*, WIPO National Seminar on Copyright Related Rights and Collective Management, Khartoum, 28 February–2 March 2005, p. 2, available online at: https://www.wipo.int > mdocs > arab > wipo_cr_krt_05 > wipo_cr_krt_05_8.

4. Arguably, this was the moment when the first identification of the need to protect folklore and the first efforts to establish certain frame for protection were made. Namely, the Stockholm Diplomatic Conference of 1967 for revision of the Berne Convention for the Protection of Literary and Artistic Works did reflect in a limited way, for the first time, the aspirations of the developing world on protection of folklore when it adopted a mechanism for the international protection of unpublished and anonymous work (Article 15(4) of the Berne Convention) – *see* Kutty, P.V. *National Experiences with the Protection of Expressions of Folklore/Traditional Cultural Expressions: India, Indonesia and the Philippines*. Geneva: WIPO, 2002, available online at http://citeseerx.ist.psu.edu/viewdoc/download?doi=10.1.1.130.6846&rep=rep1&type=pdf.

protection of human rights are often invoked in the debate on the legal protection of folklore.[5] Provisions of human rights laws are often suggested as tools for improving the existing unsatisfactory legal regime.[6] This approach opens a range of interesting questions – which of the legal regimes, intellectual property or human rights law, is more suitable? Depending on the envisaged goals of such protection, is it necessary to choose just one of these? Or, instead of selecting one, we should be thinking about the ways of integrating them?

While I believe that it is only intellectual property law that can provide the appropriate *basis* for folklore protection, I also think that we ought to be considering the ways in which human rights and intellectual property laws can be correlated and integrated to comprehensively protect folklore. Guided by that idea, this chapter will examine the different legal regimes that expressions of folklore can be dealt under and for that purpose look into both intellectual property law and human rights laws. Before proceeding on to exploring the particular legal regimes, the chapter will first briefly delineate the subject matter of folklore and answer certain vital questions that precede any protection-related debates. Then, having examined the different relevant aspects of intellectual property law and human rights laws, in order to evaluate their capability and adequateness in protecting expressions of folklore, this chapter will suggest further ways in which the search of adequate folklore protection could advance.

20.2   GETTING A GRASP OF FOLKLORE

To start with, experts have not yet agreed on the most fundamental of all question – should folklore be protected at all? With this respect, it has been pointed out that just because something is being copied, this does not automatically mean that is must be protected and that the maxim that '*what is worth copying is prima facie worth protecting*'[7] threatens to collapse the crucial distinctions between harm and wrong, and between mere loss and actionable injury.[8] At the heart of the debate on whether expressions of folklore belong to the public domain is the question of whether a given regime provides opportunities for further creation, development, cultural

---

5. Lucas-Schloetter, A. Folklore. In: von Lewinski, S. ed. *Indigenous Heritage and Intellectual Property: Genetic Resources, Traditional Knowledge and Folklore.* The Hague: Kluwer Law International, 2004, at p. 434.
6. Kuruk, P. Protecting Folklore under Modern Intellectual Property Regimes: A Reappraisal of the Tensions between Individual and Communal Rights in Africa and the United States. *American University Law Review,* 1998, vol. 48, at p. 61.
7. *Justice Peterson in University of London Press Ltd v. University Tutorial Press Ltd,* 1919.
8. Drassinower, A. Canadian Originality: Remarks on a Judgement in Search of an Author. In Y. Gendreau ed. *An Emerging Intellectual Property Paradigm: Perspectives from Canada.* Cheltenham: Edward Elgar Publishing, 2009, 150.

exchange and fair trade. Resistance to providing protection to folklore expression relies on the necessity to keep folklore expressions available as a source of further creation or knowledge. For example, when examined in the intellectual property discourse, placing folklore within a protection regime might mean that the public domain will shrink if one views the public domain as an unstructured sum of things, a kind of a zero-sum game.[9] However, this is not entirely correct. If we accept that intellectual property rights have an incentive in the sense that the reward for exploitable property rights increases the production of intellectual goods, then arguably the greater the incentive, the greater the potential returns, thus the greater volume of intangible goods created and ultimately, the greater the extent of the public domain.[10] Also, in copyright terms, the rights of attribution and integrity of the work, which essentially function to prevent plagiarism, in the long run help foster creativity. These rights do not remove works from the public domain; rather, they create a bounded or 'softly' regulated public domain, which in many ways is what the idea of the cultural commons is about.[11]

Ultimately, and regardless of the concrete type of protection we are considering, when we come to *why* folklore should or should not be protected, one must ask – is it fair that one simply takes, as from some open treasury, without acknowledging the source? Is it just that one makes a significant profit, not even using it as an inspiration to create something new on the basis of something old, but merely copying and selling? Is it fair to *'harvest without sowing, to steal the other person's labour of mind'*?[12] If not, drawing upon the various arguments and contrasting viewpoints for and against protection, one should not drop the idea of protection altogether just because the existing system may not be perfect and coming up with one that could benefit expressions of folklore overall may be difficult.[13] While recognizing and appreciating the expressed concerns, rather than dismissing

---

9. *See* Graber, C.B., K. Kuprecht and J.C. Lai eds, *International Trade in Indigenous Cultural Heritage: Legal and Policy Issues*. Cheltenham: Edward Elgar Publishing, 2012, 220.

10. W. Van Caenegen, The Public Domain: Scientia Nullius?, *European Intellectual Property Review,* 2002, vol. 6, p. 324.

11. L. Lixinski, *Intangible Cultural Heritage in International Law*. Oxford: Oxford University Press, 2013, 199.

12. Wiese, H. The Justification of Copyright System in the Digital Age. *European Intellectual Property Review,* 2002, vol. 24, No. 8.

13. With that respect, note that even authors like Browne, who passionately advocate against protection, do not dismiss the idea of some form of protection (though other than copyright) and say that 'although there are compelling reasons to be sceptical of some indigenous intellectual property rights proposals currently under discussion, I strongly support efforts to create basic mechanisms for the compensation of native people for commercial use of their scientific knowledge, musical performances, and artistic creations' – *see* M.F. Browne, Can Culture Be Copyrighted?. *Current Anthropology,* 1998, vol. 39, No. 2, 193-222, 204.

the idea of protection completely, one should seek to design such a system of protection that would annul or at least minimize the harm that it could cause to the communities from which expressions of folklore originate, to the expressions itself and to the society at large.

Further, before considering *how* expressions of folklore ought to be protected, it is of fundamental importance to establish *what* we are contemplating protecting and *who* should be the rightholder of such protection. Finding the appropriate terminology and agreeing on the basic definitions has further implications. For legal purposes, it is necessary to have a clear and shared understanding of what is legally meant or not meant by a term or terms selected for protection.[14] Equally important, the core founding definitions further impact the potential protection itself as they establish the context and connotations for understanding and interpreting the scope of potential protection. Hence, choosing the suitable definitions and terminology is one of the fundamental tasks, and certainly, one that precedes all consequent debates on the protection itself. Accordingly, describing the subject matter and establishing adequate definitions has been identified as one of the most important problems in the field.[15] Yet, this extraordinary complicated task remains uncompleted.[16]

Over the years, numerous different terms have been considered and used to describe the subject matter, such as 'folklore',[17] 'expressions of folklore',[18] 'intangible cultural heritage',[19] 'traditional cultural expressions' (TCEs), 'traditional knowledge',[20] 'indigenous knowledge' or 'indigenous

---

14. Palethorpe, S. and S.G. Verhulst (2000), *supra* note 2.
15. For example, at the Tenth Session of the WIPO Intergovernmental Committee on Intellectual Property and Genetic Resources, Traditional Knowledge and Folklore in 2006 this was listed as the first out of ten issues to be focused on in the future work of WIPO.
16. '*Compared to folklore, it is easy to define a lion, sodium chloride, an electron or the beauty of a woman, as their shape or nature can be seen and perceived*' – *see* Islam, M. *Folklore, the Pulse of the People: In the Context of Indic Folklore.* New Delhi: Concept Publishing Company, 1985, vol. 7, p. 5.
17. Term initially used but afterwards abandoned due to the negative connotation that this term was allegedly associated with.
18. The term is used in the WIPO/UNESCO Model Provisions and is nowadays often used by WIPO interchangeably with the term 'traditional cultural expressions'.
19. The term is used in the UNESCO Convention for the Safeguarding of the Intangible Cultural Heritage (2003).
20. The term 'traditional knowledge' is sometimes used as a wider term for both folklore and traditional knowledge, for example, in the WIPO Intellectual Property Needs and Expectations of Traditional Knowledge Holders: WIPO Report on Fact-finding Missions on Intellectual Property and Traditional Knowledge (1998-1999), Geneva, 2001, available online at https://www.wipo.int/meetings/en/doc_details.jsp?doc_id=994. The two terms are, however, usually used to describe two distinct concepts – traditional knowledge stands for knowledge resulting from intellectual activity in a traditional context and includes the know-how, skills, innovation, practices and similar, while folklore stands for cultural forms.

heritage',[21] to mention just a few of the most frequent ones. Despite the lively debate on this topic, no internationally agreed term exists so far, although the two terms most commonly used today are '[expressions of] folklore' and 'traditional cultural expressions' or 'TCEs'.[22]

With regards to a definition, no internationally agreed consensus on the concept of folklore exists either. And not only that, but the disagreements also concern much more fundamental questions, such as whether 'broad, non-exhaustive and non-exclusive, definitions' are indeed necessary at this moment or whether the goal should be more loosely worded terminology and definitions to avoid getting 'stuck in working on ideal definitions that could take years to adopt'.[23] In that sense, folklore is approached differently in developed countries and developing countries and indigenous groups – the former tend to adopt narrow definitions, viewing folklore as tradition, while the latter tend to prefer broader definitions, viewing folklore as a continuing and constant cultural manifestation.[24]

As confusing as the choice of appropriate term and definition when it comes to expressions of folklore may seem, this is even more so when we ask who the rightholders of folklore are and, accordingly, who should be the beneficiaries of potential protection. Namely, folklore is not created by known persons, and hence, it is commonly ascribed to 'peoples' as in a group of people, an entire community. Therefore, one of the crucial questions associated with the protection of expressions of folklore is the definition and identification of its holders.

Again, various terms have been used to describe the holders, such as 'indigenous communities', 'indigenous people', 'traditional communities' and 'cultural communities'. Most commonly, the rightholders of expressions of folklore are identified as 'indigenous peoples'. This notion has been the subject of considerable discussion and study, yet, the precise meaning of this term is not clear. Both the terms 'indigenous' and 'community' are very broad social and political concepts, and as such, are ultimately context dependant. The prevailing view today is that no formal universal definition of the term is necessary and that for practical purposes, the understanding of

---

21. Term mostly used by UNESCO.
22. For discussions of terminological issues, *see* Blakeney, M. The Protection of Traditional Knowledge under Intellectual Property Law. *European Intellectual Property Review*, 2000, vol. 22, No. 6, pp. 251-261; Niedzielska, M. The Intellectual Property Aspects of Folklore Protection. *Copyright,* November 1980, 339-346; Girsberger, M.A., In: Graber, C. and Burri-Nenova, M. eds, *Legal Protection of Traditional Cultural Expressions: A Policy Perspective, Intellectual property and Traditional Cultural Expressions in a Digital Environment*. Cheltenham, UK: Edward Elgar, 2008, pp. 123-149.
23. *See* the statements of the representatives of New Zealand and Singapore, and of Nigeria at the WIPO Intergovernmental Committee on Intellectual Property and Genetic Resources, Traditional Knowledge and Folklore, Fourteenth Session, 2009 – *see* in Antons, C. What Is "Traditional Cultural Expression"? International Definitions and Their Application in Developing Asia. *WIPO Journal*, 2009, vol. 103, at p. 104.
24. Palethorpe, S. and S.G. Verhulst (2000), *supra* note 2, p. 6.

the term provided by Cobo study[25] is regarded as an acceptable working definition by many indigenous people and their representative organizations. Similarly, the terms 'traditional community' or 'other cultural community'[26] do not appear much clearer than the concept 'indigenous peoples'. According to some,[27] these phrases are also understood in a way similar to 'indigenous' and in essence, represent the colonized people of the south. On the other hand, there is very little guidance and almost no international consensus as to which communities this tentative definition would comprise. While the reasoning behind introducing such a formulation might be explained by the need to come up with a concept that is broad enough,[28] the actual practical usefulness of such a construction is highly questionable.

In any case, a crucial question that remains unanswered is not who the rightholders are, in terms of how we should name and define them, but how we can identify them. Practically, more than one community might claim custodianship of the same or similar expression of folklore in a country. Or, through geographical proximity, common history, migration or displacement of the folklore custodians to new territories, certain renditions of expressions of folklore might well appear concurrently behind the borders of what today represents different countries. All these possibilities raise complex, context-specific questions concerning which criteria can we use to identify the exact rightholder.

It is to a certain extent understandable that, in a complex field such as this one, providing the theoretical underpinning and definitional framework within which the relevant problems should be addressed, is a complex and time-consuming process. Certain critical issues further complicate the task of defining folklore, again underscoring its complex nature. Expressions of

---

25. *'Indigenous communities, peoples and nations are those which, having a historical continuity with pre-invasion and pre-colonial societies that developed on their territories, consider themselves distinct from other sectors of the societies now prevailing on those territories, or parts of them. They form at present non-dominant sectors of society and are determined to preserve, develop and transmit to future generations their ancestral territories, and their ethnic identity, as the basis of their continued existence as peoples, in accordance with their own cultural patterns, social institutions and legal system' – see* WIPO. Intellectual Property Expectations of Traditional Knowledge Holders: WIPO Report on Fact-Finding Missions on Intellectual Property and Traditional Knowledge, *supra* note 20.

26. In order to surpass the ambiguities related to defining 'indigenous peoples' as well as to broaden the scope of potential beneficiaries, WIPO has, for example, included in the 2006 Revised Draft Articles a rather tentative definition of beneficiaries of folklore protection as 'indigenous peoples and traditional and other cultural communities'.

27. For example, *see* Oguamanam, C. Local Knowledge as Trapped Knowledge: Intellectual Property, Culture, Power and Politics. *The Journal of World Intellectual Property*, 2008, vol. 11, No. 1, at p. 35.

28. A WIPO Secretariat's commentary suggests that the term 'cultural communities' is broad enough to 'include also the nationals of an entire country' – *See* WIPO. Traditional Cultural Expressions/Expressions of Folklore: Legal and Policy Options, Geneva, 15-19 March 2004, WIPO/GRTKF/IC/6/3, at p. 17.

folklore emerge in an entire variety of different forms, encompassing a diversity of customs, traditions, artistic expressions, crafts and products, and appear in communities that are so essentially different that hardly any links can be found between them. As folklore entails diverse legal, social, anthropological and economic aspects, it seems almost impossible to accurately comprise all these different elements under one all-including definition. Of course, this problem is not unique to folklore. Concepts with long and diverse histories often elude tidy definitions, as Nietzsche captures it best – *'it is only that which has no history, which can be defined'*.[29] On account of the aforesaid, although a number of terms and definitions have been proposed over the years, there still appears to be no wider concord on certain key terms and definitions of the basic concepts in the field.[30]

20.3   PLACING THE PROTECTION OF FOLKLORE WITHIN THE RIGHT LEGAL FRAMEWORK

Expressions of folklore can be dealt with under a number of available legal regimes. In general and in brief, these different systems can principally be divided into intellectual property-based and other types of protection. The appropriateness of dealing with the subject matter under either of these regimes has been a subject of an ongoing heated debate, where different legal, socio-cultural, economic and political arguments have been used to justify the application of one or the other. Yet again, as with most other questions raised in this field, the answer seems difficult to grasp as it is neither simple nor straightforward.

Over the years, many advantages, drawbacks and justifications of particular types of protection have been pointed out. Scholars have stressed that certain intellectual property concepts, such as those of authorship and originality, are wholly inapplicable to expressions of folklore and that therefore intellectual property laws are not suitable for regulating this subject matter. In contrast, there are those who claim that the existing intellectual property standards can nevertheless be modified so as to elude these problematic points. Yet others suggest designing a new, sui generis approach, but within the intellectual property law rationale. Some are concerned with

---

29. F. Nietzsche, *On the Genealogy of Morals and Ecce Homo*, New York: Courier Dover Publications, 2003, p. 53.
30. The WIPO Intergovernmental Committee on Intellectual Property and Genetic Resources, Traditional Knowledge and Folklore (IGC), that has been meeting up since 2001, now holds regular sessions about 4 times per year. Even though it cannot be denied that much progress has been made (at least with regards to raising the global attention to the need to *somehow* protect folklore), almost twenty years since the Committee first met, there is still no consensus on the basic terms to be used in the field (*see* the Draft Articles updated at the last session held from 17 June to 21 June 2019: https://www.wipo.int/edocs/mdocs/tk/en/wipo_grtkf_ic_40/wipo_grtkf_ic_40_19.pdf).

the overexpansion of intellectual property law and consider it crucial to maintain a healthy public domain. Others are of the view that stretching intellectual property law to cover expressions of folklore is not dangerous and impossible per se but might be unfeasible from the perspective of indigenous people as the potential beneficiaries of such protection.

On the other hand, there are those who think that the answer to '*how*' should be looked for in other fields. Apart from the intellectual property systems, expressions of folklore are said to be potentially regulated on the basis of some other laws, such as laws on cultural heritage or, in particular, laws on human rights. Again, there are those who consider these laws incapable of providing a satisfactory mode of protection on their own as they can only protect certain limited aspects of folklore.

The following pages will be concerned with examining the appropriateness of these legal regimes in protecting folklore. For that purpose, the following sections will provide a summary of the possible intellectual property and human rights-based types of protection.

20.3.1   INTELLECTUAL PROPERTY LAWS

Most of the literature seems to have focused on intellectual property law when searching for the structure within which the problem of protecting folklore should be placed. This does not come as a surprise. Historically, the first attempts to protect folklore within the intellectual property regime were made in the framework of copyright law and neighbouring rights. The very notion of 'folklore' emerged from the Eurocentric precepts and was, as such, swiftly placed within the concept of copyright.[31] Such an initial classification of expressions of folklore as copyright works appears unsurprising, knowing that folklore emerges in the artistic domain, and therefore, at least, at first sight, bears a certain level of resemblance with copyright works, given that most expressions of folklore appear in the forms corresponding to the classic copyright categories – such as music, dances, crafts, tales, etc. In addition to copyright and neighbouring rights, over the years the search for adequate folklore protection has also been placed within the trademark, geographical indications of origin, sui generis and other types of intellectual property law.

However, as straightforward as this may seem, once we look at intellectual property law as it stands today, it immediately becomes clear that this field of law is not, in its current form, entirely ideal for providing protection for expressions of folklore as the subject matter appears to be far more complex than the existing categories recognize, and the inherent characteristics of expressions of folklore seem incompatible with the existing

---

31. Blakeney, M. Hans. In: Helle Porsdam, ed. *Christian Andersen and the Protection of Traditional Cultural Expressions, Copyright and Other Fairy Tales.* Cheltenham: Edward Elgar, 2006, at pp. 114.

criteria for protection. While international and national intellectual property laws can, in certain aspects, facilitate the protection of folklore, they also demonstrate a number of drawbacks which significantly limit their efficiency. This is due to the fact that the application of standard intellectual property categories to folklore generates several critical difficulties related to the protection criteria. These limitations altogether hinder the practical reach of any protection and make it rather difficult for expressions of folklore to be governed by intellectual property laws in their current forms.

20.3.1.1 Copyright

Direct protection of folklore on the basis of general copyright principles appears to be substantially inadequate. Application of copyright rules to folklore generates several critical difficulties in relation to the fixation requirement,[32] originality,[33] authorship[34] of the work and the term of protection[35] that, altogether, make it practically impossible to be governed by copyright.

---

32. Certain copyright systems require that the work, in order to be able to enjoy copyright protection, must be fixed in a material form. This requirement, however, directly clashes with the very idea of folklore which is mainly characterised by oral transmission. Consequently, an entire segment of folklore will remain unprotected as the scope of copyright application is reduced only to works materialized in a certain tangible form. This argument against the protection of folklore by means of copyright has a limited range, however, and will not present a difficulty in civil law countries, since the fixation requirement is characteristic mainly of common law copyright systems.

33. Regardless of the different levels of originality established by different copyright systems, it has now been widely agreed that expressions of folklore do not meet the required criterions for protection. This prerequisite directly collides with the very nature of expressions of folklore which are a 'result of a constant and slow impersonal process of creative activity exercised by means of consecutive imitation within an ethnic community'.

34. Copyright system is based on the idea of an individual author or group of individual authors that create a work. However, the main characteristic of folklore is that it is attributable to the community as a whole and not to an individual author. The continually changing nature of folklore, in which every generation reproduces and builds upon the creations of the previous generations, makes it generally impossible to determine the exact author of a certain expression of folklore.

35. The protection of copyright works is mainly limited to 70 years after the death of the author in accordance with the Directive for Harmonisation of the Term of Protection of Copyright and Certain Neighbouring Rights (with certain exceptions, for example the Berne Convention where the term of protection is life plus 50 years). It is difficult to imagine how this period could be measured for expressions of folklore when authors of folklore are impossible to identify. Furthermore, even if this problem could be surpassed, applying the copyright principles would mean that the expressions have already fallen in the public domain as is it very likely that the term of protection has already passed. Finally, given that expressions of folklore have existed and were being developed over a number of centuries, it does not seem sensible to protect them only for a limited period of time.

Reasons for this are multiple, but they all seem to derive from the genuinely different natures of folklore and copyright works. Three reasons are particularly instructive. First, it is the collective and anonymous nature of folklore which is in opposition to the individualistic character of copyright. The rationale behind copyright is the protection of the author's own intellectual creation or skill, labour and judgment. On the contrary, folklore is an expression of the collective spirit, and therefore, does not have an author or, to be more precise, has a multiplicity of unknown authors. Second, copyright is designed to guide the commercial exploitation of the work. Quite the opposite, expressions of folklore have not been created in order to be economically exploited but only to serve the community from which they originate and whose tradition they exemplify. Third, when it comes to damage caused by the exploitation of folklore, it is mainly of a moral nature, rather than economical.[36]

Thus, it is now commonly accepted that copyright and neighbouring rights appear to be a fundamentally inappropriate system for the protection of folklore. Certain indirect protection based on the copyright principles can be achieved in the case of collections of folklore and works derived from it. However, the real extent of such protection is rather limited and can only be used to supplement some other form of protection as it does not benefit the folklore or the community it originates from as such, but only the original elements of the newly created works.

20.3.1.2   Trademark Law

Likewise, international and national trademark law, as it currently stands, can in certain aspects facilitate the protection of folklore. However, it also has a number of drawbacks which significantly limit its efficiency.

For example, when it comes to positive protection of folklore on the basis of trademark law, fulfilling the requirements for trademark registration are fewer and simpler than the ones necessary under copyright law. Consequently, it might be easier for folklore holders to meet the criteria for trademark protection and directly benefit from trademark law, and in this respect, the use of certification and collective marks are particularly noteworthy. Furthermore, trademark rights can be renewed continually, and the benefits from their use are, therefore, not limited only for a certain period.

However, the first important restraint on the effectiveness of active trademark protection is that it is only applicable when there is commercialization of the folklore, that is when there is an attempt to use and protect them in the course of trade and in relation to certain goods. Furthermore, one self-imposing question arises in relation to this approach – should one particular person, whether natural or legal or an association of any kind, even though a member of the community from which the concerned expression of

---

36. Blakeney, M. In: Helle Porsdam, ed. (2006), *supra* note 31, at p. 298.

folklore originates, be allowed to register that expression as a trademark and consequently monopolize an element of collective culture that in fact belongs to that community as a whole? In order to address this issue, it would be necessary to have a certain administrative body that would apply for the trademark on behalf of the entire concerned community and this, in fact, requires a high level of organization as well as the consensus of the entire community on the need to register a certain trademark.

With respect to defensive employment of trademark law, trademarks might be used to prevent the unauthorized exploitation and commercialization of traditional designations. Although within the limits discussed above, trademark law can provide certain protection against offensive and deceptive use of folklore, which ultimately also benefits consumers. However, the practical effectiveness of this approach is rather limited for a number of reasons. Trademark law might only provide partial protection against offensive and deceptive use rather than the protection of general use of traditional designations. Furthermore, and very importantly, this type of protection is only triggered when a third party applies to register a trademark that contains certain traditional elements, and thus fails to provide protection in all other situations where expressions of folklore are exploited without filling a registration application. Finally, as a general observation, trademark law essentially only concerns the commercial aspect of exploitation of folklore in the course of trade, whereas folklore should enjoy protection in any case, whether it is being exploited or not and regardless of whether such exploitation is done in the course of trade and in relation to particular goods and services or not.

Evaluation of both the advantages and shortcomings of trademark law in relation to traditional designations leads to the conclusion that trademark law, in its current form, has a rather limited effect on the protection of folklore. However, it also appears that further improvement, within the boundaries of existing trademark law, is absolutely feasible. The recognition and acknowledgement of the existing limitations provide a valuable starting point for the development and adjustment of trademark law which could, ultimately, provide a more balanced and functional mechanism for protection of one aspect of folklore.

20.3.1.3 Geographical Indications of Origin

The opinions on the adequateness of geographical indications of origin in relation to folklore vary significantly. While on the one hand geographical indications of origin have been praised as having the best balance in recognizing the cultural significance and protecting the commercial value of folklore,[37] on the other hand, they were said to provide too limited, and thus insufficient, protection.[38]

A potential advantage of the protection of folklore by geographical indications of origin is that such protection could be unlimited in time. The crucial argument in favour of geographical indications of origin-based protection of folklore lays in the nature of geographical indications of origin – they are a collective right and as such, do not require that potential protection is limited in relation to certain organizational form, which would be the case with trademark protection.

On the flip side though, the main problem with the protection offered under the The Agreement on Trade-Related Aspects of Intellectual Property Rights (TRIPS) is generated by the narrowed scope of protection which has not, up to now, been equalized with the protection offered for wines and spirits. As a result, such protection ultimately depends on the public opinion in the country where protection is sought, which in turn might significantly limit the scope of protection. Furthermore, and as a general drawback of this type of protection – geographical indications of origin can only protect tangible expressions of folklore and only the tangible element of expression, while the know-how behind it remains the public domain. Finally, and essentially, geographical indications of origin cannot prevent others from making the same products as long as they use a different denomination.

Despite the disagreement on the actual effectiveness of the current scope of protection offered for folklore under TRIPS, it appears that geographical indications of origin nevertheless provide an interesting system whose elements could be valuable in developing a future model for folklore protection.[39] Within this context, it is worth noting that examples of registrations of geographical indications of origin with respect to expressions of folklore can be found in many countries.[40]

---

37. For example, *see* Gangjee, D.S. *Geographical Indications Protection for Handicrafts under TRIPS*. MPhil Thesis submitted to University of Oxford, 2002; Zografos, D. *Intellectual Property and Traditional Cultural Expressions*. Cheltenham: Edward Elgar Publishing, 2010; Kamperman Sanders, A. Incentives for and Protection of Cultural Expression: Art, Trade and Geographical Indications. *The Journal of World Intellectual Property*, 2010, vol. 13, No. 2, pp. 81-93.

38. For example, *see* Kur, A. and R. Knaak. In: von Lewinski ed. *Protection of Traditional Names and Designations,* 2004, *supra* note 5.

39. In addition to the international protection offered under TRIPS, the GIs type of protection can also be supplemented on the basis of bilateral GI agreements – an excellent example of this is Switzerland which has used bilateral agreements to protect its folklore (the Lotschental masks) – *see* Zografos, D. (2010), *supra* note 37, at p. 170.

40. For example Russia, Portugal and India; *see* WIPO Consolidated Analysis of the Legal Protection of Traditional Cultural Expressions, Geneva, 7-15 July 2003, WIPO/GRTKF/IC/5/3, at p. 53.

20.3.1.4   Sui Generis Protection

In parallel with exploring the possibilities of folklore protection under the existing intellectual property systems and aware of the fact that the existing legislative models are not entirely adequate in comprehensively dealing with the subject matter, the attention of the experts has been turned towards the potentials of creating a special sui generis system of protection within intellectual property law. The sui generis system was expected to be sufficiently close to existing intellectual property laws, mainly copyright, so as to benefit from the general principles in the amount allowed by the extraordinary characteristics of folklore, yet modified enough in order to reflect its specific features.[41]

As a response to the expressed concerns over the protection of folklore and the need to share experiences on these issues, WIPO has been developing best practices and guidelines for managing and safeguarding folklore. These guidelines are aimed at assisting communities in managing and protection their folklore against misappropriation and misuse.[42]

As a brief historical overview of the WIPO activities in relation to folklore, it is worth noting that WIPO has been active in the legal and policy debate over folklore for several decades. Past highlights include working with The United Nations Educational, Scientific and Cultural Organization (UNESCO) to adopt the Model Provisions in the 1980s and attempting to establish an international treaty. Following, under the auspices of WIPO, the WIPO Performances and Phonograms Treaty (WPPT) was adopted in 1996, providing a certain level of indirect protection for the expressions of folklore as well. In 1997, the WIPO-UNESCO World, discussing the needs and addressing issues related to intellectual property and folklore. Next, through 1998 and 1999, WIPO conducted fact-finding missions to identify the expectations of folklore holders. The results of the missions, conducted in twenty-eight countries, were published as a WIPO Report 'Intellectual Property Needs and Expectations of Traditional Knowledge Holders: WIPO Report on Fact-finding Missions (1998-1999)'. Most recently, WIPO's Member States established the WIPO Intergovernmental Committee on Intellectual Property and Genetic Resources, Traditional Knowledge and Folklore (hereinafter the '*IGC*') in 2000, which serves as an ongoing forum

---

41. 'Expressions of folklore constituting manifestations of intellectual creativity deserved to be protected in a manner inspired by the protection provided for intellectual productions, and that the protection of folklore had become indispensable as a means of promoting its further development, maintenance and dissemination' – *see* WIPO Final Report on National Experiences with the Legal Protection of the Expressions of Folklore Geneva, 13-21 June 2002, WIPO/GRTKF/IC/3/10, at p. 10.

42. Wendland, W. In: Kono, T. ed. *Managing Intellectual Property Options, Intangible Cultural Heritage and Intellectual Property: Communities, Cultural Diversity and Sustainable Development.* Antwerp-Oxford-Portland: Intersentia, 2009, at p. 87.

for discussion between the Member States, intergovernmental and non-governmental organizations on genetic resources, traditional knowledge and folklore. The IGC and WIPO Secretariat undertake a series of detailed analytical studies, surveys national experiences and fosters international policy debate, and is also working on developing practical tools for the protection of folklore, including the Draft Provisions/Articles for the Protection of Traditional Cultural Expressions that are under constant revision.

The sui generis model proposed by WIPO can certainly be appraised as a vital step towards adequate folklore protection. This is not reflected merely in the provisions which are currently being developed by IGC, but also in the wider appreciation and recognition of the issues that arise in the context of folklore protection. Wide-ranging attention, acknowledgement of the specifics of the subject matter and global efforts are imperative in developing any system for folklore protection.

Nevertheless, even the WIPO achievements entail certain limitations. First, the documents produced up to date are not legally binding upon the Member States, but merely provide for optional rules which could be implemented in the legislation of the Member States. It appears, however, that so far they had somewhat limited impact on the national legislation of Member States as these have been hesitant to incorporate the proposed provisions.[43] Further, for such a system to be fully operational and globally functions, it is not sufficient that some Member States implement some solutions. For the system to work, it is either necessary that the Member States enter into a legally binding Treaty or that they all implement the corresponding provisions in their national legislations. Also, the WIPO proposals attempt regulating both the economic and moral aspects of folklore protection, which may not be entirely necessary and will certainly not be required for all of the potential beneficiaries. This may result in a somewhat stiff and robust system which may not be fully adequate, as what is needed are soft, manageable and flexible rules. Finally, the major critique, when it comes to the WIPO instruments concerns the duration of the entire process. Leaving aside the earlier attempts, it has been well over a decade since IGC began developing the Draft Articles, and these have undergone a number of revisions since.[44] Not only do the Draft Articles not appear closer to a final text, but the debate seems to heathen even more as the discussion continues. At the same time, the parties involved in the consultations hold diametrically opposite positions.[45] This is also obvious from the proposals – some of the

---

43. Lucas-Schloetter, A. In: Silke von Lewinski ed. (2004), *supra* note 5, at p. 345.
44. At the latest session of the IGC held in June 2019, the Committee developed, on the basis of previous drafts, a further, revised text of Draft Articles, *see* online at: https://www.wipo.int/edocs/mdocs/tk/en/wipo_grtkf_ic_40/wipo_grtkf_ic_40_19.pdf.
45. *See,* for example, the WIPO Draft Report, Twenty-Fifth Session, Geneva, 15-24 July 2013, WIPO/GRTKF/IC/25/8.

solutions offered under the earlier drafts considerably diverge when compared to the recent ones. On account of all this, it seems that the efforts made by WIPO, while indisputably valuable, are far away from reaching a practically functional form.

20.3.2	HUMAN RIGHTS LAWS

The specific characteristics of expressions of folklore – for example, the fact that they are expressions through which a right to pursue cultural development, as one of the elements of the right of self-determination, is manifested, inspired the attempts to place the search for their protection within the discourse of human rights law. The final verdict as to the usefulness of these attempts has not yet been reached – as it will be summarized in the following pages, some argue that human rights laws are capable of protecting the subject matter in a comprehensible manner, while others claim that they can only add some elements to the protection but do not have the capacity, on their own, to provide satisfactory protection.

20.3.2.1 Relevant Legal Instruments in the Field of Human Rights Laws

Human rights and within them, the rights of indigenous peoples, acquired particular attention in discussions of folklore protection. When it comes to norms directly relevant for folklore within the framework of general human rights, it is possible to distinguish between the standards for the protection of intellectual property and those relevant for the protection of indigenous peoples.[46]

Within the first group, when it comes to the grounds to protect intellectual property, perhaps the most commonly quoted legal instrument is the European Convention on Human Rights[47] (ECHR). One might reasonably question what a human rights treaty has to do with intellectual property – the answer is the right of property, which appears in the ECHR.[48] Article 1 of Protocol 1 of ECHR states: '*Every natural or legal person is entitled to the peaceful enjoyment of his possessions. No one shall be deprived of his possessions except in the public interest and subject to the conditions provided for by law and by the general principles of international law*'.

---

46. Stoll, P-T. and von Hahn, A. Indigenous Peoples, Knowledge and Resources in International Law. In: von Lewinski, S. ed. (2004), *supra* note 5, at p. 17.

47. The 1950 Convention for the Protection of Human Rights and Fundamental Freedoms, as amended by Protocols Nos 11 and 14, supplemented by Protocols Nos 1, 4, 6, 7, 12 and 13.

48. Helfer, L. The New Innovation Frontier? Intellectual Property and the European Court of Human Rights. *Intellectual Property and the European Court of Human Rights. Harvard International Law Journal*, 2008, vol. 49, at p. 2.

The protection of property contained in the ECHR seems to be one of the most controversial and disputed provisions in the European human rights system with regards to its purpose, scope and extent of protection it provides. The intention of the legislators was questioned, since the cited Article does not appear in the text of the ECHR but in the Protocol, and also that it makes no mention the word 'right'.[49] While the subsequent case law confirmed that intellectual property rights constitute possessions within the meaning of Article 1 of Protocol 1 and that these rights are under the guarantee of ECHR,[50] sceptics have repeatedly expressed their concerns over the dangers of an 'arranged marriage' between human rights and intellectual property – some find this protection redundant, others fear that such protection is only secondary to some fundamental human rights, and some are concerned that the continuous proclamation of new human rights will undermine the balance of existing intellectual property laws.[51] On account of this, it appears that the ECHR may serve as a ground but not as the detailed rule for the protection of intellectual property.

Further and more specifically, within grounds for protection of intellectual property, there are several international and regional legal instruments in the field of human rights which recognize the right to benefit from the protection of the moral and material interests that derive from scientific, literary and artistic production. For example, pursuant to the 2048 Universal Declaration on Human Rights[52] (hereinafter '*UDHR*') '*everyone has the right to the protection of the moral and material interests resulting from any scientific, literary or artistic production of which he is the author*'.[53] Even though UDHR is a non-binding instrument in the field of international human rights law, it has influenced certain other documents, such as the International Covenant on Economic, Social and Cultural Rights[54] (ICESCR) and the International Covenant on Civil and Political Rights[55] (ICCPR), which are both binding upon the signatory parties.[56] Accordingly, the provisions of the UDHR that may be relevant in relation to the protection of folklore are nearly directly reflected in the ICESCR and the ICCPR.

---

49. Helfer, L. In: Torremans, P. ed. *Intellectual Property and the European Court of Human Rights, Intellectual Property and Human Rights*. London: Kluwer Law International, 2008, at p. 32.
50. Çoban, A.R. *Protection of Property Rights Within the European Convention on Human Rights*. Ashgate Publishing, Ltd., 2004, at p. 149.
51. Yu, P.K. Challenges to the Development of a Human Rights Framework. In: Torremans, P. ed. (2008), *supra* note 49, at pp. 79-80.
52. Universal Declaration on Human Rights, adopted and proclaimed by the United Nations in General Assembly Resolution 217 A(III), U.N. doc. A/810, 10 December 1948.
53. Article 27(2) of the UDHR.
54. International Covenant on Economic, Social and Cultural Rights, 993 U.N.T.S. 3, concluded on 16 December 1966, entered into force on 3 January 1976.
55. International Covenant on Civil and Political Rights, 999 U.N.T.S. 171, concluded on 16 December 1966, entered into force on 23 March 1976.
56. Currently, 156 state are parties to the ICESCR and 160 states are parties to the ICCPR.

661

Looking more closely at the relevant provisions of the ICESCR and ICCPR, it follows that Article 15 of the ICESCR is the one most directly relevant for folklore, while certain other provisions also bear potential importance for the subject, including Article 27 ICCPR (minority rights), Article 20 ICCRP (freedom of expression), Article 1 ICCRP and Article 1 ICESCR (right to self-determination).[57] Article 15 of the ICESCR provides that '*the State Parties […] recognise the right of everyone […] to benefit from the protection of the moral and material interests resulting from any scientific, literary or artistic production of which he is the author*'.[58] Such 'right to benefit' has recently been interpreted as providing the linkage between copyright and indigenous heritage[59] and thus particularly relevant within discussions on the protection of folklore expressions.

Furthermore, Article 1(1) of the ICCPR is often cited as relevant in relation to the indigenous people, as the presumed rightholders of folklore, since it lays down the right to self-determination: '*All peoples have the right of self-determination. By virtue of that right they freely determine their political status and freely pursue their economic, social and cultural development*'.[60]

Summarizing the above outlined, it has been argued that all these provisions are relevant to the claims of traditional communities, insomuch as they recognize collective rights, and may be used to require compensation for works relating to traditional knowledge and prohibit discriminatory tendencies reflected in the deliberate failure to protect folklore. In addition, provisions on self-determination are said to have the potential to be used by

---

57. Graber, C. Using Human Rights to Tackle Fragmentation in the Field of Traditional Cultural Expressions: An Institutional Approach. In: Graber, C.B. and M.B. Nenova, eds (2008), *supra* note 22, at p. 102.
58. Article 15(1)(c) of the ICESCR.
59. Committee on Economic, Social and Cultural Rights, General Comment No. 17 (2005), adopted 21 November 2005, E/C.12/GC/17, 12 January 2006. Paragraph 32 of the Comment reads that '[…] State Parties should adopt measures to ensure the effective protection of the interests of the indigenous peoples relating to their productions, which are often expressions of their cultural heritage and traditional knowledge. In adopting measures to protect scientific, literary and artistic productions of indigenous peoples, States parties should take into account their preferences. Such protection might include the adoption of measures to recognize, register and protect the individual or collective authorship of indigenous peoples under national intellectual property rights regimes and should prevent the unauthorized use of scientific, literary and artistic productions of indigenous peoples by third parties … '.
60. On right to self-determination, also relevant is the International Labour Organization Convention No. 169 which deals specifically with the rights of indigenous people – *see* for example, Cowan, J.K., M.-B Dembour and R.A. Wilson, eds, *Culture and Rights: Anthropological Perspectives*. Cambridge: Cambridge University Press, 2001; Yupsanis, A. The International Labour Organization and Its Contribution to the Protection of the Rights of Indigenous Peoples. *The Canadian Yearbook of International Law*, 2011, vol. 49, No. 1, pp. 117-176.

minority groups who are also fighting for political independence to support their right to control and dispose of their cultural resources.[61]

20.3.2.2 Suitability of Human Rights Laws for Protecting Folklore

However, the direct application of these provisions, as well as the use of human rights in general, in relation to the protection of folklore has been subject to several reservations.

First, as has been pointed out, apart from the right of self-determination whose features might be regarded as collective and could potentially serve as the basis for action by indigenous communities, human rights law provisions are intended primarily for individuals, rather than for groups.[62] Human rights theory and practice mainly perceive human rights as individual rights, and this is also the case in relation to the so-called cultural rights within the sense of ICCPR and ICESCR.[63] Accordingly, the established rights provide the basis for protecting the rights of individual authors, in their capacity as members of particular groups.[64] This, however, is in contrast to the collective nature of expressions of folklore and thus it has been argued that any attempt to provide legal protection for cultural minorities or groups cannot be efficient, as long as it is not based on a concept of group rights.[65]

On the other hand, it has also been pointed out that the individual character of human rights does not preclude them from enshrining a collective aspect as well.[66] Recent human rights theory seems to suggest that most individual human rights may have a collective dimension, without therefore becoming collective rights.[67] This has been pointed out in relation to the cited Article 27 ICCPR, which serves to protect the cultural rights of individuals in their capacity as members of indigenous people. The expressed reasoning is supported by the interpretation of the ICCPR Committee, which addressed the problematic relationship between individual and collective

---

61. Kuruk, P. (1998), *supra* note 6, vol. 48.
62. *See,* for example, Chapman, A. In: Greaves, T. ed. *Human Rights Implications of Indigenous Peoples' Intellectual Property Right, Intellectual Property Rights for Indigenous Peoples.* Society for Applied Anthropology, 1994; Evatt, E. In: Niec, H. ed. *Enforcing Indigenous Cultural Rights: Australia as a Case-Study., Cultural Rights and Wrongs.* UNESCO Publishing and Institute of Art and Law, 1998.
63. Eide, A. In: Eide, A., Krause, C. and Rosas, A. eds, *Cultural Rights as Individual Human Rights, Economic, Social and Cultural Rights.* The Hague: Kluwer Law International, 2001, at pp. 290-291.
64. Graber, C. In: Graber, C. and Burri-Nenova, M. eds (2008), *supra* note 22, at p. 109.
65. Stavenhagen, R. Cultural Rights: A Social Science Perspective. In: Eide, A., Krause, C. and Rosas, A. eds, *Economic, Social and Cultural Rights.* The Hague: Kluwer Law International, 2001, at p. 102.
66. Graber, C. In: Graber, C. and Burri-Nenova, M. eds, (2008), *supra* note 22, at p. 103.
67. *See* Kalin, W. and Kunzli, *The Law of International Human Rights Protection.* Oxford: Oxford University Press, 2009.

rights in two ways: (i) by inviting State Parties to recognize not only individual but also collective authorship; and (ii) by requiring State Parties to provide 'for collective administration by indigenous people of the benefits derived from their productions', i.e., suggesting the use of *Domaine Public Payant* or other forms of collective right management.[68] However, as valuable as it may seem in relation to clarifying the collective aspect of established human rights, this argumentation hardly clarifies the practical applicability of such rights. Rather, it merely observes the problem of protection through copyright or general intellectual property prism.

Along with the same discussion of the individual character of human rights, it has been pointed out that these, as public law rights, are essentially addressed to states and not to individuals or groups of individuals. Accordingly, their value in relation to folklore seems rather relative in that 'indigenous people are primarily concerned with their collective rights as distinct people, while international human rights law is mainly concerned with the rights of individuals against states'.[69] This is particularly evident if we look at the above-cited right to self-determination. While the quoted international instruments provide for a right to self-determination, which may be of particular interest to indigenous people, the essential problem with the protection of folklore is not how to provide a mechanism for indigenous and potentially other communities to express their right to self-determination. Rather, the essential problem is how to protect the *existing* creations. This casts doubt on whether the relevant international human rights provisions, in fact, establish a clear basis for their application to individuals or corporations which engage in unauthorized utilization of folklore.[70]

Perhaps the most important drawback related to the use of human rights as a tool for protecting expressions of folklore is the problem of its applicability and enforceability. Human rights are enforceable only to a limited extent. According to human rights theory, the recognition of human rights imposes three levels of obligation on State Parties: (i) the obligation to respect, (ii) the obligation to facilitate, and (iii) the obligation to provide.[71] Although these obligations present positive duties for State Parties, they essentially present a requirement to take all necessary steps within their own available resources to ensure effective protection of human rights.[72] In that way, the international human right standards impose a duty for states to

---

68. Committee on Economic, Social and Cultural Rights, *supra* note 59, at para. 32.
69. Suagee, D.B. Human Rights and Cultural Heritage: Development in the United Nations Working Group on Indigenous Populations. In: Greaves, T. ed. (1994), *supra* note 62, at p. 196.
70. Kuruk, P. (1998), *supra* note 6.
71. Committee on Economic, Social and Cultural Rights, *supra* note 59, at para. 15.
72. Graber, C. In: Graber, C. and Burri-Nenova, M. eds (2008), *supra* note 22, at p. 103.

provide organizational, administrative, judicial and other appropriate technical mechanisms for individuals to enforce their rights, rather than substantially providing the practical mechanisms for their implementation.

To a certain but limited extent, human rights may also be applied in private-law disputes.[73] Namely, there have been cases where judges have applied the provisions of human rights instruments horizontally, that is, in conflicts between private individuals. The provisions applied in private-law discourse concern the protection of property on the one hand, and the protection of freedom of expression, information, art and science on the other. Although not directly relevant in relation to folklore, the horizontal effect of human rights was argued to be important insomuch as it may provide the flexibility and balance within intellectual property law – as a regulator between the protective tendencies of intellectual property and freedom of expression.[74]

Finally, another obstacle to the efficient use of the quoted provisions of human rights in relation to folklore is their vagueness. Namely, it has been pointed out that the exact ambits of the provisions of ICCPR and ICESCR are far from clear.[75] Accordingly, it is not certain whether the provided principles of cultural self-determination and cultural development are genuine rights or merely political principles.[76] The provisions leave open the delicate question of how the relevant entities, as beneficiaries of the established human rights, may be identified and defined.[77] While 'peoples' may represent nationals or citizens of particular states, it has been disputed whether this concept should necessarily include indigenous communities or other groups identified on the basis of their ethnic, religious, cultural or linguistic characteristics, for example.[78]

The same problems appear in relation to the other concepts and provisions – for example, what precisely should be understood as falling under the 'right to benefit'? While the 'right to benefit' may be relevant insomuch as it provides the basis for claims of communities to a particular expression of folklore, it is not clear whether it may be imposed so as to prevent the misappropriation of those expressions by other communities or individuals. Quite the contrary, it may be argued that a vague formulation like the cited one provides sufficient ground for those who, on the basis of

---

73. *See* in Geiger, C. The Constitutional Dimension of Intellectual Property. In: Torremans, P. ed. (2008), *supra* note 49, at p. 113.
74. Geiger, C. Fundamental Rights, a Safeguard for the Coherence of Intellectual Property Law? *IIC,* 2004, vol. 35, No. 3, 268-280.
75. Macmillan, F. Human Rights, Cultural Property and Intellectual Property: Three Concepts in Search of a Relationship. In: Graber, C. and Burri-Nenova, M. eds (2008), *supra* note 22, at p. 77.
76. Graber, C. In: *ibid.*, at p. 105.
77. Macmillan, F. In: *ibid.*, at p. 76.
78. Musgrave, T.D., *Self Determination and National Minorities.* Oxford: Oxford University Press, 1997, at p. 90.

misappropriated expression of folklore, create new works, to 'benefit' from such work.

20.4 WHICH LAW FOR FOLKLORE: A SUGGESTION

On the basis of the afore discussed, it seems that the practical effectiveness of both the existing intellectual property and human rights laws is somewhat limited when it comes to expressions of folklore, even though both fields of law are certainly an indispensable contribution to the creation of a complete and well-balanced system.

Some general basis for the protection of expressions of folklore may clearly be achieved through human rights. However, overall, there does not seem to be too many links between the potentially relevant human rights and the effective and enforceable safeguarding of expressions of folklore. On very general and basic grounds, one may say that human rights law has not been designed to protect intellectual creations, and in essence, this field of law is there to provide for some core principles and values which should be protected, rather than to establish precise mechanisms on the basis of which these principles and values will be protected. Furthermore, even those provisions of the international human rights law which could be understood as relevant in relation to folklore are said to be greatly limited due to their vagueness and limited enforceability. A general lack of effective implementation and enforcement mechanisms for human rights, therefore, dictates the need to promote alternative ways of realization of folklore related rights, such as intellectual property rights.[79]

For example, the provisions of ICCPR and ICESCR briefly discussed in the previous pages are said to be important in relation to folklore as they support the characterization of intellectual property rights as human rights and to ground intellectual property rights, in general, on human rights basis.[80] As a general concern relevant for the present discussion, however, it is highly dubious whether the protection of traditional culture or folklore does or should depend upon them being characterized as human rights. As Macmillan says, not everything that requires protection and seems morally defensible automatically must mean or depend on being labelled as a human

---

79. Tobin, B. Setting Protection of TK to Rights – Pacing Human Rights and Customary Law at the Heart of TK Governance. In: Kamau, E.C. and Winter, G. *Genetic Resources, Traditional Knowledge and the Law: Solutions for Access and Benefit Sharing*, London: Earthscan, 2009, at p. 107.
80. Macmillan, F. In: Graber, C. and Burri-Nenova, M. eds (2008), *supra* note 22, at p. 77. *See also* for example: Chapman, A. Approaching Intellectual Property as a Human Right. *Copyright Bulletin*, vol. XXXV, No. 3, at p. 14; Santos, A.E. Rebalancing Intellectual Property in the Information Society: The Human Rights Approach. *Cornell Law School Inter-University Graduate Student Conference Paper*, 2011.

right.[81] In addition to this general criticism, Peter Yu, for example, has expressed specific criticism when it comes to expressions of folklore by pointing out that the development of a human rights framework for intellectual property would result in the undesirable human rights ratchet of intellectual property protection and that such framework could potentially be biased against non-Western cultures and traditional communities.[82]

On the other hand, authors have pointed out examples which demonstrate the need for human rights and intellectual property laws to operate jointly.[83] Geiger, for example, has argued that it is precisely the core values protected on the basis of human rights laws that may serve as a corrective to the overprotectiveness and therewith potential misbalance existing under intellectual property regimes.[84] When it comes to folklore, certain recent practices show an interesting approach, by focusing on the integration of human rights and intellectual property laws with the aim of protecting expressions of folklore and traditional knowledge – by basing the claim on human rights grounds and further enforcing it through intellectual property mechanisms.[85]

The discussed limitations particularly reinforce the need for complementary operation of human rights laws and intellectual property laws. I believe that it is precisely in their complementary application that we need to look for the solutions that would fit folklore protection the best. Obviously, the range of human rights laws is limited when it comes to folklore, and unless the next step is available under some set of rules, the very purpose of mechanisms established under human rights law may ultimately prove to be impractical. Unless there is a set of positive rules and enforceable mechanisms, it would be very difficult to create an operational system of protection. Therefore, even if we start from the viewpoint of human rights laws, once their practical application has been exhausted, we are inevitably directed towards intellectual property laws.

---

81. Macmillan, F. In: Graber, C. and Burri-Nenova, M. eds (2008), *supra* note 22, at p. 77.
82. Yu, P. Reconceptualizing Intellectual Property Interests in a Human Rights Framework. *UC Davis Law Review* 2007, vol. 40, 1039-1149, at pp. 1128.
83. *See* for example, Ruse-Khan, G.H. Proportionality and Balancing within the Objectives of Intellectual Property Protection. In: P. Torremans, ed. (2008), *supra* note 49, at pp. 191-194; Helfer, L.R. Toward a Human Rights Framework for Intellectual Property. *UC Davis Law Review*, 2006, vol. 40, 977; Gervais, D.J. Intellectual Property and Human Rights: Learning to Live Together. In: P. Torremans, ed. (2008), *supra* note 49, at p. 6.
84. Geiger, C. In: Torremans, P. ed. (2008), *supra* note 49, at p. 113.
85. *See* for example: http://www.washingtonpost.com/business/capitalbusiness/new-practice-focuses-on-human-rights-intellectual-property/2012/03/30/gIQARQvnpS_story.html.

20.5   CONCLUSION

The history of mankind is a history of borrowing and piracy. If you watch a Disney cartoon, purchase a hand-made Persian rug or join a Halloween party, you will be enjoying the results of hundreds or even thousands of years of continuous folklore flow, mixing, borrowing, re-shaping and evolution. One may ask – should we interfere with that at all or should folklore be left free?

Folklore should be free, but the use of folklore should also be fair. Fair folklore does not necessarily mean non-free folklore, and there certainly are certain limited aspects of every community's folklore that should be regulated without restricting the free flow and further evolution of folklore. Authors have already spoken of the importance of free culture. On the one hand, many scholars considered that broad and durable intellectual property rights might jeopardize further creation and innovation. On the other hand, others noted that simply leaving a resource in the public domain is not enough to satisfy societal ideals. Sunder concludes, and I fully agree with this, that our laws should serve to facilitate the free flow of culture but on fair terms.[86] Therefore, it is ultimately *fairness* in cultural exchanges that requires that we regulate at least certain practices and certain aspects of folklore.

The question raised in this chapter was which law could provide such an adequate basis for the protection of folklore. In addressing this issue, the available literature has mainly been looking at intellectual property law, but also at human rights laws, weighing specific limitations of each of these against their potential to protect folklore. However, I think that the correct question to be asked is not *which law*, but *which laws*.

And the answer to this question would be – all of them. First, these fields of law do not necessarily conflict when it comes to folklore. Nor do they need to be seen as mutually exclusive. Quite the contrary, it is precisely in the case of folklore where it is evident that they can work in parallel, dealing with different aspects and levels of protection, thus completing one another rather than competing with one another. Indeed, not only we do not have to choose between these, but if we want to create a comprehensive system which will effectively deal with folklore, we do not have the luxury to do so. Due to the compound nature of folklore which comprises different cultural, historical, traditional and other elements, addressing the problem of its protection requires coordinated solutions in different fields of law, thus a truly multidisciplinary approach.

Therefore, instead of asking which – given that they are all relevant in certain aspects and contribute to providing a comprehensive system in their own way – what is needed is to think about the possibilities of integrating intellectual property and human rights laws.

---

86. Sunder, M. From Free Culture to Fair Culture. *WIPO Journal*, 2012, vol. 4, No. 1, pp. 20-27, at p. 21.

While they ought to remain in the folklore debate as they are indispensable when it comes to addressing certain aspects of folklore and could, therefore, contribute to the creation of a wide-ranging, complete system, it is evident that the legal instruments in the fields of human rights law cannot, on their own, provide a solid and concrete foundation for protection of folklore, mainly due to the lack of detailed provisions concerning the essence of protection and the problems with clear enforcement mechanisms for their application. Therefore, I believe that the platform for creating the basis of any future protection, which should be complemented by provisions from human rights laws, lies within the framework of intellectual property law. Though intellectual property law, in its current form, is not the perfect solution, it still seems like it is the most effective one, and, as it follows from the ongoing WIPO work in this field, definitely the one that has most sufficient capacity and flexibility for developing a suitable system for protection of folklore.

Chapter 21

Is Taking Advantage Always Unfair? Balancing Interests in Brand Investment with Basic Rights and Free Competition Rules in the EU

Nigar Kirimova

21.1 INTELLECTUAL PROPERTY RIGHTS VERSUS BASIC HUMAN RIGHTS

It is recognized at the European Union (EU) level that Intellectual Property rights, as a type of property, constitute fundamental rights and, therefore, shall certainly be protected.[1] Nevertheless, one has to always remember that these unquestionably important rights shall be balanced with other essential human rights, and may even be limited in case of clash with the overweighting basic rights such as Free Speech (versus Copyright) or Right to health (versus Patent).

An extended academic literature has been created on the issue of interrelation between some basic rights with copyrights or patents.[2] However, trademarks, being perceived as more economic phenomena, are not

---

1. Charter of Fundamental Rights of the European Union Article 17, 2010 O.J. C 83/02.
2. *See*, for example, P. Samuelson, "Copyright and Freedom of Expression in Historical Perspective" (2002)10 J. Intell. Prop. L. 319; M. Bakhoum, "TRIPS, Patent Rights and

often considered as a potential threat to the other basic rights. Perhaps the reason for this, is the general underestimation of such Human rights as free commercial speech (included in the interpretation of Article 11 of EU Charter) and the right to conduct business (Article 16 of EU Charter), where the latter unarguably leads to the necessity to have free competition in the market. Thus, some basic rights and competition rules may and shall define limits to exclusive rights of trademarks' proprietors.

The balancing exercise is one of the most challenging and important ones when it comes to a conflict of interests. It refers to striking the best compromise between two clashing rights by relying on general public interest. However, it is not always clear what public interest is. The question shall most probably be: what is "fair" or what is beneficial for public? The latter seems to be quite an objective criterion, but the answer may vary depending on the goals and values of different societies. Thus, a clearly property-type of rights such as trademark can be limited by free commercial speech or competition rules only in a society where the latter two rights are fundamental ones.

One may question whether commercial speech, which in most cases refers to the advertising activity, constitutes one of the basic human rights because it is not explicitly mentioned in any of the legal instruments. In the United States (U.S.), this type of speech was recognized as the one covered by the First Amendment after the decision of the Supreme Court in famous *Virginia State Board of Pharmacy*.[3] The condition set up by the Court for the legal protection to be provided was that the information must be truthful and lawful. The U.S. Supreme Court has extended the notion of free speech to commercial speech due to the importance of such kind of data to the consumers and the society[4]: " … Commercial speech protection serves foundational goals and premises of our democratic system".[5]

On the other side of Atlantic, the European Court of Human rights (ECtHR) has also several times stated that commercial speech is one of the types of expressions protected by Article 10 of the European Convention on Human Rights (ECHR).[6] In the EU, where free movement of goods, persons, services and capitals are the main principles of the Single Market, together with the aim to protect consumers, including by providing them with truthful advertisements, commercial speech naturally receives special attention. "The

Right to Health: 'Price' or 'Prize' for Better Access to Medicine?" (2009). Max Planck Institute for Intellectual Property, Competition & Tax Law Research Paper No. 10-07.

3. *Virginia Pharmacy Board v. Virginia Consumer Council* (1976) 425 US 748.
4. A. Garde, "Freedom of Commercial Expression and Public Health Protection in Europe" in C. Bernard & O. Odudu (eds), *Cambridge Yearbook of European Legal Studies*, Vol. 12 (2009-2010), pp. 226-228.
5. M. Redish, "Commercial Speech and the Values of Free Expression", Policy Analysis No. 813, CATO Institute, June 19, 2017.
6. *Markt Intern v. Germany* Series A no 165 (1990) 12 EHRR 161, paras. 25-26; *Casado Coca v. Spain* Series A no 285 (1994) 21EHRR 1, paras. 35-36.

freedom of individuals to promote commercial activities derives not only from their right to engage in economic activities and the general commitment … to a market economy based upon free competition, but also from their inherent entitlement as human beings freely to express and receive views on any topic, including the merits of the goods and services which they market or purchase."[7]

Hence, trademarks, which have an economic value as any other property, give their owners the right to prevent others from the use of an identical or similar mark.[8] But the mere existence of the economic value is not enough to grant property rights.[9] Since it limits and excludes rights of others, it must always be justified.[10]

The widely known and discussed incentive, reward and investment arguments are perhaps good grounds for granting the general legal protection to trademarks and for treating them as property rights. Nevertheless, when it comes to the enhanced protection for well-known trademarks (so-called anti-dilution law), there are much more counter-arguments and this protection does not seem to be always justified.

Additional protection provided for famous marks refers to even more chances and grounds for limiting the rights of others. That is why there must be especially strong arguments and a solid public interest in order to grant such strong exclusive rights. It is hard to disagree with the additional value of famous brands, however, shall the investment in that value (made by an owner on her own interest) always receive an enhanced protection? There are not many arguments one could raise to prove public interest in such a special protection for well-known brands.

For instance, the brand owner cannot invoke the consumer interest argument, unless consumers are misled. Even more than that, the laws prohibiting legal imitation of brands, arguably, diminish consumers' choice on the market.[11] From the economic point of view, free riding is considered to be a "positive externality" which, eventually, leads to social benefits.[12]

7. A. Garde, *supra* note 3, 230, *See also* AG Fenelly, opinion of December 12, 2006, C-380/03, *Germany v. Parliament and Council,* paras. 201-203.
8. It is also considered as a positive right to use the sign exclusively, *See* S. Evans & J. Bosland, "Plain Packaging of Cigarettes, and Constitutional Property Rights" in T. Voon et al. (eds), *Public Health and Plain Packaging of Cigarettes* (Edward Elgar 2012) 53.
9. H.C. Mitchell, *The Intellectual Commons: Toward an ecology of Intellectual Property* (Lexington books 2005).
10. R. Tomkowicz, *Intellectual Property Overlaps: Theory, Strategies and Solutions,* (Routledge 2012) 17.
11. A. Ohly, "The Freedom of Imitation and Its Limits – A European Perspective" (2010) 41 IIC 506, p. 517, *See also* Recital 14 of Unfair Business Practices Directive: " … *it is not the intention of this Directive to reduce consumer choice by prohibiting the promotion of products which look similar to other product unless similarity confuses consumers as to the commercial origin of the product and is therefore misleading."*
12. D. Gangjee & R. Burrell, "Because You're Worth It: L'Oreal and the Prohibition on Free Riding" (2010) 73 MLR 282, 289.

And although one may argue that copying is ethically unfair, it has been correctly stated that Intellectual property (IP) rights shall be limited to reasonable borders "because other people have rights too."[13]

Furthermore, the problem with justifying dilution is that it causes essential risk to freedom of expression, even more than traditional infringement cases.[14] The whole concept of trademark protection bares a risk of monopolization over a word or phrase, which can otherwise be freely used.[15] There is no significant danger when it comes to "normal" trademarks, because prohibition there is limited strictly to competitors, who are in the same market. But the number of potential companies that may be affected by the anti-dilution law is unlimited, regardless of the sector of the market where they operate.[16]

It is also true that trademark owners develop an attractive style primarily for their own benefits and this shall not necessarily entail an additional protection. A café owner who invests in decorations and a cozy atmosphere of his property does not obtain better legal protection than the owner of any other ordinary café, except that he may charge clients more for giving them that esthetic pleasure.

In a way, the risk of being imitated is the price that a well-known trademark pays for its fame, just like popular singers whose style or image is often copied, to some extent, by young artists who try to enter show-business. Similarly, the owner of a beautiful garden in front of the house can claim nothing from the neighbor enjoying the view.[17]

On the other hand, one may also argue that a total absence of protection against dilution may demotivate local companies from investing in marketing and branding in a given market (a good example is the trademark legislation and the market of the Russian Federation). However, what is clear is that such a protection should not go too far. It is absolutely necessary to find a fair balance between the conflicting rights, taking into account norms of competition law.[18] Moreover, for the sake of legal certainty, such a balance should be reached from the outset, in a well-drafted legal provision.

---

13. H. Breakey, "Natural Intellectual Property Rights and the Public Domain" (2010) 73 MLR 208, 210.
14. R. Burrell & D. Gangjee, "Trade Marks and Freedom of Expression-A Call for Caution" (2010) 41 IIC 544, 547.
15. A. Chronopoulos, "Determining the Scope of Trademark Rights by Recourse to Value Judgment Related to the Effectiveness of Competition – The Demise of the Trademark-Use Requirement and the Functional Analysis of Trademark Law," (2011) 42 IIC 535, 539.
16. V. Di Cataldo, "The Trademark with a Reputation in EU Law – Some Remarks on the Negative Condition "Without due Cause," (2011), 42 IIC 833, 836.
17. D. Gangjee & R. Burrell, *supra* note 12, 289.
18. A. Chronopoulos, *supra* note 15, 70.

21.2   ANALYSIS OF THE SITUATION IN THE EU

21.2.1   THE LEGAL BACKGROUND: WHY PROTECTION OF TRADEMARKS WITH
             REPUTATION IN THE EU IS CONSIDERED TO BE EXCESSIVE?

Both EU and U.S. jurisdiction provide additional protection for trademarks that are well known. However, while in the U.S., this additional protection can still, arguably, be justified by the ultimate benefits of the consumers, the EU model of anti-dilution law seems to also add further protection for trademark owners against the "unfairness" of the competitors.

Despite the general resemblance of the EU anti-dilution law with other legislations and the international law, there are some specific characteristics that should be noted. Arguably, those small (at first glance) dissimilarities are the reasons for the excessive protection of famous trademarks in the EU. However, it shall be noted that there is an opinion in the literature that due to the particular (and differing from each other) interpretations of the concepts such as "confusion" and "dilution" on the two sides of the Atlantic, the difference between the EU and the U.S. anti-dilution law is smaller than it may initially seem to be.[19]

First, unlike many other jurisdictions, in order to obtain protection in the EU it is sufficient to prove the so-called niche fame, i.e. reputation among "specialized public" consisting only of the trading circles for a specific product.[20] Although, one may not conclude that from the legal provisions of the EU Trademark Regulation[21] or the Directive[22], this interpretation, favoring trademark owners, was given by the Court of Justice of the European Union (CJEU) in the *General Motors/Yplon* decision.[23] Consequently, the EU opted for a lower standard of niche-knowledge in contrast to the "knowledge by general public", adopted, for instance, in the U.S.[24]

---

19. M.H.H. Luepke, "Taking Unfair Advantage or Diluting a Famous Mark-A 20/20 Perspective on the Blurred Differences Between U.S. and E.U. Dilution Law" (2008) 98 TMR 789, 811-812, The author argues that application of broader concept of dilution in EU is, in fact, necessary, in order to balance it with broader interpretation of ordinary confusion in U.S. The latter includes cases of assumed sponsorship, affiliation or business connection of "related" and not only similar goods in the U.S., whereas in EU, based on the CJEU's decision in Canon it is more restricted to similar goods and services.
20. J.T. McCarthy, "Dilution of a Trademark: European and United States Law Compared" (2004) 94 TMR 1163, 1172.
21. European Union Trademark Regulation (EU) 2017/1001
22. Directive approximating the laws of the Member States relating to trademarks (EU) 2015/2436
23. CJEU, September 14, 1999, Case C375/97, *General Motors/ Yplon,* para. 24.
24. M.R.F. Senftleben, "The Trademark Tower of Babel – Dilution Concepts in International, US and EC Trademark Law (October 1, 2008)". (2009) 40(1) Int'l Rev. Intell. Prop. & Competition L., 45-77, 55.

Moreover, further loosening of the "repute" requirement in the EU is based on the fact that there is no need to prove fame throughout all the member states.[25] By using the term "repute" instead of "fame", the EU legislator implies that not so much of a quantitative, but rather qualitative approach shall be used in the assessment.[26] According to the CJEU's ruling in *Pago/Tirolmilch*,[27] reputation in even one member state might be sufficient. Therefore, due to the specific interpretation of the subject matter[28] (niche knowledge and not even in all member states), it is unquestionably easier to be recognized as a known brand and obtain additional protection for investments in the EU than in any other jurisdiction.

21.2.2   A Notion of "Taking Unfair Advantage"

Another particularity of the EU trademark law, which leads to a wider scope of protection, is that besides blurring and tarnishment, an owner of a trademark with a reputation is entitled to prevent any use that could be covered by a very unclear and wide notion of "taking unfair advantage."[29] The phrase "takes unfair advantage of, or is detrimental to, the distinctive character or the repute of the trade mark," which sets the enhanced standards of protection for famous marks in Europe, has been interpreted by CJEU as including three separate categories of infringement: (1) detriment to distinctiveness; (2) detriment to repute; and (3) taking unfair advantage.[30]

While the first two categories can be easily compared to blurring and tarnishment as known to the U.S. jurisdiction, "taking unfair advantage" was for a long time (before *L'Oreal* was decided by CJEU) an unknown animal, interpretation of which was left to national courts. Differently from the EU, "free riding *per se* is not actionable under federal law."[31]

The concept of "taking unfair advantage of, or being detrimental to distinctive character or repute of the trademark with reputation without due cause" in Europe is based on an old provision of Benelux Trademark Act.[32]

---

25. *General Motors/Yplon,* para. 28.
26. M.R.F. Senftleben, *supra* note 24, 73.
27. CJEU, October 6, 2009, Case C-301/07, *Pago/Tirolmilch*, para. 30.
28. M.R.F. Senftleben, *supra* note 24, 50-56.
29. Article 5(2) TMD and 9(2) (c) EUTMR.
30. CJEU, November 27, 2008, Case C-252/07, *Intel/CPM*, paras. 27-28.
31. D. Gangjee & R. Burrell, *supra* note 12, 287.
32. Benelux Trademark Act 19, 1962 Article 13 A.1, *See also* Uniform Benelux Law on Marks, Amended by the Protocol of November 10, 1983, amending the Uniform Benelux Law on Trademarks and by the Protocol of December 2, 1992, amending Uniform Benelux Law on marks, Article 3.2(c), available at http://www.wipo.int/wipolex/en/text.jsp?file_id=128587, *See also* M. Rijsdijk & M. Antic, "A Case of the Old and New in Benelux," (February/March 2010) WTR, 54, available at http://www.worldtrademarkreview.com/issues/article.ashx?g=29772485-f8e1-437e-806e-79378ab12eb4.

The Netherlands, Belgium and Luxemburg have always been "front runners" in that sense and adopted the concept of dilution (when association instead of confusion is enough) much earlier than any other EU member state.[33] Protection of famous trademarks against unfair advantage taken by the competitors was further elaborated in *Claeryn/Klarein*[34] and stipulated in the new Benelux Convention on Intellectual Property.[35]

In the mentioned case, the Court announced that prejudices among consumers shall be interpreted as an adverse effect on attractiveness power and ability of trademarks to increase the "desire to buy" it (degradation of trademarks) and subsequent "loss of exclusivity" (blurring).[36] Therefore, the Benelux Court provided an explanation that adverse effect on a trademark by a similar sign may occur in two cases: (1) blurring of distinctiveness; or (2) degradation of a trademark.[37]

Consequently, "taking unfair advantage" was not interpreted as a separate, third type of infringement and was considered in relation to detriment to distinctiveness and repute.[38] Thus, arguably, in applying "unfair advantage" independently, as an infringement *per se*,[39] CJEU went even further than the Benelux law.[40]

So, what does it mean to "take unfair advantage" from the distinctiveness or repute of a trademark? In distinction from blurring and tarnishment as known in the U.S. dilution theory, the focus in this category turns from the harm that can be caused to a trademark proprietor toward a competitor who obtains an advantage without his own effort.[41]

This notion is similar to the "misappropriation" and "unjust enrichment" doctrine in the U.S. jurisdiction,[42] which are normally covered by the unfair competition law provisions of the Lanham Act, rather than Trademark law. It refers to the "instances where there is clear exploitation and free-riding on the coat-tails of a famous mark or an attempt to trade upon its

---

33. P. Torremans, "Trademark Law: Is Europe Moving Towards an Unduly Wide Approach for Anyone to Follow the Example?" (2005) 10 J. IPR 127, 128.
34. Benelux Court of Justice, March 1, 1975, Case A74/1, *Claeryn/Klarein,* Nederlandse Jurisprudentie 472 (1975).
35. Law Approving the Benelux Convention on Intellectual Property (Trademarks and Designs), February, 25, 2005, Mem.2006, 1738, Article 2.20(1)(c) and (d), available at http://www.wipo.int/wipolex/en/text.jsp?file_id=217692.
36. *Supra* note 34, 4-65.
37. AG Jacobs, opinion of April 29, 1997, Case C-251/95, *SABEL/Puma*, paras. 38-39, paraphrasing the judgment of the Benelux Court in *Claeryn/Klarein*, Case A 74/1, Jurisprudence of the Benelux Court of Justice 1975, 472.
38. *Claery / Klarein, See also,* Ch. Gielen, "Trademark Dilution under European Union Law," (2014) 104 TMR 693, 726.
39. D. Gangjee & R. Burrell, *supra* note 12, 287.
40. M. Rijsdijk & M. Antic, *supra* note 32, 55.
41. I.S. Fhima, *Trade Mark Dilution in Europe and the United States,* (OUP 2011), 219.
42. F.W. Mostert (ed.) *Famous and Well-Known Marks: An International Analysis* (2nd ed. 2004 & Supp. 2007), 1-14.

reputation"[43] Since it is not *misrepresentation*, but only *misappropriation*, i.e. transfer of famous trademark's characteristics,[44] no confusion as to origin,[45] and, what is more, no association raised in consumer's minds (as in case of dilution) is needed. Competitors can be considered taking advantage unfairly even when consumers are absolutely aware that the sign is different and not related to a famous trademark.

According to Advocate General (AG) Mengozzi, in case of free riding, consumer is attracted to the sign due to the positive features taken from a trademark with reputation.[46] It is considered that a competitor takes unfair advantage when he makes his own marketing easier by associating his product with an earlier mark that has already obtained a reputation.[47] In order to prove that marketing of the competitor was easier because of some advantage taken unfairly, it is necessary to establish "some sort of boost given to the later mark by its link with the earlier mark."[48] However, there is no clear explanation in CJEU case law on how to establish that "some sort of boost" or prove that consumers wouldn't buy the same product if no earlier trademark existed or had a reputation, on which "coat-tail" the competitor is free-riding.

Despite all attempts to give a clear interpretation to the notion of "unfair advantage," it still seems to constitute "vague and undefined notions of unfair competition and free riding," at least to American lawyers and academics.[49] In fact, the idea that unfair advantage is more related to unfair competition law rather than dilution[50] was implicitly acknowledged by CJEU itself when the Court referred to the French concept of "parasitism" and free-riding,[51] which are normally known as unfair competition law terms. [52] Moreover, one would easily notice that the same "unfair advantage," but in relation to a narrower circle of cases of comparative advertising appears in the European Comparative Advertising Directive, which makes it even more complicated to see a difference between the two fields. [53]

Interestingly enough, I.S. Fhima argues that the inclusion of "unfair advantage" as a basis for a trademark infringement in the EU Trademark

---

43. AG Jacobs, opinion of July 10, 2003, Case 408/01, *Adidas/Fitnessworld*, para. 39.
44. CJEU, June 21, 2009, Case C-487/07, *L'Oreal/Bellure*, para. 41.
45. Court of 1st Instance, March 22, 2007, Case T-215/03, *SIGLA/OHIM (VIPS)*, paras. 71-72.
46. AG Mengozzi, Opinion of February 10, 2009, Case C-487/07, *L'Oreal/ Bellure*, para. 103.
47. *Ibid.*, paras. 99-101, *see also VIPS*, para. 40.
48. AG Sharpston, Opinion of June 26, 2008, Case C-252/07, *Intel/CPM*, para. 62.
49. J.T. McCarthy, *supra* note 20, 1165.
50. I.S. Fhima, *supra* note 41, 190.
51. *L'Oreal/Bellure*, para. 41.
52. *See*, for instance, WIPO, Protection against unfair competition 55 (1994) (WIPO Pub. No. 725(E)); M. LaFrance, "Passing Off and Unfair Competition: Conflict and Convergence in Competition Law," (2011) Mich. State L. Rev., 1422.
53. V. Di Cataldo, *supra* note 16, 844.

Regulation (EUTMR) was the result of failure to harmonize the Unfair Competition Law in Europe.[54] The argument is that since the project with the EU Unfair Competition Law became clearly unsuccessful and resulted in adoption of only Misleading Advertising Directive in 1984,[55] and the concept of "unfair advantage" was, arguably, first time mentioned within the framework of Trademark law in 1983,[56] it was possibly an attempt to save this provision through the backdoor.[57]

In support of this argument, in their analysis of the landmark *L'Oreal/ Bellure*, D. Ganjee and R. Burell mentioned that the provision on free-riding in the trademark law was "attempting to achieve some degree of harmonization of unfair competition law."[58] Moreover, when the project on harmonization of Unfair Competition Law was still ongoing, the Memorandum on the creation of the European Economic Community (ECC) trademark stated that a trademark use such as "attaching references or making comparisons, or for other unfair purposes"[59] falls under the scope of Unfair Competition Law rather than Community trademark law.

Perhaps, all the ambiguity and confusion with the unfair competition law was the reason why for a long time the "unfair advantage" element introduced to the trademarks law attracted very little academic attention and was rarely discussed in literature.[60] The situation had dramatically changed after *L'Oreal/Bellure*, when CJEU tried first time to give some interpretation to the notion and applied it to the case. The case and the interpretation of the "unfair advantage" will be discussed below.

Although, many commentators agree that the decision raised more questions rather than answers,[61] one may argue that it was only the first step toward development of the concept, which is still new. To be fair and precise, it also took quite some time to develop dilution theory in the U.S. and "the likelihood of harm to a mark's distinctiveness does not appear more tangible

---

54. I.S. Fhima, *supra* note 41, 190.
55. C. Wadlow, "Unfair Competition in Community Law: Part 1: The Age of the 'Classic Model' and Part 2: Harmonization Becomes Gridlocked" (2006) 28 EIPR 433, 469.
56. Opinion of the European Parliament on the Regulation, OJ C 307, 14.11.1983.
57. I.S. Fhima, *supra* note 41, 190.
58. D. Gangjee & R. Burrell, *supra* note 12, 294.
59. Memorandum on creation of an ECC trade mark, SEC (76) 2462 final, July 6, 1976, *Bulletin of the European Communities*, Supp.8/76, p.28, available at http://aei.pitt.edu/5363/1/5363.pdf.
60. I.S. Fhima, *supra* note 41, 219, Note also that in "Trademark Dilution under European Union Law"(*supra* note 37), which was published recently, Ch. Gielen has two separate Chapters on Detriment of Distinctiveness and Detriment to reputation without doing so for the category of unfair advantage.
61. J. Box, "Comments on Decision: Court of Justice of the European Union (First Chamber), 21 June 2009 – Case No. C-487/07 L'Oreal parfums et beaute & Cie SNC, Labaratoire Garnier & Cie v. Bellure NV, Malaika Investments Ltd, Starion International Ltd" (2010) 41 IIC 485, 490.

or more precisely determined than the unfairness of a 'free ride'."[62] What is clear, however, is that CJEU's interpretation broadened up, even more, the scope of protection of trademarks in the EU.

21.2.3 TRADEMARK FUNCTIONS THEORY

Besides the reasons mentioned above, the European trademark law is also special due to a very wide interpretation of the use requirement.[63] The use of a sign in the course of trade is a general pre-condition for an infringement to occur. [64] But, for trademarks not to become a weapon suppressing all possible legitimate uses, this critical requirement should be interpreted very narrowly.[65] The narrow interpretation of use is especially important in case of protection of marks with reputation, since owners of these marks may act even against non-competitors and even in absence of any confusion.[66]

However, CJEU's case law, to the contrary, has been gradually widening the concept of use, to the point that today almost any use, including merely referential one, can be considered a trademark use.[67] Following the Court's interpretation, in order to overcome the use requirement in the EU, it is enough to simply establish a link between goods and a sign.[68] Consequently, even if consumers do not consider the sign as a source of origin and are not misled, the use still can be prohibited.[69]

According to CJEU, the use of a sign can be prevented by a trademark proprietor only in case it affects functions of a trademark.[70] Typically, in most jurisdictions, the main function fulfilled by trademarks is so-called "origin function," i.e. establishing the link between a product and the company that produces it. This link is necessary for the consumers to make their choice during the search in the market and to be sure of the particular quality of the product associated with the producer. Therefore, the origin function of

---

62. M.H.H. Luepke, *supra* note 19, 827.
63. M.R.F. Senftleben, "Adapting EU Trademark Law to New Technologies – Back to Basics?" in C. Geiger (ed.), *Constructing European Intellectual Property: Achievements and New Perspectives* (Edward Elgar Publishing 2013), 147.
64. Article 5(1) and 5(2) TMD.
65. S.L. Dogan & M.A. Lemley, "The Trademark Use Requirement in Dilution Cases" (2007) 24 Santa Clara High tech. J. 541.
66. *Ibid.*
67. M.R.F. Senftleben, *supra* note 63, 147; CJEU, June 12, 2008, Case C-533/06, *O2/Hutchison*, paras. 35-36; CJEU, February 23, 1999, Case C-63/97, *BMW/Deenik*, para. 42.
68. CJEU, February 19, 2009, Case C-62/08, *UDV/Brandtraders*, para. 47.
69. M.R.F. Senftleben, *supra* note 63, 147.
70. CJEU, November 12, 2002, Case C-206/01, *Arsenal/Reed*, para. 51.

trademarks partially justifies "monopolization" in a sign by providing benefits to consumers.[71]

In addition to that, the theory of "economic functions" of trademarks has been developed in Europe. The latter includes investment, communication and advertising functions. According to that theory, those functions shall be recognized by the legislator in order to secure rights to holders' investments in creating an image for the brand, as well as give them the possibility of increasing demand by using marketing tools.[72] The economic functions of trademarks were first mentioned in the German legal literature and found their further support throughout Europe.[73] Eventually the theory was officially recognized also by CJEU and, therefore, brought about an even stronger protection for trademark owners in EU.[74]

The point here is that common law jurisdiction understands trademark law mainly as a system establishing a link between a company and consumers, aiming at avoiding any possible confusion and reducing search costs.[75]In Europe, in addition to that, trademark is perceived as an asset of enterprises and, therefore, obtains protection not only insofar as it is beneficial for consumers, but also against competitors in the market.[76]

Recognition of additional functions of trademark by CJEU resulted in very wide academic discussions and polarity of opinions. However, it seems that the concern of those who do not support the idea of economic functions of trademarks is based not on a doubt that investments in brands may bring about attractiveness (which is clearly correct), but rather the fact that protection of those additional functions, according to CJEU, is available even when no confusion as to origin is caused.

This kind of "multifunctional interpretation" given by the Court leads to the effect that any use of trademarks, including the use as a part of expression of thoughts or feelings, is likely to be always infringing.[77] Judge Jacob LJ, has explicitly stated that he has difficulties with accepting functions of investment, communication and advertising when they are not connected to the origin function. According to him, those functions are "conceptually vague and ill-defined" and will bring the result that "all comparative advertising … is likely to affect the value of the trade mark owner's

---

71. M. Strasser, "The Rational Basis of Trademark Protection Revisited: Putting the Dilution Doctrine into Context" (2000) 10 Fordham IP Media & Ent. L.J 375, 379.
72. A. Chronopoulos, *supra* note 15, 541.
73. *See*, for example, L. Heydt, "Zur Funktion der Marke," 1976 GRUR Int. 399-345 or W. Oppenhoff, "Wandel der Markenrechtskonzeption" [1973] GRUR Int. 433-436.
74. *L'Oreal/Bellure* and CJEU, September 22, 2011, Case C-322/09, *Interflora/Marks & Spencer*.
75. B. Beebe, "The Semiotic Account of Trademark Doctrine and Trademark Culture" in G.B. Dinwoodie & M. Janis (eds) *Trademark Law and Theory: A Handbook of Contemporary Research*, (Edward Elgar Publishing 2008), 43.
76. M.R.F. Senftleben, *supra* note 24, 56-57.
77. A. Chronopoulos, *supra* note 15, 541-542.

investment."[78] Thus, although there are excellent explanations for securing proprietors' rights in essential (origin) function of trademarks, there is very little, if any, justification for protection of non-origin functions.[79]

A. Banerjee radically argues that the trademark law system is, in general, not suited for protection of so-called "non-origin use." He mentions as an example, the case of Lacoste company suing the Norwegian murderer Breivik for wearing the brand's garments, and Louis Vuitton suing a student, studying art in the Netherlands, for drawing the brand's bag on a painting inspired by *Guernica* of Picasso.[80] The author seems to be desperate in asking the rhetorical question as to whether there is someone so daft as to confuse or stop using brands because the mass murderer uses the same label or because of the controversial painting of an artist? Later, he answers his own question with a famous remark from Ogilvy: "The consumer is not a moron, she is your wife."[81] However, in Europe sometimes it seems like lawmakers and some "odd judges" view us/consumers as less intelligent than we are.[82]

It is important to note that even supporters of the idea that trademarks may fulfill additional functions argue that those functions are only related to the trademarks with reputation. For instance, M. Senftleben sees the wider functions of trademarks as those appearing only at the last, third stage of the development of a trademark (first stage is reservation of sign, second-programming and the third-brand image creation).[83] Consequently, those elements are there not by default, but come with the time and effort. They are the result of certain investments, when the sign of an enterprise becomes associated with particular image or lifestyle.[84] The wider functions are not inherent in any trademark.

Nevertheless, in the *L'Oreal/Bellure*, CJEU went one-step further toward the extension of trademarks' protection in the EU. By recognizing communication, investment and advertising function in each and every, even not famous, trademark, the Court "transformed Article 5(1)(a) TDM (*Trademark Directive*) into a powerful instrument for brand image protection."[85] This way the Court erased the borders between basic protection against

---

78. *L'Oreal SA v. Bellure NV*, U.K. Court of Appeals, [2010] EWCA Civ535, para. 30.
79. A. Banerjee, "Non-Infringement – Has Trade Mark Law Gone Too Far?" (2012) 43 IIC 555, 567.
80. *Ibid.*, 555.
81. D. Ogilvy, *Ogilvy on Advertising*, (Vintage Books 1985), 170.
82. A. Banerjee, *supra* note 79, 555.
83. M.R.F. Senftleben, *supra* note 24, 46-50.
84. M.R.F. Senftleben, *supra* note 63, 141; *see also*, R. Brown, "Advertising and the Public Interest: Legal Protection of Symbols" (1999) 108 Yale L.J. 1619, 1619-1620.
85. *Ibid.*, 153.

confusion under Article 5(1)(a) TMD and the stronger protection reserved only for trademarks with reputation under Article 5(2) TMD.[86]

This development might be perceived as an opening of the backdoor for circumvention of the anti-dilution provisions. Thus, if a trademark does not have enough of repute to claim an infringement based on dilution or free riding, the proprietor can still obtain the same enhanced scope of protection under CJEU's interpretation of Article 5(1)(a) TMD. The concern here is that the existence of particular strict requirements, such as a certain reputation, specific infringement criteria or the possibility of "due cause defense" included in the anti-dilution provisions, are not required under Article 5(1)(a) TDM, which makes it easily applicable to almost any case.[87]

Moreover, taking into account that an adverse effect on *any* function under Article 5(1)(a) may lead to an infringement[88] (i.e. no proof of confusion is needed), this generous "gift" of the Court to trademarks' owners may result in elimination of almost any possibility to avoid an infringement verdict.[89] If nothing else, this kind of broad and overwhelming protection has a potential to be in conflict, at a minimum, with competition law and freedom of expression.[90]

The issue of contradiction between functions theory and other rights was addressed by AG Kokott in Viking Gas/Kosan Gas:

> not every adverse effect on those functions justifies the application of Article 5(1) of Directive 89/104. The protection of those functions on the basis of that provision, first, must not undermine the requirements of specific protective rules and, second, must respect overriding other interests.[91]

This means that even when there is an adverse effect on any function recognized by the Court, that effect shall still be balanced with other interests, including interest in healthy competition as a pre-condition to enjoy the basic right to conduct business and free commercial speech. This kind of interpretation of the functions theory obviously tries to balance trademark rights with other important principles. However, it does not make things easier as it brings about legal uncertainty for the parties and gives too much discretion to the courts.

---

86. M.R.F. Senftleben, "Function Theory and International Exhaustion – Why It Is Wise to Confine the Double Identity Rule to Cases Affecting the Origin Function" (2014) 36 EIPR 521, 520. Moreover, according to Ch. Gielen, the same result of infringement could be achieved without introducing new functions, based on origin function which is in law, if one takes into account post-sale confusion, recognized by CJEU in Arsenal decision (Ch. Gielen, *supra* note 38, 701).
87. Relaxation of even those criteria by the CJEU in practice will be discussed further.
88. M.R.F. Senftleben, *supra* note 63, 154.
89. *Ibid.*, 155.
90. M.R.F. Senftleben, *supra* note 86.
91. AG Kokott, Opinion of 7 April 2011, Case C 46-10. *Viking Gas/ Kosan* Gas, para. 59.

Therefore, the functions theory elaborated by the CJEU is very problematic in the sense that it leads to both legal uncertainty and unjustifiable expansion of protection of trademarks without reputation. "The mere fact that the trademarks may be used in this way and with these objectives does not justify the conclusion that trademark owners should be able to bring an infringement action without any showing of their marks having a reputation, without fulfilling specific infringement criteria, and without a chance for the defendant to advance a 'due cause' argument for unauthorized use."[92]

Exactly for these reasons, just before the recent legislative changes, the EU Commission has proposed the following:

> *The recognition of additional trade mark functions under Article 5(1) (a) of the Direction (Article 9(1) (a) of the Regulation) has created legal uncertainty. In particular, the relationship between double identity cases and the extended protection afforded by Article 5(2) of the Directive (Article 9 (1) (c) of the Regulation) on the trade marks having a reputation has become unclear. In the case of both double identity [under Article 5(1) (a) TMD] Article 9 (1) (a) and similarity [under Article 5 (1) (b) TMD] under Article 9 (1) (b) it is only the origin function which matters.*[93]

However, the above proposal was not adopted, and the provisions related to the double identity-type of infringement remained unamended both in the new EU Trademark Regulation of 2017 and the Directive, despite the fair criticism in academia.[94] Thus, the scope of protection provided to the trademark owners is unjustifiably stronger in the EU in comparison with any other jurisdiction (and that is not only in relation to the well-known marks!), as it goes far beyond the essential function of trademarks to identify origins of goods and services.

With regard to the application of the wider functions to dilution cases, CJEU didn't give any clarifications neither in the *Intel* (where the main discussions were about dilution of essential functions) nor in *L'Oreal*. However, according to commentaries on *L'Oreal*, it would be illogical to recognize wider functions of trademark in relation to Article 5(1)(a) without

---

92. *Ibid.*
93. Proposal of the Directive, para. 5.1(2) and Proposal for a Regulation of the European Parliament and the Council amending Council Regulation (EC) No. 207/2009 on the Community Trade mark, March 27, 2013, Document COM (2013) 161 final, 2013/0088(COD), para. 2.1(2), available at http://ec.europa.eu/internal_market/indprop/tm/index_en.htm, *see also* Max Planck Institute for Intellectual Property and Competition law, "Study on the Overall Functioning of the European Trade Mark System," (2011) *Munich: Max Planck Institute*, para. 2.214.
94. M. Senftleben, "Function Theory and International Exhaustion – Why It Is Wise to Confine the Double Identity Rule to Cases Affecting the Origin Function (November 19, 2013)". (2014) 36(8) European Intell. Pro. Rev. 521-524.

giving protection against dilution or tarnishment of those functions.[95] How dilution of investment, advertising or communication functions will differ from dilution of origin function in practice is not clear, though, and needs further interpretation. It is interesting to mention that, in contract to the EU, the U.S. trademark law, is more resistant to extension of trademark protection and, thus, it does not recognize the theory of the economic functions of trademark.[96]

To sum up, the EU trademark legislation definitely provides for much wider protection than any other jurisdiction and can barely be considered "unsatisfactory"[97] On the one hand, it obviously stimulates and incentivizes investments and, arguably, is the reason why the EU has so many brands known internationally, as opposed to Russia, for example, where almost no additional protection is offered for famous trademarks.[98] However, on the other hand, all the particularities of the EU dilution law mentioned above, such as the niche fame requirement, the protection against unfair advantage, the broad interpretation of the use requirement and the protection of several wider functions of trademarks, lead it to the situation of a conflict with some other interests, including competition in market and consumer interest in free commercial speech.

21.3 THE DANGER FOR FREE COMPETITION AND COMMERCIAL SPEECH TO FALL INTO THE BLACK HOLE OF TRADEMARK PROTECTION IN THE LIGHT OF L'OREAL DECISION

21.3.1 FACTS OF THE CASE

As discussed above, "the ECJ significantly expanded the scope of trade mark protection but provided little justification for doing so."[99] Since this kind of protection is overwhelming and has the potential to suppress free competition and free commercial speech, it is sometimes compared to the "black hole."[100]

---

95. J. Box, *supra* note 61, 488.
96. W.R. Cornish & D. Llewelyn, *Intellectual Property-Patents, Copyright, Trade Marks and Allied Rights*, (Sweet and Maxwell 2003), 591.
97. M.R.F. Senftleben *supra* note 86, p. 519.
98. Гражданский кодекс Российской Федерации (часть четвертая) от 21.12.2006 N 230-ФЗ (ред. от 23.07.2013). (с изм. и доп., вступающими в силу с 01.09.2013), ст. 1508-1509.
99. D. Gangjee & R. Burell, *supra* note 12, 282.
100. M.R.F. Senftleben, "Trade Mark Protection – A Black Hole in the Intellectual Property Galaxy?" (2011) 42 IIC 383.

The widely discussed decision of *L'Oreal/Bellure* was the last drop added by the Court to the glass already full of disapprovals, when it all spilled out and led to severe censure. In this case, CJEU has generously opened the door for protection of trademarks with reputation and, thereby, substantially limited the possibility of any legal imitation. The ruling has resulted in a burst of academic criticism[101] and was ultimately applied quite reluctantly by the national court (United Kingdom (U.K.)).[102]

The case involved L'Oreal, the proprietor of a well-known brand and a Belgian company, Bellure. Bellure started to produce replicas of some of L'Oreal's fragrances, selling them much cheaper, because it obviously did not have the same luxury image. The business model was built on the assumption that the "cost of the major fragrance brands was beyond the pocket money of many consumers. In consequence the demand was for affordable perfumes in attractive bottles and packaging, with fragrance similar to those of popular designer brands."[103]

So, Bellure was selling imitations of some of L'Oreal's brands, including "Tresor," "Miracle" and "Noa," and in some instances, it was even sold in quite similar packages and bottle designs. Moreover, Bellure presented to its retailers (not consumers) a list comparing their products to those of L'Oreal.

However, it is important to note that despite some similarities in packaging, undisputedly no confusion was probable in this case. Consumers and retailers would know for sure that they were not buying products of L'Oreal. For this reason, the imitation of the fragrances itself was not (and could not have been) challenged, and L'Oreal built its allegations around the "unfair advantage" argument.[104]

The High Court of Justice of the U.K. has referred to CJEU five questions for preliminary ruling. All the issues in *L'Oreal* can be combined into two groups: (1) imitation of bottles and packaging and (2) use of the trademarks in the comparison list.

As mentioned, the imitation of perfumes' scent (production of scent – alike products) was not challenged in the case. The reason for this is that, in contrast with the Netherlands,[105] perfume is not protected by copyrights in

---

101. *See,* for example, D. Gangjee & R. Burrell, *supra* note 12, M.R.F. Senftleben, *supra* note 100, A. Kur, L. Bentley & A. Ohly, "Sweet Smells and a Sour Taste – The ECJ's L'Oreal Decision," Max Plank Institute for Intellectual Property, Competition and Tax law Research Paper Series No. 09-12.
102. "As I have said I do not agree with or welcome this conclusion – it amounts to a pointless monopoly. But my duty is to apply it." (L.J. Jacob, *L'Oreal SA v. Bellure NV, supra* note 78).
103. *L'Oreal SA v. Bellure NV & Ors* [2006] EWHC 2355 (Ch), Lewison J, para. 34.
104. *L'Oreal/Bellure,* paras. 14-21. *See also,* D. Gangjee & R. Burrell, *supra* note 12, 283-284.
105. *Kekofa BV v. Lancome Parfums et Beaute et Cie SNC* [2006] ECDR 26 (Hoge Raad) In France the issue was under discussions until Cassation Court made it clear, that in France

the U.K., where replicas of fragrance brands constitute a fourth category of legal perfume market.[106] It is not one hundred percent identical scents, but normally a very accurate imitation based on analysis of ingredients done by companies like Bellure.[107]

Judging only from the facts of the case, and ignoring the background academic discussions on justifications of the IP system in the light of economic benefits, one could think of the business model created by Bellure as an "unfair" one, since they were simply coping without creating or, as they say, "reaping without sowing."

Fortunately (or unfortunately), in law and policy we rarely talk about objective fairness. The main concern of legislators and policy makers is (or at least, shall be) what is beneficial for a given society or a state at a certain time. The same argument of social welfare is normally the reason for limitation of some rights when they cross over other basic interests of citizens.

Thus, when IP rights clash with the basic rights, the necessity arises to balance those interests. A typical example would be compulsory licensing of standard essential patents, where the interest of society in health or further innovation "beats" the patent rights.

In the *L'Oreal case,* the conflict was between the IP right holder's interest in a broader protection of his investments on the one hand, and consumer interest in free commercial speech and competition, through which they obtain wider array of choices and better prices, on the other. Each position, of course, has its own strong arguments, which will be scrutinized below. We will first look at the issue of imitation of packages and then proceed with the legal analysis of the comparison list of Bellure.

21.3.2   LEGALITY OF IMITATION AND FREE COMPETITION NECESSARY FOR EXERCISING THE RIGHT TO CONDUCT BUSINESS

Although imitation in many jurisdictions is accepted as a positive factor in the market and "the very lifeblood of a competitive economy,"[108] the general instinct among lawmakers and lawyers is often that it is unfair and shall be considered illegal.[109] Different jurisdictions refer to this phenomena as "reaping without sowing,"[110] "ploughing with someone else's calf,"[111]

---

no copyright protection is possible for perfume (Coir de Cassation, Ste Senteur Mazal/SA Beaute prestige international, July 1, 2008.

106. *L'Oreal SA v. Bellure NV & Ors* [2006] EWHC 2355 (Ch), Lewison J, para. 4.
107. *Ibid.*, para. 13.
108. US Supreme Court, *Bonito Boats, Inc. v. Thunder Craft Boats, Inc.*, 489 US 141, 146 (1989).
109. A. Ohly, *supra* note 11, 506.
110. US Supreme Court, *INS v. AP*, 248 US 215, 239-240 (1918).

"parasitic competition"[112] or "passing-off."[113] It is important to underline that, in most cases, imitation is actionable under unfair competition provisions and on the basis of consumer confusion or, at least, association. Despite general recognition of the positive effects of imitation for consumers, including price lowering, it seems to be wrong because the profits of the imitating company are undeserved and are made at the expense of the competitor.[114]

During the case hearing, Bellure's representative acknowledged that the packaging was "a wink of an eye to existing branded product" in order "to make it sell easily for those who recognize it."[115] Moreover, the defendant accepted that the products in "lookalike" packaging cost more than those in plain packaging.[116] Therefore, Bellure was simply exploiting something that was created and developed by L'Oreal relying on its power of attraction and gained prestige, without investing in its own marketing and not even compensating the IP owner.[117]

Hence, one of the arguments against so-called free-riding, is that "brand owners spend very large sums of money to promote and protect their brand" by different means, since they consider it to be a valuable intangible asset.[118] As a result, it is simply "unfair" when companies like Bellure later build their business without any investments in marketing, relying on success and reputation of famous brands. Nevertheless, this is more of a moral than a legal argument.

Another, more economic, argument would be that this kind of imitation can be harmful to further innovation in communication and marketing tools. According to J. Drexl and complementarity theory, competition law and Intellectual property law have the "common purpose of promoting competition and enhancing consumer welfare."[119] On the one hand, Intellectual property rights exist in order to incentivize and protect innovators, because, arguably, lack of protection will result in a mass imitation and unwillingness to innovate further. On the other hand, Competition law comes to the play

---

111. A. Lobe, "Der Hinweis auf fremde gewerbliche Leistung als Mittel zur Reklame" 1 (1916-1917) 16 Markenschutz und Wettbewerb 129, 129.

112. P. Tourneau, *Le Parasitisme,* (Litec 1998).

113. C. Wadlow, *The Law of Passing-Off: Unfair Competition by Misrepresentation*, (Sweet & Maxwell 2011).

114. A. Ohly, *supra* note 11, 507-508.

115. *L'Oreal SA v. Bellure NV & Ors* [2006] EWHC 2355 (Ch), Lewison J, paras. 36-37.

116. *Ibid.*, para. 60.

117. *L'Oreal/ Bellure*, para. 50, *see also*, A.A. Machnicka, "The Perfume Industry and Intellectual Property Law in the Jurisprudence of the Court of Justice and of National Courts" (2012) 43 IIC 123, 134.

118. *L'Oreal SA v. Bellure NV & Ors* [2006] EWHC 2355 (Ch), Lewison J, paras. 79-81.

119. J. Drexl, "Intellectual Property and Antitrust Law – IMS Health and Trinko – Antitrust Place for Consumers Instead of Sound Economics in Refusal-to Deal Cases" (2004) 35 IIC 788, 793.

when IP rights are so strong that the monopoly of an IP right holder restrains innovation by other competitors and creates market entry barriers.

But even when the competition rules prevail, the desired scenario is to have a "competition by substitution" and not "competition by imitation."[120] So, some element of novelty, addition or alternative must be there. Moreover, even when competition law interferes with the field of intellectual property rights by limiting them, like in the example of compulsory licensing, an IP right holder normally gets a compensation, which was not the case for L'Oreal.[121]

However, there is a good counter-argument to this point. As stated in previous sections, it is *mainly*, but not always that competition by imitation is not allowed. As already mentioned, many jurisdictions accept that imitation is positive for competitive market, necessary also for realizing one's right to business. If that is true, then the "threshold for justifying intellectual property rights is significantly higher [and] broad anti-dilution laws, for example, are more difficult to justify because consumer interests are only marginally affected and ... there is no evident need to create incentives for the creation of luxury images."[122]

So once again, it is consumer interest that matters in the first place. Beyond any doubts, consumers are the ones who benefit when, without misleading them, companies offer products similar to the known ones but for cheaper, with no added price for a luxurious brand. Consumers definitely did not benefit from the decision on *L'Oreal*, to the contrary, the "poor consumers are losers" in this case, according to Jacob LJ, because "they are denied ... the ability to buy a product for a euro or so which they know smells like a famous one."[123]

Thus, the restriction in imitation may lead to a "pointless monopoly,"[124] as a result of which competitors' basic right to conduct business is restricted, consumers lose and the brand owner is "overcompensated for its investment ... which did not involve a major degree of creativity." [125] Therefore, "price competition, at least, in this case, turns out to be much more vital than innovation."[126] Consequently, competition law rules and permission of imitation may become a good solution to the problem monopolization.[127]

---

120. J. Drexl, "Is There a "More Economic Approach" to Intellectual Property and Competition Law?" in J. Drexl (ed.) *Research Handbook on Intellectual Property and Competition Law* (Edward Elgar Publishing 2008), 47.
121. For the discussion of theory as applied to patent law cases *see* J. Drexl, *supra* note 119, especially at 793, 806.
122. A. Ohly, *supra* note 11, 507.
123. L.J. Jacob, *L'Oreal SA v. Bellure NV*, *supra* note 78, para. 14.
124. *Ibid.*, para. 50.
125. J. Drexl, but with regard to IMS Health case, *supra* note 119, 806.
126. *Ibid.*, 803.
127. *Ibid.*, 805.

Moreover, one may argue that L'Oreal and Bellure were not even proper competitors. According to the division of U.K.'s perfume market into four categories given by Lewison J, Bellure's products were on another, lower layer of the market.[128] The fact that Bellure was creating a new, "down-market" was also admitted by CJEU.[129] Therefore, the replicas are not meant for the same circle of consumers that are brand users, but for those who are not able to afford expensive perfumes and would like to use a legal smell-alike. And even more, if a brand is a specific lifestyle, with which one wants to be associated, arguably, the given brand's consumers will not buy a cheaper fragrance of a different producer, even if it smells similarly.

The logic of free competition benefiting all consumers can be traced in the decisions of the German Court that applied Unfair Competition law to cases of legal imitation. In the case involving cheap copies of Hermes handbags, the Supreme Court stated that the distinction between the cheap imitation and the genuine bag was so obvious that consumers will not be misled.[130] As Jacob LJ said, "consumers are not stupid [and] will not see the cheap copy as being the same quality as the original."[131]

The German Supreme Court added that a mere creation of association with a brand is not illegal. In the case of legal imitation of the famous Lego brick, the patent of which had expired, the Court announced that an entrance to the market shall not be prohibited, if a new-comer makes a clear labeling, even though he benefits from the prestige of the former dominator of the market.[132] Similarly, legal imitations of Lego bricks were allowed by the Italian Supreme Court.[133]

Therefore, in case of imitation, there is a clash between two contradicting goals: protection of IP rights, including trademarks, versus promotion of fair and healthy competition in the market. It is admitted that brands have the feature of attracting consumers and, thus, constitute a valuable asset of a proprietor.[134] Nevertheless, the value does not necessarily need an absolute legal protection resulting in a monopoly. Existence of competitors in the market is in the interest of consumers because it brings about price lowering and wider choice.

So, what is important, as a result, is to keep a *fair balance* between interests of IP rights holders and the needs of society, as it is provided in Articles 7 and 8(2) of the The Agreement on Trade-Related Aspects of Intellectual Property Rights (TRIPS) and Article 3(2) European Community

---

128. *L'Oreal SA v. Bellure NV & Ors* [2006] EWHC 2355 (Ch), Lewison J, para. 4.
129. *L'Oreal/Bellure*, para. 46.
130. 2007 GRUR 795 – Handtaschen.
131. L.J. Jacob, *L'Oreal SA v. Bellure NV, supra* note 78, para. 5[63].
132. 2005 GRUR 349 – Klemmbausteine III.
133. Italian Lego case, Supreme Court, February 28, 2008, No. 5437; *see also,* A. Ohly, *supra* note 11, 516.
134. D. Gangjee & R. Burrell, *supra* note 12, 288.

Enforcement Directive.[135] This balance shall supposedly be ensured from the very outset by the legislator in order to not leave much of discretion to judges.

However, currently in the EU, striking a fair balance between securing investments in brands and free competition is not possible due to the latest interpretation of Article 5(2) of the Directive given by CJEU. The Court stated that "taking unfair advantage" from famous trademarks is an infringement *per se* and no proof of harm is needed. Thus, even if as a result of an imitation there is no damage caused and consumers only benefit, the harmless act is still considered to be an infringement.

Being so generous to trademark proprietors, the Court left aside any possibility to balance interests based on the construction of the legal provision. The latter fact leads to the result that this balancing exercise has to be done on the later stage, i.e. by applying limitations and exceptions, as it was actually done by the Court itself in *Inteflora*.[136]

21.3.3 IP RIGHTS AND FREE COMMERCIAL SPEECH

The second issue in *L'Oreal/Bellure* was the list of some of L'Oreal's brand perfumes compared to their imitations as produced by Bellure.[137] Following the decision in *O2/Hutchison*, this kind of referential use of the marks was considered to be a comparative advertising, and, consequently, a use "in the course of trade" for the purposes of Article 5(1)(a) TMD. [138] Thus, the verdict of infringement based on double identity was unavoidable in this case, given that even a simple reference to a mark was considered to be a use as a trademark.

Thus, the list, which was clearly stating that the marks of L'Oreal were different from those of Bellure, was not misleading retailers as to the origin of the products (to the opposite, clarified the same), and was not even accessible to consumers, was, according to the Court, infringing the rights of L'Oreal. This is how, by interpreting almost any kind of use as a use "in the course of trade" necessary for alleging an infringement, the CJEU created the case law, which basically blocked any possibility of balancing IP rights with

---

135. Agreement on Trade-Related Aspects of Intellectual Property Rights, April 15, 1994, Marrakesh Agreement Establishing the World Trade Organization, Annex 1C, 2169 U.N.T.S. 299; 33 I.L.M. 1197 (1994); Directive 2004/48/EC of the European Parliament and of the Council on the enforcement of intellectual property rights, April 29, 2009, O.J. No. L.157, 30/04/2004, p. 45, *see also* A. Ohly, *supra* note 11, 510.
136. *Interflora/ Marks&Spancer*, paras. 91, *see also* M.R.F. Senftleben, "Freedom of Expression and Trademarks," presented at 14th EIPIN Congress, CEIPI, Strasbourg, April 7, 2013, video available at http://www.canalc2.tv/video.asp?idvideo=11765.
137. *L'Oreal/ Bellure*, para. 23.
138. *L'Oreal/ Bellure*, paras. 52-54.

other interests, such as free commercial speech, before looking at limitations and exceptions.[139]

Another option for balancing interests in investments with free speech based on legislation (besides having narrower interpretation of the use requirement), would be a strict interpretation of Article 5(1)(a) TMD by limiting it to only the cases when a confusion of consumers takes place.[140] However, as explained above, CJEU has blocked even this possibility and stated in the same *L'Oreal* that a proprietor is entitled to prevent a use of a trademark relying on the investment, communication and advertising function, even when consumers are not confused about origins of products.[141]

Therefore, as in the case of the interpretation of Article 5(2) TMD (analyzed above), for double identity cases, the Court left the balancing exercise to the later stage of application of limitations and exceptions or even external balancing tools.

In *L'Oreal/Bellure* itself, the balancing was done by referring to the Comparative Advertisement Directive[142]. Thus, according to the Court, in the case at stake, there were enhanced trademark rights of the brand owner, on the one hand, and the right to comparative advertisement (the list to the retailers?!), on the other. Based on Article 3a(1) of the Comparative Advertisement Directive, the Court decided that the comparison list was used presenting "goods ... as imitations or replicas" and was "taking unfair advantage" from the reputation of L'Oreal and, therefore, should be excluded from the permitted Comparative advertisement.[143]

Noticeably, here again, the argument on the side of trademark owner is mainly a moral one. One may argue that even if the imitations of smells were legal, Bellure, by mentioning and comparing them to the ones of L'Oreal, clearly wanted to gain an advantage from the good reputation of their established competitor. However, a very good counter-argument to that was given by Jacob LJ who mentioned that prevention of the use of trademarks in comparative advertisements is equal to not allowing one to speak the truth.[144]

Jacob LJ made further strong statement against the over-protective trademark approach elaborated in the EU, saying that "countries with a healthy attitude to competition law, such as the U.S., would not keep a perfectly lawful product off the market by the use of trade mark law to suppress truthful advertising."[145] Sir Jacob refers to the overweighting

---

139. M.R.F. Senftleben, "Freedom of Expression and Trademarks," presented at 14th EIPIN Congress, CEIPI, Strasbourg, April 7, 2013, video available at http://www.canalc2.tv/video.asp?idvideo=11765.
140. *Supra* note 93.
141. *L'Oreal/Bellure*, para. 65.
142. Directive 97/55/EC, OJ L 290/21, 23.10.97.
143. *L'Oreal/Bellure*, para. 80.
144. L.J. Jacob, *L'Oreal SA v. Bellure NV, supra* note 78, paras. 6-15.
145. *Ibid.*, para. 20.

freedom of speech. In Europe, the basis for a limitation of excessive trademarks is freedom of expression provided by Article 10 of European Convention of Human Rights and Article 11 of the Charter of European Union.[146]

Another related argument in support of the above, is the right of consumers to receive truthful and "commercially relevant" information.[147] As A. Kur, L. Bentley and A. Ohly argue, the CJEU was not bound to the strict wording of Article 3a(1) and should have tried to reconcile that provision with free commercial speech and consumers' interest in it.[148]

As CJEU has declared in its own previous decision in *Gillette*, information provided in a comparative way should be admissible and excluded from trademark protection "if that was the only way of conveying the relevant information to the public." [149]And, in fact, in *L'Oreal* it possibly was the only way, since, as Lewison J mentioned, "a smell is very difficult to define in words so that people in the trade often use the proprietary names of fragrances to describe them."[150]

Regardless of the above, Article 3a(1) of the Comparative Advertising Directive (CAD) suggests that advertising of a replica is always illegal, even if a reference is the only way to describe a product. Interestingly enough, A. Ohly and M. Spence suggest that the inclusion of the provision in the past, had exactly the purpose of providing a special protection for the perfume industry.[151]

The latter may seem to be justifiable, due to the specificity of the perfume industry where "magnetism is created not only by the chemical structure and composition of their ingredients, but even more so by the aura of beauty and luxury surrounding them."[152] There is an opinion in literature that *L'Oreal/Bellure* "should be principally read as perfume-specific"[153]. The perfume industry is very particular due to the involvement of long research, high cost of marketing and difficulty, or in some jurisdictions impossibility, of being protected by any IP rights other than the trademark.[154]

A. Machnicka claims that giving such a broad interpretation to the relevant provision and stretching the functions theory by the Court was necessary in order to provide at least this possibility of a trademark protection for the perfume industry, since the EU failed to harmonize Unfair

---

146. *See* A. Kur, L. Bentley, A. Ohly, *supra* note 101, 4.
147. *Ibid.*
148. *Ibid.*, 5.
149. CJEU, March 17, 2005, Case C-288/03, *Gillette/ L.A.-Laboratories*, paras. 24-39; A. Kur, L. Bentley & A. Ohly, *supra* note 101, 5.
150. *L'Oreal SA v. Bellure NV & Ors* [2006] EWHC 2355 (Ch), Lewison J, para. 14.
151. A. Ohly & M. Spence, *The Law of Comparative Advertising* (Hart Publishing 2000), 165.
152. A. Kur, L. Bentley & A. Ohly, *supra* note 101, 2.
153. A. Machnicka, *supra* note 117, 138.
154. *Ibid.*, 123-127.

Competition law, and Copyright protection for scents is only available in the Netherlands.[155]

The aura of luxury attached to perfume as a result of investments and efforts of a proprietor becomes an essential element of the product together with the physical good itself.[156] So, consumers are paying not only for the perfume as a physical product but also for the image related to it.

If one agrees with the above, then Bellure's replicas were not "perfectly lawful products" as Jacob LJ said, because, although, imitation of smell itself was legal, another element of the product, namely the image surrounding it, was stolen. Imitators "sell the luxury that they do not possess."[157]

However, regardless of the historical reasons, today the general Article 3a(1) CAD is obviously applicable not only to fragrances. Therefore, it is the courts' obligation to always balance the rule set in the provision with the basic freedom of expression[158] Otherwise, as Jacob LJ mentioned, it becomes a problematic issue for important sectors of advertising, such as generic drugs, for example, where the only way to do so is to refer to famous trademarks.[159]

Following the above, one may conclude that there are some good moral and economic arguments for prohibiting look-alike packaging, especially when it applies to perfume and luxury goods. However, it is very difficult to justify the illegality of comparative advertisement based on the trademark's functions theory when marks are named for a simple reference without causing any confusion. Barring such a use means prohibiting to speak freely in the course of one's business. "It is absurd to permit imitation but forbid advertising the imitating product." [160]

To summarize, as trademarks with reputation obtain wider protection in the EU, the monopolistic rights of their proprietors start clashing with some other interests such as competition rules or free commercial speech. Thus, the excessive protection of famous trademarks in the EU creates the "black hole" phenomenon, in which the named basic rights of competitors and consumers may fall. In order to avoid that, it is necessary to provide fair balancing between protection of investments and other important rights.

Presently, because of CJEU's interpretation of existing trademark legislation, the balancing is provided by limitations and exceptions applied to trademarks, which leaves too much legal uncertainty and discretion to the courts. Moreover, this kind of balancing sometimes results in arguably aggressively extended protection of famous trademarks in Europe, as it was demonstrated with the example of *L'Oreal/Bellure*. Consequently, the better

---

155. A. Machnicka, *supra* note 117, 137-157.
156. *Ibid.*, 135-137.
157. *Ibid.*
158. *Ibid.*, 5.
159. L.J. Jacob, *L'Oreal SA v. Bellure NV*, *supra* note 78, para. 16 [26].
160. V. Di Cataldo, *supra* note 16, note No. 23.

solution would be to perform the balancing exercise at an earlier stage, i.e. based on the correct interpretation of the legal provisions.

21.4   RECOMMENDATIONS

There are at least three possible alternatives for a reconciliation of the basic rights with trademarks. The first one is the most desirable solution because the recommendation hits to the core legislative provision on protection of well-known marks in Europe and, thus, leaves almost no space for uncertainty and judicial discretion. The second and third options are mainly recommending paying a closer attention to the wording of the existing provisions and improving the situation not by re-drafting them, but rather providing an adequate interpretation of some terms.

21.4.1   Removal of "Unfair Advantage" Element and Broader Interpretation of "Detriment to the Distinctiveness"

In order to overcome the issue of excessively expanded protection of trademarks with reputation and take into account the interests in free competition and commercial speech, the first recommendation would be to remove the third category of infringement in Article 5(2) TMD, namely, "taking unfair advantage," or, otherwise, not to interpret it as an infringement *per se*.

Although it may seem as a radical solution, it will not result in any decrease of investments in branding. Arguably, the necessary protection for investments can be provided by securing trademarks only from detriment to their repute and distinctiveness, if the latter will be better interpreted. "Taking unfair advantage," as it is understood at present, is partially fulfilling the functions of the blurring in a broader sense, and partially enters into the zone of Unfair Competition law, resulting in the unjustified overprotection not fitting in the limits of the trademark law.

Although CJEU rarely compares the European "detriment to the distinctive character or to the repute" to the U.S. dilution by blurring and tarnishment,[161] most academics clearly find parallels between them.[162] In fact, AG Jacobs has openly stated that detriment to the distinctiveness shall be considered equal to what is known as blurring, in the U.S., whereas detriment to the repute is another term for so-called tarnishment.[163] This is

---

161. The rare cases of comparison were in *Adidas/ Fitnessworld*, para. 37 and *SABEL/Puma*, para. 15.
162. J.T. McCarthy, *supra* note 20, 1165; Ch. Gielen, *supra* note 38, 716; P. Torremans, *supra* note 33, p. 128.
163. AG Jacobs, Opinion to *SABEL/Puma*, para. 39.

why, Article 5(2) of the Directive was always seen as an anti-dilution provision, including blurring and tarnishment.

When it comes to the "unfair advantage," however, its interpretation as a third, independent type of claim is questionable. Despite the attempt of AG Jacobs to give clarification to the notion, and even dividing it into two sub-categories,[164] it was not until the decision of CJEU in *Intel*,[165] that the Court clearly read the Article 5(2) TMD "disjunctively," enunciating that it comprises three, and not two, separate categories of infringement. [166]

However, the interpretation of Article 5(2) TMD as including three categories of infringement is quite doubtful. As D. Gangjee and R. Burell rightly mentioned, a complete and accurate disjunctive reading of the article would allow four (not three) kinds of claims: two based on detriment and two based on unfair advantage, in relation both to repute and distinctiveness.[167] However, CJEU itself considers *distinctiveness* and *repute* as two related objects from which competitors can take unfair advantage. Thus, if a consistent interpretation to Article 5(2) is applied, the provision should be read as including only two categories of dilution: (a) taking unfair advantage of distinctiveness or repute, i.e. blurring; and (b) detriment to distinctiveness or repute, i.e. tarnishment.[168]

Consequently, it is arguable that, the "unfair advantage" in the trademark law was meant to be equal to the same or similar term (parasitism, passing off, etc.) in unfair competition law. Instead, it should rather be understood as an action done by a competitor that eventually results in whitening out, eroding or blurring of the distinctive character and reputation of a famous trademark. The issue is rather a danger of eventual blurring of the luxury image developed by a brand, if a competitor is able to raise the same image in the minds of the consumers.

Thus, the result of "taking unfair advantage" is equal to blurring under the U.S. law and by proclaiming it an independent type of claim, or infringement *per se*, CJEU, arguably, misinterpreted Article 5(2) in *Intel*. The latter mistake was a good precondition for successful argumentation of L'Oreal in the case against Bellure[169] and the Court's application of the provision, which has been so much criticized.

Another, the second misinterpretation made by CJEU in the same *Intel*, which is also a reason for the current situation in the EU, is related to its understanding of detriment to distinctiveness.

So, if we ignore the first argument, stating that Article 5(2) TMD shall be read as giving a basis for only two types of claims, and follow CJEU's

---

164. AG Jacobs, Opinion in *Adidas/Fitnessworld*, para. 36.
165. *Intel/CPM,* para. 27.
166. D. Gangjee & R. Burrell, *supra* note 12, 287.
167. *Ibid.*, note No. 27.
168. *Ibid.*
169. *Ibid.*

"disjunctive" interpretation, the term that is equivalent to the U.S. "blurring" notion will be the "detriment to the distinctive character." However, even here, following the unnecessarily burdened interpretation of the Court on how the "detriment" shall be demonstrated, this type of infringement became much narrower than the "blurring" under the U.S. law. The standard to prove a detriment was raised by the case law so high that, in practice, is almost impossible.[170]

The classic understanding of dilution by blurring is when a sign that used to bring immediate association with a particular lifestyle, is not capable of doing so any more.[171] Although most of the examples in literature, are related to the use of a mark in relation to non-similar goods or services, such as "Rolls Royce" for restaurants or cafeterias,[172] according to CJEU's decisions in *Davidoff* and *Adidas*,[173] detriment to distinctive character may take place even when the sign is used for similar goods.[174] The latter is important in the light of this Chapter and the facts of *L'Oreal*.

In paragraph 77 of *Intel*, CJEU has unexpectedly established a new rule of evidence for proving detriment to the distinctive character of trademarks.[175] According to the Court, so-called blurring in Europe can now be claimed only if a trademark proprietor is able to demonstrate *"a change in economic behavior of the average consumer of the goods or services for which the earlier mark was registered consequent on the use of the later mark, or a serious likelihood that such a change will occur in the future."* This new requirement resulted in a significant amount of academic debate given that such kind of economic evidence is very difficult to prove.[176]

Thus, "unfortunately for trademark owners," the threshold to prove the detriment to distinctiveness has been significantly raised by CJEU in *Intel*.[177] The problematic character of this high standard became obvious very soon afterward, during its application by the Dutch courts.[178] Further, the CJEU itself, arguably, was limited to its own boundaries as established in *Intel* and had to circumvent the same in *L'Oreal*. Therefore, the unjustifiably broad interpretation of "unfair advantage" and the elaboration of the "coat-tail

---

170. B. Beebe, *supra* note 75, 58.
171. *Intel/CPM*, para. 29.
172. Hearings before the House Comm. on Patents, 72d Cong., 1st Sess.15 (1932), statement of Frank Schecter, quoted in D.S. Welkowitz, "Reexamining Trademark Dilution" (1991) 44 Vand. L. Rev. 531, 539.
173. CJEU January 9, 2003, Case C-292/00, *Davidoff/Gofkid*, para. 30, *Addidas/Fitnessworld*, para. 22.
174. M.H.H. Luepke, *supra* note 19, 811.
175. *Intel/CPM*, para. 77.
176. Ch. Gielen, *supra* note 38, 721.
177. M. Rijsdijk & M. Antic, *supra* note 32, 55.
178. *See G-Star Raw v. Pepsi Raw*, The Hague District Court, December 15, 2008, Intellectuele Eigendom en Reclamerecht 2009/9; Huis & Hypotheek, Case No. HA ZA 08-96, Leeuwarden District Court, April 29, 2009.

formula" was a cry for help and a tool to circumvent a very heavy burden of proof.[179]

Some authors try to argue that the correct reading of the *Intel* decision does not require trademark owners to actually prove the change in economic behavior of consumers. Instead, the Court meant that as long as a proprietor is able to demonstrate that his mark is diluted and the similar sign is associated in minds of consumers with the trademark of the owner, there is a risk of change in the consumers' choice as a logical consequence.[180]

This kind of reading of *Intel* would have been the desirable one. Nonetheless, it seems like the Court is insisting on having the strict interpretation of blurring in the EU. In its recent decision CJEU held that "*the concept of 'change in the economic behavior of the average consumer' lays down an objective condition [and] ... the mere fact that consumers note the presence of a new sign similar to an earlier sign is not sufficient of itself to establish the existence of a detriment or a risk of detriment to the distinctive character.*"[181]

As a result of the above-mentioned development, in practice, trademark owners are advised to base their claim related to the repute and distinctive character on the "unfair advantage" provision rather than relying on the detriment to distinctiveness that was so frequently used before the *Intel* decision.[182]

As M.R.F. Senftleben correctly explains, it is very important to understand that the main concern in cases of dilution "is not the whitening away or dispersion of the mark's capacity to distinguish (distinctiveness), but free riding on and gradual erosion of the marks power of attraction (repute)."[183] Therefore, in blurring, as well as in "free riding" cases, the main danger is not that consumers will not see the link between goods and well-known trademarks any more, but rather that a trademarks will stop attracting them due to the eventual loss of *uniqueness*.

The same is true for the "detriment to distinctive character" claim under the EU law, as well as the concept of taking unfair advantage. So, the difference between the two types of claim in Europe is only that there is a better chance of success under the "taking unfair advantage," which doesn't require a proof of change in economic behavior of the consumer, and can be invoked based on a simple claim that a third party attempts to "ride on coat-tail" of a repute.

Therefore, CJEU's broad interpretation of "taking unfair advantage" is partially trying to fill the gap that appeared after its own misinterpretation of the blurring concept in *Intel*. In fact, in the issue of similar packaging,

---

179. M.R.F. Senftleben, *supra* note 63, 153, note 54.
180. Ch. Gielen, *supra* note 38, 721.
181. CJEU, November 14, 2013, Case C-383/12 P, *Environmental Manufacturing/OHIM*.
182. M. Rijsdijk & M. Antic, *supra* note 32, 55.
183. M.R.F. Senftleben, *supra* note 24, 70.

L'Oreal could have based its argumentation on the "detriment to distinctiveness," because eventually consumers will stop associating those special bottle shapes and boxes with the lifestyle and luxury aura created by L'Oreal's marketing. The argument might have or have not succeed at the later stage of balancing with due cause defense, but would definitely be within the legally predictable trademark concept of blurring. The Court's reasoning, however, has instead artificially stretched the vague notion of "free riding" due to the fact that it was not possible to rely on the heavily burdened claim of detriment to distinctiveness.

The other part of the "unfair advantage" element, as it is interpreted by CJEU, is conflicting with, and interfering in the field of unfair competition law. "Arguably, unfair advantage has more in common with unfair competition law than dilution."[184]

It is important to mention, the whole structure of Article 5 TMD suggests that the anti-dilution provisions, as well as all other harmonized rules enunciated in Articles 5(1)-5(4), apply only to the use of a sign as a trademark.[185] Any other use (such as use in comparative list, for instance), which has no purpose of identifying source of goods and services, even when it is detrimental to distinctiveness, repute or is constitutive of a free-riding, should be regulated according to the rules left to the discretion of the member states. In many EU member states this kind of use is governed by unfair competition law.[186]

One may question whether it makes a difference if a sign is protected against free riding by the Trademark law or by the Unfair Competition law. The answer is "yes," because in unfair competition law, "the test will be "Are you lying to or misleading the plaintiff's consumers?," rather than "Are you ridiculing the plaintiff's trademark? The difference is subtle but important."[187] There are also background reasons making the difference essential.

As mentioned above, Unfair Competition law in the EU is not harmonized. The reason for the painful history and eventual failure[188] lies in the tremendous difference between some rules of competition in the Member States. One of the significant disagreements is related to imitation and look-alike products. In France, for example, parasitic competition is prohibited *per se*, whereas in common law countries, that kind of competition is not necessarily considered unfair even if it is at the expense of the competitor; and Germany has a position somewhere in between those two.[189]

The clash between the attitudes toward slavish imitation is based on preferences given to either the interests of consumers (in common law

---

184. I.S. Fhima, *supra* note 41, 190.
185. M.R.F. Senftleben, *supra* note 63, 163.
186. *Ibid.*
187. A. Banerjee, *supra* note 79, 565.
188. C. Wadlow, *supra* note 55, 469.
189. A. Ohly, *supra* note 11, 508; *see also* F. Henning-Bodewig, *Unfair Competition Law: European Union and Member States* (Kluwer Law International 2006), 2.

countries) or the interests of producers (for instance, France).[190] Although those interests may most of the time co-exist, in particular cases, such as the case of *L'Oreal/Bellure*, they come into conflict. And that is exactly the moment when a member state is given the discretion to balance the interests according to the values prevailing in the country.

Thus, the lack of harmonized rules of Unfair Competition law was, arguably, a result of the desire of the member states to keep their policy with regard to unfair competition rules. Perhaps the excessive protection of perfume producers in France makes sense due to the specificity and importance of the industry in that country. In the U.K., where look-alike products are common things to buy in supermarkets, the same strict rule would be considered as depriving consumers of wider choice and better prices. Interestingly enough, at the time of discussions on harmonized rules for the EU "there was widespread agreement that the Franco-German 'classical model' of unfair competition law, defined solely by reference to the interests of competitors *inter se*, required revision to take into account the interests of consumers and other market participants."[191]

Therefore, it seems like CJEU has brought to the European level the rule against free riding, which countries such as U.K. were resisting, through the back door of the trademark law. Moreover, the broad interpretation of the trademark use concept provided by the Court for the purposes of comparative advertising, brings gradually the "non-harmonized unfair competition law under the umbrella of harmonized EU trademark law."[192] Taking into account the differences between the national legislations and traditions, "the level of protection against pure misappropriation in European Community law is surprisingly high."[193]

The problem with including the "unfair advantage" clause to the Trademark law, instead of the Unfair Competition law, is not only that the member states are deprived their discretion. The issue is also that the trademark rules are based on property rights, whereas unfair competition law considers cases from the perspective of fairness of behavior in the market.

Consequently, based on the current understanding of "unfair advantage" as a trademark infringement, there is clash between two fundamental rights – property rights versus free competition or free commercial speech. On the other side, as a category of Unfair competition law, "unfair advantage" is not able to invoke such a strong counter balance as property rights and is rather a flexible category.

Accordingly, it is not excluded that even in a jurisdiction where imitation is not welcomed, such as Germany, for example), *L'Oreal* could have been analyzed and decided differently under the rules of the Unfair

---

190. D. Gangjee & R. Burrell, *supra* note 12, 294.
191. C. Wadlow, *supra* note 55, 441.
192. M.R.F. Senftleben, *supra* note 63, 176.
193. A. Ohly, *supra* note 11, 516.

Competition law. For instance, in the case involving well-known perfumes and their cheap imitations with names directly associated with brands, the German Supreme Court stated that "vague association" is not sufficient for an obvious message to the consumers that the product is an imitation, which is a necessary requirement for the advertising being unlawful.[194]

Imitation that misleads and confuses consumers should obviously be prohibited.[195] However, there are cases when unfair advantage taken from the rival without confusing purchasers brings about positive results and advantage for the consumers.[196] The need for a proper competition and lawful free trade will always involve an element of some "free riding."[197] Following this idea, in the case of *Siemens/VIPA*, the CJEU recognized that although VIPA took an advantage of Siemens's reputation by using the same serial numbers, it was beneficial for the consumers, since it helped to easily search compatible products in the market.[198]

Therefore, since IP law is normally very inflexible and "follows a 'one size fits all' logic,"[199] in some cases, such as free-riding, where an effective balancing of interests is necessarily based on the circumstances of each case, the rules of unfair competition law should not be transposed to the trademark law. Trademark law has been expanded dramatically, hardly leaving some space for free competition or comparative advertising.[200] Therefore, the small loopholes that were left should be considered as breathing space and interpreted less restrictively. Unfair competition law, arguably, is more elastic in that sense, and would take into account not only the interests of trademark proprietors, but also consumers' interest in free competition. [201]

To sum up, the first recommendation in order to reconcile protection of investments with free competition and free commercial speech, which are beneficial for consumers, is an "internal solution"[202] to remove the element of "taking unfair advantage" from Article 5(2) TMD.[203] The functions that the provision now fulfils can be partially covered by the notion of "detriment to distinctive character" (if the restriction of "change in economic behavior of the consumers" is removed) and partially regulated by the more flexible rules of unfair competition law. The interpretation of "unfair advantage," as given by CJEU in *L'Oreal/Bellure*, is overwhelming, giving the hardly

---

194. German Federal Supreme Court, December 6, 2007 – I ZR 169/04, 2008 GRUR, 628; *see also*, B. Clark, "'Cool Water' and 'Icy Cold': Comparative Advertising for Perfume Imitations Though the Use of Allusive Product Names" (2008) J. Intell. Prop. L. & Prac. 688, A.A. Machnicka, *supra* note 117, 139.
195. A. Ohly, *supra* note 11, 513.
196. *Ibid.*, 517.
197. L.J. Jacob, *supra* note 78, para. 16 [27].
198. CJEU, C-59/05, 2006, ECR I-2147, *Siemens/VIPA*, paras. 22-26.
199. A. Ohly, *supra* note 11, 522.
200. V. Di Cataldo, *supra* note 16, 844.
201. *See*, A. Ohly, *supra* note 11, 523.
202. R. Burrell & D. Gangjee, *supra* note 14, 545.
203. For the similar opinion *see* R. Burrell & D. Gangjee, *supra* note 14, note 51.

justifiable all-embracing protection to brands, which restrains free competition and free commercial speech in the market.

21.4.2   CORRECT INTERPRETATION OF THE TERMS "UNFAIR" AND "WITHOUT DUE CAUSE" AS THE ALTERNATIVE WAYS OUT

The second option for restoring the balance with the clashing fundamental rights described above requires a closer look at, and a proper interpretation of the term "unfair advantage." Although CJEU clearly stated that the reason for the verdict was that Bellure was taking advantage *unfairly* from L'Oreal, the analysis seems to imply that any free-riding would always be "unfair" and no "fair advantage" is possible.[204] However, the wording of the provision – taking *unfair* advantage – suggests that there must be also a fair advantage.[205]

Thus, not every advantage is illegal, and even when a use of a sign has the aim to raise an association with a senior trademark, one should "take into account the benefit to consumers."[206] But since the concept is subjective and creates a higher risk of discretion,[207] the exact meaning and limits of "unfairness" should be defined for the sake of legal certainty.

Thus, arguably, according to the wording of Article 5(2) TMD, taking advantage is not prohibited as such.[208] Jacob LJ proposes that in order to be unfair the advantage should result in a harm caused to a trademark owner.[209] So, imitation shall not be prohibited as such, but only under the circumstance that it is causing some harm.[210] The same is applicable to comparative advertising.

Following this logic, AG Mengozzi, came up with a very useful two-step test: (1) the court shall identify whether a competitor is taking any advantage by raising an association with a well-known brand in the minds of consumers and (2) if yes, then the court shall assess whether that advantage is unfair.[211] Further, the AG provides a list of factors, which should be taken in to account in evaluating "fairness," including interests of consumers.

Thus, in each case, it should be decided individually, based on the facts and circumstances, if the advantage was fair or unfair.[212] Moreover, the word "unfair" shall be read narrowly with regard to comparative advertising, since

---

204. D. Meale & J. Smith, "Enforcing a Trade Mark When Nobody's Confused: Where the Law Stands after L'Oreal and Intel" (2010) 5 J. Intell. Prop. L. & Prac. 96, 103.
205. T. Cohen et al. (eds), *European Trademark Law: Community Trademark Law and Harmonized National Trademark Law* (Kluwer Law International 2010), 313.
206. AG Mengozzi, Opinion of January 31, 2008, Case C-533/06, *O2/Hutchison,* para. 55.
207. I.S. Fhima, "Trade Mark and Free Speech," (2013) 44 IIC 293, 303.
208. A. Ohly, *supra* note 11, 519.
209. L.J. Jacob, *supra* note 78, 90-94.
210. A. Ohly, *supra* note 11, 519.
211. AG Mengozzi, *supra* note 46, paras. 74-75.
212. *Ibid.,* para. 76.

it is inherent in the phenomena of comparative advertising and the latter is encouraged in the Union.[213]

Although, Jacob LJ argues that in *L'Oreal*, there was no harm to the brand, because none of the consumers attracted by the luxury image will change their preferences to a cheap replica and, even more, because telling the truth is not harmful,[214] EU Intellectual Property Office's (EUIPO) Board of Appeal tried to support CJEU's opinion by stating that free-riding is "unfair since the reward for the costs of promoting, maintaining and enhancing a particular trade mark should belong to the owner of the earlier trade mark in question."[215] Differently from EUIPO, CJEU does not even try to give a justification for the brand protection in the absence of any harm.

Unfortunately, CJEU's answer to the issue of "unfair advantage" both under the Comparative Advertising Directive and the Trademark Directive was unhelpful.[216] The Court has declared that taking advantage is harmful *per se* and no proof of damage is necessary.[217] After *L'Oreal/Bellure*, free riding became actionable as such, which is not the case in the U.S., as mentioned above[218]

As a result of the "harmless' concept of free riding"[219] developed by the Court, Europe is in the situation, where a producer of goods with a quality similarly good as one of some famous brands but more affordable prices, who does not try to mislead consumers as to the source if his products, faces significant barriers to enter the market. What do we try to protect then? A monopoly on a sign which is difficult to justify economically?! The problem with making the "free riding on a coat tail" of a competitor actionable *per se* is "that it provides a remedy without a supportable theorization of the harm."[220]

Not surprisingly, application of the "infringement automatism created in *L'Oreal/Bellure*" was problematic in subsequent cases of the Court itself, especially those including keyword advertising.[221] In the opinion of *Inteflora/Marks & Spencer*, AG Jaasiken, suggests a change from the "coat-tail formula" of CJEU to the fairness test.[222] Following this suggestion, the recommendation would be that even if Article 5(2) is going to stay as it is, including unfair advantage as an independent infringement, the courts

---

213. *Ibid. See also* J. Box, *supra* note 61, 491-492.
214. L.J. Jacob, *supra* note 78, para. 15.
215. *Mango Sport System v. Diknak* (R 308/2003-1) [2005] ETMR 5, para. 19.
216. J. Box, *supra* note 61, 492.
217. D. Gangjee & R. Burrell, *supra* note 12, 289.
218. *Ibid.*, 287.
219. M.H.H. Luepke, *supra* note 19, 816.
220. H. Farley, "Why We Are Confused about Trade Mark Dilution Law" (2006) 16 Fordham IP Media & Ent. L.J. 1175, 1214.
221. M.R.F. Senftleben, *supra* note 63, 159.
222. AG Jaaskinen, Opinion of March 24, 2011, Case C-323/09, *Interflora/Marks & Spencer,* paras. 104-105, *see also* M.R.F. Senftleben, *supra* note 63, 159.

should apply it not as such, without proof of any harm, but rather focusing on the fairness requirement. This is how the necessary balancing of interests of producers and consumers can be provided at least at the level of application of the legal provisions. This is the second possible internal solution.

However, CJEU did not follow the recommendation of AG Jaasiken. Instead of weakening the infringement criteria, the Court found the way out of the situation through the application of limitations to the rule.[223] Therefore, the balancing exercise was done at the last stage, after the application of the general rule. Consequently, other interests, such as basic freedoms or principle of free movements of goods, may outweigh the rights of trademark owners also as a "due cause" defense.[224] Although, this solution is less desirable due to legal uncertainty, it does provide for the third possible way to overcome the current situation of the "black hole" created by the trademarks' overprotection.

Initially the "due cause" defense was introduced for the cases of a trademark use in a narrow sense.[225] Based on the solely commercial need of competition to use a sign, EUIPO for a long time was following the rule developed by the Benelux court.[226] In *Claeryn /Klarein*, the Court declared that the "due cause" could be a defense only if the use of a sign is outside of the control or the defendant had an earlier right.[227] However, the recent CJEU decision in *Red Bull*,[228] makes it clear that the due cause defense is now available not only for objective need to use a sign, but also for subjective reasons if they are made in a good faith.[229]

The unforeseeable need for the *wider* "due cause" defense arose only after CJEU's elaboration on trademark use concept, which now includes decorative and referential use. [230] This broad interpretation entails a potential danger for clashes of the trademark owner's rights with artistic freedom or freedom of expression in cases such as comparative advertising or parody, as argued throughout this article.[231]

There is a large number of academic works, proposing to balance the basic right of free speech with property rights in trademark.[232] However, the question still remains whether free speech and other basic principles could be used as an external tool, guaranteed by a Constitution or other high hierarchy legal documents, or if, instead, it should be recognized as one of the

---

223. *Ibid.*, 159
224. M.H.H. Luepke, *supra* note 19, 13.
225. M.R.F. Senftleben, *supra* note 63, 167.
226. *Hollywood v. Hollywood*, Case R 283/1999-3, OHIM Board of Appeal, April 25, 2001.
227. Case A74/1, *Claeryn/Klarein* 472 (1975).
228. CJEU, February 6, 2014, Case C-65/12, *Leidseplein/Red bull,* para. 60.
229. Ch. Gielen, *supra* note 38, 727-728.
230. M.R.F. Senftleben, *supra* note 63, 168-169.
231. *Ibid.*, 170.
232. *See* I.S. Fhima, *supra* note 207, R. Burrell & D. Gangjee, *supra* note 14.

limitations to the trademark protection within the notion of "due cause" and, therefore, become an internal tool of balancing.[233] Although, in practice, CJEU already tried to use external balancing tools of harmonized legislation in cases involving comparative advertising,[234] there are at least several good reasons for advocating the second option, i.e., introducing free speech as a due cause to limit the rights of trademark proprietors.

First, arguably, commercial courts are very reluctant in applying constitutional provisions to their cases.[235] This argument is even stronger in the EU, if one agrees with the statement that "freedom of speech is more strongly protected against Government regulations in the United States, than it is, say, in Germany and under the ECHR."[236] Second, trademark is a property right also protected by constitutions and, thus, free speech loses the ability to trump it.[237]

Moreover, speech has different categorizations, including artistic, political, commercial one, and the latter is typically given less protection.[238] Since commercial speech is the one used by competitors in the market, the likelihood to overweigh the trademark rights will always be questionable.[239] Last but not least, although there are examples of successful cases where the rights of a trademark owner were limited based on Constitutional rights,[240] this possibility is not flexible and will always depend on the existence of specific provisions in external basic laws.

Consequently, "shifting the debate [on balancing rights] onto the plane of constitutional principle offers little promise and some risk."[241] The risk is mainly attached to non-flexibility and legal uncertainty.[242] Although, the issue of legal certainty cannot be solved even by introduction of internal trademark limitations, the "due cause" defense is undoubtedly a better solution with regard to flexibility concern.

Taking into account the development of technologies and the potential need for use of a brand, for instance, in cultural, teaching or research purposes, "an open-ended" due cause notion is better because it provides more elasticity.[243] Comparable to the U.S. fair use

---

233. *Ibid.*, 545.
234. O2/Hutchison and L'Oreal/Bellure, *see also* M.R.F. Senftleben, *supra* note 63, 170.
235. R. Burrell & D. Gangjee, *supra* note 14, 599.
236. E. Barendt, *Freedom of Speech* (2nd ed., OUP 2007), 54.
237. R. Burrell & D. Gangjee, *supra* note 14, 599.
238. C. Ovey & J. White, *Jacobs and White: The European Convention on Human Rights* (4th ed., OUP 2006), 319-320.
239. R. Burrell & D. Gangjee, *supra* note 14, 599.
240. German Federal Court of Justice, February 3, 2005, Case I ZR 159/02, Lila Postkarte, Gewerblicher Rechtschutz und Urhberrecht 2005, 583 and *Laugh it Off Promotions v. South African Breweries International (Finance) BV t/a Sabmark International*, [2206], (1)SA 144 (CC).
241. R. Burrell & D. Gangjee, *supra* note 14, 569.
242. *Ibid.*, 563-564.
243. M.R.F. Senftleben *supra* note 63, 171-173.

defense,[244] the due cause, as an alternative, can become a very good balancing tool. The defense should include such important interests as free speech, artistic freedom, free movement of goods, but not be limited to them.[245]

The use of a particular sign can be necessary in order to be able to communicate with consumers, to let them know what kind of product is being offered.[246] There are many cases when it is objectively impossible to communicate without referring to a trademark. A good example is the device with the registered trademark name "Segway" (a platform on two wheels moving with the power of battery and able to carry a standing person at the speeds up to 20 km/hour), which cannot be described otherwise but by naming the trademark.[247]

The same applies to perfumes. Normally, one cannot describe it and, instead, would simply name specific trademark.[248] Therefore, arguably, Bellure was merely communicating with retailers by providing the comparative list.[249] The latter should be allowed within the notion of free commercial speech as a due cause.

Interestingly enough, the condition that an unfair advantage shall take place *"without due cause"* in order to result in an infringement, was for a long time ignored by CJEU.[250] V. Di Cataldo argues that such an "overlooking" and lack of attention was done by the Court with the intent of focusing on extending rather than limiting rights of trademark holders. The author correctly states that "by ignoring the formula 'without due cause' in the interpretation of Article 5(2) of the Directive, we run the risk of upsetting the balance of the law … [and] grant excessive space to the exclusive right."[251] The whole idea of having a negative condition of "due cause" in the provision is to keep the balance and limit excessive rights of trademark

---

244. *Ibid.*, 172; *see also* M.R.F. Senftleben, "Comparative Approaches to Fair Use: An Important Impulse for Reforms in EU Copyright Law" (2013) in G.B. Dinwoodie (ed.) *Methods and Perspectives in Intellectual Property* (Edward Elgar Publishing 2014), 27-28.
245. Important to mention, that "due cause" defense is only available to TMs with reputation, which are subject of this thesis. However, another unsolved issue is balancing of interests, such as freedom of speech, with right in non-famous trademarks. M.R.F. Senftleben proposes inclusion of fair use like defense as an open-ended limitation not only for TM with reputation, but also all other exclusive rights.
246. V. Di Cataldo, *supra* note 16, 838.
247. *Ibid.*, 839-840.
248. *Ibid.*, 841.
249. Important to mention, that while use of the TM name in comparative advertising can be considered as a free speech defense, use of shapes or colors that are registered as TM is difficult to justify as "due cause," because there is no strong necessity to do so. (V. Di Cataldo, *supra* note 16, 839).
250. V. Di Cataldo, *supra* note 16, 834.
251. *Ibid.*, 835.

owners. "There is no reason to consider these interests worthy of prevailing over all possible interests of a third party to use the trade mark."[252]

Consequently, as the last, third option for reconciling interests in investments and consumers' welfare, it is recommended to pay closer attention to the limitation, which is already provided in the law. Although, this option is the least desirable from the point of view of legal certainty, it definitely ensures some flexibility for unforeseeable situations in the future.

All that has to be done is to provide a better interpretation of the phrase "due cause," which should include such significant overweighting rights and interests as free speech, free competition, free movement of goods, but not be limited to them. Without such a balance, owners of trademarks with reputation obtain a total monopoly in the market, which becomes a barrier to newcomers, reduces the accuracy of communication and changes the economic behavior of consumers.[253] Therefore, instead of maintaining the law without a rationale, as it was done in 2017 when the new EUTM Regulation was adopted, it is important to amend it, or – in this case – its interpretation.[254]

21.5   CONCLUSION

To summarize, the trademark protection in EU has reached the point when it is over-protective and started to pose a danger on the other basic rights, such as free speech and conducting free business entailing the need for free competition. The current situation is the result of CJEU's misinterpretation of existing legal provisions. Hence, the EU needs a better balance of the conflicting interests.

As a solution, it is recommended, to remove the option of "taking unfair advantage" from being an independent claim for an infringement. For this to be effective, the "detriment to distinctive character" should not be limited to the cases where the economic behavior of consumers changes and must be interpreted in a broader manner.

As the second alternative, the focus shall be made on "fairness" and harm (which is "unfair"), as important pre-conditions to invoke the anti-dilution law. And the last option would be to stop ignoring the existing negative condition of a "due cause" in the relevant provision and to cover by this defense important principles and basic rights as a justification for limitations of excessive protection of famous trademarks in Europe.

---

252. *Ibid.*
253. *Ibid.*
254. *Ibid.*, 836.

Chapter 22

Algorithmic Enforcement Online

Giancarlo Frosio

22.1   INTRODUCTION: TOWARDS ALGORITHMIC
          ENFORCEMENT

Artificial Intelligence (AI) is increasingly and pervasively affecting society. AI and algorithms play a relevant role in the Intellectual Property (IP) discourse as well. Tomorrow, algorithms will, of course, come as creators and innovators but today they are already here as enforcers. Content sanitization online will soon – and inevitably – become the sole domain of algorithmic enforcement tools. This process towards algorithmic enforcement online has been characterized by a few important recent developments.

First, emerging regulatory framework, new legislative obligations and judicial trends would like to force online intermediaries to implement architectural changes leading to sanitization of allegedly infringing content – possibly legit freedom of expression – by design. Given the unsustainable transaction costs related to manual checking of the infringing content and linking to infringing content, online intermediaries will be forced to deploy algorithmic tools to perform monitoring and filtering and limit their liability. In this context, as Lessig and others have explained, the code is the law of cyberspace.[1] Therefore, enforcement can become implicit by modifying the architecture of the Internet.[2]

Second, as a consequence, algorithmic enforcement brings about the privatization of enforcement and delegation of public authority. Automated and algorithmic copyright enforcement implies a number of policy choices, which are operated by platforms and right holders and subject freedom of expression and online cultural participation to a new layer of 'private ordering'.[3] In practice, automated filtering determines online behaviour far more 'than whether that conduct is, or is not, substantively in compliance with copyright law'.[4] A legal system switching the liability equilibrium on online intermediaries – which can more than any other manipulate Internet architecture – can actually lead to fundamental architectonical changes to limit that liability. This process might likely bring about pervasive over enforcement, which becomes invisible and leads users to get accustomed to a highly censored online ecosystem.

Third, in online enforcement of intellectual property – as well as any other content sanitization – algorithms take decisions reflecting policy's assumptions and interests that have very significant consequences to society at large, yet there is limited understanding of these processes.

Finally, but critically for the focus of our investigation, Online Service Providers' (OSPs) regulatory choices – occurring through algorithmic tools – can profoundly affect the enjoyment of users' fundamental rights, such as freedom of expression, freedom of information and right to privacy and data protection. Therefore, human right protection lies at the core of any policy debate regarding OSPs' algorithmic IP enforcement.[5] In this context, tensions have been highlighted between algorithmic enforcement and the European Convention of Human Rights (ECHR) and the Charter of Fundamental

---

1. *See* Lawrence Lessig, *The Code and Other Laws of Cyberspace* (Basic Books 1999) 3-60; William Mitchell, *City of Bits: Space, Place, and the Infobahn* (MIT Press 1995) 111.
2. *See* Joel Reidenberg, 'Lex Informatica: The Formulation of Information Policy Rules Through Technology' (1998) 76 Texas L Rev 553.
3. *See* Matthew Sag, 'Internet Safe Harbors and the Transformation of Copyright Law' (2017) 93 Notre Dame L Rev 1.
4. *Ibid*
5. On the increasing influence of human and fundamental rights on the resolution of IP disputes, *see* Christophe Geiger, 'Constitutionalising Intellectual Property Law?, The Influence of Fundamental Rights on Intellectual Property in Europe' (2006) 37(4) IIC 371; 'Fundamental Rights as Common Principles of European (and International) Intellectual Property Law' in Ansgar Ohly (ed), *Common Principles of European Intellectual Property Law* (Mohr Siebeck 2012) 223; 'Reconceptualizing the Constitutional Dimension of Intellectual Property' in Paul Torremans (ed), *Intellectual Property and Human Rights* (Kluwer Law International 2015) 115; 'Implementing Intellectual Property Provisions in Human Rights Instruments: Towards a New Social Contract for the Protection of Intangibles' in Christophe Geiger (ed), *Research Handbook on Human Rights and Intellectual Property* (Edward Elgar 2015) 661.

Rights of the European Union (EC Charter),[6] with special emphasis on filtering and monitoring measures, which would fail to strike a 'fair balance' between IP and other fundamental rights.[7]

This Chapter will map the complex conundrum triggered by algorithmic enforcement in the IP domain with special emphasis on copyright and trademark enforcement online.[8] In doing so, this chapter, first, briefly explains what algorithmic enforcement online actually is. Second, this chapter will dig into voluntary, judicial and legislative measures that have been promoting the emergence of algorithmic enforcement online. Third, this chapter will assess tensions between algorithmic enforcement and human rights, including due process, freedom of information, freedom expression, privacy and freedom of business. In conclusion, this chapter will discuss solutions for protecting human rights form algorithmic enforcement negative externalities.

22.2   WHAT IS ALGORITHMIC ENFORCEMENT?

AI refers to 'the theory and development of computer systems able to perform tasks normally requiring human intelligence, such as visual perception, speech recognition, *decision-making*, and translation between languages'.[9] Semi or fully independent decision-making lies at the core of AI revolutionary promises. This, however, brings about fundamental changes in enforcement.[10] On one side, authority shift, automation and centralization

---

6. *See* Convention for the Protection of Human Rights and Fundamental Freedoms (European Convention on Human Rights, as Amended) [1950] (hereafter ECHR); Charter of Fundamental Rights of the European Union 2012 OJ (C 326) 391 (hereafter 'EU Charter').
7. *See* Joan Barata and Marco Bassini, 'Freedom of Expression in the Internet: Main Trends of the Case Law of the European Court of Human Rights' in Oreste Pollicino and Graziella Romeo (ed), *The Internet and Constitutional Law: The Protection of Fundamental Rights and Constitutional Adjudication in Europe* (Rutledge 2016); *Akdeniz v. Turkey*, App no 20877/10, 11 March 2014; C-314/12, *UPC Telekabel Wien* [2014] EU:C:2014:192 (hereafter *UPC Telekabel*); C-360/10, *Belgische Vereniging van Auteurs, Componisten en Uitgevers CVBA (SABAM) v. Netlog NV* [2012] ECLI:EU:C:2012:85, § 36-38 (hereafter '*Netlog*'); Stefan Kulk and Frederik Zuiderveen Borgesius, 'Filtering for Copyright Enforcement in Europe after the Sabam Cases' (2012) 34 EIPR 791, 791-94; Evangelia Psychogiopoulou, 'Copyright Enforcement, human rights protection and the responsibilities of internet service providers after Scarlet' (2012) 34 EIPR 552, 555.
8. However, similar considerations – especially in connection to due process, privatized and automated decision making – can be applied *mutatis mutandis* to automated trademark and patent enforcement offline.
9. Artificial Intelligence, Oxford Dictionary, Lexico <https://www.lexico.com/en/definition/artificial_intelligence>.
10. *See* Karen Yeung, 'Algorithmic Regulation: A Critical Interrogation' (2017) 12(4) Reg. & Governance 505, 505-523 (including a taxonomy that identifies eight different forms of algorithmic regulation); Leighton Andrews et al., 'Algorithmic Regulation' (2017) LSE

characterize algorithmic decision-making and enforcement processes. First, authority over enforcement of rights shifts from public to private parties. Second, enforcement is automated as machines implement the law. Third, enforcement becomes centralized as a single action produces legal decisions for many individuals at once. On the other side, automated law enforcement brings obvious benefits in the areas of efficiency and cost savings.[11]

Algorithmic enforcement involves a large-scale collection of data, data processing by algorithms, and automatic performance. For this reason, the EU General Data Protection Regulation (GDPR) is the first legislative instrument having defined algorithmic enforcement. It characterizes 'automated individual decision-making' as a 'decision based solely on automated processing, including profiling, which produces legal' or similar effects on people.[12] The Article 29 Working Party in discussing this provision clarifies that 'a legal effect suggests a processing activity that has an impact on someone's legal rights, such as the freedom to associate with others, vote in an election, or take legal action'.[13] This would most likely encompass also effects upon freedom of receiving and imparting information as to be later discussed.

Automatic infringement assessment systems or Automatic Content Recognition (ACR) technology have been adopted by online platforms worldwide, such as in the case of Google Content ID and Vimeo Copyright Match or any other automated audio/video content identification system build on top of Audible Magic technology.[14] These technologies rely on digital fingerprinting to match an uploaded file against a database of protected works provided by right holders. Google's Content ID system applies four possible policies, including (1) muting matched audio in an uploaded video, (2) completely blocking a matched video, (3) monetizing a matched video for the copyright owner by running advertisements against it and, (4) tracking a matched video's viewer statistics.[15] The Copyright Match system functions in a similar way. Tailoring of Content ID policies is also

---

Discussion Paper no 85 <https://www.kcl.ac.uk/law/research/centres/telos/assets/DP85-Algorithmic-Regulation-Sep-2017.pdf>.

11. *See* Woodrow Hartzog, et al., 'Inefficiently Automated Law Enforcement' (2015) Mich St L Rev 1763, 1764-1765.

12. *See* Regulation 2016/679/EU of the European Parliament and the Council of 27 April 2016 on the protection of natural persons with regard to the processing of personal data and on the free movement of such data, and repealing Directive 95/46/EC [2016] OJ L 119/1, Article 22.

13. Article 29 Data Protection Working Party, Guidelines on Automated individual decision-making and Profiling for the purposes of Regulation 2016/679 [3 October 2017] 17/EN WP 251, 10.

14. *See* Audible Magic <https://www.audiblemagic.com> (providing ACR systems to web media platforms and social networks such as Daily Motion, Facebook, SoundCloud, Twitch, Vimeo and Verizon Wireless).

15. *See* YouTube, How Content ID Works <https://support.google.com/youtube/answer/2797370?hl=en>.

possible and right holders can block content in some instances and monetize it in others, depending on the amount of copyrighted content included in the allegedly infringing uploaded file. The system also allows end-users to dispute copyright owners' claims on content.[16]

In addition, online search manipulation – and so-called demotion – enforce sanitization of presumptively illicit activities online through AI tools. Although it spans multiple online allegedly illicit activities,[17] copyright enforcement has been traditionally a primary goal of search manipulation. Google has been demoting allegedly pirate sites for some time now. In 2012, Google altered its PageRank search algorithm on the basis of the number of DMCA-compliant notices for each website.[18] Shortly thereafter, in 2014, Google started to demote autocomplete predictions returning search results containing DMCA-demoted sites.[19] This algorithm, also known as Google's Pirate algorithm, changes the search algorithm so that it downgrades or deletes allegedly pirate websites, which are moved to the bottom of the search result list.

Meanwhile, online e-commerce platforms, such as Alibaba or eBay, have witnessed the widespread deployment of complex AI-powered technology to tackle online counterfeit and piracy. In 2017, twenty-seven times more goods were removed from Alibaba platforms using these technologies than were removed with takedown notices issued by IP rights holders.[20] Every day, Alibaba identifies up to 600 million product images with an accuracy rate of 98%.[21] Alibaba IPRs Protection system is based on fake product identification modelling, image recognition techniques, semantic recognition

---

16. *See* YouTube, Dispute a Content ID Claim <https://support.google.com/youtube/answer/2797454?hl=en>.

17. Search manipulation, demotion and delisting have been used to fight child-pornography. *See,* e.g., Anchayil Anjali and Arun Mattamana, 'Intermediary Liability and Child Pornography A Comparative Analysis' (2010) 5 J Int'l Comm L Tech 48. Again, these techniques have been deployed against Nicolas Suzor, Bobbie Seignior and Jen Singleton, 'Non-consensual Porn and the Responsibility of Online Intermediaries' (2017) 40(3) Melbourne U L Rev 1057-1097; Joanna Walters, *Google to Exclude Revenge Porn from Internet Searches?* (The Guardian, 21 June 2015) <https://www.theguardian.com/technology/2015/jun/20/google-excludes-revenge-porn-internet-searches>. More recently, demotion have been applied to curb extremism and radicalization. *See* Ben Quinn, *Google to Point Extremist Searches Towards Anti-radicalization Websites* (The Guardian, 2 February 2016) <http://buff.ly/20J3pFi>.

18. *See* Annemarie Bridy, 'Copyright's Digital Deputies: DMCA-plus Enforcement by Internet Intermediaries' in John A. Rothchild (ed), *Research Handbook on Electronic Commerce Law* (Edward Elgar Publishing 2016) 200.

19. *Ibid.*

20. *See* Jungong Sun, *Intellectual Property and E-commerce: Alibaba's Perspective* (WIPO Magazine, September 2018) <https://www.wipo.int/wipo_magazine/en/2018/05/article_0004.html>.

21. *Ibid.*

algorithms, product information databases, real-time interception systems, and data collaboration platforms.[22]

22.3 HOW IS ALGORITHMIC ENFORCEMENT EMERGING?

Increasingly, proactive filtering and monitoring obligations have been imposed on OSPs along the entire spectrum of intermediary liability subject-matters.[23] The discourse is increasingly shifting from liability to 'enhanced responsibility'[24] of OSPs under the assumption that their role is unprecedented for their capacity to influence the informational environment and users' interactions within it. This has happened via voluntary measures, judicial decisions and legislation, as in the case of the recent European Union (EU) copyright law reform. This, in turn, leads to the widespread adoption of automated filtering and algorithmic enforcement systems online, which have become the only option for OSPs to cope with the scale of online infringement, make costs of enforcement sustainable while minimizing liability risks.

22.3.1 PRIVATE ORDERING AND VOLUNTARY MEASURES: FROM INTERMEDIARY LIABILITY TO RESPONSIBILITY

Private ordering has been emerging powerfully as a privileged tool for online enforcement. Voluntary and private enforcement of intellectual property online through algorithmic tools – as well as broader sanitization of online content – appears a recent well-marked trend that can be explained as a paradigmatic shift from intermediary liability to responsibility.[25] In this context, policymakers – and interested third parties such as intellectual property right holders – try to coerce online intermediaries into implementing enforcement strategies through voluntary measures and self-regulation, in addition to legally mandated obligations.

---

22. *Ibid.*
23. *See* Giancarlo Frosio, 'The Death of "No Monitoring Obligations": A Story of Untameable Monsters' (2017) 8 JIPITEC 199.
24. European Commission, 'Tackling Illegal Content Online. Towards an enhanced responsibility of online platforms' (Communication) COM(2017) 555 final.
25. *See* Giancarlo Frosio and Martin Husovec, 'Intermediary Accountability and Responsibility' in Giancarlo Frosio (ed), *The Oxford Handbook of Intermediary Liability Online* (Oxford University Press, forthcoming March 2020) Ch 31; Marin Husovec, *Injunctions Against Intermediaries in the European Union: Accountable But Not Liable?* (CUP 2017) 13; Giancarlo Frosio, 'Why Keep a Dog and Bark Yourself? From Intermediary Liability to Responsibility', (2017) 25 Oxford JILIT 1-33.

This move from intermediary liability to platform responsibility has been occurring first at a theoretical level, with a special focus on intermediaries' corporate social responsibilities and their role in implementing and fostering human rights.[26] In the introduction to *The Responsibilities of Online Service Providers*, Mariarosaria Taddeo and Luciano Floridi noted that OSPs are increasingly expected to act according to current social and cultural values, which rises 'questions as to what kind of responsibilities OSPs should bear, and which ethical principles should guide their actions'.[27] Taddeo and Floridi identify three important sets of ethical problems, the organization and managing of access to information, censorship and freedom of speech, and users' privacy.[28] First, according to the authors, the issue at stake is whether OSPs bear any moral responsibilities for circulating on their infrastructures third-party generated content that may prove harmful, rather than whether OSPs should be held morally responsible for their users' actions.[29] In this respect, some authors argued that it might be desirable to ascribe moral responsibilities to OSPs with respect to the circulation of harmful material.[30]

Again, corporate social responsibility theory has been ported to cyberspace to deploy human rights principles to non-public bodies, which operate largely outside the remit of traditional human rights law.[31] Arguments have been made that obligations pertaining to States – such as those endorsed by the UN Human Rights Council declaration of Internet freedom

---

26. *See*, e.g., United Nations Human Rights Council, 'The Promotion, Protection and Enjoyment of Human Rights on the Internet' (20 June 2014) A/HRC/RES/26/13 (addressing *inter alia* a legally binding instrument on corporations' responsibility to ensure human rights). *See also* Emily Laidlaw, *Regulating Speech in Cyberspace: Gatekeepers, Human Rights and Corporate Responsibility* (CUP 2015); Dennis Broeders et al., 'Does Great Power Come with Great Responsibility? The Need to Talk About Corporate Responsibility' in Mariarosaria Taddeo and Luciano Floridi (ed), *The Responsibilities of Online Service Providers* (Springer 2017) 315-323.
27. Mariarosaria Taddeo and Luciano Floridi, 'New Civic Responsibilities for Online Service Providers' in Mariarosaria Taddeo and Luciano Floridi (ed), *The Responsibilities of Online Service Providers* (Springer 2017) 1.
28. Mariarosaria Taddeo and Luciano Floridi, 'The Debate on the Moral Responsibility of Online Service Providers' (published online 27 November 2015) Sci Eng Ethics 1, 5.
29. *Ibid.,* 10.
30. *See* Vincent Cerf, 'First, Do No Harm' (2011) 24(4) Phil. & Tech. 463, 465 (noting 'the opportunity and challenge that lies ahead is how Internet actors will work together not only to do no harm, but to increase freedom from harm'); Anton Vedder, 'Accountability of Internet Access and Service Providers – Strict Liability Entering Ethics?' (2001) 3(1) Ethics and Info Tech 67, 67-74; Herman Tavani and Frances Grodzinsky, 'Cyberstalking, Personal Privacy, and Moral Responsibility' (2002) 4(2) Ethics and Info. Tech. 123, 123-132.
31. *See* Laidlaw (n 6) (noting that ultimately, however, the largely voluntary nature of CSR instruments makes it a problematic candidate as a governance tool for IIGs and freedom of speech).

as a human right[32] – should be extended to online platforms as well.[33] In particular, the preamble of the Universal Declaration of Human Rights appears to support corporate obligations to protect human rights where it mentions that 'every individual and every organ of society' should strive to promote these rights.[34] Other international instruments to that effect have been identified in the Declaration of Human Duties and Responsibilities,[35] the preamble of the UN Norms on the Responsibilities of Transnational Corporations and Other Business Enterprises,[36] and the UN Guiding Principles on Business and Human Rights.[37] Recently, the United Nations Human Rights Council adopted a resolution on the promotion, protection and enjoyment of human rights on the internet, which also addressed a legally binding instrument on corporations' responsibility to ensure human rights.[38]

Miscellaneous reactions from international institutions and organizations reflect obvious uncertainty in addressing a complex conundrum. This also explains why – regardless of negative externalities from a fundamental rights perspective – private algorithmic enforcement has been increasingly put forward as viable – and perhaps the only sustainable – policy option. On one side, the 2016 Report of the UN Special Rapporteur for Free Expression has strong language about states pressuring private actors to voluntarily remove content. The Special Rapporteur stressed that in the information and communication technology context, 'States must not require or otherwise

---

32. *See* Human Rights Council of the United Nations, Resolution on the Promotion, Protection and Enjoyment of Human Rights on the Internet (2012). *See also* David Karp, 'Transnational Corporations in "Bad States": Human Rights Duties, Legitimate Authority and the Rule of Law in International Political Theory' (2009) 1(01) Int'l Theory 87 (noting that an argument that OSPs are expected to respect human rights is made problematic by the fact that international obligations address states, rather than private parties).
33. *See* Florian Wettstein, 'Silence as Complicity: Elements of a Corporate Duty to Speak out Against the Violation of Human Rights' (2012) 22(01) Bus. Ethics Q. 37, 37-61; Stephen Chen, 'Corporate Responsibilities in Internet-Enabled Social Networks' (2009) 90(4) J. Bus. Ethics 523, 523-536 (arguing that social networks bear both moral and legal responsibility to respect human rights because of the centrality of their role). But *see* George Brenkert, 'Google, Human Rights, and Moral Compromise' (2009) 85(4) J. Bus. Ethics 453, 453-478 (stressing the need to consider the context in which companies act before assessing their moral responsibilities).
34. *See* Universal Declaration of Human Rights, G.A. Res. 217A (III), U.N. Doc. A/810 at 71 (1948), Preamble.
35. *See* UNESCO Declaration of Human Duties and Responsibilities (Valencia Declaration) (1998).
36. *See* UN Norms on the Responsibilities of Transnational Corporations and Other Business Enterprises (13 August 2003).
37. *See* United Nations, Human Rights, Office of the High Commissioner, Guiding Principles on Business Human Rights: Implementing the United Nations 'Protect, Respect, and Remedy' Framework (2011) [hereinafter UN GPBHRs].
38. *See* United Nations Human Rights Council, The Promotion, Protection and Enjoyment of Human Rights on the Internet, A/HRC/RES/26/13 (20 June 2014).

pressure the private sector to take steps that unnecessarily or disproportionately interfere with freedom of expression, whether through laws, policies, or extralegal means.'[39] Again, the Report recommended that 'any demands, requests and other measures to take down digital content or access customer information must be based on *validly enacted law*, subject to external and independent oversight, and demonstrate a necessary and proportionate means of achieving one or more aims under article 19 (3) of the International Covenant on Civil and Political Rights.'[40] In contrast, in a Joint Declaration of the Three Special Rapporteurs for Freedom of Expression, the Rapporteurs encourage the adoption of self-regulatory solutions for the management of rights online, while, at the same time, noting this should be read in conjunction with the importance of minimum safeguards for individual liberties.[41] Again, the OCSE believes that cooperation of intermediaries might be a legitimate tool that shouldn't go too far: '[m]aking private intermediaries more transparent and accountable is a legitimate aim to be pursued by participating States through appropriate means. However, this must not lead to excessive control by public authorities over online content.'[42]

Under the umbrella of this emerging theoretical approach, algorithmic monitoring and filtering have been increasingly adopted by OSPs as a private ordering mechanism to purge the Internet from allegedly infringing content or illegal speech and as a means of protecting themselves from lawsuits as regards content uploaded by third parties. For example, in 2008, Google launched its Content ID system – an automated content screening and filtering mechanism – after being exposed to a major lawsuit brought against it by Viacom based on the unauthorized uploading and viewing of copyright-protected content onto the YouTube platform (owned by Viacom) by users.[43] Similarly, in 2014, Viacom adopted an analogous filtering system known as

---

39. Report of the Special Rapporteur on the promotion and protection of the right to freedom of opinion and expression, A/HRC/32/38, 5 November 2016, at § 85.
40. *Ibid.,* (emphasis added).
41. *See* The United Nations (UN) Special Rapporteur on Freedom of Opinion and Expression, the Organization for Security and Co-operation in Europe (OSCE) Representative on Freedom of the Media, the Organization of American States (OAS) Special Rapporteur on Freedom of Expression and the African Commission on Human and Peoples' Rights (ACHPR) Special Rapporteur on Freedom of Expression and Access to Information, International Mechanism for Promoting Freedom of Expression, Joint Declaration on Freedom of Expression and the Internet (2011) 2.b [hereinafter Joint Declaration of the Three Special Rapporteurs for Freedom of Expression].
42. Organization for Security and Co-operation in Europe, The Representative on Freedom of the Media, Dunja Mijatovic, Communiqué No.1/2016, 3rd Communiqué on Open Journalism, 29 January 2016, 2, <https://www.osce.org/fom/219391?download=true> (accessed on 16 November 2017).
43. *See Viacom Int'l v. YouTube* Inc 676 F3d 19 (2nd Cir 2012) (US) (upholding YouTube's liability in the long-lasting legal battle with Viacom by holding that Google and YouTube had actual knowledge or awareness of specific infringing activity on its website). The lawsuit was subsequently settled.

Copyright Match in the aftermath of a copyright infringement lawsuit brought against it by Capitol Records and EMI concerning several music videos that were uploaded onto the Vimeo platform by users.[44]

Meanwhile, private ordering by OSPs through the voluntary application of algorithmic filtering and monitoring mechanisms is being increasingly promoted by governments. The EU Commission's *Communication on Online Platforms and the Digital Single Market* puts forward the idea that 'the responsibility of online platforms is a key and cross-cutting issue.'[45] In other words, the Commission would like to impose an obligation on online platforms to behave responsibly by actively and swiftly removing illegal materials, instead of reacting to complaints.[46] Again, the Commission in a 2017 Communication aims at promoting 'enhanced responsibility of online platforms' on a voluntary basis through '*proactive* measures to detect and remove illegal content online'.[47] The Commission highlights how algorithmic automated enforcement should become a standard for content sanitization online by calling OSPs to adopt effective voluntary 'proactive measures to detect and remove illegal content online' by using automatic detection and filtering technologies.[48]

Algorithmic content sanitization and moderation online on voluntary basis reach far beyond IP enforcement. As an umbrella framework, the Commission recently agreed with all major online hosting providers – including Facebook, Twitter, YouTube and Microsoft – on a code of conduct that includes a series of commitments to combat the spread of illegal hate speech online in Europe.[49] Also, in partial response to this increased pressure from the EU regarding the role of intermediaries in the fight against online terrorism, major tech-companies announced that they would begin sharing hashes of apparent terrorist propaganda.[50] For some time, YouTube and Facebook have been using the Content ID and other matching tools to filter 'extremist content'.[51] For this purpose, tech-companies plan to create a shared database of unique digital fingerprints – known as hashes – that can

---

44. *See Capitol Records LLC v. Vimeo* 972 F Supp 2d 500 (SDNY 2013) (US) (denying in part Vimeo's motion for summary judgment).
45. European Commission, 'Online Platforms and the Digital Single Market: Opportunities and Challenges for Europe' (Communication) COM (2016) 288 final, 9.
46. *Ibid.,* 8.
47. *See* European Commission, 'Tackling Illegal Content Online. Towards an enhanced responsibility of online platforms' COM (2017) 555 final, section 3.3.1.
48. *Ibid.,* section 3.3.2.
49. *See* European Commission, 'European Commission and IT Companies Announce Code of Conduct on Illegal Online Hate Speech' (*Press Release,* 31 May 2016) <http://europa.eu/rapid/press-release_IP-16-1937_en.htm>.
50. *See* 'Google in Europe, Partnering to Help Curb the Spread of Terrorist Content Online' (*Google Blog,* 5 December 2016) <https://blog.google/topics/google-europe/partnering-help-curb-spread-terrorist-content-online>.
51. *See* Joseph Menn and Dustin Volz, 'Excusive: Google, Facebook Quietly Move Toward Automatic Blocking of Extremist Videos' (*Reuters,* 25 June 2016) <www.reuters.com/

identify images and videos promoting terrorism.[52] When one company identifies and removes such a piece of content, the others will be able to use the hash to identify and remove the same piece of content from their own network. The fingerprints will help identify the image and video content that are 'most likely to violate all of our respective companies' content policies'.[53] Despite the collaboration, the task of defining removal policies will remain within the remit of each platform.[54] The European Commission would like to provide a regulatory framework for these initiatives with special emphasis on tackling the dissemination of terrorist content online. In a recent Recommendation, the Commission has singled out automated filtering means as the optimal policy solution:

> Hosting service providers should take proportionate and specific proactive measures, including by using automated means, in order (1) to detect, identify and expeditiously remove or disable access to terrorist content (36) (2) in order to immediately prevent content providers from re-submitting content which has already been removed or to which access has already been disabled because it is considered to be terrorist content.[55]

A proposal for a Regulation for preventing the dissemination of terrorist content online endorses similar principles and is under consideration before the EU Parliament.[56]

22.3.2   CASE LAW: ADDRESSING THE INTERNET THREAT

This shift that leads to the widespread adoption of algorithmic enforcement tools is also reflected in jurisprudential developments. This judicial approach is apparently rooted in an 'Internet threat' narrative that focuses on the 'threat' posed by digitalization and Internet distribution and would construe OSPs as likely to inflict imminent harm unless subdued through enhanced

---

article/us-Internet-extremism-video-exclusive-idUSKCN0ZB00M> (apparently, the 'automatic' removal of extremist content is only about automatically identifying duplicate copies of video that were already removed through human review).

52. *See* Olivia Solon, 'Facebook, Twitter, Google and Microsoft Team up to Tackle Extremist Content' (*The Guardian,* 6 December 2016) <www.theguardian.com/technology/2016/dec/05/facebook-twitter-google-microsoft-terrorist-extremist-content>.

53. *See* 'Partnering to Help Curb Spread of Online Terrorist Content' (*Facebook Newsroom,* 5 December 2016) <https://newsroom.fb.com/news/2016/12/partnering-to-help-curb-spread-of-online-terrorist-content>.

54. *Ibid.*

55. European Commission, 'Recommendation on measures to effectively tackle illegal content online' C(2018) 1177 final.

56. *See* European Parliament, 'Legislative resolution of 17 April 2019 on the proposal for a regulation on preventing the dissemination of terrorist content online' [2019] P8_TA-PROV(2019)0421.

legal obligations and liability.[57] The deployment of widespread and invasive automated content screening and filtering software is seen by courts as a proportionate answer to the massive and uncontrollable threat that OSPs trigger against multiple rights online.

A decision delivered by the Brazilian Superior Tribunal de Justiça (STJ) in the *Dafra* case illustrates well the terms of this discourse.[58] In this decision, which concerned copyright-infringing videos posted on the You-Tube platform by users, the Brazilian STJ stressed the importance of imposing liability on intermediaries, stating that, 'if Google created an "untameable monster", it should be the only one charged with any disastrous consequences.'[59] The Court in *Dafra* stressed the importance of imposing liability on intermediaries saying that, 'violations of privacy of individuals and companies, summary trials and public lynching of innocents are routinely reported, all practised in the worldwide web with substantially increased damage because of the widespread nature of this medium of expression.'[60] Following this conclusion, accordingly, Google was required to set up proactive, automated filtering systems not only to remove the infringing video which was the object of the lawsuit but also to remove any similar and related unauthorized videos.[61]

In Europe, the Members States' courts have imposed miscellaneous proactive monitoring and filtering obligations that triggered the widespread deployment of algorithmic enforcement tools. In the *Allostreaming*[62] case – a landmark decision in France – the Paris Court of Appeal imposed an obligation on OSPs to block the Allostreaming – an illegal movie streaming website – and affiliated enterprises. In addition, search engines, including Google, Yahoo! and Bing, were required to proactively expunge any link to these websites from their search results.[63] The Court of Appeal remarked that

---

57. The 'Internet threat' narrative dates back quite long time. *See,* e.g., *Universal v. Corley* 60 USPQ 2d 1953. 1968 (2nd Cir 2011) (US) (where, responding to the request made by the defendants to refrain from using the DMCA as an instrument of censorship, Justice Newman replied as follows: '[h]ere, dissemination itself carries very substantial risk of imminent harm because the mechanism is so unusual by which dissemination of means of circumventing access controls to copyrighted works threatens to produce virtually unstoppable infringement of copyright'). *See also* James Boyle, *The Public Domain: Enclosing the Commons of the Mind* (Yale University Press 2008) 54-82 (discussing this very point).

58. Superior Court of Justice Fourth Panel *Google Brazil v. Dafra* [24 March 2014] Special Appeal no 1306157/SP (BR) (hereafter '*Dafra*').

59. *Ibid.*

60. *Dafra* (n 58) para. 5.4.

61. *Ibid.,* para. 5.2.

62. *See* Cour d'Appel Paris *UPC et al. v. Google, Microsoft, Yahoo!, Bouygues et Al.* [16 March 2016] (FR) (hereafter *Allostreaming 2016*) confirming TGI Paris *UPC et al. v. Google, Microsoft, Yahoo!, Bouygues et a.l* (28 November 2013) (FR). *See also* Laura Marino, 'Responsabilités civile et pénale des fournisseurs d'accès et d'hébergement' (2016) 670 JCl Communication 71, 71-79.

63. *See Allostreaming 2016* (n 62) 7.

right holders are 'confronted with a massive attack' and are 'heavily threatened by the massive piracy of their works.'[64] Hence, the Court of Appeal determined that it is 'legitimate and in accordance with the principle of proportionality that [ISPs and search engines] contribute to blocking and delisting measures' because they 'initiate the activity of making available access to these websites' and 'derive economic benefit from this access, especially by advertising displayed on their pages.'[65]

German courts have highlighted that OSPs might be bound by an obligation to set up proactive, automated monitoring and filtering if their business model is mainly based on copyright infringement. In two disputes involving the Swiss-based file-hosting service, RapidShare, the Federal Supreme Court of Germany – *Bundesgerichtshof* (BGH) – imposed monitoring obligations on RapidShare.[66] According to the BGH, although RapidShare's business model was not primarily designed for violating copyright, it nevertheless provided incentives to third parties to illegally share copyrighted content.[67] Therefore, RapidShare – and similar file-hosting services – are required to abide by more stringent monitoring duties. Thus, the BGH determined that a hosting provider is not only required to delete files containing copyrighted material as soon as it is notified of a violation by the right holder but must also take steps to prevent similar infringements by other users in the future. File-hosting services must actively monitor incoming links to discover copyrighted files and then ensure that these files become inaccessible to the public.[68] In doing so, the service provider should use all possible resources – including search engines, Facebook, Twitter or web crawlers – to identify links made accessible to the public.[69]

Furthermore, in the so-called Internet Auction cases[70] which involved trademark infringements taking place on Internet auction platforms such as eBay, the BGH repeatedly decided that notified trademark infringements imposed an obligation on these platforms to investigate future offerings,

---

64. *Ibid.*
65. *Ibid.*
66. *See* BGH *GEMA v. RapidShare* [15 August 2013] I ZR 79/12, GRUR-RR 2014, 136 (DE) (where the German copyright collective society, GEMA, sued RapidShare in Germany, alleging that over 4,800 copyrighted music files were shared via RapidShare without consent from GEMA or the right holder). An English translation is available at <https://stichtingbrein.nl/public/2013-08-15%20BGH_RapidShare_EN.pdf>. *See also* BGH *Atari Europe v. RapidShare* [12 July 2012] I ZR 18/11, GRUR 2013, 370 (DE) (in this case, RapidShare neglected to check whether certain files violating Atari's copyright over the computer game 'Alone in the dark' were stored on its servers by other users).
67. *Ibid.*
68. *See GEMA v. RapidShare* (n 66) para. 60.
69. *Ibid.*
70. *See* BGH *Rolex v. Ebay/Ricardo* (a.k.a. Internetversteigerung I) [11 March 2004] I ZR 304/01, GRUR 2004, 860 (DE) para. 31; BGH *Rolex v. eBay* (a.k.a. Internetversteigerung II) [19 April 2007] I ZR 35/04, GRUR 2007, 708 (DE); BGH *Rolex v. Ricardo* (a.k.a. Internetversteigerung III) [30 May 2008] I ZR 73/05, GRUR 2008, 702 (DE).

either manually or through software filters, if the necessary measures are possible and economically reasonable.[71] The BGH struggled in determining the exact scope of the duty of care to be imposed on auction platforms which would qualify as 'reasonable' or 'technically possible'. In the *Internet Auction III* case, the BGH determined that the investigation of clearly noticeable infringements – such as blatant counterfeit items – would pass the reasonability test, whereas a filtering obligation which endangers the business model of the Internet auction platform would be unreasonable. A later decision of the BGH determined that an obligation to manually check and visually compare each product offered in an online auction against infringement – which was not clear or obvious – would be unreasonable.[72] In contrast, offering filtering tools to trademark holders – as eBay does – in order to perform such manual checks themselves, would be sufficient for the purpose of avoiding liability under the doctrine of *Störerhaftung*.[73]

Some international courts set a threshold for proactive, automated monitoring and filtering based on the popularity and high-volume views/ downloads of the content in question. In the *Baidu* case, the Beijing Higher People's Court determined that it was reasonable to impose on Baidu, a duty to monitor and to examine the legal status of an uploaded work once it has been viewed or downloaded more than a certain number of times.[74] As per its duty to monitor, Baidu is required to inspect the potential copyright status of the work by contacting the uploader, checking whether the work is originally created by the uploader or legally authorized by the copyright owners.[75] However, the Court failed to indicate the number of views or downloads that would be sufficient for triggering this duty, thereby giving rise to legal uncertainty regarding the exact scope of an OSP's liability in relation to popular content.

The 'Internet threat' discourse – and the automated proactive content sanitization that it brings about – has also been gaining ground in multiple matters unrelated to IP infringement and enforcement. By way of example, the European Court of Human Rights (ECtHR) re-echoed this narrative in the context of hate speech rather than of copyright infringement. The ECtHR noted that, on the Internet, '[d]efamatory and other types of clearly unlawful

---

71. *See ibid.*, Internetversteigerung I (n 70) para. 46.
72. *See* BGH *Kinderhochstühle im Internet* [22 July 2010] I ZR 139/08, GRUR 2011, 152 (DE).
73. *Ibid.* The German property law doctrine of *Störerhaftung*, as codified in section 1004 of the German Civil Code, grants a proprietor a right to (permanent) injunctive relief against any person who causes an interference with his property. However, the doctrine prevents any person from being held liable as a Störer (i.e., an interferer) if that would entail an unreasonable burden upon him.
74. *See* Beijing Higher People's Court *Zhong Qin Wen v. Baidu* [2014] Gao Min Zhong Zi no 2045 (CH).
75. *Ibid.*

speech, including hate speech and speech inciting violence, can be disseminated like never before, worldwide, in a matter of seconds, and sometimes remain persistently available online.'[76] In the *Delfi* case, concerned readers' comments containing clearly unlawful hate speech had been posted below a news article published by Delfi – an Estonian Internet news provider – on its online news portal. The ECtHR was required to strike a balance between the freedom of expression granted under Article 10 of the European Human Rights Convention and the preservation of personality rights of third persons under Article 8 of the same Convention.[77] The ECtHR tackled this conundrum by delineating a narrowly construed scenario in which the liability imposed on OSPs supposedly does not interfere with the freedom of expression.[78] The ECtHR held that in a situation of higher-than-average risk of defamation or hate speech[79] if comments from non-registered users are allowed,[80] a professionally managed and commercially based Internet news portal should exercise the full extent of control at its disposal – and must go beyond automatic keyword-based filtering or *ex post* notice-and-takedown procedures – to avoid liability.[81] The ECtHR, therefore, concluded that finding Delfi liable for anonymous comments posted by third parties on its online platform did not breach its freedom to impart information.[82] In later cases, the ECtHR has clarified the issue of liability for OSPs by confirming that automated proactive monitoring obligations should not apply to 'offensive and vulgar' speech rather than hate speech nor to non-profit media outlets.[83] Still, the ECtHR singles out proactive and automated monitoring and filtering – although narrowly applied – as a privileged tool to tame the

---

76. *Delfi AS v. Estonia*, App no 64569/09 (ECtHR, 16 June 2015) para. 110 (hereafter '*Delfi AS*').
77. *Ibid.*, para. 59.
78. For detailed comments of each relevant principle stated in the decision, *see* Giancarlo Frosio, 'The European Court Of Human Rights Holds Delfi Liable For Anonymous Defamation' (*CIS Blog*, 25 October 2013) <https://cyberlaw.stanford.edu/blog/2013/10/european-court-human-rights-holds-delfiee-liable-anonymous-defamation>.
79. *See Delfi AS* (n 76) paras 144-146. A strikingly similar standard was also adopted by an older decision of the Japanese Supreme Court. *See* Supreme Court *Animal Hospital Case* [7 October 2005] (JP) <https://cyberlaw.stanford.edu/page/wilmap-japan> (finding Channel 2, a Japanese bulletin board, liable on the rationale that – given the large amount of defamatory and 'unreliable' content in threads found on its site – it was not necessary for Channel 2 to know that each thread was defamatory, but it was sufficient that Channel 2 had the knowledge that there was a risk that such transmissions/posts could be defamatory.
80. *See Delfi AS* (n 76) paras 147-151.
81. *Ibid.*, paras 152-159.
82. *See*, e.g., Lisl Brunner, 'The Liability of an Online Intermediary for Third Party Content: The Watchdog Becomes the Monitor: Intermediary Liability after Delfi v Estonia' (2016) 16 Human Rights L Rev 163, 163-174.
83. *See Magyar Tartalomszolgáltatók Egyesülete and Index.Hu v. Hungary*, App no 22947/13 (ECtHR, 2 May 2016) para. 91; *Rolf Anders Daniel Pihl v. Sweden*, App no 74742/14 (ECtHR, 7 February 2017) para. 37.

'untameable monster' or the 'Internet threat'. Also, likewise, the Baidu case mentioned above, the ECtHR linked liability and obligations to deploy automated filtering to the popularity of the alleged infringing content. The ECtHR noted that Delfi could have anticipated the posting of negative comments based on the high degree of reader interest in the news article as demonstrated by the above-average numbers of comments posted below it.

A notable exception to the global trend in enforcing proactive monitoring obligations is the decision delivered by the Supreme Court of Argentina in the *Belen* case.[84] In this case, a well-known public figure – Belen Rodriguez – brought an action against the search engines Google and Yahoo! for linking search results to third-party content which, she claimed, violated her copyright and her right to honour and privacy. The Argentinian Supreme Court repudiated the imposition of liability based on a regime of strict liability and instead adopted a test based on actual knowledge and negligence and required judicial review for issuing a notice to takedown content – except in a few cases of 'gross and manifest harm'. The Supreme Court further rejected the imposition of any filtering obligation in order to prevent infringing links from appearing in the future.[85] As a default rule, actual knowledge – and possibly negligence – would only arise after a judicial review has upheld the issuance of the notice.

22.3.3   LEGISLATION: ARTICLE 17 OF THE C-DSM DIRECTIVE

Meanwhile, legislation has been emerging to impose on OSPs allegedly infringing content filtering and monitoring obligations that can be met only through algorithmic enforcement. In particular, this is the foreseeable outcome of the recent EU Copyright in the Digital Single Market (C-DSM) Directive.[86] In this context, Article 17 of the C-DSM Directive would signal a transition of EU copyright law from the existing 'negligence-based' intermediary liability system – grounded on the principle of 'no-monitoring

---

84. *See* Supreme Court *Rodriguez M Belen v. Google y Otro s/ daños y perjuicios* [29 October 2014] R.522.XLIX. (Argentina) (hereafter '*Belen*'). *See also* Pablo Palazzi and Marco Jurado, 'Search Engine Liability for Third Party Infringement' (2015) 10 JIPLP 244; Marco Rizzo Jurado, 'Search Engine Liability Arising from Third Parties Infringing Content: A Path to Strict Liability?' (2014) 9 JIPLP 718, 718-720.
85. *See Belen* (n 84).
86. *See* Directive 2019/790/EU of the European Parliament and of the Council of 17 April 2019 on copyright and related rights in the Digital Single Market and amending Directives 96/9/EC and 2001/29/EC [2019] OJ L130/92. Given the scope of this chapter, commentary on the C-DSM reform is limited. The author, however, has discussed the reform – and related issues relevant for this chapter – extensively elsewhere. *See*, e.g., Giancarlo Frosio, 'Reforming the C-DSM Reform: a User-Based Copyright Theory for Commonplace Creativity' IIC (forthcoming March 2020); Giancarlo Frosio, 'To Filter or Not to Filter? That is the Question in EU Copyright Reform' (2018) 36(2) Cardozo Arts & Ent. L J 101-138.

obligations'[87] – to a regime that requires OCSSPs to undertake proactive monitoring and filtering of content, and would almost certainly lead to the widespread adoption of automated filtering and algorithmic copyright enforcement systems.

In an attempt to close an alleged 'value gap' of the EU online digital economy,[88] the reform *inter alia* requires OSPs to engage in a more proactive role in preventing the availability of copyright-infringing content in order to enable right holders to receive appropriate remuneration for the use of their works.[89] In sum, the C-DSM reform would require some selected 'Online Content Sharing Service Providers' (OCSSP) to conclude fair and appropriate licencing agreements with right holders,[90] which shall cover the liability for works uploaded by the users.[91] Otherwise, if no authorization is granted, OCSSPs will be liable unless, *inter alia*, they make 'best efforts' to prevent the availability of infringing works on their network.[92] In addition, service providers shall put in place 'complaints and redress mechanisms' that are available to users in case of disputes over unjustified removal of content.[93] Meanwhile, stakeholder dialogues should 'define best practices' and 'best efforts' for the sanitization of content from OCSSPs' networks.[94]

In earlier versions, the C-DSM Directive proposal referred specifically to effective technologies to ensure the non-availability of copyright-infringing works.[95] However, although Article 17 does not apparently impose anymore automated filtering obligations *ex lege*, it does so de facto. There is the high likelihood that the enhanced risks of liability for copyright infringement would compel OCSSPs to adopt automated filtering systems, such as content recognition technologies, and algorithmic enforcement

---

87. *See* Directive 2000/31/EC of the European Parliament and the Council of 8 June 2000 on certain legal aspects of information society services, in particular electronic commerce, in the Internal Market [2000] OJ L 178/1, Articles 14-15.
88. The 'value gap' refers to an alleged unfair distribution of revenues generated from the online use of copyright-protected works among industry actors along the value chain. *See* European Commission, 'Proposal for a Directive of the European Parliament and of the Council on copyright in the Digital Single Market' COM (2016) 593 final, Explanatory Memorandum, Part 1 (noting that '[e]volution of digital technologies has led to the emergence of new business models and reinforced the role of the Internet as the main marketplace for the distribution and access to copyright-protected content. ... It is therefore necessary to guarantee that authors and right holders receive a fair share of the value that is generated by the use of their works and other subject-matter.')
89. Directive 2019/790/EU (n 86) recital 61.
90. *Ibid.,* Article 17(1).
91. *Ibid.*
92. *Ibid.,* Article 17(1) and Recital 39.
93. *Ibid.,* Article 17(2).
94. *Ibid.,* Article 17(3).
95. For a discussion of the original commission proposal and potential inconsistencies with Article 15 of Directive 2000/31/EC, *see* Giancarlo Frosio, 'To Filter or Not to Filter? That is the Question in EU Copyright Reform', (2018) 36(2) Cardozo Arts & Ent. L. J., 118-123.

mechanisms, such as automated content blocking.[96] General and indiscriminate monitoring of all content uploaded by users through manual filtering would impose an unsustainable financial and logistical burden on OCSSPs, which in the words of the BGH earlier mentioned would jeopardize the OCSSPs' business model. Thus, automated filtering and blocking tools would prove to be the most efficient and cost-effective means of ensuring the unavailability of unauthorized content over online services. Actually, the assessment of 'best efforts' in accordance with 'high industry standards' and evolving technologies implies that OCSSPs may even be legally required to employ algorithmic monitoring and enforcement systems for two order of reasons.[97] First, they might be determined to be the most effective and proportionate means of achieving the unavailability of infringing content. Second, and moreover, they might reflect the prevailing industry-standard – which is increasingly becoming the case with dominant players such as Google resorting to automated filtering and enforcement systems.

An issue worth exploring is whether Article 26 of the GDPR poses any limitation to algorithmic enforcement under Article 17 of the C-DSM Directive, such as filtering and monitoring that should be implemented to make infringing content unavailable on OCSSPs' networks. As such, Article 26 might theoretically encompass algorithmic IP enforcement. Article 26 states that data subjects 'shall have the right not to be subjected to a decision based solely on automated processing', which produces legal effects or similarly affects the data subject. As already mentioned, interpreting Article 26 GDPR, Article 29 Working Party has noted that 'producing legal effects' means to have an impact on someone's rights.[98] Actually, IP algorithmic enforcement mechanisms fulfil Article 26 GDPR definition insofar they affect uploaders' freedom of expression. However, Article 26 GDPR includes also a number of exceptions to the prohibition of automated decision-making. One would be explicit consent, which actually OCSSPs might include in their terms of service. The additional exceptions provide that automated individual decision-making is allowed if:

---

96. Actually, the version of September 2018 of the C-DSM Directive included an explicit counsel to avoid the use of automated content-blocking in defining best-practices. *See* version of September 2018, Article 13(3) ('When defining best practices, special account shall be taken of fundamental rights, the use of exceptions and limitations as well as ensuring that […] *automated blocking of content is avoided*') (emphasis added). Surprisingly this reference to the avoidance of automated content-blocking systems has been deleted from the final version.

97. *See* Directive 2019/790/EU (n 86) recital 66 paras 2-3 (for the purpose of assessing whether 'best' efforts have been made and high industry standards' have been met, it should also be considered 'the evolving state of the art as regards existing means, including potential future developments, to avoid the availability of different types of content and the cost of such means for the services').

98. Article 29 (n 13) 10.

(a) necessary for the performance of or entering into a contract between the data subject and the controller; [or] (b) authorised by Union or Member State law to which the controller is subject and which also lays down suitable measures to safeguard the data subject's rights and freedoms and legitimate interests […].

Both exceptions might be applicable to Article 17 of the C-DSM Directive. Obviously, the exception at (b) covers quite clearly the scenario of Article 17 as OCSSPs have an obligation of making infringing content unavailable if no authorization has been granted by the right holders. At the same time, Article 17 also provides for the setting up of a complaint and redress mechanism to preserve users' fundamental rights and enjoyment of exception and limitations.[99]

However, in contrast, voluntary automated enforcement would not be covered by that exception, and unless explicit consent is given, might be unlawful. In this case, however, the exception (a) could still be applied if the automated filtering mechanisms are necessary for the performance of a contract between OSPs and users. In this context, the Article 29 Working Party apparently suggest that upload filters might be covered by the exception, which would reach situations in which algorithmic filters 'enables [OSPs] to deliver decisions within a shorter time frame and improves the efficiency of the process. Routine human involvement may sometimes also be impractical or impossible due to the sheer quantity of data being processed'.[100] However, as Stalla-Bourdillon has noted,[101] Article 29 Working Party seem to conclude that this might not be decisive and the processing could still be found infringing Article 26.

In any event, the inconsistency of algorithmic enforcement tools with Article 26 GDPR in the copyright domain would be residual at this stage,[102] as all OCSSPs are covered by the exception (b) under the framework of Article 17 of the C-DSM Directive. However, in content sanitization contexts other than copyright, such as those considered by the European Commission's Communication and Recommendation on Tackling Illegal Content Online that was earlier mentioned, the question might not be completely moot, and further clarification might still be needed from Article 29 or the CJEU.

---

99. Directive 2019/790/EU (n 86) Article 17(7)-(9).
100. Article 29 (n 13) 12.
101. *See* Sophie Stalla-Bourdillon, 'Data Protection and Copyright: Could Art. 29 WP Guidance on Automated Decision-Making "Help" with Filters?' (*Peepbeep!*, 30 October 2017) <https://peepbeep.wordpress.com/2017/10/30/data-protection-law-and-copyright-could-art-29-wp-guidance-on-automated-decision-making-help-with-filters>.
102. The issue might be raised in connection to voluntary automated enforcement deployed by OSPs not covered by the obligations in Article 17 of the C-DMS, if they do not obtain explicit consent to use fully automated upload filters from their users. Most likely, however, if OSPs do not have an obligation to make infringing content unavailable, they will not implement proactive automated filtering.

22.4   HOW ALGORITHMIC ENFORCEMENT AFFECTS
              HUMAN RIGHTS?

Emphasis on a responsible role of OSPs in fostering human rights – which
brings about the proactive, automated filtering as described in the previous
pages – poses considerable challenges to human rights themselves. Private
actors might be structurally unfit for purpose. OSPs are unequipped – and
lack constitutional standing – for coming down to decisions involving the
proportional balancing of rights. As Calabresi-Coase's 'least-cost avoid-
ers',[103] OSPs will inherently try to lower transaction costs of adjudication
and liability and, in order to do so, might functionally err on the side of over
blocking, in particular by deploying automated algorithmic enforcement
tools.

   Given this preliminary consideration, algorithmic enforcement online
might impinge on a trifecta of major competing fundamental rights. First,
OSPs regulatory choices increasingly taken through algorithmic tools can
profoundly affect the enjoyment of users' fundamental rights, such as
freedom of expression, freedom of information and the right to privacy and
data protection. Second, OSPs will make choices and implement obligations
dealing with blocking and sanitization of a vast array of allegedly infringing
content online that affect IP right holders and creators. Third, imposing too
strict or expansive obligations on OSPs raises further fundamental right
challenges in connection to possible curtailment of their freedom to conduct
business.

22.4.1   USERS' RIGHTS

Users' fundamental rights take centre stage in the present review. The
harshest debate surrounding algorithmic monitoring, filtering and enforcement point at how it can highly affect users' right. Obviously, algorithmic
enforcement primarily affects the due process. In addition, users' freedom of
information and freedom of expression – or freedom to receive and impart
information – can also be affected together with the right to privacy.

22.4.1.1   Due Process

While discussing Google new obligations in the aftermath of the CJEU's
Costeja decision on the right to be forgotten, Google European Communications Director candidly admitted that Google 'never expected or wanted to
make [these] complicated decisions that would in the past have been
extensively examined in the courts, [but are] now being made by scores of

---

103. *See* Guido Calabresi, 'Some Thoughts on Risk Distribution and the Law of Torts' (1961)
     70 Yale L J 499; Ronald Coase, 'The Problem of Social Cost' (1960) 3 J L & Econ. 1.

[Google's] lawyers and paralegal assistants'.[104] More dramatically, these decisions are increasingly taken by algorithms, boots and other sapient machines.

This emerging phenomenon destabilizes the very notion of due process. The principle of due process guarantees that laws and legal proceedings must be fair, and people's basic right to life, liberty and property cannot be limited without due process of law.[105] Due process refers to a fair judicial process, which includes the right to be treated fairly, efficiently and effectively by the administration of justice. It focuses on the right to a fair trial, which is guaranteed if individuals can have recourse to 'a competent, independent and impartial tribunal' and find recognition in multiple human rights conventions.[106]

As Perel and Elkin-Koren argue, algorithmic enforcement by OSPs reflects a fundamental governance shift by effectively converging 'law enforcement and adjudication powers in the hands of a small number of mega platforms, which are profit-maximizing, and possibly biased, private entities'.[107] While, traditional law enforcement involves detection, prosecution, adjudication and punishment by different public authorities, algorithmic enforcement conflates all these functions in OSPs' hands, focusing primarily on detection and prevention.[108] The convergence of law enforcement and adjudication powers challenges due process principles by affecting 'trust and accountability that are inherent to reliable systems of law enforcement'.[109]

Algorithmic enforcement raises three main due process concerns tightly related to the technical complexity of neural networks' processes: transparency, accountability and contestability.[110] Transparency refers to the disclosure of methods and processes adopted to take a decision. Accountability is

---

104. Peter Barron, *Google European Communications Director* (September 2014).
105. *See* Alfred Denning, *Due Process of Law* (OUP, 1980).
106. *See,* e.g., UDHR Article 10; ECHR (n 6) Article 6; Charter (n 6) Articles 47-50.
107. Maayan Perel and Niva Elkin-Koren, 'Accountability in Algorithmic Copyright Enforcement' (2016) 19 Stan Tech L Rev 473, 473.
108. *Ibid.,* 481.
109. *Ibid.*
110. Council of Europe, Committee of experts on human rights dimensions of automated data processing and different forms of artificial intelligence (MSI-AUT), 'Draft Recommendation of the Committee of Ministers to Member States on human rights impacts of algorithmic systems' [12 November 2018] MSI-AUT(2018)06, 6-7 <https://rm.coe.int/draft-recommendation-on-human-rights-impacts-of-algorithmic-systems/16808ef256>; Ansgar Koene et al., *A Governance Framework for Algorithmic Accountability and Transparency* (European Parliament Research Center 2019) 4-8; Aaron Rieke, Miranda Bogen, and David Robinson, *Public Scrutiny of Automated Decisions: Early Lessons and Emerging Methods* (An Upturn and Omidyar Network Report, 2018) 23-28 <https://www.issuelab.org/resources/30226/30226.pdf>; Aaron Rieke, Miranda Bogen, and David Robinson, *Public Scrutiny of Automated Decisions: Early Lessons and Emerging Methods* (An Upturn and Omidyar Network Report, 2018) 23-28 <https://www.issuelab.org/resources/30226/30226.pdf>.

the possibility of taking responsibility for the decision takes.[111] Finally, contestability is the ability to challenge the outcome of an automated enforcement decision.[112] No fair judicial process can occur if these requirements remain unfulfilled. Accountability and contestability, however, depends on transparency. If transparency of algorithmic decision-making cannot be guaranteed, neither accountability nor contestability can. Actually, there are multiple obstacles that stand in the way of a transparent algorithmic enforcement process. First, trade secrets or confidential information may be insurmountable limitations to algorithmic transparency.[113] Second, state secrets may prevent public authorities from disclosing their automated decision-making processes. For example, the tax authority will not reveal the algorithm that chooses taxpayers whose tax declarations needs to be checked.[114] Likewise, customs authorities will not reveal the pattern-match system that chooses which company needs to undergo customs check for suspect IP infringement. Third, there are technical obstacles that depend on the complexity of the deciding algorithms. In the case of fast-learning neural networks, it will be very hard to qualify the reasons leading to a certain decision outcome.

22.4.1.2 Freedom of Information and Internet Access

Algorithmic enforcement might curtail freedom of information and access to the Internet. The right to freedom of expression[115] guarantees not only the right to impart information but also the right to receive it.[116] In recent years, it has evolved towards a 'right to Internet access', which has been increasingly construed as a fundamental right.[117] Access to the Internet

---

111. *See* Perel and Elkin-Koren (n 107) 481-484; Koene et al. (n 110) 8; Ruben Binns, 'Algorithmic Accountability and Public Reason' (2018) 31 Phil. & Tech. 543, 543-556.
112. *See* Council of Europe (n 110) 6-7.
113. *See,* e.g., Mariateresa Maggiolino, 'EU Trade Secrets and Algorithmic Transparency' (2019) Bocconi Legal Studies Research Paper No. 3363178 <papers.ssrn.com/sol3/papers.cfm?abstract_id=3363178>; Rebecca Wexler, 'Life, Liberty, and Trade Secrets: Intellectual Property in the Criminal Justice System' (2018) 70 Stanford L Rev 1343, 1343-1429; Taylor Moore, *Trade Secrets and Algorithms as Barriers to Social Justice* (Center for Democracy and Technology 2017).
114. *See* Joshua Kroll and Others, 'Accountable Algorithms' (2017) 165 U Pa L Rev 633, 658; Wexler (n 113) 1367.
115. *See,* e.g., Charter (n 6) Article 11; ECHR (n 6) Art 10.
116. *See,* e.g., *Times Newspapers Ltd (nos. 1 and 2) v. the United Kingdom*, App no 3002/03 and 23676/03, 10 March 2009, § 27; *Ahmet Yildirim v. Turkey*, App no 3111/10, 18 December 2012, § 50; *Guseva v. Bulgaria*, App no 6987/07, 17 February 2015, § 36; *Cengiz and Others v. Turkey*, App no 48226/10 and 14027/11, 1 December 2015, § 56. On the public's right to receive information, *see also* Christophe Geiger, 'Author's Right, Copyright and the Public's Right to Information: A Complex Relationship' in Fiona Macmillan (ed), *New Directions in Copyright Law, Vol. 5* (Edward Elgar 2007) 24.
117. *See* on this question, Nicola Lucchi, 'Access to Network Services and Protection of Constitutional Rights: Recognizing the Essential Role of Internet Access for the

as a human right has been argued by noting that 'the Internet, by facilitating the spreading of knowledge, increases freedom of expression and the value of citizenship'.[118]

In Europe, as part of a survey among all Member States, the European Court of Human Rights (ECtHR) noted that 'it can be inferred from all the general guarantees protecting freedom of expression that a right to unhindered Internet access should also be recognised'.[119] In response to three-strike legislation proposals, the Council of Europe had already sustained that access to the Internet is a 'fundamental right'.[120] Again, in a decision of 10 June 2009 on the first HADOPI law, the French Constitutional Council, for instance, stated explicitly that '[i]n the current state of the means of communication and given the generalized development of public online communication services and the importance of the latter for the participation in democracy and the expression of ideas and opinions, [the right to freedom of expression] implies freedom to access such services'.[121] Also, the European Commission concluded that 'any limitations to access to the Open Internet can impact on end-users' freedom of expression and the way in which they can receive and impart information'.[122] Meanwhile, several international and national bodies, such as the UN Human Rights Council,[123] the ITU-UNESCO Commission,[124] the Costa Rican Constitutional Court,[125]

Freedom of Expression' (2011) 19(3) Cardozo J of Int'l and Comp L 645; Molly Land, 'Toward an International Law of the Internet', 54(2) Harvard Int'l L J 393 (2013).

118. *See* Marshall Conley and Christina Patterson, *Human Rights and the Internet* (Macmillan 2000).

119. *Ahmet Yildirim v. Turkey*, App no 3111/10, 18 December 2012, para. 31.

120. *See* Monika Ermert, *Council of Europe: Access to Internet is a Fundamental Right* (IPWatch, 8 June 2009); *Internet Access Is a Fundamental Right* (BBC News, 8 March 2010) <http://news.bbc.co.uk/2/hi/technology/8548190.stm>.

121. French Constitutional Council, Decision no 2009-580 DC of 10 June 2009, § 12.

122. European Commission Staff Working Document, Impact Assessment Accompanying the Document Proposal for a Regulation of the European Parliament and of the Council laying down measures concerning the European single market for electronic communications and to achieve a Connected Continent, and amending Directives 2002/20/EC, 2002/21/EC and 2002/22/EC and Regulations (EC) No. 1211/2009 and (EU) No. 531/2012, SWD (2013) 331 final, § 3.4.

123. UN General Assembly, Human Rights Council Resolution, The Promotion, Protection and Enjoyment of Human Rights on the Internet, A/HRC/RES/20/8, twentieth session, 16 July 2012. *See also* UN General Assembly, Human Rights Council Resolution, The Promotion, Protection and Enjoyment of Human Rights on the Internet, A/HRC/26/L.24, twenty-sixth session, 20 June 2014.

124. *See* Kaitlin Mara, *ITU-UNESCO Broadband Commission Aims at Global Internet Access* (IPWatch, 10 May 2010).

125. 'Acceso a Internet es un derecho fundamental (Nacion, 8 September 2010) <http://www.nacion.com/2010-09-08/ElPais/NotasSecundarias/ElPais2514038.aspx> (reporting the Constitutional Court declaring Internet Access essential to the exercise of fundamental rights).

or the Finnish government officially making broadband a legal right,[126] have stressed the fundamental rights nature of access to the Internet.

Accordingly, any measure that is bound to have an influence on the accessibility of the Internet, such as automated enforcement tools, might trigger States' responsibility for infringement of the right of freedom of expression. For example, within the framework of Article 10 ECHR – and corresponding Article 11 of the EU Charter – courts have found that website blocking must be weighed against a number of factors, including the effects of blocking on legitimate communication, the public interest in disabled information and whether the alternatives to accessing such information were available.[127] The ECtHR provided further guidance on the potential implications of the general public interest in information affected by algorithmic blocking and enforcement by recalling that States have limited leeway for political speech but the broader margin of appreciation in the regulation of commercial speech, however, 'the breadth of that margin has to be qualified where it is not strictly speaking the 'commercial' expression of an individual that is at stake but his participation in a debate on a matter of general interest'.[128] Also, the general public interest in information is not reduced to the political context. In effect, such interest had previously been recognized by the Court in the information on, e.g., sporting matters[129] or performing artists,[130] as well as when the material at issue related to the moral position advocated by an influential religious community.[131]

Algorithmic delisting has been notoriously posing challenges to human rights in connection to the right to be forgotten – and more broadly data protection rights – and potential tensions with the right to access information on the Internet. In 2014, the Court of Justice of the European Union ruled that an internet search engine operator is responsible for the processing that it carries out of personal data which appear on web pages published by third parties.[132] Thus, under certain circumstances, search engines can be asked to remove links to webpages containing personal data. The recognition by the

---

126. *Finland Makes Broadband a Legal Right* (BBC News, 1 July 2010) <http://www.bbc.co.uk/news/ 10461048>.
127. Akdeniz (n 7) para. 28.
128. *Ibid.*
129. *See Nikowitz and Verlagsgruppe News GmbH v. Austria*, App no 5266/03, 22 February 2007, § 25 (society's attitude towards a sports star); *Colaço Mestre and SIC – Sociedade Independente de Comunicação, SA v. Portugal*, App no 11182/03 and 11319/03, 26 April 2007, § 28 (an interview by the president of the sports club); *Ressiot and Others v. France*, App no 15054/07 and 15066/07, 28 June 2012, § 116 (doping practices in professional sport).
130. *See Sapan v. Turkey*, App no 44102/04, 8 June 2010, § 34 (a book about the Turkish pop star).
131. *See Verlagsgruppe News GmbH and Bobi v. Austria*, App no 59631/09, 4 December 2012, § 76.
132. *See C-131/12, Google Spain SL and Google Inc. v. Agencia Española de Protección de Datos (AEPD) and Mario Costeja González* [2014] ECLI:EU:C:2014:317. *See also.*

European Union of a so-called right to be forgotten has ignited critical reactions pointing at the fact that the right to be forgotten would endanger freedom of expression and access to information.[133] How a balance should be struck among these competing rights depends heavily on the jurisdiction called to decide: '[t]hings change, for example, depending on which side of the Atlantic one is. According to the European approach, privacy trumps freedom of speech; whereas the American view is that freedom of speech is preeminent with respect to privacy'.[134] In this regard, the CJEU stated that the person's right to privacy generally overrides 'as a rule, not only the economic interest of the operator of the search engine but also the interest of the general public in finding that information upon a search relating to the data subject's name'.[135] However, the CJEU also noted that this general rule should not apply if there is a preponderant interest of the general public in having access to the information 'for particular reasons, such as the role played by the data subject in public life'.[136] Although Google claims that 'the process of dealing with each delisting request is not automated',[137] AI-machine learning enforcement could be easily deployed to deal with the task and the raising transaction costs of manual enforcement that Google must face. Whether this is already the case or it will be in the future, this is a glaring example of the apparently unresolvable conundrum that algorithmic enforcement triggers. On one side, there are raising transaction costs of online sanitization that only AI could keep under control. On the other side, AI would be called to make a balancing of rights that is unfit to make.

22.4.1.3   Freedom of Expression

The active side of the right of freedom of expression, freedom to impart information, stands perhaps as the most striking example of the human rights tension that algorithmic enforcement brings about. Algorithmic filtering and automated copyright and trademark enforcement might impinge greatly on users' freedom of expression. A preliminary issue concerns the fact that

---

133. *See*, e.g., Miquel Peguera, 'The Shaky Ground of the Right to Be Delisted', 15 Vand J Ent Tech L 507 (2015); Jeffry Rosen, 'The Right to Be Forgotten' (2015) 64 Stan L Rev Online 88; Stefan Kulk and Frederik Zuiderveen Borgesius, 'Google Spain v. González: Did the Court Forget About Freedom of Expression?' (2014) 3 Eur. J Risk Reg. 389 (2014); Jonathan Zittrain, *Don't Force Google to Forget* (NYTimes, 14 May 2014) <http://www.nytimes.com/2014/05/15/opinion/dont-force-google-to-forget.html?_r=0>.
134. Taddeo and Floridi (n 7) 18-19.
135. C-131/12 (n 132) § 81.
136. *Ibid. See* Article 29 Data Protection Working Party, Guidelines on the Implementation of the CJEU Judgment on *Google Spain v. Costeja* (2014) 14/EN WP 225 (hereinafter WP29 Guidelines), <http://ec.europa.eu/justice/data-protection/article-29/documenta tion/opinion-recommendation/files/2014/ wp225_en.pdf>.
137. Gareth Corfield, *Here Is How Google Handles Right to Be Forgotten Requests* (The Register, 19 March 2018) <https://www.theregister.co.uk/2018/03/19/google_right_to_ be_forgotten_request_process>.

proactive filtering – implemented through algorithmic tools – operates *ex ante* in an automated way, rather than ex post as a result of a notice-and-take-down procedure. This shift in enforcement practices has relevant consequences on users' right of freedom to express themselves. In *Google v. Louis Vuitton*, the CJEU Advocate General reminded how general rules of civil liability (based on negligence) – rather than strict liability IP law rules – suit online content governance best from the human rights perspective. His argument – crafted in the context of trademark infringement online – stressed that:

> [l]iability rules are more appropriate, since they do not [give] trade mark proprietors general – and virtually absolute – control over the use in cyberspace of keywords which correspond to their trade marks. Instead of being able to prevent, through trade mark protection, any possible use *– including, as has been observed, many lawful and even desirable uses* – trade mark proprietors would have to point to specific instances giving rise to Google's liability in the context of illegal damage to their trademarks.[138]

According to this argument, a negligence-based system would better serve the delicate balance between protection of IP rights, access to information, and freedom of expression that online proactive algorithmic enforcement might upset. Ex post review following a notice-and-take-down mechanism embeds an enhanced safeguard for freedom of expression as long as it forces intermediaries to consider the infringing nature of the materials before deciding whether to take them down. As Van Eecke mentioned, 'the notice-and-take-down procedure is one of the essential mechanisms through which the e-Commerce Directive achieves a balance between the interests of right holders, online intermediaries and users'.[139]

In contrast, an *ex ante* mechanism based on filtering and automatic infringement assessment systems that online intermediaries might deploy to monitor potentially infringing users' activities might disproportionally favour property rights against other fundamental rights. Algorithmic enforcement's false positives might cause relevant chilling effects and negatively impact users' fundamental right to freedom of expression. Automated systems cannot replace human judgment that should flag a certain use as fair or falling within the scope of an exception or limitation. Also, complexities regarding the public domain status of certain works might escape the

---

138. Joined Cases C-236, 237 & 238/08, Opinion of Advocate General, *Google France, S.A.R.L. & Google Inc. v. Louis Vuitton Malletier SA, Viaticum S.A., Luteciel S.A.R.L., v. Centre Bational de Recherche en Relations Humaines (CNRRH) S.A.R.L., Pierre-Alexis Thonet, Bruno Raboin, Tiger, a franchisee of Unicis*, ECLI:EU:C:2009:569, § 123.
139. Patrick Van Eecke, 'Online Service Providers and Liability: A Plea for a Balanced Approach' (2011) 48 Common Market L Rev 1455, 1479-80.

discerning capacity of content recognition technologies. In the own word of the European Court of Justice, these measures:

> could potentially undermine freedom of information, since that system might not distinguish adequately between unlawful content and lawful content, with the result that its introduction could lead to the blocking of lawful communications. Indeed, it is not contested that the reply to the question whether a transmission is lawful also depends on the application of statutory exceptions to copyright which vary from one Member State to another. In addition, in some Member States certain works fall within the public domain or may be posted online free of charge by the authors concerned.[140]

Of course, as already mentioned, following the approval of Article 17 of the C-DSM Directive,[141] the implications of an increase in the general monitoring of content uploaded onto OCSSPs' services and the increased use of automated filtering and enforcement systems, raises important questions relating to the preservation of users' fundamental rights to expression and information.

22.4.1.4   Right to Privacy and Data Protection

The deployment of algorithmic enforcement technologies has effects on the proper balance between privacy and freedom of expression.[142] On one side, Courts stressed the importance of imposing obligations on OSPs that lead to the implementation of automated enforcement tools by noting that 'violations of privacy of individuals and companies, summary trials and public lynching of innocents are routinely reported, all practised in the worldwide web with substantially increased damage because of the widespread nature of this medium of expression'.[143] Again, upholding the protection of the right to privacy against freedom of expression, courts reinforce this 'internet threat' discourse by noting that, on the internet, '[d]efamatory and other types of clearly unlawful speech, including hate speech and speech inciting violence, can be disseminated like never before, worldwide, in a matter of seconds, and sometimes remain persistently available online'.[144]

On the other side, courts highlighted that the unqualified deployment of filtering and monitoring technology might also impinge on users' right to protection of personal data. The CJEU has outlined the disproportionate impact of these measures on users' privacy by concluding that:

---

140. *See Netlog* (n 7) § 50.
141. *See* Directive 2019/790/EU (n 86) recital 61.
142. *See,* e.g., EU Charter (n 6) Articles 8, 11.
143. *Delfi AS v. Estonia*, App no 64569/09, 2015, § 110.
144. *Google Brazil v. Dafra,* Special Appeal no 1306157/SP, Superior Court of Justice, 24 March 2014) <https://cyberlaw.stanford.edu/page/wilmap-brazil>.

requiring installation of the contested filtering system would involve the identification, systematic analysis and processing of information connected with the profiles created on the social network by its users. The information connected with those profiles is protected personal data because, in principle, it allows those users to be identified.[145]

In *Scarlet* and *Netlog*, the CJEU established for the first time – a 'fundamental right to the protection of personal data, which is not fairly balanced with copyright holders' rights when a mechanism requiring the systematic processing of personal data is imposed in the name of the protection of intellectual property'.[146] According to the European Court of Human Rights, which tends to be critical of systems to intercept communications, the secrecy of communication or the right to respect for private life[147] could also be impinged upon by filtering technologies, especially when those systems monitor the content of communications.[148]

22.4.2   IP Owners' Rights

Algorithmic enforcements also adjudicate IP owners' rights, which have been construed as human rights. Article 27(2) of the Universal Declaration of Human Rights (UDHR) and Article 15(1)(c) of the International Covenant on Economic, Social and Cultural Rights (ICESCR), secure to authors the benefits from the 'protection of the moral and material interests resulting from [their] scientific, literary or artistic production'. In Europe, Article 17(2) EU Charter and Article 1 of Protocol No. 1 ECHR provide a fundamental right status of intellectual property.[149] The EU Charter, unlike the ECHR, expressly listed IP protection in its catalogue of rights under Article 17(2).[150] The ECHR, however, has been interpreted as extending its Article 1 Protocol

---

145. Netlog (n 7) § 49.
146. Gloria González Fuster, 'Balancing Intellectual Property Against Data Protection: a New Right's Wavering Weight' (2012) 14 IDP 34, 37.
147. *See* Charter (n 6) Article 7.
148. *See* Kulk and Borgesius (n 7) 793-794.
149. *Neij and Sunde Kolmisoppi v. Sweden,* App no 40397/12 (ECtHR, 19 February 2013) para. 10 (noting '[a]s to the weight afforded to the interest of protecting the copyright-holders, the Court would stress that intellectual property benefits from the protection afforded by Article 1 of Protocol No. 1 to the Convention'). *See also* Christophe Geiger and Elena Izyumenko, 'Copyright on the Human Rights' Trial: Redefining the Boundaries of Exclusivity through Freedom of Expression' (2014) 45(3) IIC 316.
150. *See* Christophe Geiger, 'Intellectual "Property" after the Treaty of Lisbon: Towards a Different Approach in the New European Legal Order?' (2010) 32(6) EIPR 255; 'Intellectual Property Shall be Protected!? Article 17(2) of the Charter of Fundamental Rights of the European Union: A Mysterious Provision with an Unclear Scope' (2009) 31(3) EIPR 113.

No. 1 protection to all IP rights.[151] This European approach on an autonomous fundamental right nature of IP implies that, when balancing two competing interests both protected as human rights, States are afforded 'a particularly wide' margin of appreciation.[152] This might lead to overprotection of IP interests vis-à-vis other fundamental rights, including the users' rights and ISPs' business freedom.[153]

However, human rights protection for IP should not be overestimated. The UN Special Rapporteur in the field of cultural rights stressed that inferring that Article 15(1)(c) recognizes a human right to protection of intellectual property 'is false and misleading'.[154] According to the UN Committee on Economic, Social and Cultural Rights (CESCR), an evident distinction exists in principle between standard IP rights and human rights protection given to creators in accordance with Article 15(1)(c).[155] Thus, Article 15(1)(c) cannot be interpreted as guaranteeing IP rights or as elevating IP to human rights.[156] Also, under the EU regime, a cautionary note would be of use. In *Telekabel*, the CJEU noted 'there is nothing whatsoever in the wording of Article 17(2) of the Charter to suggest that the right to intellectual property is inviolable and must for that reason be absolutely protected'.[157] Article 17(2) of the Charter would just clarify Article 17(1), which in turn stresses that '[t]he use of property may be regulated by law in so far as is necessary for the general interest'.[158] Likewise, Article 1 of the First Protocol to the ECHR provides for restrictions of the right 'in the public

---

151. *See* in the field of copyright: *Akdeniz* (n 7); *Neij and Sunde Kolmisoppi* (n 149); *Ashby Donald and Others v. France* App. no. 36769/08 (ECtHR, 10 January 2013); *Balan v. Moldova*, App no 19247/03, 29 January 2008; *Melnychuk v. Ukraine*, App no 28743/03, 5 July 2005; *Dima v. Romania*, App no 58472/00, 26 May 2005. In the field of trademarks: *Paeffgen Gmbh v. Germany*, App no 25379/04, 21688/05, 21722/05 and 21770/05, 18 September 2007; *Anheuser-Busch Inc. v. Portugal*, App no 73049/01, 11 January 2007. In the field of patent law, *see* ECommHR, *Lenzing AG v. United Kingdom*, App no 38817/97, 9 September 1998; ECommHR, *Smith Kline & French Lab. Ltd. v. the Netherlands*, App No. 12633/87, 4 October 1990.

152. *Neij and Sunde Kolmisoppi* (n 149) para. 11. *See also Akdeniz v. Turkey,* App no 20877/10 (ECtHR, 11 March 2014) para. 28; *Ashby Donald* (n 151) para. 40.

153. *See*, eg, for a critique of the approach towards treating IP rights and other fundamental rights 'as if they were of equal rank', Alexander Peukert, 'The Fundamental Right to (Intellectual) Property and the Discretion of the Legislature' in Christophe Geiger (ed), *Research Handbook on Human Rights and Intellectual Property* (Edward Elgar 2015) 132; Robert Burrell and Dev Gangjee, 'Trade Marks and Freedom of Expression: A Call for Caution' (2010) 41(5) IIC 544; Christina Angelopoulos, 'Freedom of Expression and Copyright: The Double Balancing Act' (2008) 3 IPQ 328.

154. UN General Assembly, Report of the Special Rapporteur in the field of cultural rights, Farida Shaheed, Copyright Policy and the Right to Science and Culture, Human Rights Council, Twenty-eighth session, A/HRC/28/57, 24 December 2014, para. 26.

155. *See* CESCR, General Comment No. 17 on Article 15(1)(c) of the ICESCR, 12 January 2006, E/C12/GC/17.

156. *Ibid.*

157. *UPC Telekabel* (n 7) para. 61.

158. *Ibid.*

interest' and allows the State 'to enforce such laws as it deems necessary to control the use of property in accordance with the general interest [...]'.[159]

It is worth noting that – in the context of the tension between IP rights and other human rights that algorithmic enforcement tools are called to balance – there is a progressive perspective emerging at the CJEU level.[160] The CJEU is departing from traditional continental European fairness and personality theory approaches and increasingly opens to the welfare and cultural theory perspectives.[161] In *GS Media*, the CJEU emphasizes the need to balance property rights with competing fundamental rights, such as freedom of expression and information and users' rights. Furthermore, *GS Media* concerns itself with safeguarding the functioning of the Internet as a fundamental tool to guarantee personal realization and exchange of information and opinions.[162] In this respect, *GS Media* signals a critical moment in the evolution of the EU jurisprudence. It embraces a progressive vision of copyright and cultural policies that focuses on public interest and user's access to content, rather than on a purely individualistic and propertarian approach. This development has been steadily taking place since a 'fair balance' approach was sought in the *Promusicae* case.[163] In *UPC Telekabel*, the CJEU stated that in order to strike that 'fair balance' between competing fundamental rights, measures to be applied, such as blocking orders, must 'not unnecessarily deprive internet users of the possibility of lawfully accessing the information available'.[164] In *L'Oreal*, *Scarlet* and *Netlog*, the CJEU banned general monitoring obligations by highlighting their disproportional negative externalities over fundamental rights, such as the right to receive and impart information, the right to privacy and freedom of business.[165] Finally, a recent trifecta of CJEU decision has placed fundamental rights and exceptions and limitations – thus the public interest perspective of the copyright paradox – at the centre stage, noting *inter alia* that, in

---

159. *Ibid.*
160. This, however, should be contextualized within a counter posing long-standing move towards propertization in the field of copyright law in particular, and IP law more broadly. *See* Caterina Sganga, *Propertizing European Copyright: History, Challenges and Opportunities* (Edward Elgar 2018).
161. *See* Terry Fisher, 'Theories of Intellectual Property' in Stephen Munzer (ed), *New Essays in the Legal and Political Theory of Property* (Cambridge University Press 2001).
162. *See* C-160/15 *GS Media BV v. Sanoma Media Netherlands BV and Others* [2016] ECLI:EU:C:2016:644, paras 31 and 45.
163. C-275/06 *Productores de Música de España (Promusicae) v. Telefónica de España SAU* (2008) ECLI:EU:C:2008:54, para. 70.
164. C-314/12 *UPC Telekabel Wien GmbH v. Constantin Film Verleih GmbH* [2014] EU:C:2014:192, para. 64.
165. *See* C-324/09 *L'Oréal SA and Others v. eBay International AG and Others* [2011] ECLI:EU:C:2011:474, para. 139; Case C-70/10 *Scarlet Extended SA v. Société belge des auteurs, compositeurs et éditeurs SCRL (SABAM)* [2011] ECLI:EU:C:2011:771; C-360/10 *Belgische Vereniging van Auteurs, Componisten en Uitgevers CVBA (SABAM) v. Netlog NV* [2012] ECLI:EU:C:2012:85.

striking a balance between exclusive rights of the author and the rights of the users, a court must 'rely on an interpretation […] which, whilst consistent with their wording and safeguarding their effectiveness, fully adheres to the fundamental rights enshrined in the Charter of Fundamental Rights of the European Union [("Charter")]'.[166] Furthermore, the level of protection of human rights provided by the Charter can never be compromised by national implementations or jurisprudential application of national standards.[167]

22.4.3 OSPs, FREEDOM OF BUSINESS AND INNOVATION

Another fundamental right that comes to balancing when imposing obligations on OSPs to implement enforcement systems – possibly automated – is the freedom to conduct business as provided by Article 16 of the EU Charter.[168] In contrast to the freedom of expression, freedom to conduct business is unknown to other international human rights instrument.[169] As a consequence, 'to date the case law has not […] provided a full and useful definition of this freedom'.[170] Both the textual context and the judicial history of Article 16, therefore, point to its low-qualified nature, allowing the State a wide power to interfere with it.[171] This particularly 'weak' nature of the right[172] has arguably induced the CJEU to rule in favour of right holders, also when the Advocate General failed to find a 'fair balance'.[173]

Obviously, imposing new enforcement obligations on OSPs makes it more expensive for platforms to enter and compete in the market, thus lowering incentives to innovation. OSPs – and OCSSPs in particular under the new Article 17 of the C-DSM Directive – might be called to develop and

---

166. C-469/17 *Funke Medien NRW GmbH v. Bundesrepublik Deutschland* (2019) ECLI-:EU:C:2019:623, para. 76; C-516/17 *Spiegel Online GmbH v. Volker Beck* [2019] ECLI:EU:C:2019:625, para. 59. *See also* C-476/17 *Pelham GmbH and Others v. Ralf Hütter and Florian Schneider-Esleben* [2019] ECLI:EU:C:2019:624.

167. *Ibid.,* paras 79-80.

168. *See* Charter (n 6) Article 16.

169. Note, however, that some national constitutions have provided for the protection of the freedom to conduct a business long before these supranational developments. *See,* eg, Italian Constitution of 1947, Article 41; Spanish Constitution of 1978, Article 38; Croatian Constitution of 1990, Article 49; and Slovenian Constitution of 1991, Article 74.

170. C-426/11, Opinion of Advocate General Cruz Villalón, *Alemo-Herron and Others* [2013] EU:C:2013:82, para. 49.

171. *See* C-283/11, *Sky Österreich* [2013] EU:C:2013:28, § 46; T-587/13, *Schwerdt v. OHIM – Iberamigo (cat&clean)* [2015] EU:T:2015:37, para. 55.

172. *See* Xavier Groussot, Gunnar Thor Pétursson & Justin Pierce, 'Weak Right, Strong Court – The Freedom to Conduct Business and the EU Charter of Fundamental Rights' in Sionaidh Douglas-Scott & Nicholas Hatzis (eds), Research Handbook on EU Law and Human Rights (Edward Elgar 2017) 326-344; *EMI Records Ltd & Ors v. British Sky Broadcasting Ltd & Ors* [2013] EWHC 379 (Ch) [107].

173. *See UPC Telekabel* (n 7) para. 49.

deploy costly technology to cope with legal requirement and obligations. The CJEU emphasized the economic impact on OSPs of algorithmic filtering and monitoring obligations. The CJEU assumed that monitoring all the electronic communications made through the network, without any limitation in time, directed to all future infringements of existing and yet to create works 'would result in a serious infringement of the freedom of the hosting service provider to conduct its business.'[174] Hosting providers' freedom of business would be disproportionally affected since an obligation to adopt filtering technologies would require the ISP to install a complicated, costly and permanent system at its own expense.[175] In addition, according to the CJEU, this obligation would be contrary to Article 3 of the Enforcement Directive, providing that 'procedures and remedies necessary to ensure the enforcement of the intellectual property rights … shall not be unnecessarily complicated or costly [and] shall be applied in such a manner as to avoid the creation of barriers to legitimate trade.'[176]

22.5   HOW HUMAN RIGHTS CAN BE PROTECTED FROM ALGORITHMIC ENFORCEMENT?

In the IP domain and elsewhere, socially relevant choices online increasingly occur through automated private enforcement run by opaque algorithms, which creates a so-called 'black-box' society.[177] Algorithmic enforcement finds its primary Achilles' heel in algorithms' transparency and accountability, which remains an issue challenging from the outset efficient and democratic semiotic regulation online.[178] Setting aside, for now, more futuristic concerns regarding the displacement of human decision-making,[179] promoting algorithmic transparency and accountability is a field where

---

174. *Netlog* (n 7) para. 46.
175. *Ibid.*
176. *See* Directive 2004/48/EC of the European Parliament and of the Council on the enforcement of intellectual property rights [2004] OJ L157, Article 3.
177. Frank Pasquale, *The Black Box Society: The Secret Algorithms That Control Money and Information* (Harvard University Press 2015). *See also* Nicolas Suzor, *Lawless: The Secret Rules That Govern Our Digital Lives* (CUP 2019); Tarleton Gillespie, *Custodians of the Internet: Platforms, Content Moderation, and the Hidden Decisions That Shape Social Media* (Yale University Press 2018).
178. *See* Joshua Kroll, et al., 'Accountable Algorithms' (2017) 165 U Pa L Rev 633; Nicholas Diakopoulos, 'Accountability in Algorithmic Decision Making' (2016) 59(2) Communications of the ACM 56, 56-62; Nicholas Diakopoulos and Michael Koliska, 'Algorithmic Transparency in the News Media' (2016) Digital Journalism.
179. *See* Tim Wu, 'Will Artificial Intelligence Eat the Law? The Rise of Hybrid Social-Ordering Systems' (2019) 119(1) Columbia L Rev 1, 1-29 (arguing that hybrid machine–human systems are the predictable future of legal adjudication); Richard Re and Alicia Solow-Niederman, 'Developing Artificially Intelligent Justice' (2019) 22 Stan Tech L Rev 242; Eugene Volokh, 'Chief Justice Robots' (2019) 68 Duke L J 1135.

regulation could promptly intervene on the basis of miscellaneous scholarly proposals and suggestions.

Given the early stage of human engagement with artificial intelligence, the essential basics and the precise nature of the notion itself of algorithmic accountability are still under review. According to Wagner, there is still a high level of uncertainty regarding 'to whom' and 'for what' algorithms should be accountable.[180] An initial basic finding is that algorithms should be at least accountable to users.[181] Alternatively, it has also been argued that algorithms should be accountable for 'decision subjects'[182] or public regulators.[183]

In this respect, access to the source code might provide some accountability[184], but users – or other subjects – should be enabled to understand what the algorithm is actually doing.[185] In order to do so, however, there are technical, organizational and regulatory challenges in ensuring access to data.[186] In this context, Elkin-Koren and Perel suggest that the solution to black-box content moderation can be found in grass-root oversight through 'tinkering',[187] which would allow people to 'systematically test and record how online intermediaries respond to representatives, like-real content' submitted to the platforms.[188]

Proposals also suggest that attaching lowered online intermediaries' liability to increased algorithmic accountability might ensure more effective compliance with human rights.[189] Specific provision for ensuring algorithmic accountability might include transparency of automated decisions, external

---

180. *See* Ben Wagner, 'Algorithmic Accountability: Towards Accountable Systems' in Giancarlo Frosio (ed), *The Oxford Handbook of Online Intermediary Liability* (OUP forthcoming 2020) ch 35 (in file with the author).

181. *Ibid*; Don Norman, *The Design of Everyday Things: Revised and Expanded Edition* (Revised, Expanded edition, Basic Books 2013); Nicholas Diakopoulos, 'Algorithmic Accountability' (2015) 3 Digital Journalism 398; Cathy O'Neil, *Weapons of Math Destruction: How Big Data Increases Inequality and Threatens Democracy* (Crown 2016).

182. *See* Michael Veale, Max Van Kleek and Reuben Binns, 'Fairness and Accountability Design Needs for Algorithmic Support in High-Stakes Public Sector Decision-Making' (2018) arXiv:1802.01029 [cs] 1, 6.

183. *See* Ben Wagner, 'Algorithms and Human Rights: Study on the Human Rights Dimensions of Automated Data Processing Techniques and Possible Regulatory Implications' (Council of Europe 2018) DGI(2017)12 <https://rm.coe.int/algorithms-and-human-rights-study-on-the-human-rights-dimension-of-aut/1680796d10>.

184. O'Neil (n 181).

185. *See* Wagner (n 183).

186. *Ibid.*

187. *See* Maayan Perel and Niva Elkin-Koren, 'Black Box Tinkering: Beyond Disclosure in Algorithmic Enforcement' (2017) 69 Fla L Rev 181, 193.

188. *See* Niva Elkin-Koren and Maayan Perel, 'Guarding the Guardians: Content Moderation by Online Intermediaries and the Rule of Law' in Giancarlo Frosio (ed), *The Oxford Handbook of Online Intermediary Liability* (OUP forthcoming 2020) ch 34 (in file with the author).

189. *See* Wagner (n 183).

auditing of the algorithmic accountability mechanism, independent external body addressing complaints, 'radical transparency' of the system, irrevocable storage of the decisions, user-friendly explanation of the automated decisions, and availability of human review of the decisions.[190]

Again, from a broader perspective, Frederick Mostert stresses the point that regulators should set up a more permanent online architecture supported by 'digital due process'.[191] This 'digital due process' framework should be based on transparent and internationally agreed 'digital due process' principles.[192] Of course, these principles should eminently address rampant online algorithmic enforcement and its negative externalities on freedom of expression and data protection. Attempts to move forward in this process of 'constitutionalization' of the Internet[193] with special emphasis on the role of online intermediaries have been plenty. For example, the Manila Principles on Intermediary Liability set out safeguards for content restriction on the Internet with the goal of protecting users' rights, including 'freedom of expression, freedom of association and the right to privacy.'[194] Again, these 'digital due process' principles should build upon the UN 'Protect, Respect and Remedy' Framework as endorsed by the UN Human Rights Council together with the UN Guiding Principles on Business and Human Rights.[195]

Once these 'digital due process' principles are in place, they might be coordinated with ongoing projects, such as Ranking Digital Rights, which promotes best practices and transparency among online intermediaries by ranking Internet and telecommunications companies according to their virtuous behaviour in respecting users' rights, including privacy and freedom of speech.[196] Online intermediaries ranking high in algorithmic due process and accountability – according to the variables and solutions that I have earlier mentioned – might be exempted from the strictest enhanced liability

---

190. *Ibid. See also See* Ben Wagner, 'Ethics as an Escape from Regulation: From Ethics-Washing to Ethics-Shopping?' in Mireille Hildebrandt (ed), *Being Profiling. Cogitas ergo sum* (Amsterdam University Press 2018) (on independent external bodies); David Kaye, 'Report of the Special Rapporteur on the Promotion and Protection of the Right to Freedom of Opinion and Expression' (2018) A/HRC/38/35 <https://documents-dds-ny.un.org/doc/UNDOC/GEN/G18/096/72/PDF/G1809672.pdf?OpenElement> (on radical transparency.

191. *See* Frederick Mostert, '"Digital Due Process": A Need for Online Justice' (forthcoming 2020) (on file with the author).

192. *Ibid.*

193. *See* e.g., Dennis Redeker and Lex Gill, Urs Gasser, 'Towards Digital Constitutionalism? Mapping Attempts to Craft an Internet Bill of Rights' (2018) 80(4) Int'l Comm Gazzette 302, 302-319.

194. *See* Manila Principles on Intermediary Liability, Intro, <https://www.manilaprincip les.org>.

195. *See* United Nations, Human Rights, Office of the High Commissioner, 'Guiding Principles on Business Human Rights: Implementing the United Nations "Protect, Respect, and Remedy" Framework' (2011) A/HRC/RES/17/4.

196. *See* Ranking Digital Rights <https://rankingdigitalrights.org>.

standards. A modern system promoting due process and algorithmic accountability online should function according to a strict function based on
principles-compliance-ranking-exemption.

22.6 CONCLUSIONS

Today, privately ordered automated content moderation defines the contours
of the infosphere where social interaction occurs for billions of people daily.
The impact of online content moderation on modern society is tremendous.
In this context, socially relevant choices are delegated to automated
enforcement run through opaque algorithms. Meanwhile, AI-empowered
platforms grow increasingly omniscient as machine learning and data
analytics allows algorithmic enforcement tools – and the OSPs developing
and running them – to proactively predict and prevent the illicit use of
content.

   This development poses plenty of challenges. First, enforcement
through the private ordering and voluntary measures moves the adjudication
of lawful and unlawful content out of public oversight. Further, enforcement
would be looking once again for an 'answer to the machine in the
machine'.[197] By enlisting online intermediaries as watchdogs, governments
would de facto delegate online enforcement to algorithmic tools – with
limited or no accountability.[198] Finally, transferring regulation and adjudication of Internet rights to private automated enforcement online highlights
unescapable tensions with the preservation of fundamental rights of users,
OSPs and IP right holders. The tension between competing rights – such as
intellectual property, due process, freedom of information, freedom of
expression, freedom of business or a fundamental right to Internet access –
leads to unavoidable constriction of some rights against others depending on
policy choices. This 'conundrum' has yet to find a sustainable policy
solution. Legislators have erred so far in privileging some of the relevant
interests against others, while increasingly resorting to the mandatory or
voluntary promotion of filtering, monitoring and automated enforcement
technologies, which might fail to strike a fair balance between IP and other
fundamental rights.

   Omniscient platforms enforcing human rights through opaque algorithms evoke threatening dystopian scenarios. This is a dangerous path to
take. Algorithmic enforcement, although in its infancy, seems set to become

---

197. Charles Clark, 'The Answer to the Machine is in the Machine', in Bernt Hugenholtz
    (ed), *The Future of Copyright in a Digital Environment* (Kluwer Law Int'l 1999) 139.
    See also Christophe Geiger, 'The Answer to the Machine Should Not Be the Machine,
    Safeguarding the Private Copy Exception in the Digital Environment' (2008) 30 EIPR
    121.
198. *See* Joshua Kroll and others, 'Accountable Algorithms' (2017) 165 U Pa L Rev 633.

the standard for content moderation online, given all transaction costs involved. However, little thinking has been dedicated to the consequences of massive adoption of algorithmic enforcement. Legislators and policymakers have been promoting AI-run content sanitization online without setting up first a strong technological and legal framework for preserving human rights. Unsupervised AI pervasiveness has the capacity to lower dramatically human rights standards online that subtly, invisibly and increasingly will fade away before our very eyes.

Part IV
Rights in Information

Chapter 23

Privacy, Confidentiality and Property

Peter Jaffey

23.1   INTRODUCTION

My aim in this chapter is to differentiate between various types of legal claim that appear to overlap or are sometimes conflated. The claims are concerned, broadly speaking, with the disclosure or exploitation of the information, though the discussion sometimes goes beyond this for the purposes of comparison. More particularly, I deal with 'informational privacy' and its relation to the law of confidentiality; aspects of a wider notion of privacy not concerned with private information; aspects of the law of confidentiality concerned with commercial rather than private information, that is to say, the law of trade secrets, and more generally, claims arising from the ownership of intangibles, including information. The objective is not to provide a detailed account of the law, but to consider it broadly in order to identify the principles underlying the different claims and thereby highlight the confusion and incoherence that is liable to result from a failure to separate distinct categories based on different principles.[1] Although the principal concern is with English law, the arguments are of more general relevance.

---

1. Some of these issues are discussed in similar fashion in P. Jaffey, *Private Law and Property Claims* (Hart Publishing, 2007), Ch. 1-3. The Data Protection Act 2018, applying the General Data Protection Regulation (GDPR) (EU) 2016/679, is not discussed.

23.2 PRIVACY AND CONFIDENTIALITY

Until relatively recently, it was said straightforwardly that there was no right of privacy in English law, and there were cases that gave striking support to this proposition. In the notorious *Kaye v. Roberston*,[2] newspaper journalists entered the hospital room of the claimant where he was bedridden and recovering from a serious accident, and took a photograph which was to be published without his consent. The court described this as a 'monstrous invasion of privacy',[3] but denied that there was any right of privacy in English law.[4] In light of this case and others, the subject of privacy has long been controversial. The enactment of the Human Rights Act 1998, giving effect to the European Convention on Human Rights, revived the issue, in light of Article 8 of the Convention, which provides in paragraph 1:[5] 'Everyone has the right to respect for his private and family life, his home and his correspondence.' The law has now reached the position that, although there is still no action for breach of privacy as such, the right of privacy under Article 8 does now receive satisfactory protection, principally through the ancient action for breach of confidence, as it has been developed by the courts.

23.2.1 THE LAW OF CONFIDENTIALITY

The basis of the law of confidentiality has been a matter of controversy. In the simplest case, C confides in D, who has agreed to keep the information confidential, and the law prohibits D from divulging the secret. More commonly, although D has not made an explicit undertaking of confidentiality, it is clear that there is an agreement to keep the information confidential, but one that is unspoken and indeed need not be expressed because of the nature of the relationship and the circumstances: there is, in

---

2. [1991] *FSR* 62.
3. At 70, per Bingham L.J, using Griffiths J.'s expression in *Bernstein v. Skyviews* [1978] *QB* 479, 489.
4. The court contrived to give some protection on the unsatisfactory basis of injurious or malicious falsehood. This applied only because the court found: (1) a false implication that the photograph was consented to by the claimant; and (2) a pecuniary loss in the form of the loss of the commercial value of the story. Such a false implication is not a necessary characteristic of a breach of privacy, and the loss identified is based on the value of the claimant's story for commercial exploitation, not the value of his privacy, and the implication is that if the claimant would not have been willing to sell his story he should have no claim.
5. Subject to the proviso in para. 2.

other words, a confidential relationship, carrying with it an implied under-taking of confidentiality. In such cases, the law can, in principle, be explained in terms of agreement or contract, broadly understood.[6]

Say C confides in D1 and D1 conveys the information to D2. It is established that D2 can also incur a duty not to publish the information.[7] It is sometimes argued that D2's duty is a duty not to interfere with the performance by D1 of his duty of confidentiality, or not to induce D1 to breach it.[8] But this explanation is plausible only where D2's disclosure makes him complicit in the wrong by D1, as, for example, where D1 relayed the information to D2 with a view to D2's disclosing it. If D1 intended D2 to keep the confidence, D2's breach cannot plausibly be understood as wrongful on the ground that it procured or assisted in a breach by D1.[9] The point is even clearer where D2 eavesdrops on C confiding in D1. It may have been thought at one time that in such a case D2 incurs no duty to keep the information confidential because D2 is clearly not an accessory to a breach by D1,[10] but it is now clear that D2 can be bound by a duty of confidentiality in such a case,[11] and this surely cannot be understood as incidental to or dependent on the undertaking of confidentiality by D1.[12] On what basis, then, is D2 bound by a duty of confidentiality?

It is said that the basis of D2's duty is a principle of 'good faith' or a principle of 'unconscionability'. These ideas are of course associated with the origins of the law of confidentiality in the law of equity as opposed to the common law, but in themselves, they do not disclose any meaningful basis for a claim.[13] The basis of the claim must lie in the fact that where C has given personal information to D1 in confidence,[14] disclosing the information

---

6. As noted in W.R. Cornish, D. Llewelyn & T. Aplin, *Intellectual Property* (Sweet & Maxwell, 9th edn, 2019), 8-06. Historically the claim was governed by equity rather than common law. The difficulty at common law would have been the inadequacy of the common law remedy of pecuniary damages compared to the equitable remedy of injunction.
7. *See,* e.g., *Attorney-General v. Guardian Newspapers (Spycatcher)* [1990] *AC* 109.
8. *See,* e.g., Cornish et al., *supra* n. 6, 8-06.
9. The fact that by making the disclosure D2 destroys the value of D1's undertaking to C does not mean that D2 has induced a breach or unlawfully interfered with its performance: *See RCA v. Pollard* [1983] 1 *Ch* 135; *Douglas v. Hello!* [2003] *All ER* 996 at para. 243, per Lindsay J.
10. This may have been the position of Megarry V.C. in *Malone v. Metropolitan Police Commissioner* [1979] *Ch* 344, 375-7.
11. *Francome v. Mirror Group Newspapers* [1984] 1 *WLR* 892, *Attorney-General v. Guardian Newspapers (Spycatcher)* [1990] *AC* 109.
12. Lord Goff in *Attorney-General v. Guardian Newspapers (Spycatcher)* [1990] *AC* 109, 281 referred to the 'public interest in the maintenance of confidences', but if this does not refer to enforcing undertakings of confidence or preventing interference by third parties in the performance of such undertakings, then it is not clear what it can really mean other than, as argued below, the protection of privacy.
13. *See* further Jaffey, *supra* n. 1, Ch. 4.
14. As to information that is not personal, *see* the section below concerning trade secrets.

is liable to cause harm to C: it is liable to cause him embarrassment or humiliation or to demean him in the eyes of some people – this is why C wanted the information kept confidential.[15] The duty of D2 not to disclose the information must be based, not on D1's undertaking to maintain its confidentiality, but on duty arising under the general law not to cause C harm of this sort by revealing the information. Thus the basis of the claim must surely be, not that the information was divulged to D1 in confidence, but that the information was private. The fact that the information was divulged in confidence merely demonstrates its private nature and the fact that its disclosure is liable to cause harm to C. This seems to be the only plausible basis for the duty binding third parties. Understood in this way, the claim for breach of confidence is clearly in principle a claim in tort, though because of its origins in the law of equity it is not traditionally so described.

This understanding is confirmed by a consideration of the principal condition for a duty of confidentiality to arise. This is said to be that the information 'must have been imparted in circumstances importing an obligation of confidence'.[16] On its most natural interpretation, this means that the information must originally have been communicated or acquired in a confidential relationship in a sense explained above, that is, subject to an actual express or implied agreement to respect confidentiality. In some cases, it seems that the absence of a genuine confidential relationship in this sense was enough to preclude any legal duty of confidentiality.[17] But it now seems clear that there is no requirement of a genuine confidential relationship in this sense. Thus in *Attorney-General v. Guardian Newspapers (No. 2) (Spy-catcher)*,[18] Lord Goff said: '[I]n the vast majority of cases ... the duty of confidence will arise from a transaction or relationship between the parties ... But it is well settled that a duty of confidence may arise in equity independently of such cases'. He also said that a duty of confidence could arise when 'an obviously confidential document, such as a private diary, is dropped in a public place, and is then picked up by a passer-by'.[19] A personal diary is not a communication made subject to a confidential relationship, but it is clearly private.

A good example of this point is provided by *Hellewell v. Chief Constable of Derbyshire*.[20] Here Laws J. took the view that when the police take photographs of suspects who are subsequently convicted, although the police are free to distribute the photographs for the purpose of promoting law and order, their freedom to do so is subject to constraints to protect the suspect's privacy. It is clear here that the protection is not based on any

---

15. *See infra*, text at n. 72. Where the confidential information concerns a third party, it is the third party's privacy that is in issue.
16. *Coco v. Clark* [1969] *RPC* 41, 47, per Megarry V.C.
17. *See*, e.g., *Malone v. Metropolitan Police Commissioner* [1979] *Ch* 344.
18. [1990] 1 *AC* 109, 281.
19. *Ibid.*
20. [1995] 1 *WLR* 804.

undertaking of confidentiality given by the police, or on any confidential relationship in a sense above. The police are empowered to take the photographs without giving any such undertaking. As the judge said, the duty of confidentiality protects the claimant's right to privacy. Laws J. also said:[21]

> If someone with a telephoto lens were to take from a distance and with no authority a picture of another engaged in some private act, his subsequent disclosure of the photograph would … as surely amount to a breach of confidence as if he had found or stolen a letter or diary in which the act was recounted and proceeded to publish it.

Clearly, there is no confidential relationship between the photographer and the subject, just as there is no confidential relationship with a stranger in respect of a diary.[22]

These cases begin to reveal the transition in the law of confidentiality from the idea of an undertaking of confidentiality, arising from a confidential relationship, as the justification for a duty of confidentiality or non-disclosure, to the idea of a duty of confidentiality or non-disclosure as the remedy to protect a right of privacy. The transition is disguised by the ambiguity in the expression 'circumstances importing an obligation of confidence'. This seems originally to have been intended to refer to a genuine confidential relationship in which there was an actual, though tacit, confidentiality agreement, but was subsequently understood to mean circumstances in which it is justified to impose a duty of confidentiality, *viz.*, where disclosure would infringe a right of privacy. The same ambiguity can be found in the expression 'confidential relationship', since one might take it to refer to a situation where, by virtue of the claimant's interest in his privacy, the defendant incurs a duty of confidentiality. Thus, even before the need arose to take account of Article 8, in cases such as the ones mentioned the law of confidentiality could only be understood on the basis that its function was to protect privacy.

As the courts have acknowledged, the application of Article 8 to English private law is not a straightforward matter. As Lord Hoffmann said in *Campbell v. MGN*, Article 8 'is not directly concerned with the protection of privacy against private persons or corporations. It is … a guarantee of privacy only against public authorities'. But he went on:

> What human rights law has done is to identify private information as something worth protecting as an aspect of human autonomy and dignity. And this recognition has raised inescapably the question of why it should be worth protecting against the state but not against a private person.[23]

---

21. At 807.
22. Maybe this could not be said of correspondence.
23. [2004] *UKHL* 22, paras 49–50.

Thus, on Lord Hoffmann's view, the courts have developed the English domestic law of privacy by analogy with the Convention rather than by the direct application of it.[24] In light of Article 8, the courts have made it explicit that the claim for breach of confidence protects a right to privacy. This is well illustrated by the case of *X & Y v. News Group Newspapers*,[25] where an injunction was issued prohibiting the media from revealing the new name of the applicant who had been notorious under her original name as a convicted murderer.[26] In *Douglas v. Hello!*,[27] Sedley L.J., taking account of Article 8 and the state of the common law, said:[28] 'The law no longer needs to construct an artificial relationship of confidentiality … it can recognise privacy itself as a legal principle', and in *A v. B*, Lord Woolf C.J. said:[29] 'A duty of confidence will arise whenever the party subject to the duty is in a situation where he either knows or ought to know that the other person can reasonably expect his privacy to be protected.' He added:[30] 'The bugging of someone's home or the use of other surveillance techniques are obvious examples of such an intrusion.' Thus the defendant incurs a duty of confidentiality not because of an undertaking of confidentiality or a confidential relationship in a natural sense, but in order to protect privacy. This development was made clear by the House of Lords in *Campbell v. MGN*.[31] On the basis that a field of law should be defined by reference to the rationale for the claim, the law of confidentiality should now really be described as the law of informational privacy, i.e., the law restricting disclosure of information on the ground that it is private. In a case where there was a genuine confidential relationship, and the defendant broke the confidence – an 'old-fashioned breach of confidence' – these circumstances will count against the defendant.[32]

23.2.2 THE LIMITS OF INFORMATIONAL PRIVACY

There are two main problems that arise concerning the right to informational privacy. The first is the scope of the right: when are the circumstances private, such as to generate protection through an action for breach of confidence? In *A v. B*, Lord Woolf said that 'usually the answer to the question whether there exists a private interest worthy of protection will be

---

24. As Baroness Hale explains at para. 132, Article 8 enters private law because the court as a public authority must act in conformity with the Convention.
25. [2003] *EWHC* 1101.
26. *Cf. Venables v. News Group Newspapers* [2001] *Fam* 430.
27. [2001] *QB* 967.
28. Paragraph 126.
29. [2003] *QB* 195, 207.
30. *Ibid. See also WB v. Bauer Publishing* [2002] *EMLR* 8.
31. [2004] *UKHL* 22, paras 13-14, per Lord Nicholls; *McKennitt v. Ash* [2008] *QB* 73; *Associated Newspapers v. Prince of Wales* [2008] *Ch* 57.
32. *McKennitt v. Ash* [2008] *QB* 73; *Mosley v. News Group Newspapers* [2008] EWHC 1777.

obvious.'[33] He also quoted from the judgment of Gleeson L.J. in *Australian Broadcasting Corpn v. Lenah Game Meats*:[34]

> The requirement that disclosure or observation of information or conduct would be highly offensive to a reasonable person of ordinary sensibilities is in many circumstances a useful practical test of what is private.

One suspects that Lord Woolf may have been too sanguine in thinking that particular cases will not raise difficulty on this point. But at least it seems clear that the claimant in *Kaye v. Robertson* would have been protected. Similarly, it is surely clear that someone who is surreptitiously photographed in private by the use of a long lens camera is covered, certainly if he is dressed or presents himself or acts in a way that he would not in public.[35] In *Campbell v. MGN*, it was suggested that the 'highly offensive to disclose' test might not always be apt and that sometimes it would be better to ask simply whether there was a reasonable expectation of privacy.[36] There are some cases where it is quite clear that information is private, as, for example, with respect to information about medical treatment, whether or not a reasonable person would consider disclosure to be highly offensive. Recent cases adopt the requirement that in the circumstances, the claimant had a reasonable expectation of privacy in accordance with Article 8.[37]

Lord Woolf also quoted from the judgment of Gleeson L.J. to the effect that there is no hard and fast line between what is public and what is private.[38] An activity may not be private even though it occurs on private property and is not open to the public. On the other hand, there can presumably be a right of privacy in respect of what is said or done in a public place or is open to the gaze of strangers who happen to be in the vicinity: for example, where someone is lying injured in the road after an accident. The latter point is illustrated by the case of *Peck*, a case from the UK in the European Court of Human Rights.[39] In *Peck*, the applicant had been filmed

---

33. [2003] *QB* 195, 206.
34. (2001) 185 *ALR* 1, 13.
35. This is the position under the Press Complaints Commission Code of Practice, referred to by Woolf CJ in *A v. B*, at 209, which the Human Rights Act 1998 by s. 12 requires the courts to take account of. In *Spencer v. United Kingdom* (1998) 25 *EHRR* CD 105 before the European Commission of Human Rights, one alleged invasion of privacy was the taking of a telephoto picture of the claimant in a private garden of a hospital. It was held that the applicant had not established that there was no claim in English law, although one can have some sympathy with the applicants' view that at the time the authorities did not support such a claim.
36. At paras, 22, 94.
37. *See*, for example, *Murray v. Big Pictures Ltd* [2008] EWCA Civ 446 [24]. See N.A. Moreham, 'Privacy in the Common Law: A Doctrinal and Theoretical Analysis' (2005) 121 *LQR* 628.
38. (2001) 185 *ALR* 1, 13.
39. *Peck v. United Kingdom* [2003] *EMLR* 15.

on closed-circuit television (CCTV) used for security purposes by the local authority. The applicant as seen with a knife which he subsequently used to attempt suicide, although the suicide attempt was not caught on film. The film was subsequently shown on television in a programme about CCTV. The court held that the English law of confidentiality was inadequate to protect the applicant because it did not apply where the claimant was in a public street. This would have been indisputable as a statement of English law at one time, but following recent cases, there seems no reason to think that the applicant would not now be protected. Some cases now imply that there may even be a reasonable expectation of privacy in respect of ordinary activities in public, in the absence of a good reason for publication.[40]

An interesting case on this point is *Douglas v. Hello!*[41] Here, the claimants held a large wedding with several hundred guests and imposed a condition on everyone attending that no one other than the claimants' authorized photographers were permitted to take photographs. The restriction was enforced by tight security. This was in accordance with a contractual arrangement with OK magazine, and the intention was that the claimants would be able to select photographs that showed them at their best, to be published exclusively by OK, for which OK paid a considerable sum, reflecting the commercial value of this exclusive. An unauthorized photographer entered and took clandestine photographs which he sold to a rival magazine, the defendant Hello. The claimants asserted a right to stop the publication by the defendant. One might ask first what the position would have been if no confidentiality or security arrangements had been put in place. Would the nature of the occasion in itself have given the claimants a right of privacy? It could certainly be described as a private occasion, though possibly it is less clear whether the claimants would be said to have a reasonable expectation of privacy.[42]

What about the effect of the arrangements to secure confidentiality? Leaving aside the question of the duty imposed on people who attended by the conditions of entry, and the liability of third parties as accessories in a breach of this duty, can one infer from the fact that the claimants made these arrangements that they regarded the occasion like a private one, and is this sufficient to establish that they did indeed have a reasonable expectation of privacy even if they otherwise would not have done? There seems to be no reason why this should not be the case. If the claimants wanted to have an occasion where they could be confident that no photographs would be published so that they could feel free to look and behave as they might at

---

40. *Murray v. Big Pictures Ltd* [2008] EWCA Civ 446. Support for this appears to come from *von Hannover v. Germany* (2005) 40 *EHRR* 1.
41. Interim proceedings [2001] *QB* 967; final proceedings [2003] *All ER* 996.
42. And it would not seem apt to say, applying Gleeson L.J's formula, that it would be 'highly offensive' to publish photographs of such an occasion, as noted by Lindsay J., [2003] *All ER* 996 at para. 192.

home, say, why should they not be able to do this?[43] The fact that the claimants also intended to release specially selected photographs to preserve and enhance their public image does not seem to undermine this right, though it was suggested that the concern for privacy and for commercial exploitation of the occasion were at odds with each other.[44] In fact, it was held that there was a right of privacy, but compensation for invading the right by the release of unauthorized photographs was very modest, certainly by comparison with the commercial value of the information,[45] and this seems reasonable because, although the claimants' privacy may have been invaded, the photographs published did not embarrass them or show them in an adverse light.

The second main problem is in what circumstances the right of privacy is overridden by a countervailing public interest in disclosure. It is an issue that has already had to be addressed in connection with the public interest defence in confidentiality and copyright.[46] Some judges have suggested that it might be an insuperable problem or at least one that requires a legislative solution.[47] It is on this issue that the influence of the European Convention on Human Rights has been most apparent. Under the Convention, the scope of the public interest justification for disclosure of private information under Article 8 has to be assessed in light of the right to freedom of expression under Article 10, and conversely, the limitations on the right conferred by Article 10 have to be assessed in light of the right to privacy conferred by Article 8. The two provisions are interrelated and together provide a framework for addressing the issue. They have to be approached on the basis that neither the right to privacy under Article 8 nor the right to freedom of expression under Article 10 has automatic priority or should be presumed to be dominant. The two rights have to be weighed against each other in light of the particular circumstances, and this balancing question is treated as a matter within the discretion of the judge at first instance.[48]

It was on this issue that the House of Lords was divided in *Campbell v. MGN*. It was agreed that, although it was private,[49] information about the claimant's drug addiction and the fact that she was having treatment for it could be published by the defendant newspaper because it was in the public interest to correct the false impression, cultivated and exploited by the

---

43. Subject to any public interest justification for disclosure in respect of particular events.
44. *See*, for example, the judgment of Lord Walker in the House of Lords [2007] *UKHL* 22.
45. *See ibid.*, at para. 248.
46. *See*, e.g., the earlier case of *Woodward v. Hutchins* [1977] 1 *WLR* 760.
47. *See*, e.g., *Malone v. Metropolitan Police Commissioner* [1979] *Ch* 344, 373, per Megarry V.C.: *Wainwright v. Home Office* [2002] *QB* 1334, para. 60, per Mummery L.J.
48. *See Campbell v. MGN* [2004] *UKHL* 22, per Lord Nicholls at para. 20. *See also A v. B* [2003] *QB* 195, para. 4.
49. According to Lord Nicholls, the information ceased to be private (as opposed to being private but subject to disclosure in the public interest), because the claimant could no longer have a reasonable expectation of privacy: *See* para. 24.

claimant, that she did not take drugs. The majority held that the defendant's right to publish information in the public interest did not extend to publishing any more detailed information about the claimant's treatment, including the fact that she was having treatment at Narcotics Anonymous, nor to publishing photographs showing the claimant in the street leaving a meeting of Narcotics Anonymous. The minority thought that, given that the defendant newspaper was entitled to publish the facts of the claimant's addiction and that she was having treatment, it should also have been entitled to add supporting detail about the nature of the treatment and the photograph in order to make a more convincing and appealing story for commercial publication. Although Lord Hoffmann, one of the minority, said that the House was divided on a 'narrow point',[50] in practice, the weight attached, in balancing freedom of expression against privacy, to the commercial interest of newspapers in being free to add such background detail and photographs to a story in order to attract readers is bound to have a significant effect on what newspapers actually choose to publish.

23.2.3   INFORMATIONAL PRIVACY AND THE 'BLOCKBUSTER TORT' OBJECTION

There is now, in reality, a right of privacy in English law, and the English courts consider that the law now provides protection in accordance with Article 8; as argued above, even the old law of confidentiality could not adequately be explained except in terms of the protection of privacy. Traditionally breach of confidence is an equitable claim, but it is now described, certainly in this context, as the tort of breach of confidence. It is said that there is a tort of breach of confidence, which protects privacy, though it has also been said that there is now a tort of misuse of private information.[51] In any case, the courts have insisted that it remains the case that there is no 'freestanding' tort of privacy in English law.[52]

The discussion above has concerned informational privacy, the protection of private information against disclosure. This is of course why the appropriate remedy is an order against disclosure or publication, just as for the original case of confidentiality where the private information was initially divulged in a confidential relationship. Privacy is often taken to be a broader

---

50. At para. 36.
51. Lord Nicholls in *Campbell v. MGN* [2004] UKHL 33. *See also Vidal-Hall v. Google Inc* [2015] EWCA Civ 311.
52. For example, *Khorasandjian v. Bush* [1993] 727, 744; *Wainwright v. Home Office* [2002] *QB* 1334 (CA) para. 57, paras 96ff, [2003] *UKHL* 53 (HL), paras 16-19, 29-35; *see also* '*X & Y v. News Group Newspapers*' [2003] *EWHC* 1101, para. 14; *A v. B* [2003] *QB* 195, 206; *Murray v. Big Pictures Ltd* [2008] EWCA Civ 446. *See* generally P. Giliker, 'A Common Law Tort of Privacy?' (2015) 27 *SAcLJ* 761. J. Hartshorne, 'The Need for an Intrusion upon Seclusion Privacy Tort Within English Law' (2017) 46 *Com. L. World Rev.* 287.

concept than informational privacy.[53] In the United States (US), the right of privacy is famously said to be 'a right to be left alone',[54] and the Restatement of Torts, adopting the famous analysis by Prosser,[55] reflects the idea that the right to be left alone is a fundamental right that supports a number of more specific rights, of which a right against the disclosure of private information is only one.[56] Another specific right said to be an aspect of the general right of privacy is a right of seclusion or right against intrusion. This would appear to include rights against physical intrusion into the home and against intrusive noise or smells. On this understanding, the right of privacy appears to underlie at least part of the law of trespass, assault, and nuisance.[57] Indeed 'a right to be left alone' might seem broad enough to cover any form of harm to or constraint of the individual and so to underlie much of the law of tort. As considered further below, the right against 'false light portrayal' and the right against 'appropriation of personality' are also identified as elements of the general right to be left alone in the Restatement and are recognized in some jurisdictions in the US. Furthermore, in the US, the right of privacy has notoriously been invoked as the basis for the protection of certain liberties, for example, to use contraception, have an abortion, or form homosexual relationships.[58] In this context, privacy seems to refer to what in other contexts is described as autonomy, and is concerned with a right to be free to take certain decisions bearing on the conduct of one's life free of state interference. This is again very broad: it amounts to a general criterion for limiting the scope of civil and criminal law.[59]

Thus there is an important issue whether a right of informational privacy is an element of a broader and more fundamental right of privacy. If this is the case, the recognition of a right of informational privacy implies, in principle, the recognition of such a broader right, at least subject to countervailing considerations. Indeed the controversy over the recognition of a right of privacy in English law has involved discussion of harassment in particular as well as informational privacy. In the recent case law, some judges have been particularly insistent that no right of privacy has been or should be recognized in English law, unless introduced through legislation in Parliament, apparently mainly because they have assumed that this would

---

53. *See,* e.g., Giliker, *supra* n. 52, 767.
54. The formulation is apparently attributable to T. Cooley, *Cooley on Torts* (2nd edn, 1888), 29, although it is generally associated with the famous article by S.D. Warren & L.D. Brandeis (1890) 4 *Harv LR* 193.
55. Restatement (Second) of Torts (1977); W. Prosser, 'Privacy' (1960) 48 *Cal LR* 383.
56. *See* further S. Deakin & Z. Adams, *Markesinis & Deakin's Tort Law* (OUP, 8th edn, 2019), Ch. 22.
57. *See,* e.g., Deakin & Adams, *ibid.* In the US, it appears that many such cases actually concern intrusive means of acquiring and revealing information, and so are really a matter of informational privacy.
58. For example, *Griswold v. Connecticut* 381 *US* 479 (1965); *Roe v. Wade* 410 *US* 113 (1973); *see,* e.g., J. Rubenfeld, 'The Right of Privacy' 102 *Harv LR* 737 (1989).
59. *See* R. Wacks, 'The Poverty of Principle' (1980) 96 *LQR* 73.

have broad implications beyond informational privacy. For example, in *Malone v. Commissioner of the Metropolitan Police*,[60] where the judge said that a right of privacy could be introduced only by Parliament and not by the courts because of its very broad and indefinite character, he clearly understood the right of privacy to include a right against physical intrusion as well as a right to informational privacy. In *Kaye v. Robertson*, as mentioned above the court again insisted that the courts were unable to remedy the absence of a right of privacy, and Leggatt L.J. referred to the 'right to be left alone' in US law and the four heads of privacy that have sprung from it.[61] In *Khorasandjian v. Bush*,[62] Peter Gibson J. said simply that the argument for a right of privacy 'was not open to him in light of the decision of this court in *Kaye v. Roberston*, confirming that English law has recognized no such right'. But this was not a case of informational privacy; it was a case where the defendant had harassed and pestered the claimant, in particular by making unwanted telephone calls.

More recently, in *Wainwright v. Home Office*,[63] where the claimants had been subjected to a strip search on a prison visit, in the Court of Appeal Mummery L.J. said:

> [T]here is no tort of invasion of privacy. Instead there are torts protecting a person's interests in the privacy of his body, his home and his personal property. There is also available the equitable doctrine of breach of confidence for the protection of personal information, private communications and correspondence.

He continued:[64] 'I foresee serious definitional difficulties and conceptual problems in the judicial development of a "blockbuster" tort vaguely embracing such a potentially wide range of situations.' Similarly, Buxton L.J. insisted that all the cases where privacy had actually been protected were actions to prevent disclosure of information, and he inferred that they could all be explained in terms of breach of confidence without any need for a tort of breach of privacy:[65] 'These cases, therefore, do nothing to assist the crucial move now urged, that the courts in giving relief should step outside the limits of confidence, artificial or otherwise.' Buxton L.J. was right to reject the 'crucial move', but it would be better to say, not that this is a move from confidentiality to privacy, but that it is a move beyond informational privacy to some other supposed notion of privacy. Buxton L.J's approach is misleading as an analysis of the case law since it suggests that confidentiality supplies a basis for the claims distinct from privacy, which, as discussed above, is not the case. This point causes some inconsistency, or at least the

---

60. [1979] *Ch* 344, 372-3, Megarry V.C.
61. [1991] *FSR* 62, 70-71, per Bingham and Leggatt L.J.J.
62. [1993] *QB* 727, 744.
63. [2002] *QB* 1334, para. 57 per Mummery L.J.
64. *Ibid.*, para. 60.
65. *Ibid.*, para. 99.

appearance of inconsistency, in Lord Hoffmann's judgment in *Wainwright* in the House of Lords. Lord Hoffmann also rejected the possibility of a tort of invasion of privacy, because he denied that the law recognized or ought to recognize a 'high-level principle of invasion of privacy', but he did accept that the action for breach of confidence 'might as well be renamed invasion of privacy'.[66] The same point was reiterated by Lord Nicholls in *Campbell v. MGN*:

> In this country, unlike the United States of America, there is no over-arching, all-embracing cause of action for 'invasion of privacy' ... The present case concerns one aspect of invasion of privacy: wrongful disclosure of private information.[67]

There is a clear rationale for protecting informational privacy.[68] Most people are concerned about what other people think about them, about their reputation in the broadest sense. This is based on general self-consciousness, on disquiet at being evaluated on the basis of limited information by strangers, and on fear of prejudice. Consequently, most people behave differently in different contexts, showing more restraint in public and revealing weaknesses, sensitivities and abnormalities only in private. By enabling people to prevent the dissemination of private information, the right to privacy protects their reasonable expectations concerning the nature of their audience. The case of an express undertaking of confidentiality or a confidential relationship is covered by this principle, but the principle is broad enough to justify protection whenever it is reasonable for the claimant to assume in the circumstances that information divulged by him or information about his behaviour or appearance will not be publicized. This is the reasonable expectation of privacy that is now protected through the law of confidentiality.

This rationale is distinct and limited to informational privacy. It is not, it seems to me, derived from a broader principle that requires the recognition of a broader right of privacy of which informational privacy is merely an element. Thus there is no reason to think that in recognizing that English law has a right of informational privacy – which is now simply an accurate statement of the law – the courts have also implicitly recognized or are bound to recognize a 'right to be left alone' or some form of right of autonomy as a concrete legal right, or more particularly a right against intrusion or harassment. Furthermore, as considered further below, a right of informational privacy does not entail a right against 'false light portrayal' or a right

---

66. [2003] *UKHL* 53, paras 29-30.
67. Paragraphs 11-12.
68. There is a large literature on the nature and rationale of privacy, e.g., R. Gavison, 'Privacy and the Limits of the Law' 89 *Yale LJ* 421 (1980); Rubenfeld, *supra* n. 58; R.C. Post, 'Three Concepts of Privacy' 89 *Geo LJ* 2087 (2001), discussing J. Rosen, *The Unwanted Gaze: The Destruction of Privacy in America* (Random House, 2000); D.J. Solove, 'Conceptualising Privacy' 90 *Cal LR* 1087 (2002).

against 'appropriation of personality'.[69] The problem that persists in the case law is that if, as the courts have repeatedly said, informational privacy is an aspect of a broader concept of privacy, and is protected as such, it would appear that the rationale for protecting informational privacy extends to the broader concept, and on this basis, it is difficult to see how the development of a broader right of privacy can be resisted.[70] In my view, it should be resisted by rejecting the idea that informational privacy is an aspect of a more general principle or concept of privacy.

23.3	CONFIDENTIALITY AS THE OWNERSHIP OF TRADE SECRETS

In many cases where confidential information is protected, the information is clearly not private at all, but commercial, that is, it is a trade secret, or 'know-how' concerning industrial or commercial activities.[71] Clearly, protection for trade secrets cannot be explained in terms of a right of informational privacy. One might object that the law of confidentiality cannot, therefore, be regarded as based on privacy. But the point here is that there is a fundamental divide in the law of confidentiality that has not previously been recognized in English law. Only part of what is traditionally described as the law of confidentiality is based on a right to informational privacy. In *Douglas v. Hello!*[72] Lord Nicholls said that, following the developments discussed above, the law of breach of confidence 'now covers two distinct causes of action, protecting two different interests: privacy, and secret ("confidential") information'.

But surely what the developments discussed above indicate is that confidentiality is not itself a basis for a claim unless this is taken to refer to the original case where someone has explicitly or implicitly undertaken to keep a confidence, and a claim arises against that person or an accessory who has assisted in or procured a breach of the undertaking. In this type of case, the basis of the claim is, as mentioned above, in essence, contractual, though not conventionally so treated. In some other cases, the basis is the right to

---

69. [2003] *UKHL* 53, paras 29-30.
70. Deakin & Adams, *supra* n. 56. *See also* N. Moreham, 'Beyond Information: Physical Privacy in English Law' (2014) 73 *CLJ* 350. Moreham argues that protection for privacy should extend to physical intrusion into private space by spying and eavesdropping, though arguably this is an aspect of informational privacy. *See also* K. Hughes 'A Behavioural Understanding of Privacy and Its Implications for Privacy Law' (2012) 75 *MLR* 806.
71. A well-known example is *Seager v. Copydex* [1967] 2 *All ER* 415.
72. [2007] *UKHL* 21, para. 255. *See also* A. Schreiber, 'Confidence Crisis, Privacy Phobia: Why Invasion of Privacy Should Be Independently Recognised in English Law' (2006) *IPQ* 160.

privacy. But neither of these explains the law of trade secrets. What then is the basis of this aspect of the law?

In my view, the justification for protecting a trade secret is that it is the property of the claimant.[73] Property rights are capable of binding 'all the world', and this is why a third party is bound by a duty of confidentiality even though he did not give an undertaking of confidentiality and is not complicit in a breach of such an undertaking by anybody else. But, of course, this explanation is incomplete. Why should the claimant have ownership of the confidential information? The only plausible answer is that ownership of a trade secret is justified (in this situation) as a means of providing an incentive or reward for the creation of value. A right of ownership achieves this by securing to the owner the power to exploit the property by exclusive use, licensing or sale. On this understanding, the right to a trade secret is a form of intellectual property, in terms of both its proprietary nature and its rationale, and of course, the law of trade secrets or know-how is commonly associated with patent law and treated in this way.

In *Douglas v. Hello!* Lord Walker was particularly critical of any such analysis of trade secrets. Quoting Finn, he said:[74]

Perhaps the most sterile of debates which have arisen around the subject of information received in confidence is whether or not such information should be classified as property.

And he made it clear that in his view this was not the basis of the claim for breach of confidence in a trade secret. But this leaves obscure what the justification is for the claim if it does not lie in the enforcement of an undertaking to keep a confidence, or in the protection of informational privacy, or in securing to the claimant the value of the information he has created by way of a property right.

It seems to me that (leaving aside the contractual basis), the two different rationales for protecting confidential information are privacy and property.[75] They characteristically raise different types of issue. The justification for the first category is simply to protect against a certain type of harm, and the existence of a claim depends on whether the claimant has a reasonable expectation of privacy and whether there is a countervailing interest in the disclosure of the information. For the second category, the fundamental issue of principle is whether it is justified to give the right holder the right to all the value to be made from exploiting the information. The two different rationales support different types of legal regime. If the claimant has a right of ownership of information, designed to secure to him

---

73. *See* further Jaffey, *supra* n. 1, Ch. 3. There has been some discussion in the literature of whether the right to confidential information can or should be understood as a property right: *see*, e.g., Cornish et al., *supra* n. 6, 8-50.
74. At para. 276, quoting from P.D. Finn, *Fiduciary Obligations* (CUP, 1977), para. 293.
75. *See* further Jaffey, *supra* n. 1, Ch. 3.

the commercial value of the information, he should be able to license the use of the confidential information or sell it by transferring his right of ownership. By contrast, in the case of a right of privacy, designed to protect the claimant from personal harm caused by the disclosure of private information, the purpose of the law is not to secure to the claimant the commercial value of the information, or to empower him to sell the information or licence its use, although there is no reason why he should not be free to waive his right of privacy. For example, a newspaper that has paid for a waiver of privacy in order to be free to publish private information would not thereby acquire the right to prevent third parties from publishing the information, as would the purchaser of a trade secret. Secondly, in the case where the claimant has a right of ownership, he should be entitled to what might be called a 'use claim', that is to say, a claim for payment of a reasonable licence fee as a remedy for unauthorized use of the confidential information, as an alternative to a claim for compensation for loss caused by the disclosure of the confidential information.[76] This is justified on the basis of the claimant's right to the 'use-value' of the information, as an element of his ownership of it. But in the case of the right of privacy, there is no basis for such a claim, and the normal pecuniary remedy will be compensation for the harm caused by the disclosure.[77] The essential difference between the two categories is not the type of information or the context, but the principle underlying that category, which determines the nature of the right and its relation to the information in question, that is to say, whether it is a right of ownership of confidential information as property, or whether it is a right against a certain type of harm arising from the disclosure of information. Generally, the right of ownership subsists in respect of industrial or technical or business information or know-how, but in principle, there can be ownership of the information that is also private. As mentioned above, in *Douglas v. Hello!* one issue considered was whether unauthorized wedding photographs were protectable as a trade secret.[78] This point is considered further in the last section below.

---

76. That is, where the information is still confidential and there has been no loss to the claimant through the defendant's use. As to the use claim in general, or restitutionary or 'licence fee' damages, *see* P. Jaffey, 'Licence Fee Damages' (2011) *Restitution L. Rev.* 95. In the ownership case, the claimant can of course and normally will make a claim for compensation for loss, but this is damage to the property, which is the right to the exclusive value of the information.
77. Leaving aside the question of 'disgorgement' to remove the profits of wrongdoing, or exemplary or punitive damages: as to which *see* generally N. Witzleb, 'Justifying Gain-Based Remedies for Invasions of Privacy' (2009) 29 *OJLS* 325.
78. *See* [2003] *All ER* 996, para. 195; [2007] *UKHL* 21.

23.4 PRIVACY, DEFAMATION AND 'FALSE LIGHT' PORTRAYAL

23.4.1 PRIVACY AND DEFAMATION

The interest in privacy – that is, informational privacy – arises from people's sensitivity to other people's opinions and judgments about them. It is concerned, in a broad sense, with reputation, although there is no requirement for the claimant actually to show that his reputation has been adversely affected in anyone's eyes: it is better to say that the right of privacy is based on a legitimate concern about reputation.[79] There is an obvious question of the relationship of privacy to defamation. Consider the famous case of *Yousoupoff v. MGM.*[80] The claimant succeeded in a claim for defamation in respect of a false statement by the defendant that she had been the victim of a rape. It has been argued that such a case involves artificially stretching the law of defamation because the reputation of the claimant is not lowered in the eyes of 'right-thinking people' as the conventional test for defamation requires and that it might be better regarded as a case of invasion of privacy.[81] Indeed, it has been argued that this reveals the basic distinction between defamation and privacy, namely that the former is concerned with a reputation in the eyes of right-thinking people and the latter with a reputation in the eyes of what might be called 'wrong-thinking people', which would include people who are liable to be prejudiced against someone who has been raped.[82] The implication is that defamation and privacy should operate in parallel to deal with the protection of reputation, the distinction between the two turning on whether reputation in the eyes of 'right-thinking' or 'wrong-thinking' people is in issue, and this would avoid the need to stretch the law of defamation in this artificial way.[83]

It is no doubt fair to say that the right of privacy is often concerned with protecting against the prejudice of 'wrong-thinking' people. Private matters

---

79. *See supra*, text at n. 37.
80. (1934) 50 *TLR* 581.
81. This argument is advanced by M. Tugendhat, 'Privacy & Celebrity' in E. Barendt, A. Firth et al., eds, *The Yearbook of Copyright & Media Law 2001/2* (OUP, 2002), 13.
82. *Ibid.*
83. Alternatively privacy could be subsumed into defamation by expanding what is counted as loss of reputation. There have at various times been proposals for legislation to modify the law of defamation to protect privacy by withholding the defence of justification if the statement relates to a private matter – the claimant would sue for defamation and if the matter is private then the defendant would be liable irrespective of truth or falsity: *see* J.G. Fleming, *The Law of Torts* (LBC, 9th edn, 1998), 613. This would no doubt have served a useful purpose in providing some protection for privacy in the absence of an explicitly recognized right of privacy.

are particularly prone to be the subject of prejudice.[84] But it is not clear that this is the basis for the distinction between defamation and privacy. The problem of damage to reputation amongst 'wrong-thinking people' can also arise in respect of matters that are not private at all – an example might be the statement that the claimant at one time had an official position in a certain political party. The development of the law of privacy will leave unresolved the question of the proper scope of this aspect of the law of defamation. In any case, on one view the 'right-thinking people' test is not an accurate statement of the current law of defamation, and a statement can indeed be defamatory if it is liable to harm the claimant's reputation in any significant section of the community.[85]

More generally, this approach ignores a basic feature of privacy. By contrast with defamation, privacy is not concerned with the falsity of statements. It is concerned with protecting against loss of reputation (in a broad sense) resulting from the disclosure of true private information, for example, the true information that the claimant has been raped, or rather statements about private matters irrespective of their truth or falsity. (It cannot be relevant whether the information is true or false, because otherwise, the claimant would have to show the truth of the statement, or the defendant would escape liability by showing its falsity, and yet if the claimant has a right of privacy in respect of the information he can prevent its disclosure without having to bring its truth into consideration at all.) Thus, the point in *Yousoupoff* is not that the claimant had a grievance that was strictly a matter of privacy rather than defamation; it was that the claimant had two distinct grievances, one the publication of falsehood, and the other an invasion of privacy, namely the statement about private matters, whether true or false. Although it might seem that subsuming privacy under an expanded notion of defamation would be a compact way to bring together two forms of protection for reputation, broadly understood,[86] to the contrary, it is surely preferable for the two categories to be kept distinct, even if both are relevant in some circumstances because they have distinct rationales and raise distinct issues. The essence of the law of defamation is to protect reputation against damage from falsehoods, whereas the essence of the law of privacy is to protect reputation from being influenced by private information the disclosure of which might be unfairly prejudicial, even if true.[87]

---

84. For example, matters of sexuality or medical conditions, where people are prone to be prejudiced and to take account of irrelevant matters: *see* Tugendhat, *supra* n. 841.
85. Fleming, *supra* n. 83, 583.
86. The range of statements that would count as defamatory would have to be wide enough to encompass all types of private information.
87. And even though it would enhance the accuracy of reputation amongst entirely dispassionate and objective parties.

23.4.2 'FALSE LIGHT' PORTRAYAL

In the US, many jurisdictions recognize a tort of 'false light' portrayal. As mentioned above, the tort is recognized in the Restatement of Torts and was identified by Prosser as one of the four privacy torts derived from the 'right to be left alone'.[88] It appears that the tort is committed where the defendant depicts the claimant in a false light, and the depiction would be highly offensive to a reasonable person.[89] The claim clearly has an affinity with defamation. Often it operates in tandem with defamation, and some US jurisdictions have denied the existence of the tort on the ground that it subverts the law of defamation.[90] The development of the tort in the US raises the question whether it is a necessary aspect of a right of privacy and so should be recognized in English law by virtue of the development of a fully-fledged right of privacy in accordance with Article 8.

Some commentators in the US regard false light portrayal as an aspect of informational privacy, on the basis that informational privacy is concerned with a right to control information about oneself and that this extends to suppressing false information in some circumstances.[91] Some false light cases do indeed appear to concern the exposure of private information or at least information that would be private if it were true so that one can say that it is a private matter whether the information is true or false.[92] If a claim based on informational privacy would be available if the information were true, it would seem that there should be a claim whether it is true or not, since it should not be possible to put this in issue. Sometimes, however, the defendant may be entitled to publish the information, despite its private nature, because of a legitimate public interest in the disclosure of the events in question, but only if the account is true, or at least if the defendant has not been reckless as to its truth. In this type of case, it would seem that the claim can be explained entirely in terms of the ordinary claim for informational privacy.

In other cases of false light portrayal, it appears that the information is not the sort of information that would be thought of as private and the claim cannot be understood in terms of informational privacy in this way. For example, the case might concern aspects of the professional life of the claimant that are entirely in the public domain, and not in any sense,

---

88. *Supra* n. 55 and text following. It is also mentioned as a possible aspect of the right of privacy under Article 8 in *Mosley v. the UK* [2011] ECHR 774, para. 56.
89. With knowledge or recklessness as to falsity.
90. *See,* e.g., D. Zimmerman, 'False Light Invasion of Privacy: The Light that Failed' (1989) 64 *NYULR* 364; B.R. Lasswell, 'In Defence of False Light: Why False Light Must Remain a Viable Cause of Action' 34 *S Tex L Rev* (1993).
91. *See* the discussion in Solove, *supra* n. 68, 1109-15.
92. For example, *Time Inc v. Hill* 385 *US 374* (1967), concerning the claimants' experiences whilst they were being held hostage; *Wood v. Hustler Magazine* 736 F.2d 1084 (1984), concerning the publication of a nude photograph of the claimant in circumstances arguably implying that the publication was with consent.

private.[93] The issue here is simply whether the claimant's reputation has been damaged or he has otherwise been adversely affected by a false account of his life or more broadly whether he should be able to suppress any false statement about himself. One would think that this is, in principle, a matter that should be addressed in connection with the law of defamation. One issue may be the difficulty considered above that the false account is not liable to lower his reputation amongst 'right-thinking people'.[94] It does not seem helpful to address this issue by way of the development of a separate tort of false light privacy that circumvents the possible limitations in the law of defamation.[95] In any case, this does not seem to be an aspect of an overarching tort of privacy that also encompasses the other elements mentioned above.

23.5   PUBLICITY AND MERCHANDISING

23.5.1   PRIVACY AS THE OWNERSHIP OF IMAGE: THE RIGHT OF PUBLICITY

In the US, the general right of privacy has also been understood to give rise to a tort of 'appropriation of personality', which is committed by a defendant who without permission uses the name or image of the claimant (generally a celebrity) for commercial purposes, typically to promote the sale of a product by exploiting the claimant's appeal to consumers.[96] This is said to be based on a 'right of publicity'.[97] The idea of the right of informational privacy as a right to control personal information might lead to the misconception that this tort is an aspect of informational privacy as described above. But again this is not the case. The right to prevent the commercial use of one's public image does not relate to private information; indeed the commercial use of a public image does not involve the transmission of the information at all (unless it is understood as an endorsement).[98] That is not

---

93. *See* the case discussed in M. Stohl, 'False Light Invasion of Privacy in Docudramas: The Oxymoron which Must Be Solved' 35 *Akron L Rev* 251 (2002).
94. *See* Stohl, *ibid*. There are procedural differences between the torts that do not provide a principled basis for recognizing two different torts.
95. Lasswell, *supra* n. 90, 170, suggests that false light privacy protects against emotional disturbance whereas defamation protects reputation, but protection for reputation is surely designed to protect against emotional disturbance caused by damage to reputation (as surely is false light privacy). *See also* Zimmerman, *supra* n. 90, 431ff.
96. This is the fourth category of privacy identified by Prosser and incorporated in the Restatement of Torts. A standard example is '*Carson v. Here's Johnny Portable Toilets*' 698 F.2d 831 (1983). On the possible development of a publicity right, *see* H. Beverley-Smith, *The Commercial Appropriation of Personality* (CUP, 2002).
97. The term comes from *Haelen Laboratories v. Topps Chewing Gum* 202 F.2d 866 (1953).
98. It does not convey information about the product, or about the celebrity. An endorsement does convey information: *viz.*, that the product meets the standards of the celebrity.

to say that such a right is not justified. But it has to be justified on quite different grounds from a right against the invasion of informational privacy.

Furthermore, there is an important distinction that is often disregarded in connection with the concept of appropriation of personality. This is the distinction made above in connection with informational privacy and trade secrets, between a right against harm to the claimant, and a right of ownership.[99] The point is that it is one thing to recognize that a celebrity has a right against the use of his image for commercial purposes on the ground that the association with a commercial product or activity causes harm to an interest of his that should be protected, possibly an interest in reputation or dignity or autonomy; and it is quite another to say that a celebrity owns his image, and so is entitled to its commercial value. The latter right would be designed to enable the celebrity to license his image and realize its commercial value, whereas the former would be designed to save him from a certain type of harm. In the US, it appears that the law has moved from the former to the latter without an appreciation of the distinction.[100] This point will be returned to below, after a brief discussion of the law of trademarks, which, as will be seen, impinges on the same issue from a different direction.

23.5.2 TRADEMARKS: THE INFORMATION FUNCTION

The principal function of a trademark has always been said to be the 'origin function'. This should be understood in the following sense.[101] A trademark tells a consumer that the quality and attributes of the product bearing the mark are under the control of some person (whoever it may be) who uses or authorizes the use of the mark to signify this fact. For this reason, the consumer can infer that a product bearing a certain trademark will have the quality and attributes that he has come to associate with products he has previously encountered bearing the trademark. Thus, the trademark is a simple and powerful tool for communicating information,[102] albeit information that is vague and impressionistic and not entirely reliable. The use of a trademark to communicate information allows a producer to build up and exploit a reputation in his products, *viz.*, goodwill. This goodwill is valuable to the trader because it attracts custom. It represents the fruits of his efforts

---

99. *Supra*, text following n. 75.
100. See generally D Westfall & D Landau, "Publicity Rights as Property Rights" 23 Cardozo Arts & Ent LJ 71 (2005); D Gervais & ML Holmes, "Fame, Property and Identity: The Purpose and Scope of the Right of Publicity" 25 Fordham Intell Prop Media & Ent LJ 181 (2014).
101. As defined in the text, the origin function is not the function of revealing the identity of the manufacturer or distributor of the product, which is how it is sometimes understood. The function of a trademark is not a question of law: identifying the function is a matter of explaining social and economic practices.
102. This understanding is associated with the economic analysis of trademarks; *see*, e.g., W.M. Landes & R.A. Posner, 'The Economics of Trademark Law' 78 *TMR* 267 (1988).

in providing products that have the quality and attributes that satisfy customers.

The law of trademark infringement prohibits the deceptive use of the claimant's trademark.[103] It is only because the trademark conveys information that its unauthorized use can be deceptive. The law of trademark infringement thus reflects the information-related function of trademarks. It might seem that the law of trademarks is the counterpart of the law of defamation, protecting commercial reputation or goodwill as opposed to personal reputation. In fact, a closer commercial equivalent to defamation is injurious or malicious falsehood,[104] which concerns false statements that damage the claimant's business and products, including his goodwill. The law of trademark infringement has a different function: it is characteristically concerned not with actions that cause damage to the claimant's goodwill, but with deceptive use of the claimant's trademark by which the defendant exploits the claimant's goodwill for his own benefit, typically by diverting custom to himself. There is no equivalent in defamation. This is an example of what was referred to above as a 'use claim',[105] and it reflects the fact that the law of trademarks protects goodwill as a form of property belonging to the claimant, whereas personal reputation is not property in this sense under the law of defamation.[106]

23.5.3   THE NON-INFORMATION-RELATED 'IMAGE' FUNCTION OF A
           TRADEMARK

Trademarks can also have an important effect that is not concerned with communicating information to consumers.[107] A trademark can acquire an 'image' through advertising. The image embodies attitudes or feelings or 'values' that the producer through advertising has managed to associate with the trademark. If a trademark has such an image, consumers may be influenced to purchase the product by their attraction to the image or their desire to associate themselves with it. Insofar as a trademark operates through its image, it does not communicate information to consumers about

---

103. The law of trademarks encompasses the common law of passing off and the statutory law of registered trademarks. By preventing deception in this way, the law remedies the particular harm suffered by the trademark owner as a result of the deception, and also sustains the trademark system in general against the degradation in its efficacy as a means of communication that would result from deceptive use.
104. Injurious or malicious falsehood extends to damage to reputation but is not confined to it.
105. *See supra* n. 76.
106. Similarly, goodwill is transferable but personal reputation is not.
107. The aesthetic appearance of a trademark may in itself induce some consumers to buy the product, but a stronger effect of the aesthetic appeal would be to enhance the efficacy of the trademark as a sign communicating information about the product.

the product. This non-information-related, image-based function can be described as the advertising or merchandising function.

Trademark owners see their trademarks as embodying and protecting a mixture of goodwill and image, and therefore, serving both information-related and non-information-related functions. The concept of 'brand', although originally understood to mean a trademark having the traditional information-related function, is now generally used more broadly to refer to a trademark as the repository of the advertising image of the product as well as its reputation in the quality and attributes of the product.

In principle, the justifications for supporting the two functions are quite different. Protecting the pure trademark or origin function and the ownership of goodwill is easily justified because it merely prohibits the provision of false information and thereby sustains the ability of producers to convey information to consumers and to profit from the reputation in their products that they have established amongst consumers. But protection for the merchandising function cannot be justified in this way. It is not concerned with prohibiting deceptive statements in order to promote the supply of true information. The unauthorized use of an image cannot in itself be deceptive because its purpose is not to convey information, or at least not information about the product. With respect to the merchandising function, the question is whether it is right to recognize ownership of an image cultivated through advertising and exercising an emotional appeal to consumers. Can it, for example, be justified as a way of rewarding and encouraging the investment of the trader in the development of the image? Are such images valuable things that traders ought to be rewarded for developing?[108] In practice, however, the protection provided by the law of trademarks, even if intended to protect the pure trademark or origin function, in practice inevitably also provides protection for the merchandising function, that is, it supports trademark owners in developing and exploiting the image of their trade-marks.[109]

23.5.4   PROTECTING IMAGES FOR MERCHANDISING THROUGH THE LAW OF TRADEMARKS

A trademark's image can receive protection through the law of trademarks, as discussed above. A different issue is whether the law recognizes a

---

108. *See,* e.g., M. Madow, 'Private Ownership of Public Image: Popular Culture and Publicity Rights' 81 *Cal L Rev* (1993). *See also* Beverley-Smith, *supra* n. 96.
109. In modern times, trademark regimes have increasingly recognized that non-deceptive 'dilution' can constitute infringement, e.g., tarnishing of the trademark or blurring of its distinct. This is readily understood to be intended to protect the image of a trademark and so to support the advertising or merchandising function of a trademark, but it is also explicable in terms of the origin function, i.e., in terms of its effect in hindering communication with consumers.

merchandising right – that is, an exclusive right to use or license an image for commercial purposes – in respect of the images of celebrities, cartoon characters, or other things or events that may be appealing to consumers. In the absence of explicit merchandising rights in English law, claimants have sometimes sought to secure the exclusive right to such images through the law of trademarks, by action in passing off or by seeking to register the image as a trademark. As discussed above, an image designed for merchandising is distinct in function from a trademark, or at least a trademark in its pure trademark or origin function; by contrast with a trademark, such an image does not purport to convey information, and so its use (whether authorized or not) is not in itself deceptive. Since, as explained above, deceptiveness is the essence of trademark infringement, English law traditionally denied any protection of an image for merchandising by this avenue. However, recent passing off cases have established that although a celebrity has no general right over the use of his or her name or image, it can involve passing off if the use is in relation to goods or services and implies falsely that the celebrity endorsed them, or more generally if members of the public have come to recognize that the celebrity has licensed his or her name or image for use in relation to goods or services so that they have a sense that the use of the name or image can be official or unofficial.[110] Recent developments in the law of registered trademarks have also given increasing support to the protection of merchandising marks through trademark registration, on the ground that such a mark can become distinctive of goods or services.[111]

The approach of founding merchandising rights on trademark law has gone further in other jurisdictions. However, this has often depended on establishing deceptiveness in some artificial way;[112] in reality, deceptiveness

---

110. Support for this comes from *Irvine v. Talksport Ltd* [2003] 2 *All ER* 881 and *Fenty v. Arcadia Group Brands Ltd (t/a Topshop)* [2015] EWCA Civ 3. Earlier cases gave no support to the passing off claim: *Lyngstrad v. Anabas Products* [1977] *FSR* 62; *Wombles v. Wombles Skips* (1977) *RPC* 99; *Tavener Rutledge v. Trexapalm* [1975] *FSR* 179; and *BBC Worldwide v. Pally Screen Printing* [1998] *FSR* 665. As to how the law of passing off should develop, *see* H. Carty, 'Passing Off: Frameworks of Liability Debated' (2012) *IPQ* 106.

111. For the same reason, registration of a merchandising mark has been denied on the ground that the mark is not capable of acting as a trademark because it will not be so understood by consumers: *Elvis Presley Trade Marks* [1999] *RPC* 567. More recently *Arsenal FC v. Reed (no. 2)* [2003] *RPC* 39 suggests a turn in favour of the protection of merchandising rights through trademark registration. Similarly, according to *Hearst Holdings Inc v. AVELA Inc* [2014] *FSR* 36, a merchandising mark that has become distinctive can be protected as a registered trademark.

112. For example, it might be argued that the consumer is deceived because he mistakenly thinks that the use of the merchandising mark was authorized, i.e., a misrepresentation 'as to licensing': *see,* e.g., *Dallas Cowboys Cheerleaders v. Pussycat Cinema* 604 F.2d 200 (1979) and *'Boston Athletic Association v. Sulliva n'* 9 *USPQ* 2d 1960 (1989) in the United States; *'Pacific Dunlop v. Hogan'* (1989) 87 *ALR* 14 in Australia; and in the English courts *Mirage Studios v. Counter-Feat Clothing* [1991] *FSR* 145; *see* further P. Jaffey, 'Merchandising and the Law of Trade Marks' (1998) *IPQ* 240.

is not really an issue at all. One might argue that this is a reasonable fiction by which to make a natural extension to the law in order to generate merchandising rights in law. But the move away from deceptiveness and the promotion of supply of information means that a different justification of the claim is required and this issue is obscured by the fiction.

The right of publicity discussed earlier is a merchandising right in their image for celebrities. It was suggested that the argument for a right of publicity based on the general right of privacy was unconvincing. The argument for a merchandising right arising from the law of trademarks and goodwill is an attempt to establish the same right (although not confined to celebrities) from a different direction, and it is also unconvincing.

23.6   INTELLECTUAL PROPERTY AND THE OWNERSHIP OF INTANGIBLES

The law of intellectual property is concerned with the ownership of ideas or information or certain other types of valuable intangible.[113] An intellectual property right is a right of ownership in the sense discussed above.[114] It is designed to secure to the owner the commercial value of the intangible created, as a reward for the work and effort involved in creating it and the contribution it makes to the society, rather than to provide protection from harm or to compensate for harm to an antecedent interest.[115] Thus, an intellectual property right holder can make a use claim as explained above as well as a simple claim for compensation for harm, and he can license and sell his right.

In English law, it seems that generally intellectual property rights have not been recognized by the common law, only through a statutory regime:[116]

> [C]ourts of equity have not in British jurisdictions thrown the protection of an injunction around all the intangible elements of value, that is, value in exchange, which may flow from the exercise by an individual of his powers or resources whether in the organisation of a business or undertaking or the use of ingenuity, knowledge, skill or labour.

There appear to be certain exceptions to this, however. First, in the law of confidentiality, although the right of privacy is a right against harm, not a

---

113. This refers to 'non-exclusive' intangibles, which can be used by different people at once, not intangible transferable wealth or money.
114. *See supra* n. 73 and text following.
115. That is, as opposed to harm to the prospects of securing the benefit of the property, including damage to the property. But some aspects of intellectual property law are concerned with protecting against harm, e.g., moral rights in copyright, or copyright where it protects privacy in unpublished works, rather than with securing the value of the intangible to the right holder.
116. *Victoria Park Racing v. Taylor* (1937) 58 *CLR* 479, per Dixon J. at 509.

right of ownership of private information, as suggested above the right to a trade secret does appear to be a right of ownership, and it is recognized at common law. This may well be justified, though it has emerged from the development of a law of confidentiality that did not identify clearly the principles behind its operation or the interests that it protected. Employers can clearly impose binding obligations of confidentiality on their workers, but this does not necessarily imply that it is justified to have a right of ownership of the information developed in the business. Furthermore, if the trade secret concerns an invention, one might argue that it should be required to be patented and regulated by the statutory patent regime, which is designed to secure an appropriate return to the inventor, and accordingly limits the term of protection.

Second, in the law of trademarks, goodwill is a form of intangible property (by contrast with personal reputation, which as discussed above is not recognized as a form of property in the sense above), and it is protected at common law through the law of passing off. This is justifiable; it seems because goodwill is distinct from other forms of intellectual property in important respect alluded to above. Normally recognizing an intellectual property right has the drawback of imposing a significant cost on consumers. For example, a patent or copyright allows the right holder to exclude competitors from selling a product incorporating the protected matter and the effect is to raise prices to the consumer in order to confer a return to the right holder in excess of what he would otherwise get through the market. It is a complex question involving empirical issues to determine what sort of regime is justified, arguably a question that the courts are not qualified to answer, and this may be why it is appropriate for the recognition of intellectual property rights to be left to the legislature. But the protection of goodwill does not impose any such cost on consumers; to the contrary, the protection of goodwill also benefits consumers by facilitating the supply of information to them.

Third, in recent years there has been a tendency towards recognizing merchandising rights – rights of ownership of images whose appeal to consumers can promote the sale of products. As discussed above, one argument for this in connection with celebrities is the argument for the right of publicity recognized in US law as an aspect of the law of privacy. As pointed out above, the distinction has often been missed here between a right against harm to an interest of the celebrity caused by the commercial use of his image and the celebrity's right of ownership of his image. Neither is plausibly based on a right of informational privacy, and this is particularly clear in the case of the latter. As considered above, another argument for merchandising rights has come from the law of trademarks, through the attempt to characterize the image or a celebrity or other object of fame as a trademark. This is also misconceived because an image does not communicate information about the product, and so its use is not deceptive and does not fall within the scope of trademark infringement, at least as it is conventionally understood. Although image and goodwill are often confused, they are not the same in principle and ownership of image cannot be justified in the same way as ownership of goodwill. The effect of these two lines of argument if they were to succeed in establishing a merchandising right or a right of publicity, would be to circumvent the traditional aversion to the judicial recognition of intellectual property rights in the common law, without addressing or overcoming the objection mentioned above.[117]

Douglas v. Hello! provides an interesting set of facts to illustrate some of these issues.[118] The issue from that case discussed above was whether the claimants Douglas and Zeta-Jones had a claim against the defendant magazine arising from the publication by the defendant of unauthorized photographs of their wedding. When the case eventually reached the House of Lords,[119] the House was concerned only with the claim of the other claimant, OK magazine, which had contracted with Douglas and Zeta-Jones to publish exclusive pictures of the wedding, pursuant to which Douglas and Zeta-Jones had taken the measures to exclude unauthorized photographers.

There are a number of possible types of claim that might arise in these circumstances. The claim by Douglas and Zeta-Jones for breach of confidence based on invasion of privacy succeeded and the couple was awarded a modest sum in damages for compensation.[120] For these claimants, there was also the possibility of a claim for breach of contract against an authorized photographer or invited guest who breached an undertaking not to divulge photographs without permission, or a claim against a third party for procuring a breach of contract, but the defendant, Hello, had only taken advantage of unauthorized photographs and had not procured a breach of contract. Neither had Hello acted unlawfully with a view to causing harm to OK, so as to have committed the tort of causing harm by unlawful means.[121] The possibility of a right of ownership of the image (i.e., a right of publicity or merchandising right), not dependent on confidentiality or the privacy of the occasion, which, as Lord Nicholls pointed out might be available in the US,[122] was adverted to and rejected.[123] As argued above, there is no basis for developing such a right by analogy with the right of informational privacy, or by extension of the law of trademarks.

---

117. The various ways in which celebrities have attempted to protect and exploit their name and image are discussed in G. Black, *Publicity Rights and Image: Exploitation and Legal Control* (Hart Publishing, 2011). Black argues for a limited form of publicity right. *See also* G. Black, 'Publicity Rights and Image: Exploitation and Legal Control' (2012) 34 *EIPR* 426.
118. *See also* P. Jaffey, *Privacy, Publicity Rights, and Merchandising*, in E. Barendt, A. Firth et al., *supra* n. 81.
119. [2007] *UKHL* 21.
120. Also, there is the possibility of passing off if an endorsement can be found.
121. *See* paras 129ff, per Lord Hoffmann.
122. *See* para. 253.
123. *See* at para. 253 per Lord Nicholls; para. 285 per Lord Walker.

Also, there is the possibility of a right to the photographs as a trade secret. This was not relevant to Douglas and Zeta-Jones, who had been paid to transfer the commercial benefit of the photographs to OK, but the majority concluded that, because Douglas and Zeta-Jones had taken the undertakings of confidentiality from their guests on behalf of OK as well as themselves, OK had the benefit of the right to the trade secret which they could enforce against Hello. It was argued above that the law of trade secrets should be understood in terms of ownership of confidential information as property, but the claim was characterized simply as a traditional claim for breach of confidence, and as discussed above there was opposition to a property analysis.

Lord Nicholls, who would have denied OK's claim, took the view that when OK brought forward its own publication of the authorized photographs, knowing that Hello was about to publish unauthorized photographs, it thereby put the trade secret into the public domain, so that when Hello's unauthorized photographs appeared there could be no breach of confidence: 'the unapproved pictures contained nothing not included in the approved pictures'.[124] Lord Hoffmann, for the majority, insisted that each photograph was a separate piece of information, and its value, like a photograph, was not lost as a result of a similar photograph having been published.[125]

Lord Walker made another objection to the claim. He thought that Douglas and Zeta-Jones could not 'invest the wedding reception with the quality of confidentiality, if it did not otherwise attract it', just by taking stringent security arrangements.[126] But Lord Hoffmann's straightforward view was that any commercially valuable information was capable of being the subject matter of a trade secret, like any other industrial or commercial information.[127]

Lord Walker was also concerned that, by recognizing what was in effect a right of confidentiality in respect of any aspect of the appearance of the occasion that might be captured by a photograph, the court was verging on recognizing 'property in a spectacle'. He referred to *Victoria Park Racing v. Taylor*, which was quoted from above, in which the claimant organized a sporting event, and the defendant commentated on it from a vantage point outside the stadium. As the quotation shows,[128] the mere fact that the claimant had generated an object of commercial value was not taken to establish that he had an exclusive right to it, and was entitled to prevent the defendant commentating on it or exact a licence fee from him. In light of his discussion of the idea of 'property in a spectacle', it is difficult to see why Lord Walker should want to deny that the right to a trade secret is a form of

---

124. *See* para. 259.
125. *See* paras 122-3.
126. *See* para. 294.
127. *See* per Lord Hoffmann at paras 118-120.
128. *See also* K. Gray, 'Property in Thin Air' (1991) *CLJ* 252.

property ownership. But Lord Walker's concern points to something that does appear anomalous: if it is practicable to make arrangements that will secure the confidentiality of an occasion or 'spectacle' then (if the arrangements fail) the organizers will be able to protect it through the law of trade secrets, whereas if such arrangements are impracticable, as in *Victoria Park Racing v. Taylor*, anyone is entitled to exploit the occasion without having to pay anything to the organizers. Similarly, in *Sports & General Press Agency v. Our Dogs Publishing Co*,[129] the claimant sought to prevent the defendant from publishing photographs of a sporting event put on by the claimant, who controlled entry but had not imposed any condition of confidentiality or restriction on taking photographs. It was held that he had no right to prevent the publication of photographs or demand payment.

If the claimant does not have the exclusive right to profit from an event by publishing photographs of it, just by virtue of being the person who organized and managed it, why should he acquire this right through the imposition of confidentiality conditions on the people who attend the event? Why should so much turn, *vis-á-vis* third parties, on whether it is possible to control access and thereby impose confidentiality conditions on visitors? In fact, this argument applies to trade secrets in general. A manufacturer who discovers a new method of manufacture that can be put into use without being revealed can rely on the law of trade secrets, but a manufacturer who discovers a new method of manufacture that is inevitably revealed when the product is released onto the market has no protection unless he can get a patent.[130]

23.7   CONCLUSION

The action for breach of confidence in English law has evolved to protect the right to privacy, meaning informational privacy. The interest it protects is, broadly speaking, the interest in being free from public scrutiny in circumstances when it is reasonable to act on this assumption. The English courts insist that although the action for breach of confidence protects a right to informational privacy, there is no tort of privacy. This is because of an assumption that the recognition of such a tort would mean recognizing a more general, fundamental right to privacy going beyond the right to informational privacy and supporting the recognition of other specific new rights, for example, rights against physical intrusion, harassment, 'false light' invasion of privacy, or the 'appropriation of personality'. In fact, these are

---

129. [1917] *KB* 125, mentioned by Lindsay J, [2003] *All ER* 996 para. 222.
130. For a discussion of how event organizers attempt to prevent other traders from exploiting the event for commercial profit, *see* O.H. Dean, 'Ambushing Event Piracy' (2012) 34 *EIPR* 762.

either reducible to a right of informational privacy or are quite distinct claims that have different rationales and are based on different interests.

In addition to enforcing express or implicit undertakings of confidentiality against the parties who accepted them and third party accessories, the law of confidentiality in English law includes a law of informational privacy and law of trade secrets or know-how. Whereas the right of informational privacy is a right against a certain type of personal harm caused by the disclosure of information, the right to a trade secret is, it was argued above, a right of ownership of confidential information.

The right to informational privacy is concerned with reputation, inasmuch as it responds to a general concern with the way in which private information will affect other people's opinions. In some circumstances, a defamation claim can arise from the same events as a claim for breach of privacy. The two are distinct because defamation is concerned with false statements that damage reputation, whereas privacy is concerned with the disclosure of private information irrespective of its truth or falsity, and without any requirement to show that reputation has actually been adversely affected. 'False light' privacy is reducible in principle to either informational privacy or defamation.

The 'right of publicity' amounts to a right of ownership of image for celebrities. It is said to be a type of privacy right, but it is not based on the same principle as informational privacy, and the recognition of a right of informational privacy provides no support for the recognition of a right of publicity. The right of publicity is a type of merchandising right, and it is sometimes argued that merchandising rights can be established through the natural development of the law of trademarks. This is also unconvincing because trademarks are in principle concerned with communicating information to consumers, whereas merchandising images do not communicate information but operate purely through their inherent appeal to consumers.

For a good reason, the common law has generally avoided recognizing intellectual property rights in the intangible products of labour, leaving it to the legislature to enact an appropriate regime. The recognition of the ownership of confidential information is an exception and so would be the recognition of a merchandising right or right of publicity. According to the decision of the House of Lords in *Douglas v. Hello!*, there can be a right of confidentiality in respect of all aspects of the appearance of an occasion or 'spectacle', as a trade secret, if it is held in the circumstances such that the organizers can control access to it and take undertakings of confidentiality from people admitted, but there is no 'property right in a spectacle' as such, and so no exclusive right to the commercial value of a spectacle if it is not practicable to make such arrangements. This may be anomalous, but if so, it is an anomaly that can occur in other contexts in connection with the law of trade secrets.

Chapter 24

Developing a Right of Privacy for Corporations

Jacqueline N. Nwozo

24.1   INTRODUCTION

The development of the protection of privacy in English law has been driven by Article 8 of the European Convention on Human Rights (ECHR), the European Court of Human Rights jurisprudence on Article 8 ECHR, and the Human Rights Act 1998 (HRA), in particular, sections 2, 3, 6, and 12.[1] In view of the fact that English law now recognizes privacy protection for individuals, via the 'extended' action for breach of confidence, which has brought forth a 'tort of misuse of private information'[2] and to a much lesser extent a recognition of 'intrusion privacy protection',[3] it becomes important to ask whether English law also protects or ought to protect a right of privacy for corporations?[4]

---

1. For a detailed discussion of this development *see* Aplin, T. Filling the IP Gap: Privacy and Tabloidism in Richardson, M. and Ricketson, S. (eds) *Research Handbook on Intellectual Property in Media and Entertainment.* Edward Elgar, 2017. Chapter 15, 400-424; *see also,* Aplin, T. The Development of the Action for Breach of Confidence in a Post-HRA Era. *Intellectual Property Quarterly.* 2007: 1, 19-59.
2. Discussed in section 24.3 below.
3. *Ibid.*
4. A limited discussion of this issue appears in Mulheron, R. A Potential Framework for Privacy? A Reply to Hello!. *Modern Law Review.* 2006: 69, 679, 709-712. An extensive

This chapter argues that the extended action for breach of confidence – that is to say, the tort of misuse of private information as well as intrusion privacy protection – does not presently apply to corporations, but that it ought to be further developed in order to protect both individual and corporate privacy. Such a development would facilitate corporate autonomy and enable corporations effectively to carry on their activities without unwarranted interference.

Section 24.2 defines the concept of privacy. Section 24.3 argues that, as the English action for breach of confidence presently stands, corporations do not have a right of privacy, but that it is open to the courts to develop the law in this direction. Section 24.4 then investigates Article 8 ECHR and the associated Strasbourg jurisprudence in order to demonstrate a legal imperative for the development of a right to privacy for corporations in English law. The position in Australia, where the High Court of Australia in *Australia Broadcasting Corporation v. Lenah Game Meat Property Ltd*[5] explored whether to recognize a right of privacy that extends to corporations is examined in section 24.5, to see whether this decision from another common law jurisdiction lends weight to the development of a right of privacy in English law. Section 24.6 argues that there is a significant rationale underpinning a right of privacy in English law for corporations, namely, the autonomy rationale, which enables corporations to carry on their activities without unwarranted interference. In conclusion, section 24.7 makes preliminary recommendations on how the extended action for breach of confidence ought to be developed in relation to corporations.

24.2 DEFINITION OF PRIVACY

Arguably the earliest definition of privacy was espoused by Judge Cooley, who defined privacy as the right 'to be let alone'.[6] This definition, though proffered by Cooley, was made better known by Warren and Brandeis[7] who

---

discussion is in Aplin, T. 'A Right of Privacy for Corporations?' in Torremans, P.L.C. *Intellectual Property and Human Rights*. The Netherlands: Kluwer Law International BV, 2008.

5. *Australia Broadcasting Corporation v. Lenah Game Meat Property Ltd* [2001] HCA 63. For excellent analysis of this decision *see* Heath, W.M. Possum Processing, Picture Pilfering, Publication and Privacy: *Australian Broadcasting Corporation v. Lenah Game Meats Pty Ltd. Monash University Law* Review. 2002: 28, 162; Stewart, D. Protecting Privacy, Property, and Possums: *Australian Broadcasting Corporation v. Lenah Game Meats Pty Ltd. Federal Law Review.* 2002: 30, 177; Taylor, G. and Wright, D. *Australian Broadcasting Corporation v. Lenah Game Meats. Melbourne University Law Review.* 2002: 26, 707; Trindade, F. Possums, Privacy and the Implied Freedom of Communication. *Torts Law Journal.* 2002: 10, 119.

6. Cooley, T. *Cooley on Torts.* 2nd edn. 1888, 29 cited in Warren, S.D. and Brandeis, L.D. The Right to Privacy. *Harvard Law Review.* 1890: 4(5), 193-220, 195.

7. Warren and Brandeis, *ibid.*

declared that the protection of privacy 'is merely an instance of the enforcement of the more general right to be let alone'.[8] Although Judge Cooley's definition of privacy is limited in scope, it serves as the starting point in the development of the theoretical jurisprudence of privacy.

As the concept of privacy has developed, in addition to being defined as a 'right',[9] and a 'tort',[10] privacy has also been defined as a 'condition',[11] a 'state',[12] an 'interest',[13] a 'claim',[14] a 'value',[15] a 'form of control',[16] and an 'area of life'.[17] It has similarly been proclaimed to be 'an absolutely essential value that makes life more wholesome and worth living',[18] 'a pre-condition to personhood',[19] 'a universal concept',[20] and 'an aspect of one's humanity'.[21] Privacy has equally been defined in terms of freedom, more generally, with 'gains and losses of privacy as gains and losses of freedom'.[22]

Consequently, in comprehensively defining the concept of the individual's privacy, it is proposed that privacy is a broad concept which may be defined in two limbs. First, privacy may generally be defined as the state in which one desires to be free from unwanted interference or disturbance – intrusion – into his private sphere, which may include his physical space, or his home or his property; and secondly, privacy may be defined as a claim to

---

8. At 205.
9. Warren and Brandeis, *ibid*, 205.
10. Prosser, W.L. Privacy. *California Law Review*. 1960: 48(3), 383-424, 389. Prosser defined privacy as a complex of four torts. At 389.
11. Weinstein, M.A. The Uses of Privacy in the Good Life in Pennock, J. and Chapman, J. (eds) *Privacy Nomos XIII*. New York: Atherton Press, 1971, 88; Lusky, L. Invasion of Privacy: A Clarification of Concepts. *Columbia Law Review*. 1972:72(4), 693-710, 709; Parent, W.A. Privacy, Morality, and the Law. *Philosophy and Public Affairs*. 1983:12, 269-288, 269.
12. *Hosking v. Runting* [2005] 1 NZLR 1. Anderson J. defined privacy as a 'state of personal exclusion from involvement with or the attention of others.' At para. 264.
13. Prosser, W. *Privacy California Law Review*. 1960: 48(3), 383-424, 389.
14. Westin, A. *Privacy and Freedom*. New York: Association of the Bar, 1967, 7.
15. Gavison, R. Privacy and the Limits of Law. *The Yale Law Journal*. 1980:89(3), 421-471, 424-425.
16. Fried, C. Privacy. *Yale Law Journal*. 1968:77(3), 475-493, 483, 493; Gross, H. 'Privacy and Autonomy' in Pennock, J. and Chapman, J. *ibid*, 169; *See also* Miller, A. *Assault on Privacy*. Michigan: University of Michigan Press, 1971, 25; Beardsley, E.L. 'Privacy: Autonomy and Selective Disclosure' in Pennock, J. and Chapman, J. *ibid*; Van Den Haag, E. On Privacy in Pennock and Chapman, *ibid*; Parker, R. A Definition of Privacy. *Rutgers Law Review*. 1974: 27, 275-297.
17. *Privacy and the Law*, 1970. A Report by the British Section of the International Comm'n of Justice cited in Wacks, R. *Personal Information: Privacy and the Law*. Oxford: Clarendon Press, 1989, 14.
18. Whitman, J.Q. The Two Western Cultures of Privacy: Dignity Versus Liberty. *Yale Law Journal*. 2004: 113, 1151-1221, 1153.
19. Reiman, J. Privacy, Intimacy and Personhood. *Philosophy and Public Affairs*. 1976: 6, 26-44, 39.
20. Westin, *ibid*, 7-30.
21. Fried, C. Privacy. *Yale Law Journal*. 1968: 77(3), 475-493, 486.
22. Parker, R. A Definition of Privacy. *Rutgers Law Review*. 1974: 27, 275-296, 277.

the control of an individual's private information from being released into the public domain against the individual's wishes, thus protecting the said information from unwanted dissemination or publication.

This two limbed definition reflects a comprehensive definition of privacy, as it integrates the two fundamental privacy interests of intrusion privacy and information privacy – that is to say, limiting unwanted access to the individual, his home or his property, as well as limiting unwanted communication of the individual's private information – thereby enabling the individual to exercise autonomy within the society.[23] Indeed, these are the hallmarks of the protection of privacy and represent the core of the provisions of Article 8 ECHR, which protects the right to one's 'private life, family life, home and correspondence'.[24]

---

23. For elaboration on these fundamental privacy interests, *see* generally Warby, M., Moreham, N. and Christie, I. (eds) *Tugendhat and Christie The Law of Privacy and the Media.* 2nd ed. Oxford: Oxford University Press, 2011, Chapters 2, 5, and 10.
   Autonomy is discussed in section 24.6 below.
24. For other definitions of privacy, *see* Cornish, W., Llewelyn, D. and Aplin, T. *Intellectual Property: Patents, Copyright, Trade Marks and Allied Rights.* 9th edn. London: Sweet & Maxwell, 2019, 361; Parker, R. B. A Definition of Privacy. *Rutgers Law Review.* 1974: 27, 275-296, 277. *See also* Government Response to the National Heritage Select Committee, *Privacy and Media Intrusion,* Cmnd. 2918, HMSO, 1995; Calcutt Committee Report: *Report of the Committee on Privacy and Related Matters,* Cm. 1102, HMSO, 1990.
   For more on the general concept of privacy, *see* Roberts, J. and Gregor, T. Privacy: A Cultural View in Pennock, J. and Chapman, J. (eds) *Privacy Nomos XIII.* New York: Atherton Press, 1971; Silber, J. Masks and Fig Leaves in Pennock and Chapman, *ibid*; Simmel, A. Privacy Is Not an Isolated Freedom in Pennock and Chapman, *ibid*; Friedrich, C. Secrecy versus Privacy: The Democratic Dilemma in Pennock and Chapman, *ibid*; Spiro, H. Privacy in Comparative Perspective in Pennock and Chapman, *ibid*; Weinstein, W.L. The Private and the Free: A Conceptual Inquiry in Pennock and Chapman, *ibid*; Mead, M. *Coming of Age in Samoa: A Psychological Study of Primitive Youth for Western Civilization.* London: Cape, 1929; Anderson, D.A. 'The Failure of American Privacy Law' in Markesinis, B. (ed) *Protecting Privacy.* Oxford: Oxford University Press, 1999; Hall, E. *The Hidden Dimension.* New York: Anchor Books, 1966; Ardrey, R. *The Territorial Imperative: A Personal Inquiry into the Animal Origins of Property and Nation.* London: Collins, 1967; Hsu, F. *Americans and Chinese: Two Ways of Life.* New York: Schuman, 1953; Murdock, G.P. *Outline of World Cultures.* New Haven: Human Relations Area Files, 1963; Murdock, G.P. The Universals of Culture in Hoebel, E.A, Jennings, J.D. and Smith, E.R. (eds) *Readings in Social Anthropology.* New York: McGraw- Hill, 1955; Feldman, D. Privacy – Related Rights and Their Social Value in Birks, P. (ed.) *Privacy And Loyalty.* Oxford: Clarendon Press, 1997; Lewin, K. *Resolving Social Conflicts.* New York: Harper and Row, 1948; Murphy, R. Social Distance and the Veil. *American Anthropologist.* 1964: 66, 1257-1274; Zimmerman, D. Requiem for a Heavyweight: A Farewell to Warren and Brandeis's Privacy Tort. *Cornell Law Review.* 1983: 68, 291-365. Darling, F. Social Behaviour and Survival. *Auk.* 1952: 69 @. http://www.jstor.org/stable/4081268 Accessed on the 29/04/2019.

24.3   THE PROTECTION OF CORPORATIONS' PRIVACY
UNDER THE ENGLISH LAW OF CONFIDENCE

Under the influence of Article 8 ECHR and its accompanying Strasbourg jurisprudence, as well as the HRA 1998, English courts have interpreted and developed the action for breach of confidence in a manner that provides much fuller protection for privacy.[25] This has been achieved through the incorporation of Article 8 and Article 10 ECHR into the cause of action for breach of confidence.[26]

Article 8 ECHR provides:

1. Everyone has the right to respect for his private and family life, his home and his correspondence.
2. There shall be no interference by a public authority with the exercise of this right except such as is in accordance with the law and is necessary in a democratic society in the interest of national security, public safety or the economic well-being of the country, for the prevention of disorder or crime, for the protection of health or morals, or for the protection of the rights and freedom of others.

Article 10 ECHR provides:

1. Everyone has the right to freedom of expression. This right shall include freedom to hold opinions and to receive and impart information and ideas without interference by public authority and regardless of frontiers. This Article shall not prevent States from requiring the licensing of broadcasting, television or cinema enterprises.
2. The exercise of these freedoms, since it carries with it duties and responsibilities, may be subject to such formalities, conditions, restrictions or penalties as are prescribed by law and are necessary in a democratic society, in the interests of national security, territorial integrity or public safety, for the prevention of disorder or crime, for the protection of health or morals, for the protection of the reputation or rights of others, for preventing the disclosure of information received in confidence, or for maintaining the authority and impartiality of the judiciary.

---

25. For a comprehensive and general discussion of the status of the ECHR on UK domestic law both pre and post the HRA *see* Blackburn, R. The United Kingdom in Blackburn, R. and Polakiewicz, J. (eds), *Fundamental Rights in Europe.* Oxford: Oxford University Press, 2001, Chapter 36.
26. *See A v. B Plc* [2003] QB 195.
   On the origins of Article 8 *see* Velu, J, The European Convention on Human Rights and the Right to Respect for Private Life, the Home and Communications in Robertson, A. H. (ed.), *Privacy and Human Rights.* Manchester: Manchester University Press, 1973, 12-95 at 14-18.

The incorporation of Article 8 and Article 10 ECHR into the cause of action for breach of confidence, enabled by the HRA 1998, has had the effect of establishing an extended action for breach of confidence. Much of the focus of this action has been on the protection of private information, which has in turn brought about the establishment of a tort of misuse of private information,[27] as well as recognition for protection against intrusion,[28] although the development of intrusion protection is much more nascent.[29] Adjudicating a matter under the tort of misuse of private information entails asking the touchstone question 'whether in respect of disclosed facts there is a reasonable expectation of privacy' – which in turn usually requires a 'balancing exercise' between Articles 8 and 10 ECHR.[30]

The question to be addressed in this section, therefore, is whether the extended action for breach of confidence also provides protection for the privacy of corporations. As will be demonstrated below, the courts have not recognized the application of the extended action to corporations, but neither have they ruled out this possibility.

A case which came close to dealing with the question of whether a corporation is entitled to privacy protection is *Douglas v. Hello!*.[31] In this case, the first and second claimants, the Douglases', gave the third claimants, *OK!* magazine, exclusive rights to publish photographs of their wedding. A rival magazine, *Hello!*, published photographs of the Douglases' wedding that had been taken surreptitiously. At first instance, Lindsey J. held *Hello!* liable to all three claimants for breach of confidence. At the Court of Appeal, the defendant's appeal against the Douglases' was dismissed. The court found that the unauthorized photographs had infringed the Douglases' 'private life',[32] and awarded damages. However, the Court of Appeal upheld

---

27. *Campbell v. Mirror Group Newspaper* [2004] 2 AC 457, para. 14.
28. For the recognition of the intrusion aspect of privacy, *see Campbell v. Mirror Group Newspaper* [2004] 2 AC 457, paras 12 and 15, *Wood v. Commissioner for Police of the Metropolis* [2009] 4 All ER 951, para. 34, Eady J in *Mosley v. News Group Newspapers Ltd* [2008] EWHC 1777, para. 17. *See also Imerman v. Tchenguiz* [2011] Fam 116.
    See also Warby, M., Moreham, N. and Christie, I. (eds) *Tugendhat and Christie: The Law of Privacy and the Media*. Oxford: Oxford University Press, 2011, Chapter 10.
29. For a detailed discussion on the extended action *see* Warby, M., Moreham, N. and Christie, I. *ibid*, Chapters 5, and 10. On privacy of the individual in general, *see also* Warby, M., Moreham, N. and Christie, I., *ibid*; Cornish, W., Llewelyn, D. and Aplin, T. *Intellectual Property: Patents, Copyright, Trade Marks and Allied Rights*. 9th edn. London: Sweet & Maxwell, 2019, Chapter 9.
30. On the touchstone question and balancing exercise, *see Campbell v. Mirror Group Newspaper* [2004] 2 AC 457, para. 21; *McKennitt v. Ash* [2008] QB 73, para. 11; *Murray v. Express Newspaper* [2009] Ch. 481, para. 36.
    For more recent cases, *see* generally, *Khuja v. Times Newspaper Ltd* [2019] AC 161; *Richard v. BBC* [2019] Ch. 169; *PJS v. News Group Newspaper Ltd* [2016] AC 1081; *In re JR38* [2015] UKSC 42.
31. This case as reported as *OBG Ltd v. Allan* [2008] 1 AC 1.
32. *Douglas v. Hello!* [2005] EMLR 28 (CA), para. 95.

Hello!'s appeal against the third claimant, OK!. In the House of Lords, however, OK!'s appeal was upheld, and the order of Lindsey J. restored.

Notably, the House of Lords drew a distinction between the 'traditional' action for breach of confidence and the 'extended' action, which protects privacy. Lord Hoffmann stated: 'English law has adapted the action for breach of confidence to provide a remedy for unauthorised disclosure of personal information'.[33] Similarly, Lord Nicholls stated: 'As the law has developed, breach of confidence or misuse of confidential information now covers two distinct causes of action, protecting two different interests: privacy, and secret ("confidential") information'.[34] However, Lord Hoffmann stated that *OK!'s* case was not concerned with the protection of privacy but the commercial interest in the photographs which were taken at the wedding. To this end, Lord Hoffmann declared:

> But this appeal is not concerned with the protection of privacy. Whatever may have been the position of the Douglases, who, as I mentioned, recovered damages for an invasion of their privacy, 'OK!'s' claim is to protect commercially confidential information and nothing more ... 'OK!' has no claim to privacy under article 8 nor can it make a claim which is parasitic upon the Douglases' right to privacy.[35]

Thus, according to Lord Hoffmann, although the information in question concerned the private life of the Douglases'; for OK!, the issue was about the protection of the commercial interest in the photographs which were taken at the wedding.

Notwithstanding Lord Hoffmann's statement that OK! had no claim under Article 8, this does not preclude the possibility of privacy protection for corporations. This is because the appeal before the House of Lords concerned OK!'s commercial secrets as opposed to its private information and, arguably, there is a difference between these two types of information.[36]

Other cases have considered the extent to which business information may engage Article 8 ECHR, albeit in the context of individuals. In *Browne v. Associated Newspaper Ltd*,[37] an injunction was granted, on the basis of breach of confidence and/or misuse of private information, to restrain the defendant from publishing information relating, *inter alia*, to business activities communicated in the course of a personal relationship by the claimant, an individual. The injunction was subsequently discharged by Eady J., and an appeal to the Court of Appeal was dismissed.

In the Court of Appeal, Sir Anthony Clarke MR stated that 'although there is no authority to the effect that information relating to business

---

33. Paragraph 118.
34. Paragraph 255.
35. *OBG Ltd v. Allan* [2008] 1 AC 1, para. 118.
36. This is discussed in *R v. Broadcasting Standards Commission ex parte BBC* [2001] QB 885 below.
37. *Browne v. Associated Newspaper Ltd* [2007] 3 WLR 289.

activities communicated in the course of a personal relationship or learned in a domestic environment would be characterized as private, it appears to us that it all depends upon the circumstances of each particular case'.[38] After citing, *inter alia, Societe Colas Est v. France*,[39] Sir Anthony Clarke MR held:

> In short, each case must be decided on its own facts … without entering into a preliminary inquiry as to whether any particular piece of information should be allocated a 'business' or a 'personal' characterisation, the question to ask, in relation to each of the categories individually, was whether there was a reasonable expectation of privacy [and if so] article 8 is engaged.[40]

From the above, it is clear that the relevant enquiry is whether a reasonable expectation of privacy exists, rather than whether information can be characterized as private as opposed to business (or commercial). In view of the court's reference to the European Court of Human Rights case of *Societe Colas Est*, which established privacy protection for the corporation under Article 8,[41] it is unclear, however, whether the court's *ratio* is limited to the facts of the case – i.e., an action brought by an individual – or applies more generally to any claimant, including corporations.

Imerman v. Tchenguiz[42] is another case where business information fell within the scope of Article 8 ECHR. In this case, the claimant's wife, through her brothers (the defendants) accessed the computer system of the claimant, and without his authorization copied information, emails, and documents which he had stored there. In handing down the judgment of the Court of Appeal that, *inter alia*, Article 8 ECHR had been infringed, Lord Neuberger MR held:

> In this case, as far as we can see, there is no question but that Mr Imerman had an expectation of privacy in respect of the majority of his documents stored on the server … Many e-mails sent to and by and on behalf of Mr Imerman, whether connected with his family or private life, his personal and family assets, or his business dealings must be of a private and confidential nature.[43]

Lord Neuberger MR added:

> the fact that the documents [confidential personal or business papers] were stored on the server, which was, as [Mr Imerman] knew, owned by Robert Tchenguiz [one of Mrs Imerman's brothers] who enjoyed

---

38. Paragraph 34.
39. *Societe Colas Est v. France* [2004] 39 EHRR 17; Sir Anthony Clarke at para. 35. This European Court of Human Rights case is discussed in section 24.4 below.
40. Paragraphs 36-37.
41. As will be seen in section 24.4.
42. *Imerman v. Tchenguiz* [2011] Fam 116.
43. Paragraph 77.

physically unrestricted access to the server, cannot deprive Mr Imerman of the reasonable expectation of privacy, and the consequent right to maintain a claim for breach of confidence, in respect of the contents of any of his documents stored on the server.[44]

Although the Court of Appeal established that there was a reasonable expectation of privacy under Article 8 in relation to business information, it made this declaration specific to an individual, Mr Imerman, and was silent on whether this would also apply to corporations.

That there is a reasonable expectation of privacy in relation to an individual's business information seems to be gaining ground in English Law. This is further affirmed in the recent case of *ZXC v. Bloomberg*,[45] wherein, the Chief Executive of a company, X Ltd, made a claim for misuse of private information by a news organization which had published an article about him on their website regarding a criminal investigation by a United Kingdom Law Enforcement Body [UKLEB] into his activities. The claimant applied for an injunction to remove the article from the said website.

In holding that the claimant's Article 8 ECHR rights were engaged in this case, Justice Nicklin declared:

> In my judgment, the Claimant does have a reasonable expectation in the Information (defined in [106] above). I am satisfied that a reasonable person of ordinary sensibilities, placed in the same position of the Claimant, would consider that he had a reasonable expectation of privacy in the Information.[46]

Justice Nicklin noted:

> [T]he high-level of confidentiality that I find attaches to the Information is a very significant factor when considering whether he has a reasonable expectation of privacy in that Information.[47]

The said information Justice Nicklin referred to in paragraph [106] was as follows:

> (i) the fact that UKLEB had asked the authorities of the foreign state to provide banking and business records relating to four companies in its investigations into the Claimant ... (ii) the details of the deal that UKLEB was investigating in relation to the Claimant, including that: (a) UKLEB considered the Claimant had provided false information to the X Ltd board on the value of an asset in a potential conspiracy ... (b) UKLEB believed that the Claimant had committed fraud by false representation ... and (c) UKLEB was

---

44. Paragraph 79.
45. *ZXC v. Bloomberg* [2019] EWHC 970 (QB).
46. Paragraph 125.
47. Paragraph 125(g).

seeking to trace the onward distribution of [a substantial sum of money] ... believed [to be] the proceeds of a crime carried out by the Claimant.[48]

This case did not consider whether the corporation, itself, had a reasonable expectation of privacy, however, as seen from the above, the information in question was the business information of a corporation, of which the claimant was Chief Executive. Indeed, the Court indicated that it 'found the claimant had privacy interests in the said information';[49] it, therefore, follows that privacy interests can exist in business information. Furthermore, the Court in holding that the said information was subject to a reasonable expectation of privacy and therefore engaged Article 8 rights, thereby affirmed its presently established position that business, financial or commercial information may engage Article 8 rights of the individual. It is, however, uncertain whether the Court would have so held if a corporation had been the claimant. This is in light of the Court's observation that this case was 'a complaint about loss of autonomy and damage to reputation which are both dimensions of Article 8 ECHR'.[50] It is suggested that the rationales of loss of autonomy and damage to reputation are equally applicable to the corporation.

Although English courts have not expressly ruled out the possibility of privacy protection for corporations under the English law of confidence, they have not yet recognized it. However, if one turns to the Broadcasting Act 1996, it will be observed that English law recognizes privacy protection for corporations with respect to broadcasting matters. Privacy for corporations is a recognized legal value in English law, such that the application of the extended action for breach of confidence to corporations might represent a short leap.

In sections 110(1)(b), and 111(1) of the Broadcasting Act 1996, the right of corporations to the protection of their privacy, with respect specifically to broadcasting matters, is recognized.[51]

The combined effect of these two sections is that individuals, as well as incorporated persons, may make a fairness complaint concerning infringement of privacy on matters to the Broadcasting Standards Commission (BSC) for consideration and adjudication. Thus, it is clear from these legislative provisions along with the legislative history of the Broadcasting Act 1996 that Parliament provided privacy protection for both individual and corporate persons with respect to broadcasting matters.[52]

---

48. Paragraph 106.
49. Paragraph 131.
50. Paragraph 125.
51. The individual's privacy in broadcasting matters is also protected by the Broadcasting Act 1996.
52. The protection of the privacy of the corporation by Parliament is not unique to the Act of 1996. From the legislative history of the Broadcasting Act, it is observed that the first

The application of sections 110(1)(b) and 111(1) of the Broadcasting Act 1996 is illustrated in the case of *R v. Broadcasting Standards Commission ex parte BBC*,[53] where programme makers for a broadcasting company secretly filmed transactions in the plaintiff's store without the plaintiff's permission. The plaintiff, DSG Retail Ltd, made a complaint to the BSC that the secret filming had been an unwarranted infringement of its privacy within sections 110 and 111.

The BSC found that the secret filming had infringed the plaintiff's privacy and that the infringement was unwarranted and as such, upheld the complaint.

In light of this, the BBC[54] applied for judicial review. Forbes J. at first instance held, *inter alia*, that a body corporate as a matter of law did not have a right to privacy and as such could not bring a complaint for an infringement of privacy under the Broadcasting Act 1996. Furthermore, there could not be an infringement of privacy by the mere fact of surreptitious filming in a place to which the public had access if there was no element of seclusion in the event being filmed. Forbes J., therefore, quashed the BSC's finding.

On appeal by the BSC, the Court of Appeal reversed the holding of Forbes J. and unanimously held, *inter alia,* that on a proper construction of sections 110 and 111 of the Broadcasting Act 1996, a company could make a complaint of unwarranted infringement of its privacy, and as such, the BSC had been entitled to conclude that secret filming of transactions in the plaintiff's stores was an infringement of the plaintiff's privacy.

In delivering judgment, Lord Woolf MR declared:

> There is no dispute that a company can make a complaint. This is categorically stated in section 111(1) of the Act.[55]

Although this case specifically dealt with the corporation's privacy under the Broadcasting Act 1996, Lord Woolf MR generally recognized that a corporation could suffer an infringement of its privacy, and explained how the interference could occur. To this end, he observed:

Broadcasting Act which was enacted in 1980 [section 18(1)(b) and 19(2)], the Broadcasting Acts of 1981 [section 54(1)(b) and 55(2)], and 1990 [section 143(1)(b) and 144(2)], also provided privacy protection for incorporated persons, in broadcasting matters. It is therefore submitted, that in accordance with the provisions of the Act of 1980 and the subsequent amendments of the Acts of 1981, 1990, and 1996 noted above, it was the firm intention of Parliament to provide privacy protection for incorporated persons in matters specific to broadcasting.

This intention of Parliament is also demonstrated in the HANSARD HL law debate on the Broadcasting Bill 1980, in which the House of Lords debated the Bill before passing it to law, including the relevant sections on the protection of the privacy of incorporated persons. HANSARD [HL Debate] 15th October, 1980. *See* particularly, cc1303-4, 1310, 1312-13.

53. *R v. Broadcasting Standards Commission ex parte BBC* [2001] QB 885.
54. British Broadcasting Corporation.
55. Paragraph 34.

While the intrusions into the privacy of an individual which are possible are no doubt more extensive than the infringements of privacy which are possible in the case of a company, a company does have activities of a private nature which need protection from unwarranted intrusion [such as if an intruder] without any justification attempted to listen clandestinely to the activities of a board meeting. The same would be true of secret filming of the board meeting. The individual members of the board would no doubt have grounds for complaint, but so would the board and thus the company as a whole. The company has correspondence which it could justifiably regard as private and the broadcasting of the contents of that correspondence would be an intrusion on its privacy. It could not possibly be said that to hold such actions an intrusion of privacy conflicts with the Convention.[56]

Consequently, his Lordship concluded:

The [Broadcasting] Act extends to unwarranted interference with the privacy of a company.[57]

On the intention of the Broadcasting Act as an Act to provide protection for individual as well as corporate privacy in broadcasting matters, Hale LJ (as she then was) declared:

The provisions of the Act are quite clear. A 'body of persons, whether incorporated or not' has the right to make a fairness complaint: section 111(1) ... It is, I acknowledge, surprising that section 111(2) and (3) also refer to a 'person or body', but had the draftsman intended to confine a 'person affected' to an individual he could and, in my view, would have done so.[58]

Furthermore, on the nature of a corporation's privacy, Hale LJ declared:

There are many things which companies may (legitimately or illegitimately) wish to keep private, including their property, their meetings and their correspondence. There are still more about which they may (legitimately or illegitimately) wish to avoid publicity ... Notions of what an individual might or might want to be kept 'private', 'secret' or 'secluded' are subjective to that individual ... If this is so for an individual, I cannot see why it should not also be capable of being so for a company. The company will have its own reasons (good or bad) for wanting or not wanting to object and the secrecy of the filming has deprived it of the opportunity to do so.[59]

---

56. Paragraph 33.
57. Paragraph 34.
58. Paragraph 41.
59. Paragraphs 42-43.

Hale LJ, however, noted that the context was one of broadcasting standards and not legal rights, and this justified 'a wider view of the ambit of privacy than might be appropriate in some other contexts'.[60]

Lord Mustill, although concurring with Lord Woolf MR and Hale LJ. that the appeal be allowed, emphasized the degree to which that conclusion was dependent on the language and purpose of the Broadcasting Act 1996. He also expressed serious concerns about whether a corporation could have a right to privacy. Lord Mustill commented:

> Can a company say that it is aggrieved by an invasion of its own privacy? As a matter of ordinary language I would not have thought so ... for in general I find the concept of a company's privacy hard to grasp. To my mind the privacy of a human being denotes at the same time the personal 'space' in which the individual is free to be itself, and also the carapace, or shell, or umbrella, or whatever other metaphor is preferred, which protects that space from intrusion. An infringement of privacy is an affront to the personality, which is damaged both by the violation and by the demonstration that the personal space is not inviolate. The concept is hard indeed to define, but if this gives something of its flavour I do not see how it can apply to an impersonal corporate body, which has no sensitivities to wound, and no selfhood to protect.[61]

In spite of Lord Mustill's scepticism, he nevertheless applied the Broadcasting Act 1996 and found in favour of privacy protection for the corporation. It is noted that this case was heard on the threshold of the coming into force of the HRA when a broader understanding of privacy had not been contemplated. Indeed, Lord Mustill in his concluding statement acknowledged that:

> when it becomes necessary to consider the question [of a general appreciation of privacy] in the much wider context of human rights, as it surely will, there may well be room for more than one opinion about what the concept entails.[62]

By holding that a company can make a complaint of an unwarranted infringement of its privacy under the Broadcasting Act 1996, the Court of Appeal recognized that corporate persons have privacy interests that are worthy of protection. However, the court left open whether a corporation has a legal right to privacy under Article 8 ECHR. Lord Woolf MR declared 'in difficult cases, it is perfectly appropriate to have regard to the jurisprudence of the ECtHR, the ECJ, and of other countries'.[63] At the time *R v.*

---

60. Paragraph 44.
61. Paragraphs 46, 48.
62. Paragraph 50.
63. Paragraph 17.

Broadcasting Standards Commission ex parte BBC[64] was decided, the jurisprudence from Strasbourg and the EU had yet to recognize corporations within the scope of Article 8 ECHR. In light of the evolving Strasbourg and EU jurisprudence, where such recognition has since been established, it is argued that there is now a legal imperative for the development of a right of privacy for corporations in English law. I turn now to examine this jurisprudence.

24.4   ARTICLE 8 ECHR: JURISPRUDENCE OF THE
          EUROPEAN COURT OF HUMAN RIGHTS ON
          PRIVACY

This section traces the progression of Strasbourg jurisprudence and how Article 8 ECHR has been held to include an individual's personal undertakings; the protection of an individual's business or professional activities, and in certain circumstances, the protection of the business and professional activities of a corporation. The expansion of Article 8 to include corporations is what provides an impetus to develop the extended action for breach of confidence, under English law, to include corporations.

As indicated above, Article 8(1) prescribes that everyone has the right to respect for his 'private life', 'family life', 'home' and 'correspondence'. According to Strasbourg jurisprudence, 'private life' is a broad term not susceptible to exhaustive or restrictive definition. In *S v. United Kingdom*,[65] the European Court of Human Rights held that private life incorporates a variety of situations such as the protection of the individual's personal data,[66] physical and psychological integrity,[67] protection of a zone of interaction in a public context.[68] It is not, however, unlimited in scope.[69]

---

64. *R v. Broadcasting Standards Commission ex parte BBC* [2001] QB 885.
65. *S v. United Kingdom* [2009] 48 EHRR 50.
66. Information of an individual's health records have been held to be an aspect which affects his private life. *See Z v. Finland* [1998] 25 EHRR 371; *KH v. Slovakia* [2009] 39 EHRR 34; *Roche v. United Kingdom* [2006] 42 EHRR 30, *See also PG v. United Kingdom* [2008] 46 EHRR 51.
67. The physical and psychological integrity of an individual is an aspect of private life which protects the individual's right to personal development, and the right to establish and develop relationships with other human beings and the outside world *See Friedl v. Austria* [1996] 21 EHRR 83; *Pretty v. United Kingdom* [2002] 35 EHRR 1; *Mikulic v. Croatia* [2002] 1 FCR 720; *YF v. Turkey* [2004] 39 EHRR 34. the physical and psychological integrity of an individual can embrace multiple aspects of the person's physical and social identity such as an individual's name, or gender identification – *Bensaid v. United Kingdom* [2001] 33 EHRR 10, *Peck v. United Kingdom* [2003] 36 EHRR 41; an individual's sexual orientation and sexual life – *KU v. Finland* [2009] 48 EHRR 52; an individual's right to his image such as his photograph – *Sciacca v. Italy* [2006] 43 EHRR 20; as well as an individual's decision to or not to become a parent – *Evans v. United Kingdom* [2008] 46 EHRR 34.
68. *Von Hannover v. Germany* [2005]40 EHRR 1.
69. *Botta v. Italy* [1998] 26EHRR 241.

Initially, the scope of the protection of Article 8 ECHR was understood only to comprise an individual's personal undertakings and did not envisage the protection of the individual's activities which were of a business or professional nature, nor did it envisage the protection of the activities of corporations.[70] However, this soon shifted, as illustrated in *Huvig v. France*.[71] In this case, the applicants' private as well as business telephone lines were tapped by the police on the instruction of an investigating judge, and the applicants complained that this violated their Article 8 rights.

The European Court of Human Rights unanimously held that the tapping of both the applicants' business and private telephone lines constituted a violation of their Article 8 rights. The court declared:

> The telephone tapping complained of amounted without any doubt to an 'interference by a public authority' with the exercise of the applicants' right to respect for their ... 'private life.'[72]

In including the business telephone tapping of the applicants' as a violation of their private life, the court stated that such interference contravened Article 8 unless it was 'in accordance with the law' and 'necessary in a democratic society' for the purpose of achieving one or more of the legitimate aims referred to in Article 8(2) ECHR.[73]

As the law evolved, the question of whether the notion of privacy under Article 8 ECHR could extend to engage the protection of an individual's business premises arose. This question was tested in the case of *Niemietz v. Germany*.[74] In this case, the applicant complained that a search which had been carried out at his office had, *inter alia*, violated his rights to home and correspondence under Article 8 ECHR.

The European Court of Human Rights unanimously held that the search of the applicant's office amounted to a violation of his Article 8 rights. The understanding of Article 8 ECHR was therefore expanded to include the

---

70. The scope of privacy comprising only the personal undertakings of individuals is illustrated in such early cases as *Dudgeon v. United Kingdom* [1982] 4 EHRR 149 [relating to inquiry on homosexual conduct in private between consenting males]; *Marckx v. Belgium* [1979-80] 2 EHRR 330 [relating to limitations on the rights of a single mother and child]; *X v. Belgium* (App. No.5488/72), decided on 30 May 1974 and *Gillow v. United Kingdom* [1989] 11 EHRR 335 [on the understanding of interference with home life]; *Golder v. United Kingdom* [1979-80] 1 EHRR 524 and *Silver v. United Kingdom* [1983] 5 EHRR 347 [interference with prisoners' correspondence]; *Malone v. United Kingdom* [1985] 7 EHRR 14 [interception of postal and telephone communications].
71. *Huvig v. France* [1990] 12 EHRR 528.
72. Paragraph 25.
73. This was applied in *Halford v. United Kingdom* [1997] 24 EHRR 524, where the European Court of Human Rights declared: "'In the Court's view, it is clear from its case law that telephone calls made from business premises as well as from home may be covered by the notions of "private life" ... within the meaning of Article 8(1)'. Para. 44. *See* also *Kopp v. Switzerland* [1999] 27 EHRR 91, para. 50.
74. *Niemietz v. Germany* [1993] 16 EHRR 97.

business and professional premises of the individual. The court in arriving at its decision stated that it was difficult to clearly distinguish which of an individual's activities formed part of his business life and which did not. It indicated that an individual's business and non-business activities may be so intermixed that there was no means of differentiating between them. In developing the law under Article 8 to include the protection of the business and professional premises of the individual, the court declared on 'private life':

> The Court does not consider it possible or necessary to attempt an exhaustive definition of the notion of 'private life.' However, it would be too restrictive to limit the notion to an 'inner circle' in which the individual may live his own personal life as he chooses and to exclude therefrom entirely the outside world not encompassed within that circle. … To deny the protection of Article 8 on the ground that the measure complained of related only to professional activities … could moreover lead to an inequality of treatment, in that such protection would remain available to a person whose professional and non-professional activities were so intermingled that there was no means of distinguishing between them.[75]

The court concluded that there was no reason of principle why the notion of 'private life' should be taken to exclude activities of a professional or business nature. It added that to interpret 'private life' as including certain professional or business activities or premises would be consonant with the essential object and purpose of Article 8, namely, to protect the individual against arbitrary interference by the public authorities.[76]

On the scope of 'home' under Article 8 ECHR as appearing in the English text of Article 8, the court declared:

> As regards the word 'home,' appearing in the English text of Article 8, the Court observes that in certain Contracting States, notably Germany, it has been accepted as extending to business premises.[77] Such an interpretation is, moreover, fully consonant with the French text, since the word 'domicile' has a broader connotation than the word 'home' and may extend, for example, to a professional person's office … [78]

The court noted that it may not always be possible to draw precise distinctions between an individual's home and his business premises, since activities which are related to a profession or business may well be

---

75. Paragraph 29.
76. Paragraph 31.
77. *See* Article 13(1) of the Basic Law for the Federal Republic of Germany, which guarantees the inviolability of the home. The court noted that this provision has been consistently interpreted by German courts in a wider sense to include business premises.
78. Paragraph 30.

conducted from a person's private residence, and activities which are not so related may well be carried on in an office or commercial premises.

To this end, the court accordingly concluded:

> More generally, to interpret the words [inter alia] 'home' as including certain professional or business activities or premises would be consonant with the essential object and purpose of Article 8, namely to protect the individual against arbitrary interference by the public authorities.[79]

The court indicated that to interpret 'home' narrowly would give rise to the same risk of inequality of treatment as a narrow interpretation of the notion of private life. Therefore, the court understood 'home' under Article 8 of the Convention as encompassing an individual's private residence, as well as his professional or business premises.

This case, therefore, established that Article 8 ECHR not only protects an individual's personal undertakings but can also protect an individual's business or professional activities.[80]

In a further development, advancing from the original intention of Article 8 ECHR, which was intended specifically for the protection of the individual;[81] Article 8 ECHR was held to include a corporation's registered office, branches and other business premises. This is illustrated in *Societe Colas Est v. France*,[82] where the applicant companies, relying on Article 8 ECHR, complained that raids and seizures which were undertaken within their premises by government inspectors constituted a violation of the right to respect for their home.

The European Court of Human Rights unanimously held that there had been violations of the companies' Article 8 rights. In extending the scope of Article 8 to include the protection of corporations, the court declared:

> The Court reiterates that the Convention is a living instrument which must be interpreted in the light of present-day conditions. As regards the rights secured to companies by the Convention, it should be pointed out that the Court has already recognised a company's right under Art. 41 to compensation for non-pecuniary damage sustained as a result of a violation of Art. 6(1) of the Convention. [Therefore] building on its dynamic interpretation of the Convention, the Court considers that the time has come to hold that in certain circumstances the rights guaranteed by Art.8 of the Convention may be construed as including the right to

---

79. Paragraph 31. *See also Amann v. Switzerland* [2000] 30 EHRR 843, para. 65.
80. *See also Kennedy v. United Kingdom* [2011] 52 EHRR 4.For a discussion of how this decision impacts on the private life of employees *vis- á -vis* their employers *see* Ford, M. Two Conceptions of Worker Privacy. *Industrial Law Journal.* 2002: 31, 135.
81. *See* Council of Europe, Preparatory Work on Article 8 European Convention on Human Rights @ http://www.echr.coe.int/LibraryDocs/Travaux/ECHRTravaux-ART8-DH(56) 12-EN1674980.pdf, page 2. Accessed on 23/5/2019.
82. *Societe Colas Est v. France* [2004] 39 EHRR 17.

respect for a company's registered office, branches or other business premises.[83]

In extending the scope of 'home' under Article 8 to include corporations, the court referred to the case of *Niemietz v. Germany*[84] and reiterated that the word 'domicile' had a broader meaning than the word 'home' and extended to a professional person's business premises. The court added that in *Chappell v. United Kingdom*[85] it had held that a search conducted at a private individual's home, which was also the registered office of a corporation run by the individual, had amounted to an interference with his right to respect for his home within the meaning of Article 8. The court also referred to *Cossey v. United Kingdom*[86] noting the fact that, in keeping with the Convention being a living instrument, the court may depart from an earlier decision. The court, although acknowledging that interference by a public authority may be more far-reaching where the business premises of a juristic person are concerned, nevertheless concluded that 'the inspections in issue, on account on the manner in which they were carried out – that is to say, the inspectors simultaneous entry into the premises of the applicant companies' head and branch offices without judicial authorization, and the seizure of various documents containing evidence unrelated to the operations in issue – constituted intrusions into the applicant companies' 'homes'.[87]

It is suggested that in holding that a corporation's registered office and other business premises came within the scope of protection of Article 8 and that the manner in which the raids and seizures in issue were carried out constituted intrusions into the applicant companies' homes, the court sought to realize, guarantee and safeguard Convention rights 'in a practical, effective and dynamic manner to ensure that the interpretation of the Convention reflects societal changes and remains in line with present day conditions'.[88] In so holding, the court adopted an autonomous interpretation of 'home' in a manner which was not hindered by its meaning under domestic law.

This dynamic interpretation of Article 8 ECHR by the European Court of Human Rights in *Societe Colas Est v. France*,[89] extending the notion of

---

83. Paragraph 41.
84. *Niemietz v. Germany* [1993] 16 EHRR 97.
85. *Chappell v. United Kingdom* [1990] 12 EHRR 1.
86. At para. 41. *Cossey v. United Kingdom* [1991] 13 EHRR 622, para. 35.
87. Paragraph 46.
88. On the court's dynamic interpretation of the Convention as it relates to the protection of the corporation, *see* generally *Comingersoll v. Portugal* [2001] 31 EHRR 31, and particularly, para. 35.
89. *Societe Colas Est v. France* [2004] 39 EHRR 17.

home thereunder to corporations has been further reinforced by its subsequent judgments in *Buck v. Germany*[90] and *Sallinen v. Finland.*[91] In *Buck's* case, the court declared:

> The Court would point out that, as it has now repeatedly held, the notion of 'home' in Art.8(1) encompasses not only a private individual's home ... 'home' is to be construed as including also the registered office of a company run by a private individual, as well as a juristic person's registered office, branches and other business premises.[92]

This declaration was subsequently reiterated in *Sallinen's* case.[93]

Equally, in *Wieser v. Austria*[94] where a corporation's premises were searched, and electronic data was seized, the European Court of Human Rights found this to constitute an interference with the corporation's right to respect for its correspondence within the meaning of Article 8. In justifying its position of extending Article 8 to include a corporation's correspondence, the European Court of Human Rights recalled that in *Societe Colas Est*, it had held the search of a corporation's business premises to constitute an interference with its right to respect for its 'home'. Consequently, the Court declared:

> Having regard to its above-cited case law extending the notion of 'home' to a company's business premises, the Court sees no reason to distinguish between the first applicant, who is a natural person, and the second applicant, which is a legal person, as regards the notion of 'correspondence'.[95]

The principle in *Societe Colas Est* has been recognized and applied by the Court of Justice of the European Union. In *Roquette Freres SA v. Directeur General de la Concurrence, de la Consommation et de la Repression des Fraude,*[96] this court relied on *Societe Colas* and *Niemietz* to reject its earlier position in *Hoechst AG v. Commission of the European Communities*[97] that business premises were not included in the notion of

---

90. *Buck v. Germany* [2006] 42 EHRR 21.
91. *Sallinen v. Finland* [2007] 44 EHRR 18.
92. Paragraph 31.
93. At para. 70.
94. *Weiser v. Austria* [2008] 46 EHRR 54.
95. Paragraph 45.
96. *Roquette Freres SA v. Directeur General de la Concurrence, de la Consommation et de la Repression des Fraude* [2003] 4 CMLR 1. This case involved the requirement by the European Commission for Roquette to submit itself for an investigation concerning alleged participation in monopoly practices, and price fixing.
97. *Hoechst AG v. Commission of the European Communities* [1991] 4 CMLR 410. In this case, Hoechst AG was being investigated by the Commission of the European Communities in respect of alleged anti-competitive conduct. Hoechst AG sought annulment of the Commission's decision to investigate it, *inter alia*, on the grounds that it amounted to the inviolability of the home under Article 8 ECHR. This application was dismissed.

'home' under Article 8 ECHR. In departing from its *Hoechst* judgment, the Court of Justice of the European Union stated:

> fundamental rights form an integral part of the general principles of law observance of which the Court ensures ... The ECHR has special significance in that respect ... For the purposes of determining the scope of that principle in relation to the protection of business premises, regard must be had to the case law of the European Court of Human Rights subsequent to the judgment in Hoechst. According to that case law, first, the protection of the home provided for in Art. 8 of the ECHR may in certain circumstances be extended to cover such premises and, second, the right of interference established by Art. 8(2) of the ECHR 'might well be more far-reaching where professional or business activities or premises (Societe Colas Est v. France, April 16, 2002) were involved than would otherwise be the case' (Niemietz v. Germany, December 16, 1992: [1993] 16 EHRR 97).[98]

Equally, in *Agrofert Holding A.S. v. European Commission*,[99] the Court of Justice of the European Union declared:

> The right to respect for private life is a fundamental right which forms an integral part of the general principles of law, the observance of which the Court ensures ... The right to respect for private life is, moreover, reaffirmed in art. 7 of the Charter of Fundamental Rights of the European Union, proclaimed on 7 December 2000 in Nice ... The notion of private life may include activities of a professional or business nature of natural or legal persons. (judgment of the European Court Of Human Rights, Niemietz v Germany, 16 December 1992, (1993) 16 EHRR 97, 29 ... Societe Colas Est v France (37971/97), 16 April 2002, (2004) 39 EHRR 17, 41), these being activities which may be covered by a merger notification (see, by analogy, in respect of public procurement procedures ...[100]

The Court of Justice of the European Union, although holding that a merger notification may come within activities of a professional or business nature and within the scope of Article 8 ECHR, nevertheless, rejected the

---

98. Paragraphs 24, 29.
99. *Agrofert Holding A.S. v. European Commission* [2011] 4 CMLR 6. Herein, Agrofert sought the annulment of the Commission's decision to refuse it access to unpublished documents concerning the notification procedure of a merger which the Commission had authorized. The Commission in response invoked Article 8 of the ECHR as a fundamental right with regard to the respect for the privacy of its undertakings.
100. Paragraphs 75-76.

Commission's plea of Article 8 with respect to the privacy of its undertakings.[101] It is nevertheless submitted that the Court of Justice of the European Union in espousing the notion of private life acknowledged that a corporation, just like an individual, may have a private life protected under Article 8.

More recently, this principle of Article 8 ECHR including the protection of corporations, has been reinforced by the ruling in *Conseil National de l'Ordre des Pharmaciens (CNOP) v. European Commission*[102] where the Court of Justice of the European Union declared:

> under the case law, the protection of private life provided for in art. 8 of the ECHR must be respected and the protection of the home is extended to the premises of commercial companies.[103]

In *Schenker North AB v. EFTA Surveillance Authority*,[104] the court similarly stated:

> It must also be recalled that, in certain circumstances, art. 8 ECHR protects the right to respect for a company's business premises, and that seizure of documents under an administrative investigative procedure may constitute an interference with a company's rights pursuant to art. 8 ECHR (compare the European Court of Human Rights Societe Colas Est v France (37971/97) (2004) 39 E.H.R.R. 17, April 16, 2002, §§ 41 and 42).[105]

Additionally, the European Commission[106] has recognized that:

> Several judgments of the European Court of Human Rights have interpreted that the notion of 'private life' cannot be taken to mean that the professional or commercial activities of either natural or legal persons are excluded.[107]

It is submitted that the above cases demonstrate the jurisprudence of the European Court of Human Rights, as well as the Court of Justice of the European Union, has evolved to include the activities of the corporation

---

101. The plea was rejected on the grounds that Article 8 would not be employed to release the Commission from carrying out a concrete and effective examination, which had not been sufficiently carried out in the present case.
102. *Conseil National de l'Ordre des Pharmaciens (CNOP) v. European Commission* [2013] 4 CMLR 27.
103. Paragraph 40.
104. *Schenker North AB v. EFTA Surveillance Authority* [2013] 4 CMLR 17.
105. Paragraph 166.
106. European Commission's Impact assessment on the Proposal for a Directive of the European Parliament and of the Council on the protection of undisclosed know-how and business information (trade secrets) against their unlawful acquisition, use and disclosure. 28/11/2013 @ http://eur-lex.europa.eu/LexUriServ/LexUriServ.do?uri=SWD:2013:0471:FIN:EN:PDF Accessed on 26/5/2019.
107. At 248.

within the scope of Article 8 ECHR; and these, it is suggested, serve as important and decisive indicators of the approach to be taken in the protection of privacy for corporations in English law. It is nevertheless acknowledged that in view of the United Kingdom's proposed exit from the European Union if the United Kingdom is no longer a Member of the Union, the judgments of the Court of Justice of the European Union would no longer be binding on it. They would, however, still have persuasive value and possibly serve as a template of the development of the privacy jurisprudence of countries in Europe.

Furthermore, although the decisions of the European Court of Human Rights are not binding on English Courts, section 2(1) HRA requires courts to 'take into account' the relevant Strasbourg jurisprudence. Equally, section 6 HRA instructs that 'it is unlawful for a public authority to act in a manner which is incompatible with a Convention right'. In *R (on the application of Alconbury Developments Ltd) v. Secretary of State for the Environment, Transport and the Regions*,[108] Lord Slynn indicated that:

> In the absence of some special circumstances it seems to me that the court should follow any clear and constant jurisprudence of the European Court of Human Rights. If it does not do so there is at least a possibility that the case will go to that court, which is likely in the ordinary case to follow its own constant jurisprudence.[109]

Thus, it is argued that Strasbourg jurisprudence provides a legal imperative for the future development of a right of privacy for corporations in English law. This would satisfy the provision of Article 13 ECHR which provides that there should be an effective remedy at domestic law for the violation of the rights and freedoms set forth in the ECHR; it would also accord with the provision of section 6 HRA.

24.5   THE AUSTRALIAN EXPERIENCE

English courts are not bound by the jurisprudence from other common law jurisdictions; however, they have, on occasion found it a useful source of comparison and of some persuasive value. Thus, this section briefly investigates whether English courts may be persuaded by the position taken in Australia where the High Court in *Australia Broadcasting Corporation v. Lenah Game Meat Property Ltd* (ABC)[110] has indicated that if a tort of

---

108. *R (on the application of Alconbury Developments Ltd) v. Secretary of State for the Environment, Transport and the Regions* [2003] 2 AC 295.
109. Paragraph 26.
110. *Australia Broadcasting Corporation v. Lenah Game Meat Property Ltd* [2001] HCA 63. For excellent analysis of this decision *see* Heath, W.M. Possum Processing, Picture Pilfering, Publication and Privacy: *Australian Broadcasting Corporation v. Lenah Game*

invasion of privacy were to be recognized, it would be unlikely to apply to corporations.

In this case, an application for an interlocutory injunction was brought by *Lenah* against the *ABC*, to restrain the broadcasting of a film of its operations at a brush tail possum processing facility, which was made surreptitiously.

The interlocutory application was denied by Underwood J. in the Supreme Court of Tasmania. On appeal to the Supreme Court of Victoria, however, the injunction was allowed.[111] *ABC* subsequently brought the matter before the High Court of Australia in order to have the injunction lifted. The appeal was allowed.[112]

In response to the respondent's argument that Australian law recognizes the tort of invasion of privacy and that it was available to be relied upon by corporations, the High Court declined to so hold. Gleeson CJ acknowledged that activities such as directors meeting were activities which were private in nature. Similarly, Gleeson CJ accepted that certain internal communications of a corporation might be considered private. However, he drew a pertinent distinction between Australian law and United Kingdom law, in that the latter has the Broadcasting Act 1996. Thus:

> United Kingdom legislation recognises the possibility [of privacy for corporations]. Some forms of corporate activity are private. For example, neither members of the public, nor even shareholders, are ordinarily entitled to attend directors' meetings. And, as at present advised, I see no reason why some internal corporate communications are any less private than those of a partnership or an individual.[113]

Gleeson CJ added:

> However, the foundation of much of what is protected, where rights of privacy, as distinct from rights of property, are acknowledged, is human dignity. This may be incongruous when applied to a corporation.[114]

It is submitted that Gleeson CJ's statements acknowledge that a corporation may have a privacy interest against intrusion (e.g., into directors meetings) and against the misuse of private information (e.g., unauthorized use of the internal correspondence of a corporation). In relation to Gleeson

---

Meats Pty Ltd. Monash University Law Review. 2002: 28, 162; Stewart, D. Protecting Privacy, Property, and Possums: *Australian Broadcasting Corporation v. Lenah Game Meats Pty Ltd. Federal Law Review.* 2002: 30, 177; Taylor, G. and Wright, D. *Australian Broadcasting Corporation v. Lenah Game Meats. Melbourne University Law Review.* 2002: 26, 707; Trindade, F. Possums, Privacy and the Implied Freedom of Communication. *Torts Law Journal.* 2002: 10, 119.

111. Slicer J. dissenting.
112. Callinan J. dissenting.
113. Paragraph 43.
114. Paragraph 43.

CJ's statement that human dignity is the foundation of what is protected in privacy, it is argued that the dignity rationale is only one of the justifications for the protection of privacy. Another rationale is autonomy and, as will be discussed in section 24.6, corporations fall within this justification.

In their joint judgment, Gummow and Hayne JJ observed that commercial enterprises may sustain economic harm through methods of competition which are said to be unfair, or by reason of other injurious acts or omissions of third parties.[115] They held that in the present case, the interest involved was the profitable conduct of *Lenah's* business and that this provided an important distinction between the interest the corporation may have, and that of the individual; in which the individual may be subjected to unwanted intrusion into his personal life and seeks to protect seclusion from surveillance and to prevent communications therefrom. Gummow and Hayne JJ, therefore, declared that privacy was not a right that could be enjoyed by corporations.[116]

Callinan J, however, noted that a right of privacy for the corporation has been held to exist, in part, as a result of the above *R v. Broadcasting Standards Commission ex parte BBC* case,[117] and accepted the possibility that in certain cases, a corporation may enjoy privacy, thus:

> For my own part, I would not rule out the possibility that in some circumstances, despite its existence as a non-natural statutory creature, a corporation might be able to enjoy the same or similar rights to privacy as a natural person, not inconsistent with its accountability, and obligations of disclosure, reporting and otherwise. Nor would I rule out the possibility that a government or a governmental agency may enjoy a similar right to privacy over and above a right to confidentiality in respect of matters relating to foreign relations, national security or the ordinary business of government.[118]

Commentators have been critical of the High Court's decision that a corporation cannot enjoy a right to privacy. Taylor and Wright,[119] in particular, have argued that privacy is not necessarily a personal right of which only natural persons can take advantage; and that broadly speaking, it ought to be recognized that it is contradictory for a legal system to create fictitious persons and conversely use their very fictitiousness as a reason for denying them legal rights. According to Taylor and Wright,[120] corporations do not deserve to be side-lined from important rights such as privacy,

---

115. Paragraph 80.
116. Paragraph 84.
117. *R v. Broadcasting Standards Commission ex parte BBC* [2001] QB 885. Callinan J. at para. 326.
118. Paragraph 328.
119. Taylor, G. and Wright, D. *Australian Broadcasting Corporation v. Lenah Game Meats. Melbourne University Law Review.* 2002: 26, 707.
120. *Ibid.*

although they acknowledge that this does not mean the privacy protection of corporations should be as extensive as that for individuals. Additionally, Taylor and Wright[121] have indicated that corporations come in all shapes and sizes and are set up for different purposes. As such, it would be too simplistic and untenable to assume that their interests are always commercial. Indeed, as noted by Taylor and Wright,[122] not all corporations exist for profit making – some exist primarily to serve the public – and thus, a denial of privacy to corporations on the ground that is often stated – that they exist for economic reasons – is unacceptable. Instances of organizations not setup solely or primarily for economic purposes may include some non-governmental organizations and charities, universities, government-owned medical institutions, associations for promoting the ideals of the United Nations, associations for the advancement of international understanding, Amnesty International and other worthy bodies, such as churches, sundry voluntary associations, pressure groups, and private scholarship bodies.

More recently, however, the Australian Law Reform Commission in its report[123] has recommended that a proposed new tort for privacy should only be actionable by 'natural persons'.[124] It made this recommendation on the basis of one of the rationales of privacy – the dignitary rationale. To this end, it noted that 'an action in privacy is designed to remedy a personal dignitary interest, and as such it would be incongruous to assign the dignitary interest to a corporation'.[125] It, however, did not consider the other key rationale of privacy – the preservation of autonomy; which is a privacy rationale that arguably also applies to the corporation.[126]

It is argued that *ABC* does not have persuasive precedential value on English courts, in view of the very different legal framework that exists in England as compared to Australia. More specifically, absent from the Australian legal landscape is the equivalent of the ECHR and its jurisprudence, as well as the HRA, which has created a broader role for privacy in the legal system generally.[127] Similarly absent is the statutory protection provided by the Broadcasting Act 1996, as applied in the *R v. Broadcasting Standards Commission ex parte BBC*.[128]

---

121. *Ibid.*
122. *Ibid.*
123. *Australian Law Reform Commission Report on Serious Invasions of Privacy in the Digital Era*, 2014 @ http://www.alrc.gov.au/publications/serious-invasions-privacy-digital-era-alrc-report-124 Accessed on 2/6/2019.
124. Paragraph 10.41.
125. Paragraph 10.42.
126. The autonomy rational is discussed in section 24.6 below.
127. *Ibid.*
128. *R v. Broadcasting Standards Commission ex parte BBC* [2001] QB 885.

24.6   ARGUMENTS FOR THE FURTHER
DEVELOPMENT OF A RIGHT OF PRIVACY FOR
CORPORATIONS

Thus far, it has been argued that a right of privacy for corporations is not recognized under the English law of confidence; however, that the jurisprudence of the European Court of Human Rights, strengthened by its application by the Court of Justice of the European Union, provides significant legal impetus for the development of such a right. In arguing in favour of a right of privacy for corporations, this section will discuss the reasons why a right of privacy for corporations is important and concludes that the preservation of the autonomy is the key rationale.

Generally, the two main rationales for privacy protection are the preservation of autonomy and/or dignity.[129] These rationales may be pleaded independently or in conjunction with one another.[130] The autonomy rationale involves the ability to control one's information – the ability to decide whether and when to disclose information about oneself – as well as the ability to decide whether and when to allow access into one's space or property. Similarly, the desire to control one's private information or to allow access into one's space or property may also, in the alternative, be brought about by one's desire to maintain his dignity.

It is argued that the rationale supporting a right to privacy for corporations is the preservation of corporate autonomy. In this regard, subject to the measures set out in Article 8(2) and Article 10(2) ECHR, the corporation ought to have the autonomy to protect itself against unwarranted intrusion, as well as the autonomy to protect its private information from unwarranted interference.

---

129. For a discussion of the rationales of privacy *see* generally, Beardsley, E.L. Privacy: Autonomy and Selective Disclosure in Pennock, J. and Chapman, J. (eds) *Privacy Nomos XIII.* New York: Atherton Press, 1971; Rachel, J. Why Privacy is Important. *Philosophy and Public Affairs.* 1975:4, 324-333; Freund, P. One Concept or Many in Pennock and Chapman, *ibid.*; Negley, G. Philosophical Views on the Value of Privacy. *Law and Contemporary Problems.* 1966: 31, 319-325; Weinstein, M.A The Uses of Privacy in the Good Life in Pennock and Chapman, *ibid.*; Wong, S. The Concept, Value and Right of Privacy. *UCL Jurisprudence Review.* 1996: 3, 165-182; Westin, A. *Privacy and Freedom.* New York: Association of the Bar, 1967; Fried, C. Privacy. *Yale Law Journal.* 1968: 77(3), 475-493; Bloustein, E.J. Privacy as an Aspect of Human Dignity: An Answer to Dean Prosser. *New York University Law Review.* 1964: 39, 962-1007; Benn, S. I. Privacy, Freedom and Respect for Persons in Pennock and Chapman, *ibid.*; Neill, B. A Challenge for the Next Century in Markensins, B.A. (ed.) *Protecting Privacy.* Oxford: Oxford University Press, 1999; Fenwick, H. and Phillipson, G. *Media Freedom under the Human Rights Act.* Oxford: Oxford University Press, 2006.

130. Bloustein, *ibid.*, defined the rationale of privacy solely on the basis of the preservation of dignity.

As Westin[131] explains, autonomy enables corporations the space required to carry out their work away from the public view:

> Just as with individuals, and subject to the same process of social limitations, organizations [including corporations] need the right to decide when and to what extent their acts and decisions should be made public.[132]

As argued by Westin[133] the claim to privacy by organizations, including corporations, is much more than just the protection of the collective privacy rights of their members as individuals. Just as in the case of the individual, corporations also have the same basic need to be free from constant and immediate public exposure. As such, corporations also have a legitimate claim to resist unwanted intrusions into their privacy. A lack of privacy can threaten the autonomous and independent life of a corporation.[134]

As concluded by Westin:

> The foregoing discussion of organizational behavior suggests that privacy is a necessary element for the protection of organizational autonomy, gathering of information and advice, preparation of positions, internal decision making, inter-organizational negotiations, and timing of disclosure. Privacy is thus not a luxury for organizational life; it is a vital lubricant of the organizational system in free societies.[135]

Thus, it is submitted that a corporation can exercise autonomy in relation to its property against unwarranted intrusion, and equally, in the protection of its private information or communications from dissemination or publication; and the corporation's ability to exercise autonomy in its private sphere suggests that the autonomy rationale of privacy also applies to corporations. The autonomy of corporations in this regard is fundamental to their effective functioning in a democratic society.

The fact that only the autonomy rationale – and not also the dignity rationale – applies to corporations is not an objection since it is not unusual for a cause of action to have various rationales and for these to be selectively applicable. This is illustrated by the tort of defamation, which protects natural as well as non-natural persons, such as corporations, where injury has been suffered as a result of a false attack on reputation, character or good name.[136]

---

131. Westin, A. *Privacy and Freedom*. New York: Association of the Bar, 1967.
132. At 42. The term organization was defined by Westin as including corporations.
133. Westin, *ibid.*, 42.
134. Westin, *ibid.*
135. Page 51.
136. *See* generally, Post, R. The Social Foundations of Defamation Law: Reputation and the Constitution. *California Law Review*. 1986: 74, 691-742.

The three main rationales underpinning the protection of reputation by defamation law are identified as the dignity, honour, and property rationales.[137] It is suggested that where a corporation seeks a remedy through defamation, the dignity and honour rationales do not apply to it because the feelings associated with the said rationales, such as feelings of pain, hurt, distress, loss of honour and pre-eminence, are feelings which can only be felt by the individual. Rather, the appropriate rationale would be the property rationale on the basis that the corporation's good name and reputation are deemed the corporation's property.[138] It thus follows that the different rationales of defamation law support the different claims to defamation depending on the persons involved: the individual may claim an interest in the dignitary, honour or property rationale, whilst the corporation may only claim to have an interest in the property rationale. The fact that only one rationale applies does not preclude the corporation from its claim under defamation.

Likewise, in the case of privacy, it is argued that the rationales of dignity and autonomy are also engaged depending on the nature of the claimant; such that the dignity rationale of privacy may be claimed by the individual alone, for reasons noted above, while the autonomy rationale serves the corporation as well as the individual. The fact that corporations may only rely on the autonomy rationale ought not to hinder their ability to claim privacy protection under English law.

In further making the argument for the development of a right of privacy for corporations, it is acknowledged that a great many cases of privacy infringement pertain to the individual; nevertheless, there are some cases in which privacy invasions may affect the corporation. For such circumstances, it is important to reiterate that a corporation, although an

---

137. *See* Post, R. The Social Foundations of Defamation Law: Reputation and the Constitution. *California Law Review*. 1986: 74, 691-742; Oster, J. The Criticism of Trading Corporations and their Right to Sue for Defamation. *Journal of European Tort Law*. 2011: 2(3), 255-279, 259. On the dignitary interest, the legal remedy herein seems to involve the treatment of the injury to reputation which arguably engages feelings of distress, hurt, and embarrassment – the loss of dignity. *See also* Warren, S.D. and Brandeis, L.D. The Right to Privacy. *Harvard Law Review*. 1890: 4(5), 193-220, 194. *See* generally Descheemaeker, E. Protecting Reputation: Defamation and Negligence. *Oxford Journal of Legal Studies*. 2009, 29(4), 603-641. On the honour interest, legal remedy herein seems to involve the treatment of the injury to reputation, which arguably 'results in loss of the individual's honour and pre-eminence'. *See* Post, *ibid.*, 699, 703. On the property interest, the legal remedy seems to involve the treatment of the injury where a person suffers injury as a result of false attack on the said person's reputation or good name. This false attack on the reputation may be regarded as a property interest – a form of intangible property – on the basis that one's good name and reputation are deemed one's property which has been cultivated over time. Hence to attack or injure it without justification is to unjustly destroy the reputation. Post, *ibid.*, 693-694.

138. This accords with the position in Oster, J. The Criticism of Trading Corporations and their Right to Sue for Defamation. *Journal of European Tort Law*. 2011: 2(3), 255-279. The individual may also rely on this rationale.

artificial entity, is a juristic person established and recognized by law to carry on business, as well as other activities.[139] The concept of a corporation is such that as a result of incorporation, it becomes a *person* – a legal, non-natural person – with legal personality.[140] The consequence is that this legal person – the corporation – as established by law is recognized as having a separate legal existence and status, with a legal name, legal rights, privileges, duties, responsibilities, assets, or liabilities, much in a manner similar to a natural person.[141] As a result of incorporation, a corporation is brought to life,[142] has perpetual succession,[143] can sue and be sued in its own name,[144] including to protect its reputation,[145] can own its own property,[146] can enter into contracts,[147] and can die upon its winding up.[148]

Consequently, if a corporation is empowered by law with a distinct legal existence and the capacity to enjoy rights which enable it to come to life with its registration, to have its own name, to enter into contracts in its own name, to sue and be sued in its own name, to own property in its name, and cease to exist when it is wound up; it is reasoned that the corporation also ought to have a right to its privacy to carry on activities within its establishment, which it has been empowered by law to undertake. That is to say, a corporation ought to have a right to privacy, to protect itself from unwarranted intrusion, and also to protect its private information.

Additionally, in proposing the development of a right of privacy for corporations, it is suggested that utilizing the action for breach of confidence or other causes of action as mediums of protection for the privacy issues of the corporation, would place the corporation in a similar position as the individual was before a cause of action for the individual's privacy was established. At that time, the individual's privacy was being 'shoe-horned' into the action for breach of confidence, as well as other causes of action,[149] and this created hardship in privacy cases of the said era.[150] Shoe-horning

---

139. Such as charity activities, with regard to corporations that are charities.
140. *See Salomon v. A Salomon & Co Ltd* [1897] AC 22, a *locus classicus* for the concept of legal personality.
141. In *the case of Salomon v. A Salomon & Co Ltd*, Lord Halsbury declared that ' ... once the company is legally incorporated it must be treated like any other independent person with its rights and liabilities appropriate to itself'. At para. 30.
142. *Salomon v. A Salomon & Co Ltd* [1897] AC 22.
143. *Re Noel Tedman Holdings Property Ltd* [1967] QdR 561.
144. *Foss v. Harbottle* [1843] 2 Hare 461.
145. Section 1(2) UK Defamation Act 2013.
146. *Macaura v. Northern Assurance Co Ltd* [1925] AC 619.
147. *Lee v. Lee's Air Farming Ltd* [1961] AC 12.
148. That is to say, where it becomes insolvent, goes into liquidation, and subsequently ceases to exist.
149. Such as defamation, trespass, malicious falsehood, passing off.
150. *See Kaye v. Robertson* [1991] FSR 62. *See also,* Bingham, T. Should There Be a Law to Protect Rights of Personal Privacy? *European Human Rights Law Review,* 1996: 5, 455-462. Lester, A. English Judges As Law Makers. *Public Law,* 1993: Sum, 269-290.

corporations' privacy matters into the action for breach of confidence, as well as other causes of action, would equally create difficulties. For instance, where a corporation has been the subject of surreptitious surveillance (e.g., through phone 'hacking') this would entail inquiring, rather artificially, about the *confidential quality of information*, and furthermore, whether there is an *obligation of confidence* –rather than organically applying the touchstone question in privacy cases which is to ask *whether in view of the facts there is a reasonable expectation of privacy?* Equally, under the traditional action for breach of confidence, the obligation of confidence is lost where information has entered into the public domain. Conversely, under the extended action, information entering the public domain does not take away its quality of being private information and therefore, does not deny privacy protection. This was aptly illustrated in the case of *PJS v. News Group Newspaper*.[151] Herein, a claimant sought an interim injunction, pending trial, to restrain the defendant from publishing a story about his alleged extra-marital activities, on the basis that it would be a breach of confidence and a violation of his Article 8 ECHR rights, even though the story had been published on-line in the US, Canada, and Scotland. Lord Neuberger[152] (with whom Baroness Hale, Lord Mance and Lord Reed JJSC agreed) noted that if this case had simply been based on confidentiality, the claim for injunction would have had 'substantial difficulties'.[153] He accordingly declared:

> The publication of the story in newspapers in the United States, Canada, and even in Scotland would not, I think, be sufficient of itself to undermine the claim for a permanent injunction on the ground of privacy … However, there comes a point where it is simply unrealistic for a court to stop a story being published in a national newspaper on the ground of confidentiality, and, on the current state of the evidence, I would, I think, accept that, if one was solely concerned with confiden-tiality, that point had indeed been passed in this case.[154]

Lord Neuberger continued:

> However, claims based on respect for privacy and family life do not depend on confidentiality (or secrecy) alone … Tugendhat J … cite[d] with approval a passage written by Dr Moreham in The Law of Privacy and the Media, 2nd ed (2011), (eds Warby, Moreham and Christie), in which she summarised 'the two core components of the rights to

---

Thompson, M.P. More Judicial Support for Privacy. *Conveyancer and Property Lawyer*, 1995: September-October, 404-409. Markensims, B.S. Our Patchy Law of Privacy: Time to Do Something About It. *Modern Law Review*, 1990: 53(6), 802-809. Eady, D. A Statutory Right to Privacy. *European Human Rights Law Review*, 1996: 3, 243-253.

151. *PJS v. News Group Newspapers Ltd* [2016] AC 1081.
152. President of the Supreme Court, as he then was.
153. Paragraph 57.
154. *Ibid.*

privacy' as 'unwanted access to private information and unwanted access to [or intrusion into] one's ... personal space' ... .[155]

Lord Neuberger concluded by noting that there had been several cases where 'intrusion had been relied on by judges in order to justify the grant of an injunction despite a significant loss of confidentiality'.[156]

In view of the foregoing, it is argued that the protection of the corporation's privacy ought not to be shoe-horned into the traditional action for breach of confidence; rather, a right of privacy ought to be developed to provide full privacy protection for the corporation.

In further arguing for the development of a right of privacy for corporations, it is posited that there is a notion the corporation may become too powerful if afforded a right of privacy, on account of the concept of separate legal personality which places a veil of incorporation placed upon the corporation. This notion is defeated on the grounds that before a privacy claim can succeed, it must be subjected to the rigorous process of a balancing act between Article 8 ECHR and Article 10 ECHR in the case of *the corporation v. the press*.[157] Correspondingly, before a privacy claim can succeed in the case of *the corporation v. public authority*, a rigorous process of assessment must equally be undertaken between Article 8(1) and 8(2) ECHR. This is aptly illustrated in the case of *Bernh Larsen Holding AS v. Norway*[158] where a Tax Authority had demanded, corporations provide a copy of an entire computer server of electronic archives, to review for Tax Audit purposes. The corporations complained that this demand and subsequent seizure of the server had violated their Article 8 rights of respect for their home and correspondence, on the grounds that the server primarily contained private information of its employees, and other persons, that were not relevant to tax audit purposes.

The European Court of Human Rights held that there had been no violation of the corporations' Article 8 rights. In arriving at this decision, Court undertook a rigorous assessment between Article 8(1) and 8(2), assessing whether the interference complained of had been in accordance

---

155. Paragraph 58.
156. Paragraph 59. The said cases referred to by Lord Neuberger are: *Blair v. Associated Newspapers Ltd* (unreported) 10 March 2000 (Morland J); *West v. British Broadcasting Corpn* [2002] EWHC 3260 (Ouseley J); *McKennitt v. Ash* [2006] EMLR 10, para. 81 (Eady J); *X v. Persons Unknown* [2007] EMLR 10, para. 64 (Eady J); *JIH v. News Group Newspapers Ltd* [2011] EMLR 9, paras 58-59 (Tugendhat J); *TSE v. News Group Newspapers Ltd* [2011] EWHC 1308 (QB) at [29]-[30] (Tugendhat J); *CTB v. News Group Newspapers Ltd* [2011] EWHC 1326 (QB) at [23] (Eady J); *CTB v. News Group Newspapers Ltd* [2011] EWHC 1334 (QB) at [3] (Tugendhat J); *Rocknroll v. News Group Newspapers Ltd* [2013] EWHC 24 (Ch) at [25] (Briggs J); and *H v. A (Family Proceedings: Reporting Restrictions)* [2016] 1 FCR 338, paras 66-69 (MacDonald J).
157. For veil of incorporation, *see* Mayson, S., French, D., and Ryan, C. *Company Law*. 35th edn. Oxford: Oxford University Press, 2018. Chapter 5.
158. *Bernh Larsen Holding AS v. Norway* [2014] 58 EHRR 8.

with the law,[159] whether it pursued a legitimate aim,[160] and whether it was necessary for a democratic society.[161]

It was in view of the foregoing that the Court arrived at the conclusion that there had been no violation of the corporations' Article 8 ECHR rights, as the interference complained of was in accordance with the law, pursued the legitimate aim of protecting the economic well-being of the country, and was necessary for a democratic society. The Court arrived at this conclusion, although acknowledging the right of the corporation to its 'home' and 'correspondence' under Article 8 ECHR.[162]

As such, just as the individual in English law and the corporation in the law adjudicated by the European Court of Human Rights as well as the Court of Justice of the European Union, the corporation in English law would equally be subjected to the rigorous measures of a balancing act, which must be undertaken for the determination of a privacy violation.[163]

Thus, it is submitted that corporations do have a legitimate claim to privacy, which is worthy of full protection in English law. This right of privacy for corporations is important in a democratic society, for the preservation of the corporation's autonomy.

24.7   DEVELOPMENT OF CORPORATIONS' PRIVACY
           IN ENGLISH LAW: RECOMMENDATIONS

It is argued that a right of privacy for corporations be developed in the same manner as the individual's right was developed, namely, through the extended action for breach of confidence.

The extended action is recommended as the medium for the development of privacy for corporations because other mechanisms such as passing off, battery, trespass, defamation, and malicious falsehood, have their limitations. This is notably illustrated by *Kaye v. Robertson*.[164] In this case, the Court of Appeal held that there was no passing off because the plaintiff was not a trader; on the claim of trespass to person amounting to battery,

---

159. The requirement of 'in accordance to law' is explained in para. 123. *See also* para. 127.
160. *See* para. 135. *See also* para. 136.
161. *See* para. 158. *See also* para. 161.
162. The Court acknowledged that the word 'home' under Article 8 included the registered office, branches, and other business premises of a corporation owned by a legal person. *See* para. 104. *See also* para. 106.
163. *See also* the individual's privacy case of *In re JR38* [2015] UKSC 42, in which the United Kingdom Supreme Court did not allow Article 8 ECHR protection to be utilized to shield or cover up criminal activity.
164. *Kaye v. Robertson* [1991] FSR 62. In this case, a famous actor who was recovering in hospital, having undergone very extensive surgery due to severe head injuries sustained in a car accident, was interviewed by journalists who improperly gained access to his room, and took photographs, with a view to publish the interview. The plaintiff sought to protect his privacy, but in the absence of an independent cause of action for privacy

there was no evidence that damage had in fact been caused by the taking of photographs; on the claim of libel, it was arguable whether libel was the case; and there was no actionable right of privacy in English law. Malicious falsehood was the only ground upon which the Court of Appeal felt able to grant relief. This was on the basis that Mr Kaye had a commercial interest in the interview following his accident and that the newspaper would misleadingly damage this commercial interest if it suggested to the public that Mr Kaye had given the interview voluntarily. The court, however, felt unable to restrain the publication of the interview, and the newspaper went ahead and published the interview. It was in the face of this apparent inadequacy of the law in providing protection for Kaye that the Court of Appeal unanimously called for the recognition of a legal right to privacy.[165] It is argued that these common law mechanisms would similarly fail adequately to protect the privacy of corporations.

Existing statutory law mechanisms would also not provide full protection for the privacy of corporations as they advance protection on a specific aspect of privacy, such as, for instance, the Broadcasting Act 1996, which, although it provides privacy protection for both individuals and corporations, is restricted to broadcasting. Additionally, the Data Protection Act 1998, which provides protection of individuals' personal data, if sought to be developed, would not provide adequate protection for the privacy of corporations because it does not protect against intrusions. It is also doubtful that the Protection from Harassment Act 1997 can be developed to provide for the privacy of corporations. In *Majrowski v. Guy's and St Thomas's NHS Trust*,[166] the House of Lords declared that a corporation may be a perpetrator of harassment, but cannot be a victim; that 'a victim must be an individual'.[167] Moreover, even after these specific statutory protections had been established, the common law nevertheless had to be developed, using the extended action for breach of confidence, to provide more general protection for the individual's privacy.

It is submitted that protection of corporate privacy be developed in the same manner, using an extended breach of confidence. Following this approach, the right of privacy for corporations should be defined in two limbs. First, as the state in which the corporation is free from unwanted interference or disturbance – intrusion – into its premises or property; and secondly, as a claim to the control of the corporation's private information from being released into the public domain against the corporation's wishes,

---

at the time the plaintiff sought an injunction against the publication through malicious falsehood, libel, trespass to person, and passing off, on the grounds that he had not consented to the interview.
165. *See* paras 66, 70-71.
166. *Majrowski v. Guy's and St Thomas's NHS Trust* [2007] 1 AC 224.
167. Paragraph 19.

thus protecting the said information from unwanted publication or dissemination. As in the case of the individual, a corporation's right to privacy would
be protected under the extended action for breach of confidence and the new
methodology that this entails. In particular, the threshold test of a reasonable
expectation of privacy would equally apply to corporations. Assuming there
is a reasonable expectation of privacy and Article 8 ECHR is engaged, this
would bring on the balancing exercise between Article 8 ECHR and Article
10 ECHR. However, because corporate privacy is justified only by the
autonomy rationale, (and not also the rationale of dignity), the weight of
Article 8 is likely to be affected. It is also likely to be influenced by the type
of corporation involved.

Finally, the fact that the claimant is a corporation is likely to affect
whether harm needs to be proved and the way in which damages are
calculated. In this latter respect, a similar principle to that which guides
corporate defamation under section 1(2) Defamation Act 2013 could be
applied in the case of corporate privacy. This section provides a different
requirement of harm for profit trading persons from individuals:[168]

> For the purposes of this section, harm to the reputation of a body that
> trades for profit is not 'serious harm' unless it has caused or is likely to
> cause the body serious financial loss.

From section 1(2), it is clear that profit trading persons would have to
prove special damages. It is suggested that a similar principle could also be
applicable to the corporations in privacy cases. Accordingly, in the case of
corporations trading for profit, in a claim for a right to privacy, it would have
to prove special damages. These damages would be awarded to compensate
the corporation for the harm done to its autonomy.

24.8   CONCLUSION

In conclusion, it is argued that a right of privacy for corporations in the
English law of confidence ought to be developed. The proposition of the
development of a right of privacy for corporations in English law is
strengthened by virtue of the Broadcasting Act, which has since its inception
in its 1980 Act, to the present Act of 1996, envisioned the possibility of
infringements of privacy of the incorporated person;[169] and as such, has

---

168. Section 1(1) of the Defamation Act 2013 provides a general rule for non-profit persons
to the end that 'A statement is not defamatory unless its publication has caused or is
likely to cause serious harm to the reputation of the claimant'.
169. *See* sections 18(1)(b) & 19(2) Broadcasting Act 1980; Sections 54(1)(b) & 55(2)
Broadcasting Act 1981; Sections 143(1)(b) & 144(2) Broadcasting Act 1990; Sections
110(1)(b),&111(1) Broadcasting Act 1996.

consistently provided protection for the privacy of corporations, in broadcasting matters.[170] In addition, such a development of a right of privacy for corporations would accord with sections 2 and 6 HRA. At the European level, it is also supported by the evolution of the Strasbourg court's jurisprudence, and the jurisprudence of the Court of Justice of the European Union. Finally, it would also provide corporations with the autonomy they require to effectively carry on their activities within the law and without unwarranted interference.

---

170. Indeed, it was clearly the intention of Parliament to provide privacy protection for incorporated persons in their own right, in matters specific to broadcasting. This intention of Parliament is demonstrated in the HANSARD HL debate on the Broadcasting Bill 1980 in which the House of Lords heavily debated the bill before it was passed to law, including the relevant sections on the protection of the privacy of incorporated persons.

    See, HANSARD [HL Debate] 15th October, 1980, at 1303-4, 1310, 1312-13, and 1319.

Chapter 25

Intellectual Property, Human Rights and Climate Change

Abbe E.L. Brown[*]

25.1   INTRODUCTION

The complex relationship between intellectual property (IP) and human rights is well explored throughout this established and respected collection. A key theme is the extent to which a human rights approach to IP law – both internally and externally[1] – may deliver change. Such change could enhance the positive contribution of IP to encouraging innovation and creativity and to addressing societal challenges,[2] while also limiting the less positive

---

[*] This contribution builds on previous relevant exploration by the author in A.E.L. Brown, 'Intellectual Property and Climate Change' in *The Oxford Handbook of Intellectual Property Law* ed., R.C. Dreyfuss and J. Pila (Oxford: Oxford University Press, 2018) 958 and A.E.L. Brown, *Intellectual Property, Climate Change and Technology. Managing National Legal Intersections, Relationships and Conflicts* (Cheltenham: Edward Elgar, 2019) in particular Chapters 1 and 6.

1. R.L. Okediji, 'Does Intellectual Property Need Human Rights' *International Review and Politics* 51(1) (2018) 8-9, 25 and calling to look beyond an exceptions based approach to a more collective approach to IP arguing (6-7) that there are no structural pathways to use human rights to respond to IP's challenges.

2. F.M. Scherer, 'The Innovation Lottery' in *Expanding the Boundaries of Intellectual Property. Innovation Policy for the Knowledge Society* eds., R.C. Dreyfuss, D.L. Zimmerman and H. First (Oxford: Oxford University Press, 2001); K.E. Maskus, 'The Economics of Global Intellectual Property and Economic Development: A Survey' in *Intellectual Property and Information Wealth* ed., P. Yu (Westport: Praeger, 2006); R.M.

consequences of restricting the short-term innovation and creativity of others.[3] In arguing for a new approach to this balance, attention has been paid to access to medicines[4] and to food security.[5] In these spaces, there may be only one relevant medicine or type of seed to address particular circumstances, and solving the problem is almost invariably accepted as necessary – the challenge is how to do so without losing the benefits of IP and also while meeting the obligations of the present international legal framework (the Agreement on Trade-Related Aspects of Intellectual Property Rights (TRIPS) which is part of the WTO Agreement).[6] Climate change – a key societal challenge – has long fascinated this author because it appeared to raise a different issue. Enabling greater use of a particular wind farm technology may contribute to the reduction of greenhouse gas emissions, which can make an important contribution to responding to climate change. Yet in contrast to the medicine and seed example, there are other ways of reducing emissions, say through using less heating or travelling by public transport.[7] This could argue against the need to intervene in the powers of IP owners, given the possible negative consequences of such an intervention on encouraging innovation.

Yet writing in early 2020, evidence grows of the impact of climate change,[8] there are calls and protests (particularly from the young) for new

Sherwood, *Intellectual Property and Economic Development* (Special Studies in Science, Technology, and Public Policy (Colorado: Westview Press Inc, 1990).

3. C. Greenhalgh and M. Rogers, *Innovation, Intellectual Property and Economic Growth* (Princeton: Princeton University Press, 2010); W.R. Cornish, *Intellectual Property. Omnipresent, Distracting, Irrelevant* (Oxford: Oxford University Press, 2004); D. Vaver, 'Intellectual Property: Still a Bargain?' *European Intellectual Property Review* 2012, 34(9), 579.

4. H. Hestermeyer, *Human Rights and the WTO. The Case of Patents and Access to Medicines* (New York: Oxford University Press, 2007) Chapters 1 and 4; F. Abbott, 'Managing the Hydra: The Herculean Task of Ensuring Access to Essential Medicines' 393 and H. Klug, 'Comment Access to Essential Medicines – Promoting Human Rights over Free Trade and Intellectual Property Claims' 481 in *International Public Goods and Transfer of Technology under a Globalized Intellectual Property Regime* ed., K.E. Maskus and J.H. Reichman. (Cambridge: Cambridge University Press, 2005); Commission on Intellectual Property Rights, 'Integrating Intellectual Property Rights and Development Policy' (2002) http://www.iprcommission.org/, Chapter 2.

5. Commission on Intellectual Property Rights Integrating Intellectual Property Rights and Development Policy (2002) http://www.iprcommission.org/, Chapter 3; C. Chiarolla, *Intellectual Property. Agriculture and Global Food Security* (Cheltenham: Edward Elgar, 2011); M. Lightbourne, *Food Security. Biological Diversity and Intellectual Property Rights* (Abingdon: Routledge, 2016).

6. Annex IC of Marrakesh Agreement Establishing the World Trade Organization (1994).

7. *See*, e.g., Center for Climate and Energy Solutions, 'Reducing Your Transportation Footprint' https://www.c2es.org/content/reducing-your-transportation-footprint/ last accessed 29 October 2019.

8. Intergovernmental Panel on Climate Change, 'Fifth Assessment Report' (2014) https://www.ipcc.ch/assessment-report/ar5/ and Start of IPCC meeting to consider ocean and

attitudes to it[9] and there is a growth of climate change litigation on a variety of bases, including some with no link with technology or human rights in their legal base.[10] There are fairly longstanding arguments of the need for transformative leadership[11] and that the world is in a position of crisis.[12] There are calls in treaties and scholarship for distributive and climate justice and intergenerational equity-based approaches with greater responsibility to be taken by developed countries.[13] This is alongside calls for developing economies to embrace low carbon solutions rather than repeat the high carbon pathways taken by developed states to build their economies in the

---

cryosphere report (2019) https://www.ipcc.ch/2019/09/20/p51-srocc-opening/ last accessed 29 October 2019; *see also* 'Lancet Commission on Pollution and Health' (2017) https://www.thelancet.com/commissions/pollution-and-health last accessed 29 October 2019 and discussion in K. Cook, 'A Mutually Informed Approach: The Right to Life in an Era of Pollution and Climate Change' *European Human Rights Law Review* 3 (2019) 274.

9. *See*, e.g., Greenpeace, 'Join the School Strike for Climate' https://www.greenpeace.org/international/act/global-climate-school-strike/; A. Vaughan, 'David Attenborough on Climate Change "We Cannot Be Radical Enough"' (New Scientist 9 July 2019) https://www.newscientist.com/article/2209126-david-attenborough-on-climate-change-we-cannot-be-radical-enough/ and David Attenborough documentary, 'Climate Change – the Facts' (May 2019) https://www.bbc.co.uk/programmes/m00049b1 https://www.bbc.co.uk/news/entertainment-arts-47988337 all last accessed 29 October 2019.

10. *See* discussion in J. Lin, 'Climate Change and the Courts' *Legal Studies* 32(1) (2012) 35; H. Osofsky and J. Peel, *Climate Change Litigation: Regulatory Pathways to Cleaner Energy* (Cambridge: Cambridge University Press, 2015); note also *People of the State of New York v. Exxon Mobil Corporation* (2018) https://ag.ny.gov/sites/default/files/summons_and_complaint_0.pdf last accessed 29 October 2019; K. Cook, 'A Mutually Informed Approach: The Right to Life in an Era of Pollution and Climate Change' *European Human Rights Law Review* 3 (2019) 274 which also makes references to some cases raised against Russia and Pakistan regarding warning systems and the inadequacy of steps of the state in the light of national legislation which led to the appointment of a climate change commission – *see Budayeva v. Russia* (application nos 15339/02, 21166/02, 20058/02, 11673/02 and 15343/02) and *Asghar Leghari v. Federation of Pakistan* W.P. N. 25501/2015 and *see* http://climatecasechart.com/non-us-case/ashgar-leghari-v-federation-of-pakistan/ last accessed 30 October 2019.

11. Declaration on Climate Justice (2013) led by the Mary Robinson Foundation https://www.mrfcj.org/wp-content/uploads/2015/09/Declaration-on-Climate-Justice.pdf last accessed 29 October 2019.

12. *See*, e.g., N. Klein, *This Changes Everything* (London: Penguin, 2014). *See also* Center for International Environmental Law, 'Announcing the First Ever Global Summit on Human Rights and Climate Change' https://www.ciel.org/news/announcing-the-first-ever-global-summit-on-human-rights-and-climate-change/ and S. Duyck, 'Time to Act for Climate Justice' https://www.socialeurope.eu/time-to-act-for-climate-justice leading to the Peoples' Summit on Climate, Rights and Human Survival September 2019 and to a Declaration, all last accessed 29 October 2019.

13. Article 3.1 UNFCCC and Articles 2(2), 4(3), 4(19) Paris Agreement; W. Zhuang, *Intellectual Property Rights and Climate Change: Interpreting the TRIPS Agreement for Environmentally Sound Technologies* (Cambridge: Cambridge University Press, 2017) 79-82.

past.[14] In 2019, the First Minister of Scotland declared a Climate Emergency[15] and new legislation was proposed in New Zealand[16] calling for net zero emissions. And also in 2019 teenage activist Greta Thunberg said at the United Nations (UN) '[e]ntire ecosystems are collapsing. We are in the beginning of a mass extinction and all you can talk about is money and fairy tales of economic growth. How dare you'.[17]

Thunberg continued '[h]ow dare you pretend that this can be solved with just "business as usual" and some technical solutions'.[18] Technology was also referred to in a 2017 court decision in New Zealand, in the context of a challenge to the government's approaches to targets. One argument made was that the government's approach was irrational as there was too much reliance on star trek technology which may never exist.[19] The court considered that the evidence put before it showed a range of available technologies, and that although the plan did refer to future research, there was nothing to suggest that this was 'star trek'[20] technology. So technology has a role in climate change action, even if it will not provide a complete solution.[21]

---

14. *See* e.g., D. Shabalala, 'Technology Transfer for Climate Change and Developing Country Viewpoints on Historical Responsibility and Common but Differentiated Responsibilities' in *Research Handbook on Intellectual Property and Climate Change* ed., J.D Sarnoff (Cheltenham: Edward Elgar, 2016) 172-199; H.A. Forrest and P. Lawrence, 'Intergenerational Justice: A Framework for Addressing Intellectual Property Rights and Climate Change' in *Intellectual Property and Clean Energy: The Paris Agreement and Climate Justice* ed., M. Rimmer (New York: Springer 2018).

15. *See* speech of Nicola Sturgeon SNP Party Conference, Edinburgh (April 2019) https://www.thenational.scot/news/17603494.read-nicola-sturgeons-full-speech-from-the-snp-spring-conference/ last accessed 29 October 2019. Note also Climate Change (Emissions Reduction Targets) (Scotland) Bill 2019 referring to a 75% reduction in emissions by 2030 with net zero emission by 2045.

16. Climate Change Response (Zero Carbon) Amendment Bill https://www.mfe.govt.nz/climate-change/zero-carbon-amendment-bill with target of zero emissions by 2050 and compare Manatu Mo Te Taiao, 'About New Zealand's Emission Reduction Targets' https://www.mfe.govt.nz/climate-change/climate-change-and-government/emissions-reduction-targets/about-our-emissions both last accessed 29 October 2019.

17. UN Climate Action Summit 23 September 2019, *see* via https://www.bloomberg.com/news/articles/2019-09-23/teen-activist-greta-thunberg-to-world-leaders-how-dare-you last accessed 29 October 2019.

18. UN Climate Action Summit 23 September 2019 *see* via https://www.bloomberg.com/news/articles/2019-09-23/teen-activist-greta-thunberg-to-world-leaders-how-dare-you last accessed 29 October 2019.

19. *Sarah Thomson v. The Minister for Climate Change Issues* CIV 2015-485-919 [2017] NZHC 733 in particular [84], [88], [91], [94], [96]–[97], [179] [162(c)] (*Thomson*).

20. *Thomson* [167].

21. *See also* International Council on Human Rights Policy, 'Beyond Technology Transfer: Protecting Human Rights in a Climate-Constrained World' (2011) 79-86, 108-216 exploring technologies which can be relevant to different parts of the response to climate change.

In this context it is timely to reflect further, and with new vigour, on the extent to which new approaches should be taken to IP to maximise the contribution which technology can make to preserving the future of the planet. It is also valuable to explore the contribution which can be made to this by human rights. This chapter will set out some instances in which IP can be relevant to responses to climate change, explore human rights which are relevant to climate change and will note the increasing engagement of the fields. The chapter will suggest that there is much still to be done. Proposals are crafted with a base in Wild Law and the rights of nature to empower and bring about a new approach.

25.2   IP AND CLIMATE CHANGE

25.2.1   LEGAL LANDSCAPE

IP rights confer on their owner the power to control the activity of others in respect of the underlying innovation and creativity.[22] All states which are members of the WTO are required to have IP rights[23] and to provide court processes by which they can be enforced.[24] Most WTO Member States[25] do also have obligations in respect of climate change, notably pursuant to the Paris Agreement[26] under the United Nations Framework Convention on Climate Change (UNFCCC).[27] This provides that states are to hold 'the increase in emissions to well below 2 degrees above pre-industrial levels and to attempt to limit the increase to 1.5 degrees above pre-industrial levels'.[28] The importance of technology and its transfer is recognised, with the Paris Agreement referring to the ongoing role of the Technology Mechanism which had been established under the UNFCCC.[29] The Paris meeting also

---

22. *See*, using the UK as an example sections 25, 60 Patents Act 1977; sections 7, 7A, 8 Registered Designs Act 1949; sections 12-15, 16-26, 28-50C, 50D, 51, 216, 226-227 Copyright Designs and Patents Act 1988.
23. Articles 9, 25, 27 TRIPS.
24. Part III TRIPS.
25. WTO members and observers https://www.wto.org/english/thewto_e/whatis_e/tif_e/org6_e.htm last accessed 29 October 2019.
26. UNFCCC Paris Agreement Annex to Decision FCCC/CP/2015/L/9/Rev.1 https://unfccc.int/resource/docs/2015/cop21/eng/l09r01.pdf https://unfccc.int/files/meetings/paris_nov_2015/application/pdf/paris_agreement_english_.pdf and status of Ratification https://unfccc.int/process/the-paris-agreement/status-of-ratification both last accessed 29 October 2019.
27. UNTS vol. 1771 p. 107.
28. Article 2(1)(a) Paris Agreement.
29. Article 4.5 UNFCCC, Article 10 Paris Agreement.

saw the launch of Mission Innovation, crossing private and public actors, to accelerate green energy innovation and to make it more affordable.[30]

These instruments and indeed activities do not, however, engage directly with the fact that technologies may be the subject of IP rights in relevant countries, and that these rights would likely be owned by private entities (upon whom no responsibilities are directly imposed). This structure of responsibility is reflected at national level. Taking the United Kingdom (UK) as an example, the climate change legislation imposes obligations on states and on some public bodies to, *inter alia*, reduce emissions.[31] These laws do not engage with the prospect of technologies emerging which could make a high contribution to making these reductions, but an UK IP owner refuses to permit them to be used widely.[32]

The lack of engagement between IP and climate change at international level can seem surprising, as there is awareness of technology and IP in instruments relating to environment and climate change. The Montreal Protocol on Substances that Deplete the Ozone Layer of 1987 refers to cooperation regarding best technologies and providing technical assistance.[33] Agenda 21 (an output from the Earth Summit in 1992 which also gave rise to the UNFCCC) calls for consideration of the role of patents and other IP rights regarding access to and transfer of environmentally sound technologies regarding developing countries, and also calls for consideration of fair incentives to innovate.[34]

25.2.2 A PLACE FOR IP

From this starting point, it is useful explore the situations in which IP could be relevant to responses to climate change.[35] Patents can be relevant to development and dissemination of conventional responses such as delivering

---

30. Mission Innovation, 'Overview' http://mission-innovation.net/about-mi/overview/ last accessed 29 October 2019.
31. Sections 1, 4, 8 Climate Change Act 2008 and sections 1, 44-6 Climate Change (Scotland) Act 2009, although *see* proposed amendments introduced above [n. 16] in 2019 Bill.
32. For detailed analysis of this and the development of solutions based in statutory interpretation and legislative process, *see* A.E.L. Brown *Intellectual Property, Climate Change and Technology. Managing National Legal Intersections, Relationships and Conflicts* (Cheltenham: Edward Elgar, 2019) in particular Chapters 2, 4, 5, 6, 7.
33. UNTS vol. 1522 p. 3 Articles 9, 10; W. Zhuang, *Intellectual Property Rights and Climate Change: Interpreting the TRIPS Agreement for Environmentally Sound Technologies* (Cambridge: Cambridge University Press, 2017) 149, 152.
34. Agenda 21 https://sustainabledevelopment.un.org/content/documents/Agenda21.pdf last accessed 20 October 2019, paras 34.10, 34.11.
35. H.A. Forrest and P. Lawrence, 'Intergenerational Justice: A Framework for Addressing Intellectual Property Rights and Climate Change' in *Intellectual Property and Clean Energy: The Paris Agreement and Climate Justice* ed., M. Rimmer (New York: Springer 2018)) noting the different impact of the varying forms of IP rights.

improved renewable energy.[36] Patents could also exist in respect of more radical and controversial solutions such as geoengineering (to develop products or processes which could remove greenhouse gas emissions from the atmosphere)[37] and the development of new forms of crops through genetic engineering.[38] Designs can be relevant to the delivery of renewable energy (covering the shape of wind turbines, new light bulbs or tidal technology).[39] Copyright and database can be relevant to data sets of changes in temperature,[40] manuals and information sets[41] and also charts and maps;[42] and more aspirationally, copyright can be relevant to thought leadership and attempts to change attitudes to climate change through art and film.[43] Further,

---

36. *See* discussion in E. Lane, 'Legal Aspects of Green Patents' in *Green Innovations and IPR Management* eds., A. Kirchner and I. Kirchner-Freis (Alphen aan den Rijn: Kluwer 2013) 3-65 and European Patent Office, 'EPO Supports New Platform on Renewable Energy Innovation' (10 July 2015) https://www.epo.org/news-issues/news/2015/20150710.html accessed 29 October 2019.

37. M. Rimmer, 'Intellectual Ventures: Patent Law, Climate Change, and Geoengineering' in *Intellectual Property and Clean Energy: The Paris Agreement and Climate Justice,* ed., M. Rimmer (New York: Springer 2018) exploring concerns raised regarding manipulation of nature and additional ones regarding the prospect of the patents being owned by non practising entities.

38. M. Blakeney, 'Climate Change and Intellectual Property: Regulatory Issues' in *Genomics and Breeding for Climate Resilient Crops* ed., C. Kole, (Germany: Springer, 2013) vol. 1, 433 reviewing empirical analysis of patents in respect of drought tolerant and climate ready genes.

39. *See* e.g., UK registered design 4037878 registered 21 October 2014 'Impellor designed for turbine rotar shaft', in name of Michael French; for analysis with an Australian focus, *see* M. Sainsbury, 'The Power of Visual Appeal: Designs Law and Clean Energy' in *Intellectual Property and Clean Energy: The Paris Agreement and Climate Justice* ed., M. Rimmer (New York: Springer 2018).

40. *See* e.g., NASA, 'GISS Surface Temperature Analysis' https://data.giss.nasa.gov/gistemp/ accessed 29 October 2019.

41. *See* consideration in M. Carroll, 'Intellectual Property and Related Rights in Climate Data' in *Research Handbook on Intellectual Property and Climate Change* ed., J.D Sarnoff, (Cheltenham: Edward Elgar 2016), 384.

42. E. Derclaye, 'The Role of Copyright in the Protection of the Environment and the Fight Against Climate Change: Is the Current Copyright System Adequate' in *Research Handbook on Intellectual Property and Climate Change* ed., J.D. Sarnoff (Cheltenham: Edward Elgar 2016).

43. T. Hollo, 'Key Change: The Role of the Creative Industries in Climate Change Action' in *Intellectual Property and Clean Energy: The Paris Agreement and Climate Justice* ed., M. Rimmer (New York: Springer 2018); *see also* B. Lord, *Art & Energy. How Culture Changes* (Washington DC: AAM Press of the American Alliance of Museums, 2014) arguing that changes in energy are reflects over time in new approaches in art.

patents[44] and copyright[45] can be obtained or exist in respect of software[46] which enables power to move around the grid.[47]

The existence of these rights need not, of course, mean that IP will be an obstacle to responding to climate change. It can be argued in the traditional manner that the prospect of these rights encourages the innovation and creativity to bring these things about. There have been suggestions that prizes could complement activity in this innovation space – with the assurance that IP rights could be retained.[48] Further, IP owners may choose not to enforce IP rights in all situations, may be willing to enter into licence agreements for a reasonable fee, or there may be situations in which a potential licensee is in fact able to pay a market rate.[49] These last opportunities could be enhanced through the international marketplace provided by WIPO Green at the World Intellectual Property Organization (WIPO).[50] There are also examples of IP owners choosing to embrace sharing of IP in a more radical manner. This is done communally, such as through the copyright focussed Creative Commons[51] and the patent focussed and very relevant (although now closed) Eco-Patent Commons,[52] and also through more individual high profile declarations to encourage wider adoption of technology and growth of a market. This was done by Tesla in

44. Section 1(2)(c) Patents Act 1977.
45. Sections 1, 3 Copyright Designs and Patents Act 1988.
46. For overview of debate on this issue, *see* A. Brown, S. Kheria, J. Cornwell and M. Iljadica *Contemporary Intellectual Property Rights: Law and Policy,* 5th edn (Oxford: Oxford University Press, 2019) 429-467.
47. *See* e.g., J. Anderson, 'Using Software to Get More Renewable Energy onto the Power Grid' (Breaking Energy 8 August 2013) https://www.greentechmedia.com/articles/read/using-software-to-get-more-renewable-energy-into-the-power-grid last accessed 29 October 2019.
48. *See* discussion in M. Rimmer, 'Beyond the Paris Agreement: Intellectual Property, Innovation Policy and Climate Justice' *MDPI Laws* 8(1) (2019) 7.
49. *See also* K. Kariyawasam and M. Tsai, 'Intellectual Property, Climate Change and Technology Transfer in South Asia' in *Intellectual Property and Clean Energy: The Paris Agreement and Climate Justice* ed., M. Rimmer (New York: Springer 2018)) 8-9 exploring patent pools and clearing houses which can share information about technologies, match needs and enable agreeing of royalties.
50. WIPO Green, 'The Marketplace for Sustainable Technology' https://www3.wipo.int/wipogreen/en/ last accessed 29 October 2019.
51. Creative Commons https://creativecommons.org/ last accessed 29 October 2019.
52. *See* CEF Spotlight, 'Welcome to the Eco-Patent Commons' http://www.corporateecoforum.com/welcome-to-the-eco-patent-commons/ last accessed 29 October 2019. Note debate about the contributions of this initiative and the value of the patent made available – B.H. Hall and C. Helmers, 'Innovation and Diffusion of Clean/Green Technology: Can Patent Commons Help?' *Journal of Environmental Economics and Management* 66(1) (2013) 33-51 and M. Van Hoorebeek and W. Onzivu, 'The Eco-Patent Commons and Environmental Technology Transfer: Implications for Efforts to Tackle Climate Change' *Climate Change Law Review* 4(1) (2010) 13-29.

respect of all their patents for electric vehicles,[53] with a statement that Tesla would not sue others who wish to use them in good faith. This is, however, rather unusually defined[54] and there are views that the patents were made available to increase the installation of infrastructure such as charging points.[55] In similar vein, Toyota made a pledge in respect of patents relating to electrification and fuel cell technology. Yet this was only for a limited period and there are requirements as to on what other Toyota technology needed to be used.[56]

But even if these steps are viewed in the most open and collaborative matter, they do not remove the possibility of a legal conflict between IP rights and responding to climate change. The approaches just discussed depend on decisions taken by the IP owner. If there is a relevant IP right in a relevant country at a relevant time, and the IP owner chose to rely on their IP right, sue infringers and decline to service or indeed create a market for a relevant technology, there nothing which could be done to address this from the perspective of climate change law.

---

53. Tesla Blog, 'All Our Patents Are Belong to You' (12 June 2014) http://www.teslamotors.com/en_GB/blog/all-our-patent-are-belong-you last accessed 29 October 2019.
54. *See* Patent Pledge, 'A party is "acting in good faith" for so long as such party and its related or affiliated companies have not: asserted, helped others assert or had a financial stake in any assertion of (i) any patent or other intellectual property right against Tesla or (ii) any patent right against a third party for its use of technologies relating to electric vehicles or related equipment; challenged, helped others challenge, or had a financial stake in any challenge to any Tesla patent; or marketed or sold any knock-off product (e.g., a product created by imitating or copying the design or appearance of a Tesla product or which suggests an association with or endorsement by Tesla) or provided any material assistance to another party doing so' https://www.tesla.com/en_GB/about/legal#patent-pledge last accessed 29 October 2019.
55. *See* C. Buschmann, 'Tesla's Patent Strategy Opens the Road to Sustainability for Transport and for Itself' Techcrunch (27 March 2016) https://techcrunch.com/2016/05/26/teslas-patent-strategy-opens-the-road-to-sustainability-for-transport-and-for-itself/ last accessed 29 October 2019.
56. J. Groves, 'Toyota Releases Electrification Patents Royalty-Free' (5 April 2019) https://www.carmagazine.co.uk/car-news/tech/toyota-patent-sharing/ and K. Korosec, 'Toyota Is Giving Automakers Free Access to Nearly 24,000 Hybrid Car-Related Patents' https://techcrunch.com/2019/04/03/toyota-is-giving-automakers-free-access-to-nearly-24000-hybrid-car-related-patents/ both last accessed 29 October 2019. *See also* K. Wishart, 'Management of Intellectual Property in Australia's Clean Technology Sector: Challenges and Opportunities in an Unclear Regulatory Environment' 5.3.1 and 5.3.2 and M. Rimmer, 'Elon Musk's Open Innovation: Tesla, Intellectual Property, and Climate Change' both in *Intellectual Property and Clean Energy: The Paris Agreement and Climate Justice* ed., M. Rimmer (New York: Springer 2018).

25.2.3   Wʜᴀᴛ Cᴀɴ Bᴇ Dᴏɴᴇ Wɪᴛʜɪɴ IP Lᴀᴡ

More may be possible within IP law. There have been discussions, returning to the comparison between IP and climate change and IP and health set out above, of the possibility of a declaration on IP and climate change. This could confirm or indeed require compulsory licensing of IP at national level.[57] Prior to the UNFCCC meeting in Copenhagen in 2008, several draft documents were prepared on this point, and they ranged from requiring compulsory licensing to making no reference to IP.[58] The prospect of a compulsory licence led United States (US) senators to contact President Obama and to argue as to the risks of this for weakening IP and US industry.[59] There was also debate on the extent to which IP was in fact having a negative impact on technology transfer such that intervention could be warranted.[60] It was argued that the position differed with technology types and the countries, that in some cases there were substitutable technologies and so no negative impact, and that there were also challenges to effective technology transfer which arose from lack of local expertise and awareness of technology.[61] Others argued, however, that patenting was increasing and

---

57. *See* discussion in A.E.L. Brown et al., 'Towards a Holistic Approach to Technology and Climate Change: What Would Form Part of an Answer?' (2010). University of Edinburgh School of Law Working Paper No. 2010/32. Available at SSRN: http://ssrn.com/abstract= 1697608 or http://dx.doi.org/10.2139/ssrn.1697608, 10, 11, 15-17.

58. M. Rimmer, *Intellectual Property and Climate Change: Inventing Clean Technologies* (Cheltenham: Edward Elgar 2011), *see* extracts on pp. 55-57; for detailed consideration of the negotiations, *see* 45-54, 62 and 58-67 and records of meetings are available via http://unfccc.int/meetings/copenhagen_dec_2009/meeting/6295.php accessed 29 October 2019.

59. *See* letter Evan Bayh and others to the President, 2 November 2009 http://www.ip-watch.org/weblog/wp-content/uploads/2009/11/110209obamasenateletter1.pdf last accessed 30 October 2019. Considered by the author in A.E.L. Brown, 'Securing Access to Climate Change Technologies: Answers and Questions' (2010) University of Edinburgh School of Law Working Paper No. 2010/21. Available at SSRN: http://ssrn.com/abstract= 1622024 or http://dx.doi.org/10.2139/ssrn.1622024, 15, n 69.

60. W. Zhuang, *Intellectual Property Rights and Climate Change: Interpreting the TRIPS Agreement for Environmentally Sound Technologies* (Cambridge: Cambridge University Press, 2017) 12, 39-44.

61. J.H. Barton, 'Intellectual Property and Access to Clean Energy Technologies in Developing Countries: An Analysis of Solar Photovoltaic, Biofuels and Wind Technologies' (ICTSD Trade and Sustainable Energy Series Issue Paper, No. 2 (OCTSD, 2007) x, xi; Copenhagen Economics, 'Are IPR a Barrier to the Transfer of Climate Change Technology' (January 2009) via http://www.eurosfaire.prd.fr/7pc/doc/ 1236588421_climate_change_ipr.pdf last accessed 29 October 2019, 4-6; K. Culver, 'Low Carbon Futures for All? Strategic Options for Global Availability of Environmental Technologies' in *Environmental Technologies: Accessing, Obtaining and Protecting*, ed., A.E.L. Brown (Cheltenham: Edward Elgar 2013); W. Zhuang, *Intellectual Property Rights and Climate Change: Interpreting the TRIPS Agreement for Environmentally Sound Technologies* (Cambridge: Cambridge University Press, 2017) 12, 39-44.

that this was having a negative impact in some countries[62] and called for more sharing and collaboration.[63]

Copenhagen resulted in an Accord[64] which stressed the importance of the development and transfer of technology – but it did not refer to IP. The Accord also provided that there would be a Technology Mechanism,[65] and as noted this is became part of the Paris Agreement.[66] Work within the UNFCCC continued after Copenhagen, with a focus on technology needs identification and funding, including through the Green Climate Fund.[67] Debate on the place of IP also continued. There has been empirical analysis[68] and ongoing calls for intervention at the UNFCCC (from 2010 to 2012, Bolivia and India argued unsuccessfully for engagement with IP)[69] and at the TRIPS Council by Ecuador from 2014.[70] Since the Paris Agreement, in 2017 South Africa stated in the context of its implementation that 'climate

---

62. Work from 2001 and 2006 was submitted to WIPO Standing Committee in 2014 as part of a submission by the Third World Network, and considered in the minutes of the meeting SCP/20/10, pp. 6-7.
63. B. Lee et al., 'Who Owns Our Low Carbon Future? Intellectual Property and Energy Technologies. A Chatman House Report' (2009) https://www.chathamhouse.org/sites/files/chathamhouse/public/Research/Energy,%20Environment%20and%20Development/r0909_lowcarbonfuture.pdf, viii-ix.
64. Report of the Conference of the Parties http://unfccc.int/documentation/documents/advanced_search/items/6911.php?priref=600005735; Copenhagen Accord 30 March 2010 FCCC/CP/2009/11/Add.1 2/CP.15, p. 4 (Accord) and list of parties via http://unfccc.int/meetings/copenhagen_dec_2009/items/5262.php.
65. Article 11 Accord and UNFCCC webpage 'Technology Mechanism' https://unfccc.int/ttclear/support/technology-mechanism.html last accessed 29 October 2019.
66. Article 10(3)-(5) Paris Agreement.
67. *See* e.g., rolling workplan draft for 2019-2022 TEC/2019/19/4.
68. EPO, ICTSD, UNEP, 'Patents and Clean Energy: Bridging the Gap Between Evidence and Policy. Final Report' (2010) https://www.epo.org/news-issues/technology/sustainable-technologies/clean-energy/patents-clean-energy/study-1.html last accessed 29 October 2019 showing a variety in patenting in different countries and sectors and a willingness to licence to developing countries if requests are made and there is local expertise; K. Downey, 'Intellectual Property Rights and Renewable Energy Technology Transfer in China' *South Carolina Journal of Law and Business* (2012) 9(1) 89 considering IP was not a barrier to TT.
69. *See* N. Buxton, 'Cancun Agreement Stripped Bare by Bolivia's Dissent' (16 December 2010) http://www.tni.org/article/cancun-agreement-stripped-bare-bolivias-dissent and consideration in M. Khor, 'Climate Change, Technology and Intellectual Property Rights: Context and Recent Negotiations' (South Centre, April 2012) http://www.southcentre.int/wp-content/uploads/2013/05/RP45_Climate-Change-Technology-and-IP_EN.pdf 26 both last accessed 29 October 2019; Doha Climate Change Conference – November 2012 http://unfccc.int/meetings/doha_nov_2012/meeting/6815.php and consideration in J. De Meeus and A. Strowel, 'Climate Change and the Debate Around Green Technology Transfer and Patent Rules: History, Prospect and Unresolved Issues' *World Intellectual Property Office Journal*, 2 (2012) 179, 196-7.
70. *See* TRIPS Council Minutes https://docs.wto.org/dol2fe/Pages/FE_Search/FE_S_S006.aspx?Query=(%20@Symbol=%20ip/c/m/*)&Language=ENGLISH&Context=FomerScriptedSearch&languageUIChanged=true#, February 2014 Addendum paras 240-366 and June 2014 Addendum paras 123-248; and W. Zhuang, *Intellectual Property Rights and*

technologies need to flow, without hiding behind the issue of Intellectual Property Rights'.[71] In 2018, the European Union (EU) called for a declaration on IP and climate change to assist in climate action in developing countries.[72] A 2019 public policy piece noted that the US has been willing to impose compulsory licences in respect of innovation which could facilitate military action, and queried whether there may be more of this if the US Green New Deal proceeds.[73] In this respect, it should be noted that in parallel with these US developments, in late 2019 President Trump confirmed that he would give notice to withdraw from the Paris Agreement.[74] Finally, there have been scholarly calls for 'a more systematic approach to intellectual property and clean technologies in order to promote larger goals of climate justice, human rights, and sustainable development', and for an IP mechanism in international climate law.[75]

So there is an existing pressure base from the international perspective which could be combined with increased media and activist calls for action – although it would be unwise to assume that the pressure (and evidence) supporting the exclusivity of IP rights would decline. States do have the option to act directly within their own laws to manage elements of the conflict between IP and climate change. TRIPS permits, but does not require, exceptions with some restrictions: through the 'three step tests' in respect of

---

Climate Change: Interpreting the TRIPS Agreement for Environmentally Sound Technologies (Cambridge: Cambridge University Press, 2017) 361-4.

71. Republic of South Africa Department of Environmental Affairs, 'Full Wrap: South Africa Participates in CoP23 in Bonn, Germany' https://www.environment.gov.za/event/international/southafrica_participates_cop23bonn_germany2017 accessed 29 October 2019, p. 2.

72. European Parliament Resolution 2018/2598(RSP) para. 69 referring to the Declaration on the TRIPS agreement and public health (2001) WT/MIN (01)/DEC/2. *See also* discussion in A. Phelan, 'Climate Change and Human Rights: Intellectual Property Challenges and Opportunities' in *Intellectual Property and Clean Energy: The Paris Agreement and Climate Justice* ed., M. Rimmer (New York: Springer, 2018), section 4.3.

73. Z. Eldredge, 'Intellectual Property and Climate Change' (The Trouble, 20 September 2018) https://www.the-trouble.com/content/2018/9/20/intellectual-property-and-climate-change last accessed 29 October 2019. *See* Clean Air Act 1970 S308 42 US Code 7608 which provides for mandatory patent licensing on reasonable terms if this is necessary to comply with standards set out under the legislation; Atomic Energy Act 1954 provides that there can be compulsory licensing on fair and equitable terms if the patent, and the licensing of it, is of primary importance to achieve objectives in respect of nuclear energy section 153(a) and (d)(4). For details of Green New Deal *see* L. Friedman, 'What Is the Green New Deal? A Climate Proposed, Explained' (The New York Times, 21 February 2019) https://www.nytimes.com/2019/02/21/climate/green-new-deal-questions-answers.html last accessed 29 October 2019.

74. R. Harrabin, 'Paris Agreement: Trump Confirms US Will Leave Climate Accord' (BBC News, 24 October 2019) https://www.bbc.co.uk/news/world-us-canada-50165596 last accessed 29 October 2019.

75. M. Rimmer, 'Beyond the Paris Agreement: Intellectual Property, Innovation Policy and Climate Justice' *MDPI Laws* 8(1) (2019) 7.

all IP rights (broadly that there may be limited exceptions provided they do not unreasonably conflict with the normal exploitation of the right, and not unreasonably prejudice the legitimate interests of the IP owner, taking account of the legitimate interests of others) and compulsory licensing in respect of patents.[76] There are also introductory provisions which appear to encourage (although again they do not impose obligations) the embracing of these opportunities in respect of climate change. They refer to the protection and enforcement of IP rights to contribute to transfer and dissemination of technology in a manner conducive to social and economic welfare and to a balance of rights and obligations, and provide that states may adopt measures necessary to protect public health and nutrition and promote the public interest in sectors of vital importance to their technological development – providing that these measures are consistent with TRIPS).[77]

States could introduce commercial and non-commercial research exceptions to expedite further development of relevant improved technologies. Crown Use provisions could be introduced and relied upon, and specific reference could made in them to responding to climate change.[78] Compulsory licensing could be introduced and used if there was no meeting of market demand in respect of the patented invention once three years have

---

76. Article 9 TRIPS (referring also to Berne Convention Article 9(2)), Article 26(2) TRIPS, Article 30 TRIPS, Article 31 TRIPS in particular (b); *see also* A.E.L. Brown, 'Intellectual Property and Climate Change' in *The Oxford Handbook of Intellectual Property Law* ed., R.C. Dreyfuss and J. Pila (Oxford: Oxford University Press, 2018) 978-80 exploring restrictions on the existence or obtaining of IP rights and A.E.L. Brown, *Intellectual Property, Climate Change and Technology. Managing National Legal Intersections, Relationships and Conflicts* (Cheltenham: Edward Elgar, 2019) 35.

77. Articles 7 and 8 TRIPS, analysis in *Canada Pharmaceutical Patent* DS 114 http://www.wto.org/english/tratop_e/dispu_e/cases_e/ds114_e.htm last accessed 30 October 2019. *See* discussion of the imbalance in S.K. Sell *Private Power, Public Law. The Globalization of Intellectual Property Rights* (Cambridge: Cambridge University Press, 2003); K.E. Maskus and J.H. Reichman, 'The Globalization of Private Knowledge Goods and the Privatization of Global Public Goods' 3 and P. Drahos, 'The Regulation of Public Goods' 46 both in *International Public Goods and Transfer of Technology under a Globalized Intellectual Property Regime* eds., K.E. Maskus and J.H. Reichman (Cambridge: Cambridge University Press, 2005).

78. *See* e.g., section 55-7 Patents Act 1977, section 12 and sch 1 Registered Designs Act 1949 and consideration in A.E.L. Brown, *Intellectual Property, Climate Change and Technology. Managing National Legal Intersections, Relationships and Conflicts* (Cheltenham: Edward Elgar, 2019) 126-8 and the prospects of settlements and new approaches emerging in the context of this possibility as seen in health in England and Wales. *See* debate in Hansard vol. 661 10 June 2019 https://hansard.parliament.uk/commons/2019-06-10/debates/15AB9280-DBE7-413D-98AA-8079206FB93B/ CysticFibrosisDrugsOrkambi and NHS, 'NHS England concludes wide-ranging deal for cystic fibrosis drugs' (24 October 2019) https://www.england.nhs.uk/2019/10/nhs-england-concludes-wide-ranging-deal-for-cystic-fibrosis-drugs/ both last accessed 30 October 2019.

passed since the patent was granted[79] and to deal with national emergencies (which could be specifically stated to include responses to climate change).[80] Indeed legislation could be included for all IP rights which enabled use by others, without consent, in return for a reasonable payment. This could be argued to be consistent with a stewardship approach to IP.[81]

There has, however, been very limited introduction of IP provisions which have a focus on climate change.[82] And importantly, the prospect of this may also be less likely if a state has committed to contrary obligations, say under a trade and investment agreement that IP protection would be maximised and that no steps would be taken to support renewable energy technologies. States may be particularly reluctant to explore these just raised IP possibilities if investor state dispute settlement is available under the trade and investment agreement, as this would raise the prospect of IP owners acting directly against states.[83]

A solution already proposed is international guidance for fair, reasonable and non-discriminatory licensing of IP in respect of environmentally sustainable technologies.[84] This would intertwine several regimes. It would build on action taken at the WTO in the Basic Telecommunications reference paper; on competition law and the essential facilities doctrine;[85] on the

---

79. Section 48, 48A Patents Act 1977, Article 5A(4) Paris Convention, A.E.L. Brown, *Intellectual Property, Climate Change and Technology. Managing National Legal Intersections, Relationships and Conflicts* (Cheltenham: Edward Elgar, 2019) 128.

80. The question of what could be a national emergency is raised in the Declaration on the TRIPS agreement and public health (2001) WT/MIN(01)/DEC/2 Article 5(c) which provides that each member can determine what constitutes an emergency and refers to particular health situations.

81. H.R. Howe, 'Copyright Limitations and the Stewardship Model of Property' *Intellectual Property Quarterly* 15(1) (2011) 183, and H.R. Howe, 'Property, Sustainability and Patent Law: Could the Stewardship Model Facilitate the Promotion of Green Technology' in *Concepts of Property in Intellectual Property Law* eds., H. Howe and J. Griffiths (Cambridge: Cambridge University Press 2013), A.E.L. Brown *Intellectual Property, Climate Change and Technology. Managing National Legal Intersections, Relationships and Conflicts* (Cheltenham: Edward Elgar, 2019) 86-89.

82. For example Poland, Republic of Korea, Bosnia and Herzegovina, and Croatia, *see* consideration in WIPO Standing Committee on the Law of Patents SCP/21/4 Rev 3 November 2014, p. 6 note 30, p. 15 notes 102, 103, 106 and regarding government use *see* consideration in WIPO Standing Committee on the Law of Patents SCP/21/5 Rev 7 November 2014 Kenya and Portugal p. 4 note 23 and Thailand p. 4 note 24.

83. For exploration of risks A.E.L. Brown, *Intellectual Property, Climate Change and Technology. Managing National Legal Intersections, Relationships and Conflicts* (Cheltenham: Edward Elgar, 2019) 265-275, 285-295 – this then goes on to develop a means within trade and investment agreements by which this risk could be managed.

84. W. Zhuang, *Intellectual Property Rights and Climate Change: Interpreting the TRIPS Agreement for Environmentally Sound Technologies* (Cambridge: Cambridge University Press, 2017) 364-9.

85. *See* exploration of essential facilities in the context of IP in A.E.L. *Brown Intellectual Property, Human Rights and Competition. Access to Essential Innovation and Technology* (Cheltenham: Edward Elgar 2012) 48-51, 56-58, 95-8, 154.

UNFCCC in calling for lower rates to be paid by businesses seeking to use the IP in least developed countries and for balances to be paid to IP owners by the Green Climate Fund; and the guidelines could refer to the activities at WIPO Green. The proposal would involve the UNFCCC, the United Nations Conference on Trade and Development which has in the past issued guidance on technology transfer,[86] WIPO and WTO work together to develop the guidelines. Finally, the proposal suggested, building on the WTO's incorporation of the Basic Telecommunications reference paper, that the guidelines should be incorporated in the WTO agreement and therefore be enforced through the WTO Dispute settlement system.

These proposals warrant serious consideration. The question is whether this will be done. The next sections will explore the extent to which human rights could provide a new lens and impetus for action.

25.3 HUMAN RIGHTS, CLIMATE CHANGE AND IP

25.3.1 RELEVANT RIGHTS

Human rights treaties at international and regional level impose obligations on states to protect and ensure rights to individuals in their territory.[87] Relevant here are rights to health,[88] to life,[89] regarding environmental

---

86. Draft International Code of Conduct on Technology Transfer from 1985, *see also* UNCTAD, 'Transfer of Technology' (2001) www.unctad.org/en/docs//psiteiitd28.en.pdf last accessed 30 October 2019.

87. *See* e.g., International Covenant on Civil and Political Rights (ICCPR) 1966 UNTS vol. 999 p. 171, Article 2.

88. International Covenant on Economic, Social and Cultural Rights 1966 UNTS 993, p. 3 (ICESCR) Article 12, which includes a reference to improvement of environmental hygiene (2)(b) (considered in General Comment No. 14 (2000) E/C.12/2000/4); Charter of Fundamental Rights of the European Union 2000/C 364/01 (EU Charter), Article 35 regarding preventive health care, medical treatment and implementation of a high level of human health protection into policies; American Declaration of the Rights and Duties of Man 1948 UNTS vol. 144 p. 123 (ADRMD), Article IX; the African Charter on Human and Peoples Rights 1987 UNTS vol. 1520 p. 217 (African Charter), Article 16.

89. ICCPR, Article 6; Convention on the Rights of the Child 1989 UNTS 1577, p. 3, Article 24; Convention on Elimination of All Forms of Discrimination against Women 1980 UNTS 1980 UNTS 1249, p. 13, Article 12; European Convention on Human Rights 1951 UNTS vol. 213 p. 221 (ECHR), Article 2; EU Charter, Article 2; ADRMD, Article I; African Charter, Article 4. *See* consideration in A. Phelan, 'Climate Change and Human Rights: Intellectual Property Challenges and Opportunities' in *Intellectual Property and Clean Energy: The Paris Agreement and Climate Justice* ed., M. Rimmer (New York: Springer, 2018)) regarding the consequences of bush fires in Australia and K. Cook, 'A Mutually Informed Approach: The Right to Life in an Era of Pollution and Climate Change' *European Human Rights Law Review* 2019 3 (2019) 274-290 arguing that a focus on the right to life could deliver new informed risk management approaches to managing pollution, combining human rights and international environmental law.

protection and sustainable development,[90] to enjoy the benefits of scientific progress[91] and to take part in cultural life.[92] Also highly relevant is the UN Declaration on the Rights of Indigenous People of 2007. This engages with the importance of the land and the connection with it of indigenous people,[93] and there is a right to conservation and protection of the environment.[94] The Anchorage Declaration of 2009[95] builds on this in its call for states to respect fundamental rights of indigenous peoples to air, forest, waters, oceans, sea rights and rights recognised in climate mitigation strategies.[96] Finally, the UN Sustainable Development Goals for 2030 ('a blueprint to achieve a better and more sustainable future for all')[97] include climate action.[98]

There are arguments that an individual, human rights focussed approach can enable the best identification of the technologies which can respond to the relevant needs in a particular situation.[99] Yet a human rights approach also brings a different lens. First, there is the fact that the sustainable development goals also include industries, innovation and infrastructure.[100] Second, the European Convention on Human Rights (ECHR) includes a right to enjoyment of property,[101] which has been found by the European Court of Human Rights to cover IP.[102] The EU Charter also includes rights to the

---

90. EU Charter, Article 37: 'a high level of integration of environmental protection must be integrated into the policies of the Union and ensured in accordance with the principle of sustainable development.' *See also* Treaty on the Functioning of the European Union OJ 115 9 May 2008 132-133, Article 191; African Charter, Article 24: 'satisfactory environment'.

91. ICESCR, Article 15(1)(b). In 2009 UNESCO published the Venice Statement on the right to enjoy the benefits of science and its application, via http://unesdoc.unesco.org/images/0018/001855/185558e.pdf and https://www.aaas.org/sites/default/files/VeniceStatement_July2009.pdf last accessed 30 October 2019. This notes climate change as a contemporary challenge Article 13(c).

92. ICESCR, Article 15(1)(a).

93. United Nations Declaration on the Rights of Indigenous Peoples 2007 A/RES/61/295 (UNDRIP) Articles 25-30.

94. UNDRIP, Article 29(1).

95. Output of Indigenous Peoples' Global Summit on Climate Change https://unfccc.int/resource/docs/2009/smsn/ngo/168.pdf last accessed 30 October 2019.

96. Anchorage Declaration, recital 6, Articles 1, 11.

97. Sustainable Development Goals website https://www.un.org/sustainabledevelopment/sustainable-development-goals/ last accessed 30 October 2019.

98. Goal 13 https://www.un.org/sustainabledevelopment/climate-change/ last accessed 30 October 2019.

99. D. Shabalala, 'Climate Change, Human Rights and Technology Transfer' in M.K. Land and J.D. Aronson *New Technologies for Human Rights Law and Practice* (Cambridge: Cambridge University Press, 2018).

100. Goal 9 https://www.un.org/sustainabledevelopment/infrastructure-industrialization/.

101. ECHR, Protocol 1 Article 1; *Sporrong & Lonnroth v. Sweden* Series A No. 52 (1983) 5 EHRR 35.

102. *Anheuser-Busch Inc v. Portugal* Application 73049/01 (2007) 45 EHRR 36; *Balan v. Moldova* No. 19247/03 [2009] ECDR 6.

protection of property[103] and specifically to the protection of IP.[104] Third, there is a debate about the extent to which there is also international human rights protection of IP. There is the right to the 'moral and material reward of the author',[105] which is part of the same treaty provision as the rights regarding science and cultural life discussed above, and it has been suggested that this right can cover, among other things, copyright.[106] A UN General Comment and Special Rapporteur reports argue, however, that this should apply only to individual authors and not to corporate ones;[107] that copyright should have safeguards for other human rights; and that copyright does not equate to a human right.[108] This complex human rights base has seen action and direction in relation to climate change, which is now being discussed.

25.3.2   POLICY ENGAGEMENT

A milestone came in 2012 when the Office of the UN High Commissioner for Human Rights appointed an independent expert for Human Rights and the Environment. In 2015 this role became a Special Rapporteur, and it was extended in 2018 in a resolution referring to the Paris Agreement.[109] A July 2018 report of this Special Rapporteur[110] concluded '[t]he relationship between human rights and the environment has evolved rapidly over the past five decades, and even more so over the past five years. The greening of well-established human rights, including the rights to life, health, food, water, housing, culture, development, property and home and private life, has contributed to improvements in the health and well-being of people across

---

103. EU Charter, Article 17(1).
104. EU Charter, Article 17(2); this has been the subject of significant attention, *see* e.g., C. Geiger, 'Implementing Intellectual Property Provisions in Human Rights Instruments' in *Research Handbook on Human Rights and Intellectual Property* ed., C. Geiger (Cheltenham: Edward Elgar Publishing, 2013).
105. ICESCR, Article 15(1)(c).
106. Considered in General Comment No. 17 (2005), and Report of United Nations Office of High Commissioner for Human Rights Special Rapporteur in the field of cultural rights, 'Copyright policy and the right to science and culture' A/HRC/28/57 (Special Rapporteur 2014). *See* discussion in A. Chapman, 'Approaching Intellectual Property as a Human Right: Obligations Related to Article 15(1)(c)' *Copyright Bulletin XXXV* 3 (2001), 4 and L. Helfer, 'Human Rights and Intellectual Property: Conflict or Coexistence?' *Minnesota Intellectual Property Review* 5 (2003) 47.
107. Considered in General Comment No. 17 (2005) para. 2, and Special Rapporteur 2014, paras 26-29, 40-51, 95, 99.
108. Considered in General Comment No. 17 (2005) para. 3 and Special Rapporteur 2014, paras 94-98.
109. A/HRC/RES/34/20 and A/HRC/RES/37/8 preamble paras 7 and 8; UNHR Office of High Commissioner, 'Special Rapporteur on Human Rights and the Environment' http://www.ohchr.org/EN/Issues/Environment/SREnvironment/Pages/SRenvironmentIndex.aspx accessed 30 October 2019.
110. A/73/188.

the world'.[111] The Special Rapporteur called for this greening to be delivered more widely across states.[112]

The document appointing the Special Rapporteur referred to the Paris Agreement, however, that agreement itself engages with human rights only in the preamble. This acknowledges that climate change is a common concern of humankind and provides that parties should, when taking action to address climate change, respect, promote and consider their respective obligations on human rights, as well as intergenerational equity.[113] A draft of the Paris Agreement did refer to human rights in the body of the text but this was not included in the final version. This has been criticised, particularly given the risks from climate change for communities living in low-lying coastal areas,[114] yet there is also the view that any engagement is a positive and a starting point.[115] A contrary position, however, is that different parts of the world approach human rights in different ways, and that including the term could have been a distraction from the actual goal of addressing climate change, and perhaps an obstacle to it.[116]

International human rights policy activity reveals, then, an intersection between climate change and human rights. Elements of this have been developed in court cases at national level.

25.3.3   MOVEMENTS TO COURT

There have been findings in India that the constitutional right to life covered the right to an unpolluted environment.[117] In South Africa, courts found in planning-related cases that environmental rights are justiciable human rights

---

111. A/73/188 para. 53.

112. A/73/188 paras 54, 57.

113. Paris Agreement, para. 11 preamble.

114. S. Adelman, 'Human Rights in the Paris Agreement: Too Little, Too Late?' *Transnational Environmental Law* 7(1) (2018) 17-36, 26-27, 36; A. Savaresi, 'The Paris Agreement: A New Beginning?' *Journal of Energy and Natural Resources Law* 34(1) (2016) 16, 24-25.

115. Report of the Special Rapporteur on the issue of human rights obligations relating to the enjoyment of a safe, clean, healthy and sustainable environment (February 2016) A/HRC/31/52, para. 22. *See also* discussion in K. Cook, 'A Mutually Informed Approach: The Right to Life in an Era of Pollution and Climate Change' *European Human Rights Law Review* 3 (2019) 274-290, 280.

116. A. Huggins and B. Lewis, 'The Paris Agreement: Development, the North-South Divide and Human Rights' in *Intellectual Property and Clean Energy: The Paris Agreement and Climate Justice* ed., M. Rimmer (New York: Springer, 2018).

117. Constitution of India, Article 21; *Subhas Kumar v. State of Bihar* 1991 AIR 420; S. Jolly and Z. Makuch, 'Procedural and Substantive Innovations Propounded by the Indian Judiciary in Balancing Protection of Environment and Development: A Legal Analysis' in *Courts and the Environment* eds., C. Voigt and Z. Makuch (Cheltenham: Edward Elgar Publishing 2018); S. Sedley, 'Human Rights: A Twenty-First Century Environment' *Public Law* (1995) 386, 400.

and that the state has a positive duty to protect the environment under the Constitution.[118] In 2009 in Alaska, Kanuk (and other young people)[119] claimed that the state was in breach of its obligations under its constitution to protect a public trust resource – which the young people argued included protecting the atmosphere. The court declined to extend its approach to public trust obligations (which so far had involved requiring that problematic activity come to an end) to now require that the state took positive steps to regulate.[120] In Austria, in 2017, a first instance court in litigation involving an extension to Vienna airport had regard to provisions in the EU Charter of Fundamental Rights on sustainability and the environment, and references in constitutional law to sustainability,[121] in interpreting obligations under climate protection legislation regarding the public interest in the context of expansion of Vienna International Airport. The first instance court balanced economic development against the avoidance of environmental harm;[122] however, the Constitutional Court found that the legislation did not provide a base to take this approach.[123]

Actions continue. In the Philippines a petition[124] was made in 2015 to its Commission on Human Rights. It was against private actors (not the state) by climate change activists and individuals. The petition claimed that the private entities should be accountable for violations of Filipino rights to life, health, food and water in the Bill of Rights, and obligations of the state under international human rights treaties and instruments and at the end of 2019 Commission found that such claims could be made and should proceed under national law.[125] In *Youth/Juliana v. United States* also raised in 2015, a group

---

118. *Director of Mineral Development v. Save the Vaal* [1999] ZASCA 9 [20] regarding licensing for open cast mining and *BP v. MEC for Agriculture, Conservation, Environment and Land Affairs* [2004] ZAGPHC 18 [41 et seq] regarding a filling station in a built-up area.

119. *Kanuk v. State of Alaska, Department of Natural Resources* 335 P. 3d 108.

120. A later action by Sinnok and others was rejected on the same basis *Sinnok v. The State of Alaska* (2018) and *see* http://climatecasechart.com/case/sinnok-v-alaska/ last accessed 30 October 2019. *See* discussion in M. Rimmer, 'Northern Exposure: Alaska, Climate Change, Indigenous Rights, and Atmospheric Trust Litigation' in *Intellectual Property and Clean Energy: The Paris Agreement and Climate Justice* ed., M. Rimmer, (New York: Springer, 2018).

121. Austrian Federal Constitution BGBI I No. 111/2013 sections 1, 3.

122. *See* discussion in J. Peel and H. Osofsky, 'A Rights Turn in Climate Change Litigation' *Transnational Environmental Law* 7(1) (2018) 37, 58-59.

123. *In re Vienna-Schwechat Airport Expansion* http://www.lse.ac.uk/GranthamInstitute/litigation/in-re-vienna-schwechat-airport-expansion/ accessed 30 October 2019.

124. Petition to the Commission on Human Rights of the Philippines http://www.greenpeace.org/seasia/ph/PageFiles/105904/Climate-Change-and-Human-Rights-Complaint.pdf last accessed 30 October 2019.

125. Commission on Human Rights Press Release (26 March 2018) http://chr.gov.ph/chr-to-conduct-first-hearing-investigating-possible-contribution-of-carbon-to-climate-change-and-its-impact-on-human-rights/ including in London, *see* LSE National Inquiry on Climate Change, Commission on Human Rights of the Philippines London Hearing

of young people argued that energy policy and fossil fuel activity contributed to climate change which was in breach of the claimants' rights to, *inter alia*, life, liberty and property – in early 2020 appeals are ongoing regarding in particular the extent to which the issue should be determined by a court or is in essence more of a policy and legislative question.[126] In 2019 the Supreme Court in the Netherlands found that in the light of the rights to life and private and family life in the ECHR, the state had a positive obligation to prevent climate change and reduce greenhouse gas emissions by 25% by the end of 2020 compared to 1990 levels[127] Also in 2019, alongside the activism discussed at the start of this chapter, sixteen children aged 8-17, including Alexandria Villasenor and Greta Thunberg, raised a petition against Argentina, Brazil, France, Germany and Turkey[128] under the UN Committee on the Rights of the Child, using its optional protocol on a communications procedure.[129] The petition referred to rights to life, health and culture, obligations to act in the best interests of the child[130] and failure to prevent foreseeable human rights harms caused by climate change.[131] The next steps would be the submission of a response, evidence and an enquiry and the progress is awaited with interest.

The intersection between climate change and human rights, then, is seen in litigation as well as in policy action. There has also been some more targeted action regarding technology and IP.

(2018) http://www.lse.ac.uk/GranthamInstitute/event/inquiry/ both last accessed 30 October 2019, and the Commission on Human Rights of the Republic of the Philippines National Inquiry on Climate Change https://chr.gov.ph/nicc-2/ and Center for International Environmental Law, 'Press Release' 9 December 2019 https://www.ciel.org/news/groundbreaking-inquiry-in-philippines-links-carbon-majors-to-human-rights-impacts-of-climate-change-calls-for-greater-accountability/ both last accessed 31 March 2020.

126. *See* Complaint via https://static1.squarespace.com/static/571d109b04426270152febe0/t/57a35ac5ebbd1ac03847eece/1470323398409/YouthAmendedComplaintAgainstUS.pdf last accessed 30 October 2019, paras 130, 288, 289 and for details of the claim and its progress *see* https://www.ourchildrenstrust.org/juliana-v-us last accessed 31 March 2020.

127. *Netherlands v Urgenda Foundation* 19/00135 https://uitspraken.rechtspraak.nl/inziendocument?id=ECLI:NL:HR:2019:2007 in particular [5.1-5.4.3] and A. Noellkamper and L Burgers, 'A New Classic in Climate Change Litigation: the Dutch Supreme Court Decision in the Urgenda Case' (6 January 2020) EJIL Talk! https://www.ejiltalk.org/a-new-classic-in-climate-change-litigation-the-dutch-supreme-court-decision-in-the-urgenda-case/ both accessed 31 March 2020.

128. *Petition Sacchi et al v. Argentina et al* https://childrenvsclimatecrisis.org/wp-content/uploads/2019/09/2019.09.23-CRC-communication-Sacchi-et-al-v.-Argentina-et-al.pdf last accessed 30 October 2019 (Petition).

129. A/RES/66/138 2011 https://www.ohchr.org/EN/ProfessionalInterest/Pages/OPICCRC.aspx last accessed 30 October 2019.

130. Petition paras 13, 24-9; and CRC Articles 3, 6, 24, 30.

131. Petition paras 20, 21.

25.3.4   HUMAN RIGHTS, CLIMATE CHANGE, TECHNOLOGY AND IP

The decision at the UNFCCC to create a Technology Mechanism consolidated the place of technology in responding to climate change, and this led to exploration of the connection with human rights. A key contribution in 2011 explores the full landscape through which technology may be developed and transferred, analyses how to bring about an enabling environment, and engages deeply with the barriers which may be posed by IP rights and the steps which could be taken to manage this (to the extent there is a problem), and discusses differing forms of sharing, including through compulsory licensing.[132] In 2012, important developments came from the human rights instrumental framework. The UN Special Rapporteur in the field of cultural rights considered there to be links between the right to share in the benefits of scientific progress, the emerging right to a clean and healthy environment and rights regarding access to information, food and health, and considered that the right to enjoy the benefits includes 'an enabling environment fostering the conservation, development and diffusion of science and technology'.[133] The Special Rapporteur also noted that the power of IP 'to obstruct new technological solutions to critical human problems such as ... climate change, requires attention'.[134] The Special Rapporteur called for states to take a minimalist approach to IP protection and seek advice from WIPO on how to use TRIPS flexibilities.[135] On this, arguments have been made within the IP framework to deliver rights to life, health and to share the benefits of science through curtailing the power of the rights through compulsory licensing,[136] as well as suggesting more collaborative approaches through patent pools and capacity building.[137]

In 2015, this same UN Special Rapporteur considered that IP rights can have a negative impact on, *inter alia*, the environment;[138] that there is no

---

132. International Council on Human Rights Policy, 'Beyond Technology Transfer: Protecting Human Rights in a Climate-Constrained World' (2011) 60-78.

133. Special Rapporteur A/HRC/20/26 (Special Rapporteur 2012) Summary (c) paras 21-23, quote from Summary (d) and para. 25, and development in paras 45-55.

134. Special Rapporteur 2012 para. 56.

135. Special Rapporteur 2012 para. 74(o), (p).

136. U. Shankar, T. K. Bandopadhaya and C. Mehta, 'Climate Change and Technology Transfer: Tying the Knot Through Human Rights' *Journal of Intellectual Property Rights* 23 (2018) 27-34; A. Phelan, 'Climate Change and Human Rights: Intellectual Property Challenges and Opportunities' in *Intellectual Property and Clean Energy: The Paris Agreement and Climate Justice* ed., M. Rimmer (New York: Springer, 2018), section 4.3.2.

137. A. Phelan, 'Climate Change and Human Rights: Intellectual Property Challenges and Opportunities' in *Intellectual Property and Clean Energy: The Paris Agreement and Climate Justice* ed., M. Rimmer (New York: Springer, 2018) section 4.3.3; K. Bouwer, 'Insights for Climate Technology Transfer from International Environmental and Human Rights Law' *Journal of Intellectual Property Rights* 23 (2018) 7-21, 16.

138. Special Rapporteur A/70/279 Report of Special Rapporteur in the field of Cultural Rights 2015 (Special Rapporteur 2015), para. 3.

human right to patent protection;[139] and that the rights to share in the benefits of science and culture require 'affordability of and accessibility to technologies that are essential for a life with dignity'.[140] Most robustly, it considered that 'human rights law operates as a limit to prevent the overreaching of economic claims by patent-owners in contexts where the rights to health, food, access to technology or other human rights could be compromised'.[141] From the opposite perspective, it has been argued that the right to enjoy the benefits of scientific progress could be a base for right to technology transfer.[142]

Similar themes, this time in an intertwined approach, can be seen in the 2017 response of the Office of UN High Commissioner for Human Rights to a request from the Ad Hoc Working Group on the Paris Agreement.[143] This notes the preamble reference to human rights and considers that efforts to implement the Paris Agreement must integrate human rights throughout, with 'this [being] both a legal and moral imperative as well as sound policy'.[144] The response then refers to the technology elements of the Paris Agreement, the right to share in the benefits of scientific progress, and considers that states should encourage the development of technology and that it should be reasonably priced and shared, and transferred across countries as needed. Importantly, 'states should also take steps to ensure that global intellectual property regimes do not obstruct the dissemination of mitigation and adaptation technologies while at the same time ensuring that these regimes create appropriate incentives to help meet sustainable development perspectives'. This engagement is valuable. Yet the return to balance, without providing a suggestion as to how this could be done, is unfortunate. The same is so for the Special Rapporteur's annual report of 2019.[145] This engages with clean air and refers to measurement technologies, heating and lighting, travel and electric cars and sharing information about technologies. It does not, however, refer to IP rights.[146]

A more interventionist tone can be seen from another output of the Special Rapporteur on human rights and the environment, from 2019.[147] They then considered that '[a] rights-based approach could serve as a catalyst for accelerated action to achieve a healthy and sustainable future where all

---

139. Special Rapporteur 2015, para. 5.
140. Special Rapporteur 2015, para. 89.
141. Special Rapporteur 2015, para. 90.
142. A. Phelan, 'Climate Change and Human Rights: Intellectual Property Challenges and Opportunities' in *Intellectual Property and Clean Energy: The Paris Agreement and Climate Justice* ed., M. Rimmer (New York: Springer, 2018), section 4.2.
143. FCCC/APA/2016/2.
144. FCCC/APA/2016/2 Introduction para. 1.
145. A/HRC/40/55 (2019 report).
146. 2019 report *see* paras 65, 69, 87-90, 98-101, 110, 112(f) (h) (i), 114).
147. A/74/161 'Human rights obligations relating to the enjoyment of a safe, clean and healthy and sustainable environment' July 2019 (Special Rapporteur 2019).

energy is provided by zero carbon sources'.[148] It called for transfer of zero carbon and low carbon and high efficiency technology from wealthy to less wealthy states, and stated in the context of funding to bring this about, that 'it violates the basic principles of justice to force poor countries to pay for the costs of responding to climate change when wealthy countries caused the problem'.[149] There is no reference to IP; however, the interventionist perspective continues, with the view that investor state dispute settlement should not be available regarding climate action[150] and also that geoengineering should not be used until its consequences can be more explored.[151]

There is a strong theme, then, that technology and its affordable transfer is important. The question remains as to how this could be done – how to encourage adoption of possibilities explored in this chapter so far and how to disrupt this eternal balance. In 2019 the Special Rapporteur concluded with a reference to a statement made by Greta Thunberg about needing to act as if the house is on fire.[152] This is a valuable metaphor. Identifying the scope for conflict, calling for transfer and affordable fees, seeking to reduce the scope of human rights directly supporting IP owners, making clear that they exist alongside other human rights and identifying opportunities for possible revision of IP laws have not been enough to bring about change. National human rights requirements could be a driver in this respect and it will be interesting to see how constitution based actions in the Philippines and the US discussed above can further influence this.[153] Yet more may be needed. In 2018, a UN resolution on 'Harmony with nature'[154] called for a holistic and integrated approach to sustainable development to guide humanity to live in harmony with nature and restore health and integrity of earth's ecosystems.[155] This may provide a springboard for a new approach. The next section will look beyond a focus on the human to a focus on nature.

---

148. Special Rapporteur 2019 para. 27.
149. Special Rapporteur 2019 para. 68, including quote.
150. Special Rapporteur 2019 para. 81.
151. Special Rapporteur 2019 para. 83.
152. Special Rapporteur 2019 para. 96.
153. *See* A. Slade, 'National Courts and Their Role in the Development of International Intellectual Property Law and Policy – With Reflections on India' in *Is Intellectual Property Pluralism Functional?* ed., S. Frankel (ATRIP Intellectual Property Series) (Cheltenham: Edward Elgar, 2019).
154. UNGA 2018 A/RES/73/235.
155. Harmony with Nature, para. 8.

25.4   WIDENING THE LENS

Such an approach – 'Wild Law' – could draw on a breadth of international activist activity. In 2003 there was the Earth Charter[156] addressed to everyone (not states). This provides: '[w]e stand at a critical moment in Earth's history, a time when humanity must choose its future … [w]e must join together to bring forth a sustainable global society founded on respect for nature, universal human rights, economic justice and a culture of peace.'[157] Similar themes are seen in the Universal Declaration of Rights of Mother Earth which followed the World People's Conference in 2010,[158] and reference is made to this in 'Harmony with Nature'. This declaration was made by 'we, the peoples and nations of Earth',[159] and provides that Mother Earth has inherent rights, including to life, to be respected, clean air, integral health, to regenerate and to be free from contamination.[160]

Yet although these instruments provide a valuable different insight, the points made are highly resonant of those discussed in respect of human rights. Calls for action are not the same as delivering action. Wild Law has also, however, had a more practical focus. One key contribution has been rewriting judgments from a nature perspective.[161] Another is arguing for nature to have a place in the human-based litigation systems. This is through having standing to bring an action, and a legal personality, particularly in the context of public law challenges to activities which could have a negative impact on the environment.[162] Arguments have been made, and some successes achieved, in respect of trees,[163] coral reefs,[164] lakes and rivers (in the US,[165]

---

156. Earth Charter Initiative website http://earthcharter.org/act/ and Earth Charter http://earthcharter.org/discover/the-earth-charter/ both last accessed 30 October 2019.
157. Earth Charter para. 1 preamble.
158. *See* http://therightsofnature.org/universal-declaration/ (Rights of Mother Earth) last accessed 30 October 2019.
159. Rights of Mother Earth, para. 1.
160. Rights of Mother Earth, Article 2(1).
161. *Law as if Earth Really Mattered. The Wild Law Judgment Project* eds, N. Rogers and M. Maloney (Abingdon: Routledge GlassHouse, 2017).
162. *See also* C. Callinan, *Wild Law: A Manifesto for Earth Justice,* 2nd edn (Cambridge: Green Books 2011).
163. C.D. Stone, *Should Trees Have Standing: Law, Morality and the Environment,* 3rd edn (Oxford: Oxford University Press, 2010).
164. M. Akhtar, 'Rights for the Coral Reefs Oceans' Earth Law Centre (16 May 2019) https://www.earthlawcenter.org/blog-entries/2019/5/rights-for-the-coral-reefs last accessed 30 October 2019.
165. Lake Erie pursuant to a referendum, *see* Great Lakes Law, 'Voters Approve Lake Erie Bill of rights, Polluters Challenge it in Court' (February 2019) https://www.greatlakeslaw.org/blog/2019/02/lake-erie-bill-of-rights.html last accessed 30 October 2019.

India[166] and New Zealand)[167] and the Pacific Ocean,[168] and this introduction of a new status provides an important disruption. Yet placing new actors in the adversarial framework regarding climate change, IP and human rights, and new approaches to the judicial balances with it, would not, it is suggested, bring about the level of change sought. The question of the balance between IP and the non-IP-related human rights, and the contribution which IP can make to addressing societal challenges, would still go on.

More direct intervention is needed. It is suggested here that a Wild Law stance could empower states to take advantage of the opportunities available under TRIPS, and to decline to enter into trade and investment agreements which value property over nature.[169] Relevant instruments are useful but do not provide a solution in themselves. The Earth Charter preamble provides: '[w]e have the knowledge and technology to provide for all and to reduce our impacts on the environment'[170] and goes on to provide that everyone should promote the development, adoption and equitable transfer of environmentally sound technologies.[171] Yet it does not engage with IP. The draft Covenant on Environment and Development[172] (prepared by the

---

166. Ganges and Yamuna – pursuant to *Lalit Miglani v. State of Uttarakand Writ Petition (PIL) No 140 of 2015* (High Court March 2017) http://www.indiaenvironmentportal .org.in/files/living%20entity%20Gangotri%20Himalaya%20Uttarakhand%20High%20 Court%20Order.pdf last accessed 30 October 2019 (Supreme Court stayed the decision pending appeal). *See* discussion in E.L. O'Donnell, 'At the Intersection of the Sacred and the Legal: Rights for Nature in Uttarakhand, India' *Journal of Environmental Law* March 30(1) (2018) 135.

167. Wanganui river catchment a legal person pursuant to Te Awa Tupua /Whanganui River Claims Settlement Act 2017. *See* discussion in K. Sanders. '"Beyond Human Ownership?" Property, Power and Legal Personality for Nature in Aotearoa New Zealand' *Journal of Environmental Law* 30(2) 2018 207.

168. Institut de Recherche pour le DA(c) developpemnet, 'The Rights of the Pacific Ocean as a Legal Entity: A science based feasibility study'(2018) https://oceanconference.un.org/ commitments/?id=19759 last accessed 30 October 2019: 'The Pacific Ocean is more than water or food cellar for most Pacific Islanders. It is part of their lives, of their family, of their blood. Land, Sea and Men are a whole. The Ocean has its mana (spiritual authority) and mauri (life force). To recognise the Pacific Ocean as a legal person is in keeping with Pacific Islands cultures.'

169. *See also* M. Margil, 'Stories from the Environmental Frontier' in *Exploring Wild Law: The Philosophy of Earth Jurisprudence* ed., P. Burdon (Cambridge: Wakefield Press, 2011) exploring priorities and some changes which could be made when drafting laws 249-255.

170. Earth Charter, para. 4 preamble.

171. Earth Charter, Article 7(c).

172. For another current activist project, which does not engage with technology *see* 2018 Hague Principles on Responsibilities and Earth Trusteeship, calling for the United Nations to initiative a process towards the adoption of this http://www.earthtrustee ship.world/the-hague-principles-for-a-universal-declaration-on-human-responsibilities- and-earth-trusteeship/ last accessed 30 October 2019.

International Union for Conservation of Nature)[173] of 2015[174] provides that nature as a whole and all life forms warrant respect and are to be safeguarded.[175] It also engages with technology,[176] providing that parties should promote product designs to enhance recycling and eliminating waste (with the commentary noting that this calls for 'affirmative measures to encourage "green" technology')[177] and that parties are to encourage and strengthen cooperation for development, use, access to and transfer of environmentally sound technologies to accelerate transition to sustainable development.[178] The commentary notes, however, that if IP rights exist and are an obstacle to this (with relevant technologies noted possibly to also be in the public domain) parties should explore economic incentives to encourage transfers.[179]

The innovative thinking seen in decision-making and legislation regarding legal personality is again needed here, to provide the drive to move beyond the positions taken to IP in these otherwise innovative and radical instruments. By elevating the importance accorded to rights in respect of nature, countries can take a new approach to IP and a new means of delivering human based rights in respect of life, health, enjoying the benefits of science and to share in cultural life. It would support the stewarding, sharing approach to IP introduced above, rather than one focussed on control and exclusivity. And this can be delivered in a manner which is quite consistent with the flexibilities offered by the international IP framework and with the limited protection accorded to IP within the human rights framework, by creating increased exceptions and compulsory licensing and sharing regimes.

25.5   CONCLUDING THOUGHTS

This chapter has explored the IP, climate change and human rights landscape. It has identified potential for conflict between IP and each of climate change

---

173. An Intergovernmental Organization. Disclosure: since 2019, the author is a member of and adviser to the IUCN in relation to the marine biodiversity beyond national jurisdiction process. She was not involved in the development of the instrument discussed here.
174. Draft International Covenant on Environment and Development – Implementing Sustainability (5 ed 2015) https://portals.iucn.org/library/sites/library/files/documents/EPLP-031-rev4.pdf (IUCN Covenant) last accessed 30 October 2019.
175. IUCN Covenant, Article 2.
176. *See also* IUCN Covenant, Articles 22(1) and 30 should set targets, and use best available technology, to address pollution.
177. IUCN Covenant, Article 36(d) and commentary p. 109, referring to Article 17 and *see also* Article 56 regarding funding and commentary pp. 151-2 regarding consistency with TRIPS.
178. IUCN Covenant), Article 51, commentary p. 145.
179. IUCN Article 51, commentary p. 145.

and human rights. Innovative approaches to human rights and rights based in nature have been argued to provide a new base and momentum for a full embracing of opportunities within the IP framework. This could reduce the prospect of conflict and to preserve the positive contribution of IP to responses to climate change.

This pro-nature and climate change responsive proposal may be less pro-IP than some would like. Yet IP, in itself and in its potential implications, has been seen to be less pro-nature than many would like. Returning to the quotation at the start of this chapter, the house may be burning. This chapter has developed new ways to respond. It is time to act.

Chapter 26

Geographical Indications and Human Rights

Dev Gangjee

26.1   INTRODUCTION

Geographical Indications (GIs) are a notoriously controversial addition to the Intellectual Property canon. While a flute of Champagne or cup of Darjeeling is usually welcomed, the international legal regime governing the use and misuse of these product designations remains unpalatable to many. To the extent that consensus exists, there is an agreement that a GI is a sign with an actual or potential commercially valuable reputation. This portrayal has evident similarities with trademarks, suggesting that parallels may be drawn with the interaction between human rights and trademark law. However, it is the divergence between the distinct regimes governing GIs and trademarks, based upon the link between product and place, which is of far greater interest. This chapter begins by outlining the conceptual foundations of GI protection in section 26.2. It emphasizes their similarities with trademarks, with the consequence that human rights issues relevant for trademark law – whether such rights are included within the right to property or whether their utilization acts as a manifestation of or an impediment to free speech – are also relevant for GIs. It then proceeds to outline points of difference, which accounts for distinct regimes governing GIs in many countries. Section 26.3 further develops this by tracing the emergence of a cultural heritage preservation argument in international GI discourse, which is used as a partial justification for both the basis and scope of protection. This trend is significant because it marks a departure from the dominant discourse of unfair competition prevention, which has otherwise grounded as well as constrained the international GI regime for over a century.[1] An emerging narrative posits that to the extent that GI labelled products are cultural artefacts, the protection of these signs is normatively defensible as it sustains cultural heritage. This, in turn, is a crucial aspect of preserving distinct cultural identities, and therefore, an important goal of human rights instruments concerned with cultural rights. The extent to which GI protection could be used to satisfy cultural heritage related obligations is assessed.

26.2 GIs AS THE OBJECTS OF INTELLECTUAL PROPERTY LAW

26.2.1 WHAT IS A GEOGRAPHICAL INDICATION?

This section briefly sketches the story so far. A GI is a sign indicating a product's specific geographical origin and information associated with that origin. Article 22.1 of the Trade Related Agreement on Intellectual Property Rights (TRIPS) stipulates that:

> Geographical indications are, for the purposes of this Agreement, indications which identify a good as originating in the territory of a Member, or a region or locality in that territory, where a given quality, reputation or other characteristic of the good is essentially attributable to its geographical origin.

Unlike a trademarked product's *commercial origin* that may vary over time and place, a GI such as Bordeaux or Prosciutto di Parma is prescriptively embedded in a particular *geographical locale*. The 'substance of the concept' of GIs is that they are 'used to demonstrate a link between the origin of the product to which it is applied and a given quality, reputation or other characteristic that the product derives from that origin'.[2] The connoisseur will buy (or avoid, depending on preferences) Champagne precisely because of its regional provenance. Consequently, the legal regulation of GIs was premised upon enabling this marketplace signalling function. Both the law of trademarks and that of GIs have therefore emerged as distinct regimes for preventing unfair competition between marketplace rivals, by preventing unwarranted interference with the messages contained in such signs.[3]

---

1. The international history of GI protection is comprehensively reviewed in D. Gangjee, *Relocating the Law of Geographical Indications* (CUP, 2012).
2. WIPO *The Definition of Geographical Indications* 1 October 2002 (SCT/9/4) at para. 4.
3. In Europe, there is an enduring view that GI protection is a subset of Unfair Competition law. *See* E. Ulmer, 'Unfair Competition Law in the European Economic Community' (1973) *IIC* 188, 199-200; F. Henning-Bodewig & G. Schricker, 'New Initiatives for the

The conventional account holds that protecting the communicative integrity of trademarks and GIs serves a dual purpose. By granting exclusive rights to the sign, consumer deception or confusion as to origin is prevented, while simultaneously shielding legitimate producers against a particular species of unfair competition.[4]

An instrumentalist account by the Chicago School is the predominant theoretical justification for this exclusivity, in a marketplace characterized by information asymmetries between producers and consumers.[5] Trademarks enhance informational efficiency. They lessen consumer search costs by making products easier to identify in the marketplace while encouraging producers to invest in improving or maintaining levels of quality by ensuring that they, and not their rivals, reap the reputational rewards of that investment. In order to preserve the communicative integrity of the sign, its use by others should, therefore, be restricted. The economic analysis of GIs suggests a similar rationale,[6] with the added dimension of GIs exhibiting features of club goods, whereby the exclusivity is enjoyed by a collective entity. Where a collective reputation is at stake, institutional mechanisms are required to set and police common standards of production, ensuring that competing members will cooperate to maintain quality. Otherwise, in light of

---

Harmonisation of Unfair Competition Law in Europe' (2002) *EIPR* 271, 273; C. Wadlow, 'Unfair Competition in Community Law – Part 1: The Age of the "Classical Model"' (2006) *EIPR* 433, 440. On the continued applicability of an unfair competition framework, *see* K. Weatherall, 'Does the Unfair Competition Approach to GIs have a Future?' in I. Calboli & J.C. Ginsburg, *Cambridge Handbook on International and Comparative Trademark Law* (CUP, 2020).

4. For trademarks, *see*: *SA Cnl-Sucal NV v. Hag GF AG* (C-10/89) [1990] 3 CMLR 571, 582-583 (HAG II) (AG Francis Jacobs); *Arsenal Football Club v. Matthew Reed* (C-206/01) [2002] ECR I-10273, at [47]-[48]; and *Qualitex v. Jacobson* 514 US 159, 163-64 (1995). For GIs in the EU, *see*: *Commission v. Germany* (C-12/74) [1975] ECR 181 at para. 7, ('[T]hese appellations … must satisfy the objectives of such protection, in particular the need to ensure not only that the interests of the producers concerned are safeguarded against unfair competition, but also that consumers are protected against information which may mislead them.').

5. W.M. Landes & R.A. Posner 'Trademark Law: An Economic Perspective' (1987) 30 *J L & Econ* 265; N. Economides 'The Economics of Trademarks' (1988) *Trademark Rep* 523.

6. D. Rangnekar *The Socio-Economics of Geographical Indications: A Review of the Empirical Evidence from Europe* (UNCTA/ICTSD Issue Paper No. 4, May 2004), 13-16; C. Bramley, E. Biénabe, & J. Kirsten, 'The Economics of Geographical Indications: Towards a Conceptual Framework for Geographical Indication Research in Developing Countries'. In WIPO, *The Economics of Intellectual Property* (2009) 109; R. Teuber, 'Protecting Geographical Indications: Lessons Learned from the Economic Literature' in European Association of Agricultural Economists, *2011 International Congress, August 30-September 2, 2011, Zurich, Switzerland* (Paper No. 116081). However, as we will *see below*, historical debates addressing GI protection contain a persistent misappropriation prohibition seam. This does not sit comfortably with an origin information preservation model. Sui generis GI protection regimes grant broader protection, even when no consumers are confused, since they recognize the risk of free riding.

their functional similarity, instrumentalist theory accounts for the right to exclude in a congruent manner.

26.2.2 Similarities with Trademarks

Since GIs and trademarks share an apparent functional equivalence, countries such as the United States have persistently proposed that the former regime should be merged into the latter. GIs 'can be viewed as a subset of trademarks. [They] serve the same functions as trademarks, because like trademarks they are: (1) source-identifiers; (2) guarantees of quality; and (3) valuable business interests'.[7] The United States argues that 'both aim to prevent consumers from being misled or confused as to whether the goods they buy possess the anticipated qualities and characteristics'.[8] This correspondence has been appreciated by European courts as well. The Swiss Federal Court of Justice has observed that the 'function both of trademark protection and of protection for appellations of origin is to ensure the distinguishing function of the designation and to prevent mistaken attributions – whether regarding the manufacturer or the place of origin'.[9] Several countries have opted to protect GIs within the trademark system as certification marks or collective marks.[10] By implication, this suggests that issues arising out of the interaction between trademark law and human rights would map on to GIs as well. Two issues, in particular, are relevant here – GI rights as they implicate free speech interests and their accommodation within the right to property.

While the principal focus of this contribution is to consider the human rights implications for GIs as a sui generis regime, I shall briefly consider the extent to which the GI-trademark overlap is relevant. Regarding the nature of this interaction, Laurence Helfer has identified three trends:[11] (1) human rights language is co-opted to expand the scope of IP; (2) human rights law is an externally imposed limit upon the scope of IP protection; and (3) achieving human rights ends through IP means, where a desirable outcome

---

7. *See* USPTO 'Geographical Indication Protection in the United States' at <www.uspto.gov/web/offices/dcom/olia/globalip/pdf/gi_system.pdf> (last accessed 30 December 2019).

8. *EC – Protection of Trademarks and Geographical Indications for Agricultural Products and Foodstuffs* First Submission of the United States, 23 April 2004 (WT/DS174 and 290), para. 132.

9. *Anheuser-Busch Inc v. Budejovicky Budvar Narodni Podnik* [2001] *ETMR* 7 (Swiss FC) 82.

10. WTO *Review under Art. 24.2 of the Application of the Provisions of the Section of the TRIPS Agreement on Geographical Indications*, 24 November 2003 (IP/C/W/253/Rev.1), 13-14; WIPO, *Compilation of the Replies to Questionnaire I on the National and Regional Systems That Can Provide a Certain Protection to Geographical Indications*, 25 February 2019 (SCT/40/5), Annexe 13-18.

11. L.R. Helfer, 'Toward a Human Rights Framework for Intellectual Property' (2007) 40 *UC Davis L. Rev.* 971, 1014-1020.

(for example, improved public health) is furthered by an appropriately crafted IP regime. Although each of these trends is visible in the human rights-trademarks interface, the 'conflict or coexistence' polarization[12] is more prominent. Much of this concerns the impact of trademark rights upon the right to free speech and expression.[13] For instance, an aggressive assertion of trademark rights could inhibit parodic uses or stifle the signalling of competitive substitutability by other traders. The impact of GI protection on commercial speech is relatively unexplored, but could *inter alia* arise in the context of a generic status determination. If a state declares a formerly generic term to be a protected expression (such as parmesan for a type of cheese in several countries outside the EU), this will prohibit existing producers in that state from using the term, thereby placing limits on their commercial speech.[14] An entirely unexplored aspect is whether GIs, as expressive symbols, might themselves constitute a form of protected speech, thereby invoking the support of human rights law. It is increasingly recognized that trademarks are a form of speech – usually commercial speech – and this recharacterization would apply equally to GIs.[15]

Apart from speech-related concerns, there are human rights repercussions associated with the treatment of trademark rights as property.[16] GIs have been questionably categorized as 'private rights' akin to private property in the preamble to TRIPS,[17] and this taxonomic status has important repercussions in a 'takings' situation. The expropriation of a GI by state action could lead to demands for compensation for the loss of a proprietary interest. This argument was unsuccessfully rehearsed in the European Court

---

12. L.R. Helfer, 'Human Rights and Intellectual Property: Conflict or Coexistence?' (2003) 5 *Minn. Intell. Prop. Rev.* 47, 48-49.
13. *See* generally the contribution by Andreas Rahmatian 'Trade Marks and Human Rights' in Ch. 13 of the second edition of this volume. *See also* L.P. Ramsey, 'Reconciling Trade Mark Rights and Free Expression Locally and Globally' in D. Gervais (ed.), *International Intellectual Property: A Handbook of Contemporary Research* (Edward Elgar, 2015) 341; J. Schovsbo, 'Trademarks and Fundamental Rights in the EU' (2018) 8 *UC Irvine L. Rev.* 555.
14. Such a change of status might arguably be defensible if the limits are proportionate and supported by legitimate interests. *See* S. Damer, 'Not Confused? Don't Be Troubled: Meeting the First Amendment Attack on Protection of "Generic" Foreign Geographical Indications' (2009) 30 *Cardozo L. Rev.* 2257.
15. The US Supreme Court has confirmed that trademarks are constitutionally protected expression: *Matal v. Tam* 137 S. Ct. 1744 (2017).
16. The matter was considered by the European Court of Human Rights in *Anheuser-Busch, Inc. v. Portugal*, [2007] ETMR 24 (ECHR Grand Chamber).
17. Any determination of the property interest in GIs must be jurisdiction-specific. *See* V. Mantrov, *EU Law on Indications of Geographical Origin: Theory and Practice* (Springer, 2014) 67-76; D. Marie-Vivien, *The Protection of Geographical Indications in India: A New Perspective on the French and European Experience* (Sage Publications, 2015), Part III.

of Justice's (CJEU) *Tocai* decision.[18] An agreement between the Community and Hungary meant that the use of the Italian grape variety '*Tocai friulano*' would have to give way to the Hungarian appellation '*Tokaj*'. In the challenge to the Italian law which implemented this, a central issue was whether the law was inconsistent with the right of ownership protected by the ECHR and the Charter of Fundamental Rights of the EU. The assertion on behalf of Italian winemakers was that the right to use the denomination '*Tocai friulano*' was economic in nature and therefore equivalent to the object of property rights. While deciding that a grape varietal designation is not the same as a GI, the court nevertheless did consider this within the recognized category of 'incorporeal goods of economic value', and therefore, protectable as property. However, the deprivation was reasonable and not disproportionate. Italian wine could continue to be marketed using regional appellations and alternative names for the grape varietal.

As opposed to the GI being considered the object of property, the issue could also be approached from the opposite perspective, where a GI-related term is initially considered generic but then subsequently has regulatory restrictions imposed. Since it describes specific product characteristics to customers, it might be considered a part of the valuable commercial property of an undertaking in the form of goodwill. This argument was rehearsed when an association of German wine growers producing sparkling wine was deprived of the use of 'méthode champenoise' under EU wine regulations. This restriction was unsuccessfully challenged *inter alia* on the grounds that it 'adversely affect[ed] both [the association's] right to property and its right freely to pursue a trade or profession'.[19] The CJEU concluded that (a) the description was previously generic and open to all producers of sparkling wine, so it could not be the object of property rights, while (b) this labelling restriction did not jeopardize the very existence of the freedom to pursue a trade or profession, it was not disproportionate and corresponded to an objective of general interest pursued by the Community.

The references to rights engaging speech and property suggest that to the extent that GIs are functional isomorphs of trademarks, human rights law is engaged in equivalent ways. Yet of far greater interest is the potential for a normative human rights-based argument to sustain a sui generis GI protection regime and its transformation of the manner in which GIs have been historically conceptualized thus far.

---

18. '*Regione autonoma Friuli-Venezia Giulia v. Ministero delle Politiche Agricole e Forestali*' (C-347/03) [2005] ECR I-3785.
19. *SMW Winzersekt GmbH v. Land Rheinland-Pfalz* [1994] ECR I-05555 at para. 20.

26.2.3   Differences in Scope

At the risk of oversimplifying, the history of international GI protection can be depicted as a sequence of episodic attempts to break away from the limitations of a misrepresentation prevention regime of protection. The core rule for over a century has been a prohibition on misleading indications of origin (or quality associated with origin). This requires claimants to establish that consumers in the jurisdiction of the dispute have been misled into buying the defendant's product. Prior to TRIPS, three multilateral agreements administered by the World Intellectual Property Organization (WIPO) addressed the protection of GIs. These not only set the parameters for subsequent negotiations but also introduced two very different definitional visions – the Indication of Source (IS), corresponding to a minimalist account of protection and the Appellation of Origin (AO), which generates a more elaborate, registration-based architecture. The Paris Convention for the Protection of Industrial Property of 1883[20] introduces both in its description of industrial property[21] but regulates only the former. WIPO's suggested definition for the IS is an 'expression or sign used to indicate that a product or service originates in a country, region or specified place'.[22] Article 10 of the Paris Convention prohibits the use of signs which are false indications of source, through border measures such as seizure by customs authorities to prevent the movement of goods which are falsely labelled. By the end of the nineteenth century, the limitations of protection premised on the communicative content of the sign became painfully obvious to those seeking to protect reputed indications of source. If the test for infringement is consumer confusion or deception, it cannot apply where the sign in question becomes generic (as Champagne is in the United States), where the relevant public is unfamiliar with the product (such as traditional Bangladeshi textiles replicated externally and sold on the Australian market) or the use of the sign is qualified to avoid deception as to origin or quality ('Swiss Champagne' or 'Roquefort style cheese'). The AO subsequently emerges as a response to the limitations of a truth-telling model, with its restricted consumer protection rationale.

The Madrid Agreement for the Repression of False or Deceptive Indications of Source on Goods of 1891[23] marks the transition from the IS to

---

20. The Paris Convention for the Protection of Industrial Property, 20 March 1883 as revised at Stockholm on 14 July 1967, 828 UNTS 305 (1972). (Hereinafter, the 'Paris Convention'). Also at <www.wipo.int/treaties/on/ip/paris>, (last accessed 30 December 2019).
21. *See* Article 1(2).
22. In section 1 of the WIPO *Model Law for Developing Countries on Appellations of Origin and Indications of Source.*
23. Madrid Agreement for the Repression of False or Deceptive Indications of Source on Goods 14 April 1891, 828 UNTS 389 (Hereinafter, the 'Madrid Agreement'). Also at <www.wipo.org/treaties/en/ip/mmopecd/>, (last accessed 30 December 2019).

the AO. While marginally extending the scope of protection for the IS,[24] it more significantly afforded higher levels of protection for products of the vine.[25] Finally, the Lisbon Agreement for the Protection of Appellations of Origin of 1958[26] established an international registration system for AOs.[27] The AO is defined in Article 2(1) as [T]he geographical name of a country, region or locality, which serves to designate a product originating therein, the quality and characteristics of which are due exclusively or essentially to the geographical environment, including natural and human factors.

Both the Madrid and Lisbon Agreements introduce the notion of a link between the qualities of the product and its geographical environment, including both natural and human influences, which is what sets apart GIs as the objects of a discrete IP regime. Building on this distinctive anchor to place, Article 3 of Lisbon (1958) (now Article 11 of the Geneva Act (2015)) sets out robust exclusionary standards of protection by doing away with a 'false or misleading use' requirement and preventing misappropriation of goodwill even in the absence of consumer confusion:

> *Protection shall be ensured against any usurpation or imitation, even if the true origin of the product is indicated or if the appellation is used in translated form or accompanied by terms such as 'kind', 'type', 'make', 'imitation', or the like.*

The legal assumptions underpinning such *sui generis* protection have historically been informed by French experiences with viticultural regulation. Rules have accreted around the influential notion of *terroir*, with products of the vine as the archetypal subject matter for GI protection.[28] *Terroir* is a key ingredient in differentiating between wines by reference to a distinct origin. It causally influences the quality and in so doing, shapes the reputation of the wine. In its more geographically deterministic iteration, this concept suggests that the human and physical geography of a discrete region

---

24. Article 1(1) of Madrid states that: 'All goods bearing a false or deceptive indication by which one of the countries to which this Agreement applies, or a place situated therein, is directly or indirectly indicated as being the country or place of origin shall be seized on importation into any of the said countries'.
25. The hard-earned innovation is found in Article 4, which effectively states that products of the vine may not become generic.
26. Lisbon Agreement for the Protection of Appellations of Origin and their International Registration 31 October 1958, 923 UNTS 205 (Hereinafter, the 'Lisbon Agreement'). Also at <www.wipo.in/treaties/en/registration/lisbon/>, (last accessed 30 December 2019). The Lisbon Agreement has been extensively revised in 2015, when a WIPO Diplomatic Conference adopted the 'Geneva Act of the Lisbon Agreement on Appellations of Origin and Geographical Indications' (LID/DC/19) 20 May 2015.
27. The register can be searched at: <www.wipo.int/ipdl/en/search/lisbon/search-struct.jsp>.
28. *See* A. Stanziani, 'Wine Reputation and Quality Controls: The Origin of the AOCs in 19th Century France' (2004) 18 *Eur. J. L. & Econ.* 149; E. Barham, '"Translating *Terroir*" Revisited: The Global Challenge of French AOC Labeling', in D. Gangjee (ed), *Research Handbook on Intellectual Property and Geographical Indications* (Edward Elgar, 2016) 57.

shapes a product's qualities, making it impossible to faithfully replicate the product elsewhere. This view also finds traction with courts on occasion:

> *The two features of Champagne of prime importance for its uniqueness are the soil and climate in which the grapes are grown, and the method of manufacture by skilled personnel. The first of those elements cannot be exactly duplicated anywhere in the world, but the second can. It apparently is generally recognised among wine experts that the precise geographical location (i.e. soil and climate) for the growing of a vine is the outstanding, unchanging factor which governs the final product. Hence the predominance of place names for appellations.*[29]

and:

> *The region in which the Champagne vineyards are found is about one hundred miles east of Paris around Reims and É pernay, where there is a chalky, flinty soil and the climate is subject to extreme variations of heat and cold. It appears that these factors give to the wine its particular qualities.*[30]

According to this logic, if geographically deterministic *terroir* holds true, referring to an external product by the original's name is, therefore, a wrongful act. This is because it either misleads consumers into believing the original and replica are substitutable (i.e., based on its signalling effect on consumers) or because the external producer has illegitimately misappropriated the name, knowing that her product does not share the same history and qualities (i.e., based on producer conduct).

The contested essence of this unique link argument is summarized in a League of Nations Report as early as 1922:

> [It is argued that] some products of the vine derive their special qualities from the peculiar characteristics of the soil or climate of one particular district, and are therefore inherently incapable of being produced of the same quality elsewhere. So far as this is really true, the particular district in which they are produced may be said to have an absolute natural monopoly of their production, and it would seem that any geographical appellation in their title can never be employed properly in a 'generic' sense as the result of use or custom. Unfortunately, there is not always general agreement either as to the fact of the regional monopoly or as to the limits of the area possessing such monopoly. There is a natural tendency to exaggerate the view that the special qualities of a wine are in reality a 'regional' monopoly, and in many cases there has been keen

---

29. '*Comite Interprofessionnel du Vin de Champagne v. Wineworths Group Ltd*' [1991] 2 *NZLR* 432 at para. 10 (Wellington HC).
30. '*J Bollinger v. Costa Brava Wine Co Ltd*' [1961] 1 *All ER* 561, 563 (Ch. D) (J. Danckwerts).

dispute as to the limits of the area (if it exists) which is alone capable of producing a speciality.[31]

The legacy of these competing visions helps explain the apparent incongruity in TRIPS today. The agreement contains a single definition for GIs in Article 22.1, but two distinct levels of protection. Under Article 22, the scope of protection consists of the following three components:

- protection against uses of indications that mislead the public[32] or are false despite being literally true;[33]
- protection against uses of indications where this amounts to acts of unfair competition;[34] and
- refusal or invalidation of trademarks that contain or consist of indications, where they may mislead the public.[35]

This clutch of substantive rules seeks to preserve the integrity of consumer information by preventing misleading use, while also protecting producer goodwill and thereby enabling product differentiation in the marketplace. By contrast, protection for wines and spirits is significantly stronger and is referred to as 'absolute' protection. There are three commitments involved here:

- Members shall provide the legal means for interested parties to prevent the use of GIs for wines and spirits on such products when they do not originate in the designated place, 'even where the true origin of the goods is indicated or the [GI] is used in translation or accompanied by expressions such as "kind", "type", "style", "imitation" or the like'.[36]
- Trademarks which contain or consist of such GIs shall be refused or invalidated for wines and spirits which do not have this origin.[37]
- Coexistence in the case of homonymous indications for wines and spirits, provided misleading uses are controlled for.[38]

What remains conspicuously absent is any legislative or doctrinal explanation addressing the existence of these two levels. This explanatory gap continues to obstruct progress for those who propose that Article 23 standards should be applied beyond the restrictive confines of wines and spirits to all products.

---

31. Report on Unfair Competition, Particularly in Relation to False Marks and Indications [1922] League of Nations Official Journal 625, 630.
32. Article 22.2(a).
33. Article 22.4.
34. Article 22.2(b).
35. Article 22.3.
36. Article 23.1.
37. Article 23.2.
38. Article 23.3.

If GIs are to be protected against any references on similar goods even in the absence of consumer confusion or deception, there are limitations on the ability of physically deterministic *terroir* to justify such absolute protection. There is no disputing the importance of geographical origin for certain products such as wines, mineral water or even fruits and vegetables. However, the range of products covered by national or even international GI regimes extends to traditional crafts, textiles and jewellery, where human skills are of far greater significance. Thus, the majority of registrations pending before India's national GI Registry consist of traditional crafts and textile products,[39] while the international Lisbon register includes '*Olinalá*' for handcrafted wooden objects, '*Jablonec*' (or '*Gablonz*') for utility and decorative glassware, and '*Kraslické Krajky*' for embroidery and lace goods.[40] Such products are of greater relevance to many of the developing countries lobbying for greater GI protection as the human skills dimension gains in importance. This shift in emphasis, from natural to human factors and a broader range of products being covered, is what creates the space for a cultural heritage argument.

26.3   GIs AND CULTURAL RIGHTS?

This section explores the potential affinity between GI protection and cultural rights by considering whether cultural heritage may act as a bridging concept.[41] Whereas the previous sections have explored similarities between GIs and trademarks as well as the consequent human rights implications, the potential involvement of cultural rights is what sets GIs apart. There are a growing number of references to cultural heritage as one of the reasons advanced for GI protection. In the context of justifying a broad scope of protection preventing any evocation, or calling to mind, of a protected GI, Advocate General Pitruzella observed:

> [The] protection of such designations not only constitutes part of the strategy of the European Union economy, as expressly stated in the first recital of Regulation No 1151/2012, but also forms part of the objective

---

39. These product specifications are available in the Indian Geographical Indications Journal. For further details on the registry, *see* <www.patentoffice.nic.in>, (last accessed 30 December 2019). For specific illustrations *see* N.S. Gopalakrishnan, et al., *Exploring the Relationship Between Geo graphical Indication and Traditiional Knowledge* (ICTSD Working Paper, August 2007); N. Lalitha & S. Vinayan, *Regional Products and Rural Livelihoods: A Study on Geographical Indications from India* (OUP, 2019).
40. *See* respectively Lisbon Registration Nos 732, 66 and 22.
41. This section is based on a more detailed study in D. Gangjee, 'Geographical Indications and Cultural Rights: The Intangible Cultural Heritage Connection' in C. Geiger (ed.), *Research Handbook on Human Rights and Intellectual Property* (Edward Elgar, 2015) 544.

of safeguarding European cultural heritage, as referred to in Article 3(3), fourth subparagraph, of the EU Treaty.[42]

At the World Trade Organisation (WTO), Switzerland has observed that (in contrast to private trademarks rights) GIs 'form part of the national, cantonal or communal heritage'.[43] In the same forum, the Representative from Thailand supported extending GI protection since 'GIs were often related to culture and ancestors' traditional knowledge'.[44] Whilst introducing its sui generis GI legislation, India's position was that a GI 'is considered under the Act to be the property or heritage of all the persons engaged in the activity of creating [such] products'.[45] Cultural heritage references also appear frequently in recent scholarship on GIs.[46] Since an established justificatory account already exists for some degree of exclusive protection based on informational efficiency (section 26.2.1 above), it is worth asking why the cultural heritage basis becomes possible or necessary in international GI protection debates. In previous research, I have explored three overlapping lines of enquiry that unpack the heritage rationale:[47] (1) Since GI protection was historically associated with agricultural products, where natural conditions such as soil and climate play an important role, how was the space created for a cultural heritage argument? (2) As a practical matter, how are aspects of cultural heritage incorporated within GI protection regimes? and (3) What additional justificatory work does this heritage rationale do, to supplement the information efficiency rationale described above? What follows is a brief recapitulation of the first two issues, which clarifies the incorporation of the cultural heritage component, as the basis for any subsequent cultural rights-based claims. This section will first explain how space was created for a cultural heritage argument within GI regimes. It will then consider the potential to align GI protection with cultural rights.

---

42. C-614/17 *Fundación Consejo Regulador de la Denominación de Origen Protegida Queso Manchego v. Industrial Quesera Cuquerella SL*, 10 January 2019, ECLI:EU:C:2019:11, at para. 20 (AG Pitruzella).

43. *Review under Art. 24.2 – Switzerland's Response to the Checklist*, 16 February 1999 (IP/C/W/ 117/Add.13) 10 at footnote 11.

44. *TRIPS Council Special Session on GI Extension*, November and December 2002 (IP/C/M/38) at para. 180.

45. *See* the response to Q.13 in *Review of Legislation – India*, 8 October 2003 (IP/Q/IND/1).

46. R. Chesmond, 'Protection or Privatisation of Culture? The Cultural Dimension of the International Intellectual Property Debate on Geographical Indications of Origin' (2007) *EIPR* 379; R.J. Coombe, S. Schnoor & M. Ahmed, 'Bearing Cultural Distinction: Informational Capitalism and New Expectations for Intellectual Property' (2007) 40 *UC Davis L. Rev.* 891; T.W. Dagne, *Intellectual Property and Traditional Knowledge in the Global Economy: Translating Geographical Indications for Development* (Routledge, 2014) 20 ('Many conceptualize GIs as "publicly-oriented" rights that have particular relevance for preserving cultural heritage and conserving agricultural systems for multiple benefits').

47. D. Gangjee 'Geographical Indications and Cultural Heritage' (2012) 4 *WIPO J.* 92; D. Gangjee, *Relocating the Law of Geographical Indications* (CUP, 2012) 77-126.

26.3.1   THE SPACE FOR A CULTURAL HERITAGE ARGUMENT

As the paradigmatic example of wine suggests, GI products have historically been conceived of in 'natural' terms. Therefore, under what conditions did 'cultural' aspects begin to be recognized? A response can be usefully developed by analysing transformations in the legal regulation of wine appellations in France across the nineteenth and twentieth centuries since this regime has proved enormously influential over time. Early attempts to regulate false labelling of French wines were premised on ensuring the veracity of the place of origin. The initial *Appellation d'Origine* system developed around a notion of *terroir* that privileged physical geography – geological and climatic factors. It was thought that quality could be guaranteed and fraud prevented by merely ensuring that wines actually originated from the places indicated on their labels since physical place (immovable and locally unique 'nature') was responsible for producing the grapes that led to this quality. However, the very act of delineating such distinctive parcels of place proved economically, politically and even scientifically divisive, while the impact of human factors and production techniques on end quality came to be increasingly appreciated. Therefore, the importance of locally specific *savoir faire*, including both technical and cultural components, came into focus. Technologies and associated cultures of production – usually designed around the particularities of local conditions and capabilities – took their place alongside natural factors in the *Appellation d'Origine Contrôlée* regime which followed.[48] This called for a series of recalibrations in the articulation of the link between product, people and place, as *terroir* was broadened out.[49] One important consequence of recognizing the human dimension was the expansion of subject matter, whereby GI regimes could accommodate recipe-based products (e.g., charcuterie, cakes and pies)[50] or even textiles and crafts.[51]

All these products are conventionally understood as having cultural heritage dimensions. As far as symbolic representation goes, it is acknowledged within the legal literature that local products can be emblematic of

---

48. The matter is debated in: B. Parry, 'Geographical Indications: Not All Champagne and Roses' and D. Gangjee '(Re)Locating Geographical Indications: A Response to Bronwyn Parry' in L. Bently, J.C. Ginsburg and J. Davis (eds), *Trade Marks and Brands: An Interdisciplinary Critique* (Cambridge University Press, 2008) 361, 381.
49. Several contributions on the theme of 'Rethinking *Terroir*' can be found in R.E. Black & R.E. Ulin (eds), *Wine and Culture: Vineyard to Glass* (Bloomsbury, 2013).
50. D. Gangjee, 'Melton Mowbray and the GI Pie in the Sky: Exploring Cartographies of Protection' (2006) *Intell. Prop. Q.* 291.
51. D. Marie-Vivien, 'The Protection of Geographical Indications for Handicrafts or How to Apply the Concepts of Natural and Human Factors to All Products' (2013) 4 *WIPO J.* 191.

regions or even countries of origin.[52] This tracks the approach found within the anthropological study of food as a symbolic system, which is a well-developed field of research.[53] For instance, *rituals of consumption* (and conversely, taboos) have been well documented where a ritual meal binds people to their faith or reaffirms their relationship with other members of the same group. Additionally, *eating may be intimately linked to identity* where food serves to consolidate group membership as well as distinguish between groups. Food and drink therefore tangibly reinforces regional, ethnic or national identities. To the extent that traditional GI products (often quite literally) feed into regional or national identity formation, they are the symbolic raw material. However, critics such as Tomer Broude stress that when identity reinforcement projects draw on the tradition for legitimacy, the risk of mythmaking and associated exclusion of groups or practices is ever-present.[54] Amongst the most illuminating studies are those of Champagne and Camembert,[55] both as distinctive markers of national identity and as 'invented traditions'.[56] Despite this, an awareness of their emergence as social constructs does not detract from their potency as cultural symbols. Our collective socio-economic existence depends on social constructs, with money being a prominent example of a shared agreement to regard it as valuable.

With an increasing awareness of such social conventions, GIs came to be seen as having a cultural component. But to what extent can the operational architecture of GI protection respond to heritage recognition concerns? Protected GI status certainly helps at the symbolic or representational level, as described above, by granting exclusive rights to Ethiopian coffee or Darjeeling tea and reinforcing their status as 'national champions'. Where the symbols representing products – geographical names or logos – have cultural resonance, protecting these signs against misuse is helpful. Therefore WIPO recognizes the potential for 'the positive protection by

---

52. F. Addor & A. Grazioli, 'Geographical Indications Beyond Wines and Spirits: A Roadmap for a Better Protection for Geographical Indications in the WTO/TRIPS Agreement' (2002) 5 *J. World Intell. Prop.* 865, 865 (GIs 'convey the cultural identity of a nation, region or specific area').

53. An excellent review is provided by Sidney W. Mintz & Christine M. Du Bois, 'The Anthropology of Food and Eating' (2002) 31 *Ann. Rev. Anthropology* 99.

54. T. Broude, 'Taking "Trade and Culture" Seriously: Geographical Indications and Cultural Protection in WTO Law' (2005) 26 *U. Pa. J. Int'l Econ. L.* 623.

55. K.M. Guy, *When Champagne Became French: Wine and the Making of a National Identity* (Johns Hopkins University Press, 2003); P. Boisard, *Camembert: A National Myth* (University of California Press, 2003).

56. The standard reference point is E. Hobsbawm and T. Ranger (eds), *The Invention of Tradition* (Cambridge University Press, 1983) 1 ('"Invented tradition" is taken to mean a set of practices, normally governed by overtly or tacitly accepted rules and of a ritual or symbolic nature, which seek to inculcate certain values and norms of behaviour by repetition, which automatically implies continuity with the past').

communities of indigenous names, words and symbols as trademarks, certification and collective marks, and geographical indications'.[57]

However, GIs are not the obvious tool of choice for protecting *the content* of a cultural practice or the resulting product – e.g., the techniques for carving a wooden toy or the sparkling wine that results from double fermentation. The scope of protection under GI regimes is restricted to preventing the misuse of the geographical name of a region or an associated image, such as the ducal crown of Parma Ham or the female leaf picker's stylized profile for Darjeeling.[58] While Champagne is a protected designation, the *méthode champenoise* can be adopted by those outside the region to produce their own versions of sparkling wine. To that extent, GI protection is more akin to trademarks, than trade secrets, patent or copyright. Therefore, it is helpful to think of GI protection as a mechanism for indirectly, yet meaningfully, sustaining certain cultural practices. Legal recognition as a GI helps with place branding campaigns and if this is successful, domestic or international markets reward the producer collective. But beyond the branding and representational aspects, how else can GI protection be relevant?

As seen above, much of the interest in GIs as cultural vectors has emphasized their symbolic and commercial value, associated with the *consumption* of regional products. Yet, the procedure for formal recognition as a GI has a potentially more significant impact when identifying collectively developed *production practices*. Most contemporary GI systems are registration-based and require a product specification, also referred to as a code of practice or *cahier des charges*. This contains details such as the product's name, a product description including distinctive chemical or organoleptic characteristics, delimitation of the production area, officially prescribed raw materials and production techniques, as well as labelling and inspection requirements.[59] The product specification, therefore, becomes an important site where heritage is identified and negotiated. According to one view, the cultural significance of this process is evident at an early stage, when producer groups begin to collectively engage with the drafting of a product specification. The collective interest in the origin-linked product potentially strengthens social linkages between local actors during this process, while the promotion of an origin-linked product increases self-esteem among local actors as their identity and related way of life is

---

57. WIPO, *The Protection of Traditional Cultural Expressions: Updated Draft Gap Analysis* 9 April 2019 (WIPO/GRTKF/IC/40/8), Annex I, at para. 58.
58. *See* respectively http://www.prosciuttodiparma.com/en_UK/ and the successful Darjeeling registration application filed before the Indian Geographical Indications Registry, as published in the *Geographical Indications Journal* (1 July 2004) Vol. 1, at: http://ipindia.nic.in/girindia/.
59. For details, *see* FAO and SINER-GI, *Linking People, Places and Products: A Guide for Promoting Quality Linked to Geographical Origin and Sustainable Geographical Indications* 2nd edn (FAO, 2009-2010) 49-92.

recognized and valorized.[60] While such negotiations can develop or sustain networks of collaboration and build social capital within a region, the drafting process could also produce the exact opposite result, leading to divergences and dissent.[61] In terms of the content of the specification, the interaction between biodiversity conservation and (cultural) production techniques has been noted. A GI scheme can 'also help protecting important elements of local cultural heritage, for instance traditional production methods and recipes, endangered animal breeds, or indigenous vegetables'.[62] As Berard and Marchenay have noted, local 'breeds, plant varieties, landscapes and microbial ecosystems are all expressions of collective skills, practices and adaptations. These may vary with the type of production, which in turn depends on the social and environmental context'.[63] They refer to the chestnut groves of Ardèche in France, where chestnut production 'grew to be the defining factor in community life and cultural heritage. The sheer extent and density of the Ardèche chestnut groves shaped the landscape, testifying to a culture, civilization and local production system that were inseparable from this particular terroir'.[64] Interdisciplinary scholarship recognizes the collective, intergenerational transmission processes associated with successful GIs, concluding that 'a GI product is the outcome of the traditions and know-how of many people in the zone over a long period of time. It is tied to a community and has a heritage dimension'.[65]

Various cultural norms are associated not only with production practices but also with the oral traditions surrounding a local product. These norms can function to signal demarcations between social groups or help integrate the product with social occasions.[66] Regional specialities and well-known products can additionally act as the focal points for fairs, festivals and other cultural events which are used to promote a region's distinct identity.[67] These initiatives can be synchronized with general tourism promotion strategies which showcase local heritage.[68] By formally recognizing certain agricultural practices – for instance, free-range animals requiring open spaces or

---

60. *Ibid.*, 23.
61. London Economics et al., *Evaluation of the CAP Policy on Protected Designations of Origin (PDO) and Protected Geographical Indications (PGI)* – (Final Report for the European Commission, November 2008) 245.
62. *Ibid.*, 245-246.
63. L. Berard & P. Marchenay, *From Localized Products to Geographical Indications: Awareness and Action* (CNRS, Bourg-en-Bresse, 2008) 54.
64. *Ibid.*, 38.
65. A. Lecoent, E. Vandecandelaere & J.-J. Cadilhon, *Quality Linked to Geographical Origin and Geographical Indications – Lessons Learned from Six Case Studies in Asia* (FAO RAP Publication, 2010/04) 181.
66. *See* Ch. 3 of D. Rangnekar *Geographical Indications and Localisation: A Case Study of Feni* (ESRC Report 2009).
67. London Economics et al., *Evaluation of the CAP Policy* (n. 61), 246-251.
68. J. Suh & A. MacPherson, 'The Impact of Geographical Indication on the Revitalisation of a Regional Economy: A Case Study of "Boseong" Green Tea' (2007) 39 *Area* 518.

systems of terraced cultivation – GI specifications could help sustain traditional landscapes, experienced as libraries of local history as well as living laboratories for experimentation.[69] Therefore, heritage dimensions can be acknowledged at several stages within the GI protection process. Nevertheless, it is worth emphasizing that a product specification only *potentially* accommodates cultural practices – the choice is left to the various actors involved with the production process for any given product. The formal availability of GI registration does not ensure the incorporation of heritage elements. This will ultimately depend on how the system is used. To facilitate more effective product specification drafting, attempts are under-way to share best practices and document successful case studies, where the drafting process has been responsive to collective action dynamics, demands for the equitable distribution of economic benefits and heritage concerns.[70] It is hoped that this empirically informed, inductive and 'bottom-up' approach will help deliver tangible benefits. Thus, heritage is relevant both at the level of symbolic significance, where GIs operate as cultural resources for identity formation and within the drafting of the GI product specification when traditional modes of production are stabilized and sustained.

26.3.2   THE LIMITATIONS OF CULTURAL RIGHTS

While cultural rights are a clearly established category in international human rights law, understanding their precise relationship with cultural heritage remains a work in progress. Heritage, therefore, may not be up to the task of acting as a bridging concept, in order to integrate GI protection initiatives within a cultural rights framework. Cultural rights – used here, in the narrow sense[71] – emerged as part of the so-called second generation of human rights and include the right to take part in cultural life; the right to enjoy the benefits of the arts and scientific progress; the right to benefit from

---

69. I.B. Thompson, 'The Role of Artisan Technology and Indigenous Knowledge Transfer in the Survival of a Classic Cultural Landscape: The *Marais Salants* of Guérande, Loire-Atlantique, France' (1999) 25 *J. Hist. Geography* 216. R.L. Barsh, 'How Do You Patent a Landscape? The Perils of Dichotomizing Cultural and Intellectual Property' (1999) 8 *Int'l J. Cultural Prop.* 14.
70. For e.g., C. Bramley, E. Biénabe & J. Kirsten (eds), *Developing Geographical Indications in the South: The Southern African Experience* (Springer, 2013); FAO and SINER-GI, *Linking People, Places and Products* (n. 59); E. Barham & B. Sylvander, (eds) *Labels of Origin for Food* (CABI, 2011) 157-195.
71. In the broad sense, they include rights which could incidentally or directly relate to culture, such as the right to life, including private life; freedom of thought, conscience and religion; freedom of expression; freedom of association; the right to education and so on. *See* F. MacKay, 'Cultural Rights', in M.E. Salomon (ed.) *Economic, Social and Cultural Rights: A Guide for Minorities and Indigenous Peoples* (Minority Rights Group International, 2005) 83: 83.

one's creative (authorial) works; and the right to enjoy the measure of freedom which is indispensable for scientific research and creative activity.[72]

Commentary on cultural rights usually commences with the Universal Declaration of Human Rights 1948 (UDHR)[73] and Article 27 in particular:[74]

(1) Everyone has the right freely to participate in the cultural life of the community, to enjoy the arts and to share in scientific advancement and its benefits.

(2) Everyone has the right to the protection of the moral and material interests resulting from any scientific, literary or artistic production of which he is the author.

These commitments are re-emphasized in Article 15 of the International Covenant on Economic, Social, and Cultural Rights 1966 (ICESCR) and Article 27 of the International Covenant on Civil and Political Rights 1966 (ICCPR).

Despite their decades-long existence, cultural rights – in the narrow sense – have been relatively neglected,[75] while they continue to be controversial. Yupsanis accounts for their relative neglect by contrasting them with the categories of civil, political, economic and social rights, which were prioritized within an ideological context framed by Cold War exigencies. This resulted in a weak political commitment to enforce such rights.[76] They are also controversial primarily for three reasons. First, if the international human rights project is premised on universalist normative foundations, cultural rights emphasize the dissimilarities and distinctive features of groups, which generates normative tension. 'Universalism asserts that every human being has certain human rights by virtue of being human … human rights are inalienable and meant to protect human dignity and all persons should equally enjoy them … The relativist position reflects the empirical fact that there is an immense cultural diversity in the world, including diverse views about right and wrong. Cultural relativism, accordingly, claims that there are no universal human values and that the variety of cultures implies that human rights can, and may, be interpreted differently'.[77] A relativistic approach is also premised on the ability to identify individuals as members of a clearly defined group, as a received category, in an

---

72. A. Yupsanis, 'The Concept and Categories of Cultural Rights in International Law – Their Broad Sense and the Relevant Clauses of the International Human Rights Treaties' (2010) 37 *Syracuse J. Int'l L. & Com.* 207, 219.
73. G.A. Res. 217A (III), U.N. Doc A/810 at 71 (1948).
74. UDHR Articles 22 (an obligation for States to realize economic, social and cultural rights) and 29 (limitations) are also relevant.
75. J. Symonides, 'Cultural Rights: A Neglected Category of Human Rights', (1998) 158 *Int'l Social Sci. J.* 595.
76. Yupsanis (n. 72) 207-209.
77. Y. Donders, 'Do Cultural Diversity and Human Rights Make a Good Match?' (2010) *Int'l Social Sci. J.* 15, 16.

essentializing manner. Second, there is concern that the recognition of indigenous and minority cultural identities could lead to tensions within national polities, including separatism, tribalism or ethnonationalism.[78] Third, much turns upon the particular notion of culture which informs cultural rights. This has cycled through various iterations in recent decades.

Yupsanis identifies three distinct approaches to culture in international legal instruments.[79] In the first case, culture is perceived in material terms, as the accumulated heritage of humanity as a whole or of particular groups. Here, cultural rights would mandate equal access to this cultural capital. In the second case, it refers to the processes of scientific and artistic creativity, whereby individuals create culture. Cultural rights should, therefore, enable both the freedom to create and the freedom to access the resulting creations. Historically, culture was restricted to 'high art' under this approach. The third approach is aligned with an anthropological perspective and views culture as emergent and relational; as the sum of material and intellectual activities and practices of a group that distinguishes them from other groups. The preamble to the UNESCO Universal Declaration on Cultural Diversity 2001[80] adopts this approach, when it reaffirms that 'culture should be regarded as the set of distinctive spiritual, material, intellectual and emotional features of society or a social group, and that it encompasses, in addition to art and literature, lifestyles, ways of living together, value systems, traditions and beliefs'. Such an approach liberates culture from dependence on material objects and acknowledges practices as well as symbolic systems. This conception of culture, in turn, allows for a related notion of cultural heritage which is dynamic.

Even this limited précis suggests that cultural rights are relatively underdeveloped. Yet despite the relative neglect, potential conflict with universalist commitments and definitional ambiguities, cultural rights have experienced a resurgence as the pace of globalization, with its homogenizing tendencies, intensifies and cultural diversity is correspondingly valued.[81] Of particular interest are recent attempts to situate cultural heritage protection within a human rights paradigm. Cultural heritage is seen both as a problem for human rights and as having certain synergies with human rights goals. As Janet Blake, an experienced commentator summarizes it:

> There are obviously several elements and characteristics of cultural heritage that have strong human rights dimensions (negative as well as positive), in particular its role in cultural identity formation and affirmation, its relationship to the tricky notion of cultural diversity, the

---

78. Yupsanis (n. 72) 225-226.
79. *Ibid.,* 212.
80. (2002) 41 ILM 57.
81. W. Logan, M. Langfield & M.N. Craith, 'Ch 1: Intersecting Concepts and Practices' in William Logan, Michele Langfield and Máiréad Nic Craith (eds), *Cultural Diversity and Human Rights: Intersections in Theory and Practice* (Routledge, 2010) 4.

problem of cultural traditions or practices that contravene human rights standards, and the potential of heritage to exclude and serve as the vehicle for expressing social and political tensions.[82]

The following description emphasizes its political and ideological dimensions as well as its functional significance in group identity formation:

> Implying certain relationships between history, memory and identity ... heritage is a set of present day ideas and practices referring to and utilizing the past. As such, it has come to be valued as a versatile medium of social, cultural and political recognition, as underpinning claims for rights, as well as a potential source of cultural exchange and economic and touristic development ... Heritage is a term of the present and works by mobilizing selected pasts and histories in the service of present-day agendas and interests.[83]

Heritage is problematic for its relativistic as opposed to universalist orientation, as described above. Since 'individuals belong to cultural groups, there is the potential for a collision between the desire for cultural self-determination by one group and the claim of universal human rights principles on the part of different and competing groups or the overarching nation-state'.[84] This raises the possibility that the cultural rights of the group may conflict with the other human rights of individual members of that cultural group (e.g., where certain traditional practices discriminate against women or cause harm to children).[85] On the positive side of the ledger, heritage informs cultural identity, which in turn underpins human dignity. To take one example, UNESCO's Declaration Concerning the Intentional Destruction of Cultural Heritage 2003 states in its preamble that, with reference to monuments, 'cultural heritage is an important component of the cultural identity of communities, groups and individuals, and or social cohesion, so that its intentional destruction may have adverse consequences on human dignity and human rights'.[86] As Ziegler puts it, '[c]ultural identity is part of an individual's personality and therefore, has a close relationship with, and is an element of an emerging right to human dignity ... The partly shared rationale of cultural heritage protection and human rights might lead

---

82. J. Blake, 'Taking a Human Rights Approach to Cultural Heritage Protection' (2011) 4(2) *Heritage & Soc'y* 199, 199.
83. M. Daugbjerg & T. Fibiger 'Introduction: Heritage Gone Global. Investigating the Production and Problematics of Globalized Pasts' (2011) 22 *Hist. & Anthropology* 135, 135-136.
84. H. Silverman & D. Fairchild Ruggles, 'Ch 1: Cultural Heritage and Human Rights', in H. Silverman & D. Fairchild Ruggles (eds), *Cultural Heritage and Hum. Rts.* (Springer, 2007) 3, 4.
85. F. Francioni, 'Culture, Heritage and Human Rights: An Introduction' in F. Francioni & M. Scheinin (eds), *Cultural Human Rights* (Martinus Nijhoff, 2008) 1, 3-6.
86. Adopted by the 32nd session of the UNESCO General Conference, Paris, 17 October 2003.

to an alignment of cultural heritage with human rights, which might help raising cultural heritage to the level of subjective rights to cultural heritage'.[87] Protecting cultural heritage also facilitates the advancement of cultural diversity[88] as well as being a prerequisite for notions of development based on the freedom to participate in the cultural life of a community,[89] or development enabled by ensuring sustainable livelihoods.[90] The diversity aspect is reflected in Article 5 of the UNESCO Universal Declaration on Cultural Diversity 2001:[91] 'Cultural rights are an integral part of human rights, which are universal, indivisible and interdependent. The flourishing of creative diversity requires the full implementation of cultural rights [...]'. Ultimately, this suggests that while cultural heritage values may overlap with foundational values such as dignity and diversity associated with human rights, the detail is yet to be worked out. At present, there is limited scope for channelling cultural heritage claims through legally enforceable cultural rights.

26.3.3   INTANGIBLE CULTURAL HERITAGE AND GIS

A promising line of research in recent years has begun to explore the synergies between GI protection and the formal recognition of intangible cultural heritage (ICH).[92] This trend has been assisted by the increasing interest in protecting non-agricultural products such as crafts and textiles within sui generis GI regimes.[93] For example, Brazilian researchers identified the strategic potential for GI protection for the clay pots of Goiabeiras, from

---

87. K. Ziegler 'Cultural Heritage and Human Rights' (Oxford Legal Studies Research Paper Series; No. 26/2007) 12.
88. J. Blake 'On Defining the Cultural Heritage' (2000) 49 *Int'l & Comp. L. Q.* 61 (Artefacts associated with heritage both represent a community and are the means by which culture is transmitted across time, thereby helping to recreate the community).
89. M. Sunder, 'Intellectual Property and Development as Freedom' in N. W. Netanel, *The Development Agenda: Global Intellectual Property and Developing Countries* (Oxford University Press, 2009) 453.
90. T. Kono (ed.), *Intangible Cultural Heritage and Intellectual Property: Communities, Cultural Diversity and Sustainable Development* (Intersentia, 2009).
91. Resolution adopted on the report of Commission IV at the 20th plenary meeting, on 2 November 2001.
92. R.J. Coombe & N. Aylwin, 'Bordering Diversity and Desire: Using Intellectual Property to Mark Place-Based Products' (2011) 49 *Env't & Plan. A* 2027, 2029; S. Van Uytsel, 'When Geographical Indications Meet Intangible Cultural Heritage: The New Japanese Act on Geographical Indications' in I. Calboli & W.L. Ng-Loy (eds), *Geographical Indications at the Crossroads of Trade, Development, and Culture: Perspectives from Asia* (Cambridge University Press, 2017) 508; V. Vadi, 'ICH and Trade' in C. Waelde, C. Cummings, M. Pavis & H. Enright (eds) *Research Handbook on Contemporary Intangible Cultural Heritage* (Edward Elgar, 2018), 398, 409-414.
93. Since 2011, the EU has been considering adopting a regime for non-agricultural GIs: https://ec.europa.eu/growth/industry/intellectual-property/geographical-indications/non-agricultural-products_en (Last accessed, 30 December 2019).

the Brazilian state of Espirito Santo. The artisanal production of pots was formally recognized as ICH under Brazilian law in 2002, but it was thought that further recognition as a GI – a marketing symbol – would assist during promotion campaigns as well as provide protection in international markets.[94] A logo for Goiabeiras has now been registered in Brazil.[95] An EU report exploring the different methods of GI protection for non-agricultural products notes that the gunsmiths of Ferlacher Waffen (guns and hunting weapons) are formally recognized as part of the ICH of Austria.[96] This chapter, therefore, concludes by considering two possible avenues for further research at this intersection.

First, there is the potential for GI protection to give effect to obligations under the Convention for the Safeguarding of the ICH 2003. According to Art. 2(1):

> [ICH] means the practices, representations, expressions, knowledge, skills – as well as the instruments, objects, artefacts and cultural spaces associated therewith – that communities, groups and, in some cases, individuals recognize as part of their cultural heritage. This intangible cultural heritage, transmitted from generation to generation, is constantly recreated by communities and groups in response to their environment, their interaction with nature and their history, and provides them with a sense of identity and continuity, thus promoting respect for cultural diversity and human creativity.

An illustrative list in Article 2(2) covers domains such as oral traditions and expressions, social practices and rituals, knowledge and practices concerning nature and traditional craftsmanship. Several aspects of the definition correspond to the collective processes by which GIs are created, as well as reasons why they are valued by local communities. The Convention was preceded by paradigm shifts in the manner in which both culture and material heritage are conceived, including the acknowledgement that a material culture paradigm is incomplete. Some of the conceptual shifts included: rejecting any universal (read Western) definition of cultural authenticity in favour of a contextual appreciation; de-emphasizing permanence and materiality; a shift from static preservation associated with objects to living heritage associated with people, in ecological terms; an epistemological shift from the nation state as the legitimate guardian of cultural

---

94. E.F. da Silva & P.P. Peralta, 'Collective Marks and Geographical Indications – Competitive Strategy of Differentiation and Appropriation of Intangible Heritage' (2011) 16 *J. Intell. Prop. Rts.* 246. *See also* Insight Consulting et al., *Study on the Protection of Geographical Indications for Products Other Than Wines, Spirits, Agricultural Products or Foodstuffs* (European Commission DG Trade, November 2009) 87.
95. Registration No. IG 201003 published in *Revista da Propiedade Industrial* (RPI) No. 2126 on 4 October 2011.
96. Insight Consulting et al., *Study on Geographical Indications Protection for Non-Agricultural Products in the Internal Market* (Final report, 18 February 2013) 118.

heritage to include the community or group which actively maintains the heritage site; the related recognition of groups as rights holders; and recognition that monuments, objects, and performances were endowed with meaning by virtue of their relation to the present.[97] In terms of the outcomes sought and the corresponding obligations on signatories, Article 2(3) clarifies that 'safeguarding' means 'measures aimed at ensuring the viability of the intangible cultural heritage, including the identification, documentation, research, preservation, protection, promotion, enhancement, transmission, particularly through formal and informal education, as well as the revitalization of the various aspects of such heritage'. The commitments undertaken by signatories are further elaborated upon in Articles 11-13. These include identifying ICH with a view to safeguarding it, drawing up inventories and adopting 'a general policy aimed at promoting the function of the intangible cultural heritage in society'. In appropriate cases, such as those involving craft or textile products which have the intergenerational relevance for collective identity formation, GI protection and promotion could be one avenue for sustaining a vital community and living heritage. GI regimes could be included as one of the options within ICH recognition strategies, especially since the Convention otherwise lacks rules on preventing the misappropriation of ICH.[98]

The second possibility is less obvious but has considerable potential. Insights from ICH theorizing, methodology and practice could inform GI protection frameworks which also have to work with categories like 'tradition' and 'authenticity'. It is common to find assertions that 'at the conceptual core of GIs is a claim about authenticity and heritage'.[99] Registration as a GI is supposed to guarantee 'authenticity',[100] whereupon such symbols 'transmit and guarantee to the consumer the values concentrated therein, which may include up to hundreds of years of traditional artisan craftsmanship and the region's particular natural and environmental characteristics, which are embedded into the specific product'.[101] This aspect

---

97. *See* D. Fairchild Ruggles & H. Silverman, 'From Tangible to Intangible Heritage' in D. Fairchild Ruggles & H. Silverman (eds), *Intangible Heritage Embodied* (Springer, 2009) 1; N. Aikawa-Faure, 'From the Proclamation of Masterpieces to the Convention for the Safeguarding of Intangible Cultural Heritage' in L. Smith & N. Akagawa (eds), *Intangible Heritage* (Routledge, 2009) 13.

98. B. Ubertazzi, 'EU Geographical Indications and Intangible Cultural Heritage' (2017) 48(5) *IIC* 562.

99. K. Raustiala & S.R. Munzer, 'The Global Struggle over Geographical Indications' (2007) 18 *Eur. J. Int'l L.* 337, 346.

100. J. van Niekerk, 'The Use of Geographical Indications in a Collective Marketing Strategy: The Example of the South African Wine Industry' 1 September 1999 (WIPO/GEO/CPT/99/8) 5 ('To be part of a successful collective marketing strategy, the authenticity of geographical indications needs to be guaranteed, controlled and protected').

101. P. Zylberg, 'Geographical Indications v. Trade Marks: The Lisbon Agreement: A Violation of TRIPS?' (2002-2003) 11 *U. Balt. Intell. Prop. L. J.* 1, 3.

has also been recognized by courts: 'For consumers, the link between the reputation of the producers and the quality of the products also depends on his being assured that products sold under the designation are authentic'.[102] Inevitably, this raises questions: what are the benchmarks for authenticity? And if the GI registration process requires a stabilized, historically validated production method to be identified, how is a change to be accommodated within limits set by tradition and authenticity?

GI critics such as Broude plausibly argue that frequent claims to timeless tradition in the GI context are overstated.[103] Change is inevitable, in the face of varying consumer preferences, market forces and technological developments. This also leaves the scope for political or commercial capture, whereby industrialized production models masquerade as traditional ones. However, this does not exhaust the argument. In fact, the setting up of tradition as somehow frozen and in opposition to change is itself a strained and artificial understanding.[104] The scholarship that has developed around ICH stresses that as opposed to being fixated on the material product, it is the process and producers over time which are equally deserving of our attention; the tangible is only a manifestation of the intangible. 'While the intangible only receives expression by means of the tangible, the tangible only has meaning because of the intangible elements'.[105] Change is possible if our understanding of authenticity no longer refers:

> to a certain idea of antiquity, but designates a strong link with a specific community [...] In this sense, traditional craftsmanship becomes heritage when it is recognized as such by the individuals, the groups and the communities that create, maintain and transmit it. The skills and knowledge that are inherited from the past live in the present in the body of craftsmen that hold them and are passed on to future generations. As expressions of intangible cultural heritage, traditional craftsmanship is

---

102. ECJ, Case C-469/00, *Ravil SARL v. Bellon Import SARL and Biraghi SpA* [2003], Judgment of the Court of 20 May 2003, ECR I-05053; [2004] ETMR 22, at [49] ('Grana Padano').
103. Broude, 'Taking "Trade and Culture" Seriously', (n. 54). Broude has also argued that the very conceptualization of ICH is wooly and unhelpfully overinclusive: T. Broude, 'From Chianti to Kimchi: Geographical Indications, Intangible Cultural Heritage, and Their Unsettled Relationship with Cultural Diversity' in I. Calboli & W. Ng-Loy (eds), *Geographical Indications at the Crossroads of Trade, Development, and Culture: Focus on Asia-Pacific* (CUP, 2017) 461.
104. For an example of a series of incremental technical and commercial innovations in Italian Murano glassmaking over several centuries, *see* F. Trivellato, 'Murano Glass, Continuity and Transformation (1400-1800)' in P. Lanaro (ed.), *At the Centre of the Old World: Trade and Manufacturing in Venice and the Venetian Mainland, 1400-1800* (University of Toronto, 2006) 143.
105. L. Lixinski, *Intangible Cultural Heritage in International Law* (OUP, 2013) 19.

strongly related to the space and time where it takes place, and it is continuously transformed and innovated upon.[106]

This brings into focus the importance of intergenerational transmission and the active interpretation of the past by a specific community that is involved in identifying its traditions:

> The concept of intangibility points, among other things, to investigations focused on the workings of cultural transmission and reproduction. In contrast with material artefacts, intangible creations endure only through active, socially maintained processes of transmission from older to younger practitioners. These transmissions usually involve training and apprenticeships, sizeable investments of time and energy that must be meaningful and rewarding for this who undertake them.[107]

Thus 'tradition may be reinterpreted to such a point that some techniques, despite their significance, are lost for good. Usage and tradition alike are partly dependent on the knowledge that a community decides to pass on'.[108] As opposed to demands that the content of product techniques remains fixed, the enquiry shifts its focus to the manner in which the techniques have been acquired (the historical context of transmission) and the manner in which they are used. Recognizing the significance of intergenerational transmission, as an aspect of this continuity, creates the space for transformations within methods of production and is just one illustration of the potential for interactions between ICH recognition and GI protection. GI regimes acknowledge that production methods can evolve and supplementary rules permit the amendment of product specifications.[109] Where there is consensus amongst the community of producers that a change is legitimate and does not undermine the link to the region of origin – admittedly not always a straightforward process – and that change is congruent with the image of the GI that is being projected as well the reasons why consumers wish to buy the product, it ought to be permitted.[110]

---

106. F. Cominelli, 'Governing Cultural Commons: The Case of Traditional Craftsmanship in France' (13th International Association for the Study of the Commons Conference, Hyderabad 2011) 8.

107. M.L. Pratt, 'Thoughts on Intangibility and Transmission' in L. Arizpe and C. Amescua (eds), *Anthropological Perspectives on Intangible Cultural Heritage* (Springer, 2013) 79, 79.

108. Berard and Marchenay, *From Localized Products to Geographical Indications,* (n. 63), 32-3.

109. XF Quinones Ruiz et al., 'How Are Food Geographical Indications Evolving? – An Analysis of EU GI Amendments' (2018) 120 *Brit. Food J.* 1876.

110. For some of the controversial aspects associated with this re-negotiation, *see*: K. Gugerell, et al., 'Do Historical Production Practices and Culinary Heritages Really Matter? Food with Protected Geographical Indications in Japan and Austria' (2017) 4(2) *J. Ethnic Foods* 118; Amit Basole, 'Authenticity, Innovation, and the Geographical Indication in an Artisanal Industry: The Case of the Banarasi Sari' (2015) 18 *JWIP* 127.

Therefore an anthropologically informed, less rigid understanding of heritage, tradition and authenticity will help GI regimes to navigate processes of change.

26.4 CONCLUSION

To the extent that GIs and trademarks cover common ground, as regimes granting distinctive rights to commercially valuable signs in the marketplace, they generate similar types of interfaces with human rights. The sparse case law and commentary till date have considered whether GIs (or claims to related terminology) are covered by the right to property so that their expropriation triggers familiar legal consequences; whether the grant of exclusive rights impedes the commercial speech of those previously using a term generically; and whether restrictions on generic use might impact the right to commercial speech or on the right to freely pursue a trade or profession. However, the potential for a truly distinctive interface rests with cultural rights. The recognition of GIs as cultural symbols relevant to collective identity formation projects (Champagne symbolizing Frenchness), the collective, intergenerational human investments required for their transmission across time and the incorporation of cultural practices within product specifications all attest to the cultural heritage aspects of GI protection. Yet cultural heritage is itself a problematic fit with cultural rights; it may lack the capacity to function as a bridging concept between GIs and cultural rights, at least for the present. It may, therefore, be worth looking beyond human rights instruments, to consider whether these aspects of GI can find synergies with recent initiatives to recognize ICH.

Part V

Patents and Human Rights

Chapter 27

Expanding the Role of Morality and Public Policy in European Patent Law

Karen Walsh & Naomi Hawkins[*]

27.1   INTRODUCTION

Recent and projected advances in technology give rise to difficult questions about the interaction between patents and the public interest. Not only are there patents for inventions where the invention or its commercial exploitation is potentially immoral or against public policy, there are patents for inventions which, in their operation, have ethically problematic effects, creating public interest concerns. Patent law often takes an excessively economic approach and fails to appropriately accommodate the public interest, with important ethical consequences. The concepts of morality and public policy are ways in which the law can address the public interest balance. However, they are generally treated as conceptually distinct and legally separate. In this chapter, we argue that the analysis of morality and public policy in European patent law ought to be given more attention and

---

[*] The authors would like to thank Dr Justine Pila, Professor Charlotte Waelde, Dr Aisling McMahon and Professor Stephen Skinner for their comments on earlier drafts of this chapter. A version of this chapter was presented at the UK & Ireland Patent Scholars Network Meeting and the authors are grateful to those who provided feedback and participated in the resulting discussion. NH is supported by the UK Economic and Social Research Council (grant code ES/K009575/1).

should not be separated off from broader public interest concerns relating to the operation of the patent system. Instead, we argue that morality and public policy should be seen as part of the public interest as a whole, and that issues of morality and public policy concerns (such as access to medicine) are part of the same continuum. Employing a stronger role for human rights (specifically human dignity) in patent law has the potential to draw these areas together to make the law more coherent across these two types of potentially problematic inventions. In turn, this practice would expand the role of the public interest in patent law.

In European patent law, provisions exist to ensure that patents are not granted for inventions, the commercial exploitation of which is deemed to be generally against public policy or morality. There are additional specific provisions against the patentability of processes for cloning human beings, processes for modifying the germ line genetic identity of human beings, uses of human embryos for industrial or commercial purposes, and processes for modifying the genetic identity of animals which are likely to cause them suffering without any substantial medical benefit.

These provisions have the effect of linking patents, a predominately economic tool, and human rights. Morality and public policy have been long-standing features in national and European patent laws. The Statute of Monopolies would not allow protection for inventions that were deemed 'generally inconvenient', seventeenth century patent laws in the United Kingdom (UK) prevented patentability on inventions prejudicial to subjects, and there were explicit exceptions in subsequent laws, and from then on.[1] Their inclusion in European patent laws was never questioned.

However, explicit human rights discussions in patent law are a relatively recent development. Since human rights have become a part of patent law, the morality and public policy provisions have taken on a different role. On the implementation of the Biotech Directive,[2] human dignity became a significant consideration for biotech inventions in the European Union (EU). The provisions of the Directive were then incorporated into the Implementing Regulations of the European Patent Convention (EPC). The European Convention on Human Rights and the EU Charter of Fundamental Rights have also had an impact, with their provisions on fundamental rights and human dignity being referred to in cases raised to the Court of Justice of the European Union (CJEU) and in cases before the Boards of Appeal of the European Patent Office (EPO) respectively.[3]

---

1. Statute of Monopolies 1623, VI; UK Patent Law Amendment Act 1852, p. 427.
2. Directive 98/44EC of the European Parliament and of the Council of 6 July 1998 on the legal protection of biotechnological inventions (Biotech Directive).
3. Case C-34/10 *Oliver Brüstle v. Greenpeace* ECLI:EU:C:2011:669; T149/11 *Method and device for processing a slaughtered animal or part thereof in a slaughterhouse* of 24 January 2013.

In this chapter, we first explore the role that the morality and public policy provisions have played in European patent law and argue that these concepts be considered in more depth. Following a brief historical overview of these provisions, this chapter examines the related case law in detail.[4] The focus will be on the interpretation of the general provision and also the specific exception relating to the use of human embryos for industrial or commercial purposes. Morality is a contested concept, and there is no single European morality. Moreover, conceptions of morality and public policy can vary over time. It is therefore difficult for courts to rule on such questions, but it is nonetheless not impossible for them to do so.[5] However, as will be expanded on below, to date, morality has only been interpreted by the CJEU and Boards of Appeal in a very narrow manner in relation to patents. Although these cases have taken huge strides forward for the consideration of human rights in patent law, we argue that the conception of morality and its interpretation ought to be broader.

We then explore some of the wider public interest concerns arising from patents, including a case study on gene patents. The examination of these provisions has implications for the use of patents in accordance with the public interest, for which, we argue, the concept of human dignity is important.

In the final sections of this chapter, we explore how, through the better employment of human dignity in patent law in Europe, moral and ethical concerns can be better addressed. Given the significance and relevance of morality and ethics in modern technology that currently exists and the inevitable advances that will be made in the future, we suggest that these concepts should be considered in more detail in relation to the public interest. We argue that the principle of human dignity, which is expressly referred to in the relevant legislation, and has been drawn on by the Boards of Appeal and the CJEU, is an appropriate and sensible principle to apply in this respect.[6]

In our view, importing a deeper and more nuanced consideration of human dignity in patent law would help to address moral and ethical

---

4. We focus in this chapter on the European perspective and rely therefore on the case law and practice of the European Patent Office and the European Union.
5. Courts in this context include the quasi-judicial Boards of Appeal of the EPO.
6. Although the principle of human dignity encompasses only human morality and does not extend to non-human aspects of morality, the majority of ethical issues arising from current patent law cases have an explicit link with humans, thus the principle of human dignity assists with the resolution of moral and ethical concerns in this arena. It is possible that the principle of human dignity will not adequately address some environment concerns, or issues of animal ethics, although the involvement of humans in the patented invention in such cases may be sufficient to enliven the principle in any case (*see* for example T149/11 *Method and device for processing a slaughtered animal or part thereof in a slaughterhouse* of 24 January 2013).

concerns and support a better equilibrium between the private economic interests of patent holders and the public interest.

27.2   MORALITY AND PUBLIC POLICY IN EUROPEAN
        PATENT LAW

The provisions with which this chapter is concerned are found primarily in the EPC, the Biotech Directive and their corresponding national Patents Act provisions. There are two different types of provision in European patent law.

The first, Article 53(a) EPC, is the more general and provides that patents are not granted for inventions the commercial exploitation of which would be contrary to *ordre public* or morality.[7] The corresponding provision of the UK Patents Act, section 1(3), uses the term 'public policy' rather than '*ordre public*', but the terms equate.[8]

The second set of provisions are more specific and are found in Rule 28(a)-(d) of the Implementing Regulations of the EPC 2000. These provisions were voluntarily incorporated into the EPC following the introduction of the EU Biotech Directive.[9] Rule 28 provides:

> Under Article 53(a), European patents shall not be granted in respect of biotechnological inventions which, in particular, concern the following:
>
> (a) processes for cloning human beings;
> (b) processes for modifying the germ line genetic identity of human beings;
> (c) uses of human embryos for industrial or commercial purposes;
> (d) processes for modifying the genetic identity of animals which are likely to cause them suffering without any substantial medical benefit to man or animal, and also animals resulting from such processes.

These provisions have also been incorporated into the national laws of EU Member States as a result of the Biotech Directive and are applicable in all Contracting Member States of the EPC as a result of Rule 28. Therefore,

---

7. Article 53(a) EPC. No such exception to patentability on the basis of morality exists in United States or Australian law.
8. Chartered Institute of Patent Agents, *CIPA Guide to the Patents Acts* (8th ed Sweet & Maxwell, London 2016) (1.21). Section 1(3) PA 1977 is also mentioned in section 130(7) PA 1977 which requires that the provisions mentioned therein 'are so framed as to have, as nearly as practicable, the same effects in the United Kingdom as the corresponding provisions of the European Patent Convention'.
9. When the Biotech Directive was implemented the European Patent Organisation decided to incorporate its provisions into the Implementing Regulations of the EPC in order to have a consistent approach towards biotech patents.

national patent offices, the EPO, national courts, the Boards of Appeal of the EPO and the CJEU may all be called upon to interpret these provisions.[10]

If a patent application falls within one of these four types of invention, it is denied patentability under this provision. If an application falls outside these provisions, the application then needs to be assessed to determine whether it nonetheless falls within the Article 53(a) prohibition.[11] Furthermore, the grant of the patent can be opposed, and the validity of a patent can be challenged, on the basis of these provisions.[12]

27.2.1   THE HISTORY OF THE PROVISIONS IN EUROPEAN PATENT LAW

Modern patent law has always had an ethical dimension, which can be gleaned from the social contract on which it exists.[13] The social contract is at the core of patent law and ensures that the interests of the patentee are balanced with those of society. Patent law gives inventors an exclusive right; however, in order to balance that exclusivity against the public interest the right is limited in time and the invention must be sufficiently disclosed. These requirements ensure that the public can work the invention work once the exclusive right lapses.

Internationally, the exclusion of inventions from patenting is permitted by Article 27(2) of the Agreement on Trade-Related Aspects of Intellectual Property (TRIPS), which provides that Member States 'may exclude from patentability inventions, the prevention within their territory of the commercial exploitation of which is necessary to protect *ordre public* or morality, including to protect human, animal or plant life or health or to avoid serious prejudice to the environment, provided that such exclusion is not made merely because the exploitation is prohibited by their law'.[14] However, the inclusion of these provisions in patent laws pre-exist TRIPS.

For the UK, it could even be said that something akin to a morality and public policy provision can be seen in the 1623 Statute of Monopolies where it says that patents would not be granted if they are 'altogether contrary to the Lawes of this Realme' and further on 'soe as alsoe they be not contrary to the Lawe nor mischievous to the State, by raising prices of Commodities at home, or hurt of Trade, or generally inconvenient'.[15] Here, the current day language can be seen emerging and although it might not specifically

---

10. The Unified Patent Court will also play a role if it becomes operational.
11. T315/03 *Transgenic animals/HARVARD* of 6 July 2004, Reasons 6.1.
12. Article 100 EPC; section 72(1) Patents Act 1977 (UK).
13. European Group on Ethics in Science and New Technologies (European Commission), 'Opinion on ethical aspects of patenting inventions involving human stem cells' (2002), available at <https://publications.europa.eu/en/publication-detail/-/publication/687b0402-32b8-4b1a-905e-b7885d2a3eac> last accessed 9 August 2019, 1.18.
14. Article 27(2) TRIPS.
15. Statute of Monopolies 1623, I and VI.

mention morality or public policy, something that is contrary to the laws of the realm, something that is mischievous to the State, or generally inconvenient, demonstrates a consideration of something other than the economic interests involved in patent law and a link to something akin to morality and public policy. This interpretation has also been inferred from the Statute of Monopolies in other jurisdictions, such as Australia, where it has been argued that 'generally inconvenient' could have been intended as a broad public interest test.[16]

This language can also be seen in the UK Patent Law Amendment Act 1852, which was introduced following criticisms on the functioning of the patent system at the time.[17] It is stated in the example given of a granted patent that 'if at any Time during the said Term hereby granted it shall be made appear to Us, Our Heirs or Successors, or any six or more of Our or their Privy Council, that this Our Grant is contrary to Law, or prejudicial or inconvenient to Our Subjects in general … these Our Letters Patent shall forthwith cease, determine, and be utterly void to all Intents and Purposes'.[18] Reflections of the Statute of Monopolies can be seen in the language being used here, but this Act also goes further by explicitly allowing the revocation of a patent if it is prejudicial to society.

Explicit provisions appear in the 1883 UK Patents, Designs and Trade marks Act and then continue to be included in subsequent pieces of legislation such as the 1907, 1949 and 1977 (as amended) Patent Acts. It is clear that from very early on in patent law, in the UK at least, morality and public policy provisions are included.[19]

---

16. Statute of Monopolies 1623, I and VI. Other jurisdictions, such as Australia, do not make explicit mention of morality even today. However, the Australian Patent Act is based on the Statute of Monopolies and has this similar phrasing. It is arguable that the words 'generally inconvenient' were intended to be a broad public benefit test, incorporating considerations of the public interest, and that such considerations could be employed in excluding patents on this basis. However, there is little evidence that courts or patent offices would be inclined to rely on such public interest considerations unless explicitly directed to do so – *see* Chris Dent, '"Generally Inconvenient": The 1624 Statute of Monopolies as Political Compromise' (2009) 33 Melbourne University Law Review 415, 446; Peter Drahos, 'Biotechnology Patents, Markets and Morality' (1999) 21 European Intellectual Property Review 441, 441; Dianne Nicol 'On the Legality of Gene Patents' (2005) Melbourne University Law Review 25; Australian Law Reform Commission, *Genes and Ingenuity: Gene Patenting and Human Health Report* (Australian Law Reform Commission 2004) available at <https://www.alrc.gov.au/publications/report-99> last accessed 9 August 2019.
17. For more on the history of patent law and issues with letters patent being granted by the crown, *see*: Lionel Bently, Brad Sherman, Dev Gangjee and Philip Johnson, *Intellectual Property Law* (5th edn, Oxford, UK: OUP 2018) 394-397.
18. UK Patent Law Amendment Act 1852, p. 427.
19. The same can be said for other countries in Europe but that is beyond the scope of this chapter. *See*: Viola Prifti, 'The Limits of *"Ordre Public"* and "Morality" for the Patentability of Human Embryonic Stem Cell Inventions' (2019) 22 Journal of World Intellectual Property 2, 4.

For the EPC, discussions on this provision are seen in the *travaux préparatoires*.[20] However, what is relevant here about these discussions is that they revolve around the wording of the provision and whether terms should be defined, more so than whether or not they should be included at all. The main questions discussed were whether 'if the use of the invention is contrary to "ordre public" or morality in only one of the Contracting States, will grant of a European patent be excluded?'[21] and whether there was 'a "European" definition of morality? [or] Should national definitions be applied or is it necessary to consider what is common to them all?'[22] It was recognised that no European definition of morality existed and that it was enough to mention morality and leave its interpretation up to European institutions.[23]

27.2.2   MORALITY, PUBLIC POLICY AND HUMAN DIGNITY

From this brief historical overview, it appears that there has always been a public interest dimension to patent law, with morality and public policy being an explicit concern in modern patent legislation but implicit possibly as far back as the Statute of Monopolies.

This public interest dimension has consistently been for the benefit of society. The social contract that underpins the patent system attempts to find the balance between the rights of the patentee and society. Provisions preventing the exploitation of inventions for reasons of morality and public policy have at their core the protection of society, of human rights and human dignity especially.[24] The protection of society and human dignity in patent law has expanded greatly, especially with the introduction of the Biotech Directive and its incorporation into the Implementing Regulations of the EPC.

The CJEU has explicitly confirmed the need for patent law to take into account the link between human dignity and patent law in relation to morality in *Brüstle* (explored below at 27.3.2). Patent institutions are also beginning to recognise the role of human dignity in the interpretation of patent law, with the Technical Board of Appeal of the EPO stating that '"ordre public" must be seen in particular as defined by norms that safeguard fundamental values and rights such as the inviolability of human dignity and

---

20. Travaux Préparatoires EPC 1973, available at < https://www.epo.org/law-practice/legal-texts/epc/archive/epc-1973/traveaux.html> last accessed 9 August 2019.
21. Travaux Préparatoires EPC 1973, Article 53, Comments on the first Preliminary Draft Convention relating to a European patent law of 14 March 1961, LT 234/82 section 14 IV/2071/61 – E, 5.
22. Patents Working Party, Proceedings of the 1st Meeting of the Patents Working Party held at Brussels from 17 to 28 April 1961, section 5, IV/2767/61-E, 6.
23. Patents Working Party, Proceedings of the 1st Meeting of the Patents Working Party held at Brussels from 17 to 28 April 1961, section 5, IV/2767/61-E, 7.
24. Charter of Fundamental Rights of the European Union 2012/C 326/02, Article 3.

the right of life and physical integrity'.[25] It is clear that morality, public policy and human dignity are becoming significant concepts in European patent law.

The tension between the private interest of the inventor and the public interest is often in delicate balance in the grant of patents. The balance must be struck between providing sufficient incentive to encourage the creation of new and useful technologies on the one hand, as against the public interest in accessing those new and useful technologies.[26] Patent law has traditionally been conceived of as a tool for promoting both private and public interests, with the public interest being understood in terms of the progress of technology and economic advancement.[27] However, there is increasing recognition that a purely economic approach fails to capture important aspects of the public interest. Dreyfuss notes that 'No one is fully served by a system that depends on the market alone to encourage innovation.'[28] When the technologies in question are not merely desirable or nice to have, but are necessary for the flourishing of humanity, then the question of access goes beyond the balancing of economic incentives and has human rights implications.

Morality and ethics can be slippery concepts, which can be difficult to apply in practice. Understandings of morality, the concept of something being right or wrong, and ethics, which goes further but also includes issues of morality, can be different for different people. It can therefore be difficult for patent offices and courts to apply such broad concepts.[29] Human rights frameworks arguably provide a more concrete legal framework on which to base arguments about the implications of ethics and morality for the public interest. As van Overwalle notes, 'For patent law to be widely accepted and generally recognized as a tool fostering both private and public interest, it is vital that current patent law regimes are inextricably linked with human rights discourse, and that human rights assist in defining the utter limits of patent rights.'[30]

The place of human dignity in international human rights law has been debated for quite some time, but it has a more recent connection with patent

---

25. T149/11 *Method and device for processing a slaughtered animal or part thereof in a slaughterhouse* of 24 January 2013.
26. The justifications for intellectual property are rehearsed in detail elsewhere, and this chapter does not seek to address objections to the existence of patents per se. Moreover, we focus primarily on the traditional utilitarian justification for patents, rather than any human rights justification for the existence of patent rights: Rochelle Cooper Dreyfuss, 'Patents and Human Rights: Where Is the Paradox?' in FW Grosheide (ed.), *Intellectual Property and Human Rights: A Paradox* (Edward Elgar 2010).
27. Geertrui van Overwalle, 'Human Rights' Limitations in Patent Law' in FW Grosheide (ed.), *Intellectual Property and Human Rights: A Paradox* (Edward Elgar 2010) 241-242.
28. Dreyfuss, 90.
29. As is evident in the case law, discussed below at 27.3.
30. Van Overwalle.

law.[31] The European Group on Ethics has noted the importance of the principle of human dignity in relation to patents on human embryonic stem cells.[32] More broadly, the Committee on Economic Social and Cultural Rights has affirmed the importance of excluding from patentability inventions where their commercialisation would jeopardise human dignity.[33]

The purpose behind the public interest provisions is to protect society and ensure that there are considerations of a moral and ethical nature in patent law. Those considerations come in the form of a question as to whether the commercial exploitation of the invention is moral or against public policy. Given the importance of the balance between private and public interests in patent law, how these provisions are being interpreted is extremely important. It is only when these provisions are interpreted that we can see whether a more detailed or more expansive consideration of morality and public policy is necessary in order to protect the public interest.

27.3 INTERPRETATIONS OF THE MORALITY AND PUBLIC POLICY PROVISIONS

As has been shown above, morality and public policy have been an implicit part of patent law since the introduction of a law relating to patents, appearing explicitly in modern legislative texts. It can therefore be argued that these provisions (both general and specific) are of significant importance to patent law from a legislative perspective, and relatedly, even more so, from a societal perspective, with strong links to human dignity.[34] The

---

31. Van Overwalle, 244; Aurora Plomer, 'Human Dignity, Human Rights, and Article 6(1) of the EU Directive on Biotechnological Inventions' in Aurora Plomer and Paul Torremans (eds), *Embryonic Stem Cell Patents: European Law and Ethics* (OUP 2009); Agnieszka Kupzok, 'Human Rights in the Case Law of the EPO Boards of Appeal' in Christophe Geiger (ed.), *Research Handbook on Human Rights and Intellectual Property* (Edward Elgar 2015); Aurora Plomer, 'Human Dignity and Patents' in Christophe Geiger (ed.), *Research Handbook on Human Rights and Intellectual Property* (Edward Elgar 2015); David Resnik, 'Embryonic Stem Cell Patents and Human Dignity' (2007) 15(3) Health Care Analysis 211.
32. Opinion No. 15 of the European Group on Ethics in Science and New Technologies to the European Commission, 'Ethical Aspects of Human Stem Cell Research and Use' 14 November 2000.
33. Committee on Economic, Social and Cultural Rights, Thirty-fifth session, Geneva, 7-25 November 2005, General Comment No. 17 (2005) 'The right of everyone to benefit from the protection of the moral and material interests resulting from any scientific, literary or artistic production of which he or she is the author', GE.06 -40060 (E) 020206, (35).
34. As previously noted in footnote 6, although the principle of human dignity encompasses only human morality and does not extend to non-human aspects of morality, the majority of ethical issues arising from current patent law cases have an explicit link with humans, thus the principle of human dignity assists with the resolution of moral and ethical concerns in this arena.

provisions exist to ensure that patents are not granted for inventions whose commercial exploitation is deemed immoral or contrary to public policy.

However, whether the provisions are fulfilling that purpose depends on the extent to which they are considered at examination stage and in case law. A question thus arises as to what extent these provisions are being considered when raised before a tribunal, and whether the public interest dimension of patent law is being taken into account adequately.

The following section will examine the case law on the provisions from the Boards of Appeal of the EPO and the CJEU.[35] It will first discuss the interpretation of the general provision, and then move on to examine the specific example of the exception relating to the use of human embryos for industrial or commercial purposes.

27.3.1   THE INTERPRETATION OF THE GENERAL PROVISION

The general provision, found in Article 53(a) EPC, states that:

European patents shall not be granted in respect of:

(a) inventions the commercial exploitation of which would be contrary to 'ordre public' or morality; such exploitation shall not be deemed to be so contrary merely because it is prohibited by law or regulation in some or all of the Contracting States.

The relationship between this general provision and the specific provisions (which will be elaborated on further below) is that if an invention does not fall within one of the specific provisions but might still be potentially immoral and against public policy, the general provision will then be considered.[36] Although the specific provisions are dealt with first when appropriate, it is relevant at this point to discuss the general principles and how they have been interpreted.

When the Boards of Appeal have considered Article 53 EPC, whether part (a), (b) or (c), they have consistently suggested a narrow approach to the exceptions.

In *Oncomouse*,[37] when interpreting Article 53(a) EPC, the Boards proposed a balancing approach to determine if the invention in question was immoral. A number of factors were taken into account including the potential benefit to mankind, the suffering of the animal, harm to the environment and potential threats to evolution. The Board weighed these factors against one another and ruled in favour of the patentee given the potential benefits to

---

35. Decisions of individual national courts will not be expanded upon because the decisions of the Boards of Appeal of the EPO and the CJEU are more relevant to the focus of this chapter and should filter down into national courts as persuasive authorities.
36. T315/03 *Transgenic animals/HARVARD* of 6.7.2004 and G2/06 *Use of embryos/WARF* of 25 November 2008.
37. T19/90 *Onco-Mouse* of 3 October 1990.

mankind – the benefit was related to developments in cancer treatment. The balancing approach is considered to lead to quite a narrow interpretation of the exception as many potential benefits to mankind could outweigh harm caused to animals, as long as the benefit is *potentially* significant.[38] However, it does take into account both sides of the argument.

In *Howard Florey/Relaxin*, an even stricter and narrower test was promoted by the Opposition Division.[39] Relying on previous case law, including *Oncomouse*,[40] the Opposition Division stated that 'patents would not be granted for inventions which would universally be regarded as outrageous'[41] and also considered the Guidelines where it was stated that 'Article 53(a) EPC is likely to be invoked only in rare and extreme cases, for example that of a letter bomb.'[42] They quoted the general guidance given encouraging that a 'fair test to apply is to consider whether it is probable that the public in general would regard the invention as so abhorrent that the grant of patent rights would be inconceivable. If it is clear that this is the case, objection should be raised under Article 53(a); otherwise not'. When the case was appealed, the Board of Appeal agreed with the Opposition Division.[43]

The so-called threshold approach can generally be regarded as stricter than the utilitarian balancing approach, and it promotes a very narrow interpretation of the exceptions to patentability. Being 'universally regarded as outrageous' is a very high bar. Another relevant development by the Boards of Appeal has been the attempt to define morality and *ordre public*. In *Plant Genetic Systems*, the Board stated that:

> The concept of morality is related to the belief that some behaviour is right and acceptable whereas other behaviour is wrong, this belief being founded on the totality of the accepted norms which are deeply rooted in a particular culture. For the purposes of the EPC, the culture in question is the culture inherent in European society and civilisation. Accordingly, under Article 53(a) EPC, inventions the exploitation of which is not in conformity with the conventionally accepted standards of conduct pertaining to this culture are to be excluded from patentability as being contrary to morality.[44]

It is generally accepted that the concept of 'ordre public' covers the protection of public security and physical integrity of individuals as part

---

38. The benefit was not significant enough in the Upjohn decision, where the invention related to treating baldness.
39. *Howard Florey/Relaxin* [1995] EPOR 541 (EPO (Opposition Division)) 6.1.
40. T19/90 *Onco-Mouse* of 3 October 1990 (related to 53(a)) and T320/87 *Hybrid plants* of 10 November 1988 (related to 53(b)).
41. *Howard Florey/Relaxin* [1995] EPOR 541 (EPO (Opposition Division)) 6.2.1.
42. *Howard Florey/Relaxin* [1995] EPOR 541 (EPO (Opposition Division)) 6.2.1, referring to Guidelines for Examination then at C-IV.3.1.
43. T272/95 *Relaxin/HOWARD FLOREY INSTITUTE* of 23 October 2002.
44. T356/93 *Plant cells* of 21 February 1995, Reasons 6.

of society. This concept encompasses also the protection of the environment. Accordingly, under Article 53(a) EPC, inventions the exploitation of which is likely to breach public peace or social order (for example through acts of terrorism) or to be seriously prejudice the environment are to be excluded from patentability as being contrary to *ordre public*.[45]

National regulation does not enter the discussion in the assessment[46] and opinion polls are not considered to necessarily reflect norms of conventionally accepted standards of conduct.[47] It must be the commercial exploitation of the invention, rather than the subject matter of the patent that is contrary to morality or *ordre public*.[48] Furthermore, if the invention can also be exploited in a way which does not and would not infringe *ordre public* or morality it is not sufficient to deny patent protection pursuant to Article 53(a) EPC.[49]

These elaborations have not added much to the understanding of when something is to be considered as contrary to morality or public policy by the Boards of Appeal. Relating the definition of morality to a European consensus when one cannot be said to exist is especially problematic.

It is clear that in certain instances, not all thirty-eight EPC Contracting Member States would agree on what is moral and what is not. Indeed, perceptions of morality change over time. Why then did the Boards of Appeal define morality as they did? The Boards could be considering what they believe morality to mean, or could be ensuring that they appear to be considering morality on the surface when in reality it is not something they are entirely concerned with – a case of window-dressing.

Alternatively, the Boards may not consider themselves to be best placed to determine what is contrary to morality for the purposes of patent law. This is where the narrow interpretation of the exceptions is useful. When considering the attempts by the Boards of Appeal to interpret the general provision a consistently narrow approach can be seen, one that often comes down in favour of the patentee. Given the *raison d'être* of the EPO is to grant patents, this is not surprising.

By implementing a narrow approach towards the exceptions to patentability, it becomes easier to decide what is immoral or against public policy.

---

45. T356/93 *Plant cells* of 21 February 1995, Reasons 5.
46. Article 53(a) EPC; UK Patents Act 1977 section 1(4); T356/93 *Plant cells* of 21 February 1995, Reasons 7.
47. T356/93 *Plant cells* of 21 February 1995, Reasons 15. *See also*: Amanda Warren-Jones, 'Identifying Moral Consensus: Why Are the Patent Courts Reticent to Accept Empirical Evidence in Resolving Biotechnological Cases?' (2006) 28(1) European Intellectual Property Review 26.
48. T866/01 *Euthanasia Compositions/Michigan State*, Reasons 5.6.
49. T866/01 *Euthanasia Compositions/Michigan State*, Reasons 5.8.

For example, by having a broad definition of morality relating to 'conventionally accepted standards' tied to a narrow test relating to matters that are 'universally regarded as outrageous', only the most immoral will be rejected. If the exploitation of an invention is not so immoral that it forms a conventionally accepted standard then morality may be skipped over and Boards instead place the majority of their reasoning on another of the patentability criteria such as sufficiency, for example.

However, there are signs that this very narrow approach may be shifting. Most recently, the Board of Appeal has interpreted Article 53(a) with an explicit focus on human dignity. They found that *ordre public* had to be seen 'as defined by norms that safeguard fundamental values and rights such as the inviolability of human dignity and the right of life and physical integrity'.[50] Although the reasoning and discussion in this decision focussed on a particular aspect of the invention, which was quite odd, and it was not a very detailed consideration of *ordre public*, it does display the willingness of the Board to discuss human dignity.

27.3.2   THE INTERPRETATION OF SPECIFIC PROVISIONS

The specific provisions, contained in Rule 28 EPC, state that under Article 53(a), patents will not be granted in relation to inventions relating to specific subject matter including processes for cloning human beings, processes for modifying the germ line genetic identity of human beings, uses of human embryos for industrial or commercial purposes, and processes for modifying the genetic identity of animals which are likely to cause them suffering without any substantial medical benefit.

The specific provision which has received the most interpretative attention is Rule 28(c) – uses of human embryos for industrial or commercial purposes, or in other words, the commercial exploitation of human embryos.[51] Therefore, this part will focus on the interpretation of this provision by the Boards of Appeal of the EPO and the CJEU.[52] From the cases that have been decided, we can draw some conclusions as to the respective institution's approach towards the morality and public policy provisions.

---

50. T149/11 *Method and device for processing a slaughtered animal or part thereof in a slaughterhouse* of 24 January 2013, Reasons 2.5.
51. For examination guidance related to this provision from the EPO, *see*: Guidelines for Examination, G.II.5.3, available at: <https://www.epo.org/law-practice/legal-texts/html/guidelines/e/g_ii_5_3.htm> last accessed 29 October 2019.
52. Rule 28(d) is a reflection of Article 6(2)(c) of the Biotech Directive, as incorporated into the Implementing Regulations of the EPC. For further discussions on this topic, *see*: Viola Prifti, 'The Limits of "*Ordre Public*" and "Morality" for the Patentability of Human Embryonic Stem Cell Inventions' (2019) 22 The Journal of World Intellectual Property 2.

27.3.2.1 EPO Case Law

The first case to look directly at the human embryo exception was the *Edinburgh patent* Opposition Division decision.[53] It was decided that a broad interpretation of Rule 23(d) (as it then was) was the only appropriate way forward.[54] This was partly due to the existence of Rule 23(e)(1) which stated that the human body at various stages of its formation and development cannot constitute patentable inventions (including the discovery of a gene sequence). It was decided that if Rule 23(d) was narrowly interpreted it would exist for no reason because Rule 23(e)(1) would already exclude it.[55]

The next to discuss the exception was the *WARF* referral to the Enlarged Board of Appeal.[56] The Technical Board of Appeal said that the Opposition Division in *Edinburgh patent* had been wrong as both Rule 23(d) and Rule 23(e)(1) dealt with similar subject matter and intentionally overlapped.[57] However, more relevant here is the passage from this decision where the Board stated that the 'EPO was not and should not act as a moral censor of controversial technologies. The EPO's expertise was in the field of patents, not in resolving controversial moral and ethical issues. The regulation of controversial technologies was a matter for legislators rather than the EPO.'[58]

The Board went on to promote a narrow reading of the exception and one that was very pro-patent. It was stated that 'in cases where a provision of the EPC was capable of bearing two alternative meanings, one of which resulted in refusal of the application on ethical grounds (i.e., the broad interpretation) and one of which permitted grant (i.e., the narrow interpretation), the correct approach was to construe the provision narrowly'.[59] They went on to promote the balancing test from *Oncomouse*, weighing the moral objections against the usefulness of the invention for humanity but also referred questions to the Enlarged Board of Appeal.[60]

When the Enlarged Board of Appeal decided on *WARF*,[61] they began by referring to the legislators' intention and concluded that an invention such as

---

53. Interlocutory decision of the Opposition Division dated 21 July 2003 concerning European patent 0 695 351 (*Edinburgh patent*).
54. *Edinburgh patent*, Reasons 2.5.3, Sheet 22.
55. *Edinburgh patent*, Reasons 2.5.3, Sheet 22.
56. T1374/04 *Stem cells/WARF* of 18 November 2005 (Interlocutory Decision).
57. T1374/04, 9.
58. T1374/04, 10.
59. T1374/04, 10-11.
60. T1374/04, 12.
61. G2/06 *Use of embryos/WARF* of 25 November 2008 (*WARF*). For further discussions on the *WARF* case, *see*: Sigrid Sterckx and Julian Cockbain, 'Assessing the Morality of the Commercial Exploitation of Inventions Concerning Uses of Human Embryos and the Relevance of Moral Complicity: Comments on the EPO's WARF Decision' (2010) 7(1) SCRIPTed 84; Sigrid Sterckx, 'The European Patent Convention and the (Non-) patentability of Human Embryonic Stem Cells – the WARF Case' (2008) 4 Intellectual Property Quarterly 478.

the one concerned should not be protected. The Board appeared to reject the argument put forward by the appellant that an embryo meant '14 days or older, in accordance with usage in the medical field'.[62] They were of the opinion that as human embryo had not been defined by the legislator and that because the purpose of the legislation was to protect human dignity, a restrictive meaning of human embryo would 'undermine the intention of the legislator'.[63]

Furthermore, they stated that 'what is an embryo is a question of fact in the context of any particular patent application'.[64] Instead of the usual narrow interpretation that has been seen in relation to the exceptions, the Enlarged Board gave quite a broad meaning to human embryo in this context in the name of human dignity.[65] When considering the invention it was decided that it was immoral to destroy a human embryo. This was decided without discussing whether that would ever be permitted. They did not reason this point in relation to the invention in question and, we argue, missed an opportunity to do so.[66]

The Board implied that this decision was so clear cut that it was not necessary (or appropriate) for them 'to discuss further arguments and points of view put forward in these proceedings such as whether the standard of ordre public or morality should be a European one or not, whether it matters if research in certain European countries involving the destruction of human embryos to obtain stem cells is permitted, whether the benefits of the invention for humanity should be balanced against the prejudice to the embryo, or what the point in time is to assess ordre public or morality under Article 53a EPC'.[67] However, we argue that it was necessary and appropriate for them to do so.

Instead, the reasoning focusses on whether there had been a commercial exploitation of the invention and the immorality of the invention is assumed without further discussion. It was noted that it is not the patenting that should be questioned regarding *ordre public* and morality but the performing of the invention.[68] The Enlarged Board then equated the making of the invention

---

62. *WARF*, Reasons 19 and 20.
63. *WARF*, Reasons 20.
64. *WARF*, Reasons 20.
65. For more on the interpretation of Article 53(a), *see*: Ella O'Sullivan, 'Is Article 53(a) EPC Still of Narrow Interpretation?' (2012) 7(9) Journal of Intellectual Property Law & Practice 680.
66. This decision has been criticised for going too far and giving too broad a reading. *See*: Aurora Plomer, 'Human Dignity, Human Rights, and Article 6(1) of the EU Directive on Biotechnological Inventions' in Aurora Plomer and Paul Torremans (eds), *Embryonic Stem Cell Patents: European Law and Ethics* (OUP 2009).
67. *WARF*, Reasons 31.
68. *WARF*, Reasons 29.

with its commercial exploitation[69] linking this to the rights granted to the patentee to stop third parties from making or using a protected invention.[70] From this reading, the Board appears to be saying that making an invention that is immoral amounts to an immoral commercial exploitation of the invention regardless of its intended use. Despite the note, the focus seems to be more on the morality of the invention rather than its commercial exploitation, if viewing commercial exploitation from the perspective of intended use. This is problematic and a departure from previous jurisprudence.

As a result of the invention being deemed immoral – coupled with the link made between the commercial exploitation of an invention and the making of the invention – its commercial exploitation was automatically deemed immoral. The potential use of the invention was never considered.[71] There was no balancing test or threshold test used to determine the morality of the commercial exploitation of the invention. The result of the failure of the Board to make explicit their reasoning is a level of legal uncertainty, with parties left wondering whether this means that the use of a human embryo at any stage of development would be deemed immoral by the EPO, or just a use that results in its destruction.

In this case, the Enlarged Board are saying all the right things – that the legislators' intention needs to be taken into account, that a narrow restriction would be bad for human dignity – and considerations of morality and public policy are being highlighted, but they are not discussed or explored in any meaningful way. No guidance has been given for future cases and the implications of this can be seen below.[72]

---

69. For a discussion on the meaning of commercial exploitation, *see*: Amanda Warren-Jones, 'Morally Regulating Innovation: What Is "Commercial Exploitation"?' (2008) 2 Intellectual Property Quarterly 193. Examining Beyleveld and Brownsword's contention that this provision goes beyond its literal meaning, she discusses how 'exploitation' has been widely interpreted to include the development of the invention. This practice is seen to continue despite the Boards of Appeal in the *Oncomouse* decision stating that Article 53 'raises no question of the morality of patenting a particular invention or of the morality of that invention *per se* … Neither the making of the invention nor the process of patenting an invention can be seen as contrary to *ordre public* or *morality*'. However, Warren-Jones contends that there may be certain circumstances where this is useful, such as 'where the immorality inherent in the development of an invention must be continually repeated in order to use the invention' (p. 202).

70. *WARF*, Reasons 25.

71. There is a question as to whether it must be considered given the definitional nature of Article 6(2) Biotech Directive, however, we argue that it should be considered to ensure a well-rounded analysis. For more on the definitional nature of these provisions *see*: Aurora Plomer, 'After *Brüstle*: EU Accession to the ECHR and the Future of European Patent Law' (2012) 2(2) Queen Mary Journal of Intellectual Property 110.

72. For a similar view, *see*: Paul Torremans, 'The Construction of the Directive's Moral Exclusions under the EPC' in Aurora Plomer and Paul Torremans (eds), *Embryonic Stem Cell Patents: European Law and Ethics* (OUP 2009).

Additionally, the Board also decided that if an invention requires the destruction of the human embryo and that is not mentioned in the application, it should still be taken into account.[73] This is another broad interpretation where the Enlarged Board decided that if the invention required the destruction of a human embryo and that was not included in the application, it would still be relevant.[74] We can see here that the Enlarged Board is looking beyond the patent application to ensure that patents are not granted due to crafty drafting. This was a significant step forward for considerations of human dignity and morality in patent law.

The Enlarged Board ultimately decided that patents would not be granted on claims to products that involved the destruction of human embryos even if that method was not part of the claims. As a result, subsequent cases involving human embryos have followed suit.

In *CALIFORNIA*, the Board referred to *WARF* and made similar reference to morality.[75] The Board determined whether the invention in question necessarily involved the destruction of human embryos. It did and so the invention fell under Article 53(a) and Rule 28(c). In *TECHNION*, the Board again focussed on the manner in which the human embryonic stem cells were obtained and whether this involved the destruction of the human embryo.[76] They did mention *WARF* and the *Brüstle* decisions (which had been decided two years previously by the CJEU, mentioned in detail below); however, the focus was on the technicalities of whether that which was not claimed in the patent application – how they came to be in possession of human embryonic stem cells and whether that involved the destruction of a human embryo – was relevant to their consideration.[77] Only a few months later in *ASTERIAS*, the Board again focussed on how the human embryonic stem cells were obtained relying on *WARF* and *Brüstle* and the idea that 'if

---

73. *WARF*, Reasons 22.
74. This is especially broad when contrasted to the interpretation of the plant and animal variety exception. In *Novartis*, the Enlarged Board decided that an application that did not specifically claim plant varieties but could 'embrace' plant varieties would be allowed (G1/98 *Transgenic plant/NOVARTIS II* of 20 December 1999, Reasons 3.10). This reasoning was then also applied to animal varieties in *Transgenic Animals/HARVARD* (T315/03 *Transgenic animals/HARVARD* of 6 July 2004, Reasons 11.8). In those cases, as long as a single plant or animal variety was not claimed in the application, the exception would not apply, even if the plant or animal variety fell within the scope of its claims.
75. T522/04 *Stem cells/CALIFORNIA* of 28 May 2009.
76. T2221/10 *Culturing stem cells/TECHNION* of 4 February 2014. For more detail on the *TECHNION* case, *see*: Aurelie Mahalatchimy et al., 'Exclusion of Patentability of Embryonic Stem Cells in Europe: Another Restriction by the European Patent Office' (2015) 37(1) European Intellectual Property Review 25.
77. *TECHNION*, Reasons 26.

for implementation of an invention a human embryo was destroyed, the point in time at which such destruction took place was irrelevant'.[78]

From these cases, we can see a general avoidance of examining the detail of morality and the Boards of Appeal (following the Enlarged Board in *WARF*) focussing very narrowly on the specific aspect of how the invention was made rather than discussing the broader morality and public policy concerns of whether the use of the embryo should ever be permitted. While the immorality of the destruction of embryos is being assumed, it is not being discussed in detail. Instead, the reasoning in each of these decisions focuses on whether there was a commercial exploitation deemed to be immoral – commercial exploitation being linked to the making of the invention.

27.3.2.2   CJEU Case Law

This provision has also been interpreted by the CJEU in two well-known decisions – *Brüstle* and *ISCC*.[79] The CJEU, on the one hand, has been criticised for defining human embryo in *Brüstle* and then having to backtrack on that in *ISCC* given the incorrect scientific evidence that had been presented in *Brüstle*.[80] On the other hand, these cases, *Brüstle* especially, have considered what morality means to a greater extent in this context and have highlighted how important the discussion around human dignity is.

In *Brüstle*, the Court began its consideration on the meaning of human embryo by stating that it was 'not called upon, by the present order for reference, to broach questions of a medical or ethical nature, but must restrict itself to a legal interpretation of the relevant provisions of the Directive' but went on to explicitly consider the moral underpinnings of the Biotech

---

78. T1441/13 *Embryonic stem cells, disclaimer/ASTERIAS* of 9 September 2014, Main Request.
79. Case C-34/10 *Oliver Brüstle v. Greenpeace* ECLI:EU:C:2011:669 (*Brüstle*); Case C-364/13 *International Stem Cell Corporation v. Comptroller General of Patents, Designs and Trade Marks* ECLI:EU:C:2014:2451 (*ISCC*).
80. For discussions on the *Brüstle* and *ISCC* cases, *see*: Aurora Plomer, 'After *Brüstle*: EU Accession to the ECHR and the Future of European Patent Law' (2012) 2(2) Queen Mary Journal of Intellectual Property 110; Andrea Faeh, 'Judicial Activism, the Biotech Directive and Its Institutional Implications: Is the Court Acting as a Legislator or a Court When Defining "Human Embryo"?' (2015) 40(4) European Law Review 613; Scott Parker and Paul England, 'Where Now for Stem Cell Patents?' (2012) 7(10) Journal of Intellectual Property Law & Practice 738; Shawn Harmon, Graeme Laurie & Aidan Courtney, 'Dignity, Plurality and Patentability: The Unfinished Story of Brüstle v Greenpeace' (2012) 38 European Law Review 92; Ana Nordberg and Timo Minssen, 'A "Ray of Hope" for European Stem Cell Patents or "Out of the Smog into the Fog"? An Analysis of Recent European Case Law and How it Compares to the US' (2016) 47 International Review of Intellectual Property and Competition Law 138; Ella O'Sullivan, 'International Stem Cell Corp v Comptroller General of Patents: The Debate Regarding the Definition of the Human Embryo Continues' (2014) 36(3) European Intellectual Property Review 155.

Directive and its essential objective of protecting human dignity.[81] The Court went on to say that, given these objectives, human embryo should be regarded in a wide sense and defined it as a fertilised human ovum capable of commencing the process of development of a human being and a non-fertilised human ovum that had been stimulated by parthenogenesis.[82]

The issue with this definition was that inventions that used non-fertilised human ova that had been stimulated by parthenogenesis were capable of commencing development of a human being but did not have the capacity of developing into a human being.[83] As a result, the CJEU clarified this definition in *ISCC*. Now, in order to fall under the definition of a human embryo for the purposes of the Biotech Directive, any non-fertilised ovum stimulated by parthenogenesis must have the 'inherent capacity of developing into a human being'.[84]

Although the definition may be problematic in some other respects, in our view, by considering the moral nature of this question and its links to human dignity, the CJEU have taken strides forward for the consideration of human rights issues in patent law.[85] The Court examined the Biotech Directive in great detail and came to the conclusion that its context and aim were to 'exclude any possibility of patentability where respect for human dignity could thereby be affected'.[86] *Any* possibility denotes a very wide margin of interpretation and consideration of human dignity, which allows patent law to take this into account more regularly. In doing so, the discussion surrounding human dignity and patent law can move forward and human dignity cannot be ignored.

The CJEU has also considered the commercial exploitation of the invention. In *Brüstle*, the issue was discussed in relation to whether the use of human embryos for scientific research was a use for an industrial or commercial purpose. The Court decided on this but it did not appear to be the main focus of the decision. It was stated that the grant of a patent implied industrial or commercial application and that only therapeutic or diagnostic

---

81. *Brüstle*, para. 30.
82. *Brüstle*, para. 35.
83. It has also been argued that the CJEU should have questioned when the human embryo would be entitled to the full guarantee of human dignity. *See*: Ansgar Ohly, 'European Fundamental Rights and Intellectual Property' in Ansgar Ohly and Justine Pila (eds), *The Europeanization of Intellectual Property Law: Towards a European Legal Methodology* (OUP 2013).
84. *ISCC*, para. 28. However, the definition remains controversial as there is no consensus in Europe on the morality or patentability of human embryonic stem cell research.
85. For more on this issue, *see*: Justine Pila, 'A Constitutionalized Doctrine of Precedent and the *Marleasing* Principle as Bases for a European Methodology' in Ansgar Ohly and Justine Pila (eds), *The Europeanization of Intellectual Property Law: Towards a European Legal Methodology* (OUP 2013) 233-240. For a counter argument, *see*: Aurora Plomer, 'After *Brüstle*: EU Accession to the ECHR and the Future of European Patent Law' (2012) 2(2) Queen Mary Journal of Intellectual Property 110.
86. *Brüstle*, para. 34.

methods applied to the human embryo would be patentable.[87] This aspect of the decision deserves a little more attention. Again we see the focus on the invention rather than its commercial exploitation. The potential use of the invention was not considered and it arguably should have been.

Finally, the CJEU also followed the same route as the Boards of Appeal when it came to whether the destruction of a human embryo was involved in the making of the invention but was not mentioned in the application.[88] This is an important addition for considerations of human dignity in patent law, as discussed above in relation to *WARF*.

27.4   PUBLIC INTEREST CONCERNS BEYOND THE MORALITY AND PUBLIC POLICY PROVISIONS

Consideration of questions of morality and public policy in European patent law tends to be primarily focused on the provisions explored in the previous sections of this chapter. As we have noted, these provisions are narrow in their scope, being considered mostly at the point of patent grant, and they have been further narrowed in their interpretation. However, the public interest implications of patent law are broader, in ways that are closely linked to the concerns evident in the cases arising from these provisions. Many of the recent controversies in patent law, especially in the life sciences, are not only related to the intrinsic nature of the invention but also to the way in which it is commercialised or exploited in practice, more remote from the grant of the patent.

Many controversies relate to questions such as access to medicine, but other areas, such as the relationship between patents and access to technologies to combat climate change, are also of increasing concern.[89] We argue that a more holistic consideration of the public interest in patent law, by both patent offices and courts, would better reflect the requirements of human rights and human dignity especially.[90]

---

87. *Brüstle*, para. 46.
88. *Brüstle*, paras 50 and 51.
89. For an outline of issues relating to Intellectual Property and climate change *see* for example: Kristina Lybecker and Sebastian Lohse 'Innovation and Diffusion of Green Technologies: The Role of Intellectual Property and Other Enabling Factors. Global Challenges Report' (2015) WIPO, Global Challenges Report.
90. As set out in the Charter of Fundamental Rights of the European Union. Although this is clearly an EU instrument, the EPO has recently referred to it in decision T149/11 – *see*: Agnieszka Kupzok, 'Human Rights in the Case Law of the EPO Boards of Appeal' in Christophe Geiger (ed), *Research Handbook on Human Rights and Intellectual Property* (Edward Elgar 2015).

27.4.1   GENE PATENTS: AN ILLUSTRATIVE CASE

The recent controversy over patents on human genes provides a useful illustration of our argument in this respect. Patents on human genes have long been controversial, with the breast cancer gene patents controlled by Myriad Genetics acting as a lightning rod for public and academic concern, with *Myriad* 'emblematic of the fear that patents on human genetic material would have an adverse impact on access to useful technologies, both for research and for clinical use'.[91] The moral and ethical implications of these patents are at the core of the objections to these patents but the concerns extend beyond the scope of, and are not addressed by, the core provisions of European patent law which we discussed in section 27.3 above.

The debate about the patentability of human genes will be familiar to patent law scholars and experts.[92] Objections to gene patents on morality and public policy grounds were regularly raised in the popular and academic press by various groups[93] and there was widespread public opposition to the concept of ownership of genes.[94] There was a concern that patents on human genes would result in a lack of respect for human life and a devaluation of human dignity via commercialisation and instrumentalisation of human beings.[95] However, it is generally accepted that human dignity is not directly violated by gene patents and that any effect is indirect in nature.[96]

In Europe in the 1990s and early 2000s there were a number of opposition proceedings in relation to gene patents and early cases mooted the morality and public policy exception as a basis for overturning gene patents. However, these objections were given short shrift by the Boards of Appeal of the EPO.

---

91. Timothy Caulfield et al., 'Evidence and Anecdotes: An Analysis of Human Gene Patenting Controversies' (2006) 24 Nature Biotechnology 1091.

92. For a discussion of the law around the patenting of human genes in Europe, *see*: Aisling McMahon, 'Gene Patents and the Marginalisation of Ethical Issues' (2019) 41(2) EIPR 608; Naomi Hawkins, 'Human Gene Patents and Genetic Testing in Europe: A Reappraisal' (2010) 7 SCRIPTed 454; Naomi Hawkins, 'A Red Herring – Invalidity of Human Gene Sequence Patents' (2016) 38 European Intellectual Property Review 83.

93. Nuffield Council on Bioethics, *The Ethics of Patenting DNA: A Discussion Paper* (Nuffield Council on Bioethics, London 2002); FB Charatan, 'US Religious Groups Oppose Gene Patents' (1995) 310 British Medical Journal 1351. For a summary of moral objections to gene patents *see* David Resnik, *Owning the Genome: A Moral Analysis of DNA Patenting* (State University of New York Press, Albany 2004) 3.

94. *See* for example Tim Radford, 'Patenting DNA "Not in Public Interest"' *The Guardian* (London 23 July 2002) <https://www.theguardian.com/uk/2002/jul/23/science.genetics> accessed 29 October 2019.

95. Timothy Caulfield and Roger Brownsword, 'Human Dignity: A Guide to Policy Making in the Biotechnology Era?' (2006) 7 Nature Review Genetics 72, 73; Australian Law Reform Commission, *Genes and Ingenuity: Gene Patenting and Human Health Report* (Australian Law Reform Commission, Canberra 2004) 68.

96. David Resnik, *Owning the Genome: A Moral Analysis of DNA Patenting* (State University of New York Press, Albany 2004) 95.

In *Howard Florey/Relaxin*,[97] the Green Party opposed the Howard Florey Institute's patent for the gene coding for relaxin on three *ordre public* and morality grounds. The first of these was that the use of pregnancy for profit was offensive to human dignity, the second was that the patent in question was a patent over life and therefore immoral, and the third was that patenting DNA was equivalent to slavery.[98] Each of these arguments was rejected by the Opposition Division which held that the patent did not in fact involve the patenting of human life, abuse of pregnant women or slavery,[99] but that DNA should be treated as a chemical substance and treated in the same manner as other chemical substances, such as pharmaceuticals.

In *Breast and Ovarian Cancer/University of Utah*,[100] an opponent argued that there was a contravention of the morality provisions constituted by a failure to obtain specific consent from the donor of cells used to derive the invention to commercial exploitation of the research results, and the lack of a benefit sharing agreement. The Board was not persuaded by this argument observing that the EPC does not require either evidence of informed consent or a benefit sharing agreement and that although the Biotech Directive provides that there must have been an opportunity to express free and informed consent in accordance with national law, there was no procedure to verify this informed consent in the patent framework. The Board held that there was therefore no prohibition on the BRCA1 patent as a result of Article 53(a) EPC.[101] The socio-economic consequences of the patent were raised by another opponent, which argued that the patent would result in increased costs for patients and would also influence the way in which diagnosis and research would be organised in Europe in a way that would be clearly to the detriment of patients and doctors.[102] The group of patients suspected to carry a predisposition to breast cancer would be faced with severe disadvantages and would become dependent on the patent proprietor and, it was argued, this was contrary to human dignity. The Board also rejected this argument, holding that Article 53(a) applied only where the exploitation of the invention (as opposed to the exploitation of the patent) would be contrary to *ordre public*. It is therefore clear that these general objections on the basis of morality and public policy are insufficient under current interpretations to satisfy the requirements of Article 53(a) in relation to patents on human genes.

Although Article 53(a) is too narrow to address these objections to gene patents, ethical and moral concerns persist. The core of the objection is

---

97. *Howard Florey/Relaxin* [1995] EPOR 541 (EPO (Opposition Division)).
98. *Ibid.,* 6.1.
99. *Ibid.,* 6.3.
100. T1213/05 *Breast and Ovarian Cancer/University of Utah* of 27.9.2007, Reasons 45-47.
101. Naomi Hawkins, 'Human Gene Patents and Genetic Testing in Europe: A Reappraisal' (2010) 7 SCRIPTed 453.
102. T1213/05 *Breast and Ovarian Cancer/University of Utah* of 27 September 2007, Reasons 52.

focused on questions of access to medicine.[103] Gene patents arguably limit access to medicine through increasing prices, reducing the breadth of provision, reducing quality of testing, and reducing research.[104] These issues have clear moral and ethical implications.[105] Such concerns are evident in the United States (US) and Australian cases overturning the breast cancer gene patents in those jurisdictions and the cases at all levels make reference to questions of access to medicine. Although these concerns were evidently the key motivation for bringing the cases, the legal basis for the decisions does not relate to the ethical questions and the US and Australia decisions in Myriad 'display no real engagement with the potential healthcare implications of patents on isolated genes'.[106]

Moreover, case law to date has largely focused on invalidating or narrowing gene patents. However, overturning the existence of a patent is only one means of addressing concerns about its unethical or immoral impact. Invalidity is a blunt tool and there may be other more nuanced, targeted and effective means of addressing the ethical implications of patents, explored further in section 27.6 below.

27.5   WHAT ROLE DO MORALITY AND PUBLIC
        POLICY PLAY IN PATENT LAW?

Patents and the public interest are connected, and the creation, operation and interpretation of the patent system are linked to moral and ethical standards.[107] However, not all inventions raise morality or public policy concerns, and not all inventions which give rise to these issues do so in the same way. In our view, there is an important distinction between two different categories of concerns which can arise from inventions:

(1) Inventions where all commercial exploitation of the invention is immoral or against public policy. Examples include the invention of a new type of letter bomb or land mine. Such inventions include, for example, those traditionally deemed to be immoral as contained in the Guidelines for Examination in the EPO.

---

103. For an exploration of the nature of objections to gene patents *see*: Hawkins, 'A Red Herring – Invalidity of Human Gene Sequence Patents'.
104. Hawkins, 'A Red Herring – Invalidity of Human Gene Sequence Patents', 88.
105. Aisling McMahon, 'Gene Patents and the Marginalisation of Ethical Issues' (2019) 41(2) European Intellectual Property Review 608 and discussion in Nuffield Council on Bioethics, *The Ethics of Patenting DNA: A Discussion Paper* (Nuffield Council on Bioethics 2002 available at <http://nuffieldbioethics.org/wp-content/uploads/2014/07/The-ethics-of-patenting-DNA-a-discussion-paper.pdf> last accessed 29 October 2019.
106. Aisling McMahon, 'Gene Patents and the Marginalisation of Ethical Issues' (2019) 41(2) European Intellectual Property Review 608.
107. Peter Drahos, 'Biotechnology Patents, Markets and Morality' (1999) 21 European Intellectual Property Review 441, 441.

(2) Inventions where some, but not all, commercial exploitation of the invention is immoral or against public policy, or which raise moral or ethical concerns. Such inventions might involve technology with a dual use for moral and immoral purposes, such as CRISPR technology, which could be used for both problematic germ line gene editing and uncontroversial gene editing for research purposes. Alternatively, some commercial exploitation of the invention may raise public interest concerns through, for example, questions of equality of access. In this case, the invention is not morally questionable, but the operation of the patent system in relation to that invention gives rise to broader questions about the public interest and patent law.

The second of these categories is not traditionally treated as part of any analysis of morality or public policy in European patent law. These questions are viewed as beyond the scope of the legal provisions and therefore tend to be discussed in different academic literatures, removed from the doctrinal and textual analysis of the provisions in European patent law. However, the concerns raised in category two have important implications for the public interest.

In this chapter, we argue that morality and public policy should be viewed more broadly, and therefore that the two categories above should be viewed as linked and part of a continuum of the public interest. The analysis of the legal provisions should not be separated off from these broader questions relating to the public interest of the operation of the patent system. Employing a stronger role for human rights and dignity has the potential to draw these areas together and to make the law more coherent across these two categories. Below, we explore the nature of the concerns for each of these categories in more detail.

27.5.1   CATEGORY 1: ALL COMMERCIAL EXPLOITATION OF THE INVENTION
          IS CONSIDERED IMMORAL AND AGAINST PUBLIC POLICY

The first category identified concerns inventions the commercial exploitation of which would always be considered immoral or against public policy. Examples of this category in action have been discussed above, which will inform the discussion in this section related to the role the public interest plays in patent law.

Morality and public policy are first considered from the perspective of the general provision. The Opposition Division in *Howard Florey/Relaxin* cited an example in which Article 53(a) would be invoked – a letter bomb.[108] The context of this example is important because the Opposition Division stated, implementing a narrow approach to the interpretation of exceptions,

---

108. *Howard Florey/Relaxin* [1995] EPOR 541 (EPO (Opposition Division)) 6.2.1.

that Article 53(a) would only be invoked in 'rare and extreme cases'.[109] In the case of a letter bomb, when considering the moral and ethical implications, the answer is clear. It is possible to distinguish between the morality of the invention and the morality of the commercial exploitation of the invention. In this case, it is likely that the invention itself is immoral but so would any possible commercial exploitation of it. Therefore, the criteria of Article 53(a) would be satisfied, that is, the possible commercial exploitation of this invention, i.e., if it were to be put on the market, would be immoral. As a society, the overall consensus would likely be that selling letter bombs, for example, would be immoral.

However, considerations of morality and public policy are different when inventions are more complex and multi-layered. As expanded on above, morality has been playing a role in the case law of the Boards of Appeal of the EPO and the CJEU and is front and centre in these decisions, with the basis of these decisions being linked to human dignity. However, the role morality plays in these decisions is difficult to decipher. Both the Boards of Appeal and the CJEU appeared to have difficulty distinguishing between the morality of the creation of the invention and its commercial exploitation.

In the *WARF* and *Brüstle* decisions the general provision seemed to take on a new function. In *WARF*, it was determined that the invention was immorally made and therefore, any commercial exploitation of it was immoral. In *Brüstle*, it was determined that a human embryo ought to be widely defined and that any use that required the destruction of the human embryo was broadly condemned, that use being linked to its commercial exploitation by applying for a patent on it.

In both of these cases it was the invention that was deemed immoral and as a result any commercial exploitation of it was automatically immoral. The link to commercial exploitation in these cases is tenuous. Neither the Boards nor the CJEU considered the potential uses of the invention. Nor did they consider scientific practice at the time in individual Member States.[110]

In *WARF*, the Enlarged Board of Appeal did not use a balancing test or a threshold test to determine whether the potential benefits of the invention (its commercial exploitation) would ever outweigh the destruction of the human embryo, or whether there was an overwhelming consensus against the possible use of the invention, as previous Board of Appeal practice established in relation to the exceptions to patentability as shown above. In *Brüstle*, the CJEU defined human embryo broadly without considering current day practice surrounding research restrictions on embryos in its Member States.

---

109. *Ibid.*
110. For an overview on the differences in scientific practice in some Member States, *see*: Gerard Porter, 'The Drafting History of the European Biotechnology Directive' in Aurora Plomer and Paul Torremans (eds), *Embryonic Stem Cell Patents: European Law and Ethics* (OUP 2009) 23-26.

In both scenarios, it would have been relevant to identify and judge the potential uses of the inventions. This is because the legal requirement of the general provision is to determine whether the commercial exploitation of the invention would be immoral and against public policy. Instead, these examples show that the courts and tribunals tend to focus on the invention and then vaguely link that to commercial exploitation without discussing what the inventions could be used for and whether there would be any scenario in which this type of invention would be permitted.

It appears that it does not necessarily matter what the invention could be used for, if how it is made is immoral. This is even the case if the details on how the invention is made are not contained in the patent application. This is without doubt an expansion of the general provision, which is a huge step forward for human dignity considerations in patent law. However, despite that, we are not given an explanation as to why these inventions are immoral and why their commercial exploitation would thus always be immoral.

It can be concluded at this point that in current practice the public interest has a strong presence in patent law and the role it has taken on is beneficial from a human dignity perspective, but it is not optimal because there is very little detail in reasoning of courts as they apply the relevant concepts in patent cases.

27.5.2   CATEGORY 2: SOME BUT NOT ALL COMMERCIAL EXPLOITATION OF
               THE INVENTION IS CONSIDERED IMMORAL AND AGAINST PUBLIC
               POLICY OR WHERE SOME COMMERCIAL EXPLOITATION OF THE
               INVENTION RAISES PUBLIC INTEREST CONCERNS

The inventions with which this section is concerned fall into two broad types. First, there are inventions where some, but not all, commercial exploitation of the invention raises moral or ethical concerns. Such inventions might involve technology with a dual use for moral and immoral purposes, such as CRISPR technology, which could be used for both unacceptable germ line gene editing and acceptable gene editing for research purposes. The second type of invention is where the invention itself is not immoral but some commercial exploitation of the invention may raise public interest concerns.

At present, as discussed earlier, these types of invention fall outside the exception in Article 53(a) EPC. However, other provisions of patent law also offer opportunities to address balancing of the public interest. The majority of these provisions make no explicit reference to concepts of morality or human dignity, and the reasoning which is referred to in their application is more or less disconnected from discussions of the ethics or from human rights law concepts.

The most obvious links between the provisions of patent law and the types of invention included in this section are through the exceptions to patentability. Although Article 53(a) has been limited in scope to the extent that it is inapplicable to this category of inventions, Article 53(b) and (c) have ethical underpinnings and may also be linked to concepts of human dignity. Under Article 53(c), patents will not be granted for methods for treatment of the human or animal body by surgery or therapy and diagnostic methods practised on the human or animal body, although this exception does not apply to products for use in any of these methods.

Prior to the EPC 2000, the prohibition on patenting of medical methods was found in Article 52(4), which provided *inter alia* that 'diagnostic methods practised on the human or animal body shall not be regarded as inventions which are susceptible of industrial application'. This fiction of lack of industrial applicability was abandoned in EPC 2000, with the rationale for the exception is now clearly based on public health considerations.[111] However, the scope of this exception is very narrow, such that in vitro diagnostic method steps performed on isolated samples do not satisfy the criterion of 'practised on the human or animal body', and therefore are not excluded from patentability.[112]

Other patents in this category may be dealt with by means of the technical patentability criteria. In some cases, there is a reasonably obvious link to the public interest; for example, overly broad patents strain the patent bargain too far in favour of incentives for innovation against access. The most appropriate response to such overly broad patents is to narrow them by reference to the technical patentability criteria. The criteria of novelty, inventive step and industrial application are a 'hybrid mix of technical and legal components encompassing economic and social considerations', and their application by patent offices, and ultimately by EPO tribunals and national courts, can have important social and economic effects.[113]

The 'as such' limitations in Article 52(2) exclusions can also serve to limit the patentability of inventions which may have unethical implications. Although examples are scarce in Europe, in other jurisdictions, the product of nature doctrine[114] and the interpretation of the requirement of manner of manufacture[115] have served to limit patents on human genes with the reasoning in the cases making extensive references to ethical and moral arguments.

---

111. European Patent Office Administrative Council, 'Basic Proposal for the Revision of the European Patent Convention' (European Patent Organisation, Munich 2000) 45.
112. Chartered Institute of Patent Agents, *CIPA Guide to the Patents Acts* (8th ed Sweet & Maxwell, London 2016) [4A.07]; UK Intellectual Property Office, 'Examination Guidelines for Patent Applications relating to Medical Inventions in the UK Intellectual Property Office' (UKIPO, Newport 2016) [62]; G1/04 *Diagnostic Methods* of 16 December 2005; T1197/02 *Australian National University/Glaucoma* of 12 July 2006.
113. Aurora Plomer, 'The EPO as Patent Law-Maker in Europe' (2019) 25 European Law Journal 57, 61.
114. *Association for Molecular Pathology v. Myriad Genetics Inc* 133 S Ct 2107 (2013).
115. *D'Arcy v. Myriad Genetics Inc* [2015] HCA 35.

Defences to infringement also work to avoid problematic outcomes of patents in this area. As infringement is (currently) a matter of national law,[116] questions of infringement and defences to infringement are also a matter of national law, although there is some consistency across Europe due to changes implemented into national law in light of the Community Patent Convention. Two defences which mitigate unethical or immoral effects of patents are the experimental use exception[117] and the extemporaneous preparation of medicaments exception.[118]

In England and Wales, section 60(5)(b) of the Patents Act provides a defence to patent infringement for acts done for experimental purposes relating to the subject matter of the invention, and there are similar, although not uniformly applied, provisions in many other EPC Member States.[119] The defence is recognised as having two limbs. An act will fall within the defence if its purpose is to discover something unknown or to test a hypothesis[120] but will not be for experimental purposes if it is carried out in order to demonstrate to a third party that a product works or in order to amass information to satisfy a third party, such as a customer or a regulatory body.[121] The second limb concerns whether the conduct relates to the subject matter of the invention. Here, 'experimenting on' or 'experimenting into' a patented invention is within the scope of the defence, whereas 'experimenting with' or 'experimenting using' the patented invention is usually outside the scope of the defence.[122]

Section 60(5)(c) of the Patents Act 1977 (UK) provides a defence to infringement for the extemporaneous preparation in a pharmacy of a medicine for an individual in accordance with a prescription given by a registered medical or dental practitioner.[123] This section is also justified on public health grounds ensuring that pharmacists are able to carry out their

---

116. Although the UPC may have implications should it come into force in the future.
117. Section 60(5)(b) Patents Act 1977 (UK).
118. Section 60(5)(c) Patents Act 1977 (UK).
119. Community Patent Convention at Article 27(b). Geertrui van Overwalle et al., 'Models for Facilitating Access to Patents on Genetic Inventions' (2006) 7 Nature Reviews Genetics 143, 143; Trevor Cook, 'Responding to Concerns about the Scope of the Defence from Patent Infringement for Acts Done for Experimental Purposes Relating to the Subject Matter of the Invention' (2006) Intellectual Property Quarterly 193; Trevor Cook, *A European Perspective as to the Extent to which Experimental Use, and Certain Other Defences to Patent Infringement, Apply to Differing Types of Research: A Report for the Intellectual Property Institute* (Intellectual Property Institute, London 2006).
120. *Monsanto Co v. Stauffer Chemical Co* [1985] RPC 515 (CA) 542.
121. *Ibid.*, 542.
122. Trevor Cook, 'A European Perspective as to the Extent to Which Experimental Use, and Certain Other Defences to Patent Infringement, Apply to Differing Types of Research: A Report for the Intellectual Property Institute' (Intellectual Property Institute, London 2006) 31.
123. The corresponding provision of the Community Patent Convention is Article 27(c).

professional role and that patients obtain necessary medicines without obstruction caused by the necessity of having regard to patents.[124]

The final areas of patent law which work to mitigate outcomes contrary to the public interest in this category are compulsory licensing and crown use. Compulsory licences are often suggested as a possible solution to ameliorate the access problems potentially created by patents.[125] Compulsory licences permit individuals other than the patent owner to exploit the invention that is the subject of a patent when the patentee is unable or unwilling to do so. Although very few applications are made for compulsory licences, common wisdom provides that the mere prospect of the grant of such a licence may result in the working of an invention or willingness to license.[126]

Similar to the compulsory licensing provisions, under the Crown use provisions in sections 55-59 of the UK Patents Act a government department or a person authorised in writing by a government department may, for the services of the Crown, do certain acts in relation to a patented invention without the consent of the proprietor of the patent. These acts include, in relation to a product, making and using the product, and, in relation to a process, using the process. Section 57A of the Patents Act provides that compensation for loss of profit must be paid for the Crown use. Nothing in these provisions requires that notice must be given to the patent proprietor prior to the Crown use or that attempts to license from the patent proprietor must be made. The making, use or importation of pharmaceuticals for supply to National Health Service patients on prescription is specifically mentioned within the terms of the provisions as falling within the ambit of Crown use.[127]

Some inventions give rise to moral and ethical concerns, whether that be where all commercial exploitation of the invention is clearly immoral and against public policy (category 1) or where some commercial exploitation of the invention raises public interest concerns (category 2). At present, the legal analysis and approach to inventions in category 1, as opposed to the inventions outlined in category 2, is separate and distinct, and lacks a

---

124. Naomi Hawkins, 'An Exception to Infringement for Genetic Testing – Addressing Patient Access and Divergence Between Law and Practice' (2012) International Review of Intellectual Property and Competition Law 641; Bengt Domeij, *Pharmaceutical Patents in Europe* (Stockholm Studies in Law, Kluwer Law International, The Hague 2000) 310.

125. *See* for example William Cornish, Margaret Llewelyn and Mike Adcock, 'Intellectual Property Rights (IPRs) and Genetics: A Study into the Impact and Management of Intellectual Property Rights within the Healthcare Sector' (Public Health Genetics Unit, Cambridge Genetics Knowledge Park, Cambridge 2003) section C(2)(c); Nuffield Council on Bioethics, *The Ethics of Patenting DNA: A Discussion Paper* (Nuffield Council on Bioethics, London 2002) 54-56.

126. Lionel Bently et al., *Intellectual Property Law* (5th ed, OUP 2018) 684.

127. *Pfizer Corporation v. Ministry of Health* [1965] AC 512 (HL); Patents Act 1977 section 55(1)(a)(ii), section 55(1)(c).

coherent and connected framework. However, it is our contention that the concerns about the inventions in category 1 and category 2 are on the same continuum.

An approach to the public interest in patent law which is underpinned by the principle of human dignity will provide a cogent framework for legal analysis which will allow concerns about morality and public policy in patent law to be addressed in a consistent and coherent manner. We explore this further in section 27.6 below.

27.6   WHAT ROLE SHOULD MORALITY AND PUBLIC
            POLICY PLAY IN PATENT LAW?

Morality, public policy and human dignity clearly have a significant role in European patent law. In practice, that role is currently being discussed in very narrowly defined areas. In other areas, it is only being considered implicitly.

The use of human dignity in interpreting existing provisions of patent law provides a legal and theoretical framework for the interpretation of existing provisions in a coherent manner in accordance with the public interest. It also opens up a broader range of case law for practitioners and judges looking to interpret these provisions, which arguably answers to some extent increasing calls for an interpretation of intellectual property law which integrates human rights considerations.[128]

Human rights support both the private interest and the public interest components of patent law and provide a consistent and coherent basis for the interpretation of patent law provisions which touch on questions of morality and ethics.[129] Moreover, the concept of human dignity is sufficiently flexible and the case law recognises a wide margin of defence and respect for the plurality of diversity of moral cultures in Europe.[130] Although the application of human dignity to patent law can be criticised for being too indeterminate[131] and for allowing the importation of religious objections in a manner which lacks transparency,[132] while it may not be perfect, it adds legal content

---

128. *See* for example: Christophe Geiger, '"Constitutionalising" Intellectual Property Law? The Influence of Fundamental Rights on Intellectual Property in the European Union' (2006) 37 International Review of Intellectual Property and Competition Law 371, Duncan Matthews, 'Right to Health and Patents' in Christophe Geiger (ed.), *Research Handbook on Human Rights and Intellectual Property* (Edward Elgar 2015).
129. Van Overwalle, 257.
130. Aurora Plomer, 'Human Dignity, Human Rights, and Article 6(1) of the EU Directive on Biotechnological Inventions' in Aurora Plomer and Paul Torremans (eds), *Embryonic Stem Cell Patents: European Law and Ethics* (OUP 2009) 224.
131. Aurora Plomer, 'Human Dignity, Human Rights, and Article 6(1) of the EU Directive on Biotechnological Inventions' 209.
132. Aurora Plomer, 'Human Dignity and Patents' in Christophe Geiger (ed.), *Research Handbook on Human Rights and Intellectual Property* (Edward Elgar 2015) 485.

to concepts of morality and ethics in patent law which would otherwise be lacking.

At the same time, we recognise that the patent framework should not be the primary means of regulating the use of new technologies.[133] EU and national laws restrict the uses of new technologies on public safety grounds, such as those which regulate the clinical use of new pharmaceuticals. However, while patent law does not provide the only opportunity for regulation of new technologies, this does not mean that it should not more extensively accommodate public interest concerns. A state cannot discourage or prohibit a particular activity, for example, by prohibiting or restricting use, but, at the same time, encourage innovation in that activity by offering the opportunity of reward through the patent system; to do so is illogical and inconsistent. Full consideration of the ethical implications of particular technologies may more appropriately take place in contexts other than intellectual property law, but it does not follow that patent law should completely disregard these issues.

A patent application is frequently the first consideration of a new technology by any organ of a state and therefore, the first opportunity for an examination of the public interest issues arising from the commercial exploitation of the invention. Patent offices must not reject the opportunity to address the question of morality and public policy. The incorporation of reference to human dignity at relevant points in the patent life cycle would provide some appropriate safeguards to help rebalance the patent system in the public interest, and we explore this further below.

Section 27.5 has shown that in the identified categories the role of morality and public policy is limited. This section will make suggestions as to the role they should play in European patent law in both categories and beyond. We argue that for category one, the interpretation of morality and public policy should be more detailed and reasons should be given in the decisions of Boards and Courts to increase legal certainty. For category two, the recognition of the importance of human dignity in relevant cases, and interpretation of the relevant provisions of patent law in accordance with human dignity, will serve to better address concerns about ethics and morality. Finally, the public interest should be considered through the life cycle of the patent. We argue that these changes would not require a massive shift in practice and would bring about a more coherent approach to morality and public policy in patent law.

27.6.1   CATEGORY 1

The inventions in category 1 give rise to moral and ethical concerns relating to the subject matter of the invention and how the invention has been made.

---

133. T356/93 *Plant cells* of 21 February 1995, Reasons, 18.4.

In sections 27.3 and 27.5.1 above, it can be seen that references to morality, public policy and human dignity in patent law are rising. In the two most important cases in this area, *WARF* and *Brüstle*, morality and human dignity played a significant role. This practice is one that should continue in order to ensure that these fundamental rights are being taken into account in European patent law. However, we argue that this practice is not yet optimal and could be taken further.

Although *WARF* and *Brüstle* came to similar decisions and were both significant steps forward for considerations of morality and human dignity in patent law, the reasoning in each case focussed on different aspects. Both institutions implemented a broad understanding of human embryo and ensured that the destruction of a human embryo, even if not mentioned in the patent application, would mean that an invention would not be patentable. These decisions are extremely important and show the significance of morality and ethical considerations in patent law.

Although these decisions both represent an advance in the way in which morality, and human dignity in particular, are considered in patent law, we argue that these considerations should be developed further. The Enlarged Board in *WARF* did not find it necessary to view the practice in its Contracting Member States around the use of human embryos and whether the destruction of a human embryo was ever permitted. In fact, human embryonic stem cell research is permitted up to a point in many Contracting Member States.[134] In *Brüstle*, the CJEU defined human embryo quite broadly, which again, did not match with practice in many EU Member States.[135]

In both *WARF* and *Brüstle* the possible uses of the inventions were not given much consideration and it can be argued that they should have been. By linking commercial exploitation to the making of the invention (*WARF*), and linking the application for a patent to commercial exploitation (*Brüstle*), the potential benefits of the inventions were ignored. This is most perturbing in relation to the Board of Appeal decisions where previous practice with exceptions is to consider these potential benefits and weigh them against the consequences.

In these cases the immorality of the invention was assumed, which then influenced the final decision of the Board or Court in relation to the commercial exploitation of the invention. If the Boards of Appeal and the CJEU are going to expand morality considerations in patent law to asking whether the invention is immoral and thus all commercial exploitation of it is immoral, the reasoning behind this decision should be included.

---

134. On the lack of consensus on the ethical acceptability of human embryonic stem cell research, *see*: Gerard Porter, 'The Drafting History of the European Biotechnology Directive' in Aurora Plomer and Paul Torremans (eds), *Embryonic Stem Cell Patents: European Law and Ethics* (OUP 2009) 23-26.
135. *Ibid.*

By leaving out the reasoning behind questions relating to what is moral and what is not, there is an increase in legal uncertainty. Courts and Boards are abrogating their responsibility and shirking their duty to determine what is moral, what is not, and most importantly, how they came to that conclusion. Expanding the morality provision to an investigation as to the morality of the subject matter of the invention or how it is made places human dignity at the centre of the debate, but society is left without an explanation as to why the invention is immoral. The reasoning behind this is directly related to the final decision and should therefore be included in the final decision of the court.

Possible reasons against doing so must be taken into account. First, with regard to the Boards of Appeal of the EPO, panels consist of predominantly technical members. Given that the majority of case law at the EPO relates to very specific technological advances that are well understood by panellists who are familiar with the technology in question, the makeup of the panel is appropriate. However, when a moral or ethical concern is raised the same level of expertise is not present.

Leading on from that point, with regard to the CJEU, the Court may have been more willing to discuss matters of morality given their generalist legal perspective.[136] However, even with that generalist perspective a definition was given without having considered the practice in Member States and without providing clear reasons.

There are also some possible overarching reasons. First, it could be argued that considering possible uses of the invention is too speculative. However, numerous possible uses of the invention are often contained in the patent application so that the patentee is given protection for an appropriate range. Looking at the potential uses of an invention is something that has been done previously in cases such as *Oncomouse*. Additionally, in *Euthanasia Compositions*, abuse of the invention was found not sufficient to deny patent protection if there was a use for the invention that would not fall under Article 53(a) EPC.[137]

Furthermore, by taking into account the potential uses of the invention and weighing that against the moral and ethical implications, the Courts and Boards of Appeal would be addressing some of the broader concerns that we have addressed above. However, it must also be said that questions of access to medicine, and indeed access to other technologies, might be better addressed by attention to the flexibilities in patent law around licensing and defences to infringement, rather than the blunt tool of invalidity. These are not morality specific, but they do have moral implications. The lack of appropriate opportunity to address specific moral and ethical concerns

---

136. For multiple commentaries on generalist and specialist judiciaries in the European patent system, *see*: Christophe Geiger (ed), *Intellectual Property and the Judiciary* (Edward Elgar 2018).
137. T866/01 *Euthanasia Compositions/Michigan State*, Reasons 5.8.

related to not knowing all iterations of use could be addressed at this later stage.

Second, given the differences in opinion on moral and ethical issues among EU Member States and Contracting Member States, general rulings could be preferred as these can be implemented in any Member State without the need to determine an overall consensus. This is a fair point, but it was not followed in the *Brüstle* decision, and generally, some guidance is required for Member States to follow.

Finally, all national patent laws in Europe and all European patent laws contain a morality and public policy provision. Therefore, it is the duty of the Board or the Court to interpret this legal provision and give reasons for their decisions, be they generalist or specialist.[138] If this practice were optimised, the role of the public interest in patent law would be significantly more important and better reflect the balance necessitated by the patent social contract.

27.6.2   CATEGORY 2

The inventions in category 2 give rise to concerns which relate less to the subject matter of the invention, and more to the way in which the patent is exploited. These concerns are in relation to particular immoral types of uses of the invention, or the exploitation of the patent in ways that disadvantage particular sectors of the public, or the public generally. Existing provisions of patent law offer opportunities to address these problematic patents, as outlined in section 27.5.2 earlier. In many cases, these provisions provide an appropriate and adequate solution.

Moreover, in relation to some aspects by which the public interest is addressed, outlined in section 27.5.2, the scope for reference to human dignity is very narrow. Application of the technical patentability criteria is unlikely to draw on principles of human dignity without straining the interpretation of the legislation beyond breaking point. Similarly, it seems unlikely that principles of respect for human dignity will add anything to a consideration of whether the subject matter of the patent constitutes an invention under Article 52(2) EPC.

However, in some cases, the narrow, economically focused approach of patent law may be insufficient. The patent law bargain depends on the delicate balance between the private rights of the inventor and the public interest. There is more scope for reference to principles of human dignity in other existing patent law solutions which may be applied in relation to unethical inventions.

---

138. Even though both the Boards of Appeal and the CJEU have made statements indicating this was not something they had been tasked with, as elaborated on above.

Article 53(c) EPC exceptions of medical methods, defences to infringement, compulsory licensing and crown use all incorporate elements of the public interest, and all would be amenable to considerations of human dignity in relation to certain inventions. Although case law exploring these provisions is relatively limited, it is our contention that reference to principles of human dignity in the determination of these areas of patent law would provide a coherent link to appropriately weigh the public interest.

The obvious question which arises is then how human dignity might apply in these cases. Where there are exceptions to patentability the considerations of human dignity may arise both in the examination phase, before EPO tribunals, and potentially before the courts. In such cases, the analysis would potentially be similar to that in relation to the morality and public policy provisions as outlined above and could draw on the existing and developing case law. Article 53(c) EPC might be particularly amenable to this type of analysis, although current narrow interpretations of the provision leave very little scope for these types of arguments.

It is more complicated to conceive of the application of human dignity in relation to defences to infringement, which is a matter of national law and very rarely litigated. However, there is a clear potential for the public health considerations which underlie the extemporaneous medicament defence to draw on a human dignity analysis, should such a case arise. The compulsory licence and crown use provisions are also very rarely applied in court cases. However, there is in these cases a clear relationship between the underlying principles in these areas and questions of human dignity.

In practical terms, there is very little litigation that proceeds to trial in these areas and therefore little hope that these questions will result in helpful precedent in this area. However, increasingly, charitable and public interest cases are being brought by these groups in relation to patents perceived by these groups to be contrary to the public interest. There is therefore potential for a human dignity approach to be ventilated in such a case. Moreover, even in its absence, there is scope for these arguments to be put forward in patent negotiations, although without legal authority supporting them perhaps there is little scope for them to be decisive. Finally, particularly where there is a potential compulsory licence or crown use, there will be significant governmental involvement in negotiations. In such cases, a human dignity legal analysis would be helpful to balance the economic arguments, in support of the public interest.

27.6.3   How the Public Interest Should Play a Role in the Rest of the Patent Life Cycle

The failure of patent law to adequately respond to concerns about the moral and ethical implications of patents on particular inventions, and the wider problems of access to technologies is well recognised. Too often, patent law can be seen to be about the grant of patents in the context of economic rights and the commercialisation of inventions with scant attention paid to the broader public interest implications of those economic rights in practice.[139] However, as we have argued, importing a greater role for human dignity could help to rebalance patent law away from an excessive focus on trade, access to markets and economic incentives,[140] to more appropriately account for the public interest by addressing moral and ethical concerns.

Importantly, such rebalancing need not involve large changes in existing practice, for patent offices, patentees or patent users. The majority of patents do not raise public interest concerns and will therefore be entirely unaffected. Even in cases where patents do raise the concerns we have outlined above, the existing approach may be sufficient. However, an additional consideration of whether the existing approach reflects the obligation to respect human dignity may assist in cases where there are difficult moral and ethical questions.

A significant obstacle to the operation of human dignity in European patent law is its enforceability. Although there is evidence that the Boards of Appeal are beginning to have regard to the principle of human dignity, at least with respect to Article 53(a) EPC, the applicability of EU instruments to the EPC is limited and there is no mechanism within the EPC to require the EPO and its institutions to take into account or respect rules beyond those contained in the EPC.[141] An important exception is the Biotech Directive, however, which has been incorporated into the EPC and explicitly references human dignity. However, as the EPO is structurally insulated from the national legal systems and the EU machinery, its willingness to take into account human dignity in its granting procedures, including opposition procedures, remains to be seen.

The EPO, through its role in granting patents, is highly influential in defining and applying policy and unless the EPO moves to situate human dignity more centrally in relation to the moral and ethical aspects of patent law, progress in this area is likely to be slow.[142] However, as individual Member States of the EPC are, with few exceptions, subject to the EU Charter, there is potentially more scope for national court willingness to employ concepts of human dignity in their treatment of patent law at national level.

---

139. *See* for example: Aisling McMahon, 'Gene Patents and the Marginalisation of Ethical Issues' (2019) 41(2) European Intellectual Property Review 608.
140. Van Overwalle.
141. Plomer, 'The EPO as Patent Law-Maker in Europe' 65; *WARF*.
142. Plomer, 'The EPO as Patent Law-Maker in Europe' 73.

27.7   CONCLUSION

It is clear that morality and public policy have a significant role in European patent law. However, this chapter has shown that although great strides have been taken to ensure that human rights concerns, especially human dignity, are taken into account when the morality and public policy provisions are an issue, more can be done.

Concerns about the public interest arise in a small but significant number of inventions, be it where all commercial exploitation of the invention is clearly immoral and against public policy (category 1) or where some commercial exploitation of the invention raises public interest concerns (category 2). It has been shown that morality and public policy are considered in both categories, but not optimally. The legal analysis of morality and public policy in European patent law should be considered in more detail and should not be separated from questions of public interest relating to the operation of the patent system. More detailed reasoning in court decisions is required for category 1 and the scope for reference to human dignity in category 2 needs to be expanded.

We suggest that, in order to have a more coherent and connected approach to morality and public policy in patent law, attention needs to be drawn to the wider public interest implications of patents in practice and the potential uses of the inventions. Reference to the principle of human dignity draws these areas together and has the potential to make law more coherent across both areas. Consideration of the public interest implications of patents in this way should be applied at all relevant points in the patent life cycle. To do so would not require a huge change in practice and would help to ensure that the interests of society are balanced appropriately with those of the patentee.

Chapter 28

Personalized Medicine, Intellectual Property Rights and Human Rights[*]

Sven J.R. Bostyn[**]

28.1   INTRODUCTION

Personalized medicine is, without a doubt, the next big thing in the medical 'business' for many years to come. Personalized medicine must not be understood as the personal service one gets if one goes to the doctor, but encompasses a vast array of techniques and technologies that allow scientists and doctors to tailor medical treatment to the specific genetic makeup of the patient. Some patients may have a mutation in their genetic code that makes them unsuitable for certain treatment with standard drugs, or at least certain drugs, as they might have severe side effects, or the drugs might simply not work because of metabolites produced in the body once the 'standard' medicament has been administered, or for any other reason. The techniques and technologies will be applicable in genetic screening of patients, diagnostic testing, and treating patients with as much as possible tailor-made drugs, even though in practice that will mean that patients are what is called

* This is a substantially reworked and updated version of the chapter with the same title the present author wrote for the previous edition of this book. This Chapter has gained much in relevance in the light of the COVID-19 pandemic caused by the 2019 novel coronavirus.
** Acknowledgment: This work was supported by the Collaborative Research Program for Biomedical Innovation Law, which is a scientifically independent collaborative research program supported by the Novo Nordisk Foundation (grant NNF17SA0027784).

stratified, or classified into different groups, towards which drug and treatment tailoring can be developed.

The development of all these techniques and technologies, many of which are still in early stages or yet to be developed, presents a plethora of legal issues. There are multiple medical law issues, relating to liability, informed consent and medical ethics. There is quite a major issue of privacy and access to all that information by healthcare providers and/or insurers. However interesting, those will not be dealt with in this Chapter. This Chapter will exclusively deal with patent law issues discussed in their own right, but also in the light of human rights questions around intellectual property rights.

There are quite a few patent issues that deserve scrutiny here, and the present Chapter will critically address the most important ones, being which techniques and technologies within the field of personalized medicine can and are being patented and which are the problems which need to be addressed in this vast area of technology and how they can be tackled.

In the second instance, a critical appraisal is being made of the human rights aspects of personalized medicine. This has largely remained untouched by the academic literature. Even though there is a large volume of literature available covering the relationship between intellectual property rights and human rights, and within that category, even a substantial body of literature on the issue of access to drugs and the relationship with intellectual property rights, an investigation into the specific consequences of patenting personalized medicine on this discussion is not very well documented at this time. This Chapter hopes to provide a useful addition to a discussion which will only become more prominent in the future.

In section 28.2, we will provide some insight into the technological aspects of personalized medicine, allowing the reader to tackle the chapter on patent law issues in a more educated manner.

In section 28.3, a critical analysis of the various patent law issues will be carried out, which does not only show a number of problems facing this personalized medicine era but will also assist us in getting a better understanding of some of the flexibilities offered within the system to mitigate some of the at first sight worrying consequences.

In section 28.4, we will touch upon an issue that is largely underdeveloped in the academic literature, and that is the role of the regulatory system and in particular regulatory exclusivities, such as data and market exclusivity, in the context of personalized medicine. It will be clear from what is being discussed in that section that this introduces yet another layer of exclusive rights for marketing authorization holders of medicinal products, which brings with it another option to enforce those against third parties wishing to bring on the market generic versions of the reference product. As we will demonstrate, the traditional Trade-Related Aspects of Intellectual Property Rights (TRIPS) flexibilities are largely not applicable here, as these exclusivities are mainly not traditional intellectual property rights,[1] and to the extent that they are covered, the flexibilities are very limited indeed.

In section 28.5, we will discuss the difficult relationship between intellectual property rights and human rights in general first, to focus then later on the right to health and how to combine this right with the intellectual property rights system. It will be clear that this is always going to be a very difficult balancing exercise, indeed. We will, on that occasion, also present actions that can be taken to resolve the conundrum. Pre-empting some of the conclusions drawn in this Chapter, it should be recognized that, even though it is recognized that intellectual property rights are also a fundamental right and that their stimulation is important with a view to achieving the necessary medical innovation we need in personalized medicine, doing justice to the fundamental right to health is a moral duty, and that is no less so because the right to health is not an absolute one. At the end of the day, it is in the interest of society at large and the world community that the goal of achieving high levels of health across the world is attained, as disease knows no borders (at least in most cases). Governments and companies should, therefore, work towards improving access to drugs and high-quality healthcare. That will inevitably also have effects on the intellectual property right system. Those rights do not exist in a vacuum, and their effect can be limited in the general interest. It is in that connection that I have developed a number of actions that can and probably should be taken. Those reach from using TRIPS flexibilities in their broadest sense more widely, make more use of the patent pools, introduce a policy that discourages the use of TRIPS-plus provisions in trade negotiations, and develop a practice of linking trade and intellectual property with the right to health.

In section 28.6, we will finally draw some conclusions.

28.2   PERSONALIZED MEDICINE: WHAT IS IT?

Personalized medicine has become a common denominator for a variety of techniques and technologies which do not necessarily all relate to the treatment of patients. The term is also somewhat confusing, as it gives the impression that all of these techniques and technologies relate to the individualized treatment of a patient.

---

1. The TRIPS Agreement refers to data exclusivity in Article 39(3): 'Members, when requiring, as a condition of approving the marketing of pharmaceutical or of agricultural chemical products which utilize new chemical entities, the submission of undisclosed test or other data, the origination of which involves a considerable effort, shall protect such data against unfair commercial use. In addition, Members shall protect such data against disclosure, except where necessary to protect the public, or unless steps are taken to ensure that the data are protected against unfair commercial use.' Market exclusivity does not seem to be covered by the TRIPS Agreement.

In fact, most of the techniques and technologies understood to fall within the denomination of personalized medicine do not pertain to the treatment of an individual patient, but are based on so-called stratification strategies, i.e., technology strategies which aim at categorizing patients into a variety of patient groups, on the basis of which treatments targeted at those groups can be developed. The term personalized medicine hence encompasses a number of technologies which are, in fact, ancillary to the effective treatment of patients.

Schleidgen et al. have attempted to come to what they call an adequate précising definition[2] of what is personalized medicine:

> 'PM seeks to improve tailoring and timing of preventive and therapeutic measures by utilizing biological information and biomarkers on the level of molecular disease pathways, genetics, proteomics as well as metabolomics.'[3] The authors add that 'In medical practice, however, we will rarely witness a medical encounter where decisions are based exclusively on information of such biomarkers. Rather, in the majority of cases information from both standard biomarkers (like blood pressure) and new molecular biomarkers (for instance, the existence of a specific genetic variant) will be combined to come to a reasonable treatment decision. Therefore, we realize that PM can only be understood as an add-on to standard medical care.'[4]

The means used in these technologies consist mainly of identification of informative biomarkers and stratification of patients using genomic, proteomic and metabolomic technologies and information obtained from patients.

While it was once used to refer primarily to pharmacogenomics – the individualization of treatment based on an individuals' genomic profile, it is now more inclusive. Today, personalized medicine often refers to the consideration of individual, molecular, epigenetic and even non-molecular, characteristics of individuals in clinical decision making more widely.[5]

Another useful definition is to be found in a Report from the European Alliance for Personalised Medicine: 'Personalised medicine most frequently refers to a medical model using molecular profiling for tailoring the right therapeutic strategy for the right person at the right time, and/or to determine

---

2. For other definitions, *see* e.g., W.K. Redekop & D. Mladsi, *'The Faces of Personalized Medicine: A Framework for Understanding Its Meaning and Scope'*, 16 Value in Health Law, 2013, S4-S9.
3. S. Schleidgen, et al., *'What Is Personalized Medicine: Sharpening a Vague Term Based on a Systematic Literature Review'*, BMC Medical Ethics, 2013, 14:55, http://www.biomedcentral.com/1472-6939/14/55, p. 9.
4. *Ibid.*, p. 10.
5. G.P. Patrinos & B. Prainsack, *'Working Towards Personalization of Medicine: Genomics in 2014'*, 11 Personalized Medicine, 2014, 611-613.

the predisposition to disease and/or to deliver timely and stratified prevention. It may also involve imaging and other technologies.'[6]

It includes the prediction of disease risk, treatment response and safety profile based on genomic sequence data, but is much wider than that. It also includes what is called stratified medicine. The latter refers 'to the identification of subgroups of patients with a particular disease who respond to a particular drug or, alternatively, are at risk of side effects in response to a certain treatment. Indeed stratified medicine is already being used in the clinic. Drugs such as gefitinib and erlotinib, for instance, are being used to treat patients with non-small-cell lung cancer who have mutations in the epidermal growth factor receptor (EGFR) 3, 4, and vemurafenib is being used for the treatment of metastatic melanoma in patients with BRAF V600 mutations. By identifying those patients who have a specific molecular subtype of the disease, it is possible to provide more effective, targeted treatment. Almost certainly, stratification is an important step towards personalized medicine. Indeed it is a core element in any effort to customize healthcare based on individual differences.'[7]

The following terms and concepts are relevant for a proper understanding of the concept of personalized medicine:

> *Biomarker:* 'A characteristic that is objectively measured and evaluated as an indicator of normal biological processes, pathogenic processes, or pharmacological responses to a therapeutic intervention.'[8] A biological marker (biomarker) is simply a molecule that indicates an alteration in physiology from the normal. For example, any specific molecular alteration of a cancer cell either on DNA (deoxyribonucleic acid), RNA (ribonucleic acid), or protein level can be referred to as a molecular marker. A biomarker is defined as a characteristic that is objectively measured and evaluated as an indicator of normal biologic processes, pathogenic processes, or pharmacologic responses to a therapeutic intervention. Applications of biomarkers relevant to personalized medicine are: The biomarker would specifically and sensitively reflect a disease state and could be used for diagnosis, for predicting response to drug, and for disease monitoring during and following

---

6. '*Innovation and Patient Access to Personalised Medicine*', European Alliance for Personalised Medicine, 2013, p. 8.
7. European Science Foundation (ESF), '*Personalised Medicine for the European Citizen: Towards More Precise Medicine for the Diagnosis, Treatment and Prevention of Disease (iPM)*, Strasbourg', 2012, p. 13.
8. H. Salter & R. Holland, '*Biomarkers: Refining Diagnosis and Expediting Drug Development – Reality, Aspiration and the Role of Open Innovation*', 276 Journal of Internal Medicine, 2014, (215-228), 215.

therapy; Biomarkers can be used as drug targets in drug development; Biomarkers might serve to integrate diagnostics and therapeutics.[9]

Genomics: The study of all the genes in an organism – their sequences, structure, regulation, interaction, and products.

Pharmacogenomics: Is the use of genetic sequence and genomics information in patient management to enable therapy decisions. The genetic sequence and genomics information can be that of the host (normal or diseased) or of the pathogen.[10]

Pharmacogenomics promises to enable the development of safer and more effective drugs by helping to design clinical trials such that non-responders would be eliminated from the patient population and take the guesswork out of prescribing medications. It will also ensure that the right drug is given to the right person from the start. In clinical practice, doctors could, before prescribing, test patients for specific Single nucleotide polymorphism (SNP) known to be associated with non-therapeutic drug effects to determine which drug regimen best fits their genetic makeup.[11]

A leading example is genetic testing related to the antiviral drug, abacavir, for human immunodeficiency virus (HIV). About 5% to 8% of people of European descent, 2% to 5% of African Americans, and 2% to 7% of Hispanics have a histocompatibility gene variant, HLA-B*5701, that confers a risk of a serious hypersensitivity reaction if exposed to abacavir.[12] Presence of the variant is associated with a 50% likelihood of a hypersensitivity reaction, whereas the absence of the variant has a negative predictive value of > 99%. Because the hypersensitivity reaction can be life-threatening, the standard of practice now calls for genetic testing before the use of this drug, with the use of an alternative drug if the test is positive:[13]

Pharmacogenetics: A term recognized in pharmacology in the pre-genomic era, is the study of the influence of genetic factors on action of drugs as opposed to genetic causes of disease. Now, it is the study of the linkage between the individual's genotype and the individual's ability to metabolize a foreign compound. The pharmacological effect of a drug depends on pharmacodynamics (interaction with the target or the site of action) and pharmacokinetics (absorption, distribution and metabolism). It also covers the influence of various factors on these processes. Drug metabolism is

9. K.K. Jain, *'Textbook of Personalized Medicine'*, Springer, New York, 2009, p. 59.
10. *Ibid.*, p. 105.
11. *Ibid.*, p. 106.
12. E. Phillips & S. Mallal, *'Successful translation of Pharmacogenetics into the Clinic: The Abacavir Example'*, 13 Mol Diagn Ther, 2009, 1-9.
13. W. Burke, S.B. Trinidad, N.A. Press, *'Essential Elements of Personalized Medicine'*, 32 Urologic Oncology: Seminars and Original Investigations, 2014, (193-197) 194.

one of the major determinants of drug clearance and the factor that is most often responsible for interindividual differences in pharmacokinetics. Pharmacogenetics links genotype and phenotype.[14]

It is estimated that genetics can account for 20%–95% of variability in drug disposition and effects. Genetic polymorphisms in drug-metabolizing enzymes, transporters, receptors, and other drug targets have been linked to interindividual differences in the efficacy and toxicity of many medications.[15]

Proteomics: The term 'proteomics' indicates PROTEins expressed by a genOME and is the systematic analysis of protein profiles of tissues.[16] There is an increasing interest in proteomics technologies now because DNA sequence information provides only a static snapshot of the various ways in which the cell might use its proteins whereas the life of the cell is a dynamic process.[17]

Purely gene-based expression data is not adequate for dissection of the disease phenotype at the molecular level. There is no strict correlation between the gene and the actual protein expression. Therefore, the cell's full proteome cannot be deciphered by analysis at the genetic level alone. It is necessary to look at the proteins directly to understand the disease at a molecular level. Aberrations in the interaction of proteins with one another are at the heart of the molecular basis of many diseases. For example, genomic analysis alone may not suffice to understand type 2 diabetes mellitus as the insulin gene may be normal and the disease may arise from an abnormality at any point in the complex pathway that involves insulin and the complex proteins with which it interacts.[18]

Metabolomics: The human metabolome is best understood by analogy to the human genome, i.e., where the human genome is the set of all genes in a human being, the human metabolome is the set of all metabolites in a human being. In a systems biology approach, metabolomics provides a functional readout of changes determined by the genetic blueprint, regulation, protein abundance and modification, and environmental influence. Metabolomics is the study of the small molecules, or metabolites, contained in a human cell, tissue, or organ (including fluids) and involved in primary and intermediary metabolism.[19] Metabolites are the quantifiable molecules with the closest link to the phenotype. Many phenotypic and

---

14. K.K. Jain, *supra*, 2009, p. 69.
15. *Ibid.*, p. 69.
16. *Ibid.*, p. 121.
17. *Ibid.*, p. 121.
18. *Ibid.*, p. 122.
19. *Ibid.*, p. 129.

genotypic states, such as a toxic response to a drug or disease prevalence are predicted by differences in the concentrations of functionally relevant metabolites within biological fluids and tissues.[20] Such changes in the biochemical phenotype are of direct interest to pharmaceutical, biotech, and health industries once appropriate technology allows the cost-efficient mining and integration of this information.[21]

Drug target: Generally, the 'target' is the naturally existing cellular or molecular structure involved in the pathology of interest on which the drug-in-development is designed to act. Target identification and validation comprise the complex set of experimentation that aims to identify the key molecular drivers of disease and confirm that pharmacological modulation of that target leads to a net clinical benefit in that disease.[22] The majority of targets currently selected for drug discovery efforts are proteins.[23]

The aim of the personalized medicine is to match the right drug to the right patient and in some cases, even to design the treatment for a patient according to genotype and other individual characteristics.[24]

Even though the sequencing of the human genome has enabled the practice of medicine to enter an era in which the individual patient's genome will help determine the optimal approach to care, whether it is preventive, diagnostic, or therapeutic,[25] it would be ill-conceived to reduce personalized medicine only to genomics, as many other technologies play a crucial role in the development of what we now call personalized medicine.

Personalized medicine has developed out of the shortcomings of traditional medicine, which started from the identification of lead molecules. These were then tested in vivo. Based on those results, and after clinical trials, a drug was brought on the market. This approach has quite a high number of inefficiencies built-in. First of all, it ignores the specific circumstances of patients. One patient reacts better to a certain drug than another. Indeed, a certain drug has, in certain situations, no effect at all for a specific patient.

Second, and partly based on the previous argument, in the absence of taking into consideration the genetic constitution of patients, certain drugs are not effective at all. For instance, patients with certain genetic mutations might not be susceptible at all to the administration and use of a certain drug.

---

20. *Ibid.*, p. 130.
21. *Ibid.*, p. 130.
22. A.M. Manning, '*Target Identification and Validation*', in, J.J. Li & E.J. Corey (eds), '*Drug Discovery: Practices, Processes, and Perspectives*', John Wiley & Sons, Hoboken, N.J., 2013, p. 43.
23. *Ibid.*, p. 45.
24. K.K. Jain, '*Textbook of Personalized Medicine*', Springer, New York, 2009, p. 1.
25. *Ibid.*, p. 2.

Third, the use of drugs in the traditional manner also ignores side effects that may occur in certain patients, as apart from dosage and testing of allergic reactions, no further filtering takes place prior to the administration of a drug. Such methods obviously present further inefficiencies in the treatment of medical conditions.

Fourth, the traditional approach also missed quite a few medical conditions which may have been considered to be less prevalent, as the traditional process attempted to target the most common medical conditions.

In other words, the traditional process of development of new drugs was quite unsophisticated, and 'missed' not only a number of medical conditions but was also a very inefficient, and in part, ineffective way of treating a patient.

With the advent of gene technology, that all changed. The growing strength in computational power allowed technology to make genetic profiles of patients, thus presenting the first step into the process towards personalized medicine. On the basis of a genetic profile of a patient, it is first of all possible to derive some diagnostic conclusions, such as the predisposition for certain genetic conditions. The genetic profile of a patient also allows targeting medication in a far more superior personalized fashion. Access to genetic profiles of patients also has important consequences for future drug and therapy development. Genetic profiling can be used to study the distribution of certain mutations in (parts of) a population, thus allowing to provide a more targeted approach towards drug development. For example, certain mutations seem to be prevalent in certain populations.[26] That knowledge allows one to target a diagnostic and/or therapeutic treatment towards that population. Research has shown that for any two randomly selected individuals, the human genome shows a variation between these individuals of about 0.5% of the entire genome. The majority of these differences involve simply a single unit in the DNA code, which are referred to as SNPs. This variation can influence disease and must thus be considered in research into studying the influence of genetics on human health.[27]

Even though strictly speaking not confined to personalized medicine, other health crises such as the fight against antimicrobial resistance[28] and the urge to develop drugs for suddenly emerging outbreaks of often severely

---

26. G.S. Ginsburg & H.F. Willard (eds), *'Genomic and Personalized Medicine'*, 2nd edn., volume 1, Elsevier, 2013, pp. 12-14.
27. *Ibid.*, p. 9.
28. Antibiotic resistance is now a health crisis and affects not only people in developing countries, but is a huge problem also in the industrialized part of the world, and maybe even more there, as the overconsumption and inadequate prescription of antibiotics presents life threatening challenges to the medical profession and to patients. *See*, e.g., *'The evolving threat of antimicrobial resistance Options for action'*, WHO, Geneva, 2012, available at https://apps.who.int/iris/handle/10665/44812 (last visited 2 January 2020); C. Årdal, et al., *'Developing New Economic Models to Incentivise Antibiotic Discovery and Development Activities While Safeguarding the Efficacy of Antibiotics by Researching and*

debilitating or even lethal diseases[29] are also crucial issues, but are beyond the scope of this Chapter. What is interesting to observe in this regard is that intellectual property rights have without a doubt a negative effect on access to affordable drugs, as a patent right traditionally provided some type of monopolistic or at least some exclusionary right, but their existence, and even their non-existence for that matter, is still unable to resolve, for instance, the antibiotic resistance challenge. Those types of battles prove that intellectual property (IP) plays a certain role, but is not the only and definitely not always the magic formula that influences access to drugs. Attaining the highest level of health, and fulfilling the goals under the right to health, as explained in this Chapter, are hence not solely a matter of intellectual property rights, but deserves a holistic approach. The mission with this Chapter is, though, to discuss the relationship between intellectual property rights and human rights in the context of personalized medicine, and will therefore not discuss those other vital aspects.

28.3   PATENT LAW ISSUES

28.3.1   INTRODUCTION

Now that we have a good idea of what personalized medicine encompasses, we can also appreciate that a vast array of techniques and technologies are used, not all new and untested, but most definitely a large variety of them. That also implies that discussing the patent law framework will require an approach that goes beyond one single technology.

If we would summarize all the different techniques and technologies which are used in personalized medicine and taking into account that the present section is only covering patent issues, we could classify those technologies under the following subheadings:

- patenting of genes and gene-related inventions;
- patenting of (predictive) diagnostic methods;
- patenting of chemical molecules;
- patenting of medical treatments and of second and further medical indications (to the extent possible if we talk about a future personalized dosage for each patient group).

Advocating Their Appropriate Use', Drive-AB, 2018, available at http://drive-ab.eu/wp-content/uploads/2018/01/CHHJ5467-Drive-AB-Main-Report-180319-WEB.pdf (last visited 2 January 2020).
29. For example Ebola, Zika etc.

The above catalogue is by no means aiming to be exhaustive, as other technologies such as screening methods[30] and the use of antibodies[31] are also most relevant, but in view of the case law development and critical issues, we have decided to limit the analysis in the present section to the technologies listed above.

In what follows, we will provide a critical appraisal of the various patent issues relating to the technologies listed above.

28.3.2   PATENTING OF GENES AND GENE-RELATED INVENTIONS

First, there is the patentability of genes. Indeed, a gene may have been isolated, which is associated with a certain disease. Prototypical and almost mythical example is the BRCA1 and BRCA2 genes.[32] Or a gene could have been isolated of which it is later discovered that a polymorphism to that gene is associated with disease.

The patent law issues relating to the patentability of genes are not new, and in the view of the author, recent years have not shown much evolution in the debate or the narrative for that matter. The only exception to that assertion could maybe be the Myriad decision in the United States (US).[33] Observe the wording 'could maybe'. I am not convinced that the Myriad decision has, in fact, changed that much in the paradigm of patenting human genes in the US, but that will be discussed later. What Myriad does show, is that the US Supreme Court has over the last years restricted what amounts to the patent-eligible subject matter, and has been a showcase for a revival of judicially created exclusions.[34]

28.3.2.1   Europe

In Europe, the situation regarding the patentability of genes has been and still is relatively unchanged for a number of years. Article 5 sets out clearly that human genes are patentable, as long as that DNA sequence has been isolated

---

30. Which admittedly are often applied in combination with gene sequences, and to that extent, patent protection will in those cases cover both the screening method as a diagnostic test, and the gene sequence of interest. Patent protection covering such screening methods will in many situations be covered by discussing the patent issues relating to gene sequences and diagnostic methods.
31. On the patentability of antibodies, *see* my, *'Patenting Antibodies after HGS v Lilly: More Questions Raised than Answered'*, CIPA Journal, October 2012, 573-580.
32. *See* further subsection 28.3.2.2 for a discussion of those cases.
33. Association for Molecular Pathology, et al., *Petitioners v. Myriad Genetics, Inc.*, et al., 133 S. Ct. 2107; 186 L. Ed. 2d 124; 2013 U.S. LEXIS 4540; 106 U.S.P.Q.2D (BNA) 1972; 24 Fla. L. Weekly Fed. S 276.
34. *See also*, R.S. Eisenberg, *'Wisdom of The Ages or Deadhand Control? Patentable Subject Matter For Diagnostic Methods After In Re Bilski'*, 3 Case Western Journal of Law, Technology & The Internet, 2012, (1-65), 8.

from the human body or otherwise produced by a technical process, even if the sequence so isolated or obtained is identical to the naturally occurring DNA sequence.[35]

I have been critical in the past of the added value of the biotech directive.[36] However, I think that the legal framework set out in the directive for the patentability of human genes is a clear example of a beneficial consequence of the biotech directive. Article 5 is a clear rule which leaves no room for manoeuvre and for the kind of confusing considerations which the US Supreme Court has made in the Myriad decision. One may not agree with the stance taken by the Biotech Directive, but at least it has the advantage of clarity and legal certainty, something which is currently lacking in the US. Legal certainty is very important in the area of intellectual property law, as any lack of it will have an impact on the future of research, public and private alike, and will influence the related investment in innovation.

That does not mean that there has not been a debate, but that debate has seen very few if any new arguments apart from those already known for some time.[37] It would be beyond the scope of this Chapter to deal with these arguments and objections in detail. Suffice to say that arguments range from the rather fundamentalistic view that no patents should be granted for anything that pertains to the human being, including isolated elements such as DNA sequences or genes over the more balanced expression of concern about the consequences of gene patents for subsequent research to these who think that genes should be patentable. I have made clear in the past that I am in the camp of those who think that DNA should not be excluded from patentability outright, but we have to be aware of certain consequences, or at least potential ones.[38] As most patent applications for DNA are filed at a very early stage of the research process, it has been argued that by granting product claims for such sequences, subsequent research could be hampered.[39] It is in that connection that the term 'patent thickets' has been

---

35. *See* Article 5(2) Directive 98/44/EC on the legal protection of biotechnological inventions, OJ L 213, 30/07/1998.
36. *See*, S.J.R. Bostyn, '*A Decade after the Birth of the Biotech Directive: Was it Worth the Trouble?*', in, E. Arezzo & G. Ghidini, 'Biotechnology and Software Patent Law: A Comparative Review on New Developments', Edward Elgar Publishing, Cheltenham, 2011, pp. 221-259.
37. For a more elaborate discussion on the patentability of genes, *see* S.J.R. Bostyn, '*Patenting DNA Sequences (Polynucleotides) and Scope of Protection in the European Union: An Evaluation*', Luxemburg, European Communities, 2004, pp. 37 et seq. (hereinafter Bostyn, EC Report 2004).
38. *Ibid.*
39. At least in Europe, those potential consequences could potentially be limited due to the fact that no absolute product protection can be granted for DNA. *See* in that connection, Judgment of the Court (Grand Chamber) of 6 July 2010 (reference for a preliminary ruling from the Rechtbank's Gravenhage – Netherlands) – *Monsanto Technology LLC v. Cefetra BV, Cefetra Feed Service BV, Cefetra Futures BV, Alfred C. Toepfer International GmbH*, (Case C-428/08). For an extensive discussion of the difference between absolute

cast.[40] It must be said, though, very few if any patent thickets have been found to date in this area of technology. However, one cannot deny that a patent for a DNA sequence will have some effect on subsequent research where that DNA sequence is needed. And in view of the fact that there is no way of inventing around a DNA sequence, negative effects can be expected. Indeed, freedom to operate will be limited because of these patents to some extent, but the literature has not been able to provide much evidence that the effects of patenting in this area have, in fact, inhibited research.

28.3.2.2 The United States

In the United States of America, the patentability of genes was for many years almost evident. Recent developments in case law, and in particular the active role of the US Supreme Court in attempting to clarify the boundaries of what constitutes patent-eligible subject matter and what not has led to rather ground-breaking decisions both in the area of biotechnology and software.

The most relevant case relating to the patentability of genes is the *AMP v. Myriad Genetics* judgment by the US Supreme Court.[41]

The decision in the Myriad case can be readily summarized as follows. This case involved 'patents filed by Myriad after it made one such medical breakthrough. Myriad discovered the precise location and sequence of what are now known as the BRCA1 and BRCA2 genes. Mutations in these genes can dramatically increase an individual's risk of developing breast and ovarian cancer. The average American woman has a 12% to 13% risk of developing breast cancer, but for women with certain genetic mutations, the risk can range between 50 and 80 percent for breast cancer and between 20 and 50 percent for ovarian cancer. Before Myriad's discovery of the BRCA1 and BRCA2 genes, scientists knew that heredity played a role in establishing a woman's risk of developing breast and ovarian cancer, but they did not know which genes were associated with those cancers. Myriad identified the exact location of the BRCA1 and BRCA2 genes on chromosomes 17 and 13. [...]. Knowledge of the location of the BRCA1 and BRCA2 genes allowed

---

product protection and purpose-limited protection for gene sequences, *see also* S.J.R. Bostyn, '*Narrow Trousers and Narrow Patents, a Health Risk? Product Protection or Purpose-Bound Protection for Biotechnological Inventions*', Bio-Science Law Review, 2004/2005, 89-95. The views expressed therein were largely confirmed in a more recent European Expert Group Report, which the present author chaired: S.J.R. Bostyn, et al., '*Final Report of the Expert Group on the Development and Implications of Patent Law in the Field of Biotechnology and Genetic Engineering, European Commission, (E02973)*', 2016. 265 pp. (http://ec.europa.eu/growth/industry/intellectual-property/patents/biotechnological-inventions/index_en.htm), in particular pp. 180-264.

40. *See* for more details, Bostyn, EC Report 2004, pp. 113 et seq.
41. Association for Molecular Pathology, et al., *Petitioners v. Myriad Genetics, Inc.,* et al., 133 S. Ct. 2107; 186 L. Ed. 2d 124; 2013 U.S. LEXIS 4540; 106 U.S.P.Q.2D (BNA) 1972; 24 Fla. L. Weekly Fed. S 276.

Myriad to determine their typical nucleotide sequence. That information, in turn, enabled Myriad to develop medical tests that are useful for detecting mutations in a patient's BRCA1 and BRCA2 genes and thereby assessing whether the patient has an increased risk of cancer.'[42] Representative claims are claims 1 and 2 of US Patent 5,747,282 (the '282 patent).[43] The Supreme Court started by saying that '[I]t is undisputed that Myriad did not create or alter any of the genetic information encoded in the BRCA1 and BRCA2 genes. The location and order of the nucleotides existed in nature before Myriad found them. Nor did Myriad create or alter the genetic structure of DNA. Instead, Myriad's principal contribution was uncovering the precise location and genetic sequence of the BRCA1 and BRCA2 genes within chromosomes 17 and 13.'[44] It then held that 'Myriad found the location of the BRCA1 and BRCA2 genes, but that discovery, by itself, does not render the BRCA genes "new … composition[s] of matter," §101, that are patent eligible.'[45]

What the US Supreme Court hence held in that decision is that genomic DNA is no longer patentable. In order to be patentable, a product claimed must have 'markedly different characteristics from any found in nature.'[46]

But the Supreme Court also said that cDNA remains perfectly patentable: 'cDNA is not a "product of nature" and is patent eligible under §101, except insofar as very short series of DNA may have no intervening introns to remove when creating cDNA. In that situation, a short strand of cDNA may be indistinguishable from natural DNA.'[47]

I would assume that the Supreme Court also expects that cDNA to be 'markedly different' from any found in nature. This rather mysterious criterion will probably lead to many years of speculation in the academic literature. It is rather difficult to speculate what this exactly means, and I am not going to attempt much speculation in this Chapter. We will have to wait for further case law from the lower courts and the Court of Appeals for the Federal Circuit (CAFC) to give meaning to that criterion. Any meaning currently given to that criterion by the United States Patent and Trademark Office (USPTO) is not necessarily very valuable, as this might change relatively quickly and be overturned rather swiftly by the judiciary. The position currently taken by the USPTO in this regard is that the 'markedly different' analysis is the following:[48]

---

42. 133 S. Ct. at 2112-2113.
43. Claim 1 of the '282 patent reads: '[a]n isolated DNA coding for a BRCA1 polypeptide,' which has 'the amino acid sequence set forth in SEQ ID NO:2.'; Claim 2 of the same patent reads: '[t]he isolated DNA of claim 1, wherein said DNA has the nucleotide sequence set forth in SEQ ID NO:1.'
44. 133 S. Ct. at 2116.
45. 133 S. Ct. at 2117.
46. 133 S. Ct. at 2117.
47. 133 S. Ct. at 2119.
48. *See* USPTO MPEP 2106.04(c) The Markedly Different Characteristics Analysis.

The markedly different characteristics analysis compares the nature-based product limitation to its naturally occurring counterpart in its natural state. Markedly different characteristics can be expressed as the product's structure, function, and/or other properties, and are evaluated based on what is recited in the claim on a case-by-case basis. If the analysis indicates that a nature-based product limitation does not exhibit markedly different characteristics, then that limitation is a product of nature exception. If the analysis indicates that a nature-based product limitation does have markedly different characteristics, then that limitation is not a product of nature exception. Examiners should keep in mind that if the nature-based product limitation is naturally occurring, there is no need to perform the markedly different characteristics analysis because the limitation is by definition directed to a naturally occurring product and thus falls under the product of nature exception. However, if the nature-based product limitation is not naturally occurring, for example, due to some human intervention, then the markedly different characteristics analysis must be performed to determine whether the claimed product limitation is a product of nature exception.

It is also important to observe that the Myriad judgment did not explicitly rule on the patentability of the type of predictive diagnostic tests which was the subject of the patent, i.e., a test for the predisposition to develop breast cancer. The Supreme Court expressly stated that the decision did not deal with that matter. That is remarkable, as much of the controversy around the Myriad patent was about the diagnostic test, more than on the DNA or gene sequence as such. Large parts of the diagnostic methods were held not patentable, however, by the CAFC judgment preceding the US Supreme Court decision,[49] and a more recent Court of Appeals for the Federal Circuit judgment in a related BRCA case kept the door firmly shut for diagnostic tests which do not go beyond the mere comparing of a patient sample with a test DNA sequence without adding anything more.[50] Diagnostic tests are the subject of the subsequent section of this Chapter, and we will hence not further dwell upon the issue here.

Some may be tempted to try to 'import' the ruling of the Myriad decision into the European context. That is an ill-conceived exercise, as there is a fundamental difference between Europe and the US. Whereas the US has no statutory exceptions to the patentable subject matter in the US Patents Act

---

49. The Association for *Molecular Pathology et al., v. Plaintiffs-Appellees, v. United States Patent and Trademark Office, Defendant, and Myriad Genetics, Inc., et al., Defendant-Appellant*, 689 F.3d 1303; 2012 U.S. App. LEXIS 17679; 103 U.S.P.Q.2D (BNA) 1681, CAFC, 16 August 2012, 2010-1406.

50. *University of Utah Research Foundation, Myriad Genetics, Inc., et al., Plaintiffs-Appellants, v. Ambry Genetics Corporation, Defendant-Appellee,* 774 F.3d 755; 2014 U.S. App. LEXIS 23692; 113 U.S.P.Q.2D (BNA) 1241, CAFC, 17 December 2014, 2014-1361, 1366.

and has the judicially created exclusions to fill that gap, the Biotech Directive has laid down a specific set of rules for the patentability of biotechnological inventions in the European Union (EU). As said earlier, Article 5(2) of the Biotech Directive does explicitly allow the patentability of a gene sequence, even if the structure would be identical to the naturally occurring sequence. It speaks for itself that in Europe, there is currently no room for the application of a product of nature doctrine or any kind of markedly different characteristics analysis.

As I already said earlier, even though the decision by the US Supreme Court in the Myriad case has shifted to some extent patent practice in the US, the consequences for patenting DNA will probably be quite limited, in view of the fact that cDNA will remain patentable, and pending a clearer understanding of the markedly different characteristics analysis, it can be assumed that such cDNA would be deemed to be so markedly different, even though this is probably going to cause some degree of legal uncertainty for the next coming years.

28.3.3   Diagnostic Methods and Methods for Treatment

28.3.3.1   Introduction

A second important layer of patent protection that is sought in the context of personalized medicine is diagnostic methods. Such methods aim at identifying or stratifying a patient population. For instance, a patent can be filed for a test which aims at identifying whether a particular patient is a carrier of a specific polymorphism which is associated with the disease. If the patient would be such carrier, the test would at least reveal a predisposition to acquire the disease in question.

The Myriad case is a good example of the issue. Even though there are multiple patents relating to the testing of patients for the predisposition to develop breast cancer, several of those have in common that what is tested is the presence of a polymorphism in a patient, said polymorphism corresponding to a gene sequence which shows a predisposition to developing breast cancer.

Another type of patent in this category aims at establishing whether a patient population shows a certain uptake pattern to certain drugs, or is susceptible to have severe side effects if a certain drug would be administered. Those patents use biomarkers which patients might have in their genome, proteome or metabolome.

In what follows, we will discuss the situation in Europe and the US, respectively.

28.3.3.2 Europe

Under European patent law, unlike in the US, as we will see later, diagnostic methods on the human body are excluded from patentability (Article 53(c) EPC). In vitro diagnostic methods are patentable, however. Indeed, only those diagnostic methods which are carried out *on the human body* are excluded from patentability. It will be appreciated that the key issue here is determining when a method is carried out on the human body. The issue has been decided by the Enlarged Board of Appeal (EBA) in the G 1/04 case.[51] Unfortunately, the decision is long-winded and not very clear at all, leaving to some extent legal uncertainty and room for manoeuvre. Simplifying matters to a large extent, the standard set out, in that case, can be summarized as follows.[52]

According to the EBA, 'diagnosis in connection with the patent exemption for diagnostic methods practised on the human or animal body under Article 52(4) EPC is the determination of the nature of a medical or veterinary medicinal condition intended to identify or uncover a pathology. It includes a negative finding that a particular condition can be ruled out.'[53]

Of further crucial importance for a good understanding of the case, is to recognize the various method steps involved in the making of a diagnosis, as defined earlier.

According to the EBA, the method steps to be carried out when making a diagnosis as part of the medical treatment of humans or the veterinary treatment of animals for curative purposes include:[54]

(1) the examination phase involving the collection of data (which can entail activities such as examining, measuring, administering substances, collecting of data);
(2) the comparison of these data with standard values;
(3) the finding of any significant deviation, i.e., a symptom, during the comparison; and
(4) the attribution of the deviation to a particular clinical picture, i.e., the deductive medical or veterinary decision phase.

The diagnostic step *stricto sensu* is the step representing the deductive medical or veterinary decision phase as a purely intellectual exercise, i.e., the conclusions drawn and decisions taken by the physician on the basis of all preceding steps and information gathered.

---

51. G 1/04, Diagnostic methods, OJ EPO, 2006, 334.
52. For a detailed discussion of that case, *see*, S.J.R. Bostyn, *'No Contact with the Human Body, Please! Patentability of Diagnostic Methods Inventions after G 1/04'*, EIPR, 2007, no. 6, 238-244.
53. G 1/04, reasons 5.1.
54. G 1/04, reasons 5.

A method falls only within the ambit of Article 53(c) EPC if the claim consists not only of a step which is useful or even essential to diagnosis but also contains all steps, both the:

- diagnostic step *stricto sensu*; and
- all preceding steps (including those of non-technical character), i.e., examination, data gathering, comparison (*see* points 1 to 3 above).

The preceding steps to the diagnostic step *stricto sensu* (i.e., steps 1 to 3) must be present and must also fulfil the requirement that they are 'practised on the human or animal body'. The EBA says in this context that 'all method steps *of a technical nature* of such a diagnostic method should satisfy the criterion "*practised on the human or animal body*", i.e., the *performance of each and every one of these steps should imply an interaction with the human or animal body, necessitating the presence of the latter.*'[55]

Another requirement is added thereto, being that in order to evaluate whether all steps are practised on the human body, it is important to know that only steps of a technical nature are taken into account for determining whether the steps are carried out on the human body.[56]

This means that, for instance, a three-step method, which contains one examination step of a technical nature practised on the human body, one non-technical step not practised on the human body, and finally the diagnosis *stricto sensu* step, would under the reasoning of the EBA be excluded from patentability, as all essential technical steps of the method are practised on the human body.

Applied to personalized medicine, to the extent that the diagnostic tests used would be in vitro, based on a sample taken from the patient, it is unlikely that there would be issues with the exclusion from patent protection under this exclusion. In most cases, the diagnostic tests will be carried out on a DNA sequence obtained from the patient, and will hence not be excluded as being a diagnostic method carried out on the human body.

We illustrate the above with two examples which are relevant as they have given rise in the US to a revocation of the patent, as we will see later in this Chapter. It must be admitted, though, that the claims read quite differently.

One of the Myriad patents in Europe (EP 699754) was upheld in amended form by the Technical Board of Appeal.[57] Even though these claims are not technically 'correlation' claims as many of the US claims which will be discussed further, the claims give an illustration of what is patentable at the European Patent Office (EPO) as a diagnostic method. A relevant claim reads:

---

55. G 1/04, reasons 6.4.
56. G 1/04, reasons 6.4.1.
57. T 80/05, Method of diagnosis/University of Utah, decision dated 19 November 2008.

1. A method for diagnosing a predisposition for breast and ovarian cancer in a human subject which comprises determining in a tissue sample of said subject whether there is a germline alteration that is a frameshift mutation in the sequence of the BRCA1 gene coding for a BRCA1 polypeptide altering the open reading frame for SEQ ID NO:2 said alteration being indicative of a predisposition to said cancer.

A second example is EP 1115403, the European equivalent of the US Patent 6,355,623 that gave rise to the *Mayo v. Prometheus* case, which we will discuss further below. The claims were granted, and no opposition has been filed. Relevant claim is claim 1:

Claim 1: An in vitro method for determining efficacy of treatment of a subject having an immune-mediated gastrointestinal disorder or a non-inflammatory bowel disease (non-IBD) autoimmune disease by administration of a 6-mercaptopurine drug, comprising determining in vitro a level of 6-thioguanine in a sample from said subject having said immune-mediated gastrointestinal disorder or said non-inflammatory bowel disease (non-IBD) autoimmune disease, wherein said treatment is considered efficient if the level of 6- thioguanine is in the range of about 230 pmol per 8 x 10 8 red blood cells to about 400 pmol per 8 x 10 8 red blood cells.

28.3.3.3   The United States

As far as the US is concerned, two relatively recent US Supreme Court decisions have cast considerable doubt on the patent-eligibility of patent claims for diagnostic processes in the area of personalized medicine. These cases are *Mayo v. Prometheus* and the *AMP v. Myriad* case, which will be discussed in the subsequent paragraphs. But it suffices first to say that unlike in Europe, there is no statutory exclusion from patentability for diagnostic methods and indeed also medical treatment methods, even if performed on the human body.

In *Mayo v. Prometheus*,[58,59] the patentee had discovered the relationship between the level of a particular metabolite in a patient's blood and whether a patient could and should safely be administered additional medication. Specifically, 6–TG metabolite in concentrations in excess of about 400 picomoles per 8x108 red blood cells risked toxicity, whereas concentrations of less than about 230 picomoles per 8x108 red blood cells risked

---

58. *Mayo Collaborative Services, DBA Mayo Medical Laboratories, et al., Petitioners v. Prometheus Laboratories, Inc.*, 132 S. Ct. 1289; 182 L. Ed. 2d 321; 2012 U.S. LEXIS 2316; 80 U.S.L.W. 4225; 90 A.L.R. Fed. 2d 685; 101 U.S.P.Q.2D (BNA).

59. For a commentary on the case, *see* e.g., N. Scott Pierce, '*A Great Invisible Crashing: The Rise and Fall of Patent Eligibility Through Mayo v. Prometheus*', 23 Fordham Intellectual Property, Media and Entertainment Law Journal, 2012, 186-290.

ineffectiveness.[60] The asserted claims taught that doctors should test the metabolite levels of the patient and, if the patient's metabolite concentration was less than the 230 picomoles floor, the doctor should increase the dosage; if the concentration was greater than the 400 picomoles cap, the doctor should decrease the dosage.[61]

A subsequent judgement by the Court of Appeals for the Federal Circuit in the *Ariosa Diagnostics, NC v. Sequenom* case[62] usefully summarized the two-step test which has been introduced in the Mayo case by the US Supreme Court: 'In *Mayo Collaborative Services v. Prometheus Laboratories*, the Supreme Court set forth a framework for distinguishing patents that claim laws of nature, natural phenomena, and abstract ideas from those that claim patent-eligible applications of those concepts. First, we determine whether the claims at issue are directed to a patent-ineligible concept. Id. at 1297. If the answer is yes, then we next consider the elements of each claim both individually and "as an ordered combination" to determine whether additional elements "transform the nature of the claim" into a patent-eligible application. Id. at 1298. The Supreme Court has described the second step of this analysis as a search for an "inventive concept" – i.e., an element or combination of elements that is "sufficient to ensure that the patent in practice amounts to significantly more than a patent upon the [ineligible concept] itself."'[63]

With the above test in mind, the Supreme Court in the Mayo case started by reminding us of the judicially created exceptions to patent-eligibility, in the absence of any statutory exception: 'The Court has long held that this provision contains an important implicit exception. "[L]aws of nature, natural phenomena, and abstract ideas" are not patentable. [...].'[64]

The Court added that 'an application of a law of nature or mathematical formula to a known structure or process may well be deserving of patent protection.',[65] whilst adding that 'still, as the Court has also made clear, to transform an unpatentable law of nature into a patent-eligible application of

---

60. Mayo, 132 S.Ct. at 1295.
61. Claim 1 of U.S. Patent No. 6,355,623 reads:

    'A method of optimizing therapeutic efficacy for treatment of an immune-mediated gastrointestinal disorder, comprising:

    (a) administering a drug providing 6-thioguanine to a subject having said immune-mediated gastrointestinal disorder; and
    (b) determining the level of 6-thioguanine in said subject having said immune-mediated gastrointestinal disorder,
    wherein the level of 6-thioguanine less than about 230 pmol per 8×10^8 red blood cells indicates a need to increase the amount of said drug subsequently administered to said subject and
    wherein the level of 6-thioguanine greater than about 400 pmol per 8×10^8 red blood cells indicates a need to decrease the amount of said drug subsequently administered to said subject.'

62. *Ariosa Diagnostics, Inc., et al. v. Sequenom, Inc., et al.*, Case Nos 14-1139. -1144 (Fed. Cir. Dec. 3, 2015).
63. Slip op., at 8.
64. Mayo, 132 S.Ct. at 1293.
65. Mayo, 132 S.Ct. at 1293-1294.

such a law, one must do more than simply state the law of nature while adding the words "apply it." *See*, e.g., Benson, *supra*, at 71-72, 93 S. Ct. 253, 34 L. Ed. 2d, 273.'[66]

The fundamental question before the Court concerned 'patent claims covering processes that help doctors who use thiopurine drugs to treat patients with autoimmune diseases determine whether a given dosage level is too low or too high. The claims purport to apply natural laws describing the relationships between the concentration in the blood of certain thiopurine metabolites and the likelihood that the drug dosage will be ineffective or induce harmful side-effects. We must determine whether the claimed processes have transformed these unpatentable natural laws into patent-eligible applications of those laws.'[67]

The Court ruled that in order to be patent-eligible subject matter, a patent claim that covers a process that focuses upon the use of natural law must also contain 'other elements or a combination of elements, sometimes referred to as *an "inventive concept," sufficient to ensure that the patent in practice amounts to significantly more than a patent upon the natural law itself.* [...].'[68]

Looking at the patent claim, the Court held that:

beyond picking out the relevant audience, namely those who administer doses of thiopurine drugs, the claim simply tells doctors to: (1) measure (somehow) the current level of the relevant metabolite, (2) use particular (unpatentable) laws of nature (which the claim sets forth) to calculate the current toxicity/inefficacy limits, and (3) reconsider the drug dosage in light of the law. These instructions add nothing specific to the laws of nature other than what is well-understood, routine, conventional activity, previously engaged in by those in the field.[69]

In a subsequent CAFC judgment in a case related to the BRCA cases, the CAFC kept the door firmly shut for diagnostic tests which do not go beyond the mere comparing of a patient sample with a test DNA sequence without adding anything more.[70] That case confirmed the ruling of the CAFC 2012 Myriad decision.[71]

---

66. Mayo, 132 S.Ct. at 1294.
67. Mayo, 132 S.Ct. at 1294.
68. Mayo, 132 S.Ct. at 1294, emphasis added.
69. Mayo, 132 S.Ct. at 1299.
70. *University of Utah Research Foundation, Myriad Genetics, Inc., et al., Plaintiffs-Appellants, v. Ambry Genetics Corporation, Defendant-Appellee*, 774 F.3d 755; 2014 U.S. App. LEXIS 23692; 113 U.S.P.Q.2D (BNA) 1241, CAFC, 17 December 2014, 2014-1361, -1366.
71. *The Association for Molecular Pathology et al., v, Plaintiffs-Appellees, v. United States Patent and Trademark Office, Defendant, and Myriad Genetics, Inc., et al., Defendant-Appellant*, 689 F.3d 1303; 2012 U.S. App. LEXIS 17679; 103 U.S.P.Q.2D (BNA) 1681, CAFC, 16 August 2012, 2010-1406.

In the 2012 Myriad case, the Court held in respect of method claims relating to comparing and analysing patient DNA samples with BRCA mutation genes that:

> [T]his claim[72] thus recites nothing more than the abstract mental steps necessary to compare two different nucleotide sequences: one looks at the first position in a first sequence; determines the nucleotide sequence at that first position; looks at the first position in a second sequence; determines the nucleotide sequence at that first position; determines if the nucleotide at the first position in the first sequence and the first position in the second sequence are the same or different, wherein the latter indicates an alteration; and repeats the process for the next position. Limiting the comparison to just the BRCA genes or, as in the case of claim 1 of the '999 patent, to just the identification of particular alterations, fails to render the claimed process patent-eligible. [...]. Myriad's claims do not apply the step of comparing two nucleotide sequences in a process. Rather, the step of comparing two DNA sequences is the entire process that is claimed.[73]

When it comes to the second step of the Mayo test, i.e., the search for the 'further inventive concept to take the claim into the realm of patent-eligibility', the present author must confess that this is a rather confusing concept, if comprehensible at all. The term was cast in the Mayo Supreme Court judgment. The present author is concerned about this evolution of US case law, as it seems to be in a direct line to conflate patentable subject matter eligibility with patentability requirements. A further inventive concept could refer to two different things. It could be seen as a requirement that there must be an invention, as an invention must be the result of an inventive concept. It could also be seen as another description of the inventive step requirement.

From how the Supreme Court in the Mayo case explains the concept, it could be derived that what the Court meant to refer to was, in fact, an inventive step threshold. That can be derived from the wording '"[P]ost-solution activity" that is purely "conventional or obvious can[not] transform an unpatentable principle into a patentable process".'[74] That seems to be further supported by the interpretation given by the CAFC in the Ambry case, where it held that 'The second paragraphs of claims 7 and 8 do nothing more

---

72. Claim 1 of U.S. Patent 5,710,001, which reads: '1. A method for screening a tumor sample from a human subject for a somatic alteration in a BRCA1 gene in said tumor which comprises gene comparing a first sequence selected form the group consisting of a BRCA1 gene from said tumor sample, BRCA1 RNA from said tumor sample and BRCA1 cDNA made from mRNA from said tumor sample with a second sequence selected from the group consisting of BRCA1 gene from a nontumor sample of said subject, [...]' '001 patent col. 155 ll. 2-16.

73. CAFC, 2012, slip op., p. 57.

74. Mayo, U.S. 566, 2012, slip op., p. 13, thereby quoting *Parker v. Flook,* 437 U. S., at 589, 590.

than spell out what practitioners already knew – how to compare gene sequences using routine, ordinary techniques. Nothing is added by identifying the techniques to be used in making the comparison because those comparison techniques were the well-understood, routine, and conventional techniques that a scientist would have thought of when instructed to compare two gene sequences.'[75] A line of reasoning which is particularly relevant for the subject of this Chapter is the discussion relating to claim 21 of the '441 patent.[76] The CAFC held on this point that:

> [E]ven if claim 21 of the '441 patent were patent-eligible – a question about which we express no view – claim 21 is qualitatively different from the method claims at issue here. Claim 21 claims a method of detecting alterations in which the alterations being detected are expressly identified in the specification by tables 11 and 12. These tables expressly identify ten predisposing mutations of the BRCA1 gene sequence discovered by the patentees. Thus, the detection in claim 21 is limited to the particular mutations the inventors discovered: detecting ten specific mutations from the wild-type, identified as '[p]redisposing [m]utations,' for the specific purpose of identifying increased susceptibility to specific cancers. Claims 7 and 8 are significantly broader and more abstract, as they claim all comparisons between the patient's BRCA genes and the wild-type BRCA genes. The first paragraphs of claims 7 and 8, as we held in our 2012 Myriad opinion, claim abstract comparisons. We hold today that the second paragraphs recite only routine and conventional steps. The claims, therefore, are directed to the patent-ineligible subject matter.[77]

In other words, if there would be a specific relationship expressed between a patient's sample and a number of alterations or mutations against which the sample is tested, such might possibly fulfil the requirement that there is a 'further inventive concept'. That is as such not very logical, as the broader claims would inherently also include those mutations, which would hence be evidence in itself that the broader claims also include a 'further inventive concept'. The concept of 'abstract comparisons' used by the CAFC is, in that sense, not necessarily logical and easy to understand. In the view

---

75. CAFC, 2014, slip op., at 17.
76. Claim 21 (revised to include the language of claim 20, from which it depends) provides: 'A method for detecting a germline alteration in a BRCA1 gene, said alteration selected from the group consisting of the alterations set forth in Tables 11 and 12 which comprises analysing a sequence of the BRCA1 gene or BRCA1 RNA from a human sample or analysing the sequence of BRCA1 cDNA made from mRNA from said sample[,] wherein a germline alteration is detected by hybridizing a BRCA1 gene probe which specifically hybridizes to an allele of one of said alterations to RNA isolated from said human sample and detecting the presence of a hybridization product, wherein the presence of said product indicates the presence of said allele in the sample.'
77. CAFC, 2014, slip op., at 18-19.

of the present author, the issue of broad claims relating to the diagnostic methods could probably be an issue of enablement under 35 USC §112, which is a patentability requirement, more than an issue of patent-eligibility.[78]

Two recent decisions by the Court of Appeals for the Federal Circuit shed somewhat more light, be it not a very bright one, on the two-step test and how it is applied to inventions relating to DNA sequences in the context of diagnostic testing.

In *Vanda Pharmaceuticals Inc. v. West-Ward Pharmaceuticals*,[79] the patent relates to a method of treating schizophrenia patients with iloperidone wherein the dosage range is based on the patient's genotype.[80] The '610 patent teaches 'that treatment of a patient, who has lower CYP2D6 activity than a normal person, with a drug[, such as iloperidone,] that is pre-disposed to cause QT2 prolongation and is metabolized by the CYP2D6 enzyme, can be accomplish[ed] more safely by administering a lower dose of the drug than would be administered to a person who has normal CYP2D6 enzyme activity.' *Id.* col. 2 ll. 15-21. QT prolongation can lead to serious cardiac problems. The '610 patent refers to patients who have lower than normal CYP2D6 activity as CYP2D6 poor metabolizers. It provides examples of dose reductions for poor metabolizers compared to the dose given to someone with a wild-type genotype.[81] It will not have remained unnoticed that the claim in the Vanda case is rather similar in nature to the one in Mayo, i.e., it adjusts the dosage of a drug to be administered to a patient in the function of the formation of certain metabolites, which may be linked to a specific genotype of patients.

---

78. For a detailed analysis of the US enablement requirement in the context of DNA sequences, *see*, S.J.R. Bostyn, '*Enabling Biotechnological Inventions in Europe and the United States. A Study of the Patentability of Proteins and DNA Sequences with Special Emphasis on the Disclosure Requirement*', Eposcript Series, no. 4, EPO, München, 2001, pp. 221 et seq.

79. *Vanda Pharmaceuticals Inc. v. West-Ward Pharmaceuticals*, No. 2016-2707, 2016-2708, CAFC 13 April 2018.

80. Representative claim 1 of US Patent 8,586,610 ('the '610 patent') reads:

'A method for treating a patient with iloperidone, wherein the patient is suffering from schizophrenia, the method comprising the steps of:

determining whether the patient is a CYP2D6 poor metabolizer by:
obtaining or having obtained a biological sample from the patient;
and
performing or having performed a genotyping assay on the biological sample to determine if the patient has a CYP2D6 poor metabolizer genotype; and
if the patient has a CYP2D6 poor metabolizer genotype, then internally administering iloperidone to the patient in an amount of 12 mg/day or less, and
if the patient does not have a CYP2D6 poor metabolizer genotype, then internally administering iloperidone to the patient in an amount that is greater than 12 mg/day, up to 24 mg/day,
wherein a risk of QTc prolongation for a patient having a CYP2D6 poor metabolizer genotype is lower following the internal administration of 12 mg/day or less than it would be if the iloperidone were administered in an amount of greater than 12 mg/day, up to 24 mg/day.'

81. Slip op., at 3.

The Court of Appeals for the Federal Circuit came to the opposite conclusion in the Vanda case, however, than the US Supreme Court did in the Mayo case. The court ruled that that the asserted claims are not directed to patent-ineligible subject matter. In order to come to such a conclusion, the court reverted to some intellectual gymnastics to discern a distinction between Mayo and Vanda: 'This case, however, is not Mayo. First, the claims in Mayo were not directed to a novel method of treating a disease. Instead, the claims were directed to a diagnostic method based on the "relationships between concentrations of certain metabolites in the blood and the likelihood that a dosage of a thiopurine drug will prove ineffective or cause harm."'[82] Although the representative claim in Mayo recited administering a thiopurine drug to a patient, the claim as a whole was not directed to the application of a drug to treat a particular disease.[83] The court then further held that 'unlike the claim at issue in Mayo, the claims here require a treating doctor to administer iloperidone in the amount of either (1) 12 mg/day or less or (2) between 12 mg/day to 28 mg/day, depending on the result of a genotyping assay. The specification further highlights the significance of the specific dosages by explaining how certain ranges of administered iloperidone correlate with the risk of QTc prolongation. *See*, e.g., '610 patent at col. 4 ll. 1-15. Thus, the '610 patent claims are "a new way of using an existing drug" that is safer for patients because it reduces the risk of QTc prolongation.'[84] The Court hence held that the subject matter of claim 1 did not pertain to patent-ineligible subject matter, the first question under the Mayo test, which meant that there was no further need to examine the second step, as the claim related to patentable subject matter.

Worth observing is that Chief Judge Prost dissented, and argued that he would have held the claim as not patentable under the first step of the Mayo test: 'I would find the asserted patent claims to be directed to a law of nature. The majority finds the claims herein are not directed to a natural law at step one of the § 101 analysis, but its efforts to distinguish Mayo cannot withstand scrutiny. The majority relies on the claims' recitation of specific applications of the discovery underpinning the patent to find no natural law is claimed. But it conflates the inquiry at step one with the search for an inventive concept at step two. Once the natural law claimed in the '610 patent is understood in a manner consistent with Mayo, what remains fails to supply the requisite inventive concept to transform the natural law into patent-eligible subject matter.'[85]

---

82. Slip op., at 29.
83. *Ibid.*
84. Slip op., at 30.
85. Slip op., at 1-2 Dissenting Opinion.

In *Athena Diagnostics, Inc. v. Mayo Collaborative Servs., LLC,*[86] the invention related to methods for diagnosing neurological disorders by detecting antibodies to a protein called muscle-specific tyrosine kinase ('MuSK'). Having discovered the association between MuSK autoantibodies and MG (*Myasthenia gravis*), the inventors of the '820 patent disclosed and claimed methods of diagnosing neurological disorders such as MG by detecting autoantibodies that bind to a MuSK epitope.[87] The Court held that in the present case, claim 7 related to patent-ineligible subject matter:

> The claims at issue here involve both the discovery of a natural law and certain concrete steps to observe its operation. Claim 9, the most specific claim at issue, recites the following method to detect MuSK autoantibodies: (1) mixing MuSK or an epitope thereof having a 125I label with bodily fluid; (2) immunoprecipitating any resulting antibody/MuSK complex; and (3) monitoring for the label on the complex. '820 patent col. 12 l. 62–col. 13 l. 9. The claim then concludes in the wherein clause with a statement of the natural law, i.e., the discovery that MuSK autoantibodies naturally present in a patient sample, detected with the 125I label bound to the MuSK/antibody complex, indicate that the patient is suffering from a MuSK-related neurological disorder. Id. col. 13 ll. 2-5. As in Cleveland Clinic and Ariosa, we conclude that claims 7-9 are directed to a natural law because the claimed advance was only in the discovery of a natural law, and that the additional recited steps only apply conventional techniques to detect that natural law.[88]

With reference to the Vanda Pharmaceuticals case, the Court held that:

> We consider it important at this point to note the difference between the claims before us here, which recite a natural law and conventional means for detecting it, and applications of natural laws, which are patent-eligible. [...] Claiming a natural cause of an ailment and well-known means of observing it is not eligible for patent because such a claim in effect only encompasses the natural law itself. But claiming

---

86. *Athena Diagnostics, Inc. v. Mayo Collaborative Servs.*, LLC, No. 17-2508, 2019 U.S. App. LEXIS 3645, 915 F.3d 743, 753 n.4 (Fed Cir. Feb. 6, 2019).

87. The relevant claims of the US Patent 7,267,820 (the '820 patent') read:

> Claim 1 (not in issue): '1. A method for diagnosing neurotransmission or developmental disorders related to [MuSK] in a mammal comprising the step of detecting in a bodily fluid of said mammal autoantibodies to an epitope of [MuSK].'
> Claim 7 (in issue): 'method according to claim 1, comprising contacting MuSK or an epitope or antigenic determinant thereof having a suitable label thereon, with said bodily fluid,
> immunoprecipitating any antibody/MuSK complex or antibody/MuSK epitope or antigenic determinant complex from said bodily fluid and
> monitoring for said label on any of said antibody/MuSK complex or antibody/MuSK epitope or antigen determinant complex,
> wherein the presence of said label is indicative of said mammal is suffering from said neurotransmission or developmental disorder related to [MuSK].'

88. Slip op., at 12.

a new treatment for an ailment, albeit using a natural law, is not claiming the natural law.[89]

For step two, 'we consider the elements of each claim both individually and "as an ordered combination" to determine whether the additional elements "transform the nature of the claim" into a patent-eligible application.[...] The transformative "inventive concept" supplied by the claim elements not drawn to ineligible subject matter must be "sufficient to ensure that the patent in practice amounts to significantly more than a patent upon the [ineligible concept] itself."'[90] The court held in that regard that:

> We agree with Mayo that the steps of the claims not drawn to ineligible subject matter, whether viewed individually or as an ordered combination, only require standard techniques to be applied in a standard way.[...] Our decisions in CellzDirect and BASCOM are consistent with the principle that applying standard techniques in a standard way to observe a natural law does not provide an inventive concept.[91]

Responding to the argument by Athena that the patent did provide an inventive concept, the Court ruled that 'Athena also argues that the claimed steps were unconventional because they had not been applied to detect MuSK autoantibodies prior to Athena's discovery of the correlation between MuSK autoantibodies and MG. Even accepting that fact, we cannot hold that performing standard techniques in a standard way to observe a newly discovered natural law provides an inventive concept. This is because " [t]he inventive concept necessary at step two ... cannot be furnished by the unpatentable law of nature ... itself."'[92]

Judge Newmann dissented on the first prong of the test applied in the present case. She argued that the patent related to the patent-eligible subject matter:

> The '820 inventors did not patent their scientific discovery of MuSK autoantibodies. Rather, they applied this discovery to create a new method of diagnosis, for a previously undiagnosable neurological condition. [...] The panel majority ignores these steps, and instead holds that 'claims 7–9 are directed to a natural law because the claimed advance was only in the discovery of a natural law, and that the additional recited steps only apply conventional techniques to detect that natural law.' Maj. Op. at 12. This analysis of patent-eligibility is incorrect, for the claim is for a multi-step method of diagnosing neurotransmission disorders related to muscle specific tyrosine kinase, by detecting autoantibodies using a series of chemical and biological

---

89. Slip op., at 14.
90. Slip op., at 15-16.
91. Slip op., at 16-17.
92. Slip op., at 17.

steps as set forth in the claims. Eligibility is determined for the claim considered as a whole, including all its elements and limitations. Claim limitations cannot be discarded when determining eligibility under section 101, as explained in *Diamond v. Diehr*, 450 U.S. 175 (1981).[93]

What materializes from these cases is that the courts continue to struggle with the Mayo test set by the US Supreme Court and how that is to be applied to specific inventions. In both of the above-mentioned cases, I would have joined the dissenting opinions, and indeed, it appears that further legal uncertainty will reign for years to come in the specific area of patent law, not an unimportant one mind the reader.

28.3.4   FURTHER APPLICATIONS OF AN EXISTING DRUG

28.3.4.1   Introduction

A separate category of inventions in the context of personalized medicine is drug-related inventions. With regard to the patentability of medicaments, there are a number of different possibilities to discern and analyse.

A distinction needs to be made between the use of a new drug and the use of an existing drug. With regard to a new drug, the situation is relatively straightforward. If a new drug is developed to treat a certain patient population which has a certain biomarker, then such drug is patentable as a new molecule as such, irrespective of any specific medical indication.

What if the drug or molecule is already known in the state of the art, but is applied to a new patient population, or for a new disease? As the solution to that question is quite different in Europe and the US, we will treat both legal systems separately.

28.3.4.2   Europe

In Europe, the patentability of inventions relating to known molecules is subject to the rules pertaining to second and further medical indication patents. An understanding of the law relating to second and further medical indications requires distinguishing between them until recently prevailing legal regime and the current statutory regime.

For patents with a filing or priority date after 28 January 2011, patent claims may no longer be formulated in the 'old' regime Swiss claim formulation.[94] The new Article 54(5) EPC with the accompanying new

---

93. Slip op., at 2-4 Dissenting Opinion.
94. *See*, G 2/08, Dosage regime/Abbott Respiratory, OJ EPO, 2010, 456, reasons 7.1.4; and, Notice from the European Patent Office dated 20 September 2010 concerning the non-acceptance of Swiss-type claims for second or further medical use following decision G 2/08 of the Enlarged Board of Appeal, OJ EPO 2010, 514.

product claim formulation will be applicable only to patents for which the date of the decision to grant the patent under consideration was taken on or after 13 December 2007, which is the date on which the new EPC 2000 entered into force. If the decision to grant was taken before that date (the date of entry into force of EPC 2000), only 'Swiss-type' claims are allowed for any second or further medical use (provided these claims meet with all the other requirements of the Convention).[95] That implies that the new claim formulation will be admissible for patent applications filed before the entry into force of the EPC 2000, but for which no decision to grant has been taken at that moment. As the Technical Board of Appeal held in T 1570/09, once a new claim formulation has been introduced in a patent application that falls within the new regime, there is no reason any more to allow a Swiss claim formulation.[96]

The 'old' regime under the EPC 1973 did not provide for a possibility under the EPC to allow a product patent for a medicament that was already known in the state of the art and for which a first generic medical indication had already been claimed. In the words of the Board in T 1570/09:

> Enlarged Board of Appeal decision G 1/83 (G 5/83, G 6/83) introduced the 'Swiss-type' form claim in consideration of the fact that the provisions of EPC 1973, and in particular of its Article 54(5), allowed purpose-related product claims only for the first (generic) medical use of a known substance or composition. In other words, in accordance with the provisions of EPC 1973, claims drafted in the form of a product claim directed to a substance or composition for use in a method referred to in Article 52(4) EPC 1973 are allowable if the first medical use of a known substance or composition is novel under Article 54(5) EPC 1973. In contrast to the first medical indication of a known substance or composition in the form of such 'use-related product claims' under Article 54(5) EPC 1973, there was an absence of provisions in EPC 1973 allowing purpose-limited product claims for further specific medical indications (see G 2/08, OJ EPO 10/2010, 456, points 5.8 and 5.9 of the Reasons, and G 5/83, OJ EPO 1985, 64, point 15 of the Reasons).[97]

That particular statutory situation hence led to the introduction of the Swiss-type claim, which did not aim to protect the product for a new medical use, which was not allowed under the then prevalent Convention but was framed as a claim to the use of a substance X for the manufacture of a medicament for the treatment of disease Y. The claim was hence a

---

95. Decision of the Administrative Council of 28 June 2001 on the transitional provisions under Article 7 of the Act revising the European Patent Convention of 29 November 2000.
96. T 1570/09, Alpha-ketoglutaric acid and pharmaceutically acceptable salts thereof for use in increasing HDL plasma levels/PROTISTA, decision dated 16 May 2014, reasons 4.8.
97. T 1570/09, reasons 4.2.

manufacturing claim, and the further medical indication was laid down in the 'for the treatment of ... ' part of the claim. As such a claim does to protect the product as such, it was allowable.[98]

The new EPC 2000 introduced the possibility to claim a second and further medical indication as a product X for the use in the treatment of disease Y.[99] Such a claim is a purpose-limited product claim, i.e., the scope of protection of the product is limited to the specific purpose of the claim, which is laid down in the 'for the use in the treatment of ... ' part of the claim. This claim type was not a new invention, as it was already prevailing and allowed for the so-called first medical indication which was protectable under Article 54(5) EPC 1973 and now under Article 54(4) EPC 2000.[100] As was held in G 2/08, a decision dealing with the patentability of a medical indication claim for a new dosage, which the Enlarged Board of Appeal deemed patentable in principle, this new claim formulation is now the only acceptable claim formulation for medical indication patent claims.

An interesting question is whether both types of claims, which are currently both widely spread in still enforceable and valid patents, have a different scope of protection. The Swiss claim is a use or method claim, whilst the new claim formulation under the EPC 2000 is a product claim. That in itself already suggests a different scope.

A relatively recent decision by a Technical Board of Appeal (TBA) indeed seems to confirm that there is a difference in scope between a Swiss claim now longer allowed and a patent claim under Article 54(5) EPC 2000, which is now a product claim for the use in the treatment of a certain disease. In T 1780/12,[101] the TBA held that:

> It follows from the above analysis (see points 16 and 17) that the claims under consideration belong to different categories, i.e., purpose-limited process claim versus purpose-limited product claim and differ in addition in at least one technical feature. It is generally accepted as a principle underlying the EPC that a claim to a particular physical activity (e.g., method, process, use) confers less protection than a claim to the physical entity per se, see decision G 2/88 (supra, reasons, point 5). It

---

98. For further details, *see* G 5/83, Second medical indication/EISAI, OJ EPO, 1985, 60.
99. Article 54(5) EPC: 'Paragraphs 2 and 3 shall also not exclude the patentability of any substance or composition referred to in paragraph 4 for any specific use in a method referred to in Article 53(c), provided that such use is not comprised in the state of the art.'
100. For more details, *see*, S.J.R. Bostyn, '*Personalised Medicine, Medical Indication Patents and Patent Infringement: Emergency Treatment Required*', Intellectual Property Quarterly, 2016, 151-201; E. Ventose, '*Medical Patent Law – The Challenges of Medical Treatment*', Edward Elgar Publishing, Cheltenham, 2011; F-E Hufnagel, '*Der Schutzbereich von Second Medical Use Patenten*', GRUR, 2014, 123-127; P. Meier-Beck, '*Patentschutz für die zweite medizinische Indikation und ärztliche Therapiefreiheit*', GRUR, 2009, 300-305.
101. T 1780/12, Cancer treatment/Board of Regents, The University of Texas System, decision dated 30 January 2014.

follows that a purpose-limited process claim also confers less protection than a purpose-limited product claim.[102]

In a recent publication, I have cast doubt over the correctness of such position; as in my view, at least when it comes to direct infringement, the scope seems to be pretty identical between the so-called Swiss claims and the second medical indication purpose-limited product claims.[103]Irrespective of the legal regime applicable, both the 'old' regime and the current regime allow the patentability of what is called second and further medical indications. That is the situation where the molecule or drug is already known in state of the art, and one invents a further application of that molecule or drug. Creating an exception to the concept of absolute novelty, the further medical indication regime allows patent applicants to obtain protection for a variety of new applications of an existing drug, provided that the invention is further inventive, industrially applicable and is sufficiently disclosed. There is quite a substantial body of case law covering such further medical indication patents. Most common types are those inventions relating to a novel group of subjects,[104] relating to a new route or mode of administration,[105] relating to a different technical effect and leading to a truly new application,[106] and those relating to a new dosage regime for an existing drug.[107]

Specific for personalized medicine might be the case that the drug is not new, and it is already known for the treatment of the condition claimed. What is, in fact, invented is the use of a known drug for the treatment of a known condition for a new patient subpopulation which is defined by the identification in such patent subpopulation of a new biomarker.[108] As we have seen above, under the EPC and EPO case law, a variety of second and further

---

102. T 1780/12, reasons 22.
103. S.J.R. Bostyn, '*Personalised Medicine, Medical Indication Patents and Patent Infringement: Emergency Treatment Required*', Intellectual Property Quarterly, 2016, 151-201.
104. T 19/86, OJ EPO 1989, 24; T 893/90 of 22 July 1993; T 233/96 of 4 May 2000.
105. T 51/93 of 8 June 1994; T 138/95 of 12 October 1999.
106. T 290/86, OJ EPO 1992, 414; T 254/93, OJ EPO 1998, 285; T 1020/03, OJ EPO 2007, 204.
107. G 2/08, Dosage regime/Abbott Respiratory, OJ EPO, 2010, 456.
108. For example the case of gefitinib. 'In December 2004, gefitinib failed to show significant benefits in an overall population of patients with lung cancer in a Phase III clinical study. It could not therefore enter the European market and appeared to be a failure. But, gefitinib made a surprise comeback. The reason is that it was discovered a subpopulation of about 10-15% of lung cancer patients having tumours with a mutation in the epidermal growth factor receptor for tyrosine kinase (EGFR-TK) responded particularly well to the drug. This is because gefitinib inhibits the EGFR-TK activity that promotes the growth of certain lung cancer cells. Subsequently, in June 2009, gefitinib was granted marketing authorization for the treatment of adults with locally advanced or metastatic non-small cell lung cancer who present positive for mutations of EGFR-TK. Shortly afterwards, the drug was recommended by the National Institute for Health and Care Excellence (NICE) in the UK as a first line treatment option'. Taken from:

medical indication claims is considered to be patentable. Patent protection can be granted for a known substance when used for the treatment of a new condition, or for the same condition but in a new mode of administration. It is also possible, as per G 2/08, to protect a new dosage regime, where the prior art already contains the substance, the condition treated, and the patient group identified. The only novel feature is here the dosage regime. The question which is of particular interest in the context of personalized medicine is whether a patent can be granted for an invention where the substance is known in the prior art, the condition treated is already known, and the patient population has generically already been identified. The only novel feature is the identification and treatment of a new patient subpopulation.

From a patent law perspective, there are at first sight a number of problems with such patent. The prior art will already include the new subpopulation, as this subpopulation is part of the larger patient population which was already treated with the known drug before (be it perhaps in a different dosage). The biomarker on the basis of which the subpopulation is identified is arguably also not new, as it was always present in the population (of which the subpopulation forms part) for which the drug was already patented/used.

There has been an evolution in the case law of the EPO relating to subpopulations. The earlier case law relating to second and further medical indications claims did recognize the novelty of a new subpopulation.[109] However, in case T 233/96,[110] the Technical Board of Appeal held that if:

> the use of a compound was known in the treatment or diagnosis of a disease of a particular group of subjects, the treatment or diagnosis of the same disease with the same compound could nevertheless represent a novel therapeutic or diagnostic application, provided that it is carried out on *a new group of subjects which is distinguished from the former by its physiological or pathological status* (T 0019/86, T 0893/90). This does not apply, however *if the group chosen overlaps with the group previously treated* or the choice of the novel group is arbitrary which means that no functional relationship does exist between the particular physiological or pathological status of this group of subjects (here humans who are unable to exercise adequately) and the therapeutic or pharmacological effect achieved.[111]

Personalised medicine – patenting new drugs from old?, https://www.lexology.com/library/detail.aspx?g=325c2a8f-447d-4a59-8a6a-b9630bea1d78 (last visited 2 January 2020).

109. For example, T 19/86, Pigs II/Duphar, OJ EPO, 1989, 24, at 8 of the reasons; T 893/90, Controlling bleeding/Queen's University Kingston, decision dated 22 July 1993, at 4.2 of the reasons.
110. T 233/96, Adrenaline/Medco Research, decision dated 4 May 2000.
111. T 233/96, Headnote I.

In other words and applied to the present subject of personalized medicine, if the subpopulation identified overlaps with the group previously treated, there is no novelty. In the case of personalized medicine, the previous treatment will always have covered the entire patient population, and the now identified subpopulation which is susceptible to the newly claimed treatment will in that sense always overlap with the patient population already identified and treated before.

More recent case law has condemned that case[112] and has held that there is no basis in both aforementioned cases to support the interpretation given in the T 233/96 case. In T 1399/04,[113] the Board held in particular that 'The present Board does not see a basis for this interpretation in the relevant parts of decisions T 19/86 (points (5) to (8)) and T 893/90 (points (4.2) to (4.6)).'[114]

The standard for evaluating whether a subpopulation can be considered novel over the prior art and hence constitute the basis for a further medical indication claim is according to at least some of the recent case law the following:

> If the use of a compound was known in the treatment or diagnosis of a disease of a particular group of subjects, the treatment or diagnosis of the same disease with the same compound could nevertheless represent a novel therapeutic or diagnostic application, provided that it is carried out on a new group of subjects *which is distinguished from the former by its physiological or pathological status* (cf. decisions T 19/86, OJ EPO 1989, 28; point (8) of the reasons and decision T 893/90 of 22 July 1993 (point (4.2) of the reasons).[115]

A recent case supports the stance taken by the TBA in the T 1399/04 case, which consequently creates some confidence that the way taken in the earliest case law and confirmed in T 1399/04 and the present recent case is probably the state of the law at the EPO. In T 0734/12,[116] the Board held that 'According to the established case law of the Boards of Appeal, the use of the same compound in the treatment of the same disease for a particular group of subjects, could nevertheless represent a novel therapeutic application, provided that it is carried out on a new group of subjects which is

112. Surprisingly, the Case Law of the EPO Boards of Appeal case law handbook, edited by the Legal Research Service of the Boards of Appeal, still refers to the T 233/96 as valid case law, *see*, Legal Research Service of the Boards of Appeal, *Case Law of the Boards of Appeal*, 9th edn., European Patent Office, 2019, pp. 155-156.
113. T 1399/04, Combination therapy HCV/SCHERING, decision dated 25 October 2006.
114. T 1399/04, at 35 of the reasons.
115. *Ibid.*
116. T 0734/12, Arthritis patients with an inadequate response to a TNF-alpha inhibitor/ GENENTECH, INC., decision dated 17 May 2013.

distinguished from the former by its physiological or pathological status […].'[117]

In other words, a new group of subjects which is distinguished from the former by its physiological or pathological status can constitute novelty, and hence, can become patentable. Typically, a subpopulation can distinguish itself from a population from which it forms part generically, for instance, by not reacting to a specific drug in dosage or administration already part of state of the art or by showing a high degree of adverse side effects or even toxicity of the drug administered to that subpopulation. That subpopulation might also distinguish itself because the medical condition for which it is treated is caused by a specific genotype or a specific mutation, which might make the standard treatment known in the state of the art ineffective. These would all be biomarkers, and the patented invention has established a correlation between the known drug and those previously unknown biomarkers. As there is in line with the EPO case law discussed still room for at least a claim or novelty based on a further medical indication, research into specific subpopulations might be rewarded with patent protection.

From the above, it is clear that there is a plethora of opportunities for pharmaceutical companies to obtain patent protection in some form or another on active ingredients. As is also clear from what has been discussed above is that second and further medical use claims will become increasingly important in the context of personalized medicine. Many treatments for stratified patient groups will not necessarily require the development of a new drug, but in many cases, the use of existing drugs can suffice. The patent opportunities which second and further medical use patents provide are a very welcome (at least in the minds of those pharmaceutical companies) addition[118] to the toolbox of instruments to optimize exclusivity. But all this comes obviously at a price, literally. Patent protection maintains higher price levels for the drugs which are still under patent protection. Prices are known to drop only at generic entry. The various patents which may exist on molecules have the potential of de facto delaying generic entry. And that means, in turn, that society must wait longer to see drug prices drop.

The recent litigation in the context of second and further medical use claims (and it does not really matter of which variety that claim is) gives further evidence that generic entry can be delayed, and this goes against the interests of society who wants to see access to drugs at affordable prices and healthcare systems who equally want to be able to pay for the healthcare for their citizens. Imagine the following situation. The pharmaceutical compound, as such, is no longer patent-protected. That means that the compound may be put on the market by a generic company, absent any IP protection.

---

117. T 0734/12, at 24 of the reasons.
118. The patents filed for such second and further medical uses must obviously still fulfil the patentability requirements of especially inventive step and sufficiency of disclosure, and it is not always guaranteed that those patent applications will pass those hurdles.

Imagine now also that a patent for an earlier second medical indication for condition X is also no longer under patent protection, and is being supplied by one or more generic pharmaceutical companies. However, there is still patent protection for a second medical use of the same compound to treat condition Y. What now if a physician prescribes the generic drug for a patented medical use (in my example to treat condition Y), and the pharmacist dispenses the generic drug for that same patented use? Is there patent infringement, and if so, by whom? Even if the physician and the pharmacist might be infringers, the patent holder will have no immediate incentive to sue those for patent infringement. He might be more interested in suing the generic company. Without having the space to go into detail here, the conclusion is that the generic company is liable for infringement if he knows or should have reasonably known that at least some of the generic drugs he produces is going to be prescribed and dispensed for the use in a patented medical indication. In certain jurisdictions, a foreseeability test is being applied, according to which the generic manufacturer would not be liable to damages if he can prove that he has taken all reasonable measures with a view to prevent that his generic products are being used for the patented medical indication. In others, liability could be limited to situations where there the generic product is prepared and presented in a way that infringement is clear from the presentation.[119] The case law is rather unclear, however, which measure would be sufficient, and as we speak, there is still a lot of legal uncertainty around this thorny issue.

It will be immediately clear that any direction of the case might have important consequences for the activities of generic companies, and hence also on the accessibility of drugs. If the burden of proof for the generic company is so high that it becomes virtually impossible to avoid infringement, then the business model of generic companies comes under enormous strain. A generic company will always be aware of the fact that it is possible that its products will be prescribed and dispensed for a patented medical indication.[120] This could be because of a preferential use scheme that might

---

119. *See* e.g., *Generics (UK) Ltd (t/a Mylan) v. Warner-Lambert Company LLC* [2015] EWHC 2548 (Pat) (10 September 2015); *Warner-Lambert Company LLC v. Generics (UK) Ltd (t/a Mylan) & Ors* [2016] EWCA Civ 1006 (13 October 2016); *Warner-Lambert Company LLC v. Generics (UK) Ltd (t/a Mylan) & Anor (rev 1)* [2018] UKSC 56 (14 November 2018); Carvedilol II (BGH, Case X ZR 236/01); Östrogenblocker (Case I-2 W 6/17) (5 May 2017); Dexmedetomidin (Case I-2 U 30/17) (1 March 2018), (BeckRS 2018, 2410); Fulvestrant, OLG Düsseldorf, Urt. v. 9.1.2019 – 2 U 27/18, GRUR, 2019, 279.

120. In many cases, this will even be materialized in the fact that the generic company will operate under a so-called skinny-label, i.e., the product specification will make reference to all conditions that could be treated with the generic drug, but it will exclude the patented uses from the label. For more details; *see*, S.J.R. Bostyn, *Personalised Medicine, Medical Indication Patents and Patent Infringement: Emergency Treatment Required*, Intellectual Property Quarterly, 2016, 151-201.

be in place in a certain jurisdiction,[121] or other schemes that favour the prescription of generic drugs with a view to save costs for the national healthcare system. That might imply that it would become de facto impossible to avoid infringement, which makes the business model for generic companies no longer viable. This is definitely a cause for concern, as the role of generic companies to affect drug prices downwards is at stake. In the years to come, this issue will eventually need to be sorted out, whether by the courts or by the legislature, which could also intervene to settle the matter. It goes beyond the scope of this Chapter to dwell upon the possible solutions.[122]

28.3.4.3   The United States

In the US, as there is no statutory exception to the patentability of medical treatment methods, there is no such thing as second and further medical indication claims. Under US patent law, the treatment of a new patient subpopulation can just be claimed as a medical treatment method, which is perfectly patentable under the law. That does not mean that there are no issues, however. The Mayo case is also relevant for inventions relating to the treatment of patients. We have already seen earlier in this Chapter that Mayo is most relevant for and will have a major influence on the patentability of diagnostic tests where the test is doing nothing more than establishing a correlation between a patient sample gene sequence and a test sequence representing a mutation relevant to disease. Mayo was, in fact, not a diagnostic method but a medical treatment method. It is consequently not unrealistic to assume that Mayo could potentially have consequences for medical treatment methods. However, what made the Mayo patent-ineligible was the fact that the patent claim established the need to raise or lower the dosage of a certain drug if a certain metabolite was not produced enough or too much respectively, but the patent claim did not include the step of administering such higher or lower dose. That made the US Supreme Court decide that what was claimed was nothing more than a law of nature. By adding steps of administering the next dose, further intervention is claimed, and that might make a medical treatment claim patent-eligible subject matter even under Mayo. The present author is still in doubt whether that would be sufficient, as what the Supreme Court in the Mayo case required was that the invention also contains other elements or a combination of elements, sometimes referred to as an 'inventive concept'. Is the adding of such a subsequent new dosage administration such a step? This can be doubted,

---

121. Under a preferential use scheme, physicians could be stimulated or even be under an obligation to prescribe always a generic version of a drug if there is one, irrespective of whether there is patent protection for the drug for a specific condition or not. For more details, *see*, S.J.R. Bostyn, Intellectual Property Quarterly, 2016, 151-201.
122. I refer to my 2016 publication to that effect, *see*, S.J.R. Bostyn, Intellectual Property Quarterly, 2016, 151-201.

especially also in view of the fact that the Court said that the steps in the claimed processes (apart from the natural laws themselves) which involve well-understood, routine, conventional activity previously engaged in by researchers in the field would not make the subject matter patent-eligible. On the other hand, the US Supreme Court in the Mayo case may have hinted towards patent-eligibility of treatment claims in personalized medicine when it expressed its concern over the patent-eligibility of the claims in that case by saying that such claims 'threaten to inhibit the development of more refined treatment recommendations (like that embodied in Mayo's test), that combine Prometheus' correlations with later discovered features of metabolites, human physiology or individual patient characteristics. The "determining" step too is set forth in highly general language covering all processes that make use of the correlations after measuring metabolites, including later discovered processes that measure metabolite levels in new ways.'[123]

28.3.5 Some Further Comments

With the rather extensive patent law chapter, I have wanted to demonstrate that there is a wide array of patent possibilities for innovators to rely upon in the era of personalized medicine. Not only is DNA patentable, so are diagnostic methods, pharmaceutical compounds and further uses of such compounds. There is a wide arsenal of options to choose from. I will be the last one to argue that the sole determinant of affordability of drugs or other medical treatment related applications is IP protection. But it is equally true that no one can deny that by the very nature of a patent right or a regulatory exclusivity[124] the potential is there to influence price in a way that would not be possible in the absence of such exclusionary and exclusive rights. It is also one of the very foundations upon which the patent system and other exclusivities are based. With a view to stimulate further innovation, society makes a deal with innovators that the latter receive a temporary exclusionary or exclusive right so that they can recoup their investment, and in return, society gets access to the details of those inventions.[125] The orphan drug

---

123. Mayo, 132 S.Ct. at 1302.
124. Such as data and market exclusivity. For more details, *see*, amongst others, S.J.R. Bostyn et al., '*Effects of Supplementary Protection Mechanisms for Pharmaceutical Products*', May 2018, Technopolis Group, 169 pp, downloadable at https://www.rijksoverheid .nl/ministeries/ministerie-van-volksgezondheid-welzijn-en-sport/documenten/rapporten/ 2018/05/01/effects-of-supplementary-protection-mechanisms-for-pharmaceutical-produ cts.
125. Some of those foundational principles are laid down in, K.J. Arrow, '*Economic Welfare and the Allocation of Resources for Invention*,' in, National Bureau of Economic Research (ed.), 'The Rate and Direction of Inventive Activity: Economic and Social Factors', 1962, (609) 619-620. For more details, *see also*, S.J.R. Bostyn, '*Enabling*

system[126] provides good examples of drugs which have been developed with the aid of an incentive system and coupled with a small market size for the developer of the drug, leads to (exorbitant) prices.[127] I think it is fair to say that patent protection has traditionally had an upward effect on the price, and there is ample evidence that prices stay high during the lifetime of the patent or other regulatory exclusivities.

The very broad scope of possibilities to attain patent protection for a wide range of products and processes has, without a doubt, led to the very advanced healthcare systems we have today. Where certain patients would have had very little or no chance of survival some decades ago, the situation is rather spectacularly different today. Cancer is one of the most prominent examples. But all this innovation comes at a cost. And that is why healthcare becomes more and more unaffordable for public healthcare systems and unaffordable to patients in countries with insurance-based healthcare systems.[128] Access to affordable healthcare is, therefore, today no longer a discussion to be had in the context of developing countries, but also of the industrialized nations. That does not make the problem of affordable healthcare more important, but it makes it in any event much more widespread. And because it is that much more widespread, maybe discussions about measures to tackle the rising costs of healthcare and access to drugs across the world will get a wider audience and maybe also a more listening ear.

Biotechnological Inventions in Europe and the United States. A Study of the Patentability of Proteins and DNA Sequences with Special Emphasis on the Disclosure Requirement', Eposcript Series, no. 4, EPO, München, 2001, pp. 27 et seq.; S.J.R. Bostyn & N. Petit, *'Patent=Monopoly: A Legal Fiction'* (31 December 2013). Available at SSRN: http://ssrn.com/abstract=2373471 or http://dx.doi.org/10.2139/ssrn.2373471, 19 pp.

126. Regulation (Ec) No. 141/2000 of the European Parliament and of the Council of 16 December 1999 on orphan medicinal products, OJ 22.01.2000, L 18/1.

127. A recently reported example is Orkambi and Symkevi, for the treatment of certain categories of patients with cystic fibrosis. The drugs have been approved as an orphan drug and would have had a price of GBP 104,000 per patient, per year. The company Vertex, who has developed the drugs and brought them to market is estimated to make a profit of USD 21 billion (GBP 17 billion) over the drugs' lifetime. *See,* Isabelle Jani-Friend, *'Drug Companies Are Putting a Price on the Lives of Those with Cystic Fibrosis'*, The Guardian, 14 August 2019, https://www.theguardian.com/commentisfree/2019/aug/14/cystic-fibrosis-drug-makers-nhs-price-lives (last visited on 2 January 2020).

128. 'High prices, sometimes prohibitive prices for life-saving treatments, medicines and health technologies under patent protection could be financially unsustainable in both public and private sectors, thus leaving too many people without access to the benefits of the medical innovations', N. Boschiero, *'Intellectual Property Rights and Public Health: An Impediment to Access to Medicines and Health Technology Innovation?'*, Rivista telematica (www.statoechiese.it), n. 22/2017, at 4.

28.4 REGULATORY EXCLUSIVITIES

28.4.1 THE PRINCIPLES

Besides the 'traditional' IP rights, there is also an increasingly important role for the so-called regulatory exclusivities, i.e., data and market exclusivity. Their importance cannot be overestimated, even though they have led a rather elusive existence in the literature. It is rather surprising that these exclusive rights have not been the subject of more thorough scrutiny earlier. That is a reason for concern, as these exclusivities provide, to some extent, a stronger form of protection than any other intellectual property rights. We will explain this in what follows.[129]

It must be emphasized that those regulatory exclusivities operate in a separate legal system, outside of the traditional IP regimes, and are linked to the marketing authorization (MA) granted for a medicinal product. The rationale behind those exclusivities is that pharmaceutical companies that invest in the development and marketing of medicinal products need an incentive to protect their investment from third parties who would like to 'free ride' on their efforts. As said, as this is a legal layer entirely separate from the traditional IP system, and not linked to any patented inventions at all, the incentives are given once a marketing authorization has been granted for a medicinal product. This triggers the exclusivities, which start running as from the date of the grant of the marketing authorization. As there is no link with the patent system, the incentives are granted independent of whether the drug is a patentable invention or not.

Data and market exclusivity provide hence incentives by granting a temporary exclusive right as compensation for the development costs of the medicinal product and the generating of the clinical data.[130]

The difference between data exclusivity and market protection is the following:

- Data exclusivity is fundamentally a system whereby a generic company cannot refer to the MA dossier of the so-called reference product during the period of data exclusivity.

---

129. What follows relating to the principles of data and market exclusivity is largely taken from, Bostyn, S.J.R., et al., '*Effects of Supplementary Protection Mechanisms for Pharmaceutical Products*', May 2018, Technopolis Group, 169 pp, downloadable at https://www.rijksoverheid.nl/ministeries/ministerie-van-volksgezondheid-welzijn-en-sport/documenten/rapporten/2018/05/01/effects-of-supplementary-protection-mechanisms-for-pharmaceutical-products.
130. Governed by Directive 2001/83/EC of the European Parliament and of the Council of 6 November 2001 on the Community code relating to medicinal products for human use, OJ L 311, 28.11.2001, pp. 67-128. *See also* Regulation 726/2004/EC for centrally granted marketing authorizations.

– Market protection refers to the system whereby the MA holder has the sole right to market the medicinal product for which an MA has been granted.

As long as the data exclusivity period runs, no third party can refer to those data for purposes of filing a marketing authorization, in the rule for a generic version of the innovator product, also called the reference product. During the term of the market protection, no third party can bring the medicinal product that is bioequivalent to the medicinal product that is still protected by the market protection to the market.

The possibility of generics firms to introduce a generic version of a drug onto the market and offer it at a lower price than the original depends on the ability to avoid the time-consuming and costly different clinical trials.[131] Indeed, the basic principle is that to obtain an MA for a medicinal product, a wide variety of costly and time-consuming tests and trials must be carried out by the originator company, which is then labelled as the reference product.[132]

For a generic version of the drug, such clinical trials are not necessary as the clinical trials have been already performed by the originator company, provided the generic MA applicant can demonstrate that the medicinal product that is applied for is bioequivalent[133] to the so-called reference originator medicinal product.[134] Generic companies can simply refer to the so-called reference dossier, where all tests and trials relating to the active substance in question have been described.[135] This is a so-called abridged MA.

Data exclusivity denies, for a limited time, generics firms the right to refer to such data of the original drug – the 'reference product' – in their regulatory filings. Hence, during the duration of the data exclusivity, any abridged application submitted referring to the dossier of the reference

---

131. Article 10(1) Directive 2001/83/EC.
132. *See* Article 8(3) and Annex I, Part 2 Directive 2001/83/EC.
133. *See* Article 10(2)(b) Directive 2001/83/EC for the definition of what a generic product is: '"generic medicinal product" shall mean a medicinal product which has the same qualitative and quantitative composition in active substances and the same pharmaceutical form as the reference medicinal product, and whose bioequivalence with the reference medicinal product has been demonstrated by appropriate bioavailability studies. The different salts, esters, ethers, isomers, mixtures of isomers, complexes or derivatives of an active substance shall be considered to be the same active substance, unless they differ significantly in properties with regard to safety and/or efficacy.'
134. What is a reference medicinal product? Article 10(2)(a) Directive 2001/83 defines it as 'a medicinal product authorized under Article 6, in accordance with the provisions of Article 8.'
135. However, even though the generic company will be able to refer to the dossier of the reference product when filing an abridged MA, the so-called quality part (Chemistry, Manufacture and Control – CMC) of the generic MA dossier must still be produced and submitted. Reference is being made in Article 10 to Article 8(3) of Directive 2001/83, which prescribes the requirements for obtaining a marketing authorization.

product will not be accepted. This de facto implies that generic companies cannot file for an MA as long as there is data exclusivity on the data of the MA reference dossier.

Market protection refers to the system whereby the reference product MA holder has the sole right to market the medicinal product for which an MA has been granted. This de facto means that during that period, even though generic companies could file for an MA for a bioequivalent product during the period of market protection (provided there is no longer any data exclusivity active on the data referred to), they cannot market the product.

Data exclusivity and market protection overlap in the sense that during the period of data exclusivity, there is also market protection,[136] but there may be (and there is, in fact) a period of market protection exceeding the period of data exclusivity, in which case only the former can be invoked, as the latter has lapsed.

Figure 28.1 Data Exclusivity and Market Protection

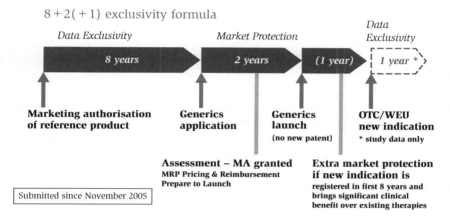

Source: European Medicines Agency.

The scheme under Directive 2001/83 and Regulation 726/2004 (the latter for centrally granted marketing authorizations), is applicable to marketing authorization applications filed as from 21 November 2005. For those filed before that date, a different regime is applicable, but in view of the cut-off date of November 2005, its effects have largely if not entirely stopped having

---

136. This is in practice merely a theoretical matter, as during the period data exclusivity, no third party can even file for a MA for the reference product, let alone prepare to market it. It is, however, important to understand that this market protection is present, as it is calculated from the notification date of the MA, and is hence relevant for calculating until when the market protection lasts, even though during the years of data exclusivity (which has the same starting date) it has no practical effect.

much practical effect today. The term of protection under the aforementioned scheme follows the '8+2(+1)'-rule.[137]

Hence, there is eight years of data exclusivity plus two additional years of market exclusivity. There are three situations where, in addition to the 8+2 years of exclusivity, an additional 1 year of market exclusivity can be obtained. These situations are the following:

- One year extension of the ten-year period in Article 10(1) in the case of new therapeutic indications which, during the scientific evaluation prior to their authorization, are held to bring a significant clinical benefit[138] in comparison with existing therapies.[139]
- One year period of data protection for new indications[140] of well-established substances.[141]
- One year period of protection for data supporting a change of classification.[142]

It is not possible to cumulate any of the above extensions, which implies that exclusivity cannot extend beyond eleven years.

The 8 refers to the eight years of data exclusivity, i.e., the period of time during which no generic applicant can refer to the data of the reference product MA in filing its MA for a generic version of the same reference product.

The 2 refers to two years of market exclusivity for the reference product after the eight years of data exclusivity have lapsed. The market exclusivity is in effect ten years from the obtaining of the MA for the reference product. During the period of market exclusivity, but in view of what has been said earlier after the period of data exclusivity, third parties can file for an MA by referring to the data of the reference product, but cannot bring the product on the market pending the market exclusivity.[143]

---

137. Article 10 Directive 2001/83; Article 14(11) of Regulation No 726/2004 (for centrally authorized medicinal products).

138. For a clarification of what is meant by 'significant clinical benefit', *see*, European Commission, 'Guidance on Elements Required to Support the Significant Clinical Benefit in Comparison with Existing Therapies of a New Therapeutic Indication in Order to Benefit from an Extended (11-Year) Marketing Protection Period', November 2007, *see* at http://ec.europa.eu/health/files/eudralex/vol-2/c/guideline_14-11-2007_en.pdf (last visited 2 January 2020).

139. Article 10(4) Directive 2001/83; Article 14(11) of Regulation (EC) No. 726/2004.

140. *See*, Guidance on a New Therapeutic Indication for a Well-Established Substance. November 2007, *see* at http://ec.europa.eu/health/files/eudralex/vol-2/c/10%20_5_%20guideline_11-2007_en.pdf, section 3.

141. Article 10(5) of Directive 2001/83/EC. For a definition of well-established substance and use, *see* Part II of the Annex to Directive 20001/83/EC as amended by Directive 2003/63/EC.

142. Article 74a of Directive 2001/83/EC, introduced by Directive 2004/27/EC.

143. *See also*, Notice to Applicants Volume 2A Procedures for Marketing Authorization Chapter 1 Marketing Authorization, December 2017, section. 6.1.2, pp. 40-41.

This means that for a reference medicinal product, the start of the data exclusivity and market protection periods is the date when the first MA was granted in the EU in accordance with the pharmaceutical acquis. New additional strengths, pharmaceutical form, administration routes, presentations as well as any variation and extensions do not restart or prolong this period. All additional strengths, pharmaceutical forms, administration routes, presentations as well as any variations and extensions have the same end point of the data exclusivity and market protection periods, namely eight and ten years after the first MA was granted, respectively. This will apply even if the new presentation has been authorized to the same MA holder through a separate procedure, national or centralized procedure, irrespective of the legal basis and under a different name.[144]

28.4.2 The Implications

One of the peculiarities of the system is that the data exclusivity and market protection start running as soon as the marketing authorization (MA) has been granted. The rights come with the MA.

From a legal perspective, the regulatory exclusivities are likely to be stronger than (other) intellectual property rights. Whilst a patent can be revoked, a regulatory exclusivity is largely unassailable as long as the underlying MA is in existence. For that reason alone, these rights have a definite appeal to them.

Second, as they are separate from traditional IP rights, most flexibilities that other IP rights could provide, such as compulsory licensing, are not necessarily *mutatis mutandis* applicable to those exclusivities.[145] Indeed, unlike traditional IP rights, there are in most countries no specific statutory regimes in place which would allow the grant of some kind of right to use the data or waive market protection. That was also acknowledged by the European Commission in 2006 during the Tamiflu crisis: 'The European pharmaceutical legislation does not foresee any exception to the above-mentioned periods of 8 year data exclusivity and 10 years marketing protection in case of emergency situations or in case a compulsory patent license has been granted by an EU Member State.'[146]

Third, unlike as is the case, for e.g., patents, where a more strict application of patentability standards can have a rather immediate effect on

---

144. *See* Notice to Applicants Volume 2A Procedures for Marketing Authorization Chapter 1 Marketing Authorization, December 2017, section. 6.1.5, p. 43.

145. *See also*, E.F.M. 't Hoen, P. Boulet & B.K. Baker, *'Data Exclusivity Exceptions and Compulsory Licensing to Promote Generic Medicines in the European Union: A Proposal for Greater Coherence in European Pharmaceutical Legislation'*, 10 Journal of Pharmaceutical Policy and Practice (JOPPP), 2017.

146. *See* European Commission, 'Letter from the European Commission to Mr Greg Perry, EGA-European Generic Medicines Association on the Subject of Tamiflu Application and Data Exclusivity in an Emergency Compulsory License Situation', Brussels, 20

the patentability of products and consequently also on the use that organizations may make of patent rights otherwise obtained, there are no such limitations possible for the regulatory exclusivities in themselves. The system itself has already foreseen in some limitations, such as the concept of the Global Marketing Authorization (GMA),[147] but apart from that, there is no further scrutiny of the scope of the right or on the award of the right. That implies that policy measures to influence the effect such rights may have cannot be found in the levers to grant them, at least to the same extent as that is the case of patents, where a policy decision could be made to interpret a certain patentability requirement more strictly, or exclude certain subject altogether from patentability. These instruments are not available under regulatory exclusivities, which makes those rights also from that perspective rather attractive indeed on the one hand, but for those on the other side of the table, such as governments trying to reduce the price of drugs, also more burdensome on the other hand. Regulatory exclusivities provide what they say on the tin, an exclusive right for a certain period of time (8+2+1 years). Any such period or exclusivity leads to delay in generic entry.

What this all means is that a more holistic approach is required when discussing the relationship between intellectual property rights and human rights. As will be seen in what follows, that discussion is largely focused on the consequences which intellectual property rights, and in particular patent rights might have on health. It is advised that any such discussion should include and take into account in the future also the effects which those other regulatory exclusivities might have in the context of, for instance, the right to health and access to medicines.

With the knowledge of the plethora of possibilities to patent pharmaceutical and biological compounds and processes and diagnostic methods, and the possibility to obtain regulatory exclusivities for authorized medicinal products, we can now move on to the second layer of this Chapter, and this is the human rights aspects of access to healthcare and drugs, and the relationship with intellectual property rights.

February 2006. The letter further states that 'Community pharmaceutical acquis does not currently contain any provision allowing a waiver of the rules on data exclusivity and marketing protection periods.'

147. The concept of GMA means that, as long as it relates to the same applicant, further indications, strengths, isomers etc., of the same active substance, will in principle not benefit from a separate period of data or market exclusivity, but will all fall within the same period of exclusivity given to the authorization of the reference medicinal active substance, apart from the limited instances where a one-year additional exclusivity can be obtained, as already referred to earlier. For more details on the concept of GMA, *see*, S.J.R. Bostyn, et al., *'Effects of Supplementary Protection Mechanisms for Pharmaceutical Products'*, May 2018, Technopolis Group, 169 pp, downloadable at https://www.rijksoverheid.nl/ministeries/ministerie-van-volksgezondheid-welzijn-en-sport/doc umenten/rapporten/2018/05/01/effects-of-supplementary-protection-mechanisms-for-ph armaceutical-products.

28.5 HUMAN RIGHTS ISSUES

28.5.1 THE FUNDAMENTALS

The relationship between intellectual property rights and human rights has always been a difficult one, and not necessarily always for good reasons. Part of the tension stems from the fact the two disciplines have for a very long time been enclosed into their own worlds, both claiming supremacy over the other. As intellectual property rights are state-granted rights, it was believed by some that they are measures of public policy and as such untouchable by any other discipline of the law. The other extreme view was that human rights are basically supreme to all other rights, and consequently, all intellectual property rights should be interpreted in the context and confines of human rights. It is clear that both extreme views were not very productive and conducive to coexistence between the two legal systems.

With Helfer,[148] I have always been quite surprised that both legal words have been so far apart. Intellectual property rights have always been recognized in the most basic of human rights instruments, *see*, for instance, Article 27 of the Universal Declaration of Human Rights (UDHR) which recognized the moral and material interests of authors in their scientific, literary and artistic productions.[149] Almost identical wording was used in Article 15(1)(b)-(c) of the later International Covenant on Economic, Social and Cultural Rights (ICESCR).[150]

Under the European Convention on Human Rights (ECHR),[151] intellectual property right has been recognized as a fundamental right by case law[152] under Article 1 of Protocol No. 1 to the ECHR:[153]

---

148. L.R. Helfer, *'Human Rights and Intellectual Property: Conflict or Coexistence?'*, 5 Minnesota Intellectual Property Review, 2003, 49.

149. Universal Declaration of Human Rights, G.A. Res. 217A, Article 27, U.N. GAOR, 3d Sess., 1st plen. mtg., U.N. Doc. A/810 (12 December 1948). For an overview of the drafting history, *see* P.K. Yu, *'Reconceptualizing Intellectual Property Interests in a Human Rights Framework'*, 40 UC Davis Law Review, 2007, (1039) 1050-1058.

150. International Covenant on Economic, Social and Cultural Rights, adopted 16 December 1966, S. Exec. Doc. D, 95-2 (1977), 993 U.N.T.S. 3, which entered into force on 3 January 1976, which recognizes the right 'to benefit from the protection of the moral and material interests resulting from any scientific, literary or artistic production of which he is the author' and 'to enjoy the benefits of scientific progress and its applications.' For an overview of the drafting history, *see* P.K. Yu, *'Reconceptualizing Intellectual Property Interests in a Human Rights Framework'*, 40 UC Davis Law Review, (1039) 1059-1069.

151. Convention for the Protection of Human Rights and Fundamental Freedoms, signed at Rome on 4 November 1950, as amended.

152. *See, Case of Anheuser-Busch Inc. v. Portugal* (Application No. 73049/01), European Court of Human Rights, 11 January 2007, para. 72; Case of *Balan v. Moldova* (Application No. 19247/03), European Court of Human Rights, 29 April 2008, para. 34; Fredrik Neij and Peter Sunde Kolmisoppi against Sweden (Application No. 40397/12), European Court of Human Rights, 19 February 2013.

153. Protocol No. 1 to the Convention for the Protection of Human Rights and Fundamental Freedoms, signed at Paris on 20 March 1952.

Every natural or legal person is entitled to the peaceful enjoyment of his possessions. No one shall be deprived of his possessions except in the public interest and subject to the conditions provided for by law and by the general principles of international law.

The preceding provisions shall not, however, in any way impair the right of a State to enforce such laws as it deems necessary to control the use of property in accordance with the general interest or to secure the payment of taxes or other contributions or penalties.

The aforementioned case law has established that intellectual property law is a form of property law and can hence benefit from the same protection as the right to entitlement to the peaceful enjoyment of one's possessions.

The drafting history of the international human rights instruments mentioned above shows that it has always been a subject of controversy to introduce intellectual property rights as human rights. Based on an analysis of the drafting history of both provisions, it is not illogical to conclude that the position of intellectual property as a human right is probably quite weak. Chapman refers in that context to 'relatively weak claims of intellectual property as a human right.'[154]

Additionally, intellectual property law has been explicitly protected under Article 17 of the Charter of Fundamental Rights of the European Union, which says: '*1. Everyone has the right to own, use, dispose of and bequeath his or her lawfully acquired possessions. No one may be deprived of his or her possessions, except in the public interest and in the cases and under the conditions provided for by law, subject to fair compensation being paid in good time for their loss. The use of property may be regulated by law in so far as is necessary for the general interest; 2. Intellectual property shall be protected.*'[155]

The Charter of Fundamental Rights of the European Union has since the Treaty of Lisbon become part of the EU legal order. Article 6(1) of the TEU[156] states that '*The Union recognises the rights, freedoms and principles set out in the Charter of Fundamental Rights of the European Union of 7 December 2000, as adapted at Strasbourg, on 12 December 2007, which shall have the same legal value as the Treaties.*' There is, in fact, already ample evidence of the Court of Justice of the European Union referring to the

---

154. A. Chapman, *Core Obligations Related to ICESCR Article 15(1)(c)*, in, A. Chapman & S. Russell (eds), *Core Obligations: Building a Framework for Economic, Social and Cultural Rights*, Intersentia, Antwerp, 2002, 314.
155. Charter of Fundamental Rights of the European Union, OJ C 364/1, 18.12.2000. For a critical appraisal of Article 17(2) of the Charter, *see* C. Geiger, '*Intellectual Property Shall Be Protected!? Article 17(2) of the Charter of Fundamental Rights of the European Union: A Mysterious Provision with an Unclear Scope*', 31(3) European Intellectual Property Review, 2009, 113-117.
156. Consolidated version of the Treaty on European Union, OJ C 326/13, 26.10.2012, pp. 13-390.

Charter in its judgments relating to intellectual property rights.[157] Not only does the Court explicitly recognize intellectual property as part of the human rights portfolio, but more importantly it invokes the Charter, in particular, to balance the right to have intellectual property rights with other fundamental rights. It was held in the C-70/10 Scarlet case in that connection that '[T]he protection of the right to intellectual property is indeed enshrined in Article 17(2) of the Charter of Fundamental Rights of the European Union ("the Charter"). There is, however, nothing whatsoever in the wording of that provision or in the Court's case-law to suggest that that right is inviolable and must for that reason be absolutely protected,'[158] and further that '[A]s paragraphs 62 to 68 of the judgment in Case C 275/06 Promusicae [2008] ECR I 271 make clear, the protection of the fundamental right to property, which includes the rights linked to intellectual property, must be balanced against the protection of other fundamental rights.'[159]

It must be said, though, that international intellectual property law statutory instruments have never made the link with human rights, the latter being entirely absent in the Berne,[160] Paris,[161] and Rome[162] Conventions.

The most recent of international intellectual property law statutory instruments, the TRIPS Agreement,[163] is equally silent on human rights and emphasizes on the private nature of intellectual property rights. However, two provisions of the TRIPS Agreement deserve mentioning here, as they are relevant for the present Chapter. It concerns Articles 7 and 8 TRIPS. According to Article 7, 'The protection and enforcement of intellectual property rights should contribute to the promotion of technological innovation and to the transfer and dissemination of technology, to the mutual advantage of producers and users of technological knowledge and in a manner conducive to social and economic welfare, and to a balance of rights

---

157. For example, C-314/12, *UPC Telekabel Wien GmbH v. Constantin Film Verleih GmbH*, Wega Filmproduktionsgesellschaft mbH; C-70/10, *Scarlet Extended SA v. Société belge des auteurs, compositeurs et éditeurs SCRL (SABAM)*; C-275/06, *Productores de Música de España (Promusicae) v. Telefónica de España SAU*.
158. C-70/10, para. 43.
159. C-70/10, para. 44.
160. Berne Convention for the Protection of Literary and Artistic Works of 9 September 1886, completed at Paris on 4 May 1896, revised at Berlin on 13 November 1908, completed at Berne on 20 March 1914, revised at Rome on 2 June 1928, at Brussels on 26 June 1948, at Stockholm on 14 July 1967, and at Paris on 24 July 1971, and amended on 28 September 1979.
161. Paris Convention for the Protection of Industrial Property of 20 March 1883, as revised at Brussels on 14 December 1900, at Washington on 2 June 1911, at The Hague on 6 November 1925, at London on 2 June 1934, at Lisbon on 31 October 1958, and at Stockholm on 14 July 1967, and as amended on 28 September 1979.
162. International Convention for the Protection of Performers, Producers of Phonograms and Broadcasting Organizations Done at Rome on 26 October 1961.
163. Agreement on Trade-Related Aspects of Intellectual Property Rights (TRIPS), Annex 1C of the Marrakesh Agreement Establishing the World Trade Organization, signed in Marrakesh, Morocco on 15 April 1994.

and obligations.' Even though Article 8(1) (which is the most relevant for our purposes) at first glance seems to have a somewhat stronger wording, the message which the article conveys remains somewhat ambiguous: 'Members may, in formulating or amending their laws and regulations, adopt measures necessary to protect public health and nutrition, and to promote the public interest in sectors of vital importance to their socio-economic and techno-logical development, provided that such measures are consistent with the provisions of this Agreement.'. The ambiguity lies in the fact that the provision seems to provide room for manoeuvre to the Member States, to then state that any such room must not lead to an interpretation that is not consistent with the Agreement.

It must moreover be added that the so-called Doha Declaration[164] refers to the right to protect the health, which as we will see further below, is also a fundamental right, be it of a different category than the fundamental rights referred to in, for instance, the ECHR. The Doha Declaration says in that connection the following:

1. We recognize the gravity of the public health problems afflicting many developing and least-developed countries, especially those resulting from HIV/AIDS, tuberculosis, malaria and other epidemics.
2. We stress the need for the WTO Agreement on Trade-Related Aspects of Intellectual Property Rights (TRIPS Agreement to be part of the wider national and international action to address these problems.
3. We recognize that intellectual property protection is important for the development of new medicines. We also recognize the concerns about its effects on prices.
4. We agree that the TRIPS Agreement does not and should not prevent Members from taking measures to protect public health. Accordingly, while reiterating our commitment to the TRIPS Agreement, we affirm that the Agreement can and should be interpreted and implemented in a manner supportive of WTO Members' right to protect public health and, in particular, to promote access to medicines for all.[165]

The explanation for this quite distinct development of both legal worlds is predominantly historical. Whilst the human rights scene evolved in the decades after the Second World War around the establishment and development of basic human rights both internationally and nationally and monitoring and enforcement mechanisms, during that same period, the intellectual property rights scene was predominantly concerned with the further

---

164. World Trade Organization. Declaration on the TRIPS Agreements and Public Health, Ministerial Conference, Fourth Session, WTO Doc. WT/MIN(01)/DEC/2. 2001.
165. *Ibid.*, paras 1-4.

elaboration and expansion of existing intellectual property rights both at the international and national level, and in a later phase, an explicit link was made between intellectual property and trade.[166,167] That is as such not surprising, at least not from the perspective of some of the intellectual property rights such as trademark and patents, which had historically always been seen in the context of industrial policy and economic development of a country, and in any event much more than copyright which had a traditional background and justification of being a natural right and more of a reward for artistic creation.[168]

The catalysts to change in that situation of living together apart were the globalization of the intellectual property rights system through the WTO and the TRIPS Agreement on the one hand and on a coming of age of the economic, social and cultural rights which, even though they were present in the international human rights framework for quite a long time, lived a rather low profile existence whilst the human rights system was trying to establish in first instance the basic and fundamental human rights and their enforcement. Probably unjustified, economic, social and cultural rights were in the earlier days seen as less of an urgency. In more recent times, whilst the basic human rights were properly developed, monitored and enforced, more attention could be given to those 'forgotten' rights. The globalization of intellectual property right system has caused a backlash of countries who were not very pleased with the new situation, thus resisting the introduction of the largely western industrialized world inspired intellectual property rights systems and enforcement.

Relevant for this Chapter (but not necessarily limited to this), the two developments, in fact, met each other at the forum of the WTO, which led to the Doha Declaration on TRIPS and Public Health, adopted by the WTO membership in 2001.[169] Also, at the level of the World Intellectual Property Organization (WIPO), a comparable debate was being held, which culminated in the WIPO Development Agenda, launched in 2004.[170] Public health, as one of the fundamental rights, took the forefront position as from then. We will discuss the relationship between the rights to health and intellectual property rights later in this Chapter.

---

166. Witness whereof the TRIPS Agreement.
167. For more details, *see* L.R. Helfer & G.W. Austin, *'Human Rights and Intellectual Property. Mapping the Global Interface'*, Cambridge University Press, New York, 2011, pp. 33-34 and further references mentioned there.
168. This is probably more the case for copyright systems in Europe than that of the US, which had a traditionally more 'industrial' approach towards copyright, hence the duality which is sometimes dubbed as droit d'auteur versus copyright systems.
169. Ministerial Declaration on the TRIPS Agreement and Public Health, WT/MIN(01)/DEC/ W/2, 14 November 2001.
170. WIPO General Assembly, Report of the Twenty-First (15th Extraordinary) Session, para. 218, WO/GA/31/15, 5 October 2004, available at, http://www.wipo.int/edocs/mdocs/ govbody/en/wo_ga_31/wo_ga_31_15.pdf (last visited 2 January 2020).

The growing attention to intellectual property rights, whether as human rights or as being the antithesis of human rights in a trade context must obviously also be seen in a political context of what the Germans would call *Realpolitik*. The development of human rights, and the positioning of human rights against intellectual property rights as human rights or otherwise is quite often the consequence of political compromise,[171] not infrequently heavily influenced by economic and social considerations. Rights, be they human rights or rights of industrial policy are not conceived and do not operate in a vacuum, but are the result of the world in which they operate and the use made of them by all actors in that world or society.

Even though intellectual property rights are held to be part of the fundamental rights according to the above-mentioned international statutory instruments, it does not necessarily mean that those intellectual property rights are deemed to be at equal footing with the other fundamental rights. In General Comment No. 17 to Article 15(1)(c) of the ICESCR, it was held that:

> Human rights are fundamental as they are inherent to the human person as such, whereas intellectual property rights are first and foremost means by which States seek to provide incentives for inventiveness and creativity, encourage the dissemination of creative and innovative productions, as well as the development of cultural identities, and preserve the integrity of scientific, literary and artistic productions for the benefit of society as a whole. In contrast to human rights, intellectual property rights are generally of a temporary nature and can be revoked, licensed or assigned to someone else. While under most intellectual property systems, intellectual property rights, often with the exception of moral rights, may be allocated, limited in time and scope, traded, amended and even forfeited, human rights are timeless expressions of fundamental entitlements of the human person. Whereas the human right to benefit from the protection of the moral and material interests resulting from one's scientific, literary and artistic productions safeguards the personal link between authors and their creations and between peoples, communities, or other groups and their collective cultural heritage, as well as their basic material interests which are necessary to enable authors to enjoy an adequate standard of living, intellectual property regimes primarily protect business and corporate interests and investments. Moreover, the scope of protection of the moral and material interests of the author provided for by Article 15, paragraph 1(c), does not necessarily coincide with what is referred to as

---

171. J. Cornides, '*Human Rights and Intellectual Property: Conflict or Convergence*', 7 Journal of World Intellectual Property, 2004, (135) 137.

intellectual property rights under national legislation or international agreements.[172]

28.5.2   THE DIFFERENT APPROACHES TOWARDS THE RELATIONSHIP BETWEEN
              HUMAN RIGHTS AND INTELLECTUAL PROPERTY RIGHTS

Despite the fact that the two legal worlds developed to meet each other, this did not take away the continued hostility between them. This ever-growing hostility was fed by the growing concern that intellectual property rights in a globalized and WTO era would interfere undesirably with human rights. Exemplary is the Sub-Commission on Human Rights resolution 2000/7,[173] where it was first recalled in paragraph 2 that 'since the implementation of the TRIPS Agreement does not adequately reflect the fundamental nature and indivisibility of all human rights, including the right of everyone to enjoy the benefits of scientific progress and its applications, the right to health, the right to food and the right to self-determination, there are apparent conflicts between the intellectual property rights regime embodied in the TRIPS Agreement, on the one hand, and international human rights law, on the other' to 'remind' then in paragraph 3 of the resolution Governments of 'the primacy of human rights obligations over economic policies and agreements' after which the Resolution requests in paragraphs 4 and 5 that 'all Governments and national, regional and international economic policy forums to take international human rights obligations and principles fully into account in international economic policy formulation' and 'to integrate into their [Governments'] national and local legislations and policies, provisions, in accordance with international human rights obligations and principles, that protect the social function of intellectual property.'

A long list of Reports and other documents have since then been produced by United Nations (UN) bodies which have all in common that they are not very positive towards intellectual property rights and the way they have been exercised.[174,175]

---

172. UN Economic and Economic Council, Committee on Economic, Social and Cultural Rights, Thirty-fifth session, Geneva, 7-25 November 2005, General Comment No. 17 (2005), The right of everyone to benefit from the protection of the moral and material interests resulting from any scientific, literary or artistic production of which he or she is the author (Article 15, para. 1 (c), of the Covenant), E/C.12/GC/17, 12 January 2006.
173. Sub-Commission on the Promotion and Protection of Human Rights (2000), *'Intellectual Property Rights and Human Rights',* UN Doc. E/CN.4/Sub.2/RES/2000/7, adopted 17 August 2000.
174. For a detailed list, *see* Helfer & Austin, *supra,* at 53-56.
175. For intellectual property law scholars and practitioners, it is quite interesting to *see* the overwhelming volume of documents produced clarifying and interpreting UN statutory instruments which can be at times vague and generic in wording. These documents and interpretations, even though not legally binding, seem to obtain at some point and in varying degree the status of non-official interpretations of UN statutory instruments, a

This approach towards the relationship between intellectual property rights and human rights starts from the primacy of human rights, and intellectual property rights have to be 'adapted' to fit into the human rights framework. Such an approach is bound to be not very effective, as it starts from a rather conflictual model between the two worlds, and it seeks very little or no reconciliation or coexistence between the two systems.[176] The conflictual model was clearly expressed in the Sub-Commission on Human Rights resolution 2000/7, where it was held that:

> actual or potential conflicts exist between the implementation of the TRIPS Agreement and the realization of economic, social and cultural rights in relation to, inter alia, impediments to the transfer of technology to developing countries, the consequences for the enjoyment of the right to food of plant variety rights and the patenting of genetically modified organisms, "bio-piracy" and the reduction of communities' (especially indigenous communities') control over their own genetic and natural resources and cultural values, and restrictions on access to patented pharmaceuticals and the implications for the enjoyment of the right to health[.][177]

Supporters of this view hold that '[I]n any principled national legal system, basic human rights to health, education and indigenous rights to their cultures take precedence over (trump) utilitarian considerations.'[178] And also that 'Intellectual property rights should be limited when necessary to protect the public health and to the degree necessary to guarantee the general welfare.'[179]

Categorizing all UN documents as belonging to the above conflictual model would not do justice to the work of the UN, which has obviously also realized that apart from the traditional human rights which were at the core of the argument in Sub-Commission on Human Rights resolution 2000/7, there are also the economic, social and cultural rights, which do recognize, at least to some extent, the existence and benefit of intellectual property rights.[180] There has been a variety of UN documents and Reports which have

---

world quite apart from the rather positivistic legal approach in intellectual property law. For more details, *see* Helfer & Austin, *supra,* 57-58 and the references mentioned there.

176. Gold calls this the subjugation approach. *See*, E. Richard Gold, '*Patents and Human Rights: A Heterodox Analysis*', Journal of Law, Medicine and Ethics, 2013, (185), 187.

177. UN Doc. E/CN.4/Sub.2/RES/2000/7, preamble, recital 11.

178. P. Drahos & J. Braithwaite, '*Information Feudalism: Who Owns the Knowledge Economy?*', Earthscan, London, 2000, p. 200.

179. Z. Lazzarini, '*Making Access to Pharmaceuticals a Reality: Legal Options under TRIPS and the Case of Brazil*', 6 Yale Human Rights and Development Law Journal, 2003, (103), p. 123.

180. Gold argues that Article 15(1)(c) of the ICESCR does recognize that benefits should be granted to inventors and other creators of scientific or creative works, but it does not state that such rights should be intellectual property rights. *See* E. Richard Gold, *supra*, 176. That is very true indeed, but quite a few UN Reports and documents have

appealed for a balance between the public interests in human rights and private interests in fulfilling people's cultural and economic rights.

An important document in this connection, clarifying the relationship between intellectual property rights (under TRIPS) and human rights, is the Report of the High Commissioner on Human Rights on the impact of the Agreement on TRIPS on human rights of 27 June 2001.[181] In paragraph 10, it is said:

> Article 15 of the Covenant obliges States parties to respect, protect and fulfil people's cultural rights. The article identifies a need to balance the protection of both public and private interests in intellectual property. On the one hand, article 15 recognizes the right of everyone to take part in cultural life and to enjoy the benefits of scientific progress and its applications. On the other hand, the same article recognizes the right of everyone to benefit from the protection of the moral and material interests resulting from any scientific, literary or artistic production of which he or she is the author. Taking these two aspects of article 15 together, ICESCR could be said to bind States to design IP systems that strike a balance between promoting general public interests in accessing new knowledge as easily as possible and in protecting the interests of authors and inventors in such knowledge.

And further in paragraphs 12 and 13:

> 12. Consequently, there is a degree of compatibility between article 15 and traditional IP systems. However, the question essentially is where to strike the right balance. Should greater emphasis be given to protecting interests of inventors and authors or to promoting public access to new knowledge? There are certain preconditions to a human rights approach to intellectual property protection which should be borne in mind. 13. First, a human rights approach requires that the public/private balance under article 15 should be struck with the primary objective of promoting and protecting human rights. This conclusion is based on the text of ICESCR itself. Article 15 should be read in conjunction with article 5 of ICESCR, which states that nothing in the Covenant can justify any act aimed at the destruction of any of its rights or freedoms or to limit a right beyond what is provided for in the Covenant. In the

---

themselves made the link between Article 15(1)(c) of the ICESCR and proprietary intellectual property rights. To the extent that one accepts the premise that UN documents and Reports can be seen as interpretative documents of inherently vague Treaty provisions, it could be concluded that those documents interpret the above-mentioned ICESCR provision as encompassing proprietary intellectual property rights.

181. United Nations Commission on Human Rights (2001) Economic, Social and Cultural Rights: *'The Impact of the Agreement on Trade-Related Aspects of Intellectual Property Rights on Human Rights'*, Report of the High Commissioner, 27 June 2001, E/CN.4/ Sub.2/2001/13.

context of article 15, this suggests that, whatever balance is struck between private and public interests in intellectual property, the balance should not work to the detriment of any of the other rights in the Covenant.

Also, the World Health Assembly has voted resolutions, strategies and plans trying to reconcile both types of rights. In its Resolution on Public Health, Innovation and Essential Health Research and Intellectual Property Rights of 27 May 2006,[182] the World Health Assembly emphasized that the Universal Declaration of Human Rights provides that 'everyone has the right freely to participate in the cultural life of the community, to enjoy the arts and to share in scientific advancement and its benefits' and that 'everyone has the right to the protection of the moral and material interests resulting from any scientific, literary or artistic production of which he is the author', after noting that 'that intellectual property rights are an important incentive for the development of new healthcare products', whilst at the same time expressing its concern over the impact of high prices of medicines on access to treatment.

The World Health Organization (WHO) Global Strategy and Plan of Action on Public Health, Innovation and Intellectual Property[183] further contributes to the exercise of balancing both the need for human rights and the importance of intellectual property rights. In doing so, the WHO Assembly emphasized that 'intellectual property rights are an important incentive for the development of new healthcare products. This incentive alone does not meet the need for the development of new products to fight diseases where the potential paying market is small or uncertain',[184] and that 'the Universal Declaration of Human Rights provides that "everyone has the right freely to participate in the cultural life of the community, to enjoy the arts and to share in scientific advancement and its benefits" and that "everyone has the right to the protection of the moral and material interests resulting from any scientific, literary or artistic production of which he is the author"'.[185]

The approach which tries to balance human rights and intellectual property rights is often called the coexistence approach. This approach 'sees both areas of law concerned with the same fundamental question: defining the appropriate scope of private monopoly power that gives, authors and

---

182. World Health Assembly (2006), *'Public Health, Innovation, Essential Health Research and Intellectual Property Rights: towards a global strategy and plan of action'*, Fifty-Ninth World Health Assembly, WHA59.24, 27 May 2006.
183. World Health Assembly (2008), *'Global Strategy and Plan of Action on Public Health, Innovation and Intellectual Property'*, Sixth-First World Health Assembly, WHA61.21, 24 May 2008.
184. Global strategy on public health, innovation and intellectual property, Annex to WHA61.21, 24 May 2008, para. 7.
185. *Ibid.*, para. 12.

inventors a sufficient incentive to create, and innovate while ensuring that the consuming public has adequate access to the fruits of their efforts.'[186]

Equally so, General Comment No. 17 to Article 15(1)(c) of the ICESCR advocated the coexistence approach. In paragraph 35, the document states that:

> The right of authors to benefit from the protection of the moral and material interests resulting from their scientific, literary and artistic productions cannot be isolated from the other rights recognized in the Covenant. States parties are therefore obliged to strike an adequate balance between their obligations under article 15, paragraph 1(c), on the one hand, and under the other provisions of the Covenant, on the other hand, with a view to promoting and protecting the full range of rights guaranteed in the Covenant] In striking this balance, the private interests of authors should not be unduly favoured and the public interest in enjoying broad access to their productions should be given due consideration. [...]. Ultimately, intellectual property is a social product and has a social function. States parties thus have a duty to prevent unreasonably high costs for access to essential medicines, plant seeds or other means of food production, or for schoolbooks and learning materials, from undermining the rights of large segments of the population to health, food and education. Moreover, States parties should prevent the use of scientific and technical progress for purposes contrary to human rights and dignity, including the rights to life, health and privacy, e.g., by excluding inventions from patentability whenever their commercialization would jeopardize the full realization of these rights. States parties should, in particular, consider to what extent the patenting of the human body and its parts would affect their obligations under the Covenant or under other relevant international.[187]

Also, the case law of the Court of Justice of the European Union shows a desire to balance the right to have intellectual property rights with other fundamental rights. It was held in the C-70/10 *Scarlet* case in that connection that '[T]he protection of the right to intellectual property is indeed enshrined in Article 17(2) of the Charter of Fundamental Rights of the European Union ("the Charter"). There is, however, nothing whatsoever in the wording of that provision or in the Court's case-law to suggest that that right is inviolable and must for that reason be absolutely protected,'[188] and further that 'As

---

186. Helfer & Austin, 2011, *supra,* 73.
187. UN Economic and Economic Council, Committee on Economic, Social and Cultural Rights, Thirty-fifth session, Geneva, 7-25 November 2005, General Comment No. 17 (2005), The right of everyone to benefit from the protection of the moral and material interests resulting from any scientific, literary or artistic production of which he or she is the author (Article 15, para. 1 (c), of the Covenant), E/C.12/GC/17, 12 January 2006.
188. C-70/10, para. 43.

paragraphs 62 to 68 of the judgment in Case C 275/06 *Promusicae* [2008] ECR I 271 make clear, the protection of the fundamental right to property, which includes the rights linked to intellectual property, must be balanced against the protection of other fundamental rights.'[189]

The coexistence approach is much more promising and workable than the conflict approach mentioned earlier. However, it equally has inherent weaknesses. An important one is that it still starts from the premise that there is a hierarchy between human rights and intellectual property rights, whilst as we have seen both the 'traditional' human rights and intellectual property rights have both been recognized as human rights in the same international instruments. However, much we can argue that there is a weak basis for categorizing intellectual property rights as human rights, the fact remains that they are considered to be human rights according to international law.[190] That also implies that setting the one against the other is not very productive. The normative setting makes both sets of rights coexist, and to some extent, in conflict also. This causes an internal tension. The discussion should probably hence focus on alleviating the tension between the two sets of human rights, and that is indeed a formidable if not impossible task.[191]

One solution to the tension between the two types of rights is to distinguish between the core minimal obligations under certain human rights and obligations outside of that core. That solution has even been suggested in General Comment No. 3 to the ICESCR which states in that connection that 'the Committee is of the view that a minimum core obligation to ensure the satisfaction of, at the very least, minimum essential levels of each of the rights is incumbent upon every State party. Thus, for example, a State party in which any significant number of individuals is deprived of essential foodstuffs, of essential primary healthcare, of basic shelter and housing, or of the most basic forms of education is, prima facie, failing to discharge its obligations under the Covenant. If the Covenant were to be read in such a way as not to establish such a minimum core obligation, it would be largely deprived of its raison d'être.'[192] Comment No. 3 then also suggests a 'progressive realization' of the rights recognized in the ICESCR.[193]

This approach is equally not without its problems, as, provided one would be able to define a number of core obligations, and General Comment

---

189. C-70/10, para. 44.
190. Somewhat confusingly, General comment No. 17 also says that 'It is therefore important not to equate intellectual property rights with the human right recognized in Article 15, paragraph 1 (c).' General Comment No. 17, para. 3. That paragraph must be seen in the context of corporate intellectual property rights discussed in the preceding para. 2.
191. Yu suggests to resolve this problem by distinguishing the human rights and non-human rights aspects of intellectual property protection, Peter K. Yu, *supra*, 1078.
192. Committee on Economic, Social and Cultural Rights, General Comment 3, The nature of States parties' obligations (Fifth session, 1990), U.N. Doc. E/1991/23, annexe III at 86 (1991), para. 10.
193. General Comment No. 3, para. 9.

No. 3 provides us at least with some of those, it simply shifts the 'burden of proof' from what is core to how much protection is then needed under for those core obligations. As one comment stated, 'it is one thing to assert that there is a core content of each of the rights enumerated in the Covenant and quite another to define its scope.'[194]

Helfer starts from this coexistence approach to developing a human rights framework for intellectual property which starts from the premise that first of all 'the minimum outcomes – in terms of health, poverty, education, and so forth – that human rights law requires of states' must be identified.[195] The framework 'works backwards to identify different mechanisms available to states to achieve those outcomes. Intellectual property plays only a secondary role in this version of the framework. Where intellectual property laws help to achieve human rights outcomes, governments should embrace it. Where it hinders those outcomes, its rules should be modified.'[196] That framework is definitely supported by the UN documentation described above.

The problem I have with this framework is that it still starts more or less from the primacy of human rights, to which the intellectual property framework has to adapt. Secondly, at the face of it, it equally ignores the discussion about the respective relationship between two human right types, i.e., the 'traditional' ones, and the more economical and industrial policy-orientated ones, which I described earlier. Helfer has in later work worked out how he sees this framework to work in practice. A three-step approach is suggested in this connection:

> (1) an evaluation of whether existing or proposed intellectual property protection rules and policies help or hinder the realization of specific human rights outcomes; (2) an assessment, to the greatest extent possible, of the relative causal contributions of intellectual property rules and policies in comparison to other factors; and (3) an identification of the legal and policy measures, whether or not consistent with the existing intellectual property regime, that will facilitate these human rights outcomes. If the assessment of these issues reveals that non-intellectual property factors are responsible for the lack of progress in realizing human rights ends, [...], state and nonstate actors should focus their lawmaking and advocacy strategies on those factors and should not treat intellectual property issues as a proxy for them. [...]. In the final analysis, however, national decision makers will need to decide whether to revise existing intellectual property protection rules and how best to

---

194. A. Chapman & S. Russell, *'Introduction'*, in, A. Chapman & S. Russell (eds), *'Core Obligations: Building a Framework for Economic, Social and Cultural Rights'*, Intersentia, Antwerp, 2002, 6.
195. L.R. Helfer, *'Toward a Human Rights Framework for Intellectual Property'*, 40 UC Davis Law Review, 2007, (971) 1018.
196. *Ibid.*

do so. It is here that the second, substantive stage of the framework's restrictive dimension comes into play. In deciding what measures to take, we urge decision makers to begin from the premise that the human rights and intellectual property regimes share the same core objective – to encourage creativity and innovation that benefits society as a whole. It is the different ways that each regime achieves this objective, which create the potential for conflicts between them.[197]

Geiger emphasizes on the social function of intellectual property rights and is of the view that all legislation regarding IP rights and court decisions on IP rights should take the social function of intellectual property into account. Such would imply that 'the objectives and conditions of the exercise of intellectual property should therefore always be examined in the light of the general interest.'[198] Support for this view seems to be found in the Charter of Fundamental Rights of the European Union, which states in Article 52(1) that:

> any limitation on the exercise of the rights and freedoms recognized by this Charter must be provided for by law and respect the essence of those rights and freedoms. Subject to the principle of proportionality, limitations may be made only if they are necessary and genuinely meet objectives of general interest recognized by the Union or the need to protect the rights and freedoms of others.

That means that IP rights cannot be granted without limitation, and they can equally not be used and enforced without limitation (and limitation is here not limited to statutory defences or exemptions). Every IP right must be put in front of the mirror of the general interest, which includes the fundamental human rights, and will require balancing if the picture would tilt away from the general interest. In other words, 'the grant of a right in the intellectual property may itself be derivative of a duty to others; that is, when the intellectual property owner acquires a legal intellectual property right, a duty to the public is simultaneously imposed on the intellectual property owner.'[199] This approach is clearly based on the coexistence of both types of rights, and seems to be very akin to the approach taken by Helfer.

What I have learned from this long-lasting debate about the relationship between human rights and intellectual property rights, or even within human rights between 'traditional' human rights and intellectual property rights is

---

197. Helfer & Austin, *supra*, 518-519.
198. C. Geiger, *'The Social Function of Intellectual Property Rights, or How Ethics Can Influence the Shape and Use of IP Law'*, in, G.B. Dinwoodie (ed.), *'Intellectual Property Law: Methods and Perspectives'*, Cheltenham, UK/Northampton, MA, Edward Elgar, 2014, (153) pp. 163 et seq.
199. E.F. Judge, *'Intellectual Property Law as an Internal Limit on Intellectual Property Rights and Autonomous Source of Liability for Intellectual Property Owners'*, 27(4) Bulletin of Science, Technology & Society, 2007, (301), 311.

that after more than fifteen years of debate and searching for a coexistence relationship (not even a marriage), there is still deep water between the two camps. Pressure on nations to introduce strict intellectual property standards under TRIPS without an immediate beneficial effect to those nations, to say the least, will continue to strengthen or at least keep alive this tension. In effect, both systems have already moved closer towards each other, not only because courts have recognized human rights as capable of limiting the scope of intellectual property rights, but also because of the fact that the continuing debate has probably led players to explore the flexibilities in intellectual property systems themselves, a feature which is quite often neglected in the debate about the relationship between human rights and intellectual property rights.[200]

Indeed, the present author holds the view that, even though human rights should obviously not be neglected in the discourse and policy of intellectual property law, full and fair play should first be given to the internal flexibilities which intellectual property right systems have built-in. In that sense, the IP systems already have a 'built-in' social function. Indeed, internal flexibilities allow policymakers, granting bodies, judges and users to take into account the social function of the IP system, as Geiger called it, in taking into account the general interest.

For patent law, those consist of exclusion of certain patentable subject matter, strict adherence and application of the patentability requirements of novelty, inventive step, industrial application and enabling disclosure and full use of further limitations such as the research exemption and compulsory licensing.[201] In the human right narrative about intellectual property rights, these internal tools are often overlooked. One may, however, not be naïve and think that those internal tools constitute the holy grail of reconciliation. The problems surrounding the compulsory licensing show that these internal tools have weaknesses.[202] Those weaknesses are often the result of pressures

---

200. I come back to these flexibilities in section 28.5.4 of this Chapter.
201. This is also the correct view of some of the most prominent defenders and promotors of access to medicine. *See*, e.g., E. FM 't Hoen, et al., '*Medicine Procurement and the Use of Flexibilities in the Agreement on Trade-Related Aspects of Intellectual Property Rights, 2001-2016*', Bulletin of the World Health Organization, 2018, 96, 185-193.
202. For example, the provision in the TRIPS agreement regarding compulsory cross licensing is likely written in such a manner as to make it very unlikely that the feature will ever be used, as it seems almost insurmountable to fulfil the conditions set under the system. *See* Article 31(l) states:

'*Where the law of a Member allows for other use of the subject matter of a patent without the authorization of the right holder, including use by the government or third parties authorized by the government, the following provisions shall be respected: [...](l) where such use is authorized to permit the exploitation of a patent ("the second patent") which cannot be exploited without infringing another patent ("the first patent"), the following additional conditions shall apply:*

   (i) *the invention claimed in the second patent shall involve an important technical advance of considerable economic significance in relation to the invention claimed in the first patent;*
   (ii) *the owner of the first patent shall be entitled to a cross-licence on reasonable terms to use the invention claimed in the second patent; and*

on international instruments to the advantage of trade and more absolutist respect of intellectual property rights. Moreover, flexibilities in the TRIPS agreement, however important they are, have limitations, not that much (or not only) by conceptual weakness, but by the way these flexibilities operate within the international trade system. Being part of an international trade agreement, it cannot be excluded that states negotiating trade agreements with third parties limit in effect the functioning of the TRIPS flexibilities, not only by negotiating stricter intellectual property provisions but also by the force of trade deals and practical implementation. For instance, it would be naïve to think that powerful trade nations would not use that leverage in negotiating less favourable terms with countries which plan to take maximum advantage of TRIPS flexibilities.

28.5.3   THE RIGHT TO HEALTH AND PERSONALIZED MEDICINE

For purposes of the present chapter, I would like to focus on two human rights recognized in the international framework, being the right to obtain intellectual property rights and the right to health. The former has already been mentioned and clarified above. The latter is enshrined in a number of international instruments.

The human right to health is recognized in numerous international instruments. Article 25(1) of the UDHR affirms: 'Everyone has the right to a standard of living adequate for the health of himself and of his family, including food, clothing, housing and medical care and necessary social services'.

The ICESCR provides the most comprehensive article on the right to health in international human rights law. In accordance with Article 12(1) of the Covenant, States parties recognize 'the right of everyone to the enjoyment of the highest attainable standard of physical and mental health'.

In Europe, Article 3 of the Convention for the Protection of Human Rights and Dignity of the Human Being with regard to the Application of Biology and Medicine states that 'Parties, taking into account health needs and available resources, shall take appropriate measures with a view to

---

     (iii) the use authorized in respect of the first patent shall be non-assignable except with the assignment of the second patent.'

     It seems very difficult if indeed possible to provide evidence that a second patent constitutes an important technical advance of considerable economic significance, not only because it is absolutely unclear what is meant by those terms, but equally because it will often be impossible to make such evaluation objectively, not in the least because it takes often a considerable amount of time and many years of exclusivity of patent protection to evaluate whether a piece of technology is indeed of any economic significance, let alone of considerable economic significance, if we would be able to understand what that term means, *quod non*.

providing, within their jurisdiction, equitable access to healthcare of appropriate quality.'[203]

The European Social Charter states in Article 11 that:

With a view to ensuring the effective exercise of the right to protection of health, the Contracting Parties undertake, either directly or in cooperation with public or private organizations, to take appropriate measures designed inter alia: 1 to remove as far as possible the causes of ill health; 2 to provide advisory and educational facilities for the promotion of health and the encouragement of individual responsibility in matters of health; 3 to prevent as far as possible epidemic, endemic and other diseases.[204]

It must be said, however, that Article 11 does not belong to the core provisions of the Social Charter to which Parties should commit, witness whereof Article 20 which lists the core provisions to which Parties should consider themselves bound, and Article 11 does not belong to that 'club' of core rights to be protected.

Article 12(1) of the ICESCR has been the subject of General Comment No. 14 on the Right to the Highest Attainable Standard of Health.[205] Important for the present chapter is paragraph 9 of General Comment No. 14 which states that 'The notion of "the highest attainable standard of health" in article 12.1 takes into account both the individual's biological and socio-economic preconditions and a State's available resources. [...]. Consequently, the right to health must be understood as a right to the enjoyment of a variety of facilities, goods, services and conditions necessary for the realization of the highest attainable standard of health.'

Another obligation under the Covenant is that Member States should, amongst others, 'provide essential drugs, as from time to time defined under the WHO Action Programme on Essential Drugs.'[206] General Comment 14 also provides more substance as to the elements that form part of the right to health. According to the said Comment, the right to health encompasses four interrelated elements, i.e., availability, accessibility (with four dimensions, being, non-discrimination, physical accessibility, economic accessibility and

---

203. Convention for the Protection of Human Rights and Dignity of the Human Being with regard to the Application of Biology and Medicine: Convention on Human Rights and Biomedicine, Oviedo, 4 April 1997 (ETS 164).
204. European Social Charter, Turin, 18 October 1961 (ETS 35).
205. United Nations Economic and Social Committee General Comment No. 14 on the right to the highest attainable standard of health (Article 12 of the International Covenant on Economic, Social and Cultural Rights). Committee on Economic, Social and Cultural Rights, Twenty-second session, Geneva, 25 April-12 May 2000, E/C.12/2000/4, 11 August 2000.
206. General Comment No. 14, para. 43 sub (d).

information accessibility), acceptability and quality (also sometimes known as the AAAQ framework).[207]

General Comment No. 3 to the ICESCR also refers to 'a State party in which any significant number of individuals is deprived of [...] essential primary healthcare, [...]' as 'failing to discharge its obligations under the Covenant.'[208]

The Right to Health is hence a recognized right under international human rights law that entails rights and obligations, one of which is, at least for the Member States of the ICESCR, to provide essential drugs to their populations. Some have interpreted this as including the obligation for WTO members to interpret and apply the TRIPS Agreement in a manner which is consistent with the right to health obligations under Article 12 ICESCR.[209]

An important question to ask oneself is how the right to attain the highest standards of health relate to the concept of intellectual property rights. No one will deny that this is not always a comfortable relationship, and various health crises, amongst others the HIV crisis, have provided ample evidence of that difficult relationship.[210] However, many attempts have been made at the UN level to arrive at a coexistence between the two worlds. The above-mentioned Global strategy on public health, innovation and intellectual property[211] attempts to implement a strategy which aims 'to promote new thinking on innovation and access to medicines, as well as, based on the recommendations of the Commission on Intellectual Property Rights, Innovation and Public Health (CIPIH) report, provide a medium-term framework for securing an enhanced and sustainable basis for needs driven essential health research and development relevant to diseases which disproportionately affect developing countries, proposing clear objectives and priorities for R&D, and estimating funding needs in this area.'[212] The elements of the global strategy, which are designed to promote innovation, build capacity, improve access and mobilize resources are the following:

(a) provide an assessment of the public health needs of developing countries with respect to diseases that disproportionately affect developing countries and identify their R&D priorities at the national, regional and international levels; (b) promote R&D focusing on Type II and Type III diseases and the specific R&D needs of developing

---

207. General Comment No. 14, para. 12.
208. General Comment No. 3, para. 10.
209. J. A. Sellin, *'Does One Size Fit All? Patents, the Right to Health and Access to Medicines'*, 62 Netherlands International Law Review, 2015, (445-473), at 452.
210. For a more detailed appraisal, *see* D. Matthews, *'Intellectual Property Rights, Human Rights and the Right to Health'*, in W. Grosheide (ed.) *'Intellectual Property Rights and Human Rights: A Paradox'*, Cheltenham, UK/Northampton, MA, USA, Edward Elgar, 2010, p. 118.
211. Global strategy on public health, innovation and intellectual property, Annex to WHA61.21, 24 May 2008.
212. Global strategy, para. 13.

countries in relation to Type I diseases 1; (c) build and improve innovative capacity for research and development, particularly in developing countries; (d) improve, promote and accelerate transfer of technology between developed and developing countries as well as among developing countries; (e) encourage and support the application and management of intellectual property in a manner that maximizes health-related innovation, especially to meet the R&D needs of developing countries, protects public health and promotes access to medicines for all, as well as explore and implement, where appropriate, possible incentive schemes for R&D; (f) improve delivery of and access to all health products and medical devices by effectively overcoming barriers to access; (g) secure and enhance sustainable financing mechanisms for R&D and to develop and deliver health products and medical devices to address the health needs of developing countries; (h) develop mechanisms to monitor and evaluate the implementation of the strategy and plan of action, including reporting systems.[213]

All the work relating to the relationship between the human right to health and the existence of intellectual property rights for medicines led, amongst others, to the UN 2008 Human Rights Guidelines for Pharmaceutical Companies in relation to Access to Medicines,[214] to the development of which the pharmaceutical industry largely refused to collaborate. The Guidelines cover issues such as transparency, management, monitoring and accountability, pricing and ethical marketing. The Preamble to the Guidelines emphasizes the role and responsibility of pharmaceutical companies to contribute to an effective right to health:

i. Pharmaceutical companies, including innovator, generic and biotechnology companies, have human rights responsibilities in relation to access to medicines; j. Pharmaceutical companies also have other responsibilities, for example, a responsibility to enhance shareholder value; k. Pharmaceutical companies are subject to several forms of internal and external monitoring and accountability; however, these mechanisms do not usually monitor, and hold a company to account, in relation to its human rights responsibilities to enhance access to medicines.[215]

---

213. Global strategy, para. 14.
214. U.N. Report of the Special Rapporteur on the right of everyone to the enjoyment of the highest attainable standard of physical and mental health, Annex to the Report: Human Rights Guidelines for Pharmaceutical Companies in Relation to Access to Medicines, UN Doc. A/63/263, 11 August 2008.
215. Preamble i-j to the Human Rights Guidelines for Pharmaceutical Companies in Relation to Access to Medicines, UN Doc. A/63/263, 11 August 2008.

One part of the Guidelines sets forth compliance with the compulsory licensing scheme within the TRIPS Agreement.[216] Another part, covering pricing, emphasizes that:

> the company should give particular attention to ensuring its medicines are accessible to disadvantaged individuals, communities and populations, including those living in poverty and the very poorest in all markets. The arrangements should include, for example, differential pricing between countries, differential pricing within countries, commercial voluntary licences, not-for-profit voluntary licences, donation programmes, and public-private partnerships.[217]

Even though these Guidelines provide a useful framework for all nations to achieve the right to enjoyment of the highest attainable standard of health, the fact the pharmaceutical industry was unwilling to participate to its drafting shows that there is still a long way to go before the marriage between human rights and intellectual property rights will be a successful affair. The industry must have thought that the Guidelines would have been too prescriptive for and interfering with their commercial business, and without a doubt fears that collaborating with these Guidelines could have led to watering down intellectual property rights have also convinced the industry not to participate. That does not mean that these Guidelines are not useful or even more not used. To the contrary, these Guidelines function as a moral mirror for society in general and the pharmaceutical industry in particular.

As past crises relating to access to drugs have shown, lessons are not always learned willingly and easily. The HIV crisis analysed in detail in Helfer and Austin[218] is a showcase of what can be achieved. A lot has been written about the problems of access to medicines and its relationship with human rights, and it is not our intention to rewrite that story.[219] Suffice to say that the debate about access to medicines as it has been held in the past retains its validity today.

Applied to personalized medicine, all the issues which have been discussed in the context of access to medicine remain equally valid. What is even more, the era of personalized medicine has made the debate more complex and multi-faceted. The 2008 Guidelines include 'active pharmaceutical ingredients, diagnostic tools, vaccines, biopharmaceuticals and other related healthcare technologies'[220] within the scope of technologies which

---

216. Guidelines No. 26-32.
217. Guidelines No. 33.
218. For a detailed account, *see* Helfer & Austin, *supra*, 90-170.
219. *Ibid.*
220. Preamble q to the Human Rights Guidelines for Pharmaceutical Companies in Relation to Access to Medicines, UN Doc. A/63/263, 11 August 2008.

should be covered by the right to enjoyment of the highest attainable standard of health.

It should also be added that there are indeed many factors that cause the lack of access to good healthcare and medicines, and it should be clear that the existence of intellectual property rights and the way how these are exercised by the right holders is only part of the puzzle. Indeed, also the Report of the UN Secretary-General's High-Level Panel on Access to Medicines confirms this: 'There are many reasons why people do not get the healthcare they need, including, *inter alia*, under-resourced health systems, a lack of sufficiently qualified and skilled healthcare workers, inequalities between and within countries, regulatory barriers, poor health education, unavailability of health insurance, exclusion, stigma, discrimination and exclusive marketing rights.'[221] It is inescapable, however, that intellectual property rights – and for that matter, also regulatory exclusivities – and especially the effect they may have on pricing, are a relevant issue that requires proper attention.

In the next section of this Chapter, I will discuss a number of actions that can be taken with a view to addressing the challenges in the context of the fundamental right to health. Whether one wants it or not, the right to health is a fundamental right that requires governments, companies and society at large to invest in attempting to attain the highest possible standard of health. That is a fundamental right and a moral obligation. And it is a task for all of us, including also the holders of intellectual property rights, whose rights are not unlimited, and should take into account the general interest.

Indeed, the existence and the use of intellectual property right has for many years already been defined by higher fundamental principles. Most developed nations have compulsory licensing schemes within the patent act, allowing governments and/or courts to step in and grant a licence in the more general interest. The patent system itself hence already contains checks, balances and limitations against the (attempted) use of patent rights which would go against the public interest. The right to health is such a general interest, and in that regard, intellectual property rights should be interpreted within the context of that right. In that context, I would like to refer again to what I said before Geiger has called the social function of the intellectual property right, which should take into account the general interest.

28.5.4   What Action Can Be Taken?

What is then the relation between the right to health as a fundamental right, the right to obtain and exercise intellectual property rights, and personalized

---

221. Report of the United Nations Secretary-General's High-Level Panel On Access to Medicines: Promoting innovation and access to health technologies, 14 September 2016, available at http://www.unsgaccessmeds.org/final-report (last visited 2 January 2020).

medicine? The easy answer would be to say that it fits neatly within the discussion around access to drugs which is linked to the right to health. Such an answer is, to a large extent correct, and it is logical to conclude that the same narratives and practices developed in the context of access to drugs are equally relevant to personalized medicine.[222]

That is not the complete answer, however. The fact that, for instance, the 2008 Guidelines include diagnostic tools, vaccines and in general other healthcare technologies, suggest that all new technologies developed in the context of personalized medicine fall within the ambit of the right to health. That is not a revolutionary position. But it demonstrates that a discussion in the context of the right to health in relation to intellectual property rights should not limit itself to a discussion about access to medicines only. As we have seen in the chapter dealing with patent protection, there is a rather wide weaponry of patent protection on a wide variety of technologies relevant to healthcare. And in personalized medicine, many of them will be cumulatively relevant. For instance, a patented gene sequence can be necessary to diagnose disease or stratification within a certain genetic profile, such diagnostic or stratification method potentially also being patented. A patented molecule or further use of such molecule might be the treatment for the condition diagnosed. There are hence a plethora of possible patent rights that need to be navigated with a view to guarantee access to adequate healthcare.

As we have said before, the right to health is not an absolute right, as no fundamental right is. That as such should, however, not be a reason to discard the right to health as being less important. It is a fundamental right, and attaining the highest possible level of health is beneficial to the entire world. In the most egoistic way, it also benefits more wealthy parts of the world, as the more the people who die from diseases because of inadequate health provision, the higher the burden on development programmes funded by such more industrialized nations. Moreover, disease knows no borders, and epidemic outbreaks of infectious diseases without adequate treatment will inevitably also affect the lives of people in the industrialized world.

Investing in access to affordable and high-quality healthcare is also a moral imperative for all of us, however, and in that way, the entire world and the pharmaceutical industry should feel morally bound to contribute to affordable access to healthcare.

A second question is then also what action can be taken to ensure that the right to health is protected, whilst at the same not ignoring the existence of intellectual property rights and the equally legitimate expectation to exercise such rights? That will be the subject of the rest of this section.

One of the most obvious ways to deal with the rather tense relationship between the right to health and the existence of intellectual property rights,

---

222. Discussing generally the ramifications of access and personalized medicine, K.A. McClellan, et al., '*Personalized Medicine and Access to Health Care: Potential for Inequitable Access?*', 21 European Journal of Human Genetics, 2013, 143-147.

and at the same time to implement our moral duty to improve access to affordable healthcare, as I already mentioned earlier in this Chapter, to optimize flexibilities present in IP systems so as to ensure that potential negative consequences relating to access to affordable medicines can be avoided or at least mitigated. The use of flexibilities was also promoted in a Resolution adopted by the UN Human Rights Council on 1 July 2016, where it was stated: 'Calls upon States to promote access to medicines for all, including through the use, to the full, of the provisions of the Agreement on Trade-Related Aspects of Intellectual Property Rights, which provide flexibility for that purpose, recognizing that the protection of intellectual property is important for the development of new medicines, as well as the concerns about its effects on prices'[223]

In what follows I will discuss some of these flexibilities,[224] the most important ones of which are possibilities relating to the application of patentability standards, the exclusion of certain subject matter of patent protection, and the use of compulsory licensing systems.

That very same UN Resolution also calls for a delinkage of the cost of new research and development from the prices of medicines, vaccines and

---

223. United Nations General Assembly, Resolution 32/15 adopted by the UN Human Rights Council on 1 July 2016 'Access to medicines in the context of the right of everyone to the enjoyment of the highest attainable standard of physical and mental health', A/HRC/RES/32/15, para. 3.
224. It is important to note that I define TRIPS flexibilities somewhat broader than this was done in the WTO Doha Declaration, where flexibilities were largely focusing on (compulsory) licensing, whilst I include also flexibilities allowed under the TRIPS Agreement in relation to patentable subject matter, the interpretation of patentability requirements, and the introduction of exceptions to infringement. Under para. 5 of the Doha Declaration 'Accordingly and in the light of paragraph 4 above, while maintaining our commitments in the TRIPS Agreement, we recognize that these flexibilities include:
    a) In applying the customary rules of interpretation of public international law, each provision of the TRIPS Agreement shall be read in the light of the object and purpose of the Agreement as expressed, in particular, in its objectives and principles.
    b) Each member has the right to grant compulsory licences and the freedom to determine the grounds upon which such licences are granted.
    c) Each member has the right to determine what constitutes a national emergency or other circumstances of extreme urgency, it being understood that public health crises, including those relating to HIV/AIDS, tuberculosis, malaria and other epidemics, can represent a national emergency or other circumstances of extreme urgency.
    d) The effect of the provisions in the TRIPS Agreement that are relevant to the exhaustion of intellectual property rights is to leave each member free to establish its own regime for such exhaustion without challenge, subject to the MFN and national treatment provisions of Articles 3 and 4.' WTO, Ministerial Conference, Fourth Session, Doha, 9-14 November 2001, Declaration on the TRIPS Agreement and Public Health, adopted on 14 November 2001, WT/MIN(01)/DEC/2, 20 November 2001. Available at: https://www.wto.org/english/thewto_e/minist_e/min01_e/mindecl_trips_e.htm (last visited 2 January 2020).

diagnostics for diseases that predominantly affect developing countries: 'Reiterates the call upon States to continue to collaborate, as appropriate, on models and approaches that support the delinkage of the cost of new research and development from the prices of medicines, vaccines and diagnostics for diseases that predominantly affect developing countries, including emerging and neglected tropical diseases, so as to ensure their sustained accessibility, affordability and availability and to ensure access to treatment for all those in need.'[225] That is a very important goal indeed and deserves all the attention it can get, but a more detailed discussion is beyond the scope of this Chapter, and it will not be further discussed. One of the most well-known flexibilities under the TRIPS system is the use of compulsory licensing, which allows countries to get access to drugs under a compulsory licence against a patent holder so as to arrive at a lower cost of supply of the drugs. Typically, the compulsory licence is granted to a generic manufacturer, who will then manufacture and sell at a cost lower than the patented product. Regarding compulsory licensing as a tool to achieve access, even though the TRIPS agreement leaves Members free to decide under which circumstances and conditions they grant compulsory licences, if a Member wishes to invoke the waiver of having to try to reach a consensual licence first, there are some requirements laid down in the TRIPS agreement. Under Article 31(b), the requirement 'may be waived by a Member in the case of a national emergency or other circumstances of extreme urgency or in cases of public non-commercial use.' What constitutes a national emergency or other circumstance of extreme urgency is not further defined. However, the Doha Declaration clarifies in paragraph 5(c) that 'it being understood that public health crises, including those relating to HIV/AIDS, tuberculosis, malaria and other epidemics, can represent a national emergency or other circum-stances of extreme urgency.'[226] I think it would be premature to decide that all personalized medicine related inventions could be subsumed under the denominator 'public health crises'. This could have as a consequence that a not necessarily inconsiderable number of personalized medicine innovations could, to the extent that they are priced at a level unaffordable to developing countries, be in effect inaccessible to those countries. As a mitigating factor, it must be added, however, that some of those innovations might also remain unavailable in the industrialized world to the extent that public or private insurers would decide not to make those diagnostic or treatment methods

---

225. *Ibid.*, para. 5.
226. WTO, Ministerial Conference, Fourth Session, Doha, 9-14 November 2001, Declaration on the TRIPS Agreement and Public Health, adopted on 14 November 2001, WT/MIN(01)/DEC/2, 20 November 2001. Available at: https://www.wto.org/english/thewt o_e/minist_e/min01_e/mindecl_trips_e.htm (last visited 2 January 2020).

available to the population. Not only for developing but also for developed nations, the right to health is confined by financial capacity.[227]

The other option is to issue a licence for public non-commercial use. I would suggest that this option is probably not sufficiently used, as it seems that this tool provides a room of manoeuvre for countries to guarantee access. One must realize, however, that this option also comes at a cost, both financially and administratively, and that such burden is not always feasible for certain countries.

An interesting study by 't Hhoen et al.[228] reveals that, in fact, the TRIPS flexibilities relating to licensing are more used than we might think at first glance:

> The aim of this study was to document the use of TRIPS flexibilities to access lower-priced generic medicines between 2001 and 2016. Overall, 176 instances of the possible use of TRIPS flexibilities by 89 countries were identified: 100 (56.8%) involved compulsory licences or public noncommercial use licences and 40 (22.7%) involved the least-developed countries pharmaceutical transition measure.[229] The remainder were: 1 case of parallel importation; 3 research exceptions; and 32

---

227. A recently reported example is Orkambi and Symkevi, for the treatment of certain categories of patients with cystic fibrosis. The drugs have been approved as an orphan drug and would have had a price of GBP 104,000 per patient, per year. The company Vertex, who has developed the drugs and brought them to market is estimated to make a profit of USD 21 billion (GBP 17 billion) over the drugs' lifetime. *See*, Isabelle Jani-Friend, '*Drug Companies Are Putting a Price on the Lives of Those with Cystic Fibrosis*', The Guardian, 14 August 2019, https://www.theguardian.com/commentisfree/2019/aug/14/cystic-fibrosis-drug-makers-nhs-price-lives (last visited on 2 January 2020).

228. E. F.M. 't Hoen, et al., '*Medicine Procurement and the Use of Flexibilities in the Agreement on Trade-Related Aspects of Intellectual Property Rights, 2001-2016*', Bulletin of the World Health Organization, 2018, 96, 185-193.

229. The least developed countries pharmaceutical transition measure refers to para. 7 of the Doha Declaration: '7. We reaffirm the commitment of developed-country members to provide incentives to their enterprises and institutions to promote and encourage technology transfer to least-developed country members pursuant to Article 66.2. We also agree that the least-developed country members will not be obliged, with respect to pharmaceutical products, to implement or apply sections 5 and 7 of Part II of the TRIPS Agreement or to enforce rights provided for under these Sections until 1 January 2016, without prejudice to the right of least-developed country members to seek other extensions of the transition periods as provided for in Article 66.1 of the TRIPS Agreement. We instruct the Council for TRIPS to take the necessary action to give effect to this pursuant to Article 66.1 of the TRIPS Agreement.' That transition period is now extended to 1 January 2033: *see*, Extension of the transition period under Article 66.1 of the TRIPS Agreement for least developed country members for certain obligations with respect to pharmaceutical products. Decision of the Council for TRIPS of 6 November 2015. Geneva: World Trade Organization; 2015. Available at: https://docs.wto.org/dol2fe/Pages/FE_Search/FE_S_S009-DP.aspx?language=E&CatalogueIdList=228924,135697,117294,75909,77445,11737,50512,1530,12953,20730&CurrentCatalogueIdIn

non-patent-related measures. Of the 176 instances, 152 (86.4%) were implemented.[230]

That study suggests that TRIPS licensing flexibilities are first of all invoked and used, but also and consequently that they are an important policy lever to guarantee access to medicines at affordable prices. TRIPS-plus provisions which now become increasingly used in trade agreements could put the practice of TRIPS flexibilities into jeopardy, though.[231]

The TRIPS Agreement also allows the Member States to exclude some of the earlier described inventions from patent protection. Article 27(3)(a) states in that connection that Members may exclude from patentability 'diagnostic, therapeutic and surgical methods for the treatment of humans or animals.'[232] To the extent that members would do that indeed, which would cover at least some of the personalized medicine treatments, quid with products used in such treatments? There is a good reason for asking this question, as a practice under the EPC is that one will not claim, for instance, the treatment method, but the product used in such treatment. That is possible under the EPC, as there is a specific provision in the Convention creating an exception to the basic principle of novelty (*see* Article 54(4) and (5) EPC, already discussed earlier).[233] In the US, which statutory framework does not provide such exception to the principle of novelty, medical treatments are simply patentable. This Chapter has not endeavoured to undertake an analysis of the statutory provisions of Members, but there is clearly room for manoeuver here, at least in the abstract.

In that same context, flexibilities within national patent systems also allow for room of manoeuvre. For instance, genetic diagnostic methods are susceptible to compulsory licences for reasons of public health under Belgian law.[234] Even though the procedure is unnecessarily burdensome, complex and, in practice, very difficult if at all efficient to apply, it shows that members states still have room for legislating on issues of compulsory licensing outside of the areas of 'health crises', simply by introducing a new category.[235] There have also been calls to introduce an exemption from liability for infringing gene patent claims, but these have not made it into

---

dex=1&FullTextHash=&HasEnglishRecord=True&HasFrenchRecord=True&HasSpanishRecord=True (last visited 2 January 2020).

230. *Ibid.*
231. I will discuss TRIPS-plus practices, its consequences and potential remedies further in this section.
232. Observe that the provision is formulated more broadly than the EPC, which only excludes patentability of those methods if they are performed ON the human body.
233. *See* subsection 28.3.4.2.
234. Article XI.38 Belgian Code Economic Law.
235. As TRIPS does not give a list under which conditions compulsory licences can be granted, that leaves room for members to develop policy.

statute.[236] There is equally research which suggests that some gene patents have very little or no impact on the development of genetic testing by public funds as those patents seem to be ignored.[237]

Further talking about flexibilities within the patent system, in Switzerland, since 1 January 2019, some important amendments to the patent act have entered into force. We limit ourselves here to the so-called therapeutic freedom exemption. Under the G 2/08 decision of the EBA, a second and further medical indication of a known substance is patentable as a 'product for the use in the treatment of … '. This is now a purpose-limited product claim. That claim protects the delivery and use of the product, and according to the Swiss government also the prescription of a known and no longer protected drug for a new and patented medical indication.[238] The new Article 9(1)(g) Swiss Patent Law,[239] according to which the therapeutic freedom of physicians is guaranteed, and the delivery, use and prescription of a drug for a patented medical indication for an individual patient will not be held to be a patent infringement.[240] This is a rather pioneering new exemption in Europe, as it casts in statute the concept of therapeutic freedom of the treating physician, a concept that is silently recognized in patent law of several EU Member States but not in any patent statute. It goes without saying that such a provision could potentially have far-reaching consequences for patenting personalized medicine. I support the introduction of such exemption, as it gives absolute freedom to medical practitioners to prescribe the treatment which is best for the patient, without being constrained by patents, which was at least one of the key reasons why in Europe medical treatment methods are excluded from patentability and why in the US medical practitioners are exempted from patent infringement liability under US patent law 35 U.S.C. 287(c).[241] But for the specific area of

---

236. *See* e.g., J.M. Mueller, '*Facilitating Patient Access to Patent-Protected Genetic Testing*', 6 Journal of Business & Technology Law, 2010, 83-101.

237. N. Hawkins, '*The Impact of Human Gene Patents on Genetic Testing in the United Kingdom*', 13 Genetics in Medicine, April 2011, 320-324.

238. *See*, Felix Addor, Christine Vetter, '*Der Schutz der medizinischen Behandlungsfreiheit vor patentrechtlichen Verletzungsklagen*', sic!- – Zeitschrift für Immaterialgüter-, Informations- und Wettbewerbsrecht, 2014, Sondernummer 4/125 IGE, p. 3, to be found on https://www.sic-online.ch/fileadmin/user_upload/Sic-Online/2014/documents/245.pdf (last visited on 2 January 2020).

239. Enacted by 'Anhang Ziff. 2 des BG vom 18. März 2016, in Kraft seit 1. Jan. 2019 (AS 2017 2745, 2018 3575; BBl 2013 1).'

240. Artikel 9 Absatz 1 PatG: 'Die Wirkung des Patents erstreckt sich nicht auf: g. Handlungen im Rahmen einer medizinischen Tätigkeit, die sich auf eine einzelne Person oder ein einzelnes Tier bezieht und Arzneimittel betrifft, insbesondere die Verschreibung, Abgabe oder Anwendung von Arzneimitteln durch gesetzlich dazu berechtigte Personen.'

241. 35 U.S.C. 287(c): 'With respect to a medical practitioner's performance of a medical activity that constitutes an infringement under section 271 (a) or (b), the provisions of sections 281, 283, 284, and 285 shall not apply against the medical practitioner or against a related healthcare entity with respect to such medical activity. […]' *See also*,

personalized medicine, where the individual prescription to the individual patient may be the invention indeed, such exemption may have quite important consequences. That the new exemption comes very timely is also evidenced by the recent case law on patent infringement for second medical use patents which has engulfed many European countries, but which has proven to be a difficult problem to solve.[242] My analysis of the case law seems to suggest that it can indeed not be excluded that physicians and pharmacists potentially expose themselves in prescribing a generic drug for a patented medical use and dispensing a generic drug for such patented use to a patent infringement claim.

The issues relating to personalized medicine maybe teach us an important lesson on how patent-eligible subject matter has been evaluated in the past. Apart from calls to exclude large categories from being patent-eligible subject matters, other suggestions have been and should be explored. For some time already, there has been a discussion about the consequences of gene patents, and in particular their scope. As a consequence of the concept of absolute product protection,[243] it has been argued that product patents for genes were too broad and were capable of creating what has been called patent thickets.[244] It would lead us too far to integrate that entire discussion, which is still ongoing, into this Chapter.[245] What the advent of personalized medicine shows is that the discussion on broad gene patents was maybe not the real problem after all. Research has not been able to provide evidence of structural patent thickets in the area of gene patents. One of the arguments I have developed in the past against the abolition of absolute product protection for genes was that the consequential purpose-limited product protection might lead to a rather scattered patent landscape, where a multiplicity of patent owners hold patents for relatively narrow distinctive patents relating to a specific gene and adjacent diagnostic and

---

S.J.R. Bostyn, *'Medical Treatment Methods, Medical Indication Claims and Patentability: A Quest into the Rationale of the Exclusion and Patentability in the Context of the Future of Personalised Medicine'*, Intellectual Property Quarterly, 2016, 203-230.

242. For a detailed appraisal of the infringement issues, *see* S.J.R. Bostyn, *'Personalised Medicine, Medical Indication Patents and Patent Infringement: Emergency Treatment Required'*, Intellectual Property Quarterly, 2016, 151-201.

243. Absolute product protection protects every use of the protected product and every way of making the product. *See* for Europe, G 2/88, cited earlier.

244. *See*, M.A. Heller & R.S. Eisenberg, *'Can Patents Deter Innovation? The Anticommons in Biomedical Research'*, 280 Science, 1 May 1998, 698-701; R.S. Eisenberg, *'Genes, Patents, and Product Development'*, 257 Science, 14 August 1992, 903-908; On the issue of patent thickets, *see also*, Bostyn, EC Report 2004, pp. 113 et seq.; G. Van Overwalle (ed.), *'Gene Patents and Collaborative Licensing Models: Patent Pools, Clearinghouses, Open Source Models and Liability Regimes'*, Cambridge University Press, Cambridge, 2009.

245. *See* S.J.R. Bostyn, *'Narrow Trousers and Narrow Patents, a Health Risk? Product Protection or Purpose-Bound Protection for Biotechnological Inventions'*, Bio-Science Law Review, 2004/2005, 89-95; Bostyn, EC Report 2004, pp. 56-66.

therapeutic tools. These patent holders will try to maximize the return on their investment, which could show in their licencing policies. This could lead to a situation where access to these patented tools, which will all form part of the personalized medicine weaponry, becomes particularly difficult, and maybe even more difficult than in a situation where those various patents would be in the hands of a single patent holder, who would in view of that position be more inclined and less averse of providing licences under very reasonable terms. Hence, the era of personalized medicine may face a situation where access to those diagnostic and therapeutic tools becomes more expensive and consequently difficult. This would be an unwelcome situation and in the context of a human rights narrative even more reason for concern.

And finally, it is the view of the present author that a response to the challenges as to access to personalized medicine should start from an integrated approach, looking at the full spectrum of options and possibilities to ensure that as many people as possible have access to the better and more effective treatment personalized medicine will be able to provide, and not limiting oneself to human rights as the remedy to guarantee access to possibly patent-protected personalized medicine products and treatments.

One of the unresolved problems that can be identified is the following. It is all very well to argue that TRIPS flexibilities can be invoked in the context of access to medicines in relation to the right to health, but as can be seen from the UN documentation and the literature, that is always the case in relation to developing countries. Indeed, much of the discussion focuses on those countries. And also the most recent Report of the UN Secretary-General's High-Level Panel on Access to Medicines[246] does exactly that, and the solutions it suggests are largely limited to the effect they may have on access to medicines in developing countries. There is nothing inherently wrong with this, and indeed, promoting access to medicines in developing countries is not only commendable but also absolutely necessary. But as we have established earlier in this Chapter, the problem of access to medicines is not limited to developing countries but becomes increasingly also a problem in the industrialized world. If policy and even more importantly the pharmaceutical industry could eventually find themselves in solutions providing TRIPS flexibilities (meaning in effect limited enforceability of patent rights, or not obtaining patents at all in case of invoking of exclusions to patentability) as a moral duty, it is far less likely, if indeed at all feasible, that those same stakeholders would accept those same instruments in the fight for access to affordable medicines in the industrialized world. And that risks the acceptance of any of such measures. If they would be supported in

---

246. Report of the United Nations Secretary-General's High-Level Panel on Access to Medicines: Promoting Innovation and Access to Health Technologies, September 14, 2016, UN Secretary-General and Co-Chairs of the High-Level Panel, available at http://www.unsgaccessmeds.org/final-report (last visited 2 January 2020).

some parts of the world, how could it then be explained that they would not be supported in other parts of the world? In other words, invoking TRIPS flexibilities is a positive evolution, but fails to be a holistic approach. Having said that, it is not easy to see how a genuinely holistic approach, equally applicable across the world would not only be conceivable but even more desirable, in view of the rather large differences between states and regions, even more so in the context of access to medicines.

It must also be admitted that TRIPS-plus provisions in bilateral agreements may make things much more complicated, as countries might be forced under such provisions to adopt statutory instruments to limit the use of TRIPS flexibilities, and retaliatory action may be part of trade agreements with nations using a wide range of TRIPS flexibilities as set out above. In that regard, I would agree with a recommendation formulated in the Report of the UN Secretary-General's High-Level Panel on Access to Medicines[247] where it was held that:

> Governments and the private sector must refrain from explicit or implicit threats, tactics or strategies that undermine the right of WTO Members to use TRIPS flexibilities. Instances of undue political and commercial pressure should be reported by the WTO Secretariat during the Trade Policy Review of Members. WTO Members must register complaints against undue political and economic pressure which includes taking punitive measures against offending WTO Members. Governments engaged in bilateral and regional trade and investment treaties should ensure that these agreements do not include provisions that interfere with their obligations to fulfil the right to health. As a first step, they must undertake public health impact assessments. These impact assessments should verify that the increased trade and economic benefits are not endangering or impeding the human rights and public health obligations of the nation and its people before entering into commitments. Such assessments should inform negotiations, be conducted transparently and made publicly available.[248]

Another recommendation of the same Report I would like to think is a useful addition to the weaponry for the fulfilment of the right to health is to improve policy and national coherence between trade and intellectual property on the one hand and the right to health on the other, which is also something that would be useful in industrialized nations. Too often, trade and intellectual property are seen as crucial for economic development and employment creation, but the burden such policies might put on the cost of the health system can be crippling:

---

247. *Ibid.*
248. *Ibid.*, p. 9.

Governments should strengthen national level policy and institutional coherence between trade and intellectual property, the right to health and public health objectives by establishing national inter-ministerial bodies to coordinate laws, policies and practices that may impact on health technology innovation and access. Appropriate member/s of the national executive who can manage competing priorities, mandates and interests should convene such bodies. The deliberations and decisions of such groups should operate with a maximum of transparency. Civil society should be financially supported to participate and submit their shadow reports on innovation and access to health technologies.[249]

Another layer of solutions is in the use of patent pools. Patent pools are instruments which provide access to patented technology amongst the members of the pool, and they have the potential to lower the cost of access. A very good example in this regard, and very relevant in the context of the present Chapter, is the so-called Medicines Patent Pool (MPP).[250] The MPP is a UN-backed public health organization working to increase access to, and facilitate the development of, life-saving medicines for low- and middle-income countries. What it does is to negotiate with patent holders access to the patented technology so that generic companies can produce and distribute the patented drugs under a voluntary licence agreement negotiated by the MPP. The licences also provide the freedom to develop new treatments such as fixed-dose combinations and special formulations for paediatric use. The Pool focusses currently on HIV,[251] tuberculosis and hepatitis C, but it would be to the advantage of society at large if the number of conditions that becomes subject to licences by the MPP would expand.[252] But that will also require external funding.

The reason why the MPP is an important instrument is that a voluntary licence is from an economic and societal point of view always more beneficial than a compulsory licence, which is in any event against the volition of the licensor (=patent holder), and will hence bring with it considerable economic costs. The compulsory licensing system within TRIPS, as one of the flexibilities within the system, has clearly proven to work for conflicts in the area of HIV, but any more expansive use of

---

249. *Ibid.*, p. 10.
250. https://medicinespatentpool.org/. The MPP was founded by Unitaid in 2010, which serves as sole funder for the MPP's activities in HIV, hepatitis C and tuberculosis.
251. E. F.M. 't Hoen, *'Private Patents And Public Health: Changing Intellectual Property Rules for Access to Medicines'*, Health Action International, Amsterdam, 2016, 75.
252. That is also the advice given in the Report of the WHO Expert Committee on Selection and Use of Essential Medicines, 2019 (including the 21st WHO Model List of Essential Medicines and the 7th WHO Model List of Essential Medicines for Children), WHO, 2019, p. 20, available at https://www.who.int/medicines/publications/essentialmedicines/en/ (last accessed on 2 January 2020).

voluntary licensing in the context of the MPP would be very much welcomed with a view to guarantee access to affordable healthcare.

To the extent that room is given to use TRIPS flexibilities in the form of (compulsory) licensing, and even patent pools, it will be necessary to also include the regulatory framework, and in particular data exclusivity and marketing protection into the discussion. As we have seen earlier, as these regulatory exclusivities are separate from traditional IP rights, most flexibilities that other IP rights could provide, such as, compulsory licensing, are not necessarily *mutatis mutandis* applicable to those exclusivities.[253] Absent any 'fix' to that problem, marketing authorization holders with still active regulatory exclusivities would be in a position to obstruct the putting into effect of a compulsory licence. Such licence would typically be granted to a generic company, but that manufacturer would not be able to file for generic marketing authorization (a requirement to put any drug on the market) and/or not be able to market the product in the presence of such exclusivities. That means that those exclusivities could potentially frustrate the putting into effect of any compulsory licence or effective patent pool, largely reducing the practical effect of the use of TRIPS flexibilities. With a view to putting the right to health into effect, that should not be allowed. Statutory changes are called for, which introduce a system whereby a data and market exclusivity waiver should accompany any compulsory licence for medicinal products or any other medical products which are subject to prior regulatory authorization and where some form of exclusivity is granted to the holder of such authorization. Similarly, as part of a patent pool, right holders should as a condition to enter the pool also be willing to waive their exclusivities, absent which the patent pool remains without practical effect.

28.6   CONCLUSIONS

The route towards a fruitful and peaceful coexistence between intellectual property rights and human rights is a long and steep one. The perfect marriage is yet to be formed in that context.

Does the emergence of personalized medicine present new problems and issues that deserve our attention? The answer to that question is definitely yes. Personalized medicine presents many issues partly also because it is an amalgamation of known and new technologies, which present us with new questions. We have seen in this Chapter that there are many challenges ahead but also that personalized medicine presents us also with many exciting opportunities to provide effective treatment to patients with a

---

253. *See also*, E F.M. 't Hoen, P. Boulet, & B.K. Baker, '*Data Exclusivity Exceptions and Compulsory Licensing to Promote Generic Medicines in the European Union: A Proposal for Greater Coherence in European Pharmaceutical Legislation*', 10 Journal of Pharmaceutical Policy and Practice (JOPPP), 2017.

view to ensure that more people get a proper cure for debilitating and lethal conditions.

One fundamental question which we have to ask ourselves is the following. Assuming that all those technologies would be patent-eligible subject matter, can we invoke the same arguments as the ones that have been invoked in the context of HIV drugs? That is not at all certain, as, unlike the case of HIV drugs which was classified as a 'public health crisis', a national emergency and essential medicine, it can be asked whether the same is true for personalized medicine. Admittedly, the concept of essential medicine is a vague one, as it could be argued that all medicines in the absence of alternative treatments for a specific disease are essential. Applying this to personalized medicine, the entire idea behind it is exactly to provide medical treatment which is effective. If a patient has a polymorphism making 'traditional' treatment not effective or even counter-indicated, there is an argument in saying that a personalized medicinal treatment can equally be considered an essential medicine, as there is no alternative in the absence of a personalized medicinal treatment. To that effect, there is an argument for saying that the rules and models developed for essential medicines might find application also in the field of personalized medicine. Whether the criterion of public health crisis/national emergency would be fulfilled is an entirely different matter. As personalized medicine will in most cases deal with the identification and/or treatment of a patient with a specific genetic makeup, it targets in the first instance known medical conditions for which no proper treatment was found in a certain patient population. Starting from that knowledge, it is probably difficult to contend that all personalized medicine treatments would attempt to cure health crises, even though it is not entirely excluded that in certain specific cases this might be the case. One could, for instance, think of the situation where an entire population is the carrier of a certain polymorphism making 'traditional' treatments ineffective for that population. Such an eventuality would likely legitimize a categorization as a health crisis, and it would be rather logical to apply similar exceptions as for other health crises. But saying as a general rule that access to personalized medicine should be given invoking the same exceptions as for health crises seems to be reaching too far.

Additionally relating to compulsory licences, it might equally show necessary to contemplate an expansion of the presently available compulsory licensing scheme in the TRIPS agreement. The present system not only allows some Member States to apply such licensing for the supply of the own population with certain life-saving drugs in case of medical emergency but also for the production of such drugs for export towards least developed countries which have no production means. The present system might require an expansion to other areas of personalized medicine which would today not be readily covered by the system. The availability of drugs for a patented medical indication would likely be covered by the present system. However, the present system does not seem to provide for the making available of genetic screening and diagnostic products, methods and tests.

However, by claiming that such more expansive compulsory licensing systems should be put in place for genetic screening, stratification methods and for diagnostic testing, the question can be asked whether that is not unduly taking away incentives for innovation. There will never be a situation where there is unlimited access to healthcare, whilst there is patent protection. Also, developed wealthy nations struggle with providing access to their citizens for all newly available treatments, and there is a growing number of reports of treatments which are not available in certain developed nations because of the prohibitively high cost to the health system. The most radical solution to this is obviously abolishing patent protection for medical products and tests, but that is a solution which has very little support. Other solutions could be licences as of right, i.e., an automatic licence to the medical profession to perform the diagnostic methods and tests and prescribe the treatment, but especially for a treatment with a patented product, that seems to be particularly problematic, as the producer/patent holder of such products will normally not be interested in bringing a product on the market in countries where there would be a policy in place which makes that the availability of a medical treatment product would not lead to a recoup of the investment made in the innovation. This would be different if at a global level the same strategy would be applied, but that is very difficult if ever possible to achieve, due to the high diversity of healthcare systems in the world, going from purely government-led and financed systems such as the UK National Health Service (NHS) over systems with private partners to virtually exclusively private insurance-based healthcare systems.

That brings us to the third pillar of possible action. It would be short-sighted if one would think that the choice is only between more or less human rights and less or more intellectual property rights. The innovations that will be brought on the market in the field of personalized medicine have to be looked at from a global approach. Not only is there an important role in human rights and intellectual property rights, but there are many other factors which can guarantee or limit access to these innovations.

Having said that, it should also be recognized that doing justice to the fundamental right to health is a moral duty, and that is not less so because the right to health is not an absolute one. At the end of the day, it is in the interest of society at large and the world community that the goal of achieving high levels of health across the world is attained, as disease knows no borders (at least in most cases). Governments and companies should, therefore, work towards improving access to drugs and high-quality healthcare. That will inevitably also have effects on the intellectual property right system. Those rights do not exist in a vacuum, and their effect can be limited in the general interest. It is in that connection that I have developed a number of actions that can and probably should be taken. Those reach from using TRIPS flexibilities in their broadest sense more widely, make more use of the patent pools, introduce a policy that discourages the use of TRIPS-plus provisions in trade negotiations, and develop a practice of linking trade and intellectual property with the right to health.

Additionally, there is the regulatory framework which likely needs to be amended to fit more neatly within the current scientific development. Under the current framework, the regulatory scheme is entirely separate from the patent law framework, and for many reasons, that is a good thing. However, it becomes a problem if that regulatory system is, in fact, making it more likely that medical practitioners of pharmacists infringe patents, or that generic manufacturers cannot avoid infringement even if they exclude from their market authorization protected medical indications, allowing them to bring the off-patent drug on the market for all other non-patented medical indications. As it stands now, it is not excluded that in a number of jurisdictions the regulatory system, in fact, forces physicians and pharmacists to prescribe and dispense the generic version of a drug, which is as such no longer under patent protection, but for which there is still a medical indication protected. That would bring those physicians and pharmacists in a situation that they will infringe the medical indication patent. Similarly, to the extent that the generic manufacturer, despite excluding the patent-protected medical indication from the market authorization (so-called skinny labelling), would produce medicaments which would be prescribed for the patented medical indication, it is likely that such generic manufacturer will commit an indirect or contributory infringement, and that could not be avoided, as it would have been instigated by the regulatory system which insists that the generic version of a molecule is prescribed and dispensed. It is clear that these are good reasons to call for an adaptation of the regulatory system to ensure at least that infringement is no longer 'organized' by that system. Whether that is feasible or not is yet to be seen, but the possibilities need to be explored.

Moreover, relating to data and market exclusivity, marketing authorization holders benefitting from such exclusivities should not be able to use those levers in cases where the underlying patents are also the subject of a compulsory licence or part of a patent pool. As patent law and regulatory exclusivities are separate legal regimes, under the current legal framework, right holders could enforce those exclusivities even in case of a compulsory licence, or when the patents are part of a patent pool. The statutory framework should be amended to ensure that in cases of compulsory licensing, regulatory exclusivities could not prevent third parties from producing, obtaining authorization and marketing the products made under such compulsory licence, or where the products are part of a patent pool.

There is also the role of the state as a subsidizer of innovation. The state could take the opportunity to require players who receive government funds for developing new technologies to abide with certain rules relating to sharing of the results of the research and dissemination of the results.[254] The framework suggested by Pogge to classify all essential medicines as a public good hence ensuring that medicines are available at production cost, whilst granting a specific type of patent to the companies who have developed these essential medicines, is yet another way to deal with the problems faced.[255] Under this framework, the specific type of patent thus granted rewards those companies, out of public funds, in proportion to the impact of their invention on the global disease burden., That would incentivize those pharmaceutical companies to ensure that access to their drugs is available to the highest possible degree, as that would lead to a higher impact and hence a higher reward. Additionally, these companies would, under this suggested frame-work, allow generic manufacturers to make copies, so as to create an even larger impact and ensure that all patients get treatment, which would, in turn, lead to a higher reward. Even though the Pogge model looks appealing, it can be questioned whether it is feasible and viable in an economic era of austerity where there is more and more pressure on governments to downsize the state, hence making it unlikely that the funds to subsidize the rewards would be available.

Human rights are there to continue playing a crucial role in finding the balance between the interests of patent holders to obtain a return on the investment they have made into new and more advanced medical treatments, the need to maintain incentives to stimulate and foster innovation and the interest of society to gain access to such innovative treatments. But however important they are, they should not be used to claim supremacy over intellectual property rights. Furthermore, they are only one element in the mix of instruments that can and should be used with a view to ensuring that medical treatments are available to the widest possible number of people on this globe, as we all share the same right to attain good health.

---

254. An interesting collaborative model is described in, A.K. Rai, et al., '*Pathways Across the Valley of Death: Novel Intellectual Property Strategies for Accelerated Drug Discovery*', 8 Yale Journal of Health Law, Policy & Ethics, 2008, 53-89.

255. Thomas W. Pogge, '*Human Rights and Global Health: A Research Program*', 36 Metaphilosophy, 2005, 182-209.

Chapter 29

Human DNA and Stem Cell Research: Ethical and Religious Concerns over Patenting Biotechnological Inventions in Malaysia

Ida Madieha bt Abdul Ghani Azmi & Majdah Zawawi

29.1   INTRODUCTION

Human samples, including DNA, are routinely collected by medical practitioners for treatment and subsequently for research by medical research institutes in Malaysia. Facilities that offer biobanking of human samples are mushrooming in Malaysia, including umbilical cord banking, blood blanks, as well as tissue samples. This includes the Malaysian Cohort Biobank and the Universiti Kebangsaan Malaysia Medical Molecular Biology Institute Biobank (UKMMC-UMBI) and private companies such as the Cryocord Malaysia and StemLife Berhad. In 2015, the Malaysian government released the Guidelines on the Use of Human Biological Samples for Research outlining the types of research involving human biological samples and the need for institutional review board/independent ethics committee (IRB/IEC) approval. The increasing use of human DNA for research ultimately raises further issues as to the subsequent patenting and commercialization of the research output involving such samples.

The biotech revolution has indeed challenged many of the basic norms of ethics and morality thus making it necessary to revert to religious views in order to provide for a framework in which ethical determination can be made. Many of the reports show that consultations with religious groups such as Christianity, Judaism and Islam were made in order to determine the ethical aspects of biotechnological inventions. While the patenting of human DNA does not attract a barrage of ethical concerns, the use of human embryonic stem cells for research does as it challenges human dignity. The stigma left by the aftermath of the Nuremberg Trials has left mankind to find it reprehensible to conduct research on human subjects. It therefore poses further questions on whether or not embryos are "humans" and whether research should be done using embryos. These questions cannot be easily answered by mere reference to scientific findings and of course the law lags behind. Hence, the need for legitimization and support from religion becomes crucial. This challenges the basic premise of ethical inquiry in that it should be free from religious precepts and has resulted in diverging views in Europe where the notion of respecting the "ordre public and morality" originated from. On the one hand is the view that this only excludes inventions likely to induce riot or public disorder or to lead to criminal or other generally offensive behavior. While, on the other hand, the European Group on Ethics in Science and New Technologies,2000[1] and 2002[2] was of the view that such determination should be left to the national courts and patent offices. In which case, religious views would definitely play a role.

In Malaysia, the incorporation of the "ordre public and morality" as a yardstick for the determination of patents brings into question the extent of religious views in patent law. The Islamic position is particularly important as it is the official religion of the country[3] and it is the religion of the majority of the citizens.

This chapter analyzes the patentability of biotechnological inventions particularly those resulting from human embryonic stem cell research. At the same time, the Malaysian practices on research involving human DNA are also considered. The chapter puts forward the position that since the United Kingdom (U.K.) and Europe have considered ethics and morality as a factor

---

1. "Ethical Aspects of Human Stem Cell Research and Uses", European Group on Ethics in Science and New Technologies to the European Commission on November 14, 2000, available at http://ec.europa.eu/european_group_ethics/publications/docs/dp15rev_en.pdf.
2. Opinion on the Ethical Aspects of Patenting Inventions Involving Human Stem Cells, Opinion No. 16, available at <http://ec/eu/europa.eu/european_group_ethics/publications/docs/avis16_complet_en.pdf.
3. Article 3 of the Malaysian Constitution states that "Islam is the religion of the Federation". Other religions may be practiced freely in the country. While the majority of the citizens are Muslim Malays, there are other races who have also embraced Islam. Other ethnic groups include the Chinese, Indians and the indigenous groups.

in determining the patentability of biotechnological inventions, then Malaysia, in having adopted similar provisions into the patent laws in the country, could also rely on the ethical position to do the same. In doing so, the Islamic position would be relied on to provide an ethical basis for such a determination.

29.2   THE PATENT LAW IN MALAYSIA

The current Malaysian Patent Act 1983 is similar in many respects to the U.K. Patent Act 1977 and the European Patent Convention. The incorporation of morality into the Patent law took place in 2000 as a result of the need to comply with Article 27 of the Trade-Related Aspects of Intellectual Property Rights (TRIPS) Agreement.[4] The Article allowed Member States to "exclude from patentability, inventions which is necessary to protect ordre public or morality." This included "the prevention of the commercial exploitations in order to protect human, animal or plant life or health or to avoid serious prejudice to the environment."

The Malaysian legislators, however, decided to make it a ground for refusing a grant of invention. Section 31(1) of the Patents Act 1983 provides that a grant of patent may be refused if the "performance of that act would be contrary to public order or morality". Alas, the Act does not define what is meant by "public order or morality."

The European Directive of Biotechnological Patents instead took a different approach. It clearly states that such inventions are considered to be unpatentable. Article 6 of the Directive took the position further by specifically laying down the following to be considered as unpatentable:

(a) processes for cloning of human beings;
(b) processes for modifying the germline, identity of human beings;
(c) uses of human embryos for industrial or commercial purposes.[5]

Article 5(1) mentions that, " ... the human body, at the various stages of its formation and development, and simple discovery of one of its elements, including the sequence or partial sequence of a gene, cannot constitute patentable inventions." Article 5(2) further allows, "an element isolated from the human body or otherwise produced by means of a technical process, including the sequence of a gene," to constitute a patentable invention, "even if the structure of that element is identical to that of a natural element."

---

4. The refusal of patents on the ground of morality was included into the Act via the Patents (Amendment) Act 2000.
5. The Directive also includes processes for modifying the genetic identity of animals which are likely to cause them suffering without any substantial medical benefit to man or animal and also animals resulting from such processes.

Indeed Malaysia has commonly sought guidance from the U.K. and Europe on many legal positions due to her being historically related particularly to the U.K. legal system. To this very day, the position in the U.K. as well as Europe could be influencing the legal position in Malaysia. The Civil law Act even allows importation of the English Common law so far as there is a lacuna and such position is suited to the local circumstances.[6]

However, it is clear that ethical decision-making in this delicate area needs to also take the religious aspects as a consideration. In doing so, venture made into the Islamic position should indeed be done to assist in the determination of whether biotechnological inventions particularly those resulting from the use of human embryos should be patentable. The incorporation of "ordre public and morality" could refer to the Islamic position as a basis for ethical decision-making as Islam is the religion of the Federation and it should be taken as a guiding principle in determining the patentability of biotechnological inventions.

Admittedly, the U.K. and European position on morality is currently more comprehensive and elaborate than the Malaysian position. This is understandable as there has been no attempt in Malaysia to examine what should be the approach taken to settle ethical debates within the patent system. As such, the current chapter explores the Islamic position on such a crucial matter.

29.3   THE POSITION OF ETHICS AND MORALITY IN ISLAM

There is a need to first understand some basic concepts in Islam[7] before venturing further into the subject of ethics in Islam in general and how it affects the determination of Islamic law or the Shari'ah in particular. The basic foundation in Islam is the concept of Tauhid or the belief in the Oneness of Allah and the temporariness of this world. Each Muslim has a unique and personal relationship with their Creator.[8] Man has been created with the sole purpose of worshipping Allah.[9] While submitting to Him, Allah in His infinite Mercy will endow upon us His Grace and Beneficence. This

---

6. Section 3(5)(1)(a).
7. Al-Attas has explained that when speaking of din or religion, indeed there are many forms of religion. However, he says, "the one in which is enacted total submission (istislam) to God alone is the best." And Allah Himself has declared in Surah Ali Imran (3), verse 85 that, "Verily the Religion (al-din) in the sight of Allah is Islam." For further reading *see* Syed Muhammad Naquib al-Attas, Islam. The Concept of Religion and the Foundation of Ethics and Morality. IBFIM: Kuala Lumpur, 2013, p. 13.
8. Muhammad Abduh, The Theology of Unity, Trans. Ishaq Musa'ad and Kenneth Cragg, Islamic Book Trust: Kuala Lumpur, 2004, p. 45.
9. This has been mentioned clearly in the Qur'an in Surah al-Dhariyat (51), verse 56 which translates, "I have only created Jinn and Men, that they may serve Me."

is done through the process of rewarding every good deed. Due to the temporal nature of this world, Allah has offered guidance to the right path (Siraat al-Mustaqim)[10] through His commandments in the Holy Qur'an and through the teachings of Prophet Muhammad s.a.w.[11] Allah has placed mankind on this earth as test—which is to follow the right path. The temporal nature of this world also means that a person will be answerable for all his deeds in this world in preparation for a lasting world in the Hereafter. This is an important underlying concept in Islamic ethics.

Life is a test because each human is also given a free will.[12] He may choose whether he wants to follow the right path, for which Allah has shown guidance, or to follow one's nafs or desires and stray away from it. In keeping to this path, mankind is reminded that they must care for not only their relationship with Allah (hablu minallah) but also their relationship among fellow human beings (hablu minnanas) as well as with other beings that share the earth and also the environment.

The relationship with Allah is established through specific[13] and general[14] acts of worship. Meanwhile, the relationship between humans are of two types:

(i) Al-ahkam al-akhlaqiyyah—ethical or moral ways of dealing with each other in order to ensure a peaceful co-existence based on mutual respect. Failure to observe any ethical precepts are not punishable in this word but will be an object of concern for the Hereafter. Aside from catering to the relationships between humans, al-ahkam al-akhlaqiyyah also deals with the ways in which man has to deal with the environment, through maintaining what is known as the Sunnatullah. Allah has created the running of the earth in a specific way, i.e., according to the fitrah or nature of every being.[15]

---

10. *See* Surah al-Fatihah, verse 5 where man asks Allah to "Lead us to the right way".
11. The teachings of Prophet Muhammad s.a.w. is the final prophet. Teachings of previous prophets are also recognizable. However, these teachings have either been incorporated into the teachings of Islam and any teachings that have been deviated from cancelled by the teachings.
12. Muhammad Abduh, The Theology of Unity, p. 62.
13. Specific acts of worship are known as ibadah khususiah which includes the five pillars of Islam—saying the Syahadah, praying five times a day, fasting in the month of Ramadhan, paying alms or zakat and doing the pilgrimage when one has enough means to do so. Nevertheless, non-fulfillment of these types of worship are not punishable in this world. Each individual will have to answer to it in the Hereafter.
14. Meanwhile general acts of worship include all good deeds done with the intention of pleasing Allah and has a very wide scope.
15. For every action there will be a resulting reaction. For example, when a seed is planted and nurtured, it will grow; it takes in the sun light and carbon dioxide to produce oxygen. Humans need oxygen in order to survive. If we deprive the seed from sun light, it will fail to grow; it cannot make its own food without the sun. As a result, the carbon dioxide will not be utilized and no oxygen will be released. Therefore, if the Sunnatullah is disturbed, there will be very serious repercussions on humans. For further reading *see* Lekha

Hence, humans as the Khalifah or Vicegerents of Allah has the responsibility of making sure that the Sunnatullah is maintained in order to ensure that the environment is well cared for. This is to ensure that the benefits of this world will be passed on to the next generations.

(ii) Al-ahkam al-qanuniyyah—the legal ways of dealing with matters. In a legalistic way it may also be referred to as the Shari'ah or the Divine Law which "is to be implemented to regulate society and the actions of its members rather than society dictating what laws should be."[16] The break of a legal relationship will have legal consequences in this world.

The determination of what is ethical and what is legal is found in the main sources of Islamic law or the Shari'ah, i.e., the Holy Qur'an and the Sunnah of the Holy Prophet s.a.w. However, in recognition of the changing times, the applications of the Qur'anic and Prophetic rulings may be done through ijtihad or juristic opinion.[17] When forming these juristic opinions, the jurists must ensure that the main objectives of the Shari'ah (al-Maqasid al-Shari'ah) are fulfilled and realized. These main objectives of the Shari'ah stem from the premise that the Shari'ah aims at regulating the conduct of human beings by promoting beneficence (maslahah) and avoiding or preventing evil (mafsadah).[18]

The role of the Muslims and Muslim jurists will then be to determine whether a particular act complies to the Maqasid al-Shari'ah and in doing so declares such acts as permissible (mubah) which is also signified as being halal, permissible but not encouraged (makruh), beneficial (mandub) or totally impermissible (haram).[19] The collective decisions of these jurists may then become ijma' (a collective ijtihad) and should be followed by all Muslims within that territory. The views of the jurists that is the result of ijtihad are known as a fatwa. While an individual fatwa is not binding on other Muslims, a collective fatawa (plural of fatwa) could result in an ijma' of the ulama' or jurists of the day and could be binding on Muslims.

Laxman, Abdul Haseeb Ansari and Majdah Zawawi, "The Islamic Approach to Conserving Biodiversity for Global Sustainability: An Exploration", Advances in Environmental Biology, Vol. 8:3, (Special 2014), 751.

16. Seyyed Hossein Nasr, The Heart of Islam, HarperSan Francisco: New York, 2002, p. 117.

17. The "mujtahid" are the jurists who have specific educational background which include the learning of Arabic, Qur'anic Sciences, the Sciences of Hadith as well as various other subjects that equip them to interpret the Holy Qur'an. However, in coming up with their individual ijtihad they have the responsibility of conducting a thorough research on related aspects of the position in which they wish to give their opinion. Usually, their opinions are sought as and when is necessary. As such in issues of the new sciences, they will usually seek the aid of scientists or physicians who are experts in a particular area.

18. Ibn Ashur, Treatise on Maqasid al-Shariah, translated by Mohamed al-Tahir ibn Ashur, IIIT, London, Washington, 2009, 116.

19. Muhammad Hashim Kamali, Principles of Islamic Jurisprudence. Second Revised Edition, Ilmiah Publishers: Petaling Jaya, 2000, p. 321.

In today's modern world, every Muslim state has its own Council of Muslim Jurists that is responsible in determining the status of emerging problems of the Muslim community. There are even councils at the international level which are known as the Council of the Islamic World League as well as the International Fiqh Academy. These juristic views may then be adopted as laws when it is legislated by the respective state legislative assemblies. Nevertheless, there are juristic views that are not legislated and remain a general ethical guide.

It is based on this premise that the following discussion on the status of human embryonic stem cell research is made.

In relation to medical ethics, in determining ethical choices, the rights and responsibilities of the individual are intertwined with that of other individuals as well as the society or the "ummah." In other words, these ethical choices should not be serving the individuals alone, or humans only but also the environment. From the writings of traditional scholars on medical ethics, the practice of medicine—as an art and science, was pursued with the fullest commitment to discover scientific accuracy and truth, coupled with a recognition of the purposive nature of that pursuit as an extension of man's relationship with God.[20] It is for these reasons that most traditional scholars trained in medicine would also be trained in law and theology so that the pursuit of science would not be divorced from religion.

The prominence given to "akhlaq" (ethical values) particularly in relation to medicine, could be seen in the construction of the physician's Oath in Islam that puts the welfare of the patient and the avoidance of harm at the forefront.[21] From the Oath, values such as compassion, charity, wisdom and solidarity are seen as central to any pursuit of medicine and practice. Whenever there is a conflict between religious tenets and scientific inquiry, the Muslim scientist would always ground his decision on dharuriyyah (necessity). For example, when al-Nafis had to decide whether cadaver dissection would offend what is considered as morally impermissible, he found it justifiable to establish vital facts (like the heart's ventricular structure) that made effective treatment. This could in no way mean that there is an absolute or unqualified right to pursue anatomical curiosity regardless of results.[22] It is justified only so far as it is necessary (dharurah). This allowance is based as an exception to the general rule that is usually made in order to ensure that the maslahah or benefit of the ummah is secured.

The heavy reliance on the doctrine of necessity or dharurah in order to benefit the maslahah of the community is often used to justify recent advances in biomedical issues is understandable. However, the reliance on

---

20. *Ibid.*, 11.
21. Wahaj D. Ahmad, Ahmad El-Kadi and Bashir A. Zikria, 'Oath of a Muslim Physician', (1988) 20 Journal of the Islamic Medical Association of North America, 11 (DOI: http://dx.doi.org/10.5915/20-1-13050).
22. *Ibid.*

the concept of dharurah must be done cautiously and must also bear the need to arrive at a balanced approach in life. This is due to the need to ensure that the balance of the Sunnatullah is not disrupted. This has been clearly mentioned in Surah al-Furqan (25), verse 2, which mentions:

> He to whom belongs the dominion of the heavens and earth, no son has He begotten, nor has He a partner in His dominion. It is He who created all things and ordered them in due proportions. Yet have they taken besides Him gods that can create nothing but are themselves created: that have no control or hurt or good to themselves; nor can they control death nor life nor resurrection.

This concept of maintaining balance as created by Allah (Sunnatullah) is also mentioned in Surah al-Taghabun (64), verse 3, which also says:

> He has created the heavens and the earth in just proportions and has given you shape, and make your shapes beautiful; and to Him is the final goal.[23]

The Holy Qur'an contains several verses that describe the creation of the earth, universe and all living creatures as signs from which we can learn from and draw lessons.[24] One of the important messages that can be drawn from these verses is that the universe and the whole creation are created in the best proportion and in a balance which should not be disturbed.[25] It is also clear from the Qur'an that human does not have the power to create

---

23. Other Qur'anic verses that discusses the creation of the earth in due proportion would include, Surah al-An'am (6), verse 73.
24. Surah Yunus 10: 6 reads: "Verily, in the alternation of the night and the day, and in all that Allah hath created, in the heavens and the earth, are signs for those who fear Him".
   See also Surah al Baqarah: 164:

   > Behold! In the creation of the heavens and the earth; in the alternation of the Night and the Day; In the sailing of the ships through the Ocean for the profit of mankind; In the rain which Allah sends down from the skies, and the life which He gives therewith; To an earth that is dead; In the beasts of all kinds that He scatters through the earth; in the change of the winds, and the clouds which they trail like their slaves between the sky and the earth—(Here) indeed are Signs for a people that are wise.

25. *See* Surah al Nahl 16: 3: "He has created the heavens and the earth for just ends: Far is He above having the partners they ascribe to Him!"; Surah al Rum 30: 22: "And among His signs is the creation of the heavens and the earth and the variations in your languages and your colours; verily in that are signs for those who know"; Surah al Shura 42: 29: "And among His signs is the creation of the heavens and the earth, and the living creatures that He has scattered through them and He has power to gather them together when He wills"; Surah al Jathiyah 45: 22: "Allah created the heavens and the earth for just ends, and in order that each soul may find the recompense of what it has earned, and none of them be wronged"; Surah al-Taghabun 64: 3: "He has created the heavens and the earth in just proportions, and has given you shape, and made you shapes beautiful; and to him is the final goal."

life[26] and that all the creations are signs of the powers as well as blessings of God.[27]

In this regard, considerable similarity between the utilitarian approach as exemplified by the Warnock Report,[28] or by many contemporary literature[29] and the religiously based ethic of maximizing public benefit from biomedical interventions in Islam could be found. The main difference, however, is in the existence of a Hereafter for which each individual is to be answerable to for all actions that affront the rights of others but also that disrupts the balance of Sunnatullah or the balance of creation that has been mentioned in the above verses of the Holy Qur'an.

29.4 PROMOTING BENEFICENCE (MASLAHAH) AND GENETIC RESEARCH

In promoting beneficence (masalih is the plural for maslahah) which are the main objectives of the Shari'ah (Maqasid al-Shari'ah) there are three tiers that must be taken into consideration, which would include the following:

(i) Maslahah Dhururiyyah: the essential requirements in human life, the absence of which will affect human life. It is both essential for the community collectively and individually. Al-Ghazali in his book al-Mustasfa, Ibn al-Hijab and al-Shatibi described the daruri category as consisting of the preservation and safeguarding (hifz) of religion (din), life (nafs), intellect ('aql), lineage (nasab) and property (mal).[30]

(ii) Maslahah Hajiyyah are the complementary things that are needed in life but does not essential for human existence.

(iii) Maslahah Tahsiniyyah: the desirable or embellishments.

The discussion now concentrates on the first type of maslahah, i.e., Maslahah Dhururiyyah which according to Al-Shatibi as comprising of five essential requirements that is crucial to human existence which includes the

---

26. *See* Surah al-Furqan 25: 2: "He to whom belongs the dominion of the heavens and the earth; no son has He begotten, nor has He a partner in His dominion: It is He who created all things, and ordered them in due proportions. Yet have they taken besides Him, gods that can create nothing but are themselves created: that have no control or hurt or good to themselves; nor can they control death nor life nor resurrection."

27. Surah al An'am 6: 73: "It is He who created the heavens and the earth in true (proportions): the day He saith, 'Be,' Behold! It is. His Word is the truth. His will be the dominion the day the trumpet will be blown. He knoweth the unseen as well as that which is open. For He is the wise, well-acquainted (with all things)".

28. Report of the Committee of Enquiry into Human Fertilisation and Embryology (1984).

29. For an illustration of contemporary literature on the law and ethics of medical research, *see* Aurora Plomer, The Law and Ethics of Medical Research: International Bioethics and Human Rights, Cavendish Publishing: UK, 2005.

30. *Ibid.*, 118.

protection and preservation of life (hifz al-nafs), religion (hifz al-din), intellect (hifz al-'aql), progeny (hifz al-nasl) and property (hifz al-mal).

Al-Shatibi added that the preservation of these fundamental universals is achieved in two different ways: (1) by establishing and strengthening them and (2) by averting all harm that might affect them.[31] Ibn Ashur added that the preservation of human souls (hifz al-nafs) means to protect human lives from being ruined either individually or collectively. This is because according to him, the society or the human world ("alam") comprises the individuals of the human species and every single soul has its specific characteristics that are essential for the existence and survival of the human world. One of the higher objectives of the Shariah is the Protection of human life. The sanctity of human life must be respected regardless of religious affiliation, race, color or ethnic grounds as is explicit in the Qur'an (al Maidah: 35):

> On that account: We ordained for the children of Israel that if any one slew a person (take away life) unless it be for murder or for spreading mischief in the land, it would be as if he slew the whole people. And if anyone saved a life, it would be as if he saved life of the whole people.

Meanwhile, the protection and preservation of religion (hifz al-din) is aimed at protecting the religion from being misunderstood and misapplied. This protection is also crucial in ensuring that all acts do not contradict the Shari'ah. It also ensures that all human acts are in line with the Sunnatullah. This helps avoid environmental disasters that wreak havoc on human lives.

As for the preservation of the intellect (hifz al-'aql) means the protection of the intellect from acts which could corrupt the human intellect or disrupt the human brain. This is because any disorder of the intellect leads to serious corruption consisting of improper and perverted human conduct. Next is the preservation of lineage would refer to the preservation of descent or lineal identity (nasab), as neglecting these aspects results in the harmful consequences of the undermining of the social order and family break-down.[32] Finally, the preservation of property (hifz al-mal) means protecting the wealth of the community being ruined and from shifting to the hands of the others without compensation. It also means protecting the different constituents of that wealth which is valued in the Shari'ah from being destroyed for no return.

The Maqasid al-Shari'ah or the main objectives of the Shari'ah is to ensure that these five essentials in human lives are preserved and protected. It has thus been submitted that a reliance on the Maqasid al-Shari'ah could help in determining the ethical position of biotechnological inventions particularly the appropriateness of using human embryos for stem cell research.

---

31. *Ibid.*, 120.
32. *Ibid.*, 121, 122.

Using the "maqasidi" approach, the position of research on human embryos sits within two of the objectives of the Shari'ah: the protection of life (hifz al-nafs) and the preservation of lineage (hifz al-nasl)—the first and third of the hierarchy of maqasid. In such a situation the need to preserve and protect life would definitely take priority over the protection of lineage. In determining the status of using human embryos for stem cell research, the question would thus have to be, what is the purpose of such a research? In order to be permissible under the Shari'ah, the reason would have to be in line with the aim of finding cures for life-threatening diseases. Research on human embryonic stem cells has the potential of resulting in cures and treatments for many untreatable diseases and genetic disorders. If viewed from this perspective, then the general position would be permissible.

Nevertheless, there is the issue of the destruction of the human embryo when doing research. This will be the subject of the next part of the discussion.

29.5   LIMITS OF SCIENCE: BIOETHICS AND LESSONS FROM THE HOLY QUR'AN

This is true to the Qur'anic pronouncement that the creation of man is considered to be the best[33] and that other living creatures are created as sustenance for humans.[34] However, man cannot simply act as he wills, as he is responsible to maintain the balance in which the whole universe is created.

Most Muslim scholars take recognition of the Qur'anic message and adopt an approach that resolves in the spirit of reconciliation between science and religion. The mainstream view among the scholars is that the door to scientific inquiry must not be closed but should be monitored according to religious dictates. The most important limit to scientific inquiry is that it must not bring about a result that goes against God as the creator of creation.[35]

Thus, in the views of Yusuf al-Qardawi:

---

33. "Man is created in the best of creation": Surah al Tin 95: 4.
34. Surah al Isra' 17: 70: "We have honoured the sons of Adam; provided them with transport on land and sea; given them for sustenance things good and pure; and conferred on them special favours, above a great part of our creation". This concept known as takhlif essentially means that nature and all creations are for human, *see also* 15: 15-34.
35. Surah Fatir 35: 1: "Praise be to Allah who created (out of nothing) the heavens and the earth who made the angels messengers with wings—two, or three, or four (Pairs): He adds to Creation as He pleases: for Allah has power over all things"; Surah Al Ra'd 13: 16: Say: "Who is the Lord and Sustainer of the heavens and the earth?" Say: "(It is) Allah." Say: "Do ye then take (For Worship) protectors other than Him, such as have no power either for good or for harm to themselves?" Say: "Are the blind equal with those who see? Or the depths of darkness equal with light?" Or do they assign to Allah partners who have created (anything) as He has created, so that the creation seemed to them similar? Say: "Allah is the creator of all things: He is the One, the Supreme and Irresistible."

If it becomes possible through research to clone organs such as the heart, liver, kidneys or others, which may benefit those who are in dire need of them, then, this is permitted by religion and the researcher or scientist will receive the reward from Allah. This is because the research will confer benefit on humanity without loss to others or infringing upon them. Therapeutic cloning with this noble research pursuit is permissible and it is encouraged. In fact, in some circumstances, it may become mandatory to enhance this research in accordance with the need and man's research capability and accountability.[36]

It should be clear however that the purpose of science should not just be for the sake of inquiry alone. Applying the concept of beneficence or Masalih here, one of the lessons that can be drawn is that for any scientific inquiry, there should be clear indications that it would benefit mankind. Sardar, for example, views that science and technology are related to a set of ten basic Islamic values, which include (Tawhid) unity of God (ibadah) worship and trusteeship (khilafah). Islam is opposed to the concept of science for science's sake.[37]

29.6   ISLAM AND EMBRYO RESEARCH

The main concern with human embryonic stem cell research is the destruction of embryo to harvest the stem cells. The permissibility of destroying embryos depends substantially on the ontological status of embryo in Islam. The discussion must begin with the division in the status of an in vivo embryo if compared to the in vitro embryo.

The issue relating to in vivo embryos that have been implanted was explored by Mahdi Zahra and Shaniza Shafie in the context of pre-implantation of Genetic Diagnosis.[38] Central to the authors' analysis is the Quranic injunctions on development of embryo, among others (Al Hajj: 5):

> O mankind! If you are in doubt about the Resurrection, then verily, We have created you from dust, then from a Nutfah (mixed drops of male and female sexual discharge), then from 'alaqah (a clinging clot of blood), then from a little lump of flesh that We may make it clear to you (Our Power and Ability to do what We will). And We cause whom We

36. Yusuf Al-Qardawi. Hadyul Islam Fatawi Mu'athirah. Darul Qalam, Kuwait 2001. Translated by Gema Insani Press, October 2002, cited in Musa Mohd Nordin, "An Islamic Perspective of Assisted Reproductive Technologies", (2012) 11 Bangladesh Journal of Medical Science No. 4, Editorial, 252-257.

37. Pervez Hoodboy, Islam and Science: Religious Orthodoxy and the Battle for Rationality, S Abdul Majeed & Co: Malaysia, 1992.

38. Mahdi Zahra and Shaniza Shafie, "An Islamic Perspective on IVF and PGD, with particular reference to Zain Hashmi, and Other Similar Cases", Arab Law Quarterly, Vol. 20 (2006), Pt 2.

will to remain in the wombs for an appointed term, then We bring you out as infants.

This verse and other verses of the Holy Qur'an reinforce the view that the embryos developed gradually in the mother's wombs in various stages.[39] From the above ayah, Muslim scientists believe that the nutfah represents the blastocyst which embeds within the endometrium. The 'alaqah is described as the stage where it clings to the inner uterine wall like a leech. The mudghah is the stage where the chewed lump of flesh resembled accurately the appearances of the somites.[40]

As the above view describes the gradual development of embryo within the mother's womb, three authentic Hadiths further reiterate the gradual development of embryo:

"The creation of every one of you [mankind] is formed in the womb of his [/her] mother for forty days as a nutfah (mixed drops of male and female sexual discharge), then a alaqah" (clot or a piece of thick, coagulated blood) for similar period, then a mudghah (little lump of flesh) for a similar period, then to it an Angel is sent, the Angel blows ruh (spirit or soul or breath of life) in it.[41]

If forty-two nights have passed over the embryo, Allah sends an angel to it, who shapes it and creates its hearing, vision, flesh and bones. Then he [the angel] says, "O Lord, is it male or female? And your Lord decides what he wills.[42]

---

39. *See also* Surah al Mu'minun 23: 12-14: Man We did create from a quintessence (of clay); Then We placed him as a drop of sperm in a place of rest, firmly fixed; Then We made the sperm into a clinging clot of blood; then of that clot We made a chewed lump; then We made out of that lump bones and clothed the bones with flesh; then We developed out of it another creature, So blessed be God, the Best to create! Surah al Mu'min 40: 67: It is He who has created you from dust then from a sperm drop, then from a leech-like clot, then does he get you out (into the light) as a child; then lets you (grow and) reach your age of full strength; then lets you become old, though of you there are some who die before—and lets you reach a Term appointed; in order that ye may learn wisdom; Surah al Qiyamah 75: 36-40: Does man think that He will be left uncontrolled (without purpose)? Was he not a drop of sperm emitted (in lowly form)? Then did he become a leech-like clot; then did (God) make and fashion him in due proportion. And of him He made two sexes, male and female. Has He not (the same) power to give life to the dead?; Surah al Zumar 39: 6: "He makes you in the wombs of your mothers, in stages, one after another".

40. Musa Mohd Nordin, "An Islamic Perspective of Assisted Reproductive Technologies", (2012) 11 Bangladesh Journal of Medical Science No.4, Editorial, 252-257.

41. Sahih al Bukhari, Kitab al Qadar; Sahih Muslim, Kitab al Qadar; as translated by Mahdi Zahra and Shaniza Shafie, 'An Islamic Perspective on IVF and PGD, with Particular Reference to Zain Hashmi, and Other Similar Cases' (2006) 20 Arab Law Quarterly, No. 2, 152.

42. Sahih al Bukhari, Kitab al Qadar; as translated by Mahdi Zahra and Shaniza Shafie, 'An Islamic Perspective on IVF and PGD, with Particular Reference to Zain Hashmi, and Other Similar Cases' (2006) 20 Arab Law Quarterly, No. 2, 152.

Two women from Bani Hadhil had a fight; one of them threw a stone on the other and caused her to die together with the fetus in her womb. The dispute was brought before the Prophet (pbuh) Who ruled that the diyyah (blood money) for the fetus is ghurrah (1/20 of a normal diyyah) and a full diyyah for the woman to be paid by the tribe of the guilty woman."[43]

Based on the three authentic Hadiths, three spectrums of opinion are formed:

(1) the most strict view is that the embryo attains its "human status" from the moment of conception. This view emerges from the Malikis and al-Ghazali from the Shafi'i school;

(2) the middle view is that the embryo attains its "human status" only when the embryo starts to develop its human features such as eyes, ears, limbs, skin, flesh and bones. This view is the most popular view and is adhered by the Hanafis, Shafiis, Zahiris and some Hanbalis; and

(3) the most liberal view is that the embryo attains its "human status" only after ensoulment which takes place at the 120 days. Prior to the 120 days, thus, the removal and destruction of the embryo would not entail any liability.

Yet in other verses of the Koran, the beginning of a human is described to be that of 'alaqah. In Chapter 23, verses 12-14 the Holy Qur'an teaches:

We created (khalaqna) man of an extraction of clay, then we sent him, a drop in a safe lodging, then We created of the drop a clot, then we created of the clot a tissue, then We created of the tissue bones, then we covered the bones in flesh; thereafter We produced it as another creature. So blessed be God, the best of creators (khaliqin)!

This verse has been taken by some Muslim scholars as the earliest point in which an early embryo is considered to be beginning its life.[44] This was also the stand of the Malaysian Fatwa Council in its 2005 fatwa.[45]

The ensoulment process is clearly described in the Quran in Surah 32: 9: "And breathe into him of His spirit." Some scholars believe that ensoulment is the point in which the embryo in-vivo is considered to be a human being, as far as legal capacity is concerned, albeit at an incomplete

---

43. Sahih al Bukhari, Kitab al Tub; Sahih Muslim, Kitab al-Qasamah, *see also* Al Zuhayli, Wahbah. Vol. 6, 362-363 as cited and translated by Mahdi Zahra and Shaniza Shafie, 'An Islamic Perspective on IVF and PGD, with Particular Reference to Zain Hashmi, and Other Similar Cases' (2006) 20 Arab Law Quarterly, No. 2, 152.

44. *See* Majdah Zawawi, An Ethico-Legal Analysis of Assisted Reproductive Technologies in Malaysia: Balancing Rights and Responsibilities, PhD dissertation submitted to Ahmad Ibrahim Kulliyyah of laws, International Islamic University: Malaysia, November 2006.

45. Majlis Fatwa Kebangsaan ke 66, February 22, 2005.

stage or known as ahliyyah al naqisah.[46] At this stage, the embryo does not have the legal capacity to exercise any rights but only to receive responsibility especially from the mother.

The above discussion illustrates the views of traditional Muslim jurists based primarily on the little knowledge of human embryonic development that was available to them during those times. Meanwhile, the views adopted by the Fatwa Councils are based on information obtained from experts in the medical field and is therefore more current. If taken from that perspective, it could be surmised that while ensoulment is an important stage where the embryo is recognized as having a legal status, it does not mean that prior to ensoulment the embryo is totally devoid of recognition as being "human" and that anything can be done to it. Some contemporary scholars believe that the process of ensoulment is only a metaphysical concept. Even though ensoulment comes much later in the process of the development of the embryo, the embryo is respected from the onset of fertilization and acquires consideration as a human fetus after implantation.[47]

A middle view, which is the majority view, is that an embryo does not attain its human status at least until it starts to develop its human-like physical attributes; to which the Hadith attributes this to occur on the fortieth day. This can only occur if the embryos are allowed to develop within the uterus of the mother. Hence, the status of in vitro embryos has a slightly different position. Due to this, many Muslim scientists have accepted the view that the current practice in which embryo research is allowed up to the fourteenth day from fertilization to be acceptable within Shariah perspective. At least three Islamic Fiqh (Jurisprudence) Councils have given permission for the use of the surplus embryos from IVF laboratories for ESC research.[48] However, most scholars believe that it is not permissible to consciously generate pre-embryos either by conventional IVF techniques or by Somatic Cell Nuclear Transfer (SCNT) for ESC research.

As early as the 1990s, the Muslim scholars have deliberated on the permissibility of research on human embryo. One such occasion is the First International Conference on Bioethics in the Muslim World held in Cairo

---

46. *See* Yasien Mohamed, "Fitrah and Its Bearing on Islamic Psychology", The American Journal of Islamic Social Sciences, Vol 12:1, (1995), 12 as cited in Majdah Zawawi, An Ethico Legal Analysis of Assisted Reproductive Technologies in Malaysia: Balancing Rights and Responsibilities, PhD dissertation submitted to Ahmad Ibrahim Kulliyyah of Laws, International Islamic University Malaysia, (November 2006).

47. Musa Mohd Nordin, "An Islamic Perspective of Assisted Reproductive Technologies", (2012) 11 Bangladesh Journal of Medical Science No.4, Editorial, 252-257.

48. *See* the Council of Islamic Fiqh Academy of Muslim World League, 2003: 17th session in Makkah, December 13-17; Fiqh Council of North America, International Institute of Islamic Thought, Graduate School of Islamic and Social Sciences, Islamic Institute news release August 27, 2001; and Aly A. Mishal, "Stem Cells: Controversies and Ethical Issues", Jordan Medical Journal, Vol. 35:1, (May 2001), 80-82; as cited in Musa Mohd Nordin, "An Islamic Perspective of Assisted Reproductive Technologies", (2012) 11 Bangladesh Journal of Medical Science No.4, Editorial, 252-257.

from December 10-13, 1991. In the Conference the following practice guidelines may be summarized:

(1) cryopreserved pre-embryos may be used for research purposes with the free and informed consent of the couple;

(2) research conducted on pre-embryos is limited only to therapeutic research. Genetic analysis of pre-embryos to detect specific genetic disorders is permissible. Hence diagnostic aids should be provided for couples at high risk for selected inherited diseases. The treated embryo may only be implanted into the uterus of the wife who is the owner of the ova and only during the span of the marriage contract;

(3) any pre-embryos found to be genetically defective maybe rejected from transfer into the uterus after proper counseling by the physician;

(4) research aimed at changing the inherited characteristics of pre-embryos (e.g., hair and eye color, intelligence, height) including sex selection is forbidden;

(5) sex selection is however permitted if a particular sex predisposes to a serious genetic condition. One of the first couple to use the technique of sex selection was hoping to escape a neurologically debilitating disease known as x-linked hydrocephalus, which almost always affected boys. Embryonal sex selection would make possible the weeding out of other serious x-linked disorders including hemophilia, Duchene muscular dystrophy and fragile X syndrome;

(6) the free informed consent of the couple should be obtained prior to conducting any non-therapeutic research on the pre-embryos. These pre-embryos should not be implanted into the uterus of the wife or that of any other woman;

(7) research of a commercial nature or not related to the health of the mother or child is not allowed; and

(8) the research should be undertaken in accredited and reputable research facilities. The medical justification for the research proposal must be sound and scientific and conducted by a skilled and responsible researcher.[49]

The recommendation of the 1991 Conference is a clear example of how the concept of dharurah or necessity works in allowing the research to be done on embryos before the fourteenth day after fertilization sets in. It is ONLY allowed in cases where it is necessary. Although the fatwa allowed research to be done on embryos with the free informed consent from the couple, it limited the type of research, in that it must be for therapeutic purposes. The fatwa clearly prohibits research on embryos for purposes of tampering with the inherent characteristics of the embryos. There is one contradiction in paragraph (6) of the fatwa which allows research to be done

---

49. Musa Nordin, *ibid.*

for non-therapeutic purposes if the informed consent is obtained from the couple. It is submitted that this goes against the rest of the paragraphs and therefore needs to be revised as it goes against the basic principles of necessity as discussed earlier.

Prior to this fatwa, the 1990 Majma' al Fiqh al Islami meeting[50] gave an express prohibition on the creation of embryos that would be more than what is safe for implantation into the womb at a single treatment.[51] The Committee of Islamic Medical Science to the Islamic Fiqh Academy of Jordan in 1992[52] also does not recommend the creation of extra embryos except in special circumstances. The Committee was of the view that in the instance of divorce/death, the embryos must be kept until the end of storage period then allow to perish but no embryos may be intentionally discarded, destroyed or donated. These two fatwas reflect the concern over the safety of the woman in cases of multiple pregnancies as well as the obvious respect given to human embryos. However, these fatwas cannot be said to contradict the 1991 fatwa because that fatwa could be considered as being the exception to the general rule. Therefore, it could be surmised here that while research on human embryos may only be permitted in cases of necessity in order to find cures and therapies for life-threatening diseases. Even then, the research cannot go beyond forty days. The current position of limiting research to fourteen days after fertilization is well within the permission given.

Another ground in which the Muslim scholars have based on to permit embryo research is by drawing a distinction between an in vivo embryos and in vitro embryos. The latter would only survive if it is implanted in a woman's womb and thus should not be treated the same as an embryo in a natural environment. The inviolability and sacredness of the former are not the same as the latter. Hence, if respect for a human embryo entails the avoidance of action which may results in the destruction of an embryo in a woman's womb, the position is not the same with the destruction of an excess fertilized embryo.[53] This indicates, according to Siddiqi, that there is a distinction between potential life and actual life,[54] in these words:

---

50. 17th Meeting, 1990.
51. Cited by Umar ibn Muhammad ibn Ibrahim Ghanim, Ahkam al Janin fi al Fiqh al Islami, 2001; "Dar al Andalus al Khadra", Jaddah 262.
52. In its 5th meeting November 5-December 17, 1992.
53. The ratio of the reasons making people liable to pay "blood money" (diyat), if someone destroys a live embryo in the womb of a woman does not cover embryos produced in vitro and therefore provides further support to the permissibility of the use of human embryos produced using the in vitro techniques. Dr. Seyyed Mohammad Fatemi, Dr. Mirghasem Jafarzadeh and Dr. Marefat Ghaffari, "Muslim's View on the Moral Aspects of the Patentability of Human Embryos: Appraisal of Shariah with Special Reference to Shi'i Fiqh", available at <http://ipgenethics. group.shef.ac.uk/workshopabstract.htm>.
54. "Embryo Reduction: Islamic View", Islamic Online Fatwa Bank, July 14, 2001, <www.islamonline.net>. *See also* Christl Dabu, "Stem Cell Science Stirs Debates in Muslim World Too", <http://csmonitor.com>.

The core question is whether an embryo, which is formed within a few days after an artificial fertilization and is not yet in the womb of its mother be considered a human being, with all the rights of a human being? … if these embryos were treated as full human, it would have been forbidden to produce them in excess and destroy them later. No one treats them as humans. Destroying such embryos is not called and cannot be called abortion.[55]

The distinction between in vivo embryos and in vitro embryos is further seen in the distinction between the accrual of legal capacity and rights over embryos as discussed earlier. Embryos are accorded with the right to live upon fertilization. It is accorded with ahliyyah al wujub al naqisah that is, incomplete legal capacity. In which the fetus enjoys principally two rights: the right to life and the right to inheritance but this right operates only once he/she is born.[56] The destruction of an in-vivo embryo also would mean amount to abortion which is prohibited by all Majority of the ulama in normal circumstances except if life of the mother is in danger.

The views of individual Muslim scholars also state that research on embryo should only be done in narrow and exceptional circumstances which is again based on the concept of dharurah. For example, Siddiqui views that the use of embryonic stem cells should be very heavily limited. In his opinion, the isolation of stem cells should only be allowed from frozen embryos that were created for the purpose of in vitro fertilization and would otherwise have been destroyed. Full consent of the donors must be obtained. Safeguards must also be created against monetary compensation to embryo donors and against the creation of embryos in excess of what is required for in vitro fertilization.

Gamal I. Serour opines that research on human embryos should be limited to therapeutic research. Research of a commercial nature or unrelated to the health of mother or child is not allowed. Cryopreserved pre-embryos may be used for research purposes with the free informed consent of the couple. Non-therapeutic research may be conducted on excess pre-embryos with the free informed consent of the couple, to improve the treatment of infertility, contraception, reproductive medicine, genetics, cancer, and embryology. These treated pre-embryos are not to be transferred to the uterus of the wife or that of any other woman. He frowned upon the creation of human embryo just for the purpose of research. He views that creating embryos solely for research purposes is not a reproductive liberty. It is an act of liberty in the use of one's reproductive capacity.[57]

---

55. Dr. Muzammil Siddiqi, "An Islamic Perspective on Stem Cells Research", <http://IslamiCity.com>.00

56. Yasien Mohamed, Human Nature in Islam, A.S. Nordeen: Malaysia, 1998, 129.

57. Gamal I. Serour: "Reproductive Choice: A Muslim Perspective", in John Harris and Soren Holm (ed.) The Future of Human Reproduction: Ethics, Choice and Regulation; Clarendon Press (1998) 191-202.

Abdulaziz Sachedina opines that the Shariah treats a second source of cells, those derived from fetal tissue following abortion, as analogically similar to cadaver donation for organ transplantation in order to save other lives, and hence, the use of cells from that source is permissible.[58]

He concludes that:

(1) The Qu'ran and the Sunnah regard the perceivable human life as possible at the later stages of the biological development of the embryo.

(2) The fetus is accorded the status of a legal person only at the later stages of its development, when perceptible form and voluntary movement are demonstrated. Hence, in earlier stages, such as when it lodges itself in the uterus and begins its journey to personhood, the embryo cannot be considered as possessing moral status.

(3) The silence of the Qur'an over a criterion for moral status (i.e., when the ensoulment occurs) of the fetus allows the jurists to make a distinction between a biological and a moral person, placing the later stage after, at least, the first trimester of pregnancy.

On the gradual formation of a human being, Abdul Aziz Sachedina quoted two views from Muslim scholars:

Ibn Hajar al-Asqalani (d.1449) says:

"The first organ that develops in a fetus is the stomach because it needs to feed itself by means of it. Alimentation has precedence over all other functions for in order of nature growth depends on nutrition. It does not need sensory perception or voluntary movement at this stage because it is like a plant. However, it is given sensation and volition when the soul (nafs) attaches itself to it."[59]

Ibn al Qayyim, Al Tibyan fi Aqsam al Qur'an (Cairo, 1933, page 255): "Does an embryo move voluntarily or have sensation before the ensoulment? It is said that it grows and feeds like a plant. When ensoulment takes place voluntary movement and alimentation is added to it."[60]

---

58. Abdulaziz Sachedina, "Testimony of Abdulaziz Sachedine, PhD., University of Virginia, Islamic Perspectives in Research with Human Embryonic Stem Cells", in Michael Ruse & Christopher A. Pynes (ed.) The Stem Cell Controversy: Debating the Issues; Prometheus Books (2006) New York.

59. Ibn Hajar al Asqalani, Fath al Bari fi Sharh al Sahih al Bukhari, Kitab al Qadar, 11: 482 quoted by Sachedina, 254.

60. Ibn al Qayyim, al Tibyan fi aqsam al Qur'an (Cairo, 1933), p. 255 as quoted by Sachedina, 256.

Based on these two views, Sachedina's interpretation of Islam is that it permits the use of five-day-old blastocysts to produce embryonic stem cells.[61]

Therefore, the general views of the Muslim jurists are that research on embryonic stem cells may be permitted as a necessity to search for cures and therapies for therapeutic purposes only. Even then, most Muslim scholars are not in favor of allowing the creation of embryos for the purpose of research and would limit the permissibility of research on excess embryos from IVF treatment which has been subjected to the informed consent of the couples.

Aside from Muslim jurists and the Fatwa Committees, Muslim scientists have also explored the permissibility of such research at various international fora. One of it is a Workshop on Ethical Implications of Assisted Reproductive Techniques (ART) for the treatment of Infertility which was conducted in Al-Azhar, Cairo, 2000 that has accepted not only research done on leftover embryos but also allows the use of non-reproductive cloning to produce stem cells that would be of benefit to others. This opinion represents a major shift in the stand of Muslim scientists as far as genetics is concerned. In an earlier Symposium of Medical Jurisprudence held in Jeddah in 1987, it was recommended that leftover embryos are not to be used but discarded. Usage of leftover embryos for research would only be allowed if the parties agree but before they reach the fourteen days stage. The creation of embryos is strictly prohibited. This difference in approach is based on the premise that creation embryos through somatic cell nuclear transfer technology should be allowed because these embryos were not created from germ cells but from somatic cells. Hence, this could eliminate the need to rely on leftover embryos. Even then, these embryos may only be created, again, out of necessity or dharurah, with the intention of benefitting the community for therapeutic purposes. It cannot be misused for purposes that fulfill only Hajjiyyah (complementary matters) or Tahsiniyyat (desirable matters). This would also mean that the result of such a research must be able to benefit the public as a whole.

There seems to be a divergent view when it comes to the creation of embryos for research purposes through somatic cell nuclear transfer technology. As seen above, fatawa given in the 1990s only allowed research on left-over embryos for therapeutic purposes. While the later Muslim scientists and jurists go further to allow creation of embryos by way of somatic cell nuclear transfer technology as an opportunity to cease doing research on embryos left-over from fertility treatments.

These differences of opinion exist so long as the said country has not adopted one particular stand on this issue. Atigetchi,[62] referred to Egypt as

---

61. *See* LeRoy Walters, "Human Embryonic Stem Cell Research: An Intercultural Perspective", in Michael Ruse & Christopher A. Pynes (ed.) The Stem Cell Controversy: Debating the Issues, Prometheus Books (2006) New York.
62. Dariusch Atigetchi, Islamic Bioethics: Problems and Perspectives, 2007, Springer, 248.

one such country. While one renowned professor from Al-Azhar University tolerates non-reproductive cloning and believes it right to use precious supernumerary embryos—but only within the first fourteen days—for research for the benefit of others instead of leaving them to die. On the other hand, the President of the Egyptian Medical Syndicate, oppose the usage of embryos for research, as the conceived being is already a human being. The divergent viewpoints could well explain the differences in national countries' approaches to stem cell research.[63]

The Fatwa Committee of the Majlis Ugama Islam Singapura (Islamic Religious Council) concurs with the opinion of the Singapore Bioethics Advisory Committee to use stem cells from embryos below fourteen days for the purpose of research, which will benefit mankind, is allowed in Islam. This is with the condition that it is not misused for the purposes of human reproductive cloning, which would result in contamination of progeny and the loss of human dignity.[64] In the deliberation of the Fatwa Committee, Islam does not place any judgment on an embryo, which is not fully formed. An embryo is only considered as a human life after it is four months old when the soul is introduced into the embryo. Thus, an embryo below four months, regardless of whether it was created in vivo or in vitro, is to be considered as a living being undergoing the growth process. However, it is not yet considered as the beginning of human life with the existence of a soul.[65]

The question now comes as to which position should influence the patentability of inventions resulting from human embryo research? If there exist diverging views, which view should then be taken? Usually, the position in a particular Muslim country needs to be determined by the Government of the day. In doing so it is also necessary to look into the commercialization of the human body and human body parts.

---

63. *Ibid.*, 248.
64. Singapore Bioethics Advisory Committee, Ethical, Legal and Social Issues in Human Stem Cell Research, Reproductive and Therapeutic Cloning, G-3-G-71.
65. The Committee formed its view based on the opinion of Dr. Muhammad Sulaiman al-Asyqar, who is of the view that an embryo which is not formed or is not in a woman's womb, will not be placed any judgement on it. In his view: "Islamic law does place any form of judgement on an embryo which is not formed. Verily, I have explained in detail my opinion during my forum discussion on birth. In that forum, decision had to be made that Islamic law does not place any judgement on a woman's fertilized egg except after it is in the womb. There is no judgement on it before it is in the womb. A similar opinion was given by the Fatwa Institution of Darul Ifta, Saudi Arabia, where, for as long as there is no soul in an embryo, the sperm and the egg are judged to be living things adapting to their specific conditions. They are considered as components of the fertilization process. They have not reached the stage of a complete human being." *See* The Fatwa the Majlis Ugama Islam Singapura, Fatwa Committee Special Meeting, Thursday, November 22, 2001, "Ethical, Legal and Social Issues in Human Stem Cell Research, Reproductive and Therapeutic Cloning", A Report from the Bioethics Advisory Committee, Singapore.

29.7   COMMERCIALIZATION OF HUMAN BODY AND
        HUMAN BODY PARTS

Another limit in which Muslim scientists would have to avoid is the religious proscription against the commercialization of human body and human body part. In an earlier work, it has been pointed out that the patenting of human body or parts of human body should not be allowed as it may offend the classical views on the commercialization of human body parts. This view is formed based on the viewpoint of several Muslim scholars who openly opposed any form of commercialization of the human body for fear that it would offend human dignity.[66]

According to Resnik, the basic argument for property rights to embryonic stem cells is capitalistic and utilitarian in nature.[67] It is further postulated that, "property rights should be granted in order to promote the progress of science, technology, medicine, business and the industry."[68] The Shari'ah on the other hand views that human beings are defined by their relation to Allah. In Islam, humans did not evolve from apes. Instead, Allah created humans as mentioned in Surah al-Tin (95), verse 4, "Indeed, We created man in the best of forms" and in another verse in Surah al-Taghabun (64), verse 3, "He fashioned you in the best of images." And even more profound is Allah's declaration in Surah Sad (38), verse 72, "I breathed into Him (Adam) of My spirit." In relation to the creation of humans, Seyyed Hussein Nasr explains:

> Human beings therefore reflect the Divine attributes like a mirror, which reflects the light of the Sun. By virtues of being created as this central being in the terrestrial realm, the human being was chosen by God as His Vicegerent (khilafat Allah) as well as His servant ('abd Allah). As servants, human beings must remain in total obedience to God and in perfect receptivity before what their Creator wills for them. As vicegerents they must be active in the world to do God's Will here on earth.[69]

The essence of commercialization is the ability to claim ownership over something and monopolize the benefits over that matter in return for monetary benefits. The promotion of scientific inquiry and research is not done only to benefit those who will be able to pay for it. Instead, it is done to benefit the society, in order to gain Allah's blessings or Barakah. As such, any research that results in an invention that would benefit the society cannot be monopolized by one person or group of persons.

---

66. Al Hidayati, Part II, at 34, cited in Mohammad Naeem Yasseen, "The Rulings for the Donation of Human Organs in the Light of Shari'ah Rules and Medical Facts", 5, Part 1, (February, 1990), 49-87, at 51.
67. David B. Resnik, "The Commercialization of Human Stem Cells: Ethical and Policy Issues", Health Care Analysis Vol. 10 (2002), 127-154, Available at www.ualberta.ca.
68. *Ibid.,* 138-151.
69. Seyyed Hossein Nasr, The Heart of Islam, p. 276.

As for the sale of human body parts or matters extracted from it, al-Marghenani states, "it is not permitted to sell a human being's hair or utilize it in any way, because humans are highly dignified, therefore no part therefrom should be undignified or demeaned."[70] Al-Kasani has also stated that human bones and hair should not be sold out of respect for human organs. According to him to sell them would be demeaning and it is humiliating.[71] Nevertheless, the donation of human organs is permitted on the basis of necessity or dharurah.[72]

A closer analogy could perhaps be taken from the position on the sale of human germ cells such as ova and sperm. The general position in regard to the sale of ova, sperm and embryos is very clear in that it is prohibited to sell these materials.[73] On the same note, the patenting of inventions stemming from research using human embryo should also be viewed with caution for fear that the practice may encourage the commercialization of human embryos.

Whatever the position taken, it remains to be questioned whether the patent office should take a different position than that of the religious authorities in relation to embryo research. Should the religious authorities allow such research, then correspondingly the same position should be taken by the patent office. Would the patenting of the result of the research is offensive to human dignity when in the first place the research was justified by the religious authorities. These issues require further deliberation by the Muslim scholars.

29.8 MALAYSIAN PRACTICES ON RESEARCH INVOLVING HUMAN EMBRYO AND STEM CELLS

In Malaysia, a Code of Practice was formulated to provide guidance to physicians and hospitals involved in Assisted Reproductive Technologies (ART).[74] Part IV(b) of the Guidelines is important as it relates to storage of gametes and embryos. According to this part, anyone consenting to the storage of their gametes or of embryos produced by them must:

---

70. Al Bada'i, Part V, 142, cited in Yasseen, *ibid.*, at p. 51.
71. Al Hidayati, *ibid.*
72. For further reading on the status of organ donation in Islam, *see ibid.*
73. Majdah Zawawi, "Donated Materials in Assisted Reproductive Technologies: An Ethico-Legal Analysis of ART Legislations Worldwide." Journal of Medical Ethics and History of Medicine, Vol. 3:2 (2010).
74. Ministry of Health, Malaysian Code of Practice and Guidelines for Assisted Reproductive Techniques (ART) Centres, 2002. *See also* the Malaysian Medical Council Guideline, Assisted Reproduction, October 19, 2005.

(i) specify the maximum storage (maximum of three years);
(ii) dispose of the gametes or embryos if they die or are incapable of varying or revoking their joint consent.

Emphasis is made for the attainment of consent from the couple undergoing the ART treatment concerning the storage and disposal of embryos or for research.[75] A couple undergoing ART should be asked for instruction concerning the storage and disposal of embryos. Specific instruction must be obtained from the couple and informed consent duly obtained. It was further provided that no research or experimentation shall be performed on or using any human oocyte.[76]

Part V of the Guidelines meanwhile specifies that the termination and disposal of gametes and embryos must refer to the couple's written consent. In the absence of instructions, the embryos are then stored for a maximum period of three years before they are destroyed. If the couple consents to it, the Guideline also allows research on leftover embryos provided that the research does not exceed the fourteen days requirement.

The Code of Practice acknowledges that the human embryo is given special status. Hospitals and private healthcare are to decide carefully whether or not to dispose, how to dispose and whether to use it for research purposes. The Center then should decide the culture period, the method that is to be used to terminate development and the procedure to ensure that embryos do not continues to develop after fourteen days or after the appearance of the primitive streak. The Code stipulates that all research must have license from the Ministry of Health. Licenses will only be granted for the following types of research projects:

- to promote advances in the treatment of infertility;
- to increase knowledge about causes of miscarriage;
- increase knowledge on causes of congenital disease;
- develop better contraceptives;
- develop methods for detecting presence of gene or chromosome abnormalities before implantation;
- increase knowledge about serious diseases; and
- to allow such knowledge to be applied in developing treatments for serious disease.

The Code of Practice contains several specific prohibitions.[77] First, the keeping or using an embryo after the fourteen-day period or after the appearance of the primitive streak is not allowed. So is the placing an embryo in a non-human animal and replacing a nucleus of a cell of an embryo with a nucleus taken from the cell of another person, another embryo or a subsequent development of an embryo altering the genetic structure of any

---

75. Paragraph 9 on "Storage and Disposal of Gametes and Embryos".
76. Paragraph 14 on "Prohibited/Unacceptable Practices".
77. Paragraph 10.4 on "Prohibitions".

cell while it forms part of an embryo. It was also specifically mentioned that embryos that have been appropriated for research must not be used for any other purposes.[78]

In 2007, the Health Ministry introduced the Guidelines for Stem Cell Research in Malaysia.[79] Among the policies is that the Ministry of Health will undertake to encourage and promote stem cell research in Malaysia. Second, all stem cell research must pass through an institutional review board and an institutional ethics committee to prevent unethical research and unethical use of stem cells. Third, research on stem cells derived from adult stem cells is allowed in accordance with existing guidelines. Fourth, the use of fetal tissues from legally performed termination of pregnancy is also allowed in accordance with existing guidelines. Fifth, the use of non-human stem cell lines is also allowed (mice and primates). Sixth, the use of embryonic stem cell lines (from sixty-four cell lines) for therapeutic purposes should be allowed. Seventh, the creation of embryos either from ART or SCNT specifically for the purpose of scientific research is presently prohibited.

The Health Ministry Guidelines was formulated taking into consideration a national fatwa that has also been released on Therapeutic Human Cloning and Stem Cell Research in 2005.[80] The fatwa states:

(i) That therapeutic human cloning is permitted (diharuskan) if for—medical treatment—through the creation of certain cells or replacing damaged organs taking into account the limits permitted by the Shari'ah.

(ii) The use of embryos leftover from IVF for research purposes is permitted (harus) on two conditions:
   (a) The couples had consented.
   (b) Before the embryo reaches the stage of 'alaqah.

(iii) Research on pre-embryo for purposes other than for therapeutic purposes is also permitted provided that:
   (a) The couples consented.
   (b) The embryo is not implanted into any womb.

(iv) Research on pre-embryo to detect any predisposition to any genetic diseases for high-risk couples is allowed and only embryos that were determined to be clear from any of such diseases could be implanted in the womb of the mother during the marital term.

(v) Any genetic treatment on pre-embryo to change the natural characteristics of the pre-embryo such as hair, hair color, intelligence, height including sex determination is not allowed. However, sex

---

78. Paragraph 10.5.
79. "National Organ, Tissue and Cell Transplantation Policy", Ministry of Health, June 2007.
80. Majlis Fatwa Kebangsaan ke 66; February 22, 2005.

determination is allowed if is linked to predisposition to fatal genetic diseases.

(vi) Any type of research for commercial gain or that which has no relation to the health of the mother or the fetus—is not permitted.

(vii) Research done must be:
(a) legal with a clear research proposal;
(b) for scientific purposes;
(c) carried out by qualified research personnel who are trustworthy and responsible.

(viii) Sources of stem cell permitted:
(a) excess embryos (consent obtained from parents);
(b) aborted fetus as a result of natural abortion or from medical treatment that is allowed under the Shariah and is carried out with the consent of the family members; not from the aborted fetus that is carried out deliberately without any causes accepted by the medical fraternity and Shariah.

(ix) Stem cell created from SCNT is not permitted based on sadd al-zara'I (blocking the means of evil).

With this fatwa, one could infer that there is no blanket approval for stem cell research as the Malay word "diharuskan" refers to mubah in Arabic which means: "something which is permitted" and not: "something which is promoted or encouraged". Second, it would appear that research must be for therapeutic purposes only which must be on legitimate grounds and not for commercial purposes. Third, the Malaysian Fatwa Council requires that such research must be legal and conducted in a responsible manner. However, the first statement allowing therapeutic cloning would have to be made more consistent with the last stand on the creation of stem cells through somatic cell nuclear transfer. If the latter practice is not allowed, the first statement in relation to the permissibility of therapeutic cloning would have to be clarified further.[81]

29.9   RESEARCH ON HUMAN DNA

The last few years have witnessed an important expansion of human DNA sampling and data collecting. The formation of a DNA bank involves collecting hundreds of thousands of blood samples from volunteers. The development of DNA bank can be regarded as a large study of the role of

---

81. These views are based on the presentation by the author and Majdah Zawawi entitled, "The Legal Position of Research on Human Embryo: A Comparative Study on Selected Jurisdictions" at the Workshop on Guidelines on Stem Cell Research and Transplant, Kementerian Kesihatan Malaysia Hyatt Regency Hotel, April 22, 2007. According to a clarification from of the officers of the Malaysian Fatwa Council, the first statement in relation to therapeutic cloning was referring to the practice of PGD with particular reference to the case of Zain Hashmi.

nature and nurture in health and disease. This activity has strategic importance for genetic research, clinical care and future treatments. DNA bank can help unlock the disorders such as heart disease, arthritis, cancer, diabetes, and Alzheimer's disease.

Human DNA, tissue or cell collections and the attached databases have been extensively exchanged for scientific purposes. However, the status of such collections and databases is not well defined and most institutions have no written policies or agreements regarding this activity. There are also clear ethical and legal concerns that have not been properly addressed.

First, the rules for exchanging and sharing of information and material are not clear. Should DNA bank data be made available to pharmaceutical companies as well as biotechnology companies and academic researchers? No one party will be permitted to have exclusive access to the data, and strict controls must be in place on how the data can be used.

Removing identifiers (including coded numbers) for a sample is mostly appreciated by patients who appreciate privacy; however, it may prove to be otherwise by patients whose genetic coding is important in getting down to the history of the disease, in determining the right treatment. For example, the DNA stored in a bank is privately secured but once submitted for research, it will be anonymous and no longer identifiable by its owner, meaning chances are, nobody would know who would be most likely to carry which disease in future as the research is done anonymously through using a specific DNA of a person. This calls for ethical reasoning in which the patient's consent should be obtained should scientists decide to do a thorough investigation of the diseases in discussion.

Second, there is the possibility of multiple uses of the same sample in different and unforeseen research project. Different research has different objectives and the outcomes would be the ultimate goal of helping to save another person's life based on the studied gene criteria. If a DNA is known for its helping characteristic in one individual but proves to be adverse in another, perhaps the question of gene selection would fall into place where scientists can now segregate between the good and the bad genes in accordance with an individual's compatibility. This is hoped to help individuals or patients to enjoy a life of knowing that their future maladies are curable and not only be subjected to research of unknown progress and treatment.

Third, the existence of a DNA bank allows sharing of samples among collaborators, including international collaborators and commercial entities in predicting a disease among patients in a different continent from their own. Once collected and banked, the sample of DNA can be a great guide for scientists all over the world for the benefits of other patients from different world continents. For example, a disease potent in a society might differ in potency in another. By having samples of DNA of the diseases, scientists can now predict the best possible treatment for its patients without having to go through a rigorous process of long-winding research. This will shorten the time span for treating patients.

29.10   MALAYSIAN GUIDELINES ON THE USE OF
          HUMAN BIOLOGICAL SAMPLES

The collection and biobanking of human DNA in Malaysia is now subjected to the Malaysian Guidelines on the Use of Human Biological Samples. Under the Guidelines, DNA falls under the definition of human biological material, that refer to all biological material of human origin, including organs, tissues, bodily fluids, teeth, hair and nails, but not established cell lines.[82] Further, the deposit of such DNA in a biobank is explicitly covered by the Guidelines. The termbiobank refers to a biorepository where activities of receiving, processing, preservation, storage or distribution of human biological samples and cells are undertaken. Biobank can also be used for the procurement or testing of human biological samples and cells.[83]

In the Guidelines, it was conceded that generally tissues are collected during surgery and may be used for research. In such an instance, the patient is rarely informed of the prospective use and handling of the tissue samples. The purpose of the Guidelines was therefore to establish uniform practices among the research institutes in the collection, storage and use of such materials for research. Three specific instances of tissue collection were mentioned in the Guidelines; i.e., (i) stored/archived human biological materials; (ii) biological samples prospectively collected during routine investigation or treatment and (iii) planned prospective collection for biobanking purposes.[84]

Stored/archived human biological samples are very useful for research. While the initial collection of the tissue samples are only for routine treatment, it would be ideal if consent is obtained from the original patient if they are used for research purposes. A second consent should also be sought from the institutional research board or institutional ethics committee (IRB/IEC). In lieu of the practicality of attaining the consent from the specific patient, it is also possible to get a waiver from the IEC/IRB.[85]

Biological samples are also routinely collected from patients undergoing routine investigation or treatment. In such an instance, there must be an explicit separate consent to the use of such samples for research. Such informed consent must be taken before or after the surgery/procedure. The

---

82. Malaysian Guidelines on the Use of Human Biologiocal Samples for Research, Ministry of Health Malaysia, 2015, at p. 4.
83. *Ibid.,* at p.4
84. *Ibid.,* at p. 5.
85. *Ibid.,* at p. 6

attainment of consent is independent of consent for surgery. Patient is free to opt for the use of his samples for research and can withdraw anytime.[86]

For prospective collection, the issue of informed consent becomes more critical. In such an instance, the Guidelines specify that a multi-layered consent must be obtained prior to conducting the study. The consent sought must be for different purposes such as (i) the specific planned research; (ii) for storage and future use (iii) for access to medical records and information for data relevant to the biobanking; and (iv) for re-contacting the subject for more data.[87]

The new Guidelines emphasize the growing role of the IRB/IEC whose approval must be sought for every study involving human biological materials. Even the process of anonymization must be proceeded with the approval and consent of the IRB/IEC.

For vulnerable groups, consent must be sought from the next of kin, guardian or legal representatives.[88]

Under the Guidelines, the institution that establishes the biobanking facilities is in full custody of the samples. Strict rules apply with regards to the use and sale of the samples to the third party for gain. If there is potential commercialization of these samples, the patient must be informed.

Among matters to be included in the patient information sheet are the purpose of the research and possible future research, the type and amount of tissue to be taken, the manner of collection, the duration of storage, the potential use of the samples. The patients are also to be informed as to any identifying information, privacy issues and the right to withdraw and arrangement for disposal of tissues and data.[89]

29.11   CONCLUSION

It must be admitted that the convergence between the current patent law and the position in Islam may seem difficult, but it is submitted that it is possible. The Patent Office could refer to the fatwa issued by the National Fatwa Committee. Aside from that reliance could also be made to the Code of Practice and Guidelines applicable to the recent biomedical advances, including Guidelines on Stem Cell Research issued by the Ministry of Health.[90] Their guidelines on Stem Cell Research in Malaysia could be commended as they result from deliberation of committees comprising of members from different religious groups. These guidelines could be seen as adopting a rather strict approach to research on human embryos, despite the

---

86. *Ibid.*, at p. 7
87. *Ibid.*, at p. 8
88. *Ibid.*, at p. 8
89. *Ibid.*, at p. 9.
90. Pekeliling Ketua Pengarah Kesihatan Bil 1/2006.

permissive tone of the National Fatwa Committee. The extraction of stem cells from embryos is currently not allowed, nor is embryonic stem cell therapy.[91] While research involving stem cell lines is allowed if not encouraged,[92] provided it complies with the existing International/National guidelines on ethical conduct of research.[93] The importation of such tissues could only be made through institutions recognized by the Ministry of Health and in accordance with Guidelines on Importation and Exportation of Human Tissues and/or any Body Part.[94] In addition, the creation of embryos from either ART or SCNT specifically for the purpose of scientific research is presently prohibited.

For future reference, the Patent Office could indeed rely on the Islamic position to better determine the types of inventions that poses a threat to "ordre public and morality" in Malaysia and could be declared as unpatentable instead of merely refusing the grant of invention.

The hesitation expressed by the Guidelines on Stem Cell Research issued by the Malaysian Ministry of Health could be taken as a sign that a majority of Malaysians, especially the Muslims do not feel comfortable with the notion of using human embryos for research purposes. Despite the rather permissive tone of the National Fatwa Committee on the creation of embryos through somatic cell nuclear transfer technology, the Guideline remains strict in its prohibition on the creation of embryos either by way of normal fertilization or by way of SCNT, solely for the purpose of scientific research. Does this mean that Malaysia will lose out on the benefits promised by the use of human embryonic stem cells. Perhaps not. In fact, it has lead researchers to revisit the use of adult human stem cells as the ethical clout is less permeating.[95]

Any research on human DNA meanwhile would be subjected to the Malaysian Guidelines on the Use of Human Biological Samples that regulates not only the collection of samples but also the deposit of the samples in biobank. The Guidelines emphasizes the need to obtain proper consent from patient not only at the point of collection, but later on if the samples are being used for research and other purposes. The insistence on

---

91. *See* 9.6 National Organ, Tissue and Cell Transplantation Policy, Ministry of Health, June 2007.
92. *See* 15.1 National Organ, Tissue and Cell Transplantation Policy, Ministry of Health, June 2007.
93. *See* 15.2 National Organ, Tissue and Cell Transplantation Policy, Ministry of Health, June 2007.
94. *See* 11.2 National Organ, Tissue and Cell Transplantation Policy, Ministry of Health, June 2007.
95. *See* for example the discovery of Mesenchymal Stem Cells, which are reported to have the potential for self-cell therapy, based on the concept of ex vivo manipulation of cells and their re-implantation into the donor. For further reading *see* Arnold I. Caplan, "Mesencymal Stem Cells", Journal of Orthopaedic Research, Vol. 9:5 (1991), 641-650. For more recent works on this topic *see also* Bianco et al. "Mesenchymal Stem Cells: Revisiting History, Concepts and Assays", Cell Stem Cell, Vol. 2 (April 2008), 313-319.

multi-layered consent by the Guidelines is highly ambitious and may be difficult to be reconciled with current practice that only seeks blanket consent from patients at the point of collection. Nevertheless, the formulation of the Guidelines is timely at a time when human biological samples, including DNA, are routinely collected, deposited and researched on.

Chapter 30

Gene Patents and Human Rights

Geertrui van Overwalle[*]

30.1 INTRODUCTION

Over the last decade, the relationship between intellectual property rights (IPRs) and human rights has gained wide academic attention.[1] In this expanding stream of research, scholars have also started to explore the particular relationship between patent law and human rights law in more depth.[2] The present chapter will examine a specific theme within that research stream, and focus on the interplay between patent law, as applied to human genes and genetic diagnostic methods, and human rights.[3]

---

[*] The present research was supported by the Vancraesbeeck Fund. Special thanks to Erik Claes for his valuable comments on an earlier draft of this chapter, and to Isabelle Huys, Amandine Leonard and Lodewijk Van Dycke for their valuable research assistance.

1. *See*, e.g., A.E.L. Brown, *Intellectual Property, Human Rights and Competition,* Cheltenham, Edward Elgar, 2012; W. Grosheide (ed.), *Intellectual Property and Human Rights. A Paradox,* Cheltenham, Edward Elgar Publishing Ltd, 2010; L.R. Helfer & G.W. Austin, *Human Rights and Intellectual Property. Mapping the Global Interface,* Cambridge, Cambridge University Press, 2011. Of possible interest is also F.M. Abbott, C. Breining-Kaufmann & T. Cottier (eds), 'International Trade and Human Rights. Foundations and Conceptual Issues', *Studies in International Economics. The World Trade Forum* 5, Ann Arbor, The University of Michigan Press, 2006.
2. *See* the Chapters 24-27, in the present volume.
3. Recent papers reflecting on the interplay between human gene patents and human rights which the interested reader might wish to consult, include E.R. Gold, 'Patents and Human Rights: A Heterodox Analysis', *Global Health and the Law* (Spring 2013): 185-198; S.

Patents on human genes have a long and turbulent history and trigger considerable debate to this very day. In Europe, the lenient granting policy of the European Patent Office (EPO) on human genes was challenged in 1995 in a case relating to a patent claiming the gene encoding human relaxin. The subsequent debate came to a formal standstill in 1998, with the promulgation of the EU Biotechnology Directive officially confirming the patentability of human genes.[4] However, the controversy revived with the grant of a series of patents for the screening of breast cancer genes (the so-called BRCA patents) to the US-based company Myriad Genetics in the years 2001-2004.[5] For many geneticists, the patenting of genes remained questionable and even unacceptable from a principled point of view. Arguments included that the identification of a gene or a mutation, or the link between a genetic defect and a disease, is not an invention but a discovery. The counterargument that isolated DNA does not exist in nature, and thus makes its sequence patentable, was often viewed as a legal twist that does not convince.[6] In the US, the BRCA patents also sparked discussion about the patentability of human genes and genetic diagnostic methods.[7] The debate came to a temporary pause with a verdict of the Supreme Court in the Myriad Genetics case on 13 June 2013,[8] where it was ruled that claims on isolated DNA are

---

Kumar, 'Gene Patents and Patient Rights', *Whittier Law Review* 35 (2013-2014): 363-372; J. Pila, 'Intellectual Property Rights and Detached Human Body Parts', *Journal Medical Ethics* 40 (2014): 27-32; A. Plomer, 'Human Dignity and Patents', in *Research Handbook on Human Rights and Intellectual Property,* C. Geiger (ed.), Edward Elgar, 2015, 479-495.

4. *See* Article 5, Directive 98/44/EC of 6 July 1998 of the European Parliament and of the Council on the legal protection of biotechnological inventions, *Official Journal L* 213, 30/07/1998, p. 0013, discussed in detail further (available at http://eur-lex.europa.eu/legal-content/EN/TXT/?uri=CELEX:31998L0044, last visited 11 February 2015).

5. The BRCA patents were later subject to opposition and appeal procedures at the European Patent Office (EPO). The claims survived albeit with narrower scope. For a detailed report and analysis of the breast cancer case in Europe, and a comparison with the proceedings in the US, *see also* G. Matthijs & D. Halley, 'European-Wide Opposition Against the Breast Cancer Gene Patents', *European Journal of Human Genetics* (2002): 783-784; G. Matthijs, et al., 'The European BRCA Patent Oppositions and Appeals: Coloring Inside the Lines', *Nature Biotechnology* 31, (2013): 704-710. Also *see* E.R. Gold & J. Carbone, '*Myriad Genetics. In the Eye of the Policy Storm*', *Genetics in Medicine*, 2010, S39–S70.

6. *See* S. Aymé, G. Matthijs & S. Soini (on behalf of the European Society of Human Genetics (ESHG) Working Party on Patenting and Licensing), 'Patenting and Licensing in Genetic Testing. Recommendations of the European Society of Human Genetics', *European Journal of Human Genetics* 16 (2008): S3–S9.

7. *See* National Research Council – Committee on Intellectual Property Rights in Genomic and Protein Research and Innovation, *Reaping the Benefits of Genomic and Proteomic Research. Intellectual Property Rights, Innovation, and Public Health*, S.A. Merrill & A.-M. Mazza (eds), *National Research Council (US)*, Washington, National Academies Press, 2006 (available at http://www.nap.edu/catalog/11487.html, last visited 4 March 2015).

8. Available at https://supreme.justia.com/cases/federal/us/569/12-398/, last visited 4 March 2015.

invalid.[9] However, this judgment did not draw the debate to a halt.[10] On 22 May 2019, a draft bill was introduced in the US Congress. The draft states that criteria for patentability should not rely on judicially created exceptions, such as the doctrine that human genes would be 'natural phenomena'. According to some scholars, the draft bill would overrule the Supreme Court's verdict in the Myriad Genetics case and render human genes patentable.[11] In Australia, the BRCA patents spurred wide debate as well. In contrast to the US, the Australian Federal Court of Appeal upheld a claim on isolated DNA from the BRCA1 gene in a judgment from 5 September 2014.[12]

As is sufficiently well known, the debate on the legitimacy of patents for human genes and genetic diagnostic methods was intensified by the fact that Myriad Genetics licensed the breast cancer test exclusively to a limited number of commercial genetic laboratories within specific geographical regions at a high cost.[13] This highly restrictive and expensive licensing policy gave rise to a strong and worldwide concern about the possible

---

9. For a detailed overview of facts and submissions, *see* the well documented *BRCA Gene Patenting Case archive* of the Duke Center for Public Genomics (available at http://www.genome.duke.edu/centers/cpg/Myriad/, last visited 4 March 2015). For a comparative US-Europe analysis, *see* I. Huys, G. Van Overwalle & G. Matthijs, 'Gene and Genetic Diagnostic Method Patent Claims. A Comparison under Current European and US Patent Law', *European Journal of Human Genetics (EJHG)* 19, no. 10 (2011): 1104-1107, and the references cited there; Nicol D., et al., 'International Divergence in Gene Patenting', *Annual Review of Genomics and Human Genetics* 20 (2019): 519-541.

10. For details, *see* S. Kumar, 'Gene Patents and Patient Rights', *Whittier Law Review* 35 (2013-2014): 363-337.

11. For details, *see* K. Servick, 'Controversial U.S. Bill Would Lift Supreme Court Ban on Patenting Human Genes.' Science Magazine Website, 4 June 2019. http://www.sciencemag.org/news/2019/06/controversial-us-bill-would-lift-supreme-court-ban-patenting-human-genes, last visited 5 September 2019.

12. Available at http://www.judgments.fedcourt.gov.au/judgments/Judgments/fca/full/2014/2014fcafc0115 (last visited 5 March 2015). For details on facts and submission of the Australian case, *see* D. Nicol et al., *The Innovation Pool in Biotechnology: The Role of Patents In Facilitating Innovation,* Centre for Law and Genetics Occasional Paper No. 08, Tasmania, 2014: review the Australian and US cases in Chapter 6 (*see* particularly pages 166 to 170) and addendum (pages 279a-281a). Also *see* K.M. Meadt, 'Gene Patents in Australia: A Game Theory Approach', *Pacific Rim Law & Policy Journal.* 22, (2013): 751. For a comparison between the US and the Australian verdicts, *see* D. Nicol et al. 'International Divergence in Gene Patenting', *Annual Review of Genomics and Human Genetics* 20 (2019): 519-541; R. Cook-Deegan, 'Australian Court Upholds Patents on Isolated BRCA1 DNA', *Genomics Law Report,* 30 September 2014 (available at http://www.genomicslawreport.com/index.php/2014/09/30/australian-appeals-court-upholds-patents-on-isolated-brca1-dna/, last visited 4 March 2015).

13. For more details, *see* I.R. Walpole, et al., 'Human Gene Patents: The Possible Impacts on Genetic Services Healthcare', *Medical Journal of Australia* (2003): 256-283.

detrimental effects of gene patents on research, clinical applications and patient care.[14]

The *research objective* of the present chapter is to (re)assess the legitimacy of patent protection for human genes and genetic diagnostic methods, by examining the current state of patent law and practice through the lens of human rights. In this regard, the present study will focus on two *research questions*. A first research question is: What is the attitude of European patent law and practice vis-a-vis the patenting of genetic elements of human origin – such as human genes, human proteins and genetic diagnostic methods – and how has the position of European patent law and practice evolved over time? A second research question is: What human rights come into play in the discourse on the patenting of human genetic material and how have those rights been applied in the practice of the EPO, and been interpreted by European patent courts and in legal doctrine?

The *normative starting point* underlying the present study is that human rights are valuable and necessary complements of patent rights. Patent law is an autonomous legal system of its own kind with an intrinsic raison d'être. Human rights are valuable and necessary complements of the patent system, as they serve as a counterbalance of patent rights centring too one-sidedly on trade, access to markets, economic calculus and increasing wealth.

Looking at the gene patent controversy through the prism of human rights as complements, the present chapter sets forth the *hypothesis* that human rights contribute to settling the debate in two ways. First and foremost, human rights provide a profound argument to limit the coming into existence of patents for human genes, gene products and genetic diagnostic methods. Interrogating the concept of human dignity is highly relevant in this regard, as the respect for human dignity introduces certain limits on the patentable subject matter in order to safeguard the rights of human beings. The right to informed consent comes to the fore as well in this context. Second, human rights offer a foundation to limit questionable behaviour in the exercise of patent rights in the field of human genetics. More specifically, the human right to access to health care plays a vital role in the dispute on patents and licenses for genetic diagnostic methods.

---

14. For a more detailed and in-depth analysis of the alleged – upstream and downstream – problems in the current patent landscape in the area of human genetics – such as anti-commons, patent thickets, blocking patents, translational gap, etc. – empirical evidence documenting their appearance and a description of their (alleged) impact, *see* G. Van Overwalle, 'Of Thickets, Blocks and Gaps: Designing Tools to Resolve Obstacles in the Gene Patents Landscape', in *Gene Patents and Collaborative Licensing Models. Patent Pools, Clearing Houses, Open Source Models and Liability Regimes*, G. Van Overwalle, (ed.), Cambridge, Cambridge University Press, 2009, 381-463. Also *see* I. Huys, G. Matthijs & G. Van Overwalle, 'The Fate and Future of Patents on Human Genes and Genetic Diagnostic Methods', *Nature Reviews Genetics* 13, no. 6 (May 2012): 441-448 and the references cited there.

The *focus* of the present study is restricted to Europe. Even though the gene patenting debate has attracted worldwide attention, analysis from a global perspective would be most welcome; the present study is limited to the European continent. A first reason is that European patent law has certain peculiarities which are different from the US and Australian patent law. A second reason is that human rights have a particular history in Europe, and universal human rights instruments seem to have resonated more vigorously and have been made more exacting on the European continent, compared to the US.[15] A third and even more compelling argument for restricting this study to Europe is the call of contemporary authoritative intellectual property (IP) scholars, to move away from the internationalization of the discourse and focus on creating domestic dialogues.[16] The study will not zoom in on the justiciability of relevant human rights, nor on their adjudication in practice by the various (quasi)judicial bodies.

The present chapter will apply the following *method* of analysis. The second section will offer a basic introduction into the technicalities of human genetics for the non-informed reader. The third section will provide a comprehensive overview of current European patent law and practice in the field of human genes and genetic diagnostic methods. Therefore, this section includes a description and analysis of the norms currently set forth and applied in this field. Relevant legal sources that will be discussed include the European Patent Convention (EPC), the EU Biotechnology Directive and the case law of the European Patent Office (EPO). Next, a critical analysis of their reception in scholarly literature. The fourth section will examine those human rights which are pivotal in investigating the relationship between the human rights pantheon and the application of patent law in the area of human genetics. In this regard, three components come to the fore: human dignity, the right to informed consent and the right of access to health care. Therefore, this section entails an examination of the general rules relating to these rights and values, and an analysis of the way they are enshrined in universal and European human rights instruments and documents and in European patent law and practice. The last and fifth section, will compare the outcome of the conducted analysis with the hypothesis developed at the start, and provide conclusive insights on the relationship between European patent law, as applied in the area of human genetics, and European human rights law. In addition, some critical afterthoughts and paths for future academic research will be presented.

---

15. For a brief insight on the intersection between liberty rights and the right to bodily integrity in the US, and the relevance of the due process clause in that discussion, *see* S. Kumar, 'Gene Patents and Patient Rights', *Whittier Law Review* 35 (2013-2014): 363-37.
16. *See* E.R. Gold, 'Patents and Human Rights: A Heterodox Analysis', *Global Health and the Law*, Spring 2013, 185-198: 'Far from abandoning the ideals of human rights, we strengthen them by enabling the discourse over how best to construct a domestic innovation system that is responsive to human rights concerns within the forum best suited to that discussion: domestic patent law' (p. 193).

30.2   HUMAN GENETICS

For the non-informed reader, we provide some preliminary explanation on a few concepts which are vital to understanding the current human gene patent debate.

The science of genetics studies revolves around heredity: human genetics is the study of the heredity in human beings. The human genome – the entirety of human genetic information[17] – contains some 22,000 genes, which form the basis of human inheritance. The substance of genes is DNA. Each and every gene is composed of deoxyribonucleic acid molecules or DNA molecules. Each DNA molecule consists of units of four nucleotide bases, more in particular, adenine (A), thymine (T), cytosine (C) and guanine (G), linked together via a sugar-phosphate backbone. The linear order of nucleotide bases in a DNA molecule is referred to as a sequence.[18]

DNA is called 'native', 'chromosomal' or 'genomic' DNA. Native DNA refers to the DNA molecule that is properly folded and functional, for instance, in a natural cell. Chromosomal DNA refers to the DNA as present in chromosomes, which are dens structures composed of packaged DNA molecules (packed into twenty-three pairs of chromosomes) associated with several other proteins (like histones). Chromosomal DNA is also referred to as genomic DNA (gDNA).[19] Genomic DNA may be transcribed to generate RNA. In turn, RNA may be spliced to create a sequence of exons (coding sequences), called the messenger RNA (mRNA). This mRNA may be translated into a protein. DNA that is obtained by reverse transcribing mRNA is called 'complementary' DNA (cDNA).[20] DNA in a cell can be isolated or extracted from a cell by breaking open the cell wall, removing membrane lipids and other proteins (like the histones) and finally purifying the DNA from reagents or salts used in the first steps of isolation. In most cases, the isolation process thus results in a purified DNA molecule. DNA that is not present in a cell but that resides outside a cell (or that is synthetically produced), does not undergo the isolation process but may still have to be purified from its environmental contaminants, resulting in purified DNA. In sum, isolated DNA is, in most cases, also purified DNA, but purified DNA is not always isolated DNA.

Genes play an essential role in guiding the production of polypeptide chains that form proteins.[21] Exons are DNA segments that are necessary for the creation of a protein, in other words, that code for a protein. Introns are

---

17. B. Alberts, et al., *Molecular Biology of the Cell,* 2nd ed., Garland Publishing, 1989, 483 (The 5th revised edition has been published in 2007, with featuring authors B. Alberts, A. Johnson, J. Lewis, P. Walter & M. Raff).
18. *Ibid.,* 95.
19. In contrast to extra-chromosomal DNA.
20. *Ibid.,* 183.
21. *Ibid.,* 100.

DNA segments lined up between the exons, not coding for proteins.[22] Only cDNA is likely to contain an uninterrupted chain of nucleotide sequences that code for proteins.[23]

Recombinant DNA technology is a technique to move DNA from one organism to another organism, where the inserted DNA will give rise to the production of a protein. For example, the gene that encodes for human insulin can be isolated from human cells, inserted into a bacterium such as *E.coli*, after which the bacterium can be reproduced, creating many identical copies of the insulin gene and manufacturing (almost) the same protein as it does in a human cell in large quantities. Recombinant insulin was one of the first medical recombinant DNA products and was so to speak one of the showpieces of gene technology. Other examples of proteins which have been produced by means of recombinant DNA technology are human growth factor, human interferon, tissue-type plasminogen activator or t-PA and erythropoietin (EPO).[24]

Genetic testing relates to identifying changes in chromosomes or genes to find changes that are associated with inherited disorders.[25] More narrowly, medical genetic testing aims at probing genetic material for disease-associated geno- or karyotypes.[26] Recent debates have mainly focused on genetic diagnostic methods, in other words, on medical genetic DNA/RNA testing.

30.3   HUMAN GENETICS AND PATENT LAW

Over the last decades, international and European patent law and practice have gradually tailored themselves – in a less or more subdued voice – to accommodate patents for various types of genetic elements from human origin, ranging from human genes to human proteins, and methods for detecting human genes.

---

22. *Ibid.*, 102.
23. *Ibid.*, 183.
24. For details on these and other examples, *see* G. Van Overwalle, *The Legal Protection of Biotechnological Inventions in Europe and in the United States. Current Framework and Future Developments,* in *Leuven Law Series,* University Press, 1997 and the references cited there.
25. *See* http://www.ghr.nlm.nih.gov/handbook/testing/genetictesting, last visited 7 February 2015.
26. J. Sequeiros, 'Regulating Genetic Testing: The Relevance of Appropriate Definitions', in *Quality Issues in Clinical Genetic Services*, U. Kristoffersson, J. Schmidtke, J. & J.-J. Cassiman (eds), Berlin-Heidelberg, Springer, 2010, 23-32.

30.3.1 HUMAN GENES

From an international perspective, the TRIPS Agreement[27] does not explicitly treat the patentability of human genes. On the basis of Article 27(1) TRIPS Agreement and the proclaimed principle of non-discrimination with regard to technology, it is generally assumed that biological material, including human genes, can be regarded as a patentable subject matter under international IP law.

On the European scene, patent law did not contain an explicit rule concerning the admissibility of patents on human body material in general, or human genes, in particular, for a long time. Article 52 EPC quite generally stated that a European patent shall be granted for any invention which is new, involves an inventive step and is susceptible of industrial application. As a matter of routine, the EPO granted patents for subcellular fragments, like DNA sequences, genes, plasmids and vectors without a great stir, provided they met the conditions of novelty, inventive step and industrial applicability. A classroom example in this regard is the patent granted for the DNA sequence of alpha-type interferon in 1984, which includes a claim on 'A DNA sequence selected from DNA sequences of the formula. ATGGCCTCGCCCTTTGCTTTACTGA[…]AGGAA, said DNA sequence being for use in cloning or expressing said sequence in bacteria, yeasts or animal cells and in selecting DNA sequences that code for an alpha-type interferon'.[28]

The lenient EPO granting policy was first formally challenged when a patent was granted for a DNA fragment encoding human H2-preprorelaxin.[29] In the subsequent decision of the Opposition Division of 1995, the EPO argued that '[…], the allegation that human life is being patented is unfounded. It is worth pointing out that DNA is not "life", but a chemical substance which carries genetic information and can be used as an intermediate in the production of proteins which may be medically useful'.[30] The EPO closed in stating, that '[…], neither does the opposed patent offend

---

27. Agreement on Trade-Related Aspects of Intellectual Property Rights (TRIPS Agreement), Annex 1C of the Marrakesh Agreement Establishing the World Trade Organization, signed in Marrakesh, Morocco on 15 April 1994 (available at http://www.wto.org/english/tratop_e/TRIPS_e/t_agm0_e.htm, last visited 11 February 2015).

28. Claim 32 of European patent with publication number 32.134 entitled 'DNA sequences, recombinant DNA molecules and processes for producing human interferon-alpha like polypeptides', granted on 15 August 1984 (B1). The middle part of the DNA sequence is represented here as '[…]' and has been omitted here for reasons of space.

29. *See* European patent with publication number 112.149 entitled 'Molecular cloning and characterization of a further gene sequence coding for human relaxin', granted on 10 April 1991 (B1), of which claim 1 reads as follows: 'A DNA fragment encoding human H2-preprorelaxin, said H2-preprorelaxin having the amino acid sequence set out in Figure 2'.

30. EPO Opposition Division, 18 January 1995 in *Howard Florey Institute* (on file with the author). For a more extensive analysis, *see* S. Sterckx & J. Cockbain, *Exclusions from Patentability. How Far Has the European Patent Office Eroded Boundaries,* Cambridge

against widely-accepted moral standards of behaviour by promoting slavery, the sale of women etc., nor is there a clear consensus amongst members of the public in the Contracting states that patenting human genes such as that encoding H2-relaxin is immoral. In view of this, the patent is not considered to offend against article 53 (a) EPC'.[31] An explicit reference to 'human dignity' was not made in the decision of the Opposition Division itself but in the later summary of this decision in the verdict of the Technical Board of Appeal. The Technical Board of Appeal said that the Opposition Division concluded that under Article 53(a) EPC 'an invention concerning a human gene was not an exception to patentability because it would not be universally regarded as outrageous: it did not amount to patenting life because DNA as such was not life but one of the many chemical entities participating in biological processes; no offence to human dignity had occurred as the woman who donated tissue was asked for her consent and her self-determination was not affected by the exploitation of the claimed molecules'.[32]

In a bid to resolve the controversy on gene patents and to harmonize Member States' legislations on this point, a Directive on the legal protection of biotechnological inventions was adopted by the European Parliament on 6 July 1998.[33] At the same time, the Directive also represented a subtle attempt, the EU having no authority over the EPO, to steer the granting policy of the EPO indirectly.[34] The EU Biotechnology Directive posits that the human body at the various stages of its formation and development, as well as the simple discovery of one of its elements including the sequence or partial sequence of a gene, cannot constitute a patentable invention (Article

---

University Press, 2012, 119-122 and 271. Also *see* J. Pila, 'Intellectual Property Rights and Detached Human Body Parts', *Journal of Medical Ethics* 40 (2014): 27-32.

31. EPO Opposition Division, 18 January 1995 in *Howard Florey Institute* (on file with the author).

32. Summary of the decision of the Opposition Division of 18 January 1995 in *Howard Florey Institute,* as presented in the later decision of the Technical Board of Appeal (*see* EPO T 0272/95, 23 October 2002 – Relaxin/Howard Florey Institute, available at http://www.epo.org/law-practice/case-law-appeals/pdf/t950272eu2.pdf, last visited 7 February 2015). The opposition was rejected by the Opposition Division, setting forth the aforementioned line of reasoning. The opponents then filed a notice of appeal. The appellant's arguments were turned away on the basis of the then implemented EU Biotechnology Directive, which clearly allowed the patenting of genes (Article 5 EU Biotechnology Directive, Rule 23 EPO Implementing Regulations).

33. *See* Article 5, Directive 98/44/EC of 6 July 1998 of the European Parliament and of the Council on the legal protection of biotechnological inventions, *Official Journal L* 213, 30/07/1998, p. 0013, discussed in detail further (available at http://eur-lex.europa.eu/legal-content/EN/TXT/?uri=CELEX:31998L0044, last visited 11 February 2015).

34. The EU Biotechnology Directive was incorporated in the EPC in 1999 thus providing for the EPO more detailed guidelines with regard to the patenting of human genes. More in particular, the Directive was inserted as Rule 23 of the Implementing Regulations to the EPC, which was inserted by decision of the Administrative Council of 16 June 1999, and which came into force on 1 September 1999.

5(1)), whereas an element isolated from the human body or otherwise produced by means of a technical process, including the sequence or partial sequence of a gene, may constitute a patentable invention, even if the structure of that element is identical to that of a natural element (Article 5(2)).[35]

Thoughtful reflection on Article 5, teaches that in Europe – as in many other jurisdictions[36] – two principles are relevant in the context of patent law and human genes: isolation and function.[37] The first principle, isolation, has been introduced in an attempt to overcome the discovery exclusion. Jurisdictions that recognize the principle of isolation hold the view that if a DNA sequence is isolated from the human body for the first time, it is regarded as having no previously recognized existence. In the same line, Article 5 specifies that an invention based on 'an element isolated from the human body or otherwise produced by means of a technical process, including the sequence or partial sequence of a gene', which is susceptible of industrial application[38] is not excluded from patentability, 'even if the structure of that element is identical to that of a natural element'.[39] The possible reason why isolated genes are not excluded from patentability is that the legislator takes the view that an isolated gene contains technical information, in the sense that the aspect of 'isolation' is considered to be the result of 'technical processes used to identify, purify and classify it, techniques which human beings alone are capable of putting into practice and which nature is incapable of accomplishing by itself' (Recital 21, EU Biotechnology Directive).[40]

---

35. For a detailed analysis of the Article 5 regime, *see* S.J.R. Bostyn, *Patenting DNA Sequences (Polynucleotides) and Scope of Protection in the European Union: An Evaluation*. European Communities, Luxemburg, 2004; S.J.R. Bostyn, 'Patentability of Genetic Information Carriers', *Intellectual Property Quarterly* (1999).

36. *See* the judgments from the US Supreme Court (13 June 2013) and the Australian Federal Court of Appeal (5 September 2014) in the Myriad Genetics case (references above). Also *see* I. Huys, G. Matthijs & G. Van Overwalle, 'The Fate and Future of Patents on Human Genes and Genetic Diagnostic Methods', *Nature Reviews Genetics* 13, no. 6 (May 2012): 441-448.

37. *See* I. Huys, G. Matthijs & G. Van Overwalle, 'The Fate and Future of Patents on Human Genes and Genetic Diagnostic Methods', *Nature Reviews Genetics* 13, no. 6 (May 2012): 441-448. In the same sense, (as regards isolation) J. Pila, 'Intellectual Property Rights and Detached Human Body Parts', *Journal of Medical Ethics* 40 (2014): 27-32.

38. Cf. Article 5 (3) EU Biotechnology Directive; Rule 29 (3) Implementing Regulations to the EPC.

39. Article 5 (2) EU Biotechnology Directive; Rule 29(2) Implementing Regulations to the EPC.

40. Also *see* I. Huys, G. Van Overwalle & G. Matthijs, 'Gene and Genetic Diagnostic Method Patent Claims. A Comparison under current European and US Patent Law', *European Journal of Human Genetics (EJHG)* 19, no. 10 (2011): 1104-1107.

The second principle, function, has been introduced in Europe to make sense of the industrial applicability requirement.[41] In Europe, a function for the isolated genetic sequence(s) has to be proposed in the patent application to be acceptable. This means that when a patent claims a sequence of a gene used to produce a protein, the application has to specify which protein is produced or what function it performs.

Part of the debate, but less so, is nowadays also centred around the requirements[42] of novelty and inventive step for receiving gene patents[42] and the appropriate scope of its protection. An analysis of these debates is beyond the scope of the present chapter.

30.3.2   HUMAN PROTEINS

The TRIPS Agreement, nor the EPC provide explicit guidance as to the patentability of human gene products, resulting from recombinant DNA technology. Based on EPC practice and case law, and later backed up by the EU Biotechnology Directive, European patents have been granted for the majority of recombinant DNA products. European patents were issued for the production of recombinant alpha-type interferon, gamma-type interferon, tissue-type plasminogen activator or t-PA and erythropoietin (EPO).[43] An instructive example is the patent granted for alpha-type interferon. An examination of the description and patent claims of this patent show that protection has not only been granted for a well-defined DNA sequence[44] but also for a recombinant DNA molecule, a host transformed with the said recombinant DNA molecule, alpha-type interferon produced by the said

---

41. The US Patent and Trademark Office (USPTO) Guidelines state that the utility that is attributed to the claimed product must be specific, substantial and credible, meaning that it can be used to produce a useful protein or that it can hybridize near and serve as a marker for a disease gene.

42. For an in-depth and comparative assessment of the inventive step requirement as applied to human genes, *see* T. Minssen, *Assessing the Inventiveness of Bio-Pharmaceuticals under European and US Patent Law (A Comparative Study With Special Emphasis on DNA & Protein-Related Inventions)* (Doctoral Dissertation, Faculty of Law, Lund University), Göteborg, Ineko AB, October 2012. For an interesting analysis of other threshold requirements and scope, *see* G. Van Overwalle, 'Policy Levers Tailoring Patent Law to Biotechnology. Comparing U.S. and European Approaches', *University of California (UC) Irvine Law Review* (2011): 435-517 and the references cited there.

43. For further details (relating EP numbers, title, short description, relevant claims), *see* G. Van Overwalle, 'Biotechnology and Patents: Global Standards, European Approaches and National Accents', in *Genetic Engineering and the World Trade System,* D. Wüger & T. Cottier (eds), Cambridge University Press, first published 2008, 77-108.

44. *See* above.

transformed host for a process for producing the recombinant DNA molecules, a process for the transformation of the host and a process for the production of alpha-type interferon.[45]

30.3.3 GENETIC DIAGNOSTIC METHODS

From an international perspective, and based on Article 27(3)(a) of the TRIPS Agreement, it is generally accepted that national patent legislatures can exclude diagnostic methods for the treatment of humans from patentability. It was agreed that this exclusion shall not apply to products, in particular, substances or compositions, for use in any of these methods.

On the European scene and long before the TRIPS Agreement came into being, the EPO decided to exclude diagnostic methods from patent protection when 'practised *on* the human or animal body' (Our italics). The exclusionary provision in the EPC is constructed more narrowly than its TRIPS counterpart, implying that the *only* methods excluded from patent protection are diagnostic methods practised *on* the human body. Unfortunately, the EPO legislator did not define the term 'diagnostic method', so it was left to the courts to delineate the exact scope of the exclusion and to decide to what extent DNA testing was patentable.[46] The ongoing debate on the scope of the exclusion of diagnostic methods came to a halt with an authoritative EPO ruling in 2005.[47] The decision clearly confirms that practising a diagnostic method requires *several* method steps due to the inherent and inescapable multi-step nature of such a method, contrary to surgical or therapeutic methods which can be achieved by a single step. It is accepted that the method steps to be carried out when making a diagnosis as part of the medical treatment of humans include: (i) the collection of data (examination phase), (ii) the comparison of found data with standard values (comparison phase), (iii) the finding of any significant deviation (i.e., a

---

45. For further details (relating EP numbers, title, short description and relevant claims), *see* G. Van Overwalle, 'Biotechnology and Patents: Global Standards, European Approaches and National Accents', in *Genetic Engineering and the World Trade System,* D. Wüger & T. Cottier (eds), Cambridge University Press, first published 2008, (77), 88-89.

46. For a more detailed analysis of the EPO case law on diagnosis in general, and in relation to human genetics, *see* D. Thomas, 'The EPC and the Granting Policy and Case Law of the EPO', in *Gene Patents and Public Health,* G. Van Overwalle (ed.), Brussel, Bruylant, 2007, 61-71; D. Thomas, 'Patentability Problems in Medical Biotechnology', *International Review of Intellectual Property and Competition Law (IIC)* (2003): 847-994; S. Sterckx & J. Cockbain, *Exclusions from Patentability. How Far Has the European Patent Office Eroded Boundaries,* Cambridge University Press, 2012, 152-160; G. Van Overwalle, 'IPR Issues and High Quality Genetic Testing', in *Quality Issues in Clinical Genetic Services,* U. Kristoffersson, J. Schmidtke, J. & J.-J. Cassiman (eds), Berlin-Heidelberg, Springer, 2010, 251-265.

47. EPO Enlarged Board of Appeal G1/04, 12 December 2005 *Diagnostic methods* (available at http://www.epo.org/law-practice/case-law-appeals/recent/g040001dp1.html, last visited 11 February 2015).

symptom), and (iv) the attribution of the deviation to a particular clinical picture (the deductive medical decision phase). The EPO ruling further holds that only methods including *all* steps are excluded from patent protection: only those methods are excluded, pertaining to the diagnosis for curative purposes as a purely intellectual exercise representing the deductive medical decision phase (the diagnosis for curative purposes *stricto sensu*), *as well as* to the preceding steps which were constitutive for making the diagnosis (examination, data gathering and comparison), *and* the specific interactions with the human body which occurred when carrying out those of the said preceding steps which were of a technical nature. A method for obtaining intermediate findings of diagnostic relevance does not fall under the exclusionary provision and is patentable.[48] The EPO requires that all method steps of a technical nature of a diagnostic method should satisfy the criterion 'practised on the human or animal body'. In other words, the performance of each and every one of these steps should imply interaction with the human or animal body, necessitating the presence of the latter. If, on the other hand, some or all of the method steps of a technical nature are carried out by a device without implying any interaction with the human body (e.g., by using a specific software program), these steps may not be considered to satisfy the criterion 'practised on the human or animal body'. By the same token, this criterion has not complied with either, in respect of method steps carried out *in vitro* in a laboratory, such as method steps carried out *in vitro* by diagnostic devices known as DNA microarrays.[49]

Current EPO case law thus suggests that genetic diagnostic methods carried out *in vivo* are unpatentable, whereas genetic diagnostic methods not carried out on the human or animal body, but practised *in vitro* are considered patentable.

30.4   GENE PATENTS AND HUMAN RIGHTS

Overlooking past and present European patent law and practice in the area of human genetics leads to conclude that over time a quite open and liberal framework was crafted, providing patent protection for many achievements in the area of human genetics, ranging from patents for human genes, over human gene products, to *in vitro* genetic diagnostic methods.

In view of the seemingly never-ending critique on the grant of patents on human genes, this section aims at (re)assessing the current state of play through the lens of human rights. In his seminal paper, Helfer sets forth two distinct approaches to qualify the relationship between IP and human

---

48. *Ibid.*
49. *Ibid.*

rights.[50] The first school of thought takes the view that IP and human rights are in fundamental *conflict*.[51] Strong IP protection is undermining, and therefore, incompatible with, a broad spectrum of human rights obligations, especially in the area of economic, social and cultural rights.[52] Resolving this conflict lies in recognition of the *primacy* of human rights law over IP law, and in viewing IP as an instrument designed to fulfil human rights objectives. In this view, human rights have absolute priority over patent rights, and human rights have normative predominance. In the same line of reasoning, patent rights are seen as instrumental rights, which serve the interests and needs that citizens identify, through the lens of human rights, as being fundamental. IPRs, in general, and patent rights, in particular, are pressed into service on behalf of human rights. Property rights come to serve human rights.[53] The second way of thinking claims that IP and human rights are essentially compatible and can *coexist*.[54] IP and human rights focus on the

---

50. L. Helfer, 'Human Rights and Intellectual Property: Conflict or Coexistence?', *Minnesota Journal of Law, Science & Technology* 5 (2003): 47 (available at http://scholarship .law.duke.edu/cgi/viewcontent.cgi?article=2635&context=faculty_scholarship, last visited 24 January 2015). Also *see* R. Helfer & G.W. Austin, *Human Rights and Intellectual Property,* Cambridge University Press, 2011, 64-80 and the references cited there. Also *see* E.R. Gold, 'Patents and Human Rights: A Heterodox Analysis', in *Global Health and the Law*, Spring 2013, 185-198; P.L.C. Torremans, 'Copyright (and Other Intellectual Property Rights) as a Human Right', in *Intellectual Property and Human Rights,* P.L.C. Torremans (ed.) Edward Elgar, 2008.
51. Gold recently referred to this first approach as the 'subjugation approach', *see* E.R. Gold, 'Patents and Human Rights: A Heterodox Analysis', in *Global Health and the Law*, Spring 2013, 185, 186.
52. This approach can be witnessed in Resolution 2000/7, which stipulates that 'Actual or potential conflicts exist between the implementation of the TRIPS Agreement and the realisation of economic, social and cultural rights', *see* United Nations, Sub-Commission on the Promotion and Protection of Human Rights, Resolution 2000/7, 'Intellectual property rights and human rights', 17 August 2000 (available at http://www.un.org/en/ ecosoc/docs/resdec1946_2000.asp, last visited 4 March 2015).
53. An exponent of this school of thought can be found in P. Drahos, 'Intellectual Property Rights and Human Rights', *Intellectual Property Quarterly* (1999): 349-371; P. Drahos & J. Braithwaite, *Information Feudalism,* Earthscan, 2002 (a soft copy of the book is freely available at https://www.anu.edu.au/fellows/pdrahos/books/Information%20Feudalism .pdf, last visited 5 March 2015); H. Brennan, R. Distler, M. Hinman & A. Rogers, 'A Human Rights Approach to Intellectual Property and Access to Medicines', *Yale Law School and Yale School of Public Health Global Health Justice Partnership Policy Paper, No 1.,* August 2013 (available at http://papers.ssrn.com, last visited 4 March 2015) who claim that 'Judicial articulation of the relationship between the right to health and intellectual property law might also legitimize broader political actions that *prioritize* the right to health over intellectual property protection' (My Italics); S.T. Rosenberg, 'Asserting the Primacy of Health over Patent Rights: A Comparative Study of the Processes that Led to the Use of Compulsory Licensing in Thailand and Brazil', *Developing World Bioethics* 14, no. 2 (2014): 83-91.
54. Gold equally referred to this approach as the 'coexistence approach', *see* E.R. Gold, 'Patents and Human Rights: A Heterodox Analysis', in *Global Health and the Law*, Spring 2013, 185, 187.

same fundamental question and share the same goal. Both human rights and IP rights aim at enhancing the welfare and the benefit for society.[55] Both legal regimes equally try to define the appropriate scope of private rights, while safeguarding the public interest.[56]

In the present chapter – and in previous work[57] – we have put ourselves in the line of recent scholarly writings going beyond the conflict and coexistence literature.[58] The present chapter agrees that human rights' law has normative primacy over IP law, in the sense that it is imperative to take into account human rights discourse in a patent law context. Patent law should be assessed from a human rights' perspective. Human rights should feed into patent law in a moderate, *complementary* manner. Patent law is an autonomous legal system of its own kind, with an intrinsic raison d'être. More, in particular, patent law is an instrument, a legal tool, aiming to serve both private and public objectives, both reward for innovation and societal well-being through the production of new goods and services. Human rights are valuable and necessary complements of the patent system. Human rights serve as a counterbalance of patent rights centring too one-sidedly on trade, access to markets, economic calculus and increasing wealth, rather than on increasing well-being.[59] For patent law to be widely accepted and generally recognized as a tool fostering both private and public interest, it is vital that current patent law regimes are inextricably linked with the human rights discourse, and that human rights assist in defining the utter limits of patent rights.

---

55. This is the view taken by C. Geiger, '"Constitutionalising" Intellectual Property Law? The Influence of Fundamental Rights on Intellectual Property in the European Union', *IIC* 37, (2006): 371-500.
56. A clear exponent of this attitude is reflected in the International Covenant on Economic, Social and Cultural Rights (ICESCR), adopted by the General Assembly, Resolution 2200A (XXI) of 16 December 1966, and entered into force on 3 January 1976 (also available at http://www.ohchr.org/EN/ProfessionalInterest/Pages/CESCR.aspx, last visited 4 March 2015).
57. *See* G. Van Overwalle, 'Human Rights' Limitations in Patent Law', in *Intellectual Property and Human Rights. A Paradox,* W. Grosheide (ed.), Cheltenham, Edward Elgar, 2010, 236-271.
58. Other commentators that have developed frameworks that go beyond the conflict-coexistence approach and focus on patent law are L.R. Helfer, 'Toward a Human Rights Framework for Intellectual Property', *U.C. Davis Law Review* 40 (2007): 971-1020; A.E.L. Brown, *Intellectual Property, Human Rights and Competition,* Edward Elgar, 2012; P.K. Yu, 'Reconceptualizing Intellectual Property Interests in a Human Rights Framework', *UC Davis Law Review* 40 (2007): 1039-1149.
59. In the same sense: F.M. Abbott, 'TRIPS and Human Rights: Preliminary Reflections', in *International Trade and Human Rights. Foundations and Conceptual Issues,* F.M. Abbott, C. Breining-Kaufmann & T. Cottier (eds.), Ann Arbor, The University of Michigan Press, 2006, (145), 145: 'Human rights represent the values for establishing a global constitutional balance between the interests of the public and the private holders of IPRs'; E.R. Gold, 'Patents and Human Rights: A Heterodox Analysis', in *Global Health and the Law,* Spring 2013, 185-198, at 193.

Before exploring the interface between patent law and human rights in more detail, let us focus on human rights instruments in some more depth. In terms of international human rights conventions, the foundational document which shaped or 'constitutionalized' the human rights regime is the Universal Declaration of Human Rights of 1948 (UDHR).[60] However, the UDHR is just a declaration, lacking enforceability. The rights of the UDHR were further developed and given greater specificity in the International Covenant on Civil and Political Rights (ICCPR)[61] and the International Covenant on Economic, Social and Cultural Rights (ICESCR),[62] both of 1966. They were given enforceability in those states which ratified the Covenants. As of today, 2020, the US has still not ratified the ICESCR.[63]

At the European level, a two-layered human rights regime has been developed over time. First and foremost, human rights were recognized in the framework of the Council of Europe. Discussions resulted in constitutional documents such as the European Convention for the Protection of Human Rights and Fundamental Freedoms in 1950 (ECHR)[64] for civil and political rights, and the European Social Charter in 1961 (ESC-1961)[65] for

60. Universal Declaration of Human Rights, adopted and proclaimed by the General Assembly of the United Nations on 10 December 1948 (available at http://www.un.org/en/documents/udhr/, last visited 26 February 2015).

61. International Covenant on Civil and Political Rights, adopted and opened for signature, ratification and accession by General Assembly resolution 2200A (XXI) of 16 December 1966; entry into force 23 March 1976, in accordance with Article 49 (available at http://www.ohchr.org/en/professionalinterest/pages/ccpr.aspx, last visited 26 February 2015).

62. International Covenant on Economic, Social and Cultural Rights, adopted by the General Assembly, Resolution 2200A (XXI) of 16 December 1966, and entered into force on 3 January 1976 (available at http://www.ohchr.org/EN/ProfessionalInterest/Pages/CESCR.aspx, last visited 26 February 2015). The Optional Protocol to the International Covenant on Economic, Social and Cultural Rights (available at http://www.ohchr.org/Documents/HRBodies/CESCR/OProtocol_en.pdf, last visited 4 March 2015), which entered into force on 5 May 2013 (*see* http://op-icescr.escr-net.org/about-op-icescr, last visited 5 March 2015) introduces the possibility for the Committee to receive and consider communications submitted by or on behalf of individuals or groups of individuals. At present three such communications have been submitted (*see* http://www.ohchr.org/EN/HRBodies/CESCR/Pages/PendingCases.aspx, last visited 5 March 2015), but none of them relates to the issues at hand in the present chapter. Of further possible interest is General comment No. 21, relating to the right of everyone to take part in cultural life (Article 15(1)(a) ICESCR). Even though the Comment confirms that the concept embedded in Article 15(1)(a), on the one hand, and Article 15(1)(b) and (c), on the other hand are closely intertwined, the Comment mainly discusses Article 15(1)(a) ICESCR.

63. The US undersigned the ICESCR on October 1977, but still not ratified (*see* https://treaties.un.org, last visited 7 March 2015).

64. Rome, 4 November 1950 (available at http://www.echr.coe.int/Documents/Convention_ENG.pdf, last visited 25 February 2015).

65. Turin, 18 October 1961 (available at http://www.coe.int/t/dghl/monitoring/socialcharter/Presentation/TreatiesIndex_en.asp, last visited 26 February 2015).

economic and social rights, as revised in 1996 (ESC-1996).[66] Second, within the specific confines of the European Union, the attention for human rights dates back to the late 1960s.[67] The current point of departure is the Treaty on the European Union (TEU), and the Treaty on the Functioning of the European Union (TFEU), undersigned on 13 December 2007 entered into force on 1 December 2009 and most recently consolidated in 2012.[68] The most comprehensive constitutional human rights document at EU level is the Charter of Fundamental Rights of the European Union of 2000 (European Charter), most recently consolidated in 2012.[69] The relation between the TEU/TFEU and the European Charter has been established in Article 6(1) TEU, which stipulates that 'The Union recognises the rights, freedoms and principles set out in the Charter of Fundamental Rights of the European Union of 7 December 2000, as adapted at Strasbourg, on 12 December 2007, which shall have the same legal value as the Treaties'.

The interplay between the two human rights layers at the European level has been arranged for in Article 6(2) TEU, which states: 'The Union shall accede to the European Convention for the Protection of Human Rights and Fundamental Freedoms. Such accession shall not affect the Union's competences as defined in the Treaties'. Article 6(3) further adds that 'Fundamental rights, as guaranteed by the European Convention for the Protection of Human Rights and Fundamental Freedoms and as they result from the constitutional traditions common to the Member States, shall constitute general principles of the Union's law'.[70] However, the foreseen accession scheme was barred by the Court of Justice of the EU (CJEU) in December 2014 in Opinion 2/13.[71] In the May 2016 *Avotins v. Latvia*

---

66. Strasbourg, 3 May 1996, (available at http://www.coe.int/t/dghl/monitoring/socialcharter/Presentation/TreatiesIndex_en.asp, last visited 26 February 2015). All EU Member States have ratified the ESC, either in its original or in its reviewed version.
67. Human rights were not explicitly mentioned in the European Coals and Steel Community, nor in the European Economic Community Treaties, but the European Court of Justice took them into account for the first time in the *Stauder* case (European Court of Justice, Case 29/69, *Stauder v. City of Ulm*, 1969, *E.C.R.* 419). *See* O. De Schutter, *International Human Rights Law,* Cambridge University Press, 2014, 26.
68. Document 2012/C 326/01, *Official Journal of the European Union C-326,* 26 October 2012 (available at http://eur-lex.europa.eu/legal-content/EN/TXT/PDF/?uri=OJ:C:2012:326:FULL&from=EN, last visited 3 March 2015).
69. Document 2012/C 326/02, *Official Journal of the European Union C-326,* 26 October 2012 (available at http://eur-lex.europa.eu/legal-content/EN/TXT/PDF/?uri=OJ:C:2012:326:FULL&from=EN, last visited 3 March 2015).
70. Article 6 only mentions ECHR and does not include any explicit reference to the ESC. It remains to be seen to what extent the ESC is (to be) taken into account in the EU context.
71. When delivering its opinion on the draft Agreement on the accession of the European Union to the European Convention for the Protection of Human Rights and Fundamental Freedoms, the CJEU identified problems with regard to its compatibility with EU law. *See* Opinion of the Court (Full Court) of 18 December 2014, Opinion pursuant to Article 218(11) TFEU – Draft international agreement – Accession of the European Union to the European Convention for the Protection of Human Rights and Fundamental Freedoms –

judgment, the European Court of Human Rights (ECtHR) reacted to Opinion 2/13 by reluctantly upholding the *Bosphorus* doctrine, which claims that human rights protection under EU law is presumed to be equivalent to the protections guaranteed under the ECHR.[72] The decision of the ECtHR has not ended the debate, and the relationship between the ECtHR and the CJEU remains unclear.[73] The intricate details of this debate will not be surveyed in the context of the present contribution.

The legal basis to take account of human rights in patent law is twofold. First, in scholarly research – more in particular in earlier work of ours – it has been substantiated that human rights enter the gate of patent law via the public interest concept: factoring in human rights in patent law can be achieved via the reassessment of the notion of public interest in patent law.[74] Indeed, a contemporary interpretation of the public interest component of the patent system can offer a legal foundation to introduce the human rights discourse into patent law. Second, jurisprudential decisions have suggested that Article 53(a) EPC can act as a specific legal gate of entry to discuss human dignity and the right to informed consent in patent law.[75]

Compatibility of the draft agreement with the EU and FEU Treaties. Opinion 2/13 (available at http://curia.europa.eu/juris/celex.jsf?celex=62013CV0002&lang1=en&type=TXT&ancre, last visited 4 March 2015). The CJEU concluded that the agreement on the accession of the European Union to the European Convention for the Protection of Human Rights and Fundamental Freedoms is not compatible with Article 6(2) TEU or with Protocol (No 8) relating to Article 6(2) of the Treaty on European Union on the accession of the Union to the European Convention on the Protection of Human Rights and Fundamental Freedoms. For some preliminary, critical comments, *see* S. Peers, 'The CJEU and the EU's Accession to the ECHR: a Clear and Present Danger to Human Rights Protection' (available at http://eulawanalysis.blogspot.be/2014/12/the-cjeu-and-eus-accession-to-echr.html, last visited 4 March 2015).

72. L. Glas & J. Krommendijk. 'From Opinion 2/13 to Avotiņš: Recent Developments in the Relationship Between the Luxembourg and Strasbourg Courts.' *Human Rights Law Review* 17, no. 3 (2017): 567-87. https://doi.org/10.1093/hrlr/ngw047; P. Gragl. 'An Olive Branch from Strasbourg? Interpreting the European Court of Human Rights' Resurrection of Bosphorus and Reaction to Opinion 2/13 in the Avotiņš Case: ECtHR 23 May 2016, Case No. 17502/07, Avotiņš v Latvia.' *European Constitutional Law Review* 13, no. 3 (2017): 551-67. https://doi.org/10.1017/S1574019617000165.

73. M. Kuijer. 'The Challenging Relationship between the European Convention on Human Rights and the EU Legal Order: Consequences of a Delayed Accession.' *The International Journal of Human Rights* (2018) https://doi.org/10.1080/13642987.2018.1535433; A. Masiero. 'The Accession of the European Union to the European Convention on Human Rights Four Years after Opinion 2/13: Should We Lose Hope?' *European Criminal Law Review* 9, no. 2 (2019): 222-50. https://doi.org/10.5771/2193-5505-2019-2-222.

74. For more details on how human rights can be factored in in patent law via a (re)assessment of the notion of public interest, *see* our earlier work: G. Van Overwalle, 'Human Rights' Limitations in Patent Law', in *Intellectual Property and Human Rights. A Paradox,* W. Grosheide (ed.), Cheltenham, Edward Elgar Publishing Ltd, 2010, 236-271.

75. *See* further, the introduction of the concept of human dignity, and the right to informed consent in EPO case law regarding Article 53 (a) EPC, more in particular the relaxin and BRCA cases.

The next section will scrutinize the UDHR, the ICCPR, the ICESCR, some other international conventions, as well as the ECHR, the ESC, the TEU, TFEU and the European Charter and their resonance in patent law as regards human genetic inventions.

Special attention will be drawn to foundational human values, pertinent civil and political rights (so-called first-generation human rights) and economic, social and cultural rights (so-called second-generation human rights).[76] Three human rights concepts come to mind as bearing high relevance in the interplay between human genetics, patent law and human rights: human dignity, usually considered as a value underlying human rights and serving as guidelines for interpreting human rights;[77] the right to informed consent, an attribute to various first-generation human rights; and the right of access to health care, commonly considered as a second-generation human right.

30.4.1   HUMAN DIGNITY[78]

30.4.1.1   In General

Human dignity appears as a pivotal concept in a variety of international conventions. The UDHR already underlines in 1948 that 'recognition of the inherent dignity and of the equal and inalienable rights of all members of the human family is the foundation of freedom, justice and peace in the world' (Preamble). The UDHR further proclaims that 'All human beings are born free and equal in dignity and rights' (Article 1).[79] The ICCPR of 1966 equally

---

76. *See* O. De Schutter, *International Human Rights Law*, Cambridge University Press, 2014, 18-21. The present chapter will not address solidarity rights (third generation) encompassing, i.e., the right to development, the right to peace, the right to environment and the right to humanitarian assistance. On third generation rights, *see* P. Alston, 'A Third Generation of Solidarity Rights: Progressive Development or Obfuscation of International Human Rights Law?', *Netherlands International Law Review* (1982): 307-322.

77. Cf. J. Fierens, 'La dignité humaine comme concept juridique', *J.T.,* 2002, 577-582; G. Hermerén, 'European Values, Ethics and Law. Present Policies and Future Challenges', in *Jahrbuch für Wissenschaft und Ethik,* 2006, (5), 8-9 and footnote 10 in particular: 'A distinction is sometimes made between values and human rights. ... I would be inclined to think that we have agreed on certain human rights and codified them in international documents, because these human rights promote or protect certain important values'.

78. Parts of this section are based on G. Van Overwalle, 'Human Rights' Limitations in Patent Law', in *Intellectual Property and Human Rights. A Paradox,* W. Grosheide (ed.), Cheltenham, Edward Elgar, 2010, 236-271.

79. Also *see* Article 22 UDHR ('Everyone, as a member of society, has the right to social security and is entitled to realization, through national effort and international cooperation and in accordance with the organization and resources of each State, of the economic, social and cultural rights indispensable for his dignity and the free development of his personality') and Article 23 UDHR ('(1) Everyone has the right to work, to free choice of employment, to just and favourable conditions of work and to protection

stipulates that 'in accordance with the principles proclaimed in the Charter of the United Nations, recognition of the inherent dignity and of the equal and inalienable rights of all members of the human family is the foundation of freedom, justice and peace in the world' (Preamble) and further recognizes that 'these rights derive from the inherent dignity of the human person' (Preamble). The ICCPR further sets forth that 'all persons deprived of their liberty shall be treated with humanity and with respect for the inherent dignity of the human person' (Article 10(1)).

The concept of human dignity equally appears in more specific international treaties focusing on research on and use of the human body and the human genome, more in particular in the Universal Declaration on the Human Genome and Human Rights of 1997,[80] which underlines that 'The human genome underlies the fundamental unity of all members of the human family, as well as the recognition of their inherent dignity and diversity. In a symbolic sense, it is the heritage of humanity' (Article 1).

On the European scene, the notion of human dignity has no literal equivalent in the ECHR,[81] the constitutional human rights treaty which came about in the bosom of the *Council of Europe*. However, the notion is well established in the case law of the European Court of Human Rights.[82]

Within the Council of Europe, a more specific regulation is concluded, namely the Convention for the Protection of Human Rights and Dignity of

---

against unemployment; (2) Everyone, without any discrimination, has the right to equal pay for equal work; (3) Everyone who works has the right to just and favourable remuneration ensuring for himself and his family an existence worthy of human dignity, and supplemented, if necessary, by other means of social protection; (4) Everyone has the right to form and to join trade unions for the protection of his interests').

80. Universal Declaration on the Human Genome and Human Rights, 11 November 1997 (Available at http://portal.unesco.org/en/ev.php-URL_ID=13177&URL_DO=DO_TOP IC&URL_SECTION=201.html, last visited 11 February 2015).

81. *See*, however, the Protocol to the Convention for the Protection of Human Rights and Fundamental Freedoms concerning the abolition of the death penalty in all circumstances, Vilnius, 3 May 2002 stipulating in its Preamble 'Convinced that everyone's right to life is a basic value in a democratic society and that the abolition of the death penalty is essential for the protection of this right and for the full recognition of the inherent dignity of all human beings' (available at http://www.echr.coe.int/Documents/Convention_ ENG.pdf, last visited February 2015). Also *see* Part I-26 and Article 26 of the ESC-1996, which relates to dignity at work, and is not relevant in the context of the present chapter.

82. *See*, e.g., European Court of Human Rights (ECHR), 22 November 1995 (*S.W. v. United Kingdom*), *Publ. Cont., Series A*, vol. 335-B, § 44, where the Court underlined that 'the abandonment of the unacceptable idea of a husband being immune against prosecution for rape of his wife was in conformity not only with a civilised concept of marriage but also, and above all, with the fundamental objectives of the Convention, the very essence of which is respect for human dignity and human freedom' (available at http:// hudoc.echr.coe.int/sites/fra/pages/search.aspx?i=001-57965, last visited 11 February 2015). Also *see* ECHR, 22 November 1995 (*C.R. v. United Kingdom*), *Publ. Cont., Series A*, vol. 335-C, § 42, etc. (available at http://hudoc.echr.coe.int/sites/fra/pages/search.as px?i=001-57955, last visited 11 February 2015).

the Human Being with regard to the Application of Biology and Medicine of 1997 (Oviedo Convention).[83] The Oviedo Convention announces that 'Convinced of the need to respect the human being both as an individual and as a member of the human species and recognising the importance of ensuring the dignity of the human being' (Preamble), and warns that 'the misuse of biology and medicine may lead to acts endangering human dignity' (Preamble). The Oviedo Convention equally stipulates that signatory states 'shall protect the dignity and identity of all human beings and guarantee everyone, without discrimination, respect for their integrity and other rights and fundamental freedoms with regard to the application of biology and medicine' (Article 1). The Additional Protocol to the Convention on Human Rights and Biomedicine, concerning Genetic Testing for Health Purposes from 2008,[84] reaffirms the fundamental principle of respect for human dignity and the prohibition of all forms of discrimination, in particular those based on genetic characteristics (preamble). The Protocol aims to protect the dignity and identity of all human beings and guarantee everyone, without discrimination, respect for their integrity and other rights and fundamental freedoms with regard to genetic tests (Article 1). Genetic tests are which are carried out for health purposes, involving analysis of biological samples of human origin and aiming specifically to identify the genetic characteristics of a person which are inherited or acquired during early prenatal development (Article 2).

At the *EU* level, the TEU explicitly recognizes human dignity and stipulates: 'The Union is founded on the values of respect for human dignity, freedom, democracy, equality, the rule of law and respect for human rights, including the rights of persons belonging to minorities. These values are common to the Member States in a society in which pluralism, non-discrimination, tolerance, justice, solidarity and equality between women and men prevail' (Article 2).[85]

The notion of human dignity is further implemented *expressis verbis* in the European Charter which recalls that 'Conscious of its spiritual and moral heritage, the Union is founded on the indivisible, universal values of human dignity, freedom, equality and solidarity; it is based on the principles of democracy and the rule of law' (Preamble). The European Charter also

---

83. Convention for the Protection of Human Rights and Dignity of the Human Being with regard to the Application of Biology and Medicine – Convention on Human Rights and Biomedicine, Oviedo, 4 April 1997, entered into force December 1 1999 (available at https://rm.coe.int/CoERMPublicCommonSearchServices/DisplayDCTMContent?docum entId=090000168007cf97, last visited 4 March 2015).
84. Strasbourg, 27 November 2008 available at https://rm.coe.int/CoERMPublicCom monSearchServices/DisplayDCTMContent?documentId=0900001680084816, last visited 4 March 2015).
85. Article 2, TEU (available at http://eur-lex.europa.eu/legal-content/EN/TXT/?uri= CELEX:12012M/TXT, last visited 4 March 2015). The principle of human dignity is further echoed as it relates to an international context in Article 21.

stipulates that 'Human dignity is inviolable. It must be respected and protected' (Article 1). Noteworthy is Article 3, entitled 'Right to the integrity of the person', which stipulates under paragraph (2): 'In the fields of medicine and biology, the following must be respected in particular: (a) … (b) … (c) the prohibition on making the human body and its parts as such a source of financial gain'. The European Charter is legally binding on all members of the EU.

Notwithstanding the unprecedented expansion and ubiquity of particularly human dignity in the human rights discourse, scholars have recently voiced criticism in putting human dignity front and centre. Human dignity is invoked by all sides alike in the debate on genetics, thus neutralizing to some degree its normative function.[86] Furthermore, the meaning of human dignity remains elusive and defies definition, and an increasing 'thinning of the concept of human dignity into an abstract indeterminate concept' can be observed in the wave of bio-rights instruments.[87] Last but not least, the interlocking of different human rights texts and the intricate legal architecture of dual supra-national courts implicated in judicial review of the texts makes for a complex and uncertain legal environment to ascertain the exact meaning and scope of application of 'human dignity' at the European level.[88]

30.4.1.2   In Patent Law

Moving beyond the human dignity discourse and its discontent, we now focus on the relationship between human dignity and patent law. This relationship can be explored from two sides. First, from the *human rights looking at patent law* perspective. Do the surveyed human rights documents say something about human dignity and (the use of) patents? Do human rights texts point to the application of human dignity in patent law and practice or provide instructions or guidelines as to the scope of patent law? On the international level, this seems to be the case. The relationship between human dignity and patent law, and the extent to which the respect for human dignity can limit patent law, was subject of a debate in the UN Committee on Economic Social and Cultural Rights of the United Nations, which monitors

86. T. Cottier, 'Genetic Engineering, Trade and Human Rights', in *Biotechnologies and International Human Rights,* F. Francioni (ed.), Oxford-Portland, Hart Publishing, 2007, (275), 289. Cf. R. Brownsword, 'Ethical Pluralism and the Regulation of Modern Biotechnology', in *Biotechnologies and International Human Rights,* F. Francioni (ed.), Oxford-Portland, Hart Publishing, 2007, 45-70.

87. A. Plomer, 'Human Dignity and Patents', in *Research Handbook on Human Rights and Intellectual Property,* C. Geiger (ed.), Edward Elgar, 2015, 479-495.

88. We fully agree with Plomer on this point. *See* A. Plomer, 'Human Dignity and Patents', in *Research Handbook on Human Rights and Intellectual Property,* C. Geiger (ed.), Edward Elgar, 2015, 479-495.

the International Covenant on Economic, Social and Cultural Rights (ICE-SCR).[89] However, the implementation of the ICESCR was hampered by unclarities about the definition and scope of rights.[90] An attempt to interpret some concepts and the scope of the ICESCR, more, in particular, Article 15 which is highly relevant in the context of the present chapter, the UN Committee issued General Comment No. 17.[91] The Committee confirms that States should prevent the use of scientific and technical progress for purposes contrary to human rights and dignity, including the rights to life, health and privacy, e.g., by excluding inventions from patentability whenever their *commercialization* would jeopardize the full realization of these rights.[92] Although not explicitly referring to patents, the European Charter stands in the same line of thinking, where it prohibits in Article 3(2)(c) making the human body and its parts as such a source of *financial gain*. In contrast, the Oviedo Additional Protocol remains rather silent on this point.[93] In sum, although an analysis of international and European human rights texts does not provide a clear and explicit answer to the question whether or not patents on human genes contravene the principle of human dignity, human rights documents do speak of concepts which are closely intertwined with the essence of patent law, such as commercialization and financial gain when discussing human dignity.

The second point of view is the *patent law looking at human rights/human dignity* perspective. Does patent law say something about human rights? Does patent law point to the existence of human rights in general and human dignity in particular? And here, the answer is yes: patent discourse does refer to human rights principles, even though the connection between patent law and human dignity is quite recent. That should not come as a surprise, as developments in human genetics and subsequent debates on patentability have mainly emerged over the last two decades.

On the European level – within the confines of the *Council of Europe* so to speak, as the EPC has been convened within the Council of Europe – human dignity was introduced in patent law via EPO case law in the relaxin

---

89. Adopted by the General Assembly, Resolution 2200A (XXI) of 16 December 1966, and entered into force on 3 January 1976 (available at http://www.ohchr.org/EN/ProfessionalInterest/Pages/CESCR.aspx, last visited February 11, 2015).

90. *See* P. Alston, 'Out of the Abyss: the Challenges Confronting the New U.N. Committee on Economic, Social and Cultural Rights', *Human Rights Quarterly* (1987): 332-384; A.R. Chapman, 'A "Violations Approach" for Monitoring the International Covenant on Economic, Social and Cultural Rights', *Human Rights Quarterly* (1996): 23-66.

91. General Comment on Article 15(1)(c) of the Covenant (General Comment no. 17), Committee on Economic Social and Cultural Rights, Geneva, 7-25 November 2005, para. 32 [E/C.12/GC/17 12 January 2006] (available at http://www.ohchr.org, last visited February 11, 2015).

92. *Ibid.*, para 35.

93. The present chapter does not further unravel the possible impact of the Protocol on the patent discourse and welcomes further research on this point.

case in 1995,[94] with Article 53(a) EPC serving as the legal gate of entry to introduce human dignity in patent law. From 2004 onwards, human dignity was explicitly brought to the fore again, during the various BRCA proceedings before the EPO.[95] The argument was raised by some of the parties that socio-economic consequences of the patenting of the claimed subject matter should be considered by the Board. The fact that patients, suspected to carry a predisposition to breast cancer, would be faced with severe disadvantages and would become dependent on the patent proprietor, was considered contrary to human dignity. Hence, human gene patents were to be excluded from patent protection on the basis of Article 53(a) EPC.[96] In their epoch-making judgment of 2007, the EPO Technical Board of Appeal argued that 'It is important to note that Article 53(a) EPC refers to the "exploitation of the invention", not about the "exploitation of the patent".'[97] The Board stated that 'No arguments or evidence have been brought forward to the Board showing that the publication or exploitation of the claimed probes, vectors and cells is contrary to "ordre public" or morality'.[98] In other BRCA related cases, the EPO Technical Boards of Appeal followed the same line of reasoning[99] and turned down the human dignity argument.

On the *EU* stage, the notion of human dignity explicitly emerged in patent legislation for the first time in the proposal for an EU Biotechnology

---

94. *See* above.
95. For details of the various proceedings, *see* G. Matthijs, et al., 'The European BRCA Patent Oppositions and Appeals: Coloring Inside the Lines', *Nature Biotechnology* 31 (2013): 704-710.
96. EPO Technical Board of Appeal, 27 September 2007 (T 1213/05) related to European patent with publication number 705902, entitled '17q-Linked breast and ovarian cancer susceptibility gene', point 52 (available at http://www.epo.org/law-practice/case-law-appeals/advanced-search.html, last visited 17 March 2015).
97. *Ibid.*, point 53.
98. *Ibid.*, point 56.
99. Cf. EPO Technical Board of Appeal, 13 November 2008 (T 0666/05) related to European patent with publication number 705903, entitled 'Mutations in the 17q-linked breast and ovarian cancer susceptibility gene', where it was stated: 'This Board, in a different composition, already in decision T 1213/05 (*supra*) has dealt with the socio-economic and ethical consequences of the patenting of diagnostic methods involving the use of human genetic material. The Board in the present composition follows decision T 1213/05 (*supra, see* especially points (52) and (53)) and, on this basis, rejects Opponents' objection under Article 53(a) EPC' (point 82). Cf. EPO Technical Board of Appeal, 19 November 2008 (T 0080/05) related to European patent with publication number 699754, entitled 'Method for diagnosing a predisposition for breast and ovarian cancer', where it was said: 'This Board, in a different composition, already in decision T 1213/05 (*supra*) has dealt with the socio-economic and ethical consequences of the patenting of diagnostic methods involving the use of human genetic material. The Board in the present composition follows decision 1213/05 (*supra, see* especially points (52) and (53)) and, on this basis, rejects Respondent IV's objection under Article 53(a) EPC' (point 65). (All decisions are available at http://www.epo.org/law-practice/case-law-appeals/advanced-search.html, last visited 17 March 2015).

Directive in 1988.[100] Conceived as being against *ordre public* and morality as laid down in Article 53(a) EPC, the proposal stated that 'processes for modifying the genetic identity of the human body for a non-therapeutic purpose which is contrary to the dignity of man' are unpatentable (an implicit reference to cloning, chimera production, etc.). The provision was implemented to preserve human genetic integrity, and more in particular, in an attempt to exclude the patenting of processes eliminating flaws or enhancing human potential (eugenics) making use of patented gene sequences. The notion was also implemented in the final EU Biotechnology Directive of 1998,[101] yet only as a recital. Recital 16 stipulates that 'patent law must be applied so as to respect the fundamental principles safeguarding the dignity and integrity of the person' and that 'it is important to assert the principle that the human *body*, at any stage in its formation or development, cannot be patented'. In turn, recital 38 echoes the first proposal and underlines that 'processes, the use of which offend against human dignity, such as processes to produce chimeras from germ cells or totipotent cells of humans and animals, are obviously also excluded from patentability'. That the formal reference to the principle of respect for human dignity is made in a Directive on patents, can be seen as an indication of the concern aroused by developments in the fields of human genetics and medicine. However, its scope of application is narrow, as it mainly focuses on experiments revolving around the human body, rather than on the use of elements of the human body such as genes outside of the context of human enhancement and/or eugenics.

In the run-up for the EU Biotechnology Directive, the link between human dignity and patent law was also explored in depth by the European Group on Ethics in Science and New Technologies (EGE),[102] and its predecessor, the Group of advisers to the European Commission on the ethical implications of biotechnology (GAEIB). The task of the Group is to examine ethical questions arising from science and new technologies and on

---

100. Proposal for a Council Directive on the legal protection of biotechnological inventions, October 1988, *Official Journal EC C,* 13 January 1989, 10/3. The proposal was eventually rejected by the European Parliament on 1 March 1995 (*see Official Journal EC C,* 20 March 1995, 68/26).
101. Directive 98/44/EC of 6 July 1998 of the European Parliament and of the Council on the legal protection of biotechnological inventions, *Official Journal EC L* 213/13 of 30/07/1998 13 (available at (available at http://eur-lex.europa.eu/legal-content/EN/TXT/?uri=CELEX:31998L0044, last visited 11 February 2015).
102. The EGE is a neutral, independent, pluralist and multidisciplinary body, composed of experts appointed by the Commission for their expertise and personal qualities, representing a broad range of professional competences in different disciples such as, biology and genetics, medicine, pharmacology, agricultural sciences, ICT, law, ethics, philosophy, and theology. For further information, *see* http://erawatch.jrc.ec.europa.eu/erawatch/opencms/information/country_pages/eu/euorganisation/europeanorg_mig_0043 (last visited 8 February 2015). Also consult http://ec.europa.eu/archives/bepa/european-group-ethics/index_en.htm (last visited 8 February 2015).

this basis to issue Opinions to the European Commission in connection with the preparation and implementation of Community legislation or policies. Examining the various opinions of the GAEIB/EGE clearly demonstrates that this advisory body supports the integration of a human rights approach in patent law, especially in the context of human genetics. In its first Opinion on this issue (Opinion 3 of 1993),[103] the GAEIB admitted that in pursuit of its economic and social objectives, it is essential for the Community to harmonize patent law relating to biotechnology. The GAEIB underlined that the need to protect human dignity does not contravene patenting, in the sense that 'there are no ethical objections to the patenting of biotechnological inventions per se'.[104] However, 'genes and partial gene sequences whose functions are unknown should be made expressly unpatentable to end the international debate on the matter'.[105] In its second opinion on this topic (Opinion 8 of 1996),[106] the GAEIB brings to mind Article F(2) of the Treaty on European Union,[107] underlining that 'The Union shall respect fundamental rights, as guaranteed by the European Convention for the Protection of Human Rights and Fundamental Freedoms signed in Rome on 4 November 1950 and as they result from the constitutional traditions common to the Member States, as general principles of Community law'.[108] In the same Opinion, the GAEIB underlines that the EU Biotechnology Directive takes place in an aim to actualize and adapt patent law to the specific case of biotechnological inventions which, when they are based on elements of human origin, involve the issue of fundamental rights of the human person. More, in particular, the GAEIB takes the view that whatever is the nature of the biotechnological invention involving elements of human origin, the Directive must give sufficient guarantee so that refusal to grant a patent on an invention in so far as it infringes the rights of the person and the respect of human dignity should be legally founded.[109] The affirmation of citizens' rights in the European Union implies that the economic advantages derived

---

103. GAEIB, Opinion no. 3, 30 September 1993, *Ethical Questions Arising from the Commission Proposal for a Council Directive on Legal Protection for Biotechnological Inventions, Referring to Article F2 of the Treaty of the European Union* (available at http://ec.europa.eu/archives/bepa/european-group-ethics/docs/opinion3_en.pdf, last visited 8 February 2015).
104. GAEIB, Opinion no. 3 – Part III. Opinion.
105. *Ibid.*
106. GAEIB, Opinion no. 8, 25 September 1996, *Ethical Aspects of Patenting Inventions Involving Elements of Human Origin,* para. 1.6. (available at http://ec.europa.eu/archives/bepa/european-group-ethics/docs/opinion8_en.pdf, last visited 8 February 2015).
107. GAEIB, Opinion no. 8, Preamble: 'Having regard to the Article F2 (Human Rights) to the Common Provisions of the Treaty on European Union'.
108. Article F(2) of the Treaty on European Union, *Official Journal of the EC C,* 191, 29 July 1992, pp. 1-112 (available at http://eur-lex.europa.eu/legal-content/EN/TXT/?uri=CELEX:11992M/TXT, last visited 10 March 2015).
109. GAEIB, Opinion no. 8, para. 2.1.

from biotechnological developments should in no way affect the respect for ethical requirements.[110] Reference is explicitly made to the respect for human rights and fundamental freedoms,[111] the respect for 'fundamental rights of the human person'[112] and respect for human dignity.[113]

Let us now cast a look on legal doctrine and the thorny issue of human dignity and patent law Article 53(a) EPC set a lot of academic tongues wagging. There is relative consensus about the fact that Article 53(a) EPC provides the legal basis for the EPO to act as a 'moral tollbooth'[114] or a 'moral censor',[115] and to carry out an ethical assessment. However, there is wide disagreement on the exact interpretation and scope of Article 53(a) EPC and the subsequent ethical assessment. One stream of legal doctrine – most recently supported by high-level case law, albeit in a case on human stem cells, rather than on human gene patents[116] – often seems to read Article 53(a) EPC as meaning that an *invention* which runs counter to *ordre public* and morality should be excluded, thus providing a pretty wide gate of entry for ethical considerations. Another – minority – string of academic literature stresses that it is only when the *commercial exploitation* of an invention runs counter to *ordre public* and morality, the invention should be excluded from patent protection,[117] thus suggesting a rather narrow gate of entry.[118] As we

110. GAEIB, Opinion no. 8, para. 2.7.
111. GAEIB, Opinion no. 3, 30 September 1993, *Ethical Questions Arising from the Commission Proposal for a Council Directive on Legal Protection for Biotechnological Inventions, Referring to Article F2 of the Treaty of the European Union* (available at http://ec.europa.eu/archives/bepa/european-group-ethics/docs/opinion3_en.pdf, last visited 8 February 2015).
112. GAEIB, Opinion no. 8, 25 September 1996, *Ethical Aspects of Patenting Inventions Involving Elements of Human Origin,* para. 1.6 (available at http://ec.europa.eu/archives/bepa/european-group-ethics/docs/opinion8_en.pdf, last visited 8 February 2015).
113. GAEIB, Opinion no. 3, para. 2.2.3; GAEIB, Opinion no. 8, para. 2.1; EGE, Opinion no. 16, 7 May 2002, *Ethical Aspects of Patenting Inventions Involving Human Stem Cells,* referring to Article 1 of the European Charter (*see* http://ec.europa.eu/archives/bepa/european-group-ethics/docs/avis16_en.pdf, last visited 8 February 2015).
114. R.E. Gold, 'The Moral Tollbooth: a Method that Makes Use of the Patent System to Address Ethical Concerns in Biotechnology', *The Lancet* 359 (29 June 2002): 2268-2270.
115. *See* S. Sterckx & J. Cockbain, *Exclusions from Patentability. How Far Has the European Patent Office Eroded Boundaries,* Cambridge University Press, 2012, 289-290.
116. *See* the judgment of the Court of Justice of the European Union (Grand Chamber) in the in the famous Brüstle case, 18 October 2011 (Case C-34/10) (Reference for a preliminary ruling under Article 267 TFEU from the Bundesgerichtshof, Germany, made by decision of 17 December 2009, received at the Court on 21 January 2010) (available at http://curia.europa.eu, last visited 4 March 2015).
117. In the same sense, *see* R. Moufang, 'The Concept of "Ordre Public" and Morality in Patent Law', in *Octrooirecht, ethiek en biotechnologie – Patent Law, Ethics and Biotechnology,* G. Van Overwalle (ed.), Brussel, Bruylant, 1998, 63-77; R. Moufang, 'Patenting of Human Genes, Cells and Parts of the Body – the Ethical Dimension of Patent Law', *International Review of Intellectual Property and Competition Law* (1994): 487-515.
118. For an excellent analysis of the scope of the concept of 'commercial exploitation' in Article 53 (a) EPC, and an overview of arguments supporting either a broad or narrow

have argued before,[119] rather than an invitation to look backwards (how was the invention developed? what happened exactly during the research leading to the invention?), Article 53(a) EPC invites us to look forward (how will the invention be valorized? what is the impact of the commercial exploitation?)

In that regard, questions about the compatibility of human gene patents and human dignity, should not focus on the conflict between human dignity and scientific research but should focalize on the possible conflict between human dignity and the commercial exploitation of that research via patents. The discussion on the legitimacy of research should be clearly distinguished from the debate on the legitimacy of appropriating rights, such as patents, on the results of that research. Or as Plomer states, solving questions on the moral permissibility of research in the field of human genetics on the back of patent law, and letting patent tribunals and courts – in particular the Court of Justice of the EU – imposing their view on research when called to judge on patents, is a worrying development.[120]

When applying a forward-looking (patent) oriented approach, rather than a backward-looking (research) oriented interpretation of Article 53(a) EPC, and subsuming the commercial exploitation of research results under the commercial exploitation of a patent, Article 3(2)(c) European Charter – which prohibits making the human body and its *parts* as such a source of financial gain – appears to be highly relevant.

We develop our thinking on the relationship between Article 53(a) EPC and Article 3(2)(c) European Charter in two steps. In a first step, we assess Article 3(2)(c) European Charter in the wider context of patent law, more in particular in view of the narrative underlying the rationale of patent law. At first sight, Article 3(2)(c) of the European Charter and patent law seem opposed to one another, but on closer inspection, they are not. The major

---

perspective, *see* Hellstadius, Å., *A Quest for Clarity. Reconstructing Standards for the Patent Law Morality Exclusion* (PhD Stockholm University), Stockholm, April 2015.

119. *See* G. Van Overwalle, 'Legal and Ethical Aspects of Bio-Patenting: Critical Analysis of the EU Biotechnology Directive', in *Death of Patents*, P. Drahos (ed.), Oxon, Lawtext Publishing, 2005, 212-227. In this chapter, we argued that Article 6(2) EU Biotechnology Directive does not seem to aim at limiting the *patent* implications of certain biotech inventions, but wishes to exclude certain fields of *research* as such. We took the view there – as we do here – that patent law should take into account ethical concerns and that patent law can and should act as a 'moral tollbooth' (dixit R.E. Gold, 'The Moral Tollbooth: A Method that Makes Use of the Patent System to Address Ethical Concerns in Biotechnology', 359 *The Lancet*, 29 June 2002, 2268-2270), but that patent law should only do so to the extent that it concerns matters which are directly and inextricably linked with *patents* and the exercise of patents; patent law should not interfere when *research* is ethically undesirable. Since a direct link is missing between ethics and patents in Article 6(2), we defended the view that this provision had to be abolished and that the exclusions had to be treated in research regulations.

120. A. Plomer, 'Human Dignity and Patents', in *Research Handbook on Human Rights and Intellectual Property*, C. Geiger (ed.), Edward Elgar, 2015, 479-495.

objective of IP law in general, and patent law in particular, is to offer protection to the inventor against free riding and to encourage the development and disclosure of knowledge and innovation with a view to fostering scientific, technical and social progress in the interest of society at large. In order to pursue this objective, inventors are given the opportunity to recoup their investments by way of a patent right.[121] Patent law institutionalizes patents as an instrument for the right holder to recover his investments in research and development. The underlying idea is that without this exclusive right, inventors would not be encouraged to make such investments.[122] Financial motives are seen as a very important factor that thrives innovation: in patent law thinking the dominating motivation for innovation seems to be profit-making;[123] in other words: patent law puts the profit motive front and centre.[124] Comparing the underlying rationale of patent law and Article 3(2)(c) of the European Charter may lead to the conclusion that patents on human genes should be prohibited, as they may aim at and result in financial gain, either by exploiting the invention or permitting others to exploit the invention in return for royalties. However, patent law allows but does not force a patent holder to aim for financial gain by commercializing his/her patent. Pursuing financial gain is left to the discretion of the patent holder. One can imagine an inventor applying for patent protection, and then dedicating his/her invention to the public domain. When applying such a line of action, patents would not be compromising the prohibition of financial gain as laid down in Article 3(2)(c) of the European Charter.

In a second step, we compare Article 3(2)(c) of the European Charter with Article 53(a) EPC. At first sight, Article 3(2)(c) of the European Charter and Article 53(a) EPC seem quite different and might have a distinct impact in the field of human genetics, but in the end, the difference is not that relevant. Article 3(2)(c) of the European Charter suggests that *any* commercialization of human genetic material implying financial gain is prohibited, whereas Article 53(a) EPC states that *only* when the commercial exploitation of an invention relating to human genetic material runs counter to *ordre public* and morality, patent protection should be prohibited. On the one hand,

---

121. *See* G. Van Overwalle & E. van Zimmeren, 'Functions and Limits of Patent Law', in *Facing the Limits of the Law*, E. Claes, W. Devroe & B. Keirsbilck (eds), Berlin-Heidelberg, Springer, 2009, 415-442 and the references cited there.

122. Economic studies on this presumption are, however, inconclusive. In fact, the effect of patents on innovation and diffusion depends on particular features of the *patent regime*. *See* for a brief explanation: OECD, *Patents and Innovation: Trends and Policy Changes* (Paris: OECD, 2004) (available at http://www.oecd.org/dataoecd/48/12/24508541.pdf) 9-10.

123. In the same sense, R. Moufang, 'Patenting of Human Genes, Cells and Parts of the Body – the Ethical Dimension of Patent Law', *International Review of Intellectual Property and Competition Law* (1994): 504.

124. Cf. G. Van Overwalle, 'Inventing Inclusive Patents. From Old to New Open Innovation', *Kritika: Essays on Intellectual Property*, vol. 1, P. Drahos, G. Ghidini & H. Ullrich (eds), Edward Elgar, 2015, 206-277.

the European Charter seems more stringent and allows less room to allow for patents than the EPC. But, in light of the discretion of a patent holder to commercialize his/her invention or not,[125] it is difficult to argue that those provisions provide a stable and undisputed basis to exclude patents for human genes as a matter of principle. On the other hand, it does follow crystal clear from both these Articles that when patents are taken with no intent for financial gain – e.g., to apply a sharing ethos and to serve as a legal basis to establish copyleft like licenses,[126] or to dedicate the invention to the public domain – patents are not to be prohibited. Only, and only when it can be ascertained that the commercial exploitation will run counter to *ordre public* and morality, only then, the invention should be denied patent protection. Admittedly, it is quite difficult to predict at the moment of the application of the patent, what kind of valorization strategy will be applied. Hence, without a preview of the future, it is almost impossible to apply Article 53(a) EPC adequately.

More theoretical reflection and academic inquiry would be welcome to study the relationship between Article 3(2)(c) of the European Charter and Article 53(a) EPC, and their impact on the patenting of human genetic material. In the unlikely case that the outcome of that research would point out that the EU equivalent of Article 53(a) EPC, namely Article 6(1) of the EU Biotechnology Directive,[127] is not in line with Article 3(2)(c) of the European Charter, the annulment of the EU Biotechnology Directive could be considered on the basis of Article 263 TFEU.

---

125. In this regard, it is important to bring to mind the essence of the contemporary definition of a patent right, which can be found in international and domestic legislation, and which is widely commented upon in basic IP textbooks: a patent is not circumscribed as a *positive* right to *exploit,* but as a *negative* right to *stop* others from using or making the patented invention. *See,* e.g., Article 28 TRIPS Agreement, entitled 'Rights Conferred': '1. A patent shall confer on its owner the following exclusive rights: (a) where the subject matter of a patent is a product, to prevent third parties not having the owner's consent from the acts of: making, using, offering for sale, selling, or importing for these purposes that product'. This reasoning explains the reluctant position of the EPO Technical Boards of Appeal in denying certain inventions patent protection. In the same sense, S. Sterckx & J. Cockbain, *Exclusions from Patentability. How Far Has the European Patent Office Eroded Boundaries,* Cambridge University Press, 2012, 289-291.
126. *See* G. Van Overwalle, 'Inventing Inclusive Patents. From Old to New Open Innovation', *Kritika: Essays on Intellectual Property,* vol. 1, P. Drahos, G. Ghidini & H. Ullrich (eds), Edward Elgar, 2015, 206-277.
127. Article 6 (1) reads as follows: 'Inventions shall be considered unpatentable where their commercial exploitation would be contrary to ordre public or morality; however, exploitation shall not be deemed to be so contrary merely because it is prohibited by law or regulation'.

30.4.2.1   In General

In human rights literature pertaining to diagnostic testing and further research and development, the right to informed consent is widely discussed.[129] On an international level consensus is growing that sources of tissue should consent to the secondary use of their tissue.[130] However, opinions differ on how the right to informed consent should be qualified. One school of thought claims that the right to informed consent is an accessory right of another – fundamental – human right, more, in particular, the prohibition of torture and inhuman or degrading treatment or punishment. This – major – right is guaranteed in the UDHR, which proclaims that 'no one shall be subjected to torture or to cruel, inhuman or degrading treatment or punishment' (Article 5). In the same line of reasoning, the ICCPR proclaims that 'no one shall be subjected to torture or to cruel, inhuman or degrading treatment or punishment', and that in particular 'no one shall be subjected without his free consent to medical or scientific experimentation' (Article 7). The prohibition of torture is also articulated in the ECHR,[131] which states that 'no one shall be subjected to torture or to inhuman or degrading treatment or punishment' (Article 3). The right is equally expressed in the European Charter, stating that 'no one shall be subjected to torture or to inhuman or degrading treatment or punishment' (Article 4).

     Other human rights scholars take the view that the right to informed consent is an accessory right of the right for respect of physical integrity, which is, for example, proclaimed in the European Charter: '1. Everyone has the right to respect for his or her physical and mental integrity; 2. In the fields of medicine and biology, the following must be respected in particular: (a) the free and informed consent of the person concerned, according to the procedures laid down by law, (b) the prohibition of eugenic practices, in particular those aiming at the selection of persons, (c) the prohibition on making the human body and its parts as such a source of financial gain, and (d) the prohibition of the reproductive cloning of human beings' (Article 3).

---

128. This section is largely based on G. Van Overwalle, 'Human Rights' Limitations in Patent Law', in *Intellectual Property and Human Rights. A Paradox,* W. Grosheide (ed.), Cheltenham, Edward Elgar, 2010, 236-271.
129. For further information on this issue, the interested reader might turn to C. Trouet, *Van lichaam naar lichaamsmateriaal. Recht en het nader gebruik van cellen en weefsels,* Intersentia, 2003 and the references cited there. Also *see,* C. Trouet, 'Informed Consent for the Research Use of Human Biological Materials', *Medical Law* 22, no. 3 (2003): 411-419.
130. *See* C. Trouet, 'Informed Consent for the Research Use of Human Biological Materials', *Medical Law* 22, no. 3 (2003): 411-419.
131. Rome, 4 November 1950 (available at http://www.echr.coe.int/Documents/Convention_ENG.pdf, last visited 11 February 2015).

Yet another school of thought claims that the right to informed consent is an accessory right of the right to respect for his or her private and family life, home and communications (Article 7 European Charter), the latter right implying respect for physical integrity and personal autonomy.[132]

Not awaiting the outcome of academic debates on the exact legal basis of the right to informed consent, this right has been given an autonomous basis in the context of human health and genetics in the Oviedo Convention, which stipulates that 'An intervention in the health field may only be carried out after the person concerned has given free and informed consent to it. This person shall beforehand be given appropriate information as to the purpose and nature of the intervention as well as on its consequences and risks. The person concerned may freely withdraw consent at any time' (Article 5). Furthermore, the Oviedo Convention stipulates that 'When in the course of an intervention any part of a human body is removed, it may be stored and used for a purpose other than that for which it was removed, only if this is done in conformity with appropriate information and consent procedures' (Article 22). As was equally demonstrated in US case law, more in particular in the trendsetting *Moore* case, sources of human biological materials have a right to informed consent on the further use of their bodily material.[133]

30.4.2.2   In Patent Law

The link between the right to informed consent and patent law is quite recent. The debate emerged at the event of modern medicine, as new medical developments have increased the use of human tissue and encompassing human genes, especially for research purposes and subsequent innovation. Various patent legislators tried to give something to hold on to people, who in the framework of diagnosis or treatment, give body material, which material is subsequently being used for scientific research and forms the basis of a new drug or therapy, for which patent protection is requested and granted. Most prominent in this regard, is recital 26 of the EU Biotechnology Directive stipulating that 'if an invention is based on biological material of human origin or if it uses such material, where a patent application is filed, the person from whose body the material is taken must have had an opportunity of expressing free and informed consent thereto, in accordance with national law'. Recital 26 attempts to embed the general principle of free and informed consent of the donor of body material as proclaimed in Article 22 of the Oviedo Convention, in the context of biotech-patenting.[134]

---

132. Cf. C. Trouet, *Van lichaam naar lichaamsmateriaal. Recht en het nader gebruik van cellen en weefsels*, Intersentia, 2003, 503 p.

133. *John Moore v. The Regents of the University of California*, Supreme Court of California, decided 9 July 1990, 793, *P2d*, 479.

134. Article 22 (Disposal of a Removed Part of the Human Body): 'When in the course of an intervention any part of a human body is removed, it may be stored and used for a

Discussions emerged on the binding nature of recital 26 on national authorities in the EU Member States.[135] In the past, the EGE[136] has already explicitly expressed the view that the ethical principle of informed and free consent of the person from whom retrievals are performed, must be respected. The EGE has underlined that this principle includes that the information of this person is complete and specific, in particular on the potential patent application on the invention which could be made from the use of this element. An invention based on the use of elements of human origin, having been retrieved without respecting the principle of consent will not fulfil the ethical requirements.[137] In addition, the Council of Europe has issued an Additional Protocol relating to the informed consent requirement in the framework of the use of human tissue outside the traditional physician-patient relationship (so-called further use), e.g., in the framework of scientific research.[138] Free and informed consent is also required in those circumstances[139] on the basis of the right to dignity and integrity.[140] Informed

purpose other than that for which it was removed, only if this is done in conformity with appropriate information and consent procedures.'

135. *See* G. Van Overwalle, 'Legal and Ethical Aspects of Bio-Patenting: Critical Analysis of the EU Biotechnology Directive', in *Death of Patents,* P. Drahos (ed.), Oxon, Lawtext Publishing, 2005, 212-227.
136. On the EGE and its predecessor, the GAEIB, *see* above.
137. GAEIB, Opinion no. 8, 25 September 1996, *Ethical Aspects of Patenting Inventions Involving Elements of Human Origin,* para. 1.6 (available at http://ec.europa.eu/archives/bepa/european-group-ethics/docs/opinion8_en.pdf, last visited 8 February 2015).
138. Council of Europe, Additional Protocol to the Convention on Human Rights and Biomedicine, Concerning Biomedical Research, Strasbourg, 25 January 2005, *European Treaties Series,* no. 195 (available at http://conventions.coe.int/Treaty/en/Treaties/Html/195.htm, last visited 11 February 2015). The Additional Protocol entered into force on 1 September 2007 (*see* http://conventions.coe.int/Treaty/Commun/ChercheSig.asp?NT=195&CM=&DF=&CL=ENG, last visited 18 February 2015). Also *see* Council of Europe, Steering Committee on Bioethics, Explanatory report to the Additional Protocol to the Convention on Human Rights and Biomedicine, Concerning Biomedical Research, Strasbourg, 25 January 2005 (available at http://conventions.coe.int/Treaty/EN/Reports/Html/195.htm, last visited 11 February 2015). Similarly, Council of Europe, Recommendation Rec(2006)4 of the Committee of Ministers to Member States on research on biological materials of human origin, 15 March 2006 (available at http://www.coe.int/t/dg3/healthbioethic/texts_and_documents/Rec_2006_4.pdf, last visited 11 February 2015).
139. *See* Article 14 (1) of the Protocol: 'No research on a person may be carried out, without the informed, free, express, specific and documented consent of the person'; *See* Article 10 (2) of Recommendation 2006(4): 'Information and consent or authorisation to obtain such materials should be as specific as possible with regard to any foreseen research uses and the choices available in that respect'.
140. *See* Article 1 of the Protocol: 'Parties shall protect the dignity and identity of all human beings and guarantee everyone, without discrimination, respect for their integrity and other rights and fundamental freedoms with regard to any research involving interventions on human beings in the field of biomedicine'. *See* the Preamble of Recommendation 2006(4): 'Biomedical research that is contrary to human dignity and human rights

consent is also required for any foreseen potential further uses, including commercial uses, of the research results, data or biological materials.[141] In 2001, the Court of Justice of the European Communities (CJEC) voiced the view that reliance on the fundamental right of human integrity was 'clearly misplaced as against a directive which concerns only the grant of patents and whose scope does not, therefore, extend to activities before and after that grant, whether they involve research or the use of the patented products'.[142] The Court furthermore stated that '[t]he grant of a patent does not preclude legal limitations or prohibitions applying to research into patentable products or the exploitation of patented products, as the 14th recital of the Preamble to the Directive points out. The purpose of the Directive is not to replace the restrictive provisions which guarantee, outside the scope of the Directive, compliance with certain ethical rules which include the right to self-determination by informed consent.'[143]

In 2007, the EPO dealt with a similar argument in one of the BRCA cases and stated that 'the EPC contains no provision establishing a

---

should never be carried out'. For more, *see* C. Trouet, 'New European Guidelines for the Use of Stored Human Biological Materials in Biomedical Research', *Journal of Medical Ethics* (2004): 99-103.

141. *See* Article 13.2.vii of the Protocol, which stipulates: '2. The information [for research participants] shall cover the purpose, the overall plan and the possible risks and benefits of the research project, and include the opinion of the ethics committee. Before being asked to consent to participate in a research project, the persons concerned shall be specifically informed, according to the nature and purpose of the research: ... *vii. of any foreseen potential further uses, including commercial uses, of the research results, data or biological materials'* (My Italics). Also Article 13, Nr. 74 of the Memorandum of the Protocol, stipulating that 'indent vii [of Article 13 § 2] requires the researcher to disclose to the potential participant any foreseen commercial use of data, research results or biological materials to be obtained from the potential participant during, or prior to, the research. The requirement in this indent does not reflect any endorsement or condemnation of research conducted with commercial applications in mind. Rather, it acknowledges the fact that the motivation for participation in biomedical research for many persons may be out of solidarity, and information on foreseen commercial uses of their contribution to the research may be important to them in making a decision on whether to take part or not. Additionally, *recital 26 of Directive 98/44/EC of the European Parliament and of the Council of 6 July 1998 on the legal protection of biotechnological inventions states that* whereas if an invention is based on biological material of human origin or if it uses such material, where a patent application is filed, the person from whose body the material is taken must have had an opportunity of expressing free and informed consent thereto, in accordance with national law' (My Italics).

142. Court of Justice of the European Communities, 9 October 2001 (Case C-377/98) concerning the application for annulment of the EU Biotechnology Directive by the Kingdom of the Netherlands, supported by Italy and Norway (document D174) (point (79).

143. *Ibid.*, (point (80).

requirement for applicants to submit evidence of a previous informed consent or a benefit-sharing agreement'.[144]

One can argue that informed consent is also required for patenting, which falls under commercialization. The Additional Protocol to the Convention on Human Rights and Biomedicine, Concerning Biomedical Research holds a great attraction to apply the free and informed consent in the context of the application for a patent on human genes. However, given the negative attitude of both the EPO Boards of Appeal and the CJEC towards integrating an informed consent requirement in patent law[145] and the fact that implementation of an effectively informed consent requirement in the context of patent applications might prove to be rather cumbersome in daily clinical practice, it may take some time before this requirement will be turned into action.

30.4.3   Right of Access to Health Care

30.4.3.1   In General

The right of access to health care is a fundamental principle that is traditionally qualified as a socio-economic right.[146] However, some authors suggest that the right to health care falls under the right to human dignity.[147] The present chapter opts for the first view and will examine the right of access to health care as an autonomous human right.

The right to access to health (care) often also covers the right to access to medicines: the specific discussion on access to medicines is usually conceived as a component of the right to health (care).[148] Closely related to the debate on the right to health (care), is the discussion on the right to *equal* access to health care. The latter aspect will not be dealt with here.[149]

The right of access to health care is proclaimed at the international level in the UDHR, which stipulates that 'Everyone has the right to a standard of

---

144. EPO Technical Board of Appeal, 27 September 2007 (T 1213/05) related to European patent with publication number 705902, entitled '17q-Linked breast and ovarian cancer susceptibility gene' (point 48).
145. *See* their decisions in the relaxin and the BRCA case, above.
146. *See* H. Brennan, R. Distler, M. Hinman & A. Rogers, 'A Human Rights Approach to Intellectual Property and Access to Medicines', *Yale Law School and Yale School of Public Health Global Health Justice Partnership Policy Paper, No 1.,* August 2013 (available at http://papers.ssrn.com, last visited 4 March 2015).
147. *See* J. Pila, 'Intellectual Property Rights and Detached Human Body Parts', *Journal of Medical Ethics* 40 (2014): 27-32.
148. *See* H. Brennan, R. Distler, M. Hinman & A. Rogers, 'A Human Rights Approach to Intellectual Property and Access to Medicines', *Yale Law School and Yale School of Public Health Global Health Justice Partnership Policy Paper, No 1.,* August 2013 (available at http://papers.ssrn.com, last visited 4 March 2015).
149. For an interesting and in-depth analysis, *see* M. San Giorgi, *The Human Right to Equal Access to Health Care,* Intersentia, 2012.

living adequate for the health and well-being of himself and of his family, including food, clothing, housing and medical care' (Article 25(1)). The right is equally guaranteed in the ICESCR, which claims that '1. The States Parties to the present Covenant recognize the right of everyone to the enjoyment of the highest attainable standard of physical and mental health' (Article 12). States are, therefore, required to strike an adequate balance between the effective protection of the moral and material interests of authors and States parties' obligations in relation to the right to health.[150]

At the European level, the right to health (care) was not stipulated in the ECHR but was taken up both in the ESC-1961 and the reviewed ESC-1996. The latter sets forth: 'Everyone has the right to benefit from any measures enabling him to enjoy the highest possible standard of health attainable' (Preamble, Part 1-11). The ESC-1996 further stipulates: 'With a view to ensuring the effective exercise of the right to protection of health, the Parties undertake, either directly or in co-operation with public or private organizations, to take appropriate measures designed *inter alia*: (1) to remove as far as possible the causes of ill-health; (2) to provide advisory and educational facilities for the promotion of health and the encouragement of individual responsibility in matters of health; (3) to prevent as far as possible epidemic, endemic and other diseases, as well as accidents' (Article 11). Closely related to the right to protection of health, is the right to access to health care, equally proclaimed in ESC-1996, and setting forth that 'Anyone without adequate resources has the right to social and medical assistance' (Preamble Part 1-13). The Preamble is further elaborated in Article 13, entitled 'The right to social and medical assistance', which sets forth: 'With a view to ensuring the effective exercise of the right to social and medical assistance, the Parties undertake: (1) to ensure that any person who is without adequate resources and who is unable to secure such resources either by his own efforts or from other sources, in particular by benefits under a social security scheme, be granted adequate assistance, and, in case of sickness, the care necessitated by his condition; [...]'.

In the same vein, the Oviedo Convention takes the right to health to heart in putting forward that 'Parties, taking into account health needs and available resources, shall take appropriate measures with a view to providing, within their jurisdiction, equitable access to health care of appropriate quality' (Article 3).

At the *EU* level, the TFEU states that the Union shall have the competence to carry out actions to support, coordinate or supplement the actions of the Member States, and more, in particular, the protection and improvement of human health (Article 6(a)). The TFEU equally stipulates that in defining and implementing its policies and activities, the Union shall take into account 'requirements linked to the promotion of a high level of employment, the guarantee of adequate social protection, the fight against

---

150. General Comment no. 17, 2005, para. 39 (e) (*see* above).

social exclusion, and a high level of education, training and protection of human health' (Article 9). The TFEU further underlines in a specific title devoted to public health, that a high level of human health protection shall be ensured in the definition and implementation of all Union policies and activities (Article 168(1)). Last but not least, the TFEU declares that Union policy on the environment shall contribute to the pursuit of the objectives of preserving, protecting and improving the quality of the environment, and the protection of human health (Article 191(1)).

In contrast to the TFEU, which remains rather silent with regard to the particular right of access to health care, the European Charter clearly stipulates that 'Everyone has the right of access to preventive health care and the right to benefit from medical treatment under the conditions established by national laws and practices. A high level of human health protection shall be ensured in the definition and implementation of all the Union's policies and activities' (Article 35).

30.4.3.2   In Patent Law

On the global level, the relationship between the right of access to human health (care) and patent law has recently been formally recognized in the TRIPS Agreement.[151] The TRIPS Agreement clearly stipulates in Article 8(1) that Members may, in formulating or amending their laws and regulations, adopt measures necessary to protect public health and nutrition, and to

---

151. A cascade of academic papers and books has emerged on the relation between the right to health and patent law, in particular the TRIPS Agreement, with a focus on developing countries. The interested reader might care to consult R. Abbott, 'Balancing Access and Innovation in India's Shifting IP Regime', *Whittier Law Review* 35 (2014): 341 (available at http://papers.ssrn.com, last visited 4 March 2015); H. Brennan, R. Distler, M. Hinman & A. Rogers, 'A Human Rights Approach to Intellectual Property and Access to Medicines', *Yale Law School and Yale School of Public Health Global Health Justice Partnership Policy Paper, No 1.,* August 2013 (available at http://papers.ssrn.com, last visited 4 March 2015); C. Chamas, B. Prickil & J.D. Sarnoff, 'Intellectual Property and Medicine: Towards Global Health Equity', in *Intellectual Property and Human Development. Current Trends and Future Scenarios,* T. Wong & G. Dutfield (eds), Cambridge, Cambridge University Press, 2011; include E.R. Gold, 'Patents and Human Rights: A Heterodox Analysis', *Global Health and the Law* (Spring 2013): 185-198 and the references cited there (in particular footnotes 10-16); N. Kaur, 'Understanding Patent Law from a Human Rights Perspective', 12 May 2013 (available at http://papers.ssrn.com, last visited 4 March 2015); W.P. Nagan, 'International Intellectual Property, Access to Health Care, and Human Rights: South Africa v. United States,' *Florida Journal of International Law* 14, no. 2 (2002): 155-191; G. Shaffer & S.K. Sell, 'Transnational Legal Ordering and Access to Medicines', in in *Patent Law in Global Perspective,* R.L. Okediji & M.A. Bagley (eds), Oxford, Oxford University Press, 2014; J.A. Sellin, *Access to Medicines: The Interface Between Patents and Human Rights. Does One Size Fit All?*, in *School of Human Rights Research,* Intersentia, 2014.

promote the public interest in sectors of vital importance to their socio-economic and technological development, provided that such measures are consistent with the provisions of the Agreement. Furthermore, the Doha Ministerial Declaration of 14 November 2001, explicitly stipulates that the TRIPS Agreement can be implemented and interpreted in a manner supportive of public health, by promoting both access to existing medicines and research and development into new medicines.[152]

One measure to safeguard public health from the potential hindering effects from patents is a compulsory license.[153] In case a patent holder refuses to grant licenses, a court or government can grant a compulsory license to a third party without the authorization of the right holder. The Declaration on the TRIPS Agreement and public health of 14 November 2001, supports the use of such compulsory licenses, where it specifically states that each Member has the right to grant compulsory licences and the freedom to determine the grounds upon which such licences are granted.[154]

For countries with no or insufficient manufacturing capacities the condition in Article 31(f) of the TRIPS Agreement, that products made under a compulsory license must be 'predominantly for the supply of the domestic market', proved to be a stumbling block. At the Ministerial Conference in Doha in November 2001, the WTO Members were not able to reach an agreement on the way to create extra flexibilities enabling those countries to profit from the compulsory licensing system. The negotiations on this issue remained deadlocked for almost two years. On 30 August 2003, the General Council then agreed on a Decision allowing a waiver from the obligations set out in paragraphs (f) and (h) of Article 31 of the TRIPS Agreement with respect to pharmaceutical products in the interest of the above-mentioned countries.[155] The Decision also comprised safeguards to prevent that the products were diverted from the markets for which they were intended. More than two years later, on 6 December 2005, the General Council finally agreed to permanently amend the TRIPS Agreement by inserting a new Article 31*bis* and an Annex to the TRIPS Agreement, containing definitions, required

---

152. *Ministerial Declaration,* adopted on 14 November 2001 (WT/MIN(01)/DEC/1), more in particular Point 17 (available at http://www.wto.org/english/thewto_e/minist_e/min01_e/mindecl_e.htm, last visited 18 February 2015).

153. *See,* E. van Zimmeren & G. Van Overwalle, 'A Paper Tiger? Compulsory License Regimes for Public Health in Europe', *International Review of Intellectual Property and Competition Law (IIC),* (2011): 4-40.

154. *Declaration on the TRIPS Agreement and Public Health,* adopted on 14 November 2001 (WT/MIN(01)/DEC/2), more in particular Point 5 (b) (available at http://www.wto.org/english/thewto_e/minist_e/min01_e/mindecl_TRIPS_e.htm, last visited 18 February 2015).

155. Decision of the General Council of 30 August 2003, *Implementation of Paragraph 6 of the Doha Declaration on the TRIPS Agreement and Public Health* (Document WT/L/540 and Corr. 1, available at http://www.wto.org/english/tratop_e/TRIPS_e/implem_para6_e.htm, last visited 18 February 2015).

29.7   COMMERCIALIZATION OF HUMAN BODY AND
HUMAN BODY PARTS

Another limit in which Muslim scientists would have to avoid is the religious proscription against the commercialization of human body and human body part. In an earlier work, it has been pointed out that the patenting of human body or parts of human body should not be allowed as it may offend the classical views on the commercialization of human body parts. This view is formed based on the viewpoint of several Muslim scholars who openly opposed any form of commercialization of the human body for fear that it would offend human dignity.[66]

According to Resnik, the basic argument for property rights to embryonic stem cells is capitalistic and utilitarian in nature.[67] It is further postulated that, "property rights should be granted in order to promote the progress of science, technology, medicine, business and the industry."[68] The Shari'ah on the other hand views that human beings are defined by their relation to Allah. In Islam, humans did not evolve from apes. Instead, Allah created humans as mentioned in Surah al-Tin (95), verse 4, "Indeed, We created man in the best of forms" and in another verse in Surah al-Taghabun (64), verse 3, "He fashioned you in the best of images." And even more profound is Allah's declaration in Surah Sad (38), verse 72, "I breathed into Him (Adam) of My spirit." In relation to the creation of humans, Seyyed Hussein Nasr explains:

> Human beings therefore reflect the Divine attributes like a mirror, which reflects the light of the Sun. By virtues of being created as this central being in the terrestrial realm, the human being was chosen by God as His Vicegerent (khilafat Allah) as well as His servant ('abd Allah). As servants, human beings must remain in total obedience to God and in perfect receptivity before what their Creator wills for them. As vicegerents they must be active in the world to do God's Will here on earth.[69]

The essence of commercialization is the ability to claim ownership over something and monopolize the benefits over that matter in return for monetary benefits. The promotion of scientific inquiry and research is not done only to benefit those who will be able to pay for it. Instead, it is done to benefit the society, in order to gain Allah's blessings or Barakah. As such, any research that results in an invention that would benefit the society cannot be monopolized by one person or group of persons.

---

66. Al Hidayati, Part II, at 34, cited in Mohammad Naeem Yasseen, "The Rulings for the Donation of Human Organs in the Light of Shari'ah Rules and Medical Facts", 5, Part 1, (February, 1990), 49-87, at 51.
67. David B. Resnik, "The Commercialization of Human Stem Cells: Ethical and Policy Issues", Health Care Analysis Vol. 10 (2002), 127-154, Available at www.ualberta.ca.
68. *Ibid.,* 138-151.
69. Seyyed Hossein Nasr, The Heart of Islam, p. 276.

one such country. While one renowned professor from Al-Azhar University tolerates non-reproductive cloning and believes it right to use precious supernumerary embryos—but only within the first fourteen days—for research for the benefit of others instead of leaving them to die. On the other hand, the President of the Egyptian Medical Syndicate, oppose the usage of embryos for research, as the conceived being is already a human being. The divergent viewpoints could well explain the differences in national countries' approaches to stem cell research.[63]

The Fatwa Committee of the Majlis Ugama Islam Singapura (Islamic Religious Council) concurs with the opinion of the Singapore Bioethics Advisory Committee to use stem cells from embryos below fourteen days for the purpose of research, which will benefit mankind, is allowed in Islam. This is with the condition that it is not misused for the purposes of human reproductive cloning, which would result in contamination of progeny and the loss of human dignity.[64] In the deliberation of the Fatwa Committee, Islam does not place any judgment on an embryo, which is not fully formed. An embryo is only considered as a human life after it is four months old when the soul is introduced into the embryo. Thus, an embryo below four months, regardless of whether it was created in vivo or in vitro, is to be considered as a living being undergoing the growth process. However, it is not yet considered as the beginning of human life with the existence of a soul.[65]

The question now comes as to which position should influence the patentability of inventions resulting from human embryo research? If there exist diverging views, which view should then be taken? Usually, the position in a particular Muslim country needs to be determined by the Government of the day. In doing so it is also necessary to look into the commercialization of the human body and human body parts.

---

63. *Ibid.*, 248.
64. Singapore Bioethics Advisory Committee, Ethical, Legal and Social Issues in Human Stem Cell Research, Reproductive and Therapeutic Cloning, G-3-G-71.
65. The Committee formed its view based on the opinion of Dr. Muhammad Sulaiman al-Asyqar, who is of the view that an embryo which is not formed or is not in a woman's womb, will not be placed any judgement on it. In his view: "Islamic law does place any form of judgement on an embryo which is not formed. Verily, I have explained in detail my opinion during my forum discussion on birth. In that forum, decision had to be made that Islamic law does not place any judgement on a woman's fertilized egg except after it is in the womb. There is no judgement on it before it is in the womb. A similar opinion was given by the Fatwa Institution of Darul Ifta, Saudi Arabia, where, for as long as there is no soul in an embryo, the sperm and the egg are judged to be living things adapting to their specific conditions. They are considered as components of the fertilization process. They have not reached the stage of a complete human being." *See* The Fatwa the Majlis Ugama Islam Singapura, Fatwa Committee Special Meeting, Thursday, November 22, 2001, "Ethical, Legal and Social Issues in Human Stem Cell Research, Reproductive and Therapeutic Cloning", A Report from the Bioethics Advisory Committee, Singapore.

balance.[166] Human rights can and should act as an external correction mechanism[167] and can and should play a complementary role regarding patent law in that they 'mobilize[s] a moral and interpretative force which patent law cannot generate by itself'.[168] It is important that current patent law regimes are linked with human rights discourse, and that human rights assist in defining the utter limits of patent rights in general, and in the field of human genetics in particular.

The *hypothesis* set forth in the present chapter that human rights actually contribute to settling the gene patent controversy has not been confirmed. *First*, human rights instruments have not provided a straightforward basis to limit the coming into *existence* of patents for human genes and genetic diagnostic methods. The human dignity concept as enshrined in Article 3(2)(c) of the European Charter has not resonated in EPO and CJEU jurisprudence to the extent that it was considered a clear and unambiguous argument to limit the coming into existence of patents for human genes, gene products and genetic diagnostic methods. On the contrary, European jurisprudence has taken the view that the concept of human dignity is not opposed to patents for human genes; this view was supported by European advisory and legislative authorities. More theoretical reflection and academic inquiry would be welcome to study the relationship between Article 3(2)(c) of the European Charter and Article 53(a) EPC, and their impact on the patenting of human genetic material. In the unlikely case that the outcome of that research would point out that the EU equivalent of Article 53(a) EPC, namely Article 6(1) of the EU Biotechnology Directive, is not in line with Article 3(2)(c) of the European Charter, the annulment of the EU Biotechnology Directive could be considered on the basis of Article 263 TFEU. In addition to the human dignity issue, the free and informed consent requirement as embedded in the Additional Protocol to the Convention on Human Rights and Biomedicine, concerning Biomedical Research did not resonate either in the context of the application for human gene patents. Both the EPO Boards of Appeal and the CJEU took a negative stance towards integrating an informed consent requirement in patent law. The fact that the implementation of an effectively informed consent requirement in the context of patent

---

166. External correction mechanisms constitute useful tools for cases at the intersection of two branches of law, *see* A. Brown, *Intellectual Property, Human Rights and Competition,* Edward Elgar, 2012; I. Govaere & H. Ullrich (eds), *Intellectual Property, Market Power and the Public Interest,* P.I.E. Peter Lang S.A., 2008; L. Helfer & G. Austin, *Human Rights and Intellectual Property,* Cambridge University Press, 2011; C. Geiger, 'The Social Function of Intellectual Property Rights, Or How Ethics Can Influence the Shape and Use of IP Law', in *Intellectual Property Law: Methods and Perspectives,* G. Dinwoodie (ed.), Edward Elgar, 2013.

167. *Ibid.*

168. E. Claes, 'Patent Law, Human Rights and Human Dignity: A Reply to Geertrui Van Overwalle', comments presented at *Ethics and Human Rights in Bio-Law,* Workshop organized at the Centre for Intellectual Property Rights, University of Leuven, 31 May 2007 (On file with the author).

applications may prove to be rather cumbersome in daily clinical practice further aggravates the situation.

Second, human rights instruments have not directly offered a foundation to limit questionable behaviour in the *exercise* of patent rights in the field of human genetics on the European level, either. On the basis of Article 3(2)(c) European Charter, and even more so, Article 53(a) EPC, the EPO is (made) responsible for assessing the discrepancy between certain inventions offered for patent protection and *ordre public* and morality, including respect for human dignity and access to health care. An adequate reading of Article 53(a) EPC suggests that when carrying out such a morality assessment, the EPO should focus on (future) questions related to the commercial exploitation of the invention, rather than on (past) issues relating to research and development of the invention. At the moment of the grant, it is difficult to ascertain the commercial exploitation of the invention. Subsequently, the EPO can continue maintaining a reluctant approach at this stage, and provide patent protection for inventions which do not seem to contravene Article 53(a) EPC at first sight. However, in later stages, when it becomes clear that the patented invention is marketed and exploited in a manner that runs counter to morality and human dignity or jeopardizes the right to access to health care, the EPO should resume its full responsibility – e.g., in the context of an Opposition procedure or a procedure before the Technical Boards of Appeal – and investigate the impact of the commercial exploitation of the patent (claims) on human dignity or access to health care. In case the commercial exploitation of the patent (claims) at stake can be proven to hinder access to health care, the EPO should resolutely invalidate the patent (claims) at hand. In the Myriad Genetics case, the EPO, time after time, refused to assess the alleged hindering effects of the BRCA patents in the framework of an assessment of Article 53(a) EPC and the right to access to health care. It could be argued that such behaviour boils down to flagrant denial of justice ('Rechtsverweigerung').

The upcoming Unitary Patent Package does not address the interrelationship between human rights and patents in its foundations' documents.[169] However, it is conceivable – at least in principle – that the Unified Patent Court develops a more favourable attitude in factoring in human rights concepts in patent law when dealing with patent cases in the area of human genetics.

---

169. Regulation (EU) No. 1257/2012 of the European Parliament and of the Council of 17 December 2012, Implementing Enhanced Cooperation in the Area of the Creation of Unitary Patent Protection, *Official Journal of the European Union* – L 361/1, 31 December 2012, is based on the objectives set forth in Article 3 (3) TEU. The Council of Europe Agreement on a Unified Patent Court, Brussels, 11 January 2013, recalls 'the primacy of Union law, which includes the TEU, the TFEU, the Charter of Fundamental Rights of the European Union, the general principles of Union law as developed by the Court of Justice of the European Union'.

In retrospect, two afterthoughts come to mind. *First*, the present chapter may have given too much weight to the human rights discourse, in the sense that high aspirations have been allotted to human rights and the idea that human rights instruments carry deep universal ethical values. Future research may reassess the assumption that human rights are permeated with deep ethical values in more detail, and pay more attention to the open and complex texture of the human rights narrative. This afterthought may assist in further shaping and deepening the relationship between patent law and human rights, and making the interplay between those two fields of law more attuned.

Second, as an alternative to assessing patent law through the lens of human rights law in an attempt to bring more shade and nuance to the gene patent debate and provide a more profound legal foundation to patent law restrictions, patent law could be re-assessed through the prism of legal philosophy, more in particular, the 'Law as integrity' theory.[170] The 'Law as integrity' theory, put forward by Ronald Dworkin,[171] could provide a valuable alternative prism to reflect upon values and objectives justifying patents for human genes. Rather than infusing values and principles from the human rights pantheon into patent law to moderate the possible sharp effect of contemporary patent law – and in that way instrumentalizing human rights – it might be interesting to revisit and adjust the values and principles underlying patent law in general and gene patents in particular, turning to the 'Law as integrity' theory for guidance. In such an analysis, the question whether patent rights should be awarded to human genetic material would not mainly depend on whether such patents would fuel innovation, but rather on the degree to which such patents would contribute to global values such as fairness or distributive justice, or to values such as preservation of human diversity and equal respect of each uniqueness.[172] Plugging the discussion on patents for human genes, into the 'Law as integrity' discourse, might assist not just in *correcting* some negative effects of patent law in the area of human genetics, but might assist patent law in general in *re-framing* the underlying objectives of patent law and re-assessing the principles on which it is grounded, including the incentive to invent/incentive to disclose tandem

---

170. The author is very grateful to Erik Claes for having suggested this avenue of thinking, during one of the many exchanges of ideas they had on the theme of patent law and human rights.
171. R. Dworkin, *Law's Empire*, Harvard University Press, 1986. For a critical approach, *see* T.R.S. Allan, 'Dworkin and Dicey: The Rule of Law as Integrity' *Oxford Journal of Legal Studies*, 1988, 266-277.
172. E. Claes, 'Patent Law, Human Rights and Human Dignity: A Reply to Geertrui Van Overwalle', comments presented at *Ethics and Human Rights in Bio-Law*, Workshop organized at the Centre for Intellectual Property Rights, University of Leuven, 31 May 2007 (On file with the author).

and the private-public interest balance on which it is founded.[173] Future research could provide a much more extended analysis to work out precisely how the 'Law as integrity' theory might be applied in the context of patent law and human genetics, and patent law more generally, thereby enriching the stream of academic conversation which started exploring similar avenues of thinking.[174]

---

173. See G. Van Overwalle & E. van Zimmeren, 'Functions and Limits of Patent Law', in *Facing the Limits of the Law*, E. Claes, W. Devroe & B. Keirsbilck (eds), Berlin-Heidelberg, Springer, 2009, 415-442.
174. More in particular, A.E.L. Brown, *Intellectual Property, Human Rights and Competition*, Edward Elgar, 2012, at 212-220 and E.R. Gold, 'Patents and Human Rights: A Heterodox Analysis', in *Global Health and the Law*, Spring 2013, 185-198.

Index

INFORMATION LAW SERIES

1. Egbert J. Dommering & P. Bernt Hugenholtz, *Protecting Works of Fact: Copyright, Freedom of Expression and Information Law,* 1991 (ISBN 90-654-4567-6).
2. Willem F. Korthals Altes, Egbert J. Dommering, P. Bernt Hugenholtz & Jan J.C. Kabel, *Information Law Towards the 21st Century,* 1992 (ISBN 90-654-4627-3).
3. Jacqueline M.B. Seignette, *Challenges to the Creator Doctrine: Authorship, Copyright Ownership and the Exploitation of Creative Works in the Netherlands, Germany and The United States,* 1994 (ISBN 90-654-4876-4).
4. P. Bernt Hugenholtz, *The Future of Copyright in a Digital Environment, Proceedings of the Royal Academy Colloquium,* 1996 (ISBN 90-411-0267-1).
5. Julius C.S. Pinckaers, *From Privacy Toward a New Intellectual Property Right in Persona,* 1996 (ISBN 90-411-0355-4).
6. Jan J.C. Kabel & Gerard J.H.M. Mom, *Intellectual Property and Information Law: Essays in Honour of Herman Cohen Jehoram,* 1998 (ISBN 90-411-9702-8).
7. Ysolde Gendreau, Axel Nordemann & Rainer Oesch, *Copyright and Photographs: An International Survey,* 1999 (ISBN 90-411-9722-2).
8. P. Bernt Hugenholtz, *Copyright and Electronic Commerce: Legal Aspects of Electronic Copyright Management,* 2000 (ISBN 90-411-9785-0).
9. Lucie M.C.R. Guibault, *Copyright Limitations and Contracts: An Analysis of the Contractual Overridability of Limitations on Copyright,* 2002 (ISBN 90-411-9867-9).
10. Lee A. Bygrave, *Data Protection Law: Approaching its Rationale, Logic and Limits,* 2002 (ISBN 90-411-9870-9).
11. Niva Elkin-Koren & Neil Weinstock Netanel, *The Commodification of Information,* 2002 (ISBN 90-411-9876-8).
12. Mireille M.M. van Eechoud, *Choice of Law in Copyright and Related Rights: Alternatives to the Lex Protectionis,* 2003 (ISBN 90-411-2071-8).
13. Martin Senftleben, *Copyright, Limitations and the Three-Step Test: An Analysis of the Three-Step Test in International and EC Copyright Law,* 2004 (ISBN 90-411-2267-2).
14. Paul L.C. Torremans, *Copyright and Human Rights: Freedom of Expression – Intellectual Property – Privacy,* 2004 (ISBN 90-411-2278-8).
15. Natali Helberger, *Controlling Access to Content: Regulating Conditional Access in Digital Broadcasting,* 2005 (ISBN 90-411-2345-8).
16. Lucie M.C.R. Guibault & P. Bernt Hugenholtz, *The Future of the Public Domain: Identifying the Commons in Information Law,* 2006 (ISBN 978-90-411-2435-7).

17. Irini Katsirea, *Public Broadcasting and European Law: A Comparative Examination of Public Service Obligations in Six Member States,* 2008 (ISBN 978-90-411-2500-2).
18. Paul L.C. Torremans, *Intellectual Property and Human Rights: Enhanced Edition of Copyright and Human Rights,* 2008 (ISBN 978-90-411-2653-5).
19. Mireille van Eechoud, P. Bernt Hugenholtz, Stef van Gompel, Lucie Guibault & Natali Helberger, *Harmonizing European Copyright Law: The Challenges of Better Lawmaking,* 2009 (ISBN 978-90-411-3130-0).
20. Ashwin van Rooijen, *The Software Interface between Copyright and Competition Law: A Legal Analysis of Interoperability in Computer Programs,* 2010 (ISBN 978-90-411-3193-5).
21. Irini A. Stamatoudi, *Copyright Enforcement and the Internet,* 2010 (ISBN 978-90-411-3346-5).
22. Wolfgang Sakulin, *Trademark Protection and Freedom of Expression: An Inquiry into the Conflict between Trademark Rights and Freedom of Expression under European Law,* 2011 (ISBN 978-90-411-3415-8).
23. Stef van Gompel, *Formalities in Copyright Law: An Analysis of their History, Rationales and Possible Future,* 2011 (ISBN 978-90-411-3418-9).
24. Nadezhda Purtova, *Property Rights in Personal Data: A European Perspective,* 2012 (ISBN 978-90-411-3802-6).
25. Brad Sherman & Leanne Wiseman, *Copyright and the Challenge of the New,* 2012 (ISBN 978-90-411-3669-5).
26. Ewa Komorek, *Media Pluralism and European Law*, 2012 (ISBN 978-90-411-3894-1).
27. Joris van Hoboken, *Search Engine Freedom: On the Implications of the Right to Freedom of Expression for the Legal Governance of Web Search Engines,* 2012 (ISBN 978-90-411-4128-6).
28. Natali Helberger, Lucie Guibault, Marco Loos, Chantal Mak, Lodewijk Pessers & Bart van der Sloot, *Digital Consumers and the Law: Towards a Cohesive European Framework*, 2012 (ISBN 978-90-411-4049-4).
29. Tatiana-Eleni Synodinou, *Codification of European Copyright Law: Challenges and Perspectives,* 2012 (ISBN 978-90-411-4145-3).
30. Heather Ann Forrest, *Protection of Geographic Names in International Law and Domain Name System Policy*, Second Edition, 2017 (ISBN 978-90-411-8839-7).
31. Sari Depreeuw, *The Variable Scope of the Exclusive Economic Rights in Copyright*, 2014 (ISBN 978-90-411-4915-2).
32. Vikrant Narayan Vasudeva, *Open Source Software and Intellectual Property Rights*, 2014 (ISBN 978-90-411-5228-2).
33. Frederik J. Zuiderveen Borgesius, *Improving Privacy Protection in the Area of Behavioural Targeting*, 2015 (ISBN 978-90-411-5990-8).
34. Paul L.C. Torremans, *Intellectual Property Law and Human Rights*, Fourth Edition, 2020 (ISBN 978-94-035-1304-1).

35. Irini A. Stamatoudi, *New Developments in EU and International Copyright Law*, 2016 (ISBN 978-90-411-5991-5).
36. Lodewijk W.P. Pessers, *The Inventiveness Requirement in Patent Law: An Exploration of Its Foundations and Functioning*, 2016 (ISBN 978-90-411-6731-6).
37. Susy Frankel & Daniel Gervais, *The Internet and the Emerging Importance of New Forms of Intellectual Property*, 2016 (ISBN 978-90-411-6789-7).
38. Axel M. Arnbak, *Securing Private Communications: Protecting Private Communications Security in EU Law – Fundamental Rights, Functional Value Chains, and Market Incentives*, 2016 (ISBN 978-90-411-6737-8).
39. Christina Angelopoulos, *European Intermediary Liability in Copyright: A Tort-Based Analysis*, 2017 (ISBN 978-90-411-6835-1).
40. João Pedro Quintais, *Copyright in the Age of Online Access: Alternative Compensation Systems in EU Law*, 2017 (ISBN 978-90-411-8667-6).
41. P. Bernt Hugenholtz, *Copyright Reconstructed: Rethinking Copyright's Economic Rights in a Time of Highly Dynamic Technological and Economic Change*, 2018 (ISBN 978-90-411-9103-8).
42. Manon Oostveen, *Protecting Individuals Against the Negative Impact of Big Data: Potential and Limitations of the Privacy and Data Protection Law Approach*, 2018 (ISBN 978-94-035-0131-4).
43. Tatiana Eleni Synodinou (ed.), *Pluralism or Universalism in International Copyright Law*, 2019 (ISBN 978-94-035-0355-4).